GOLD AND IRON

GOLD
AND IRON

Bismarck, Bleichröder, and the Building of the German Empire

FRITZ STERN

Vintage Books
A Division of Random House
New York

FIRST VINTAGE BOOKS EDITION,
September 1979

Copyright © 1977 by Fritz Stern

All rights reserved under International and Pan-
American Copyright Conventions. Published in the
United States by Random House, Inc., New York,
and simultaneously in Canada by Random House of
Canada Limited, Toronto. Originally published by
Alfred A. Knopf, Inc. in February 1977.

LIBRARY OF CONGRESS CATALOGING
IN PUBLICATION DATA

Stern, Fritz Richard, 1926-
   Gold and iron.

   Reprint of the 1977 ed. published by Knopf,
New York.
   Bibliography: p.
   Includes index.
1.   Bismarck, Otto, Fürst von, 1815-1898.
2.   Bleichröder, Gerson von, 1822-1893.
3.   Statesmen—Germany—Biography.
4.   Bankers—Germany—Biography.   I.   Title.
[DD218.2.S85   1979]   943.08'092'2
[B]   79-11462
ISBN 0-394-74034-3
987

Cover Painting: *Das Ballsouper* by Adolph von Menzel
(Nationalgalerie, Bildarchiv Preussischer Kulturbesitz)

To Peggy

Money is the god of our time, and Rothschild is his prophet.

—Heinrich Heine

The history of the House of Rothschild is of greater importance for world history than the domestic history of the state of Saxony; and is it a matter of indifference that that is the history of a German Jew?

—Theodor Mommsen

The great questions of the day will not be settled by speeches and majority decisions—that was the great mistake of 1848 and 1849—but by blood and iron.

—Otto von Bismarck in 1862

The German Empire has been built more truly on coal and iron than on blood and iron.

—John Maynard Keynes

CONTENTS

ILLUSTRATIONS

GUIDE TO ABBREVIATIONS

Archives

AI	Alliance Israélite, Paris
BA	Bleichröder Archive, Baker Library, Harvard University
BLHA	Brandenburgisches Landeshauptarchiv, Potsdam (German Democratic Republic)
DZA	Deutsches Zentralarchiv (German Democratic Republic)
FA	Fürst von Bismarck Archive, Friedrichsruh
GFO	German Foreign Office: Politisches Archiv, Bonn
HHSA	Haus-, Hof-, und Staatsarchiv, Vienna
HN	Paul von Hatzfeldt Nachlass, care of Dr. Gerhard Ebel, Bad Nenndorf (German Federal Republic)
HS	Fürstliches Hohenzollern Haus- und Domänenarchiv, Sigmaringen (German Federal Republic)
MAE	Ministère des Affaires Étrangères, Correspondance Politique, Paris
PRO: FO	Public Records Office, Foreign Office files, London
SA	Schönhausen Archive: a separate part of Fürst von Bismarck Archive, Friedrichsruh
RA	Archives de Rothschild frères, Paris

Published Works

AHR	*American Historical Review*
APP	Historische Reichskommission, *Die Auswärtige Politik Preussens, 1858–1871* (Vols. i–vi and viii–x, Berlin, 1932–1939)
CEH	*Central European History*
DDF	Ministère des Affaires Étrangères, *Documents diplomatiques français*, 1st series, 1871–1900 (16 vols., Paris, 1929–1959)
DPO	Heinrich Ritter von Srbik, ed., *Quellen zur deutschen Politik Österreichs, 1859–1866* (5 vols., Oldenburg, 1934–1938)
FBPG	*Forschungen zur brandenburgischen und preussischen Geschichte*

GP	Johannes Lepsius and others, eds., *Die grosse Politik der europäischen Kabinette, 1871–1914* (40 vols., Berlin, 1922–1927)
GW	Hermann von Petersdorff and others, eds., *Bismarck: Die gesammelten Werke* (15 vols. in 19, Berlin, 1923–1933)
GWU	*Geschichte als Wissenschaft und Unterricht*
HZ	*Historische Zeitschrift*
JEH	*Journal of Economic History*
JMH	*Journal of Modern History*
LBY	*Leo Baeck Institute Year Book*
OD	Ministère des Affaires Etrangères, *Les origines diplomatiques de la guerre de 1870–1871* (29 vols., Paris, 1910–1932)
SBHA	*Stenographische Berichte über die Verhandlungen des Landtages, Haus der Abgeordneten*

INTRODUCTION

This is a book about Germans and Jews, about power and money. It is a book focused on Bismarck and Bleichröder, Junker and Jew, statesman and banker, collaborators for over thirty years. The setting is that of a Germany where two worlds clashed: the new world of capitalism and an earlier world with its ancient feudal ethos; gradually a new and broadened elite emerged, and Bismarck's tie with Bleichröder epitomized that regrouping. It is the story of the founding of the new German Empire, in whose midst a Jewish minority rose to embattled prominence. It is a record of events and of the interests and sentiments that shaped these events; it is a record largely told by contemporaries, in thousands of hitherto unused letters and documents. It is also the story of the fragility of that Empire and its ruler, of its hidden conflicts, and of the hypocrisy which allowed a glittering façade to cover the harsh and brutal facts below. The ambiguity of wealth—its threat to tradition and its promise of mobility—is part of this record, and so is the anguished ambiguity of Jewish success, so striking, so visible, so delusive. It is a study of a society in motion, and mobility was its essence and its trauma.

Bismarck represented the old Prussia—aristocratic, agrarian, hierarchic —but it was he who sought to combine the modern elements of the society with the old traditions of the monarchy. In this endeavor he needed Bleichröder. The two men personified the historic encounter between old nobility and new presumption, between men of rank and birth and men of wealth and aspiration. The two men and the form of their collaboration also symbolized the anachronistic forms of Germany's modernization. The great themes of the nineteenth century—the impact of capitalism, the struggle between democracy and authoritarianism, nationalism and imperialism, the rise of Jewry and of its nemesis, the new anti-Semitism—were reflected in their work. It is the intersection of their lives that affords a new perspective on their era and a view of a living society to set against the generalities and abstractions of received opinion.

Bismarck's work is known—or thought to be known. A monumental hero, a brooding presence to generations of Germans, Bismarck has been studied many times, but his relations with Bleichröder have, until recently, been excised. Bleichröder was a household word to his contemporaries, connoting enormous wealth, power, and mysterious influence. But Bleichröder faded from consciousness with his death, although his career had a decisive bearing on Bismarck's life and on the course of German history. Bleichröder was Bismarck's private line to the practical world and Bismarck was Bleich-röder's principal link to the dignified world of Prussian politics.

Gerson Bleichröder, the chancellor's banker, rose from obscurity to the pinnacle of German society: often called the German Rothschild, he was the first Prussian Jew to be ennobled without converting to Christianity. His rise dramatized the power of money and the limits of that power; it showed the hostility that money and mobility engendered. He built up his position gradually, capitalizing at first on his intimate ties with the Rothschilds; he rose ever further by virtue of his services, both professional and personal, to Bismarck, to the state, and to the German elite.

Bleichröder's career mirrored the pervasiveness of capital: its influence on policy and public opinion and its attractiveness to an elite that seemed to forswear it. As his confidant, Bleichröder had immediate access to Bismarck. He was in charge of the chancellor's fortune, and he was given, and he sought, political assignments requiring his particular mixture of expertise and discretion. Europe knew him as Bismarck's secret agent, and his diverse roles give us a new view of Bismarck's reign and of the governing class of Germany at a time when the Reich became the dominant power of the con-tinent. Bleichröder's career illuminates those aspects of Bismarck's rule previously slighted or ignored. It shows that Bismarck in the public and private realm fully understood the magnitude of money and that even in his much-vaunted and much-studied diplomacy economic weapons as instruments of policy were never far from his mind. He had learned his lesson early: he needed funds to wage the first two wars of unification, funds that the parlia-ment he defied refused him and that Bleichröder helped to raise.

Bleichröder also served Bismarck's entourage and the old Prussian elite generally. To him that elite acknowledged its needs, appetites, and ambitions. They did so covertly, as money remained the great taboo. They appealed to his influence, which they resented. He was a convenience and an embarrass-ment; he too could have sighed: "Why should our endeavor be so loved, and the performance so loathed?"[1] Bismarck was least troubled by his concern with money: he would have understood an historian's interest in his role as one of Germany's largest landholders, in his investments in politically sensitive securities, in his reticence as a taxpayer. The record examined con-firms neither the Simon-pure naïveté that German historians ascribed to him nor the profiteering that scandalmongers of the Empire charged him with. He made no illicit profits but neither did he think that the intelligence which his office brought him should be excluded from his considerations as an investor.

The Bismarck-Bleichröder tie reflected the connectedness between gov-ernment and capital, diplomacy and finance, public and private interests. In Bleichröder's relations with his clients, who encompassed the elite of Germany, there were no neat separations between public and private realms; it was one great web of mutual interest, advantage, need. These links were sensed by the great novelists of the nineteenth century and brilliantly inferred in the analysis of Marx: inferred analytically, not documented empirically. These same links, disguised, denied, or belittled by the principal actors and by the ethos of the time, were ignored by subsequent historians, and hence this unorthodox side of the German past has remained largely uncharted.

In the story of Bleichröder I have been able to reconstruct some of these links. They attest economic power, but not in the way in which economic power has in recent years been assumed or dogmatized. One is struck by the penetration of economic power, its ubiquitous presence, but also by its limits and indeed by its inferiority as compared to the power of the state. Bleichröder's career is of course but one instance, though an instance at the highest level of the German polity; it is an instance complicated by his Jewishness which made the banker most especially subservient to the unique hero-dictator. It is then in many ways an unusual and extreme case, but the history of the Bismarck-Bleichröder relationship suggests the primacy of politics, not economics. Bismarck is dominant and Bleichröder is useful: at his discretion, Bismarck accepted Bleichröder's advice, heeded his wishes, afforded protection. So did the German government generally. The history of Bleichröder confirms Max Weber's contention that " 'Economically conditioned' power is of course not identical with 'power' as such."[2]

Bleichröder thirsted after power and profits—and after what both were to give him: respectability and acceptance. In the new world of the mid-nineteenth century, the symbols of success changed as well: the palaces and temples of the time were banks, cast in stone and marble, exuding solidity and power. Bleichröder belonged to the group of merchant bankers who marshaled the funds for the great monuments of nineteenth-century progress. He financed mines, railroads, and the St. Gotthardtunnel; his charity enabled Robert Koch to apply his new discovery of the tuberculosis bacillus to the treatment of the sick. He floated loans to governments and he was a marginal participant in colonial affairs. His clients and collaborators included much of the business and political elite of Europe, and his interests embraced every continent. Both Bismarck and Bleichröder belonged to a world governed by notables; but that world was passing, and even in the economic realm Bleichröder came to be overshadowed by the growth of corporate banks and great industrial magnates, and his traditional usefulness as creditor to states was gradually supplemented, as modern states devised their own means of raising funds.

For all his loyalty to Bismarck and the new Reich, Bleichröder never forgot—or was allowed to forget—his religious origins and responsibilities. His ten-year effort to orchestrate the influence of western Jewry so that the Great Powers would compel Rumania to grant civic equality to its Jews records his sense of mission, his successes, and his ultimate failure.

Bleichröder lived simultaneously in many worlds. In some, the price of success was discretion and anonymity; in others, he needed visibility and prominence. He cultivated an aura of ostentatious mystery. His conduct was dictated by his function and station in society, and yet, as with most successful men, his role and his passions coincided.

He cherished secrecy and sought recognition. He was an indefatigable hunter after titles, distinctions, honors; instinctively he knew that money needed respectability, and Jewish money doubly so. He was no worse than his contemporaries, than *nouveaux riches* anywhere. In the hands of plutocrats this quest for respectability often turned to dazzling vulgarity, to the reification of tastelessness. Bleichröder's life described this yearning for acceptance and his social presence exemplified the anxious snobbery that was the very stuff of bourgeois society.

Bleichröder's career takes us from Bismarck's chancellery to the furthest limits of German imperial penetration in China and Mexico, and yet at the heart of the story is Bleichröder's Jewishness, which shaped his life, enhanced his sufferings, divided him from his peers and progeny. As Thorstein Veblen said of young intellectual Jews: "They are neither a complaisant nor a contented lot, these aliens of the uneasy feet: but that is, after all, not the point in question."[3] The ambiguity of Jewish success was embodied in his career: by virtue of his wealth and service he was allowed to rise to the top; by royal fiat and on parchment he was an equal to Prussian nobles—and yet in his mature years he became the magnet for all the malice, frustration, and resentment that festered in German society.

His life demonstrated the fateful conjunction of anticapitalism and anti-Semitism. There were other men of wealth in Germany, but it was Bleichröder who became the symbol of wealth and, to many, the symbol of the inequities of a system rent with social conflict. In 1889, in a private memorandum to a fellow senator, Dr. Rittscher, the police chief of Lübeck, warned against a new repressive law proposed by Bismarck, because "it would spread dissatisfaction with existing conditions, even within the circles of the bourgeoisie, within the liberalising philistines, and hasten more than we would like the bloody decision, which I think will have to come, as to who should govern: Bebel or Bleichröder, because that is the question, property or poverty, since the time of the Gracchi."[4]

There had always been what might be called respectable anti-Semitism, perhaps no more than a prejudice against the insinuating presence of a money-making, money-centered clannish group, but in Imperial Germany Bleichröder helped to bring this latent sentiment to the fore. More: the simultaneity of his secret power and social pomp enraged the new anti-Semites of the 1870s, who, unlike the more circumspect, traditional anti-Semites, believed that Jewish power had become a mortal menace to German life and who demanded that the state should revoke or restrict the rights of Jews. In the early 1870s, a time of unprecedented economic depression, accompanied by charges of corruption and fraud, Germans of many persuasions insisted that Jews were at the heart of an international conspiracy that was corroding the German character and the European order. Bleichröder became the chief hostage of this new anti-Semitism: even the most imaginative anti-Semites could not have invented this figure, at once so powerful and so vulnerable. His progeny was corrupted by what had spurred him on: wealth and prominence. The Bleichröder story illuminates the rise, travail, and ultimate decline of German Jewry, and the endemic quality of many forms of anti-Semitism in German society. Legal emancipation coincided with new economic opportunities; released from their disabilities, Jews performed great economic feats: they were immeasurably useful and they were immeasurably resented. In Bleichröder's time patterns were set and silences begun that lasted for a long time.

The central theme of the book, however, is the joint work of Bismarck and Bleichröder. The scope of their collaboration was immense; in different ways they helped to shape the destinies of Germany at the moment of its great upsurge of power. Their lives and careers instruct us about the character and functioning of that new society. They were its representative men.

For all his importance and prominence, Bleichröder has remained an "unperson" in German historiography. Bismarck loomed in superhuman dimension; at recent reckoning, over 7,000 works have appeared about him. This is the first study of Bleichröder. It may be pardonable exaggeration to say that Bleichröder is everything that has been left out of German history.

For a long time the memory of Bleichröder was an embarrassment. He represented so many lingering taboos—money-grubbing, influence-peddling, Jewish-ness. Even in his lifetime it was his vilifiers who magnified his role and power; the elite whom he served preserved a decorous silence. The Bismarcks pointed the way: after thirty years of collaboration, after countless conversations and a voluminous correspondence, Bismarck omitted Bleichröder's name from the first two volumes of his memoirs. In the third volume, slated for publication only after William II's death, Bleichröder's name is mentioned once, as somebody's emissary.

Of course, there was a vast inequality between Bismarck and Bleichröder in life, but that inequality was greatly magnified after their deaths. German historians lifted one man to apotheosis and consigned the other to oblivion—and the two processes were linked. The editors of Bismarck's collected works published not a letter of Bismarck's to his banker; mention of him was rare and aseptic. The editors seem to have been restrained in their efforts to uncover the traces of Bismarck's tie to Bleichröder. This process of excision persisted until 1945.

Historians—whatever their persuasion or intention—reflect the values of the society in which they write, and German historians for the half century after Bismarck's death had every incentive to neglect Bleichröder. The favorite historiographical focus in those decades was narrowly political or intellectual; social and economic history was long a stepchild of German scholarship. The Jewish question was hardly ever touched by German historians.[5] If Bismarck had a Jewish banker and confidant, then it was something that belonged to his private realm, marginal to the public figure. The will to neglect was easily satisfied: the record of Bleichröder's role was hard to find and hence could respectably be overlooked.

In recent times German historians have turned to studies of social and economic phenomena, and some of the most important and promising work of the profession has been done in these fields. Contemporary historians are no longer embarrassed by the presence of bankers or of economic appetites; if anything, they would be alarmed by their absence. But historians today have other interests, and perhaps other taboos as well: they seek to transcend the individual, pragmatic element in history in search of the structure of a society and of the broad, anonymous forces that appeared within that structure, according to its fundamental commands and strictures. They shun biography and their fascination with the structure often dulls their concern for the spirit that animated it; nor is the spirit of a society quantifiable. Belief in the historic role of individuals is not in vogue today and the study of the elite is slighted in favor of classes and causes previously neglected.

Bleichröder and his fellow bankers appear in the accounts of recent historians as representatives of certain economic interests. As individuals they tend to remain unpersons, or types, in a new effort to make history a science by purging it of the intangible ephemera, of the habits, attitudes, and moral stance that give society its particular character.

But Bleichröder would have remained an unperson for yet another reason. Even if historians in the last eighty years had been more hospitable to a study of him, the traces of his life had largely disappeared. The record was scattered, buried in often inaccessible archives. It was only after many different sources had been uncovered and many diverse bits of evidence put together that something of the contours of a career emerged.

So interesting has been this search after Bleichröder and his long forgotten relationship with Bismarck that a brief account of it may be useful. The search was triggered by the appearance in New York of the remnants of the private archive of Gerson Bleichröder; the business archive was taken over by the Aryan successors of the bank in the 1930s and lost during the Second World War. This private archive contained thousands of letters addressed to Bleichröder, covering the years from the mid-1860s to his death in 1893, with a few documents from before and after. The material had never before been used; the correspondence included many letters from the Bismarck family and from Bismarck's secretaries. The rest came from eminent statesmen and diplomats, from leading officials and bankers of the German Empire, from Disraeli and Leopold II, from the Rothschilds and the Oppenheims, from the Jews of Jassy and from William I, from friends and supplicants. They were candid letters, destined for Bleichröder's eyes alone. They were full of news and fears and hopes, gossip and innuendos, hints of portentous events: they were the authentic record of a generation of Europeans speaking to their banker, in whose integrity, discretion, and intelligence they put the utmost stock, and from whose benevolent interest they expected to draw tangible and intangible benefits. (Not all letters were important or symptomatic; perhaps only a small percentage was. But they all had to be read, and it was the totality that illuminated the particulars.) One voice was largely absent: that of Bleichröder himself. The centrality of his role could be inferred, but the actual record of his work and the imprint of his character were absent. The Bleichröder Archive, in short, was a tantalizing, even frustrating beginning. Bleichröder was still an unperson.

And thus the quest for Bleichröder started: In the beginning, as I make clearer in the Acknowledgments below, the search was conducted jointly by David S. Landes and myself. There were two principal sources: the extensive correspondence of Bleichröder with the House of Rothschild in Paris, covering the entire span of his career, but at its most candid in his early personal letters to Baron James de Rothschild, who died in 1868. They were housed in the attic of the old Rothschild Bank and most generously put at our disposal. The second great find was various files of Bleichröder's letters and statements to Bismarck and the Bismarck family, a large part of which reposed above the stables of Prince Bismarck's estate in Friedrichsruh.

The entire Bleichröder-Bismarck correspondence—some of it of course also preserved in government files—consists of well over a thousand letters, only a handful of which has ever been used. The bulk of the letters concern routine business, though Bleichröder always mixed ordinary reports about Bismarck's finances with observations about the political economy of Germany and Europe, with reports about his own activities or intentions, and with digests of political intelligence he received from his many sources. The correspondence touched on a multitude of subjects, private and public. It is one of the most revealing records of nineteenth-century German history.

It was an odd circumstance that these two richest sources remained in their historic locations: in the rue Laffitte and at Friedrichsruh, where Bleichröder had often visited. The Rothschilds and Bismarck: the glittering poles of his existence.

And still, the record was inadequate; individual histories emerged, but not a comprehensive or continuous story. I could find echoes and traces of Bleichröder's activities in the governmental archives of East and West Germany; police records proved informative as well. The unpublished reports of his friends among the French and Austrian ambassadors in Berlin complemented the story, as did his correspondence with Disraeli, located in Disraeli's old home in Hughenden Manor. Even the holdings of the Alliance Israélite in Paris shed valuable light—and if nothing else, this may be the only book on Bismarck that has used the files of the Alliance. There were other finds, and occasional disappointments, either because material had been lost or access to some archive was denied.

It was a constant search after remaining traces. Each clue would suggest new places to look, and in the end I may have overlooked some hidden hoard. Gradually I could piece together some of the elements of the Bismarck-Bleichröder relationship. Some aspects remain obscure, and much evidence was lost during World War II. I have read a vast number of letters and documents, and it is a token of my respect for the reader that not more of these found their way into the book. I have given preference to the unpublished over the published, and I have tried throughout to focus on the revealing rather than the routine. And yet no one is more aware of the incompleteness of the record than myself: so much of Bleichröder's role depended on confidentiality and was conducted in conversation. We hear occasional echoes of these conversations; if anything, it is surprising how many letters which the senders asked to have burned survived, how many traces of the *éminence grise* could be recovered.

The historian must integrate his new sources with existing literature. In this way the sources acquire meaning and prevailing scholarly opinion acquires necessary correction. The literature on Bismarck and on Europe's history is huge; to this awesome record of scholarship I owe much, as my notes suggest; I am also aware of how much I had to omit, which I regret.

In the end one finds that the best letters and the fullest set of documents are partially mute. They take for granted a particular context—shared assumptions, time-bound conventions—which the historian must simultaneously extract from and bring to these voices. I have tried, in G. M. Young's phrase, to hear the past speak.

But there remained something beyond the massive scholarship, invaluable though it was, that I could consult. There was the sense that my subject and my sources constituted a story, inherently dramatic and poignant: the rise of Bleichröder, his struggle to translate unimaginable wealth into respectability, his public honors and his private humiliations, the Germanism which he embraced and the Jewishness which he could not evade, and the precipitous decline of his family. It is a story of Bleichröder's rise set against the background of the triumphant new Germany. It is a long story, but it was a crowded scene that surrounded this sedate banker; his life encompassed many worlds. To recall those worlds, the facts by themselves were insufficient; I had to infer or imagine what these facts once represented. To be faithful to that aspect of my work, I found inspiration in the great novels of the last century, for, as Lionel Trilling said: "The novel, then, is a perpetual quest for reality, the field of its research being always the social world, the material of its analysis being always manners as the indication of the direction of a man's soul."[6]

The organization of the book reflects its character and scope: the first part deals with the rise of the two protagonists, with Bleichröder's help in Bismarck's daring policy of unifying Germany. The second part reconstructs their joint efforts to shape the policies of this new Germany. Their collaboration dramatizes in specific detail the concatenation of different realms and subjects: of finance and politics, of domestic and foreign policy, of private and public concerns, of personal ambitions and historic currents. It touched important aspects of European diplomacy, colonialism and imperialism. In the third part I deal with the omnipresent element of the Bleichröder story: his Jewishness in relation to German society, to German politics, to the Jewish community, to his family—to his own self. He described a pinnacle of Jewish success: in clear weather the peak stands out with grandeur; in stormy times it is the first to attract lightning. Both perspectives are real and both are worth pondering.

I hope the book does more than offer new facts or revise impressions. It should convey something of the atmosphere of imperial Germany, something of the responses of a society suddenly in the throes of a dimly understood social transformation. It is not only the functioning of a society that is meant to be depicted here, not only the daily *do ut des*, the reciprocity of services, to use a favorite phrase of Bismarck's. Something of its spirit should emerge as well. There are attitudes, clusters of ideas and prejudices, gestures that bespeak manners, silences that express values as clearly as do sermons or patriotic speeches. The atmosphere of imperial Germany seemed to exude a kind of sentimentalized self-righteousness, copious hypocrisy, distressing servility, though the personages of our story may have been so accustomed to these characteristics as to have been unaware of them. We are perhaps more conscious of them than were the contemporaries. It was Nietzsche who said: " 'I have done that,' says my memory. 'I cannot have done that,' says my pride, and remains inexorable. Eventually—memory yields."[7] Society screened memory and reality, and here is a record of what was screened out and how.

There is, I fear, an inherent bias to the book: by focusing on money and Jews, the book touches the raw nerves of German society. Perhaps money and Jews brought out the worst in that society. Neither Bleichröder nor Bismarck was the focus of virtue or good will and in a few, very few instances, some of Bleichröder's clients will appear more in their roles as debtors and speculators than as the eminent diplomats or public servants they also were. It is not necessarily flattering to view a society from the top down. Bleichröder's career exemplified some of the deep ambiguities of German society that in many accounts are treated rather flatly, if at all. It is a commonplace to speak of the triumph of capitalism in the second half of the last century; but the peculiar character of German society was shaped by the intrusion of capitalism in some sectors and the resistance to it in others. It is not unusual to speak of anti-Semitism in imperial Germany, but this book depicts its political appearance in the context of the rise of the German Jews and recalls that in the last century they managed as great a leap forward as any minority has ever achieved in European history.

It is not an easy story to write or an edifying one to ponder. It is overladen with the tragedy of later developments. I have tried to listen to the society as it then was, as it revealed itself privately, candidly, almost naïvely. There were ominous signs in that society, and I have so recorded them; I believe they would be adjudged ominous even without our hindsight that they were harbingers of disaster. We also hear the beginnings of that great silence before evil that accompanied Germany's terrible decline in the first half of the twentieth century. The book may help to explicate the catastrophes that have shaped our own historical experience; but that was not its principal intent. Finally we must note that a great embarrassment has covered the study of German-Jewish relations, and it could not be otherwise. It is hard to recapture the days when Germans and Jews shared an identity of interests and even an identity of attitudes—for all the antagonisms that divided them.

Oftentimes German Jews have been portrayed as innocent victims of discrimination, craven in their submission to authority. But at some time and place there were also exemplars of success among them, no more immune to hubris than their gentile peers.

Other societies in the grip of triumphant and embattled capitalism betrayed similar characteristics—or so in magnificent indignation Ibsen, Shaw, and the great novelists of an earlier time recorded. "American traditions," wrote Richard Hofstadter a generation ago, "show a strong bias in favor of equalitarian democracy, but it has been a democracy in cupidity rather than a democracy of fraternity."[8] In Germany—in part for reasons that the book suggests—it was cupidity without democracy, and hence without a beneficent or reformist impulse from the political realm.

Life does not resemble what Shaw once called "a moral gymnasium," where the forces of good and evil are neatly arrayed. Nor is the historian some kind of moral umpire. But there are distinctions, and the historian must point to them. "We cannot establish by actual count that there were more villains in real life at one time than at another, but we can say that there was at one time better reason, more practical use, for villainous dissembling than at another."[9] This is not a book about villains, but about a society in which individual acts of self-righteous hypocrisy appeared so regularly as to suggest that these forms had been lifted into a governing system. Hypocrisy lapsed into self-deception, and the self-deception of Germans and Jews, both in their joint efforts and in their relations to one another, had awesome consequences for the world. Here is a record of certain strains of this society: here are the voices, candid and unreflective, of the time but portentous nevertheless. It is the record of men sowing the wind, not knowing that a later generation would reap the whirlwind.

PART ONE

THE HAZARDOUS RISE
1859–1871

CHAPTER 1

First Encounter:
Junker and Jew

To be a good philosopher, one must be dry, clear, without illusion. A banker who has made a fortune has one character trait that is needed for making discoveries in philosophy, that is to say, for seeing clearly into what is.
                                        —Stendhal, as attributed by Nietzsche

In the Mark [Brandenburg], everything is a question of money because there is none around—money sanctifies person or cause.
                                        —Theodor Fontane, *Der Stechlin*

Opposites attract—partly by complementing each other. Otto von Bismarck and Gerson Bleichröder were cast in radically different molds, originally lived in different worlds, and aspired to different stations: but their lives intersected, and for thirty-five years they proved useful to each other. As masters of their respective crafts, both men altered the lives of others—one visibly and dramatically, the other invisibly but none the less deeply. The statesman who had to circumvent the Prussian Constitution in order to bolster a conservative monarchy needed the help of the ingenious banker who as a Jew had to circumvent the social hierarchy of the day in order to climb to aristocratic respectability. Gradually collaboration turned into something akin to friendship, and it is their extraordinary relationship that forms the core of this book.

At birth, the social distance between Bismarck and Bleichröder could hardly have been greater. Each had to rise above his station and his ancestral prejudices until the two men helped to create a world that could accommodate and that gradually came to depend upon their collaboration.

Bismarck was born in 1815, a few weeks before the Battle of Waterloo, on the ancestral estate of Schönhausen in the old Mark Brandenburg. The Bismarcks had lived in the Mark for centuries, long before the Hohenzollerns came to rule it. A century before Otto's birth, Frederick William I of Prussia had warned his heirs against the likely insubordination of some Junker families, and the Bismarcks, he warned, were among "the worst."[1]* The Bis-

---

* Superior figures indicate notes beginning on page 551.

marcks were not among the first families in Prussia, as measured by their own canons of service or wealth; but they had a heritage of pride and belonged to the rulers, not the ruled.

Bleichröder was born of Jewish parents in Berlin in 1822—ten years after an edict of the government had promised Prussian Jews immediate emancipation, a promise that was fully redeemed only a half-century later, under Bismarck's government. The experience of centuries of oppression, of oppression which the oppressors thought attested their virtue as certainly as the villainy of their victims, was not to be overcome by a half-hearted decree. The march out of the ghetto was slow, and the attitudes that had sustained the ghetto lingered on. Gerson was born into a social group that for centuries had been depressed and was popularly thought to be depraved; it was also a group that was to rise to unimaginable heights, as Gerson's own life was to demonstrate. Bismarck was born at the top, but of a class that all over Europe had been rudely challenged in the preceding twenty-five years and that was to find itself continuously threatened by the twin revolutions of the nineteenth century—by the industrial and the egalitarian revolutions— and that would have declined more precipitously and more openly if Bismarck had not saved it, often against its own wishes. In later years, Bismarck raised Bleichröder into the ranks of the Prussian nobility, and Bleichröder helped Bismarck to become a wealthy man in an increasingly materialistic age. To neither man did success come easily.

Gerson may have had an easier time of youth and early manhood than his more famous contemporary. Gerson's life was circumscribed by certainties: by the commands of his faith, which enjoined the strictest filial devotion, by the necessity of hard work in a competitive and largely hostile world, by the limited aspirations that stretched out before him. In older, traditional societies, one's reach into the future was usually determined by one's reach into the past: instant mobility was the exception—which was why Napoleon's crowning of himself as emperor became the great symbolic legend of the nineteenth century. Few Jews had ancestors they knew anything about: one knew about one's grandparents and one knew about the common descent from Adam and Abraham; the interval was marked by the obscurity of the Diaspora.

Like many Jewish names in German-speaking territory, the name of Bleichröder probably derived from a town's name, Bleicherode in the Harz, in the Prussian province of Saxony. The town is some miles east of Göttingen; in today's political geography, it is just inside the border of East Germany. When and whence the Bleichröders first came to the Harz is unknown; until the eighteenth century, most Jews had no family name. They were known as their father's sons. We have only a few traces of the family before Gerson's father's time. The first Bleichröder to appear in the records of the state was Gerson's grandfather, Gerson Jacob, born in the 1740s, who as a young man went to Berlin, having received the right of residence because the Jewish community needed him as a gravedigger. He tried his hand at other enterprises but failed at all of them. His one success—and an important one—was his marriage to Suse Aaron, the daughter of a Berlin *Schutzjude* (protected Jew). To appreciate the importance of this leap requires a brief look at the infinitely complicated picture of preemancipation Jewry.[2]

In those days, a closed, hierarchical Christian society regarded Jews as a religious and social excrescence; state action corresponded to general sentiment. The mass of Jews lived on the margins of that society, in their own communities, speaking their own dialect, wearing their own garb, eating their own food—and suffering their own disabilities. Thus kept in their place, they were sanctioned to perform only those services that gentiles shunned or did less well. Hence the bulk of Jewry engaged in moneylending and in a variety of peddling, of endless buying and selling—and always in an atmosphere of suspicion between seller and buyer, Jew and gentile. The Christians reproached the Jews for their exclusive concern with matters of money, and Moses Mendelssohn, himself an eminent philosopher, exclaimed in exasperation: "They bind our hands and then complain that we do not make use of them." Both sides recognized the deep gulf that lay between them. "The outside world," as one recent historian has put it, "did not overly occupy the Jewish mind."[3]

A few Jews rose above the lowly mass. For particular usefulness to the state, they were granted the status of protected Jews, exempted by the state from many, though not all, of the disabilities it had imposed on the rest of Jewry. Protected Jews paid fewer dues and enjoyed greater mobility. A handful of Jews rose still higher; their special services, usually as bankers and lenders to dynasts, earned them the place of *Hofjude*—court Jew. Gerson Jacob married the daughter of a protected Jew; his grandson, Gerson, was often seen as the last of the court Jews.[4]

Of Gerson Jacob's four children, it was Samuel who made the most of his maternal connections. In 1803 he opened a Wechselstube, or exchange office, on the Rosenthaler Strasse, a rather remote corner of Berlin. As an entrepôt between West and East, Berlin was always flooded with diverse currencies; within the old Holy Roman Empire a host of currencies circulated, and the French occupation of Berlin that began in 1806 brought an even greater need for exchange facilities. Samuel Bleichröder's shop also functioned as a Lotterie-Geschäft, that is, as an agency for the sale and redemption of lottery tickets. The state ran lotteries as the main device for raising funds for its honorable charges, such as army widows and disabled soldiers. Gradually Samuel expanded his business and like many Jewish jobbers of the time began to give himself the more grandiloquent title of banker. By the time Gerson was born, his father had become a fledgling merchant-banker; by the late 1820s, he had established the first connections with the Rothschilds—connections that were destined to lift Samuel, and later Gerson, far above the rank of most other Berlin bankers. A generation later, it was the Rothschilds who brought Bleichröder and Bismarck together.

The Rothschilds have been a legend since Waterloo or since the old Meyer Amschel died in 1812, leaving a vast fortune and five able sons to multiply it. Meyer Amschel had been a dealer in coins, medals, and antiques in the *Judengasse* of Frankfurt; during the revolutionary upheavals, he saved the fortune of Prince William of Hesse. His sons founded a dynasty of inter-national bankers; they established their courts in Vienna, Paris, London, and Naples, leaving the oldest to maintain the ancestral house in Frankfurt. The Rothschilds institutionalized international banking, and under their aegis European capital became fully mobile. Their own wealth surpassed that of all rivals, and with it they could mobilize additional funds as well. As they were ensconced in their five cities, speaking all foreign tongues with the same Yiddish accent, they clung together, invested in one another's business, and intermarried with one another's family. Theirs was a commercial equivalent of the Napoleonic dynasty, which had also started with an upstart from the margins of society and had also relied on fraternal loyalty to rule an empire. The commercial variant was no doubt less glorious than the Napoleonic Empire; it was also less bloody and more enduring. Throughout the nineteenth century it was the model of fabled wealth and luxury, of elegance and power. The Rothschilds described the pinnacle of plutocracy, and they were aped, envied, and detested.* The Rothschild dynasty still flourishes in Paris and London, and although their power has shrunk, their operations still encompass the world, their history still captures the imagina-tion of the multitudes.†

The exact date of Samuel's first connection with the Rothschilds is buried in obscurity; according to one source, it was 1828, when Anselm von Rothschild (the son of Baron Solomon of Vienna) visited Berlin and added Bleichröder to the short list of acceptable agents for Rothschild interests.[5] From Bleichröder's letters to the Paris and London Rothschilds we know that by the early 1830s Samuel received regular commissions from the Rothschilds, gradually pushing aside earlier and more venerable correspondents, like the Mendelssohns.

This is not the place for an analysis of Samuel's relations with the four Houses of Rothschild (Naples hardly figured in Berlin).** In the 1830s the

---

* And detested by all manner of people. As early as 1832, writing from Paris, the radical German poet Ludwig Börne suggested that the Rothschilds should formally be crowned mon-archs of Europe; it would make their invisible empire visible, and as monarchs themselves they would not float onerous loans: "It is always the same game which the Rothschilds play in order to enrich themselves at the expense of the country they exploit." Ludwig Börne, *Sämtliche Schriften* (Düsseldorf, 1964), III, 482–491.

† Books on the Rothschilds appear with considerable regularity and usually for motives that the Rothschilds could appreciate: profit. The best-known work is still Count Egon Corti, *The Rise of the House of Rothschild 1770–1830*, and *The Reign of the House of Rothschild 1830–1871* (New York, 1928), from which the more popular writers copiously borrow. For a scholarly economic history, see Bertrand Gille, *Histore de la Maison Rothschild*, 2 vols. (Paris, 1965–1967). The subject is inherently dramatic; films and musicals have demonstrated the Rothschilds' entertainment value, and Virginia Cowles, *The Rothschilds: A Family Fortune* (New York, 1973), adds splendid pictures to a familiar story. But a full history of the Rothschilds, based on now available archival sources, and depicting their political and economic role in Europe, their social presence, and the response to them in different countries remains to be written. It is a magnificent subject.

** Such an analysis will be presented by David S. Landes's history of the Bleichröder Bank. For this section I have relied on his draft chapters dealing with the bank in the years before 1845.

Berlin market came to life, and Samuel bought and sold securities for the Rothschilds. Their orders usually specified that he should buy below the market price and sell above it—a feat that the Rothschilds chose to regard as routine. He also was their agent in executing regular arbitrage operations between Paris or London and Berlin. Arbitrage—the buying and selling of securities or moneys on more than one market in order to take advantage of price differences—depends on an exact knowledge of the market and perfect timing: the smallest change in price means the difference between profit and loss. The Rothschilds were the best-informed men of Europe; they collected intelligence faster than did their governments. To do so required minute attention to the collecting and dispatching of news. One had to know the right people everywhere, and, in the days before rapid communications, one had to devise one's own system of couriers and carrier pigeons to speed news from place to place. Accordingly, Samuel in the 1830s often pleaded with the Rothschilds to include him in their network of rapid news; he complained that their letters from Paris took six days, whereas by a different routing it could be done in five. The Rothschilds only gradually came to appreciate the importance of the Berlin market.

Samuel tried his best to solicit their interest, especially in German railroad issues, which in the late 1830s and early 1840s triggered the first boom on the Berlin market—followed, inevitably, by the first bust.[6] Nor did Samuel forget to remind the Rothschilds of his own growing importance: in September 1838 a clerk signed a letter for him, with the explanation that Bleichröder had felt "constrained to accept" an invitation to take part in the opening of the Berlin-Potsdam railroad. On the next day, Samuel himself reported that the two-mile trip from Potsdam to Zehlendorf had been less rapid than expected: it had taken thirty minutes one way and twenty-six the other. Still, Samuel was enthusiastic, and no doubt honored to have been invited to the opening of the first railroad in the Prussian kingdom. He encouraged the Rothschilds to buy shares of the Potsdam-Berlin railroad; a few months later, he was trying to liquidate their holdings because his happy expectations had been disappointed. Instead of the anticipated dividends, the company faced additional expenses. Undaunted, Samuel sought to entice Rothschild funds into other German railroads—a fact that earned him a prominent place on one or two boards of directors.[7] The Bleichröder-Rothschild correspondence illuminates one other aspect of those early days of stock market operations: the modesty of profit expectations. Samuel correctly assumed that the Rothschilds would be interested in operations that promised a profit of 1 percent in a short time, or of 3 to 4 percent over a period of some months. The motto of the day was closer to the Chinese proverb that a journey of a thousand miles begins with a single step than to the American hope of getting rich quick. The Rothschilds (and their agent, Samuel) did not like to miss a single step.

Even this early record from the 1830s and 1840s makes it clear that the Rothschilds in all their branches were an insufferably haughty dynasty; they knew that their custom was a priceless gift to a struggling banker in

Berlin. Samuel had to beg for every favor and participation; he had to offer every advantage. Worse, Baron James of Paris—who, after the death of Nathan Meyer in London in 1836, had become the dominant Rothschild— occasionally accused Samuel of neglect of Rothschild interests, with the invariable, implicit threat that the Rothschilds could find other agents in Berlin. Samuel assured him that he worked only for the Rothschild Houses (unlike other Berlin houses) and that hence, even for selfish reasons, he was totally devoted to their interests. When the Berlin market suffered a severe setback in 1840, Samuel offered to sacrifice a part of his commission in order to execute James's orders. Three years later, after another tongue-lashing, Samuel protested that he had not only spent many a sleepless night pondering Rothschild's wishes, but that he had given up his own commission and some of his own money in order to please Rothschild.[8]

The few surviving pieces of Samuel's correspondence with the Rothschilds indicate the other services that he rendered them. As early as 1831, he sent them news of political developments—explaining, when appropriate, their bearing on the market. He reported on the king of Holland's anticipated response to the Five Powers' decision concerning the new state of Belgium; he informed the Rothschilds on the Russian treatment of the Polish rebellion of 1831. He reported on the ravages of the cholera, and in 1848 he supplied the Frankfurt House with news about the Berlin revolution. After giving a very precise recital of Berlin's revolutionary *journée*, he reassured them that the securities and the gold which he had purchased for them were safe: *"The esteemed gentlemen need have no fears because there is no reason to be concerned for private property."*[9] It was a shrewd as well as an illuminating remark to make: the fate of private property was central to the revolution and to the Rothschilds.

The correspondence reveals yet another tie between Samuel and the Rothschilds: their unashamed Jewishness. The very first letter of Samuel to the London House ended with a postscript in Hebrew letters; the language of letter and postscript was German, but this was German as Samuel Bleichröder spoke it—with a heavy Yiddish accent. From time to time, Samuel— and Gerson after him—would resort to the same method which simultaneously assured the confidentiality of the message (censors were thought to be primitive in those days) and reiterated the special kinship between the correspondents.[10] Samuel took it for granted that the Rothschilds were particularly interested in all matters pertaining to Jewry; thus in July 1840 he reported to the Paris House that the new Prussian king, Frederick William IV, had graciously received the Executive Board of the Jewish Community in Berlin, had listened to a "very beautiful speech" by the spokesman of the group, and had then replied in roughly these words: "I take pleasure in recognizing that you count among my best citizens, and I shall never forget how patriotically the Jews, particularly the Berlin Jews, felt.—I am not out of some dark age and you will always find with me the just recognition of your deserts."[11] There was often a kind of unarticulated rivalry among Jews of different nationalities, as if they were saying to each other: our gentiles are at least as good as yours.

Other services followed as a matter of course. The Rothschilds expected Samuel to scurry around for *objets d'art* that might suit the Rothschilds' taste and purse. Nor did Baron James object when Samuel begged him to accept "graciously, a small cask of the freshest caviar," which he was dispatching via his son-in-law B. Wolff.[12] The Rothschilds liked the better things in life—the more so if they were free or economical.

The Rothschilds were the making of Samuel; he knew it, and he was never allowed to forget it. To be the Rothschild agent or correspondent in Berlin was not only a challenge to Samuel's ingenuity and a promise of ever greater profits and kudos to himself; it was also, to some extent, a recognition of Samuel's past achievements and character. He was known for his rectitude and intelligence.[13] Like all exacting dynasts, the Rothschilds wanted subordinates who were slavishly loyal and yet smartly enterprising. Deference alone was not enough; deeds had to match words, and Samuel came to be adept at both. He tried his hand at elegant phrases, as when he introduced his seventeen-year-old son, Gerson, to Baron Anselm Solomon of Vienna, who happened to be in Paris:

. . . May I once and for all be permitted to be able to put before you, in all brevity, my deepest, most heartfelt thanks for the kindnesses I have enjoyed through your goodness, for it is you, most honorable Herr Baron, who picked me up out of the dust: you, most noble one, have put me in the position of being able to nurture a large family.

As long as I live, therefore, your picture will live in my heart, and my last breath of life will be devoted to you, my benefactor.

May you then have the goodness now to carry over your favor and benevolence to my son. . . .[14]

In the private banking world of those days, personal ties were of the greatest importance. Common ventures depended on mutual trust, and that trust had to be established by direct personal knowledge.

Gerson entered his father's business in 1839. We know little of his early years in the firm. He worked diligently, and in 1843 he was given the power to sign for the firm (*Prokura*); Samuel assured Baron James in Paris that this was done because of Gerson's "fair-mindedness and his efforts and devotion on behalf of your esteemed interest."[15] In 1847 he became a partner, and in 1855, when Samuel died, Gerson became the head of the firm. His younger brother, Julius, also worked in the bank; by 1860 he relinquished his role in the family business and founded his own bank. For a few years, the brothers were silent partners in each other's bank, but by 1870 that link ceased.

On the whole it was an auspicious time for Gerson to begin his own career. At midcentury, the Prussian economy enjoyed its first modern boom, triggered by railroads, the metallurgical industry, and the growing availability of capital. In the 1850s German industry developed at an unprecedented pace: "the decade saw the decisive breakthrough of modern capitalistic enterprise in Germany."[16] A new form of economic organization, the joint-stock corporation, became the favorite vehicle for growth. In the 1850s joint-stock banks made their first appearance and eventually were to surpass the power of even the greatest of private bankers. For a long time, however, the joint-stock and private banks cooperated. By coincidence, Gerson's lifelong associate, friend, and sometime rival, Adolph Hansemann, entered his father's business, the joint-stock Disconto-Gesellschaft, in 1856, a year after Gerson's independent career began.

Gerson helped to finance the great expansion of the 1850s, and he profited from the ensuing boom. His most important asset was still his tie with the Rothschilds, which he cultivated even more diligently than his father had. But he also gradually established himself as a powerful figure in his own right. He formed syndicates with other banks to establish new investment companies, and in the same fashion he entered the metallurgical industry and promoted several railroad lines, including the Thuringian Railroad. He was named official banker of the Cologne-Minden and the Rhenish Railroads. In 1859 the Prussian prince regent (later William I) invited him to the opening of the famous railroad bridge across the Rhine at Cologne—which Gerson had helped to finance.[17]

More and more frequently, he collaborated with the Cologne House of Sal. Oppenheim Jr. and Company, run by the exceptionally enterprising brothers Abraham and Simon Oppenheim.* In 1853, against the wishes of the Prussian government and the Frankfurt Rothschilds, the Oppenheims together with the brilliant entrepreneur Gustav Mevissen, and with the help of French capital, had taken a leading part in the founding of one of the first joint-stock banks, the so-called Darmstädter Bank; two years later, Abraham Oppenheim urged Gerson to join the Darmstädter in founding another bank, which perhaps could be run by Julius Bleichröder. Oppenheim added: "In any case, this suggestion will prove to you that I have unlimited confidence in your person and your capacity, and I have no doubt that my colleague thinks as I do on this matter. . . ." Gerson declined the flattering invitation, but the Oppenheims continued to express to Gerson their esteem for "your intelligence, your insight, and your method of dealing with things."[18] In 1859, during the Franco-Austrian war, Gerson became a co-founder with the Hansemanns of the so-called Prussian Consortium, a syndicate of banks organized to raise 30 million taler for the financing of the Prussian mobilization. The government, in turn, was beginning to recognize Bleichröder's importance.[19]

Men's external careers are usually better documented than their internal

---

* Sal. Oppenheim was founded in Cologne in 1801—four years after the new French rulers had lifted the 350-year-old-ban on Jews residing in Cologne. The House of Oppenheim established itself quickly as a foremost Cologne banking firm; by mid-century, because of its vigorous promotion of new industrial ventures and because of its international ties, it had become an enterprise of European standing—such as Bleichröder was to become by the 1870s. See Dr. Alfred Krüger, *Das Kölner Bankiergewerbe vom Ende des 18. Jahrhunderts bis 1875* (Essen, 1925), pp. 64–72.

growth. Perhaps this is peculiarly true of businessmen; indeed there has always been a presumption that they have no life of the sentiments. Would any of Thomas Buddenbrook's friends, for example, have suspected the seething anguish beneath his sober imperturbability? We know little of Gerson's inner life; a few letters survive, a few nostalgic recollections from the 1880s, prompted by widowhood and the loneliness of old age. Who would have saved whatever intimate letters young Gerson might have written? We know that after a careful inspection of eligible young ladies and in accordance with the wishes of his father, he decided to marry a banker's daughter, Emma Guttentag, from Breslau, a city with a large and distinguished Jewish community, with which Samuel had many contacts. If Gerson suffered even the faintest stirrings of Sturm und Drang, of a desire not to become a respectable *Biedermeier* and to strike out along new paths, the ethos of his people and of his time would not have encouraged him to indulge such feelings. Work was thought to cure all; Tolstoi's Levin once said, "I want to enrich medicine with a new word: '*Arbeitskur.*' "[20] Gerson immersed himself in work, at the expense of almost everything else, perhaps even of his health. Bismarck, as we will see, had the leisure and the pain to try to find himself; Gerson was early cosseted by duty, and his reward was his success.

But one realm of fragility Gerson could not avoid: his Jewishness made him permanently vulnerable. Indeed, the greater his triumphs, the greater the uncertainties and the attacks. He sought and was sought by the gentile world; the more he entered it, the more he was made to realize that he lacked the traditions and qualities that that society held in the highest esteem. His Jewishness defined his life—far more than Bismarck's *Junkertum* served to define his. Hence Gerson's biography will be treated below in the context of the German-Jewish relationship, of what I have called the anguish of assimilation.

Bismarck's youth was more tempestuous. He had thrown himself headlong into life, impatient of restraint, disdainful of his class and its ideals, bemused by his fellow men. He was born to what Bleichröder could never attain: an aristocratic heritage, an immediate and unquestioned opening to the highest levels of society. The Jewish bourgeois was far more impressed by these advantages than Bismarck, whose ambition soared beyond his birth. Of a romantic temper, steeped in Shakespeare and Byron, with a fierce ironic wit, he thirsted for some noble purpose or heroic life and, while waiting, squandered his time on boorish dissipation. "My ambition strives more to command than to obey," he wrote his father in 1838, and this ambition and his will to power made him loathe and abandon his career in the Prussian bureaucracy.[21] He discarded religious sanctions as well and abandoned the nightly prayers which had been his habit since childhood. The death of a young woman he adored—the wife of his best friend—and his own subsequent marriage in 1847 to Johanna von Puttkamer sobered him down.

In the same year, Prussia's political life emerged from the doldrums, and Bismarck entered the arena with relish—and exceptional connections.

He had tried the life of a country squire—and found it insufferably dull. Still, throughout his life, in moments of exasperation or despair, he dreamed of the pleasures of the bucolic life, of retiring to Schönhausen, the ancestral estate. His attachment to Schönhausen—and later to Varzin and Friedrichsruh—was genuine and unflagging. He loved nature; he loved being the master of his own land, the lord of some peasants; he loved the independence and community of that kind of life. But the management of estates was a tedious task, and the return often meager enough. "Experience has led me away from the delusion about the Arcadian happiness of a landowner incarnate, with double-entry bookkeeping and chemical studies," he wrote in 1847.[22] At times Bismarck affected magnificent indifference to money and would with obvious pride apologize for his spendthrift and irresponsible habits. But those were moments of exuberance, which after his marriage became less and less frequent. Mostly, he had a keen appreciation of money, as did his fellow landowners. Even as a young man he thought he needed "a large fortune in order to enjoy state service so that I can appear at will with the brilliance I consider decent but also so that I can easily renounce all advantages of office as soon as my official functions prove incompatible with my convictions or my taste."[23]

After his entry into public service his need for funds increased, and his time to manage them diminished. His earlier disdain for money matters disappeared, and the accompanying antibusiness and anti-Semitic sentiments declined as well. Jews and money-grubbing had appeared as one to him, and he once apologized for his "Jewish accounting nature [*Berechnungswesen*]" to his friend Hermann Wagener, from whom he sought to collect some debts.[24] His letters from the 1830s and 1840s attest his easily aroused prejudices; but he had no particular ideology about the Jews, and his intervention against them at the United Diet in 1847 was merely a defense of the status quo. Jews, he thought, should play no role in the public administration of a Christian state. For the rest, he did not like them, and he rather relished not liking them. It was one more way of being antiliberal, of being provocatively candid.

In 1848 Bismarck's world came close to collapse. There had been isolated tremors of revolution before; Restoration Europe had been haunted by the specter of Jacobinism resurgent. In 1848 the revolutionary forces triumphed everywhere: in Milan, in Paris, in Vienna, and even in Berlin. In Prussia, as in the other German states, the demands were twofold: unity and freedom, and the hope was that somehow the two could be achieved simultaneously and by peaceful, deliberative means. On all specific questions—the role of Austria and her non-German possessions, for example, or the nature of the suffrage—there was uncertainty and division: only the ideal of a single, united, liberal-constitutional Germany shone forth as a beacon to action. To Bismarck, this ideal, with its liberal and anti-Prussian intentions, became anathema, as was the road of revolution to attain it.

In Bismarck's memoirs, admittedly his own variety of poetry and truth, the Revolution of 1848 is accorded the principal place in his political development. It was a searing experience for him, and he remembered it as such. If anything, historians, concerned with correcting the flamboyant exaggerations of his account, have slighted the psychological impact of the upheaval on him. The Revolution gave Bismarck (like Marx) a new élan and a new direction. The death of a woman he loved brought a new religious commitment to his life; the near-death of his monarchy left him with a new political resolve. The first had taught him the powerlessness of all men; the second the frailty of most men. Both together gave him a stronger sense of his own duty and destiny.[25]

Revolutions test men's fortitude and vision; they create a vacuum of power, where unimagined alternatives fleetingly appear realizable. They break the mold that contains the fears and aspirations of a people. They dramatize politics; they make visible the link between the public realm and the ordinary lives of subjects and citizens. Revolutions reward the unconventional. Whatever foolishness Bismarck may have committed on the way, his first impulse in 1848 was to rush to Berlin, to insinuate himself into the presence of the king, to assert his will, and speak his mind—all this in defiance of the usual courtesies and restraints, in order to inculcate firmness in the king. He was going to save the monarchy from the mob, and from itself.

This is not the place to analyze the Revolution or Bismarck's thoughts and actions during it. He was appalled by the facile defiance of the public order, by the physical and symbolic violations of that order. What embittered him most was the instant retreat of the authorities; in his first parliamentary speech, two weeks after the Revolution, he said: "The past is buried; and it is a matter of more poignant grief to me than to many of you that no human power can raise it up again, since the Crown itself has thrown the earth upon its coffin."[26] At the very least he refused to do what so many of the king's men did: to celebrate what they called a new union between the monarch and his people. What he remembered in his memoirs was his threat to kill a vacillating fellow landowner, his utter contempt for a frightened minister like Ernst von Bodelschwingh, his injunction to his monarch that a king must be able to sleep. He probably embellished his own importance and steadfastness; perhaps he, too, vacillated between impractical schemes of counterrevolution and crying fits, such as put an end to his speech to parliament. But it would be hard to deny that Bismarck emerged from the Revolution of 1848 infinitely strengthened, with a clearer sense of himself and a greater contempt for others. (What audacity to write to his pietistic mother-in-law, who had expressed concern for some Hungarian revolutionaries who had been executed: "In you, my dearest Ma [*Mutschchen*], still spook Rousseauistic educational principles which brought Louis XVI to the point where out of disinclination to bring about in legal ways the death of one individual he became responsible for the disappearance of millions. . . . The soft compassion with the *body* of the criminal carries the greatest blood guilt of the last sixty years.")[27] Bismarck had felt no compassion. He had discovered his own sang-froid. And he now felt—and expressed—that loathing of parliaments and parliamentarians that became a characteristic of his later life. He sensed in his ebullience in crisis that at the right moment and in the right place, the drama of politics would afford him supreme moments of total engagement, of feeling alive. But he also understood that the defeat of the Revolution had been a respite, that the battle for Prussia's survival as a conservative monarchy would have to be fought again and won by different, by more daring means.*

The Revolution fed Bismarck's ambition and formed his political realism. He had attacked the king for his pusillanimity in face of the barricades. He had nothing but contempt for the Frankfurt Assembly. He astounded both right and left when in December 1850 he defended the king for bowing before the military might of Austria and Russia and thus abandoning his own scheme of German unification. He did not feel what others called "the humiliation of Olmütz": "According to my conviction, Prussian honor does not consist in Prussia's playing the Don Quixote all over Germany for the benefit of mortified celebrities from parliament. . . . I look for Prussian honor in Prussia's abstinence before all things from every shameful union with democracy. . . ."[28] The king had few defenders in those days.

In 1851 Frederick William IV appointed Bismarck Prussia's delegate to the German Confederation at Frankfurt. Bismarck had become accustomed to public life, but in the early months of his new assignment he was still afraid of his own restlessness. He wrote his wife Johanna: "You are my anchor at the good side of the river bank; if it snaps, then may the Lord have mercy on my soul." That anchor held—though in the same year he confided to his close friend Hans von Kleist Retzow that "the chief weapon with which evil assaults me is not the desire for external glory, but a brutal sensuality. . . . Whenever I am alone and unoccupied I have to struggle against visions of an abyss that come from a depraved fantasy. . . ."[29]

During his seven years in Frankfurt, he grew more serious and no longer cultivated his eccentricities of spirit. In that patrician town, with its rich traditions, its historic wealth, and its cosmopolitan atmosphere, he settled down to sustained responsibility, and the mask of the Pomeranian squire dropped away. He was now playing before a larger audience—and for higher stakes.

Within a few weeks of his arrival in Frankfurt, Bismarck was entertained by the famous Amschel Meyer Rothschild, almost eighty, and the eldest of the five brothers. To his wife Bismarck mocked Rothschild's accent and the Jewish construction of German sentences, but he was pleased to have been invited and was impressed by Rothschild, "a real old Jew haggler

---

* In his memoirs he added this observation: "It has, perhaps, proved better for our future that we had to stray plodding through the wilderness of internal conflicts from 1848 to 1866, like the Jews before they entered the Promised Land." The parallel between Germans in their disunity and Jews in their Diaspora is not without interest in our context. *GW*, XV, 33.

[*Schacherjude*]," and by "the tons of silver, by the golden spoons and forks." And still he saw in him "a poor man in his palace, childless, a widower, cheated by his people and badly treated by his elegant frenchified and anglicized nephews and nieces, who inherit his treasures, without gratitude and without love."[30] Rothschild's orthodox Judaism pleased him, as a sign that he was genuine, unwilling to pretend to be anything but what he was. Bismarck warned his wife nevertheless: "Don't be afraid of this city's men of eminence; according to wealth, Rothschild is the most eminent, and take from *all* of them their money and their salaries, and then one would see how barely eminent each one is intrinsically; money doesn't do it, and for the rest—may the Lord keep me humble, but here the temptation to be satisfied with oneself is great."[31] Humility toward his fellow men was never one of Bismarck's traits; but neither did his restlessness allow him any but the most fleeting moments of self-satisfaction. He thought himself humble before God and the judgment of history. But even in his relations to God, it was he who defined the terms: he spurned the mediation of church and minister. And yet throughout his life and despite all manner of excesses in his anxious aggressions against his own health or against his domestic enemies, he retained a measure of moderation, and a clear sense of responsibility in matters of statecraft, especially in questions of war and peace.

The Confederation, headed by Austria, provided neither Prussia nor its envoy with the power and prestige that Bismarck thought was their due; he bridled at Austrian pretensions and overreacted to every slight, intended or unintended. But as a diplomat he was in a subordinate position, and his Berlin superiors would not heed his pleas for a more assertive policy. His political anger may have colored his personal views about Frankfurt life; he found it all "horribly boring," and he thought diplomacy an appalling piece of charlatanry.[32] Frustrated, he continually annoyed and challenged his Austrian colleague, he ridiculed the envoys of the smaller states ("even with only their shirts on, they don't lose the sense of being ambassadors to the Confederation"), and he complained about the loose morals of the more worldly ladies of Frankfurt.[33] Bismarck had always been attracted to power and intelligence, and there was none of the former and very little of the latter at the Confederation or indeed anywhere in official Frankfurt. Amschel Meyer and his adopted son, Carl Meyer, had both, and unsurpassed wealth and international connections to boot. No wonder he found them worthy objects of his attention. And no wonder they sought to cultivate Bismarck; throughout their history, the Rothschilds have prided themselves on picking winners before they had been recognized as such. They had already picked Disraeli (and Heine); in time, they would discover Winston Churchill.

But after a few months of cordiality, Bismarck had a violent quarrel with the Rothschilds in their capacity as the official bankers of the Confederation. The Rothschilds had always been closest to the Austrian government, which had been the first to bestow honors and benefits upon their house. In 1852, on a relatively minor matter, Austria and Prussia clashed at the Confederation, and the Rothschilds were caught in the middle. The

Confederation urgently needed funds to pay the crew of the tiny German fleet—that ghostly reminder of the liberal hopes of 1848. Ignoring Prussian opposition, Austria, on behalf of the Confederation, asked the Rothschilds for an immediate loan of 60,000 gulden. Reluctantly, old Amschel Meyer obliged—and Bismarck's instantaneous wrath descended on him. In the ensuing recriminations between Bismarck and the Austrian envoy, the latter repeatedly accused Prussia "of taking refuge in the most ignominious and disgraceful of all means—lodging a protest against the Confederation with the Jew." Bismarck countered at once that it was not Prussia's fault if "the Confederation had been dragged through the mud by negotiations with the Jew," but Austria's for applying to a Jew for unconstitutional help. It is instructive to note how quickly both Prussia and Austria demoted the respectable Rothschilds to the status of "Jews": obviously close contacts with Jews remained potentially debasing.

Bismarck's anger persisted; he suspected the Rothschilds of being more frightened of Austria than of Prussia. He dismissed their entreaties and refused their invitations; he appealed to the Prussian prime minister, Otto von Manteuffel, to appoint the gentile rivals of the Rothschilds, the House of Bethmann, as Prussia's court bankers. The Prussian Treasury was more circumspect than Bismarck; they balked at offending the Rothschilds, who had been helpful with loans in the past.[34] After a few months the Austrian ambassador left Frankfurt, and Bismarck thought himself the victor. Quickly reversing his policy toward the Rothschilds, he now wooed them. He regretted their special ties to the indigent Hapsburgs, he realized that Austrian efforts on behalf of Frankfurt Jewry had helped to cement this relation. At the next opportunity, he had Prussia appear as the champion of these Jews, and he repeatedly counseled his government to press the Rothschilds, "this most powerful money power" in South Germany, into Prussian service—much to the annoyance of Karl von Bodelschwingh, Prussia's finance minister, who disliked them.[35]

In 1853 Bismarck endorsed the government's suggestion that the Frankfurt Rothschilds be appointed Prussian court bankers. More than that, he urged that Baron Meyer Carl be given the Prussian Red Eagle, third class. "I have often had occasion to convince myself," he wrote Manteuffel, "that the heads of this financial power would value a distinction conferred upon them by Prussia, since they are not merely very receptive to personal honors but they also regard official marks of the good will of governments, especially of those governments whose financial house is in order, as an important support of their credit." The Rothschilds received the coveted title and Baron Meyer Carl the Red Eagle—but in a form especially designed for Jews. The traditional base of the eagle was a cross; for the Rothschilds (and subsequent Jewish recipients), the heraldic office designed an oval base. Bismarck warned against discriminatory decorations because "all more or less emancipated Jews, and the Rothschilds are such with the exception of the very aged Amschel, will lose all inclination to adorn themselves with a decoration that will have become a stamp of Judaism."[36] Meyer Carl responded just as Bismarck had foreseen: he refused to wear the Jewish eagle.

The personal relations between Bismarck and Carl Meyer, however, remained cordial and unclouded.

In 1858 Prussia's prince regent (later William I) appointed Bismarck ambassador to St. Petersburg. Dissatisfied though he had been in Frankfurt, Bismarck was irked that the regent was putting him on ice up north, while replacing him at Frankfurt with an incompetent successor, Count Usedom.[37] Before he left Frankfurt in March 1859, he asked Baron Meyer Carl for a reliable banker in Berlin. According to legend, he specified that it had to be a Jewish banker. Perhaps Bismarck did say that, knowing that it was unlikely that a Rothschild would recommend anyone else and knowing also that in the field of banking, the Jews of Berlin had established themselves in the leading place. Moreover, a Junker often boasted of a Jewish banker. Perhaps Bismarck thought the Jews uniquely talented bankers, all driven by the same ambition as the Rothschilds; in any case, he wanted a banker who would in no way disturb his own close connections with the Rothschild dynasty.

Baron Meyer Carl suggested Gerson Bleichröder, their subservient and successful agent in Berlin. Bismarck accepted the recommendation, and before he departed for his new assignment, he formally appointed Bleichröder as his banker.[38] He had undoubtedly heard of Bleichröder before, probably as early as 1851, when as a member of the Prussian Diet and rapporteur of one of its commissions, he had examined the operations of the Seehandlung (the government bank) and of the *"Seehandlungsjuden,"* as he put it sneeringly.[39] The two men may even have met in the 1850s. Bismarck must have known something of Prussian finances; in 1856 he was sounded out on whether he would accept the ministry of finance. With characteristic modesty, he intimated his ignorance but thought he could do as well as the incumbent, Bodelschwingh.[40]

Bismarck had no reason to be ashamed of his new banker. By 1861 Bleichröder had bought an elegant and spacious mansion at Behrenstrasse 63, in the very heart of Berlin, within a few minutes' walk of the castle and of Bismarck's future residence at the Wilhelmstrasse. Earlier, Bismarck and his father had lived at Number 60, across the street from Bleichröder's bank.[41] Some of the older bankers in Berlin, such as the Mendelssohns, for example, still overshadowed Bleichröder, but his star was rising as his tie to the Rothschilds became ever more important. When in Berlin, the Rothschild clientele —men of power and wealth and talent—did their banking at the House of Bleichröder in the Behrenstrasse. Even such renowned anti-Semites of later years as Richard Wagner and his wife-to-be, Cosima Bülow, banked there. Cosima received gifts from her father, Franz Liszt, via the Rothschilds in Paris and Bleichröder in Berlin. By the early 1860s Bleichröder's sedate office in the center of Berlin was already crowded with *Prominenz*, with dignitaries from the court, the diplomatic service, the arts, and the international business community.[42]

Bleichröder began his services for Bismarck at once.* He collected

---

* At the very time when Bismarck was leaving Berlin for St. Petersburg—that is, at the time he entrusted Bleichröder with his affairs—he was importuned by a very different kind of

Bismarck's official salary and other income, paid his obligations at home, and established accounts for him abroad. He also invested some of Bismarck's still-meager capital; a part of the income Bleichröder transferred to Bismarck's continuing account with the Rothschilds at Frankfurt. Bismarck and Bleichröder also began the habit of corresponding with each other. Like the Rothschilds, like all sensible bankers, Bleichröder was avid for political news, and Bismarck obliged him occasionally. It was a return for Bleichröder's services. Their earliest relations—of no great importance for either man—will be discussed below. Their paths had intersected, but until Bismarck's return to Berlin in 1862, both men pursued their separate ambitions, each aware, however, that he had found a useful partner.

Before 1862 what mattered most to Bleichröder was his intimate tie to the Rothschilds, especially to the Frankfurt and Paris branches, and that tie alone set him apart from the other bankers in Berlin. It certified, as it were, his integrity and his intelligence, and reputation obviously enhances business. All his life Bleichröder remained in the service of that exacting dynasty, and it was in that service that he learned the effusive but never quite spineless subservience and loyalty that came to characterize his relations with Bismarck.

The Prussian government also came to acknowledge Bleichröder's virtues. In 1858 it awarded him the order of the Red Eagle, fourth class.* In 1861 the Prussian minister of commerce proposed that Bleichröder be given the title of Kommerzienrat. (It was a title given to eminent businessmen; in the 1860s, we know of thirty-one Berlin businessmen so honored, though there may have been a few others as well.) As was customary in such promotions, the minister requested a confidential report from the Police Präsidium and received from it a glowing confirmation of his own estimate. Bleichröder, the report specified, was the sole owner of a large banking establishment, employing twenty-two clerks. He belonged in the seventeenth income class, with an annual tax of 700 Reichstaler on an annual income of 23,333⅓ Reichstaler (roughly $16,000 at the time). The report concluded that Herr Bleichröder, "of unblemished moral character, is in political matters a loyally devoted *Bürger* of H.M. the king and enjoys in wide circles the highest reputation." The minister's suggestion was endorsed.[43] By the time he was thirty-nine Bleichröder had acquired his first order and his first title. The crown—the source of all public honors—had begun to single him out. He had already surpassed his father.

---

banker. A man named Levinstein—presumably also Jewish—offered him a thinly disguised bribe of 30,000 taler a year if he would represent Austrian as well as Prussian interests at his new post. Bismarck tried to extract a written bid, and when that failed, he ordered Levinstein out of his room, offering in fact to throw him down the staircase. The offer obviously implicated the Austrian government. Bismarck came to learn the many uses a discreet banker offered his governmental patrons. *GW*, XV, 142–45.

* Abraham Oppenheim at once asked Bleichröder whether the order had been given in the special form first created for Baron Meyer Carl. Bleichröder's answer is not preserved, but it is probable that the eagle came in the same non-Christian version. In the portrait of Bleichröder he is seen wearing the ribbon of the order, but not the order itself. Oppenheim to Bleichröder, 27 Sept. 1858, BA.

Of course, Bleichröder was a loyal servant of the crown. The Prussian monarchy and Prussian Jewry had for some time lived on relatively easy terms; the monarchy protected and suffered the Jews, and the Jews suffered and served the monarchy. By the 1840s, however, the Jewish issue became entangled with the gradual awakening of political life in Prussia, and the Jews played a notable role in the German revolutions of 1848 and in the German liberal movement thereafter. They were in the forefront of the economic expansion of the 1850s, and in some fields and places, such as banking in Berlin, they had won for themselves a position of preeminence. The growth of Prussian power presented the Jews with great opportunities. By the alacrity with which they exploited these opportunities, they in turn accelerated Prussia's growth.

Bleichröder knew that his welfare and that of his fellow Jews was indissolubly linked to their relations with the Prussian state. The uncertain and impoverished condition of East European Jewry made that all too apparent. Hence Bleichröder was a loyal subject of his Prussian monarch, despite the social disabilities that official Prussian society still imposed. But Bleichröder had other loyalties as well, and it was his good fortune that until the mid- or late 1860s these rarely conflicted. He had a narrower but fiercer loyalty to his fellow Jews, and he still felt very much a part of a separate and not equal caste, the very discrimination against which inspired a sense of solidarity and a touch perhaps of superiority. His loyalty to Jewry was formally demonstrated by his having been elected in the 1860s to the Executive of the Jewish community in Berlin. His intense, unquestioned identification with and loyalty to Jewry facilitated his cosmopolitan loyalties, personified in Bleichröder's case by his ties with the Rothschilds. In the early 1860s these three loyalties could still coexist harmoniously, but the crosscurrents within Prussia and Europe threatened to tear them apart.

CHAPTER 2

Bismarck's Struggle for Survival

Child! Child! Forbear! As if goaded by invisible spirits, the sun-steeds of time bear onward the light car of our destiny; and nothing remains for us, but, with calm self-possession, firmly to grasp the reins, and now right, now left, to steer the wheels here from the precipice and there from the rock. Whither he is hasting, who knows? He hardly remembers whence he came.
—Count Egmont, in Goethe's *Egmont*, Act II

With confidence in God put on the spurs and let the wild horse of life fly with you over stones and hedges, prepared to break your neck but above all without fear because one day you will in any case have to part from everything dear to you on earth, though not for eternity.
—Bismarck to his bride Johanna, March 7, 1847

Bismarck and Bleichröder had met at a critical time in the fortunes of their country. In the late 1850s and early 1860s the politics of Prussia—and of the world—gathered a new momentum. The forces of nationalism were on the march again, while in Russia and America a new struggle for emancipation had begun. In Europe dramatic changes were taking place, symbolized by new rulers, new aspirations, and decisive battles. The old order, created in 1815 and precariously restored in 1849, seemed on the wane again; no one knew what the new order would be like. Only the historian writing with hindsight—often erroneously—sees logic and inevitability; at the time, people grope, improvise, and react. This is particularly true at a time of great fluidity and change, such as prevailed when Bismarck came to power.

But some things contemporaries understood all too clearly. In the late 1850s Austria—the bulwark of the old order in central Europe—suffered repeated reverses. Austria's ill-starred intervention in the Crimean war against Russia had left her diplomatically isolated—and redeemed rather sooner than expected Prince Schwarzenberg's warning in 1849 that Austrian ingratitude toward Russia would astonish the world. In 1859 Austria lost Lombardy to the nascent Italian state, backed by Napoleon III's armies. The multinational empire was out of tune with the new nationalism, and its economy was growing at its own slow and uneven rhythm; the smaller neighbor to the north was steadily gaining on Austria. From mid-century the old empire faded, amidst bursts of revival, amidst a great cultural efflorescence, amidst enough strength to give substance to the ancient glory—so that the decline over decades was dignified and at times disguised.

The example of Italian unification was not lost on the Germans. By 1859 various groups in Germany, mostly middle class in composition, began to clamor for German unification, preferably under the aegis of a liberal Prussian monarchy. Plans abounded, and most of them reflected a new realism, consonant with the strong economic impulse that informed the new nationalism. Unity and freedom was the battle cry, and freedom usually signified the hope for a constitutional regime of laws (but not parliamentary sovereignty), a Rechtsstaat, which would protect its citizens from all arbitrary acts of state. Many groups also pleaded for industrial freedom, for the final end of all guild restrictions on the exercise of a trade. The proponents insisted that economic freedom would unfetter the individual and allow the same full development of his potential that an earlier generation had expected from spiritual freedom.

Events in Prussia seemed to justify the high hopes of the reformist nationalist groups. The accession in 1858 of Frederick William's brother, William, as regent, and in 1861 as king, was generally hailed as yet another "new era" in Prussian history. William was an austere, eminently practical ruler; the ethos of the Prussian army had formed his mind and personality. He seemed imbued with the new realism, and he dismissed his brother's mystical, reactionary camarilla. But almost at once, the new era ended in an old conflict, as king and parliament found themselves at loggerheads.

William's very practicality precipitated the constitutional conflict: he had decided on a drastic reorganization of the Prussian army, found unprepared during the Austro-French war of 1859. Seconded by his minister of war, Albrecht von Roon, and stiffened by the ultraconservative chief of the military cabinet, Edwin von Manteuffel, William demanded that the regular army be augmented in size and importance, at the expense of the popular national guard. It was hard for moderates and liberals alike to swallow the downgrading of the national guard—which had been the special pride of the bourgeoisie ever since the great reformers Boyen and Scharnhorst had created the new military order a half-century earlier. The regular army was the preserve of the feudal class; in the national guard the nontitled, the sons of the middle class, could win an officer's commission and wear an officer's uniform. To be sure, the old system had grown inefficient, but William wanted to seize the opportunity to strengthen not merely the army but the militaristic element generally.

The heart of the reform was a lengthening of the term of military service in the regular army from two to three years—a change that entailed heavy costs. The opposition deputies also wanted a strong Prussian army, but they balked at the money, and they balked at the dismantling of an earlier system. They sensed—correctly—that the king's plan would make Prussia an even more authoritarian state than it already was. William acknowledged that more than military efficiency was at stake; in 1859 he explained that only in the third year did the recruit "understand the dignity of the soldier's coat, the seriousness of his calling, [only then did he] imbibe the *Standesgeist*."[1] But it was precisely this caste spirit—in all its narrow arrogance—that the moderates in parliament did not want the soldiers to imbibe.

At first both government and opposition temporized. In 1860 the government withdrew the army bill and asked parliament to pass a "provisional" bill that provided the necessary funds for reforms but not the specific authorization for changes in the military system. A majority consented. The passage of that bill has been called "one of the most fateful events in German history. It made Prussia an absolute and militaristic state for more than another half-century."[2] But temporizing could not avert the conflict which neither side wanted. In 1861 the more resolute liberals formed the Progressive party, which in December scored an unprecedented triumph in the elections. Thus bolstered, they refused to pass the government's budget, which included appropriations for the three-year term. They banked on the traditional power of the purse; the government would not be able to govern without a budget. But William stuck to his guns, dissolved the chamber, dismissed his moderate ministers—and looked for a solution. The prospects were dismal. On March 11 Bleichröder wrote a personal letter to Baron James in Paris, referring to his earlier coded telegram about the dissolution of parliament:

> According to my innermost conviction, the country will remain entirely quiet during this dissolution, but the new house will be composed of even more democratic elements, if that is possible, and if, as I fear, there will be no compromise in the army question, then in three months we will have another dissolution and at the end a change in the electoral law, with a reactionary ministry or the entire abolition of the chamber. . . . I have not seen the finance minister in the last few days but will do so as soon as it is opportune in order to find out about possible finance operations and will then report at once.[3]

Bleichröder's summary was concise and prescient—and showed his own conservative leanings.

The conflict deepened. The king insisted on his absolute prerogative over the army, the opposition on the inviolability of its budgetary rights. Beyond that, liberals sensed that the conflict would determine the very nature of Prussian society in the future. The liberal deputies were largely lawyers and bureaucrats by profession; their electorate was the propertied classes, favored by Prussia's three-class voting system. Men of affairs voted liberal because they wanted national unification, economic freedom, and a moderate constitutional monarchy. The analogy to Charles I and to the Long Parliament was popular at the time; certainly William had no doubt that a king and his subjects were "clean different." His opponents, however, had little stomach for anything that smacked of civil war. For that, they had too great a stake in the existing society; they hoped to prevail by legal means, by remonstrance, and by refusing to pass budgets. The bloody successes of foreign revolutions—whether English or French—frightened most of the Prussian liberals.

No doubt there was another reason for their hesitancy. The liberals found themselves in happy agreement with the commercial policy of the government, and they voted with near-unanimity for the Franco-Prussian commercial treaty before it was even formally signed.[4] Charles I and the Long Parliament clashed on every issue; William and his parliament at least agreed on economic issues. Such agreement blunted the drive of William's opponents, but they nevertheless found themselves in a deadlock, inadvertent to be sure, but nonetheless hopeless.[5]

In September 1862 the king, discouraged and exasperated, threatened to abdicate. Roon persuaded him to entrust Bismarck with one last effort. William reluctantly consented, and Roon telegraphed Bismarck to return from France, where he had been Prussian minister since the spring of 1862 and where that summer—while Prussian affairs were near collapse—he regained his health and spirits in a passionate, if harmless, encounter with the young and charming Katherine Orlov, wife of the Russian ambassador in Brussels. Summoned by Roon, Bismarck returned to Berlin, in exceptionally fine fettle. His diplomatic assignments in St. Petersburg and Paris had deepened his knowledge of European affairs, but ever since his days in Frankfurt he had longed for the top Prussian post. Already in 1851 he had written to Ludwig von Gerlach that Prussian diplomacy was so organized that only the position of king, Generaladjutant, or foreign minister would satisfy the ability and ambition of an adult.[6] For years he had thirsted not so much for position as for authority, for legitimate power, to direct the fortunes of Prussia in a more intelligent and incisive manner. At the age of forty-seven, the longtime aspirant moved from the wings to the stormy center of Prussian politics.

To have been called to power at the height of the crisis suited Bismarck perfectly. He could deal more easily with antagonists than with colleagues or with equals, and parliament's recalcitrance restricted even the king's freedom of choice. Bismarck was relatively free and quite alone—but to do what?

Everything profound loves a mask, said Nietzsche, and every great ruler has something of De Gaulle's sense that power should be enveloped by mystique. Bismarck was a genuinely complex figure who, though more often baffling by his candor than his disguise, proved unfathomable to his contemporaries. He has eluded most historians as well. The worst is to see his life backwards, beginning as it were with his success. For this perspective slights his years of struggle, when he was groping his way to solutions—years of particular importance, too, for his relations with Bleichröder.

It is hard to summarize in brief Bismarck's aims or hopes when he became the king's first minister.[7] As with all great leaders, character and policy were inextricably intertwined; men do not come in compartments—least of all so titanic a person as Bismarck. In 1862 his achievement was ahead of him; what prepared him for greatness was his unconventional intelligence, his ability to improvise, his exuberant self confidence, his boundless energy, his overweening will, and his indomitable courage. Even then he had the faults of his virtues: at the beginning of his career he was arrogant and cheerfully misanthropic; at the end, he was contemptuous of men, cynically misanthropic, ready to use people as tools to be discarded after use. Above all, he set a prize on realism. He had a fund of pragmatic knowledge, acquired in life and politics, and he had total disdain for theorists or sentimentalists, for men with but a partial or inflexible vision. His bent for practicality made him appreciate a banker who combined worldwide interests with single-mindedness of purpose.[8]

Bismarck had no specific program when he assumed office in 1862. He intended to preserve the authority of the Prussian monarchy at home and to increase its power abroad, for he saw in its strength the best protection against recurrent revolution and disorder. At Frankfurt he had become convinced of the inadequacy of the German Confederation, which was Austrian-dominated and hence injurious to Prussia's interests. In 1856 he wrote to the Prussian premier that "because of Vienna's policies, Germany is too small for both of us."[9] But he also realized that Austrian power no longer matched Austrian pretensions in Germany.

Bismarck had no scruples about exploiting Austrian weakness and isolation. Nor was he unaware that Austria was making desperate efforts to overcome her isolation. Prussian conservatives—Leopold von Gerlach, for example, Bismarck's original sponsor at court and a man of inflexible principles in religion and politics—thought that the German Confederation and the settlement of 1815 were the sacrosanct bulwark against German revolutionaries. Most people at the time thought that the lines were drawn between the national-liberal elements that wanted unification and the monarchical-Prussian forces that wanted to preserve the status quo. Bismarck came to change the equation: perhaps nationalism could be made to serve the monarchical cause. By pursuing what he called "unsentimental politics [ungemütliche Interessenpolitik]," by replacing Austria as the dominant power in Germany—perhaps by means like these, Prussia's aristocratic-monarchical order could be preserved.[10] That was his general direction, and his principled unprincipledness was to estrange former friends and win over former enemies. No doubt circumstances favored his design: Austria was declining and German nationalism was growing. But perhaps no other man could have exploited prevailing winds and currents with equal dexterity.[11]

In the fall of 1862 Bismarck might well have chosen any number of paths—provided they led to a clear and immediate strengthening of Prussia. He made no bones about his unconventional views. A few weeks before assuming office, he told Disraeli: "I shall seize the first best pretext to declare war against Austria, dissolve the German Diet, subdue the minor States, and give national unity under Prussian leadership."[12] In November and December

1862 he repeated these warnings. He told Austrian diplomats that he was immune to terms like "fratricidal war," that Austro-Prussian relations had to improve or they would have to deteriorate, perhaps to the point of war. "We must have the necessary air [*Lebensluft*] for our political existence."[13] He startled the French ambassador, Count Talleyrand, by another candid preview of his possible intentions: Prussia would leave the Confederation rather than allow Austria to use it as an anti-Prussian vehicle; such a rupture would lead to war, "at the first signs of which, we will occupy them [Hanover, Hesse, and Saxony] militarily. We will draw a line of demarcation between North and South Germany and behind that line we shall take our position." Asked what Napoleon would do if things "heated up" in Germany, Talleyrand replied that it would be hard for him to "remain cool."[14]

Bismarck understood the great variety of aspirations that characterized German society at the time. He realized the political importance of economic interests; in 1851 he had already written to his friend Leopold von Gerlach that Prussia should concern itself in time with the material questions in Germany: "The authority which takes the initiative in these matters, be it the Confederate Diet, the Zollverein, or Prussia, will obtain a great advantage in the sympathies of the people concerned. . . ."[15] He believed that most people put material concerns ahead of political loyalties, and he would have recognized the force of Ranke's observation that men "always strive after two things above all else—after honor and wealth," though Ranke's contention that there should be a higher goal in life might have struck Bismarck as mere piety.[16] Bismarck urged that Prussia should abet "the consolidation of the healthy North German elements through the bond of material interests," even at the expense of South German membership in the Zollverein.[17] He had warned against Austrian efforts to enter the Zollverein and bend it to its protectionist needs, and he had fought every Austrian attempt to place German commercial policy in the hands of a Frankfurt majority. He shared the prevalent views of successive governments that Prussia should aim at greater commercial freedom abroad, and he strongly favored the Franco-Prussian trade treaty of 1862 which promoted freer trade and integrated Prussia still further into the dynamic economic life of western Europe. He at once grasped the political implications of this treaty with France and on Christmas Day 1862 drafted a memorandum to persuade William of its desirability.[18] Bismarck was particularly solicitous of the economic needs and desires of the leading classes, most of whom favored the treaty. He knew that material prosperity enhanced the power of the state—and enfeebled the revolutionary fervor or ideology of the possessing classes.

The Junker, who had once managed his own estates and always maintained a healthy appetite for greater profits and more land in his own possessions, and the diplomat, who had dined with the Rothschilds and had seen their power in international affairs, was not quite so much an economic illiterate as he and later German historians have been wont to make out. To be sure, he was more absorbed by the workings of European diplomacy than by the incidence of taxes and tariffs or the fluctuations of the market, but he was not so oblivious of the realities of the nineteenth century as to depreciate the role of material things in his own and his nation's life.

In power, Bismarck had few assets besides the seeming hopelessness of the royal cause and the uncertainty of his opponents. Few people thought he would last; most believed his recklessness would bring him to fall. He had promised William to uphold the army bill, including the three-year term, and to govern even without a properly authorized budget. But from the beginning and behind the scenes he sought a compromise. For all his bluster and contempt for parliament, he did not want to go back to naked absolutism, if it could be avoided. He was not persuaded of the need for the three-year term, and within weeks of his accession to power he seems to have favored an ingenious plan that his friend Roon sought to launch: to allow some soldiers to "buy" their way out of the third year—a system that had an analogue in France. What led one close student of this scheme to suspect Bismarck's hand in it was the devilish quality of it: on the one hand it offered parliamentarians a face-saving formula (and their sons the welcome prospect of shorter service), while at the same time it provided the government with additional and substantial revenue independent of all parliamentary interference. It would have confused and divided the opposition. But William, backed as always by his ultrareactionary friend Manteuffel, rejected the scheme. Bismarck had to look for other solutions.[19]

Bismarck had few friends or allies. The king was suspicious of this hotspur, this mercurial figure who in a day could think of more visions and stratagems than William could accommodate in a year. The crown prince shared the general liberal distrust of Bismarck and noted: "Poor Mama, how bitterly the designation of precisely this mortal enemy of hers will grieve her."[20] Many of Bismarck's colleagues feared him and wondered where this imperious master might lead them to.

Bismarck and Roon were friends; for the rest, Bismarck had contempt for what he saw around him: capable rivals, incapable colleagues, obstructing ideologues in parliament. He spoke sneeringly of "Usedomia" in reference to one of the king's chief diplomats. But despite Bismarck's exasperation with his colleagues, he had to wait a decade or so before he could install his own creatures. (And even then he admitted that he would rather negotiate the most intractable issues with any hostile foreign power than to reach an agreement with a Prussian war minister.)[21] In the interim, he needed expert advice outside the usual channels of government. He needed men of broad perspective and intelligence, men eager to serve but not replace him.

This need proved to be Bleichröder's chance. But in September 1862 and for some time afterward, Bleichröder had no inkling of what was in store for him—or for Bismarck. He remained reticent and skeptical. His main concern was business, and Bismarck's seeming recklessness threatened to exacerbate the constitutional conflict and to weaken the economy.

Bleichröder had friends and sympathies on both sides of the constitutional conflict. Several of the leading parliamentarians were his friends and clients; his coreligionists generally favored parliament against king and held no particular brief for the military party, with its anachronistic views that the army and its feudal exclusiveness were sacrosanct. Prussian Jewry was liberal: of the 160 Jewish electors (*Wahlmänner*) chosen between 1858 and 1866, 92 percent voted liberal.[22] Bismarck's parliamentary opponents were men of means who had a stake in society—and hence some of Bleichröder's natural friends and associates had become reluctant opponents of the regime.[23] On the other hand, Bleichröder had excellent connections with the Ministry, even with the court, and his clients included members of the most blue-blooded nobility.* Like most bankers, Bleichröder had a predisposition to be close to the government, to support it, to remain *regierungstreu*. As Bismarck singled him out for trust and distinction, this predisposition turned into settled policy.

In the early months after Bismarck's accession to power, Bleichröder was a privileged observer—and fortunately for posterity, he shared his impressions and Bismarck's confidences with his most cherished contact in the world, Baron James in Paris. The daily business letters between the Behrenstrasse and the rue Laffitte were supplemented by Bleichröder's personal letters, written in his own, ornate hand. They were sometimes in code, or protected from ubiquitous censors by the transliteration of key words or names into Hebrew letters. They supplied Baron James with the kind of intelligence that a banker-statesman could appreciate and use—and the kind that he received from well-placed persons the world over. Bleichröder's confidential letters to Baron James are an important gauge of his views of Bismarck's early fortunes and of his relations with the chancellor. They are a unique record of a banker's impressions of a turbulent time. They also illuminate Bleichröder's unequal relationship to the last survivor of the five sons of Meyer Amschel, and they intimate his gradual conversion to complete Bismarckianism.†

On September 24, 1862, almost immediately after Bismarck's return to Berlin, Bleichröder wrote Baron James:

We are in the middle of a ministerial crisis! Herr von Bismarck-Schönhausen as minister-president is occupied with the formation of a new cabinet. Roon, the war minister, remains, and this is proof enough that

* As early as 1861, Bleichröder was importuned for money by Prince Charles, the son of Frederick William III and a member of the ultraconservative clique in Berlin. Kühlow's notes, BA.

† Rothschild often charged Bleichröder with little special commissions, like recommending a particularly good gardener or finding a pheasant specialist who could collect the best of the species near Prague and bring them by train to Paris, with Bleichröder responsible for itinerary and all details. For his troubles and expenses, he would occasionally receive a fine pâté de foie gras or some other delicacy. In that delightful and yet precise gift-exchanging world of the mid-nineteenth century, the selection of appropriate gifts and the execution of commissions must have been a time-consuming business for Bleichröder.

the conflict between Chamber and Crown will *not* be solved by the change of ministry. . . . Count Bernstorff and von der Heydt have been dismissed from their posts. As for the new ministry, nothing positive is known, but it appears as if we were to get an entirely reactionary ministry. Bodelschwingh is often mentioned as minister of finance. . . .*

The crisis, he added, had depressed the market, especially in Prussian bonds.[24]

A week later, Bismarck appeared before the budget committee of the Diet and hinted at the direction his efforts would take. He would buy acquiescence at home by gains abroad. He spoke of "favorable moments" in foreign policy which had so often eluded Prussia and which had to be seized to augment her strength: "Her borders under the treaties of Vienna are not favorable for the healthy existence of the state. The great questions of the day will not be settled by speeches and majority decisions—that was the great mistake of 1848 and 1849—but by blood and iron."[25] To Bismarck, this was a simple truism, the distillation of his experiences; to the liberal deputies and their supporters among the public, they were fighting words. Bismarck came to be regarded as a reactionary and militaristic *Provisorium*. At the time no one could forecast the daring, revolutionary character of this "reactionary" regime.

For some time, Bleichröder remained critical of Bismarck's stance. He could see no solution to the ever-deepening crisis, and like everyone else, he heard a spate of often contradictory rumors about the likely dismissal of the new ministry, the dissolution of the Chamber, and the vacillations of the court. In those early days, Bleichröder saw Bismarck but rarely, and hence knew little more than most informed people in Berlin. The uncertainties that hung over Prussian politics continued to depress the otherwise ebullient business community, and Bleichröder was troubled.

By the end of 1862, however, Bleichröder had gained special access to Bismarck, and his letters to Baron James began to reflect Bismarck's confidences. No doubt these letters were also intended to impress Baron James with Bleichröder's new importance—and hence the recurrent prediction in them that Bismarck's ministry was about to fall acquires a special significance. It would have served Bleichröder's interests better if he could have assured Baron James that his newly found source was enjoying a measure of stability.

In late December 1862, Bleichröder reported that "according to the

---

* How Bodelschwingh regarded this call to join the ministry can be gleaned from a hitherto unnoticed letter which he wrote, probably to Bismarck, on September 27, acknowledging an inquiry whether he would be ready to serve in the new government. He was pleased by the turn of events which he took "as clear evidence for the will to offer decisive resistance against democracy and parliamentary regime—for which God may give His blessings. The high seriousness of the situation and the physiognomy of the Diet, now entirely unmasked, are certainly designed to frighten one off from entering the ministry and if one thinks of oneself or one's family to restrain one from doing so . . . but the king by God's Grace has by right to count on all his subjects who with fidelity bend themselves before God's order and will." DZA, Merseburg: Zitelmann Nachlass.

personal information from Herr von Bismarck" the conflict with the Chamber would not be resolved in its next session either. On January 18, a few days after the opening of the new session, he insisted that "a change in the cabinet is much discussed, but not in a liberal direction. The resignation of Bismarck seems close at hand, the entry of von der Heydt (whom Bismarck refused to have) into the cabinet as finance minister in the making, but *no* change in the system." The king, he reported, was still ailing, and more than ever toying with the idea of withdrawing from the affairs of state. A week later he wrote, "Our political situation looks gloomy . . . the present ministry is unpopular to a degree that has rarely ever been seen in Prussia before." The alternative to Bismarck's dismissal was the dissolution of the Chamber, followed by the promulgation of a new and restrictive electoral law, which would mark the final break with the Constitution.[26] Bleichröder was right in signaling even at this early date that Bismarck was trying to break out of the three-class voting system, by which the propertied—who happened to be liberal—had a preponderant representation, at the expense of the lower classes. Bleichröder's letters attest the uncertainty and bewilderment of Bismarck's contemporaries, who no more than the minister-president himself could divine how the government was ever going to extricate itself or Prussia from the existing deadlock.

By January 1863 yet another crisis erupted: the Poles, long suffering under harsh Russian rule, rebelled, and instantly Bismarck sought to help Russian repression. Bismarck's precipitous action in mobilizing some Prussian forces and in concluding an agreement with the Russians (the so-called Alvensleben Convention) angered the French and British; it also aroused Prussian liberals who did not relish their country's role as Russia's jackal in the suppression of valiant Poles seeking their freedom. Bismarck, on the other hand, was worried that Alexander II might succumb to the reformist party in Russia and would make concessions to the Poles, who would thus become emboldened to cause trouble in the Polish provinces of Prussia. Bismarck, like Marx, like most Germans, felt a peculiar fury against the Poles.

During this crisis, Bleichröder supplied Baron James with regular news about Prussia's military and political dispositions. "Herr von Bismarck, with whom I conferred," was the usual source for these authoritative reports. Bismarck had not counted on quite such a storm of protest from the Western powers or from his domestic foes, and he used Bleichröder to reassure the French and to express his amazement that Napoleon might consider the Alvensleben Convention as a "*casus belli.*"[27] The Russians finally canceled the military provisions of the Convention and suppressed the Poles on their own. But Bismarck's position had been shaken, and on February 21 Bleichröder predicted that the crisis would lead to the fall of the government in a few days. "Well-informed sources" told Bleichröder that Bismarck had not been the author of the Convention at all, but that William's military cabinet had concluded it "without his knowledge." An unlikely story, inspired probably by Bismarck himself, who on February 27 told the same canard to the

British ambassador, Sir Andrew Buchanan.[28] In those days of crisis, Bismarck was far from celebrating the Convention as he did later in his memoirs and as historians have generally done until recently.[29] Bismarck's brilliant stroke, as his attempt to use the Polish revolt in order to win Russian friendship has often been called, nearly cost him his post, and Bleichröder promised Baron James to telegraph him in an elaborate code the news of Bismarck's resignation and of his replacement, by either a reactionary or a liberal.[30] According to Bleichröder's information from "the king's private cabinet," Bismarck had offered his resignation, which was being seriously considered. If Bismarck were to go, Bleichröder added, the market would react bullishly. Bleichröder also reported that the Diet had attacked the Alvensleben Convention and had repudiated Bismarck's policy, 246 to 57.[31] In turn, Bismarck accused the opposition of ignorance and treason. He wanted to prorogue the Diet, but the cabinet overruled him; only Roon supported him and wrote him a letter, full of despair about the divisions within the cabinet, and about "E" (that is, Count Fritz Eulenburg, minister of the interior), who either was taking the matter too lightly or was unwilling to "burn all his bridges behind him." In time, his friends, "Noah, Wolfsheim, Jacobi and the other scoundrels, with or without foreskin, will betray him and leave him in the lurch." Roon ended: "You, I, and Bodelschwingh are most deeply involved in this business, and I would not want to go on living if we suffer a fiasco out of—impotence."[32]

Bismarck's fall seemed imminent, but Bleichröder knew that the king would have to scuttle his policies along with the chancellor: "There are no capable men of the same persuasion as the present minister."[33] Bleichröder's reports make it abundantly clear that Bismarck had blundered and for a time had worsened his own position. Perhaps he had worsened it so much that the king could find no other man to pick up the pieces. The immediate crisis waned, as the Russians ruthlessly suppressed the Poles and William retained his embattled premier.

Bleichröder's reporting of the crisis had been swift and accurate. He had supplied Baron James with the same intelligence and at least as promptly as the Berlin embassies had supplied their respective foreign ministries.[34] It is a fitting commentary on the Bismarck-Bleichröder relationship that it was precisely in those weeks of crisis that Bismarck first turned to Bleichröder as a confidant and special conduit. During that time, Bismarck and Bleichröder "conferred" regularly, often several times a week. Bleichröder did not hide the fact of his new intimacy, and crowed to Baron James: "In order to get some clarity in matters of foreign policy, I took the occasion to visit Herr von Bismarck," "I took occasion today to confer for a long time with my well-known source," or, more laconically, "The Ministry received no noteworthy dispatches today."[35]

Bleichröder came to think of himself as a secret collaborator of Bismarck's, as a special adviser to the chief of the Prussian government. Bismarck in turn knew that any information he conveyed to Bleichröder would find its rapid way to Paris and London, and thus he supplied Bleichröder with bits of selected truths. The full truth he kept to himself. He regarded Bleichröder's contacts with the Paris Rothschilds (who in turn were close to the French government) as a useful supplement to his regular diplomatic ties with Paris, the more so as he considered his ambassador in Paris, von der Goltz, anything but a friend. Count Robert Goltz had his own political ambitions, and he had his own conception of Franco-Prussian relations—two capital sins for which Bismarck could not forgive him.[36]

By the spring of 1863, Prussia's constitutional conflict had become still more intense, and Bleichröder was correspondingly gloomy: "From a non-partisan point of view, our politics at home can only be considered pretty wretched." The deadlock persisted; the king would not give up the army reforms and the Diet rejected the budget authorizing them. The Diet repudiated the Ministry with crushing majorities—on one important occasion in May 1863 by a vote of 295 to 5—"the king is furious at these happenings, and the camarilla incites him against the people's representatives."[37] Bismarck hoped that the liberal deputies would weary of their opposition, especially if he could demonstrate that they, not the government, were isolated from the people. Meanwhile he excoriated the deputies publicly—and privately complained to his friend John Lothrop Motley about this "House of clichés": "These babblers really can't govern Prussia, I have to offer resistance, they have little wit and too much smugness, [they are] stupid and presumptuous."[38] By the spring of 1863 Bismarck had established a virtual dictatorship. He defied parliament, harassed the liberal press, and sought to purge the bureaucracy; he confided to friends that the Constitution might have to be abandoned altogether.[39] In the meantime, he bent the Constitution to his own purposes and with a mere pretense of legality decided that the state could continue to collect taxes as in previous years, even though the Diet had not approved a budget. He was playing a daring and inscrutable game, expecting to win several advantages at once. By infinitely complicating the situation at home, he made himself indispensable to William; the king could sacrifice Bismarck only if he sacrificed his principles as well. As for parliament, Bismarck treated its members with contempt, hoping thus to make them contemptible. Meanwhile Prussia's role in Germany was also being compromised. How to break out of this enfeebling conflict? In the end would king *and* parliament come to accept him?

Bismarck ran great risks at the time. In his memoirs, he recalled that in the spring of 1863 friends suggested that he should transfer the estate of Kniephof to his brother because of the Diet's formal injunction that ministers would be liable with their persons and their property for unconstitutional expenses.[40] There is no doubt that the opposition would have liked to strip Bismarck of his office and his property—if they could find a means at once effective and peaceful.

To Bleichröder, as to most observers at the time, Prussian politics seemed destined to go from bad to worse. The situation appeared hopeless. "Allow me to give you a short sketch of our somber internal conditions," he wrote Baron James on May 17, "conditions which unfortunately are suited to open doors to a foreign enemy, conditions which [will] undermine Prussian power, if they last a long time." The conflict between Diet and crown had reached a new height, but the government would neither appear before the Diet nor dissolve it. By ignoring the Diet it "hoped to win the support of the public. I believe that the government deceives itself rather badly, because seven-eighths of the population sides with the Diet and longs for a change in the cabinet." But such a change was unlikely, because the crown believed that the Diet had gone too far "and that conciliatoriness was tantamount to weakness." Hence there was no way out, and "under these conditions, of course, trade and commerce suffer terribly."[41]

In the ensuing weeks the positions hardened still further. On May 22, in an address to the king, the Diet protested the government's continued violation of the Constitution and warned that "Prussia stands almost alone in Germany, even in Europe. . . . Every further negotiation [with the ministry] strengthens our conviction that a chasm separates the advisers of the crown and the country, a chasm which can be overcome *only by a change of personnel*, and even more, by *a change of system*."[42] Bismarck of course thought that a chasm existed between the Diet and the country. Even moderate liberals talked radical, and Hermann Baumgarten wrote to the historian Heinrich von Sybel that the opposition had been too meek: "People who hold constitution, law, and reason in contempt must be made to quake. One has to arouse their intense fear that one day they will be slain like mad dogs. . . . Let Bismarck win even for a short time, and the revolution, I think, is inevitable." Sybel replied that the Ministry could be intimidated not by words, but by force, by the threat of disloyal soldiers.[43]

On May 24 Bleichröder sent another summary of the conflict to Baron James, because, as he put it—prophetically!—Prussia's internal conditions "will play a not unimportant role in the politics of Europe. The harsh conduct of the Diet regarding the army reforms has made the government stubborn and the king, surrounded by reactionary councillors, has chosen the extreme feudal direction, despite his thoroughly upright character." (The "despite" with its implied contrast between feudal reaction and upright character was one of the few indications of Bleichröder's own disposition, conservative-conciliatory, not reactionary-bellicose.) The government, Bleichröder added, persisted in its unconstitutional stance, but would not dissolve the Diet until the king was ready to impose a new electoral law, which "for the time being he can *not* be persuaded to do." Bleichröder's letters suggest that Bismarck sought to persuade the king to promulgate such a law—further indication that Bismarck was contemplating a coup d'état in the spring of 1863.[44] Bismarck told Bleichröder correctly that the Diet would not be dissolved and that the king was "in bitter struggle" with himself as to what policy to adopt. "The fate of Prussia lies in the hands of the monarch," Bleichröder wrote, discounting perhaps the power and resourcefulness of his esteemed friend.

Bleichröder added that "a very large part of the population sides with the Diet, but on the other hand, a great many prudent people think the

Diet is *going too far*."[45] If prudent *Bürger*—and most likely Bleichröder included himself in that category—thought that the legal, nonviolent, but dogged defense of the Prussian Constitution was going too far, then the liberals in the Diet were doomed indeed. At the same time, the liberal leader, Viktor von Unruh, deprecated "the well-to-do bourgeois [who] are politically apathetic. . . . But if the well-to-do middle class and the rich citizen have no political nerve and steadiness, then it is clear that political oppression must constantly increase until the lower classes take up the fight."[46] Like Sybel, like so many liberals, Unruh was afraid that if the liberals failed, the country—and the liberals—would face the dismal alternative of absolutism or revolution. Bismarck, on the other hand, counted on the political conservatism of the masses and hoped to isolate the liberal parliamentarians and prove to the nation how unrepresentative its representatives really were.

The pathetic hope of so many Prussian liberals of the time that the conflict would be resolved naturally, by the death of William and the accession of the liberal crown prince, Frederick William, married to a daughter of Queen Victoria, was a perfect illustration of their view of politics. But Bleichröder pointedly noted that "while the public generally believes that the heir to the throne pursues a thoroughly liberal direction, he and his wife are traveling through the Altmark during Whitsuntide, in order to pay visits to the chiefs of the feudal party there!"[47]

On May 27 the Diet was prorogued, and on June 1, despite the perfect calm in the country, the king, invoking his emergency powers, issued a press edict aimed at silencing all opposition papers. Even the crown prince was alarmed—and quickly muzzled. After the crown prince had protested the press laws, Bismarck told Bleichröder that the crown prince would "under no circumstances" repeat his disavowals. Bleichröder was also alarmed. He assumed that "the rather strict press law" would soon be followed by an edict limiting the constitutional rights of assembly and finally by "comprehensive disciplinary proceedings against civil servants." At its next meeting, the Diet would disapprove of these repressive measures; it would then be dissolved, and elections would be held under a new electoral law, imposed by the king. "Should this not succeed either, then one goes so far here as to believe that a coup d'état would take place. With all these happenings, the country remains entirely quiet, and, as mentioned often before, the danger lies only in external events!"[48] Others hoped that the quiet might be deceptive, and even moderate liberals, like Heinrich von Treitschke, believed that "the revolution is now only . . . a question of an opportune moment. . . . The monarchy of divine grace needs a salutary, frightfully serious chastisement."[49]

Bleichröder's reporting of the hardened conflict at home had been accurate and remarkably dispassionate. His letters also offer clues to his own views. Like Bismarck, Bleichröder was a practical man, mistrustful of abstract principles. Nothing in his education or experience would have led Bleichröder to recognize the ties between a struggle over budgetary rights and personal freedom—if indeed he particularly esteemed the latter. To Bleichröder—as to other men of substance—the struggle was a public nuisance, brought on by the ambition and obstinacy of a few men. Bleichröder thought that politics was a conflict of personalities; the policies of the crown had always been determined by the inclination of monarchs and the intrigues of their advisers, rarely by a clash of issues. He disapproved of parliamentary obstructionism and of extreme feudal reaction. He probably disapproved of a coup d'état. Along with many other businessmen, he wished the conflict might be resolved so that the nation could resume its march to prosperity.

Of that march, Bleichröder knew better than most that Bismarck was a committed partisan. Bleichröder knew of Bismarck's economic interests, both personal and governmental, his concern for free trade and Prussian commercial hegemony in Germany. Bismarck saw Prussian prosperity as an instrument of power; to Bleichröder it was an end in itself. But Bismarck's policies and his support of the economic counselor Rudolf von Delbrück pleased most businessmen, and even outspoken liberals were adherents of Bismarck's economic policies. There was common ground as well as conflict between Bismarck and his opponents—and this fact emboldened Bismarck and enfeebled his opponents.[50]

Bleichröder was a man of peace because peace was the precondition of prosperity. He was also a prudent man. Would any successor to Bismarck bestow the same exclusive confidence in Bleichröder as Bismarck had done in his first year of office? Had any other Jewish banker ever been received so regularly and so solicitously by a Prussian chancellor? Among politically accommodating businessmen Bleichröder was probably preeminent—and for good reason.

In June 1863 Bleichröder reported that the king would soon leave for Karlsbad, where he would most likely meet with Francis Joseph, as indeed he did.[51] During that eventful summer, Bleichröder seems to have suspended his private correspondence with Baron James, probably because each of them was away at one of those great spas, where amidst natural splendor the European elite strenuously pursued its health and social contacts.*

Prussia's domestic crisis deepened, and, as Bleichröder had predicted, foreign complications threatened to exacerbate it. In the summer of 1863 Austria, sensing Prussia's weakness, pushed its own scheme for strengthening the German Confederation under Austrian leadership. As a first step, Emperor Francis Joseph invited his fellow princes in Germany to convene in Frankfurt to consider the Austrian proposals. William thought it his duty to go; Bismarck—in one of the supreme crises of his early career—was determined that he should not go. Bismarck feared Prussian isolation and submission at Frankfurt, persuaded the king to decline, and put forth his own counterplan that called for a Prussian-Austrian condominium and a popularly

---

* A friend of Bleichröder's and an associate of Baron James, Victor Benary, once urged Bleichröder to visit the Baron in Ostend: "You know how good and necessary it is to talk with Baron James from time to time. It helps business more than twenty letters." Benary to Bleichröder, 1 Aug. 1865, BA.

elected national parliament. He remained true to his earlier idea that Austria would have to pay for Prussian collaboration or lose it, and in the meantime, by his proposal for a national parliament, he sought to rally German nationalism to the Prussian colors. The rivalry between the two powers entered a new and critical stage, and Bleichröder reported on September 28, having just conferred with Bismarck, that "the German question still lies in the future, but the present position of Prussia vis-à-vis Germany and especially Austria is untenable in the long run and must certainly give rise to complications."[52] Bismarck may well have inspired Bleichröder's warning to Baron James. The Rothschilds, with their intimate ties to the Austrian dynasty, could play an important role in shoring up the tottering finances of the Austrian Empire. It was best to advise them early and often that Prussia intended to exploit Austrian weakness for the sake of its own greatness. Bismarck emerged from the crisis strengthened, as even some of his domestic opponents grudgingly supported his defiance of Austria. At the very least he had preserved Prussia's freedom of action.[53]

But a new crisis over Schleswig-Holstein had erupted and forced Bismarck to change his course abruptly. The long-smoldering question of the two duchies had flared up anew when in March 1863 King Frederick VII of Denmark promulgated a constitutional decree which would have tied Schleswig closer to Denmark despite various guarantees that the two duchies would not be separated. The fate of these duchies had inflamed German nationalism in 1848; the defeat of the Revolution crushed the liberals' great cause in the north as well. The Treaty of London of 1852 restored the duchies to Danish rule but stipulated that their special joint status should be retained, just as Holstein remained a member of the German Confederation. Despite the Treaty of London, the Danes hoped to create a unitary state. The Frankfurt Diet, prodded by the smaller German states, had worried about the question throughout the spring and summer of 1863. Bleichröder had mentioned the affair in a different context: on May 1 he confided to Baron James that "our ministry has projected a major loan of 50 million taler for naval purposes, but . . . this was reduced to 30 million for the defense of the Baltic ports." The government delayed making the request to the Diet, knowing that it would be rejected in any case. Bleichröder sensed the seriousness of the new crisis and reported that Bismarck had told him that the Danish affair could "lead to serious complications later," but not for three months because armaments would not be ready.[54] It was an ominous warning.

The crisis over the two duchies deepened in the fall of 1863. At the end of September, Bleichröder reported that the Frankfurt Diet was about to threaten Denmark with military action for violating the Treaty of London. He expected Denmark to prove unyielding and added that the market was depressed.[55] In November the Danish parliament passed a constitutional law incorporating Schleswig into Denmark, and two days later Frederick VII died unexpectedly, without a direct heir. The succession issue now compounded the conflict over the duchies. The Danes, their nationalism fully aroused, proclaimed Christian IX as the new king, who at once signed the constitution incorporating Schleswig. Most Germans, on the other hand, insisted that under their ancient law the German prince of Augustenburg had the best claim to become ruler over the two duchies. The issue in all its complexity boded ill for the peace of Europe.

Bleichröder reported that the prince of Augustenburg had visited Berlin but had failed to enlist Bismarck's support. For the rest, "the stock market was swept by a great panic concerning the Schleswig-Holstein affair, and stocks lost 3½ percent, without arousing any buyers' interest."[56] The business community was afraid of military complications and reacted accordingly. For those halcyon days, it was a sizable drop.

In the winter of 1863–1864 Bleichröder saw Bismarck regularly, but his reports to Baron James dwelt mostly on Bismarck's need for money. Bleichröder said little about the premier's intricate policy—perhaps because he knew little about it. Few people could divine Bismarck's aims. It was a time of unprecedented difficulty for him. He had to fight the Danes without jeopardizing Prussia's favorable diplomatic position; he had to contend with German nationalism and all the smaller German states that had rallied to Augustenburg; he had to fend off an alliance between Austria and German nationalism. He had to struggle for the support of William, who if anything was pro-Augustenburg, whereas Bismarck saw no benefit in Prussia's installing a liberal German prince in the northern provinces. The shoals to be avoided were clearer than the shores to be reached. He gradually devised a policy that trapped the Austrians into a common front with Prussia, thus isolating them from the other German states. The ultimate fate of the two duchies was unclear; perhaps annexation by Prussia was an early goal of Bismarck's. His success depended on the apparent clarity and logic of each move and on the inscrutability of his final aims.

During this crisis, Bismarck had no allies at home. He was universally distrusted. Most Germans favored the Augustenburg candidacy, which Bismarck opposed. As an alternative to Augustenburg, most Prussians would have welcomed Prussia's annexation of the two duchies, but Bismarck could never avow that aim publicly without jeopardizing Austria's support and antagonizing Europe. For a while Bismarck posed as the champion of the Treaty of London—a position that earned him good will abroad, but not at home. At no other time was Bismarck so wrongly vilified as during this campaign. Nor could he defend himself, without injuring his chances of success. He clung to his post and policy, and when his triumph took shape at last, his star shone all the brighter for having been obscured before.

For his enterprises abroad, Bismarck needed money—a truth at once obvious to Bismarck and totally ignored by later historians. The Prussian state had continued to collect taxes even without an authorized budget, but the imminent war with Denmark and the likely complications beyond that war, which only Bismarck could dimly perceive, required additional funds which could not be covered from the regular income. Wars were expensive even then, and Bismarck's diplomacy, as we shall see, also liked to boast of a full treasury. A triumph abroad, Bismarck assumed, would successfully weaken the opposition at home, but the continuing hostility of the Diet threatened to deprive him of the funds he needed. He was determined to break out of this vicious circle.

In his search for money he needed help and advice. His own cabinet was divided, and most of its members followed the ineffectual counsels of the finance minister, Karl von Bodelschwingh, who objected to any further step beyond constitutional legality. Bodelschwingh was old, timid—and principled: no wonder Bismarck grew impatient with him. In his memoirs he spoke of Bodelschwingh and Count Itzenplitz, the commerce minister, "as unable to direct their ministries. . . . Bodelschwingh, who according to his personal beliefs constituted the extreme right wing of the ministry, usually cast his vote with the extreme left," because he depended on the advice of his liberal councillors. "I could not expect any support for my policy from these two ministers—because they neither had any understanding for my policy nor a measure of good will for me as a premier younger than themselves, who had originally not belonged to the service."[57]

Bismarck was determined to raise money where he could; legal niceties did not trouble him. As far as he was concerned, the fate of the nation could not be made dependent on some ill-conceived law or constitution, but on power. Put differently, considerations of power and considerations of law were separate and unequal realms to Bismarck. He was willing to resort to unauthorized loans or to the equally unconstitutional alienation of state property. The question was simply how to mobilize the necessary funds in order to exploit the great possibilities which he sensed existed abroad.

In those two years of urgent need, Bismarck depended more and more heavily on Bleichröder. He sought his advice and used his connections. The Rothschilds were of extraordinary importance to Bismarck. He might have wished to have the Frankfurt Rothschilds in Berlin—as the most fitting and promising place in Germany for a member of that dynasty—but he was willing to rely on Bleichröder, who also was formally connected with the Cologne-Minden Railroad, in which the state had an important financial stake. The principal reason for Bismarck's growing reliance on and indeed intimacy with Bleichröder was his trust in the banker's judgment and intelligence. One of Bismarck's chief assistants of that time, Robert von Keudell, wrote that by 1864 Bleichröder, "a man of unusual capabilities," belonged to the inner circle of lieutenants. "His intelligence was as lively as it was penetrating, his memory reliable, his heart staunch and loyal." Bismarck ordered Keudell to keep Bleichröder briefed on "the state of foreign policy, insofar as it was not to be kept secret, so that he could rapidly and correctly understand those revelations" which Bismarck chose to make directly to Bleichröder. The chancellor expected much of this information to be communicated to Baron James, who, still according to Keudell, "always had free access to the Emperor Napoleon, who allowed him to speak openly not only on financial but on political questions as well. This made it possible to send information to the emperor through Bleichröder and Rothschild, for which the official route seemed inappropriate." As a consequence, Bleichröder used to call on

Keudell almost daily; he began to feel "like an auxiliary of the Foreign Office, and he started calling Bismarck 'our highly esteemed chief.' "[58]

Bleichröder saw Bismarck regularly in those two years, often as much as once or twice a week. Keudell could not possibly have known all that transpired between these two men in the privacy of Bismarck's office. Affairs of state were discussed along with Bismarck's personal investments—a subject that will be treated separately in Chapter 5. Bleichröder conveyed as well as received political news. There was no record of their conversations and only traces survive in Bleichröder's letters to friends, especially to Baron James. In those critical years, Bismarck spent more time in Berlin than later, so that Bleichröder could count on seeing the premier whenever urgent business required it; direct correspondence was therefore rarer.[59] Bismarck kept his associates in separate compartments; only he himself knew *all* aspects of his policy. Keudell was unaware—or unwilling to admit when he wrote his memoirs in 1901—that from November 1863 on, Bleichröder not only conducted occasional diplomatic maneuvers on Bismarck's behalf but played a central role in raising money for Bismarck's ventures.

In November 1863 Bleichröder first suggested to Bismarck that the Prussian state could sell its rich coal mines in the Saar area to a private company.[60] The Prussian state controlled a large part of the national coal output, owning most of the Saar mines and some of the largest in Silesia. The liberal business community in the Saar opposed the monopoly and on practical and ideological grounds would have liked a diminution of the state's role. The sale of the Saar mines had already been rumored in 1861, when it was said that the Paris Rothschilds had offered 20 million taler for them. The story was quickly denied, but recurred with extraordinary persistence.

Bismarck knew that Napoleon coveted the Saar coal basin. The French emperor had referred to it explicitly when Bismarck called on him in late October 1862 in order to sound him out about the chances—and the price— of French neutrality in case of a German war. It is unlikely that Bismarck told anyone of these Napoleonic dreams, which in any case he had sought to puncture at once by insisting that William would never consent to the cession of a single German village.[61] Occasionally William proved a stubborn obstacle to Bismarck's plans, but more often he provided a magnificent excuse that Bismarck could hide behind.

There is no indication that the Rothschilds were interested in the Saar mines in 1863. The subject had come up casually in Bleichröder's correspondence with Baron James. There were, however, numerous German companies that would cheerfully have bought the mines from the Prussian state, leaving it with sufficient funds to carry on its nonconstitutional life. On the other hand, the sale of the mines would deprive the state of the annual yield. During the constitutional conflict, the government raised the production of coal and derived about 2 million taler annually from this source.[62] But the rumors persisted. Time and again in 1864, French newspapers reported that the Saar mines were to be sold, and William was annoyed when Austrian papers picked up the same canard, trying to discredit Prussia in German eyes by suggesting that these mines in the German borderland would pass into French hands. The king, a man of simple honor, was furious at stories that suggested another Plombières—when Italy had paid Napoleon for his help by ceding Nice and Savoy. The question of the mines was shelved, for the moment. Bismarck returned to the subject in 1866, in part precisely because he assumed that a Prussian victory over Austria would have to be paid for by compensations to France. But that occurred two years and one war later.

Still, Bismarck needed money for the approaching war with Denmark. On December 7, 1863, Bleichröder wrote Baron James that the government would ask the Diet for a loan of 10 million taler, which the Diet would probably reject. The government would then raise the money by asking for a voluntary loan. Two days later, the government did ask the Diet for 12 million taler for likely military expenditures in connection with the Schleswig-Holstein affair. It acknowledged that a war chest of 21 million taler existed, but because of possible further complications—presumably beyond the war with Denmark—this reserve needed to remain intact.[63] A commission of the Diet deliberated on the government's request and proposed that first of all a petition should be sent to the king warning him against Bismarck's "anti-German policy," which, the commission disingenuously argued, he might be unaware of. Bismarck warned the Diet against such a petition and taunted the deputies with the threat that they would be responsible if in the coming war Prussia faced tiny Denmark with an inferior force. On December 18 the Diet accepted an address to the king, criticizing Bismarck's likely adherence to the London Treaty and cautioning the king against a policy that "threatens to harm the country for a long time to come. Because of the nature of the ministry, we must be afraid that in its hands, the requested means would *not* be expended in the interests of the duchies or of Germany, would *not* benefit crown or country."[64] Bismarck's spectacular successes in 1864 and 1866 made a mockery of these brave words. No wonder that liberal self-confidence collapsed so completely in those two years.

To Baron James, Bleichröder wrote on December 21 that the Diet's likely rejection of the loan would cause the government "great embarrassment." The Diet's commission hinted that the government could cover its needs from the state treasury, but Bleichröder remarked that such an attempt "would be a great burden for the government."[65] The commission also advised that the state could live on its own by alienating some of its property—the very idea that Bleichröder was later to realize for Bismarck.

The commission's report to the Diet quoted Bismarck as having said that he wanted to use legally appropriated funds for the Danish venture, "*but if these were refused, then he would take them wherever he could find them.*"[66] The deputies were outraged, for they were still unaccustomed to Bismarck's brutal candor.

On January 22, 1864, the Diet rejected the loan by a vote of 275 to 51, with the explanation that it disapproved the government's intended policy, which was at variance with the will of the rest of Germany and which could only result in Prussia's fighting a war in order once again to hand over the duchies to Denmark. The more militant deputies opposed Bismarck *tout court*; four days before the vote, Theodor Mommsen had written to a friend that he found the prospect of Bismarck's continued rule—"this *Spottgeburt* of filth and fire"—unbearable, and added that it would probably lead him to resign his Prussian professorship.[67] Other deputies hinted that for a "more national" policy of annexation funds might be forthcoming. In any case, the deputies misjudged Bismarck. To restore the status quo was but one of his alternatives. In their less flexible minds they could never grasp that Bismarck harbored several alternatives, hoping to realize the most desirable one that political conditions would allow.

The Diet's rejection of the loan had deeper reasons, and the Austrian ambassador, Count Károlyi, reported home that the clash between the government and the opposition reflected

> the sorest spot not only of the political but of the social divisiveness which is inherent in the internal life of the Prussian state, to wit, the passionate hatred of different estates and classes for each other. This antagonism, which did not originate with the three-year-old struggle, which indeed dates back far beyond the year 1848 and which places in sharp opposition army and nobility on the one hand and all other industrious citizens on the other, is one of the most significant and darkest characteristics of the condition of the Prussian monarchy.[68]

Even then, the two states were banking on each other's political bankruptcy.

The big question remained: Where could Bismarck find the necessary money? The likelihood of war steadily increased. In late December, Bleichröder could still assure Baron James that his "good source," as he always referred to Bismarck, "did not think there would be a war, unless the Austrian foreign minister, Count Rechberg, were to be dropped, and a liberal regime were to succeed him." William and Prussian conservatives generally wanted peace. They had no wish to be dragged into a war with Denmark for what appeared to be non-Prussian aims.[69] A month later, Bismarck told Bleichröder that "the foreign situation is *not good* and so confused that no person could predict the outcome with certainty."[70] At the time, Bismarck posed as the defender of the *status quo ante* but threatened that if the European powers interfered with the imminent Austro-Prussian occupation of Schleswig, he would feel free to embrace a more radical solution. By his seemingly conservative stand, Bismarck made it easier for the British to rest content with pious pro-Danish statements. Lord Palmerston, though pro-Prussian, was full of bluster about England's concern for little Denmark. Palmerston's policy was bluff, Queen Victoria was staunchly pro-Prussian, and the British cabinet was divided on the Danish question to the end. The result was inaction, and Bismarck's pose made it easier for Palmerston to maintain his verbal virtue.[71]

Bismarck discussed the various alternatives for raising money, including an offer from a South German consortium, headed by the Frankfurt banker Raphael von Erlanger, who had offered the Prussian government 15 million taler, despite the fact that several deputies had explicitly warned private bankers that parliament would not honor loans extended to the government without parliamentary authorization.[72] Bleichröder assured Baron James that "the idea of a loan payable to the crown, as suggested by Erlanger, has been totally rejected." Bleichröder seems to have urged that the government mortgage the bonds of a loan, already authorized by the Diet for railway construction, but not yet issued. The bonds should be mortgaged to bankers who would supply the government with immediate funds and sell the bonds later to the public.

In his letter to Baron James, Bleichröder correctly announced that the crown prince had already left for the northern army, and that the king would follow soon. He predicted that internally the military operations would be followed by further restrictions of the press and by a new electoral law.

On February 1 Bismarck launched the Austro-Prussian invasion of Schleswig, under a favorable European constellation. He had persuaded the Austrians to join this two-pronged attack against the Danes and against the smaller German states that sought to install the prince of Augustenburg. Both powers invoked the London Treaty as the basis for the joint attack, a stance that tended to neutralize Britain. Bismarck was waging war together with Austria, traditionally a more powerful state, but here his junior ally, with ill-defined aims and little prospect of attaining even these. He had entered the path to supreme success, though he could not divine the dangers and detours he would encounter on the way.

On February 3 Bleichröder saw Bismarck again, and on Rothschild's instructions warned him again against Erlanger. All the Rothschilds detested this Erlanger, who "was in his early days an employee, and subsequently the confidential representative of the Rothschilds," and who then turned independent and developed his own successful House, which in the 1850s often and by preference cooperated with other Rothschild rivals and enemies, like the Pereires and the Foulds.[73] The Rothschilds bore implacable hatred toward all their former employees turned rivals, and in this instance Bleichröder seems to have been instructed to ask Bismarck that a "polemical article" against Erlanger be placed in the Prussian press. Bismarck rejected this extraordinary idea, but Bleichröder reassured Baron James that "in any case [the government has been] carefully briefed about Erlanger."[74]

But Bismarck still needed money. At the same meeting, he told Bleichröder that Bodelschwingh continued to oppose a loan, whereas he wanted 12 million taler from somewhere. A decision would soon be taken. Bodelschwingh continued to balk at placing an unauthorized loan, the more so as he insisted that he had "50 million taler at his disposal," though the source of that wealth remained obscure. The Berlin market meanwhile was lifeless, and Bleichröder believed that "at the moment, the capitalists here have kept 20 to 25 million taler uncommitted, pending a clarification of the situation."[75]

These sums would be available for the first attractive issue, such as a new Russian loan the Rothschilds were contemplating at the time.*

During the first hectic weeks of the Danish war, Bismarck frequently saw both Bodelschwingh and Bleichröder.[76] Bismarck's later insistence that he left all economic matters to his ministers was a convenient pose, but in fact he was deeply concerned that Prussia should have the sinews of war.[77]

On February 25, Bleichröder reported that Prussia and Austria had accepted the English proposals for an international conference, but that military operations would continue and that Prussia hoped for some "brilliant deeds such as the storming of the Düppel trenches. . . . These seem to be needed for the *gloire* of the army." Once again Bleichröder correctly sensed the mood of Prussia's ruler, for a fortnight later Roon pleaded with the king that the army must "*win some major victory* in this campaign," and Manteuffel said simply: "In the present state of military affairs, there exists no more important military object than the glory of the Prussian army."[78] The *gloire* was needed for domestic purposes. The people, one hoped, would rally to a victorious army and turn their back on obstructionist parliamentarians.

Bleichröder predicted that at the projected conference Prussia would support a personal union of the duchies with the Danish crown rather than the claims of Augustenburg, as the rest of Germany desired. The dispatches from France, he continued, were "favorable and the relations are once again most friendly, so that an alliance of France, England, and Sweden has become unthinkable." And in the manner of the master whom he had just left, he added: "The German states, though *not* satisfied with Austro-Prussian policy, will calm down and at the most protest."[79]

And still, every day brought fresh news and dangers. Occasionally Bleichröder transmitted some urgent news to Bismarck in writing instead of orally. Thus, in mid-March, he informed Bismarck that the Austrian press reported that "Denmark had refused the conferences!!! Garibaldi's disappearance from Caprera, reported yesterday, would be of great importance, if true."[80] Bleichröder was right about Garibaldi's disappearance—three weeks later he surfaced in England and, much to Queen Victoria's displeasure, began to set out for a triumphant speaking tour throughout Britain on behalf of "poor little Denmark."[81] Garibaldi's program was clear: to wrest Venetia from Austria; hence Austria's enemies were Italy's friends. Had Bleichröder and Bismarck already discussed Garibaldi's potential usefulness against Austria? Why else this hurried note about Garibaldi's sudden and mysterious disappearance?

In early March the Prussian Bank, the Seehandlung, seems to have initiated a secret agreement with Erlanger. Baron James was enraged and

---

* This Russian loan precipitated one of the sharpest contretemps between Bleichröder and Baron James. On February 23 Baron James accused Bleichröder of being indiscreet in this matter, and two days later Bleichröder replied: "Neither in this nor in any other affair which involves the interest of your house have I committed an indiscretion—this be sworn with the holiest of oaths." He urged Baron James to trace the source of this leak to other bankers, such as Kapherr in St. Petersburg and Robert Warschauer in Berlin.

denounced Bleichröder in what apparently was another stinging letter. Bleichröder replied on March 14, in detail and innocence. Even Bismarck had not known of this agreement with Erlanger, "was highly annoyed," and would rebuke Bodelschwingh. Bleichröder moreover had followed Baron James's suggestion to sound out the Frankfurt House about Bismarck's proposal that an already authorized loan of nearly 20 million taler be mortgaged against later issue. Frankfurt had replied that Paris would "remain completely aloof" from such a venture.

> In your interest and so as not to prejudice the government here I did *not* inform my good source [Bismarck] of this refusal. On the contrary, I tried to make him believe that your esteemed Houses would cheerfully lend their support to Prussian finance operations. If I erred in this matter, I could expect *dissatisfaction from my good source*, from you surely only thanks for safeguarding your interests, and as between your good will and that of my good source I did not hesitate a moment.[82]

The less so, one assumes, as to admit that the Rothschilds had refused to help would have injured Bleichröder's own position. The Rothschilds rarely liked to finance foreign wars; but they liked it no better if rivals vied for business they had spurned.

Bleichröder assured Baron James that he had once more told Bismarck that the Rothschilds objected to any Prussian dealings with Erlanger. Bismarck understood the Rothschilds' jealousy, blamed Bodelschwingh for the negotiations, but also mentioned a new offer by Erlanger, to raise 15 to 20 million taler as an advance against a loan which the Diet might authorize later. Bleichröder replied that such an extravagant offer exposed "Erlanger's fraudulence in the clearest manner." Moreover, Erlanger and his fellow financiers apparently put little stock in the explicit warning (already noted) of the Prussian Diet that it would repudiate all private loans to the government which had been contracted without its approval. We know that Bismarck took Erlanger's offer seriously and told the cabinet about it.[83] In the end, as we shall see, he found money elsewhere—and perhaps he exaggerated Erlanger's eagerness in order to stimulate among the money powers the kind of rivalry he liked to stimulate and exploit among the European powers.*

Prussian and Austrian troops continued to make headway against the heavily outnumbered Danes. On April 18 the Allied troops finally gained their "glorious" victory, by storming the trenches of Düppel in eastern Schleswig. Germans thrilled to this first victory in two generations, though

---

* Bleichröder must have persuaded Baron James of his innocence, for relations quickly resumed their unequal intimacy. To attest his loyalty still further he bought and presented to his Paris master in May 1864 an exceptionally rare fifteenth-century bijou "as a feeble token of my deep gratitude." 5 May 1864, RA. Such gifts serve to brighten even the closest of business relations. They reflected more, however. There was substance as well as perfect form in Bleichröder's letter welcoming Baron James's approaching visit to a German spa because it would give Bleichröder a chance "to give proof in person of my love and devotion."

they were still suspicious of Bismarck's mysterious diplomacy. A week after Düppel, an international conference opened in London in hope of finding a solution that would satisfy the various participants in the struggle. Diplomacy did not avail, and by the end of June hostilities were resumed. By this time, the outcome—the defeat of the Danes—was a foregone conclusion.

It was a time of the most intricate maneuvering for Bismarck. In the spring and summer of 1864 political problems were pressing on him from every side, and still he worried about the material basis for his various strategies. He needed money and he needed help—even after the Danes were beaten in July. Few people at the time—and still fewer historians later—realized the heavy burden which the financing of the war placed on Bismarck's unconstitutional regime. "The entire summer of 1864, the ministers were concerned with the question of how to cope with the decline of liquid funds due to the Danish war."[84]

In early May, Bismarck told Bleichröder that the cabinet was deadlocked over the further mortgaging of the earlier 4½ percent Prussian loan.[85] Alarmed by the bearish effects of higher discount rates abroad, Bleichröder urged Bismarck that the necessary operations be carried out "as soon as possible."[86] For more than a month and despite almost daily conferences between Bismarck and Bodelschwingh, no decision was taken.

On June 12 a ministerial council took place, at which the ministry decided unanimously neither to recall the Diet nor to ask for a loan until all other means to cover the extraordinary war costs had been exhausted. On all other issues, the cabinet was divided. A majority of the ministry—five votes against three—decided to cancel pending tax credits and thus raise funds before calling the Diet. A different majority resolved that it would be "impossible" to float a loan authorized by the Diet for the building of a Silesian railroad and divert it to other purposes. The majority of the ministry also decided against trying to obtain a loan without the Diet's authorization. No decision was taken on whether, when the time came, it would be preferable to convene the old or call for the election of a new Diet.[87]

A crown council held the next day, in the presence of the king, continued the debate. First, Bodelschwingh announced that until the end of May, the costs of the Danish war had amounted to 17 million taler and had been covered by past surpluses, amounting in 1863 to 5,300,000 taler, and a state treasure of 16 million taler. Bodelschwingh mentioned other sources of possible income, such as had been discussed and rejected on the preceding day. He urged, however, that before the treasury was entirely depleted, the Diet be asked to authorize a loan to meet the additional costs of the Danish war. The minister of the interior, Count Eulenburg, had urged a similar course in April 1864.[88]

Bismarck and Roon violently opposed this plan. They wanted to float a loan without the Diet's authorization, by resorting to emergency powers. Bismarck explicitly referred to the offers of various bankers who demanded only the signature of the finance minister or at most of the entire ministry, and he insisted that one of them be accepted. A major war might break out and "the article of the Constitution could not mean that the king in such an eventuality would be compelled either to submit to the conditions of the Diet or to give up the country to the enemy." In short, he wanted to make sure that in case of future wars governments would be able to bypass parliament rather than have to meet parliamentary terms for necessary funds. Bodelschwingh and most of the ministers rejected this further flagrant violation of the Constitution of 1850 and, as the finance minister emphasized, of the state debt law of Frederick William III of 1820, which prescribed the approval of the estates for the contraction of new debts. "As long as the ministers of His Majesty must consider themselves bound by their oath to maintain the Constitution, it cannot be considered compatible with this oath to accept a state loan without prior authorization of the Diet." Bodelschwingh also opposed Bismarck's other subterfuge, the use of authorized loans for railway construction for entirely different purposes. The majority of the council seems to have supported Bodelschwingh against Bismarck. No decision was reached, but the king ordered the collection of outstanding tax credits and the use of other available funds.[89]

A little later, Bismarck thought of saving 4,500,000 taler in three months by a reduction of troops. This would have obviated other measures, and foreign opinion would have been impressed by Prussia's ability to finance a major war from regular income. In this way, "nobody would be able to form an opinion about the financial strength of Prussia. The credit of Prussia's finances would be raised in a brilliant manner, and the position of the government would be strengthened anew."[90]

That Bismarck was worried about foreign estimates of Prussian solvency was amply demonstrated by the fact that the day after the inconclusive crown council, he called in the Austrian chargé d'affaires, Count Chotek, and for his benefit drew a cheerful picture of Prussian finances. Bismarck admitted, as was widely rumored anyhow, that some of his colleagues wanted to go to the Diet again and request a loan. He was opposed: "In the first place, no financial necessity exists." Even without the state treasure of 40 million taler, which Bismarck said had remained untouched, "the councillors of the crown had at their disposal 35 million taler without even asking anybody," and he itemized the various reserves. In addition to this total of 75 million taler—apparently a happy fantasy of Bismarck's which Bodelschwingh certainly did not know about—the Prussian government, he boasted, had been offered "considerable funds" from private bankers in western Germany and Holland.

He admitted that there were also political motives for not calling the Diet: "Bismarck added confidentially, 'Ah, if one could only get rid of this whole dirty business known as parliamentary constitutionalism.'" At the end of this at once so candid and so mendacious interview, Bismarck assured Chotek that if a renewal of the war necessitated summoning the Diet, and if it again refused a loan, "an immediate change of the Constitution would appear justified. He had the satisfaction of knowing that in this all his colleagues—even the particularly anxious and legalistic minister of justice—agreed with him."[91] Bismarck's calculated chat with Chotek attests his wish to impress Austria with Prussian prowess, military and financial. Throughout this period of tangled Austro-Prussian relations, when every means of policy ranging from alliance to war was simultaneously contemplated, Bismarck strove to dazzle and confuse Austria by a display of Prussian power and initiative. He realized that Prussia, though smaller, was potentially stronger than the seemingly richer Austrian Empire. Bismarck's triumph over Austria was consciously won against a background of economic superiority.[92]

But Bismarck's ministry was still worried about money. While the chief was in Karlsbad, together with William and Francis Joseph, the Prussian ministers met again on July 6. Eulenburg reported that the threat of dwindling reserves had led him to go to Karlsbad to plead with William for an early request to the Diet for a loan. The king replied—and the answer had a Bismarckian flavor to it—that if the Diet were to be recalled, he would feel compelled to return to Berlin, despite his doctor's urgent warning against an interruption of his *Kur*. The ministry, then, had to choose between the king's and the treasury's health and unanimously chose the former. Bodelschwingh continued to fret. He was afraid that the government would procrastinate until its last reserves had been exhausted.

The cabinet rehearsed all the old arguments, with Roon taking the place of his absent friend and master. He insisted that "in case of urgent [financial] need for the continuation of the war a state loan could be contracted on the basis of articles 63 and 103 of the Constitution, even without the approval of the Diet, in the manner of a provisional decree which would constitutionally have full legal power." Roon's argument was rejected by all present, and it was decided to prepare the convocation of the old Diet for no later than August. At that time, the government would request a loan to cover the expenses of the war, but would reject all participation in the Diet's proceedings pertaining to other questions and would set the Diet a deadline for action, after which it would be dissolved. Roon agreed to this plan, which, if implemented, would have brought about a complete fiasco. Bodelschwingh and his colleagues apparently sought to defend the Constitution to the point of wrecking it altogether.[93] On July 12 Eulenburg gave the cabinet a draft of a memorandum to the king concerning the reconvening of the Diet, but the urgency had diminished.[94]

Between the two cabinet meetings, the war against Denmark had entered the final stage. On June 26 the armistice had ended and Austro-Prussian troops resumed their invasion of Denmark. On July 8 a new cabinet was formed in Copenhagen for the express purpose of seeking peace. In the preliminary peace of Vienna of August 1 and in the final treaty of October 30, the Danish king ceded Schleswig-Holstein and Lauenburg to Austria and Prussia.

The Danish war was over. Bismarck had scored his first great triumph: he had humbled and defeated Denmark without provoking the Concert of Europe. He had hitched Austria to Prussian aims and had pulled her away from her remaining and natural friends, the southern and middle German states. Bismarck's liberation of the duchies, so dear to the hearts of German patriots, had weakened and divided his opposition at home. But the triumph over Denmark settled very little. The most intractable problems remained: What should be done with the duchies? What was to be done with the Confederation? How was the internal conflict in Prussia to be resolved?

Bismarck had won a first round, deviously, brilliantly, barely. The domestic conflict had spurred him on in the adventure abroad—and had impeded him in its pursuit. He was still governing unconstitutionally, that is without a budget that authorized expenditures. He was still in a precarious and lonely position, more hated by far than loved. And he still had a desperate need for money. In the meantime, he had found a resourceful and shrewd adviser in Bleichröder, who in turn found that to be ensconced between Bismarck and the Rothschilds was a uniquely favorable position. He would spare no effort to keep and strengthen that position.

CHAPTER 3

Between the Throne and the Gallows

In the year 1866, he [Bleichröder] put at my disposal the necessary money for war. That was an undertaking which, under the circumstances of those days, when I was almost as close to the gallows as to the throne, compels gratitude.

—Bismarck in retirement

The war had brought Prussia glory and Bismarck some grudging admiration among a few of his erstwhile enemies. The war had not resolved any of his difficulties. It had created new ones. It had not solved the constitutional conflict; it had not solved the dualism in Germany; it had depleted Prussia's treasury. More than that: the war had hastened the moment when the two great powers in Germany would have to settle their conflict one way or the other: peacefully or by war. The war against the Danes had brought the two German rivals together; the division of the spoils would determine whether the alliance had been a step toward some form of peaceful reconstruction of Germany or a mere postponement of the fratricidal war. The duchies had been ceded to Austria and Prussia. Their disposition could not wait forever. The military operations had been simple; the aftermath was excruciatingly difficult.

In the summer of 1864 Bismarck himself did not know the way—later historians who have attributed a kind of clairvoyance to him notwithstanding. His aim remained constant: the aggrandizement of Prussia in Germany (of which the annexation of the duchies would be but symbolic rather than substantive) and the preservation of Prussia's social and political system. In his means he was forever flexible, forever fascinating. His very greatness as a statesman depended upon his ability to temporize, to seek and sometimes to prepare the right moment, the sudden opportunity, which he then exploited with daring speed and skill. Long-range planning would perforce have narrowed choices. Bismarck elevated the perfectly human reluctance to make choices into a supreme political virtue. His genius was at its best in devising "a strategy of alternatives."[1]

The early years of Bismarck's rule, which were also the most difficult, made the greatest demands on him and thus revealed the magnitude of his character. It may be far-fetched, yet illuminating, if in thinking of Bismarck in that phase of his life one recalls a quality that Keats, after a disquisition with Dilke on various subjects, once defined for men in realms other than statecraft: "Several things dove-tailed in my mind, and at once it struck me what quality went to form a Man of Achievement, especially in Literature, and which Shakespeare possessed so enormously—I mean *Negative Capability*, that is when a man is capable of being in uncertainties, mysteries, doubts, without any irritable reaching after fact and reason. . . ."[2] Bismarck's mind was divided between certainties and uncertainties, but few statesmen could have lived with as many dangerous uncertainties for as long as he did.

The fundamental question was the reconstruction of Germany—an issue held over from 1848, understood by Bismarck in the 1850s at Frankfurt, postponed from the first clash over the Congress of Princes in 1863. Put at its simplest, the question was: Would Germany be reconstituted with or against Austria? Would Austrian weakness and her growing troubles with the Magyars make her accept Prussian hegemony in the North or would her debility offer Prussia a propitious moment for war? If the latter, then Bismarck had to be sure that the favorable diplomatic constellation would hold, that Napoleon III would not seize the moment of Prussia's attack in order to demand "compensations" along the Rhine, that England and Russia would not intervene in so drastic a reordering of Europe. If there was to be a showdown, then Prussia's diplomatic and military preparations had to be intact and superior to Austria's. Nor was it easy to walk through the minefields of European politics while at home the Diet was still at war with the government, and the constitutional conflict no closer to a solution.

This much historians have acknowledged. What they have ignored is one specific consequence of the constitutional conflict for Bismarck's statecraft: his constant worry about money. The Prussian treasury was the poorer for the expenses of the Danish war; the Diet proved recalcitrant when asked to replenish the coffers. In the two hardest years of his political life, between 1864 and 1866, Bismarck needed money for the Prussian state in case of war, and sought to deny money to Austria so as to obstruct her preparation. The major works on Bismarck overlook this mundane fact—and thus could more easily ignore Bleichröder's signal role.*

Bismarck was both magnificently daring and scrupulously prudent. In his dealings with Austria, he advanced and retreated, bullied and conciliated, grasped and delayed opportunities—until everything had ripened. The availability of money was not the only reason for that flexibility of means, for what has so well been called his "diabolical simultaneity" in dealing with Austria.[3] But it was one crucial element, and one that he could never acknowledge publicly without revealing Prussia's weakness. No doubt he wished he did not have that extra worry. Perhaps at times he thought it

* As an example, consider Otto Becker's standard work, *Bismarcks Ringen um Deutschlands Gestaltung,* edited and supplemented by Alexander Scharff (Heidelberg, 1958), which in its 832 pages on Bismarck's policies from 1862 to 1870 says almost nothing about the struggle for funds—and mentions Bleichröder once (p. 797), as a transfer agent in the early 1870s!

undignified, as a poet might resent the exigencies of practical life. But Bismarck understood that the historic price of unconstitutionality was fiscal stringency, and he coped with the consequence until he could conquer the cause.

Denmark had surrendered the duchies to Austria and Prussia on August 1, 1864. Bismarck wanted them for Prussia and found German nationalist-liberal sentiment for the Augustenburg dynasty an execrable nuisance. As early as May 1864, Bleichröder wrote Baron James that while the fate of the duchies was still "totally confused, public opinion is being strenuously manipulated and mass petitions are sent to the king pleading that Schleswig should after all be given to Prussia."[4] If this were done, he continued, Prussia's internal situation would improve, the Diet would make generous concessions to the government, "and particularly the loan would be approved."[5]

The future of the duchies, however, could be decided only in conjunction with Austria. Under what circumstances and for what price would Austria continue the alliance with Prussia? Would the old plea of conservative solidarity against "the revolution," which Bismarck had intoned so often, disarm Austria once more? Or would the long dualism in Germany, the rivalry of the two major powers within the Confederation, finally have to be settled by blood and iron, as Bismarck had so often predicted, beginning with his years at Frankfurt?

Bismarck held most of the trumps. He was on the offensive, Austria on the defensive. He knew he wanted the duchies and Prussian hegemony in North Germany. Austria had no plans for the duchies and found this fickle ally that wooed and bullied her by turns hard to fathom. Bismarck sought to keep Austria dependent on Prussia, while cultivating Prussia's relations with the rest of Europe. The key figure was Napoleon III, champion of nationalities but presumably also guardian of German disunity: Could Bismarck persuade that "sphinx without secrets" to continue an anti-Austrian course so as to complete the work of Italian unification, while accepting Prussian hegemony north of the Main? In the summer of 1864 Prussia had more friends and fewer enemies than Austria. Austria, moreover, was on the brink of bankruptcy, and Prussia was potentially rich, provided Bismarck could devise means to tap Prussian wealth. Isolated and financially exhausted, Austria had to face the wily machinations of an infinitely resourceful challenger.

In August 1864, at the celebrated Schönbrunn Conference, Bismarck suddenly suggested that Austria should consent to Prussia's annexation of the duchies, and in return Prussia would aid her, if and when a favorable moment arose, in the reconquest of Lombardy.* It would have been a great

---

* He had made a similar suggestion as early as January 1864, and at the end of February Bismarck sent to Vienna General von Manteuffel, who told his hosts, "Give us a free hand in Schleswig-Holstein, and we will help you reconquer Lombardy in the next war." Károlyi to

reactionary program, anathema to all liberals and nationalists alike, but would have corresponded to one of Bismarck's projected futures: the conservative alliance of the two German powers (presumably backed by Russia), with Austria content to find its destiny in southeastern Europe, while leaving Prussia to dominate the north. In Schönbrunn, Count Rechberg, the Austrian foreign minister, took Bismarck at his word and sought to nail Prussia's commitments in such a way that it would not get the duchies until Austria had received its prize. This had not been Bismarck's intention: he thought Austria should pay at once, Prussia later, if ever. When the Austrians would not accept this, he dropped the scheme, and for two years no definitive solution concerning the duchies was reached.

The presumption of Schönbrunn was peace and the continuation of the alliance. The duchies remained under an Austro-Prussian condominium. Bleichröder was skeptical and two weeks after the conference warned Baron James

> that the great intimacy with Austria has reached its term and a chill will follow. Schleswig's future is still deeply veiled. My good source still thinks that we must reach an understanding with them [the French] and keep Schleswig-Holstein for Prussia. Russia would not object, and Austria and England would remain silent, however unhappy they might be. For the time being this ideal is frustrated by the will of the monarch, who, because of the crown princess, is inclined toward the duke of Augustenburg.[6]

It was a Bismarckian message *par excellence*, a blend of candor and design: Bismarck wanted the French to think that his alliance with Austria was shaky, that he coveted the duchies and needed the French—but there was more between him and the duchies than a sentimental king egged on by his English daughter-in-law. Still, the king needed education, as did Bismarck's colleagues.

Bleichröder's prognosis was quickly confirmed. Commercial issues suddently threatened Bismarck's balancing act with Austria. At the end of June some of the middle states accepted the renewal of the Zollverein; Austria was chagrined and hoped that the possibility of her eventual entry into the Zollverein would be formally reaffirmed. For political reasons Bismarck wanted Austria placated in form, though not in substance, and if Austria cherished "this utopia," as he called it even to Count Rechberg, then Bismarck was willing to pretend it had a flicker of life left.[7] On matters of substance Bismarck was unyielding: despite Austrian dismay, he insisted on the conclusion of an Italian commercial treaty, because in this instance "the future material interests should not be damaged by political considerations."[8]

Rechberg, 28 Feb. 1864, HHSA: PA. Preussen. The best discussion of Schönbrunn is Walter Lipgens, "Bismarcks Österreich-Politik vor 1866: Die Urheberschaft des Schönbrunner Vertragsentwurfs vom August 1864," *Die Welt als Geschichte* X (1950), 240–262.

Bismarck was determined to consolidate Prussia's economic leadership in Germany, both because it further weakened Austria's position and because it brought material benefits to the Prussian bourgeoisie and might dampen its constitutional fervor. At the same time, he hoped to keep Austria in line, and the conservative, pro-Prussian Count Rechberg in power. He urged Rechberg to place political above material interests and to preserve the Austro-Prussian alliance: without it "our monarchs [might not be] equal to their subjects."[9] It was a distinction he did not himself believe in.

But Bismarck's colleagues failed him: while he was recovering his strength in Biarritz, politicking with Napoleon and frolicking with Katherine Orlov, they slammed the door against even the possibility of later negotiations concerning Austria's entry into the Zollverein. At the end of October, consequently, Count Rechberg fell, a victim of the anti-Prussian party in Vienna, which claimed that Rechberg's policy had borne no fruit.

Rechberg's dismissal created new uncertainties and rendered less likely the survival of the alliance. Vienna became restive, and so did Bismarck. But did he at that time aim at an ultimate break with Austria, as many historians have claimed, or would he have been content to gain his immediate and minimum ends without war? The record is ambiguous. On the one hand, we see Bismarck's brutality toward Austria, consonant with his oft-expressed view that a final showdown between the two German powers was inevitable. On the other hand, he took extraordinary pains not to precipitate a war, and he engaged in many maneuvers in order to reach a peaceful solution. Some historians have argued that the latter were feints; perhaps so. Bleichröder took them seriously, and his important role in the ensuing two years supports the view that Bismarck would have been satisfied to gain the duchies without war and to defer the reconstitution of Germany until a later time.

Bleichröder was needed in domestic matters, too. Whatever course Bismarck finally chose abroad, peace or war, he would need money, whether he bought or fought for the duchies. And if he needed money, he needed Bleichröder with his excellent connections in the whole world of finance. Bismarck came to call on Bleichröder for other missions as well, and he did this the more avidly as his official staff, including most of his key ambassadors, came close to sabotaging his efforts in this period. Count Goltz in Paris and Count Usedom in Florence, in particular, were opposed to his policies and his person. The loyal Bleichröder with his shrewd intelligence and international ties proved a welcome complement. Bismarck needed Bleichröder to mobilize Prussian funds; he used him as well in order to deny funds to Austria. He employed him in what probably was his favorite scheme to obtain his minimum demands: the purchase of Schleswig from Austria, which would aggrandize Prussia *and* humiliate Austria. At times, Bleichröder took the initiative and hoped to win Bismarck's support for some particular enterprise that promised to combine profit and patriotism.

Two days after the Danes had signed the preliminary peace of Vienna, Bleichröder wrote Bismarck: "I approach you in deepest admiration in order to wish you and the Fatherland Hail and Good Fortune on the occasion of the victories which were won by the determination of His Majesty the King, by the wisdom of Your Excellency, by the heroic feats of the loyally united great German powers." In order to bring prosperity to the newly liberated population, for so long exploited and "considered as fellahs" by the Danes, Bleichröder urged the creation of a Schleswig-Holstein Landesbank with the primary aim of providing easy credit. The bank, with the right to issue notes, would also help in the collecting of the prospective war indemnity and in the building of the important Nord-Ostsee Canal. The Rothschilds and the Hamburg House of Salomon Heine had already pledged their support, and hence the enterprise—so useful to Prussia and presumably so profitable to its sponsors—could be organized at once. Bleichröder asked Bismarck to advise "the appropriate quarters to facilitate the execution of my project."[10] The bank was never founded, but the attempt to do so brought together Hansemann of the Disconto-Gesellschaft and the Frankfurt Rothschilds, who had only recently been bitter rivals, and Bleichröder's letter demonstrated anew his expectation of reciprocal favors and services. More than that, Bleichröder's suggestion sprang from his obvious belief that Prussia's material initiative in the duchies would bring with it political preponderance as well.*

No sooner had the war ended than the Prussian ministry returned to the troublesome question of its financial resources. In the summer and fall of 1864 Bismarck was mostly away from Berlin, and Roon shouldered the heavy burden of political business as well. The financial question weighed heavily upon him, the more so as he found Bodelschwingh exasperatingly incompetent. In July Roon consulted his best friend, the historian Friedrich Perthes, as to whether the government should convene the Diet and ask for war subsidies. "Bismarck and I are decidedly against it because one cannot let the king solicit these people for money a second time; by granting it, they have the opportunity of rehabilitating themselves in the eyes of the unreflective multitude; by denying it, they would dangerously impair the credit of Prussia in a political as well as in a financial sense." The other ministers, Roon continued, wanted the Diet called, speculating that the opposition either would be intimidated or, if still recalcitrant, "would ruin parliamentarism in Prussia forevermore."[11] Roon prevailed because the government did not need any immediate loan or credit. It had spent less than a quarter of the state treasure, wrote Bleichröder, and "because of the high

---

* A few months later Bleichröder begged the king for support of a similar scheme in the Prussian province of Posen, which contained most of Prussia's Polish subjects. The plan called for the establishment of an agricultural bank which by issuing shares would raise capital with which to buy land in order to sell it to peasants and tenants and to build roads and canals on behalf of local communities. In his petition Bleichröder stressed that this project "aims at the strengthening of the Prussian-national element in the Grand Duchy of Posen." Bleichröder's petition has been cited as proof of his desire to promote the *Germanisierung* of Posen; it is also possible that he stressed that element in order to gain the king's support for a profitable venture. In any case, he knew that the creation of banks in potentially troublesome areas could have useful political consequences. Bleichröder to King William, 19 Jan. 1865, Berlin-Dahlem, Preussisches Geheimes Staatsarchiv, Rep. 90, no. 1186.

revenues, our coffers are full."[12] A month later, Roon counseled gradual demobilization in order to save money "so that we will not fall into the hands of a . . . disorderly Diet."[13] In the preparation of the budget for 1865, Roon again quarreled with Bodelschwingh, and in the fall of 1864 he thought of resigning. Bleichröder heard of serious differences in the cabinet, and wrote Baron James that Bodelschwingh's resignation was expected shortly.[14] Neither minister resigned, and their unwilling collaboration continued.*

The regular session of the Diet opened in January 1865. The battle lines remained the same, but the balance of power and prestige had changed decisively. "Many deputies yearned for a settlement," and Bismarck and Roon were willing to test the possibility of a compromise.[15] Two issues were still at stake: the army reform and parliamentary control over the budget. The military victory had dazzled many deputies; their resoluteness had weakened while the king's had become more dogged and invincible than before. The opposition deputies still balked at surrendering the one basic right to which they had clung since the beginning of the constitutional conflict: the right to appropriate funds and approve their disbursement. A loan to the government would further weaken the Diet's nominal control. The liberals once again bravely protested the many acts of tyranny and arbitrary rule, but they had little hope of redress. Amidst frustration and frequent outbursts of temper, the Diet's session dragged on to its predictable end by dissolution: the session achieved nothing except to render parliament still more futile and irrelevant.

The king's opening address, drafted and read by Bismarck, was conciliatory in tone, but not in substance. The great victories, the king claimed (and worse, believed), had been due to his reorganization of the Prussian army. In fact, the new measures had not yet been implemented and the military successes had been the work of the old army. The king now urged the Diet to accept the reforms, to render their implementation constitutional and thus to liquidate the constitutional conflict. But the liberal majority, though split on other issues, could not yield on this point, and William, duly pressed by the imperious Manteuffel, vetoed a genuine compromise, favored by Roon and Bismarck, i.e. the dropping of the three-year term of conscription. On March 27, by an overwhelming majority, the Diet rejected the 1865 budget and accepted its commission's conclusion that the proposed military appropriations should be reduced, while social and educational expenditures needed to be increased. A month later the Diet rejected the military reorganization bill in its entirety. For a time Roon succumbed to despair, worn out by all the futile fighting: "I have the feeling, nay the certainty,

---

* On October 30, 1864, Roon wrote Manteuffel that he might resign, hinting that Manteuffel should be his successor. Manteuffel declined, explaining that he could have had political positions earlier, but that he would not take them except under conditions incompatible with modern constitutionalism. "But aside from all that, *Your Excellency entered the boat with His Majesty and must now help to steer it*—I shall gladly continue to row." *Denkwürdigkeiten aus dem Leben des General-Feldmarschalls Kriegsministers Grafen von Roon*, 4th ed. (3 vols.; Breslau, 1897), II, 300–301.

that one must *act*." And if action proved unfeasible, then "I can only prophesy for myself Strafford's fate [Charles I's minister, executed in 1640] and the onrushing revolution will triumph over the flag . . . then *finis Borussiae*. . . . I am at the end not of my strength but of my patience and sang froid. And hence I am dispensable, and it is time to go."[16]

In early April, Roon as naval minister introduced a bill authorizing the government to spend 19 million taler for naval purposes, including the fortification of Kiel, in the next six years, 10 million to be covered by a new loan. Since 1848 the navy had been the dream project of liberal patriots. Bismarck once more confronted his liberal opponents with an unpalatable choice: surrender your dreams or your principles, veto the navy or vote credits to the government, even if its policy is unconstitutional. Reluctantly, the majority prepared to scuttle the naval appropriations, and triumphantly Bismarck denounced them for their loss of "maritime ambition," for their failure to exploit Prussia's victory, which had given it a condominium over Kiel, which Prussia alone meant to fortify and keep. Bismarck mocked the deputies' "negative impotence. . . . If you conquered Düppel . . . with the rejection of the loan we demanded then, then I have hopes that out of your rejection of a loan now, a Prussian fleet will emerge."[17]

In May Bodelschwingh gave the Diet a résumé of the extraordinary expenses incurred during the Danish war. The total bill came to 22,500,000 taler, of which less than half had been taken from the state treasure, the rest from surplus income. The government asked the Diet's retroactive sanction for this use of the state treasure, made necessary by the Diet's rejection of the government's earlier request for a loan. Once more the Diet had to choose between surrendering its principles or rejecting support for a victory which had proved as popular with the deputies as with the people at large.[18]

Doggedly, the Diet denied all demands for money. With overwhelming majorities, it rejected the naval appropriations, the funds needed for military reform, and on June 13 declared that the government's recourse to the state treasure without the Diet's authorization had been unconstitutional and that the ministry would be held accountable for these funds. On the same day, Bismarck delivered a scathing attack against the opposition, implicitly accusing the deputies of treason for obstructing the king's foreign policy and facilitating the work of Prussia's enemies. He knew that many of the liberal deputies had thrilled to Prussia's victory; to accuse them of a lack of patriotism would hurt their persons and their political fortunes. On June 17 Bismarck closed the Diet, lamenting that "instead of achieving the much-desired agreement, the end of the session leaves once again the impression of the mutual alienation of those forces which had been called together to collaborate."[19]

The session ended on a particularly bitter note. A fortnight before, Bismarck had challenged Rudolf Virchow, the distinguished scientist and one of his chief opponents, to a duel, because Virchow had questioned his veracity. Even Bleichröder was shocked at this anachronistic extravagance and told Keudell of his misgivings; Keudell sent him several notes about the intricate behind-the-scene negotiations to call off the duel, and Bleichröder hurriedly informed Baron James when the duel had been canceled.[20] Bismarck's irritability reflected his uneasiness about the continued conflict. He had scored one triumph and still parliament held out; in the summer of 1865 Bismarck did not know for certain that he would be able to carry off another great victory without the Diet's financial support. And how many victories would it take until parliament accepted the military reform and compromised its other demands? Bismarck's dilemma persisted: in order to gain victories abroad which would finally compel the Diet at home, he needed money, which the Diet was unwilling to give him. And in the meantime could he drag his timid and unimaginative councillors further along unconstitutional paths in the search for new and necessary funds?

Bismarck's search for funds was carried out against the background of ever worsening relations with Austria. In November 1864 Austria's new and inexperienced foreign minister, Count Mensdorff, thought he could force Bismarck's hand by proposing that the duchies be converted into a new principality, preferably under Augustenburg; if the Prussian government would not curb its annexationist appetite, then Austria would have to be compensated by equivalent territorial gains, either in Silesia or from the Hohenzollern possession in Württemberg.[21] For weeks and months, Bismarck eschewed giving a definite answer, hoping that Austria would weary or that the international situation would prove even more auspicious. In the meantime, he spoke of "magnificent money equivalents" that would be able to restore the Austrian currency.[22] Territorial compensations, he insisted, were nonnegotiable, because William would not hear of them. In February he finally specified Prussia's conditions for tolerating Augustenburg's rule. The new state would in effect have to become a Prussian protectorate, and its army and navy would have to be amalgamated with and subordinated to the Prussian army. Two days before he delivered these exorbitant demands, he wrote Goltz a letter defending his policy of trying to preserve the Austrian alliance. It could still yield benefits.

> I think it more useful to continue for a while the present marriage despite small domestic quarrels, and if a divorce becomes necessary, to take the prospects as they then prevail rather than to cut the bond now, with all the disadvantages of obvious perfidy, and without *now* having the *certainty* of finding better conditions in a new relationship later.[23]

The quarrels became ever more explosive. Austria found neither Bismarck's conditions nor the existing condominium palatable. If the Austrians showed any initiative of their own—such as permitting, let alone encouraging, Augustenburg agitation in Holstein—Bismarck, with his customary insolence, posed as the injured. With a wily, ruthless partner like that, it was indeed hard to preserve the marriage. By turns, Bismarck bullied and threatened, conciliated and charmed, alternated between mystifying vagueness and baffling candor. The Austrian diplomats in Berlin, Counts Károlyi and Chotek, never quite fathomed Bismarck's game. They were reasonable and conventional men—and no match for Bismarck's cunning. If ever husband kept wife on tenterhooks, alternating embraces with rebuffs, declarations of loyalty with feints of outrageous flirtations, it was Bismarck in his treatment of Austria. Lacking Bismarck's aggressive resourcefulness, Vienna left him the initiative.

Austria's first reaction to Bismarck's demands was stunned surprise. Francis Joseph told Baron Werther, the Prussian ambassador, that they were "totally unacceptable."[24] At the same time, Count Moritz Esterhazy, minister without portfolio in the cabinet and highly esteemed as a keen political mind, confided to Werther that Prussian annexation seemed inevitable, that an honest and open annexation was preferable to the disguised form proposed, although it would leave Austria humiliated. To Werther's rejoinder that only a monetary, not a territorial, compensation would be possible, Esterhazy replied that if the former "were high, he would not reject it," though the emperor considered such a scheme dishonorable.[25]

At the same moment, Bleichröder began secret negotiations with an influential friend in Vienna, Moritz Ritter von Goldschmidt. In 1820, at the age of seventeen, Moritz Goldschmidt accompanied his distant relative, Salomon Rothschild, from Frankfurt to Vienna, and for more than half a century was the senior associate of the Rothschild Bank in Vienna. As the Rothschilds' closest collaborator, Goldschmidt had received important favors and dispensations from Metternich, whom he saw frequently, and from the court, dispensations without which a Jew's life in Vienna was still burdensome. (His son remembered particularly his exemption from wearing a still-compulsory yellow badge.) Goldschmidt was on excellent terms with all the Rothschilds, and many of his relatives worked in the different Rothschild banks.[26] He and Bleichröder had been friends for years; both were *hommes du monde*, with entry to their respective courts and to Europe's international elite, and both were faithful Jews who regarded their Jewishness as a special bond between them. It was to Goldschmidt, then, that Bleichröder turned at the end of February in order to see whether the two of them could arrive at some kind of "compensation formula" that would satisfy Austria and give Prussia the duchies.

Bismarck knew of and encouraged Bleichröder's initiative—he may indeed have commissioned it. Bleichröder's efforts, duly authorized, were part of Bismarck's strategy. Bismarck had many lines open simultaneously: this was one of them, and if the peace-loving banking brethren could devise a plan which would satisfy Bismarck's minimum ambitions without war, that might prove a welcome *Provisorium*. Rumors of such a deal abounded: "The idea of a financial transaction, aired in the newspapers since January [1865], had gained ground, especially in banking circles."[27]

Bleichröder and Goldschmidt had a long and intimate correspondence, of which, unfortunately, only Goldschmidt's letters have survived. On March 1, 1865, Goldschmidt wrote, agreeing with his "most esteemed friend" that the difficulties between Vienna and Berlin arising from the duchies were mighty; "and I do not see how these can be eliminated, however much trust you have in our (!!!) mutual good will to collaborate in this endeavor. What can *our* collaboration, dear friend, effect in such a world matter?"[28] He complained that Bleichröder's hints about material compensations were vague and concluded, "You have to express yourself clearly, because with obscure phrases one cannot do such business. Tell me clearly *what is wanted*. I will transmit to the right person in the right manner without anyone talking about it, that I can vouch for with deepest conviction." Bleichröder quickly dispelled Goldschmidt's bemused skepticism—a sure sign that he invoked his "good source" as the instigator of his *démarches*.

A week later, Goldschmidt offered to come to Berlin if chances for successful negotiations existed. He wanted to know what Bleichröder meant by a "fat sum" as compensation, "because it would have to be fat to overcome the immense reluctance against a cash settlement, which would not be very honorable." He admonished him again not to be so "diplomatically mysterious." A piece of Schleswig-Holstein, as Bleichröder had hinted, would be useless for Austria. "A piece of Silesia *en échange* would be more acceptable."[29] On March 9 Goldschmidt wrote: "I am working, dear friend, in the vineyard of the Lord! Whether it will prove useful, we shall soon find out! The mood is more conciliatory!"[30] The stumbling block was the emperor's sense of honor. Goldschmidt consulted with Baron Werther and acted as an intermediary between him and Austrian Finance Minister Ignaz von Plener. Werther had mentioned "40 million florins as *his* idea without instruction from his government," while Goldschmidt thought 60 million a negotiable sum. In any case, he urged Bleichröder to persuade "his resourceful and almighty master, who has superabundant means at his disposal," to give up Hohenzollern (a Prussian Catholic enclave in Württemberg), without the dynastic castle.[31] Would William ever consent to giving up his dynasty's ancestral home—as Victor Emmanuel had done when he ceded Savoy to Napoleon?

On March 14 Keudell wrote Bleichröder that Werther had reported that he had seen Goldschmidt and had mentioned "30 to 40" million, but that he would be instructed not to mention any sum in the future. Bleichröder apparently pleaded with Keudell that the negotiations be pursued more actively, only to be told that "an offer cannot be made from here. If the other side wants financial compensation, let them mention the sum."[32] Bismarck was a shrewd bargainer and seemed disinclined to build Austria golden bridges to renunciation.

Werther reported to Berlin that thanks to Goldschmidt's mediation he had discussed monetary equivalents with Plener. No figures were mentioned, but Plener had said that cash compensation would have to be "much higher" than the Austrian war costs, estimated at 25 million florins, including prewar expenses.

> Plener deplored in advance the outcry that a compromise through cash compensation would evoke in Austria and all of Germany and argued that therefore the compensation would have to be very high. . . . The idea of cash compensation is beginning to gain ground here, especially

among the *haute finance*, which knows the depletion of the Austrian state coffers and which must often come to the rescue.

When William read Werther's report, he said, "The matter of cash compensation could be furthered if the Kaiser knew that a land-trade is against my honor, so that it is honor against honor—and gold is certainly more malleable than human right."[33] At Werther's suggestion, Goldschmidt mentioned 40 million florins to Plener, who replied, "Too little." Goldschmidt worried that Werther's reports to Berlin might disguise the fact that this particular sum had been Werther's own initiative.[34]

Concurrently with these feelers in Vienna, Bismarck made conciliatory overtures in Berlin. On March 11 he quite spontaneously referred to the county of Glatz in Silesia as a possible object of compensation, though William objected, and the local Diet would have to consent to such a transfer.* A few days later, he returned to the subject and told Károlyi that he would favor territorial compensation, even Glatz, but that William had "a certain sentimentality of the conscience" and hence opposed this cession. He suggested, nevertheless, that the Austrians whip up local enthusiasm for such an annexation. "I will happily close one eye."[35] But the two monarchs were genuinely stubborn men, particularly when they felt their honor was at stake. "Their personal relations were excellent," Bleichröder reported to Baron James, but on the issue of the duchies neither would budge.[36]

Shortly after his friendly talk with Károlyi, the wind from Vienna changed, and Bismarck stiffened in anger. The Austrians began to favor the Augustenburg solution. Bismarck was furious at this implicit violation of Austro-Prussian collaboration, and the Bleichröder-Goldschmidt negotiations abruptly ceased. Three weeks later, Károlyi complained to Bismarck about Roon's insistence before the Prussian Diet that Kiel would always serve as a Prussian base, and Bismarck shot back: "I can assure you that Prussia won't retreat; only a lost war, only an Austrian army of 300,000 men, victoriously entering Berlin, could change our resolve."[37] Prussia and Austria inched closer to war, and even William began to feel betrayed by his imperial ally. Bismarck had done his work too well, however, and in the spring of 1865 the king assumed a more intransigent stand than Bismarck, who hesitated to plunge Prussia into war. At the crown council of May 28, Bismarck even urged the elimination of the more troublesome points in the February conditions, perhaps because Prussia's financial house was not yet in order. But William refused, and there was some justification—as well as theatrics—in Bismarck's exclamation to Count Chotek in early June: "I am not Prussia; Vienna must not delude itself on that score."[38]

* Chester W. Clark, *Franz Joseph and Bismarck: The Diplomacy of Austria before the War of 1866* (Cambridge, Mass., 1934), p. 226, argues that Bismarck's support of territorial compensation at the very time when negotiations for selling the duchies were going well was a ruse. By holding out Glatz, he made it unlikely that the emperor would accept cash. Perhaps, although it is also possible that by talking of both forms of compensation, he wanted to appear reasonable and put the blame for the necessity of a cash settlement on the king. It is just remotely possible that he was honestly raising both possibilities.

By June 1865 Bismarck's relations with Austria and with the Prussian Diet had reached a new low. The two conflicts intersected: as the two nations drifted ever closer to war, Prussia needed financial strength far beyond anything needed in the Danish war. The Diet's definitive rejection of help, leading to its dissolution in mid-June, underlined the simultaneity of the threats. On June 19—two days before William's departure for his fateful stay in Karlsbad—a crown council was convened in order to discuss what was to be done with the Diet, and the king posed three alternatives: immediate dissolution, dissolution in the fall of 1865, or a reconvening of the present Diet and immediate dissolution if it proved recalcitrant. Roon favored early dissolution, followed by a royal appeal to the nation, and if that, too, failed, then a new electoral law would have to be promulgated. Eulenburg warned that such a plan might weaken the monarchy and bring about the danger of universal suffrage. There was no safe course.

Bismarck remarked that "for a long time it had been his conviction that with the existing Constitution Prussia could not be governed for any length of time and that a major and far-reaching alteration of it was unavoidable."* The only question was when to strike the blow. Continue to allow parliament to "wither away," he urged, and at the same time harass the opposition and prosecute liberal deputies. Too many elections merely fanned the spirit of opposition and implied that the government was dependent upon a favorable majority. Hence Bismarck wanted to reconvene the present Diet in January 1866, dissolve it at its first misstep, and hold the next elections as late as possible. Finally, Bismarck pointed "to the opportunities which a complication of the foreign situation could yield, and noted that it might be advisable by proper financial operations to weaken the present inclination of the money market toward an Austrian loan." William supported Bismarck's exposition. In short, just before Bismarck had to decide whether to force a break with Austria or not, he had once more to face an uncertain ministry and to grapple with the presumed incompatibility of the Constitution with the envisioned destiny of Prussia and with the grave financial consequences of the domestic deadlock.[39]

Throughout June and July Bismarck pursued his double game: to raise money for Prussia and to deny it to Austria. In 1864 a nearly bankrupt Austria had been helped by a major loan, largely arranged by Adolph Hansemann and supported by the Berlin market.[40] Bismarck did not want a similar operation in 1865, when he thought war between the two countries seemed probable, perhaps imminent. In early June he told Bleichröder that the "actual break with Austria" might not come for months. Prussia would not force the issue or send an ultimatum; if Austria wanted war, however, Prussia would be ready.[41] Such warnings might deter Bleichröder or the Rothschilds from helping Austria. A few days later, Bismarck saw Paul

---

* On June 20 Count Chotek analyzed Prussia's political troubles by saying that the government and the upper house had followed policies that did not correspond "to the customary conduct of these bodies in constitutional states." But, he added, Prussia was far from being a constitutional state. Chotek to Mensdorff, 20 June 1865, HHSA.

Mendelssohn-Bartholdy, a leading Berlin banker, ostensibly to ask him how the business world would react to a war with Austria, more likely to warn him that in the event of war, Prussia could beat Austria in four weeks.[42]

Bismarck's aggressive intentions were reflected by his growing impatience with Prussian finances. In early July he wrote Roon that "through our own money operations [we need] to paralyze those intended by Austria and thus work for the preservation of peace." He discussed the several schemes for raising money, all of which Bodelschwingh opposed because of "his tenderness for . . . the Diet." If money were not forthcoming: "I should have to explain to His Majesty that I would have to suspend our enterprise in foreign policy."* The danger of war was growing, and the new Austrian government would not prove conciliatory: "Its more conservative position at home will demand a more forceful one abroad, just as with us."[43] It was one of the few times that Bismarck admitted the intimate connection between his regime's internal repression and external bellicosity, a connection that for decades was to characterize—and poison—German political life.

From late June, William and Bismarck were in Karlsbad—on Austrian soil—while the dangers of war increased steadily. The conditions for such a showdown were singularly auspicious for Prussia: foreign powers were benevolent or otherwise engaged, Austria's finances were in disarray, its armed forces had to be reduced, and it did not have sufficient funds to wage a war.[44] The king, too, had finally made up his mind that Austrian obstruction in the matter of the duchies was sufficient cause for war. Why then in the ensuing weeks did Bismarck hesitate and, though always ready to go to war, keep a line open for yet another peaceful resolution of the conflict? The question has been a central one in the Bismarck literature, and recently a new answer has been given, which confirms my contention that throughout the four years of Bismarck's struggle with parliament the availability of state credit was a foremost concern for him.[45] Throughout July Bismarck sought to obtain "the necessary funds for a possible mobilization without contracting a loan."[46] He bombarded Roon and Fritz Eulenburg with letters demanding action and hectored Bodelschwingh and Itzenplitz, complaining that his earlier warnings had not been heeded. In this as in all important matters, Bismarck had various schemes that he wanted pursued simultaneously; their constitutionality did not bother Bismarck, who could boast to Eulenburg that the king too wanted money and that he too thought that his duty to maintain the monarchy was greater than his duty to the Constitution. Besides, "if the latter was in any case untenable, then [according to the king] not conforming to its regulations was a preparation for its abolition."[47]

It was precisely in these hectic weeks, when the issue of war and peace hung in the balance and would be partly determined by the flow of credit,

---

* Some weeks earlier, Bismarck had received and underscored a quote from an Austrian official to the effect that "because of its lack of credit the Austrian government would temporarily have to give up its great power position." This was a fatality that Bismarck was determined to avoid. Quoted in Rudolf Stadelmann, *Das Jahr 1865 und das Problem von Bismarcks Deutscher Politik* (Munich and Berlin, 1933), p. 17.

that Bleichröder proved immensely valuable to Bismarck. He was so valuable that he had a major conference with Bismarck in Karlsbad of which, unfortunately, we know no more than what Bismarck wrote to Eulenburg at the time. Bismarck alluded to one possible operation by which Bleichröder would mobilize the Rothschilds to head a consortium to lend money to the Seehandlung, which in turn would advance the money to the government.[48]

But Bleichröder also reported on the successful completion of his most important endeavor of those years. In mid-July the government and the Cologne-Minden Railroad signed an agreement that provided the government with large amounts of money. The agreement was the outcome of protracted negotiations, in all of which Bleichröder was involved as both the company's banker and one of its directors (as his father had been before), and also as Bismarck's confidant. The story is sufficiently complex and important to warrant a short summary.

The railroad had an extraordinary history, illustrative of some of the most important aspects of German economic and political developments. The line had first been proposed in 1833 as a means of bringing cheap Ruhr coal to the Wuppertal. It was completed in 1859, with the decisive help of Bleichröder, who in that crisis year raised the necessary funds, and with the encouragement of Baron August von der Heydt, a Ruhr banker who had long been interested in the railroad and who, as commerce minister since 1848, was the chief proponent of state control and eventual state ownership of the entire Prussian railroad network. For the Cologne-Minden Railroad, Heydt negotiated successive agreements whereby the government guaranteed an interest rate of 3½ percent on the railway bonds, purchased one-seventh of the original shares, and received in turn the right to amortize further shares, so that eventually the state would be the sole proprietor of the railroad. In 1854 the state agreed to suspend its right of amortization until 1870. In the 1850s and 1860s railroads were the most important area of German investment; most of them proved profitable, and their shares dominated the German stock markets.[49]

With the beginning of the New Era, Heydt's policy of promoting state ownership was undermined by private interests and by public acceptance of laissez-faire Manchesterism. Within the government, Heydt was opposed by Karl von Bodelschwingh, finance minister and cabinet colleague since 1851, with whom he had always been at odds. While still in office, Heydt's policies were losing ground, and with his departure from power in 1862, a temporary reversal in German railroad policy set in. Sensing this, Bleichröder submitted a long memorandum to the government in December 1862, suggesting that in return for an immediate compensation from the company, the government cease its guarantee and renounce its rights to eventual ownership. Instead of having to contract loans in 1870 to buy the line, Bleichröder argued, the state should surrender these rights at once and thus gain free and immediate use of 14 million taler, which Bleichröder concluded "could even now find a more useful disposition or, alternatively, could serve to augment the state treasure."[50]

Bleichröder's memorandum was addressed to the minister of commerce, Count Heinrich von Itzenplitz, who referred it to his chief councillor, Wolf. Wolf denounced Bleichröder's suggestions as likely to enrich the stockholders at the expense of the state. Wolf claimed the state would lose 30 million taler by surrendering its various rights, whereas Bleichröder's scheme provided for a compensation of only 10 million taler and the immediate freeing of another 4 million taler of state funds. Wolf deemed the gap between compensation and likely loss outrageous and urged the rejection of the offer. In July 1864 Itzenplitz asked to see Bleichröder's original proposal again, and in the spring of 1865 he solicited and received another expert opinion, with still another schedule of payments, which would have netted the state 17 million taler in cash. The idea of such an arrangement, then, was a familiar one, and the final negotiations, which were largely conducted by Bleichröder and A. Oppenheim of the Cologne banking house, proceeded rapidly. On July 18, 1865, a contract between the government and the company was signed, subject to ratification by the king and the stockholders, whereby the government renounced its right to purchase the stock of the railway in exchange for 13 million taler.[51] In addition, the government was no longer obliged to maintain a guarantee fund for certain minor lines associated with the Cologne-Minden Railroad, and it could sell the negotiable securities that made up the fund. Of the 13 million taler that the company was required to pay, 3 million taler were to be paid in cash by October 1, 1865, 2,705,000 taler by January 2, 1866, and the rest in newly created shares.[52]

The contract may not have been as favorable as Bodelschwingh and Itzenplitz had wanted—quite aside from the fact that both ministers had scruples about concluding a contract that they suspected violated the Constitution. But it had come in the nick of time, and Bismarck and Roon were exultant. On his way to Gastein, William held a decisive council at Regensburg on July 21, at which Prussia's policy toward Austria was once more reviewed. Bismarck could counsel a tough line because the financial outlook had become so much brighter. On the same day, he wired to the crown prince: "After the decisions taken by His Majesty at the council in Regensburg, the financial means for complete mobilization and for a one-year military campaign are available; the amount is circa 60 million taler."[53] A week later, Roon exclaimed to Bismarck's old friend, Moritz von Blanckenburg:

We have money, enough to give us a free hand in foreign policy, enough, if need be, to mobilize the whole army and to pay for an entire campaign. This gives our stance vis-à-vis Austria the necessary aplomb so that we may hope that they will give in to our reasonable demands without war, which none of us wants. . . . Whence the money? Without violating a law, primarily through an arrangement with the Cologne-Minden Railroad, which I and even Bodelschwingh consider *very advantageous*.[54]

The Austrian chargé, Count Chotek, wrote Count Mensdorff that despite the possibility of war, Prussia had taken no untoward military moves; only in the financial realm had the state made extraordinary preparations, of which the principal move was the agreement with the Cologne-Minden Railroad. "These financial operations . . . can be justified only by an urgent political necessity, not from an economic point of view, and [it is doubtful] that the Diet will approve them." The Prussian treasury had accumulated "such an important supply of money as one usually keeps in readiness only in anticipation of a war."[55] The government considered the agreement a part of the constitutional conflict, especially since earlier negotiations with various bankers had collapsed because they had demanded that the loan be constitutionally contracted.

Actually the highest law of the land, the Constitution, had been broken by the alienation of prospective state property, and the Diet attacked the contract later. Roon's enthusiasm, however, may have sufficed to smother Bodelschwingh's scruples. It is doubtful whether Bodelschwingh felt anything but relief that the steady importuning of Bismarck and Roon might now cease for a while.

After the first few days of negotiations with the Austrians, Bismarck sensed that they were serious in seeking an alternative to war. He proved conciliatory himself—at the same time as he realized that the hard cash from the Cologne-Minden contract would not be available for some time and that indeed the treaty had not even been ratified by its stockholders. Meanwhile news from home continued to disappoint Bismarck. Bleichröder reported that on July 17 Baron Carl Meyer von Rothschild had negotiated with Otto von Camphausen, the president of the Seehandlung, concerning the possibility of taking over 9 million taler of the Prussian loan of 1859, which had remained unissued in the coffers of the Seehandlung. Rothschild, acting also for Bleichröder, offered to take them at 98, then 98½; finally he offered 99 and even 99½ for half the outstanding sum. To Bleichröder's dismay, Camphausen stuck to his demand for an offer at par. Negotiations collapsed, and Camphausen placed the shares in small quantities and at par with Berlin bankers. Bleichröder told Bismarck that he thought it "a financial mistake" to have rebuffed foreign help in favor of local money, which in view of the political crisis should have been kept in reserve.[56] As late as August 8, Bismarck wired Berlin from Gastein, inquiring most urgently how far the financial operations had progressed and "when the money would be available."[57]

On August 10 Bismarck wrote Eulenburg that he was working toward an accommodation with Austria, especially since in case of a rupture, "we would need time to make money and secure France." He was hoping to gain "a stopgap tolerable for us . . . with which for the time being we can live with honor without the [possibility of] war running away from us. . . ." So certain was he of reaching an accommodation with Austria that he asked Eulenburg to tell Bleichröder "that if any part of my account with him is still invested in securities, which I don't know here, he should by no means unload these because of some premature fear of war."[58] An extraordinary linkage—at least to us who are so used to having statesmen pretend that they would eschew any "conflict of interests." If Bismarck was making peace with Austria, he certainly did not mean inadvertently to lose personal money on the deal; that he thought this to be a totally unobjectionable desire emerges from the fact that he asked Eulenburg to transmit the message to Bleichröder.

By mid-August Bismarck's diplomacy had triumphed. He had exploited Austria's reluctance to go to war and extracted an acceptable agreement. The Convention of Gastein, as it came to be known, divided the "indivisible duchies" and entrusted Prussia with the administration of Schleswig, Austria with Holstein. At Austria's request, the two powers retained joint sovereignty; in practice this meant little, but it afforded Bismarck countless opportunities to interfere in Holstein (which was the southern duchy that Prussians had to traverse to get to Schleswig) and thus antagonize Austria. The duchy of Lauenburg was sold to Prussia, which also received special military and naval rights in Holstein.

The settlement, which was no more than another *Provisorium*, had brought Prussia some gains, Austria none, except time.* Many Prussians hailed Gastein as an Olmütz in reverse, and Austrian sympathizers lamented that Austria "had made the Gastein Treaty entirely for the benefit of Prussia."[59] The Convention was wrapped up in a show of monarchical solidarity when rulers and ministers met at Salzburg and Ischl in mid-August. But Prussian appetite, whetted by Lauenburg, grew with the eating.

In his confidential letters to his colleagues, Bismarck stressed the financial uncertainties as a major motive for a conciliatory policy: "The conditions of our financial and military preparations made it desirable not to force the break prematurely."[60] No doubt this was true, as this whole story of his campaign for funds makes clear—and yet it was a functional explanation as well. Staunch friend though he was, Eulenburg had not always supported Bismarck in his schemes for raising money; he should be instructed in the consequences of financial pusillanimity, to say nothing of Eulenburg's colleagues. Goltz, too, should tell the French that money had been an important consideration in reaching Gastein—lest the French should think that Bismarck had suddenly embraced an entirely new, pro-Austrian policy.

In the weeks and months before Gastein, Bleichröder had been exceptionally active on Bismarck's behalf. In return, Bismarck appointed him transfer agent for the money that Prussia paid Austria for the purchase of Lauenburg. The Convention stipulated 2,500,000 Danish Reichstaler, which the Prussian treasury paid Bleichröder in Prussian silver currency and which he transmitted to his Austrian counterpart, the Rothschilds at Vienna.[61]

* Still, some critics of Bismarck, like Goltz, thought the Convention more favorable to Austria than Prussia. Otto Graf zu Stolberg-Wernigerade, *Robert Heinrich Graf von der Goltz* (Berlin, 1941), pp. 172ff. Radowitz even thought Gastein "wretched. . . . An Austrian triumph." Hajo Holborn, ed., *Aufzeichnungen und Erinnerungen aus dem Leben des Botschafters Joseph Maria von Radowitz* (Stuttgart, 1925), I, 76

Goldschmidt encouraged Bleichröder to charge a 1 percent commission and congratulated him on the profit made and "the extra kudos won."[62]

The tensions and uncertainties in central Europe continued after Gastein, and Bleichröder's services were still very much needed. Both Prussia and Austria knew that the Convention had merely been a war postponed, a temporary agreement that still demanded a final settlement. In the breathing spell secured, both sides sought to mend their fences at home and abroad.

At Gastein, Bismarck had kept open the two basic alternatives of his policy toward Austria—accommodation or war. He was still willing to bide his time, to see whether Austria would yield peacefully what he knew Prussia could wrest from her violently, though not without danger. He probably sensed that in most respects time was on Prussia's side, because the sheer weight of her material power and preeminence could not but undermine Austria's position in Germany.[63] But Bismarck's predisposition was to hasten the process, the more so as Prussia's internal condition made an early external victory imperative.

For some time, Bismarck hoped that the Austrians might continue their concealed retreat initiated at Gastein. Already at Gastein, he thought that the sale of Lauenburg might set a useful precedent. He did not bargain with the Austrian emissary, but readily accepted all demands, because "our means allow us to pay the whole amount in one lump sum, and I like to prove to you that one can do good business with us."[64] He wrote Bodelschwingh, hinting that the Austrians might sell Holstein as they had Lauenburg.[65]

But the situation changed constantly. A month after Gastein, Bleichröder's associate, Julius Schwabach, wrote the Paris Rothschilds that "the Entente Cordiale between Austria and Prussia seems already badly damaged. . . . It is not impossible that in a short time the struggle will recommence."[66] And in mid-September Bismarck assured Usedom that the Gastein Convention was "of a provisional character," that the question of the duchies had not been solved, and that Prussia's necessary and irrevocable demands had not been fulfilled.[67]

Throughout the crisis of the summer, Bismarck had kept an uneasy eye on the Tuileries. The sudden rapprochement of Prussia and Austria at Gastein surprised and angered the French, and Bismarck at once sought to restore intimate ties with France. He knew that Napoleon held the key to his own future plans. The enmity of Austria and Prussia—at a time of British and Russian preoccupation outside Europe—made Napoleon into a kind of arbiter who at any moment could turn accomplice. To Napoleon all options were open, and Bismarck knew that Napoleon could play the same inscrutable game as himself in order to extract the best possible terms.

After Gastein, Bismarck returned to his favorite and invigorating Biarritz, where he and the emperor enjoyed a political vacation. His talks with Napoleon covered all subjects, but it is unlikely that he sought a formal pledge of French neutrality in a coming German war. The time was not ripe for such a demand. Both in Biarritz and later in St. Cloud, Bismarck answered the emperor's specific question about the future of Holstein by saying that Prussia would obtain it from Austria through "financial compensation or money equivalents."[68] Bismarck was realist enough to know that Napoleon would accept Prussian annexation only for some kind of compensation, which would redound to Napoleon's prestige at a time when the Mexican fiasco had cost him dearly. Bismarck hinted at French-speaking territories, Belgium or Luxembourg, for example, that might make suitable compensations.

Before returning to Berlin, Bismarck went to a hunt at Baron James's at Ferrières, and the two men talked privately for two hours. Apparently Bismarck also told Baron James that he hoped to buy, not conquer, Holstein, and having thus reassured the two powers of France, he returned to Berlin.[69]*

During Bismarck's stay in Biarritz he received a long and urgent letter from Bleichröder. The message was clear: Austria's financial plight, worse even than generally known, should be turned to Prussia's advantage, peacefully. Bleichröder drew a somber picture of Austria: new expenses exceeding the already anticipated "gigantic deficit"; efforts at obtaining help from the international banking world unsuccessful because financiers had their "misgivings" about Austrian solidity and about Hungarian loyalty to the Hapsburgs. Potential lenders were themselves caught "in the calamity in which the principal money markets of Europe find themselves at the present time, on the one hand because of the flowering of manufacturing for exports and on the other hand because of the reckless speculation in transatlantic funds and raw materials. . . ."

Consequently, Bleichröder advanced the startling idea that the Prussian state should help Austria and "through a pecuniary and certainly most welcome help chain its southern ally even more to the lofty policy which Your Excellency is pursuing for Germany's welfare. . . . Because of the most recent finance operations, the Royal Prussian Government has *at this moment*" the necessary funds: 42 million taler without even touching the state treasure, of which 30 million had come from the Cologne-Minden transaction.† The sum might appear inadequate, but even half of it

> offered at the right moment will add to the cold calculation of diplomatic convenience the warm glow of gratitude and determine the [Austrian] cabinet to enter most willingly into negotiations concerning the cession of the Schleswig-Holstein provinces. In my mind I can al-

---

* A couple of weeks later, he received a welcome memento from his stay at Ferrières. As Baron James wrote Bleichröder: "At the recent visit of Count Bismarck he pronounced some of my wines as good, and hence I have taken the liberty of sending to your address a crate of Burgundy and a crate of Bordeaux, with the request that you transmit these in my name to Count Bismarck." Baron James to Bleichröder, 18 Nov. 1865, BA.

† The original agreement had stipulated for 13 million to be paid by the railway; the additional 17 million mentioned by Bleichröder presumably consisted of moneys locked in the guarantee fund that the state had established to cover possible interest payments on the railway bonds. Now that the government was freed of this contingent liability, it could reduce the guarantee fund to 2 million and dispose of the rest as it saw fit.

ready foresee that the cabinet in Vienna cannot allow the northern question to remain open much longer without endangering its internal administration; it *must* resolve the northern question before the much more complicated question of its southern frontier enters into the no longer distant and much-feared stage.

Bleichröder concluded his remarks, "dictated by the sentiment of patriotism," by pointing out that now that "public opinion in Germany has purged itself and has recognized that the principle of nationality stands higher than any particularistic interest, an interest which a pretender [Augustenburg] elevated by a democratic agitation could justify least of all," it was high time to settle the Schleswig-Holstein question "definitively."[70]

Bleichröder's letter—to which Bismarck's answer has not survived—is remarkable for several reasons: it suggests something of his habitual analysis of economic-political issues, which he saw as inseparable; it suggests as well the strength of his pacific inclinations and his expectation that Bismarck shared these sentiments. Bleichröder's proposal was ingenious and extravagant; its adoption would certainly have been the surest token of Bismarck's interest in finding a peaceful solution. Perhaps Bleichröder felt a faint proprietary interest in the money he had helped raise for Bismarck, and he wanted to make sure that it should be spent not for war but for peace, "for buying Austria out."[71] Bismarck never sought to find out whether Austria would have sold her German pretensions for a paltry 21 million taler, and the idea, however sound in some ways, bespeaks the rather excessive faith that Bleichröder may have had in the power of money.

Bleichröder's diagnosis of Austrian needs was correct. The Austrian government was making tremendous efforts to cut expenses, reduce the deficit, and thus create the proper conditions for an indispensable loan. In the fall of 1865 Vienna was not looking to Prussia for succor. It tried in more promising places, and still met rebuffs and unacceptable demands. The Vienna Rothschilds refused outright, as did the London Rothschilds. Baron James negotiated with the Austrians for some time, but insisted on harsh economic and political terms—such as a more accommodating Austrian policy toward Italy. The Austrians preferred to settle with a rival banking group (the Habers, the Crédit Foncier, and the Comptoir d'Escompte), which extracted a heavy financial price but without political strings. The Austrians contracted for 90 million gulden, but at such high interest rates that they would receive only 61½ gulden out of every 100. Even this arrangement depended on the French government's permission to place the loan on the French market; Napoleon's permission was widely regarded as a significant pro-Austrian gesture.[72] The loan secured, Vienna became less interested in selling Holstein. Three days after Napoleon's approval, Goldschmidt wrote Bleichröder that "in the Holstein purchase business there is *absolutely nothing* to be done."[73]

By the fall and winter of 1865, Austro-Prussian relations had once more deteriorated to the point where war seemed inevitable—unless Austria yielded to Prussia's imperious demands. Vienna was disheartened by its staggering difficulties at home, especially its struggle with Magyar nationalism, and it became disillusioned with Bismarck's intermittent bellicosity. Mensdorff sighed, "Does nothing grow on this wretchedly prepared soil of our foreign policy?"[74] The Austrians knew that Bismarck was bent on a showdown, not only from his actions, but from his letters, which they occasionally intercepted.[75]

But Bismarck faced tremendous hurdles as well. By December, Roon believed war to have become inevitable, and he thought that he and Bismarck "might break their necks on this perilous path."[76] To risk a foreign war while locked in a conflict at home was perilous indeed. The relation between domestic conflict and foreign aggression was close and complex. The antagonism at home undoubtedly entered into Bismarck's decision to force the issue abroad, but the principal question remained, whether a people divided on everything but its desire for peace could face a war, and most immediately whether an unconstitutional government hated by large parts of the prosperous section of society could find the necessary financial means even to risk a war. Opinion in Prussia was sharply divided on this point.

To be sure, the liberal opposition was split on the government's foreign policy; some deputies had already succumbed to the magnetism of power and success. Count Chotek reported in October that "the more intelligent majority of the Prussian people" now supported Bismarck's foreign policy, and a month later he commented regretfully that "in the domestic question Count Bismarck is constantly gaining ground."[77] But Bismarck's ever more frequent violations of the Constitution made it hard even for moderate liberals to rally to him completely.

On January 15, 1866, Bismarck opened another session of the Diet, without much hope for reconciliation. The government did not resubmit the military bills, because after earlier "fruitless negotiations . . . it cannot now expect any salutary results."[78] It would, of course, maintain the new military system. The Diet in turn appointed a commission to investigate the constitutionality of the Cologne-Minden Railroad contract. One of the sharpest legal minds of the opposition, Eduard Lasker, a friend of Bleichröder's, directed the inquiry, and the outcome was a foregone conclusion. To allow the government to sell state property without parliamentary approval was tantamount to giving it a blank check and would render nugatory parliament's budgetary rights. The report was unambiguous: "The contract is considered illegal because the government, without the Diet's approval, alienated state property in order to have money for a possible conflict; one member has heard that the same was to happen with the Saar mines."[79] The commission held all parties to the agreement accountable, because the legal issue had been so plain as to make ignorance of the law an inadmissible plea. Bismarck abruptly closed the Diet twenty-four hours after the submission of the report.[80] It was bad enough, from his point of view, that the majority of deputies still clung to its vow, "Not a penny to this Ministry," without running the risk of having to disgorge the millions it had just acquired without parliamentary approval.[81] It was rumored that Oppenheim would ask the government to return the money from the Cologne-Minden Railroad if the Diet formally annulled the agreement.[82]

Government and opposition had clashed over other issues as well. A large majority of the deputies branded the purchase of Lauenburg a violation of the constitutional provision that the king needed the Diet's approval to become a ruler over foreign lands. Bismarck's rebuttal was a masterpiece of taunting obfuscation, designed once again to show up the opposition's impotence. A worse crisis ensued when the Prussian Supreme Court, duly packed for the occasion, set aside lower court decisions and ruled that deputies could be held accountable for speeches given in parliament. The decision, incompatible with the Constitution and ruinous to parliamentary life, threatened to usher in a period of despotism veiled by legal sham, which would destroy both liberty and respect for law. With the prosecution of Karl Twesten for speeches he had delivered in parliament against the corruption of the judiciary, the anger of the opposition reached its height—and the ignominy of the government its depth. No wonder that Bleichröder reported: "Prussia's internal affairs are in bad shape and the gulf between government and Diet is becoming ever greater. The recently announced verdict of the Supreme Court . . . is creating the most painful sensation in all responsible circles."[83] In closing this shortest of all parliamentary sessions, Bismarck once again blamed the Diet for the persistent deadlock and warned that it had entered a path which "would lead to still more serious conflicts and would in the future render even more difficult the resolution of existing conflicts."[84]

And yet the conflict had to be resolved. It was undermining Prussian prestige in Germany, and it left Bismarck at the mercy of uncertain and ad hoc expedients whenever extraordinary funds were needed. Among the king's partisans, there was no consensus on how to end the conflict. Some, like Manteuffel, still favored a coup d'état; others, like Goltz, wanted a change of system: a more liberal regime with himself perhaps as chancellor, and a policy that would attract German nationalists everywhere. Bismarck recognized the possibility of yet another course: he could deflect domestic passion by heating up the quarrel with Austria. He could, as it were, merge the two crises, hoping that they would cancel each other out. It was a time-honored device, to be sure, and one that Bismarck recognized as early as December 1862 when he spoke of the affinity of the liberals for his national cause. He had explicitly disclaimed in the Diet that his aggressive foreign policy was a means in his fight against parliament. Yet the denial merely suggests that both sides were aware of the temptation of the course.

A few days after the Diet had been prorogued, a fateful crown council took place at which it was decided to press for war unless the Austrians were ready to surrender. "There are moments in foreign policy that do not recur," Bismarck had told the Diet earlier, and he finally persuaded the king that the prospect of an Italian alliance and of French benevolent neutrality represented such an exceptional moment.[85] Bismarck and his supporters argued that "a forceful appearance abroad and a war undertaken for Prussia's honor would have a beneficial effect on the solution of the internal conflict."

Bodelschwingh agreed, but hoped that war could be avoided, and the crown prince still warned against a fratricidal war.[86] The external conditions for solving the German question were favorable, but Bismarck's will to seize these conditions was hardened by his certainty that a triumph over Vienna would bring in its train a triumph in Berlin as well. With the calamitous end of the Diet, Bismarck suddenly quickened his pace: he now pressed for immediate decisions and needed immediate victories. His political future, and that of his country, hung in the balance.

The next four months were excruciatingly hard for Bismarck, and his nerves nearly collapsed. To lead Prussia to a showdown with Austria without running the risk of foreign, especially French, intervention put the greatest strain on even Bismarck's unrivaled resourcefulness. He had to isolate and provoke Austria and yet keep a line open to Vienna in case his diplomatic maneuvers threatened to fail. At any moment his plans could have been crossed and destroyed by the coalescing of his enemy with jealous neutral powers, by a successful conspiracy at home, or by a weakening of the king's trust or resolution. It was a time of tremendous risks, and Bismarck was set to fight fire with fire. He was willing to risk all, to use every means, however revolutionary, to reach his end. It was a time, too, when his former friends at home, even his best Junker friends, deserted him, appalled by his daring and unprincipled policies. His old liberal enemies detested his restoration of absolutism, though some were seduced by his new German policy and many were dazzled and bewildered by his virtuosity, his genius. "And still," wrote Rudolf Haym, the liberal writer, in May, "who can fail to recognize the luck and talent of this man, with all his presumption and frivolity?"[87] The mood of the country, however, was overwhelmingly antiwar and anti-Bismarck.

Bismarck's political maneuvering depended upon Prussia's military readiness—and for this he could rely on the brilliant support of Roon and Hellmuth von Moltke, Prussian chief of staff. But political and military ingenuity was not enough. An army still marched on its stomach, and money had to be mobilized as well as men. In this field, Bismarck was less sure-footed than in political affairs and hence all the more exasperated by the incompetence and pettifogging of Bodelschwingh. At the end of March 1866, when the cabinet for once was united, Roon remarked, "Bismarck's neurotic impatience and Bodelschwingh's bureaucratic niceties and worries have made sure that not all discords have disappeared."[88] Because of Bodelschwingh, "Prussia's financial preparedness did not even remotely correspond to its military readiness."[89] But Bodelschwingh's task was immensely difficult, for the Diet would not budge from its opposition and the Berlin money market, shaken by a worldwide contraction, became nervous as war approached. New means would have to be found, and here, too, Bismarck had to try different paths before he found the right one, but the terrain was less familiar to him.

Hence Bleichröder proved of great help to Bismarck in these hardest months of his life. In the months before the war, Bleichröder was active on all fronts and fell in with his chief's bellicose as well as pacific plans. Bleichröder would have preferred a peaceful outcome of the crisis, as did the business community of Germany and indeed of Europe. And yet he was to be remembered and honored only for his help in mobilizing funds for war.

From mid-February 1866 on, Bleichröder's correspondence with Goldschmidt reflected renewed, intense uneasiness about a possible war. On February 18 Goldschmidt consoled him with the thought that wars do not break out so abruptly, but he added a telegraphic code so that Bleichröder could inform him at once of any dramatic development. "You must always exert yourself in favor of conciliation," Goldschmidt wrote him. "I do the same, and write me diligently how things are at your place. You know that I am careful and discreet."[90] Baron Anselm also asked for Bleichröder's news. In late February the Berlin banker was far more pessimistic than his Viennese friends, and his fears give some credibility to the story that right after the crown council of February 28, he warned his friend Count Hohenthal, the Saxon minister in Berlin, that the council had debated the question of a sudden invasion of Saxony, but that it had agreed to postpone the attack until "the instant war was decided upon in principle and before mobilization took place."[91] Was Bleichröder's warning, if delivered, carried out at Bismarck's instigation? The evidence is ambiguous, but that Bleichröder was greatly worried is beyond doubt.

At the eleventh hour, Bleichröder and Goldschmidt revived their earlier hopes that a compensation formula for the duchies could be found. The idea cropped up elsewhere, too, and even Bismarck mentioned it intermittently in March, adding the preposterous suggestion that Austria should send a compensation proposal in the form of an ultimatum which might budge William's stubborn opposition.[92] (The Austrians might well have wondered whether this was a trap for William or for them.) Most of the time Bismarck pursued bellicose plans. Still, the two bankers, troubled by the business paralysis induced by the threat of war, seized every opportunity of promoting peace and in March sought support for Mensdorff's policy of avoiding war. Goldschmidt suggested that if some territory, such as Glatz, were added to a cash settlement, the Austrians might accept the deal. He urged Bleichröder "to do all that is possible. . . . [W]ar would be too criminal and a curse . . . for Germany." Goldschmidt promised to submit any serious, even if informal, offer of money and territory directly to the emperor.[93] A few days later, Goldschmidt despaired of helping: "We are both too unimportant to interfere in *such* situations."

As hopes for peace faded, nationalist passions spilled into this correspondence, hitherto so matter-of-fact and disinterested. Goldschmidt was angry with Prussia, the aggressive power, and inconsolable at the thought of a fratricidal war. "The public bitterness against the originator [Bismarck] of these desperate conditions grows daily here, and if, God forbid, war comes, then it will be fought here with great energy and universal support, even if we don't have any money." Despite Bleichröder's rejoinders, Goldschmidt insisted that all provocation came from Bismarck. He denied that Austria had begun to move troops. "I tell you frankly that the war is being deliberately planned and the world thrown into misfortune—by Bismarck. . . . With patience one could have won in time what nobody here will be bullied into giving up."[94] Pride, fear, and anger filled Goldschmidt's letters—and his anger fastened on one man.

Many others in Europe, and in Prussia, felt the same indignation at Bismarck's provocative game. At the end of March, an international cabal, known as the "Coburg intrigue," involving some of Bismarck's colleagues, tried to persuade William to dismiss the reckless character who was misleading him.[95] At the heart of this intrigue was the sentiment expressed by Lord John Russell to Queen Victoria: "There is but one remedy—one certain . . . [way] of preserving peace—it is the dismissal of Count Bismarck by the king."[96] As a part of it, the *Kölner Zeitung* on April 1 suggested that Prussia trade Glatz for Holstein.[97] The idea found an immediate, favorable echo among many Prussians.* Rumors about Bismarck's dismissal made the rounds again, and people took note of his powerful enemies. On April 4, for example, the king's son wrote to one of Bismarck's ministers that "Rothschild is moving heaven and earth [against] Bismarck, that the financiers are trembling."[98] Bismarck had ample reason to appreciate Bleichröder's loyalty: it was a rare commodity at that time.

In mid-February Bleichröder began his new quest for money, turning first of all to his most powerful connection, Baron James. If the Rothschilds had embarked on a pro-Prussian policy, other bankers would have followed suit. But no such signal appeared. Bleichröder wanted to know whether the Rothschilds would head or join a consortium to buy the 8 million taler's worth of shares of Cologne-Minden, which the Prussian government wanted to sell. The Rothschilds, knowing that any such operation would fill Prussia's war chest, refused. Some four years earlier, apropos of an earlier Prussian solicitation, Baron James had already explained to Bleichröder that "it is a principle of our Houses not to advance any money for war and even if it is not in our power to prevent war, then our minds at least can be easy that we have not contributed to it."[99]

But more than pacific sentiment was at work. The world market was depressed, share prices had begun to falter everywhere, and every rumor of war sent them diving. Baron James complained of economic stagnation and Napoleonic posturing: "L'Empire, c'est la baisse," he punned, referring to Napoleon's celebrated promise, "L'Empire, c'est la paix." The London Rothschilds were violently opposed to any help to Prussia, and most bankers in Paris—and Berlin—thought that in case of war, Austria's chances were very much better than Prussia's.[100] In short, Bleichröder was rebuffed.

In a letter of mid-February to Baron James, Bleichröder also made a

---

* Even Roon's friend Friedrich Perthes urged that Prussia explore the possibilities of such a trade on top of a cash settlement: "Does Austria really want more than a fig leaf, big enough . . . to cover a sound piece of money with it?" Prussia should give her the fig leaf, be it Hohenzollern or Glatz. Roon, *Denkwürdigkeiten*, II, 409–410. But Bismarck sought a fig leaf for only one purpose: to cover his own aggressiveness, his drive for a final showdown with Austria. His principal aim by this time was to appear as the injured party.

cryptic reference to the Saar mines. "The Saarbrücken affair does not find support in the highest quarter [by which Bleichröder usually meant the king] and therefore is *not* likely to be carried out."[101] This remark suggests that in his talks with Baron James, Bleichröder had raised the possibility of a sale of the government coal mines, presumably to the Rothschilds, as had been rumored since January.[102] A week later, Count Károlyi reported that a leading financier, not from Berlin (probably Baron Oppenheim from Cologne), had told him that Prussia would soon force the issue of war with Austria, and that he had been asked to find a buyer for the government's Cologne-Minden shares. The banker had also alluded, somewhat mysteriously, to "the intended sale of another magnificent property that belonged to the Prussian government. He added most confidentially that the whole negotiation had taken place with Count Bismarck alone, without the knowledge of the ministers of finance and commerce."[103] Bismarck was negotiating on his own concerning that other "magnificent property," the Saar mines.

On March 9 Bleichröder wrote Bismarck that his financial memorandum was ready for immediate submission to him.[104] On March 12 Bodelschwingh summoned Bleichröder to discuss the memorandum, which unfortunately seems to have been lost.[105] Immediately after submitting and discussing his memorandum, Bleichröder returned to Paris.[106] On March 16 rumors circulated in Berlin that the government was negotiating the sale of the Saar mines, and it is probable that Bleichröder had gone to Paris to discuss this question with Baron James. Abraham Oppenheim meanwhile appeared in Berlin to talk about the creation of a new company which, with the participation of the government, would take over these mines.[107] On the next day, the Prussian ministers met in order to review the ever worsening relations with Austria. They were told that "Austria won't take money for the duchies"—and the very fact that this was considered important news indicates that a financial settlement had been taken seriously in Berlin. "The procurement of money creates difficulties. The placing of the Cologne-Minden shares can be done only at a loss. Sale of Saarbrücken suggested. Third possibility is to call the Diet and get a loan, but then a great German program and a German parliament."[108] The last resort, then, was to cajole the Diet into submission by adopting a liberal, nationalist program. No doubt, Bismarck would have preferred raising money without once more soliciting the Diet.

On March 23 Goltz fervently warned Bismarck against pursuing his policy bent on war. Prussia's internal dissensions and the hostility of Europe made such a conflict dangerous. In Paris the pro-Prussian sentiment had suddenly evaporated; everyone was against Prussia, except the emperor. Goltz added: "You must know better than I—I only believe I can divine it— that Rothschild refused you the Saarbrücken coal business."[109] Bismarck minuted: "It has not been offered to him."

Goltz's letter crossed with one from Bismarck, in which the chancellor explained that Prussia was holding back from matching Austrian military preparations because it sought to avoid mobilization until "the financial operations had been carried out, before these are rendered more difficult by the great tension which our military preparations would produce." Bismarck added confidentially that he had entered discussions with Baron de Rothschild, who had explained to Bismarck's "agent" (Bleichröder) that some weeks before, he would have been ready to make a deal with Prussia, but not under present, tense conditions—and especially not after a conversation he had had with Goltz! Bismarck reminded Goltz "how carefully the relations with Rothschild have to be tended."[110] No wonder that Goltz answered in some heat that the collapse of the Rothschild negotiations had had nothing to do with his conversation, but that the unreliable Bleichröder had spread this version to cover up his own failure, which stood in sharp contrast to his earlier optimism about his mission. Rothschild had told Goltz long ago that while the Prussian constitutional conflict lasted, he would give a loan only if the crown prince countersigned it. His more recent refusal, Baron James added, reflected his unwillingness "to furnish the means for war," least of all for an Austro-Prussian war that would so clearly injure his own interests.[111] Bleichröder apparently returned from Paris with empty hands, enriched only by one more enemy, Goltz, who detested what he considered the man's obtrusive meddling.

The need for money became more acute as military preparations went into high gear: on March 28, after a long struggle, Bismarck finally persuaded William to increase the strength of the army and to buy horses for half the field artillery.[112] Diplomats still explored the steadily diminishing possibilities of peace, while the Austrian and Prussian, and soon the Italian, armies began to rumble to their appointed places, in ever increasing numbers. As war drew closer, Bismarck extended the issues of the conflict. The fate of the duchies had poisoned Austro-Prussian relations; the future organization of the German nation would provide the occasion and the meaning of the war.[113] At the conference on March 31 the Prussian Ministry heard that "Bismarck will set in motion the German question," and on April 9 he made his revolutionary proposal for a reconstitution of the German Confederation and the establishment of a national parliament, elected by universal suffrage.[114] The day before, he had concluded a military alliance against Austria with Italy, hardly a conservative power. In pushing Prussia into war, Bismarck reached out for a number of revolutionary means, offending thereby his conservative friends and bewildering and often frightening his liberal enemies.

During these hectic days and weeks, Bleichröder took particular pains to collect and distribute information. The day before the Italian alliance was signed, the French chargé in Berlin, Eduard Lefebvre de Béhaine, answered a query of Bleichröder's: "Our neutrality is most well-meaning, and we in no way compromise the advantages that you will eventually be able to draw from it. . . . Seeing Bismarck so often, you are in a better position than anyone to know the heart of things for the present and the future."[115] At the same time, Bleichröder sent reports to Baron Rothschild in London, explaining, for example, that the panic on the London market, which allegedly was due to a Prussian-Italian alliance, was at the very least premature, because so far only drafts of such an alliance had been exchanged. He added that people were working hard to unseat Bismarck, but these efforts were likely to fail because they would constitute a moral defeat for the king.[116]

While Bismarck was pursuing his revolutionary policies, his finance minister dragged along, paralyzed by his own timidity. At the end of March, Bodelschwingh began selling the government's Cologne-Minden shares on the open market, but he could not sell them all at once without incurring a loss. In fact, his efforts to mobilize funds for war coincided with the onset of a severe economic contraction, manifested by a decline in production and in share prices and by a growing scarcity of credit.[117] On March 24 he informed his colleagues that he might raise 40 million taler, but that thereafter the state would need a loan, presumably approved by the Diet.[118] At the same time, Count Vincent Benedetti, the French ambassador in Berlin, thought that the Prussian government would have to pursue a prudent course until its financial operations had been completed. If these succeeded, Benedetti predicted that the treasury would have about 100 million francs, enough to start a war with.[119]

The market meanwhile began to sag, partly because of the threat of war. For Bleichröder it was a difficult time. Baron James had instructed him to sell his Prussian securities if he thought "war would come"; after the conclusion of the Prussian-Italian alliance, Bleichröder began to sell the Rothschild holdings, only to receive a stinging rebuff from Baron James that his actions contradicted his reassuring news: "You give no proof that you are protecting our interests, and we expect to hear from you what caused you to sell. We wired you this morning that we do not accept your last sale." On April 18 Bleichröder reported an easing of the political situation which had led him to stop all sales for Baron James's account.[120]

Bismarck still thought of the sale of the Saar mines. On April 3, Saar businessmen urged William not to countenance such a move, and on the next day the government denied that it was even contemplated, but left the petition unanswered.[121] In fact, Bismarck suddenly became more interested in this project and adduced altogether new arguments. He now feared that the extension of Prussian aims would stimulate Napoleon's appetite for territorial compensations, and especially for the Saar. On April 20 Bismarck recommended that Prussia's Saar mines be sold to a joint-stock company with the state as the principal shareholder, and on April 30 he wrote his fellow ministers that in case of war, France might exact a price for her support, if Prussia suffered reverses, and for her neutrality, if Prussian victories brought gains beyond the duchies. Napoleon was likely to ask for the border of 1814, which included the Saar. "He never indicated a desire for *German* territory beyond these frontiers." Because military vicissitudes could lead to a cession of this territory, it was important that the state should not also lose its mine property, which Bismarck estimated at 60 million taler. Hence he urged that the mine property be so "metamorphosed that even in case the territory is ceded, it [the property] would remain in our hands."[122]

On May 2, at a ministerial conference, Bismarck repeated his arguments for the transformation of property rights so that the Prussian state, which would be the principal shareowner in the new corporation, would not lose its property in the event the land had to be turned over to France. Bismarck defended this scheme, even if the prospective buyers would pay less than fair value for their share. It should be considered an insurance against total loss, and given the value of the property and its exposed location, the premium was not too high. Roon agreed, but all other ministers, especially Bodelschwingh and the minister of Justice, Count Leopold von Lippe, objected, and the matter was dropped.[123] Nationalistic German historians, including Gerhard Ritter, have insisted that Bismarck would never have ceded an inch of German territory to Napoleon. The ministerial conference proves the opposite, the more so as Bismarck would have been loath to speak lightly of territorial concessions when he knew that his enemies, especially Goltz, opposed his policy precisely because of this possibility. If he had wanted to, he could have pressed the original, fiscal motive for the sale of the mines, but he had adduced the far more important political motive for such a change.[124] Bismarck knew that his daring policy involved far greater risks than the possible cession of a strip of German land.

Still, he sought to reassure the indignant C. F. Stumm, a Saar mine owner of impeccably conservative views, who on May 8 protested the sale of the mines or the cession of the land. Bismarck told him it had never been contemplated, and apparently came to believe this untruth himself.[125] The rumors would not cease, and in mid-May Bleichröder heard from Goldschmidt that Vienna believed the Saar mines had been sold for 90 million taler.[126]

On May 3, at another crown council, William reviewed Prussia's relations with Austria, which had deteriorated steadily since the last council of February 28. Duly instructed by his clever mentor, he blamed Austria's bellicosity for this and urged strong countermeasures to protect Prussia from sudden peril. He proposed general mobilization; Moltke and the crown prince concurred, but Eulenburg and others objected because "of political considerations." Partial mobilization was decreed.[127] Eulenburg's objections were reasonable enough. "Almost the entire country was against the war," wrote Rudolf von Delbrück. "The liberal party accused the much-hated government of pushing for a war without necessity. For many conservatives, the alliance between Prussia and Austria was an article of faith."[128] Bismarck was execrated as a tyrant who in fratricidal war sought an escape from internal conflict.[129]

The stock market suffered a "panic" on May 2 because of rumors of impending Prussian mobilization.[130] When the rumors proved correct, the market dropped still further. May 12 was "a black day," and blacker days were to follow.[131] Prussian woes coincided with economic reverses in France and England, and on May 11 Prussia had to raise its discount rate to 9 percent. A few days later, inclement weather damaged some crops.[132] Corporate and civic bodies sent petitions to Berlin pleading for peace, and the Berlin Chamber of Commerce, an important and venerable group, begged the king not to risk "the material fruits of decades of peaceful work. . . . Neither

Prussian honor nor external danger nor the economic future of the country requires a war."[133]

Bleichröder probably shared these views, but he knew it was too late. In the early days of May he wrote to Lionel in London that Prussia, afraid of an Austrian attack, would mobilize still further. King and crown prince had given up their opposition to war, no efforts were made anymore to curb the passions, the Diet would soon be called in order to vote appropriations, which it was likely to do, and on June 2 he reported that his "good source" had indicated to him there was no alternative to war.[134]

Certainly his friends desired peace. Moritz von Goldschmidt wrote poignant letters lamenting the coming civil war which Bismarck was instigating and countered Bleichröder's rebuke that his letters were dictated by Austrian patriotism.

> For forty-five years I have lived in the country I love, where all my sons were born. And you? Are *you* perchance pro-*Austrian*? Let us write each other as honest practical men, each as he must feel and think. I do not blame you for thinking and feeling Prussian, but we must both be *just* and that an injustice is being done *us* . . . [by Prussian allegations of Austrian aggressiveness] all Europe says and knows; only your premier does not say it. He wants to aggrandize Prussia and to leave us and Germany behind. I have seen all this clearly for months, but I could not grasp the monstrosity of the unleashed civil war.

A few days later, he poured out his heart again. Why this frivolous indifference to the welfare of Europe? "One is inciting a dangerous game with human passions. Once war breaks out, we will, I fear, witness horrible things; the monarchs don't have the brute masses in their hands anymore once the war takes their bread and offers them misery and starvation instead." The only person who could benefit would be that "wretch Napoleon . . . that infamous sphinx."[135]

At the same time, Bleichröder received other news from Vienna, less wounding to his Prussian heart. Victor Benary, who had been with the Paris Rothschilds and now was director of the Austrian Creditanstalt, wrote his "esteemed friend" that "financially it looks so rotten that I believe literally in the bankruptcy [*Pleite*] of Moritz von Goldschmidt." Later letters make it clear that Goldschmidt served as a cover name for Austria, Schwabach for Prussia. Benary too must have thought Austrian censorship quite witless. On May 22 he wrote that he did not think last-minute peace efforts would avail and added:

> As a patriot I would regret it if your friend should become soft at the last moment. I am convinced Prussia will emerge from this war with unimaginable greatness. I am, as you know, a democrat and no supporter of Bismarck, but under present circumstances I would support

him in elections and in everything else. Such an opportunity to deal with the *Kleinstaaterei* and to drive Moritz von Goldschmidt [Austria] out of Germany won't recur.[136]

Throughout May and June Benary sent the gloomiest accounts of Austrian finances to Bleichröder; some of these found their way to Bismarck.[137] Bleich-röder's information strengthened Bismarck's suspicion that Austrian military preparations were being hamstrung by inadequate finances. The suspicion was amply confirmed in battle.[138]

On May 7 a man named Julius Cohen fired at Bismarck from close quarters, but the chancellor escaped unhurt, as by a miracle, he thought. The Diet was dissolved two days later, and a sense of panic spread throughout Prussia. Only the strongest nerves and the most impregnable self-confidence could have survived such tumult and antagonism. Bismarck's nerves had recovered; his whole being acquired the perfect concentration of the athlete ready at last for that long-prepared race that would decide everything.

For Bodelschwingh, the pace was too swift and the dangers too over-whelming. Roon sent him estimates of likely expenses: the mobilization of all nine army corps would cost 24 million taler, and more than 6 million additionally each month.[139] Bodelschwingh was terrified and in his helpless-ness wandered distractedly in the Tiergarten; in the end he regularly called on Adolph Hansemann, the head of the Disconto-Gesellschaft, for comfort and advice.[140]

Bodelschwingh finally accepted two emergency measures. In response to a severe scarcity of credit, the government decreed on May 18 the establishment of public credit institutes, designed to offer loans against various goods up to 25 million taler. It also abolished all existing restrictions on the rate of interest.[141] The first measure was clearly unconstitutional, and neither measure restored business confidence. The printing of the credit certificates was delayed until the end of June; their use, moreover, aroused a great deal of opposition and occasional cries of "Don't accept illegal money."[142] No wonder that Bodelschwingh wrote Bismarck on May 20 that he had neither enough money for a war nor even enough to guarantee sufficient funds beyond the next two months.[143]

A falling market made it difficult to sell the securities owned by the government, and efforts to discount them abroad failed as well. A representa-tive of the Seehandlung sought such an arrangement in Paris, but as Goltz, with ill-disguised satisfaction, wrote Bismarck, no one would accept the Prussian propositions. Goltz himself had talked to Baron James, who re-fused to commit his liquid funds at such a critical moment and added that he saw in the proposal a device for circumventing the Diet. Prussian credit must be low indeed, he concluded, and Goltz lectured Bismarck that the negotiations had shown "how infinitely difficult it would be for the royal government to realize a loan, which on the other hand it would find indis-pensable in case of war."[144] Bismarck did not need Goltz's or Baron Roth-schild's advice, though he did need the latter's money.

Bleichröder also came to suffer Baron James's ill humor. At the end of May, Baron James sharply rebuked Bleichröder for being more interested in purveying political news than in safeguarding Rothschild's economic interests. It must have been a stinging letter, which Bleichröder answered with a new dignity.[145]

As Prussia drew ever closer to war and as its credit seemed more and more in jeopardy, the government's final resource, as we shall see, was the money made available by Bleichröder's arrangement with the Cologne-Minden Railroad. He had furnished the sinews of war.

CHAPTER 4

A Banker's Share
in Bismarck's Triumph

If there is to be revolution, we would rather make than suffer it.
—Bismarck, 1866

Eighteen sixty-six was Bismarck's Year of Triumph. It was also the decisive year for Prussia, for Germany, for central Europe. In one battle—at Königgrätz—Austria's position in Germany was demolished, and Prussia emerged as Germany's hegemonial power. The center of Europe was revolutionized by a conservative statesman acting on behalf of a militaristic monarchy. The union of such vast economic and military power under an authoritarian and anachronistic government in the heart of Europe was to have fatal consequences for the history of the world. The next such decisive year in the history of Germany was 1945—when in the wreckage of the Reich, Prussia was annihilated.

For decades, 1866 was celebrated as Bismarck's achievement—and that celebration had its pernicious consequences, too. In the last decade or so, it has become fashionable to depreciate Bismarck's role, virtually to excise him, and to see the results of 1866 as the culmination of broad, anonymous forces that pushed an economically progressive Prussia into a position of leadership over a backward and divided Austria. No doubt, the constellation of forces was there; Bismarck did not create the conditions that allowed Prussia to win a victory over Austria, but he fashioned the circumstances by which Prussia could dare to enter such a war and successfully assimilate the fruits of her victory, without provoking foreign intervention. He had to parry the threats of such intervention, just as he had to parry the wishes of William and the military to humble Austria and extract from her even more than her total withdrawal from Germany.

Before they are won, overwhelming victories are but uncertain visions. Before the decisive battle, Bismarck had to guard against overwhelming defeat, which all of Europe was predicting for Prussia. Once more, he tempered recklessness with prudence, brutality with moderation. It was his willingness to use all possible means, to ally himself with men and to adapt ideas that had been anathema to him, that lent substance to his flexibility.

In his major trial, Bismarck needed bridges to new worlds, even to revolutionary underworlds. Bleichröder proved to be such a bridge to some of Bismarck's erstwhile opponents in parliament; his very tie with Bismarck symbolized and deepened Bismarck's understanding of the power of economic forces. But the faithful banker also proved a covert connection to revolutionaries who needed to be paid in secret funds. In short, Bleichröder was helpful to Bismarck in ways that have not hitherto been understood—and that illuminate Bismarck's ruthless exploration and exploitation of all means to success. After the victory, Bleichröder was allowed to share in some of its fruits.

The fratricidal war that everybody expected was slow in coming. On both sides there remained powerful advocates of peace and compromise; even those few leaders, notably Bismarck, who had decided that war had become all but inevitable had to leave retreats to peace open and in any case sought to provoke the future enemy into taking the fatal step of unleashing the war.

In those last hectic weeks when the issue of war and peace hung in the balance, Bismarck sensed the awesome implications for himself and his country of the impending war. The bullet that missed him in May had stirred thoughts of his own mortality, and over and over again in the next few weeks he was to acknowledge that he would choose death on the battlefield over defeat. The intimations of death were only in small part hyperbole. Nor were they new. Days after his accession to power, his king had said to him: "There at the Opernplatz, under my windows, they are going to cut off your head and, a little later, mine."[1] Bismarck recognized the dangers facing him, and he knew that he was approaching the supreme crisis. He summoned all his caution—and his indomitable courage—to reach a safe end. He knew he was risking the future of the Hohenzollern dynasty. If he won, it would be assured; if he lost, Austria had already planned the truncation of Prussia. If he won, he could shape the future of central Europe and could discipline, perhaps harness, the revolutionary forces of the modern age. If he lost, he feared chaos would ensue when incompetent reaction would confront impetuous revolution.

The approaching struggle, then, was for incalculable stakes, and Bismarck was resolved to rally every form of support. For years he had impressed his king and nation—indeed all of Europe—with his apparent reactionary views, and since his accession to power he had warned all who would listen against "the Revolution," a broad and sinister term that covered a multitude of sins from socialism to moderate constitutionalism. Time and again he had invoked the principle of monarchical solidarity, especially in order to keep his Austrian partner in line for as long as convenient. In the weeks before and after the outbreak of the war, he reached out to the very forces he had appeared to detest—in order both to frighten his enemies and to bolster his own defenses.

Bismarck had repeatedly tried to capture German nationalism for his own ends: in April 1866 his plans for a new German Confederation included a national parliament that would be elected by universal suffrage, according to the franchise designed by the Frankfurt Assembly of 1849. This intended bombshell did not go off: most people found Bismarck's sudden conversion from an oppressor of parliaments to an originator of them risibly transparent. Still, Bismarck's appeal among liberals had grown as he drew closer to their goal of German unity and as his economic policy satisfied liberal interests as well as liberal ideas. The way to cooperation between Bismarck and his liberal opponents was blocked by his defiance of the budgetary rights of the lower chamber: to this principle even the most easily seduced liberals clung, for without the power of the purse, parliament would have lost all justification.

Bismarck needed to split the solid front of his opposition, because he realized that it would be difficult to borrow as long as the liberals, so closely related to the business community, denied him parliamentary support. He needed liberals as well in order to rally German public opinion to his side, to make plausible his credibility as a spokesman of German nationalism. And beyond the immediate crisis, he realized—and thereby distinguished himself from most men of his class and convictions—that he needed them to govern the enlarged Prussia or the unified Germany of the future. A modern state required some form of representation.

He gradually approached the Prussian liberals, hoping to woo and separate some of them from the ideologues who would always remain his enemies. He made sweet overtures to the moderates, against a background of muffled battle drums. Perhaps he hoped to kill the liberals by embracing them.

The banking world had always stood as an intermediary between the government and the liberal business community. Even more than other groups, bankers longed for domestic peace, and as the crisis approached, some of them put pressure on both sides to end the conflict. In mid-May, for example, Abraham Oppenheim told Bismarck of the Rhinelanders' desire for peace, but added that if war was inevitable, it should be preceded by peace at home. Bismarck replied, as Oppenheim immediately informed Bleichröder, that he agreed and had accordingly asked the king to relieve him of his post, because his hated person stood in the way of reconciliation. He had suggested a successor, the prince of Hohenzollern, and had asked only to be undersecretary in the Foreign Office.[2]* Bismarck's account was colored by his dramatic imagination; the exaggeration, however, attested his desire to end his conflict with the liberal deputies. As his ties with his oldest Junker friends snapped—his fatherly friend Ludwig von Gerlach broke with him on May 16—he sought to bridge the chasm of the constitutional conflict.

On May 29 Bismarck saw Karl Twesten, whom but some months before he had tried to send to prison. Five years earlier, Twesten had described Austria as the greatest enemy of German unification and had admitted that in foreign policy "the common view that the king's subjects have limited intelli-

---

* As early as February 14, 1866, Bismarck had told the French ambassador that Prussia might have to appeal to German nationalism and call for a German parliament. In such a case, he would himself recommend that the king appoint another ministry, headed by Goltz. Somewhat later, Bleichröder reported to Baron James that the market had been alarmed by a rumor that Goltz was about to replace Bismarck, who in turn would become ambassador in Paris. OD, II, 299; Bleichröder to Baron James, 28 Feb. 1866, RA.

gence has some justification." He was eager to meet Bismarck more than half-way. He told him that the Diet would grant all necessary funds if the government would acknowledge parliament's full and inviolable control of the budget.[3] Soon it would be more important for the liberals to be able to grant appropriations than for the government to receive them. The liberals had to share in the prospective victory or lose out altogether. Bismarck needed insurance against Prussian reverses; the liberals needed insurance against a Prussian victory.

Two days after his talk with Twesten, Bismarck received—at last—Bodelschwingh's resignation, after working for it, he said, for a whole year![4] Bodelschwingh, unable to find funds for a war he abhorred, had suffered a nervous collapse. Bismarck at once appointed von der Heydt, an old enemy of Bodelschwingh's. The two men, Bismarck told the king in 1862, so hated each other that they would not sit in the same cabinet for one day.[5] Heydt, a former liberal, had turned conservative and was suspect to both parties, though he had excellent connections with the business and especially the banking community. To a liberal enemy of Heydt's, Bismarck defended his choice by saying: "That man will get us money, and we need that."[6] In later years Bismarck referred to him as "Gold-Onkel." Heydt had resigned as finance minister in 1862 because he would not condone the proposed violation of the Constitution; he returned to office on the condition that after the prospective war, parliament be asked for an indemnity for all unauthorized expenses of the government. Bismarck agreed, and Heydt set out to raise the necessary funds for the approaching war, realizing that the contracting of debts without parliamentary approval remained illegal, and that if the war were lost or the monarchy defeated, the personal consequences for the responsible minister would be grave indeed.[7]

From the first, Heydt consulted Bleichröder and Hansemann. He had known Bleichröder for many years; most recently they had both been on the board of the projected Baltic–North Sea canal, designed to promote trade and Prussia's maritime power.[8] (Bismarck was one of the first to recognize the political and economic potentialities of the canal and worked hard to realize them.)[9] Much more important, just two weeks before his appointment, Heydt had asked Bleichröder whether his firm in Elberfeld could obtain a loan of 100,000 to 150,000 taler "even under present circumstances," because it had exhausted its current credit. The "circumstances" were a deep, sudden crisis that had hit the market, especially the cotton trade, and had brought Elberfeld close "to complete stagnation."[10] Bleichröder immediately promised the funds, and Heydt gratefully acknowledged his help.[11] Heydt had experienced the difficulties that scarce credit caused to entrepreneurs. He discovered that the state faced similar problems, and in both instances he called on Bleichröder for help.

At the crown council on the day after his appointment, Heydt, despite these difficulties, urged that hostilities be begun as soon as possible. He was afraid that the continued antiwar agitation of the progressives and the ultramontanes might infect the population. It was time for war. The king and Bismarck agreed, but cautioned that Austria must appear as the aggressor.[12] Heydt thereupon asked Hansemann to form a consortium to buy the treasury's single greatest asset, its Cologne-Minden Railroad shares. Hansemann at once consulted Bleichröder, with whom he had collaborated intimately for more than a decade. Their banks were practically adjoining, they saw each other daily, and Hansemann had the highest respect for his colleague. "Bleichröder was the greatest intelligence among all private bankers of those years," wrote the official biographer of Hansemann.[13] The two men readily agreed to offer the government a price of 110; the shares were in demand right then and traded at 117.[14] The rest of the consortium, seeking to exploit the government's desperate need, insisted on a price of 105, and Hansemann had the unpleasant task of telling Heydt that only he and Bleichröder had been willing to make a reasonable bid. Heydt decided to sell the shares gradually, and, after the first Prussian victories, at ever increasing prices, through the Seehandlung. Bleichröder's original coup in arranging for the Cologne-Minden Railroad contract now supplied the necessary funds. Bismarck never forgot that Prussia's bankers —except Bleichröder and Hansemann—had failed him on the eve of war. In 1889, when lamenting the underdeveloped entrepreneurial energy and patriotism of German capitalists, he recalled: "At an earlier time, there was almost no possibility of covering Prussian war loans by national capital, as the example of 1866 made clear, and the Berlin *haute finance* did not feel strong enough as regards capital to muster the courage to risk what they had for the sake of the nation."[15]

Heydt was right in pointing to the agitation against the war. As the war approached, the anti-Bismarck mood mounted, and the market tumbled. Petitions for peace arrived in Berlin from every major city in Prussia, save Breslau, and the will for peace produced some very un-Prussian incidents during the mobilization for war in May.[16] Marx and Engels predicted a revolution in Berlin and a mutiny of the troops.[17] Bismarck must have sensed the truth of Treitschke's remark to him: "I find it terrible that the most important foreign minister whom Prussia has had for decades should at the same time be the most hated man in Germany; I find it sadder still that the most promising ideas for reforming the Confederation that were ever proposed by a Prussian government should have been met by the nation with such humiliating coldness."[18] And Bleichröder received an outraged letter at the end of May from Count Baudissin, who wrote from Schleswig and warned that "the enmity of the governor [Edwin von Manteuffel] toward the premier has become an open secret." Manteuffel's administration, moreover, injured Prussian interests and spread hatred of Prussia. "Everybody is agreed," Baudissin continued, "that the bigots must resign from political leadership and that with the heroes of the *Kreuzzeitungspartei* no great program can be executed."[19] The feudal party was losing its confidence in the "new" Bismarck and beginning to obstruct him.

In early June the two powers finally moved to war. Austria placed the issue of the duchies before the Confederation, and Bismarck, branding this step a violation of the Gastein Convention, ordered Prussian troops into Holstein.

At the same time, he presented a pseudodemocratic program for the unification of Germany without Austria, and on the fourteenth the Diet of the Confederation accepted an Austrian motion for mobilization against Prussia. Two days later, Prussian troops invaded Hanover and Saxony. The die was cast.

At the outbreak of the war, nervousness turned to apprehension and panic. The Prussian citizenry did not want war, and few people anywhere thought that Prussia could triumph over Austria. Prussia had not been in a major campaign for half a century; with its own house divided, it was now battling what still seemed a formidable empire. Hours before the war began, Abraham Oppenheim wrote Bleichröder:

> Now that war appears totally unavoidable, we must face the melancholy possibility that we might be unfortunate in the first stages and that hence the Austrians might perhaps advance as far as Berlin, in which case the city might possibly be exposed to plundering. As soon as you, dear friend, come to fear such a misfortune, we would beg you to send us by mail the securities you hold for us, stating as value 20,000 taler, but do so only if you are certain that hostilities on the Berlin-Cologne route have not yet broken out.

A week later, after some minor skirmish in which the Austrians had been successful, Oppenheim wrote an even more alarmed letter. The Austrians, he wrote, were spreading "shameless lies" about Prussian plundering in enemy territory, obviously as preemptive apologies for when "they begin to burn and plunder when they will come into enemy territory. Therefore I beg you, dear friend, to take all precautionary measures, you are more exposed than anyone else because people know your connection with v. B." And this time he instructed Bleichröder to send their securities by the next mail—if the roads were still safe—giving as value 25,000 taler, and to add any of his securities that he might want. It might even be better to send them by messenger the same evening: "Alas! These are very sad times!"[20]

They were also very trying times—especially for Bismarck. Bleichröder urged him to bend every effort to make peace at home. Two days after the war had broken out, Bismarck and Bleichröder agreed that the latter should arrange a meeting between Bismarck and the liberal deputy Viktor von Unruh. Bleichröder assured Unruh that Bismarck wanted the meeting because he was resolved to end the constitutional conflict by taking conciliatory steps. But Bleichröder—like his master—thought that a powerful threat might reinforce pleas for compromise. Accordingly, he warned Unruh that the mobilization of war funds without the Diet would require such desperate measures as compulsory loans and the devaluation of the currency, which "would result in the ruin of Prussian industry, perhaps for a generation." Unruh's initial suspicion that Bleichröder, not Bismarck, had taken the initiative for this meeting was dispelled by a hastily produced handwritten letter of Bismarck's to Bleichröder. Bleichröder conceded that he had urgently counseled Bismarck to talk to liberal leaders. His doubts allayed, Unruh eagerly accepted the invitation, as Bleichröder informed Bismarck. The two men met on June 20, and Bismarck was prepared for Unruh's irrepressible desire for conciliation.[21]

Unruh protested his unconditional loyalty to Prussia now that the war had broken out and bemoaned "the absolute indifference" of the populace. He reminded Bismarck of their earlier talk in 1859, when Bismarck had said that Prussia was totally isolated and had but one ally, the German people. To secure that ally now, the Constitution would have to be restored. Bismarck agreed, as he had in his earlier conversation with Twesten, but complained that "everybody thinks he can do everything. He, too, is only human." The king had objected to Twesten's proposals for an affirmation of parliamentary rights as an end to the conflict, but Bismarck knew that "an early resolution of the conflict was necessary." Even after a military victory, he would resign rather than continue the conflict with parliament. (A day after the decisive battle of Königgrätz, he reiterated this promise to the crown prince, and he redeemed it a month later.) He told Unruh, as he had told Twesten, that he would have been willing to resign from the premiership if only a suitable successor could be found. Unruh concurred that there was none, because from "1849 to 1858 and from 1862 until now, reactionary regimes had successfully seen to it that in the high reaches of the bureaucracy there is no liberal to be found who possesses the requisite energy and endurance and at the same time enjoys general confidence."[22] In effect, Unruh was telling Bismarck he was indispensable—and by doing so, Unruh gave Bismarck a preview of what might be called a national-liberal mentality of unconscious submissiveness. Bismarck was going to exploit it for several decades to come.

Bleichröder was pleased by the conversation and immediately wrote Baron James: "A resolution of the internal question has not yet taken place, but the first steps have been taken."[23] No doubt Bismarck wanted it known abroad that he was building his bridges to all factions in Germany.

In fact, Bleichröder kept sending Baron James reassuring news—whether he really felt that confident or not we have no way of knowing. On June 19 he wrote Baron James: "The mood of the country has shifted significantly in the last four days in favor of the government and it is not improbable that the [new] Diet, to be convened shortly, will grant the government the requisite funds."[24] (The liberals were in fact beginning to feel—and exaggerate—their impotence; they now thought that Bismarck could wage a war without parliament "and not only for a year. . . . Absolutists and Junkers have all the luck on their side.")[25] A few days later, Bleichröder submitted a long memorandum to the Paris Rothschilds about Prussia's political and financial prospects. He predicted the early end of the internal struggle and the Diet's authorization of war credits, and he urged the Rothschilds to subscribe if a loan were opened to foreigners, because Prussian finances were brilliant and its public debt was small, considering the state's vast properties.[26]

On June 30 Bismarck and the king left Berlin in order to join the Prussian armies in Bohemia. Bismarck had made every possible preparation, and now the fortunes of war would decide. He left neither untroubled nor unarmed:

the day before, Bleichröder had given him a hoard of gold coins: 50 Friedrichs d'or, 50 gold Napoleons, 50 Austrian ducats, and enough silver coins to make 1,000 taler in all. Bismarck went off to battle with $7,500 (in today's value) in his pockets.[27] Never before or after did Bleichröder give him such an assortment of immediately negotiable coins. Presumably Bismarck meant to be ready to meet all eventualities. A man certain of a lightning victory would not have traveled with his pockets full of gold. Did he have visions of captivity, did he fear himself wandering alone on desolate battlefields, as Frederick II had done? Gold would be useful—and a comfort.

The suspense was quickly over. Moltke had prepared the decisive battle in meticulous detail, by the revolutionary use of modern communications, and still convinced, as Bismarck was, "that strategy, whether employed in diplomacy or military operations, was not an exact science."[28] On July 3, in the neighborhood of Königgrätz, nearly half a million men fought desperate engagements. By nightfall the Austrians had lost a quarter of their army, and the rest was retreating back to Vienna.

Bismarck had felt apprehensive all day. "He felt," as he admitted later, "that he was playing a game of cards with a million-dollar stake that he did not really possess. Now that the wager had been won, he felt depressed rather than elated, and as he rode through the fields filled with dead and wounded he wondered what his feelings would be if his eldest son were lying there." No quarters had been prepared for him anywhere, and as he looked for a place to sleep, he slipped and fell into a manure pit.[29]

It had been the decisive battle of midcentury. Nothing would ever be the same, not in Germany, and not in Europe. On the evening of the next day, when told of what had happened, the papal secretary of state, Cardinal Antonelli, exclaimed in horror: "Casca il mondo" (The world is collapsing).[30] The world that had been so painstakingly restored in 1815 and that assumed a Hapsburg hegemony over central Europe—a hegemony that depended on the containment of revolutionary forces—was destroyed.

The impact on Prussia was intoxicating—and devastating.[31] On July 4 Bleichröder sent Bismarck a letter of fulsome adulation about the victory, and his letter can stand as a token of Prussian submission:

> I dare to importune you with these lines at a moment when fervent prayers of thanksgiving rise to the Almighty for the mercy which he showed our fatherland through the victory of the magnificent army of His Majesty over our hereditary enemy. Suffused with the deepest feeling of admiration for Your Excellency, I dare to express it by way of heartfelt congratulations for the next political success of Your Excellency and make bold to beg you to place my humblest congratulations at the feet of His Majesty. I shall give effect to my gratitude by diligent efforts on behalf of our wounded soldiers.[32]

Even allowing for the rhetoric of the time, the greatness of the moment, and Bleichröder's sense of having had a share in the great enterprise, this is remarkable hyperbole. Bleichröder's letter may also serve as an early instance of the boundless and rather demonstrative patriotism of some Prussian Jews, who outdid their gentile fellow citizens by enthusiastic loyalty to the new state. The cosmopolitan, peace-loving Bleichröder brought his offerings to the Prussian altar of victory.

Bleichröder's letter had a functional side as well. He reported that an important French personality in Berlin (Benedetti, perhaps, who did not leave Berlin for Prussian headquarters until July 8 and who was a client of Bleichröder's) had made "worrisome remarks" which suggested that the French "begrudge us the fruits of our victory and that they are afraid that their monopoly of 'gloire' could suffer from the most recent phase of world history." Bleichröder predicted that French passivity would end very soon— as it did by the end of the day. He also anticipated Bismarck's response, to wit, that these French "pretensions" would have to be rebuffed, and pointed to the force that Bismarck himself would threaten the French with: "Our national consciousness has mightily risen and the people will enthusiastically throw themselves against anyone who tries to obstruct the goals of the present movement."

Bismarck did threaten Napoleon with the full wrath of German nationalism. In warding off all foreign intervention, Bismarck was determined to marshal every revolutionary force in Germany and Europe in order to attain his ends, and when his Russian friends questioned his revolutionary gestures, he gave the characteristic reply: "If there is to be revolution, we would rather make than suffer it."[33]

Bismarck had allied himself with foreign revolutionaries even before the outbreak of the war. His alliance with "revolutionary" Italy—already an indignity to his conservative friends—was supplemented by his close contacts with Hungarian revolutionaries. Bismarck fully intended to mobilize and unleash every subversive force within the enfeebled Austrian Empire: the Hungarian émigrés, still nursing their defeat of 1849, were the most promising ally against Austria, and Bismarck had in fact established contact with them soon after his accession to power.[34] By March 1866 Bismarck's minister in Florence, Count Usedom, was in constant touch with the leaders of the Hungarian movement, including the famed Louis Kossuth, planning the establishment of Hungarian military legions on Prussian and Italian soil, destined to strike "at the heart" of the Austrian Empire.* Bismarck also conferred directly with several agents of a Hungarian National Committee. Throughout June, plans for Hungarian legions to be formed in Italy and Prussia progressed apace, although Bismarck complained to Usedom on June

---

* In a dispatch to the Italian General La Marmora of June 17, Usedom used the famous "stab-in-the-heart" phrase to incite an Italian thrust against Austria, with the help of Hungarian revolutionaries. In 1868 Usedom's dispatch was made public in Italy, and Bismarck sought to distance himself from Usedom and the Hungarian enterprise; at a still later time, he pretended that he had encouraged Hungarian revolutionaries only after Napoleon's intervention on July 4. GW, VI¹, 401–409, XV, 271; and Eduard von Wertheimer, Bismarck im Politischen Kampf (Berlin, 1930), pp. 280–281.

10 that "he had no considerable sums of money at his disposal" and that therefore the Italian government should advance the necessary funds. Later on, the Prussian government would pay back half.[35]

Bleichröder recognized the potential importance of this weapon; just before the battle of Königgrätz, he wrote to Baron James that despite Prussian superiority, the war might take a long time, because Austria could not afford another compromise unless "Hungary makes a revolution, of which indeed there are some signs."[36] On July 5, immediately after the battle of Königgrätz, after Austria's request for an armistice and Napoleon's detested offer of mediation, Bismarck received two leaders of the Hungarian movement, Count Czaki and Major von Komaromy at Horitz. (There was a certain poetic justice to Bismarck's use of Hungarians to counter Napoleon's threats. Napoleon himself had encouraged the formation of Hungarian legions on Italian soil during the Franco-Austrian war of 1859. In this, as in even more important matters, Bismarck proved an apt pupil of Napoleon.)[37] He gave the exiles a draft for 400,000 taler, payable by Baron Werther, his deputy for foreign affairs in Berlin. One hundred thousand taler were to be taken from the royal Legationskasse, i.e., from Foreign Office funds, 300,000 to be collected by Bismarck's assistant Lothar Bucher from Bleichröder. According to Bismarck's order, Bucher was to deliver this handsome sum, now suddenly available, to the two leaders, who would be staying at a Berlin hotel under assumed names.[38] The money was earmarked for the recruitment of a Hungarian Legion, destined to enter Hungary and disrupt the Empire. (At the same time, Bismarck urged the Italians to land Garibaldi's volunteers in Dalmatia, to foment revolution among Austria's South Slavs.)[39]

Bleichröder acknowledged Bismarck's order on July 8, indicating that he had paid the requested sum and implying that he would apply the Saxon contribution against it.[40] On June 20 the Prussian army had imposed a daily contribution of 10,000 taler on the defeated Saxons in exchange for their continuing fiscal autonomy.[41] Bleichröder collected this money, and against the sum advanced Bismarck the secret funds for the Hungarians. A few weeks later, Bismarck informed Heydt that the Saxon money had already been spent on the Hungarian Legion because "the pressure that it will exert on Austria is of such great importance for the conduct of the war and for peace that payments could not have been delayed."[42] Bleichröder's involvement in the Hungarian venture has never before been revealed. His friends in Vienna would have been distressed by this collusion.

Bleichröder also became involved in one of the darkest chapters of Bismarck's German war: the treatment of Frankfurt-am-Main. The city, which had joined forces with Austria, was loathed by Prussian officialdom and by William himself, for they regarded it as a hotbed of democracy and anti-Prussianism. The Frankfurt press did in fact vilify the Prussian regime with relish. On July 16 Prussian troops occupied the city, and on the next day the commanding general imposed a punitive indemnity of 6 million gulden, payable in two days. It was paid, and on July 18, Bismarck decreed what was assumed to be an additional indemnity of 25 million, which was less than William had wanted.

On the same day, Bleichröder asked Bismarck to appoint him transfer agent for this indemnity, just as he had been charged with the Saxon payments.[43] Meanwhile, the new commanding general in Frankfurt, Manteuffel, had tried to cow the city by threatening it with plunder or by hinting at it. The Frankfurt citizenry thought a "new Hun raid was beginning and that the ruin of Frankfurt had been decided upon."[44] On July 22 Bleichröder wired Bismarck that the 31 million indemnity was producing "a cry of horror" throughout South Germany. He warned that the sum was too high and that "the actual evildoers would not be much affected by it," presumably because the well-to-do, not the journalists and agitators, would have to pay.[45] Bleichröder also wrote Keudell that the indemnity was "a bit steep."[46] The fate of Frankfurt—the high indemnity as well as the threat of Prussian looting—evoked foreign protests, and the resultant furor embarrassed Bismarck.[47] On July 25 he telegraphed Bleichröder that the city's indemnity was only 25 million because the 6 million already paid would be credited to its account.[48]

On the same day, a delegation of Frankfurt citizens, headed by Baron Carl Meyer, arrived in Berlin for negotiations. Rothschild's effort to notify Bleichröder of his trip was forbidden by the Prussian authorities in Frankfurt.[49] The reception in Berlin, however, was solicitous, and Baron Carl Meyer returned to Berlin a second time and on August 6 and 7 saw Bismarck. Bleichröder reported to Baron James that Bismarck had offered to rescind the indemnity and to make other concessions if the city freely accepted Prussian annexation.[50] Bismarck sent a note to this effect to his deputy in Frankfurt.[51]

Bleichröder's role in this dishonorable enterprise had been honorable. He had wanted to serve Bismarck and himself by collecting and remitting the initial indemnity. After the second indemnity was decreed, however, he did not hesitate to warn Bismarck against the excessive severity. It must have taken some courage to speak out against Prussia and for Frankfurt and the Rothschilds, for in the minds of most Prussians the two were identical. Bismarck's subordinates were not encouraged to criticize his actions. Bleichröder apparently did not collect the indemnity.

On July 18 Bismarck telegraphed Bleichröder from Brno asking for a fair rate for converting Prussian taler into Austrian money.[52] Presumably this would help Bismarck fix the amount Austria would have to pay as war indemnity. The next day, Keudell wrote his "esteemed friend" from Nickolsburg: "Perhaps it is of interest for you that I personally foresee a peaceful phase. The affair isn't closed, but seems to be going nicely. The moment when all is closed can hardly escape the public; at such a time, a notice [to you] would be worthless."[53] Obviously news at this stage, four days before the conclusion of an Austro-Prussian armistice, was valuable indeed. To know that Bismarck's close adviser thought peace was coming—even though he warned that he could be wrong and that further "martial fury" might ensue—was important to a banker. Bleichröder acknowledged Keudell's "cherished lines" and told him that the stock exchange had already moved into a "peace market" and that a collapse of peace talks would of course lead to a severe drop in prices. He begged Keudell to keep him informed.[54]

Bleichröder always reciprocated favors. He supplied Bismarck and his friends with exquisite cigars and asked whether other "*raffraichissements*" would find favor in their eyes. He liked being the purveyor of exotic luxuries to his mighty friends, especially while they were exposed to the rigors of war.[55] For the less fortunate ones, for the wounded and their families, Bleichröder showed remarkable largesse—and in his efforts became acquainted with Johanna von Bismarck, who organized aid for the victims of her husband's war.[56] She came to know him so well that a year later she was already making fun of his grandiloquent phrases.[57]

In late July and August, Bismarck had but one aim, to effect a victorious peace on every front or to destroy all who would deny him such a peace. Ever since his talks with Twesten and Unruh and his promise to Heydt, he was determined to end the constitutional conflict. The defeat of the Progressives in the elections, fortuitously held on the day of Königgrätz, was a favorable omen; as Bleichröder wrote Bismarck right after these elections—in a manner that combined fawning with counsel—"the so-called Progressive party has become discouraged, and therefore the resolution of the [constitutional] conflict would require only minor concessions from the kindness of His Majesty."[58] Against conservative opposition—the intensity of which he later exaggerated— Bismarck persuaded the king and his ministry to open the newly elected Diet on August 5 with a conciliatory speech from the throne and a request for an indemnity for government expenses which, incurred without parliamentary authorization, had been "without legal basis."[59] In his hour of triumph, Bismarck met the moderate liberals halfway: the patent violation of the Constitution was acknowledged; the question of military reforms, imposed by the king in defiance of the Diet, was not even mentioned. Bismarck needed liberal support in Prussia so that in the face of continuing threats of foreign intervention, he could count on—and boast of—the full support of national Germany.

While extending an olive branch to a parliament that needed but such a gesture in order to submit, Bismarck settled affairs with foreign powers as well. In quick succession, he negotiated a treaty of federation with the North German states, a military alliance with the three South German states, and a definite peace with Austria. Prussia annexed Hanover, Hesse-Kassel, Nassau, and Frankfurt, despite William's misgivings about Bismarck's toppling of the Guelphs in Hanover, the oldest reigning dynasty in Germany. Bismarck, the archconservative, on the other hand, was overthrowing—or threatening to overthrow—princely houses with an abandon that no German revolutionary would have dreamed possible. He was forced to respect the integrity of Saxony, though in brutal negotiations with the neighboring state he exacted a heavy indemnity and its acceptance of Prussian hegemony in North Germany. Prussia had thus become the dominant power in all of Germany.

In completing his state-building, Bismarck had to elude Napoleon's intermittent demands for territorial compensation. Until Austria had signed a preliminary peace, Bismarck had been ready to ignite every nationalist mine in the Austrian Empire; now he threatened Napoleon with the full force of the democratic nationalist movement in Germany. (Bleichröder warned Baron James that Berlin "was not in a mood to yield even an inch of German soil," and none was lost.)[60] Bismarck, "the White Revolutionary," as Henry Kissinger has called him, grasped the power of German nationalism, harnessed that power to Prussian conservative ends, and thus thwarted Napoleon's desire for compensation and dealt his prestige a disastrous blow.[61] The Bismarck of the 1860s acted with extraordinary quickness, flexibilty, and utterly open-minded realism.

Prussia's triumphs, achieved with such seeming ease, endowed Bismarck with sudden, unbelievable popularity. The hated tyrant had become the nation's greatest idol. In the face of that transformation, the Prussian Diet quickly capitulated. The liberals split—with more than half the former opposition succumbing to Bismarck's success, disguising their surrender by rationalizations about the priority of power and unity over freedom, of the "logic of facts and events" over ideas and ideals. Other liberal deputies remembered that he had promoted liberal economic interests, that he had facilitated the free unfolding of a new capitalistic order. In early September 1866 the Prussian Diet, by a vote of 230 to 75, accepted the government's indemnity bill. The constitutional conflict was ended. The unpolitical German had begun to play his fatal role.[62]

There remained the task of giving permanent form to Prussia's hegemony in North Germany. The new Confederation had to satisfy the Prussian king and the king's party and his royal cousins on the smaller thrones of northern Germany, it had to satisfy the wishes of an admittedly docile populace, and it had to prove attractive to the South Germans, who, despite their suspicion of the illiberal Prussians, would eventually have to join a similar, enlarged union. In the fall of 1866, despite a nervous collapse that he had suffered earlier, Bismarck became the principal architect of the new North German Confederation. Its constitution, which also served the new Reich after 1871, was a masterpiece of intricate obscurity. Put simply, the new Confederation was dominated by Prussia; its representative body, the Reichstag, had a democratic franchise but hardly a democratic function; even its budgetary power was severely limited. The locus of sovereignty was left uncertain. The newly founded National Liberal party, which wanted parliamentary rights with at least a modicum of substance, extracted some concessions from Bismarck.

Above all, the National Liberals, representing *Bildung und Besitz* (education and wealth), welcomed the economic provisions of the Constitution. Bismarck had lavished particular care on these so that they would "remove those disadvantages to the material welfare of the German people which had arisen from its political disunity."[63] The Confederation provided for a common economic order; with and partially for the National Liberals, Bismarck created the institutions of an unfettered market economy that were to bring prosperity to Germany's middle classes and industrial power to the nation.

Bismarck had reason to be pleased with a constitution that would give him far greater power than he had ever enjoyed in Prussia. In the new Confederation he would be the only minister, unencumbered by a cabinet of potential dissidents. Nobody was completely satisfied with the new structure of North Germany. Bismarck alone had few regrets.

Bismarck succeeded then in so modernizing the Prussian state that it could preserve its anachronistic conservative character. For liberals, the constitution of 1867 marked a step back as compared to the hopes of 1848 or even to the Prussian Constitution of 1850. But there was progress in the material realm. Here was forged that fatal and unprecedented union of constitutional absolutism with democratic trappings, of political nonage and economic growth, that characterized the development of a powerful but illiberal Germany.

Bismarck's triumph in Germany and Europe was complete. He had split his opponents at home and formed a new majority for his rule. He had defied or duped all Europe; he had created a new order without fully destroying the old. No one, he thought, had divined his game in time, and he exulted: "But I have beaten them all! All!"[64] Beaten, too, was the dream of a liberal, humane Germany, and born was a mighty, militaristic country that would idolize power even when that power was unrestrained by intellect or moral realism.

We might boggle at Bismarck's identification of the victory with himself, an identification that became the principal illusion of the Bismarck cult. No man shapes history—and yet Bismarck, Napoleon, and Lenin did fundamentally alter the course of their countries' history. Most times, Bismarck was excessively diffident about the chances of human hands affecting destiny, but in the years from 1862 to 1866 he had felt and suffered the trials of the lonely leader who embarks on an unclear venture along a dangerous path, where few men followed because few understood him, and many opposed because they were partisans of the old way. His enemies had been legion, his supporters a handful of men—friends like Roon or instruments like Keudell and Bucher. He was, as I have suggested, intensely aware of the possibility and penalty of failure. The penalty, he said, would have been death: either self-prescribed as in his vision of death on the battlefield or death as the penalty for waging an unsuccessful revolution. Or were these dramatic inventions of an overwrought mind—would failure have meant no more than disgrace or the end of a public career? But would that not have been death, too? No matter; in later, safer years, he relished the thought of having escaped death, and he harbored a special gratitude to those few men who had helped him in this time of peril.* Among these, Bleichröder was a preeminent figure.

Bleichröder's services had been duly requited. "The world says that the

---

* How common this feeling of supreme danger was can be gleaned from a letter which Roon wrote to Perthes on June 26, 1866: "So very often I appear to myself (and when I say 'I' here I don't mean my own person but rather the personification of the present government) as a tightrope walker, who carries a heavy, shifting dead burden on his neck across Niagara Falls, knowing that every misstep or slip, even only an unbalanced shifting of the weight, will

war brought you a great deal of money," wrote Goldschmidt to Bleichröder in August 1866.[65] It had undoubtedly brought him that—and much else. He had done well in the past half-decade, as had his "good friend" in whose shadow his own fame spread. The most precious achievement in a rich period was the establishment of this special relation with Bismarck—and that was destined to endure and grow deeper.

---

lead to the carrier's fall into the abyss, knowing that everything depends on strong nerves and sure-footed steps, and that still more depends on the will of Him who keeps nerves and muscles efficient and without whom not a sparrow falls from the roof." *Denkwürdigkeiten aus dem Leben des General-Feldmarschalls Kriegsministers Grafen von Roon*, 4th ed. (3 vols.; Breslau, 1897), II, 141.

CHAPTER 5

Bismarck's Purse and Bleichröder's Place

Pomeranian estate owners [*Gutsbesitzer*] have always had their House Jew.
I am a Pomeranian estate owner and have Bleichröder.

—Bismarck

"Which vice do you hate most?" "Servility."

—Karl Marx, 1860s

The victories of 1866 benefited both Bismarck and Bleichröder. In the private realm, each man desired what the other possessed. Bismarck wanted ample means in order to indulge his passion for land, while Bleichröder wanted a secure place in Prussia's traditional-hierarchical society. Bismarck facilitated Bleichröder's social rise; Bleichröder promoted Bismarck's economic well-being and taught him something about the modern economic world. In that sense, he assisted Bismarck in his role as partial modernizer.

The collaboration of the two men—which became acknowledged fact after 1866—epitomized the larger regrouping of German society at the time. The economy was changing, and aristocrats sought to expand or at least maintain their economic position, while businessmen, often plutocratic upstarts, sought to secure social status. In his private life Bismarck paralleled his public achievement: by having Bleichröder at his side, by thus recognizing the importance and value of the business world, he promoted the reconciliation of agrarian and capitalistic, of noble and middle-class, interests. Bismarck created favorable conditions for capitalism, and Bleichröder facilitated the survival of a precapitalistic social order.

In the first four decades of his life, Bismarck had more experience in surviving debts than in choosing investments. He acquired wealth as he acquired fame—in public service. The triumphs of 1866 marked the turning point for Bismarck in the private as well as in the public realm.

It was an amiable custom of the nineteenth century, inherited from earlier times, that victorious statesmen and generals should be rewarded by grateful monarchs and nations. Virtue may be its own reward: success breeds rewards. Acclaim is fleeting; a hereditary title or a large monetary gift is a lasting testimonial. Having just "escaped the gallows," Bismarck now received honors and riches.

After the war with Denmark, Bismarck was made a count. After the six-week war in 1866, a submissive Diet—on behalf of a grateful nation—voted Bismarck a gift of 400,000 taler (a little more than $2 million in 1974 currency). It was a handsome gift; lesser gifts were made to Roon and Moltke. For Bismarck it was the beginning of his large fortune, though some years later, he said it had gone against his grain to accept the money from the Diet: "I did not want to take any money from people with whom for so many years I quarreled so bitterly. . . . But in the end I did succumb to the temptation."[1]

Bismarck never denied his fondness for money—it would have seemed false and stupid to him to do so. Only more delicately minded later historians excised that side of him, as they excised his own references to his tumultuous youth or his "hatred" for his mother.[2] Money provided independence, comfort, privacy; he would have agreed with Heinrich Heine that money had to be valued as the only means to freedom.[3] As a young man, Bismarck had experienced indebtedness, the fate of many of his fellow Junkers. He had no intention of neglecting his investments or his estates; like most men who have once felt the pangs of penury, Bismarck could never bring himself to relax, to think that he was a multimillionaire able to afford losses, taxes, or the consequences of mismanagement. In his attitude toward money, as toward power and diplomacy, Bismarck was utterly realistic. He also thought that property was the "supreme legitimation for participating in things political."[4] The management of money was an index to character: sobriety was a virtue, profligacy or neglect a vice. Genteel poverty and overbearing plutocracy were equally unattractive to Bismarck.

He had learned the hard way. In the late 1830s his father's debts and his own large and variously contracted debts forced him out of his bureaucratic career, which in any case he did not relish, and brought him back to the management of ancestral and debt-ridden estates.[5] After his father's death in 1845, Bismarck inherited Schönhausen and Kniephof. He leased Kniephof to a tenant, and after his entry into politics, he leased Schönhausen as well. By the time he was in Frankfurt, he seems to have reduced his indebtedness and, with Rothschild's help, had for the first time invested in the stock market.

Bleichröder entered Bismarck's service in 1859—in a subordinate position. He collected Bismarck's salary, which as ambassador to St. Petersburg was 33,000 taler, from which Bismarck had to pay most of his own moving and entertainment expenses.[6] No wonder he complained that in reassigning diplomats the state was levying a forced loan on them.[7] In these early years, Bleichröder essentially acted as transfer agent, receiving and disbursing funds. Any surplus between income and expense Bleichröder transmitted to the Frankfurt Rothschilds, with whom Bismarck still retained a large account. Judging from the surviving accounts in the so-called Schönhausen Archive—now quartered in an attic above the present Prince Bismarck's riding stables—it seems unlikely that Bleichröder then invested any of Bismarck's funds. It was a time of largely routine bookkeeping, and the record suggests that in the beginning it was Bleichröder who asked and Bismarck who granted various favors.

In the very first letter we have from Bleichröder to Bismarck he thanks Bismarck for having supplied him with information about the prospective Russian loan. In January 1861 he again thanks Bismarck for his information and laments that his letters are sent by regular mail "which, given the often valuable content of these letters, seems not always advisable."[8] It was the old refrain: Bleichröder wanted expert news, expeditiously and confidentially delivered.

Very quickly, however, the Bismarck-Bleichröder relationship became one of give and take. In 1861, for the first time, Bismarck asked Bleichröder's advice, which, rather ironically, considering his later successes, turned out to be poor. Bismarck wanted to know whether he should sell his shares of the Berlin Brewery, also known as Tivoli; the Frankfurt Rothschilds must have bought them, but Bleichröder was on the board of the company and hence well acquainted with its affairs. Bleichröder counseled against a sale, on the assumption that shares would greatly appreciate once they were formally introduced on the market. The business was "entirely healthy," with a likely dividend of 6 to 7 percent.[9] A little later, Bleichröder assured his friend Abraham Oppenheim that he expected a dividend of 5 to 6 percent. By November Oppenheim wrote Bleichröder angry letters about the sudden drop in the price of shares (from 75 to 50 in one day), about the "offenses" that management must have committed and concealed from Bleichröder. The situation was "wretched," and Oppenheim was furious that the company was now asking its principal shareholders to raise further capital when but a few months earlier they had still been assured of the total financial soundness of the enterprise.[10]

In January 1862 Bleichröder wrote Bismarck a five-page letter, telling him that the company had paid no dividends and would pay none, that in fact its "chief trouble" was a shortage of capital. The company would soon call a meeting at which the principal, original shareholders would be asked to invest further sums, proportionate to their original investments; if this should be refused, "the business will succumb to bankruptcy." The main shareholders—the Rothschilds of Frankfurt, Oppenheim of Cologne, Goldschmidt of Frankfurt—had already agreed to contribute the additional capital; the other principal shareowner, S. E. Günzberg, of St. Petersburg, had so far refused. "I would be very grateful if in your own interest and that of the other shareowners Your Excellency would summon Mr. Günzberg . . . and urge him not to persist in his refusal, which would bring ruin to an enterprise that is intrinsically healthy and viable, but which needs some additional assistance." Bleichröder added that his own experts had pronounced the prospects of a refinanced company as healthy. He begged Bismarck to forgive him his "boldness" in asking for his help; he was doing it for everybody's welfare but would remain beholden to Bismarck for help.[11] We have no way of knowing whether the Prussian ambassador did summon Günzberg to his office. But the company survived and Bismarck forgave Bleichröder his presumption, though it may have seemed to him only another instance of a man pushing his interest.*

In 1862, Bismarck assumed the premiership in Berlin—at less than half his ambassadorial salary. He now received 15,000 taler a year, plus a modest official residence. Bleichröder took care of the routine accounts of the Bismarck family, transmitting regular payments for household expenses of 500 or 1,000 taler at a time. Bismarck's salary was insufficient for his expenses, which in addition to the family's needs—he had three children—included occasional help to his father-in-law and other relatives. At this time, Bleichröder seems not to have collected Bismarck's income from Schönhausen, estimated at 3,500 taler, or the much smaller amount from Kniephof.[12] It is known that Bismarck entertained frugally, but he liked to live well. In July 1863, for example, Bleichröder paid a bill of 203 taler to Moët et Chandon for champagne, and two years later Bleichröder listed his various payments to the Paris Rothschilds on Bismarck's account, which Bismarck in his own hand identified as money spent in Biarritz. The total for that vacation came to 10,550 francs (say, $20,000 in 1974 funds), and despite the fact that Biarritz had been a political vacation, there is no indication that Bismarck received any reimbursement for this rather extravagant expense.[13] In 1866 Bismarck's total expenses, as listed by Bleichröder, amounted to 27,000 taler, although some of the items may have been capital expenditures or loans.

In the beginning Bleichröder's functions were essentially those of a private paymaster. The Frankfurt Rothschilds remained in charge of Bismarck's investments; in one of the few remaining balance sheets from the Rothschilds, it appears that on June 30, 1863, Bismarck's balance with them was 82,247 gulden.[14] Bismarck must have had a reason for leaving his account in Frankfurt; at the height of the constitutional conflict, he may have thought it prudent to leave his mobile wealth in safe hands—outside Prussia. Bleichröder, on the other hand, must have yearned to replace the Rothschilds as Bismarck's investment counselor. Although bound to them by ties of business and loyalty, Bleichröder coveted Bismarck's custom. He was eager to prove his special solicitude, to offer favors and services that the older House might no longer think of granting. One special courtesy—a harsher term could also be used—was to grant Bismarck free stock options and in this way promise him a good chance of profit at no cost or risk. In May 1863, for example, he wrote Bismarck that he "was holding at the disposition of Your Excellency" 1,000 taler's worth of Berlin-Anhalt Railroad shares at 148¾ and another 1,000 taler's worth of Rheinische Railroad at 102¾ until September 30. In short, Bleichröder gave Bismarck a five-month option to buy these shares at a fixed price. Bismarck declined.[15] Eleven months later, on a day when Bismarck made a cash deposit of 27,000 taler (the source of that money is not given, but Bleichröder noted that he would credit it with 5 percent, whereas the Frankfurt Rothschilds seem to have given Bismarck only 4 percent interest), Bleichröder again offered Bismarck a sixty-day call on 40,000 taler's worth of railroad shares, and again

---

* Six years later, Bleichröder sent Bismarck a gift of several kegs of Tivoli beer, hoping that they would leave no "aftertaste [Beigeschmack]." Bleichröder to Bismarck, 12 Oct. 1868, SA.

Bismarck put in the margin "nein."[16] In September 1864 he offered a 100-day option on 20,000 taler's worth of shares of the Prussian Bank, which Bismarck took up on October 1 and sold eight months later for a profit of 1,100 taler.[17]

Bleichröder's solicitude and Bismarck's interest in the stock market were attested in other ways. By the winter of 1863, for example, Bleichröder supplemented his oral reports with repeated letters about the state of the market; in December 1863 he sent similar reports to Carl Ludwig Zitelmann, Bismarck's amanuensis for internal affairs.[18] The health of the market and the views of the Rothschilds and of the business world generally were matters of great importance to Bismarck, in both his public and his private roles.

Eighteen sixty-six was the critical year for Bismarck's private finances—and for Bleichröder's management of them. Bleichröder's annual statement mirrored the extreme fluctuations of that year: Bismarck's balance varied sharply, and so did the rate of interest which Bleichröder credited him with, proportionate to the official discount rate. From May 11 to July 13 the rate was 9 percent; by December, it had fallen to 4 percent. In December 1866 Bleichröder made the first major investments for Bismarck: he bought 6 percent United States bonds for 21,623 taler, Saxon bonds at 5 percent (which Bleichröder helped to place on the market) for 24,875 taler, and shares of the Friedrich Wilhelm Nordbahn for 16,075 taler.[19] The end of the Civil War marked an auspicious moment for United States investments, and the Rothschilds generally became heavy buyers of American securities.

For Bleichröder the most important change of that year was Bismarck's decision to close his account with the Frankfurt Rothschilds. The exact date is not clear; the transfer of funds from Rothschild to Bleichröder must have taken place gradually, with the final transfer of 57,000 taler taking place in July 1867. We have no way of knowing why Bismarck finally switched from the Rothschilds to Bleichröder, but the fact that the change occurred at the end of the constitutional conflict in Prussia, just when Frankfurt lost its independence, is surely more than a coincidence: with Bismarck's position in Berlin triumphantly secure, there was no possible advantage to keeping his funds elsewhere. Bleichröder now became even closer to Bismarck than before.

Bismarck's confidence in Bleichröder's judgment was exemplified in yet another way. In July 1867, shortly after his own return from Paris, Bismarck inquired about the prospects of the market. Bleichröder replied that the Berlin market had become unsettled as a consequence of bellicose rumors from Paris, "where alarmists have been set loose." He added that, whatever the political significance of these reports, he expected the market to be depressed, and hence he urged Bismarck to sell his securities insofar as this could still be done at profit or "with minor losses."[20] Immediately upon receipt of this letter, Bismarck instructed Hermann von Dechend, head of the Prussian Hauptbank, to sell the remaining securities which the Bank held in Bismarck's name—presumably from the public gift of that year.

> Although I do not believe in any dangerous political complication. . . .
> I do believe that influential people in Paris are working *à la baisse* and
> that hotheads there are writing dispatches and inspiring newspaper arti-

cles. I do not consider it unlikely therefore that we are facing a time of market disquiet during which securities could be sold only with difficulty and during which it may well be that I will want some cash.*

In mid-July Bleichröder repeated his warnings with greater specificity: the French government, he reported, had decided on major army reforms even without parliamentary authorization, and the Austrians were also ordering new armaments. There were thunderclouds everywhere, he complained, and the apathetic market would soon go bearish. It was time to sell. Two days later, Keudell transmitted Bismarck's authorization for the sale of his railway shares. After both Dechend and Rothschild had sent their funds and after Bleichröder's sale of Bismarck's securities, Bismarck's balance with Bleichröder in mid-July was 194,000 taler.[21]

At the time of these major investment changes, Bismarck was already living on his new estate, in Varzin. In transmitting the 400,000 taler that a subdued Diet had voted, William urged Bismarck that the money be used for the purchase of an entailed estate that would forever belong to the Bismarcks and would serve as a memorial to his greatness.[22] Bismarck readily obliged, and in April 1867 he bought from Count Blumenthal the *Herrschaft* Varzin near Köslin in Pomerania. The nation's gift proved insufficient, and Bleichröder had to advance additional funds.[23] The advance was short-term, and it would seem that Bleichröder lent Bismarck the money without interest—his private gift. Later that year Bismarck sold the old paternal estate of Kniephof to his nephew, without letting familial sentiments depress the price unduly.[24]

Varzin was immense: at purchase it comprised 22,500 *Morgen* (or about 14,171 acres), half of them forest, much of it cut over. The estate also included seven villages.[25] Still, it was not enough, and Bismarck immediately sought to "round out" his holdings. To a friend he confessed that every evening he felt a ravenous hunger to annex the adjoining estates, but in the morning he could view them calmly.[26] Gradually he acquired almost half as much land again. Bleichröder came to share the financial worries that the chancellor's acquisitive habits produced.

Bismarck's heart was in his estates. He loved his new retreat and, pleading ill health, lived there for months on end. To Americans, he boasted of having become "the country squire of Varzin," inviting his friend Motley to come to see him in the "backwoods," only half a day by train from Berlin.[27] Invitations, though, were rare, and mostly the Bismarcks were by themselves; trees, he wrote, meant more to him than humans, and he rudely told his ministers to leave him alone, "de me f . . . la paix."[28] In the summer of 1867 Bismarck camped out in Varzin, alone, without family or furniture. In a touching letter that has survived in the Bleichröder Archive, old Puttkamer,

---

* It is odd that the editors of the *Gesammelten Werke* date this letter "Varzin, 6 June 1867." On that day, Bismarck was in Paris, visiting the World Exposition. It would seem virtually certain, especially in light of Bleichröder's letter of July 4 and Dechend's answer to Bismarck of July 8, acknowledged in a further letter of Bismarck to Dechend, July 11, that Bismarck's letter should have been dated July 6, when he was in Varzin. *GW*, XIV², 725–726, 730–731.

Bismarck's father-in-law, promised to dispatch clean linen and napkins there, so "there would be no scarcity" when the family came.[29]

But there was more to Varzin than riding, hunting, and endless beech forests. Bismarck took the business side of his holdings seriously, and complained of "the restless life of the *Gutsbesitzer*."[30] He had two aims: to enlarge his holdings and to make them pay. "Everything had to be run economically," his forester recalled.[31] He always had his eye on profitable manufacturing enterprises that could contribute to the meager yield his tenant farmers (*Pächter*) produced. In all these endeavors, from the buying of new lands to their profitable operation, Bismarck turned to Bleichröder for advice and assistance. In 1868 Bismarck negotiated with the brothers Moritz and Georg Behrend from Köslin a twenty-year lease for a burned-down mill that he had bought and wanted to convert to a paper mill.[32] A year later, Bleichröder acknowledged Bismarck's order to establish a credit line to the Behrends of 25,000 taler. The total sums Bismarck advanced were to be far greater.[33] In later years Bleichröder was often called upon to deal directly with the Behrends, whom Bismarck entrusted with other ventures as well and with whom relations became increasingly difficult. The Behrends were either Jews or converted Jews. Johanna was not always happy when in the late 1860s, "Bleichröder and Behrend have to eat there on business."[34]

Bleichröder was skeptical of Bismarck's land hunger and his assumption that estates could be turned into paying propositions. In the fall of 1868, with Bismarck again planning to make additional purchases around Varzin, Bleichröder cautioned:

> Although I am honored with taking care only of your capital investments, I respectfully point out . . . that the estates, despite cheap purchase price, yield only 2¾ percent and that hence it is financially absolutely necessary to invest the funds earmarked for securities at as high an interest rate as possible. . . . If I may presume to make . . . a suggestion concerning the lands [*terrains*] to be acquired, it would be that none of the existing securities should be sold but that a 4 percent mortgage should be given to me. In this way Your Excellency would not lose any of the high interest rate that securities afford.[35]

A year earlier, he had offered to take a 45,000-taler mortgage at 4½ percent.[36] At the prevailing discount rate of 2 to 2¼ percent, such a mortgage would be no burden on the lender, Bleichröder assured Bismarck.[37] It is noteworthy that Bleichröder thought it necessary to give this assurance, to say in effect that a loan on these terms would be no particular favor to the chancellor. Did he have reason to think that Bismarck might mind being too beholden to his banker—or was Bismarck afraid others would mind for him?

Bleichröder wanted Bismarck to understand that by satisfying his ravenous land hunger he was not acting as "economic man," but that because he (like nineteenth-century gentry generally) saw a special virtue in land he incurred special burdens. Economists would measure that special virtue by the difference between the rate of return on land as against other investments (of comparable risk). In Bismarck's case, the difference between investing in land or in "mobile" wealth, assuming Bleichröder's figures to be roughly accurate, would have been many thousands of taler a year. By Bleichröder's rough figures, Bismarck's annual return from Varzin should have been about 12,500 taler. But the noneconomic factors outweighed such considerations: to a Bismarck, "mobile" wealth afforded none of the tangible pleasure, none of the psychic return of security, that rooted or landed wealth provided. On the other hand, German landowners, Bismarck included, always tried to squeeze as much profit out of their holdings as possible, at the expense often of the state and the rest of the population. They were determined to retain their anachronistic ways, so closely related to their status, and to prosper as well.

At Bismarck's insistence, Bleichröder sold some of his securities (Tivoli included) and offered some important homilies in return: "The disposition of our materially minded century is to squeeze as much interest from capital as possible. . . ." Bleichröder's formulations were sometimes unintentionally entertaining, and the enunciation of this general law with its faintly pejorative note about Mammon must have amused Bismarck. Bleichröder continued that "the time of mortgage bonds [Pfandbriefe] seems to me to be over, and our high-interest-bearing railroads, too, will in some years suffer the same fate as turnpikes and will barely yield 3 to 4 percent." Russian finance experts, he continued, had understood this and were attracting foreign, mostly French, capital to build their railroad at a higher but perfectly safe rate of interest.

He added further that if Bismarck were able to buy new land at a genuinely low price, then it too would appreciate—because the king had finally given some encouragement to a plan by Baron von Senfft-Pilsach, as modified by Bleichröder and his associates (especially Oppenheim in Cologne and Hansemann's Disconto-Gesellschaft in Berlin) to found a company that would lease or buy "the lands of our monarchy" and thus drive up the price of land. Bleichröder promised to give Bismarck further details of this project at his forthcoming visit to Varzin, after his visit to Paris.[38] Bleichröder's aside was of calculated importance; his trip to Paris—in the company of Hansemann and Oppenheim—had to do with the founding of a German equivalent of the Crédit Foncier, which would mobilize large amounts of capital in order to allow peasants or landowners to buy, rent, or improve land. There was much bureaucratic opposition to this plan, and Bleichröder took an early and seemingly innocent occasion to awaken Bismarck's interest in a scheme that would benefit him, too. A year later, Bismarck's unflagging support for the founding of a Prussian mortgage bank, the Preussische Central-Bodenkredit-Aktiengesellschaft, proved decisive.[39]

Between 1866 and 1870, Bleichröder's principal concern was with Bismarck's security portfolio. With the chancellor's consent, he bought and sold—and it was this function that provided the opportunity for ever closer contacts and exchanges. Bleichröder proposed and Bismarck approved a conservative portfolio. Gradually Bleichröder revamped Bismarck's investments. In 1868 he sold nearly 6,000 taler's worth of Tivoli Brewery and nearly 77,000 taler's of Pomeranian mortgage bonds. At the same time he transferred 20,000 taler to Bismarck's legal representative, Gustav von Wilmowski, either for new land or for new credits to the Behrends. For the rest, Bleichröder added a sizable holding of Russian mortgage bonds, which repeatedly in the next few years he exchanged for new issues of the same kind, which Bleichröder could offer at 3 to 5 percent discount. Frequent conversion, then, yielded a good profit.[40] Bleichröder also managed to secure Bismarck some short-term profit on other investments: in July 1869, for example, he bought $40,000 worth of 6 percent United States bonds for 49,725 taler and sold them five months later for 52,874 taler. (This meant a 6 percent capital gain in five months as well as 6 percent interest.)[41] It is an odd coincidence that during the Franco-Prussian war, as we shall see below, Bismarck showed a remarkable appreciation of America's role in the world.

Bismarck's portfolio changed in content and value—the latter depending on his other needs. In 1869 the portfolio was worth 138,500 taler; in February 1870 it had temporarily shrunk to 86,023 taler; much of the balance had gone to the Behrends and further land purchases. In the late 1860s it was not uncommon for Bismarck to have very large overdrafts on his account with Bleichröder, sometimes ranging from 50,000 to 80,000 taler. These overdrafts were of course more than covered by Bismarck's securities. But Bleichröder seems to have lent Bismarck short-term money without interest, a favor that he was unlikely to have extended to anyone else. The subject was not broached in any of Bleichröder's letters, and we may assume that by mutual consent a delicate silence covered this issue.

Bismarck and Bleichröder conferred regularly, in and out of Berlin. Between meetings, they corresponded, directly or through Bismarck's aides. From Bleichröder's letters to Bismarck and to the Rothschilds, we know that they discussed more than Bismarck's private affairs. Indeed, there was no hard and fast line between private and public realm. The subjects they discussed, the news they exchanged, necessarily covered what might be called the political economy of Europe—hence these were matters that concerned Bismarck, the statesman and the investor. They talked of war and peace, of the prospects of the stock market, but also of specific matters, such as Bismarck's worry in 1868 about "price increases and the lower employment figures in industry which prevail in Prussia also. As soon as the weather improves, the government will energetically push railroad construction and look for means to reduce the price of bread."[42]

In those years, Bismarck's horizon steadily widened, and his grasp of economics—that is to say, of the interconnectedness of things—deepened. Bleichröder transmitted to him the best financial intelligence of the period: by virtue of Bleichröder's investments, Bismarck perforce became concerned with the economic progress of the United States, of Russia, of German railroads. He learned about the capital market, and as one of Prussia's large landowners he learned about land credit, timber sales, and paper manufacturing in a continually fluctuating market. Under expert guidance and with the most pressing incentive—his own profit—the chancellor came to appreciate the intricate nature of an agrarian-commercial world.

At times Bismarck affected to neglect the affairs of state and withdrew to Varzin, nursing his injured health. The more time Bismarck spent rusticating in his favorite estate and lovely park, cut off from frantic Berlin, the more important was Bleichröder's easy entrée. When matters of state oppressed Bismarck, and his underlings in Berlin were told to withhold disagreeable mail, he still cherished a concern for his own affairs. He painstakingly examined Bleichröder's statements. His interest in his private affairs was minute and constant, as his contemporaries knew. In 1869, apropos of recurrent rumors that Bismarck's ill health would force his resignation, the Austrian chargé, Baron Münch, wrote his foreign minister: "But all reports agree that in Varzin Count Bismarck is devoting the greatest attention and activity to the conditions of his fortune and that he is making his landed estate more profitable."[43]

At times of crisis—and who in Europe knew better than Bismarck when there was a real as distinguished from a rumored crisis—Bismarck sought to protect his capital, to move defensively. Of course Bleichröder's news —and, more importantly, his own—informed Bismarck's investment decisions. Such prudence seemed anything but culpable to Bismarck. If he had felt any scruples—or expected others to feel any moral unease at this mixing of private and public business—he would, at the time of Gastein, not have asked Eulenburg to instruct Bleichröder about his securities but would have done so directly, nor in July 1867 would he have given Dechend market instructions based on political explanations. As we will see, he exercised the same care in the management of his funds at the time of the outbreak of the Franco-Prussian war. A few months later, he pooh-poohed the idea that one could make money by using political knowledge. And in a way he was right: he was merely using it to save money, and he was always indignant at statesmen (the French foreign minister, Gramont, for example) who combined policy and speculation in such a way as to make the former serve the latter.[44]

Only a very naïve observer—or a German historian affecting contempt for money—would be surprised to learn that at times of great political crisis Bismarck found time to think of his investments. Was he profiting from his unique position in order to protect his wealth? Bismarck would have felt that to ignore the intelligence his position brought him would be tantamount to self-injury. The idea that power should be resolutely unprofitable, that public and private interests might be incompatible because the latter might corrupt the former, did not occur to Bismarck or to other nineteenth-century giants. Power, they knew, brought pain and tribulation as well as exhilaration and possible fame; it certainly should command deference and loyalty, and if these proved profitable, *tant mieux*. Profit was no threat to their integrity nor impoverishment an acceptable reward for service to king and country.

For Bleichröder, the growing intimacy with Bismarck was invaluable. To be Bismarck's banker and confidant—and to be known as such—certified

Bleichröder's special status. But there were also certain immediate, practical advantages that Bleichröder drew from this close relationship. Like the Rothschilds, like any financier, Bleichröder put a special premium on being abreast of major developments, on knowing a few hours or days ahead of his competitors the likely climate of the market. Because of his double role as Bismarck's investor and adviser, Bleichröder had ample reason for supplying the chancellor with a steady stream of news about the political economy of Europe. In conversation or correspondence Bismarck would have to offer some comment of his own, some comfirmation or denial of a report. In short, by transmitting news to Bismarck, Bleichröder was also continually soliciting news from him. And for Bleichröder to know the thoughts or the disposition of the most influential actor on Europe's stage was of incalculable importance. Both men were perfectly candid about this aspect of their relationship. At the end of 1869, for example, Bleichröder counseled Bismarck not to sell his securities, but hedged: "If, however, Your Excellency should expect troubles in the Near Eastern question or other political complications, then I would indeed sell all Your Excellency's securities."[45] Bismarck was equally candid; he once defined his relationship with Bleichröder to Lord Odo Russell, the British ambassador in Berlin in the 1870s, when Russell had been instructed to find out whether the British government should consider Bleichröder as a well-informed source. Bismarck said: "Are you aware of the fact that Bleichröder administers my private fortune? If so, do you believe that I would mislead him?"[46]

Gradually something more than a mere business relationship ripened. Bleichröder must not only have been efficient and successful, as well as pleasingly subservient and solicitous; he must have been congenial as well, for their relations deepened in these years and even Johanna formed personal ties to him. Some of the Bismarck clan—Otto's cousin and collaborator, Bismarck-Bohlen, for example—used Bleichröder as banker and investment counselor. Others had to deal with Bleichröder because Bismarck referred all financial matters to him. Occasionally Bismarck handed Bleichröder personal letters from his family, with appropriate instructions noted at the top. Thus there survive in the Bleichröder Archive two letters from old Puttkamer to his "dear son," full of affection and fond hopes of seeing him and his boys in Varzin, while also informing him of his need for 17,600 taler, for which he would pay 5 percent interest. Bleichröder was the intermediary.[47] The clan probably looked on Bleichröder as it did on money: a necessary evil. Johanna's cousin Bernhard von Puttkamer wrote Bismarck about some compromise in an inheritance question, adding: "I did this with the greatest pleasure because I know of nothing more disagreeable than strife and discord within the family on account of cursed Mammon."[48]

Bleichröder's letters to Bismarck—always a composite of candor and flattery, of substance and froth—attest this growing intimacy and mutual concern. Each was worried about the other's health. In those four years, Bismarck suffered repeated bouts of nervous exhaustion or irritation, which in the fashion of the day were treated by strenuous cures or prolonged rustic rests. The Iron Chancellor, even then, was a frequent victim of psychosomatic ills, and the magnificent exterior and lucid mind hid brittle nerves and a troubled spirit.* Bleichröder's anxiety was touching, and his expression of it—even allowing for the greater extravagance of the times—a little fulsome or bizarre: "The news about Your Excellency's condition gave me infinite pleasure and together with thousands of others I send a daily prayer to the Creator [*Weltenschöpfer*] for the strengthening of Your Excellency's health." Or a year later: "May my daily prayers to the Creator be heard and may He very soon let Your Excellency completely recover and regain strength—to the joy of the noble family and friends and as a blessing for our fatherland."[49] Prayers were regularly supplemented by appropriate delicacies to speed Bismarck's recovery: endless caskets of specially shipped caviar, sturgeon, pâté, and an occasional wine to wash them down. Bleichröder also arranged for the doctor to send him direct telegraphic bulletins from Varzin concerning Bismarck's health.[50] In the fall of 1869 Bleichröder underwent a serious eye operation and for some time afterward suffered from an inflammation of the eye. He cited his infirmity as cause for his silence. After this, the Bismarcks always inquired after his health. At least in suffering there was a kind of equality. Twice in those years, in the fall of 1868 and 1869, Bleichröder spent some days in Varzin, and he probably visited Bismarck for shorter periods there as well. The visits were private. The fact that they had taken place was a secret Bleichröder showed little reticence in revealing.

Bismarck's triumph in 1866 also transformed Bleichröder's life. He had been Bismarck's helper in the dark, uncertain days. As Bismarck became the dominant statesman of Europe, Bleichröder's prominence grew as well.

Bleichröder owed his successes to a conjunction of happy circumstances. After 1866 Berlin became Germany's national center; Bismarck had wanted it so and had indignantly rejected court suggestions that the new Reichstag should meet in Potsdam or Frankfurt. Only from its own capital could Prussia exert the necessary force to assimilate Germany to Prussian supremacy.[51] And in this newly important Berlin, Bleichröder was known to be wealthy, hence within limits powerful; he was known to be Bismarck's confidant, hence certified as knowledgeable and reliable; he had close ties to the Rothschilds, hence an international eminence. He was constantly gaining more wealth, more connections, more dignity. But none of this was automatic or painless. He had to work unceasingly to win his place.

Bleichröder's rise after 1866 illustrates dramatically the interlocking nature of Germany's new order. It was Bleichröder's simultaneous success in different realms—in the banking world, in Bismarck's world, in the world of

* Bismarck's family had an intuitive sense of the nature of some of his ailments. In a letter to Bismarck that was part personal and part business and hence ended up in Bleichröder's hands, Johanna's cousin Bernhard congratulated Bismarck on his improved health and added: "May God grant that it stay this way even here in Berlin when you will be sitting amidst the cares for our affairs and where the big, brave yak-yakkers of the Chamber [*Kammermaulhelden*] will strive to annoy you. In your place I would simply let them prattle and punish them by contempt." Bismarck tended to do that—but he also punished himself by his intense anger at most opponents. Bernhard von Puttkamer to Bismarck, 25 Nov. 1868, BA.

European finance and of the Rothschilds, in the tightly ordered world of the Prussian court—that gave him his preeminence. He helped to bring these worlds closer together, and his success in one realm reinforced his claim in another. Money begets more than money; it begets influence and some— limited—forms of power. But for Bleichröder, as for European financiers generally, wealth was not enough; in a traditional-hierarchical society, it was status and public acceptance that mattered. Bleichröder's spreading importance symbolized the triumph of capitalism itself, and yet Bleichröder's story also demonstrates the limits and travails entailed in that triumph.

After 1866 Bleichröder's intimacy with Bismarck was a celebrated fact of social and political life. He was known as a man of shrewd judgment, integrity, and prudence, blessed with a Midas touch. If anything, popular imagination already began to exaggerate Bleichröder's influence. He was rightly reputed to be the best-informed man in Berlin, precisely because he lived and worked in so many diverse realms. He had friends, clients, creatures everywhere, visibly and invisibly. He spun his web of contacts. He had much to offer and needed much in return. He had influence sometimes, political power never. And for every rung of the ladder, he had to fight or jockey. The power of capitalists is a common theme; the precariousness of their success in some societies is often ignored.

The base of Bleichröder's importance was his bank, and it flourished throughout the decade of the 1860s. Its history will be written at another time; for the purposes of this book a few salient facts must suffice. It continued to belong to the Prussian Consortium, a group of leading bankers (including Hansemann's Disconto-Gesellschaft and the Frankfurt Rothschilds), who habitually worked together on state loans and other affairs. The bank became an ever more important presence in the world markets; Bleichröder gradually emancipated himself from being a mere appendage of the Rothschilds. Alone or together with other houses, S. Bleichröder founded or funded various other enterprises, ranging, as we have seen, from breweries to railroads to the Prussian Mortgage Bank. One of the greatest projects that Bleichröder and Hansemann cooperated on was the financing of the immensely important and expensive St. Gotthardtunnel.[52] By the late 1860s and early 1870s, this type of promotion was destined to become even more important and profitable.

Gerson was the head of the bank; it was his empire and his responsibility. A staff of clerks, headed by the loyal Lehmann, who had already served under Gerson's father, helped him. In 1868 Gerson made his cousin Julius Schwabach a partner. From 1855, when old Bleichröder had died, until 1870, Gerson's brother Julius, who ran his own small bank in Berlin, had an interest in the family business; the two brothers were sleeping partners in each other's firm. A few letters from Julius to Gerson give us a picture of the annual profits of S. Bleichröder for the 1860s. In 1863 the net profit was 18,661 taler; in 1867, 43,464 taler; in 1868, 54,940 taler; and in 1869, 80,761 taler.[53] In seven years, the profits increased more than four times; it was a respectable rate of growth. At the end of the decade, the original contract between the brothers expired. Julius wanted to continue the relationship, but Gerson decided to end their respective participations.* The bank's profits were only part of Bleich-röder's income; in 1861 the police had estimated his private income as being 23,333 taler.[54] By the end of the decade, he is likely to have made at least 100,000 taler a year.

The Rothschilds remained Bleichröder's models and most coveted associ-ates. Baron James retained his special place, although Bleichröder was also in constant touch with the London and Frankfurt Houses. They often collab-orated, and in addition, Bleichröder plied Baron James with confidential news that emanated from "the good source."

He also plied him with presents. In 1864 Baron James must have men-tioned some particular antique he coveted, and Bleichröder at once sent it as a gift. "I am very partial to this sort of antique," wrote Baron James in reply,

> because otherwise, I confess, my dear Herr Bleichröder, that I would not have accepted it because the piece is really too valuable. I hardly dare to give you any further orders to buy things for me, otherwise I would ask you now to keep an eye out for old paintings or other antiques there be-cause the war against the poor Danes probably has brought many beauti-ful and interesting pieces on the market.[55]

In 1867 the two men met at Wildbad, and in the same year Bleichröder presented Baron James with an option for a rare collection of paintings, includ-ing Cranachs and Breughels, which had very nearly gone to Prince Orlov.[56] Bleichröder's efforts to please Baron James remained, but the old subservience gradually diminished. In 1868 Baron James died, and Bleichröder hastened to his funeral. James, a legendary figure who came to believe in his own legend, had already been the patron of Gerson's father, and it seemed natural for the son to preserve feelings of deference, even subservience, toward this older man. With Baron James's son and successor, Baron Alphonse, the relations became less burdened with Bleichröder's own modest beginnings. Bleichröder's growing independence—and his basking in Prussia's glory—annoyed the Rothschilds at times.

The Rothschilds had no reason to like Bismarck, but they had to reckon with and respect him. (It is hard to imagine the Rothschilds liking anyone; util-ity was their sole criterion.) Even Moritz von Goldschmidt had come to recog-nize the frightful genius who had thrust his country into the first rank of Euro-pean powers: "It is indisputable," he wrote in August 1866, "that your premier has become the top man of the present situation by virtue of his own energy and

---

* In his effort to persuade Gerson to continue the relationship, Julius wrote: "The death of our so deeply beloved father left each of us in his own sphere of activity. Whether it was his benevolent intention to separate us in later years, by having you sign alone for the business of S. Bleichröder and thus to separate us in financial and social position as well, I do not dare to say. In any case, I believe that each of us up to now has found his own way to his own satisfaction and I shall hope that whatever the future will bring, our beloved and honored deceased will be able to look down on his two sons with contentment." Julius to Gerson Bleichröder, 29 Nov. 1869, BA.

will power."[57] Bismarck's ill health was always a subject of much gossip, and Bleichröder had to supply authentic information. In November 1866 he denied the insistent rumors of Bismarck's "incurable disease," and a month later reported: "The Minister-President is in the best of shape but extremely busy."[58] At another time, in 1868, he sent this characteristic message: "The condition of the good source, whom I visited today, is decidedly better, even though he is still very feeble and receives no one."[59]

The Rothschilds may have wearied of Bleichröder's boasting, but they knew that his contacts could be put to profitable use. The aftermath of the Austro-Prussian war furnished further proof. Angry that Saxony's integrity had to be preserved, Bismarck imposed a heavy indemnity on Austria's ally. All the pleas of the Saxon finance minister and chief peace negotiator, Baron von Friesen, were unavailing. His argument that Saxony had already paid 2,500,000 taler for the dubious privilege of Prussian occupation fell on deaf ears; his insistence that Saxony's military expenditures would be higher in the new North German Confederation than in the prewar budget was met by the Prussian negotiator's laconic answer that such payments were a privilege for Saxony.[60] No wonder Bleichröder wrote Baron James a little later: "In the annexed territories, as in Saxony, sentiment toward Prussia is pretty malevolent, understandably enough, and it will take a long time until things take a friendlier turn."[61] On October 18 Bleichröder called on the hapless Friesen.[62] To Friesen's surprise, Bleichröder knew of the imminent signing of the treaty, and prompted by Baron James, he offered Friesen an advance against a later loan that might be needed to cover the indemnity.[63] Four days later the treaty was initialed, and Saxony agreed to an indemnity of 10 million taler, 9 million to be paid in cash. Baron James was most anxious to secure the loan, and Bleichröder hurried to Dresden to press Rothschild's offer, but met with reluctance and local competition.[64] Bleichröder hoped to get the loan at 95 plus commission, which would have been, he thought, a "brilliant arrangement"[65]; he apparently was successful, and he invested Bismarck's own funds in the loan. The Saxons were also pleased, for in February 1870 the king awarded Bleichröder a high decoration, and Friesen sent congratulations and thanks for "the important support which you gave, especially in connection with . . . the Saxon loan of 1866."[66] Bleichröder helped the Saxon government to pay the contribution ahead of schedule, and he thus facilitated the rapid rapproachement of Prussia and Saxony, which became an important pillar of the new Confederation.[67]

Bleichröder's name was often linked with the fate of another victim of the 1866 war: he apparently administered or helped to administer the confiscated treasure of the Hanoverian dynasty, the interest of which, the Welfenfond, constituted a large secret fund for which Bismarck was accountable to the king alone. Until 1872, Bleichröder's friend Keudell supervised the Welfenfond payments in the Foreign Office, the largest beneficiary of its revenues. All records, even of the Legationskasse, were lost during World War II, and hence most of Bleichröder's secret payments on Bismarck's behalf cannot be reconstructed.[68]

Bismarck's various interests were always closely enmeshed, but not always to Bleichröder's satisfaction. Aware that he spoke directly or indirectly for the banking community generally, Bleichröder felt no compunction in complaining to Bismarck if his interests had been disappointed. Implicitly, he too must have assumed that what was good for the House of Bleichröder was good for the state of Prussia.

One example from the late 1860s must suffice. In 1869, in order to raise new capital and attract funds from abroad, the Disconto-Gesellschaft (presumably together with Bleichröder) had planned to found an international consortium for a 100 million-taler lottery on behalf of the four biggest German railroads, in three of which Bismarck was a shareholder. There was strong parliamentary opposition to such a venture, and Bleichröder urged Bismarck to return to Berlin.[69] Bismarck's absence, however, was deliberate; he hid behind ill health in order to avoid political unpleasantness. To Motley he explained his continued absence: "I would like to wait and see whether the Diet would not do me the favor of killing some of my colleagues; if I am among them, then they too benefit from the indulgence which is granted me."[70]

The bill was defeated. Bleichröder was furious and with rare rhetorical flourish complained to Bismarck: "The engines which foiled the project are labeled envy, doctrinaire theorizing, but above all weakness of the ministers in charge. . . . The two houses [of parliament] have been given a right to meddle with specific government matters, and thus they have gained an ascendancy over the ministers in charge which very soon will manifest itself in the budgetary question."[71] It took courage to accuse Bismarck's ministers of the crime of crimes, the extension of parliamentary power. Bleichröder saw Bismarck a few days later in Varzin. By the end of the month Heydt had been dismissed, and Camphausen, until then head of the Seehandlung, was appointed his successor. The response to Camphausen, Bleichröder reported, was "very, very favorable." The new finance minister, who had originally favored the lottery loan, should defend it, if only to resist parliamentary aggrandizement. Even Camphausen, however, could not rescue a project that, according to Bleichröder, had been killed by the Diet's "long-winded theorizing," which Bismarck also always detested.[72]

On other occasions, Bleichröder had better luck in trying to enlist the government's help. Also in 1869, and largely because of Bleichröder's tireless behind-the-scenes activity, the government signed a secret agreement with the German equivalent of the Reuter News Agency, called the Wolff Telegraph Bureau. Bleichröder contributed funds to Wolff and in exchange was entitled to receive news on a preferential basis. The details of the government's treaty and of Bleichröder's role belong to the story of his extensive relations with the Fourth Estate generally, which will be discussed in Chapter 11.

Like the Rothschilds, Bleichröder wanted all governmental business, however small, provided the terms were favorable. Even routine transactions yielded commissions and some profit. Bleichröder grew richer and richer in the late 1860s. A certain kind of power accrued to him as well: his resources allowed him to bestow or withhold various forms of help to governments, companies, and individuals. Not all money was equal: Bleichröder's money had a special cachet and hence was especially valuable. He could in effect decide the fate of a person or a charity or even a company. But there was a rub to it all: he was also dependent on the good will of governments and of the socially prominent. This dependence hobbled his power. Hence his was an endless pursuit of wealth and prominence, carried on indefatigably and quite deliberately. Every profit, every title, every friend, helped to establish or maintain Bleichröder's place in the world. There was no fixed goal, there was hardly time for a contented look backwards to realize how far, how immeasurably far, he had traveled.

Wealth was not enough, nor was its pursuit an end in itself for Bleichröder. Wealth was a necessary but not a sufficient condition for his becoming an accepted part of the governing elite of Germany. Wealth without social distinction was but a flawed achievement. Social prominence, in turn, was an incalculable asset in business. The pursuit of wealth and distinction was identical and mutually reinforcing. Great new wealth always seeks distinction—and the newer the wealth or the lower the social origin of its possessor, the more anxious and desperate the search. Perhaps the search was harder in Germany than elsewhere because feudal and anticapitalistic sentiments were more strongly entrenched there than in France or England, to say nothing of America. And it was hardest undoubtedly for a German Jew, who bore the stigma of old and new Mammon worship. The irony was that while many a Jew was jealous of the intrinsic respectability that gentiles, especially noble gentiles, possessed, many a gentile nobleman was covertly jealous of the wealth that Jews seemed preeminently clever in amassing. Mutual desire led to close collaboration, even friendship, and occasionally to the illusion that the hostility and the jealousy had ceased altogether. But old families could never give up their disdain for new wealth; it was too much a part of their shrinking patrimony.

Bleichröder's rise to respectability, his struggle for a place in society, is but an instance of this universal effort to legitimize new wealth. Most of the great novelists of the last century—Balzac, Dickens, Trollope, and Theodor Fontane, for example—made this struggle a central theme of their work, and social scientists have recently rediscovered it. In Bleichröder's case we can follow the struggle, both on and off stage. We have a factual record of what it took for a Jewish banker in Berlin, under in some ways ideal circumstances, to establish himself. The special burden of Jewishness, as it affected his whole life, will be discussed in the last part of this book. Here we shall sketch a succession of portraits to show how Bleichröder, the wealthy man and the patriotic servant, received formal recognition which in turn brought him a wider range of clients and dependent friends, which in turn benefited his business and led to still greater social prominence and political visibility. To a Prussian conservative (perhaps to many a European moralist) the story was one of the infinite venality of men and society; it is also the story of infinite hypocrisy: of grabbing and crying at the same time. Bleichröder was not a moralist; he was content to make his way—upward and without troublesome thoughts about the intrinsic value of the climb.

For centuries, grateful governments had eased the passage of the rich into the kingdom of man by distributing formal signs of recognition: titles and medals. The Prussian government systematically exploited its subjects' hunger for decoration. The politically reliable were rewarded, the dissident would go bare. The rich could expedite their rise—some would say, buy it—by making large gifts to communal charity. Such purposeful charity was a kind of voluntary tax. The state meticulously scrutinized Bleichröder's qualifications on all these points.[73] On New Year's Day, 1866, Bleichröder was accorded the title Geheimer Kommerzienrat, a further, rare distinction which meant that in future he would be addressed as "Herr Geheimrat." Before the award, the Berlin police scrutinized Bleichröder's record, and the chief wrote a long report, supporting the new title. He explained that the integrity of Gerson's father had led the Rothschilds to appoint him their deputy in Berlin; Gerson had continued in that role but had achieved "greater independence." The House of Bleichröder "is now regarded as the greatest banking house in Berlin. . . . Politically, Bleichröder belongs to the strict conservative party, he is devoted with unshakable loyalty to the Royal House; he enjoys the high esteem of the College of Elders of the Berlin Merchants." The rest of the sentence, "and distinguishes himself by many qualities of the heart," was struck out, probably by Itzenplitz, the minister of commerce, who had to approve the police report and pass it on to Bismarck. (Did Itzenplitz think that bankers, especially Jewish bankers, had no qualities of heart?) Bleichröder's patriotic charity, his generous aid to the families of Prussian soldiers during the Danish war, was especially commended. The report concluded: "What, if any, other services Gerson Bleichröder has had the opportunity of rendering to the royal government must be known to Your Excellency." Details about Bleichröder's "other services" reached Itzenplitz from the most authoritative quarter, from Bismarck himself. In a formal letter, in which the key passages were corrected in Bismarck's own hand, the Premier supported this further distinction to Bleichröder because "since I assumed my present office, Kommerzienrat Bleichröder has rendered me commendable political services." Bleichröder's connections with the Rothschild Houses had given Bismarck "intelligence which I could use to advantage in the interest of the state and his connections have afforded me a channel for the transmission of entirely confidential information and influences. I would consider it therefore desirable to grant him the proposed distinction as recognition." Bismarck further assured Itzenplitz that William I would also favor such an award because "during this year's stay in Karlsbad [His Majesty] repeatedly summoned Kommerzienrat Bleichröder and deigned to listen to him about financial and stock market questions."[74]

In March 1867 the king contemplated another decoration for Bleichröder and again solicited the views of the well-informed police. A new report praised Bleichröder's many contributions to the committee aiding the families of draftees in 1866 and emphasized his "outstanding position in the Berlin financial world, his very considerable wealth which enables him to follow his charitable inclinations, and the great eagerness with which he participates in every patriotic enterprise as in every charitable institute." Bleichröder had made "sacrifices" for charity, and the report concluded: "This in every sense irreproachable conduct has earned him the respect of the widest circles and makes him worthy of another decoration. As such I would suggest the Kronen Orden, third class," which the king duly bestowed on him.[75] Among many others, the minister of the interior, Count Eulenburg, sent Bleichröder his informal, cordial congratulations.[76] This was the highest decoration that businessmen were likely to receive.[77]

Foreign governments followed suit. In 1869 the king of Italy awarded him the officer's cross of the St. Mauritius and Lazarus Order; the czar of Russia bestowed the Order of Stanislav, second class, in recognition of Bleichröder's help in founding the Russian Mortgage Bank. For every foreign decoration, Bleichröder needed and received William's approval.[78]

Bleichröder's new title was a fitting and pleasing recognition of his rising importance. It confirmed in formal dignity what the world of European bankers and diplomats knew, that Gerson Bleichröder had become a major figure in the new center of power in Berlin. Prussia had given him all that a businessman—let alone a Jewish businessman—could aspire to at the time. At formal functions, his chest was no longer hopelessly bare, and letters could now be addressed to him as "Ritter hoher" and "höchster Orden," though there was some doubt whether the Prussian decorations alone justified the term "Ritter."[79] On the long and precarious ladder of social prestige, he had moved up several rungs.

Behind the scenes, Bleichröder was tireless in his hunt for titles or medals.* But it must be remembered that it was a common chase—which the state sponsored, society tolerated, and all but the proudest and most independent participated in. Bismarck had already discovered in the 1850s that even the most distinguished members of the new money aristocracy, the Rothschilds, thirsted for decorations. The desire never slackened. In the Bismarck Archive, among the Bleichröder papers, survive two letters of November and December 1863 from Carl Meyer von Rothschild, the head of the Frankfurt House, to Bismarck, begging for a royal favor: "Your Excellency knows my old, proven, and unbounded devotion to your person, and knows how attached I have always been to Prussian interests, even though my great and protracted services have not in any way been noticed in any *prominent* fashion." Thus began the first letter, recalling how with all his "strength and energy and with the full weight of [his] far-reaching influence," he had supported the Franco-Prussian trade agreement, which was very unpopular in Frankfurt. He listed his other efforts as well: "I now turn to you, full of confidence in Your Excellency as a *noble, magnanimous*, and *all-powerful* representative, and do not doubt that Your Excellency in just appreciation of the facts known to Yourself will kindly think of me and grant me a dignified token of the all-highest recognition. . . . No more deserving or grateful person could receive such an honor," because

---

* In the fall of 1865, after and because he had served as transfer agent in the Lauenburg sale, he had solicited Goldschmidt for an Austrian decoration. Goldschmidt cautioned him against pushing his luck too far: "Let me say to you in all candor that the Lauenburg affair was too trivial to demand a decoration." Baron Anselm would not recommend it, but Bleichröder could try it through Count Chotek or Bismarck. As for Goldschmidt himself, he was no "hunter after titles or decorations," and Bleichröder should not bother the Prussian government on his behalf. He should instead try to get his son an appointment as consul in Paris. Eventually, Goldschmidt's son did become consul in Paris—and Bleichröder received his Austrian decoration in 1872. Goldschmidt to Bleichröder, 25 Sept. 1865, BA.

his unsurpassed loyalty to Prussia would endure. A few weeks later, at New Year's, Carl Meyer transmitted his wishes: "May heavenly Providence always watch over Your Excellency and may you experience only days of the brightest joy and of boundless good fortune in the circle of your family, may it be my lot always to enjoy Your Excellency's high favor and gracious protection and to be able to count myself among your most faithful admirers and servants." The prospective Honors List (*Ordensfest*) would be an appropriate time for the king to grant him an honor "on which I put such great and justified value." He mentioned his most recent services and pleaded for a higher decoration which would be consonant with the honors bestowed on him by all the other rulers within and without the German Confederation.[80] The Rothschilds were a world power, a universally recognized dynasty upon whom many monarchs had bestowed favors. And still they cravenly asked for the next highest medal.* Bleichröder was a mere upstart by comparison. Supplicants asked for these distinctions privately—and often denied publicly that they were interested in such things. Even in a servile society, servility was thought a weakness.

Wealth, a great bank, an intimate tie with Bismarck, titles and medals—all of these opened Bleichröder's way into Prussian society. His physical presence matched his new importance: he was a man of stature in the literal sense. Tall, with a large head and an intelligent, open face, of substantial, but not corpulent, circumstance, he moved with relative ease in the higher realms of society. Dress and decorum were impeccably conservative, as were of course his views. His appearance exuded propriety. His conversation lacked wit and sparkle, but was sustained by an intelligence that all his contemporaries respected. His speech was given to flourishes and occasional epigrams. His detractors saw and heard what they wanted to see and hear; they spoke of his Talmudic physiognomy and they insisted that he lapsed into a German-Jewish dialect, into a sing-song *jüdeln*. In fact, he seems not to have had any of the commonly defined "Jewish features"; in moments of excitement, the typical expressions of his youth probably did break forth, but on the whole he cut a respectable figure, and even failing eyesight, which in the 1870s gradually led to blindness, did not remove him from the social scene.

By the late 1860s he had already built up a network of clients and friends; he would bestow material favors on them and they would often pay him back in the coinage of an older society: by accepting his invitations, by reciprocating them, by encouraging others to come to the banker's house, to accept a Jew's hospitality.

A few examples must suffice. Obviously Bismarck's entourage had to reckon with Bleichröder's presence. Some did so with relish and to advantage,

---

* But were not always comfortable with it. In 1861 Baron James had received a Prussian decoration; he thanked Bleichröder for his congratulations and added: "I would ask you, however, and I am counting on you to comply, not to say too much in the newspapers about my receiving a decoration as a Jew because in that way one could provoke a polemic against the Jews which would do harm rather than good." Baron James to Bleichröder, 19 Nov. 1861, BA.

like Robert von Keudell. Others may have been more reluctant.* But Bleich-röder had his connections everywhere, even in the camp of Bismarck's enemies. From 1868 to 1876, for example, Bleichröder rented an apartment in his house to Count August Eulenburg, Hofmarschall of the crown prince, with whom Bismarck had tenuous relations.[81] In time, Eulenburg became a friend and client. Within the Prussian court, Bismarck feared none more than Queen Augusta, and Bleichröder had close relations with her Oberhofmeister, Count Nesselrode, whom Bismarck detested.[82] In 1867 Nesselrode had borrowed 50,000 taler at 5 percent for three months. A year earlier, during the Austro-Prussian war, he had informed Bleichröder that the queen, "amidst general satisfaction," had nominated him to the board of some war charity. Later he supplied Bleichröder with confidential reports. In May 1867, for example, he wrote that Baron Loë, the Prussian military attaché in Paris, had just arrived in Berlin, where he was likely to spread "evil rumors about French armaments" because "he seems to me to want war urgently." Nesselrode asked for information so that he could counter these maneuvers. The rest of the letter dealt with his investments. In July 1867 he wrote from Windsor Castle, again about his investments, and added: "People here believe that the peace will last, although the domestic conditions here strike me as very serious because the social and workers' questions must lead to terrible conflicts." Three days later, he reported that Franco-German relations seemed to have worsened, that some people in England thought that the superiority of the Prussian needle gun over the chassepot ought to be exploited: "Whether under these circumstances it wouldn't be advisable to sell my shares, I leave to your judgment." He added that some Englishmen feared a revolution in their country.[83] We do not know whether Bleichröder shared this gloom, but Nesselrode's letter came precisely at the time when for political reasons Bleichröder urged Bismarck to sell his securities. Nesselrode's letter is clear evidence, moreover, that members of the Prussian court thought it normal to use their political information for their own financial ends—and that they too regarded war as a likely depressant of the market.

Other high officials repaid Bleichröder's personal kindnesses by supplying him with confidential information that would be directly useful to his business interests. This became routine under the Empire, but even earlier Bleich-röder had his special informants. A key figure was Major A. von Brandt, whom Count Waldersee recalled as a "*bon vivant*," and as such he was obviously in particular need of Bleichröder's help.[84] Brandt called him "my esteemed friend," and wrote him in great detail about prospective government operations in Berlin real estate. "I was assured," wrote Brandt, "that I could get information at any time. Just ask me definite questions at the right moment."[85]

---

* In April 1866 Lothar von Schweinitz, Prussian military attaché in St. Petersburg and special adjutant of William, returned to Berlin with an urgent message from Alexander II, designed to prevent an Austro-Prussian war. He first saw William and then looked for Bismarck: "When I came to the Wilhelmstrasse, I found at first only Keudell and with him Herr Bleichröder, which then still struck me as novel and offensive. Bleichröder occupied a position of confidence with Bismarck at that time, although as Bismarck once said to me later, 'I never had a thought in common with him.'" *Denkwürdigkeiten des Botschafters General von Schweinitz* (Berlin, 1927), I, 202.

Bleichröder also maintained his relations with the liberal, parliamentary world. He cultivated his friendship with Lasker, the tiny Jewish deputy who by his intelligence, industry, and oratory played a leading role in German politics. In the decade after Königgrätz, he and his National Liberal colleagues helped Bismarck in the construction, first, of the North German Confederation, later of the Reich. Bleichröder and Lasker addressed each other as friends, and Berlin gossip apparently spoke of close business relations. In December 1869 Lasker wrote Bleichröder about rumors that "I am supposed to be receiving thousands from you annually, for I don't know what services, and to be concerned particularly with your financial operations. . . . I have always regarded our relations as purely personal and have ever been honored especially by the tie of personal friendship." He offered his continued advice on purely personal matters but wanted to avoid anything that might suggest "partiality that was in any way connected with [my] parliamentary activity." Lasker, it would appear, was more scrupulous in his insistence on the separation of public office and private profit than some of Bleichröder's conservative clients, Bismarck included. Unaccustomed as he was to such high-minded reticence, Bleichröder a few weeks later offered Lasker a munificent position, which Lasker apparently had once wanted. Now he declined: "My general impression is that a position such as the one offered would limit my freedom, and full unlimited freedom is my life blood."[86] Lasker's refusal saved Bleichröder potential embarrassment, for in another few years Bismarck had come to hold Lasker in such passionate hatred that any intimate link between the two might have jeopardized Bleichröder's relations with the chancellor.

By the mid-1860s, Bleichröder was already well acquainted with some of the Prussian diplomats abroad. A special contact was the Prussian minister to Bern, von Röder, a friend of Keudell's and something of a protégé of Bleichröder's. In May 1867 Röder wrote Bleichröder from Bern:

> Only now, my esteemed friend, because as such you have always shown yourself to me and my family, do I get a chance to thank you with all my heart for all the kindnesses, benevolence and true sympathy you showed me during our stay in Berlin. I hope you got to know us well enough to realize . . . that I think of you often and of the sympathetic words of friendship with which you encouraged me in dark moments. May God bless you for it, as I thank you.

Röder's predicament remains obscure, but clearly Bleichröder had helped and befriended him. The letter suggests yet another side of Bleichröder; he could be solicitous, almost avuncular, to men of middling station who needed him. In 1870 in a more familiar, tangible gesture, Bleichröder offered help and the promise of employment to Röder's son, who was just out of school and out of luck, apparently by virtue of some occupational hazard that befell young aristocrats in those days.[87]

At first Bleichröder's return was Röder's gratitude. From 1868 on, however, Röder took an active interest in the negotiations concerning the building of the St. Gotthardtunnel. Röder's pun in 1870, *"Wir gehen Gotthardlich hier wacker vorwärts*," was undoubtedly welcome news for Bleichröder.[88] The recipients of Bleichröder's benevolences often turned up in useful places and important posts.

In the years between the Austrian war and the French war, Bleichröder's home was already frequented by foreign diplomats who, like bankers, needed to be "in the know." Unlike mere bankers, they were aristocratic and socially prominent; they set the fashion.[89] They gave further respectability to Bleichröder.

The diplomatic corps in Berlin looked on Bleichröder as a vital source, certified by his access to Bismarck. Now that Bismarck spent many months away from Berlin, diplomats were starved for news. In October 1868, for example, Bleichröder visited Bismarck in Varzin and immediately briefed his foreign friends. The Austrian ambassador, Count Wimpffen, sent his government a full report of Bleichröder's impressions of the chancellor's health and dispositions.[90] Bleichröder also informed the French military attaché, Lieutenant Colonel de Stoffel, who by virtue of his intelligence and charm had secured for himself a unique position in the Bismarck household as well as in Berlin society. He was a client and debtor of Bleichröder's, who tactfully refrained from reminding him of the outstanding loan. Stoffel transmitted Bleichröder's message to his friend Franceschini Pietri, Louis Napoleon's secretary. He first drew a portrait of Bleichröder:

> an important banker of Berlin, correspondent of Rothschild and *homme d'affaires* of Bismarck. Of low origins, he has acquired, by force of perseverance and practical sense, a considerable position. He is the only Jew whom Bismarck receives familiarly, the only one with whom he is willing to dine. He employs Bleichröder as a hunter after news and assigns him certain confidential missions, etc. It is noteworthy that nearly all Prussian governments of the last 100 years have employed a Jew (already in the time of Sieyès) as a more or less occult instrument. Without being precisely an intriguer, Bleichröder aspires to play a role and to take the place of his precursors, among whom the Jew Ephraim shines in first place. Let me add that he is a gentle man, of kind manners, with whom I am in continual and cordial relations.[91]

It was not enough to have friends in the highest quarters, wealth, influence. Bleichröder's social presence had to be publicly displayed. The world had to know that Bleichröder had arrived.* The ambition for such a presence had

---

* A novel could be written about Bleichröder's social rise—the theme is a common one. Anthony Trollope's *The Way We Live Now* (first published in 1874–1875) deals with Augustus Melmotte, a man of foreign (and Jewish) origin and of incalculable fortune (". . . money was the very breath of Melmotte's nostrils, and therefore his breath was taken for money"), to whom even the highest succumb—until he is discovered to be a bankrupt swindler. But the intricacies and stages of Melmotte's climb are reminiscent of Bleichröder's struggle: " 'Everybody goes to them,' said Lady Pomona, and enumerated the titled dignitaries he had reduced to puppets." As Trollope puts it: "It is true all this came as it were by jumps, so that very often a part of the world did not know on what ledge in the world the great man was perched at that moment. . . . The great man did not quite know himself where, from time to time, he was standing. But the world at large knew . . .—and the world worshipped Mr. Melmotte." (London, 1969), pp. 295, 190, 299–300.

been there before: did he not have the glittering example of the Rothschilds before him? All the world marveled at the elegance and sumptuousness of Rothschild feasts, where royalty and nobility mingled with wealth and talent and an old and a new world met convivially and perhaps to a purpose.[92] To attract *Prominenz* and to entertain them lavishly was a rich man's dream. Bleichröder set out to realize that dream. His ascent was slow, and the higher he climbed, the less sure-footed he became. There was no want of malicious tongues to wag about his faux pas.

The difficulties began at home. His wife was neither beautiful nor brilliant and even less used to high society than Gerson. Their Jewishness laid them the more open to social slights and heightened their insecurity, though the 1860s was a relatively calm period, when old-fashioned anti-Semitic prejudice was on the wane and the new anti-Semitic ideology had not yet made its appearance. In this halcyon time, Bleichröder and some of his fellow bankers of the Jewish faith entered Berlin society.

Bleichröder capitalized on his unique advantage that set him apart from all rivals. As Bismarck's confidant he was especially worthy of cultivation. Normal social life, after all, was not intended for pleasure or scintillating conversation; it was an essential part of the network of intelligence and, less openly, a brokerage place for certain types of appointments.

In January 1868 the Bleichröders scored their first social coup: they gave a formal luncheon for Bismarck and the leading diplomats of Berlin. Bismarck hardly ever went to a private home; Johanna routinely declined. Elaborate consultations preceded the event; the seating order alone was a great problem. Keudell advised Bleichröder to place the chancellor below all the ambassadors and next to the Countess Wimpffen.[93] The Benedettis were also there and the Italian ambassador, Count Lounay. It was a gala affair, nicely indicative of Bleichröder's standing at home and abroad. No wonder the diplomatic corps took still greater notice of Bleichröder after this demonstrative proof of his familiarity with the chancellor. No wonder, too, that Bismarck's ministers, such as Count Eulenburg, invited Bleichröder to dinners in their turn.[94]

The luncheon had required a great deal of behind-the-scene help. The record of these maneuvers happens to have been preserved and illuminates Bleichröder's social network. Keudell, who called Bleichröder "my most esteemed friend," was the impresario. Keudell's holidays at Menton had recently been rendered still more agreeable by a new pair of field glasses and by a Rothschild introduction to the Lyon Railroad line, both provided by Bleichröder.[95] For the question of protocol, Keudell needed the help of the royal master of ceremonies, von Röder, who happened to be the brother of Bleichröder's friend, the Prussian minister in Bern. It was still a very small world—with its social apex the court itself.

Bleichröder's social career continued apace, acclaimed, abhorred, but never quietly accepted. Bleichröder was unstinting in making the "correct" purchases; in 1868 he bought two carriage horses from the Brunswick ducal stud for 150 Louis d'or.[96] In February 1870 Baroness von Spitzemberg, the very clever daughter of Württemberg's premier, Varnbüler, and wife of its minister in Berlin, recorded in her diary:

Ball at the banker Bleichröder whom together with his wife I met there for the first time. They gave a great, extremely brilliant ball in their new [she must have meant newly renovated] and magnificently furnished home in the Behrenstrasse, to which they invited almost only people of the highest society, to the exclusion of their own relatives, and that is really terribly wretched. Lovely place to dance in the yellow-white oblong ball-room from which various doors open into the salons and a corridor disguised as a winter garden, a mass of big and charming bouquets, and other nice surprises in the cotillion, as well as a sumptuous supper combined to make it a most pleasurable feast so that people danced with great gusto till three in the morning.[97]

Under the Empire, the Bleichröder balls became even more sumptuous and exclusive—but did the host ever feel at home at them?

CHAPTER 6

The Third War

In time one will realize to what extent the three [wars] were undertaken for reasons of internal *politics*. For seven years one enjoyed and exploited the great advantage that all the world believed that only Louis Napoleon waged wars for internal reasons. Purely from the point of view of self-preservation, it was high time that one waged the three wars.
— Jacob Burckhardt, October 12, 1871

The North German Confederation was a halfway station on the path to German unification. It was as far as Bismarck could push in 1866 without risking a war with France. But there was something incomplete about a German edifice that excluded the three South German states of Bavaria, Württemberg, and Baden. The principle of nationalism, triumphantly introduced into central Europe in 1866, militated for a wider union; the logic of state-building and the force of economic interests pointed to a larger German state as well. Bismarck had always known—and experienced afresh in 1864 and 1866—that nothing forges the links of unity as rapidly as the fires of a foreign war. Napoleon III had done much for him in the two previous wars, more than he had meant to do; France now blocked any further extension of North Germany. There was only one service left that Napoleon could perform: at a propitious time for Bismarck, to become the (diplomatically isolated) aggressor against whom the whole nation could be rallied.

There was no timetable, no certainty when this would happen. But in the late 1860s there was a presumption for war in Europe, and military preparations on all sides lent urgency to the premonition of war. Europe knew that Bismarck had instigated and won two wars, and in the process had established Prussian hegemony in northern Germany. There was reason to fear that he might provoke another war—at the right moment—in order to unite all of Germany under the Prussian aegis. Napoleon, in turn, might try to restore his battered prestige at home and France's supremacy on the Continent, perhaps in alliance with Austria, commonly suspected of nurturing revanchist feelings.

Bismarck was content to wait, and in 1867 he rebuked Moltke's wish for a preventive war. Still, there can be little doubt that he, too, thought that a Franco-Prussian war would be necessary at some time in order to complete the unification of Germany and to establish a new balance of power in Europe.

But he was in no hurry, hoping to consolidate his earlier gains and certain that time was on his side. Hence he did his best to reassure Europe that he wanted and expected peace.

In this, too, Bleichröder helped him, and in a multiplicity of ways. Bleichröder's own interests—and those of the banking community generally—favored peace. When war did come, he proved infinitely resourceful and extraordinarily patriotic.

During the years of peace, Bleichröder's activities and far-flung correspondence reflected the uncertainty of the international situation. His letters mirrored the common German belief in the *Primat der Aussenpolitik,* which in his case, with his business ties to the outside world, seemed natural. Still, his preoccupation with foreign affairs, at a time when the institutions of the new North German Confederation were being forged, tacitly bespoke an equally common German downgrading of domestic politics. Political realities, financial self-interest, and a certain kind of vanity led Bleichröder to cultivate his connection with the *Grosse Politik.*

The first major crisis broke over the future of Luxembourg—that small duchy governed by the House of Orange and garrisoned by Prussian troops. During and immediately after Prussia's war against Austria, Napoleon, alternately tempted and rebuffed by Bismarck, had hoped to find some compensations for France. As soon as peace was restored and Prussia had gobbled up its gains, Bismarck turned a deaf ear to Napoleon's reminders of earlier, vague hints concerning the borders of 1814, or even the annexation of Belgium. In exasperation, the French decided to settle for Luxembourg; Bismarck gave them devious encouragement but feigned difficulties at home. Bleichröder knew better, and in March 1867, with the crisis at its height, he wrote to Baron James: "Leading circles here are deaf on the subject of the cession of Luxembourg."[1] The information must have been destined for Napoleon, who must have wondered whether Bismarck or Bleichröder was the better source from Berlin. A few weeks later, Bleichröder received word from Paris that everyone there expected Bismarck to precipitate another war. The French, his correspondent added, would try to postpone it because their new guns were not ready.[2]*

Goldschmidt in Vienna also cautioned against another war; late in April he reported Austrian pleasure at Bismarck's acceptance of an international congress to settle the Luxembourg affair.[3] From Paris, Emil Brandeis, the Rothschilds' amanuensis in German matters and a friend of Bleichröder's, warned of France's feverish rearmament and huge purchases of arms. Everything, he thought, would depend on the conference that was to open in London on May 7.[4] On that day, Keudell sent Bleichröder a confidential note, to be

---

* At the very time when the French feared a Prussian attack, the British feared French aggression, and the *Times* complained on April 10, 1867: "What, indeed, does France want more than France? . . . No country has greater natural advantages thrown into her lap. . . . Her anxieties, if they are not assumed, can have no real foundation in history, and can only have the support of wild and visionary forecasts. But if we are to forecast the distant future, does the boldest prophet venture to speak of an aggressive Germany?"

destroyed immediately. There was "sure hope" that the conference would bring peace, but Bismarck was "wounded by the assumption that [Prussian] armaments had a warlike tendency." The army was merely being brought up to its normal strength.[5] The conference ratified what had been decided beforehand: Luxembourg remained under Orange rule, but without its Prussian garrison. Napoleon gained nothing, not even this consolation prize that he had settled on after Bismarck's other promises had evaporated. In mid-May Brandeis wrote: "The public is in a very bad temper about France's humiliation and . . . will seek a revenge soon, in the fall or at the latest at the beginning of next year."[6]

That same summer of 1867, from Marienbad, Bleichröder sent Bismarck a long account of the international situation. He stressed Napoleon's weakened position at home, which the prospects for a bad harvest did not help.

On the other side, the Austrian state is on the eve of the great bankruptcy. . . . The only means of holding off the bankruptcy, for Austria to climb down to a momentary position of small power status, is not thinkable given the prevailing beliefs, and one will resort to the favorite means of the printing press but therein lies the greater danger. . . . Given these gloomy prospects, would they not risk a last effort to unite with France against Prussia? Would not Napoleon, *pressed at home,* greet this ally with open arms?

Bleichröder's letter ended with the lament: "A dark shadow of general distrust afflicts the European stock markets and I fear trade and industry will suffer from this for a long time."[7] The close relation between domestic unrest and foreign bellicosity—which present-day historians often treat as a new insight—was a commonplace to Bleichröder and his friends. Bleichröder's trusted assistant Friedrich Lehmann echoed his premonitions and warned: "I can regard the present *hausse* therefore only as a welcome means for cleaning out, not for increasing, [financial] commitments."[8]

Bleichröder had been essentially correct in his rapid résumé to Bismarck. In 1867 and again in 1869–1870 the two victims of Bismarck's successes, Austria and France, seemed close to an alliance and the air was full of intermittent scares. Bleichröder was right, too, that the economic climate would suffer because markets, like men, abhor uncertainty.

In October 1868 Bleichröder tried to persuade Bismarck to make a gesture for peace—and even in its absence, assured foreign diplomats of Bismarck's irenic intentions. After a trip to Paris, Bleichröder wrote Bismarck that the prospects for peace for that year were excellent, but that agitation in France continued unabated, and hence "a more enduring peace might be in the offing if we would soon settle the North Schleswig question."[9] The Germans had agreed to a French demand that the final boundary between Denmark and Schleswig be fixed by a plebiscite, and the French wanted the Germans to honor this provision of the peace treaty. Bismarck had no intention of meeting this demand with its democratic overtones, and he must have been annoyed at Bleichröder's repeated reminder that the French deemed the matter important.

A few weeks later, Bleichröder paid a much-noted visit to Varzin, and Bismarck took great pains to stress his peaceful intentions, even if these did not include a plebiscite in Schleswig. The Austrian ambassador in Berlin at once reported to Vienna:

> After his return from Varzin, where he spent a few days with Count Bismarck, Mr. Bleichröder told me last night, confidentially, that the prime minister was very peacefully minded and believed in the maintenance of peace. [But] Bleichröder is . . . not at all satisfied with Bismarck's health, especially because of the great irritability of his nerves. He believes that his excessive confidence in peace must be explained in part psychologically by his illness, i.e. by his purely personal need for quiet.[10]

Napoleon received the same message, via the French military attaché in Berlin, Stoffel: Bleichröder had come to Stoffel with the secret message that Bismarck was more peaceful than ever, that Prussia did not want to go beyond the North German Confederation at this point, and that the unification of Germany would come naturally, by itself, sooner or later, and without particular efforts. Bismarck, the report continued, was looking for a way to reestablish the fullest confidence between France and Prussia and thought that perhaps a meeting between William and Napoleon might serve the purpose and "reassure the minds of Europe and bring to an end this distressing stagnation of business." Stoffel was uncertain whether this message represented genuine soundings by Bismarck or whether "his Jew is carried away by his passion to play a political role."[11]

Stoffel's letter was published, without authorization, three years later— to Bleichröder's embarrassment and to the malicious delight of his enemies.[12] What of its substance? Clearly Bleichröder returned from Varzin impressed by Bismarck's desire for peace, which coincided with his own interests in a period of calm in which business could prosper again. Did Bismarck *charge* him with talking to Wimpffen and Stoffel? Or did he rely on Bleichröder's disciplined indiscretion to get the message to the proper people—the more authoritative, perhaps, for coming from a private source? Certainly Bismarck knew that his intimacy with Bleichröder would have diplomatic reverberations, and there is no evidence that he minded Bleichröder's foreign ties—quite the contrary. For Bleichröder in turn these opportunities to play the special envoy proved invaluable.

Perhaps even more than his messages, Bleichröder's financial moves were carefully scrutinized. In March 1869 he speculated à la baisse, and Münch, the Austrian chargé in Berlin, complained that "it was the House of Bleichröder that first threw shares on the market. The chief of this house, as is well known, enjoys very good relations with Count Bismarck." Bleichröder admitted to Münch that he had seen Bismarck before and after his sudden sales, and that on both occasions the chancellor had given him "the most peaceful assurances about the world situation." But reports from London and Paris had been alarming. Münch thought the government uninvolved: "An obviously semiofficial article in the *Kreuzzeitung* condemned this *baisse* speculation." But he was dismayed that Bleichröder had sold chiefly Austrian shares; a sudden fall of prices would have a "very penetrating effect on the economic conditions of our country," and he warned that at some other time, such speculation could be used for political purposes.[13] Perhaps Bleichröder had wanted to demonstrate Austrian vulnerability as a persuasive argument against the recurrent scheme of a Franco-Austrian alliance.

But 1869 was a troubled year in many respects. As so often in German history, a kind of utopian optimism had given way to excessive pessimism. The high hopes of 1866 for completing the work of German unification had been disappointed by the resurgence of South German particularism and the continued antagonisms of democrats everywhere to Prussian Junkerdom. The 1868 elections to the Zollverein parliament proved a disaster to the national cause, and the Bavarian elections a year later confirmed the strength of anti-Prussian sentiment.[14] All of these setbacks threatened to damage Bismarck's position. By 1871, he had to submit a new army budget to the North German Reichstag, and even in Prussia the effects of disappointment could have unsettling results.

Bleichröder was marginally involved in a controversial effort to restore the German momentum. In October 1869 Eduard Lasker planned to raise in the Diet the question of the early entry into the North German Confederation of Baden, the most pro-Prussian southern state. He asked Bleichröder to solicit Bismarck's views, and Bleichröder entrusted the mission to Keudell, who was on his way to Varzin. Bismarck's answer was unequivocal opposition, as Keudell told the French chargé, Lefebvre de Béhaine, "il n'y a pas de question badoise. The North German Confederation had enough to do with internal matters, and the entry of Baden or of the other South German states was not even desirable, let alone planned."[15] In February 1870 Lasker did introduce an interpellation concerning Baden's entry, and Bismarck reacted with extraordinary ferocity: he maligned Lasker for meddling in foreign affairs, he cast aspersions on the Baden government as if it had been in collusion with Lasker, and his ill-tempered response bespoke in part his unwillingness to have any parliamentary intrusion into his own realm of foreign policy.[16] Bismarck's rebuff has often been cited by older German historians as proof of his essential peacefulness. He had, however, ample reasons to shun this particular escape from stagnation: the admission of Baden would have alienated Bavaria, and, by violating the Treaty of Prague, would have united all Europe against Prussia. Above all, Bismarck knew that to be useful a war had to have the appearance of being a defensive war; if war, then Prussia's enemies would have to be provoked to begin it. Baden was not an auspicious occasion.[17]

The chancellor's secret efforts, beginning in January 1870, to have the king of Prussia assume the imperial title indicated his anxiety lest his machine stall too long. In May the Austrian ambassador reported that Bismarck's imperial scheme had been shelved because of South German opposition, but he added, "I don't exclude the possibility of surprises, which appear with certainty in the policy of the Chancellor."[18]

The peace of Europe was indeed about to be shattered by one of Bismarck's surprises. Tension had built up for some time, and Keudell told Bismarck that the international business community was weary of uncertainty. Bismarck replied that "even Bleichröder [had] asked him recently to bring about a war in order to clarify the situation. This view, however, was reprehensible. . . . Nobody can assume the responsibility for the outbreak of a struggle which perhaps would be only the first in a series of racial wars."[19] Bleichröder's *démarche* seems out of character, and we have only Bismarck's word for it; perhaps Bleichröder had said no more than that if there was to be a war anyhow, the sooner it was got over with, the better. At the same time, however, Bismarck warned his ambassador in Paris that the German nation could never be confined to the status quo if its national development demanded an organic change. In such a case, "the interference of foreign powers would be unacceptable to us." Even the risk of war would be preferable to the thwarting of the national will.[20]

In the winter of 1869–1870, then, Bismarck was troubled by the immobility of German politics, and he was on the lookout for a crisis—the resolution of which, by war or diplomacy, would yield Prussia yet another victory. Spain afforded a chance for mischief. A revolution in 1868 had deposed Queen Isabella, and the Spanish Cortes had trouble filling a throne that was more distinguished by its past glory than present power or stability. For the French, the vacancy proved a persistent embarrassment. Napoleon, battling to retain his authority while liberalizing his Empire, could not afford another foreign setback. He had no candidate of his own, but a republican or Orleanist solution would be a disaster for him.[21] The Cortes found a solution still more distasteful to him: by September 1869 the provisional leaders favored Leopold of Hohenzollern-Sigmaringen, a young Catholic prince married to the sister of the king of Portugal and brother of Charles, recently made prince of Rumania.[22] The Hohenzollern-Sigmaringen family was skeptical, as was William I, the nominal head of the family. Leopold knew of his brother's troubles with the Rumanian throne; rumors were already current that he wanted to resign in disgust.[23] Their father, Karl Anton, realized that it was costly to the family coffers to supply princes for impoverished countries.[24]

The Spaniards, however, were not easily discouraged, and by February 1870 they found a powerful ally in Bismarck. The fact that he backed the candidacy, against the wishes of his sovereign, is now beyond question; the motives remain a subject of controversy. According to one recent historian, Bismarck "deliberately set sail on a collision course with the intent of provoking either war or a French internal collapse."[25] Perhaps, but all we know for certain is that he pushed the candidacy, despite William's annoyance, and presumably did so because it was likely to bring harm to France, hence gain to Prussia. Or could Spanish waters refloat the German ship? The trouble was that both Berlin and Paris saw the Spanish problem from the perspective of their own embittered domestic scene.

Bismarck tried to conceal his championship of the candidacy and for the rest of his life mendaciously denied it. His principal assistants, Keudell, Bucher, and Hermann von Thile, played a major part in the dangerous but secret game; despite the undocumented assertion of some historians, Bleichröder seems not to have been privy to it.[26] His friend Major Brandt warned him about the candidacy in the spring, but Bleichröder had failed to realize the importance of the news. Nor did he worry about Brandt's sudden inquiry in May 1870 concerning the means by which Major Kiss of the Hungarian Legion had received large Prussian subventions in 1866. Brandt added that he was traveling to Paris "in deepest incognito."[27] Bleichröder was accustomed to this conspiratorial tone among Prussian officials.*

At the end of June he twice assured Baron Alphonse that "in political matters there was nothing new."[28] On June 26 he wrote a long letter to Bismarck about various financial operations, including the introduction in Paris in a few days of a new issue of the Prussian Mortgage Bank. The letter began: "The political realm offers no cause for disquiet."[29] Bismarck underlined the "no" and put a question mark in the margin, knowing full well that the Spanish bomb was likely to explode at any time. In his quick reply, Bismarck revealed none of his doubts; on the contrary, he wrote, "I would consider it an important success if we could attract French capital to any appreciable extent to this country. Along the Rhine this has already been the case for a long time and in large measure, to the great advantage of industrial enterprises." He gratefully acknowledged Bleichröder's gifts of beer and champagne, lamenting, however, that his present *Kur* left him tired, disturbed his sleep, and enforced temporary abstinence. He concluded with the hope that after the *Badesaison* Bleichröder would visit the Bismarcks in Varzin.[30]

It is remarkable that a few days before the Spanish denouement Bismarck should have been so eager to lure French investments to Prussia. He might have wanted French capital in Prussia to divert it from a potential French ally, such as Austria; he might have wanted to trap French capital in Germany so that in case of war, an indemnity might be more easily collectable. In any case, in peace or war, it would have been to Prussia's advantage to have French capital investments. Later, even in private, Bismarck always pretended to have been totally surprised by the outbreak of the war. Some years later he wrote Bleichröder: "I would remind you how clear the horizon still appeared to be in June 1870."[31] At the time—as witness the question mark in the margin —he knew better.

Bleichröder discovered the threat to peace at the latest on July 5 when he wrote Baron Alphonse a personal letter, reporting the Spaniards' choice of a Hohenzollern and German fears that France might object.[32] Bleichröder's instant recognition of this threat confirms what we now know: it took neither

---

* Repeatedly Bleichröder acted as cover man for the transfer of secret funds for political purposes. By the nature of the assignment, few records have survived. For example, Keudell, the trustee of the Legationskasse, instructed Bleichröder in January 1868 to transmit 750 francs to Paris, where "on highest authority" and in top-secret fashion, Keudell was to disburse it. No one in the Bleichröder bank or at Rothschilds' should have an inkling of the true reason for this transfer: "I leave it to your kind judgment what little cloak you want to cover this matter with." There would be similar payments later, Keudell added. Keudell to Bleichröder, 29 Jan. 1868, BA.

expertise nor genius to predict French reaction to a Hohenzollern on her southern borders. Hence Bismarck must have known since February that he had embarked on a risky course.

Napoleon had already warned the Paris Rothschilds, who had immediately mobilized all their contacts to save the peace. They transmitted Napoleon's messages to Prime Minister Gladstone and repeatedly warned Bleichröder that the situation was grave.[33] On July 8, Bleichröder informed the Foreign Office, and he wrote Bismarck directly: "Rothschild in Paris writes me letters as if the war between France and Prussia had already broken out." He also cited French reports that England, Austria, and Italy agreed with French policy concerning Spain.[34] He ended nevertheless with a patriotic flourish that would have dismayed his Paris friends: "There is great excitement here, and one wonders whether, if the Cortes elect the Hohenzollern prince, war with France would be inevitable; for to do France's bidding and to give in—nobody thinks of that!"[35]

The same nationalistic bravado characterized French utterances. On July 6 the French foreign minister, the Duc de Gramont, had given a harsh warning to Prussia and Spain that France would not tolerate a hostile prince on its southern border. Even before his speech, the Berlin markets fell drastically. Bleichröder wrote the Rothschilds that on the sixth stock prices had already dropped by 2 percent.[36] It was a difficult time for bankers, and Bleichröder sought authoritative advice on what to do. On July 9 he wrote his best-informed client, Bismarck, full of solicitude for his material well-being. "On my part I do not believe in the extreme seriousness of the political situation [Bismarck put an exclamation mark next to that clause] and have therefore not yet done any selling on Your Excellency's account. Should I be mistaken, however, and should Your Excellency think that many more unpleasant incidents are to be expected, I respectfully beg you to warn me by a single syllable."[37] That syllable arrived the next day from Varzin in the form of a letter from Johanna, who began:

> My husband, who is very busy with coding and uncoding, asks me to answer your letter of today in this way: he does not indeed believe in war because despite all the frivolity of some people he thinks it improbable that anyone would suddenly attack us [über uns herfallen] because Spain did not vote the way one wanted it to. But he thought that there could still come moments when the belief in war would be stronger than now, and since he needs money here anyhow, it might be a good idea to sell the railroad shares. But you would be a better judge of the stock market than my husband; perhaps the market is not as jittery as some of the diplomats are. But it is just as impossible to predict the political decisions of irritated people of either sex as it is to predict the weather.[38]

The Prussian government had not interfered and would not interfere in other people's business, but if France armed, Prussia would have to do likewise, and if France attacked, Prussia would have to defend herself. Johanna ended this strange Sunday epistle by reminding Bleichröder that her husband had dictated the letter himself—amidst constant interruptions, a few words at a time. Indeed the message to Bleichröder was almost identical with Bismarck's coded telegram to the Foreign Office of the same day.[39]

Bleichröder's letter and Bismarck's answer were very much in character. By discovering Bismarck's estimate of the situation, Bleichröder could make authoritative dispositions of the chancellor's funds and his own. On the next day, Monday, Bleichröder reported to the Paris Rothschilds: "the rapid decline of all quotations."[40] On the same day, he apparently instructed his London agent, Worms, to sell his holdings, which was done at a loss.[41]

In those last days of peace, Bleichröder received a host of messages and must have felt that same heightened tempo and confusion that bewildered European chancelleries at the time. On July 10 or 11, for example, he received from his friend Brandt, now lieutenant colonel on the General Staff and stationed in Brussels, a handwritten note sent to Brandt by Count Waldersee, the Prussian military attaché in Paris, on July 8, a few hours before Waldersee's return from Ems to Paris. (Bismarck had ordered his return to Paris so that he could embolden some of the scared Prussian diplomats at the Paris Embassy and check closely on all possible French military moves, especially on the railroads.)[42] Waldersee wrote Brandt that "all hell has broken loose in Paris" and that he must hurry back: "For me it's a matter now of keeping my eyes open. Above all leave me B and S [presumably agents in Brandt's employ]." He also needed the assurance of having sufficient funds—could Brandt see to that? ". . . I do not believe in war but [expect] a few very agitated weeks." At the bottom of this letter, Brandt scribbled a message and asked Bleichröder to destroy the document upon receipt: he asked Bleichröder to credit him with 10,000 francs at Oppenheim in Cologne and told him that he had asked his chief (Moltke?) and Keudell whether he should return to Germany. He added apropos of Waldersee's letter: "Do you recall that I told you and warned you months ago about this project? You and S. [Schwabach] were incredulous."[43] On July 12 William's Hofmarschall, Count Perponcher-Sedlimitzky, wrote Bleichröder from Ems: "Situation still very serious and a solution not yet in sight."[44]

Bismarck made no effort to save the peace. "Politically," he wrote on the tenth, "a French attack would be very beneficial to our situation."[45] Still he realized that William and Prince Leopold might turn his bold game into a hideous defeat by renouncing the Hohenzollern candidacy under French duress. In one of his still enigmatic maneuvers to avert a Prussian humiliation, he enlisted Bleichröder's help.[46] On July 12 he telegraphed the Foreign Ministry that Prince Leopold could decently maintain his candidacy only on the condition that, if France now attacked Germany, Spain would join Germany in the war against France. The Foreign Ministry—through Bleichröder—should inform the press that Leopold had already accepted this and planned to act accordingly. Bleichröder received the message, and several papers carried this ambiguous story.[47] Was it planted to frighten the French or to present Leopold with an honorable means of escape, saddling Spain with the onus of having pulled back before French threats?

On the same July 12, William ordered Bismarck to Ems; en route,

Bismarck stopped off in Berlin and immediately summoned Bleichröder. It was in Berlin that Bismarck learned that Leopold had renounced the candidacy and that William had so informed the French ambassador; it was so stunning a reversal of Bismarck's expectations that he was reluctant to believe it; Bleichröder, however, confirmed the news. The faithful gathered around Bismarck; his son Herbert was there, and Roon and Moltke joined them. According to Herbert's diary, Moltke became red in the face "because he had now made the trip [to Berlin] for nothing, and the war, which he had already firmly planned [*den er schon fest ins Auge gefasst hatte*] seemed to recede into the distance again. . . . Old Roon was dejected too." Bismarck expressed the ill mood of the company: "Until just now I thought I was standing on the eve of the greatest historical events, and now all I will get from it is the unpleasantness of the sudden interruption of my *Kur*." To Herbert, who was serving in the army at the time, he said (in French): "I would urge you to work hard because there is not going to be a battlefield promotion." In the evening, Bleichröder was instructed to spread the news of the renunciation at the same time as it was being done officially.[48]

For Bismarck, July 12 had been a tumultuous day. Thoughts of resignation alternated with plans for one more effort to humiliate France or goad her into war. By the thirteenth, the situation had changed dramatically. Leopold's withdrawal could have given France a diplomatic victory of pleasing magnitude; by asking William for guarantees against any future renewal of a Hohenzollern candidacy, the French—unwittingly—furnished Bismarck with the means of turning threatened humiliation into a renewed challenge to France that forced her to attack Prussia. William had rebuffed the French request, and Bismarck edited William's account so as to make it appear a humiliating defiance of France. Bismarck's fabled telegraphic style alone would not have sufficed to get him out of the trap which he had set for France and which on July 12 and 13 threatened to catch him.[49] By overreaching himself, Napoleon extricated Bismarck from his own improvisation. As the best recent historian of the Franco-Prussian war put it: "Thus by a tragic combination of ill-luck, stupidity, and ignorance France blundered into war with the greatest military power that Europe had yet seen, in a bad cause, with her army unready and without allies."[50]

Driven by fear of the domestic consequences of any compromise, Napoleon had given Bismarck what the latter had long adjudged to be necessary: a French attack that would rally the nation, unify Germany, and strengthen Prussia's leadership. The world at large—as well as the Germans—perceived the war as an act of French aggression; hence the diplomatic prospects for Germany were auspicious. But few thought that the outcome was a foregone conclusion.

The Berlin stock market greeted the outbreak of the war with near-panic. Such stalwarts as the Cologne-Minden shares dropped nearly 30 percent below the July 1 price; other shares did equally poorly. The government's efforts to raise a 100 million-taler loan through public subscription proved unsuccessful; despite Hansemann's warnings, the terms of the loan (5 percent at 88 percent of nominal value) had not been made sufficiently attractive. Other state obligations already in the market were selling at lower, that is, more advantageous, prices. The loan was undersubscribed; at a later time, nationalist publicists attacked Bleichröder and other bankers for their lack of patriotism, for investing their funds in foreign, allegedly even in French, securities rather than in the new German loan. By the end of October, Hansemann formed a consortium that would offer 20 million taler to the public in Berlin and London. (Hansemann's Disconto-Gesellschaft signed for 4,300,000 taler, Bleichröder and the Frankfurt Rothschilds signed for 3 million each.) This issue proved a great success—but then it had been carefully prepared and had been preceded by great Prussian victories.[51]

Bleichröder was no friend of war, and he had even less cause for exultation at its outbreak than did his compatriots. His closest contacts abroad were with France, and he probably shared the admiration for things French that was common among the central European bourgeoisie, most fervently among Jews. But patriotic exultation came with the great German victories, and by August 13 Count Wimpffen, the Austrian ambassador, lamented the "overweening mood of victory" that gripped Berlin and nullified all political reason. "In a place where self-confidence has ever been more noticeable and more tangible, one encounters this national characteristic today in such heightened form that for the observer the thought of a still further escalation is difficult to conceive and more difficult still to bear."[52] At the same time and for some months thereafter, Goldschmidt pleaded with Bleichröder for Prussian moderation; otherwise Austrian neutrality would be jeopardized.[53]

By early September—after the fall of Sedan and the surrender of Napoleon—most Germans began to think that heaven had decreed their triumph, that Providence had punished the wicked French for their sins, and that the German nation, now at the point of final unification, had manifested incomparable moral virtue.[54] Bleichröder was not free from such hubris; even his lucid mind was occasionally beclouded by nationalistic frenzy. He was becoming ever more an Establishment figure, and it is small wonder that he embraced Establishment ideology. He too bowed before German success, perhaps more demonstratively for being a Jew, for being an outsider whose patriotism had always to be proven afresh. The war completed his conversion to nationalism, the more because he profited from the triumph of the new nation.

Wars traditionally afford great opportunities to the few, even as they bring sadness and deprivation to the many. The Franco-Prussian war, the first total war according to the historian Michael Howard, proved no exception. New needs called forth new talents; the enterprising could rise more rapidly than in peacetime. Bleichröder had already scored in the Austro-Prussian war; in the four-year interval between the two wars, he attained a position of influence and intimacy, a kind of "takeoff" point, that enabled him to play a major role in the new war. His easy access to Bismarck, to Bismarck's staff and to King William's court provided him with an incomparable base from which to operate. By war's end, he had made tremendous strides in every realm.

Throughout the war, his presence was everywhere in evidence. He lavished gifts on the powerful and charity on the deprived and bereaved. He became a kind of private Red Cross: he helped Johanna von Bismarck to organize wartime charities, and he helped the British ambassador to look after French prisoners of war. He proved useful to various branches of the Prussian government and to other German courts. Throughout the war, Bismarck and his top aides were in the field; Bleichröder sought to fill the vacuum in Berlin, supplying news, offering services, acting as a go-between. He retained his contacts with the Rothschilds abroad, strained though they were by the difficulties of wartime correspondence and by his identification with the Prussian cause. He had friends who doubled as informants in the Prussian headquarters, and the height of his wartime career came with his celebrated call to Bismarck's side in Versailles.

From the beginning of the war, he was charged with occasional missions of the greatest secrecy. We have intimations of these assignments, but they were rarely committed to paper. Bleichröder had carried out similar tasks in the Austro-Prussian war; in this longer war, the needs were greater, Bleichröder was better known, and his friend Keudell was Bismarck's right-hand man in dealing with agents and other secret work.[55] Bleichröder became a useful cover agent to transfer funds to persons or groups that had agreed to do Prussia's work. It was obviously preferable to channel money through private sources—examples of similar conduits in our own day are not exactly rare. Bleichröder was reimbursed through the Legationskasse, supervised by Keudell, who meticulously destroyed most records.[56] Bleichröder's connections with the Welfenfond was another reason why he was a convenient agent.

Bleichröder's missions attest Bismarck's determination to use all means to weaken the enemy and to restrain a potential enemy, such as Austria-Hungary. Thus, in early August, Bleichröder was ordered to pay 3,000 gulden to a Hungarian journalist, Jacob Cohn, who in return had promised the Prussian consul general in Budapest "to propagate a prescribed program."[57] In mid-August Keudell instructed the Foreign Ministry that Bleichröder in utmost secrecy should pay 100,000 francs to an Italian agent or professional revolutionary who would start operations against Nice, which the French had taken from the Italians in 1860. The Foreign Office at first demurred, but by October Bleichröder paid some reliable troublemakers in Italy for anti-French activities in Nice. One of Bismarck's favorite young diplomats, Friedrich Holstein, had inspected the reservoir of Italian revolutionaries and had thus prepared the way for Bleichröder to renew his contacts with the revolutionary underworld.[58] Also in August, the Prussian ambassador in London, Count Bernstorff, forwarded to the Foreign Ministry a letter from Algiers, signed only with initials. A committee against French rule had been formed and needed funds: "There are hardly any [French] troops left, this is the moment. Money! Money!"[59] It is not clear whether money was sent, but the request and Bernstorff's transmission suggest that people once again assumed that Bismarck was ready to explode all possible mines in the enemy camp. In any case, they exploded: by mid-September, there was an insurrection in Algeria, and the French lacked troops to deal with it.[60]

Bleichröder's most important role as Prussian agent involved Bismarck's complicated wartime dealings with Bavaria. The largest kingdom in southern Germany, with the oldest dynasty and proudest monarch, Bavaria required his special solicitude if she were to consent to German unification and if King Louis were to be persuaded to offer the imperial title to William. Bismarck recognized that he had to deal not only with the shrewdly calculating Bavarian government but with the elusive, erratic, and already disturbed monarch, then only twenty-five years old.

At the very beginning of the war, the Bavarian government needed money and instructed its Berlin representative, Baron Pergler von Perglas, to find out from Bismarck whether Prussia could secretly advance 3 million gulden (1,700,000 taler) in order to help finance Bavaria's mobilization costs. Perglas, a devout Catholic and a friend of the Bavarian prime minister, had misgivings about Prussia. The order from Munich was repeated in the most urgent terms on July 29 at 9:00 a.m., and Perglas found it impossible to call on Bismarck at that time: "At nine a.m., I would not have been able to get to Count Bismarck who is up for much of the night and usually sleeps late in the morning." Accordingly he wrote an urgent plea to Bleichröder and asked to be admitted at once in order to discuss "a government secret." Bleichröder obliged, and promised Perglas to play the intermediary between Bismarck and Perglas. More, he offered to help Bavaria in case Bismarck should refuse. By 11:20 in the morning, Bleichröder could report to Perglas that Bismarck had agreed—and on August 1 a heavily guarded train carried 3 million gulden in silver bars and coins from Berlin to Munich. It is not clear whether it was Bleichröder who advanced the money or not. However, on September 3 King Louis awarded him the "Comthurkreuz of the Royal Service Order [*Verdienstorden*] of the Holy Michael," in explicit recognition of his help in obtaining the loan and "to encourage similar affairs in the future."[61]

In mid-November the Prussian minister in Munich sent Bismarck a "top secret" telegram reporting that King Louis "was in great financial embarrassment" because of his passion for monumental buildings and the theater. The king, without telling anyone in his government, was sending his personal emissary, Count Max Holnstein, to Versailles to discuss his financial needs, which, if met, would prompt Louis to accept the proclamation of William as emperor. Bismarck promised the king a yearly gift of 100,000 taler, with Holnstein receiving 10 percent of the sum.[62] Bleichröder transferred the money to King Louis and to Holnstein, who had an account with Bleichröder. The Legationskasse reimbursed Bleichröder out of the Welfenfond.[63] Holnstein informed Louis, who at once wrote William the famous Kaiserbrief (drafted for him by Bismarck), urging the Prussian king to assume the imperial German crown. (A dispatch informing Bismarck of Louis's sending the "desired" letter had to be censored for William's eyes; he would have balked at such methods.) Obviously the transfer agent had to be totally discreet: Prussia's annual gift to Louis remained a well-kept secret during the entire Bismarck era.[64]

As late as the 1950s, conservative German historians were unhappy about this gift to royalty with its split for the royal assistant. Thus Otto Becker wrote:

"The readiness with which he [Holnstein] took the clandestine present does admittedly not bear witness to an other-worldly idealistic faith. Still the undeniably disagreeable impression is attenuated by the fact that Bismarck *offered* what he took. . . ."[65] It is doubtful whether Bleichröder or Bismarck suffered any such qualms about the arrangement. They knew that noblemen also had to live, and that the anticipation of profit could speed, perhaps sweeten, but rarely shape major political decisions.

Throughout the war, Bleichröder played his multiple roles, only more energetically than before—and the strain took a toll of his health. He needed to maintain his position in Berlin and in the European capital market, he tried to preserve his links to the Paris Rothschilds, and he strengthened his ties with Bismarck and Bismarck's entourage. Once again, he sought to mobilize the international ties of the banking community in order to establish peace— and throughout the war, his public and private charity demonstrated his prominence and patriotism. For Bleichröder, these were concurrent and mutually reinforcing activities; we must consider them briefly and consecutively.

Bleichröder's solicitude extended even to the enemy. At the request of the British ambassador, Lord Loftus, Bleichröder acted as paymaster for the 300,000 French soldiers imprisoned in Germany. To make these monthly payments to the prisoners of war "occupied the whole time" of Loftus's assistant and proved even more exacting for Bleichröder.[66] He advanced the very large sums involved; Lord Loftus expected to collect them from the Paris Rothschilds, acting as agents of the French government.[67] After the overthrow of Napoleon in early September, Bleichröder wrote anxiously to the Rothschilds; he assumed that any French government would "recognize this act of pious charity," but, just in case, he reminded the Rothschilds that he would hold them responsible for his payments, and he asked for their confirmation.[68] In May 1871, after the fighting had been over for three months, Bleichröder asked the London Rothschilds for credits so that he could continue his payments to the 200,000 prisoners still in his care.[69] During the war Bleichröder went even further in his efforts: "I also transmit to the poor prisoners letters and cash presents from relatives from all over France, and without exaggeration on my part, I may say that the task assigned to me nearly absorbs all my resources. Nevertheless I do it willingly, and where I can help with my own resources, I do it."[70] Bleichröder's letter was transmitted to the French government, in hopes that it would collaborate with a new German committee, headed by the Duke of Ratibor, which sought to assist German prisoners in France.

Bleichröder had informed Bismarck of Lord Loftus's request, and Bismarck, in turn, appointed an official intermediary between the Loftus-Bleichröder mission and the German armies. Beichröder had assured Bismarck that his new responsibilities would serve German interests as well; Bismarck probably did not see it in that light. He had been angered by British eagerness to take over French interests in Berlin and had scorned their offer to do the same for Prussia in Paris. He demonstratively picked America instead.[71] For Bleichröder this act of charity provided a new and intimate link with the British ambassador and preserved valuable ties with France. Bleichröder also went to great lengths to reassure various French notables of the whereabouts of their missing or imprisoned relatives.

It was difficult to maintain correspondence between Berlin and Paris. At first, Bleichröder and the Paris Rothschilds carried on their daily correspondence, sending letters and occasional telegrams via banking houses in Brussels and Amsterdam. Bleichröder continued his reports about the Berlin stock market; in July and August the Rothschilds sent anxious inquiries concerning the whereabouts of Rothschild friends or relatives. Bleichröder urged the Rothschilds to sell some of their Cologne-Minden shares, and on the day of Sedan and the day after, he sold for their account 1,250 shares at 128. In late July the price had been 95.[72] In the first weeks of the war, Bleichröder still sent occasional political news; on August 19, for example, he wrote Baron Alphonse that "the position of Austria has become dubious again," meaning that she might still join France against Prussia. To fool gentile censors he put the word *Haltung* (position) in Hebrew letters—assuming that they would be too stupid to make correct inferences from the rest of the sentence. Letters now took three to five days, whereas in peacetime they had taken two days.

Bleichröder was curiously insensitive to the feelings of the Paris Rothschilds. Despite his own close identification with the German cause, he assumed that the Rothschilds would be willing, and able, to continue routine business relations with him, even as he was with them. Business as usual was his motto, escalated patriotism notwithstanding. By late August, Brandeis made it clear that the Paris House wanted to terminate its German business and could not carry out Bleichröder's orders in Paris because "no one knows how far things will go."[73] A few days later, the imperial regime was overthrown, and the Paris Rothschilds had reason enough to fear for their safety without risking popular fury if it were discovered that they continued dealings with the advancing enemy. Three days after the proclamation of the Republic, Brandeis wrote what apparently was a final letter for 1870: "the Barons are convinced of your amicable feelings, but under present circumstances it is best to let things take their course and to do nothing."[74]

But Bleichröder kept writing his reports; after September 1 he sent them via the London Rothschilds. After September 15 they no longer reached Paris. On September 20 the Germans closed their ring around Paris; the Rothschilds had chosen to remain inside the besieged city. Bleichröder's letters accumulated in London and reached their destination in February of the next year.[75] The Rothschilds received occasional news via balloon from their foreign, especially English, friends, but their direct tie with Bismarck's proud banker was severed. It is unlikely that Bleichröder's epistles, with their occasional patriotic flourishes, were missed by the Rothschilds, who in a cold, hungry, and politically turbulent Paris shared their compatriots' misfortune.

Bleichröder also tried to alleviate the sufferings of his compatriots; charity, he knew, begins at home. He also knew what was expected of him.

His largesse, already celebrated in peacetime, was vastly expanded during the war. The needs were greater, the public mood engendered sacrifice, and the likely rewards were greater, too. When Countess Bismarck sponsored a league for the support of draftees' families, Bleichröder became its treasurer.* The League was under the patronage of Queen Elizabeth, widow of Frederick William IV, and the protection of William; its members consisted of eminent ladies, Christians and Jews, nobles and nonnobles. Bleichröder's prominent position as treasurer was another and costly indication of his importance. Queen Elizabeth thanked him for his gifts.[76] In December 1870 the king appointed him treasurer of the newly founded Wilhelm-Stiftung, designed to help wounded or sick soldiers—another expensive honor for Bleichröder.[77]

At the beginning of the hostilities, the king's reader and intimate companion, Hofrat Louis Schneider, asked Bleichröder, whom he remembered as "a rich man of patriotic convictions," to finance the publication of a regular newssheet, featuring songs and poems for soldiers, to be distributed gratis to the troops. Bleichröder agreed and offered to pay for a book of songs as well. He sponsored twenty-three issues of ephemeral uplift, which, Schneider reported, provided great joy to the soldiers. Bleichröder had requested anonymity, but must have been pleased when Schneider conveyed to him William's thanks for this "renewed proof of your patriotic conviction. His Majesty the King added that he of course knew you personally and that therefore he was not at all surprised by your offer." The king had always wanted a permanent collection of poems and songs "because it promises not only momentary usefulness but might perhaps be the only thing which will survive the war and remain for all time a testimonial of today's wonderful lifting of spirits."[78] Later the king thanked him directly.[79] For Bleichröder, the vain and garrulous Schneider became a valuable correspondent from William's headquarters and eventually wrote a public eulogy of his patriotic generosity.[80]

Bleichröder lavished new energy on his private charity as well. He had always been a purveyor of luxuries to men of prominence who appreciated them but who often by nature or necessity tended to be frugal. During the war, his Santa Claus activities became phenomenal and immensely time-consuming. The war occasioned hardships even at the top, the steady succession of German victories notwithstanding. After the first weeks of fighting, Bismarck's son Herbert was badly wounded, and it took weeks in Bad Nauheim to nurse him back. Johanna was at his side, distressed at his pains and high fever; Bleichröder showed his solicitude by sending exotic gifts, and Johanna wrote him long letters of thanks, full of details about her family's condition. At the end of September, still from Nauheim, she wrote,

> You have once again heaped the most sumptuous sweets upon us and for these I want humbly to express our heartfelt joy and thanks. . . . God grant that Paris soon be humbled, that peace be concluded, and that our

---

* *Der Berliner Haupt-Unterstützungs-Verein für die Familien der zur Fahne Einberufenen*, in its broadsheets of August and November 1870, appealed to the public for generous contributions to be sent to the treasurer, Geheimer Kommerzienrat Bleichröder.

armies—especially my husband and my son Wilhelm—can soon turn homewards. For several weeks now I have been without news from the latter and therefore am very anxious about him.

The long letter also thanked him for all his work for "their" relief society. She concluded, as always in this period, with cordial greetings to Bleichröder's wife.[81] Two months later, she wrote from her father's estate at Reinfeld, thanking Bleichröder for the cigars her father had gratefully received. Her husband, she added, had written that he was well, "but still no peace prospects. Unfortunately. No news from Wilhelm for three weeks."[82]

The news from the battlefields was good, but Bleichröder heard of the suffering, too, and of the growing impatience for a final victory. Louis Schneider wrote from Pont à Mousson in August, "I am writing this in the terrible surroundings of the dead and the dying from the battles of 16th and 18th, and ask your pardon therefore if my hand shakes. . . ."[83] In September, after the fall of Sedan and the capitulation of Napoleon, it looked for a moment as if peace might be restored, but the provisional French government refused the steep territorial demands that Prussia envisaged.[84] The war continued, and German headquarters was established first at the Rothschilds' château in Ferrières and then, on October 5, in Versailles. What irony, for Bleichröder, to have the Germans installed at Ferrières, amidst the unbelievable splendors that Baron James had amassed. Schneider was the first to write him "from the fairylike, magnificent castle of the French Bleichröder—Baron Rothschild."[85] Even Bleichröder, himself not a stranger to flattery, must have smiled at this hyperbole. What Schneider and others concealed was the raucous anti-Semitism that the Rothschild Palais inspired among the conquerors. The J. R. (James de Rothschild) in the various heraldic emblems, for example, was maliciously referred to as *"Judaeorum Rex."*[86] Roon spoke of the *"Judenkönig"* whose country estate was more luxurious than anything he had ever seen.[87] "But not even the vast halls of Ferrières could house Moltke's staff, the royal retinue, Bismarck's officials, and a crowd of *Schlachtenbummler* which, once the war had bogged down, swelled enormously. . . . It was an interesting, glittering, gossiping community, but hardly a happy one; and as the weather grew bleaker and peace came no nearer, its happiness grew still less."[88] The fact that Moltke and his lieutenants were bitterly angry at what they thought Bismarck's inept interference with the serious business of war and that Bismarck harbored equal disdain for the intrusion of the military "demigods" poisoned the atmosphere and made the long wait outside Paris more intolerable still. Their conflict was a harbinger of later, deeper antagonisms between the Prussian army and the civilian leadership.

Bleichröder did his unceasing best to raise the spirits of these inconvenienced heroes. "We are hungry," wrote Bismarck, "because H.M. has forbidden all requisitioning for headquarters and there is nothing to buy."[89] They ran out of wine because of William's self-denying order, and at first the Rothschilds' concierge refused to sell even one bottle from the great wine cellar. The entourage was furious at the rich Jew's inhospitality. Members of Bismarck's staff had to go wine hunting, but other necessities of life were harder to come by in an impoverished and largely hostile country, while rail connections with Germany were terribly overburdened.[90] Bleichröder sought to make up for these deprivations, and he became a self-appointed purveyor of delicacies to the Prussian retinue. It gave him pleasure to know that the king, the chancellor, and their choice lieutenants ate his victuals, drank his cognac, and smoked his cigars—all of them of exquisite quality. If the way to a man's heart is through his stomach, Bleichröder should have been the best-loved man at headquarters.

He was not. Perhaps his solicitude was too exigent. Time and again he would press Schneider or Keudell, demanding to know what their respective masters lacked. When told, he would immediately set out to find and, more difficult, to send the desired items. William—that legendary figure of simple tastes—wanted larks, lobster, and turbot as well as special beer. It all would arrive miraculously, within days of the request.[91] There were of course gradations in giving, and the lower echelons had to be satisfied with lesser gifts. Still Keudell reported that he had distributed Bleichröder's cigars among Bismarck's assistants, Abeken, Bismarck-Bohlen, and Hatzfeldt, who now "daily blow the trumpets of your praise."[92] Count Perponcher and Prince Anton Radziwill of the king's retinue and Count August Eulenburg of the crown prince's staff were also among Bleichröder's beneficiaries.[93] Only the enemies of Bismarck, the men of the General Staff under Moltke, were without Bleichröder's presents; he lacked entrée to the group. In their eyes he had a double mark against him: he was a Jew and a Bismarck creature, and the two were at times contracted into one contemptuous phrase, *"des Kanzlers Privatjude."*[94]

Bleichröder's beneficiaries also indulged in occasional anti-Semitic remarks, but in their own way they reciprocated his kindnesses. Most of them became part of Bleichröder's incredibly good network of intelligence; he received letters and telegrams from the field and remained one of the best-informed men in Berlin. A few of them, Keudell in particular, pressed his interests at critical moments.

Bleichröder and Keudell carried on an active and revealing correspondence during the war. Their close ties and mutual regard shine through letters that carry the familiar address: "Most esteemed friend." Bleichröder discussed Berlin affairs, the mood of market and populace, secret information that he had received from Paris or neutral capitals. Keudell in turn would give a full account from the field and often served as intermediary between Bismarck and Bleichröder because direct contacts were sparse during the war.

On August 5 Bleichröder wrote that commercial conditions were poor, but the newly issued Prussian loan was doing well—which turned out not to be the case. He also reported that there remained a danger of pro-French moves in Austria and Italy. In mid-August, after the first Prussian victories, Bleichröder's tone became more ebullient: "The market is developing brilliantly," while in France there is "ruin in every corner of the country."[95]

Keudell's answer gave Bleichröder an entirely different picture. On August 16, from Pont à Mousson, near Metz, where German troops had just crossed the Moselle and where he had arrived but a few hours before, Keudell wrote "amidst the thunder of battle"—the costly battle of Vionville. He found the market's bullishness premature. "We *must* weaken France in the peace to come, so that in a year's time it will not start a war again and so that our people who have shown themselves so admirably willing to make sacrifices will not lose faith in us and will not think that the monarchy represents their interests poorly and thus receive an impetus toward a republic." All other powers were jealous, he said, and hence there could be no peace without a "very heavy struggle, not only against the French people, who after all will be aroused against the conqueror, but also against the neutrals, quite aside from the difficulties and delays that might be created by the possible removal of Louis [Napoleon]. . . . For all these reasons *no* confidence" in an early or easy end of the war.[96]

In short, this was not to be a lightning war, à la 1866, where triumphant armies swiftly achieved limited aims. This was not the kind of "moderation" that Bleichröder's friends pleaded for and that he too may have expected. Keudell's letter clearly reflected Bismarck's thoughts, as witness Bismarck's message of August 11 to the czar. The fact that Keudell repeated the rather absurd alternative of hard peace or republicanism at home suggests that it must have been an *idée fixe* of Bismarck's at the time.[97] Bismarck and Keudell were continuously together, except for the very evening after Keudell wrote the letter, when Bismarck, having been informed that his son Wilhelm had been killed and his son Herbert wounded, rode into the night until the next morning —to find Wilhelm unscathed and Herbert thrice wounded.[98]

Keudell's warning that the war would last a long time was of immediate importance to Bleichröder. It is of present-day interest as well. In the last few years, Bismarck's role in the annexation of Alsace-Lorraine has again become a controversial subject. Bismarck's contemporaries had sensed the new militancy: already on August 10, Friedrich Engels wrote of the "national fury" that had seized Germans and "the cry for Alsace-Lorraine [that is heard] everywhere."[99] Had Bismarck fanned this "national fury" or was he driven by it, had he planted annexationist stories in the government press or did he reluctantly accept what public opinion and the military demanded? (In later years, he himself claimed to have been pushed.) The degree of Bismarck's involvement is still in dispute, but few would deny that by mid-August Bismarck had freely and finally resolved on the annexation of Alsace-Lorraine despite the certain cost.[100]

The renewed interest in Bismarck's motives notwithstanding, it has gone unnoticed that his determination to punish France, to cripple her alleged desire for aggression, stiffened precisely in the week that the war had touched him most intimately, in the fate of his two sons. On August 16 and 18, moreover, the German armies narrowly missed crushing defeats, and suffered heavy losses.[101] There is an important difference in tone and substance, for example, between his still vague instructions to his ambassador in St. Petersburg on August 11 and his tough insistence on territorial gains in his note to Bernstorff in London ten days later: "Public opinion in England will understand that we must prevent as best we can an early repetition of the immense sacrifices which this war has imposed on our people, from the palaces to the cottages." The French, he added, would be bitter "even if they emerge from this war *without* territorial losses." An enemy that cannot be turned into a friend must be made less powerful, and this, he concluded, could be done only by the surrender, not the destruction, of French forts.[102]

Bismarck may have partly believed his own allegation that the people's sacrifices had engendered popular hopes, which, if disappointed, would weaken monarchical sentiment. But he did his best to fan these hopes, to translate a limited cabinet-style war into a war between nations—only to recoil a few months later when he realized the ferocity of the war *à outrance* which he had helped to unleash. The parallel to the war aims crisis of the next war—which partly grew out of the annexation of Alsace-Lorraine—is inescapable. In order not to disappoint a deliberately aroused people, the governments in both wars insisted on peace conditions that necessarily prolonged the war and heightened both losses and expectations. Bismarck had battled against such an escalation of aims in 1864 and 1866, but in 1870, when the dangers were greater, he deliberately fostered it. It proved his most fateful error.

For the sake of these aims Bismarck rebuffed French overtures for peace —overtures in which Bleichröder was to play his part. After the battles of August 16 and 18 the tide turned decisively against the French, and imperial troops staggered to their doom. On September 2, with the surrender of Napoleon and his army at Sedan, France suffered the worst defeat in her long history. Bismarck repeated to General Wimpffen, the French plenipotentiary, what he had been saying—and, in view of his earlier Francophilia, one is tempted to add, learning—during the preceding weeks, that is, that the French were a perennially aggressive people, that German sacrifices must lead to better protection against such an enemy.[103]

Bismarck's political rationality returned in calmer moments, but Sedan unhinged the German public mind in a way that Bismarck's earlier, subterranean press agitation could never have done.[104] Nor was that mind easily healed, as the notorious Sedan-Feiern or annual celebrations of later decades showed ad nauseam. In Paris, the capitulation of Sedan precipitated the proclamation of a republic; a Provisional Government of National Defense was installed, with Léon Gambetta, the young, fiery radical, its leader and inspirer and Jules Favre in charge of foreign affairs. The new government wanted peace, provided it could be had with honor; an ignominious peace, like a long war, would put in deepest jeopardy the social fabric of France. Favre's famous vow—not "an inch of her soil or a stone of her fortresses"— was irreconcilable with German aims. Favre called on Bismarck at Ferrières on September 18, but Bismarck's truculence ended all hopes. With the lucidity of the doomed, Favre realized that the only alternative left was to wage a war of total effort, and the only hope was the intervention of Europe.

Against this somber background, Bleichröder tried to play the peacemaker. The intermediary was Alexander Mendel, Schwabach's father-in-law, a Dutch or Belgian citizen and cosmopolitan *homme d'affaires*, with excellent French contacts, including good relations with Gambetta. In August Bleichröder had sent Keudell a letter from Mendel, "my most reliable man in Paris

... in his heart [he] is a good German, even if he is Dutch."[105] On September 10 Bleichröder telegraphed Keudell that "my informant" had returned to London with instructions from Gambetta to open negotiations. "If chief wants to talk with Mendel which in any case considered correct telegraph immediately together with instructions for route." The reply came forthwith: "Chief will receive your friend; recommend new Berlin pass, route via Nancy."[106] On September 12 Bismarck received a letter from Bernstorff in London, enclosing a report that Mendel had just received from Paris, full of gloom because the present government could not conclude peace. Mendel's unidentified source predicted that Paris, faced with republican chaos, would not defend itself, though "Paris is not France—New York, for example, also is the seat of a foul populace, which does not prevent America from being a great and noble nation."[107] Moritz Busch, Bismarck's press secretary, noted on top of Bernstorff's letter, "used for the press." Mendel's somber report made happy reading in the official German papers.

After Bleichröder had arranged a meeting with Bismarck, Mendel took one more quick trip to Paris to find out directly "what sacrifices they will accept."[108] His visit in Ferrières was as futile as Jules Favre's had been. Keudell liked Mendel; Moltke's men, on the other hand, abused him, the more readily for thinking him a Bleichröder agent.[109] Gambetta had given Mendel a return pass to Paris, but General Verdy du Vernois persuaded him not to risk such a trip, but to surrender the pass to him. Eventually Mendel obliged, and one of Moltke's officers noted: "We hope to make good use of it."[110]*

Bleichröder kept Mendel in reserve. His aims were simple: he wanted peace, he wanted to be the first to know when peace was in the offing, and he wanted to collect the indemnity that Germany was likely to impose on France. The last two promised large profits, and he implored Keudell's help. He asked Keudell, for example, to send him a coded telegram when peace was near, but Keudell reminded him that private telegrams from headquarters were forbidden: "My first dispatch about 'a few cigars' [code word for peace prospects] was transmitted because it was followed by 'for the Chief,' but yesterday the enclosed telegram was returned as undeliverable."[111] In mid-October Bleichröder asked the deputy head of the Foreign Office, Thile, to telegraph Bismarck that Mendel, after an interview solicited by the French minister of the interior, believed that "large cigar shipments" would have an effect on the French. Bismarck must have wondered what gibberish his banker-confidant was suddenly spouting, until Keudell properly interpreted the message; on the telegram Keudell scribbled that Bleichröder had asked him to use that code, but that he had refused.[112] Strictly speaking, this was not true, as we have seen, but Keudell was probably embarrassed to be the only one who under-

---

* A month later, Bismarck referred to the recent visit by an intermediary of Gambetta's who had asked him whether the Germans would recognize the Republic. "Not only the Republic, but, if you want, a Gambetta dynasty; only it must bring about an advantageous and certain peace." In telling the story, Bismarck added: "Indeed, any dynasty, whether Bleichröder or Rothschild," whereupon these two men became the subject of further conversation. GW, VII, 385.

stood Bleichröder's code; in this way their intimacy became public knowledge.

Throughout the fall, Bleichröder transmitted Mendel's reports to Thile, who in turn would send them by coded telegram to Bismarck. On October 25 Mendel reported: "Gambetta telegraphed that all talk was useless. Favre will not accept any [territorial] cessions." But it was Gambetta who by organizing the nation-in-arms gave substance to Favre's intransigence. In early November Mendel warned the Germans that the government at Tours thought that peace was impossible, that new, well-supplied armies were entering the field, and that "desperation drives people to arms against their will." Later that month, Bleichröder transmitted further news of growing French resistance.[113]

Not that Bismarck needed Bleichröder to apprise him of the seriousness of the situation. German troops had won a string of victories, but peace seemed as elusive as ever. The strain of waiting—first for the fall of Metz, then of Paris—took its toll in the collective tempers at Versailles. The enmity between Bismarck and the military grew, and the dispute concerning the bombardment of Paris added a new focus of controversy.

Occasionally Bleichröder received intimations of the glum atmosphere. Just before the fall of Metz, Keudell wrote on Bismarck's instructions that the chancellor "would be pleased to assign to you the collection of the war contribution, insofar as he can dispose of this, if the situation develops far enough to allow discussion. But no dove is visible on the horizon." French resistance had stiffened, and people were settling down for an unhappy winter in Versailles.[114] Bleichröder began to share everyone's impatience and wrote Keudell on October 28: "Heartfelt congratulations on the capitulation of Metz. God grant that I may soon be able to congratulate you on the ceremonial entry into Paris. But [even] anticipating all happy occasions, how do we get to an actual peace?" Perhaps it would be best if Favre were to go—as if that were in German hands!—because Gambetta was softer and "already accepted Alsace."[115]

Bleichröder wanted peace, a ceremonial entry into Paris, and Alsace as well. He, too, had been swept up by the chauvinist illusions of the day—and to such an extent that he probably no longer recognized the contradictoriness of his wishes. How different from his friend Moritz Goldschmidt, who now boasted of his pro-German sentiment but pleaded for Prussian moderation, and sighed: "When will the blessed 'shalom' come?"[116]

Even though peace was remote, the question of who would eventually collect the indemnity kept cropping up—sometimes almost teasingly on Bismarck's part. Thus, in early November, at Bismarck's behest, Keudell wrote Bleichröder "that the Vienna Rothschilds offered their services for the collection of French contributions; what is your opinion on this? As a rule we would prefer to use native [i.e., German] firms . . . if it comes to that." (Bismarck exaggerated, because the Vienna Rothschilds had merely offered to act as intermediaries with the Paris House, if the latter's services were required for the financial arrangements of a peace agreement.)[117] But, Keudell added, prospects were grim: "In short, there is no pleasant news I can report."[118]

For some time, the tone in Versailles remained glum. In mid-December still, Keudell confessed that no one knew how long Paris could hold out: "I see no signs of the beginning of the end."[119] Worse still, since early December, William and Bismarck were "in a condition of highest nervous irritability, [because of] the question concerning the imperial title, the bombardment of Paris and the [French] sorties." William was getting on Bismarck's nerves, and Bleichröder was enlisted in an effort to lessen the pressure. The Wolff Telegraph Bureau—with which Bleichröder had close ties and for which he had hoped to gain special privileges during the war—was sending its reports to Schneider, who read them to the king, who bothered Bismarck about various items. Bismarck thought at least that annoyance could be cut off at its source. He assumed that Schneider did not pay for these reports and he certainly should not receive them gratis: "The Federal Chancellor," wrote Keudell, "demands that an organization that receives such important contributions from the government [as Wolff] should not cause difficulties for it." During these trying weeks, when William balked at Bismarck's various maneuvers to unify Germany, the chancellor generally tried to restrict the king's supply of news.[120]

In mid-December Keudell acknowledged Mendel's further reports and conceded that "Gambetta has indeed accomplished astounding feats, and hence delayed peace." Further mobilization in Germany would be necessary "unless we are lucky and Paris falls within the next four weeks."[121] At the same gloomy time, Bleichröder wrote Bismarck a direct report on Gambetta's putative peacefulness and on French difficulties in raising funds in London, "despite the undeniable sympathy in England for France. The last note of Your Excellency . . . annoyed London. Here one is annoyed at the procrastination in the bombardment of Paris or, as rumors allege, at its complete cancellation."[122] Bismarck hardly needed Bleichröder to discover everybody's irritation; he knew that the world had turned against him, that foreigners thought him recalcitrant and harsh, and that Germans—wrongly—suspected him of leniency toward Paris.[123] What is remarkable is that Bleichröder felt free to tell him all this; such candor at a trying time is a tribute to both men.

Bleichröder also wrote Bismarck about his personal finances. During the early phase of the war, Keudell had served as intermediary between chancellor and banker, and as early as September 5, after Prussia's great victories had driven the market up and at a time when Bismarck realized that peace was still far off, he informed Bleichröder that "the chief empowers you to sell from his holdings whatever you deem correct." Bleichröder sold all or most of Bismarck's Russian mortgage bonds, and by November thought of repurchasing them. Bismarck thought there was no hurry in buying them back, especially as he could buy a new issue of them in 1871. The chancellor, Keudell added, did not expect that Russia's denunciation of the Black Sea clauses of the Treaty of Paris would lead to war, but "should he change his views, he would let you know." On his own responsibility and after a quick résumé of conditions in France, Keudell added: "Hence if I were speculating I would not yet buy."[124] The news from Versailles was bearish for a long time. Keudell's letter is further proof that Bismarck thought it important and unobjectionable to have his banker properly briefed. Obviously he would not share state secrets with him, but neither did he want him to make costly decisions in the dark.

Bismarck's concern with his private finances and with Bleichröder's management of them varied with his mood; when he was nervous and depressed, Bleichröder's occasionally oblique requests irritated him. Certainly Bismarck's staff stood in dread of his bad humor, and it may have been some sudden unpleasantness that prompted Keudell in mid-December to write Bleichröder that he could no longer bother Bismarck with business affairs; Bleichröder should write to him directly.[125] Bleichröder did, and told the ill-tempered chancellor that he had temporarily invested the proceeds from the Russian mortgage bonds in the new German Loan, which would appreciate until the new issue of mortgage bonds was ready. In the same letter, Bleichröder announced a shipment of some beer and cigars—comestible dividends from a grateful banker.[126]

At Christmas, the mood in Versailles became more querulous still. Despite further calamitous reverses, French leaders vowed to fight on. In the German camp the antagonisms between Moltke and Bismarck intensified, and the opening on January 5 of the bombardment of Paris, which the chancellor had for so long demanded, did little to assuage embittered feelings and conflicts. Moltke was perfectly willing to wage a long war provided it ended with a punitive peace. Bismarck wanted a quick end, because once again the specter of European intervention loomed large. Discord and frustration prevailed in Versailles, and even the proclamation on January 18 of the reluctant William as German emperor did not dispel the heavy clouds. A few days later, a relatively impartial observer noted: "I have never yet known such bitterness against any man as prevails against Bismarck at this point."[127]

The vanquished broke before the victor's embarrassments became apparent. Throughout January, Bleichröder heard from Mendel that Paris was close to surrender, though the French armies in the field were still formidable threats.[128] On January 23 Keudell alerted Bleichröder that the fall of Paris might be close at hand: "Instinct tells us that the people can't hold on much longer, but we have deceived ourselves so often that no one trusts instincts anymore. . . . I recommend that as soon as a crisis occurs you ask the Chancellor by telegraph for permission to come here. I cannot give you the desired assurance."[129] That night Jules Favre appeared at German headquarters, hoping to negotiate an armistice that would relieve the starving capital and prepare conditions for peacemaking.

Peace was in the offing at last. The war had brought heavy casualties to France and Germany. It had toppled one emperor and created another. It had humbled France and marked the end of her military preponderance. The passage of that preponderance to the new German Empire—or, as a member of the House of Commons put it, "Europe had lost a mistress and gained a master"—filled Germans with hubris and fear. That terrible amalgam was a legacy of Bismarck's Third War, and one which in subsequent years he could control but no longer exorcise.

CHAPTER 7

Hubris in Versailles

How hard the conquerors have been, and what a mistake in a great nation like Germany to give up all direction of its affairs to one bold unscrupulous man.

—Lord Granville, March 1, 1871

For five long months the Germans had waited for a French surrender. It had taken six weeks to trap the emperor and topple the Empire, but an insecure Republic refused German terms, afraid that a humiliating peace would arouse in Frenchmen something of the revolutionary fervor of 1793. For the Germans, with every passing day of what appeared to them as futile resistance, the desire to punish hardened. Meanwhile, they waited and plotted and bickered. These were excruciating months for the French; they were a trial to the Germans as well.

It was a strange place, this Prussian-German headquarters outside Paris —different from any Prussian encampment before. It contained a new mixture of Prussian militarism and German nationalism, a combination uneasily managed by an embattled Bismarck. To the outside world, the scene at Versailles exuded triumph and glory, as centuries of German disunity and French preponderance came to an end. A new Reich had been forged in the fires of war.

But inside headquarters, it looked different. The besiegers succumbed to a siege mentality. It was not only a new Empire that was being born; something of its spirit was being prefigured as well. Perhaps it was the unexpected, unaccustomed length of the war, perhaps it was the multiplicity of dangers and decisions that confronted Germany's leaders, but a coarsening, even a certain brutalization of spirit came to permeate the Germans at Versailles. The phobias of the future suddenly appeared in those months— to fade away in the first few years of peace under the Empire.

The clearest conflict at headquarters was between Bismarck and Moltke, between the statesman who insisted on the primacy of politics and the strategist who demanded that in wartime the military must have total autonomy. To Bismarck, war was an instrument of policy, and peacemaking his own prerogative; to Moltke, any political interference in strategy was a threat to his proper realm of responsibility. The conflict embittered headquarters and led Moltke to withhold vital information from Bismarck, even as Bismarck tried to withhold information from William. It was a conflict that was to beset and finally destroy the very Empire that both men were then creating.[1]

But there was antagonism between monarch and chancellor as well; when Bismarck had finally cajoled the South German states into accepting a German empire, with its barely veiled Prussian hegemony, William balked at his new title of German Emperor. The king of Prussia wanted the title of Emperor of Germany—or nothing. At the moment of triumph, after William had been proclaimed German Emperor in the Hall of Mirrors at Versailles (and not in the midst of his own people), he stepped down to shake hands with his fellow dynasts and trusted aides—with all in fact except Bismarck, the architect of the new Germany. It was more than Bavarian particularism that made Prince Otto, King Louis's brother and heir to the Bavarian throne, lament the great celebration: "I cannot even describe to you how infinitely sad and hurt I felt during the ceremony. . . . Everything was so cold, so proud, so glittering, so showy and swaggering and heartless and empty. . . ."[2]

As the paladins of the new Reich were at war with one another, it was easier for them to succumb to a composite of chauvinism, xenophobia, and anti-Semitism that seemed to attest a brutalization of spirit. Even Bismarck had changed: the prescient diplomat of 1866 had come to believe, at least for the moment, in the omnipotence of power—or how else to account for his admission to Lord Odo Russell, special British emissary to Versailles, that "the more completely France was vanquished the better in the end for Germany and the more lasting the peace"?[3] This new vision determined policy: the peace Bismarck demanded would perpetuate France's weakness. The annexation of Alsace-Lorraine cemented the enmity it was supposed to be the consequence of. Bismarck himself lived to regret this harshness—and solicitously blamed it on the military. At the time, he favored it, and in part because he thought that foreign triumphs would redound to Prussian glory and weaken all remaining opponents of Prussia's authoritarian regime.

At Versailles, Bismarck needed German parliamentarians—and when they appeared, they were denigrated. Ludwig Bamberger, eminent leader of the loyal National Liberals, was immediately dubbed "the red Jew."[4] There was an insistent, harsh anti-Semitic tone at Versailles: at no other time in his life did Bismarck speak so often, so freely, so scathingly of the rootlessness of Jews, of their hustling, of their omnipresence. (He complained that almost all or at least many of the members of the French Provisional Government were Jews: "almost certainly, Gambetta, too, judging from his physiognomy.")[5] Here, too, prejudice hardened into policy.

Bleichröder knew little of all this. For him Versailles was the seat of power, and he stood in awe of all that it represented. He probably knew little of the uglier side of German power and wanted to know less. Nor is there any evidence that he injected a note of caution or moderation into the elaboration of German war aims. He shared Bismarck's harshness, and, like so many other Germans, the triumph of German arms instilled in him an uncritical admiration for power and a terrible respect for all things military.

Bleichröder was unlikely to have heard of the anti-Semitic mutterings so common in Versailles at the time. But he must have known that somewhere in the German war machine there was a harsh anti-Semitic core—and a callousness to the sufferings of "lesser breeds," like Jews and Poles. He knew because the victims indirectly begged for his intercession. The incident, small in itself, but portentous in its implications, deserves attention.

It was in late December that Bleichröder discovered just how harsh Bismarck's men could be. On the twenty-third, Dr. Philippson, rabbi in Bonn and editor of a major Jewish paper, forwarded to Bleichröder a letter from the grand rabbi of Metz, Lipman, reporting that the German prefect of Metz had just decreed the immediate expulsion from the city of all Poles, most of whom were Jews. Appalled by the brutality of this mid-winter expulsion of men, women, and children, amidst wartime scarcity of transport, Lipman had pleaded with the prefect, Guido Henckel von Donnersmarck, who cited higher orders and rejected Lipman's request to appeal those orders. The government's aim, he explained, was "to Germanize Lorraine" and hence remove "those elements that were contrary to the German spirit. And he told me, nobody was more opposed to that spirit than the Poles." Philippson implored Bleichröder "to make use of his great influence," so that the chancellor would either delay the execution of the order or would at least exempt women and children from it.[6] There is no record of Bleichröder's action, though in later years he often intervened on behalf of his coreligionists. Polish gentiles were of course also affected by this order, because Germans even then considered Poles as enemies whose anti-German "spirit" justified all manner of brutality. There is an almost uncanny quality to the incident: at the birth of the new Empire, the first victims of chauvinistic brutality were Poles and Jews; they were also the last victims of a united Germany.

Throughout January, Bleichröder was in Berlin, waiting for other news. At last, on the twenty-eighth, a three-week armistice was signed, and the city of Paris was saddled with an indemnity of 200 million francs, a foretaste of far greater exactions. Bleichröder yearned to be on the spot so that he could advise Bismarck on how such large sums might best be collected and transferred—and to make sure that he got a lion's share in the financial operations involved. His unrivaled knowledge of the money markets of Europe and his excellent contacts with the Rothschilds obviously commended him to Bismarck.

By chance, Bleichröder was much talked about in headquarters just then—and not only because he had sent some exotic fish from the Adriatic which Bismarck devoured with relish between his arduous negotiations with Favre.[7] In those hectic days, when, as one general observed, "there was a multitude of people who tried to reduce the power of this great tyrant to a minimum," Bismarck and his embattled entourage ridiculed Bleichröder in jokes that reeked of Christian barnyards.[8] On January 30, for example, they talked of Parisians who would now try to leave their city, such as a Rothschild who allegedly had already received his safe-conduct. Bismarck immediately suggested, and not in jest, that he should be arrested as a *franctireur*, whereupon his cousin exclaimed: "Then Bleichröder will come running and prostrate himself on behalf of the whole Rothschild family." Bismarck replied, "Then we will send both to Paris, where they can join the dog hunt."[9] The reference was to the famine inside Paris. Two days later, talking about the indemnity from the city of Paris, Bismarck said, "Well, in the first place, Bleichröder should go into battle. He must get into Paris right away, so that he and his coreligionists can smell each other and talk with the bankers. . . . He does want to come?" To Keudell's reply that he wanted to come in a few days, Bismarck said, "Please telegraph that we need him immediately."[10]

Bleichröder did want to come—desperately. And alone. He had anxiously warded off other bankers who thirsted for the same call. For Bleichröder, it combined what he most coveted: the lure of profits and the taste of power. Once he received the call, he made no secret of his summons to Versailles—although he concealed his assiduous solicitation of it. His friends helped with the cumbersome travel plans. General Chauvin, head of the Prussian Telegraph Service, suggested the itinerary, and Major Brandt, now attached to headquarters, sent him an official order requesting German military and civilian authorities to grant all help, including the use of military trains, to Bleichröder and his two or three companions, who were traveling to Versailles "on official business."[11] Armed with this and other orders, and assisted by his own little retinue, he set out on the long, circuitous voyage to Versailles, where he arrived to have dinner with Bismarck and Herbert on February 7.[12]

Bleichröder was formally entrusted with two tasks in Versailles: to help arrange for the payment of the 200 million francs levied on Paris and to negotiate with the French concerning the much larger indemnity to be levied on the whole country. In both matters, he was to collaborate with another expert, great industrialist and friend of Bismarck, Count Guido Henckel von Donnersmarck, of whose political activities Bleichröder had so recently heard. On February 8 the two experts met their French counterparts in a mixed commission that was to arrange for the payment of the Paris indemnity that was due three days later.[13] Bleichröder suggested a satisfactory arrangement, involving a guarantee by the London Rothschilds. A few days later, Lieut.-General von Stosch wrote the Intendant-General of the Army, that Bleichröder was brimming with enthusiasm "at two [Paris] Rothschild bills of 2 million taler each, showed them to me repeatedly and asked whether anything more beautiful existed. He was all enthusiasm to see so much money in such small pieces of paper."[14] He probably was enthralled that two "such small pieces of paper" were the easily acceptable end products of the strenuous efforts of the Rothschilds to raise huge sums in a matter of days.

These two pieces of paper represented the power of bankers and of money—and a completed transaction between conqueror and conquered. Bleichröder knew that vastly greater sums were yet to be raised and transferred and that at each step of the way, the participating bankers could make great profits. He acknowledged receipt of the 4 million in a curt business note to the Paris Rothschilds, written from Versailles, and informed them that he was starting a special account for this indemnity, charging it ¼ percent.[15] Again, a modest foretaste of bigger things to come.

That a victorious Germany would exact a tremendous indemnity from France was a foregone conclusion after the first successful battles in August 1870. On August 13 the well-informed Austrian ambassador in Berlin, Baron Wimpffen, had written Vienna "of the firm intention to demand from France 2 billion war indemnity."[16] France would be forced to pay for the war she allegedly started, and her tribute was intended to persuade the South German states that Prussian glory spelled profit as well.

Wimpffen must have heard authoritative talk in Berlin about such an indemnity. He could have added that there were good historical precedents: the obvious model was the compensation extracted from France in 1815: 700 million francs, to cover the damages and costs imposed on the Allies by twenty-three years of revolutionary and Napoleonic aggression.[17] There was also the 10 million-taler indemnity collected from Saxony in 1866, after six weeks of battle. By mid-August the Prussian leadership was already planning to adjust historic precedent to the glittering opportunities of the moment.

Apparently, it was the victim—represented by Jules Favre—that first linked the subject of indemnities and annexations. Favre hoped that hard cash could save French territory; the Germans, however, had made up their minds that they wanted annexation *and* indemnity, twin instruments in order to weaken France for decades to come. The subject first came up in September, in Bismarck's initial negotiations with Favre, who allegedly offered him 5 billion francs if only France could keep Strasbourg and Alsace. Such a sum may well have been higher than anything Bismarck had even dreamed of—but for the moment he declined all further talk on the indemnity. (If the French were accommodating on that subject, it was important to stress the other.) "But I said to him," reported Bismarck to his son, "that we will talk about the money later, first we want to determine the German frontier."[18]

But Bismarck did not drop the subject from his mind—nor would aroused German greed have allowed him to do so. Three days after his conversation with Favre, he sent to the state ministry an official memorandum (which curiously enough was omitted from his collected works) and rebuked premature planning with the assurance: "It will be our task at the peace negotiations to strive for as large a contribution as possible and one that will suffice for all purposes; the total sum will have to be determined by agreement." The division of the spoils among the interested parties was a domestic affair, to be settled by the government later.[19] It may well be that Bismarck dispatched that memorandum in order not to have the Prussian ministry arrive at prematurely low figures. The ministry repeatedly discussed the subject and appointed a special subcommittee to study the German costs that would determine the total amount of the indemnity.

As we saw, Bleichröder was also forging his plans for the anticipated indemnity. For him, the main thing was that after Germany had exacted a heavy indemnity from France, German bankers—with himself in the lead—should be the intermediaries between France and Germany, probably to the exclusion of French bankers. But even among German bankers there was bitter, behind-the-scenes competition building up. In October 1870 Abraham Oppenheim wrote to Bleichröder, urging that they should cooperate in all matters pertaining "to the business of the war contribution." Bleichröder seems to have agreed—perhaps to forestall a separate Oppenheim initiative. Indeed Oppenheim thought or hoped that Bismarck would want Bleichröder to play a subordinate and less visible role: "precisely because of the intimate relations that exist between you and v.B. (because these relations with you are well known and might be interpreted in other ways)." Oppenheim urged Bleichröder to write Bismarck along these lines so that Bismarck would entrust Oppenheim with the principal responsibility for the indemnity—the more so as Oppenheim had familial ties with the Paris banking family, the Foulds. Bleichröder should also assure Bismarck that "at his first sign, you would therefore be ready to proceed along with me to headquarters to develop our plans to him orally." Alternatively, Oppenheim offered to write directly to the king—who had encouraged him to do so whenever serious matters arose. It is unlikely that Bleichröder felt such self-denying delicacy, nor did he necessarily want to have a companion in Versailles. Nor did Bismarck feel any such compunction as Oppenheim had imputed to him.[20] Oppenheim assumed to the end that the two men would travel together, but he took the disappointment well. On learning of Bleichröder's invitation to Versailles, he wired him congratulations: "Please have no further hesitations on my account. Wish you a happy and pleasant trip. Keep me informed. Letter follows."[21] In fact, many letters followed, and Oppenheim never gave up hope that he too would be summoned to the seat of power, whether at Versailles or Berlin. His bags were packed.

By the time Bleichröder arrived at headquarters, the question of the indemnity—the total amount and the modalities of payment—was being discussed in various quarters.

On February 8, while the French people went to the polls to decide whether to continue the war or accept a harsh peace including a heavy indemnity, the Prussian state ministry met again to determine just how harsh the indemnity was to be. When all demands were listed at the session, they totaled roughly 1 billion taler (or 3 billion francs), of which 95 percent was earmarked for the army, which wanted to be reimbursed not only for wartime costs but for prospective peacetime expenses to get the army completely battle-ready again and to fortify Germany's new frontier. The finance minister, Camphausen, remarked that the military estimates were a bit high but hinted that soon there would be more to calculate than the tangible losses Germany had incurred: "The German nation had after all suffered so many additional losses in blood and material goods which are beyond all accounting that it is entirely justified to assess the price of the war generously and in addition to the estimated sum to demand an appropriate surcharge for the incalculable damages. The State Ministry concurred," according to the laconic protocol, marked secret and immediately forwarded to Bismarck.[22] The military were prompted by more than ordinary greed; a billion taler would give them immunity from parliamentary niggardliness for years to come. Camphausen's notion of collecting for intangible as well as tangible losses, if known, would certainly have eased the allied task of rationalizing German reparations at Versailles.[23]

Bismarck's ministers, however, merely furnished the approximate itemization; he himself would set the total. Nor would his decision rest on the estimate, however generous, of German costs. He was to set the total by his estimate of France's capacity to pay. This was variously estimated, and depended in part on how the money was to be collected.

Bleichröder at times counseled moderation and, soon after his arrival in Versailles, told the grand duke of Baden "that the monetary conditions in France were so bad that he thought it would be impossible for the French to pay the 4 billion war indemnity already mentioned earlier."[24] Bleichröder was widely known to think 5 billion too high.[25] Henckel von Donnersmarck favored the higher figure, and indeed, far more astronomical figures floated around Versailles. Bleichröder told the military that Favre had rejected Bismarck's suggested figure of 8 billion.[26] Bleichröder's own conservative views were reinforced by a judicious letter which Abraham Oppenheim wrote him on February 14:

If the newspapers have been driveling up to now about 7 to 8 billion francs, that is to be excused on the ground that these are people who have no accurate notion of what that is, a billion francs. We, as men of finance, however, will be guilty of a serious crime if we sing the same song and do not take into account what so rich a country as France is in a position to do, after so bloody a war, in which her financial resources have been used in an utterly irresponsible way, without succumbing to total ruin. My personal view is that we, if we be moderate and want to have the gratitude of the neutral powers, must be content with 3 billion francs plus compensation for the cost of maintaining war prisoners. Four billion francs, however, should be the outside limits of our demands and would probably be accepted by the French without grumbling. These 4 billion could be raised by the French only on very onerous conditions and would add a charge of at least 250 million francs to their annual budget. When one adds to that how much of France has been laid waste by the war, how many families have lost the greater part of their fortunes, and what further expenditures are required to recover bit by bit from the calamities of war, one is surely not out of line in predicting that it will take them at least ten years to get back on their feet. The task of raising so large an indemnity without plunging the country into a financial crisis that would ruin it completely is really no small matter.[27]

Similar words of caution reached Bleichröder from Paris. The official link between the Rothschilds and the Bleichröder Bank was resumed around February 10, when Brandeis requested news about the Berlin market. Schwabach obliged and added that "Mr. Bleichröder has been called to Versailles as . . . a member of a commission which is to deal with the financial side of the indemnity."[28] On February 17 Brandeis wrote Bleichröder directly, pleading for reasonable demands and arguing that even 1 billion francs would be too much.[29] Bleichröder replied that he had heard that there was abundant money in Paris, adding, "I would like to talk with you soon."[30]

At the same time, Bleichröder received a similar plea for moderation from his trusted secretary, Friedrich Lehmann, replying to a letter of Bleichröder's that had apparently spoken of 7.5 billion francs. Lehmann acknowledged Bleichröder's contention that France herself would benefit from such a crippling blow because it would reconcile her to a peaceful role and to disarmament (would Bleichröder have seen similar advantages for Prussia if the shoe had been on the other foot?) but added: "In all honesty, however, I do not think it *fair* [in English and in italics in original] that young Germany should set the sum of the contribution higher than absolutely necessary in order to cover its actual costs of war. . . . For this purpose I consider 800 to 1,000 million taler (3 to 3.75 billion francs) a very high estimate." To make still greater demands on France would embitter her and put Germany "on the precipitous path of either a permanently defensive posture or of a conqueror-state; the blessings of peace then would not be ours, and the burdens of Germany will not be lightened." He warned against "going astray in deference to public opinion, which is manufactured anyhow. The desire to give Germany her due should not be the cause for doing 'too much.' "[31] Oppenheim and Lehmann gave prescient advice; they were afraid hubris would dictate a settlement that would disregard the economic consequences of the peace. We do not know how far Bleichröder shared these sober views; even if he had, he could not have prevailed against the others.

While the Germans were bickering over the terms of the indemnity, the French had to put together a government that would negotiate the peace. The elections had returned a solid majority for peace and for a monarchical restoration; in the absence of a generally acceptable royal claimant, Adolphe Thiers was elected executive head of the French government on February 18. Thiers was the grand old man of French politics, the very type of self-made man in politics that the Germans—to their detriment—had never been able to produce. From the 1820s on, he had opposed authoritarian regimes and under the Orleanist monarchy which he had helped to establish, he had risen to ministerial eminence (at the age of thirty-five; at thirty-six he became a member of the French Academy). His ideal was a constitutional monarchy, with a conservative social order as its base. In February 1871, as the acclaimed savior of a defeated France, he had to contend with rapacious conquerors and to forestall rebellious radicals. He needed peace with the foreigner in order to prevent an upheaval at home. The history of France—of which he was an ardent chronicler—had already demonstrated the links between war and revolution.[32] The Germans then paid small heed to these considerations; in 1918 they were to beg for a moderate peace because anything else, they threatened, might bring Bolshevism to Germany.

Three days after his assumption of office, Thiers made the melancholy journey to Versailles. He had no hopes for German magnanimity, but even this sober realist, at first treated with great courtesy, was shocked by Bismarck's tone and terms. The negotiations lasted six days; the record of them is unfortunately scant.[33] Their outcome was not a foregone conclusion, though Thiers's will to peace was great and his country's capacity for renewed battle virtually nil. Tempers in Versailles were often close to the breaking point. Bismarck had most of the trumps in his hand, but he was pushed by his own military and worried about last-minute foreign intervention. No wonder the crown prince found him "to the last degree peevish" and feared lest he "may not once again, after his own usual fashion, take up such a line of policy that fresh wars will be stirred up."[34]

Two closely related issues dominated the negotiations: the amount of the indemnity and the extent of the annexations. Thiers apparently anticipated a total of 5 billion, but recoiled when Bismarck—for tactical reasons—wrote 6 billion on a piece of paper. He jumped "as if he had been bitten by a mad dog" and loosed a torrent of rhetoric, culminating with: "C'est une indignité."[35] At this point Bismarck—angered—switched to German. To a French objection that 6 billion was an incalculable enormity and that if someone had started counting out 6 billion francs one by one in the time of Jesus, he still would not be finished, Bismarck replied that "he had provided for that" by bringing an expert (Bleichröder) who had started counting at the Creation.[36] He assured Thiers that "two of our most important financiers had devised a procedure by which this tribute, so burdensome in appearance, will be paid by you without your being aware of it."[37] Did Bismarck really think that the pound of flesh could be excised without a stab of pain? In any case, the two sides had to agree on the proposed procedure of payment—and not only on the total amount. The Germans wanted to dictate the terms of payment (and the stipulation that German bankers would play the dominant role); France had to worry about her economic survival *and* the need to pay as rapidly as possible: the step-by-step evacuation of troops from northern France was going to be tied to the progressive payment of the indemnity, so that the French had an incentive to liquidate this burden swiftly.

Bleichröder and Henckel von Donnersmarck tried to persuade the French that the bloodletting would indeed be painless. For this purpose they were sent to Paris on February 23 with their special safe-conducts, and they negotiated with Favre and his experts. Favre later recalled his session with the German plenipotentiaries, of whom Bismarck had spoken so glowingly: "M. Black Schröder [*sic*] and the Count de Heukel [*sic*] . . . whose immense fortunes, vast renown, and incontestable cleverness put them in the first rank" of bankers. But Favre and his colleagues were not persuaded by "the ingenious systems" that they proposed and that would have left the two bankers and their German partners to collect the indemnity and settle with the German government. Favre records the "painful impression" left by

> these two princes of Prussian finance, always smiling, voices of honey, embroidering their speech with a persuasive, almost affectionate politeness, [who] did their best to prove to us how much they wanted to carry out a colossal operation with our billions. They kept at it a long time, with an answer to every objection, except those that politeness prevented us from uttering.[38]

The meeting reached no agreement, and Henckel returned to Versailles, afraid that the peace talks would collapse altogether.[39] Bleichröder tarried in Paris long enough to see his friend Emil Brandeis, and then also returned to Versailles.

Bismarck and Thiers bitterly disputed the questions concerning the indemnity and the new frontiers until a few hours before the signing of the peace preliminaries. Bismarck was furious with French objections and procrastinations, partly because the English government was making last-minute efforts to force a reduction of the projected indemnity.[40] Thiers demanded that Baron Rothschild be called to their final meeting, and when at last he appeared, Bismarck vented his accumulated anger on the hapless Rothschild, whom he had come to detest in the last few weeks and whose French speech and loyalty he unreasonably resented. (As far as Bismarck was concerned at that moment, any Rothschild was but a Jew from Frankfurt.) Bleichröder later told the crown prince: "Count Bismarck would seem to have conducted himself during the negotiations with monstrous brusquerie and intentional rudeness, and by such behavior to have in particular deeply shocked the Paris Rothschild, who in the first instance addressed him in French."[41] Whether because of or despite Bismarck's abysmal rudeness, the peace preliminaries were signed on the evening of February 26, hours before the expiration of the armistice. The indemnity was fixed at 5 billion, but the French were left to find their own way to pay. That much they had salvaged—probably to Bleichröder's chagrin.

In most of the world, the satisfaction that the war was over was greater than the distress at the harsh terms. Even in Germany, however, there were dissenting voices: the crown prince thought that German demands including the indemnity were harsh—and so did the socialist August Bebel.* A

---

* On March 4 the *Economist* commented: ". . . to exact huge sums of money as the consequence of victory suggests a belief that money may next time be the object as well as the accidental reward of battle. A flavor of huckstering is introduced into the relations between States which degrades the character of statesmen, and is sure sooner or later to infect the character of the people." In some ways, the indemnity stood for something worse than huckstering—for the brutal exploitation of power, which also was to degrade the character of statesmanship.

British protest came too late: Bismarck met it with news of Thiers's acceptance.[42] Many years later, Bismarck told the Reichstag that in case of another war the French would never be as considerate to a defeated Germany as the Germans had been in the matter of the indemnity: "So moderate a victor as the Christian German does not exist in the world anymore."[43] If this was moderation, the French could hardly have believed it. But the Germans, Christian and non-Christian alike, exulted in their victory.

Bleichröder had his share of glory. The German press reported on his presence in Versailles, and one paper wrote: "Mr. Bleichröder, a small Bismarck in this field, knew how to deal with the French, who became ever more timid."[44] He had helped to saddle the French with a staggering burden. He had won neither for himself nor for German bankers a monopoly on the financial operations that were to follow. A hot competition among Europe's leading bankers ensued.

Bleichröder remained at Versailles for another week or more; all in all, he was at his residence on the Avenue de St. Cloud for more than a month. He obviously relished his important role—perhaps too obviously. In this all-gentile, all-aristocratic company, in this military camp where civilians were slighted and Jews infinitely more so, Bleichröder must have cut a curious figure. Did he know it? Would he have been more modest, less boastful, if he had realized the antagonism all around him? Or did he sense, perhaps unconsciously, that the presence of a Jew, whatever his achievements and his presents and however self-effacing, would be the butt of unkind jokes? He seemed impervious to slights and gossip: he did his job and relished his intimacy with the great, assuming perhaps that they in turn would requite service with respect, if not with gratitude.

Oftentimes during that month he dined and talked with Bismarck. He saw the new emperor and the crown prince, met with the South German ministers, and even ventured into the lair of the military "demigods." He thought himself a member of officialdom, free to enjoy the attendant privileges. For a short while his Berlin house was allowed to use the military telegraph to transmit stock-market quotations to him; later, the military indignantly refused.[45] Still, he knew how things fared in Berlin, and there were many in Versailles who quietly sought his news and thoughts about the market. Some, like Hatzfeldt, used Bleichröder's contacts with the Rothschilds to send money to relatives in Paris.[46]

There remained a strong anti-Semitic undercurrent in Versailles. Bronsart von Schellendorff, an intimate of Moltke's, thought Bleichröder's presence an indignity and angrily wrote in his diary:

Now he [Bismarck] confers eagerly with the Jew Bleichröder, his banker, whom he let come here for *official* discussions concerning the war indemnity to be demanded from Paris. One wonders for what purpose we have an institution like the Prussian Bank if the Chancellor's *Privatjude* and not one of its officials operates as adviser in state business. . . . Bleichröder was at the General Staff this morning. In his buttonhole he wore an artistically arranged rosette of many colors, which attested the knighthood [*Ritterschaft*] of many Christian orders. Like a true Jew, he bragged about the private audiences he has had with the king, about his other exclusive connections, about the credit people like him and Rothschild can command, etc. About the political situation and the inclinations of Count Bismarck he was sufficiently informed; now he wanted to enlist the help of the General Staff and gain access even to Count Moltke.[47]

On February 25, after the big fight with the French negotiators, Bleich-röder dined with Bismarck and the other advisers. The Baden minister Julius Jolly recalled the occasion: "The conversation was extremely interesting. The most different tendencies and desires were expressed: the most brutal *Borussentum* represented by the Count Renard, who was there by chance, the heroic self-esteem of the banker Bleichröder with his incomparable Jew-physiognomy. . . . The cosmopolitan delicacy of Count Henckel."[48]

On February 26, after the peace preliminaries had at last been signed and Thiers and Favre had departed, Bismarck "in high good humor" dined with his entourage, including the Bavarian prime minister, Count Bray, and Bleichröder. It was a victory celebration, and after dinner even the rivals came, including Moltke, to tender their congratulations and to conclude their own peace with Bismarck.[49] It was an historic moment, and a man less vain than Bleichröder would have found the company and the occasion exhilarating.

A few weeks earlier his secretary in Berlin, Friedrich Lehmann, lamenting Bleichröder's long stay in Versailles, mused that the sojourn, with the threat of renewed warfare hanging over it, could not "count among the chief pleasures of life. I can only wish therefore that your willing self-sacrifice will be rewarded by a rich measure of honors."[50] Bleichröder no doubt cherished similar thoughts. Before he left Versailles, he received the Iron Cross, second class, in recognition of services just rendered. Having warmly congratulated him on this well-deserved honor, Mendel could not help adding: "May you never have to bear a different cross! Amen!"[51] Public honors aside, Bleichröder knew that his prestige among his peers had soared. From Vienna, the sometimes sardonic Goldschmidt wrote to Bleichröder about his "great, glorious and, one may indeed say, world-historical trip. . . . I believe you that the stay in Versailles offered plenty of things of the *highest* interest and left you with unforgettable memories for life. Only the elect experience such things."[52] Greater honors followed aplenty, but it is doubtful whether Bleichröder ever relished anything more than his month in Versailles, at the very center of power and high society.

PART TWO

BANKER FOR AN EMPIRE

CHAPTER 8

A New Baron in
a New Berlin

Mr. and Mrs. Veneering were bran-new people in a bran-new house in a
bran-new quarter of London. Everything about the Veneerings was spick and
span new. All their furniture was new, all their friends were new, all their
servants were new, their plate was new, their carriage was new, their harness
was new, their horses were new, their pictures were new, they themselves were
new, they were as newly married as was lawfully compatible with their having
a bran-new baby, and if they had set up a great-grandfather, he would have
come home in matting from the Pantechnicon, without a scratch upon him,
French-polished to the crown of his head.

—Charles Dickens, *Our Mutual Friend*

Before union, the atmosphere and ways of living in the various parts and
principalities had been regional and European; the changes afterwards were
gradual and not complete. Except in Brandenburg. To that nucleus of Prussia,
to that poor flat country of marches and poor sandy soil and the city set
among parade grounds and sparse pines, to that border province of garrisons
and unwieldy estates worked by Slav day-labourers and Huguenot artisans
and ruled by the descendants of Teutonic Knights, Bismarck's successful wars
and the foundation of the Empire brought at once a tide of big money, big
enterprise, big buildings, big ideas which blurred demarcations between
castes, swelled military and domestic discipline into Wagnerian displays and
atrophied the older traditions of economy, frugality and probity. Tradespeople were coining money, the middle classes were getting rich and the rich
became opulent. The pay of the bureaucracy remained lean, but its members
were puffed with self-importance. Sons of bankers entered guard regiments
instead of their fathers' firms, and the sons of brigadier generals resigned
commissions in favour of marriage to an actress or an heiress. Uniforms,
no longer the livery of duty, were worn like feathers, to strut the owner
and attract the eligible. Men still toiled, but they also spent and glittered.

—Sybille Bedford, *A Legacy*

The new Empire was born in blood and exultation. Victory and
unity, suddenly achieved, gave Germans a new sense of their
power and importance. Triumph appeared in dramatic-heroic guise, and Germans felt that their lives and collective destiny had been transformed. No
longer did they see themselves as a people of poets, dreamers, and thinkers: in
the early 1870s they discovered that they had entered the path to power and
world eminence, that in military and political terms they had ceased to be
Europe's anvil and had become its hammer instead.

It was a heady experience, and the mood was jubilant. "I feel as if every day were Sunday," wrote one young scholar.[1] What most enthralled the people at the time was the defeat of France, which for centuries already had been united and had appeared to the world as the repository of martial glory. Instantaneously, the Germans transformed their military victory into an instrument of divine justice: God had punished the frivolous, decadent French. It was harder for the German people to celebrate their own political unification—because that particular revolution had come from above, had not been their feat, but had been orchestrated by Bismarck and had as its symbol the Hohenzollern dynasty, which was quickly endowed with the imperial nimbus of the Hohenstauffen. It was easier for Bavarians to revel in the defeat of France than in the newly established hegemony of Prussia. The emphasis on German military prowess had an obvious and important consequence: it gave new prestige to the state and to the traditional servants of the crown. German officers were the heroes of the day, but they came overwhelmingly from the old landed aristocracy in Prussia, from the Junker class, and hence precisely at the moment of Germany's modernization the anachronistic and economically declining elements of a modern society were once more exalted.

The new pride was both spontaneous and carefully cultivated. After centuries of disunity, of suffering often shameful defeats, there was a kind of national intoxication with victory. Even so cosmopolitan and sensitive a witness as the Baroness Spitzemberg noted in her diary in March 1871: "What a peace for us Germans! More magnificent and more glorious than any we have ever concluded! United in one Reich, the greatest, the mightiest, the most feared empire in Europe, great not alone through its physical power, greater still through its culture and through the spirit which permeates its people."[2] In a few months, Germans had suddenly grown taller by inches and had come to walk with a prouder bearing. Just before the end of the Empire, Max Weber noted "the striking lack of grace and dignity in the overt bearing of the German."[3]

The victory had to be eulogized publicly as well as privately. Every city, every state, vied with one another in the production of spectacles and mementos of the great victory, and it was natural that Berlin should have pride of place. Overnight it had become the political center of the continent. It was in Berlin, on a perfect summer day in June 1871, that the nation's great victory parade took place: an endless procession of military prowess, led by Moltke, Bismarck (in uniform, of course), and Roon on horseback, followed in solitary splendor by the venerable William, followed in turn by his sons and the princes of the realm—with 42,000 men marching behind—complete with laurel wreaths, triumphal arches, and enthusiastic crowds. Baroness Spitzemberg remembered that "the proudest sight for a German heart was the noncommissioned officers from all the army corps who marched ahead of the troops, carrying the eighty-one French flags and eagles."[4] The city paid 150,000 taler for the parade—a modest foretaste of the mounting price of patriotic pomposity.[5]

After the parades were over, except for the annual Sedan-Feier which kept alive the memory of French humiliation, German artists took their turn to celebrate the new Empire in a rash of monumental paintings, buildings, poems, all imitative of earlier heroic styles. They sought to give their people a kind of instant apotheosis of their triumph. Everything exuded power and success, and a new national bombast belied earlier sobriety and Biedermeier restraint. In truth, a new nation had been born, and the dissonant voices who, like Nietzsche, feared that the great victory might lead to the extirpation of the German spirit were not heard.[6]

Berlin was the heart of this new Empire. It too suddenly became aware of its new importance; it became a *visible* metropolis. But just as unification had been prepared undramatically for decades before 1870, so the city of Berlin had long before begun its change, but its self-perception had not kept pace with the actual changes. For some time the city had ceased to be a sleepy, distinguished Residenzstadt, where only the court and the state's old elites were dominant. By 1871 it became clear that Berlin embodied the elements of the new society: people came to realize that Berlin had been and continued to be a dynamically expanding city, a growing center of banking, trade, and industry. A new Berlin had grown around and on top of the old Berlin.

Population figures tell a part of the story: in the 1850s the city grew by 20 percent; in 1861, after the incorporation of a few outlying districts, the city had a population of 529,000; by 1871 it was 824,000, and two years later, 900,000. By 1877 it exceeded a million inhabitants. In seventeen years Berlin had doubled its population and thus became one of the fastest-growing capitals of Europe. (The Jewish population of the city had grown even faster; it was 18,900 in 1860 and 53,900 in 1880.)[7]

Berlin had become a city of opportunity, and thousands of East Prussians fled impoverished farm conditions—in order to take impoverished industrial jobs. Berlin became a magnet for the discontented or ambitious provincials, much as Paris had been throughout the century. It also became a magnet for Jews, including many from eastern Europe, who found Berlin an open city for advancement in trade, commerce, and, increasingly, in the professions.

The city began to feel its importance. In 1870, even before the founding of the new Empire, the theater season was enlivened by a popular farce, *Berlin wird Weltstadt*, and the title became a city byword.[8] Its unpaved streets, its rather staid cultural life, and its sprawling, unplanned character belied the notion of a world metropolis, a *Weltstadt*; a *Geldstadt*, a city of new money, on the other hand, it had become. With its enviable geographical location, now fully exploited by rail and water, Berlin became a commercial metropolis, with a steadily expanding industrial sector. Berlin under the Empire remained a strange mixture of the parvenu and the provincial. For all its importance, it never caught up with the cosmopolitan vitality and elegance of Paris or London.

In a phrase of striking ambiguity, Walter Rathenau once called Berlin "Chicago on the Spree."[9] It was the last thing that most Berliners would have wanted to hear. They had relished being called the Sparta of the North; under the Empire, Chicago may have been closer to the mark, however wounding the comparison was to a people that from the 1870s on had been warned against the Americanization of Germany and that would have preferred to give up Sparta for being a latter-day Athens.

Like Chicago, Berlin was a city of dynamic capitalism. Unlike Chicago, it had older classes that resented the ferment in its midst. Capitalism has its own pace; it has its intoxicating advances and its catastrophic reverses, and at each swing of the cycle people believe that the new direction is destined to last. In the early 1870s the exuberance of victory and the sudden influx of 5 billion French francs in the form of the reparations launched an unparalleled boom and speculative excitement. These were the *Gründerjahre*—years of delirious promotions and creations. The new spirit found a dramatic focus: the stock market. Built in the early 1860s, in lavish neo-Renaissance style, the Berlin Börse in the early 1870s became the universally discussed arbiter of hopes and expectations. For a short dramatic moment—before the inevitable crash—the stock market became Everyman's Temple of Temptation. The speculative extravaganza completed the Germans' new perceptions of themselves: it was in this moment of capitalism in caricature that Germans came to realize the degree to which the new economic system had come to dominate their society. They experienced a shock of recognition from which they never fully recovered—and from that time forward, anticapitalism was a strong force in German life.

As money poured into Berlin, its physiognomy changed, and it, too, began to mirror the social discords of the new order. Capitalist desire swept the city, and Berlin became a city of extremes: the rich built themselves palaces in the west while the poor lived in proletarian barracks, *Mietskasernen*, as they were called, in the east. The gaudiness of the rich was in stark contrast to the crampedness of the poor; there was neither harmony of style nor harmony of classes in the new Berlin. Decades later, an observer was struck by a city where one could find "all styles in cheap and expensive ugliness. . . . Here is an Assyrian temple beside a patrician mansion from Nuremberg; a bit further on is a glimpse of Versailles, then memories of Broadway, of Italy, of Egypt—terrible abortions of a polytechnical beer-imagination."[10] But these contrasts were the essence of the *Gründerzeit*, which for decades Berliners remembered with distaste.*

The social life of the city was marked by the uneasy interplay between the newly rich and the old elite; the poor were kept in less than benign neglect. The court was still the pinnacle of society; the old aristocrats still clung to their posts in the upper reaches of government, bureaucracy, and

---

* In the enthusiasm of August 1914, when so many intellectuals thought that the war would bring about a cultural regeneration as well, Friedrich Meinecke recalled: "After 1870, the intellectual and political life of the nation was disfigured by cruder features of materialism and egotism. . . . We recall today with a sense of shame the plebeian orgy of the *Gründerzeit*, the heedless arrogance with which a trivial liberalism waged the Kulturkampf, the not infrequent callousness and short-sightedness with which one encountered the demands of the fourth estate which of course were often cast in immeasurably crude fashion; and not least do we regret the aesthetic insensitivity with which one tolerated that the old, lovable, modest-elegant Germany of our youth, the quiet charm of our old cities, gardens, and utensils fell victim to the cheap glitter of mass industry and mass taste." Friedrich Meinecke, *Die deutsche Erhebung von 1914: Aufsätze und Vorträge* (Stuttgart and Berlin, 1914), pp. 19–20.

the much admired and much displayed officer corps. These were the pillars of the old order. The dynamism of the city, its power and its wealth, however, was contributed by the new classes, by the bankers, industrialists, and magnates of commerce and industry.

The rich coveted the traditions of the old elite, who in turn despised and coveted the wealth of the new upstarts. The rich hoped to trap the older dignitaries by their wealth—and at the same time to emulate the old by attaining titles and decorations. It was a time of tension and uneasy, gradual amalgamation between the old and the new classes. It was a time of changing values and above all, a painful time of changing self-perceptions. Somehow the power worship that Germans had learned in measuring themselves vis-à-vis the rest of the world permeated their domestic life as well. There it jarred with older values and interests; the old Prussian elite, rooted in its estates, dominant in state and society, had lived by a simple code of honor, frugality, duty, and self-discipline. They could not deny the realities of power or the temptation of wealth. But they found the new style threatening and repugnant, and their repugnance was at once genuine and self-serving. It gave some legitimacy to their insistent claims to continued prerogative. The old classes resented modernity, and modernity appeared in Germany in a particularly swift and garish fashion. But they also resented having to share their power and their privileges with the new elites that a modern society produced, "with brand-new service nobility, with plutocrats both ennobled and not-ennobled, with garment district Jews [*Kleiderjuden*], both baptized and nonbaptized, even at times with academicians, both washed and unwashed [*gekämmten und ungekämmten*]."[11]

In sum, Berlin was a raw and changing city. It neither was nor became a bourgeois city—just as the Empire was not a bourgeois country. The bourgeoisie proved unable, to some degree unwilling, to set up their own code of values or their own style of life; they aped their impoverished betters. In imperial Berlin, not the black coat of the bourgeois but the king's uniform became the mask of distinction; even Bismarck always appeared in parliament in his cuirassier coat. "In today's Germany," wrote Robert Michels in 1914, "there is no socially independent bourgeoisie with pride in itself."[12] For reasons of politics and history, the German bourgeoisie, even in its decades of unsurpassed economic power, paid obeisance to the values of its earlier aristocratic antagonists, now economically insecure and often dependent upon bourgeois wealth and assistance for adequate survival.

Germany's failure at *embourgeoisement* had a special bearing on the condition of its Jews. Perhaps it facilitated their rise, which under the Empire was spectacular. It also facilitated their vilification. A Germany that half-denied its capitalistic-bourgeois self proved spiritually less tolerant of the rise of Jewry than did some of its bourgeois neighbors.

Bleichröder returned to Berlin from Versailles in March 1871, a few days before William's historic entry. Bleichröder had scored his own triumph; he had been present at the creation of the Reich, the only Jew to have been a participant in the great decisions. His Iron Cross was a reminder of past excitement. His several constituencies—his fellow bankers and his fellow Jews—would have to accord him still greater respect. At forty-nine, he had achieved much. He was Berlin's most renowned private banker and one of its wealthiest citizens; he was Bismarck's adviser and the counselor of much of the elite.

During the next two decades, Bleichröder grew more powerful, more prominent, and more visible. Under the Empire, industrial capitalism determined the face and growth of society; to an extent greater than elsewhere, German bankers had a controlling influence over the policies of the major industrial enterprises. In the early 1870s the new economic style, symbolized by the get-rich-quick mentality of the stock market, became an acknowledged, if much lamented, fact of German life. Because more and more people recognized the centrality of capitalism in German life, Bleichröder's own role was more widely perceived as well as calumniated.

After 1871 Bleichröder became more deeply enmeshed with the modern world of industry. He helped to reorganize the Silesian coal complex known as Laurahütte, and he promoted the new corporate form of the great Hibernia mine in the West. He thus had a major interest in the mining industry, which belonged to the fastest-growing sector of the economy. He also expanded his connections with various railroads. The companies with which he was most closely identified weathered the crash of 1873 far better than most other enterprises. He was adventurous yet prudent, and he made money in good times and held on to it in bad times. He also maintained and increased his share in the international loan market. In short, he was a major force in the various branches of Germany's economic life. Few major decisions in the economic realm could have been taken without his participation in some form.

In pursuit of his diverse interests he had to work closely with fellow bankers; large undertakings on a national or international level were almost always the work of a consortium, and Bleichröder had to be watchful lest rivals steal a march on him. In connection with the French indemnity payment, even Bleichröder's closest associates—such as Hansemann's Disconto-Gesellschaft—sought to cut him out of an arrangement that promised profit and prestige. The flavor of habitual rivalry can be inferred from a story Julius Schwabach recalled to Bleichröder during the critical indemnity negotiations: the banker Speier always told of a broker who, having made a profit of 40 gulden, claimed to have earned 500 gulden. When questioned, the broker explained: Forty gulden I earned, 460 gulden the other broker did not earn, altogether I made 500 gulden.[13]

But Bleichröder was not in business for himself alone. Banking, as David Landes put it, is always other people's money, and Bleichröder needed clients just as clients needed him. He was a banker to ministers, diplomats, generals, men of distinguished birth—they all flocked to him, attracted by his shrewdness, certified, proven integrity, and unsurpassed knowledge of the political-economic scene. Bleichröder exemplified what Walter Bagehot wrote in 1873:

"I can imagine nothing better in theory or more successful in practice than private banks as they were in the beginning. A man of known wealth, known integrity, and known ability is largely entrusted with the money of his neighbors. The confidence is strictly personal."[14]

To special customers, to customers who could help him, Bleichröder could extend extraordinary favors. To a few he could give lucrative directorships; others needed to have their fortunes salvaged. All clients could count on his advice, and some could buy shares in new issues at low subscription prices. To all, he offered the psychic, pecuniary reassurance of his solicitude: in expert fashion, he took care of what many people in imperial Germany still scoffed at and what none could do without: their money.

Bleichröder had connections and interests everywhere: as long as he enjoyed his intimacy with Bismarck, most Germans of means or ambition would hesitate to affront him. His own circle of associates and his own sphere of influence defined the interlocking nature of German elites. As one historian wrote recently:

> Politically and from the point of view of social history it became of the greatest importance that the trend toward concentrated, big business in industry and, above all, in the banking world placed a small leadership group of entrepreneurs, managers, and financiers on the captain's bridge [*Kommandobrücke*] of the German economy who controlled the decision-making process in the central realm of the economy. Their social integration in the feudalized social hierarchy of the empire corresponded to their authoritarian styles of conduct and of thought.[15]

Put differently, when Bleichröder appeared on that captain's bridge, he had the additional advantage of knowing, or at least of pretending to know, what course Bismarck was embarked on. He was a major link between the economic and political realms, and, if anything, it was easy to exaggerate his importance, especially for those who were powerless in both realms. To the powerless or the paranoid—and the two have a certain affinity—Bleichröder appeared as a nefarious wirepuller *par excellence*.

Bleichröder's life described a central story of the nineteenth century: the career of the rich bourgeois in all its luxurious wretchedness. He exemplified the precariousness of the German plutocracy: they hungered after wealth and status—and discovered that the former did not confer the latter. It was easier for a poor man to become rich than for a rich man to become honorable. Berlin was full of plutocratic parvenus; it was full, too, of Jews who were the pariahs among plutocratic parvenus. They had two strikes against them, and hence their desire to be socially acceptable was, if anything, still greater than that of their gentile confreres.

Bleichröder's life is almost an "ideal type" (in Weber's, not in any normative, sense) of the plutocrat's striving for acceptance. The story of Bleichröder is the story of many a rich bourgeois, but at least his was played out in a world-historical setting. In describing Bleichröder's rise, we must not measure him by our standards—his brother Julius's, with his more modest style of life, will suffice. Nor must we forget that Bleichröder was not a particularly reflective man; he was a doer, an activist, and he had a robust adaptability to existing conditions that some might call opportunism. Bleich-röder's success depended less on opportunism, which always suggests a degree of scheming, than on his having developed the same intuitive sense of what would advance his cause in society as he had perfected in the economic field.

The irony, of course, was that the higher Bleichröder sought to climb the more visible a target he became for all those who envied, feared, and despised the rise of Jewish plutocrats. By the early 1870s Bleichröder had become a household word for all the diverse elements of Berlin society. In the pages of *Kladderadatsch*, a Berlin humor magazine with a national circulation and mostly Jewish writers, Bleichröder became a symbol for the class of newly prominent. The references were rarely flattering, but they were kinder than in most other chronicles of the new morals. The satirists knew that Bleichröder would be recognized instantly as an individual and as a type. In the early 1870s Bleichröder finally became what so many had flatteringly called him earlier: the Berlin Rothschild. He lacked their dynastic past, he commanded less wealth, but he now gained the notoriety to which he prob-ably was more sensitive than the older exemplars of Jewish wealth and mysterious influence.[16]

So much of Bleichröder's life was symbolic of the Imperial style. His residence remained in the heart of old Berlin, at Behrenstrasse 63—a massive and ornate building which housed both business and private quarters. In the prewar years he had rented one floor to the Swedish minister and several rooms to Count Eulenburg; after the war he needed the whole building and moved his private offices to what had been the Swedish minister's salon, with a large window facing the Behrenstrasse.[17]

It was a busy street, full of stately mansions and grand offices.[18] To the west was the Wilhelmstrasse, a street of old palaces and new power. Bismarck lived and governed there, and Bleichröder was within a few steps of the chancellor's office. The crown prince's palace reached from Unter den Linden to Behrenstrasse, and adjoining it were lesser mansions in which old and distinguished families lived.[19] Magnus and Warschauer, both eminent Jewish bankers, had their residence there, and Hansemann's Disconto-Gesellschaft built its monumental headquarters a few houses away from Bleichröder. To the east, again not too far to walk, was the Berlin stock exchange, to which in the old days Bleichröder himself used to go. Like Nathan Rothschild's traditional pillar at the London stock exchange, so Bleichröder had his own, centrally placed niche. Now his associates frequented it.[20]

Bleichröder, then, was roughly equidistant from the Börse to the east and Bismarck to the west. This, too, was a symbolic location, evocative of both his origins and his aspirations. *Börsenjude*, often associated with east European provenance, was a common epithet of the time.[21] The closer he moved to Bismarck, the easier his access to the offices at the Wilhelmstrasse, the more he removed himself from his erstwhile exclusive identification with the stock market.

But Bleichröder wanted ever greater recognition of his rising eminence; in a society that had very clearly marked rungs of honor and prestige, he wanted to rise, never to stand still. In prewar years, he had received the highest title that commoners could aspire to: he had been made a Geheimer Kommerzienrat and was addressed as "Herr Geheimrat"; he had the requisite medals to go with that title. But in the aftermath of the Franco-Prussian war there was a special largesse for the nation's heroes. William rewarded the architects of victory, Bismarck, Roon, and Moltke, with new titles and large gifts. During his entire reign, William created but one prince: Bismarck in 1871. Bismarck at once grumbled that he had fallen from being a rich count to being a poor prince. Bleichröder dreamed of a similar fall.

He knew that there was something beyond bourgeois distinctions: the jump to hereditary aristocracy. It was the dream of all rich or prominent commoners; by law, such elevation conferred equality with the oldest blue-blooded nobility. In fact, such presumed equality was a fiction, and the old aristocrats looked down on the new, even as the new looked up to the old and down on the commoners. In the Second Empire, social mobility really meant the rapid movement of the eye—this infernal looking up and looking down, that was society. Bleichröder knew that the Rothschilds had been ennobled two generations before, that the Austrian Empire, in fact, had ennobled rich Jews since the end of the eighteenth century, and that smaller German dynasties could be persuaded or bribed to do the same. In Prussia great wealth, combined with service to the state and munificence to charity, did on rare occasions receive such honors, but the Prussian nobility was far less ready than its French or English equivalents to replenish its ranks and coffers in such commercial ways. In Prussia it was a rare honor at best; an unconverted Jew had never yet been raised to hereditary nobility.

In 1872 Bleichröder was so honored. Ennoblements were royal prerogative, and William cherished this remaining bit of power. In this case, the initiative came from Bismarck, who orally urged William to bestow the title on Bleichröder. Thus no written request of Bismarck's exists, and all we know is that on March 8, 1872, William formally signed Bleichröder's patent of hereditary nobility. It could hardly have come as a surprise to Bleichröder: six months earlier, Schwabach had written Bleichröder that he had heard his patent of ennoblement had already been signed in Bad Gastein.[22] A little earlier, his father-in-law had written to him: "That you, dear Gerson, were ordered to a dinner of His Majesty I read in the newspaper, and I hope that these distinctions will contribute to your health."[23] The king's official memorandum as well as Bismarck's letter to the Prussian minister of the interior announced that Adolph Hansemann had been similarly honored.[24] (This linkage led people—and historians—to believe that Hansemann was Jewish, too, which he was not.) The formal patent was impressive indeed, beginning: "We William, King of Prussia, by the Grace of God" and proclaiming Bleichröder's admission to the nobility along with his direct descendants present and future. As outward sign he was to add the coveted "von" to his name, and he was thereafter to be the equal of all noblemen, including those who were born into the nobility. The usual phrasing of the royal proclamation was changed in only one, significant particular: the explanation that the monarch sought to show benevolence to all subjects but was moved to single out those "who, sprung from good families, distinguished themselves by loyalty and salutary services toward us . . ." was amended by deleting "good families" and substituting "public-spirited activities" for "salutary services."[25] Even the king could not pretend that Bleichröder had sprung from what Prussians would call a good family.

The royal act was sensational enough, in some ways even more sensational than contemporaries could have known. During the balance of the 1870s, William raised only one other banker to the nobility; during his entire reign, he created but 131 new nobles, most of whom already had familial ties with the nobility and almost 90 percent of whom were Protestant. William's ennoblements, it has been argued, strengthened the exclusiveness of the old nobility and thus sharpened class divisions.[26] Germany's Jewish newspaper, *Allgemeine Zeitung des Judentums*, emphasized the uniqueness of the ennoblement:

> It is the first time in Prussia that an Israelite who has direct descendants has been ennobled. Bleichröder's ennoblement anyhow is [only] the second case of an Israelite being ennobled in Prussia (the first one concerned the Freiherr Abraham von Oppenheim in Cologne).* Prussia does not allow for individual ennoblement [*persönlicher Adel*]. The last king rejected—though in a most gracious fashion—the request for ennoblement by a world-famous Israelite, Meyerbeer.[27]

In one leap Bleichröder had become the most celebrated Jew of Germany.

Ironically, he owed his unique position to the threatened plight of his fellow aristocrats. It was general knowledge at the time, and Bismarck confirmed it later, that Bleichröder and Hansemann were ennobled because they had undertaken to salvage the fortunes of Prussian Junkers who had been caught in the collapse of Dr. Strousberg's railway projects in Rumania.[28] The British ambassador put it succinctly to Lord Salisbury: "His Majesty rewarded their exertions by making them barons."[29] Many a great nobleman, beginning with Prince Putbus, soon dubbed Prince Kaputbus, the dukes of Ratibor and Ujest, and Count Lehndorff, had assumed personal liability for Strousberg's venture and by 1870–1871 stood on the verge of bankruptcy.[30] Most of them were favorites of William. (The incredible intricacies of Strousberg and the Rumanian tangle are taken up in Chapter 14.) Bleichröder worked hard indeed to extricate Prussian nobility from the unanticipated consequences of their capitalist appetites.

Certainly that was the main reason for William's willingness to suspend

---

* Abraham Oppenheim had no sons to inherit the title.

ancient prejudice. No doubt Bleichröder's earlier services made it easier for the monarch to overcome his scruples, but only Bismarck's personal intervention could have dispelled them. Bleichröder was grateful:

> . . . I hasten to approach Your Highness with the warmly rising sentiments of my gratitude, for after all it was Your Highness who recommended me and my family for this distinction. In all candor I may confess to Your Highness that I am greatly pleased with this distinction for myself and my family, and yet I put the greatest weight on the continuation of Your Highness's benevolence, for which in most sincere humility I beg you. It will be my life's task to serve Your Highness at all times in loyalty and devotion and thereby to justify your confidence which greatly honors me.[31]

Some months earlier, upon having been made a prince, Bismarck thanked William in a similar vein:

> To satisfy Your Majesty is an indispensable need of my heart, and I require it in order myself to be able to enjoy success. May the feeling of personal loyalty to the ancestral lord of country and fief which my ancestors bequeathed to me become part of my children's heritage because God's blessing rests upon it in this time of dissolution and doubt. . . .[32]

These were more than verbal gestures at moments of gratitude: despite their different backgrounds, both Bleichröder and Bismarck believed in this form of personal attachment and fidelity, which even then was on the decline in German society. It strengthened and protected the bond between them.

For Bleichröder, the leap to aristocracy was indescribably pleasing. Suddenly he was called Herr von Bleichröder (or better still, Baron von Bleichröder—which many people in Germany and abroad called him, even though "Baron" was not a Prussian title), and the three-letter word must have been the psychic equivalent of all his wealth. He lost little time in discovering just how far this new honor would take him.* He formally in-

---

* Nor did *Kladderadatsch* lose any time in ridiculing his new honor and in satirizing his new detractors. Immediately after his ennoblement, *Kladderadatsch* carried a little notice under the heading: "More Vanished Persons: Gerson Bleichröder and Hansemann, later to be identified still further, have disappeared without trace from our circle [*Kreis*, which also means county] and our League. We regret their loss all the more as they belonged always to the ornaments of our class [*Stand*]." Signed: "*Die Bürgerschaft Berlins*." 24 March 1872.

A week later, *Kladderadatsch* had its mythical feudal Baron von Prudelwitz write to the equally mythical Baron von Strudelwitz: "So it happened after all, what in Austria, that state artificially put together by jobbers, had happened long ago, but what in organic [*naturwüchsig*] Prussia one thought impossible. So ennobled, after all, and right away two Jews at once—one a Jew by *birth*, the other a Jew by profession [*Beruf*]. Evil beginning! Old Christian principle violated, tradition denied, a crack in the wall which until now was unbridgeable for *Semites*, dogma of 'accursed nation' of 'pariahs of society' forever destroyed. . . . Let my name be Itzig if

quired whether the court would now receive the Bleichröders, that is, whether they had formally become "*hoffähig.*" The answer was yes.[33] But between being formally admitted to court society and being an accepted part of it, there was a world of anguished difference. Even for gentiles, there were fifty-six gradations of *Hoffähige* at the court of William II![34] No wonder Princess Marie Hohenlohe once sighed: "Nothing surpasses the Free Masonry of so-called society."[35] Bleichröder's eagerness also found expression in his immediate submission of a heraldic emblem which bore the iron cross set in the white center of the black, white, and red background.[36] The colors were those of the new Reich; the iron cross was Prussia, and the emblem was Bleichröder's synthesis of the two.

In the fall of 1872 Bleichröder received still another honor. The post of British consul general in Berlin fell vacant when Freiherr Viktor von Magnus, a distinguished fellow banker, died. It was an honorific post and unpaid, but it offered yet another avenue of information and carried a good deal of prestige as well. Bleichröder had worked with the British Embassy during the late war, and he was already a close friend of the ambassador, Lord Odo Russell, who was the star of the diplomatic corps in Berlin: charming and shrewd, Russell was the favorite of Bismarck and the court. (His father had been British minister to Berlin from 1836 to 1841—after nearly ruining his life and marriage by a wild infatuation, apparently, with the widowed daughter of Baron Salomon von Haber, a well-known Jewish banker of Karlsruhe.)[37] In September 1872 Lord Russell wrote to the Foreign Office that though "there is no necessity" to appoint a new consul general because the embassy could attend to all necessary work,* he

> entirely agrees with Lord Granville that very great advantages to the commercial and industrial interests of England can be obtained by the appointment of a Person of wealth and consideration in the Town of Berlin to whom native official and commercial authorities are more readily accessible than to Diplomacy. He thinks that no one could better realize these advantages than the banker Baron Bleichröder, who is not only the Rothschild of Berlin, but also one of Prince Bismarck's most intimate friends and advisers in financial and commercial matters. Baron Bleichröder, who holds an exceptionally good position in Berlin society,

---

I am not right, but I see it coming: Jews will be ennobled and nobility will be jewified [*verjüdelt*]. . . . Just wait and you'll live to read about the Comtesse de Contocurrente, about circumcised ducat-dukes and mosaic princes! The golden age of knighthood gives way to . . . *siècle de Louis d'or.*" The real aristocrats—and not the liberals' caricature of them—probably sounded more vitriolic and less witty. *Kladderadatsch,* 31 March 1872.

* A recent study shows that the British Foreign Office had little, if any, interest in commercial matters, and among many instances of this neglect cites that "when in 1879 Lord Odo Russell suggested the need for a commercial expert on the staff of the Berlin Embassy, an Undersecretary at the Foreign Office was discouraging—he was, Salisbury explained, 'severely orthodox and rather looks upon all traders as an old maid looks upon all men—as being in a conspiracy to surprise him into some illicit favor.'" D. C. M. Platt, *Finance, Trade, and Politics in British Foreign Policy, 1815–1914* (Oxford, 1971), p. xx.

is often personally consulted by the Emperor and the Crown Prince and is generally trusted and respected by the governing and commercial classes of Prussia. Lord Odo Russell has only just been privately informed that Baron Bleichröder would willingly accept the post of Unpaid Consul General. . . .[38]

In early October Granville authorized Russell to appoint Bleichröder and "to send civil refusal to Mendelssohn Bartholdy," who had also volunteered his services.[39] A few days later, Lord Russell called in Bleichröder "to ask [him] to do the English Government the great favor 'of accepting the post.' "[40]

Bleichröder not only beat out Mendelssohn, a distinguished rival, for the British post, but in the same month the Austrian government offered to appoint him its consul general in Berlin. He consulted Bismarck about this embarrassment of riches, adding that he had already accepted the British offer, but that the Austrian post would have "the striking advantage that one would always be exceptionally well informed about the financial operations of the neighboring country." Bismarck counseled him to stick with the British, and until his death in 1893 he remained Her Majesty's consul general and as such particularly close to the British Embassy in Berlin.[41] Other governments heaped honors on Bleichröder as well; between 1870 and 1873, he petitioned the police chief of Berlin repeatedly in order to apply for royal permission to accept and wear decorations from the Bavarian, Saxon, Austrian, Italian, and Brazilian crowns.[42]

At roughly the same time, the Prussian government recognized Julius Schwabach's deserts, and in 1871 the police chief noted in his first recommendation for an order: "Among the men who quickly and without visible pretension not only do a great deal of good here but could also serve as models in the solid, decent conduct of their business, the banker Julius Schwabach occupies a preeminent place." Six years later, suggesting a still greater honor, the police chief estimated that Schwabach's annual income was between 204,000 and 240,000 marks and that he was most generous to charities and totally blameless in every respect, having kept himself consistently aloof from "*Gründungen*." In 1878, the forty-seven-year-old Schwabach was made a Geheimer Kommerzienrat.[43]

We have seen what importance Bleichröder attached to his social standing: as he climbed higher, he was more concerned than ever to adopt the proper style of life, to conduct himself *standesgemäss*, according to his station. In the winter his home was one of Berlin's most lavish and most talked-about places of entertainment. In the summer he moved his family to the fashionable suburb of Charlottenburg, even as his father had moved to the more prosaic Pankow.[44] Unlike his father, Gerson regularly took the waters at a great spa—in Ostende or Marienbad, Kissingen or Schlangenbad—and his children were left in the hands of various servants, including Bleichröder's trusted assistant Siebert, who in the early 1870s was also the deputy who arranged Bismarck's landed operations according to Bleichröder's instructions.

In June 1873, just a year after his ennoblement, Bleichröder acquired

Gütergotz, an old seigneurial estate near Berlin that had been the country seat of the renowned Roon. Roon, also recently rewarded by William, wanted to sell Gütergotz in order to buy himself a larger retreat farther away from the bustle of the new capital.[45] Roon had bought the old *Gut* in August 1868 for 135,000 taler, had modernized the estate, enlarged the park, and renovated the manor house (also referred to as Schloss); he now sold the estate to Bleichröder for 1,290,000 marks—three times as much as he had paid. It is unlikely that the parsimonious Roon could have invested anywhere near the differential in improvements on the house. Despite improvements, despite the very large jump in real-estate values between 1868 and 1872, it is fair to suppose that Bleichröder was paying an additional premium for the fact that it was the field marshal's house he was buying.[46]

Bleichröder's country seat was to the southwest of Berlin, approximately fifteen miles from the center of the city, and about five miles from the royal palaces at Potsdam. The location was perfect and strategic, the manor house had been remodeled at the beginning of the nineteenth century by none other than the famed architect David Gilly, and the symbolic significance of Bleichröder's acquisition of Roon's seat is striking.[47] It epitomizes a chapter of German social history: the bourgeois, indeed the Jewish bourgeois—or in this instance, the Jewish nobleman of one year's standing—buying up the landed estates of old nobility and famed warriors, and acquiring or emulating the views and values of their landed predecessors.[48] The final arrangements of the purchase of Gütergotz kept Roon and Bleichröder in cordial correspondence, and Roon once remarked: "I noted with pleasure the familiar, graceful signature again because I hope I can infer from it the happy healing of your eye ailment."[49]

Bleichröder enjoyed his new property and spent much time there. He took the greatest pleasure in his flowers, and his gardener was as important to him as his chef. For years, he presented William and Augusta with rare specimens from his own garden: gifts from one gentleman farmer to another. Whether in Gütergotz or away, he kept close watch on the harvest, and his man Siebert reported whether the crops, especially rye, had been brought in safely.[50] But he cherished some bizarre projects as well. At great expense, he had various masons gather nearly 2,000 stones and rocks from the battlefields of victorious Prussian armies, especially in France, and ship these barren trophies to Gütergotz for the construction of some patriotic monstrosity. He hoped to entice William to inspect the collection—or was the royal visit perhaps the true reason for this extravaganza? Certainly enough effort went into arranging the visit, and the good offices of the king's entourage had to be mobilized again. William originally agreed to come in the summer of 1875, but his visit materialized only two years later.* He stayed for only an hour,

---

* Obviously Gütergotz was Bleichröder's Ferrières; Baron James had also been anxious to have the emperor visit his new château. Napoleon's visit occurred in December 1862, shortly after Ferrières had been completed, and was much more of a state visit: "The Emperor was accompanied by M. Fould, Count Walewski, Lord Cowley, Generals Fleury and Ney . . . [at the nearest station] the Baron's equipages, in blue liveries and yellow, awaited His Majesty, who

but Bleichröder was radiant and reported to Bismarck: "I did not want to fail to inform Your Highness that last Friday I had the good fortune to receive His Majesty at Gütergotz when he passed through. His Majesty is entirely well. . . ." The two men had discussed the Near Eastern crisis.[51] Afterward Louis Schneider, the king's reader, officially informed Bleichröder of the king's "pleasure at your comfortable home. He was particularly pleased with the visible pleasure of your esteemed wife. . . ." The press carried the news of the emperor's visit, and Bleichröder received congratulations from various friends, including Moritz von Goldschmidt in Vienna.[52]

Ordinarily Bleichröder spent quiet weekends and parts of the summer at Gütergotz. Decades later, his erstwhile assistant Carl Fürstenberg recalled that

> in Gerson Bleichröder's manor house things were very quiet. I used to meet there a few of Bleichröder's acquaintances from the Foreign Office, from time to time also a foreign diplomat and high administrative officials with their wives. Countless times I walked up and down the Gütergotz Lindenallee with the blind Gerson, arm in arm, talking with him about business affairs, about foreign policy or about financial relations with foreign countries, always imbibing the seasoned wisdom of this man.[53]

During the winter season in Berlin, the Bleichröders entertained on a lavish scale. Their balls were great events, Lucullan feasts which Berlin society talked about with often malicious relish. The letters and memoirs of the time attest the extraordinary sumptuousness of these festivities at a time when competitive entertainment was the fashion. Money was no object—and yet money alone was clearly insufficient. What really mattered was who would attend.

Even before his ennoblement, a fair sampling of the highest society appeared. Some of his clients, after all, found it difficult to snub him. After his ennoblement, the circle of prospective guests widened greatly. The Princess Bismarck and her children, the Radziwills, the Spitzembergs, Berlin's

---

took his seat in an open carriage, with four blood horses and postilions. . . . At a quarter to eleven the Emperor arrived at the Château, and the Imperial flag was at once raised on one of the towers. After looking over the interior of the edifice, the Emperor took a walk in the park, where he planted a cedar to commemorate his visit, and then returned to the Château for breakfast. The service of silver plate, made from models which were immediately destroyed to preserve it unique, was accompanied by the celebrated service of Sèvres porcelain, every plate of which bears an authentic picture by Boucher, signed with the B. . . . After breakfast a numerous shooting equipage awaited the guests, who proceeded to the great park, which covers 1,500 hectares (3,700 acres), entirely surrounded with walks, and containing three farms. The sport was splendid, and about 1,000 head of game were killed." *The Times*, 10 Dec. 1862; also *Le Monde Illustré*, 27 Dec. 1862. On a visit to the château, in September 1974, I was told that when the emperor climbed the grand staircase, he stopped and sniffed something—apparently odors from the kitchen. After the emperor's departure, Baron James ordered that the kitchen be moved to an underground location outside the château, to be linked with it by an underground tunnel. It is not clear whether Napoleon ever reinspected the now odorless château.

foreign diplomats, and many others came, but those who stayed away rankled host and guests. Marie von Bunsen, of mixed Anglo-German stock and thoroughly at home in Berlin's best society, remembered her first, glittering season in 1877–1878:

> Brilliant, too, was the Bleichröder feast. . . . The social position of the Bleichröders was so to speak superior, but still not edifying. Almost the entire aristocratic-governmental Berlin went there, but apologized for it afterward. The entire banquet table was full of the choicest of choice things. One ate from silver; the most luxurious things would be placed before one. Afterward [the violinist Pablo de] Sarasate played as well as [the court pianist] Essipoff, and then there was dancing.[54]

The same occasion was recorded more maliciously by Ottmar von Mohl, who mentioned that Bleichröder was *"persona grata"* to Bismarck, but added:

> His not very handsome person and a few faux pas in social matters had, however, made him unpopular in German circles in Berlin. His ball was heartily attended by foreign diplomats who welcomed the princely *souper*, but it was shunned by native society, especially by the officer corps, with which Bleichröder was on such bad terms that some commanders ruled the house off limits.[55]

On other occasions, socially requisite officers in their decorous uniforms were in ample evidence, for, as a contemporary saw it, "above all, the emperor's uniform was respected; no party was considered successful without an officer's presence."[56] Attendance at Bleichröder's was never without its controversial character. As Fontane said of a Berlin financier in his novel *L'Adultera*, "On the stock market he was taken unconditionally as a person of quality, in society only conditionally."[57]

The trouble was that Bleichröder cared desperately to be taken unconditionally. Despite his acknowledged fame and importance, he yearned for full social acceptance as well. Better than most, he knew of the hollowness of most aristocratic pretensions: he knew of their scandals, financial and marital, he knew of their dependence on the likes of him, and he knew that in wealth and perhaps in intelligence he surpassed them all. Still, he admired their style of life and their values and sought to emulate them.

The ambiguity of acceptance was undoubtedly hard on Bleichröder— and there was worse to come. He sensed the wrath of some Junkers who like Bismarck's erstwhile friend Ludwig von Gerlach scorned the "Jew-lovers" more than the Jews themselves; Gerlach entered in his diary in February 1873: "These days a magnificent ball given by the Jew Bleichröder, where the Princess Bismarck with her daughter and both sons were the principal persons; that is, the daughter and the grandchildren of the pietists [*Stubenprediger*] of fifty years ago."[58] To most of the old nobility, this type of fraternizing smacked of betrayal, and they latched on to the Bismarcks' relations with Bleichröder as both cause and justification for their embitterment against the chancellor. For the whole reactionary *fronde* against Bismarck that was forming in the early 1870s, Bleichröder symbolized the perfidy of the "liberal Empire." As we will see, the new anti-Semitism, unleashed in the mid-1870s, had Bleichröder as its visible focus though Bismarck often was the real target.

Bleichröder pursued his career, glittering to the outside but painful within. The attacks on him never ceased. His luck in the public realm had no analogue at home; disappointments and infirmity set in early. Already in the late 1860s his eyesight gave him trouble; by the end of the 1870s he was totally blind—a familiar, pathetic sight, as he walked on the arm of an assistant, hurrying to some appointment or merely promenading along the fashionable Tiergarten. His private life became increasingly painful. Like Bismarck, he turned more inward in the decades of success, and gradually a kind of loneliness set in. Both men became more embittered in the last decade of their public lives. What had begun as a functional and on Bleichröder's part an often sycophantic relationship gradually ripened into the association and friendship of two aging men whose struggles and triumphs lay behind them. Success had become routine, and all that was left to them was their work, which, different though it was, brought them together again and again.

CHAPTER 9

Imperial Style in Politics and Economics

My sleep is no relaxation, my dreams continue my waking thoughts, that is, if I go to sleep at all. The other day I saw a map of Germany in front of me, and on it one decayed spot after another appeared, and then peeled off.

—Bismarck to Lucius von Ballhausen, 1872

I n its appearance the new Empire was a monolith of power: a rapidly expanding industry and a large army made Germany the dominant nation of the continent. But the new power brought new conflicts: every new factory that opened increased the ranks of the dissident proletariat; every increase in industrial wealth weakened the hold of the older agrarian-aristocratic elite on the nation's government. There were widening cracks in the monolith, cracks that were disguised and denied, but that resulted from a dynamically changing society pressing against a relatively rigid political order.

The new Empire underwent a process of partial modernization: its economy changed, but its preindustrial classes clung to power and sought to perpetuate their preeminence by coopting and intimidating the new industrial classes. Germany was a society in transition, as all modern societies are; the transition was swifter but less complete than elsewhere; and above all, German society understood itself less well than did other societies. In retrospect, the course of imperial history seems clear—so clear, in fact, that some historians have forgotten that to most citizens of the new Reich the future was anything but clear, that they were painfully groping for some new stability.

In the late 1860s Bismarck had said that it would be enough to put Germany in the saddle; she would know how to ride. In the new Empire he learned that Germany did not know how to ride, at least not in the manner or direction he thought desirable. To govern the new country proved unexpectedly difficult. Bismarck had sought to give a hybrid society a hybrid constitution: the new Empire was neither a pure autocracy nor a constitutional monarchy; it defied easy definition. Critical contemporaries and recent historians often likened Bismarck's regime to Bonapartism or to a plebiscitary dictatorship; the precise term is less important than the reality. Bismarck set policy: there was no rival in the Reich with the same vision and the same responsibility for all policies, foreign and domestic; but Bismarck was dependent on the support of his monarch and on the acquiescence of the several states of the Empire; he had to contend with a host of extraconstitutional pressures and intrigues. Most important, he needed the approval of the Reichstag for his domestic policies. It was an endless balancing act, punctuated by threats that he would resign or reconstitute the Empire.[1]

After 1871 Bismarck was the great hero, but premature apotheosis prepared neither Bismarck nor the nation for the inherent conflict of modern politics. The years of struggle, of dramatic victories snatched from mortal danger, were gone; the routinization of conflict proved more trying. In the 1860s he had to deal with enemies; after 1871 he had to contend with men or groups officially designated as friendly. He found that less congenial. After 1871 his mastery of events diminished, as did his patience and his energy. His recurrent threats of resignation were functional, but they also expressed genuine discouragement and despair. The pleasures of power faded, the attractiveness of office diminished—on personal as well as substantive grounds. (In 1880 he complained that for the last ten years he had felt no "personal joy" in the execution of his duties, "only [the feeling] of duty toward God and man, and of a duty moreover which I fulfill not with any love for the task but under the coercion of my conscience.")[2] Still, he clung to power and destroyed rivals, and his style of leadership exacerbated all political conflicts.

Bismarck had no grand strategy in the Empire; he sought survival. His tactics at home were like his tactics abroad; if anything, he was more ruthless at home. For the Great Powers of Europe, he felt a certain respect, if only for their historic role in the past. For his enemies at home, he had no such respect: they had no historic roots or justifications; they were little men, trying to obstruct his designs. He transferred to the domestic scene the amoral methods of foreign policy: he sought to bully, to manipulate, to cripple his opponents, and he pursued his opponents at home with a ferocity and a contempt that he could ill afford abroad.

In the early years of the Empire, Bismarck governed in concert with the National Liberals, the largest party in the Reichstag and representative of middle-class interests and ideals. Between 1867 and 1873, government and parliament established the framework of a liberal economy. The policies of the Reich were designed to facilitate the economic pursuits of the bourgeoisie. Bismarck also collaborated with the National Liberals in a campaign against political Catholicism, organized in the Center party; he feared the power of organized Catholicism in German politics and resolved to crush it at its first appearance. In the course of what came to be called the Kulturkampf, he cemented the loyalties of Catholics to their party. At the same time, his close dependence on the National Liberals, which to him was but a tactical and temporary device, precipitated a break between him and the Conservative party, which represented the interests of his friends and fellow Junkers. In his memoirs he entitled the chapters dealing with the domestic history of the Empire: "Kulturkampf," "Break with the Conservatives," "Intrigue," and of these conflicts, the break with the Conservatives hurt him the most. He felt betrayed by the very group that without him would have succumbed to its own pigheadedness. Their desertion rankled but could not be ignored; the social and political order that Bismarck envisioned depended on the continued preeminence of the old agrarian class.

In the struggles of the 1870s, the economic component of politics became ever more important and more visible. The central events of the decade were the great boom symbolic of the dynamic forces in German society, followed by the great crash of 1873 and a protracted depression. In the wake of the crash, a divisive debate ensued as to its causes and possible remedies. For years, Bismarck groped for a new economic policy until he gradually put together a comprehensive program and a new conservative alignment that proved so radical a transformation that many people sensed in it the second founding of the Reich.

At a time of economic uncertainty, Bleichröder's role became steadily more important. His knowledge of German finance and industry was unsurpassed, as were his connections with the world of business, at home and abroad. Practical economics was his métier, and he was on an intimate footing with Germany's master: these were the props of his ever expanding influence.

Men in power listen to people who are useful, knowledgeable, and—perhaps by virtue of the constituencies they represent—influential or powerful. Bleichröder qualified on every score, and he continued to enjoy immediate access to Bismarck. Between them, the public and personal business remained intertwined. Bleichröder's private letters about Bismarck's financial affairs often included comments on political and economic development. Their conversations also touched on all aspects of domestic and foreign policy. In this unofficial manner he supplemented his official reports and memoranda, which would necessarily be seen by many eyes.

Bleichröder had many avenues to power. His creatures, clients, friends, and protégés were everywhere: in the government and at court, in parliament and in the press, in every party save the Socialist. Some of these connections were the outgrowths of his business, others the products of assiduous cultivation. He had a passion for being important, for being in the know. He collected secrets as the Rothschilds collected *objets d'art* and for the same reason: to dazzle his contemporaries.

As a consequence, people sought him out. He was the great dispenser of news—for the men of power in Berlin, for the Rothschilds, and for foreign diplomats. In 1878 the British ambassador wrote to his foreign minister: "Herr von Bleichröder, as your Lordship is aware, is Prince Bismarck's banker and Confidential Agent, and enjoys the Chancellor's confidence in a higher degree than any one in Berlin."[3] All the Rothschilds now thanked him for his intelligence and begged for more; many notables agreed with Karl Anton, prince of Hohenzollern-Sigmaringen, who wrote to a friend: "Bleichröder is uncommonly well informed, and despite all diplomatic reticence, he is very communicative. . . . An outstanding and politically very nimble man."[4] In

1882 a cabinet minister noted that Bleichröder's contacts extended to the "very center of His Majesty's entourage."[5] Bleichröder's correspondence, all personally attended to, was in itself an awesome task: daily letters to most of the Rothschild Houses and scores of letters to business partners, clients, and officials throughout the world. Bleichröder also received a steady flow of visitors; ministers and diplomats called, and so did the economic elite. As a rule, Bleichröder waited only upon Bismarck. It was a tribute to Bleichröder's energy that he could cultivate so many ties—and make his millions as well. He ran a multiple business: as a broker in profits and power.

There were psychic as well as practical reasons for Bleichröder's ceaseless efforts to build up his presence in Berlin. To some extent, he played the game for its own sake; he enjoyed being an insider when in so many wounding ways he was condemned to remain an outsider. He enjoyed the pretense of being a kingmaker. But his easy access to power elevated his place in the business world. As economic conditions worsened, he agitated in government circles for a different economic policy. To achieve his ends he used the traditional means of behind-the-scenes influence and experimented with modern efforts of persuasion. He had no clear-cut political credo: he was a conservative who feared the socialist threat; he favored the principles of a free economy but had no hesitation calling for state intervention when it was useful for business. His first principle of politics was loyalty to Bismarck, and loyalty included the readiness to tender and sometimes press advice on him.

Needless to say, a great many Germans resented Bleichröder's position, including the very notables and officials who protested their great friendship for him. Bismarck's authoritarian style gave Bleichröder his aura of importance, and Bismarck's other aides minded the meddlesome presence of the chancellor's Jew. Insecure in their jobs and the chancellor's pleasure, they saw in Bleichröder an Iago who could poison the master's mind against them. In 1885, for example, Prince Hohenlohe, German ambassador in Paris, feared for his post because "Bleichröder, Henckel, etc., used the newspapers against me and would do so again."[6] There were many other notables who were afraid of Bleichröder's power to make or break their careers. At times, they exaggerated his influence.

[i]

At the very beginning of the Empire, Bleichröder recommended policies that were at odds with those proposed by Bismarck's official advisers. The immediate task in the early 1870s was to create an imperial bank that would supplant the thirty-two banks of issue that still survived from preunification days. In May 1872 Bleichröder wrote to Bismarck that "it would be highly desirable that the chancellor at any given time should also function as chief [of such a bank], desirable because, at least according to my modest views, there are many moments when the political judgment of financial questions is more important than the material judgment."[7] Bismarck listened, but the government left the initiative to the National Liberals in the Reichstag, who under the leadership of a former banker, Ludwig Bamberger, in late 1874 prepared the appropriate legislation. Some of it conformed to Bleichröder's notions, including the reserve powers of the chancellor; other aspects did not, and he wrote to Bismarck: "Your Highness has so often had the kindness to hear me in financial matters that I am taking the liberty of submitting a few short observations about the burning question of the bank because I have the matter very much at heart." Specifically he warned that under the proposed legislation the stockholders would have inadequate representation and that the credit supply could too easily be choked off.[8]

The proponents of the Reichsbank as well as Bismarck's leading ministers, Rudolf von Delbrück and Otto von Camphausen, were partisans of the gold standard. Bleichröder was not. He was afraid that its adoption would jeopardize a flexible supply of money. The proponents were dazzled by the universal sway of gold; Bleichröder believed that the gold standard would lead to a fluctuating rate of interest that would be raised sharply and perhaps abruptly whenever it was necessary to discourage withdrawal from the Reichsbank's bullion reserves. He feared the bane of the businessman's existence: a cyclical money and credit policy that contracted the money supply in time of recession and increased it in time of expansion. Hence he urged the broadest possible bullion basis and, contrary to the dominant view at the time, he was a consistent bimetallist.

He knew how to appeal to Bismarck on this highly technical issue. In 1874 he warned him that the early introduction of an exclusive gold standard would make Germany dependent on the British gold market, which the British defended by raising discount rates. At such times Germany would have to follow suit, but "our industry," he noted, "unlike England's, is not sustained by great capital but steadily needs, as is well known, the credits of bankers and banks. . . ." By making money dearer, the gold standard would threaten industry. "Even now our industry is no longer capable of successfully competing with foreign producers because wages and money rates are too high. . . ." Bleichröder reminded Bismarck that there are "too few practical men in the Reichstag. . . . Certain circles are dominated by the desire to tailor our conditions to the British pattern." (Bismarck also doubted the competence and patriotism of doctrinaire parliamentarians.) Bleichröder urged Bismarck to consult the longtime director of the Prussian Bank, Hermann von Dechend, who would give similar advice: "Your Highness should not take amiss my request and should credit it to my love of the fatherland."[9]

In October 1876, in a long memorandum, Bleichröder again warned against demonetizing silver altogether and pointed to the Reichsbank's inadequate gold reserves. The adoption of the gold standard would probably necessitate a large gold loan from Britain and would in any case threaten a rise in the discount rate, which would further injure "our badly suffering industry." With minor editorial changes, Bismarck dispatched the memorandum to Dechend, now president of the Reichsbank.[10] A year later, Bleichröder complained that the Reichsbank had raised the discount rate to 5½ percent in order to stem the increased outward flow of gold: "The bank's practice of constant fluctuation must be controlled in some way; otherwise our industry cannot possibly compete with foreign countries."[11]

Bleichröder was a consistent critic of Germany's monetary policy. He did not prevail, because his views ran counter to conventional wisdom. He had arrived pragmatically at principles of monetary policy well in advance of his age. Events proved him right, and later he could hope to speak with still greater authority on even more critical issues.*

[ii]

The first three years of the Empire witnessed an unprecedented economic boom. Germany was in the grip of excitement: it seemed as if an era of unlimited riches had begun. Banks financed this great expansion, and in three years as many ironworks, blast furnaces, and machine-production factories were founded as had been created in the preceding seventy years. New joint-stock corporations were founded and capitalized at 2.8 billion marks, almost as much as the total capitalization of all joint-stock corporations in the preceding forty-four years. Prosperity came in the wake of unification: Germany seemed destined to triumph and prosper in every realm, and "Berlin became the center of the German economy."[12]

The boom marked an acceleration of the economic upswing that had begun in 1867; it was fed by the French reparations of 5 billion francs, which facilitated the early retirement of public debts and thus provided Germany with a sudden supply of vast liquid funds. Easy money, an ebullient public, and a new law permitting the founding of joint-stock corporations without difficulties—all of these aroused appetites and led to frenzied activity.

It was a time of genuine expansion, of fraudulent promotions, and of a gray area of recklessness where the lure of profits overwhelmed normal prudence. The era was quickly dubbed *Gründerzeit*, a time for founding empires, both political and economic. A speculative fever gripped Germans of all classes, and Germany's elites were suddenly stirred out of their economic lethargy and the slower rhythms of their lives; they were educated to economic opportunity as never before.

* Bleichröder's opposition to the gold standard occasioned a violent exchange in the Reichstag between Bismarck and Ludwig Bamberger, the virtual founder of the Reichsbank and a single imperial currency; in 1879 a note from Lord Odo Russell predicting that Germany would adopt a dual standard was leaked to the press. The report was false, and Bamberger, denied informal information from the government, raised the issue in parliament, prefacing his remarks by suggesting that Lord Russell must have received his information from Bleichröder. Bismarck lashed out at Bamberger that this was a shameful insinuation, "since because of scandalous and contemptible trials it had become universally known that this same bank house serves as my personal banker and business administrator." Bismarck in turn cast aspersions on Bamberger's banking connections, and the whole incident proved embarrassing to the principals and deeply worrisome to Bleichröder, who brooded about it for days. Hans Fürstenberg, ed., *Carl Fürstenberg Die Lebensgeschichte eines deutschen Bankiers 1870–1914* (Berlin, 1931), pp. 77–79, mistakenly dates the incident as having taken place in 1876. See also Karl Helfferich, ed., *Ausgewählte Reden und Aufsätze über Geld- und Bankwesen von Ludwig Bamberger* (Berlin, 1900), pp. 102–110.

Reputable houses and prudent bankers resisted the lure of quick promotions. As early as September 1871 one of Bleichröder's assistants wrote him about all the businesses spawned by the *"Gründungsphantasie"*; it is clear that from the beginning Bleichröder kept his distance from the promoters.[13] (The struggle between unscrupulously rising new money and honorably declining old money was of course a familiar nineteenth-century story and is a key theme of *Buddenbrooks*.) Bleichröder's major creation was the Vereinigte Königs- und Laura-Hütte (usually known as Laurahütte), a joint-stock corporation organized out of the privately held coal mines and ironworks of Count Henckel von Donnersmarck. It was a solid enterprise that weathered all manner of storms. Bleichröder was centrally involved in the creation in 1873 of the huge West German coal complex known as Hibernia; he helped found the Reichs Continental Eisenbahnbaugesellschaft, which in turn organized the Weimar-Gera and the Posen-Kreuzburg railroads. The railroads did badly, but on the whole, Bleichröder suffered less grievously from the crash than did other banks and entrepreneurs.[14]

Rectitude and prudence saved Bleichröder and his clients from the worst kind of economic reverses. As a consequence, he emerged relatively unscathed in wealth and reputation, though the demagogues of the day tried to taint him with the brush of fraudulence. (In an internal memorandum in 1877 the Berlin police praised Bleichröder's partner, Schwabach, for having kept himself aloof from all shady promotions.)[15] Once more, Bleichröder had played his cards shrewdly.

He had anticipated a crash and had warned Bismarck that the sudden collapse of the Vienna market in May 1873 was likely to affect Berlin as well. By the summer and fall of 1873, the stock markets of New York and Berlin suffered calamitous losses, credit became scarce, and businesses began to fail. In the early days of 1874 sixty-one banks, 116 industrial enterprises, and four railroad companies announced their bankruptcies.[16]

To the surprise of many people, Bleichröder included, the crash turned into the longest and most pervasive depression of the century.* Prices, profits, and dividends dropped precipitously; production declined and unemployment increased.[17] The losses people suffered were catastrophic and often had a crippling effect on families for decades to come. The literature of this disaster is surprisingly scant—in part, perhaps, because loss of money in the mid-1870s presupposed earlier speculation, and the moral code still frowned on open acknowledgment of this.†

The crash and ensuing depression had a profound effect on German

---

* In early 1873 Marx predicted that the downturn in the economic cycle would mark the beginning of a "universal crisis. That crisis is once again approaching, although as yet but in its beginning stage; and by the universality of its theatre and the intensity of its action it will drum dialectics even into the heads of the mushroom-upstarts of the new, holy Prusso-German empire." But Marx was too optimistic about the consequences of disaster, and his Communist followers have often succumbed to the same folly. The depression, as we shall see, drummed anti-Semitism and anti-Socialism into German heads and not Marxian dialectics. Karl Marx, *Capital. A Critical Analysis of Capitalist Production* (New York, 1947), p. xxxi.

† The Bleichröder Archive is full of correspondence from distinguished clients bemoaning their sudden losses. Occasionally there would run through a client's laments a reproach against

society. It dramatized, as nothing before had, the changed nature of that society: it demonstrated that Germany had become a capitalistic country, despite the precapitalistic ethos that still prevailed.[18] Among the public at large there was a strong tendency to translate the crash into moral terms, as punishment for wrongdoing. (When Tony Buddenbrook heard that her husband was bankrupt, "all the vague and terrible things that were involved in the word and that she had already sensed as a small child rose up in her. 'Bankrupt'—that was more dreadful than death, that was a catastrophe, ruin, shame, disgrace, misery, despair.")[19] Conservative and Catholic critics turned this moralizing tendency into a full-scale attack against laissez-faire Manchesterism, blaming liberals and Jews for the plight of the country. Capitalism of course survived, but it was a curiously suspect or devalued capitalism; in Germany after 1873, in good years and in bad years, there was always a powerful anti-capitalistic sentiment—which the left and the right shared. At the same time, the long crisis led to the mobilization of economic interests, which also demanded a change in the government's liberal policy.

Crisis and discontent posed a great and at first incomprehensible challenge to Bismarck. He was already troubled about the fiscal condition of the Reich and the growing tension between the Reich and the member states, notably Prussia. His own health was appallingly bad, and his offer of resignation in May 1875 may have been the most genuine of his career.[20] William refused, and gradually Bismarck put together the pieces of a new program for the fiscal and economic policies of the Reich. Slowly he sensed how he could ride the storm of discontent in order to create a new political alignment that would unite agrarians and industrialists, conservatives and right-wing liberals, and bring the Catholic Center to join the new and distinctly antiliberal coalition that would govern the Empire henceforth. It took Bismarck four years to see all the possibilities of this new, illiberal course. The economic crisis provided the occasion for the change, but the political-cultural traditions of Germany and Bismarck's own predilections favored the emergence of this particular solution—which in turn was to shape the course of German history for disastrous decades to come.

Bismarck's ministers, most notably Delbrück and Camphausen, retained

---

Bleichröder—how could you have allowed this to happen to me or, worse, how could you have encouraged me in such dangerous ventures? Sometimes total strangers wrote Bleichröder, and one such instance may stand for many: in 1875 Bleichröder received several pleas from a philosophy professor, Katzenberger, who had bought some Reichscontinental shares at 90 for a widowed cousin; now they stood at 13. He turned to Bleichröder, who had been one of the principal promoters of the Reichscontinental company, because his friend had told him of Bleichröder's "nobility of mind . . . that you are not only a financial authority but a humane benevolent nature." Was there nothing Bleichröder could do—after all, that poor widow with the proverbial brood of destitute children would never have bought these shares but that "the finest houses" of Berlin had stood behind the company. Bleichröder's answer evoked further pleas by Katzenberger and the promise that in return for favors "I put my pen entirely at your disposal for all important journals." Katzenberger to Bleichröder, 7 Sept., 23 Oct., 7 Nov. 1875, BA. A recent testimony of the effects of the depression can be found in Theodor Lessing's autobiography, *Einmal und Nie Wieder* (Gütersloh, 1969), which makes clear that his ill-matched, desperately unhappy parents had to stay married because his father had lost his mother's dowry—and hence divorce was unthinkable.

their faith in liberal economics, as did the great majority of the National Liberals. The laissez-faire economists blamed the depression on overproduction and assumed that in due course, demand, both foreign and domestic, would recover. They saw no need for abandoning Germany's free-trade course, which included a law eliminating the remaining duties on iron goods. The representatives of agriculture, which still exported grain, also favored free trade and wanted the lowest possible price on iron goods. In short, free trade had formidable support.

The German metallurgical industries were the hardest hit, and their representatives clamored for tariffs, arguing that German industry needed a monopoly of the domestic market, inadequate though that was. The defenders of German industry arrived at an economic program with but one tenet: protectionism, which was made to appear in the guise of economic nationalism. The nation needed to be "protected" from foreign competition, and gradually the term "national" acquired a xenophobic and an anti-Semitic tinge as well and legitimized the purely material demands of German pressure groups.

In the spring of 1874 the major steel producers organized. Representatives of Bleichröder's giant creations in the east and west, Laurahütte and Hibernia, joined this first pressure group to represent the whole of Germany.[21] Bleichröder was not indifferent to the welfare of these companies, but as a banker he had other interests to defend as well, and these did not call for protectionism. He seemed content to have some of his friends enter the fray; he himself remained on the sidelines. In July 1874 he was still optimistic about recovery and wrote Bismarck that "commercial life is extraordinarily quiet; the stock market still does not want to recover; but I think in the late fall prices must improve because the public has gotten into the habit of preferring to eat and drink well rather than to sleep well"—a somewhat earthy description of stock-market addiction.[22]* But Bleichröder was wrong, and by 1875 the agitation became too intense for him to remain aloof. In the spring of that year, one of his closest associates, Wilhelm von Kardorff, became a leader in the protectionist drive. Like Bleichröder, Kardorff had a stake in various branches of the economy; unlike Bleichröder, Kardorff was a deputy in the Reichstag and had considerable influence. He was resolved to use that influence and to fight on every front: in parliament, in the public arena, and in the promotion of new pressure groups. He was in the closest touch with Bleichröder, who was something of a patron-tutor to him.

Bleichröder's intimate connections with this leading German politician, hitherto undocumented and surmised only by their enemies at the time, warrant a brief digression. Six years younger than Bleichröder, Kardorff was born into the petty nobility of Mecklenburg; his father had died before his birth. Kardorff studied law and, in 1855, heavy debts notwithstanding, bought the sizable Rittergut at Wabnitz in Silesia. He settled on his estate of 1,200 acres

---

* And one in striking contrast to the early motto of the Buddenbrook firm: "Attend with zeal to thy business by day; but do none that hinders thee from thy sleep by night." Thomas Mann, *Buddenbrooks. Verfall einer Familie* (Berlin, 1928), p. 58.

and indulged his costly passion for hunting and racing.[23] In 1866 he entered politics to counteract the new conservative opposition to Bismarck, and thus prefigured his entire later career as an ardent, if not always uncritical, supporter of Bismarck. He helped shape the economic legislation of the North German Reichstag. By the early 1870s he became a leading member of the Free Conservatives, that party or group of notables closest to Bismarck and to Bleichröder's interests.

Kardorff became deeply involved in the *Gründertum* of the early 1870s, as Bleichröder used Kardorff's name to lend respectability to his own creations. In 1871 he was made board chairman of Laurahütte. He also participated in the founding of the Posen-Kreuzburg Railway and of the Prussian Mortgage Bank, both Bleichröder creations. In short, Kardorff came to have both agrarian and industrial interests—and thus was singularly attuned to the politics of the Second Empire. By being involved in both branches of the economy, he also managed to suffer losses in both.

In a biography of his father, Kardorff's son acknowledged the great losses his father sustained, but he failed to mention that he had the closest relations with the "leading German banker," as he called Bleichröder.[24] In fact, Bleichröder and Kardorff were exceptionally close; they corresponded in great detail about their common interests, and Kardorff received and usually followed Bleichröder's recommendations. He kept Bleichröder abreast of his protectionist campaign and occasionally asked him to convey messages to Bismarck. In tone and substance, the correspondence bespeaks Kardorff's solicitude to oblige Bleichröder; the banker was the dominant partner of the relationship.*

One reason for this dominance was the fact that Bleichröder repeatedly had to rescue Kardorff from his creditors. As early as July 1871, Kardorff asked Bleichröder for a 20,000-taler mortgage because he was reluctant to borrow from the Boden-Kredit company of which he was a director.[25] In the crash of 1873 he lost a great deal of money and piled new debts on old. What good, he lamented in 1875, were his parliamentary successes on behalf of protectionism if people were determined to bankrupt him? For great services rendered, the fatherland was rewarding him by putting a pistol to his head.[26] Bleichröder helped, and so did the minister for agriculture, Karl Rudolf Friedenthal, who wrote Bleichröder, "Much as I always like to follow your suggestions to help Kardorff out of any embarrassment, I have to set myself certain limits and abide by them, because my income level is essentially different from that of my esteemed friend, von Bleichröder."[27] In the end, Friedenthal contributed a 12,000-mark mortgage and Bleichröder an appropriately higher sum.†

---

* Not socially, of course. Kardorff wrote bemused letters to his wife about Bleichröder's feasts. "Was at a great concert and ball at Bleichröder's last night; after the concert, there was a gigantic supper. Then the ball—with few men; notably the officers were scarce. Princess Bismarck talked with me for quite a long time: he, of course, was not there; otherwise diplomats, ministers, and all the big shots were present en masse. S. von Kardorff, *Wilhelm von Kardorff: Ein nationaler Parlamentarier im Zeitalter Bismarcks und Wilhelms II, 1828–1907* (Berlin 1936), p. 149.

† In 1873 the German Mark replaced the Prussian taler at the rate of 3:1.

But things moved from bad to worse for Kardorff, who had no income save his various fees from directorships and the yield of his estate; members of parliament received no remuneration because Bismarck had wanted to avoid a class of professional politicians or of propertyless men in politics. He gave up racing and in 1877 had to sell his stables. By 1886 his huge debts forced him to think of selling Wabnitz. He was at the height of his parliamentary influence; the elections of 1887 had at last returned a pro-Bismarck majority, and Kardorff was its virtual leader. He also was the principal champion of the fight to lower taxes on rural distilleries in order to benefit the agricultural classes, himself and Bismarck included. All of these activities led Kardorff to think that the government would wish to show its gratitude; its opportunity came when in desperation he decided to sell his estate to the crown prince's adjacent domain. He expected 900,000 marks, a sum that his neighbors regarded "as dumping." His party colleague and now minister of agriculture, Lucius von Ballhausen, offered only 800,000. "That spells complete ruin for me," he wrote Bleichröder; he warned that he would have to resign his seat. "I suppose he [Bismarck] will not be able to do anything for me, but I know that he will feel my absence in the Reichstag." Perhaps his own parliamentary efforts might save him: "Given the prospects for [favorable legislation for] the distillery interests, after I brought about a coalition between Conservatives and National Liberals, I consider it very probable that I will get 900,000 marks, if in the meantime people do not break my neck. . . ." Such an open acknowledgment of the connection between personal profit and parliamentary activity is rare. Kardorff's despondency facilitated candor; he wrote Bleichröder: ". . . I am fed up with my life and with the trouble and worries I have had for years, and I even despair of still being useful to my wife and children because for years everything I have tackled has gone wrong."[28]

To the end, Kardorff hoped that Bleichröder could prod Berlin into making a generous offer; instead Bleichröder negotiated a new mortgage arrangement, by which he would lend Kardorff another 100,000 marks, with the provision that Kardorff would receive no revenues from his estate until all mortgage payments had been met.[29]

In the spring of 1875 Kardorff, now an ardent protectionist, set out to persuade the textile interests to champion tariffs. He also wrote a major protectionist pamphlet, "Against the Current." In early June 1875 Kardorff attacked the finance minister, Camphausen, on the floor of the Prussian Diet and reported to Bleichröder that two other ministers, Friedenthal and Eulenburg, had gone out of their way to demonstrate their friendly feelings, a fact that he interpreted to mean (correctly) that Bismarck was not displeased with the attack on Camphausen.[30]

Nor did Bleichröder's other friends mince words about the calamity that had befallen German industry. In June 1875 Oppenheim wrote him that the depressed condition of the stock market was "a reflex of the complete paralysis of our mercantile and industrial condition."[31] The crisis was worsening, as was the despondency; there was a growing demand for relief, for a change in the economic policy of the Reich.

Most of the proponents of protectionism were loyal supporters of Bismarck. They wanted a change of policy and, perhaps, the removal of some of the most committed free-traders. But in late June 1875 an entirely different attack was launched: the *Kreuzzeitung,* the venerable mouthpiece of Junker and agrarian interests, for which Bismarck himself had once upon a time written, ran a series of articles on "the Bleichröder-Delbrück-Camphausen era and the new-fangled German economic policy." The polemic, discussed below in Chapter 18, accused Bismarck of selling out German interests to Bleichröder's, that is, to Jewish, interests—and of doing so at a profit to himself. The *Kreuzzeitung* thundered against the corruption of a bankrupt liberal system and pilloried Bleichröder as "the great financial and economic *spiritus familiaris* of the new Reich . . . the intellectual author of our entire economic policy." He was the mastermind of what the *Kreuzzeitung* called a Jew-policy: "The term '*Judenpolitik*' . . . is unfamiliar to the German public" because the Jews hide their dominance, but "Jews actually govern us now."[32] The implication was inescapable: the rulers of Germany were the tools of Jews—and who but Bismarck was the ruler of Germany?

The article was a bombshell. Written by Dr. Franz Perrot, a self-styled financial expert, and carefully worked over by the editor, Nathusius, the article brought into the open the long-smoldering resentment that old Conservatives harbored for Bismarck and the Jews. The *Kreuzzeitung* insisted that it was advocating neither an economic program nor economic interests; it merely wanted to expose the giant Jewish conspiracy which, with Bismarck's connivance, had wrecked the health of the national economy.

In all his political life nothing so embittered Bismarck as this attack from his fellow Junker. He saw the attack as monumental ingratitude, born of envy and stupidity. Bismarck as *Judenknecht,* as enslaved to Jews by golden chains—that was the charge. He never forgave it.

Bleichröder had even more reason to be appalled by this onslaught. The *Kreuzzeitung,* after all, was not a minor scandal sheet but the mouthpiece of the Prussian nobility, even if the paper had latterly fallen on difficult days. It was still widely read by some of Bleichröder's clients. Bleichröder could hardly take the same line as Kardorff, who wrote him: "I have been very amused by the *Kreuzzeitung* articles: Such polemics can only help us and bring the *Kreuzzeitung* ever nearer to the category of those papers that decent men are ashamed to read."[33]

Bleichröder was not amused. On the day the article appeared, Bleichröder wrote Herbert von Bismarck—so as not to intrude on the ailing chancellor. He enclosed the article, "unsurpassed in its impudence. The author seems less concerned with compromising individuals than with newly inciting a religious hatred which belongs to a sad and somber past." Still, the article fastened on his person, "preaching contempt," and clearly deserved to be brought before court. "I believe, however, to be acting in accordance with your father's spirit, if I meet these contemptible attacks with contemptuous silence." Could Herbert, "at an appropriate moment," solicit and transmit his father's views?[34]

Two days later, Herbert sent a four-page answer, approved and probably dictated by his father. The article, he wrote, was an effort to raise the declining circulation of the *Kreuzzeitung,* and a suit would simply play into the editor's hands. To ignore the attack, however, would invite repetition. Hence Bleichröder should write an article himself, disavowing the flattering notion "that the financial policy of the German Empire, in part or in whole, is a result of your counsels. You could also express your regret at lacking all influence on the financial policy of the Empire because if you had such influence, you would use it to recommend a different course in many questions. The insipid lies of the *Kreuzzeitung*," Herbert suggested, "could receive no more convincing refutation" than if Bleichröder were to insist that his own views had been different from official policy but had been inconsequential because he lacked all power. Herbert concluded by saying that he left precise formulations to Bleichröder, but thought the important thing was to declare publicly his disagreement with the present financial policy "in a courteous manner and without wounding the representatives of this policy."[35]

It would be hard to imagine a more humiliating, callous reply than Herbert's, even without the gratuitous reminder to Bleichröder to observe the decencies. The Bismarcks could not bring themselves to express a shred of sympathy or solidarity or regret that so faithful a servant had been so wretchedly abused. To the *Kreuzzeitung* insult Bleichröder was now to add the self-injury of denying that he had any influence on the government's economic policies. Friends proved no kinder than foes, and still Bleichröder acknowledged Herbert's letter without visible trace of anger or resentment. Indeed the answer was embarrassingly fawning, at least in tone: "With pleasure . . . I thank you for the friendly and detailed response to my letter." In substance he demurred and explained that the *Kreuzzeitung* attack seemed to have so little resonance (it was but a week old!) that it deserved no formal denial.[36] Was Bleichröder so subservient in spirit that he did not feel the insult of Herbert's reply or was he pretending not to notice it, *de faire bonne mine au mauvais jeu*?

In substance, the Bismarcks had not been wrong. Bleichröder had been a consistent critic of the Reich's monetary policy, and after Herbert's letter and in view of the ever worsening economic conditions, he became even more outspoken in his criticism of the government's policies. But then Bismarck himself was turning against his erstwhile friends and closest associates, such as Delbrück. The continuing depression and the antiliberal campaign became the occasion for a general reappraisal of economic policy.

It was an ironic coincidence to see Bleichröder score the same policies as had his *Kreuzzeitung* traducers. Bismarck began to heed Bleichröder's warnings, and in October 1875 he told a close friend that Bleichröder "had repeatedly and severely criticized some of Delbrück's and Camphausen's measures, and if his opinions and predictions would be published now, he would emerge as a great *Finanzpolitiker*. But Bleichröder declines to have this done lest such revelations would have disadvantageous effects on his business."[37] In the same month, Bismarck dispatched his first highly critical missive to Delbrück, complaining about the incompetence of theorists, jurists, and learned academics who would harm "real" interests.[38]

By the fall of 1875 Bleichröder favored retrenchment. He insisted, for example, that the directors' fees to Laurahütte board members be reduced; Kardorff was skeptical of such self-denying measures. Right after the *Kreuzzeitung* attacks, Kardorff spoke of resigning from Laurahütte, largely owing to internal disputes, but also because he felt that resignation would be politically advantageous. Presumably he was worried that his political role could be seen as a projection of his economic interests. Still, he hesitated to resign because his friends owned nearly a million shares, and "they would be alarmed by my resignation."[39] (And he needed the income.) Bleichröder's mood was grim, and his associates shared his gloom. Baron Abraham von Oppenheim acknowledged that he shared Gerson's

> pessimistic attitude entirely, and I do not see whence an early recovery should come. We did not—alas!—reduce our security holdings and must await better times. I have been in business now for almost fifty-six years and cannot recall such a protracted crisis ever before. According to my view, the national wealth of Germany has shrunk by one-third, and therein lies the chief calamity. . . . Complying with your request, I must inform you that Rhenish industry is still totally languishing and that vast sums are being lost.[40]

A few days later, Bleichröder warned Bismarck about the distressing conditions, though "for me they are less surprising, because I could assess in advance the consequences of certain measures, and these aftereffects, I predict, will continue." He discounted reports of English and French prosperity because "given the financial life of Europe, it is practically impossible that a state like Germany should be suffering while its neighbors prosper." In time, if the present trend continued, he warned, there would be a general European depression—and there was.[41] A few weeks later, Baron Carl Meyer von Rothschild complained to Bleichröder that stock-market prices were low everywhere: "The whole world has become one city."[42]

Meanwhile, Rhenish industrialists, with Baron von Oppenheim as their spokesman, had petitioned William to retain the last remaining iron duties, scheduled to lapse in 1877. William, though sympathetic to their plea, deferred to Delbrück's masterly analysis of the futility of protectionism. Imports were a minimal component of the German market, and hence tariffs would make very little difference. "A protectionist current is sweeping through the greater part of Europe," and Delbrück warned that if free trade were abandoned, "decades of furthering international trade would prove abortive and the German economy as a whole would suffer, even if special interests draw short-term advantages."[43]

Neither Delbrück's opposition nor Bismarck's and Bleichröder's aloofness could dampen protectionist ardor. In January 1876 the Central Association of German Industrialists (with the subtitle "for the promotion and protection of national enterprise [*Arbeit*]") was established. Kardorff was its first president.[44] The Association had as its main credo the demand for tariffs. Whatever his reservations—and Bleichröder's many letters to Bismarck from 1874 to 1878 make it clear that he saw the key to recovery in a different monetary policy, not in tariffs—Bleichröder was inevitably drawn ever closer to the protectionist agitation. As an economic leader, he had to follow his battalions. The clamor grew as the economic news worsened.

Kardorff's letters to Bleichröder recorded the woes of the Laurahütte: a shrinking market, greater competition from the Ruhr, lower profits, and the need to reduce production and dismiss workers.[45] Baron Meyer Carl von Rothschild wrote that "trade and industry are dying. . . . In my forty years of experience, I have never lived through such times and . . . one cannot perceive the source of any improvement, since there is a kind of solidarity of depression in all places which ruins the best combinations."[46] (It also ruined Rothschild's health: "When stock prices decline, my pains increase; I would prefer it the other way around.")[47] Rothschild hoped that the government would "intervene soon in order to help trade and industry because we are moving toward a major catastrophe. . . ."[48]

In April 1876 Rudolf von Delbrück, head of the Imperial Chancery and once Bismarck's most esteemed lieutenant, resigned for reasons of health, an explanation few people believed. Certainly Bismarck had grown critical of Delbrück's policies and his "overbearing and obstinate character."[49] Delbrück was dropped, the victim of Bismarck's displeasure, of Bleichröder's criticism, of the protectionists' special anger, and of William's suspicion. He had been the principal target of the *Kreuzzeitung* and of the conservatives as well. The reactionary blast was more important than has hitherto been realized.

Delbrück's removal weakened the ranks of free traders while the continuing depression emboldened the well-organized protectionists. Bismarck remained undecided and received contradictory reports. In July 1876 the leader of the Free Conservatives, Lucius von Ballhausen, unofficially submitted the party's electoral manifesto to Bismarck for approval, a remarkable tribute to the closeness of the party to the chancellor. Lucius wrote: "The current in the country is conservative. People are surfeited with reforms and partially blame the persistent economic disturbance on the new legislature, on tariff and commercial policy. The elections will result in Conservative gains."[50]

At roughly the same time, the Conservative party reorganized and, by embracing an unideological platform designed to promote agrarian material interests, hoped to become more popular and thus more acceptable to Bismarck. But he had not forgotten the *Kreuzzeitung* attack. In February 1876 he denounced in the Reichstag "the most shameless and most mendacious calumnies against men in high office" that the paper had been guilty of. He called for a boycott of the paper because "everyone who subscribes and pays for it participates indirectly in calumny and mendacity." Three weeks later, Bismarck's former friends and neighbors, the most prestigious Pomeranian pastors and Junkers, signed a declaration siding with Bismarck's traducers, not with him. Bismarck never forgave the *Deklaranten,* as they came to be called, and he remained deeply suspicious of the new party.[51]* Still, the elections of 1876 confirmed Lucius's prognosis: the trend was away from the National Liberals and toward a strengthening of both conservative parties.

During the two years of uncertainty, Bismarck was ever more receptive to Bleichröder's advice. Bleichröder had become a permanent and privileged adviser on economic policy, and his friends and associates, in turn, urged him to use his influence. In September 1876, for example, Abraham Oppenheim wrote Bleichröder, welcoming his prophecy of "a change in our commercial policy; it is a vital necessity for our country if the iron industry is not to succumb to entire ruin, and you would deserve well of the country if you could bring to bear your weighty influence with the Chancellor. But there is no time to lose."[52] Meyer Carl from Frankfurt warned that if the remaining iron duties were allowed to lapse, "the present debacle would only get worse so that our economic conditions would face a still more dismal future."[53] Bleichröder probably agreed, but a royal council decided that the remaining iron duties should end in January 1877. Camphausen clung to the earlier, free-trade decision, even though he expected that the iron industry would further decline and the government would be blamed.[54]

In January 1877 Bismarck asked Bleichröder for a report on conditions in the Ruhr. The prospects were grim, Bleichröder replied. A further drop in coal prices would lead swiftly to a new decline in production, to the dismissal of 10,000 workers, and to a further cut by one-third of workers' wages.[55] Troubled, the government sponsored a bill imposing some retaliatory measures against French export premiums.† In April 1877 agrarians and free traders in the Reichstag defeated this half-hearted effort. Bleichröder wrote Bismarck that "the decisions of the Reichstag . . . have evoked great pain in the afflicted provinces. In the industrial realm, we shall still suffer great calamities." He also took soundings on how Camphausen's position might be affected by this defeat of the government at the hands of free traders.[56]

By the time of the government's defeat, Bismarck had left Berlin. He stayed away for more than a year, first in Friedrichsruh, then in Varzin, with

---

* The editor of the *Norddeutsche Allgemeine Zeitung,* Emil Pindter, wrote Bismarck of his paper's publication of the new program; instantly Bismarck shot back a warning that the new party, judging from its adherents, would mark but a strengthening of the *Kreuzzeitung* party, and hence if the *Norddeutsche* supported the new party it would appear as if it had "joined the reactionary opposition." The government, Bismarck continued, had no business opposing the new party, "even though through its very founding the new party detracts from and perhaps damages the [free] conservative *Fraction* which is the government's surest support." Pindter to Bismarck, 12 July 1876, Herbert von Bismarck to Radowitz, 14 July 1876, GFO: I.A.A.a. 50, Vol. II.

† Bismarck objected to early drafts of this bill and explained that retaliatory measures were not the answer to the sharp practices of foreign countries: "In every contractual agreement with foreign countries, the greater honesty and the greater cumbersomeness and the greater openness of our administration easily put us at a disadvantage in comparison to the more skillful and more disciplined administrations abroad." Bismarck to Hofmann, 27 Oct. 1876, GFO: I.A.A.a. 50, Vol. I.

occasional forays to spas.* His health was shattered, as were his nerves; he had been living beyond his means. He had a catalog of organic and psychosomatic illnesses: rheumatic ills, excruciating pain, facial spasms, shingles. A year earlier, he had already complained to a friend:

> I have been suffering twelve months during the year. . . . For a year, my doctors have threatened me with the penalty of death if I do not give up my responsibilities. . . . I sleep only in the daytime from eight to noon or one, whence the time to work, especially with others? . . . I am discourteous to all the world, a matter which prodigiously increases the number of my enemies, over and above the number that results naturally from politics and from the duties which I discharge on behalf of my country.[57]

In his celebrated nights of sleeplessness he endowed his enemies with his own intelligence and toughness. "I have spent *the whole night hating*," he once announced.[58]

He hated by day as well. He imagined enemies everywhere. He thought Empress Augusta an implacable and powerful enemy, ready to promote her political views and wishes by putting pressure on her husband. Before he left Berlin, his self-pitying horror at the maneuvers of Empress Augusta reached new heights; "her intrigues," he confided to a friend, "border on high treason."[59] He despaired of his ministers, of their incompetence and disloyalty; he sensed that many of the people he respected, Bleichröder included, held his ministers in low esteem. Worse, he knew that the economic policy of the government had failed to overcome the depression—a fact of which he was often reminded. Finally he was angry at the many guttersnipes, some titled, who vilified his relations with Bleichröder, alleging that they were tainted by excessive profit and corruption. He had fought these worthies in public trials (as we shall see in Chapter 18), and some of them had been dispatched to jail. And still he was furious at the traducers themselves and at the silent minority that stood behind them, his very own Junker friends.

As in his other major decisions and shifts, the change came gradually. He wanted to strengthen the finances of the Reich and lessen its dependency on recalcitrant, narrow-minded member states; just before he left Berlin, he complained: "Prussia is in greater need of Germanization than Germany of Borussification."[60] He sensed the need for a new economic policy and the possibilities for a new political alignment that could be based on economic interests and not on principles or ideologies. At first he had no clear plan for the reconstitution of the Reich, but through improvisations, through the conjunction of his half-formulated plans with sudden and unexpected events, he proceeded with a series of measures that so transformed the Reich as to have

---

* In November 1877 a telephone was installed between Varzin and Berlin; no wonder that the old factotum of the Bismarcks, Jenny Fatio, wrote Bleichröder: "Politics provides much disquiet, little satisfaction, and an enormous amount of work for the Prince." 4 Dec. 1877, BA.

been called the second founding of the Reich. In 1878 he spoke of the psychological roots of reaching a decision: "It is as if suddenly the needle stops, and the scale stands still, without one knowing how this steadiness suddenly came about after such a long swinging back and forth." Once the needle had come to rest, he "was unyielding to influences from above and below."[61]

Throughout those months—while the needle was still oscillating—Bleichröder handled a host of matters that were of urgent importance to Bismarck, quite aside from his routine concern with Bismarck's finances and estates. Bismarck listened carefully to Bleichröder's advice in economic matters and came to share Bleichröder's nondoctrinaire protectionism. Neither man held any particular brief for the liberal idea of the state as a night watchman; both men believed that the state, especially the Hohenzollern state, had a more positive role to play.

We have seen that Bleichröder was not an economic ideologue. As a man of multiple interests and the closest foreign ties, he certainly did not fall in with the loud, uncritical clamor of the protectionists. He shared with Bismarck a certain distrust of doctrinaire positions, a distrust that Bismarck already voiced to the king in the fall of 1876 when he complained of "the doctrinaire reports" of Camphausen and commerce minister Heinrich von Achenbach rejecting the retention of iron duties.[62] Bleichröder never thought of protectionism as a virtue in itself or even as a major cure for worsening ills; his reticence bears out recent scholarly conclusions that economic motives or necessities were not the sole or even predominant determinants of the new policy.[63] Bleichröder never tired of telling Bismarck that "cheap money was a principal factor in the competitive capacity of industry."[64]

Bismarck's entourage remained divided. His old ministers favored the old course, including free trade; new advisers, notably Christoph von Tiedemann and Baron Friedrich von Varnbüler, were enthusiastic protectionists. In June 1877 Varnbüler wrote Bismarck that every day he was becoming more certain "that with the continuation of the existing free-trade mania we move closer to economic ruin."[65]

The official champions of protectionism happened to be close to Bleichröder. Varnbüler, a prominent Free Conservative in the Reichstag, was Bleichröder's client. He, too, was worried over the decline in his Laurahütte shares, and he asked Bleichröder how to pick an investment that would be both safe and likely to appreciate: "I keep aloof from speculations in the literal sense; they inhibit one's innocence if one wants to work politically."[66] Innocence is a wondrous thing, and Varnbüler seemed untroubled by having economic interests that would benefit if his agitation for protectionism proved successful. The protectionist issue was so important that when another associate of Bleichröder's, Senator Gustav Godeffroy from Hamburg, a stronghold of free trade, converted to protectionism, State Secretary Ernst von Bülow reported it to Bismarck on Christmas Day 1877.[67]

Bleichröder acted as a key link between the new Association of German Industrialists and Bismarck. The chief executive of the Association was a former government official, Wilhelm Beutner, whom Bleichröder met and established close ties with just before the first, full meeting of the Association in June 1877.[68] One of Bleichröder's functions was to solicit Bismarck's views on prospective moves. Thus Bleichröder wrote Herbert that the Association planned a protectionist petition to William, with a copy to the chancellor; if Bismarck had any objections, Bleichröder would try to dissuade the Association's president.[69] Herbert replied that Bismarck had no objection but asked Bleichröder to avoid "*any* pressure in his [Bismarck's] name . . . because he must remain in a passive stance vis-à-vis the president."[70] Herbert's letter signaled Bismarck's growing friendliness to the protectionists and reassured Bleichröder and his friends in the protectionist camp. The meeting, bringing together five hundred industrialists from all over Germany, was an unprecedented display of economic power. The petition, carefully addressed to the emperor rather than to a hostile Reichstag or to a divided government, led to the creation of commissions of inquiries which in turn facilitated Bismarck's adherence to protectionism.[71] Right after the meeting, Varnbüler wrote Bismarck urging a new tariff that would also yield new revenues for the Reich, but added that Camphausen would oppose such a measure.[72]

Bismarck moved slowly in the fall of 1877; as so often in the critical moments of his career, he experimented with several alternatives before settling on a definite course. Eighteen seventy-eight changed all that. It proved a decisive year when Bismarck's own plans for a far-reaching transformation of German politics coincided with dramatic events outside Bismarck's control, such as the accession of Leo XIII and two assassination attempts on William. Bismarck exploited every event to his own advantage.

The great transformation involved nothing less than the scuttling of Bismarck's tacit alliance with the National Liberals, and his attempt to create a new coalition based on Conservatives, right-wing National Liberals, and Centrists. For weeks Bismarck tried to persuade the leader of the National Liberals, Rudolf von Bennigsen, to enter the ministry on Bismarck's terms. The effort failed, and suddenly a very different wind began to blow. In February 1878 Bleichröder wrote Bismarck that the public expected great agitation on domestic matters in the new session of the Reichstag, but there was "unanimity that without Your Highness's presence, the anticipated reforms will not pass."[73]

Bismarck appeared, and dramatically unveiled the new course. The occasion was minor: on behalf of the government, Camphausen defended a higher tax on tobacco, abjuring any hidden intention of creating a Reich monopoly on tobacco. Bismarck rose in order to declare that he did indeed want such a monopoly as part of a general revamping of imperial finances. At one and the same time, Bismarck repudiated Camphausen and broke with the National Liberals—for whom a state monopoly was anathema. As Bismarck spoke, Leo XIII was elected pope to succeed the uncompromising Pio Nono. Bismarck's break with the National Liberals made a rapprochement with the Center easier and more urgent.

Meanwhile, Bleichröder made overtures to Bennigsen, asking him to discuss Bismarck's economic program; in mid-March Bleichröder opened an account for Bennigsen, but the Hanoverian intermediary who arranged for their initial contacts warned Bleichröder that Bennigsen would be "uncommonly reserved." After all, Bismarck's break with the National Liberals had just taken place.[74] On the other hand, Bismarck always hoped to split the National Liberals, keeping Bennigsen on his side.

The new course required new men. The old guard with its liberal sympathies departed. Camphausen was the first to offer his resignation—and Bleichröder was ready with a candidate: "Count [Botho] Eulenburg (Hanover)," he wrote Bismarck, "is reasonably well qualified for the functions of the Prussian finance minister and possibly for the vice-chancellorship; even if he did not go through a strict school of finances, it will not be difficult for him to make himself at home in this field, especially if in the more important questions he avails himself of knowledgeable experts, as I am sure he would."[75] Bleichröder's recommendation of an archconservative is suggestive; he must have had reason to think that Eulenburg would be sympathetic to Bismarck's new economic program. (Three weeks later, Botho Eulenburg replaced his liberal namesake, Friedrich Eulenburg, as minister of the interior. In his memoirs, Bismarck had unkind words for both men.)[76] For the finance ministry Bismarck tried to get Lucius von Ballhausen, calming his misgivings about inexperience by saying: "The finance ministry is the simplest in the world: if someone as incompetent as Bodelschwingh could head it for eight years, anybody can run it."[77] Lucius demurred, no one else could be found, and finally the totally inexperienced Arthur Hobrecht was dredged up.[78] It was never easy to find suitable ministers, and a year later Bismarck complained to the king: "Applications for ministerial posts are not very numerous in any case; the salary is too low compared to the external demands and only a *rich* man can be a minister without getting into financial difficulties."[79]

During the upheavals of 1878 Bismarck needed Bleichröder's help in all manner of questions; Bleichröder, in turn, needed Bismarck's benevolence more that year than at any other time during the Empire. As a consequence, the two men saw each other whenever possible and corresponded for the rest of the time.[80] They collaborated on the widest range of issues.

In early 1878 Bismarck wrote Bleichröder that government officials in Stettin had appealed to him on behalf of Johannes Quistorp, whose factories were threatened by the failure of the Stettin Bank. Apparently, the fate of 10,000 workers was at stake, and Bismarck wanted to help, if possible, both because "I personally know and esteem the director of the business and because of my official interest in preventing the unemployment of so many people." Bleichröder replied that Quistorp's affairs were "among the most complicated and difficult that I have encountered in my business life." To salvage Quistorp would entail about 1,500,000 marks—very much more than the 100,000 to 200,000 marks Bismarck had mentioned; Bleichröder doubted the wisdom of such help. Quistorp employed only some seven or eight hundred workers—hardly the ten thousand that had been adduced as proof for the need to help the failing business. The exchange illustrated Bismarck's willingness in principle to use state funds in support of a failing business and his reliance on Bleichröder's expeditious help rather than on his own cumbersome bureaucratic machine.[81]

In May 1878 Bleichröder urged the creation of new national commissions representing economic interests. The effect of such a corporatist plan would be to lessen the influence of parliament on the resolution of economic questions; Bismarck liked the idea and at the same time wrote the finance minister that he would always battle for "healthy sanity" as against partisan tactics: "The scholars [*Gelehrten*] without a business, without property, without trade or industry, who live off salaries, fees or dividends, will in the course of years have to submit to the economic demands of the producing people or lose their parliamentary seats."[82]

Throughout the spring of 1878 Bismarck hoped to find a way to speed the departure of these doctrinaire deputies. Bleichröder knew that Bismarck was thinking of an early dissolution of the Reichstag, but he warned the chancellor against a dissolution over a secondary issue because that could endanger "our economic reform."[83] Accidents came to Bismarck's assistance: two assassination attempts on William furnished Bismarck with the perfect weapon against National Liberals. William's wounds made Bismarck ponder a future government under the crown prince. What better way to protect oneself against such a liberal ruler and the terrible prospect of what Bismarck dubbed "a Gladstone Ministry," composed of all his putative enemies, than by forging a new conservative coalition?[84]

No sooner had the king been wounded than Bismarck ordered his ministers to submit a stiff anti-Socialist law; he himself remained in Friedrichsruh. (The assassin was generally believed to have been a Socialist—wrongly, but the allegation sufficed to depict the entire party as plotters of subversion.) The mood for repression was right; as Bleichröder wrote Bismarck: "The dastardly attempt [has produced] boundless excitement," and monarchical devotion had never been stronger. Bleichröder also thought that the deed had been committed by a Socialist.[85] Bismarck had found an issue on which he could not lose: if the anti-Socialist bill were accepted, the National Liberals would have had to sacrifice their principles and the Socialists would have lost their chance for untrammeled agitation; if the bill were defeated, the National Liberals could be pilloried as being soft on socialism, heedless of the public order, while the Socialists would have won a mere reprieve. Bleichröder clearly understood Bismarck's policy; just before the vote, he wrote: "Tomorrow the bill against socialist excesses will unfortunately be defeated by a great majority. I am afraid that this will seal the break with the National Liberals."[86] Bleichröder was right—on both scores.

Bismarck's war against the National Liberals was facilitated by the second assassination attempt of June 2. This time the eighty-one-year-old monarch was badly hurt; but Bismarck's first reaction was, "Now we dissolve the Reichstag," and only then did he inquire about William's condition. The country was outraged, and Eduard Lasker remembered that "now a veritable paroxysm of indignation and horror took hold of the entire German people."[87] Nine days later, Bismarck dissolved the Reichstag in order to launch a "law-and-order" campaign which would play up the Red scare in order to defeat the National Liberals.[88]

Better than any other episode during his reign, Bismarck's struggle against the National Liberals demonstrated his willingness to apply the tactics of international conflict to domestic rivals. He had tried to press the National Liberals into continued service at his command; when that failed, he was determined to seek a new alliance and to smash his former supporters. He mobilized all his forces for a deeply divisive campaign; August Bebel remembered it as being waged with "a hitherto unprecedented ferocity." In the midst of it, Bennigsen complained about "the undignified and disgusting form . . . which seems an inseparable evil associated with politics and the party system. At the moment we Germans are responsible for the worst in this realm in Europe, and to date I at least have discovered nothing about the educational virtues of universal suffrage, unless it be education to demagogy and general brutality."[89] The second election of 1878 was the decisive campaign in the projected transformation of the Reich.

[iii]

Following his master, Bleichröder threw himself into the campaign as he had never done before and was never to do again. In some ways, he was at the height of his influence; Bismarck's liberal advisers were on the way out, and qualified successors had not been found. More than that: Bleichröder's connections and money helped as well. The election was fought on issues he cared about: anti-Socialist legislation and the new economic program. For Bleichröder, other motives were at work too: at the time of the second assassination attempt, his son had been accused of conduct unbecoming to a soldier, as we shall see below, and it was important for the father to prepare the ground for an eventual pardon. Finally, the electoral campaign coincided with the meeting of the Congress of Berlin, at which Bleichröder expected Bismarck to play the decisive role in helping Rumanian Jewry. It was a good time, then, to manifest one's loyalty to Bismarck and the state—the two, of course, being identical in Bleichröder's mind.

The Association of German Industrialists also plunged into the campaign with the greatest vigor ever. It wanted to turn the election into a plebiscite on protectionism.[90] Just before the election, the head of the Association asked Bleichröder for his "views and wishes so that I may have the right directives for our debates." Beutner also told Bleichröder that the government should help the wool industry. In regions with important wool interests, "the enemies of the government" had scored important gains: "If the government did something to gain support there, the elections would surely have a very different outcome."[91] Bleichröder urged the Association immediately to found a literary bureau to promote the cause of its candidates. He contributed 5,000 marks to begin with, and four editors were hired the next day.[92]

Bleichröder's involvement did not go unnoticed. Early on, Prince Hohenlohe called on Bleichröder and stayed ninety minutes,

listening to his Talmudic wisdom. . . . What I minded in the whole talk was the realization that Bleichröder does seem to have influence on Bismarck's commercial policy after all. He acts as if he were part of the government, notwithstanding his assurances of humility. Apropos of the elections, he told me that he had received instructions from Bismarck, just as if he, Bleichröder, could fix the elections. Thus he asserts that Bismarck does not want to have Lasker and Bamberger in the Reichstag anymore. . . . It seems to me as if Bleichröder's selfish, Jewish policy in commercial matters has been responsible for the fall of Delbrück and for various other ill-prepared financial schemes of recent times.[93]

Bleichröder must have been better informed than Hohenlohe—or the latter would not have been struck by Bismarck's particular enmity against Lasker and Bamberger. Perhaps Bleichröder was a bit overbearing as he "whispered secrets" into the ears of listening officials, as another Bismarck aide remembered it.[94] But the substance of Bleichröder's report was correct.

Bleichröder also gave unstinting support to Herbert's first bid for a seat in parliament. Herbert ran in several districts, including Lasker's; he did not expect to defeat the veteran parliamentarian, but as Bleichröder put it: "his running amply attests that the opposing candidate L. is not *persona grata* to the government."[95] By helping Herbert, Bleichröder was also supporting the main efforts of the Association of Industrialists: the defeat of Lasker and Bamberger, both free traders and both Jews. The Association asked Bleichröder to "rap the knuckles" of Lasker's supporters, and Bleichröder in turn asked the Association to support Herbert. Bleichröder fashioned Herbert's links to the Association and generally acted as one of his chief campaign managers.[96]

Bleichröder knew that the Bismarck family was carrying on an embittered personal feud against his old friend Lasker. He also knew that Bismarck had gladly used Lasker's great talents at an earlier time and was now repaying him with exceptional abuse and anti-Semitic innuendos. A hitherto unknown letter of Herbert to his prospective brother-in-law, Count Rantzau, makes clear that the Bismarck clan had singled out Lasker as the chief enemy. In telling Rantzau how to instruct the press, Herbert wrote: "It is especially important that Lasker and [Eugen] Richter [leader of the progressives] should always be put on the same footing as 'preaching insurrection,' and carefully prepared excerpts from their inflammatory speeches must be dished up over and over again." By emphasizing the liberal—or as "Lasker's rump should now be called, *progressive*"—indifference to the lot of the lower classes, the newspapers should hammer home the theme that Lasker and his associates "are working in the service of the Socialists." The Bismarcks were extraordinarily adept at the unsavory tactics of modern campaigning.[97] Bleichröder could never have protected Lasker against Bismarck's wrath, but to have joined the attack against an old friend and distinguished parliamentarian of exceptional probity suggests a boundless subservience or at the very least an indifference to the claims of friendship. In short, Bleichröder treated Lasker as others were to treat Bleichröder.[98]

At Herbert's behest, Bleichröder also mobilized his influence with the press. Having already intervened with the *Berliner Tageblatt*, Bleichröder was told by Herbert to see to it that some paper carry a denial of a recent "lie" that he belonged or was close to the Conservative party: "I have never said anything about this; rather I have always said that in these grave times what mattered was not the adherence to a particular parliamentary group, but defense against all subversive parties. I shall probably *not* join *any* parliamentary group, certainly not the German-Conservative group."[99] Until election day and indeed until the end of all runoff elections, Bleichröder labored on behalf of the Bismarcks, negotiated with them directly or through Rantzau, and supplied the press with pro-Herbert material.[100] Despite all efforts, Herbert lost everywhere. The chancellor was furious and blamed the defeat in Lauenburg on the "mendacious electoral campaigns of the Liberals," though they would never have been successful, he asserted, if the public authorities, and especially the Landrat, had been more active in countering oppositional slander. Herbert pretended to be satisfied with his defeat because it rid him "of the filth which necessarily clings to parliamentarism."[101] He nevertheless decided to run in yet another district. Bismarck instructed Count Eulenburg and the local Landräthe to rally the progovernment voters.[102] Herbert lost again.

At the beginning of the campaign, Bleichröder thought of running for the Reichstag himself. It is not clear whether the initiative for this venture came from Bleichröder, from Beutner, or from Hugo Blank, director of the Harz machine works, who wrote to Bleichröder on June 30 that he had been happy to hear of his willingness to accept the candidacy in the Braunschweig district. A complication had arisen, Blank added, because the National Liberal incumbent had unexpectedly decided to run again. Blank and his "industrial friends" favored Bleichröder's candidacy nevertheless, if they could expect a good showing.[103] Bleichröder accepted, provided there was "a considerable chance that the voters would concentrate their ballots on my person."[104] Bleichröder became the Association's candidate.

There was something neatly symbolic about Bleichröder's running against a National Liberal—even in those days when party labels and party affiliations meant much less than later. Indeed the burden of campaigning was so much lighter in those predemocratic days that Bleichröder announced that he could not deliver an electoral speech because his health required an early rest. He submitted several manifestos, accepting the call:

I need hardly add that all ambition is foreign to me, and that if despite all my accumulated obligations I submit to this sacrifice, it is done only for the interest of our German fatherland. Given my relations to the imperial government, it is self-evident that I shall strive to support it with all my strength in its efforts to preserve the order of state and society [*die Ordnung der staatlichen und bürgerlichen Gesellschaft*]. On the whole, my political standpoint is that of the Free Conservatives.

Another time, he wrote:

My political and economic outlook is rather precisely characterized by the relations which for many years I have had with our imperial chancel-

lor, Prince Bismarck. The tasks which I would want to see fulfilled by
the next Reichstag are: the recognition that a law against the rapid
increase of the Social Democrats is necessary; the departure from free
trade and the establishment of a light protective tariff on the basis of which
trade and industry will be seen to flourish; and in connection with that,
the taking over by the Reich of the railroads in order to impose uniform
and cheap railway rates.[105]

By mid-July Bleichröder abandoned his candidacy. Blank advised withdrawal because "you wanted to appear as a candidate only if you could assume
with reasonable certainty that you would have a majority. . . ." Too many people, however, had rallied to the incumbent before the "economic candidate" had
appeared. Bleichröder's candidacy, however, had forced his rival to support
the government's anti-Socialist law and economic program, and this, Blank
thought, constituted "an indirect success" for Bleichröder.[106] Bleichröder had
to be content with this limited victory. His willingness to embark on a parliamentary career is remarkable, especially in light of Rudolph Meyer's satirical
attack on him which had appeared in 1877 and with which he was almost certainly familiar. Concerning Bleichröder's possible appearance in parliament,
Meyer wrote: "Anyone who has seen Mr. Bleichröder even once understands
that [the very thought of] his personality in parliament would arouse only
mirth. Despite all the vanity of his race, which was his too, he understood
that . . . and renounced all parliamentary laurels."[107] In that extraordinary
year of 1878, Bleichröder was willing to take the plunge, and for historians it
is a source of regret that he did not pursue a career which would have forced
him to abandon his typically covert role and would have given his person
and his views much greater exposure. Bleichröder's disappointment, if any,
must have been mitigated by his preference to play the *éminence grise*; moreover, the political limelight might have hurt his business.

Bleichröder—and his friends—had ample reason to be satisfied by the
election. Bismarck's new enemies, the National Liberals, lost 100,000 votes
while the conservative parties won their first resounding success in the new
Reich. The Free Conservatives nearly doubled their vote and with 785,000
votes reached the height of their electoral strength in the Second Empire. The
protectionist cause had done well, too. As one of Bleichröder's closest journalist friends wrote him: "The result can satisfy us even though a modus
vivendi with the Catholic party will be necessary to get a reliable majority. . . .
The colossal number of social-democratic votes is totally horrible."[108]

Bismarck's electoral victory was great, as was the renewed defeat of
German liberalism. It was a victory won by a campaign of ruthless vilification;
the example set and the results achieved did great harm to the political future
of Germany. The French chargé in Berlin appreciated the importance of the
moment:

A German Caesarism—the ideal of this great authoritarian and in his
mind more and more connected with the end of Germanic unity—should

[now] be close to realization. It is true that this order of things apparently can exist only with Prince Bismarck, that he is the only one capable of directing and dominating it; was this not proven in the political struggle that has just ended, where his personality united scattered and indecisive forces and was the principal element of his victory?*

The victory opened the way to the conservative reconstitution of the Reich. Bismarck immediately extracted from the new Reichstag a law suppressing all Socialist activities, though the party could still participate in elections. Cowed by threats of yet another dissolution, the National Liberals, Lasker included, voted for the anti-Socialist law, distressed by the new illiberalism—and their own impotence. For the Socialists, the struggle for survival inaugurated the "heroic period" of their history; the party vote increased steadily, and the anti-Socialist campaign proved a worse fiasco than the Kulturkampf.†

The anti-Socialist campaign was but one element in the reconstruction of the Reich. The protectionists clamored for tariffs, and in the new Reichstag could muster a bare majority. In July 1878 Bleichröder urged Bismarck to present parliament with a clear preview of the government's projected economic program. "The vital interests of industry" demanded such clarification— but Bismarck put in the margin that he himself did not know what the program would be.[109]

Bismarck hesitated because "the vital interests of industry" were not his sole or even preeminent concern. He wanted to devise a program that also would have the support of agrarian-conservative interests and that would strengthen the fiscal independence of the Reich. It was only in the fall of 1878 that the agrarians, frightened by the import of cheap Russian and overseas grain, began to ask for protection as well. The components of Bismarck's new policy now emerged: a comprehensive tariff would satisfy both indus-

---

* C. De Moüy to Waddington, 22 Oct. 1878, MAE: Allemagne, Vol. 25. The French Embassy in Berlin sent daily reports to Paris about Germany's internal conditions; these reports were of an unusually high caliber, understandably so, given the unique importance of German developments to the French. These reports were not included in the *Documents Diplomatiques Français*, and this rich source has hitherto not been used. St. Vallier was a close friend of Bleichröder's and during his tenure as ambassador in Berlin from 1878 to 1882 his reports often included information from or about Bleichröder.

† While defending the anti-Socialist law, Bismarck acknowledged his much earlier relationship with Ferdinand Lassalle—and did so in terms that have some bearing on his relationship with Bleichröder. Lassalle, he told parliament, "was not the type of man with whom one could make definite arrangements about the *do ut des*, but I regret that his political stance and mine did not allow me to have much contact with him; I would have been happy to have someone else of this talent and brilliance as a fellow landlord on a neighboring estate." There was something here of the *grand seigneur* boasting that he could select his friends among the most unlikely people, regardless of class or religion. If he could relish the company of a Jewish socialist who could offer him little, he could stick to a Jewish banker who could offer him much. In the same speech he avowed that he had come to recognize "the social-democratic elements as an enemy against which state and society are in a condition of self-defense," when Bebel or Liebknecht in 1871 hailed the Commune "as the model of political institutions and acknowledged the gospel of these robbers and murderous arsonists." *GW*, XI, 606–610.

trialists and agrarians and bring them together in a common policy; at the same time, tariffs would bring new revenue to the Reich, which financially had been living off indirect taxes and annual contributions from the member states. In addition, Bismarck now sought new indirect taxes and state monopolies on such items as tobacco and salt.

Gradually Bismarck's program took shape. For three years he had withstood the protectionist agitation. Now that some agrarians also cried protection, he moved quickly. It has been argued that his conversion to protectionism came when he realized that such a policy would benefit him as a large landowner. Certainly Bismarck was not above considering his own economic interests in the shaping of economic policy, but there is very little evidence to suggest that in this particular case his own prospective interests played any role.[110]

Political considerations were paramount: he wanted to satisfy all major economic interests of the Reich and align them behind a new economic program. The iron industry had proven its power to sway public opinion, to persuade people that only tariffs would save it. Bleichröder had done his share in this first assertion of sheer economic power.[111] But Bismarck wanted to preserve agrarian-conservative power as well. With the "productive" elements on his side, he could more confidently battle the ideological or doctrinaire opponents of his regime.

By the fall of 1878, then, Bismarck began to see that the particular demands of agrarians and industrialists could be made to serve far greater schemes than they themselves envisioned. It was only when several motives came together and when the chances for a total reconstitution of the economic and political order seemed auspicious that Bismarck moved—with a dexterity and a brutal resoluteness that recalled his maneuvers of the 1860s.

In mid-December he unveiled his program to the Federal Council. He now insisted that there should be a general tariff on virtually all imports and an increase in indirect taxes that would add further revenue to the Reich.[112] In early 1879 Bismarck made his final plans with Tiedemann and Varnbüler. After this major strategy session in Friedrichsruh, Bismarck received the French ambassador St. Vallier and gave him one of his bafflingly candid accounts of his plans. First of all, he wanted to put imperial finances on a solid footing:

> Every year I have to play the role of mendicant in order to ensure the necessary operation of the Empire's services: I have to beg Brunswick and Mecklenburg for charity: is that tolerable and must I lose my time and exhaust myself being a laughingstock for the representatives of these little countries who immediately play the role of being arbiters of the world's destiny and keep me in suspense so that for once in their wretched life they can enjoy the voluptuous sensation of believing themselves important?

He wanted Germany to emulate France's reliance on indirect taxes; he also had come to recognize that agriculture, with which he was most familiar, needed protection, as did industry. The need for uniform railroad rates would require the state's acquisition of several railroads.

This, then, was the totality of his program. The details would depend

> on the dispositions I shall encounter in the Reichstag and the public; I shall act like a navigator who has set his course and encounters adverse winds; he more or less modifies his route; he uses more or less coal; he avails himself of the sails more or less, following the caprice of the storm, but as for the end of the voyage, he never changes. I shall act like him, and now you know my aim; as for the means of reaching it, I reserve the choice, depending on the game of the adversaries and the liveliness of the battle.[113]

The battle promised to be difficult, and Bleichröder helped to enlist the necessary ally. Bismarck needed the support of the Center, with its stable electoral support and growing sympathy for protectionism. But the legacy of the Kulturkampf was heavy, and the gulf between the towering Bismarck, who suspected clerical intrigue everywhere, and the tiny, unassuming Ludwig Windthorst, the tenacious leader of the Center, the defender of Guelph interests, and Bismarck's foremost parliamentary foe, seemed unbridgeable—until Bleichröder brought them together.

Bleichröder and Windthorst had drawn close a few months earlier; for Bleichröder, Windthorst represented one of the few Center leaders who had opposed the anti-Semitism that had developed in the party during the Kulturkampf; for Windthorst, Bleichröder was interesting as Bismarck's confidant. In March 1878 a Jewish banker friend in Hanover, Louis Meyer, wrote Bleichröder that Windthorst wanted to talk with him: "Concerning the purpose of the conversation, he said nothing—as one would expect from an old diplomat. . . . I can take it for granted that he has something on his mind." Meyer opened a credit at the Bleichröder Bank for Windthorst so that "without being conspicuous, he could come visit you more often than before."[114] Windthorst did come often; "every Sunday, when Windthorst was in Berlin, he would call on Herr von Bleichröder, in fact right after going to mass in the Hedwigskirche."[115] It is an intriguing picture—the devout and worldly Windthorst flitting from church to banker. Windthorst even called on Bleichröder in various spas, and in the 1880s attended some of his formal functions.

From that moment on, Bleichröder became ever more concerned with the affairs of the deposed Hanoverian dynasty.* The exiled King George died in June 1878. Soon thereafter, Louis Meyer wrote to Bleichröder that the king's death had removed the original reason for the sequestering of the

---

* And, characteristically enough, with the Guelph underworld as well. When in the late 1860s the deposed King George tried to arouse foreign sympathies in his cause, he relied primarily on Oskar Meding, a journalist, who for a time edited a pro-Guelph paper in Paris. Just before the outbreak of the Franco-Prussian war, Bismarck won Meding over to the Prussian cause; he promised him a pension in return for defection, and later paid him for publishing documents incriminating to the Guelph cause. In 1878 Meding, heavily in debt again,

royal property, and he proposed that the two bankers should mediate between the Prussian government and the Hanoverian dynasty. If the confiscated millions remained in Prussian hands, then, Meyer warned, the Hanoverians, though loyal to the Reich, would once again shift their sympathies to the royal underdogs. He added: "I think it advisable for the time being not to talk with Mr. W———t"—presumably because of his longstanding enmity with Bismarck.[116]

Bleichröder followed a different path. In March 1879 he arranged for an historic meeting between Bismarck and Windthorst. For years Bismarck had detested Windthorst as the skillful defender of popish and Guelph interests in the new Empire. "Everybody," Bismarck remarked, "needs somebody to love and somebody to hate. I have someone to love and someone to hate. I have my wife to love and Windthorst to hate."[117] But times were changing, Bismarck needed votes for his new economic program, and Windthorst thought that the death of King George might facilitate a reconciliation between Guelphs and Germans.

The initiative for the meeting came from Windthorst, who told Bleichröder of his desire to see Bismarck. Bismarck was skeptical but finally yielded to Bleichröder's entreaties.[118] Bleichröder knew that Bismarck needed votes, and Windthorst monetary satisfaction for the deposed Hanoverian dynasty, and he hoped that two such practical men could work out a limited bargain. He was right. During their interview, Bismarck agreed to regular payments from the Welfenfond (the interest collected from the confiscated property) to the recently widowed Queen Mary of Hanover, and then Bismarck raised the question of tariffs, insisting that the survival of German agriculture depended on them. The landless liberals could not fathom this, but Bismarck hoped Windthorst could—after all, the Center party represented rural Germany.

The interview proved to be a turning point. Windthorst was delighted with Bleichröder's "kind intervention"; a bridge for further meetings had been built and "a satisfactory understanding" could now be anticipated.[119] Windthorst wrote Bleichröder that he was confident that "the chancellor's benevolent views and your own prudence" would assure a settlement for Queen Mary. He also hinted at the quid pro quo: "Since my departure from Berlin I have not been able to do anything in the tariff matter. . . . Upon my return to Berlin I will take the liberty of calling on you in order to inform myself about the state of affairs."[120]

Although Bismarck and Windthorst had agreed in principle about payments to Queen Mary and her two daughters, negotiations dragged on. Bleichröder did all he could—behind the scenes—in order to hasten their conclusion.

---

turned to Bleichröder for help. He promised Bleichröder journalistic services and also offered his assistance in mediating between the Guelph dynasty and the German government. By this time, Bismarck warned Bleichröder against helping Meding, whom he thought incapable of living within his income. Bleichröder did help, and Meding wrote a flattering article about him. Meding to Bleichröder, 3 and 29 Dec. 1878, 26 Jan. 1879, BA; Herbert von Bismarck to Bleichröder, 2 March 1879; Meyer to Bleichröder, 5 Jan. 1879, BA.

He informed his friend Eulenburg, the crown prince's Hofmarschall, about the interview, and Eulenburg, in turn, told his court about "this exceedingly important conversation. . . . There is the urgent wish here that there be a tangible success in this move concerning the widow and daughters, and one hopes as well that this rapproachement will have happy results for our general conditions."[121] In mid-May Windthorst was still waiting for a definite arrangement and looked to Bleichröder for help.[122] On July 2 Windthorst learned that Bleichröder had delivered 100,000 marks to the queen, and 15,000 marks to each of the princesses—minus his commission of ¼ percent.[123] This was the first semiannual installment; Bleichröder made regular payments thereafter, drawing on the Welfenfond. In short, Bismarck met Windthorst's wishes—less than two weeks before the decisive vote on the government's reform projects.*

Bleichröder's initial mediation between Bismarck and Windthorst bore important fruit. Shortly after their first private meeting, Windthorst went to Bismarck's parliamentary soiree for the first time—and was received "as if a Kulturkampf had never occurred!"[124] Tongues began wagging about the new course, and Louis Meyer and Bleichröder congratulated themselves on their work.[125] Bismarck had struck up a tactical alliance with an erstwhile foe in order to destroy his erstwhile allies, the National Liberals. The new economic program was now close to passage, and Bleichröder's role had been important—at least as important as his earlier mediation between Bismarck and the liberal leader Unruh, which also took place on the eve of a great conflict.

Shortly after Bismarck's meeting with Windthorst, St. Vallier predicted an early victory for Bismarck:

It is a common enough error among newcomers and superficial observers in Berlin to take for real the parliamentary system as it exists here; with more experience and reflection, one quickly recognizes that Germany is endowed with a fine and beautiful façade, remarkably embellished on the surface, faithfully representing a picture of a parliamentary and constitutional system; the rules are correctly applied, the customs observed, the external prerogatives respected; the play of parties, turmoil in the corridors, lively debates, stormy sessions, defeats inflicted on the government and even on the powerful Chancellor (only in matters of course that he considers of secondary importance), in short everything is done that can give the illusion and make one believe in the gravity of

* Until now, it had been assumed that Bismarck agreed to help Queen Mary because of pressure from England; Disraeli did appeal to him personally in order to circumvent a more formal step by Queen Victoria. Disraeli's plea, however, came a week after the historic meeting between Windthorst and Bismarck. Bismarck had more reason to oblige Windthorst than Disraeli, though no doubt he was pleased to satisfy both men with one gesture. Cf. Hans Philippi, "Zur Geschichte des Welfenfonds," pp. 204–212 and 235–246. Philippi makes no mention of Bleichröder's or Windthorst's role in this matter, nor does Stewart A. Stehlin, *Bismarck and the Guelph Problem, 1866–1890* (The Hague, 1973), pp. 200–201.

the debates or the importance of the votes; but behind this scenery, at the back of the stage, intervening always at the decisive hour and having their way, appear Emperor and Chancellor, supported by the vital forces of the nation—the army dedicated to the point of fanaticism, the bureaucracy disciplined by the master's hand, the bench [*magistrature*] no less obedient, and the population, skeptical occasionally of their judgments, quick to criticize, quicker still to bow to the supreme will.

In sum, he asserted, once Bismarck had made up his mind and had received the emperor's approval, "the vote [on reforms] must be taken as certain."[126]

The outcome probably was certain, and perhaps the rest was shadow-boxing, but it included a vicious scene. In the Reichstag debate, Lasker warned against the fiscal and political consequences of the government's plans. Bismarck lashed back in one of the most offensive sallies of his parliamentary career. About Lasker and his colleagues, he cited Scripture: "They sow not, neither do they reap, they toil not, neither do they spin, and yet they are clothed. I shall not say how, but at least they are clothed. Those gentlemen whom our sun does not warm, whom our rain does not wet —unless by chance they forget their umbrellas at home when they go out," lack all practical experience in the nation's economic life. Parliament—he implied—was composed of ignorant parasites while property-owning ministers had a much better grasp of the needs of the people.[127] It was a preposterous extravagance, though Bismarck firmly believed in the substance of the charge, and it was one of the few times that the president of the Reichstag timidly sought to rebuke him, only to have Bismarck upbraid him and threaten parliament with dissolution. Even Bismarck's supporters regretted "his great irritability and violence."[128] To his foreign foes, he was at times magnanimous; to his critics at home, never.

The National Liberals had become his favorite foes. He preferred an agreement with the Center—even when the Center insisted on an amendment that negated his efforts at strengthening the Reich's fiscal independence—rather than collaboration with the National Liberals who would have accepted his fiscal scheme. Partly as a consequence of Bismarck's yielding to Centrist demands, three men, who had been close to the earlier political course, resigned: Adalbert Falk, champion of the Kulturkampf; Karl Friedenthal, the minister of agriculture; and the recently appointed minister of finance, Arthur Hobrecht. Bismarck resented the timing of these resignations but, as St. Vallier noted, "he firmly follows his own path . . . breaking and littering the ground with men who, having served him once, have become useless to him or show themselves resistant to his all-powerful will."[129]

Bismarck found conservative replacements for the vacant posts: he appointed Karl Bitter as minister of finance, Lucius von Ballhausen as minister of agriculture, and Robert von Puttkamer as Falk's successor. St. Vallier characterized all three "as creatures who will be docile and obliging instruments of the Prince-Chancellor." Observers believed that by picking someone "as bereft of reputation as Mr. Bitter . . . the Prince intends to control the ministry himself or rather to have it controlled by one of his most influential [*les plus écoutées*] advisers, Monsieur de Bleichröder, whose position as banker and whose religion do not allow him to take a visible part in the conduct of the affairs of state."[130]

Bismarck's triumph came in mid-July, but even at the sight of victory he remained an unforgiving enemy. He blamed the National Liberals for forcing him to work with the Center. Among National Liberals, he charged, "destructive forces slumber," which a mere defeat could turn into "angry passion." He could not work with such men. In lecturing the National Liberals, he also expressed some of his deepest thoughts about politics: in both foreign and domestic realms, he said, it is always

> as if one were walking in a strange country with strangers whose next actions are unknown; if one person puts his hand in his pocket, then the other already pulls out his revolver, and if the other fires, then the first shoots, and at such moments nobody can stop to ask whether the pre-conditions of the Prussian Penal Code concerning self-defense apply, and since the Prussian Penal Code is not valid for politics, then, alternatively, one is prepared for aggressive defense very quickly indeed.[131]

It was a fitting epitaph for Bismarck's campaign and expressed his sense that politics is the continuation of war by other means. (He so liked the image of the two strangers that a few weeks later he repeated it to a close friend as being applicable to European politics.)[132]*

In the short run, his tactics paid off brilliantly. On July 12 a coalition of Centrists, Conservatives, and right-wing National Liberals adopted his program—and if he had wanted to, he could have exclaimed, as he had in 1866: "I have beaten them all." He had scored, as St. Vallier put it, "one of the most substantial triumphs of his political career" and in a field in which his enemies thought him ignorant.[133]

Bismarck had strengthened the unitarian aspects of the Reich with the help of particularists like the Centrists and the old Prussian Conservatives. He had forged a political alliance between industrialists and agrarians, between rich *Bürger* and Junkers—an alliance that was destined to shore up German agriculture and thus preserve the social basis of Prussian conservatism. He had divided his enemies. He had neutralized or violated doctrinaire positions and rewarded material aspirations; he would have been happy to reduce German politics permanently to *Interessenpolitik*, where economic interests could be heard and bought off and where all other matters could be left in

---

* In his memoirs Bismarck alluded to the identity of domestic politics and foreign war—and attributed the thought to his opponents of the 1870s: "This rejection of everything that is fitting and honorable is vaguely connected with the sentiment that the interest of party—which is made to appear as the interest of the fatherland—must be measured by a different standard from the standard of private life and that the commands of honor and tradition can be differently and more loosely interpreted than would be true even against foreign enemies in the conduct of war." *GW*, XV, 351.

his hands. To do away with ideological politics, to transform politics into a marketplace of competing interests—that was his ambition. But the turn to conservatism sharpened the ideological tenor of future politics; the Puttkamer regime came to prescribe a new ideological orthodoxy, tinged with more than a hint of anti-Semitism. The great depression had been a catalyst to force Germany back into molds of development that had been set in earlier decades. The liberal interlude—singularly rich in legislative achievement—came to an end, and the new political system became more rigid and more repressive.

Throughout this period Bleichröder had been his loyal lieutenant. He had also been an intermediary between Bismarck and the first well-organized pressure group in German politics. At the birth of what has come to be called corporate capitalism, Bleichröder acted as a kind of lobbyist-adviser, although in his own mind he no doubt appeared as a knowledgeable voice representing not particular interests but a program for the benefit of the entire nation. By the end of the year, Bleichröder exulted to Bismarck: "Industry enjoys great liveliness in all its branches, especially the mining industry because of America's great demand." Prices will rise soon, he said, and wages will follow suit.[134] To Herbert, he wrote: "Industry is becoming more active every day, and I hope that the next few years will make the free-trading gentlemen feel in their bones how foolish they were with their free-trade system."[135] To make sure that free traders would suffer for their sins, Bismarck insisted that none of them "should be proposed for a decoration." The protectionist stalwarts, Tiedemann and Varnbüler, on the other hand, received appropriate orders. In the new phase of the Reich, conservatives garnered most of the honors.[136]

[iv]

In spirit and substance, the new economic program marked Germany's departure from its brief, liberal course. In the 1850s and 1860s laissez-faire thought had been popular among educated and commercial classes, but the veneration of the state was an older, stronger habit, and Germans never really adopted the liberal suspicion of the state. Unification had vindicated the authoritarian state; the boom, bust, and corruption of the early 1870s were quickly interpreted as a moral judgment on liberals. Interest groups clamored for "national" protection; influential academics, organized in a League for Social Reform, demanded an end to Manchesterism and a new activist state.[137] The old liberalism was declining—even in England—and Bismarck came to believe that a program of what he called state socialism would forestall revolutionary or democratic socialism.

Bismarck had always been an interventionist and a paternalist; economic necessity, political calculation, and personal predilection combined to set his course in the late 1870s and throughout the 1880s. He set a new tone as well as policy: the new Reich should appear not only as tax collector, oppressor of socialists, or rival of old dynasties, but as a beneficent agent, as a protector of the nation in the social realm—hence shield the workers from the ravages of occupational accidents, sickness, and old age. The state should offer succor—so that the subjects would be grateful.

Bismarck's new interventionist course was anticipated by his long fight to have the Reich acquire the country's railroads and organize them into an efficient national system—as a functional and symbolic demonstration of the newly found national unity. At the time of unification, railroads had remained subject to the individual states, each of which had its own excellent system, usually a mixture of state-owned and private lines. There were hard, practical reasons for Bismarck's plan: nationalization would automatically mean uniform rates and performance; it would permit more effective use of the railways in case of war, and the experiences of 1866 and 1870 had demonstrated their strategic importance. Lasker's revelations in 1873 about corrupt practices involving railroads were used—against his intentions—as an argument for state control, as was the sharp drop in railroad shares after the market collapse. Railways were too serious a matter to be left to the market or to the particularist forces within the Reich. The long-drawn-out controversy concerning the railroads demonstrated the limits of Bismarck's powers, even in an area he judged important. Rebuffed repeatedly, Bismarck's policy won a partial success in 1879. Although the nationalization debates have been called "a turning point" in the history of Germany's development, the actual history of his policy has not received an adequate, modern treatment.[138]

It is Bleichröder's role in Bismarck's railroad policy that concerns us here—and that so far has been totally ignored by historians. His role, it should be said at once, was concerned almost exclusively with the execution, not the conception, of policy. There is no indication that in the early 1870s Bleichröder either favored or opposed nationalization. (A one-time railroad expert, Franz Perrot, asserted that in August 1871 Bismarck and Bleichröder had opposed his scheme of nationalization.)[139] Bleichröder's first and quite characteristic intervention came in July 1873, when, at Bismarck's insistence, parliament created a new imperial agency for railroads (Reichseisenbahnamt) —ostensibly to work toward greater uniformity of rate structure, though actually to promote eventual nationalization. Bleichröder objected to the proposed head, who had the closest ties to another bank. He wrote Bismarck that the rumored appointment of Friedrich Wilhelm Scheele as head of the new agency had created a "sensation" in financial circles. Scheele was known as a man who "despite all intelligence sometimes succumbs to his passion and imagination, a quality which for an executive in a leading position could not be called a happy one." The same circles feared that Scheele, who as head of the board of directors of the Disconto-Gesellschaft received annually some 30,000 taler as his share of profits, would accept a 5,000-taler state appointment only if some continuing arrangement with his old bank could be made. Bleichröder was not troubled by a conflict of interest as such, but minded if the head of a government agency, charged with important financial matters, had an exclusive tie to a rival bank. He warned Bismarck that similar misgivings would appear in the Reichstag, "particularly since the selection of

Mr. Scheele would create an entirely unusual, preponderant position for the Disconto-Gesellschaft in the Reich, which is already represented in the Reichstag through its director, Mr. Miquel. I myself of course have no judgment of Mr. Scheele and have only sought to express the view of the public."[140] A fortnight later, Bismarck answered laconically and in his own hand: "Nothing new in the political realm since June. I am feeling better physically though still not well. Your letter concerning the Eisenbahnamt arrived *two months* too late."[141] Not a very full answer—nor an entirely truthful one: Scheele had first been approached two weeks, not two months, before Bleichröder's letter, and King William had also boggled at confirming the appointment of someone so closely linked with the Disconto-Gesellschaft.[142] Bismarck seemed untroubled by such scruples. Eight months later, Scheele resigned his office, exasperated by the obstacles which private railroads and individual states put in his way.[143]

As his successor, Bismarck appointed Albert Maybach, who had years of experience with railroads and who became one of the few men whom Bismarck respected. But Maybach, too, ran into heavy opposition; parliament refused to give his office supervisory power over all German railways. Even before the bill was presented, David Oppenheim wrote Bleichröder that the Reich government seemed determined to ruin all railroads by endless regulations so that in the end the Reich could acquire the railways cheaply. (David, also known after his conversion to Christianity as Dagobert, was the red sheep of the banking family: from 1841 to 1843 he had been a cofounder and editor of the *Rheinische Zeitung,* a progressive paper which published some of Marx's early writings; in later life he was active in the Rhenish Railway, the enterprise closest to his brothers.)[144] Later he wrote: "Around here, Prince Bismarck is seen as the intellectual author of this infamous draft for a new railroad law. . . . That one could dare to bring such a proposal to the light of day is a sad sign of the times, characterized as it is by a complete failure to perceive the necessity of promoting all economic interests."[145] A year later, at Bismarck's insistence, the Prussian Diet passed legislation that provided for the sale of Prussian railroads to the Reich. There was a storm of protest against such a centralist proposal—and Bismarck's own colleagues, especially Camphausen and Achenbach, opposed the plan. Oppenheim raged against the proposed "expropriation," which in a formal sense was not envisioned: "Even though I neither can nor want to believe that this project of the great statesman—which gambles recklessly with the economic and financial ruin of the German Reich—will be implemented in the next decade, still it is lamentable that with his project Prince Bismarck, unconsciously, plays into the hands of Socialism and Communism." It is a dish, he said, cooked "in Communist bouillon."[146] It is a pity that Oppenheim's polemics did not reach the ears of Bismarck, who a little later delighted in leveling similar charges at his enemies. It was an extravagant charge, but then Oppenheim had learned about the science of socialism and the art of polemics from Marx himself.

Bismarck's Prussian colleagues were reluctant to surrender the profitable lines to the Reich and unwilling to buy up private ones. The other states of the Empire also opposed the Reich's acquisition of Prussian lines. Bismarck chafed at the constant sabotaging, and Bleichröder's insinuations fed his suspicions: "I spoke to the commerce minister [Achenbach] ten days ago," wrote Bleichröder in December 1877,

> and submitted to him my ideas about the Stettin railroad affair; since then, he has not been in touch with me at all, even though he seemed delighted that I had offered him a new way to solve this question. Your Highness will understand that in this matter I can do no more and simply have to wait until the commerce minister brings up the subject. I am only afraid that this delay will injure the progress of this affair.[147]

Four days later, Bismarck wrote an angry letter to Achenbach about railway matters in general, and on December 23 insisted that if the Prussian ministry opposed his railway plans—which, Bismarck added, were absolutely essential for Prussia's defense—he would have to resign his office.[148]

Bismarck attached the greatest importance to the railroad question. He saw it as an overriding national issue—which particularists, including Prussian ministers, treated from a narrowly selfish perspective. He met repeated rebuffs in his reform proposals; finally, in March 1878, his chief opponent in the Prussian ministry, Achenbach, resigned; in the fall of that year Bismarck created a Prussian ministry of public works, entrusted it to Albert Maybach, and charged it with railway affairs. The plan now was to buy Prussia's remaining private lines and add them to the Prussian system—so that at least in the largest German state a uniform system would satisfy the demands of defense and efficiency. The implementation of this plan encountered endless difficulties, and Bleichröder was forever complaining about various delays and obstructions.

Bleichröder had a very practical interest in the execution of Bismarck's plans. Beginning in 1875 and 1876, he bought up—as discreetly as possible and with a certain amount of Rothschild financial support—shares of companies that he expected to be nationalized. To do this rapidly and yet without driving the price up was a delicate maneuver, the daily tactics of which he seems to have entrusted to Carl Fürstenberg, who a few years later began a legendary career as head of a rival bank.[149] But there must have been great risks involved as well: the prospects of the railroads were poor, their only hope was some form of nationalization, and Bleichröder knew that the government was sharply divided on that issue. No sooner had the Prussian Diet adopted its first law about selling its railroads to the Reich than Baron Meyer Carl wrote Bleichröder that their common creation, the Posen-Kreuzburg line, could hardly be in worse condition: "The best solution would be for the state to buy the lines, because in private hands they will not flourish and only the landowners with property adjacent to the lines benefit from them."[150] In the summer of 1877 Hans wrote his father that the market was bullish "with the exception of our wretched German railroads which slowly but surely seem to be moving toward bankruptcy [*Pleite*] as their end goal."[151] In the same year, Bleichröder's creation, the Continentalbau-Gesellschaft, suffered a 6 million-mark loss, as Moritz von Goldschmidt noted with great acerbity.[152] And still Bleichröder placed his bets on early nationalization, bought in railway stock, and kept warning Bismarck that his ministers were obstructing his policy.

Bismarck, too, had an intensely personal interest in the success of his policy. A very large part of Bismarck's private fortune was invested in rail-road shares precisely during these years of anticipated nationalization. Three days after the law authorizing the Prussian state to sell its lines to the Empire had been promulgated, Bismarck instructed Bleichröder to buy 30,000 marks' worth of 4½ percent preference shares in the Berlin-Stettin Railroad and an equal amount of 4¼ percent Berlin-Anhalter Railroad.[153] As it turned out, the Berlin-Stettin line was the first to be nationalized in Prussia some years later. Over the next eight years, as we will see, Bismarck bought and sold on a consecutive basis more than a million marks' worth of railroad shares—at some points, roughly half of his liquid capital was invested in these shares. Such investment was the clearest commitment to his own policy of nationalization, because failure or even undue delay in nationalizing could have cost him money.

In his frequent letters to the Bismarcks, Bleichröder never alluded to their common financial interest in the matter, but Bleichröder could count on Bismarck's intense concern, and a direct mention of their financial stake would have been gratuitous. There was no end of trouble with the Ministry, and in his many private letters Bleichröder briefed Bismarck about these machinations. In an eleven-page letter in December 1877 he complained:

> While, since the beginning of his official duties, Minister Maybach has expressed to me his view that the nationalization [*Verstaatlichung*] of certain private lines was absolutely necessary for the completion of the national economic reforms and that he felt called upon to bring this matter to a resolution in the next session of the Diet, he has in the mean-time constantly complained of the resistance which he has encountered in the Finance Ministry, which makes it impossible for him to succeed in the railroad question. Nevertheless, in the last few weeks, the finance minister has shown greater compliance, and I succeeded in arranging for conferences between the commerce minister and the executives of the Berlin-Stettin Railroad [and several other lines]. But after the finance minister raised new objections, these negotiations had to be postponed.

The rest of the letter dealt with the Berlin-Stettin Railroad, in which both men were stockholders. If the line were to be nationalized, the Prussian state would pay the shareholders in Prussian state obligations; the projected rate of interest would depend on the customary rate of return of the line. In the case of the Berlin-Stettin line, both the finance and the commerce ministers had agreed to a 5⅓ percent interest rate (the earlier rates had varied between 4 and 8½ percent). In the meantime, Bleichröder added, the directors of the railroad had cut the dividend for January 1 because of declining net income. As a consequence, the ministers decided not to ask the Diet for its authorization for the purchase of the railroad but for its acceptance of the principle of nationalization. Bleichröder was furious, because such a delay would lead to further wrangling about a lower interest rate and thus might end with the shareholders' rejection of the whole plan. Bleichröder urged that Maybach should defend the principle of nationalization *and* demand a 5⅓ percent return for Stettin; if that proved unfeasible, then Maybach could still settle for 5 percent or 4½ percent. Approval of the principle alone was not enough. "With his well-disposed benevolence, Your Highness will surely excuse these forthright explanations and will give credence to my assertion that they were not dictated by selfish interest but are based on the conviction that the nationalization of the railroads must take place simultaneously with the tax reforms anticipated for the spring, because without these the year 1879 would be another year lost for commerce and industry."[154] Bleichröder had certainly made himself clear to Bismarck; Herbert wrote his brother Bill: *"Der Bleiche* was very upset about Maybach, insisted that he could not understand him at all, and that by fall one could either not get the railroads at all or much more expensively! On the other hand, he praised Hobrecht!"[155]

In late January 1879 the budget commission of the Diet accepted the principle of further nationalization, and on the same evening a member-friend wrote Bleichröder: "The Commission thinks it incompatible with the honor of the government to ruin the private lines through its economic regulations in order to buy them cheaply."[156] But at the time nobody knew the timing and the likely terms of the government's purchase of railroads. Rumors abounded about divisions within the government and jockeying among stockholders. It was during this uncertainty that some of Bleichröder's other distinguished clients began to bombard him with requests for confidential news about the precise prospects of nationalization. In December 1878 Prince Henry VII of Reuss inquired about the likely nationalization of some specific lines and in May 1879 asked whether he should not sell his Cologne-Minden shares at 119 since Bleichröder had predicted that nationalization would drive up the price only to 115. In July 1879 Count Lehndorff asked for similar information and in August of that year Count August Eulenburg reported that he had seen Maybach who had given him authentic information on the projected terms for the nationalization of the Rhenish and Anhalt lines. Accordingly, Eulenburg asked Bleichröder whether an additional purchase of Rhenish shares "would be worthwhile." A few months later, Eulenburg reiterated his interest in railroad shares, but added that everything depended on nationalization and the prospects for that "are known only to you." Meanwhile Bleichröder kept Bismarck informed and in June 1879 reported that the shareholders of the Stettin railroad had accepted the government proposition.[157] He warned, however, that Maybach had told him that Finance Minister Hobrecht seemed unwilling to support further state acquisitions.[158] A month later, Hobrecht was out of office, and the more pliant Karl Bitter took over the finance ministry.

And still there was trouble: in November 1879 Maybach finally introduced the first specific nationalization bills in the Diet; while Bismarck thundered from afar that he would resign if the bills were rejected, Maybach had to contend with the strong opposition *in situ*. Attack, he thought, was the best defense. He acknowledged that stock-market financiers opposed the bill; they stood to lose an object of speculation. "I believe," he declared, "that the stock exchange serves as a *poisonous tree* [*Giftbaum*] in this field and throws its fatal shadow on the life of the nation." Maybach was outraged that, despite the strictest secrecy, there had been market speculation in the securities of railroads to be nationalized. This much he said in public; in private, he knew perfectly well that Bleichröder and his clients had been informed of the government plans. There was a storm of protest against his "poisonous tree" speech, and he retracted the metaphor. And yet he said no more than what most Prussians at the time felt—and even the noble speculators in railroad issues would have affected disdain for the stock market.[159]

Bleichröder must have felt especially aggrieved at Maybach's sally. His own operations in shares of the Berlin-Stettin line were well known to Maybach —and to the interested public at large. (As early as December 1877 a journalist friend wrote to Bleichröder complaining that the *Berliner Börsen-Courier* published "so malevolent an article about your recently inaugurated relations with the commerce minister concerning the Berlin-Stettin Railroad as to be almost beyond belief in the light of the many favors you have extended to Davidssohn [the editor of the *Courier*]."")[160] But Bleichröder was more troubled by Maybach's dilatoriness than by his rhetoric, and he continued his lament to Bismarck.

Bleichröder's greatest difficulty came with one of the smaller railroads: the Rhein-Nahe line of less than eighty miles, linking the Rhine and the Saar basin. It was a single-track line, which the military had long wanted to have converted into a double-track line, but the shareholders refused, calculating that their money-losing line would be nationalized only if the military became convinced that there was no other way to get the second track. Bleichröder remembered the beginning: "In the month of May 1880 I was honored by a visit from Finance Minister Bitter, who, demanding the strictest discretion, informed me of the desire to nationalize the Rhein-Nahe Railroad because Field Marshal Count Moltke considered it important strategically and thought a second track absolutely necessary."[161] By June a correspondence ensued between Bleichröder and Bitter in which the former made his propositions: he reported that the nominal capital of the railroad amounted to 27 million marks (or 270,000 shares at a par of 100), of which approximately 50,000 shares were still in the hands of the original investors, who had no desire to sell at a loss. For nationalization, the state would need the support of two-thirds of the shares voted; past experience had shown that not all shareowners voted, and hence the state needed 130,000 shares. Bleichröder proposed that the state should offer a price of 25 marks per share— the price having varied between 11 and 30 in the previous three years.

Bleichröder had already bought 30,000 shares at 18¾; he had persuaded friends who owned 22,000 shares to accept a price of 25—hence there remained the necessity of buying about 75,000 shares, which Bleichröder offered to do in the course of four to five months. He added unambiguously that the whole operation would be done for the account of the Ministry and that the profit that would arise from buying the shares below 25 would clearly accrue to the government and would in fact reduce the total cost of acquiring the railroad. Bitter accepted these propositions but fixed the top limit at 24.[162] Bleichröder pleaded for the greatest discretion, because any possible leak would drive prices up. Seven weeks later, he reported that despite "enormous difficulties" he had been able to buy another 12,000 shares, that his friends now held 36,000 shares, and the minister held 10,000 shares. More were needed, but the price had risen to 22½, and Bleichröder feared that leaks must have stimulated rival purchases. In fact, he had had to sell some of the stock he had already bought in order to prevent further price rises. In September, after some further behind-the-scenes maneuvering on Bleichröder's part, the company shareholders accepted the government's plan.[163]

The greatest difficulties, however, remained: as Bleichröder reconstructed the record, he called on Bitter repeatedly in December in order to find out when the government would submit the requisite bill to the Diet. Bitter assured him that the necessary steps would be taken at once and that he was confident of the final outcome, since both the war minister and the emperor supported the proposal. On the other hand, Bitter rejected Bleichröder's contention, according to Bleichröder's account, that the profit that had been made in the operation should accrue to the government. Bitter insisted that the government could not engage in such a deal and that the profit should remain with Bleichröder—who had also taken the risk. The two men agreed to resolve the issue after the vote in the Diet.

In the Diet, however, the minister for public works, Maybach—whom Bleichröder had met in Bad Homburg in July 1880 and whom he had duly informed of the operations—suddenly lashed out against "the great speculation" in Rhein-Nahe shares which "disgusted" him. It had driven the price unreasonably high—to the benefit of latter-day speculators, not of honest men who had invested their money in the construction of the line and had lost a part of their investment. Maybach thus jeopardized the Diet's vote, and a Centrist opposition leader echoed the charges: most of the shares had been bought by "a few great bankhouses," and "hence if today we accept twenty-four as the price then we do nothing but nurture the poisonous tree, as the minister has rightly called it."[164] Bleichröder became worried that he might get stuck with shares that would plummet without nationalization. He wrote: "As far as I am concerned I believe I can appeal to the fact that the whole operation, as the correspondence shows, was not carried out on my account but bona fide for the account and in the name of the government, and losses which result from the nonacceptance of nationalization must be debited to the government and not to my House." The Diet could still be prevailed upon to accept the proposed treaty if Maybach "could be instructed to speak for nationalization in the Diet in such a way that no doubt concerning the position of the entire Ministry could remain."[165] A year later, the line was nationalized at a price of 24.

We do not know who garnered the profits, though it is a reasonable inference that for bureaucratic reasons the Finance Ministry would have found it difficult to account for such a windfall. Hence it is likely that Bleichröder—with whatever reluctance he could conjure up—kept the approximately quarter of a million marks of capital gains. By that time he must have felt he had earned them: we have no evidence that he had so much difficulty or so large a profit margin in any other railway operation. (The margin in this instance was approximately 30 percent over a period of twenty-two months.)

Bismarck was content with far more modest profits. In November 1880, and in May 1881, Bleichröder bought for Bismarck about 140,000 marks' and 22,600 marks' worth of Rechte Oder Ufer Railroad; in June and August of 1881 he sold the same shares for about 146,000 marks and 25,000 marks, respectively. In the case of the smaller amount, his gain in three months was nearly 10 percent. (The line was finally nationalized in 1882.) During the next two years—and at a smaller rate of profit—he bought and sold about 170,000 marks of the Cologne-Minden Railroad. In July 1883, on Bismarck's oral "instructions," Bleichröder bought in six separate transactions 400,000 marks of the Upper Silesian Railroad, which was nationalized six months later, with Bismarck making a profit of just over 2 percent.[166] This type of operation was essentially a matter of what bankers call interest arbitrage: the railroad shares would be exchanged for Prussian consols, and this was a way of buying the consols at a slight discount.

Bismarck bought these shares at a time when it was general knowledge that Prussian railroads would be nationalized. The average investor, however, could not be certain when they would be nationalized or on what terms. Bismarck knew more about these matters than almost anyone else; and what is more, he had the power to put pressure on his ministers, though as we have seen, in railroad matters he often had great difficulties. By our standards, it was an odd time for a prime minister to invest in railroad shares; in some instances, it involved what we call inside knowledge; at no time was a major or improper profit involved. Bismarck, however, may well have felt that he was putting his money at the disposal of the government, since his vote as shareholder would support government policy. We can be certain that his own heavy investments sustained his intense interest in the nationalization of railroads.*

Bleichröder played a major role in the nationalization of Prussian railroads. The practical aspects of nationalization were complicated, even after the Prussian cabinet and Diet had accepted the principle. Every takeover required a separate act, requiring lengthy negotiations with the Diet and

---

* His interest in the nationalized railroads was all-embracing. In 1881, for example, he urged Maybach that on nationalized railroads political pamphlets attacking the enemies of the government ought to be made available—just as on private lines "progressive" papers were on sale. He never missed a propagandistic trick. GW, XIV², 926–927.

the approval of the shareholders. Bleichröder's advice proved useful in the former realm; his intricate market operations proved important in the latter. The Ministry needed a discreet, efficient, and resourceful banker who could carry out its program by buying the requisite number of shares before nationalization. No doubt, Bleichröder found the enterprise profitable. At the very least, he earned huge commissions, and in some instances significant gains were involved as well.

Above all, Bismarck's scheme succeeded: he was determined that the railroads, the sinews of a nation's economy in peace and of its defense in war, should belong to the Prussian state. In 1876 the state owned 4,683 kilometers of track; by 1890 it had bought an additional 14,000 kilometers for more than 2.8 billion marks.[167] There were hardly any private lines left; the state operated a model system, efficient, reliable, and economical. The power of the state was greatly enhanced by running what became the largest enterprise in Prussia, now safely shielded from the threats of would-be strikers. All in all, Bismarck had reason to be satisfied with his success and with Bleichröder's assistance: the nationalization of private enterprise proved a boon to the state and to the erstwhile owners of unprofitable lines.

[v]

For Bismarck, the great shift of 1878–1879 was but a beginning for a new conservative reordering. He envisioned a positive program of social legislation that would reintegrate the lower classes and thus protect the nation from social conflict and partisan strife. The new program needed parliamentary approval, and he hoped that the coalition which had voted the economic reforms would support his other schemes as well.

But the new dispensation proved less stable and less loyal than had the National Liberals in the early 1870s. Bismarck was still without a majority in the Reichstag, and he still had to battle the particularist elements in the upper house. For every legislative act, for every piece of fiscal reform, he needed to shop for support. For a decade he alternately fought and wooed parliament and toyed with its emasculation. He often spoke of the need to alter the electoral law; at moments of anger and frustration, he also thought the Reich might have to be undone, the army unleashed. Sometimes, these threats were functional, as weapons against his opponents; at other times, he was probably serious about a coup d'état. To General von Schweinitz, German ambassador in Russia, he said in 1886: "It could certainly happen that I might have to destroy what I created."[168]

Bismarck liked to think that the national parliament was unrepresentative of the people—an illusion to which autocratic rulers are peculiarly vulnerable. Impotent it might have been, but unrepresentative it was not. The divisions mirrored in parliament were real, though Bismarck himself had deepened them. Tirelessly, he searched for expedients to win new support: by cajoling or humoring the rulers of the other German states, by material favors to some of the aggrieved groups, and always by manipulating the press. In all of these endeavors, Bleichröder played his customary role as counselor and aide.

In the 1880s Bleichröder's role slightly shifted: he had to function more as a lobbyist and a petitioner than as an adviser. His personal tie with Bismarck remained as strong as ever, despite his break with Herbert, described in the next chapter. Bleichröder's relations with Holstein became cool, as did Holstein's with Bismarck. There was a turnover in Bismarck's entourage, and Bleichröder had to make his adjustments. Bismarck's new amanuensis and son-in-law, Count Rantzau, came to be a Bleichröder confidant, and Bismarck's new subordinates, Hatzfeldt at the Foreign Office and Karl von Boetticher at the Ministry of the Interior, were particularly close to Bleichröder. ("God be with you," wrote Boetticher, "and reward you for your friendship, so selfless and so self-sacrificing. . . . Please maintain in the future this friendship which makes me so very happy"—and solvent.)

Bleichröder's own political views were still in conformity with the new orthodoxy of the government. He too was conservative, interventionist, and antisocialist. Indicative of his espousal of state paternalism was a letter he wrote to Herbert in December 1879, pleading for immediate state intervention in Upper Silesia, where unemployment, hunger, and disease had suddenly struck: "Our government, regrettably, shows itself to be rather indifferent to this emergency, and yet it seems to me a political necessity—quite aside from all sentiments of humanity—to take care of such an unfortunate province, in order not to give the Socialists a means to make capital for themselves and their unworthy purposes." He thought millions of marks should be spent to provide jobs and food.[169]

Bleichröder appears to have been untroubled by Bismarck's hostility to parliament; he even participated in the campaign against the left-liberals, despite the fact that they were the only group in German politics to protest the new wave of anti-Semitism which the government promoted and profited from. At the Reichstag election of 1881, for example, Lasker noted that "the reactionaries had placed the Jewish question at the center of their movement in order to lean on religious fanaticism and to bend to their purposes the widespread repugnance against Jews." Julius Bleichröder helped Lasker to organize a special Jewish effort to back liberals with money—Gerson shunned this oppositional effort.[170] He still thought that the government and, above all, "his friend" were the best bulwarks against anti-Semitism. He still saw the world through the perspective of the court Jew.

Another episode tells the same story: in December 1884 a Reichstag majority composed of left-liberals, Centrists, and Socialists rejected Bismarck's request for the funding of a new position in the Foreign Office. The intent had been to register opposition to Bismarck's foreign and, especially, colonial policy. Bismarck was outraged, and a close colleague wrote: "I have never seen the Prince so upset and I am afraid he will draw serious consequences from this. . . . He emphasized repeatedly that he would welcome a *Putsch* by the Socialists, one should allow material for further conflicts to accumulate." Two days later, in a private letter to Bismarck, Bleichröder reported that the recent episodes in the Reichstag have created in leading business circles . . . a great cry of indignation against parliament, i.e., against the leaders of the Progressive party and the Center, and there is unanimity that, if there were a new election now, the Berlin business community would do all in its power to make sure that men like Ludwig Löwe [Berlin deputy for the progressives], Virchow, and their ilk would not be re-elected. The business community of the Reich is so outraged by the ignominy which the fatherland has suffered because of the rejection of the small funds deemed necessary by Your Highness that perhaps the moment has now come when sacrifices would joyously be made.[171]

Bleichröder's letter was a token of the general indignation at parliament's refusal; some business groups even offered Bismarck the necessary funds for the creation of the new post. Bleichröder thought dissolution might be the proper punishment for parliament, while Bismarck preferred tougher responses.

Bismarck's turn to conservatism encompassed his plans for the creation of pseudorepresentative bodies that would weaken the Reichstag and for social legislation that would lure workers from their socialist loyalties. Bismarck had long toyed with the idea of constituting a National Economic Council to advise the government. Bleichröder had proposed such a plan in 1878, as had the Association of Industrialists. In the fall of 1880 Bismarck assumed the Prussian Ministry of Commerce and proposed the creation, by royal fiat, of such a council. In early 1881 it met; in opening its deliberations, Bismarck reminded the members that they had greater competence and more practical experience than did government bureaucrats or parliamentarians. They represented the productive, practical, knowledgeable elements of the population, and they should help the Prussian government to formulate laws in realms they knew best.[172] The antiparliamentary intent of Bismarck's creation was obvious, and hence the Reichstag opposed a similar body for the Empire. Little came of Bismarck's plan, which consciously harked back to earlier corporate institutions—and adumbrated the later role of experts and technocrats in more complex societies.[173]

The first proposal before the Prussian Council was Bismarck's scheme for accident insurance for workers. This marked the beginning of Bismarck's ambitious social legislation, which he had fashioned at the same time as the anti-Socialist law. In true conservative fashion, he hoped simultaneously to repress subversion and remove its causes. "If the worker had no more cause for complaint, then the roots of socialism would be drained off," he remarked at the end of 1878.[174] Bismarck's aim was unambiguously political: in the grim moments of dependency, the lower classes should come to know the state as a source of succor and should not have to rely on indigent family, on indifferent employer, or on a socialist party. St. Vallier recognized the magnitude of Bismarck's program: "[It] is more comprehensive, more audacious, more dangerous than the others; he wants to fight the socialists by borrowing their aims and by making the state the pivot of all workers' organizations."[175]

Bismarck's "state socialism," as he once called his program, came naturally to someone who had always believed that the state had a moral responsibility to take care of its own, and that Christian paternalism demanded that the rich look after the poor.[176] In rural life noblesse oblige remained a still-functioning ideal. But the political motive was equally strong—and lessened the impact of the disinterested considerations.

Like so many later corporatist reformers, Bismarck placed too much faith in a kind of vulgar Marxism or economic determinism. Workers wanted more than bread, more even than security; and that more could best be supplied by their own party, which managed to combine idealistic appeal with deterministic analysis in a decidedly non-Marxian fashion. The Social Democratic party grew, despite Bismarck's efforts at suppression and concession, and his policies have often been adjudged failures. Correctly? Did they not help to mold the revisionist temper of the party and the docility of the workers —and did this temper and docility not greatly benefit Bismarck's Reich? Whether in the long run they were beneficial to Germany's political development is another question.

Though solicitous of the poor and willing to extend the sphere of the government, Bleichröder opposed the plan for accident insurance advanced by a Westphalian industrialist, Louis Baare. In a letter to Bismarck, Bleichröder objected that Baare's proposal covered only accidents that occurred on the job—Bismarck's marginalia denied that. Next, Bleichröder criticized Baare's provision for a pension, whereas what an incapacitated worker really needed was some small capital; Bismarck's marginal comment was: "He runs through that?? [*Das schlägt er todt??*]" Bleichröder admitted that he was offering this unsolicited advice because of his own close ties to a major insurance company, Nordstern, of which he was a director.[177] Bismarck disliked insurance companies, and they in turn feared he would nationalize them. He disregarded Bleichröder's warnings.[178]

In 1885 Bleichröder helped Bismarck's chief forester, Peter Lange, to prepare a detailed memorandum on the existing insurance provisions for agricultural workers on Bismarck's estates. A year later, the accident insurance law was extended to agricultural workers, and in 1889 an old-age plan, designed for workers of all kinds, was passed and completed Bismarck's program.[179] Bismarck's comprehensive social legislation was his greatest achievement of the 1880s and made Germany the undisputed leader in the field.

Bismarck found it difficult to persuade a recalcitrant Reichstag to sanction additional income to cover mounting expenses. At least he now had competent ministerial support: in June 1882 Bitter resigned as finance minister and Bismarck appointed Adolf von Scholz as his successor. Bismarck came to think of Scholz as his first loyal finance minister, and his close ties with Scholz weakened Bleichröder's influence somewhat.[180]

Still, some of Bismarck's pet schemes were repeatedly defeated. Bleichröder was suspected of sabotaging an unearned-income tax proposed for Prussia in 1883; as Holstein noted at the time: "on purely financial questions, particularly those relating to the stock exchange, the chancellor has no fixed opinion of his own, but bases it on the expositions of Scholz and Bleichröder. The two men are hardly ever in agreement, and Prince Bismarck almost invariably sides with Scholz. . . ."[181]

The disagreement between the two men came out forcefully in May 1884 after Scholz introduced legislation for a business and turnover tax.[182] Three days later Bleichröder wrote Bismarck an eight-page letter attacking the new proposal, which had already depressed stock prices by 2 to 10 percent. Bleichröder inveighed against the form of the new tax law even more than against the proposed rate. "The two fundamental pillars of mercantile business that constitute the merchant's pride—honor and discretion—are attacked in the most sensitive way by providing for the permanent submission of the merchant's books. . . ." The projected rate of taxation compounded the prospective disaster. This type of obstruction, Bleichröder said, will force "frightened capital" to seek unshackled markets abroad. Smaller transactions will dry up, and hundreds of families will suffer:

> a certain affluence [*Luxus*] . . . will probably vanish. Whether this is a blessing for our economic conditions I dare not judge. . . . From my forty-six years of practical experience I do know that German metropolises have gradually attracted the business of Europe precisely because of the freedom of movement which we have enjoyed and that the prosperity of our country has greatly benefited from this. . . . Your Highness will forgive this candid declaration of mine; as a result of my many years of experience, which I am always glad to put at the service of the fatherland, I can foresee the consequences of this move.[183]

Bismarck obviously knew that this was not disinterested advice; on the other hand, as a later generation might have put it, what was bad for Bleichröder was likely to be bad for German business altogether. As a matter of fact, the business community set up a public howl, much as Bleichröder had done privately. In June the upper house passed the bill, nevertheless. Bismarck was sufficiently troubled to think that a bad dream he had had—wherein he was traveling along a lake that suddenly became wildly agitated, leaving him with the choice of drowning or retreating—might have been prompted by his proposed stock-market tax.

In May 1885 the Reichstag passed the stock-exchange tax; Bleichröder remained unreconciled and told Bismarck that the tax was driving investments abroad: "Bismarck knows that as well as I do," Bleichröder told Holstein,

> and was equally opposed to the stock-exchange tax, but when the *Kreuzzeitung* and the *Reichsbote* hinted that Prince Bismarck was showing undue deference to the financiers, he deemed it wiser to stop protesting. I said to him: "Your Highness need not say a word. I understand Your Highness; I have the same idea. Sometimes in my dreams I see a second *Reichsglocke* [anti-Semitic paper that had attacked Bismarck's connections with Bleichröder] rising before my eyes."[184]

The threat, then, of anti-Semitic insinuations was strong enough to over-rule other considerations—or so it would seem from Bleichröder's account. It also provided another reason why Bleichröder's influence on fiscal matters declined in the conservative era of the 1880s.

[vi]

But his usefulness in some areas remained great indeed. Bismarck's exasperation with an obstructionist Reichstag led him to put greater reliance on the Bundesrat, the body that represented the government of the member states of the Empire. In the 1870s he had to fight it, too, but in 1879 he remarked that if he had no choice but to "strengthen twenty-five particularist governments or the power of the Reichstag, then he would choose the former."[185] In April 1880 the Bundesrat defeated some minor legislation, and Bismarck promptly offered his resignation.* William spurned it, but Bismarck used the occasion to strengthen his power over the Bundesrat and even toyed with a radical revision of its composition that would have given Prussia a permanent majority in it.[186] In any case, Bismarck sought to forge still closer relations with the other dynasties and on repeated occasions warned them that only the close collaboration of all German governments could stem the subversive tide.[187]

But Bismarck knew that ideological appeals were best supplemented by more tangible services as well, and in this realm Bleichröder proved useful as before. He had himself cultivated close relations with other German governments and dynasties—partly to solicit their business and partly to enhance his own position. Governments, after all, still floated their own loans, and dynasts still gave out decorations.

At certain critical moments in Bismarck's relations with German dynasts, Bleichröder with his discretion and financial fluidity played a vital, if covert, role. At times he acted as transfer agent, often in connection with the Welfenfond; at other times he obliged Bismarck by being particularly accommodating to the wishes of needy rulers.

We have already noted Bleichröder's considerable involvement in the fate of the deposed Hanoverian dynasty. The same constellation of Windthorst, disgruntled Guelphs, British royalty, and, marginally, Bleichröder marked the protracted dispute concerning the succession to the Brunswick throne. A Guelph laid claim to it, Queen Victoria backed her royal relative, but Bismarck was resolved to bar the Guelphs from a throne in Germany as long as they refused to renounce their claim to Hanover, which Prussia had annexed in 1866. In 1881 the Prince of Wales (later Edward VII) asked Bleichröder

---

* Bismarck's threat was taken seriously; one of Bleichröder's friends, General Chauvin, wrote him: "The news of the Chancellor's resignation has shaken me deeply. Let us hope that it will still be possible to retain the irreplaceable one in his position. Who besides him could develop Germany further and maintain the peace of the world? How small these so-called political greats are when compared to this giant." Bleichröder's sentiments were identical. Chauvin to Bleichröder, 9 April 1880, BA. Bleichröder received many such pro-Bismarck effusions; some no doubt were sincere; others probably were sent in the hope that via Bleichröder they would reach the dispenser of favors and positions.

for a memorandum on the Brunswick question which he in turn could give his mother. After consultations with Windthorst, Bleichröder submitted a memorandum and had several conversations with the prince. But nothing came of it, and the matter was not settled until 1913.[188]

Far more important was Bleichröder's connection with the Bavarian dynasty. He continued to pay King Louis the annual subsidy of 300,000 marks from the Welfenfond. But this sum proved much too low for the king's celebrated "building mania, [which] was a symptom of his illness."* Attractive, artistically inclined, mentally unbalanced, Louis sought to emulate Louis XIV's great architectural feats, even as he had an erotic fixation on the mistresses of the last Bourbons while rebuffing all advances from would-be mistresses of his own entourage.

Rumors of Louis's incipient bankruptcy had reached Berlin intermittently since 1876, and Bleichröder was often mentioned as a possible Maecenas— once removed. By early 1884 the king's debts had mounted to over 7 million marks, and his most ambitious schemes were just getting under way.[189] Louis finally had to send an emissary, Regierungsrat Phillip Pfister, to Bismarck to solicit help. On February 9 Pfister arrived in Friedrichsruh, incognito, and found Bismarck ready to help, though by what means remained unclear. Seven million marks was a formidable sum. Bismarck inquired whether William would be willing to bail out his royal cousin, and at the same time he suggested to Pfister that perhaps Bleichröder could raise the necessary funds. Despite William's ambiguous offer of help, Bismarck asked Franz von Rottenburg, a leading member of the chancellery staff, to persuade Bleichröder to come to the rescue. According to Holstein, "Bleichröder, speechless with delight, embraced him [Rottenburg] the moment he revealed his mission." At the same time, Herbert wrote Holstein: "I regret that the Bavarian financial affair has got into Bleichröder's hands because I look on the filthy Jew as an evil in himself and am sorry for anyone who is or will be forced to enter into business relations with him."[190] (Did Herbert really feel sorry for his father?) Holstein and Herbert were certain that Bleichröder coveted the Bavarian assignment; Holstein thought he wanted a Bavarian title or the Grand Cross, and his whole, venomous picture is of a man "always conspicuous for his lack of modesty."[191]

Hence Holstein discounted Bleichröder's remonstrance to Hatzfeldt that he would accept the Bavarian business only in order to please Bismarck. Allegedly Bleichröder even said: "What has the king of Bavaria got that he could give me?" This is almost certainly what Bleichröder said or felt: the days when bankers, even Jewish bankers, had to grovel before royal thrones were gone. Kings could still command preferential treatment but not the suspension of prudence.[192] No banker would jeopardize 7 million marks in order to get one more title or decoration.

Bleichröder proceeded cautiously. On February 10 he negotiated with

---

* For a sympathetic picture of the unfortunate king, see the memoirs of the Bavarian ambassador in Berlin, Hugo Graf Lerchenfeld-Koefering, *Erinnerungen und Denkwürdigkeiten* (Berlin, 1935), pp. 152–175. Lerchenfeld's silence about all financial aid bespeaks his own discretion and the general secrecy that surrounded the subject for many decades.

Pfister in Berlin, and the Bavarian counselor returned to Munich with a million marks in easily negotiable securities from the Berlin government and a promise from Bleichröder to submit a definite proposal.[193] Within a week, Bleichröder made an offer of a 3 million-mark loan, which Louis gratefully acknowledged, but he postponed acceptance until he had heard from a South German consortium that was contemplating a credit of up to 10 million marks.[194] The consortium declined, and in mid-March Pfister returned to Berlin with a plea from Louis to Bismarck to intercede with Bleichröder for a 6 million-mark loan. Bismarck's reply pointed to his own interest in the matter: he promised Louis all his support; if he failed it would not be for "want of effort but [because] of the limits which circumscribe my power and my means." At the same time, he warned the king against renewed liberal agitation in the Bundesrat and clearly hoped to earn Bavarian loyalty in exchange for Bleichröder's financial help.[195]

On April 6 Pfister inquired whether and under what conditions Bleichröder would lend Louis 8 to 10 million marks on the basis of "agnate consent," that is, with the legal co-responsibility of his male relatives. Bleichröder asked for still further assurances, and on April 10 Pfister informed him that the Bavarian finance minister, "recognizing the magnitude of this matter for Crown and Country," had taken over the negotiations hitherto carried on privately for the king. A solution eluded him, too, and Bleichröder was petitioned afresh. Bleichröder's response was unambiguous: "What material bases" or guarantees would such an agnate consent entail? What material security against default would he have?

> That the modest interest rate and provision envisioned by you contains nothing attractive at a moment when first-rate negotiable Russian securities with chances of appreciation offer 5½ to 6 percent interest, you will easily understand, and hence you will believe me that my readiness to conclude the arrangement which you propose rests almost entirely on my desire to be accommodating to His Majesty, your King.[196]

After months of negotiations, the Bavarian finance minister finally concluded an agreement with a South German consortium for 7,500,000 marks. Pfister thanked Bleichröder most warmly.[197] Pfister's letters give the lie to Holstein's accusation that Bleichröder had made unbearable demands, thus arousing the king's anger. For Holstein—and for others—Bleichröder could do no right: he was both sycophant and Shylock.

Holstein was malevolently wrong in saying that Bleichröder sought the loan business at all costs. Four months of negotiations, followed by failure, hardly sustain the picture of the desperately anxious banker. He was willing to help—under proper conditions. Bismarck wished to help Louis—and apparently preferred to do so through his own banker rather than through his monarch—in order to put Louis under renewed obligation to follow his lead in German politics. In the end the Bavarians managed to help themselves—for a short time. The story ends on a bizarre note. Two years later, a new and more desperate need arose, and the king, close to madness, charged agents of his to break into the Rothschild Bank in Frankfurt. The men traveled to Frankfurt but preferred to return without discharging the unusual royal order.

Bleichröder was a ubiquitous presence in the politics of the Second Empire. In Bismarck's shadow, he became adviser and lobbyist, confidant, king-maker, and financial utility man; at a later time, pressure groups, government commissions, or agencies would handle such business. In the final phases of politics by notables, Bleichröder sought to play a major role, and succeeded in doing so. His own harvest was fame and abuse in about equal measure, but prevailing hypocrisy and his own self-protective vanity made him more conscious of the public glory than the private indignities.

CHAPTER 10

Greed and Intrigue

Why, there's no remedy; 'tis the curse of service.
Preferment goes by letter and affection,
And not by old gradation, where each second
Stood heir to the first.

—Iago (*Othello*, I, 1)

Hypocrisy is the tribute that vice pays to virtue.

—La Rochefoucauld

I have always seen that rectitude is the raw material of which hypocrisy
is made!

—Balzac, *Cousine Bette*

Bleichröder lived in the dignified world of imperial Germany—
amidst the splendor of nobility and the awesomeness of power.
He also lived in the subterranean part of that world—a world whose existence
the rulers of society scarcely acknowledged, but one in which their fortunes
and their careers were nevertheless made and unmade. Bleichröder knew that
these two worlds were continuous, that many people who lived in the sun-
light of acclaim needed him for the shadier side of life.

In all societies, in all human affairs, there is a gap between appearance
and reality, between a prevailing code and actual conduct. Perhaps in imperial
Germany the gap was extraordinarily large, partly because the code was
especially strict and at ever greater variance with the material facts of
existence. The code was aristocratic; the reality was the rise of new money.
The code prescribed honor, courage, rectitude, and duty; it prescribed
austerity, a certain "iron frugality," or the affectation thereof; it condemned
the marketplace, the excessive regard for money, the notion that money could
buy everything, even distinction.[1] (This of course is a particular version of an
old European code, of which Lionel Trilling has said: "What is in accord with
this ethos is noble; what falls short of it or derogates from it is base. . . .
We might observe that the traits once thought appropriate to the military life
are definitive in the formation of the noble self. It stands before the world
boldly defined, its purposes clearly conceived and openly avowed.")[2] Financial or sexual irresponsibility was deemed incompatible with this code. The

visible violation of the code constituted a "scandal," and in extreme cases could be expiated only by exile or by a duel; the latter served as a reminder that honor was thought more precious than life. Every scandal was a potential blot on caste and code.

Codes have ever been violated—in stealth. Perhaps in Imperial Germany the rhetoric of rectitude was stricter and more strident than elsewhere and the denial of reality more pervasive. The very rectitude bred hypocrisy, and hypocrisy brought with it a false and bitter tone. There was the invocation of highmindedness and the whisper of malice; there was, as we will see, a suspicion of widespread intrigue and cupidity. This subterranean spirit had many sources: there *was* corruption and the temptation of new wealth; there was as well the misanthropic fallout from an illiberal, authoritarian regime that was itself fearful. The sway of sentimentality was a residue of noble apirations corroded by fear.

For our purposes, the perception of money is central. In Germany, as elsewhere, the howl against it was universal. "Materialism" was evil, and denounced by the churches; it was also repulsive, and denounced by moralists. It was exploitative, and as such a threat to the unity of the nation. Money had also become the battleground of competing classes. Threatened by the parvenus of the new system, the old agrarian classes reasserted their prejudice against money-grubbing—at the very time when economic realities forced them to reckon with the marketplace. Their code legitimized their continued moral hegemony, but increasingly they had to violate it in order to protect their own. By 1895 Max Weber spoke of "the economic death struggle of the old Prussian Junkerdom."[3] It was impossible to ignore the facts of life: the servants of the state were paid in Prussian austerity and had to live amidst German plutocracy.* The newly rich bought the old manorial estates.[4] As one fictional Junker put it at the end of the century, when reminded of the joys of living on ancestral soil: "Who knows, in the next generation, the Jew may already have it."† With threats like these, the Junker learned to battle for their own with a desperate tenacity, all the while insisting that they remained

---

* In 1894 Theodor Fontane observed: "The civil servant sinks ever lower through no fault of his. A hundred years ago and even up to fifty years ago, he was in a superior situation through his office and education, and in his financial condition, modest though it was, he did not lag behind; now he is surpassed tenfold in point of money and consequently in all other aspects. Because—a few shining exceptions notwithstanding—property is decisive in all questions of education as well." *Briefe an seine Familie* (Berlin, 1924), II, 302.

† Money is the theme of this novel about a noble Prussian family in the 1870s and 1880s. An army major exclaims: "Damned money! Always money!" And the head of the family, a retired cabinet minister, replies: "Less the innocent metal than the sinful people." The black sheep of the family who has gone into business once explains to his aristocratic brother that his children should have "what beats everything else today, what replaces the weapon of past epochs, what subjugates everything, what opens all doors—money. . . . The sword has become useless, our battles today are fought on the stock market, in trade, commerce, industry." To the reply that the German nobility must not aim at becoming stock jobbers, the aristocratic businessman warns: "Nobility does not have to become stock jobber, but it can overcome indolence, can adapt itself to changes brought about by time, in short it can enter productive callings, otherwise it will go to ruin." Georg Freiherrn von Ompteda, *Eysen: Deutscher Adel um 1900*, I (Berlin, 1902), 38, 42, 364–366.

the sole guardians of simple, rustic virtue. Anti-materialism will always have a strong appeal, not least to the propertied themselves, but the desire to excise money from public discourse was probably also a means of blunting the grievances of the propertyless and exploited. The rich and the poor, said Anatole France, have an equal right to sleep under the bridge—and an equal obligation not to talk money.

The whole tone of German society depended on this saving of appearances, on refinement—on what Germans called *"der gute Ton"* and *"Dekorum wahren."* Decorum demanded that much of real life had to be banished below stairs.* Education had to be censored so that the crude realities of life could be excised. ("I remember that my [parents] instructed my tutor not to use any arithmetic examples in the textbook in which money or profit was mentioned; such examples were actually crossed out by their own hands.")[5] Conversation had to be banal and uplifting—and doubly so when ladies were present. Money was always considered an affront to sensibilities, especially to the sensibilities of ladies and of the young. (Again, this was a variation on a European trait. As Dickens put it: "The question about everything was, would it bring a blush into the cheek of the young person?")[6] Base or bourgeois people talked about money and the means of making it; cultured people or nobles talked of harvests and full barns, but not of stocks and bonds. One spoke of money, if the subject was unavoidable, with embarrassed pain. In *Buddenbrooks*, Thomas Mann called this affectation "pious greediness."[7]†

Life in imperial Germany was expurgated. The existence of monetary or erotic passions was acknowledged in cryptic phrases, raised eyebrows, gestures or double entendre. An open avowal of any kind of lust would have altered the very nature of that society and its notions of civilization. In imperial society, in art and literature, in everyday, upper-class life, a kind of systematic sentimentalizing of reality took place; Fontane once complained

---

* Consider as but one example an exchange, which I found in the archives, between the head of the Prussian archives, Heinrich von Sybel, and Bismarck. Sybel wrote Bismarck on behalf of a young historian, Max Lehmann, who had found in widely scattered parts of the archive some twenty letters from Field Marshal Blücher which he wanted to publish. Sybel acknowledged that they contained some harsh expressions but no facts that had not been known: "A not very happy correspondence between Blücher and Hardenberg [head of the Prussian government at the time] concerning the shattered finances of the former was at once excluded by Dr. Lehmann." Money was automatically excluded. Bismarck objected to the publications, nevertheless—and the letters remained unpublished. Sybel to Bismarck, 4 and 10 Nov. 1876, GFO: I.A.A.a. 50, Vol. II.

† Or consider Fontane's Jenny Treibel who protests *ad nauseam*: "everything is worthless [*nichtig*]; but the most worthless thing is what all the world so greedily presses for: tangible possessions, property, gold . . . I for one stick to the ideal and will never renounce it." Her old suitor, whom she had abandoned for a man of means saw through the pretense: "She is a dangerous person and the more dangerous because she does not know it herself and sincerely imagines she has a tender heart, and above all a heart 'for the higher things.' But she has a heart only for the tangible, for everything that is substantial and bears interest. . . . They all constantly liberalize and sentimentalize, but that is all farce: when the time comes for showing one's true colors, then the motto is: Gold is trump and nothing else." Theodor Fontane, *Frau Jenny Treibel* (Berlin, 1905), pp. 32 and 96.

of this "beautifying forever," this *Verniedlichung*.[8] It is an odd fact of German life that the greatest exposers of this false sentimentality were Jews: Heine, Marx, and Freud.* And yet it would be simple-minded not to sense the connections between the achievements and aspirations of that society and the denials, even the merely verbal denials, of its appetites.

No one in imperial Germany knew more about the vulnerability of people than did Bleichröder. He was forever being importuned for help, advice, financial salvation. He served the vanities and ambitions of the system. He was a convenience for the needs of the elite and an embarrassment to its values. Above all, in its endless dealings with him, the elite had to be honest: to deceive a banker is as self-defeating as to deceive an analyst. Both are paid to deal with reality.

This peculiar position of Bleichröder as the agent that mediated between reality and appearance held true not only in the field of finance but in the very precise and circumscribed field of politics. Here, too, there was a code of conduct: it abhorred intrigue, corruption, venality, place-hunting. The Bismarck legend of the day disguised the Bismarck reality—which Bleichröder knew so well. The legend suggested rule by a benign genius according to the unwritten rules of rectitude and merit; to describe the reality, contemporaries, both German and foreign, often spoke of the corroding Byzantinism of Bismarck's rule.[9]

Bleichröder was privy to the secrets of the Empire; he participated in and profited from them. In a society less anxious to save the appearances, he could have carried on most of his work in the open; the secretiveness of the Empire made him appear even more "meddlesome" and sinister than he was. In the Byzantine atmosphere of Bismarck's Reich, he was seen and vilified as a mysterious wirepuller, as the evil demon behind thrones and policies. He was sufficiently of his time to abet the rumors of his great importance. Throughout it all, he was shielded by Bismarck, who trusted him and at whose bidding he did his least savory deeds.

Bleichröder's major tie was with Bismarck; everything else followed from that link. But other functionaries of the Reich needed him, just as he needed them. Through their eyes—as well as through his own—he must have sensed something of the "curse of service" under which Bismarck's creatures labored.

---

* The most apt example comes from *Civilization and Its Discontents*, in which Freud wrote: "A great poet may permit himself, at least in jest, to give utterance to psychological truths that are heavily censured. Thus Heine: 'Mine is the most peaceable disposition. My wishes are a humble dwelling with a thatched roof, but a good bed, good food, milk and butter of the freshest, flowers at my windows, some fine tall trees before my door; and if the good God wants to make me completely happy, he will grant me the joy of seeing some six or seven of my enemies hanging from these trees. With my heart full of deep emotion I shall forgive them before they die all the wrong they did me in their lifetime—true, one must forgive one's enemies, but not until they are brought to execution.' " Sigmund Freud, *Civilization and Its Discontents*, 4th impression (London, 1949), p. 84.

Bismarck was an exacting, moody, potentially misanthropic master. He was hard on himself and harder still on others. Governing had become a frustrating and endlessly complicated business; obstruction, rivalry, intrigue everywhere—or so he thought. In the seventies his health was wretched, and his exasperation as ruler sharpened the pains and afflictions of his body, which heightened his anger, which affected his political style. It was an endless story of mutually reinforcing complaints. Only a very strong man could have survived the toll. A close associate thought him "a bound Prometheus." To the same man he confided that "his was really a dreamy, sentimental nature."[10] The dominant note of the decade was suffering compounded by self-pity, with the robust and ebullient spirit of the past breaking through occasionally. He was irrepressible enough not to succumb to his own weaknesses. He kept alive the many facets of his character. Perhaps his shifting moods and roles kept him from being bored with himself.

He had few friends and no equals; the world treated him as a superior being, and this not only by virtue of his genius but by reason of his self-created role as sole authority in the new Reich, subordinate only to the monarch and even that more in theory than in practice. As he wrote to Roon on the latter's retirement in 1873 and repeated in almost identical words time and again: "It will be lonely in my office—more so as time goes on; old friends die or become enemies, and one does not acquire new ones anymore."[11] That prophecy, too, had a self-fulfilling quality. Convinced that most friends were potential rivals or enemies, he treated them according to their alternate roles—and compounded his loneliness. As an admirer put it, in true Germanic fashion: "Fate struck him with the olympian loneliness of the genius."[12]

Many of his Junker friends turned against him. Some had already done so in 1866, when they watched incredulously as Bismarck played the revolutionary adventurer at home and abroad. The liberal era of the new Reich, marked by so-called Manchesterism and ensuing corruption, by the Kulturkampf, by administrative reforms at Junker expense, angered many more conservatives. Bismarck's collaboration with Jews and liberals confirmed their sense that he had become a traitor to his class and principles. Bismarck, on the other hand, could never forgive *their* treason. He was certain that "he would never get over the loss of his old political friends, the old-conservative Junker."[13]

His continued struggle with the court and with his archenemy, Empress Augusta, was equally galling. Behind every difference with William, he suspected Augusta's intrigues; it was widely known that she cultivated close contacts with his political opponents, but she could do little more than occasionally warn her husband against Bismarck's schemes. Still, he was plagued, especially in the 1870s, by obsessive thoughts about "the conspiracy of petticoats [*Weiber*] at the top."[14] Even in the 1880s, when he seemed less worried about Augusta's near-treasonous activities, his morbid suspicions of the court and of the crown prince never left him. In the 1870s he had but one friend at court, Count Heinrich Lehndorff, and in the rest of

Berlin society Bismarck's friends "could be counted on the fingers of one hand."[15]

Bismarck's loneliness, real and imagined, worsened his misanthropic treatment of subordinates, although intermittently he could still charm and captivate them. Some of his subordinates may have exaggerated the slights received in order to justify their own self-pity. Still, the evidence of hardship is incontrovertible. As early as 1868, a critic of Bismarck, Franz von Roggenbach, wrote of the "widespread dissolution" brought about because "all established order is replaced by the morose arbitrariness of a single man and . . . gradually all instruments begin to break down because he had deadened them by misuse and coercion."[16] Five years later, an admirer complained: "Bismarck is unfortunately often clinically irritable, and even if he often has to suffer from the indolence and inadequacy of his colleagues as well as from court intrigues—still to work with him is also difficult enough."[17] Years later, Holstein, admittedly a protégé turned sour, wrote in his diary:

It is a pity the Chief's mistrust—he calls it pessimism—grows steadily greater. . . . suspicion, boredom, neglect, are the acids which would corrode any attachment between him and other people. . . . He kills his pleasure in other people by analysis and suspicion, by feeling annoyed when they contradict him and by wearying of them. His relations with men must be judged by the principle that governs the sentimental liaison: the newer the better.

In 1885 Holstein lamented that Bismarck treated people "not as friends, just as tools, like knives and forks which are changed after each course."[18] Even the loyal Bleichröder once complained to Hohenlohe that Bismarck "has no consideration and squeezes people like a lemon."[19] Certainly Bismarck contributed to the harsh undertone of German society: his own contemptuous distrust of others, his often intolerant authoritarianism, injected a special kind of poison into Germany's public life.

With age, success, and no restraining political tradition, Bismarck grew capricious and contemptuous. No wonder Count Paul Hatzfeldt once complained to Bleichröder that the chancellor always appointed nonentities to important posts.[20] It was perhaps harder to be his friend than his enemy.

Bismarck's entourage was not the happy little band of devoted assistants that has sometimes been depicted. There were jealousies and animosities galore; there was fear and anger, the more rankling for having to be concealed. There was an excessive burden of work because Bismarck had concentrated so much work in his hands; in the Reich, he had not even titular colleagues. He spent months on end away from Berlin, and the members of his staff, whether with him in Varzin, Friedrichsruh, or in some spa, or without him in Berlin, were overworked auxiliaries.[21]

To belong to Bismarck's entourage, then, was a painful privilege. In the early years of the Empire, amidst various storms and scandals, there was the added danger that the Bismarck rule might not last long, that Bismarck might soon be overthrown or resign.[22] In the 1880s, on the other hand, it appeared as if the Bismarck rule would be perpetuated in a Bismarck Dynasty, that there would be no end of Bismarcks. Neither prospect lent a sense of security to subordinates.

Nor did it help that the Bismarck entourage consisted of family as well as outsiders. His preferred aide, of course, was his adored Herbert, his eldest son, born in 1859. In political matters, Herbert came to be closest to Bismarck. The younger son, Bill, also served as amanuensis; after the marriage of Bismarck's daughter to a rather nondescript civil servant, Count Kuno von Rantzau, he too was pressed into service. In fact, Rantzau was chained to the Bismarck household so that the parents could enjoy the company of their only daughter. Rantzau's correspondence, which included a regular exchange with his friend Bleichröder, was important because his letters usually were dictated verbatim by Bismarck.[23] Bismarck's family, in turn, had to collaborate with his other aides, among them Count Hatzfeldt and Friedrich von Holstein. These two were able diplomats and hence were especially close to Bismarck's principal passion, but both also served for short periods as personal aides. When Keudell ceased being a member of the inner circle, Holstein gloated over his departure and its allegedly disastrous consequences for Bleichröder.[24] There was also a succession of regular assistants: Lothar Bucher, Hermann von Thile, Franz von Rottenburg, and Christoph von Tiedemann.

Bleichröder was perforce involved with all of them. At one time or another each of them corresponded with him at Bismarck's behest. They all knew how close Bleichröder was to Bismarck, and some may even have exaggerated the intimacy. In 1884 Holstein wrote in his diary, "Apart from Bleichröder, Herbert is the only influence that counts."[25] The exaggeration attests the grievance: many of Bismarck's men were bitterly jealous of the Jew who was—almost—in their midst. Any confidant would have been suspected; a Jew—innately sinister—was worse.

Oftentimes they needed him. As long as Bismarck used his services and protected him, they could not openly abuse or snub him. But among themselves they could rant against him and indulge their ill temper and boorish tongues. They feared his influence and suspected him of vile intrigues. (Rottenburg, for example, feared that Bleichröder could ruin his career as Bismarck's chief secretary; as a consequence he courted and detested him and told Holstein: "Bleichröder is a first-rate gravedigger.")[26] Behind his back they called him "filthy Jew" and "Jewish swine," and behind each other's back they wrote to him as "esteemed friend." And how often did Bleichröder's correspondents implore him to keep their letters confidential, indeed to conceal the fact that a correspondence existed! Furtive letters because one was ashamed to be openly associated with this—alas, indispensable —man. It seems likely that Bleichröder was largely oblivious of the hypocrisy, the concealed meanness with which people were using him.

Relations between some members of the inner circle and Bleichröder deteriorated as the years went on. The most spectacular—and in a sense, most honest—break came later with Herbert. Mostly strains grew worse, as Holstein in particular suspected Bleichröder of carrying on conspiracies, of influence peddling, and of illicit profiteering—sins that Holstein was suspected of, probably with more justification. Bleichröder was often the victim of projective indignation. As Holstein spread venom against Bleichröder, he was projecting on Bleichröder some of the less savory practices and characteristics of himself and his circle.

If Bleichröder was so objectionable, why could he not he ignored, why did he have to be courted in secret and vilified in semipublic fashion? Bismarck's protection was but a partial answer. He was enormously useful to Bismarck's subordinates, most of whom lived beyond their means. German aristocrats had a preeminent position in government, and the foreign service was virtually their private domain. But salaries were low and private wealth was rare, while the style of life had become more cosmopolitan and luxurious.* Unlike their British cousins, these aristocrats had mastered neither the art of marrying wealth nor the technique of making it. Their noble impecuniosity troubled their roles as representatives of the Reich. No wonder that one diplomat remembered his beginnings in the diplomatic service in the 1870s as being full of tensions and animosities and anti-Semitic attitudes. The old nobility looked down on their affluent successors among the newly titled: "The poorer he is, the harsher his negative position; then he has nothing but his old escutcheon left as the remnant of former glory."[27] To be socially prominent was expensive—and became more so all the time.[28]

Bleichröder was needed then, and at times he advertised his spectacular usefulness. It is an instructive coincidence that the recently published private correspondence of Herbert von Bismarck opens with a letter of 1872 from Fritz Holstein to his friend Herbert, inveighing against Bleichröder's alleged habit of opening fictitious accounts for people of influence. Holstein explained that Bleichröder had assured him that under proper supervision capital deposited with him should double every year. Holstein assumed that the offer meant: "Every year he would add as much, as long as I can be useful to him."[29] In the next letter, he struck a noble pose: "I want to be rid of that Jew money at last."[30] It is inconceivable that Bleichröder promised anything like Holstein alleged. Herbert certainly knew that Bleichröder's favorite client did not fare this well. Could Holstein—out of a mélange of bad motives—have misconstrued some enticing remark of Bleichröder's? Did he want to plant suspicions in Bismarck's mind—suspicions that Bleichröder was shortchanging him or that Bleichröder would use any unsavory

---

* German ambassadors abroad received higher salaries than officials at home, but their expenses were far greater. The highest-paid post was in St. Petersburg, where in 1872 the ambassador received 40,000 taler. German ambassadors were always paid less than their English, French, Russian, and Austrian counterparts. But British diplomats suffered likewise: "Few men could have lived on the salaries they were paid. . . ." Harold Nicolson claims that in 1919, after ten years, his actual salary after tax deduction was £89 annually. Zara S. Steiner, *The Foreign Office and Foreign Policy, 1898–1914* (Cambridge, 1969), pp. 174–175; Rudolf Morsey, *Die oberste Reichsverwaltung unter Bismarck, 1867–1890* (Münster, 1957), p. 113.

means to penetrate Bismarck's circle? Or did Holstein perhaps *wish* to believe that some such Jewish magic existed?

Most needy contemporaries exaggerated Bleichröder's potential for amassing wealth. After the revelations of the *Gründerzeit*, it was widely held that Bismarck had drawn huge benefits from Bleichröder's manipulations. Even a public trial did not fully stop these allegations. By the mid-seventies, Bleichröder was widely charged with sinister maneuvering for the sake of greater profit, influence, and eminence.

The early years of the Empire were riddled with crisis and scandal. Whiffs of intrigue and corruption drifted from and about the highest places. No single event so rocked Berlin society as the Arnim affair, which after years of rumors about malfeasance and insubordination and months of publicized inquiries and trials ended with the utter ruin of Count Harry von Arnim, a prominent German diplomat. The affair was rich in drama and involved a threat to Bismarck's authority and to his relations with William; it was partly played out in the underworld of the Fourth Estate, with paid newspapermen doubling occasionally as amateur spies and newspapers publishing confidential documents. Finally, it featured financial irregularities, as Arnim was suspected of conducting diplomatic maneuvers in order to suit his stock-market speculation (which, it was charged, he did jointly with the French foreign minister, the Duc Decazes). Behind the scenes of this drama, Bleichröder played an important though not very edifying role, calculated to inflame prejudices against Arnim.

Harry von Arnim, nine years younger than Bismarck and like him of old Prussian nobility, had been Prussia's representative at the Holy See from 1864 to 1871, during one of the most dramatic periods in the history of the modern papacy.[31] Arnim delighted at being at the center of things and for the same reason rejoiced at his appointment as one of Germany's two principal negotiators in Brussels to hammer out the final peace treaty with the defeated French. In all his assignments, Arnim tried to steer an independent course, to the detriment of colleagues and the anger of superiors. By all accounts, he was a charmer and enjoyed excellent relations with the Emperor and with Augusta's circle. His competence and ambition brought him the post as Germany's first ambassador to defeated France. Bismarck had grudgingly made the appointment, afraid that Arnim would prove "frivolous and unscrupulous" and—worst of all—defiantly independent.[32] Bismarck's fears proved justified and inspired his own actions, which enraged Arnim. Here were two men in unequal positions, convinced of each other's enmity and error, against a background of mounting political intrigue, launched on a collision course. Bystanders fed suspicions, and the principals exacerbated every possible issue.

To begin with, Bismarck suspected Arnim of delaying negotiations with Thiers concerning the final payment of the indemnity in order to indulge his own financial speculations.[33] Bismarck was the more willing to believe Arnim culpable because he remembered him as a spendthrift and greedy youth.[34] He punished Arnim by removing the negotiations from his control.

There were substantive disagreements as well. Bismarck (and Bleichröder) supported Thiers, assuming that he could ensure sufficient internal stability to make France meet its obligations under the peace treaty and hoping that a republican form of government would isolate France diplomatically. Arnim believed Thiers and the republic to be doomed and in his reports to William openly argued that German interests and the social peace of Europe would best be served by a return to monarchical rule. Nor did he change his tune when events had proved him wrong. "His fears had been exaggerated, his prophecies had been false, his prejudices exposed. But he did not recant; he admitted neither faults nor mistakes."[35]

Worse, Arnim always thought himself the king's envoy and bridled at Bismarck's control of foreign policy. Bismarck, on the other hand, saw in Arnim's independence the sure signs of insubordination and disloyalty and thought that his personal authority and the institutional order of the Reich were at stake. He took Arnim's position as a personal challenge—and thus made certain that it became one. By the fall and winter of 1872, chancellor and ambassador were already embattled.

Enter Bleichröder, who for some time had nurtured his own personal resentment against Arnim. Bleichröder was desperately anxious to play the leading role in all aspects of the French indemnity payment. Arnim obstructed Bleichröder's efforts, and in July 1872 called Hansemann to Paris for the express purpose of dealing with the French government concerning payment of the last billion of the 5 billion indemnity. Bleichröder complained to Bismarck: "Since I was sufficiently aware under what auspices Hansemann went to Paris, I preferred for the time being not to concern myself with the whole financial question in Paris."* Less than a week later, Bleichröder wrote Bismarck another personal letter—from Paris. He had wanted to form his own judgment on the spot: "The terrain is being sufficiently worked over by H. von Arnim's friends, Haber, Henckel, Hansemann, to make the trip from a financial point of view unrewarding," but at least he saw Thiers repeatedly and thus could gather his personal impressions of French affairs. Bleichröder reported that Thiers, attacked as being subservient to Germany, needed to be strengthened, because any successor to him would be worse. Politics aside, Thiers, after all, was a man Bleichröder was reasonably close to. With appropriate flourishes—and a somewhat embarrassing reminder of "their" days in Versailles—Bleichröder ended a letter that manifested clearly enough *his* displeasure at Arnim's views and policies.[36] From then on, Bismarck and Bleichröder had their independent and complementary quarrels with Arnim.

Both men were concerned to have Arnim closely watched. Bismarck's entourage received candid reports from Holstein, Arnim's disaffected secretary, and in 1872 Bismarck sent Rudolf Lindau to the embassy in Paris as a kind of press attaché to counteract prevailing anti-Thiers sentiments and,

---

* Bismarck scribbled on Bleichröder's letter "H. Arnim!"—as obviously being the part that most concerned him. Bleichröder to Bismarck, 4 July 1872, FA.

allegedly, to keep an eye on Arnim. The forty-three-year-old Lindau (a descendant from an originally Jewish family) was a seasoned writer and worldwide traveler; in earlier years he had edited the English newspaper of Yokohama, Japan. Bismarck was to be so impressed by his understanding of French politics and of the French press that in 1879 he appointed him as head of the press bureau in the Foreign Office.[37]

Bleichröder did no less: in the winter of 1872 he placed Emil Landsberg, a German-Jewish journalist in Paris, on the payroll of the Wolff Telegraph Bureau. In October 1873 Bleichröder first praised Landsberg to Bismarck as "my correspondent who for years has informed me with proven objectivity and whose reports, based on years of experience in Paris, distinguish and commend themselves by their true German loyalty."[38]

Landsberg sent these reports in the expectation that Bleichröder would include him in some of his lucrative ventures. Landsberg frequently reminded Bleichröder not to forget him, averring that of course he would take his losses, if such should occur. "I do not believe that the House of S. Bleichröder would ruin me through rash operations." The first investments went badly, and Landsberg had to warn Bleichröder not to credit him with any "false profit." But if he wanted to let him participate in another fling, "I will set no limits to your well-tested kindness." Bleichröder did apparently invest fictitious funds for Landsberg. For years, he begged Bleichröder to include him in his financial operations, to recommend him, as he put it in the last letter we have from him, "to the goddess of the stock market [*Börsengöttin*], whose high favor you enjoy."[39]

Landsberg sent Bleichröder detailed reports but only about things "the authenticity of which I can vouch for." He knew how to protect his sources and himself and repeatedly reminded Bleichröder that no one in Paris knew— or should know—of their private correspondence.[40] He submitted a running commentary on French events, decrying the popular notion that a monarchical restoration would be desirable. He warned Bleichröder not to believe the Orleanist Rothschilds in their prediction of a restoration. Actually we now know that they, too, had decided that the conservative republic would be the least divisive government for France.[41]

Landsberg had exceptionally close relations with Arnim, though he never neglected to talk to Arnim's underlings, including Holstein.[42] In time, Arnim would have reason to regret his intimacy with someone who gradually became a kind of double agent.

At first, Landsberg merely kept Bleichröder apprised of Arnim's activities. In October 1873 he alerted Bleichröder to the fact that the ambassador considered him "one of his most embittered enemies." It was this letter, which also contained a full survey of French affairs, that Bleichröder first sent privately to Bismarck. Thereafter Landsberg's letters—with or without his signature—were often sent to the chancellor.[43] Bleichröder undoubtedly deserved the epithet, having his own reasons for hating Arnim, even before he heard of Arnim's intimacy with rival Jewish bankers. In fact, Arnim could not divine how great Bleichröder's enmity was or how far it would go.

In an undated letter, almost certainly from the winter of 1873–1874, Landsberg confirmed Bismarck's principal suspicion: he reported that Arnim still thought that Bismarck would have to retire in a few months and that either Manteuffel or Arnim would take his place. Obviously Arnim wished to hasten Bismarck's demise—on the principle, as Bismarck put it in his memoirs, *ôte-toi, que je m'y mette.*[44] (A few months earlier, the British ambassador in Berlin had noted that Arnim was "ready for any amount of intrigue to further his plan of succeeding Bismarck as German chancellor.")[45] Just before Bismarck finally persuaded William that Arnim would have to go, Landsberg reported that the French government was puzzled by Arnim's isolation and ineffectuality.[46]

By the end of February 1874, William agreed that Arnim should be recalled and given the less important post at Constantinople. Arnim balked at the demotion, and the battle between Arnim and Bismarck was joined: "A deficient David fought a brilliant Goliath—and lost."[47]

Landsberg now regularly reported on Arnim, for whom "as a person" he felt some sympathy.[48] Arnim was most reluctant to go to Constantinople— despite the constant and presumably selfish urging of his financial brethren, Erlanger, Bamberger, and Baron Hirsch, who insisted that with their help he could recoup in Turkey financially what he had lost in Paris politically. Hirsch, of course, was deeply involved in the building of Turkish railways and would have welcomed Arnim's assistance there. But Arnim's eyes were on the Spree, not the Bosporus, and he was planning at most for a short stay in Constantinople. Worse, Arnim let it be known that he could mobilize public opinion against Bismarck: "It seems that he possesses documents, especially from his time in Rome, of which he is very proud and in which he had sketched out for the chancellor a whole strategy against the Catholics."[49]

Landsberg had warned Berlin, and on April 2 a Vienna paper, *Die Presse*, published some of Arnim's dispatches from the time of the Vatican Council, designed to contrast Arnim's farsightedness with the chancellor's myopia. Arnim denied any responsibility for the publication of these "Diplomatic Revelations." Bismarck's response, however, was predictably swift; he demanded that the king authorize Arnim's immediate retirement from the service. He now needed as much information on Arnim as he could get, and Landsberg proved indispensable. A month before the "Diplomatic Revelations" shocked Europe, Bleichröder had sent Bismarck one of Landsberg's reports, identifying him: "The author is a reporter recently appointed by our Telegraph Bureau. If Your Excellency should need special information, I should be happy to arrange for this." He also begged Bismarck to destroy the report—which for once Bismarck seems to have done.[50] Bismarck accepted the offer, and Landsberg was so informed. He was flattered and troubled by this new prominence. He stopped signing his name and wrote: "As you can see, I now prepare my letters in such a way that you can make any desired use of them." But in a confidential enclosure, he begged Bleichröder to be prudent, not to make a habit of handing his letters over, and not to reveal their origin. "I have the greatest admiration for Bismarck but by no means the ambition to be noticed by him or to enter his services. . . . Totally hateful would be the idea of indirectly engaging in police duties. . . . *My* Bismarck is *you*, and I only wish to be useful to you. If I can serve the fatherland at the same time, all the better; but incognito, *s'il vous plaît*."[51] A little later, he implored Bleichröder not to let Bismarck have his letters: "When two such prominent people as A. and B. have a falling out, it is best for the likes of us to remain at a respectful distance." What would happen, Landsberg warned, if the two were reconciled and Bismarck showed Arnim Landsberg's letters?[52] Bleichröder was less prudent, but knew that Bismarck could never be reconciled.

Landsberg's subsequent letters suggest that he intuited what Bismarck wanted to know or was replying to specific questions from Bleichröder. He warned that Arnim was becoming ever more desperate and was preparing an appearance in Berlin in order "to dare one last charge" at the court. Bismarck's downfall was his goal.[53]

After Arnim had needlessly escalated the controversy concerning the earlier *Presse* revelations, Landsberg was convinced of the count's "bottomless unreliability, self-importance, and scheming nature." He was now lost, but might fall back on an earlier plan to found a major newspaper in Berlin, with the help of Hansemann or Henckel von Donnersmarck. But these men would hesitate to spawn a paper whose only banner now would be "Mort à Bismarck." Landsberg also insisted that Arnim's relations with the French foreign minister, the Duc Decazes, had been at the extreme border of permissible intimacy. Never before had Landsberg written so venomously about Arnim.

That letter, duly copied and without signature, was the first extant communication which Bleichröder ever sent to Herbert von Bismarck.[54] Landsberg was instantaneously asked for details about Arnim's allegedly illicit relations with Decazes. His reply hinted at shared financial interests: "The two saw each other much more frequently than official business demanded; in the Turkish [Sadiok-Pascha] and in the Lesseps affairs, Decazes sent almost hourly bulletins to his friend, who then conferred again with Erlanger, Hirsch, etc.—was that in the line of duty?" All of this seemed related to market speculations, "but it is impossible to prove it."[55] Again, this confirmed Bismarck's earlier suspicions about Arnim's financial conniving, which he had already communicated to William; a few months later, Bismarck repeated the story without a trace of doubt and said to a friend, "Arnim had worked the market together with Decazes through the Hirsch Bank."[56]

Bismarck and Bleichröder kept asking for definite information about the authorship of the "Diplomatic Revelations." Landsberg was evasive, saying that people in Paris suspected various journalists, himself included, ". . . but were I to be publicly so identified, I would not tarry with a denial."[57] Pressed again, he refused to divulge whatever more he might know. "This indeed is in the interest of my relations with you: only somebody who knows how to keep silent at the right time picks up good information. After some reflection you will have to agree with me and won't reopen this subject."[58]

During the summer of 1874 Landsberg visited Bleichröder in Bad Homburg, and Bismarck was at once informed of the gist of their conversation. Arnim had told Landsberg that he was planning one last foray into German politics; he would try to submit to William a plan for ending the Kulturkampf. To Bismarck this must have been astounding proof that Arnim remained a danger and an indefatigable intriguer. Bleichröder also informed Bismarck of how close Landsberg had been to Arnim:

> . . . Dr. L. did indeed pass on Count Arnim's documents to the old *Presse*, but it will be in everybody's interest to spare Dr. L. and not to compromise him in any way, because otherwise his connections with Count Arnim would be cut off at once. Dr. L. believes he will receive further news from the Count in the very near future, and though he is very coy about passing on this information to Your Highness, I nevertheless believe that I will get it from him.

Bleichröder promised Bismarck details about Arnim's incriminating recklessness once both men had returned to Berlin from their respective spas.[59] Bleichröder's agent had provided valuable evidence against Arnim.

In the meantime, Bismarck had found yet another accomplice in his struggle—Arnim himself. In early June Holstein had discovered that eighty-six diplomatic documents were missing from the Paris Embassy. Arnim acknowledged having retained some of these and furnished Bismarck with yet another challenge—and an opportunity to destroy a rival.[60]

On October 4, 1874, Arnim was arrested on charges relating to the missing documents.[61] On the day of Arnim's arrest, Bleichröder assured Bismarck that Landsberg would provide further news, but added "once more the urgent request to Your Highness that all news that I submit in this connection should be received solely by Your Highness and the author should in no way be identified; because I had to promise this with my word of honor to Landsberg."[62]

Landsberg's coveted incognito was not maintained. The final culprit in revealing it publicly was Arnim, not Bleichröder, because a search of Arnim's house turned up some notes and letters linking Arnim and Landsberg. A few days earlier, Bleichröder had sent Landsberg some money; on the day of the arrest and because "of these entirely changed circumstances," Landsberg immediately hastened to Berlin, "most ready" to be of service.[63] The prosecution hoped to discredit Arnim by proving that he had lied in denying authorship of the "Diplomatic Revelations." For this Landsberg would be a star witness. For some time it appeared that Bleichröder would also have to be a government witness, much to Bismarck's displeasure; in the end, the prosecution did not call him. On December 11, Landsberg testified that he had transmitted the notorious article to the *Presse*, though he categorically refused to divulge who had given the documents to him, citing legal provisions whereby a witness need not offer testimony that by divulging secrets would harm a man's trade.[64]

The court accepted many of the defense arguments and found Arnim guilty of only one offense, for which he was given a three-month prison sentence. The verdict was unexpectedly lenient, but both sides planned appeals.[65]

After Landsberg's testimony and before the verdict was pronounced, Bismarck summoned Landsberg for a secret meeting.[66] At first he reproached him for his reticence at the trial, but turned affable later. Landsberg returned to Paris, proud of his interview with the chancellor, and told Hohenlohe that he had done everything he could to protect his professional honor ("*Standesehre*") but implied regret at not having done more against Arnim.[67]

The Arnim drama dragged through several more scenes, each characterized by Arnim's unrelenting self-destructiveness and Bismarck's undiminished hatred. (As one knowledgeable observer put it: "To intrigue is always dangerous, and to intrigue against Bismarck was bound to go badly.")[68] At first, it was thought necessary that Bleichröder should testify at the next trial, though Bismarck still balked at the prospect.[69] Landsberg's services were also unexpectedly dispensed with. Arnim meanwhile prepared his final defense, and Landsberg warned Berlin that Arnim was removing further secret documents from Paris to a safe place in Switzerland.[70] A few weeks before Arnim's self-justificatory *Pro Nihilo* appeared, Landsberg warned of some such vengeful act against Bismarck, though he was not sure because "his connection with the Count ceased some time ago."[71] Berlin, forewarned, immediately confiscated the anonymous *Pro Nihilo*, which was a diatribe against Bismarck and the emperor. After its publication, even William could no longer shield this former servant of his crown. A new trial for treason was started. Arnim was sentenced to five years' imprisonment but elected to end his life as an exile abroad. That Arnim faced a hard and humiliating existence, Bleichröder knew—because Schwabach happened to meet him in a Swiss spa and poignantly described his loneliness.[72]

It had been a sordid affair, and Bleichröder's role in it had not been glorious. Ever anxious to serve Bismarck—and armed with private grievances against Arnim—Bleichröder contributed to the latter's downfall by having Landsberg simultaneously act as a spy for Bismarck and as a trusted agent of Arnim's.

For his nefarious services, Landsberg was amply rewarded: financial advantages aside, Bleichröder introduced him to Arnim's successor in Paris, Prince Hohenlohe, whom Landsberg once feared as "a passionate Jewhater."[73] After their first interview—ten days after Hohenlohe's arrival in Paris—Landsberg was impressed that the new ambassador was "integrity incarnate," and Hohenlohe in turn thought him "a clever, rather decent journalist."[74] The two men established a friendly relationship, and Hohenlohe used him repeatedly as an unidentified agent and as a means of planting stories in the press. Landsberg continued to brief Bleichröder on all sorts of news from Paris.[75]

The Arnim affair had tarnished everyone—and left a legacy of rancor. Arnim's aristocratic friends remembered what they regarded as Bismarck's vindictiveness; Bismarck remembered the extremes to which rivals would go.

Some people's lives were permanently darkened. Holstein, for example, was suspected of having spied on his superiors, at Bismarck's behest or in order to curry favor with him. We now know this to have been untrue as well as superfluous, but rumors persisted and undermined Holstein's social standing.[76] The affair made Holstein still more misanthropic, and he and the Bismarck entourage generally resented Bleichröder's meddling in what after all was an embarrassing, insiders' feud. It is doubtful that they knew the full extent of Bleichröder's involvement or of Bismarck's complicity in it.

Holstein's dislike of Bleichröder, which he had already venomously expressed to Herbert von Bismarck in 1872, deepened during the affair. It is ironic, then, to read in a Landsberg "privatissimo" to Bleichröder this appreciation of Holstein, written at the time of Holstein's appointment to the Berlin Foreign Office: "You know Baron H. personally; it may, however, be news to you that—how should I say it?—he has a lively interest for affairs of the stock market. I do not know it from him, but I know it just as certainly." Despite his many other and better connections, Bleichröder should find Holstein eminently useful, "only always remember in dealing with him that by nature he is an incurable pessimist, a temperament trait that already cost him a lot of money here." Landsberg added that Holstein had no idea that the two men corresponded, and hence Bleichröder should never divulge their relations. Landsberg was right: for all his self-proclaimed horror of "*Judengeld*," Holstein often consulted Bleichröder even on financial matters. Holstein's growing hatred of Bleichröder was well known in Berlin. Publicly, Holstein spoke of Bleichröder with contempt; privately, and unbeknownst to all, he wrote friendly, intimate letters to him, buried until now in the Bleichröder Archive. Holstein, a bachelor with few friends, was single-mindedly political. Like Bleichröder, he always wanted to be in the know; unlike Bleichröder, he cherished his own political ambitions. Around 1884 Holstein became estranged from the Bismarcks; he was fearful of Rantzau's influence on the chancellor and began to distrust even his old friend Herbert.[77] Hence his hatred of Bleichröder grew fiercer—and served as a remaining tie with Herbert.

Part of Holstein's malevolence, then, was fear—fear that Bleichröder could undermine his position. For that very reason the break was hardly open. In the incomplete Bleichröder Archive, there is in fact a gap between the warm, whimsical letters of the 1870s and early 1880s—including six letters for the month of January 1880 alone—and the intimate letters addressed to "Verehrter Freund" after 1890, that is, after Bismarck's dismissal robbed Bleichröder of his political power.* Even in the interval, however, Holstein would ask to see Bleichröder, and they would have what in more tranquil times Holstein called their "pleasant chats."[78] Put in the best light,

---

* The last Holstein letter in the Bleichröder Archive is dated 8 Feb. 1893, two weeks before Bleichröder's death, and addressed to his son Hans. Holstein discussed the question of whether Bleichröder should be told of the gravity of his condition; Holstein counseled yes, once the acute attack was over. It says something about their relationship that Holstein felt free to voice an opinion on this most sensitive of matters.

Holstein was an irrepressible gossip and a hypocrite; in the worst light, he appears as a false man who vilified and courted Bleichröder at one and the same time, and the more he vilified him in public, the more he courted him in private, and vice versa; by doing both simultaneously, he very likely contributed to his own discomfort and confirmed his own misanthropy.

The Arnim affair was the most celebrated scandal of the 1870s. There were many others; and most of them suggested an illicit relation between money and politics. The smell of corruption hung heavy over the new Reich, and charges were leveled at the men at the very top, at Bismarck and Bleichröder. Many of them proved to be inventions—calumnies designed to discredit political opponents. The charges against Bismarck were usually wrong; he was more prudent than most.

The initial attack on *Gründertum* came from a liberal friend and coreligionist of Bleichröder's Eduard Lasker, and its principal target was Bismarck's friend of thirty years' standing and a high official in the Prussian state ministry, Hermann Wagener. In February 1873, in a speech in the Prussian Diet that was hailed as a "bombshell," Lasker exposed all manner of collusive behavior between public servants, especially in Itzenplitz's Commerce Ministry, and railroad builders and singled out Wagener for his participation in the founding of the Pommersche Zentralbahn. The case of Wagener, he added, belonged to the notorious "System Strousberg," which the Commerce Ministry had done a great deal to nurture.[79]

Hours before Lasker's speech, Bleichröder wrote Bismarck that "with but few exceptions almost all members of the Diet are against Lasker's proposals; members of his own party will vote against him, and hence his motions for the creation of a commission of inquiry will be defeated."[80] Actually Lasker's speech was well received, although his motion was not voted on. The charge was intensely embarrassing to Bismarck, who had pushed Wagener's appointment against William's wishes and who relied on him as an expert on social policy and as a link with the Prussian Conservatives.[81] (He told Lasker, who disclaimed all intention of attacking Bismarck: "Your bullet came so close that it missed me only by a hair's breadth.")[82] A year before Lasker's speech, Bismarck had written to Wagener: "You are the only one in my entourage with whom I speak frankly and openly and when I cannot do that anymore, I will drown in my gall."[83] Though aware that others had sinned more, Bismarck could not protect him, and in October 1873 Wagener, who, ironically enough, was a great critic of Manchesterism, had to resign his post. In a civil suit arising out of the railway's bankruptcy, he was sentenced to 1,800,000 marks' damages, and economic disaster now followed his political debacle. Bismarck maintained his contact with him and at first gave him special assignments in the field of social policy. In the fall of 1876 Wagener's financial plight became worse and Bismarck expressed his willingness to help but encountered—or alleged to have encountered—unbudgeable opposition.[84] Wagener let it be known that he could divulge information embarrassing to the chancellor. Bismarck always insisted that his relations with Wagener had been correct and complained of the man's ingratitude.[85]

The Bleichröder Archive throws light on their last painful contacts. In November 1876 Johanna wrote Bleichröder that "Mrs. Wagener just visited me, in dire straits, because she is threatened with dispossession on account of 5,000 marks that her husband is to pay at once, but he cannot possibly do it. The situation seems to be very bad, and my husband instructs me to ask you to send this sum to Geheimrat Wagener right away and for the moment to put it on our bill."[86] In the next three weeks, Wagener repeatedly came to Bleichröder for advice and asked for an advance of 24,000 to 27,000 marks against mortgages which he owned on land contiguous to the Bismarck estate at Reinbeck.[87] In the winter of 1876–1877, Bleichröder reached an agreement with Wagener, protecting him from the worst consequences of his bankruptcy.[88] Three years later, Bleichröder received his thanks: Wagener notified him that on behalf of another man he held a claim of nearly 900,000 marks against Bleichröder-related interests, and before he pressed suit, he wanted to give Bleichröder a chance to settle the affair amicably. He had become an embittered ingrate, full of insolent self-pity, "shocked that nobody felt the contradiction that princely personages, the highest dignitaries of the crown, are measured by different standards from me, the small *bürgerliche* official, and that occurrences which were considered criminal in my case left no mark on the position of these gentlemen."* However cantankerous Wagener was, Herbert Bismarck's colorful epithet in 1881 that he was *"ein ausgemachter Schweinehund"* said perhaps more about Herbert's lack of comprehension and compassion than about Wagener.[89]

Wagener had a point, and Bleichröder knew all about this double standard. The dignitaries of the crown had developed an extraordinary appetite for material gain. Speculation and the desire to get rich quick are contagious; Wagener had a mild case compared to many others.

Count Paul von Hatzfeldt-Wildenburg, charming scion of an ancient family, was a discreet example of this passion for profit. Despite grave irregularities, financial and marital, in his personal life, despite intermittent indolence that earned him the sobriquet *Der faule Paul*, Hatzfeldt rose to eminence in Germany's diplomatic service, ending his career at the Court of St. James's. He was one of the few Catholics to do so.[90] "The best horse in my stable," Bismarck used to say of him—in a typical Bismarckian phrase.[91] Recognition came fitfully—or so Hatzfeldt thought. In his letters to his wife, written during the Franco-Prussian war, he complained bitterly that amidst the general scattering of decorations, he and his fellow civilians in Versailles had been entirely forgotten: "In general I laugh at decorations. . . ."

---

* In his polemic about promotion and corruption, Rudolph Meyer, who shared Wagener's social outlook, made the same point. "It was horrible to see the hypocrisy with which the deputies, almost all of whom knew the *Gründerei* and the professional *Gründer* in their midst, listened to Lasker's revelations about the misdeeds of three notorious dilettantes"—Wagener included. Rudolph Meyer, *Politische Gründer und die Corruption in Deutschland* (Leipzig, 1877), pp. 117–118.

The frontispiece of the book shows a later Hatzfeldt in full dress uniform with a chest studded with medals and ribbons.[92] He was a complicated man, who better than most men exemplified the difficulties of being a public servant under Bismarck.

Or perhaps it is only that in Hatzfeldt's case we have portions of correspondence that allow us an unusually frank view of the man and his career. He happened to be a friend, client, debtor, and importuner of Bleichröder, and a substantial record of their extraordinary relationship has survived.

Paul was the son of Countess Sophie Hatzfeldt, who in her celebrated friendship with Ferdinand Lassalle had imbibed some of his socialist ideas. She shed them in due course and certainly never practiced them with the family fortune; her son never fell for them, though he may have inherited something of her taste for extravagant friendships. A lifelong friend of his contemporary Holstein, he was also an early protégé of Bismarck's. His rise in the diplomatic service in the 1860s was rapid and bespoke Bismarck's confidence.[93] He was clearly a shrewd observer and a man of considerable political intelligence. In an age of excellent linguists, his French shone; his marriage to an American, Helene Moulton, was unusual.

Hatzfeldt had been Bleichröder's client before the Franco-Prussian war; during the war he was attached to Bismarck's personal staff, and his stay in Versailles was brightened by many a Bleichröder cigar.[94] The two men met again and conversed often at headquarters in February 1871. During Bleichröder's stay in Versailles, Hatzfeldt mused to his wife, apropos of the many dishonest ways he could make money, as the French were doing: "We are not so corrupt as they are here. At the same time I must say that I should like to earn some money in some honest manner, and I am racking my brains to think of some way to do so. All one has to do is to get a good idea or to discover some good investment. One ought to be able to do that now. . . ."[95] It was the intonation of a refrain often to be heard by Bleichröder—and one that for a while chimed in with the prevalent desires of all Berlin.

A few months later, Bleichröder had placed Hatzfeldt on the board of directors of his best-known promotion, Laurahütte. The advantages of initial membership on the board were considerable: subscription rights to shares at low issue prices and substantial directors' fees. Early dividends were high. In the first six months, through the sale of shares to the public, the consortium made a profit of 349,724 taler, and Hatzfeldt's share on his 5,000-taler investment was 1,165 taler. A gain of more than 20 percent in less than six months was gratifying even in those glamorous times: Bleichröder may even have advanced Hatzfeldt the original 5,000 taler.[96]

The quick profit sharpened Hatzfeldt's greed: *l'appetit vient en mangeant.* In November 1871 he bought an expensive manor near Wiesbaden, the Sommerberger Hof; next he asked Bleichröder's help in finding him a suitable residence in Berlin, not above 2,500 taler in rent: "If I could raise my income proportionately, I would be more inclined to accept a higher rent. Perhaps another favorable deal like the Laurahütte beckons soon, and in your usual kindness you will think of getting me a place on the board of directors."[97] Bleichröder obliged immediately. In January 1872 he offered Hatzfeldt a seat on his new creation, the Deutsche Reichs- und Continental-Eisenbahn-Baugesellschaft, to join, in addition to Kardorff, Baron Carl Meyer von Rothschild of Frankfurt, Moritz Ritter von Goldschmidt, and other dignitaries.[98] Kardorff and Hatzfeldt brought aristocratic panache to these enterprises.

But Hatzfeldt's desires outpaced Bleichröder's resources. By early February 1872 he urged Bleichröder to buy shares for him in order to capitalize on the likely recovery of suddenly depressed prices. His real aim, though, was higher:

> Would it not be possible for me to try to get a railroad concession? You probably have many such projects before you and you could recommend one or the other of these. I would also count on your advice concerning the ways and means to go ahead with the railroad. I fail to see why I could not succeed as well as Mr. von Kardorf [sic] in this kind of enterprise, in which one can always anticipate a considerable advantage.[99]

As luck would have it, this failed to come off; a year later, on the day of Lasker's speech, another noble speculator, Count Frankenberg, sighed: "To-day everybody who had failed to get a railroad concession must rejoice."[100] On the other hand, Bleichröder realized a profit of 20,000 taler for him, mostly by subscribing to a new stock issue which yielded 26 percent almost at once. Hatzfeldt's thanks were mixed with new importunities, not all of which Bleichröder could satisfy.

Still Hatzfeldt's letters and suggestions came pouring in: scheme after scheme, running more and more into real-estate speculation. The fraction of the correspondence that has survived is a record of imaginative, mounting greed—a perfect symptom of the age. Nor did Hatzfeldt go unrewarded. His total gain in the years 1871–1873 probably came close to 100,000 taler—not a bad record for an impecunious aristocrat and civil servant who could barely afford 2,500 taler for annual rent.

Hatzfeldt benefited enormously from Bleichröder's benevolence. What did Hatzfeldt do for him? As Bleichröder put it, he "brought glory" to one of Bleichröder's first banquets, in 1872, and even produced other nobles for the occasion. Hatzfeldt also did little commissions for Bleichröder in Paris: he selected him a cook and brought him a string of pearls for 12,000 francs for possible purchase. He sent him news from Paris, where in 1872 he found "complete demoralization . . . many people but no individuals." He tried discreetly, but not effectively, to further Bleichröder's interests in Paris. But above all, he was an ornamental figure for Bleichröder's promotions. A Jewish consortium welcomed a gentile count in their midst.[101]

But there was a limit to Bleichröder's benevolence, a limit he probably intuited when tangible risks began to outweigh intangible advantages. Bleichröder's alarm bells went off early; in 1873 Hatzfeldt's account showed a debit of 129,409 taler, and to a routine letter, Schwabach appended: "I would welcome it if the more favorable monetary conditions which now prevail would offer you an opportunity to reduce your debit balance."[102]

Hatzfeldt had apparently fallen into the convenient habit of overdrawing his account; by the time it reached 129,000 taler—probably about ten times his annual salary at the time—Bleichröder, who usually carried overdrafts at a mere 4 percent, began to worry. Hatzfeldt was in fact borrowing large sums without the formality of negotiating or financing a loan.

Bleichröder acknowledged that earlier Hatzfeldt had sent him a 50,000-taler mortgage, and that Bleichröder's "principles" had forbidden him to deal in them.[103] Repeatedly Bleichröder urged Hatzfeldt to reduce his deficit, until finally, in March 1875, he wrote in clear exasperation that Hatzfeldt had *promised* to pay him back as soon as a certain mortgage had been realized, which, Bleichröder understood, had now been done.[104] At the same time, Bleichröder demanded his resignation as director of the Laurahütte, presumably because Hatzfeldt, appointed minister to Spain in 1874, had become too obviously an ornament in absentia. Exposing corruption was *en vogue*, and Bleichröder had to ward off public criticism.[105] Hatzfeldt resigned his directorships but added peevishly that circumstances often prevented one from meeting one's obligations punctually, as Bleichröder must have discovered when he did not grant Hatzfeldt the participation promised to him in some big operation. "In any case it deserves some consideration that for my part I did not miss an opportunity to be useful and accommodating to you as far as I was able."[106] The debt was reduced, but a year later Bleichröder had still to plead for the repayment of a debt amounting to nearly 50,000 marks.[107] With the help of an intermediary, Bleichröder finally negotiated a schedule of repayments, but less than a year later, in September 1877, Hatzfeldt defaulted again.[108]

Hatzfeldt felt neglected in Madrid, thought that Berlin officialdom did not appreciate him, and yearned for a gesture of recognition. Ambition drove him, bouts of indolence hobbled him; his intelligence marked him for superior posts, but Bismarck sought other qualities besides intelligence in his ambassadors. Smelling intrigue everywhere, Hatzfeldt intrigued and wished he did not have to. He was discouraged because "everything I have touched has turned against me." Hence Bleichröder's help with his material difficulties was all the more appreciated. During Bismarck's prolonged illness and attendant absence, relations with Berlin became still worse: "I have come to the point where I express no views anymore, unless I am explicitly asked to do so."[109] Hatzfeldt was chafing at the bit. He wanted "promotion and recognition," and none seemed in the offing. "After all I have achieved here in four years in often quite difficult situations, after I alone brought this country to a rapprochement with us," such official indifference paralyzed the desire for any further initiative. "It is really almost beyond comprehension that the Prince [Bismarck] decides always to pass up his best and most loyal supporters and to fill the highest posts with nonentities on whose support he cannot even count." He had no illusions about his chances for the embassy in Vienna and little hope for Constantinople: "I know unfortunately too well that with us it avails nothing to have accomplished something, that in the end a vacancy is given to some protégé of the Crown Prince, or some Prince who knows nothing about the business receives priority." If nothing turned up, he would have to leave the service altogether, if he could afford to. Would Bleichröder be willing to help? Could he plead his case with Bismarck?[110] By this time Bleichröder had become his advocate and financial patron.

All during the spring of 1878 these intimate complaints continued, as did the pleas for intervention. It was a bad time to bother Bismarck, who was still suffering pain and insomnia from a severe case of shingles. Bleichröder wrote to Herbert in Varzin:

> I see from the papers that very soon the position of Prince Reuss in Constantinople will become vacant, and I humbly beg you to ask your father whether this vacancy could not be filled through Count Hatzfeldt. Count H. seems to have a great liking for the post, and after all that I have heard about him from Spain—and what in any case you and best of all your father can properly assess—he has managed to gain for himself a very good standing in Madrid and is popular in all circles.[111]

Twenty-four hours later, Herbert acknowledged the letter at length and with thanks but added that his father was still too weak to pursue such matters energetically.[112] Bleichröder had done his best; his intervention proves that he thought it entirely proper to recommend a candidate for a high diplomatic post and that Bismarck, *père et fils*, also regarded the request as routine. As weeks went by, Bleichröder received Hatzfeldt's missives of growing impatience and gratitude. Had Bleichröder really become his principal protector in Berlin? In any case, the poor count had to work another year until he could move to the eastern Mediterranean, where politics were more turbulent— and far more important to Bleichröder's far-flung interests—than in the Spanish backwaters.

Hatzfeldt's career suffered from widespread rumors, even in the press, concerning his marital and financial troubles.[113] In early 1879, acknowledging these rumors, Bleichröder sent Bismarck a five-page letter on Hatzfeldt's complicated affairs, which he had recently taken over: "Never in my many years of business experience has anyone made it so hard for me to straighten out his affairs." Even Hatzfeldt's mother was pressing claims; still, an arrangement with all his creditors had nevertheless been proposed whereby Hatzfeldt could retain 25,000 to 29,000 marks out of his salary of 40,000, sufficient to live decently in Constantinople "and to meet fully his social obligations as ambassador." To which Bismarck appended on the margin "hardly necessary"—a strange comment coming from a former ambassador who himself had complained of the financial burden. But then Bismarck had contempt for the Porte and social life there.[114]

Yet Hatzfeldt was never out of sight or trouble. No sooner had he gone to Constantinople than rumors started that he might inherit the post of the suddenly deceased Ernst von Bülow, state secretary for foreign affairs. At the time, Bleichröder pushed another friend, Prince Hohenlohe, for this post and spoke to Bismarck in this vein, but here, too, the chancellor anticipated financial difficulties. An ambassador's salary was much higher than that of a state secretary, and Hohenlohe, also in debt, had to decline, much to Bleich-röder's regrets.[115] After Hohenlohe's refusal, Bleichröder wrote Herbert a long report on Hatzfeldt's affairs: "I have extended large advances to Count Paul in order to preserve an experienced and skilled man in the service of the government. . . ." The prospects of solvency had improved, provided the much-discussed Countess Helene did not indulge in further extravagances. "If she would live more quietly with her parents and take better cognizance of her husband's financial circumstances, then Paul could live far more com-fortably."[116] Herbert might have bridled at such familiarity, but his reply two days later betrayed nothing of the sort. "You are indeed performing a service for our country if you prevent the enforced resignation of so eminently competent an official as Count Hatzfeldt."[117]

Rumors and intrigues flourished, for at stake was the top, if underpaid, position in the Foreign Ministry. In the Bismarck entourage it was suddenly whispered that Bleichröder had decided to push Radowitz, who had served him in the Rumanian affair, for the job and hence had done everything to worsen Hatzfeldt's financial plight. Indeed he had said to Hohenlohe and others that he did not think Hatzfeldt qualified for the post, and the ever suspicious Holstein wrote Herbert about Radowitz: ". . . it would give me a peculiar feeling if a protégé of Bl. [sic] should direct the Foreign Office. How far Bl. [sic] influence goes and where it ends, you can judge better than I."[118] At approximately the same time he wrote to Bleichröder: "In the H. affair I would say that the public interest—the only aspect that concerns outsiders—is concentrated on the hope that he, our friend, will become free. How the rest of the family adjusts itself is a purely private matter."[119]

In August 1880 Bleichröder reported to Bismarck that Paul's affluent brother, Prince Hatzfeldt, whom Bismarck had asked to help Paul, had offered certain concessions that would require Bleichröder, however, to ad-vance about 450,000 marks at 4 percent, to be repaid over eighty years. Bleichröder would oblige if Bismarck still wanted Hatzfeldt as state secretary. Prince Hatzfeldt had also raised the question of a 450,000-mark property—the so-called Tichy estate in Berlin—that Paul had bought with mortgages that would soon fall due. The Hatzfeldts hoped that the state could buy the property or that Bleichröder could take over the mortgages. Bleichröder had appealed to Albert Maybach, who had replied that the state could do nothing for three years. Was there perhaps a public fund that could help Hatzfeldt?

Herbert added some sarcastic marginalia on the letter and then answered the next day in a seven-page letter of his own. The gist of it was that he would write to Maybach, urging him to buy the Tichy property now. More he could not do, but he encouraged Bleichröder to persevere. The Prussian state refused to buy the property at Bleichröder's price, which was purchase price plus interest.[120]

In the summer of 1880 the Bismarck entourage became ever more con-cerned with Paul's insolvency; Herbert estimated the total indebtedness at 850,000 marks. Some people alleged that Bleichröder had turned his back on Hatzfeldt, while others complained that the Bleichröder-Hatzfeldt axis was already too intimate.[121] Bleichröder kept urging Paul's appointment. The fact that at Princess Bismarck's suggestion, Hatzfeldt had left his daughter Helene in charge of the Bleichröders while he went to Friedrichsruh caused tongues to wag. A newspaper predicting Hatzfeldt's early appointment concluded: "The eldest daughter of the Ambassador is residing again at the house of Geheimrat von Bleichröder." Other papers reported that the eighteen-year-old was about to marry one of Bleichröder's sons![122] Such a happy end to the Hatzfeldt tangle was not to be. A Hatzfeldt-Bleichröder marriage—with Hatzfeldt's debts and Bleichröder's Jewishness mutually forgiven—might have pleased the elders, but not the principals.

By 1882 Bismarck had to make a permanent appointment; Bleichröder reassured Hatzfeldt that *der Freund*, as he always referred to Bismarck, still held him in high esteem. In July 1882, after Paul's marriage was dissolved, "as much as it could be by the laws of the Roman Catholic Church," he received a temporary appointment as state secretary.[123] In October, having thoroughly annoyed Herbert and others by his vacillations and alleged indolence, he received the regular appointment as state secretary.[124]

At last, Bleichröder's "partner," as Moritz Busch referred to the new appointee, had become the head of the Foreign Office.[125] The two men saw each other frequently, and Bleichröder's long labors now paid off in this intimacy. Holstein, too, was pleased, though his "wet nurse" cooing over Hatzfeldt's every move exasperated Herbert.[126] Hatzfeldt's tenure was not to last long; he had to be pushed upstairs in order to make room for Herbert— with whom Bismarck now wanted to run the Foreign Office jointly. With what some people thought indecent haste, Hatzfeldt in 1885 was dispatched to the Court of St. James's, where he was welcomed for his charm and because "he is almost unique among his sport-abhorring countrymen in his passionate devotion to lawn tennis."[127] It was the top assignment for a German diplomat. In the meantime, Hatzfeldt begged Bleichröder to assure his predecessor in London, Count Münster, that it had not been Hatzfeldt's intention to push him out of London.[128] For Bleichröder, the substitution of his great foe Herbert von Bismarck for his difficult friend Hatzfeldt was a sorry trade.

Bleichröder still had to look after Hatzfeldt's chaotic finances, though others now shared in the burden. Paul still suffered occasional, mild relapses of his earlier speculative fever. Bleichröder had to caution him: "I do not think Your Excellency should engage in any new projects."[129] Paul's former wife and son also importuned Bleichröder, who continued to manage Hatzfeldt's portfolio and at times balked at extending new credits. If all his clients had been like Hatzfeldt, so time-consuming and so demanding, Bleichröder would never have become rich.

But there were ample rewards—and these too show up in the correspondence that has survived. Their intimacy was attested in many ways. Herbert complained of it to Rantzau, since a story Bleichröder leaked to the London Rothschilds could only have had Hatzfeldt as its source: "It shows that despite all mutual injuries H. must be on a very intimate footing with Bleichröder if (on his return from Varzin), even during a stay of only a few hours in Berlin, he passes him information."[130]* On the night that Hatzfeldt left for his new post in London, he dined with Bleichröder.[131]

From London, there continued a sporadic but unusually candid correspondence. Hatzfeldt apparently needed someone to whom he could pour out his bruised feelings about real or imagined ill treatment, about his enemies' intrigues against him, about Berlin's chicanery and incivility. The two men also exchanged news and views about their particular spheres of activities and about the political world at large. Hatzfeldt's letters touched on the personal realm, on his troubled, rocky marital and financial life. In 1889 he wrote Bleichröder privately of the prospective engagement of his daughter to the son of the duke of Ujest, which was to be preceded by Paul's own remarriage. Herbert Bismarck, however, warned his father that such a remarriage would saddle Paul with colossal new debts and ruin him completely. Paul did in fact ask Bleichröder for further help on account of his wife's debts. The Bismarcks apparently objected to both marital alliances and were the only ones to withhold their congratulations on the engagement. Hatzfeldt was summoned to Friedrichsruh, where he had to ask for Bismarck's approval for his own prospective remarriage and to furnish renewed reassurance about his finances. Bismarck consented and agreed to request William II's approval.[132]

For all his help, Bleichröder occasionally demanded immediate, tangible returns. At such moments he could be remarkably insistent. In April 1888, for example, Hansemann and the Disconto-Gesellschaft suddenly threatened Bleichröder's preeminent position in Egyptian affairs. Bleichröder mobilized all his connections against these interlopers; he dispatched a special emissary to Hatzfeldt and sent urgent missives as well. (The details of the Egyptian affair will be discussed in Chapter 15.) "I urgently beg Your Excellency to be disposed to do everything in the interests of my house that is at all possible." One way would be for Hatzfeldt to tell the London Rothschilds that "you do not place any great weight on Hansemann and his connections with the Foreign Office, while I have the personal friendship of the Chief, which I can vouch for as complete truth." An odd request to make of the German ambassador, but Hatzfeldt's own interests would also benefit: Bleichröder had already assigned a portion of the new Mexican issue to him and would of course do the same if the Egyptian affair had the proper outcome.[133] It did.

Bleichröder's ties with Hatzfeldt were closer and of longer duration than those with any other member of the Bismarck entourage. For Bleichröder it was also a costly and complicated relationship. In its essence it embodied the reciprocity that characterized all his private dealings with public figures.

.   .   .

* Hatzfeldt was widely suspected of leaking information to Bleichröder; when Bleichröder once boasted that he knew the contents of an important letter from William to Prince Karl Anton of Hohenzollern-Sigmaringen, a confidant of the latter immediately assumed that Hatzfeldt had drafted the letter. Felix Bamberg to Prince Karl Anton, 5 Oct. 1883, HS.

Bleichröder's ambition necessarily extended to the emperor as well. The court after all was the social summit, and the monarch, though made pliable by his awe of Bismarck, retained considerable influence on governmental decisions. In difficult moments Bleichröder petitioned the king on behalf of his family or of his coreligionists. In ordinary times, he was the discreet dispenser of favors to William and his aides.

Bleichröder could not claim the honor of being royal banker; that position was already taken—by a fellow Jew, Baron Meyer-Cohn. Bleichröder had to content himself with lesser services; he made generous contributions to various patriotic charities, and every Christmas he sent William the choicest caviar and live sturgeon. On special occasions—after the second assassination attempt on William, for example—Bleichröder sent tables laden with flowers from Gütergotz, and the emperor gratefully accepted the "renewed proof of [Bleichröder's] thoughtfulness."[134] Prussian parsimony, however, set limits to Bleichröder's largesse: in the winter of 1878 he repeatedly sent William some caviar, but Count Perponcher in thanking him asked that no more be sent, because the delicacy was being reserved exclusively for the emperor and hence the supply was ample.[135] In turn, William paid Bleichröder a formal visit in Gütergotz and repeatedly received him, usually in the informal atmosphere of some spa. Audiences at the royal palace were rare; formal invitations by Empress Augusta marked the height of Bleichröder's social career.

Bleichröder also cultivated close relations with William's entourage—and found himself on exceptionally close terms with Louis Schneider, William's reader, and above all, with Count Heinrich Lehndorff, William's general adjutant, who "for decades was William's most intimate confidant." As such, he also did more than anyone else to maintain close relations between William and Bismarck.[136] William II recalled that his "grandfather's aides-de-camp all felt the greatest respect for Count Lehndorff, but they also adored him, for, in his implicit devotion to his sovereign, and in his imperturbable and distinguished manner, he was an example to them all."[137]

In appearance and in character, Count Heinrich Lehndorff was the prototype of a distinguished Prussian officer. . . . He was considered the handsomest officer at the Berlin court. . . . He was linked to the king-emperor, whose aide and later general adjutant he was for more than twenty years, by an old-Germanic fealty [*Mannestreue*], which had nothing saccharine or subservient in it, but was for him the natural fulfillment of a duty dictated by family tradition and genuine reverence. He was anything but a careerist. His ancient nobility [*Uradel*] and his daily service with the emperor satisfied his ambition. He neither wanted nor sought anything else.[138]*

---

* For a moving and illuminating evocation of Count Lehndorff's grandson and namesake, also a man of charm and fortitude, who participated in the attempted coup against Hitler on July 20, 1944, and subsequently was hanged by the Nazis, see Marion Gräfin Dönhoff, *Namen die keiner mehr nennt* (Düsseldorf, 1962), pp. 81–94.

This is the way Count Kessler, one of the most sensitive of observers, evoked him.

Bleichröder saw another side. Like Hatzfeldt and August Eulenburg, Lehndorff was deeply concerned with making money. For twenty years, Bleichröder was his banker and adviser and as such centrally involved in his versatile speculations in land and securities. Lehndorff asked Bleichröder's help in some clever real-estate operations that would enable him to profit from the building of the Berlin Stadtbahn. In November 1878 Lehndorff urged Bleichröder to solicit Maybach's views and possible help in connection with his interests; at another time he asked for confidential information on the likely nationalization of the railroads. Bleichröder was also asked to enlist the help of the Berlin chief of police, Guido von Madai. In 1885 Lehndorff begged Bleichröder to persuade the income tax authorities that they had made a mistake when they placed him in the twenty-eighth instead of the twenty-sixth bracket.[139]

As a consequence, Lehndorff and Bleichröder saw each other all the time and corresponded actively when either was away from Berlin. Business was the principal but not the exclusive concern. Lehndorff supplied intimate news about the court, about the emperor's health and plans, about his political views. Bleichröder provided the financial and political news. Lehndorff often intervened on Bleichröder's behalf—whether it was a matter of passing on a petition to the emperor or of arranging a visit. Above all, Lehndorff gave him something that was rare among Bleichröder's influential and aristocratic clients: his enduring friendship and private proof thereof. In 1877, lamenting a lapse in their correspondence, he wrote that he wanted to know about Bleichröder's well-being "because I am fond of you and because I wish you the best and like to hear the best from you." When Bleichröder had been particularly helpful in promoting a lucrative prospect, Lehndorff wrote: "You know that I cannot complain about my fate, but one thing is sure: that if everything is to have a good ending, then my pecuniary condition has to be improved. That you are willing to think about this and work on this prompts the heartfelt thanks of your old friend Lehndorff." When Bleichröder's wife died in 1881, Lehndorff was at the house, wanting to extend his "truly most sympathetic hand."[140] There were few men who rewarded Bleichröder's unflinching help with such humanity.*

Lehndorff's royal master also stood in need of Bleichröder's discreet assistance. In 1884, at the venerable age of eighty-two, William bestirred himself to take care of a lady friend. In a handwritten note to Bleichröder— surely a great rarity at that time—the emperor informed him that a Mr. de Karsky, "whose wife I have known for a very long time," was interested in a railroad project that was to redeem his fortune after unsuccessful real-estate speculations had left him in dire straits. Karsky had asked William to

---

* Not that Lehndorff did not use his wit at Bleichröder's expense. At a gala dinner at Bleichröder's, where the host's colleagues and coreligionists were, as always, carefully screened out, Lehndorff remarked to his dinner partner: "If it were not for the master of the house, the party would be far more exclusive than one normally finds these days." A. von Brauer, *Im Dienste Bismarcks* (Berlin, 1936), p. 208.

intervene with Bleichröder: "In the light of the interest which I confer on the family Karsky, also in the light of the gifts which the Emperor Alexander II gave to the family in earlier times, I recommend your support of this railroad project and request information as to what you are going to do in this matter. Address your answer to me with the notation, to be opened by my own hands." Signed William, Imp. and Rex.[141]

Bleichröder must have known, as did most of Berlin society, that William had always been fond of pretty women, that in his youth he had for six passionate years pursued Princess Elisa Radziwill until the court decided that she was ineligible, that he had married Augusta in consonance with protocol, not inclination, and that he lived with her for sixty years a relatively loveless life. People knew that young ladies brightened his otherwise somber day of royal duty—how they did it is perhaps of greater concern to the twentieth century, which likes to have its sex spelled out, than it was to William's contemporaries, who knew that love took many pleasing forms.[142]

Bleichröder examined the railroad project, which was to link Petrokov with Kutno via Lodz in Russian Poland, and discussed it with William, who put considerable pressure on him. The ubiquitous Holstein got wind of this secret contact and alerted Herbert, who replied: "Whatever had His Majesty to write to Bleichröder about? I never thought that such a relationship existed."[143] At the Three Emperors' Meeting at Skiernievice in the fall of 1884, William bestowed special attention on Karsky and encouraged Alexander to be similarly solicitous.[144] Meanwhile Mme. Karsky wrote poignant letters to Bleichröder: "Is the friendship that you had the kindness to pretend to cherish for me at an end on the first occasion that I turn to you for help—this would really be a sad and cruel lesson for life to teach me." William also was surprised, she added, that so far Bleichröder had done nothing for her.[145]

The Karskys soon went beyond the original railroad project; they dreamed of building new tramways in Moscow and of exploiting a new mine at Kremenetz. For the mine, they needed a minimum of 60,000 marks, but "if the support of the Palace [William] and your kindness should go so far as to lend us all the necessary capital, i.e. 180,000 marks, then our fortune would be assured."[146] When Bleichröder still hesitated, she pleaded with him repeatedly, in somewhat faulty French, and in a manner reminiscent of many a novel of the time: "Do you have the courage to refuse me—this loan would assure us and our poor boys a comfortable living—believe me . . . if I did not have children I could never bring myself to beg anything from any-body—but I am a mother. . . . My poor husband is ill. . . . Ah! If you knew how painful it was to beg and how wretched I am. . . ." Worse to follow: in the next letter, from Montreux, her husband was at death's door and her son, hardly of age, had committed the madness of marrying "an old maid of thirty-two, ugly and poor"; she too had nearly died, and only her friend (William) and her doctor saved her.[147] In August 1886 William wrote a final plea: "If you can help, I am certain that you will, because apparently the situation of the family is really very difficult, but whether any security exists to cover the help requested of you, I do not know."[148] And here the matter rested at last; there is no indication that Bleichröder obliged the emperor, and the Karskys must have discovered that even imperial protection could not overcome great imprudence. Bleichröder was witness to many such dramas of impoverished, well-connected nobility—though none with so mysterious a hold over so powerful a benefactor.

For all his involvement in the web of Berlin intrigue, Bleichröder escaped any fatal entrapment. However much some of Bismarck's creatures resented his influence, they bowed to its reality and knew that Bleichröder's protector was the most powerful man in Germany. Only one man dared to break openly with Bleichröder—and that was the chancellor's son.

No man was closer to Bismarck than his son Herbert; hence no one in Bismarck's entourage was more important to Bleichröder than Herbert. After years of friendly, even intimate contacts, the tie between them snapped, and Herbert became Bleichröder's implacable enemy, abusing him viciously, as only he could afford to do. The reasons for the break, hitherto not known, derived from the one personal crisis which fleetingly divided father and son.

Herbert was a handsome, clever man, and in his youth a rather spirited and witty companion. He was his father's greatest pride, his intimate collaborator, and finally his heir apparent. Turning his back on a military career originally envisioned, Herbert entered the diplomatic service instead, thus opting for years of success and servitude under his father's domination. The son was undoubtedly torn between admiration for his father's genius—and no one but Herbert was privy to Bismarck's innermost thoughts and calculations—and resentment at always being in the shadow of that genius. The dominant note of Herbert's relationship to his parents was dependency masked as solicitude. He was indispensable to them, and by meeting their affective and practical needs, he carved out for himself a purpose and a sense of mission. And yet this self-assigned role entailed a heavy psychic burden and probably cramped his own manhood. How else can one interpret the tinge of filial fear that Herbert's letters to his brother and brother-in-law still betrayed in the 1880s? Thus he once confided to Rantzau that he planned to take one-day excursions away from his official post in Dresden: *"Please do not say anything about this there* [in Varzin]. Because Papa could find it a dereliction of duty."*

In the 1870s Bleichröder's relations with Herbert reflected his intimacy with the father. Herbert wrote Bleichröder hundreds of letters, usually on behalf of Bismarck. Gradually a direct relationship developed as well. We saw how solicitous Bleichröder was of Herbert when the twenty-one-year-old was injured in the French campaign. The gifts Bleichröder sent then were but

---

* Herbert von Bismarck to Count Rantzau, 2 Sept. 1880, in SA. I discovered a special folder of Herbert's letters to Rantzau while working in the archive in June 1967. These letters, many of great political importance, were not included in Walter Bussmann's edition of Herbert's political correspondence, published in 1964. Neither was Herbert's extensive correspondence with Bleichröder referred to in that edition.

harbingers of the later favors to the whole family: caviar, pheasants, grouse, pâté for the father, Dutch delicacies for the mother, cigars and eighty-year-old sherry for father and son—they arrived in a steady stream, and Herbert usually acknowledged them. How often he assured Bleichröder that the family, while consuming these presents, "was thinking much of the benevolent giver"![149] The bulk of his correspondence with Bleichröder, however, consisted of political or personal communications from his father.

A further link soon supplemented the official tie. Bleichröder lavished great care on Herbert's small fortune. He solicited Herbert's advice and opinion and in many subtle ways flattered the much younger person by treating him as an equal in age. Herbert reciprocated by showing Bleichröder special regard, often addressing him as "Verehrtester Herr von Bleichröder," a special bit of flattery. Herbert readily accepted Bleichröder's help in his bid for a Reichstag seat in 1878. Oftentimes in the 1870s Herbert dined with the Bleichröders or graced their banquets; and when he had to miss an occasion, he sent elaborate apologies.

Behind Bleichröder's back, Herbert undoubtedly made fun of him; everybody did.* He probably resented Bleichröder's intimacy with his father, and his anti-Semitism was sufficiently strong that Holstein could denounce to Herbert Bleichröder's machinations and his "accursed Jew money," without fear of giving offense. And still the intimacy between Herbert and Bleichröder became particularly marked at the end of the 1870s, when the chancellor's prolonged bouts of illness saddled Herbert with still heavier responsibilities.

At the same time, Herbert himself headed for the worst crisis of his life; when he emerged from it, he was a changed and shaken man, with his relations to Bleichröder obliterated. The cause was love—a passion Bismarck had once understood all too well and which now, in his late sixties, he feared as an uncontrollable force which could uproot his son's loyalty. For years Herbert, one of Germany's most eligible bachelors, had been in love with the beautiful Elizabeth von Hatzfeldt (distantly related to Paul), who was unhappily married to the Prince Carolath. In the spring of 1881 Elizabeth finally divorced Carolath, in the firm expectation that Herbert would marry her. Newspapers speculated about the forthcoming marriage. Nor was there any doubt that Elizabeth and Herbert were deeply in love.

But the lovers had reckoned without Bismarck, who was to stop at nothing to wreck his son's intentions. In scene after scene, amidst "sobbing tears," the chancellor threatened his son with every conceivable calamity, including disinheritance and suicide. When Herbert wanted to visit Elizabeth, who had fallen ill in Venice, Bismarck declared that "he would go along,

---

* He seems to have taken malicious pleasure in humiliating him, too. According to one eyewitness, Herbert once told Bleichröder that he had spoken to the Paris Rothschilds about the major banking houses of Europe and of course mentioned Bleichröder. Rothschild was said to have replied: " 'Bleichröder? What is Bleichröder? Bleichröder is the one percent which I let him have.' Bleichröder had a sour expression but said nothing." The story has often been told, but is only once linked to Herbert, and illustrates what arrogant masters Bleichröder had to serve. See Brauer, *Im Dienste Bismarcks*, p. 207.

he cared more for me and the prevention of the marriage than for the whole Reich, for all his commitments, and for the rest of his life." If any Bismarck talked to Elizabeth, it would be the chancellor himself.[150]

Bismarck subjected his favorite son to the kind of ruthless bullying that he had previously practiced on his worst enemies. The tactic worked again, but at a price that perhaps even the father had not reckoned with. Torn between filial obligations and a great love, threatened with disinheritance, disgrace, and virtual poverty if he married a divorcée, Herbert floundered helplessly, until Elizabeth, aware that he would never marry her, contemptuously called off all contacts between them.* Herbert was consumed with regret, remorse, and, perhaps, occasional relief that at least the torturing uncertainty was resolved.

Why had Bismarck inflicted this horror on his son? It is generally agreed that he was troubled by his son's marrying a divorcée and outraged by the fact that Elizabeth had the closest family ties to some of his most embittered enemies. Her sisters were married respectively to Baron Walter von Loë and to Count Alexander von Schleinitz, both leading members of the anti-Bismarck *fronde*. As such, they were close to Empress Augusta, whom Bismarck always regarded as his most dangerous enemy. He warned Herbert that his "sense of honor could not allow his name to be linked in marriage with everything that is called Hatzfeldt, Carolath, Loë, etc."[151]

Yet none of this seems to explain Bismarck's rage. To be sure, Bismarck would have loathed such connections, but could the ingenious diplomat not have found a way to banish the prospective in-laws from his and Herbert's presence? The driving force in this drama, I suspect, was the father's boundless jealousy, his sense that his son's complete dependency on him might weaken in the company of this elegant and worldly woman. Her unfortunate relations alone could never have provoked this violence in Bismarck—the real threat was Herbert's independence. Perhaps still other emotions and recollections played their unconscious part: his own infatuations with spirited and married women and his own fidelity to Johanna, utterly dependent and utterly dull. Should his son find happiness in a sudden leap to a different, sumptuous world of cosmopolitan taste? Whatever jealousies and fears assailed Bismarck, the fact remains that he made no effort to screen them or subject them to other considerations, such as the likely cost of this enforced denial to Herbert. Somehow the episode suggests not only Bismarck's ruthless egoism but something of his own vulnerability.

It certainly left Herbert shattered. In the weeks of anguished indecision, he felt like someone torn to pieces by four horses pulling in different

---

* Herbert wrote his best friend: "My father has nothing except the great property of the two entailed estates." *Aus 50 Jahren. Erinnerungen des Fürsten Philipp zu Eulenburg-Hertefeld* (Berlin, 1923), p. 95. By a recent provision, the estates could not be inherited by someone who had married a divorcée. It is odd that Herbert would pretend to a friend—perhaps even to himself—that his father had no other assets besides the estates. At the time Bismarck's investments amounted to about a million marks. Did Herbert mean to exaggerate the material obstacles to the marriage in order to evade the emotional difficulties?

directions. He dared not rail against the author of his misfortunes; indeed he felt guilty at having caused his father such a violent upset. At the same time, he felt guilty at having misled the princess—deceived her, as many alleged. And, no doubt, he felt deepest guilt at somehow having failed himself, at having had a chance to fashion his life and his happiness and having failed to grasp that chance, at not having been a man. To justify his sacrifice he had to glorify his father still more, and the psychological burden of it all must have been enormous. A few months after the break, he wrote to Eulenburg that he sought escape through hard work but that this intensified his disgust with "human scum: My father is absolutely right when in moments of exhaustion and office fatigue he says, 'I am tired of driving swine.'" Whatever incipient misanthropy the young Bismarck may have nursed before the crisis, it was magnified many times during it; it was burned into his being, and he could no longer rid himself of what he called "the boundless contempt for human kind, the disgust for the pack one has to govern with."[152] And the immediate victim of this new misanthropy was Bleichröder—on whom Herbert now seemed to fasten all his hatreds and all his frustrations.

His outrage was not unjustified, though he vilified Bleichröder without ever acknowledging the true cause of his hatred. Bismarck had mobilized Bleichröder in order to convey some kind of warning to the princess—and Bleichröder had stooped to serve the chancellor even in this wretched enterprise. We have but hints of Bleichröder's role: on April 13, before the divorce had been promulgated, Bleichröder sent Bismarck a letter from his "confidant," asked that it be returned, and added that he was at Bismarck's "hourly disposal. Perhaps there is another way that could lead to the desired end, but about this I could report only orally to Your Highness."[153] Bismarck clearly authorized further efforts, and in the Bleichröder Archive on Bleichröder stationery we find the copy of a telegram dated April 23 and apparently sent from Bleichröder's secret agent, Ledermann by name, whom he had dispatched to Venice, reporting that the Princess Carolath had returned the letter to him, unopened, because "she wants no interference from third parties and Prince Bismarck could after all write to her directly." The agent wanted to know whether he should try again, giving Bismarck's name as sender. The date was April 23, 1881—the very day the decree of divorce was granted. We have another signed letter of Bleichröder to Bismarck, dated the next day, to the effect that Mr. L. would leave (Venice) unless the chancellor had different instructions. There is an undated memorandum in the Bleichröder files, also on Bleichröder stationery, containing bits of information about Prince Carolath, gathered by a banker friend in Breslau. Prince Carolath had agreed to return 118,000 marks to the princess as the remainder of her dowry and to pay her 24,000 marks annual alimony. Finally there is reference to some confidants of Prince Carolath who might be able to persuade the prince that the decree of April 23 should not be allowed to become effective.[154]

The fragments that survive suggest that Bleichröder not only sought to gather information about the Carolaths' activities and finances but conveyed to both, certainly to the Princess Carolath, Bismarck's desire that the divorce should not take place or that it should be revoked after it was granted. It was callous of the chancellor to enlist Bleichröder in this type of intrigue, and it was foolish of Bleichröder to follow Bismarck's summons with his usual alacrity. Bleichröder was to pay for his indiscretion—and for Bismarck's deceitful intriguing as well.

In July 1881 Herbert wrote a barely civil letter to the Bleichröder bank. With it he returned a letter of Bleichröder's, sending him a statement of his account, which showed a debit of 3,309 marks arising from an earlier credit given him in Naples. Herbert replied furiously that at the end of March he had already asked the bank to pay out his balance, a request he thought would be understood as tantamount to closing his account. The Naples credit should have been charged to his father's account: "I request that this be done now and that the enclosures be *burned* because since the end of March of this year I do not possess an account with your bank." In the Bleichröder files is a signed letter from Bleichröder to Herbert, written before this peremptory note had arrived, but never dispatched.[155] Herbert's unusual request to have Bleichröder's letter and account burned clearly signified the final break. There was no direct communication between them ever again.

Herbert never confided the reasons for this break to anyone, and historians to this day have been unaware of it. Perhaps Herbert told no one because to do so would implicate his father. Instead he pursued Bleichröder with unabated hatred. Bleichröder knew the true reason but apparently confided it only to one man, to State Secretary Boetticher, who in his unpublished *Nachlass* left a memorandum about "Bismarck's relation to Bleichröder." In it he mentioned Herbert's enmity and added that Bleichröder had given as one reason that Count Bismarck "resented Bleichröder because the latter had thwarted his marriage to the Princess Carolath."[156] Bleichröder's knowledge of the affair and perhaps his complicity in it was known to a few of his contemporaries. Thus Kardorff wrote him in June 1881: "It seems to me that in political matters we are still ailing because of Herbert and Venice; at least the renewed illness of the Chancellor must be essentially blamed on this."[157]

Bleichröder had to bear the full brunt of Herbert's anger, sharpened by his coarse and brutal anti-Semitism. To the whole entourage he now poured out his venom about "the disgusting Bleichröder. . . . [T]he fellow gets more impudent all the time. Hang him!"[158] To the receptive Holstein he wrote: "I look on the filthy Jew as an evil in himself. . . . [T]hat stinking brute Bleichröder."[159] And even Rantzau, with his close relations to Bleichröder, wrote Herbert, *"Der Bleiche ist ein Schweinehund."*[160] Herbert's hatred did not diminish with time; the entourage had to devise elaborate stratagems so that Herbert would not be present when Bleichröder called on his father.[161] Stories about Herbert's deliberate rudeness to Bleichröder made the rounds: such heroic pranks as setting off firecrackers while the blind Bleichröder was waiting in the Chancellery. And no one apparently suspected that it was an injured man who sought relief by injuring another.

It would be wrong to conclude that Herbert's frustrated marriage was solely responsible for his hatred of Bleichröder. It merely quickened his previously conceived disdain, just as it inflamed his previously controlled anti-Semitism.* But what had been tolerable before became unbearable now. Herbert loathed Bleichröder's influence over his father; he was jealous of their intimacy. Bleichröder's intervention in the spring of 1881 had epitomized that intimacy—and Herbert must have felt betrayed by his father. Such feelings he probably hid from himself, and what was allowed to emerge was his rage against Bleichröder. It was in some ways the rage of the powerless, the very prototype of what Nietzsche defined as that corrosive, modern force, *ressentiment*: the hatred of the impotent.

If Herbert had been conscious of his complicated feelings, he might have exacted Bleichröder's head from his father as his reward for renunciation. Bismarck might have obliged, because affection for the son would have outweighed loyalty to a servant. The request was probably never made, and there is no reason to suppose that Bismarck ever knew that Herbert had discovered Bleichröder's nefarious role in thwarting his love.

Bleichröder worried about his relations with Herbert, and Holstein noted: "Bleichröder hates Herbert von Bismarck because he knows he has no more implacable enemy."[162] Bleichröder finally asked Bismarck to reconcile him with Herbert, but to no avail. The chancellor intimated that Herbert's violence had caused him trouble in official quarters, too, but that he was powerless to effect a change.[163] Both Herbert and Bleichröder had been used and abused by Bismarck. What would he have gained from reconciling his victims? To the end, then, Bleichröder had to suffer the exaggerated retribution of his indiscretion, which Herbert always placed in the context of anti-Semitism.

Did Bleichröder take the lesson to heart? We have no reason to suppose so. Service to Bismarck had become second nature to him, and the line between service and subservience was thin. Subservience even took precedence over prudence. Bleichröder was unhappy at Herbert's hatred, but he survived it.

And still, was it sheer coincidence that in the summer of 1882 Bleichröder showed an intimate solicitude for Bismarck which surpassed even Bleichröder's exaggerated norms? In May Bleichröder sought to present Bismarck with a special horse—though at the time Bismarck had not yet resumed riding ("the Scotch cob is a calm and splendid creature . . . and awaits its presentation"); Bill assured Bleichröder of his father's interest, provided the price was right. But the gift horse—for that was probably Bleichröder's intention—did not pass inspection. Bismarck feared that it would not respond properly in the country and "was a bit lazy to boot." In

---

* Was it unrelated that six years later, as state secretary, he sought to block the admission of a Jew to the Foreign Office—only because he was a Jew? By doing so, he broke with a slightly more flexible policy in effect before, but argued that Jews always became pushy when placed in high positions, and that the rest of the carefully selected staff would object if a "Jew boor" (*Judenbengel*) be added just because his father had "jobbered together" a great deal of money. Morsey, *Reichsverwaltung*, pp. 121–122.

August Bleichröder sent another "infinitely calm and well-trained" cob to Varzin.[164]

Bismarck's health was alarmingly bad that summer. In June, in two long addresses to the Reichstag, he had berated deputies for placing vacations ahead of the nation's business—and then disappeared for six uninterrupted months in Varzin. Bleichröder had always been deeply concerned about Bismarck's health, and had taken it as self-evident that the chancellor's entourage would keep him informed about it. (As early as 1872, Lothar Bucher had sent him an accurate diagnosis: "You know how spiritual and somatic conditions are reciprocally related with the Prince. Excited or annoyed by affairs, he becomes more vulnerable to colds and lapses in his diet, and when he has physical complaints, any kind of work makes him impatient.")[165] In July 1882, in a handwritten note, Bismarck assured Bleichröder that his strength was recovering "but the facial pains do not yield."[166]

Bleichröder at once consulted a leading Berlin internist, Professor F. T. Frerichs, who in the past had attended Bismarck. Frerichs prescribed new pills for Bismarck's facial pains, and Bleichröder bought and dispatched them to Varzin. More, Frerichs—who out of his concern for Bismarck called on Bleichröder several times a day—"agrees with me that it would indeed be desirable for Your Highness's nerves if Your Highness could still resolve to go to Gastein or Wildbad." In short, Bleichröder and Frerichs urged him to foresake Varzin in favor of a more strenuous *Kur*, designed to speed his recovery. At the same time, Bleichröder reported that "the diagnosis which Frerichs makes for Your Highness is, thank God, a favorable one, as he knows the full normality of all Your Highness's organs." Bleichröder sent Bismarck Frerichs's pills and medical advice, a special Bohemian glass goblet, and his own wishes for Bismarck's nerves—as well as "my most fervent prayer to the Creator [*Weltenschöpfer*] that He may keep Your Highness in splendid health for many, many years to the great joy of Your Highness's admirers."[167] Bismarck accepted the gifts and rejected the advice; he remained in Varzin and returned to Berlin in December—with a full, white beard, a sign of how he had suddenly, terribly aged. The following year a much younger doctor, Schweninger, by a combination of strict regimen and psychological reassurance, effected a miraculous recovery.

No doubt, Bismarck appreciated Bleichröder's expensive solicitude. He could handle a great deal of adulation. Herbert, on the other hand, was fuming and wrote Bill: "The disgusting Bleichröder, who puts his nose into everything, wrote yesterday on Frerichs's behalf. . . . It is really too impudent, this aggressive ingratiating [*Anschmeisserei*]. Also today suddenly appeared a horse, with a bow-legged israelite groom. . . . Pretty soon the Jew will send a crate of coronets; the fellow gets more impudent all the time. Hang him!"* Bismarck in fact kept the horse for a few weeks; in October

---

* Bleichröder did not send a crate of coronets, but at the time of Bismarck's seventieth birthday had a medal struck, with Bismarck's—much younger—portrait on one side and his coat of arms on the other. He gave Bismarck ten gold medals, twenty-five silver ones—and had 10,000 struck in bronze to be sold for some Bismarck charity, much to Bismarck's delight. Norman Rich and M. H. Fisher, eds., *The Holstein Papers* (Cambridge, 1957), II, 227.

Rantzau assured Herbert "the Jew-horse . . . traveled to Berlin yesterday in order to be returned to his gracious giver." For all this verbal *Schneidigkeit*, or mindless virility, Herbert and Holstein thought Rantzau soft on Bleichröder and worried about "his subjective . . . feminine nature."[168] Furtive malice was the universal psychic escape for Bismarck's underlings.

Bleichröder's foes detested his "meddlesomeness," his constant intriguing, his Jewish "pushiness." But was he guilty of anything his companions did not also practice? No doubt he lacked any great delicacy of sentiment, but in the spiteful, intrigue-ridden, hypocritical world of Bismarck's Germany, a truly sensitive Jew could never have risen to the top.

The German cult of friendship, rightly celebrated as an important facet of German culture, played a great role in Bleichröder's life. Perhaps the rich and powerful rarely have friends, but Bleichröder had the misfortune to experience the decline of genuine friendship. Few men in Bismarck's Germany could have had so many protestations of friendship as did Bleichröder, and few men could have been so utterly without friends as Bleichröder—if friends are measured by their loyalty and honesty. The last word belongs to Bismarck, who, some months before his dismissal, when Alexander III bemoaned that Russia had "but one sincere friend," the Prince of Montenegro, initialed the report with the laconic: "But who has?" It is hard to imagine that he was thinking only of the international realm.[169]

CHAPTER 11

The Fourth Estate

I have been employed as a press bandit.
—Count Wilhelm Bismarck to Holstein, July 16, 1883

No one can hope to bribe or twist,
Thank God! the British journalist,
But, seeing what the man will do
Unbribed, there's no occasion to.

—Humbert Wolfe

Wilhelm Bismarck's complaint, "I have been employed as a press bandit," epitomized his father's relations with the press.[1] From the very beginning of his political life, Bismarck recognized—and exaggerated—the power of the press. Publicly he spoke of its "monstrous mendacity," and covertly he tried to bend it to his own purposes.[2] He thought most journalists failed creatures, irresponsible scribblers and literati who were ignorant of politics and scurrilous in their attacks on him. It was a field where he sought to fight fire with fire—or to use his own favorite maxim: "*A gentilhomme, gentilhomme / A corsair, corsair et demi.*" Anticipating none, Bismarck encountered few gentlemen among the press. He chose his weapons accordingly.

Throughout his reign, the press grew in importance. More people read more papers with greater coverage, owing to increasing literacy, cheaper newspapers, and a growing concern with political affairs, stimulated in part by Bismarck's dramatic successes. It was an unexamined commonplace of the second half of the century that the press molded public opinion, both in its reports and in its comments. Voters were swayed by what the press reported, and so were politicians. By 1890 the press was a far more significant force in German life than in 1862, and Bismarck treated it as he treated all objects of importance: as something to be fought, manipulated, cajoled.

Bismarck's assessment of the press was not atypical. The liberals of Europe thought the press of fundamental importance and its freedom a cherished bulwark against tyranny. Conservatives came to use the press, regretting its power and lamenting that unprincipled journalists wielding such power were an example of democracy at work. Bismarck's disdain for journalists was also widely shared. Journalists (and stockbrokers) were thought poisonous products of modernity—and Jews held a prominent place among both groups. Jew or non-Jew, the journalist was a favorite figure of abuse; in the popular mind he was often deemed a writer or teacher *manqué*, hence peculiarly vulnerable to temptations of all sorts. Journalists were either venal or subversive, or both.[3] The classic portrait of the power and corruptibility of the press was Balzac's *Lost Illusions*, and the prejudices lingered on long after the reality had begun to change.

For decades, German historians assumed that the great chancellor had been impervious to modern deformities, such as money and journalism.[4] Bleichröder knew better. He was aware that Bismarck used his office, his underlings, and his family in order to plant stories, refute articles, blacken opponents. Bismarck watched the press like a hawk, and one subordinate remembered his injunction: "Every press attack must be smashed, every insult must be avenged."[5] Bismarck's last resort in dealing with the press, both at home and abroad, was bribery, often financed through the Welfenfond and often carried out by the supple Bleichröder.

Bleichröder, of course, had his own abiding concern with the press. Until mid-century it had specialized in commercial and financial news; bankers and journalists had a common interest in getting news swiftly, and a scoop could bring fame or profits. During Bleichröder's lifetime the press became an increasingly important source of news; his personal network of intelligence gathering no longer sufficed. Newspapers could also mold commercial opinion: a favorable story could ensure the success of a new flotation; an unfavorable story could ruin it. Rival financial groups fought out their battles in the pages of the press. Bleichröder appreciated the importance of fashioning the right kind of climate; after the early 1870s he also became a frequent target of abuse, and hence he, too, needed to cultivate as many friends among the Fourth Estate as possible. And he, too, had a vast array of means at his command.

Bismarck and Bleichröder, then, had separate and complementary concerns with the press. Their first joint venture, which lasted for decades, had to do with Prussia's foremost news agency, founded in 1849 by Bernhard Wolff, a German-Jewish physician turned pressman. Days after the Prussian state telegraph line from Berlin to Aachen had been completed, Wolff established an agency to transmit commercial news between Berlin and the Rhineland. Gradually he added political news as well, and in the great economic boom of the 1850s this link between Berlin and the West became increasingly important and profitable.

In 1849 Wolff had beaten a rival entrepreneur by a few days. Julius Reuter, born in Kassel in 1816 as Israel Beer Josaphat and a convert to Christianity in the 1840s, when he married Ida Maria Magnus, the daughter of a Berlin banker, had worked in the Paris news agency established by Charles Havas (according to some accounts, a Jewish immigrant) in 1835; in 1849 Reuter wanted to establish the line that Wolff founded. Undaunted, he installed an ingenious pigeon service between Aachen and Brussels, thus linking German and French facilities. In 1851 Reuter moved to London and established his first office there.[6] In time, Reuter surpassed all his rivals, and in 1871 the duke of Saxe-Coburg-Gotha ennobled him; Baron Julius de Reuter and Baron Bleichröder became friends.

Wolff meanwhile expanded his operations throughout Germany. He spun a network of suppliers and recipients that gradually extended to foreign posts as well. In his Berlin Bureau he employed Lothar Bucher, the ex-revolutionary of 1848, who had spent years of exile in London and who in 1865 was appointed one of Bismarck's principal aides.[7] Bucher's successor was Paul Lindau, the well-known littérateur, whose memoirs depict the operations of the bureau. The staff sifted incoming reports, edited them, and dispatched them to their German customers; important news was sent to foreign subscribers as well. Wolff's men knew what was going on in the world hours before most other people did, an asset that Bleichröder came to appreciate.[8]

For some time, Wolff had collaborated with his foreign analogues, Reuter of London and Havas of Paris. In 1865 Havas intended to establish rival offices in Berlin and sought to buy out Wolff's business. Wolff appealed to the king for help, lest Prussia become dependent on foreigners for news.[9] A single individual, Wolff warned, could not compete with foreign companies; "patriotic financiers" were needed to put his business on a secure footing. He emphasized the political importance of keeping the news agency Prussian and insinuated that the king would find it a valuable personal instrument if his policy should ever diverge from that of his ministry. William rebuffed that suggestion, but, backed by Bismarck, he urged "patriotic financiers" such as Bleichröder to effect "the consolidation of [Wolff's] enterprise."[10] Encouraged by the government, Bleichröder, Viktor von Magnus, C. D. von Oppenfeld, Dr. Ferdinand Salomon, and two others founded a new joint-stock company, the Continental Telegraph Company. They contributed the original capital, some 330,000 taler out of a projected total of 2 million taler in shares, and appointed Theodor Wimmel and Richard Wentzel as the legally responsible heads for ten years. A separate agreement bought Wolff's Bureau and retained him as the general manager of the new firm, which was to "distribute on a professional basis telegrams of political, commercial, and financial content," expand the existing network, and acquire any new telegraphic devices.[11]

The company proved immediately useful to Bismarck during the Austro-Prussian war, and it also served as an important weapon to ward off anti-Prussian agitation in the newly annexed province of Hanover.[12] But Havas and Reuter still coveted their rival's business. In February 1869 Julius Fröbel, a Munich publisher and an ex-radical sentenced to death in 1848, who had served Austrian interests until 1868, warned Bismarck that Havas and Reuter were about to buy out the Continental Telegraph Bureau. By alerting Bismarck, Fröbel added, he was violating his own interests because Reuter had made him "grand offers"; the prospective merger, however, would benefit French interests. Bismarck's office began an elaborate and obscure campaign to thwart such efforts.[13] A few days later, Keudell wrote Bleichröder that Bismarck recommended the quick sale of the Telegraph Bureau "in your [Bleichröder's] interests," adding that he would offer Bismarck's reasons for the extraordinary advice the next day—orally.[14] (What a bane to the historian these oral communications are!)

In any case, Bismarck reconsidered. With Keudell the active intermediary, the Prussian government moved to forestall the foreign takeover. On April 19 Wolff warned Bleichröder that Keudell's promised intervention might come too late, because Havas and Reuter had served an ultimatum, threatening to sever all contractual agreements that enabled Wolff to obtain foreign news. On April 23 Keudell told Bleichröder to deal directly with General Chauvin, the head of the Prussian Telegraph Service, and Delbrück in order to get binding government commitments for not selling the agency.[15] Meanwhile, Havas and Reuter raised their offer from 650,000 to 700,000 francs, and Wentzel begged Bleichröder to persuade the government to back the existing enterprise and thus to combat foreign, including Hanoverian, interests; "it is a matter of serving the fatherland and checking enemy agitation."[16]*

By June 1869 Bleichröder's efforts proved successful: negotiations with Havas had broken down earlier, and the Prussian State Ministry and the Continental Telegraph Company signed a formal contract which for decades was carefully concealed from the public. The heart of the agreement was the government's grant of a virtual monopoly position to Wolff in return for far-reaching control over the activities of the company, control that could turn into censorship. The government promised to give the company's political dispatches precedence over all private telegrams and agreed to the creation of special company offices adjacent to the main telegraph office in Berlin. Obviously a competitor without such privileges would be at a serious, probably hopeless, handicap. The government further agreed to lend the company 100,000 taler, interest-free in the first year, and to contribute another 100,000 taler as outright gifts in 1871 and 1872. In return, the company promised to supply the government and any official designated by it with all incoming dispatches save stock-market and commercial news. (Bleichröder apparently received every kind of information.) Furthermore, it would expand its network and would supply upon demand all North German officials abroad with its political dispatches, and at the government's request it would give "the greatest possible publicity" at home and abroad to any telegraphic messages. "All telegrams of a political nature which the Telegraphic Bureau of the

---

* During these negotiations Wolff demonstrated his particular usefulness. In April 1869 he sent Bleichröder a confidential report from Paris that the imperial regime would win the elections because of Napoleon's "gigantic efforts," but the governmental deputies would no longer support the regime "through thick and thin. . . . [Hence] I am confident about the maintenance of peace." Bismarck, too, received private reports from the Wolff agency. Perturbed by the tenor of some of them, he inquired about their provenance and was told that they had originated with the pro-Austrian journalist Dr. Emil Landsberg, in Paris, whose reports Wolff obtained indirectly and forwarded to a select few, but did not publish. Wolff to Bleichröder, 26 April 1869, BA; Bleichröder to Bismarck, 27 April 1869, DZA: Merseburg: A.A.I. Rep. 4. Nr. 721.

Continental Telegraph Company wants to relay are subject to a prior control by officials specially designated by the royal government." In case of purposeful violation, the government could demand the appointment of a new head for the political direction of the Telegraph Bureau. The government also had the right to demand the dismissal of unreliable agents and was to have its own observer on the board of directors. The contract was to run for ten years.[17]

There had been shrewd bargaining on both sides, and the contract gave the Prussian government a most important propaganda weapon—the more important for being secret, for a long time unsuspected, and hence beyond parliamentary cavil.[18] As a recent study put it, the connection with Wolff "put into Bismarck's hands a very effective, indeed decisive instrument for influencing the press, which also afforded him control of the sources of news transmission."[19] It is remarkable that even in the heyday of economic liberalism in Prussia a mixed monopoly of this sort could have been created. (Traditions change slowly in Germany; in 1844 a foreign observer had noted: "The preparation, manufacture, and sale of political intelligence are as much a royal monopoly in Germany as those of tobacco in France. . . .")[20] In 1891 Eugen Richter condemned the original establishment of the monopoly, but he was unaware of the attendant secret prerogatives of the government. Bleichröder was untroubled at having promoted an agreement so prejudicial to the principle of a free press. He was a government man, and banker and chancellor probably felt only pleasure at having forged this new instrument for their mutual benefit. The company, in turn, could now negotiate an agreement with Havas and Reuter which in effect divided the world into different spheres of interest; Wolff received the exclusive right to "exploit" central and eastern Europe.[21]

Bismarck disposed of various powerful instruments in dealing with the press. The most notorious of these was the Welfenfond, consisting of the annual income from the sequestered funds of the Hanoverian crown which Bismarck could expend without public accounting. The fund was popularly known as the reptile fund because of Bismarck's reference to some Hanoverian journalists as reptiles. Throughout Bismarck's reign, opposition leaders assumed that Bismarck was using his fund to feed "the reptiles," in short, to bribe journalists and papers of every stripe. The fund became a symbol of Bismarck's corrupting influence on German society; the actual use may have been more modest, indeed more in keeping with what all governments did at the time—and subsequently.*

---

* The full history of how governments sought to influence or subvert foreign nations by subsidizing foreign papers will probably never be told. But even partial studies would reveal something about the expectations of such governments and their assessment of the relative importance of particular individuals and of public opinion generally. An unreliable example is provided by A. Raffalovitch, . . . *L'Abominable Vénalité de la Presse, D'Après les documents des archives russes (1897–1917)* (Paris, 1931).

In 1873 the British ambassador referred to this "secret service fund [which Parliament had handed over to Bismarck] for his *irresponsible* use. . . . It is a subject of curiosity to many to know, but nobody ventures to ask how Prince Bismarck spends the interest of those sixteen millions of Thalers or two millions and four hundred thousand Pounds."[22] Bleichröder was more knowledgeable than most contemporaries. It is probable that he invested or helped to invest the principal that had been sequestered; it is certain that he was one of the main disbursers of the interest.[23]

Bleichröder's friend Keudell supervised the Welfenfond receipts in the Foreign Office, the largest beneficiary of its revenues.[24] Keudell knew Bleichröder to be discreet when it mattered; hence he employed him as a trusted go-between. We have only one set of accounts from the fund, and it shows that in the last nine months of 1869 Bleichröder transmitted more than 30,000 taler, most of which went to his friend Major von Brandt, who at the time carried out secret intelligence work. Bleichröder was thus responsible for the transfer of more than 30 percent of total expenditures.[25] Bleichröder also acted as cover man for much smaller sums; in 1868, for example, Keudell instructed Bleichröder to transmit 750 francs to Paris, where "on highest authority" and in top secret fashion Keudell was to disburse it. Additional payments would follow, Keudell added.[26]

During the Franco-Prussian war Bismarck had used the press to inflame Prussian annexationism in regard to Alsace-Lorraine; he was also most solicitous of promoting—by all means, including subvention—pro-Prussian sentiment among neutrals. As always, Bleichröder helped. The war had sharpened Bismarck's appreciation of the power of the press, and in the new Empire, as the mass press became financially independent through advertisements, his manipulation of it became more important and more difficult.

Both Bismarck and Bleichröder were satisfied with the wartime performance of the Wolff Agency. Both men had received preferential treatment, and Bismarck had even tried to order Wolff not to deliver its dispatches to the king. After the war Bleichröder remained chairman of Wolff's board and his friend Richard Wentzel was the director. Wentzel continued to supply Bleichröder with a regular flow of financial, political, and court news. "A wakeful eye is at your service," he assured him in 1871, and the Bleichröder Archive attests Wentzel's assiduous transmission of all manner of news, both to the Berlin office and to Bleichröder on holiday. He sent confidential news regularly and ordinary news with such dispatch that Bleichröder often received it ahead of anybody else.[27] Time and again, high personages, the emperor included, complimented Bleichröder because he had managed to convey some particular news before anyone else had done so, and often Wentzel had been his source.

The preservation of the Wolff Agency as a semigovernmental yet independent company was not an easy task. Foreign agencies still sought an international cartel, and the German government was divided on whether to retain the tie to the company. In November 1874 Julius Reuter again urged

Bleichröder to accept a merger of the three agencies. He offered him shares in the new company or £60,000 in cash for his investment in Wolff and promised that each of the three original companies would maintain its complete political independence.

Reuter and Bleichröder had collaborated during the Franco-Prussian war and thereafter met in various spas.[28] The directors of the Continental Telegraph Bureau favored Reuter's proposition but delegated Bleichröder to solicit Bismarck's views. Bleichröder officially inquired whether Bismarck had any objections to the projected fusion. If Bismarck did, Bleichröder promised he would try to overrule his colleagues; as consolation, however, the government would have to renew its agreement with the company at once and not wait until its expiration in 1879. It would have to ensure that the same privilege of preferential dispatch of telegrams as had existed under General Chauvin would be continued under the new chief of telegraph.[29] Three days later Bülow, the state secretary in the Foreign Office, wrote Bleichröder that Bismarck, urgently concerned about this matter, had instructed him to discuss it with Bleichröder.[30]

In the end, Bismarck refused to renew the treaty prematurely—on the extraordinary ground that he could not bind the Prussian government far beyond his own likely tenure. More characteristically, he added that the contract offered few advantages to the government, which, if the new international company should injure its interests, would still possess sufficient resources to eliminate it.[31] In short, Bismarck saw no reason to pay Bleichröder's price, and Bleichröder opposed fusion although his conditions had not been met—proof positive that the connection was beneficial to him.[32]

The government's agreement with the Wolff Agency was to expire in 1879. In 1876 Tiedemann officially argued against renewal; two years later, a commission of government experts took up the question. Bleichröder's friend Bülow insisted that the company was "of the very greatest political importance for the . . . government. . . . [I]t has always subordinated itself to the political influences of the government in the most loyal and, for the latter, most convenient, fashion. It asks the government about every doubtful telegram and unconditionally follows the government's instructions." The core of any new agreement would still have to be the government's willingness to grant the company preferential treatment in the transmission of telegrams, whereas the company would have to accept the government's right to confirm and dismiss the chief editor of the bureau.[33] Bülow was far more appreciative of the bureau's place in the government's press policy than Bismarck had been in 1875.

Bülow's death in October 1879 removed the strongest defender of the status quo. Bismarck insisted on clearer rights of prior censorship and still greater powers over the administration of the bureau.[34] Worried, Bleichröder sought at least to retain existing privileges, and he asked Holstein for help. But Holstein replied from Varzin that Bismarck had already

shot his bolt when he ordered preferential treatment of political telegrams reestablished, as it exists now, and did so against the wishes of other officials who wanted the privilege completely eliminated. To do more would be awkward for him because, as you know, the suspicion of speculation attaches itself all too easily to such support. That is why, at this point, the proper way for you is [to go] through the state ministry; after all, you have your connections there, as everywhere.[35]

A formal agreement was not reached; Bismarck and his advisers made demands that proved too exacting even for the docile Wentzel and Bleichröder. An informal agreement prolonged existing arrangements. Bismarck continued to think that the Wolff Bureau had special obligations to heed his wishes.[36] It remained one of his instruments—the more useful for being informally dependent and hence beyond the reach of any parliamentary control.[37]

In 1872 Bleichröder established a further covert link between the German government and the press. For years he had been in touch with a German journalist in London, Dr. Max Schlesinger (another journalist with a medical degree), who, since the early 1850s, had edited a weekly bulletin, *Englische Correspondenz*, which supplied English news to German newspapers. Schlesinger also informed and influenced the British press on German affairs. He had begun as a pro-Austrian agent; in the first few weeks of the Franco-Prussian war, when influencing British public opinion was a matter of high urgency to Berlin, the government thought of buying his paper.[38] In 1872, through Keudell's good offices, Bleichröder sought to persuade Bismarck that the Prussian government should buy the *Englische Correspondenz*, which Schlesinger was anxious to sell.

Bismarck agreed and in a top secret letter to his finance minister, Camphausen, gave his reasons:

> There is no doubt that politically it would be valuable not to let the *Englische Correspondenz* fall into hostile hands, not to have its columns open to particularist, clerical or socialist influences; the *Englische Correspondenz* is almost the sole source of news about English politics and as such has an important influence on public opinion in all German-speaking countries of Europe.[39]

In short, Schlesinger's paper fitted into Bismarck's post-1871 priorities as far as the press was concerned: he now concentrated on influencing German, not foreign, opinion, and in this effort the *Englische Correspondenz* could play an important role.[40]

With Camphausen's approval, although in Bismarck's absence, a secret agreement between Wolff and the Prussian government was signed, followed by an agreement between Wolff and Schlesinger. Bleichröder helped to negotiate both agreements. They stipulated that the Wolff Bureau should pay Schlesinger 50,000 taler "on behalf of the [Prussian] State Ministry," which thereby would acquire sole ownership of the *Correspondenz*. Financial supervision and political control of Schlesinger's enterprise were vested in the Wolff Bureau, subject to the government's instructions. In exchange, Wolff's earlier debt of 50,000 taler to the government was annulled. Thus, the Welfenfond, which had originally supplied Wolff with the funds, indirectly made possible the acquisition of this foreign medium.[41]

For Bleichröder, Schlesinger became a valuable contact in London.* Schlesinger kept Bleichröder reliably apprised of London intelligence concerning politics, diplomacy, and finance, and his reports underlined the interconnectedness of politics and finance: he sent Bleichröder confidential reports on England and the Russo-Turkish war; as early as 1877 he indicated that under certain circumstances England was likely to seize Egypt and that hence Egyptian securities might appreciate. A few days later, he boasted that his advice had "been worth 6 percent between friends," and he was sorry Bleichröder had not taken advantage of it.[42] At other times, as in May 1878, he philosophized about the chances of an Anglo-Russian war. Nobody knows, he wrote, not even Jehovah or Jupiter, and the motto for the day is "to fear the worst and hope for the best."[43]

But Schlesinger proved a bad investment. His newssheet from England continued to print antigovernment stories. Bismarck believed that Schlesinger "obtained his information not from Münster [the German ambassador in London] but from Beust," the Austrian ambassador.[44] By February 1876 the German government was so annoyed that it considered legal steps against Schlesinger; the original contract designated Prussian law as final recourse, despite Schlesinger's English citizenship. Berlin recognized, however, that if Schlesinger balked at a Prussian court decision, he would have to be prosecuted under English law—with attendant and unfortunate publicity—since presumably no one in England knew of the close ties between the German government and Schlesinger. The government even thought of a "protective arrest" of Schlesinger in Berlin, that is, without court action, in order to induce him to surrender his rights.[45] Bismarck was annoyed at his underlings who had concluded the original agreement: "frivolously negotiated" was his marginal note on a copy of the treaty.[46]

The Prussian government delegated Bleichröder to lure or summon Schlesinger to Berlin; whether Bleichröder knew that the government had thought of arresting Schlesinger is unclear. In any case, Bleichröder assured Bismarck's assistant in the Foreign Office, Lothar Bucher, that he had written to Schlesinger and had made "obscure insinuations" concerning some misunderstandings that had arisen between Berlin and its London agent. Schlesinger indicated great surprise at these alleged "deep-rooted differences," but agreed to come to Berlin as soon as his health permitted it.[47]

In the meantime, the German Foreign Office drew up a list of particulars

---

* Schlesinger's first extant letter in the Bleichröder papers—obviously many had preceded it—thanked his friend for some rare caviar: "It arrived anonymously, but next to the All-Knowing above, a well-informed journalist uncovers all good and evil that is perpetrated in this world." Schlesinger to Bleichröder, 30 Dec. 1874, BA.

against Schlesinger. In essence, he stood accused of spreading stories that were hostile to German interests: in 1874 he had printed only pro-Gladstone stories, ignoring critical stories about him; the pro-Gladstone line changed abruptly when the prime minister published an anti-Vatican pamphlet. In 1874 Schlesinger reported only unfavorable comments from the British press about various Protestant meetings in Britain which had expressed their sympathies with Bismarck's struggle against the ultramontanes. He had suppressed the many favorable notices. In short, the government thought Schlesinger sided with the Catholics against the Berlin government—a line that would certainly be in accord with Austrian interests. Finally, he was charged with selectively reporting anti-German references in the British press, blowing up British reports that German fears of French rearmament might lead to a preventive strike by Germany. The Berlin Foreign Office concluded that Schlesinger must have received such impressions from "anti-German sources" and that his selective reporting exemplified his antigovernmental course. No wonder that Bismarck and the German government were furious at having spent scarce resources on such a man.[48]

In March 1876 Bismarck and Bleichröder discussed the Schlesinger affair and agreed that Wentzel and Bucher should be deputized to handle the case.[49] A month later, Bleichröder produced Schlesinger in Berlin and urged Bucher to call him to order. Bucher angrily replied that earlier Bleichröder had thought that Bucher's intervention would be "harmful," because Schlesinger "could not be reached through his sense of honor and that whatever I would say to him he would sell to Count Beust." Bismarck must have been annoyed to learn that Bleichröder now spoke so scathingly of his erstwhile protégé; Bucher wrote Bleichröder:

> The Prince entrusts me to ask you respectfully to try to persuade Schlesinger, as you have repeatedly offered to do, that in the future he should either edit the *Correspondenz* in a manner consonant with the clear interest of the German government or submit to a dissolution of existing relations, be it through return of the purchase price or through surrender of the paper's administration. His Highness believes that if anything can be attained without a legal suit, you are the only one who can attain it, considering the origin of these relations.[50]

Bismarck's message was unambiguous: Schlesinger had been Bleichröder's invention, and Bleichröder must now cope with this wretched creature.

Bleichröder had no trouble choosing between Bismarck and Schlesinger, the more so as he had sent out his son Hans to inquire about Schlesinger in London and received alarming confirmation of Bismarck's suspicions: "You, dear father, are not *au courant* about his acquaintances; the fellow plays *absolutely* no role here. . . . [H]e is extraordinarily clever and may have *important* political influence, but he is not popular because no one trusts him entirely."[51]

Bleichröder made Schlesinger sign a new protocol pledging that "in accord with Dr. Schlesinger's personal conviction, the spirit and stance of the *Englische Correspondenz* should follow the principles of German policy, support German goals, and avoid anything that could obstruct the efforts of the leading statesmen of the German Reich and of the Prussian state." Dr. Wentzel was appointed as arbiter in case of any future disagreements. By having to pledge himself to give his "whole devotion and personal strength" to his enterprise, Schlesinger was implicitly reprimanded for having less than fully engaged himself earlier.[52] Put baldly, censorship and subservience were being simultaneously exacted—and subsequent correspondence makes clear that Bleichröder and the government were not content with Schlesinger's protestations.* Bleichröder and Bucher combined efforts to find a suitable "collaborator" for Schlesinger; in the end, the least expensive candidate was chosen. It was a time of stringency for the Welfenfond.[53]

In matters of substance, Schlesinger had been brought to heel. Bleichröder now suggested stories for Schlesinger to plant in British papers, and then quote in the *Englische Correspondenz* for his German audience. Thus in April 1876 Schlesinger cited several English papers as praising Bismarck's plans for nationalizing railroads, plans that Bleichröder of course had a major stake in as well.[54]

But peace was short-lived. Less than two years later, the Berlin government was angry at Schlesinger's growing deficit. Officials complained that he had converted a profitable business into a losing venture, even if the initial deficit amounted to only £30 per quarter. Camphausen repeatedly warned Bismarck about this drain on the Welfenfond and added in an aside of more general import: "I asked the State Ministry for a decision concerning the use of this year's revenue from the sequestered capital, but State Minister Bülow urged that this await [your] presence." In short, the Welfenfond was considered Bismarck's private domain. Camphausen added that the number of subscribers to the *Englische Correspondenz* had dropped by nearly 50 percent, and income had shrunk accordingly; only the expenses continued to mount.[55]

Schlesinger's explanations for this decline were unlikely to win him friends in Berlin. In addition to poor business conditions and the growing competition from telegraph companies, he blamed "the prescribed political line," which had led subscribers to complain that the *Correspondenz* had become "purely Bismarckian, . . . a party organ. . . . The decline of the *Correspondenz* is not my fault. . . ."[56] He was no doubt right—German newspapers did not need Schlesinger to get the Bismarck line.

Bleichröder transmitted these excuses to a government that was far from persuaded by them. At their most charitable, Berlin officials believed that Schlesinger's health was failing; he complained of nervous ills which often kept him from work. But charity was a rare commodity in Berlin. Bismarck's adjutant and chief protectionist whip, Christoph von Tiedemann, believed

---

* Certainly Schlesinger began to talk like a loyal Bismarckian. He thanked Bleichröder for good news about the chancellor's health, "which today is more valuable than the health of all the other two-legged creatures in Europe (and, as far as I know, in Asia, Africa, and America, too)." Schlesinger to Bleichröder, 9 May 1879, BA.

that Schlesinger and a certain Karl Marx, "with his unpatriotic, Jewish-inter-
national conscience, . . . were servants of the British government"; Tiedemann
neglected to say whether he thought them servants by conviction or corruption.
"They like to defend English commercial interests in German free-trade journals."[57] The connection with the *Englische Correspondenz* lapsed in 1881 with
the death of Max Schlesinger, a minor but colorful and versatile figure in
European journalism.

Bleichröder's many relations with the press were facilitated by the fact
that so many members of the Fourth Estate were fellow Jews.* Bismarck once
complained to St. Vallier, the French ambassador, "that the press of the
German Reich is almost entirely in the hands of the Jews"—and thus
acknowledged what most Germans thought but relatively few articulated.[58]
The charge was of course a stock in trade of anti-Semites who saw the press
as an instrument of Jewish domination of the world.[59] There is a crucial
difference, however, between the historical fact of a large Jewish *presence* in
the press and the anti-Semitic claim that that presence implied *domination*
or the exploitation of the press for Jewish purposes. Jews flocked to the new
professions and brought a special literary penchant for journalism—which
they would have exercised in older professions, if these had not still been
barred or inhospitable to them. On the whole, the Jewish journalists in Germany were far too divided among themselves and far too timid to turn the
press into an instrument for their own interests, though their mere presence
aroused and confirmed feelings of envy, fear, and hatred.

We have already noted Bleichröder's close contacts with Emil Landsberg.
Another Bleichröder friend who combined press work with irregular diplomatic assignments was Dr. Felix Bamberg, a man of such varied careers as
to demonstrate again how open nineteenth-century society really was. A
Hegelian by early training, Bamberg became a friend of Heine's in Paris,
then gradually switched from literary to political concerns and in 1851, at the
age of thirty-one, became Prussian consul there. Bismarck came to know
him in Paris and in 1862 thought him "an honest, thoroughly reliable man";
he used him to keep an eye on the ambassador, Count Goltz, whom Bismarck
feared as a would-be rival.[60] In the aftermath of the Austro-Prussian war,
Bamberg urged Bismarck to increase Prussian subsidies to the French press
in order to counteract the flow of Austrian gold, but Bismarck rejected these
pleas.[61] During the Franco-Prussian war Bamberg was in charge of press
affairs at Prussian headquarters, and after the war he was attached as political
adviser to General Manteuffel, commander of the German army of occupa-

---

* European diplomats often referred to this fact. In 1869, for example, the French
ambassador in Vienna complained that the press there was in Jewish hands and manifested "an
anti-Catholic and pseudoliberal fanaticism" which obstructed Beust's pro-French policy and
favored instead a pro-German line. Quoted in Henry Contamine, "Dépêches diplomatiques ou
consulaires et histoire intérieure: L'Exemple de l'Autriche-Hongrie (1867–1914)," *Revue
d'histoire diplomatique*, LXV (1961), 215–230.

tion. By the late 1870s he complained bitterly to Bleichröder that certain gentlemen in Berlin had rewarded his great services by transferring him to the unimportant post of consul in Messina—with a cut of 1,300 taler in salary.[62] In his embittered isolation, he prepared a biography of his friend Friedrich Hebbel and wrote a standard history of the Eastern Question. He also cultivated close relations with Prince Karl Anton of Hohenzollern-Sigmaringen, with whom he corresponded on political affairs and for whom he bought objets d'art. Bamberg in fact established the link between Karl Anton and Bleichröder. Bleichröder and Bamberg were the same age, they often served the same ends and masters—and, at least at birth, they shared the same religion. Like many Jews, Bamberg may have converted to Christianity, although baptism did not annihilate his deeper identity with his Jewish brethren, as manifested, for example, in a letter to Bleichröder conveying warm wishes for the Jewish holidays.[63]

Bleichröder had a host of other friends and acquaintances among journalists. He was sufficiently important that pressmen vied for his attentions —and he was sufficiently ambitious and vulnerable that he sought all the covert influence he could get. The editor of the renowned Neue Freie Presse in Vienna, Michael Etienne, begged Bleichröder for confidential news and pledged total discretion. "At the moment, there exists no other paper on our continent that can compare to it in influence and strength of position."[64] In 1880 a competing paper, the Wiener Allgemeine Zeitung, was founded, and its editor, Theodor Hertzka, whom the Rothschilds certified as entirely "responsible," sought to cultivate Bleichröder's acquaintance and did so in a formula that had countless variations: "You will understand my deep desire to remain in contact with someone who is at the source of events as you are."[65]

Bleichröder gave and received—incessantly. Journalists asked for information and interviews; even so distinguished an editor as Leopold Sonnemann of the Frankfurter Zeitung pleaded with Bleichröder for news. Often individual journalists would ask for financial advice or help as well, and Bleichröder often obliged. Publishers asked for subventions, too, especially if they could claim to serve the country's interests. Thus in 1877 Rudolf von Gneist, a leading jurist, appealed to Bleichröder for funds to maintain a weekly sheet, Social-Correspondenz, dedicated to fighting Social Democracy and promoting an understanding of the "true" problems of the lower classes.[66]

Bleichröder in turn made countless demands upon editors and correspondents. He sought their intelligence almost as solicitously as they sought his. More important, he watched the press unceasingly—and any unfavorable mention in any respectable paper almost invariably evoked a prompt query or rebuke. If the offense was grave enough, the paper was punished by having all Bleichröder advertisements canceled. This happened to the Vossische Zeitung, which in 1876 had displeased Bleichröder.[67] Editors, Sonnemann included, had to plead professional confidentiality in order to ward off Bleichröder's demands for the source of offending stories. Often he intervened on behalf of others, either at their behest or on his own initiative. The Bismarcks pressed him into service. Others did the same: he was such a convenient, powerful go-between.

Bleichröder also needed to plant various stories, in support of particular policies, such as bimetallism, railroad nationalization, or tariff reform. He sought to rouse public opinion on Bismarck's behalf. Finally—and routinely —he solicited favorable notices concerning his own financial operations and, especially in the early years of his career, those of the Rothschilds. Time and again, he arranged for appropriate news regarding his major issues, whether it be mortgage bank bonds, Russian funds, or Mexican bonds.

Sometimes he would go to extreme lengths to obtain favorable publicity—and oblige an old friend. In the winter of 1890–1891 he financed a trip to Mexico by Paul Lindau, a well-known writer and playwright, who at the time was entangled in a scandal involving an actress. In return, Lindau promised to write "arresting descriptions" of the country, at the very time when Bleichröder was promoting Mexican securities. Lindau wrote personal reports to his benefactor and published thirty-four newspaper articles and, finally, a book. None of Lindau's biographers mentions Bleichröder's subvention of this Mexican venture.[68]

It would be wearisome to describe all of Bleichröder's far-flung relations with the press. A few additional examples will suffice. In the 1870s he corresponded regularly with Leopold Sonnemann, publisher of the *Frankfurter Zeitung*, which was *the* independent paper in South Germany. Sonnemann, a member of the Reichstag from Frankfurt, was that rare person in imperial Germany, a bourgeois democrat, far to the left of men like Lasker and Bamberger, opposed to the Socialists, though convinced of the need radically to improve the lot of the working class. He was also Jewish, anti-Prussian, and a proponent of Franco-German friendship—it would be hard to imagine a combination more distasteful to Bismarck. Twice Bismarck went to extreme lengths to injure Sonnemann: in October 1878, in the Reichstag, he accused him of being a servant of France, and in 1884 he ensured his electoral defeat by urging that the Right should support Sonnemann's rival—a Social Democrat.[69]

The few surviving letters from Sonnemann to Bleichröder bespeak the former's interests: in 1875 he argued against full-scale protectionism and for a peaceful foreign policy: "If you have an opportunity to work in that direction, do it." In 1877 he reported that Krupp had taken him to "shops where otherwise only the highest military personnel go." War production, especially on account of Russian purchases, was booming, but other sectors barely broke even. Sonnemann hoped to expand his correspondence with Bleichröder, despite their obvious political differences and despite the fact that he had not printed the kind of pro-Russian stories that would have favored Bleichröder's Russian issues.[70] Instead the relationship broke down in the 1880s. In December 1880 Bleichröder confided to Bismarck that "the heirs of the *Kölnische Zeitung* intend to sell the paper, and I hear simultaneously from another source that the well-known Socialist Sonnemann intends to buy the paper, even though the enormous price quoted today is 2 million taler."

If Bismarck wanted it, he and some friends would buy the paper instead. In fact, the heirs changed their mind, but it was unwarranted for Bleichröder to have labeled Sonnemann a Socialist—and thus to flatter Bismarck's prejudices.[71]

Bleichröder was exceptionally close to several leading papers in Berlin, and his enemies assumed that he could plant political stories in these papers at any time it suited him. He regularly exchanged news with Ferdinand Salomon and Friedrich Dernburg of the liberal *National-Zeitung*, owned by Bernhard Wolff. Holstein once suggested to Herbert that he use the paper to trap Bleichröder: "Bleichröder knows that your father never reads the *Nat. Ztg* [sic] and uses it therefore *sans gêne*." In short, the *National-Zeitung* could be used to undermine Bleichröder's influence with Bismarck, who allegedly referred to it as a "Jew-paper."[72]

Bleichröder had constant contacts with the leading financial journals, especially with the *Berliner Börsen-Courier* and the *Frankfurter Börsen- und Handelszeitung*.[73] The editors of these papers sent Bleichröder a steady stream of information dealing with the nationalization of specific railways. Bleichröder was also exceptionally close to the *Berliner Börsen-Zeitung*, which was edited by Killisch von Horn, a veteran stock-market reporter. (An anti-Semitic contemporary wrote of Horn: "By merit and success, he surpassed all his colleagues, though he was not even of Semitic but only of German descent.")[74] In 1877, in one of his first letters, Killisch promised a favorable notice on a Bleichröder venture and at the same time inquired whether he could see him right away: "Because I know that in the last few days you conferred with the commerce minister concerning the Berlin-Stettin Railroad matter, I would like to get a directive from you on how I should best handle myself in this matter."[75] It is not clear whether he was referring to himself as editor or speculator: he was both, and Bleichröder's confidential news about the prospective nationalization of a major railroad was clearly of intense interest to him. Two years later, and with a different railroad, Killisch speculated successfully on the market and realized a profit in four days.[76] No wonder he always began his letters to Bleichröder with: "Most esteemed benefactor."

Even the best relations with journalists had their limits—if only because rival potentates of the market could press their claims as well. The surest guarantee of having power within the Fourth Estate was to own a paper, as other bankers did. Bleichröder's associate and sometime rival, the Disconto-Gesellschaft, for example, took over the *National-Zeitung* from Wolff and *Die Post* from the bankrupt Strousberg; the delicacy of German biographers inhibited Hansemann's biographer from mentioning his connections with newspapers. In the 1880s the direct ownership of newspapers through banks declined.[77]*

Bleichröder contemplated the buying of newspapers many times during

---

* It is a remarkable fact that no serious study of the relations of capital and press exists. The relations were close, as Marxists assumed; the slow development of a strong, critical, and independent press must have confounded the Marxist view—and helps to explain the rise of European reformism.

his career. In 1870, just before the Franco-Prussian war, Wilhelm Betzold, a clever man of Jewish descent with an adventurous career already behind him, suggested to Bleichröder that they should found an international journal of finance; the Rothschilds, who employed Betzold, were also interested.[78] At other times Bleichröder toyed with buying the *Kölnische Zeitung* and actually did rescue the once flourishing *Allgemeine Zeitung* in Augsburg and enabled it to survive as a weekly in Munich, known to be close to the Free Conservative cause. Bismarck occasionally planted a story in its columns.[79]

Bleichröder's most important connection was with the *Norddeutsche Allgemeine Zeitung*, which had been founded in 1861 by a fiery German democrat, August Brass, who had fought on the barricades of 1848 and had lived in exile thereafter. Brass's chief assistant was Wilhelm Liebknecht, a democratic socialist. A year later, Bismarck became premier—and the *Norddeutsche* quickly became his favorite mouthpiece. Brass rallied to Bismarck out of conviction; if the conversion was facilitated by other means, we have no record of it. Bismarck's stable of associates was full of coopted former revolutionaries; it was one way of dampening the revolutionary fire in Europe. He even thought of hiring Karl Marx. In Germany, more than in other countries, literary talent was on the left, and Bismarck was certain that he could bend talent to his own purposes; if in the process he could impoverish his enemies, *tant mieux*.

In 1872 Brass sold the *Norddeutsche* for 300,000 taler to a Hamburg combination of the brothers Ohlendorff and the Norddeutsche Bank, headed by Bleichröder's friend Senator Godeffroy. Emil Pindter became the new editor, and he too had something of a stormy past and had lived many years in exile.[80] By the time he became editor, he was fully domesticated, concerned chiefly with titles and decorations.[81] For Bismarck, the paper became a kind of house organ, and he continually planted stories in its columns.*

Pindter was a friend of Bleichröder's and Wentzel's as well as a pliant tool of Bismarck's. The Bismarcks used the paper for their own purposes and planted their own stories—and did so with particular frequency and venom during the embittered campaigns of 1878 and 1879. As the merest example of Bismarck's mode of operations, consider his instructions, sent via Herbert to Rantzau:

> Furthermore you should call in Pindter and give him a dressing down for the article . . . against Bennigsen; *nothing* should be said against

---

* In November 1880 St. Vallier, on request from Paris, reported on the German government's control of the press. Control, he wrote, was all in Bismarck's hands, a monopoly that corresponded to the peculiar character of the Constitution and to the political temperament of the chancellor. This arrangement "has its correlate in the secret funds for the press [*Reptilienfond*] which the chancellor reserves for his own undivided and uncontrolled use. He thus possesses a powerful instrument which is always efficaciously used." As for what papers were willing to receive his stories, St. Vallier replied that it would be easier to list those that were *not* willing, i.e., the Socialist and the Catholic papers, though even the latter at times shared everybody else's readiness "to draw from the reptile fund and to serve the views of the All-Powerful Master." The *Norddeutsche Allgemeine Zeitung* had always been "the most faithful" embodiment of his thoughts. St. Vallier to Comte Horace de Choiseul, 16 Nov. 1880, MAE: CP: Allemagne.

him, that article was *extraordinarily* displeasing to my father, and if attacks against Bennigsen do not cease, he will complain to the owners of the paper regarding the editors—on the other hand, he looks in vain for any attacks on Forckenbeck—and those can never be sharp or frequent enough.[82]

For Forckenbeck, read Lasker or Richter or any of the left-liberal leaders as well. Bismarck certainly expected Pindter to dance to his vitriolic tune. After Bismarck's dismissal, Pindter served the new rulers and began to attack Bismarck.[83]

On rare occasions Bismarck and Bleichröder gave Pindter contradictory instructions. In May 1880 the paper carried a story critical of Jews, and Bleichröder's friends at once assumed that it had been inspired by Bismarck. Bleichröder reassured them that the story would soon be forgotten but a few months later insisted that Pindter publish a warning about "the specter of reaction" in Germany.[84] This was also the occasion for Bismarck's explanation to his reactionary minister, Puttkamer, that "as far as the Jewish question is concerned . . . it is a mistake to assume that with us the *rich* Jews exercise a great influence on the press. It may be different in Paris." It is the property-less Jews who cause trouble in the press, he said.[85] Bismarck's general exhortations on this subject are discussed in Chapter 18.

In the same year, Bleichröder came very close to buying the *Norddeutsche*. Ohlendorff offered him half ownership of the paper for 400,000 marks, but requested that he keep this option to himself, because Pindter also wanted to acquire the paper and Ohlendorff would not sell to him. Bleichröder replied that his acceptance depended on Bismarck's approval of a change of policy—that is, the paper would no longer attack particular personalities (here Bleichröder may have been referring to Lasker) and would no longer be partial to the anti-Semitic movement. To Bleichröder's dismay, Ohlendorff approached Bismarck directly on this; Bismarck accepted Bleichröder's wishes and ". . . indeed indignantly rejected the frequent allegation that he was involved in the declining [anti-Semitic] affair." Tiedemann gave further assurances to Bleichröder, but negotiations broke down; in 1884 Bleichröder once more toyed with the same project but abandoned it.[86]

There was something strangely symptomatic about Bleichröder's relationship with Pindter. They collaborated closely; they had many associates in common; they served the same master. Over a period of nearly two decades, they helped each other, saw each other, and Pindter often enough protested his warm feelings for the benevolent Bleichröder. Behind each other's back, things were different. Bleichröder was willing to negotiate the purchase of Pindter's paper without consulting him; Pindter confided his bemused contempt of Bleichröder to his private diary and to sympathetic listeners like Holstein.

It was a rough, competitive world, this world of journalism. Bleichröder did well in it. A part of the press attacked and vilified him; the more reputable papers were mindful of his influence and importance. They obliged him, as he did them. In the last years of Bismarck's reign, as we shall see, Bleichröder's relations with the press deteriorated. He became a frequent object of suspicion, and, more important, his financial projects were attacked on political grounds. He had to develop new, subterranean arrangements. As Bismarck's star faded, so did Bleichröder's.

CHAPTER 12

The Prince Enriched

Bismarck was the greatest despiser of principle that ever existed. . . . Genius, savior of the state, and sentimental traitor. Always me, me, and when things did not work anymore, lament about ingratitude and north German, lachrymose sentimentality. Where I sense Bismarck as instrument of divine providence, I bow to him; where he is simply himself, Junker, and dike-reeve and advantage seeker, I find him totally unsympathetic.

This mixture of superhuman and sly dodger [*Übermensch und Schlauberger*], of state founder and horse-stable tax shirker, of *heros* and tear-shedder, in whose mouth butter would not melt, fills me with mixed feelings and prevents any pure admiration from arising in me.
—Theodor Fontane to his daughter, January 29, 1894, and April 1, 1895
(on Bismarck's eightieth birthday)

In the summer of 1871 Bismarck appeared to be at the pinnacle of his career and fortune. The hero of his country, he was about to become the arbiter of Europe. He had toppled kings and an emperor; he had destroyed and created states. Not since Napoleon had a single man had such a revolutionary impact on the life of Europe—and still he managed to appear as the bulwark of conservatism.

Success, like failure, takes its toll. After 1871 Bismarck suffered, knowing that the great deeds were done. Like other mortals, he began to worry about personal things, about his health, his wealth, the pleasurableness of his career. As with other mortals, only more so, his anxieties reinforced one another and threatened to undermine his formidable constitution. Less common was the fact that for so long power had been Bismarck's opiate: it eased his pains and lessened his extravagant self-pity. Gradually he became accustomed to the opiate, to power, and its effects diminished at the very time when his power had become routinized, that is, less heady and glorious. In the earlier years he had enjoyed the uncertain game; the results meant less to him.

Even in the pecuniary world he was afraid that triumph would be costly. In March 1871 William wrote Bismarck that he wished to elevate him to the rank of prince; Bismarck's first thought (if we are to trust his memoirs) was that the honor exceeded his means. He remembered the earlier "princes with inadequate incomes such as Hardenberg and Blücher," and he was afraid that his sons like theirs would not be able to sustain the title. (In 1814 Blücher was made a prince and received huge gifts; in the next few years, he gambled away his rewards and piled up ever greater debts. It was an odd comparison to leap to Bismarck's mind.)* In any case, as Bismarck went to the king to refuse, the king, with tears in his eyes, embraced him—and Bismarck had no choice but to accept. "Ever after," he wrote in his memoirs, "I have never lost the feeling that as a count one can be well off without becoming unpleasantly ostentatious but as a prince if one wants to avoid the latter one *must* be rich."[1] It was Bleichröder's task to make Bismarck—financially—a respectable prince.

The sovereign also presented Bismarck with another gift in the form of the ancient Sachsenwald near Hamburg in the duchy of Lauenburg, a state domain valued at the time at a million taler, comprising 15,625 acres of forests and 1,250 acres of mostly meadow lands. The new gift, which came to be known as Friedrichsruh, made Bismarck—and still makes his great-grandson—one of the largest landowners of Germany; in 1976, the Bismarck estate around Friedrichsruh was still reckoned at 17,290 acres. But at first the new estate cost Bismarck additional money. The estate had no proper residence, and the one place "where one could establish oneself if one did not want to live in a haunted hunting lodge in the middle of the wild forest" had been sold. Bleichröder advanced 87,500 taler at 4 percent in order to restore that particular land.[2] Also in 1871, "out of [my] private funds and without entering it in [my] bank's accounts," Bleichröder lent Bismarck 25,000 taler—for an undisclosed purpose. The loan was paid back thirteen years later.[3]

To the outside world, the new prince seemed fortunate indeed. Even his brother thought him lucky, full of *Erdenglück,* and Bismarck, once a prolific and unrivaled letter writer, overcame his reticence, his *"Tintenscheu,"* the product of his office and of a creeping misanthropy, to set his brother straight. In a letter for the ostensible purpose of congratulating him on his birthday, Bismarck wrote: "I was lucky in what I tackled officially, less so in my private ventures. . . . It is better for a country to have it this way than to have a minister who has the opposite experience. In my own financial affairs I have no luck, perhaps no aptitude, in any case, no time to concern myself with them." Varzin, he complained, devoured money, and even the newly received Sachsenwald so far had produced nothing but expenses, though in time it should yield 30,000 taler a year. For the present he had to live off his salary and the leasing of Schönhausen. He thought himself a poor, harassed prince who no longer had the physical strength to endure his psychic burden; to boot, he received and refused daily requests for loans or gifts of thousands of taler.[4]

* The reader will recall that in 1876 Bismarck refused permission to have some of Blücher's letters published—even after their financial aspects had been purged. See Chapter 10. Theodor Fontane also linked Blücher and Bismarck; he remembered that Blücher had once complained to his king that no one wanted to play cards with him anymore, and Frederick William III replied that he was known to cheat, to which Blücher replied: " 'Yes, Your Majesty, a little cheating is the best.' That has been Bismarck's principle, too: 'a little cheating' (i.e. a lot) has always seemed to him the most beautiful thing." Theodor Fontane, *Briefe an seine Familie* (Berlin, 1924), II, p. 300.

Perhaps Bismarck exaggerated his troubles in order to ward off any incipient fraternal envy.

Certain it is that throughout 1871 he was especially worried about his finances. There is perhaps nothing like a gift of a million taler, plus the exacting honor of being made a prince, to make one ponder one's fortune. Perhaps he did regret not having more time to supervise it, but as it was he devoted a great deal of time to the details of his affairs and accounts. At times he was meticulous to the point of pettiness, and yet his attention was sometimes ill-focused, so that something of the "penny-wise, pound-foolish" quality hung about his conduct of financial affairs. Johanna, too, "concerned herself very thoroughly with the economic conditions" of the estates.[5]

In 1871 Bismarck had a further reason for financial concern and annoyance. In December 1870, while he was in France battling for the new Germany, the Prussian income tax commission had dared to put him in a higher bracket, the nineteenth, instead of the eighteenth, with an estimated annual income of between 32,000 and 40,000 taler, instead of 24,000 to 32,000. (The per capita income in Germany in 1871 was 116 taler.) In March 1871 Johanna filed a complaint, and in July Bismarck, with Keudell's help, drafted various remonstrances which—characteristically enough—concluded that he should not even be retained in the eighteenth bracket. The remonstrances were late, but Bismarck explained that "in the last years the affairs of state did not allow me to care for my own."[6]

The documents of Bismarck's fight with the tax authorities provide some clues to his wealth and political stance. The official tax assessment from the county of Köslin gives a detailed picture of the holdings in Varzin and the two smaller estates near it. Varzin alone embraced 5,752 acres, of which 4,000 acres were forest; the other two estates contained 8,062 acres. According to Bismarck's reckoning, total income from these estates for 1870, including a brick and a lime factory, amounted to 15,286 taler. He also owned Schönhausen, comprising 856 acres; the tax commission's inclusion of Kniephof—which he had sold in 1868—outraged Bismarck: "But that is an error that should not occur!" Likewise he was furious about the commission's estimate of the fair value of his residence in Varzin: "Equally arbitrary is the rental equivalent of 500 taler. I do not believe one could scare up a tenant for fifty. The Commission can have it for that price; on the other hand, the maintenance costs paid to artisans of every kind to keep up this rickety building exceed 500, as attestable through bills." In the next angry memorandum Bismarck added apropos of the 500-taler rental: "You need city unfamiliarity with rural conditions to think of such a thing. . . . The Commission seems to think that the Pollnower region is used by pleasure-seeking tourists for summer holidays!" With the aid of similar barbs and devices, Bismarck argued that his taxable income, including his 12,000-taler salary and 4,000-taler compensation as duke of Lauenburg, which was to be discontinued in 1872, and his rent-free residence in the Wilhelmstrasse (reckoned at 2,000 taler), amounted to about 24,500 taler and not 32,000 as assessed, although he added that he anticipated greater income from his estates in future years.

Keudell obtained the advisory opinion of Dr. C. Dietrici, a civil servant in the judiciary, who scrutinized Bismarck's projected remonstrance. He cautioned that the assessment of 4,533 taler as the net income from Varzin would constitute a return of only 1.12 percent of the original royal gift of 400,000 taler spent for Varzin—to say nothing of the 100,000 taler Bismarck had added. Such a claim would put his total income just above the sixteenth bracket, which he had already accepted in 1865! He also inquired whether the prince owned any "interest-bearing investments," which Bismarck denied with a penciled "none" next to it. (But what else were the securities that Bleichröder held for him?)

Dietrici warned against straining the credulity of the tax commission; in October 1871 it accepted Bismarck's plea and placed him once again in the eighteenth bracket.[7] The windfall in reverse, however, lasted but a few years; in 1876 he was raised to a higher bracket, and in 1877, under a more finely calibrated system changed to marks, he was placed in the thirty-first bracket, with an estimated income of 204,000 to 240,000 marks—and 6,120 marks to pay for taxes.[8] (On the other hand, heavier communal taxes were assessed on the basis of income tax rates.) Bismarck challenged the tax authorities again in 1880, with the result that in 1890 he was still in the thirty-first bracket. Taxpaying is universally unpopular, but aristocrats, and not only in Germany, thought tax resistance a noble protest against bureaucratic tyranny.*

Bleichröder helped Bismarck in his struggle with the tax authorities, as he had helped him in the acquisition of a proper residence for his new estate in Friedrichsruh. His services, varied and exacting, were constantly needed. The richer Bismarck became, the more diversified his interests were and the more worried he was about money. At no time or place—neither in the middle of a political crisis nor on vacation, neither in Berlin nor on his estates, neither in sickness nor in health—did Bismarck ever relax about the management of his wealth, and as a consequence Bleichröder's role was even more important after 1871 than it had been before.

At a trial in 1877 Bleichröder defined his own responsibilities:

> When Prince Bismarck received his Prussian ministerial appointment some fifteen years ago, he commissioned me to take charge of all his financial affairs. I was to take care of all his income and all his expenses, to buy and sell his domains and his securities. The Prince instructed me that in the choice of investments I should look more for basic safety than for profit.[9]

In addition, Bleichröder had to manage mortgages, deal with troublesome lessees, facilitate the sale of Bismarck's chief crop, timber, and perform other

---

* Bismarck followed the traditions of his fellow Junkers, as these were harshly characterized by a later renegade: " 'As much as possible from the state, as little as possible to the state!' was their motto. They were modest only in their taxpaying. They reckoned that the expenses for their fancy horses, for their parks, for their hunts, for tutors and governesses, etc., belonged to the necessary household budget." Hellmut von Gerlach, *Von Rechts nach Links* (Zurich, 1937), p. 36.

chores. He was also the Bismarcks' everyday banker. It was a time-consuming commitment for Bleichröder, and he and his subordinates did endless and exacting service for no direct financial reward. Bismarck had ample reason to be grateful for Bleichröder's efforts, although the mounting insinuations of the 1870s and 1880s to the effect that Bismarck was drawing illicit or extravagant profits from his connections with Bleichröder were unfounded. Bismarck resented these attacks and attributed them to the envy of his former Junker friends—each of whom, he thought, would have liked to have a clever Jew banker of his own.

Throughout the Empire, Bleichröder maintained the closest contacts with Bismarck, his family, and his circle of subordinates. When Bismarck was in Berlin, Bleichröder saw a great deal of him; he had immediate access. Bleichröder was a regular visitor in Varzin and Friedrichsruh—visits that he did not allow to go unnoticed. In the long intervals when Bismarck nursed his health away from Berlin, he and Bleichröder corresponded regularly, either directly or through his wife, his sons Herbert and Bill, his son-in-law Count Rantzau, or his successive secretaries. Among the latter Bleichröder succeeded in having particularly friendly relations with Rottenburg and Tiedemann, though with neither was he so intimate as he had once been with Keudell.

Bismarck had no choice but to be concerned about his supplementary income. His salary of 63,000 marks a year (including his Lauenburg pension) covered but a third of his living expenses, and even a rent-free residence in the Chancellery did not help much. Bismarck thought his was a frugal style of life, and still, the state did not even provide the essentials. He devoted a good part of his life to making sure that his supplementary income would comfortably cover his needs. And in the process he heeded an old German proverb he once cited in the Reichstag: "Sentiment stops where business begins."[10]

In fact, Bismarck's cash income from the government rarely amounted to more than 53,000 marks a year. The government deducted 9,000 to 10,000 marks for various taxes, plus further charges for Bismarck's purchases of the pleasures of life, especially caviar, French wines, and old port, which having been ordered abroad were often paid by the German embassies on the spot.* The Bismarcks lived well and entertained often, though always cheaply. Bismarck's official lodgings were simple (some thought hideous), and he dazzled his guests with his presence, not with victuals. His own extravagant consumption of food and drink is well known, and he himself warded off any suggestion that his limited funds could be spent differently: "Whoever is interested in furnishing is not interested in food; the essential thing is to eat well."[11]

But Bismarck took care of his own. His sons received occasional sub-

---

* In the first quarter of 1873, for example, the Legationskasse deducted 2,275 taler for port wine, 56 taler for caviar, and the usual 175 taler for his income tax. (Bleichröder statement, 1 April 1873, SA.) A quarterly purchase of fifteen to twenty pounds of caviar was by no means unusual—to which must be added the regular gifts of the same delicacy which Bleichröder sent the prince whenever a particularly fine shipment had reached him from St. Petersburg.

sidies and gifts, and in 1879 he ordered Bleichröder to remit 3,000 marks a quarter to his just-acquired son-in-law, Count Rantzau, perhaps as a dowry in installments or in payment for Rantzau's secretarial services.

Berlin gossips knew that Bismarck spent far more than the state paid him, and many professed to see in Bleichröder the secret source of the chancellor's wealth. The Jew's machinations allegedly yielded Bismarck extravagant profits.* Bismarck, it was widely rumored, used his unrivaled knowledge in order to make killings on the stock market. The possibilities were there, for if anyone could have played the market with the likelihood that his hunches could at times become "self-fulfilling prophecies," it would have been Bismarck. No wonder, then, that the envious enemies of both men invented fabulous tales. By contrast, the truth, until now shrouded in uncertainty, is prosaic. True to their character, Bismarck and Bleichröder put together a conservative portfolio that would appall any "growth-oriented" financier of today.

In any case, the bulk of Bismarck's wealth was in land, much of it the fruit of his political labors. Most of his additional income came from his estates. But that income fluctuated, because it was subject to all sorts of vagaries, the efficiency of tenants, the market for timber, the cost of repairs. In most years, he managed to have a net profit, but it varied from year to year and required constant attention. It was an absurdity of German historians to think that Bismarck would be unconcerned with this aspect of his life—or to ignore that the conduct of his private affairs broadened his economic horizon. What follows is the fullest account of Bismarck's finances to date—and perhaps the fullest for any modern statesman.

Bismarck's capital investments were Bleichröder's special fief; he had full powers over Bismarck's investments, but hardly ever used them. Before changing the prince's portfolio, Bleichröder almost invariably consulted him. Their correspondence is full of Bleichröder's particular suggestions about prospective moves or of reports about transactions completed "according to Your Highness's instructions." On several occasions the initiative came unambiguously from Bismarck, and in all instances he responded to Bleichröder's queries and suggestions. Obviously it was in Bleichröder's interest to consult Bismarck: it gave the banker unrivaled intelligence and a kind of preemptive pardon for any mistakes he might commit.

Between them, they devised a portfolio that was geared to combine maximum safety with the highest yield. Bismarck was not involved in any of the great promotions of the early 1870s—nor is there a shred of evidence to suggest that Bleichröder tried to involve him. There were never any Laurahütte or Hibernia shares in Bismarck's account; hence he missed out on the windfalls that Hatzfeldt and Kardorff benefited from, but he was also spared the consequences of the ensuing crash. In the 1870s (and intermittently thereafter, to the present day) the charge has been made that Bleichröder managed to

* The charge was first made in the French press during the Franco-Prussian war, when one paper reported on "Bismarck's avarice which had brought together colossal sums . . . through wretched speculations . . . with Mr. Bleichröder." The same paper—characteristically—dwelt on Bismarck's sexual extravagance: "People say there are about fifty illegitimate children of his in Berlin." Moritz Busch, *Tagebuchblätter* (Leipzig, 1899), I, 384.

credit Bismarck with a huge paper profit via shares of the Prussian Boden-Credit company. Bleichröder denied the charge under oath, and there is nothing in the Bleichröder archives to suggest that there was any truth to the allegation.[12] For Bismarck, Bleichröder preferred to buy safe securities at favorable issue prices or at a time when they were unreasonably depressed in price. Hence, Bleichröder was pleased when he could effect a 1 or 1½ percent gain over purchase price, even over a period of several years. On occasion he did better than that and managed a 5 to 10 percent gain in a matter of months. A rough estimate of Bismarck's account suggests that Bleichröder obtained a 4 percent capital gain in most years, regardless of the state of the market.

Despite his needs, Bismarck sought to reinvest as much of his capital gains and of his interest as possible. Thus his assets rose from 125,864 taler (roughly 377,000 marks) in 1871 to 560,000 marks in 1880—and 1,200,000 in 1890.[13] In the 1880s he established trusts for some of the estates and also transferred funds to Johanna and Herbert.

Because of these special accounts and because some of Bleichröder's statements were lost, it is hard to reconstruct all of his investments. The major categories should suffice. In 1871 over 70 percent of Bismarck's investments were in Russian securities; nearly 49,000 taler were in Russian mortgage bonds which Bleichröder—since the late 1860s the main source of Russian securities in the Berlin market—had been able to buy some months earlier at issuance for 41,500 taler. Such quick appreciation was unusual. Another 42,000 taler were invested in the Anglo-Russian loan of 1871 and in Khursk-Kharkov Railroad obligations. Of domestic securities, he held 28,600 taler of 4½ percent Bergisch-Märkisch Railroad preference shares and a small balance in Prussian state papers. In the second half of 1871, these investments yielded 3,360 taler in interest, or 5.3 percent on an annual basis.[14]

Despite the prevailing opportunities of the Gründerjahre, Bleichröder stuck to German and European securities offering 4 to 5 percent yield, though Russian shares gave a higher return than their nominal rate of 4 to 5 percent. Bismarck had sold his American securities with their 5 to 8 percent yield.[15]

Bismarck's foreign investments have always been a subject of great curiosity because it was assumed that he would have been tempted to speculate in this, his favorite, domain. In the early years he did just that. In 1872, the year of the Three Emperors' Conference in Berlin, Bleichröder invested nearly 85,000 taler of Bismarck's capital in Austrian securities.[16] Policy and portfolio coincided at that point. The Austrian economy had recovered from the ravages of the two preceding decades, but the boom was short-lived, and Bleichröder's purchase of these securities was not well timed. In May 1873 came the celebrated crash in Vienna which sent shock waves through the economies of Europe.[17] On June 10 Bleichröder and Bismarck conferred, and on the next day all of these Austrian securities were sold at a profit of 300 taler.

Six weeks later, from Marienbad, Bleichröder wrote Bismarck one of his long reports about general conditions:

The Austrian financial troubles, commonly called the Vienna *Krach,* derived from overspeculation . . . the wise men of the market, who a few weeks ago believed that the end of the catastrophe was at hand, now all agree that it is only the beginning of the end. The speculative mania, grown to an incredible extent, had seized all groups of society in the capital as well as in the provinces. . . .

The Austrian *Krach*, he added, would affect the German market as well, despite divergent patterns of development; there had been some over-speculation in Germany,

in real estate . . . in particular; if I may put it drastically, people [here] proceeded somewhat fraudulently, though it must be stressed that in comparison to Vienna, Berlin as the capital of all Germany can expect a rapid and enormous growth. Land, houses, and rents, however, have gone up in price so quickly that a setback was bound to occur, which is likely to bring painful losses especially to the leading elements of society who will be forced to liquidate.[18]

In August 1874, in a handwritten letter from Varzin, Bismarck sent some extraordinary instructions:

At my departure [a few weeks earlier] you touched on the question of selling my Russian securities and advocated a postponement of same. I beg you now to proceed with this, nevertheless, without hurrying the matter, just as the market quotations seem to make it advisable. I want to get out of the Russian securities . . . [all of them], but, as I said, without undue hurry. The alternative investment we can contemplate after the operation has been completed, perhaps mortgage bonds. Given your promise I count on your kind visit when we can discuss details. It is not necessary, however, to wait with the beginning of the operation.[19]

Three days later, Bleichröder sold all Russian securities for 98,500 taler —roughly 13,000 taler more than they had cost.[20] Bismarck had no particular need for cash, and Bleichröder, worried about this sudden liquidation, inquired point-blank whether Bismarck feared a political upheaval. He received this none too reassuring answer:

A question such as the one you put to me concerning political weather prognosis is never safe to answer; I would remind you how clear the horizon seemed to be even in June 1870. In any case, I do not see any danger today for the maintenance of peace either, and particularly not from the country you mention. If I wanted a change in my investments, it was not because I was afraid of a threat to peace, but because I thought the price of those particular issues was high, and because I would have found it hard to decide to sell *after* a decline had set in.[21]

Bismarck understood the psychology of investment and knew that in market operations, as in high policy, timing was everything.

Three years later, the Russo-Turkish war broke out, and Russian securities dropped sharply. Bismarck used to brag that Bleichröder had complimented him on his early liquidation and alleged that his reasoning had been simple: when in 1874 he had heard the news that Count Peter Shuvalov had been made ambassador to London he calculated: "If in times like these the Russians send away the brightest man they have, then one can bet ten to one that they are on the verge of some stupidity. Hence it was time to sell Russian state securities." On the following morning, he remembered, he had sent Bleichröder telegraphic instructions.[22] Bismarck's prosaic foresight in 1874 was better than his poetic hindsight three years later: Bismarck had sold his securities not a day after Shuvalov's transfer but three months later; Shuvalov, moreover, was a great success in London, while his previous assignment in Russia, as head of the third division of the police (administration and security), would hardly have given him a decisive voice in foreign policy.[23]

Russian securities had dropped even before the outbreak of the war. Johanna, Herbert, and the maid Jenny Fatio retained their Russian holdings, and in the fall of 1875 the two women lamented the decline of their Russian issues.[24] At the same time, Bleichröder informed Herbert that he had postponed some planned repurchase of his Russian securities "because the disturbances in Herzegovina cause a certain worry" about Russian investments.[25] Obviously political intelligence had a great bearing on the market.

In later years, Bismarck claimed that after 1874 he never again bought any foreign securities, asserting that "such things cloud the clear perspective of a foreign minister and should not really be."[26] Actually he forgot that self-denying principle in June 1885, when he instructed Bleichröder to invest 200,000 marks in the latest Anglo-Russian loan. Ironically, the Russian shares appear to have been bought from a special account, consisting of a national fund raised by public subscription for Bismarck's seventieth birthday in April 1885.[27] A week later, alarmed by Bleichröder's worries about Russian policies, Bismarck sold these shares, without loss.[28] In 1889 Bismarck did invest heavily in Egyptian and Mexican securities.

Between 1874 and 1889, with the one exception just noted, Bismarck's funds were invested in domestic securities. Three types predominated: governmental obligations, especially Prussian consols and, after 1877, German *Reichsanleihe*, both yielding 4 percent; mortgage bonds mostly of the Prussian Mortgage Bank, with which Bleichröder had the closest ties; and, between 1876 and 1884, various railroad securities.

By 1889 Bismarck's portfolio consisted principally of government securities, i.e., German *Reichsanleihe*. In 1889–1890 the last great changes in the prince's investments took place. In the summer and fall of 1889 he sold some *Reichsanleihe* and bought 251,000 marks of Egyptian loan and 232,000 marks of Mexican 6 percent loan, both, of course, issues that Bleichröder had a special interest in. The greatest transaction in the history of Bismarck's capital occurred between March 8 and 14, 1890, in the days of his final crisis, while he was battling the young emperor for his political life and lost. In that week, he liquidated 750,000 marks in government securities and invested nearly half that amount in Egyptian loan.[29]* Was the liquidation connected with the provocative Army Bill which he planned to introduce to a Reichstag that was certain to reject it?[30] Was Bismarck thinking of staging a coup d'état, as has often been alleged, which would have dissolved the Reich and hence depressed its obligations? Or, more likely, was this Bismarck's final speculation—a speculation against his own downfall? Did he assume, as he had alleged much earlier in Shuvalov's case, that an empire that let its ablest men depart would soon commit political follies? He did think it "very strange [that] the Emperor names His best general [Caprivi] a chancellor and His best chancellor a field marshal."[31] This time he was triply right: the market reacted to his dismissal with a violent, if brief, drop in prices,† the Egyptian loan appreciated further, and the Reich did embark on its new course of unbridled power and folly.

His last speculations proved successful. In June 1890, on Bleichröder's suggestion, Bismarck sold his Egyptian holdings, at a profit of 33,000 marks or a 5 percent gain achieved in three, respectively nine, months.[32] In July 1891 the prince inquired whether it would not be prudent to liquidate his Mexican holdings. He had read that Mexico was in the throes of a great speculative boom; perhaps he thought that to have survived one *Gründerzeit* was enough for a lifetime.[33] Bleichröder's Mexican venture proved profitable for Bismarck.

The last extant statement of Bismarck's securities dates from December 31, 1890, and shows a portfolio worth 1,215,831 marks, or $300,000 at the time. The total would have been greater still if he had not earlier transferred several hundred thousand marks to Herbert and 300,000 to Johanna. In addition Bismarck had placed major sums in other accounts, some in trusts connected with the several estates. There were also additional securities bought with the funds collected for his seventieth birthday, the interest of which Bismarck designated for various charities. When Bleichröder died in February 1893, reputedly the richest man in Germany, he left his favorite client's affairs in good order, with a total fortune of many millions.

Bismarck was not a Berliner, not a person who enjoyed the life of the metropolis. ("I would much rather live in the country," he once said to the Reichstag members, "than among you, charming though you are.")[34] Nor was he a Junker at home on his estates, his vision limited to the nearest church steeple or to the prospects of the next harvest. In fact, Bismarck needed his

---

* There had been a sharp drop on the Berlin market—for financial, not political, reasons —for some weeks before Bismarck's dismissal. On March 9 the leading financial weekly, *Der Aktionär*, XXXVII (1890), 157, noted: "Last week . . . a regular panic dominated [the stock exchange]. . . . The improvement that appeared at the end of the week was . . . to the largest part due to the intervention of others, and in the first place one recognized the House of Bleichröder." It may be relevant to note that on March 5 *Der Aktionär* carried a lead article commenting on the much-improved state of Egyptian finances, in which Bleichröder had long been interested.

† The bearish elements were encouraged by the fact that "the first House of the city, whose connections with the Chancellor are well known, served their purpose by making great sales." *Der Aktionär*, XXXVII (23 March 1890), 197. Bleichröder had obviously known for some days before Bismarck's dismissal that his position had become precarious.

several lives: he needed to recuperate from the struggles in Berlin in the peace of his estates. Berlin alone would have killed him; a solely bucolic life would have bored him to death.

No other statesman of modern times spent as much time away from his capital and duties as did Bismarck. Varzin and Friedrichsruh became alternate chancelleries—without appointments, meetings, speeches, and with only one or two trusted secretaries. Friedrichsruh at least was reasonably accessible; Varzin was a cumbersome day's trip from Berlin.[35] Even in his favorite surroundings he was never fully cut off from politics. In a moment of insouciance reminiscent of Franklin D. Roosevelt, he confided to his daughter: "Politics does not leave me entirely in peace even here. . . . But since I do not have anyone here who complicates the business, Europe is always taken care of, combed and brushed, in ten or fifteen minutes at breakfast."[36] In the early years of the Empire, he withdrew for months on end to Varzin; later he favored Friedrichsruh, to which he retired permanently in 1895.

After 1871 Bismarck owned three huge complexes: Schönhausen to the west of Berlin; Varzin in Pomerania, not far from the Baltic; and Friedrichsruh (also called by its old name, Sachsenwald) near Hamburg. The three estates together comprised approximately 40,000 acres and an investment of at least 5 to 6 million marks. The enlarged Varzin consisted of about 20,000 acres, including seven neighboring estates, and Friedrichsruh measured nearly 17,000 acres.[37] Both Varzin and Friedrichsruh had primitive homes but vast and stately forests teeming with game, and the princely Sachsenwald with its fine timber was to yield a considerable income. Bismarck had one of the largest holdings of uncut timber in Germany and thus became acquainted at first hand with some of the problems of finding and keeping markets at home and abroad.

Bismarck loved these estates and thought landowning possessed a special virtue and nobility that no other way of life had. The standard biographies of Bismarck, especially by German authors, dwell touchingly on his love of nature, on his passion for trees, on his happy (and sometimes not so happy) seigneurial relations with his peasants—on everything connected with the estates, except their management. Some mention Bismarck's self-avowed land hunger, his hot desire to annex his neighbors' lands as he saw them every evening, but few admit the endless care he lavished on the operation of his immense holdings.[38]

Bleichröder knew how infinitely intricate the administration of these estates was. In fact, he discovered that investing Bismarck's funds was easy compared to helping him run these estates profitably. Bleichröder took care of the legal and financial aspects of new purchases; he controlled the several accounts that were attached to the entailed estates; he collected and dispensed funds from the estates; he negotiated with troublesome tenants; and he supervised the stewards. (In 1867, Ernst Westphal was appointed head forester of Varzin, and after two years received full powers over the estates.[39] A few years later, Peter Lange received a similar charge for Friedrichsruh— and both men were in constant touch with Bleichröder.)

Bleichröder's help was the more important and the more appropriate because Bismarck did not engage in the traditional ways of agriculture; his income did not depend on grain growing and cattle, but on the sale of timber and on manufacturing enterprises that were run on his estates. It was a felicitous choice because after 1870 overseas competition steadily depressed grain prices. He also thought it a choice that redounded to the national good: the industrial worker, he once argued in the Reichstag, carried the marshal's baton in his knapsack; the agrarian worker had no such prospect and hence to promote rural industry was salutary—and would reduce emigration.[40]

As early as 1871 Bleichröder had arranged for the purchase of two estates contiguous to Sachsenwald, Aumühle and Friedrichsruh, two villages which even today form the heart of the Bismarck property. The prince was pleased with both the price and the rapidity of the operation.[41]

Aware of Bismarck's insatiable appetite, Bleichröder occasionally suggested additions. In November 1873—two years after the acquisition of Friedrichsruh!—he wrote Bismarck that "a competent source" had informed him that Count Blumenthal's Janowitz estate, adjoining Varzin, might be for sale. "At present, the asking price is one million taler, with a down payment of 200,000 taler. I do not know the estate, but the information sent to me suggests that Count Blumenthal would let himself be talked down considerably in his demand." If Bismarck were interested, Bleichröder would gladly negotiate. Bismarck replied at once, in his own hand and over four pages: "The Janowitz estate [Herrschaft] exceeds altogether my means and my needs, though I would gladly have acquired some individual parts of it. . . ." The present value—muddled because of some wrangle over timber rights—was 600,000 or 700,000 taler: "Too much for me; I am better off if I pay my debts, and if I buy, I prefer Chorow at this time, which would require 60,000 taler cash and would cost 100,000 taler."[42]

In the course of the next few years, Bismarck acquired Alt- and later Neu-Chorow near Varzin, with Bleichröder arranging the details, including the intricate retirement and replacement of outstanding mortgages.[43] In 1882 he bought yet another estate, Schöningstedt, for 264,000 marks, for which Bleichröder again gave him a 4 percent mortgage, plus 1 percent annual amortization.[44] At the end of 1883 Bleichröder submitted a complete list of the mortgages he held for Bismarck, most of them additions to his Varzin estate. The original cost had been 948,000 marks; the remaining total was 844,000 marks. Interest was 4 percent, and on most of the mortgages the rate of amortization was exceptionally low. In short, Bleichröder tied up a million marks in mortgages—something that he probably did for few, if any, of his other clients—so that Bismarck could buy new lands without liquidating his other investments, which yielded a larger return than the cost on Bleichröder's mortgages.[45]

It was also Bleichröder's task to open and manage several separate accounts which Bismarck assigned to different estates. The most important of these, the entailed estate Majorat Schwarzenbeck-Sachsenwald, Bismarck created in August 1872, in a handwritten letter to Bleichröder, instructing him to transfer specific securities totaling 40,000 taler to this new account: "If you find it expedient to sell any of these securities, you are not hindered from doing so by this order, and the amount realized or the securities bought in their stead should replace those sold."[46] Similar accounts were opened and closed at various times, and they paid for improvements, mortgage interest, and occasional enlargements.

Bismarck watched every aspect of his far-flung interests. Of his managers and inspectors he demanded strict economy and fullest information: "A landed property about which I do not know anything holds no interest for me, and the yield [Rente] from a share of stock is higher than from real estate."[47] In later years, Johanna assumed greater responsibilities, much to Herbert's worry: "Since she has become old and enfeebled, she does the entire household alone —all the books, all the bills, the entire correspondence with suppliers, the relations to servants—everything depends on her."[48]

There were endless chores for Bleichröder, too. In case of special worry, Bismarck delegated him to audit the books of a particular estate. In 1880 Bismarck again asked him to scrutinize various accounts:

You were . . . so kind as to hold out the prospect of your assistance in the auditing of the books and expenses connected with the running of my estates [Wirtschaften]. I would like to avail myself of your benevolence, if you had somebody who for this purpose could come to Varzin now. The estate there, so far as it is under Westphal, i.e., the forest and the farm Varzin, are running well. About the running of the [adjoining] farm Puddiger-Misdow, however, which is administered by Mr. Ritsch . . . I get no news and hear secondhand that a 5,000-mark advance against *future* delivery of rye has been contracted. Such deals, for someone who can get money from me at any time, are peculiar and uneconomical. In case you are willing to accede to my wish, I am enclosing full powers which cover all my officials, but for the time being I *mean* only Puddiger-Misdow because I receive no news from them. I have so far looked forward to your visit in vain, but will be happy whenever it takes place. I am afraid I will have to go to Berlin earlier than is healthy for me; but I will have to counter the [political] objections there which render my duties more difficult. The *faux frais* of my work exceed the *legitimate* need for exertion and I do not have much strength left.

In a postscript he added: "Out of decency, Varzin should also be audited, but begin with Puddiger."[49]

Bleichröder's trusted agent Siebert surveyed all the different estates and submitted detailed reports; Bismarck's later inquiry concerning Schönhausen established that from 1873 to 1878 the prince's expenses there exceeded his income by 27,153 marks.[50] Lange and Westphal probably resented Bleichröder's supervision, but they had no choice but to cooperate courteously.

In 1882 Lange and Bleichröder collaborated closely in order to arrange for the proper insurance for Friedrichsruh. After he had at last bought a livable residence at Friedrichsruh in 1879—an old inn which he left so unrenovated that the rooms still had their numbers on the outside—Bismarck insisted that home and furnishings be adequately insured.[51] A tedious correspondence ensued, and Bleichröder not only had to collate the itemized objects to be insured, but had to shop around for an insurance company that would offer Bismarck better terms than the previous one. Bismarck assessed every item himself; the house in Friedrichsruh was to be insured at 120,000 marks and the furnishings at 80,000 marks. Bill wrote Bleichröder, "[My father] wants to take the precaution . . . of itemizing every individual article at such an amount that the total constitutes 80,000 marks. In that way he wants to avoid having those articles lost by fire assessed through an estimate of the surviving articles because this could unduly reduce or bring to naught payments to be made."[52] In most realms, Bismarck was a prudent Junker.

But not in all. In his relations with Georg and Moritz Behrend, whose manufacturing operations provided most of the Varzin revenues, Bismarck was neither lucky nor prudent. His association with them began in 1868, lasted beyond Bleichröder's death, and proved to be a source of constant trouble for Bismarck and Bleichröder.* The Behrends, owners of a pulp mill and paper plant in Köslin, twelve miles from Varzin, were Jewish, though Moritz decided "to have himself and his family baptized; his son Ernst served his year with the horse artillery and became a reserve officer—and enjoyed a high repute with the Prince's family and was often invited to eat with them."[53]

In 1868 Bismarck acquired a burnt-down mill, called Fuchsmühle, near Varzin. In its place he built a pulp mill to manufacture paper from his timber; he leased this mill for 4,550 taler a year to the Behrends. In April 1870 Bismarck and the Behrends signed a contract for the construction and leasing of a pulp mill and paper plant, called Hammermühle. A third mill, the Campmühle, was added later. Bismarck often took visitors on a tour of these plants, proud of their modern machinery—but only his intimates knew how much time-consuming trouble he had with his tenants.†

Bleichröder knew, because he was in the thick of it. Time and again, he tried to extricate Bismarck from his greedy credulity; Bleichröder's warnings notwithstanding, Bismarck poured additional funds into the mills, while the Behrends were always on the brink of defaulting. The first crisis occurred in July 1876, with the bankruptcy of an associate of the Behrends', W. Abel, Jr. Bleichröder immediately warned Bismarck, then in Bad Kissingen, that the Behrends might also face insolvency and noted that the semiannual lease payment of 7,000 marks for the Fuchsmühle was overdue; he had therefore stopped all payments to the Behrends. Bismarck soon heard about the threatened calamity firsthand: in the middle of his *Kur*, Georg Behrend appeared in order to

---

* It also provided some splendid anecdotes. A Behrend told the story that Bismarck once asked a factory inspector (a type of official with whom he usually quarreled) how large his salary was, and when told it was 1,000 taler, Bismarck remarked: "Well, then you depend on bribes." Or so Behrend told a friend of Friedrich Engels, who relayed the story to August Bebel as proof of Bismarck's brutality. Letter of 11 Oct. 1884, Karl Marx and Friedrich Engels, *Briefe an A. Bebel, W. Liebknecht, K. Kautsky und Andere*, Part I (Moscow, 1933), p. 361.

† Theodor Fontane once commented on the incongruity of "the Prince as papermaker [*Papiermüller*]. It is really very curious; actually he cannot bear all this writing business, and least of all printed paper, and now he establishes a paper mill." *Effi Briest* (Berlin, 1895), p. 105.

plead his cause. Bleichröder recommended extreme caution; the projected third mill, Campmühle, should be abandoned now.[54] Herbert indicated that Bismarck was willing to grant the Behrends a moratorium on their debts, provided his legal counsel, Councillor Drews, and Bleichröder agreed. "You know the prince's benevolence toward the Behrends, especially toward Moritz Behrend," explained Drews to Bleichröder. Drews saw no way of salvaging the Behrends' fortune: "You, Herr Geheimrat, foresaw the end years ago already."[55] But the troubles never ended.

Bismarck heeded neither Bleichröder's warning against "leaping to the financial aid of Behrend" nor his recommendation that Bismarck should buy the mill machinery, at a price made advantageous by the prospective bankruptcy. Bismarck demurred: "Given my circumstances, I prefer leasing [Pacht] to running the operations myself, regardless of the much lower profit." Bismarck was reluctant to run an additional business or to increase his debts. In the end, Bismarck, determined to prevent a Behrend bankruptcy, if possible, instructed Bleichröder to continue the contractual payments for the Campmühle.[56]

In the two days that Bismarck spent in Berlin, en route from Kissingen to Varzin, he saw Bleichröder at length, and Bleichröder wearily wrote him a few days later: "Your Highness may remain assured that I turn my mind to this important matter almost hourly and that I am zealously concerned to discover a way to satisfy the interests of Your Highness in all respects and at the same time to take account of Your Highness's benevolence for the Behrends."[57] Bismarck meanwhile urged the Behrends to consult Bleichröder on how to raise more capital, even though the latter would not advance any money himself "so as to prevent any misunderstanding."[58] Or perhaps to prevent losses for himself?

In a twelve-page letter Bismarck reported new woes. Moritz Behrend—the good Behrend—might quit the business altogether, leaving it to the unreliable Georg to run. Or the brothers might split the business, provided Moritz could raise 75,000 taler, for which he was willing to pay 10 percent interest but could find no creditor even at that rate. In all events, Moritz would suffer from "Georg Behrend's next bankruptcy, which given his extravaganzas can hardly fail to come about."[59] Bismarck had no solution—and his deep concern was manifest in the very length of the letter. How many twelve-page letters was he wont to write in those days?

In the end, a temporary solution was found. Georg Behrend remained a lessee and a source of trouble, whereas Moritz received large loans for the completion of the Campmühle.

The next crisis occurred in October 1877 when the first director of the Ritterschaftliche Privatbank in Stettin died suddenly and under mysterious circumstances. Bleichröder immediately warned Bismarck that the bank might suffer bankruptcy and engulf Georg in the same disaster. The bank owned 1,600,000 marks of questionable notes from Behrend, and if these were suddenly called, Behrend would be insolvent and his creditors might seize the Fuchsmühle.[60] Behrend escaped insolvency but so depleted his capital that in December he had to shut down operations in the Hammermühle.[61]

Baron James de Rothschild.

Gerson von Bleichröder,
from an 1888 painting by Emile Wanters.

Otto von Bismarck in 1864.

William I, German Emperor.

William I, King of Prussia, accompanied by Bismarck, Moltke, and their entourage on the morning of the Battle of Königgrätz, 1866.

France warning Prussia in an 1867 *Punch* cartoon: "Now you're big enough. You mustn't get any bigger. I'm telling you that for your own health."

Ferrières, the château of Baron James de Rothschild.

The façade of the Bleichröder bank, Behrenstrasse 63, Berlin.

Gerson von Bleichröder
in the 1850s.

Adolph von Hansemann.

Count Henckel
von Donnersmarck.

The great hall of the Bleichröder bank. A portrait of Gerson hangs at right.

Field Marshal von Moltke
viewing Paris during the
Franco-Prussian War.

Bismarck and his
aides at Versailles
in 1871; left to
right, Abeken,
Keudell, Bismarck,
Delbrück, Hatzfeldt,
Bismarck-Bohlen.

Bismarck "negotiating"
with Jules Favre
and Adolphe Thiers,
in a painting
by Carl Wagner.

A contemporary French cartoon showing Bismarck and William I, at left,
counting the French indemnity; and, at right, the pillage of Alsace-Lorraine.

Another French cartoon depicting Favre and Thiers
doing the Germans' work after the Treaty of Paris in 1871.

A cartoon (*circa* 1875) ridiculing the anti-Jewish polemics of the Prussian *Kreuzzeitung*. The insert depicts Bleichröder Rex with Delbrück, Bismarck, and Camphausen in attendance.

An 1889 drawing by E. Thiel of the floor of the stock exchange, published in *Illustrierte Zeitung*, a widely circulated periodical. Note the stereotypical Semitic features of many of the traders.

Johanna von Bismarck.

Herbert von Bismarck.

Bismarck and William II at Friedrichsruh, October 30, 1888.

Bismarck with his family and friends at Friedrichsruh in 1893.
From left, at the end of the table: Herbert von Bismarck, Frau Lenbach,
Countess Rantzau (Bismarck's daughter), Johanna Bismarck, and Bismarck.
Standing between Frau Lenbach and Countess Rantzau is Wilhelm von Bismarck.

Benjamin Disraeli, Lord Beaconsfield.

Sir Moses Montefiore, from an 1874 painting by George Richmond.

The Congress of Berlin, 1878.

"Devour it, beast, or die!" The reference is to Bismarck's insistence
that the Reichstag pass his anti-Socialist law in 1878 or be dissolved.

Reichstags-Prognostikon.

Friß, Vogel, oder stirb!

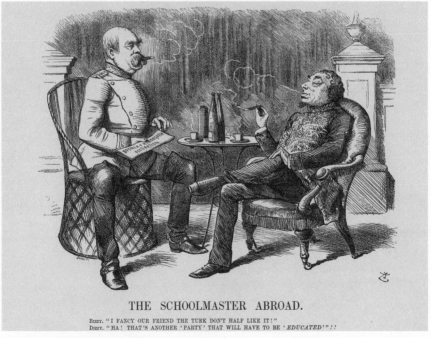

THE SCHOOLMASTER ABROAD.

Bizzy. "I FANCY OUR FRIEND THE TURK DON'T HALF LIKE IT!"
Dizzy. "HA! THAT'S ANOTHER 'PARTY' THAT WILL HAVE TO BE 'EDUCATED'"!!

Punch cartoon of Bismarck and Disraeli during the Congress of Berlin
discussing the Austrian occupation of Bosnia-Herzegovina.

Heinrich von Lehndorff.

Below, right:
Paul von Hatzfeldt.

Josef Maria von Radowitz.

Friedrich von Holstein.

Gerson von Bleichröder on his deathbed, 1893.

Paul von Schwabach.

Georg von Bleichröder, a great sports
enthusiast, at the wheel of his automobile.

Hans von Bleichröder, Jr.,
listening to a radio
with friends in 1927.

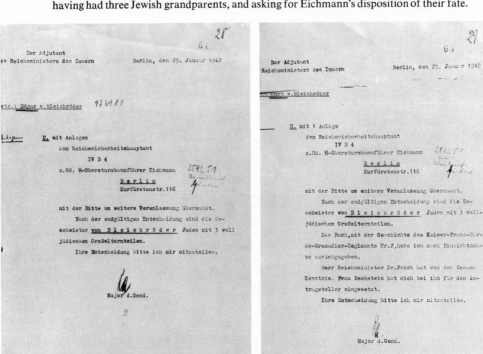

One of Bismarck's last letters to Bleichröder, written three weeks before the latter's death.

A Ministry of Interior memorandum informing SS Obersturmbannführer Adolf Eichmann that Edgar von Bleichröder and his brother Curt were Jews, having had three Jewish grandparents, and asking for Eichmann's disposition of their fate.

Meanwhile Bismarck lent ever larger sums to Moritz; he added 150,000 marks to the originally anticipated 225,000 marks. Bleichröder repeatedly objected to policy and procedure, but Bismarck mostly overruled him. Bleichröder probably saw it as a matter of throwing good money after bad; Bismarck wanted his mills and for some reason hesitated to break with the Behrends and look for new tenants.[62]

In the late 1870s hardly a month passed without a new Behrend crisis. Bismarck worried about the two brothers quarreling: "We hear reports about Georg Behrend that arouse suspicion, to wit that he manufactures cardboard at a net price of 27 marks and sells it for 12 marks, only so as to underbid his brother Moritz, who, I believe, sells for 15 marks per piece. . . ." Other rumors made the Bismarcks fear that Georg "will very soon suffer a great bust [*dass er sehr bald eine grosse Pleite machen wird*]"—using on this appropriate occasion a popular Jewish expression for bankruptcy.[63] Bleichröder replied that Georg had already been forced to grant virtual control over the Fuchsmühle to a consortium of bankers, including the eminent Berliner Handelsgesellschaft; his personal affairs would soon be headed for another catastrophe.[64]

There was no end of trouble with the Behrends. In July 1879 Georg was late paying his semiannual rental of 6,906 marks for the Fuchsmühle, and Bismarck finally resolved to sue him. Herbert sent Bleichröder the necessary instructions, but a few days later Georg paid and the occasion for drastic action disappeared.* Later that year, Georg sought to add a steam boiler to the mill; at Bismarck's request, Bleichröder inquired and discovered that the Berlin Handelsgesellschaft opposed the new venture, thought Georg penniless, hoped to terminate its relations with him, and urged that "everybody should be warned against entrusting money to him."[65] In December the existing steam boilers broke, and on Christmas Day Herbert wrote Bleichröder a long letter on behalf of his father, explaining that the boilers, ruined by Georg's neglect, would be out of commission for a long time.[66] And still Bismarck rejected Bleichröder's advice to terminate his arrangements with Georg; he preferred "not to proceed aggressively . . . but to remain passive . . . because the present situation of Georg Behrend would before long and by itself prove to be untenable."[67]

In fact, Bismarck advanced more money, and new troubles arose. In 1888 the mill was flooded and inoperable, and Behrend informed Bleichröder that therefore he could meet his obligations only partially and at an uncertain date. Bismarck was furious, gave tough instructions to Bleichröder, but, on appeal from Georg, reversed himself in two days' time. In October 1889, in the middle of the night, the mill at Aumühle burned down, with Bismarck a witness to the scene.[68]

It is a curiously accommodating Bismarck that emerged from this record

* Bleichröder to Bismarck, 7 July 1879, SA, with Bismarck's draft reply on the back of Bleichröder's letter, and Herbert's identical letter to Bleichröder of the same date, BA. This and other instances warrant the conclusion that most of the business letters to Bleichröder written on Bismarck's behalf by his sons and son-in-law were in fact drafted or dictated by Bismarck himself.

of decades of troubled transactions. Still, Bismarck greatly profited from his connections with the Behrends. The basic annual rental amounted to 78,018 marks, exclusive of additional interest charges. At a later time, Moritz Behrend, in order to raise funds for a venture of his on Lake Erie, converted his Varzin mills into a joint-stock corporation that paid Bismarck 87,105 marks annually, a figure more closely resembling one that Bismarck once mentioned.[69] The Behrends also bought some of Bismarck's timber in Varzin and paid for their use of water. All in all, they constituted the single largest source of Bismarck's income.

Yet Bismarck not only had to endure Georg's galling unreliability but suffered calumny on account of his relations with all the Behrends. The anti-Semites seized upon this further proof of Bismarck's involvement with Jews, alleged that he lent the Behrends funds at 8 percent interest, and proclaimed that the Behrends enjoyed a monopoly as sole suppliers of paper to the Imperial Post Office and the Imperial Railways—a story that later historians repeated, without documentation. (In 1881 Bismarck assured the Behrends that he "very strongly disapproved of this fight against the Jews, be it on the basis of religion or, worse, on the basis of [racial] descent.")[70] The Bleich-röder archives make no mention whatever of a lucrative contract between Behrend and the imperial government. Would Bismarck have had to be so concerned about Georg Behrend if his finances rested on such a solid basis?

Bismarck's love of trees was celebrated.* The passion was genuine, as was his very considerable expertise about the care and feeding of forests. His love was also something that served his image as an authentic German; few of his compatriots realized that his forests constituted a principal source of income as well.†

In 1879, defending a proposed tariff on timber, Bismarck complained to parliament that no one interested in money would grow timber anymore; in time, forests would become deserts—except for a few *"Holznarren"* (timber nuts) like himself "who have pleasure in seeing forests grow without reckoning the cost to the last penny of interest."[71] Bismarck may have been a timber nut, but in real life—as against parliamentary speeches—he saw no contradiction between love and profit.

Over the years, Bismarck received more money from his timber than from his salary. Accordingly he was most concerned that his product should find a ready and reliable market. In 1882 he decided to sell only by special purchase order with definite payment schedules arranged. His customers in

---

* He shared that passion with Disraeli, whom he admired, but not with Gladstone, whom he detested. To the latter, he sent this malicious message in 1887: "Tell him that while he puts the ax to trees, I am eagerly planting them." Arnold Oskar Meyer, *Bismarck. Der Mensch und der Staatsmann* (Leipzig, 1944), p. 448; Robert Blake, *Disraeli* (London, 1966), pp. 410, 414.

† In 1882 he was particularly worried about the returns from his timber. About a large and dying stand of recently planted Douglas firs he remarked to his finance minister, Adolf von Scholz: "My sons should not be angry about this! Other fathers have left their sons with far greater losses on account of horses, cards, women, and other things—hence I do not deserve any great reproaches for my mistake in forest management." *GW*, VIII, 456.

Sheffield might object, both because of price and quality and, as he wrote Bleichröder, because "Englishmen do not want to accept other modalities; they are used to defining commercial conditions by themselves."[72]

Bismarck's chief customer, however, was Friedrich Vohwinkel, a German wholesaler whose business brought him into indirect contact with Bleichröder. In 1882 Bismarck's forester from Friedrichsruh wrote Bleichröder: "As you know from the administration of the Prince's finances, Mr. Friedrich Vohwinkel from Gelsenkirchen receives a steady supply of wooden pit props for mines from the Sachsenwald. The Prince's administration is therefore very interested that Mr. Vohwinkel, who always pays promptly, should retain his own markets." Among them was the huge coal mine, Hibernia, which was to give out new contracts for timber in a short time. "Since . . . the decision as to who should receive the contract is in your hands, I am taking the liberty as representative of our princely administration of submitting the humble request to you that you should choose Mr. Vohwinkel again."[73]

Bleichröder was a director of Hibernia, as were his son and Schwabach after him. No doubt his influence was great, though normally he would hardly bother himself with Hibernia's purchase of wooden pit props. For Bismarck's chief customer, however, he intervened—successfully. Lange renewed his plea in 1886, pointing out that Vohwinkel had been Bismarck's customer since 1878 but future purchases would depend on Hibernia's continuing to buy its timber from him and on advantageous terms. "Prices are already so depressed," he wrote, "that in case of further reduction I am afraid I might lose this valuable connection." And the connection *was* valuable: Vohwinkel had already paid "a full million" to the prince's estate, without there ever having been a disagreement. Bleichröder always obliged, and a year later Lange thanked him for his help: "Because of it, we were able to keep our best customer, and we were spared the embarrassment of having to search for other reliable markets which could have been found only with difficulty. His Highness . . . has been pleased to take cognizance of the favorable business position for which we have you to thank."[74] A few days after the chancellor's dismissal, Lange again appealed to Bleichröder on behalf of Vohwinkel, adding that the Friedrichsruh oak timber was more suitable for Hibernia than for any other mines. Within three days Bleichröder had a reply from Hibernia indicating that there should be no difficulty about renewing Vohwinkel's contract, considering his satisfactory performance in the past.[75]

There is something neatly paradigmatic about Bleichröder's role in retaining Bismarck's tie with Vohwinkel. It was Bismarck's closest business connection with the Ruhr industrialists, and one that was of enormous importance to him. After all, Vohwinkel paid him more than the state did. Nor was the connection between Junker and industrial interests without political significance: Vohwinkel was a leading member of Louis Baare's hyperactive Chamber of Commerce in Bochum, which in 1873 began its drive for iron ore duties. Hibernia—Bleichröder's creation and Bismarck's indirect customer—belonged to the same pressure group.[76] Bismarck had ample reasons to heed their insistent demands.

Bismarck had other sources of income on his estates, but of relatively minor importance. There was a notorious explosives factory, Pulverfabrik Rottweiler, which at first yielded 10,900 marks annually and by the late 1880s nearly double that amount.* Bismarck derived some income from distilleries on his estates, though the Bleichröder accounts give no particulars. Likewise his Friedrichsruh estate contained a source of mineral water, which was bottled and sold under the appropriate name of Bismarck-Quelle. None of these represented a major financial return, though they all added to the income from the three estates.

Bismarck's accounts were enormously complex. They absorbed a good deal of his and Bleichröder's time, and they remain difficult to disentangle despite the evidence now in our hands. Some of the semiannual statements Bismarck checked most carefully, identifying the purpose of many of the items listed. Bleichröder sent the Bismarck family, their longtime servant Engel, or their general factotum, Jenny Fatio, lump sums of 6,000 marks for household expenses. In 1878 these apparently amounted to 156,000 marks; in 1879 they rose to 185,000 marks, and in 1883 fell to 138,989 marks.[77]

For the year 1884 we have a complete listing of Bismarck's account with Bleichröder; at year's end Bismarck's debits amounted to 526,692 marks and his income to 408,425, leaving an unfavorable balance of 118,267, which Bleichröder carried at 4 percent per annum. Among the debits were 119,500 sent to the Bismarck household; there were also the annual 12,000 marks sent to Count Rantzau and a smaller amount to Bill. Some payments were made directly to various purveyors, including a single payment of 4,000 marks for wine. The forester of Friedrichsruh received 110,000 marks, presumably for purchases, repairs, and incidental expenses connected with the proper running of the estate. Bismarck also spent 18,500 marks for the rebuilding of the Behrend mills and 120,000 marks for mortgage interests and amortization.

The income ledger for 1884 may not have been typical, although the proportions probably changed relatively little over the years. The largest item came from the various Behrend leases, amounting to 85,300 marks; Vohwinkel that year paid 76,242 marks. Bismarck's interest from investments came to 56,613 marks and his salary to 52,294 marks. Varzin's forester Westphal sent in 35,000 marks, and Pulverfabrik Rottweiler brought in a meager 10,910 marks. The balance seems largely to have been sales of securities, recorded as income. These figures attest Bleichröder's central involvement in the major sources of Bismarck's income.

---

* Alfred Vagts, "Bismarck's Fortune," *CEH* (1968), I, 216–217, makes much of the possible impropriety of Bismarck's having an interest in munitionmaking. The interest was fixed, though in later years the lease increased in value. Hence—contrary to Vagts's opinion— sudden booms due to profitable wars did not benefit Bismarck, quite aside from the fact that all his other investments would have suffered from the outbreak of war. Vagts failed to mention Bismarck's important tie with the Ruhr magnates, through Vohwinkel.

Six months later Bismarck made his own rough calculations on Bleich-röder's elaborate six-month statement and jotted down that Varzin (including the Behrends) had yielded 118,769 marks, Schönhausen 22,000 marks, Friedrichsruh (including Vohwinkel) 86,538, his salary 26,324 marks, and interest payments 7,618 marks—the last item being unusually low. During the same six months Bismarck paid out 53,000 marks for mortgage amortization and interest, 20,200 to the Behrends for construction work, and 37,000 and 15,000, respectively, to the foresters of Varzin and Friedrichsruh. Personal expenses amounted to 62,000 marks.

In connection with another bout of trouble with the tax authorities, Bismarck asked Bleichröder for a statement of his average annual *net* income from his three estate complexes for the years 1887 to 1889. Bleichröder supplied the figures: Varzin (including Behrend leases), 125,200 marks; Friedrichsruh, 130,400; Schönhausen, 9,800. Considering that Varzin plus the Behrends represented an investment (including the original gift) of nearly 3 million marks and Friedrichsruh of well over 3 million marks, the returns were relatively meager, almost certainly less than 4 percent annually. Still, in his declining years, Bismarck's income from his estates clearly rose, and his heavy investments in them began to pay off.*

Bismarck's ouster from office meant that his salary ceased at once and that he went on pension at one-third pay. His total annual allowance was reduced to 27,000 marks, which included his pension as Lauenburg minister; he also lost his rent-free Berlin residence.[78] Was it Prussian order or imperial vengeance that led the Legationskasse to demand that Bismarck return at once the difference between salary and pension for the last ten days in March 1890? Bismarck himself sneered: "By such means the Prussian state has become great."[79]† Was it chicanery or exactitude that led the government to collect 586.40 marks "for work done in the last year" on Bismarck's official quarters in Berlin?[80] Bismarck was often accused of monumental pettiness; his newly emancipated underlings had learned some lessons all too well.

In office, Bismarck had spent much time on his investments. In retirement, money was but a secondary passion. He found that managing his multimillion fortune was just as unsatisfactory as handling his meager inheritance had been half a century before. Power and politics were the ruling passions of his life—without them, money had little to offer his psychic economy.** His last coup was to put his political passion to profit: he sold his memoirs, in advance, for 100,000 marks a volume—the highest amount a German publisher had ever paid a prospective author.[81]

---

* A few weeks after his fall from power, in a conversation in Bleichröder's presence, Bismarck complained to a visiting forester that "'none of my estates with the exception of Schönhausen yield me anything—only Schönhausen has good soil.' Herr von Bleichröder smiled incredulously and even the Prince did not seem all too serious about his remark." *GW*, IX, 29.

† In the Bleichröder Archive is an unsigned note about his pension, concluding: "His Highness has to repay 1,500 marks for salary from March 21 to the end of March." Bismarck explicitly authorized the reimbursement. Chrysander to Bleichröder, 1 June 1890, BA.

** Indeed it was in retirement and a month after Bleichröder's death that Bismarck recalled how much he owed to his banker: "He relieved me of the great worry how to invest

It was inevitable and perhaps fitting that right after Bismarck's death rumors spread about the magnitude of his estate. Finally the *Hamburger Nachrichten,* a paper that had been especially close to the fallen chancellor, reported "authoritatively . . . [that] the total capital and cash value of the estate came to less than 2,500,000 marks and that this amount was burdened with major, annual obligations and expenses for his heirs."[82] We now know that Bismarck left close to triple that amount—despite the fact that in the last years of his life he transferred funds and land to Herbert. Had the prince known about this depreciation of his fortune he would have smiled, knowing that it was probably meant to discourage greedy tax assessors. But perhaps he would have wanted posterity to know that he had done better than that— and certainly Bleichröder would have wanted it known that Bismarck's fortune had multiplied many times in his lifetime.

Bismarck was never satisfied with his private ventures. Perhaps he thought that if he had ever turned his intelligence, ambition, and boundless egoism to material pursuits, he could have become a titan in business. As it is, he did reasonably well. His success in his private ventures—as in his political career—marked him as the Junker modernized. Bismarck succeeded in business and politics because of his extraordinary adaptability to modern opportunities and because of his relentless, even ruthless pursuit of his own.

As we have seen in this account of Bismarck's finances, Bleichröder was a monumental convenience to Bismarck, but he was not a means to illicit riches or dubious speculations. On the other hand, Bismarck was impatient with certain pieties of his contemporaries: in promoting his interests, he at times ignored conventional morality; he bent and perhaps occasionally even shaped the law to suit his purposes; he intimidated bureaucrats, and he evaded tax authorities. Still, in his private egoism, we are astounded by the pettiness, not the magnitude, of his rapacity.

Bismarck's sang-froid in material matters was exemplified by his decision to use a publicly raised seventieth birthday present in order to repurchase Schönhausen II, the much larger part of the ancestral estate which had been sold in 1830. The price was a million and a half. The thousands of donors had assumed that Bismarck would use their offerings (called Otto pence in allusion to the Peter pence collected by popes) to create a patriotic charity. But they had reckoned without Bismarck, whose friends in the fund-raising committee insisted on the purchase of Schönhausen II. The press reported dissent in the committee, but such stalwarts as the duke of Ratibor (to whom Bismarck

---

and administer my funds safely and advantageously, at a time when my official duties would scarcely have allowed me to deal with this alone; he collected all the income from my estates etc. and in exchange granted me a virtually unlimited right to draw from him my running expenses. His statements always arrived punctually and not one of them ever needed any correction." *GW*, IX, 336.

had been most helpful in the Rumanian tangle) persuaded thirty-four members to vote for Schönhausen, while six voted against it. Accordingly, half the funds or 1,150,000 marks went to the repurchase of the ancestral home; the remaining 350,000 marks came from a group of wealthy patrons, headed by Bleichröder and the banker Mendelssohn.[83] In this way Schönhausen was reacquired, without encumbrance, and much to Bismarck's pleasure. Bleichröder had worked hard at the reacquisition, which even then was designated as Herbert's fief, and remarked to Holstein: "An odd state of affairs. The family has *me* to thank for Schönhausen, Herbert will inherit it one day, and yet I risk being thrown out if I want to visit him."[84]

With the rest of the money, Bismarck was willing to endow a national charity. In a private letter to William I, Bismarck explained that he envisioned a foundation in support of secondary school teachers because their "teaching is the nursery of our national sentiment. The idealistic consciousness which infuses the teaching profession . . . is the moral counterweight to the materialism of our time." The seat of the foundation, he continued, would be Schönhausen, not Berlin, "in order to remove [it] from all contact with the Berlin city administration and all possible influence from it." Bismarck's epistle —with its pious denunciation of materialism—did not mention that a fraction of the funds collected would also be used for the establishment of a trust for the care of the indigent on Bismarck's estates. Nor did it mention that the principal of these trust funds, administered by Bleichröder, was partly invested in mortgages on Bismarck's estates, thus retiring some of the mortgages Bleichröder had held.[85]

Bismarck had decided on this division of the spoils without consulting Johanna or his sons. Especially his sons "thought the contribution of the great Jew-bankers dreadful." Herbert was incensed, because his father's decision scandalized the crown prince's court and many people in South Germany. Few people agreed with the Bavarian ambassador in Berlin, who celebrated Bismarck's acceptance of a public gift for private benefit as an act of "moral courage." Lesser men, he thought, might have pretended to be too "high-minded" for such a gift, "but it was not Bismarck's style to play such a comedy in front of the world."[86]* The acquisition proved unexpectedly intricate and required Bleichröder's unstinting help. For months letters passed back and forth, and however much Herbert loathed Bleichröder and pretended to abhor the deal, he was the main beneficiary and fell heir to the much-enlarged estate almost immediately.

Bismarck's friends and foes (many people were both) often referred to the coincidence of his own economic interests and his commercial policy. Thus Holstein noted in 1884: "It cannot be denied that in matters like duty on wood, spirits, etc. the Chancellor does take into account his own interests, and this fact has been used against him before now. But in every one of these

---

* By an odd psychological coincidence, it was while discussing with Countess Spitzemberg the reacquisition of the ancestral home that Bismarck suddenly mentioned his mother and made the famous remark that "she had been intelligent but cold to the very heart." Rudolf Vierhaus, ed., *Das Tagebuch der Baronin Spitzemberg* (Göttingen, 1960), p. 218.

questions his interests are identical with those of a great mass of citizens, so he is by no means taking up the cudgels just for himself."[87] In 1879 Bismarck warned the war minister against the deleterious domestic effects of overestimating the quality of American timber.[88] In 1887 his colleague Lucius noted that every time the distillery tax was discussed, Bismarck quickly calculated how the tax would affect his own business "and thus get a practical picture of the extent of the proposed rates."[89] Ludwig Bamberger reported that at a party at the Bismarcks' in March 1883 someone mentioned the low price of timber in Germany and Bismarck casually noted that he no longer cared because he sold all his wood to England. Bamberger added maliciously, "Soon thereafter came the bill proposing an increase in duties on timber."[90] Bamberger did not know that Bismarck's assertion about his English market was largely a mendacious anachronism.

It has recently been said that "the list of material favors, administrative and legislative, which Bismarck obtained for himself and sometimes for his peers, is nearly endless."[91] Certainly Bismarck's concern over a possible "conflict of interest" between his private and public activities was at best intermittent; he invoked the principle when there were other reasons why he did not want to do something. The Bleichröder Archive does not adduce any further evidence for Bismarck's alleged adoption of public policies in order to promote private interests. We saw that Bismarck invested in his own railroad policy, but his decision to nationalize the railroads was obviously independent of his investments. On the other hand, it is true, as Holstein alleged, that Bismarck stood to benefit from certain taxes of the late 1880s, especially the duty on timber, and that he sought to tailor the distillery tax to his own needs.

Bismarck could be outrageously imperious in dealing with local authorities who ran afoul of his expectations that the interests of the large landowners should determine local road or tax policy. Bleichröder seems not to have had anything to do with Bismarck's celebrated hectoring of officials. But at the end of the chancellor's tenure, Bleichröder was again witness to Bismarck's reluctance to pay taxes. How strongly Bismarck felt about the Prussian income tax can be gleaned from a major Reichstag speech in 1882, in which he argued that it was the Prussian tax that was driving so many Germans into emigration, just as the state collector drove many a defaulting citizen to suicide. Bismarck's extravagant allegation tells us more about his own view of the levying of direct taxes by "our urban, scientific, bureaucratic, law-giving circles who are ignorant of the real conditions" than it does about the causes of large-scale German emigration.[92]*

In March 1890, when the tax commission informed Bismarck that

---

* A year later, Bismarck petitioned the king for yet another tax exemption. The original dotations of 1866 and 1871 had been converted into entailed estates at Varzin and Friedrichsruh. By William's order, the stamp tax of 3 percent customarily paid for such deeds had been waived. In 1883 Bismarck wanted to make sure that the rather considerable additions to these estates, which normally would be subject to tax, would also be exempt. On the recommendation of two of his ministers, the king agreed. Scholz and Friedberg to William, 23 April 1883, DZA: Merseburg: Geh. Civil Cabinet, Rep. 89H, XXIII, 12ff.

he was in the thirty-first bracket, with an estimated income of between 204,000 and 240,000 marks, and an annual tax of 6,120, there were only about 1,500 people in all of Prussia with an estimated income exceeding 100,000 marks. (The reader will recall that the much higher communal taxes were based on the assessment of income taxes.) He had been in that bracket since 1877. After his dismissal, and his loss of salary and rent-free dwelling, Bismarck thought of appealing his tax status, and Bleichröder was asked to furnish him with information about his income. Bleichröder submitted a review for 1890: the total income came to 332,000 marks (27,000 marks pension and 40,300 marks interest; the rest from the estates). It would seem incontrovertible, then, that Bismarck's income exceeded the official estimate by 90,000 and that he should have been in the thirty-third bracket, with a tax of 9,000 marks. At this point, Bismarck dropped the projected appeal to the authorities. There is no record to suggest that he sought to correct these belittling figures. The discrepancy between official estimate and actuality probably afforded him pleasure.[93] To paraphrase Bismarck: By such means, the Prussian Junker became wealthy.

CHAPTER 13

The World of Banking and Diplomacy

Later on, diplomatic reports were again discussed, and the Chief, who seems in general to have a poor opinion of them, said: "For the most part, they are just paper smeared with ink. . . . As for using them someday as material for history, nothing of any value will be found in them. I believe the archives are open to the public at the end of thirty years—but it might be done much sooner. Even the dispatches which do contain information are scarcely intelligible to those who do not know the people and their relations to each other. In thirty years' time who will know what sort of a man the writer himself was, how he looked at things, and how his individuality colored them? And who has really an intimate knowledge of the people mentioned in his reports? One must know what Gorchacov or Gladstone or Granville had in mind when making the statements recorded in the dispatch. . . . The main points always lie in private letters and confidential communications, also oral ones, and these never find their way into the records."
—Moritz Busch, February 22, 1871

In an offshoot of the *Times* yesterday I saw some remarks of Bismarck on "despatches" and "State Papers," which the Ranke school might weigh to their great profit. He looks on such materials as of very little value. "What," he asks, "would all the current despatches tell of my real policy or that of Gladstone or Thiers?" Surely they tell even less of national feeling, of those impulses which (and not the policy of statesmen) really—and with Lord Beaconsfield's and Ranke's good leave—make history.
—J. R. Green to E. A. Freeman, November 20, 1878

I telegraphed to you that Prince Bismarck has sent me a private personal and secret message through Bleichröder, his Secret Agent. . . .
—Lord Ampthill to Lord Granville, November 26, 1881

For over twenty years Bismarck was the dominant statesman of Europe. His domineering will and Germany's strength gave him a unique position among Europe's leaders—in fact, no statesman since has surpassed his tenure or his impact. And during all those years, somewhere—not at his side and yet not in his shadow—stood Bleichröder, his special aide, his "Secret Agent," in foreign affairs.[1] Europe recognized him as such.

It, too, was a unique relationship in Europe, unique in duration, compass, and intensity. No other servant of Bismarck's lasted as long; with none did he have those many hours of candid talk, closeted in Berlin or at some Bismarck retreat. Thirty years of wide-ranging talks, of habitual *tours d'horizon,* of favors asked, granted, ignored. We have no record of those conversations, no tapes; we hear echoes of them in their correspondence and in their conversations with other notables.

There were a host of different functions that the two men performed for each other. They ran the gamut from private to public affairs, official and unofficial business, financial and diplomatic considerations. Each assumed a succession of roles: Bleichröder spoke as Bismarck's banker, as transmitter of information, by designation and by passion; he spoke as Bismarck's agent in dealing with particular statesmen, as his unofficial ambassador-at-large, as a representative of his own interests or those of the German banking community; at times he pushed his own clients for high office, and at other times he pleaded the cause of persecuted Jews abroad. He asked for favors for himself so that his own role or business would be enhanced: a word from Bismarck at the right time could give Bleichröder the decisive edge over foreign or domestic rivals. All of these subjects were continually touched upon—in conversation or correspondence—and in a way that a more bureaucratic world would abhor.

Bismarck found the ubiquitous banker a splendid supplement to his official entourage: "Through Bleichröder I am accustomed to receive important political news from Paris or St. Petersburg, usually eight days earlier than through my ambassadors."[2] But it was more than speed that commended Bleichröder's services: Bismarck learned to see the world through the eyes of his banker who had his own connections with the new powers of the world, with the Rothschilds and with a whole web of competing and cooperating banks. More than that, he charged Bleichröder with special missions abroad, missions of a delicacy or a tentativeness that were best accommodated outside official channels. Europe listened, because Bleichröder's special relationship to Bismarck was universally known.

For Bleichröder these conversations were priceless. They gave him that special aura of distinction, importance, all-knowingness. They gave him practical advantages as well: from them he gleaned the dispositions and outlook of the dominant statesman of his time, and he could make his own financial dispositions accordingly. His easy entrée to Bismarck implied equally easy entrée to the lower echelons of power, and Bleichröder could count on being listened to and often helped in his routine *démarches* to the Foreign Office or to embassies abroad. He wanted to be an *éminence grise et riche*—and the rest of Bismarck's entourage had to accept his place, at times defer to him, even compete for his favors.

The Bismarck-Bleichröder relationship exemplified the many overlapping interests between finance and diplomacy, between domestic and foreign affairs, between private and public concerns. It also suggests that in Bismarck's eye, diplomacy was too serious to be left to diplomats—and it shows that bankers needed a political sense, a second vision, just as sailors need a meteorological sense. All of this was obvious to Bismarck and Bleichröder and remained unspoken: they became habituated to thirty years of reciprocal relations, but none of it will give much satisfaction to those who see the world in discrete compartments. The Bismarck-Bleichröder relationship underscores the difficulty, perhaps futility, of reconstructing the past, even the diplomacy of the past, from diplomatic records alone. Nor does it conform to the vision of some modern historians or ideologists who see the past as a neat structure, within which one element, usually the socioeconomic element, has "primacy." Least of all does the relationship bear out the once fashionable view that cast international bankers in the role of villains, as wirepullers bent on war. The reality, at least as far as Bleichröder's role would suggest, was a good deal less melodramatic; it shows a world more complex, more intertwined, more variegated, more fascinating, and less certain than people have assumed. The particular relationship of Bismarck and Bleichröder enjoins prudence about the construction of grandiose systems. Still the preliminary remark may be in order that while the relationship was always mutually beneficial, while Bleichröder could and did apply pressure, even at times frantic pressure, power always resided in his great friend, the balance was always tipped in Bismarck's favor.[3]

In the nineteenth century, diplomacy was still the preserve of the privileged. Most diplomats were aristocrats because it was assumed that only the scions of ancient families would have the natural elegance, the inborn discretion, bearing, and cosmopolitanism, that the task required; only they could be sure of instantaneous entrée to the highest society of the country to which they were being sent.

But diplomacy was the preserve of the privileged in more than rank or status: the whole realm of foreign policy—of what the Germans call *die Grosse Politik* or the French *la haute politique*—was considered superior to other realms, and especially to the grubbiness of domestic politics. It was "high" because the players were models of distinction and the stakes were ultimately war and peace. In a world of shrinking pomp and mystery, the men flitting in and out of the Wilhelmstrasse or the Quai d'Orsay or Downing Street felt themselves to be great actors in an historic drama—in the drama that determined the fate of nations. In their plumed hats and dress uniforms, in their guardianship of that mystical treasure, the National Interest, they thought they were playing a role of unsurpassed importance.

Diplomacy was a world of glitter and mystery. Beneath the glitter of imperial visits and formal conferences was the mystery of the true designs of nations, the ambitions of rulers. Diplomacy was not only the rare moment of decision; it was the routine search for clues—clues in ambiguous statements, in press campaigns and economic dispositions, in an imperial phrase or gesture, in armaments and troop movements. Beneath the glitter was a world at best of partial knowledge and continuous search for temporary resolutions to conflicting demands. Diplomats believed that but for their skill the nations of Europe would clash; they were the doctors of a world system that without their little adjustments would plunge from malady to malady. Like their fellow aristocrats in the army, they pictured themselves as the defenders of the nation's security. In the meantime, they led great lives, perched in dignity on the edge of often imagined disaster. Diplomacy and warfare remained the noble professions—and both offered their practitioners the lure of glory.*

Diplomacy was Bismarck's life. For him the primacy of foreign policy was not some kind of academic tenet: his world and his passion were foreign affairs. Under the shield of diplomacy, he had led Prussia into three insulated wars; after 1871 he realized that a united Germany could hardly expect to fight such safely circumscribed wars again. His Germany had been created by diplomacy and war, and his nightmare was its destruction at the hands of a victorious coalition. He wanted peace and ever increasing power—because international affairs was not a static system and because he knew that after centuries of defeats and disunity, his own people would forgive internal disappointments for external glory. To Bismarck, then, diplomacy was the essence of survival.

Diplomacy presupposed a vision of the interconnectedness of things: Europe was cramped, and every move of every power had a hundred distant repercussions—and even small countries could cause great upheavals. Above all, the scene changed continually, at least on the surface; there were always new issues and crises that threatened the precarious balance of forces. Interests and alliances shifted, and it was Bismarck's aim to anticipate and guide these changes as much as possible.

Foreign affairs was Bleichröder's field, too. He also had a stake, actual or potential, in nearly every country in Europe and in many beyond. He negotiated with foreign governments; he formed alliances with or against other bankers or syndicates in other countries. Financiers, with their international ties, were statesmen in mufti. Foreign governments and bankers needed his support, and he needed their business. The list of his clients was long, and necessarily his interests intersected with the interests of the state.

Bleichröder was the archetype of that much-esteemed, much-vilified being, the international banker. These bankers were the modern analogues of ancient potentates—and at times expected similar deference.† They marshaled their millions and sent them out as earlier potentates had dispatched their men.

---

* How pleasantly virtuous and important ambassadors felt in their role is reflected in these words by one of Bleichröder's friends in the French Embassy in Berlin. Fondly recalling his life, the Comte de Moüy wrote: "I found in it . . . the powerful and varied interest of the great affairs of state, the charm of an active existence, of great travel, of constant relations with that part of society that is at once the most elegant and the most correct in the world, the attraction of important duties which I undertook and better than all the rest, the conviction of serving only one's fatherland above and beyond all parties." Comte Charles de Moüy, *Souvenirs et Causeries d'un Diplomate* (Paris, 1909), p. iii.

† International bankers enjoyed an extraordinary prestige—as long as they were successful. Sir Edward Malet, Britain's ambassador in Berlin in the late 1880s—and as such a man of frequent contacts with Bleichröder—left this description of the (short-lived) glory of the original owner of the mansion that the British Embassy had bought: "The house was built by a banker of vast wealth, named Strousberg, who for a time blazed like a comet in the financial world, and at his zenith he built this fine house in the most aristocratic street in Berlin. He was

Bleichröder needed to know the lay of the land before he committed his money; he, too, made his dispositions in accordance with short-term outlook and long-term prospects for peace or war. A loan to Russia on the eve of war would run risks that a similar loan at a more auspicious moment would not. Like many successful people, Bleichröder developed a passion for something that was essentially functional: he wanted to know everybody and everything, to be a part of the great diplomatic world, and in the process, no doubt, he also acquired that shrewd judgment on which so many people complimented him, and his own power of combination, a kind of second sight from visible fact in the present to likely consequences in the future.

Bleichröder always wanted peace, and his desire was well known. The British ambassador in Berlin once noted that "Bismarck's indifference to the prospects of a Turco-Greek War greatly alarmed Bleichröder who, as a Banker, is a man of Peace." Peace brought prosperity; war spelled uncertainty, which the stock market abhors, as nature abhors a vacuum. Apropos of the military budgets of Austria and Germany Bleichröder's friend Goldschmidt once wrote: ". . . I can only bitterly lament . . . that for the benefit of our brass [*bunte Kragen*] billions are taken away from industry and from useful production and that the people's welfare is sacrificed to militarism." We have no similar utterances from Bleichröder, and we know of course that at an earlier time he financed wars. But his preference for peace was unambiguous and dictated by his worldly wisdom and self-interest.[4]

The workaday Bismarck—unlike the Olympian or aseptic master chess player depicted by diplomatic historians or in carefully pruned collections of documents—had a pragmatic sense of the interconnectedness of high policy and every aspect of domestic policy. Precisely because of his greater practicality, perhaps because of his own involvement in the economic life of the nation, he appreciated the perspective on international affairs that his banker had to offer him. For Bismarck, economic matters were at once a barometer of a nation's health and disposition—a barometer over which he sometimes had limited power. But he also knew that in deciding issues of war and peace, sometimes at least "passions are stronger than calculations."[5]

Bismarck's breadth of vision reflected the multiplicity of his posts: he

---

not destined to enjoy it. . . . I think it must have been in the autumn of 1874. . . . [that] I arrived, fasting and wanting warmth, at the hotel of 'The Three Kings' at Basle. I found all the personnel of the hotel ranged in the hall, and as I approached an individual, who appeared by his assumption of importance to be the manager, he requested me to stand aside, I edged into a corner, supposing that a king or at least a prince was immediately behind me. As I looked a waiter advanced with a lighted candelabrum, descended the steps into the street, and returned ushering in a little elderly man in a very beautiful fur coat, followed by a comely young lady of Jewish type. They went upstairs, preceded by the candelabrum-bearer; the waiters dispersed. I emerged from my corner. I addressed the porter, who seemed to have regained the stolid aspect which became his calling, and asked him who it was who had just arrived. He seemed surprised at my question and replied, 'It is Herr Strousberg.' The name did not enlighten me. I said, 'Who is Herr Strousberg?' The porter seemed more and more surprised. 'Don't you know,' he said, 'Herr Strousberg, of Berlin, the great financier?' " We will hear of Strousberg's misadventures in the next chapter. Sir Edward Malet, *Shifting Scenes. Or Memories of Many Men in Many Lands* (London, 1901), pp. 166–167.

was prime minister, foreign minister, and at times commerce minister; the British ambassador described him as the "German Dictator," the source of power over all domains.[6] Like other statesmen, he may on occasion have talked as if the domestic and foreign realms were separate or separable, but he knew that the world was not that simple, not for him and not for his foreign protagonists. Diplomacy was the art of obtaining possible ends abroad within the clear constraints at home. The two were in constant interaction, and Bismarck knew as well that war and revolution were deeply intertwined: the Commune had reminded him of that historic lesson. The two realms most clearly intersected in economic matters. He always assumed that the state should promote business interests at home and abroad, wherever it could do so without injuring competing, higher interests.

Bismarck was therefore concerned with Bleichröder's principal business, the placing of foreign loans. The stability of Europe depended in part on a variety of loans that advanced countries made to less developed countries—to use the terminology of our day. Even great powers were utterly dependent on foreign credit, as Russia and Austria-Hungary continually demonstrated. By comparison with London and Paris, the Berlin capital market was very limited, with heavy demands from domestic enterprises that needed capital to finance their expansion.[7] A limited amount of capital, then, had to be invested wisely, according to the best economic and political criteria. Bismarck knew that the investment of German capital abroad was a source of power, influence, and prestige for Germany. It also enlarged German markets. On the other hand, he was concerned at times lest Germany invest capital abroad that it needed at home or that might give a foreign power (specifically Russia) a strategic or political advantage. In short, the movement of capital into and out of Germany always had a political dimension. Bleichröder lived with these questions and kept Bismarck informed. Bankers wanted their government's blessings for a particular transaction, not for patriotic reasons alone, but because in case of trouble they needed their government's support. Bismarck kept the closest scrutiny on economic issues.

Bleichröder's reports reflected the multifaceted aspects of any given operation. Consider a long letter he wrote in 1880, warning Bismarck that the British were buying huge quantities of Prussian consols, that they were thereby driving up the price so high that German investors, used to higher rates of interest than the British investor, would begin to liquidate their holdings and begin to invest their money abroad. In his quaint way, Bleichröder added: "There is no way of sounding a veto against the present movement; but, according to my unimportant view, there is one means to dam in the rapid rise in consol price"—accelerate the nationalization of railroads, which required the issue of new consols, and thus enlarge the market of these securities. "From the political point of view these English purchases are welcome because they express the confidence that the English public has in German politics and German peacefulness." The message was unambiguous despite some stylistic imprecision; Bismarck's notation at the end of the letter, though unclear, seems to say that Bleichröder's letters should be forwarded to Maybach "for political instruction."[8]* As we know, both Bismarck and Bleichröder had other reasons for speeding up the nationalization of railroads.

Bismarck knew that foreign policy—in its formation and in its effects—was the result of myriad factors. From the very beginning of his career, he had understood the economic aspects of politics, both foreign and domestic, and given his realistic, even Hobbesian, outlook on these relations; he became adept at using weapons that a later age called "economic warfare." Long before the vocabulary had been invented, Bismarck (and Bleichröder) used the substance. For Bismarck, war and peace, hostility and alliances, were not clear opposites, but there was a vast gray area of presumed hostility where Bismarck knew that economic policies were like so many weapons in his hands. The scale of weapons ranged from the imposition of crushing indemnities on beaten foes to the floating of loans to potential friends—and Bleichröder was involved in celebrated instances of both. In between the extremes were tariffs selectively applied—preferably to please interests at home and punish interests abroad—or import prohibitions, or a *Lombardverbot* that prohibited the central bank from accepting some particular foreign security as collateral. At times Bismarck pretended that these commercial policies should be considered as purely economic incidents, with no implications for diplomacy.[9] But basically he knew them to be the fiscal analogues of war and alliance, and he valued their expert application accordingly.

Bismarck always kept an eye on the economic and financial conditions of other countries. In April 1879 he was worried over an Austro-Russian war and told the French ambassador apropos of some credit Russia hoped to obtain in France: "No Russian loans this spring, and peace is assured; money lent to Russia and anything is possible." In 1882 he was alarmed because ". . . France owns more gold than it needs."[10] At other times, he cautioned his ambassadors against thinking that a country's incipient bankruptcy would necessarily make it peaceful. Money was the sinews of war—but empty coffers offered no guarantee of peace. Countries could go to war for profits. Meanwhile diplomats watched stock markets and financiers watched diplomats. The market fluctuated according to its perceptions of political news; by doing so, it became a political datum in itself. As Bismarck once observed, a drop in securities prices, inspired by fear of war, would often enhance that very fear.[11] Bleichröder supplied Bismarck with a running commentary on the economic aspects of politics or the political aspects of the market. As an example, consider his letter in August 1877, during the Russo-Turkish war, when he reported "an interesting stock-market phenomenon, that with Turkish victories prices advanced significantly because speculators remain convinced that Rus-

---

* Three months earlier, at a time when consols were depressed, Bleichröder made a similar plea to the finance minister, urging the internationalization of Prussian loans by facilitating their purchase in London and Amsterdam. For years, Bleichröder advocated this and the Finance Ministry opposed it—partly because it ran counter to Prussian tradition and the self-sufficiency of Great Powers. Heinrich Steubel, *Das Verhältnis zwischen Staat und Banken auf dem Gebiete des preussischen Anleihewesens von 1871 bis 1913* (Berlin, 1935), pp. 34–37.

sian weakness would keep Austria-Hungary out of the conflict and that peace will thereby be brought closer."[12] *

Bleichröder's role in supplying and interpreting economic news was the more important because most ambassadors omitted this kind of grubby intelligence. They concentrated on the dispositions of the leading players and relegated economic matters to the—untitled—stepchildren of the diplomatic service, to the consuls. The distinction between high politics and low economics was institutionalized in the German Foreign Office, which had two unequal sections: the political department and the commercial-legal section, which was so far below the other in prestige and influence that it even tolerated (converted) Jews.[13]†

In Bismarck's world, then, Bleichröder was a welcome supplement to official channels—the more welcome, of course, because he could not possibly be suspected of harboring his own political ambitions or of wanting to become a rival of Bismarck. (Among his other creatures, "any attempt at independence or initiative he [Bismarck] stamps out at once.")[14] Hence Bismarck used him freely and continuously as a special emissary, as an additional and informal link to foreign powers and statesmen. Statesmen always like to have a multiplicity of contacts—to solicit reactions, to convey hints, to reinforce threats or allay fears. Sometimes Bleichröder would be formally charged with such missions; mostly, he was Bismarck's principal *unofficial* spokesman, hence easily disavowable by all interlocutors. The convenience of such an informal supplement is obvious: the formal channels, however delicately used, carried the danger of solidifying reactions or limiting later maneuverability. Conversely, the word of a trusted third party could add further weight to official exchanges. Bleichröder was important precisely because he was "irresponsible." Bleichröder, needless to say, relished the role, and Bismarck knew that his vanity and self-interest kept him an indefatigable aide.

Two examples must suffice here. In October 1887, when German-Russian relations were especially tense, Rantzau reported to Herbert Bismarck that

Papa [had given] Bleichröder a long lecture that Shuvalov [Russian ambassador in Berlin] is deluding himself by thinking that we are afraid

* Of course, he also supplied others with the same kind of news. Lord Ampthill reported in 1882 that "while calling on Bleichröder I saw a telegram come in from the Paris Rothschilds asking for immediate news of the true state of the Emperor's health, who has a slight cold,—and I asked Bleichröder what effect French Financiers expected from the Emperor's death upon the Paris Bourse. 'A general "baisse" of from ten to fifteen percent,' he replied. . . . 'because of the uncertainty of Bismarck's tenure of office under a new reign.' " Paul Knaplund, ed., *Letters from the Berlin Embassy* (Washington, 1944), p. 283.

† In this respect the British diplomatic corps was no better, perhaps even worse, than the German. British consuls with their economic preoccupations were always at the bottom of the pile, and proper diplomats showed magnificent contempt for British commercial interests or visiting businessmen. A young British consul in Brazil recalled that in 1907, addressing his superior, the British minister there, "I ventured a remark that I did not see why in time (mind you) members of the Consular Service might not be as acceptable to God and man as are Officers in the Navy and Army. . . . Delicately putting his monocle in place as though the place was sore, [the minister] stared and ejaculated, 'My dear Campbell, is a Consul ever any*body*?' " Quoted in D. C. M. Platt's pioneering *Finance, Trade, and Politics in British Foreign Policy 1815–1914* (Oxford, 1968), p. xxii. A similar work for Germany is much needed.

of a Russo-French attack and that he can therefore make impertinent demands on us; we want to avoid war because of the financial and economic disadvantages connected with it . . . but we are not afraid of war, we have 3 million trained soldiers, etc. Papa hopes that Bleichröder will repeat all this to Shuvalov.[15]

On an earlier occasion, Holstein wrote Herbert, the most jealous of Bleichröder's foes, that in a given crisis, Britain had suddenly become more conciliatory: "Also Malet [British ambassador in Berlin] has an adviser in Bleichröder whose cunning and knowledge of the Prince's character are undeniable—whatever else one might think of him."[16]

"Knowledge of the Prince's character" was perhaps the most coveted intelligence in Europe's chancelleries. Statesmen were always guessing about Bismarck, because his style of diplomacy relied on deliberate ambiguity— which Bleichröder could help to explicate. In an age of secret diplomacy, Bismarck was exceptionally secretive; he kept his own subordinates in the dark. He also preferred not to write about delicate subjects and once asked William II to burn a letter because it touched on "things and questions I do not usually entrust to paper but discuss orally as long as their *actual* development has not occurred."[17] Bismarck talked with many tongues, always "sincerely," that is, always parceling out partial truths. Often ambiguity was punctuated by flashes of candor—and still his underlings or foreign partners could not divine his aim or policy, often, of course, because he himself had not set on a definite course but was pursuing many lines simultaneously. Ambiguity or a kind of intimidating inscrutability was a constant weapon; at other times, Bismarck could bully, threaten, woo, plead—and Bismarck's style kept foreigners off balance. No wonder Europe often referred to him as the sphinx; people also noted that a pair of black stone sphinxes stood as sentries to the entrance stairs of the Wilhelmstrasse.[18]

Universally known as the confidant and private banker of that sphinx, Bleichröder became a much-sought-after person. At the time of the Congress of Berlin, when Bleichröder gave his sumptuous dinner for the statesmen of Europe, Disraeli wrote to Queen Victoria: "Mr. Bleichröder . . . is Prince Bismarck's intimate, attends him every morning, and according to his own account, is the only individual who dares to speak the truth to His Highness."[19] Disraeli almost certainly embellished on Bleichröder's embellishment, but he caught the essence of how Bleichröder wanted to appear to the world. And, by and large, the world saw him in those very terms—and thus helped to make him what he hungered after. As we will see, Thiers, Disraeli, Leopold II, and a succession of Russian finance ministers sought to use the same special conduit. The Berlin diplomatic corps regularly attended him and invariably cited him as one of their principal sources.*

---

* It is an interesting fact that the massive German publication of prewar diplomatic papers, *Die Grosse Politik der europäischen Kabinette 1871–1914*, has but three—insignificant— references to Bleichröder; the *Documents diplomatiques français* has many more, and the archives of the German and French Foreign Offices make it clear that he was a major figure on the fringes of officialdom.

But Bleichröder acted as special emissary to the German world as well—especially to Bismarck's ambassadors and to the regular retinue at the Foreign Office. Bismarck kept them in the dark, too; many of them he distrusted, and some he still feared as rivals. They were told what they needed to know—no more; they, too, had to guess at Bismarck's particular design at a given time. None of them had the kind of access to Bismarck over a long period that Bleichröder had, and as a consequence they all flocked to him: Hatzfeldt, Münster, Hohenlohe, Radowitz, and Holstein—and they all felt demeaned in doing so. But there was no escaping Bleichröder. A permanent official of the Foreign Office, Arthur von Brauer, recalled that "to converse with the old Bleichröder was always a pleasure. One had to overlook his Jewish manner. But his intelligent and perceptive head knew a great deal, and he combined things with a fine political sense." One of Bismarck's most distinguished ambassadors, first in London and then in Paris, Count Münster, had a most active and candid correspondence with Bleichröder and thanked him profusely for his news—at once more authoritative and more expeditious than the meager reports he received officially.[20]

Holstein was driven frantic by Bleichröder's role and presumed influence; Herbert was enraged by the intimacy between his father and Bleichröder, an intimacy that most specifically covered the very field in which Herbert was being groomed as his father's successor. But Bleichröder had been his father's confidant when Herbert was still a boy in knee pants.

Herbert, then, had his most special reasons for loathing Bleichröder's "filthy meddling," and always assumed that the close link between his father and Bleichröder was due to Bleichröder's seductiveness, to his false servility. Worse, Herbert, Holstein, and the others thought that Bleichröder used his influence in order to make or break Bismarck's creatures. (Holstein noted: "Rottenburg privately hates Bleichröder, but fears him still more, and thinks he will be ruined if ever Bleichröder says a word to the Chancellor against him. Only yesterday he said to me: 'Yes, Bleichröder is a first-rate gravedigger.'") Herbert and Holstein were forever complaining that Bleichröder corrupted venal men, their own friends and relatives (like Rantzau) included. More, they suspected that Bleichröder was using his mysterious hold over Bismarck as well as his unlimited funds in order to build up a web of toadies. In 1887 Herbert, told that Bleichröder was spreading rumors about his wanting to leave Berlin, wrote Rantzau: "That Bleichröder would prefer to have someone here whom he could pay I entirely believe: but for the time being his intriguing won't do him any good."[21] Rantzau concurred and assured Herbert that he would try to do something most malevolent to this "detestable swine of a *Bleichen*. . . . when that beast comes day after tomorrow" to see Bismarck.[22]*

---

* Others saw the venial sins of Bleichröder and were no doubt closer to the mark in describing Bleichröder's manner of recruiting friends. In 1880 one of Bismarck's most trusted aides in the diplomatic service, Radowitz, wrote in his diary: "The much-knowing Bleichröder, who likes to give the impression however that he knows even more about Bismarck's thoughts than is possible, has repeatedly come to see me in order to say that '*Der Chef*' (as he too is accustomed to call him) was satisfied with the support which he received from Stolberg and me during the summer and he does not consider it a matter of doubt and indeed had definitely heard Bismarck say that I should become the successor to State Secretary von Bülow."

There was of course another reason for the affinity between diplomats and Bleichröder: most of them were impoverished nobles and were compelled by their respective countries to live beyond their salaries—and often beyond their means. The great diplomatic posts were still distributed in rough accordance with the *Almanach de Gotha*; wealth no longer was. In 1877 Count Münster threatened to resign when the Reichstag refused to raise his salary by 30,000 marks to 150,000 marks. Even in the early part of this century it has been said authoritatively of the British Foreign Service that "it was natural that diplomacy remained the occupation of gentlemen; few men could have lived on the salaries they were paid."[23] Hence money was a constant, nagging worry for most ambassadors with their heavy representational responsibilities. Many chose to become Bleichröder's clients: one more way to emulate the chancellor. All of them were grateful for his advice. They were especially drawn to someone who knew the state of the market and the state of Europe equally well—and sensed the interaction between the two. Obviously this aspect of their relationship heightened their candor as well: all his clients had a stake in Bleichröder's "all-knowingness."

For Bleichröder these multiple roles were of unsurpassed importance—to his *amour-propre* and to his business. He reaped advantages from his roles, but the record also tells of unprofitable ventures assigned to him, of occasional rebuffs when Bismarck's government would not budge from its position despite his pleas. In short, despite his ties to government, he had his full measure of professional disappointments: of being shut out of international consortia, of having his interests swamped by those of a rival power. The occasional failures, the intermittent contretemps with Bismarck or the Rothschilds, served to keep him on his toes. He had become the wealthiest banker in Berlin, with the most distinguished connections—and he struggled to preserve and enlarge his role.

Before turning to some of Bleichröder's specific assignments in foreign affairs, it may be useful to sketch the political context of his operations and to offer a general summary of what Bleichröder's contacts and correspondence reveal, not so much about the facts of diplomatic history but about the "unspoken assumptions" of the time. How did Bleichröder's contemporaries perceive the world around them?

Here the barest reminder of the structure of politics must suffice.[24] The balance of power in Europe shifted with the unification of Germany, and Berlin became the dominant capital of the Continent. There were still five Great Powers (Russia, Austria-Hungary, Germany, France, and Britain), with

---

Radowitz added, throwing a characteristic light on both of them: "The degree of certainty with which *Der Bleiche* expects this I could also gauge from the fact that for the New Year he sent me one of his expensive fresh sterlets which it is his wont at this time of year to import in carloads from Russia to distribute to the political personalities he most highly esteems. In any case I enjoyed the taste of this tender homage." And so did countless others. Hajo Holborn, ed., *Aufzeichnungen und Erinnerungen aus dem Leben des Botschafters Joseph Maria von Radowitz*, II, *1878–1890* (Berlin and Leipzig, 1925), p. 114.

Italy ever struggling and rarely making it.* Of the Great Powers, France had a permanent grievance against Germany, and Bismarck's worst nightmare was that France would someday become the heart of a new coalition against Germany. Bismarck's diplomacy reassured Europe that Germany was a satiated, hence peaceful, nation (there were too many troublesome foreigners within her borders at is was), and at the same time he sought to wage a continuous battle for the expansion of German influence. As the most powerful country in Europe, Germany was watched with distrust, and Bismarck wanted Germany feared, not loved, because fear was the best deterrent. No one took his benevolence or peaceful intentions for granted; and there was always enough saber rattling amid the protestations of peace to remind Europe of Bismarck's bellicose past and Germany's powerful present.

Bismarck was concerned with the substance, not the form, of power. Visible supremacy or continued expansion would have prompted other nations to bury their rivalries in common fear of Germany. He alternatively exploited and moderated the rivalries of others; it was one way to make other powers dependent on German diplomacy.

Of the Great Powers, France was considered the most volatile because of its instability at home and its grievances abroad. Britain was thought of as an imperial power whose major interest lay in the Near East and India and whose internal stability could be assumed except when Bismarck's special enemy, the relentlessly moral Gladstone, threatened to foist radical principles on the British polity. Austria and Russia had shaky domestic systems and conflicting foreign interests. There was growing appreciation of Russia's huge economic potential that would need a great deal of foreign capital for its realization. Bleichröder wanted Germany to supply that capital.

During the two decades of Bismarckian diplomacy, the particular crisis areas and the alignments often shifted. Until 1875 the dangers of a renewed Franco-German war dominated European diplomacy. After 1875 the Eastern Question emerged as the principal threat to peace. The decaying Turkish Empire could no longer contain the nationalist aspirations of its Balkan subjects; the Empire was doomed to dissolution, and Russia, Austria, and England sought the major spoils of successorship or hoped at least to deny them to others.

In the first phase, Bismarck reached back to the Three Emperors' League —more as an ideological reaffirmation of conservative solidarity than as a tangible commitment to joint action.† In the second phase, he sought to play "the honest broker"—a role that was symbolized by his presidency of the Con-

---

* Other nations sought the trappings of greatness, without possessing the substance. They were rebuffed, sometimes brutally, as when Bismarck complained about the Spaniards' *Ambassadomanie* and told them: "Appoint an ambassador, that is of no concern to me, but don't ask me to send you one; I will not do it now or later." St. Vallier to Waddington, 24 April 1878, MAE: Allemagne, Vol. 23.

† As Bleichröder correctly informed the Paris Rothschilds on the last day of the Three Emperors' Meeting: "One merely came to an accord concerning one's peaceful intentions, and I don't believe I am wrong—though I would ask for your discretion—that the three potentates merely gave their respective promise to work together on all major political questions." Bleichröder to Rothschild, 12 Sept. 1879, RA.

gress of Berlin in 1878. Bleichröder, an old canard has it, warned Bismarck that there was no such thing as an honest broker, and Bismarck discovered that Russia, dissatisfied by his mediation, turned anti-German. A combination of Russian expansionism and French revanchism was a mortal threat to Germany.

In 1879 Bismarck broke with his own preference for a fluid situation in European politics and concluded a firm defensive alliance with Austria-Hungary. William violently objected to any estrangement from Russia, and Bleichröder warned Bismarck that "to ally ourselves with Austria-Hungary is to attach ourselves to a cadaver."[25] Gradually, Bismarck added other countries to his new web of alliances and hoped to build up an entente with France. His principal hope was still to contain Austro-Russian rivalry in the Balkans. As new conflicts arose in the East, Bismarck was forced to take sides, while England took Cyprus and Egypt. In the early 1880s, still on a conciliatory course toward France, he followed an intermittently hostile one toward Britain over colonial issues. By the mid-1880s, an alliance between Russia and France became a more likely prospect, precisely because Germany had drifted into a position as Austria's protector. At the end, his diplomacy became more and more enmeshed with his political difficulties at home, and the aging chancellor, burdened by the sudden accession of the impetuous young William II, grasped at various improvisations, none of which seemed consonant with the political forces at home and abroad. Even Bleichröder opposed Bismarck's anti-Russian policy out of principle and out of self-interest—and sighed for the days when the master seemed truly sovereign.

The historian's hindsight rarely does justice to the uncertain foresight of past generations. Bleichröder was one of those men whose success depended on the correct assessment of the future; his friends and clients wrote to him with extraordinary candor, and from his correspondence—from the thousands of letters hitherto unused—we can reconstruct something of the milieu, of the political outlook, of the style of judgment of his world. These letters throw a new light on the premises and values of that generation.

The fact that some of Europe's leading diplomats and statesmen wrote Bleichröder so regularly and so candidly suggests already one element of their perspective: despite—and in some ways, because of—the secrecy at the top, the world was still thought to be securely knowable. Politics was thought to be made by relatively few men—hence news about these few men, about their prospects, their health, their plans, became precious. Even alliances were thought to be uncertain because, as Bismarck once put it to Lord Odo Russell, they "sometimes depended on the lives of single individuals."[26] Certainly the correspondence shows the role that the personal animosities of statesmen played. Bismarck, the much-vaunted *Realpolitiker*, allowed his piques and hatreds to transcend national boundaries; his dislike of Gorchacov or Gladstone almost dictated his policies.

Contemporaries knew that international politics was unpredictable, and the correspondence from those peaceful years between the Franco-Prussian war and the emergence of rival blocs in the 1890s describes the volatility and tension of the time. To these observers, the peace of Europe was never assured for very long. The shadow of war hung over western, then over eastern, Europe, and as soon as a crisis loomed there was fear that it would lead to war. Bleichröder's correspondents would have been astounded by this later characterization of their world: "Men were too busy growing rich to have time for war. . . . They came to believe that peace and security were 'normal,' and anything else an accident and an aberration."[27] On the contrary, these men thought they were condemned to pursue their wealth in the shadow of war. Contemporaries lived with the constant threat of war breaking out somewhere, but the prospect—partly because of the nature of warfare, partly because of its perpetual presence—held less terror than it did at later times.

In that world of security amidst great foreign tension, the hunt for clues never ceased. Given the general acceptance of everybody's *inclination* to threaten everyone else—the basic rule of what has come to be called international anarchy, where every option seemed morally and politically open though in fact it probably was not—every move deserved close scrutiny. One could never relax. As the French foreign minister wrote to Bleichröder in 1883: "I agree with you that nothing threatens the peace of Europe at the moment; but the unforeseen always plays a very big role in human affairs; it is wise not to trust the present absolutely." A year later, Count Münster complained that even when the horizon seems clear, a sudden storm could bring mortal danger.[28] And Bismarck delighted in warning Bleichröder and others that wars sometimes occur when least expected; he was fond of citing 1870 as an illustration—somewhat disingenuously perhaps.

This extreme jumpiness sometimes froze into particular nightmares, as when a succession of responsible Englishmen kept dreading Russia's march to India or when leading statesmen, including Disraeli and St. Vallier, worried about a German annexation of Holland.[29] One could ignore these sudden escalations and fixations of fear—as most historians have—if they did not offer some clues to how diplomats formed their responses and made their decisions. These recurrent fears help to define a climate where sunshine was always thought to be a temporary aberration and where for any actual storm a score of storms had been erroneously predicted. To change the metaphor: one assumed that international politics was determined by men, not by blind forces, and the prevalence of these phantasmagorias seemed to confirm that assumption. One paid very little attention to what historians call the underlying conditions, and this fascination with the surface of things—which people probably always have—was one of the conditions for the state of habitual and perhaps agreeable tension.

What is extraordinary, then, about this candid correspondence of professionals concerned equally with their country's welfare and their own is the atmosphere of fear and the collective neglect of the deeper or "underlying" causes of war. The correspondence reflected the fragility of the international order and the widespread apprehension that states will defend their prestige, their standing, with the same determination as some more tangible interest and that they were always likely to calculate that a defeat or a diplomatic setback could have a domino effect. Bismarck eloquently warned against pursuing prestige politics, against paying a heavy price for the appearance of success. Great powers, he thought, could dispense with such posturings, but they rarely did, and Bismarck, despite his own dicta, knew that prestige was an element of power and as such had to be especially protected. Count Münster once wrote to Bleichröder: "In these times everyone wants to be tough [*schneidig*]. Toughness, a word I hate, is simply a confusion between brutality and energy."[30]

Bankers and diplomats talked about war and feared it—and always hoped for peace. Did they exaggerate the dangers that beset them? The Bleichröder correspondence seems to suggest this. It is too full of wars that never took place. But Europe had always lived with war, and no one guaranteed to this particular generation immunity from the common scourge. The all-pervading fear may also have been functional: it may have generated countervailing forces against the threatened war.

The fear may have been functional in yet another way: it reassured the diplomats of their usefulness; the illusion of danger may have been a professional equivalent of the search for adventure. Another reason suggests itself as well: in a hypernationalist age, the fear of war could be used against domestic agitation. Bleichröder's correspondents belonged to the privileged elite; some explicitly, all implicitly, were afraid of the internal foe, of nihilists, anarchists, and socialists. Bismarck was a master at conjuring up foreign dangers—and yet in this circle of professionals, there was no sympathy for the nationalist agitators who exaggerated foreign dangers in order to stifle radicalism at home. Of their common detestation for democracy, let alone socialism, there can be no doubt. But they seem to have thought that peace was a better prospect for prosperity and for containing the revolution than was war or chauvinism.

Moreover, there is little in these letters to suggest an awareness, let alone a conniving, at what has been called the social-imperial impulse. The world of Bleichröder's German contemporaries was Europe-centered, and the new colonialism and the division of Africa and Asia appeared marginal. If, as has recently been contended, imperialism was central to the German elites even before 1890, then the chief actors of the time were hardly conscious of it— because in their intimate correspondence with their banker they would certainly have unburdened themselves. To be sure, Bleichröder became involved in Samoa and the Congo and he participated in the supervision of Ottoman and Egyptian finances; in the late 1880s he became interested in the economic future of a developing country like Mexico. But to think that Bleichröder's contemporaries in the 1870s and 1880s were particularly concerned with the lure of empire is a mistake—or else they concealed it from one another. On the contrary, the actual imperial race in Africa, in the South Seas, and in Indochina was but marginally discussed in their letters. They were Europe-centered—to a fault, perhaps.

France was the country that engaged Bismarck's and Bleichröder's interests most strongly and most consistently. Born in the year of Waterloo, Bismarck remembered the havoc that French arms and French revolutionary ideas had once wrought; neither the defeat of 1870 nor the Commune nor republican instability dispelled Bismarck's sense of the power and the threat of *la grande nation*. He knew France well, had spent some of the happiest moments of his life there, and was fond of conversing in French, which he had mastered with the same suppleness that characterized his German. For Bleichröder, France was the home of the Paris Rothschilds, who had given his father's firm its first distinction. For him the connection with Paris was his single most important tie abroad. He, too, knew France well and had a special intimacy with French diplomats and statesmen.

For Bismarck, France, defeated, divided, and resentful, was a far more troublesome neighbor than Imperial France had ever been. All certainty had disappeared: Would Thiers and his conservative-republican interregnum last, would a monarchical restoration replace him, or would France drift into unpredictable chaos, Jacobinism, and a new military dictatorship? Which regime would be most capable of unifying the nation and finding allies in Europe in order to translate the desire for revenge—which Bismarck took for a given fact—into practical reality?

For years, Bismarck's attention was riveted on France, the more so as his principal subordinates (the military commander, General Manteuffel, and the German ambassador, Count Arnim) proposed and pursued policies in opposition to his own. Bismarck regarded Thiers as the best that Germany could hope for, because Thiers would be strong enough to pay off the indemnity in the time specified and yet not strong enough to mount a revanchist policy. It was this presumptive danger of revenge that led Bismarck to contemplate or at least to threaten a preemptive strike of his own. He worried about France until 1877, when his hope for a moderate republic was realized and when new dangers in the East began to distract him. For some years thereafter, he sought an entente with France, only to return to renewed bellicosity in the last three years of his rule.

Bleichröder was also deeply drawn into French affairs. His relations with the Rothschilds had suffered because of his close tie to Bismarck. They still appreciated the value of the link, but they were annoyed at their agent's conversion to Prussianism and his subservience to a tyrant who was feared and detested in France.

For Bleichröder, the indemnity was the touchstone of his financial and political success. In February 1871 he had been at Bismarck's side in Versailles, and he hoped to use that honor as a steppingstone to the next, profitable task: the collection of that vast sum. Europe had never seen so complicated a financial transaction; the political ramifications made it still more complicated. Put simply, the sooner France paid the indemnity the sooner German troops would end their occupation of French territory. The intricacies of this unprecedented affair and the intrigues that attended it are authoritatively depicted in David Landes's essay on the indemnity.[31]

As Landes points out, the payment of the indemnity really comprised two questions: How could the French raise the money and how could they "deliver it to Germany without upsetting the international balance of payments . . ."? The Germans prescribed what kind of money and paper they would accept (bullion and the drafts on major bankers) and what not. The first billion was due a month after the Thiers government had crushed the Commune and returned to Paris. The French government had to decide how to raise the money (it opted for successive loans as against a capital levy or taxes), how to transfer the sum, and how to do it all in one short month. It had to depend on the old private banking houses of Europe, and the latter competed among themselves, jockeyed for position, in the most extraordinary scramble of intrigue and rivalry, all in an atmosphere of catch-as-catch-can and against a relentless deadline. Bleichröder hoped that his ties to Bismarck and to the Paris Rothschilds would give him a decisive edge; but others, including his longtime associate Adolph von Hansemann of the Disconto-Gesellschaft, tried to beat him out. The frantic competition of bankers was paralleled by negotiations between the two governments, and these were complicated by the fact that the Germans spoke with many voices, as Manteuffel and Arnim carried on their own negotiations. Despite Bleichröder's entreaties, the Paris Rothschilds distributed that first loan all over Europe in such a way that Bleichröder received only a very small portion. He had the satisfaction that most of the bankers' drafts on Berlin banks, handed by the French to the German occupation authorities, were made out to Bleichröder—a reminder of his standing and a source of small profit, as measured by earlier expectations.[32]

In the midst of that first round over the indemnity, Bleichröder's eye trouble became much worse and he had to yield temporary command to his cousin and partner, Julius Schwabach, who was tougher and more outspoken than Bleichröder himself. Schwabach, however, made no move without consulting Bleichröder, and fortunately his letters from the summer of 1871 survived intact.

As if the intrigues and rivalries of bankers were not sufficiently exasperating for Bleichröder—whose ailment Schwabach soothingly diagnosed as purely "nervous"—he was drawn into the jealousies within German officialdom. Bismarck never trusted his subordinates, and his suspicions were still greater when military men played politics. The commander of the German occupation troops in France was Edwin von Manteuffel, who had already opposed Bismarck's policies in the 1860s. Accredited to Manteuffel as French plenipotentiary was the Comte de St. Vallier, and their contacts, while both men were at Nancy in the spring and summer of 1871, bespeak a degree of mutual respect and personal warmth that must have been rare between victor and vanquished even in the nineteenth century, and that is quite unheard of in ours. They were both aristocrats, both fiercely old-fashioned, and both were probably concerned lest German harshness should feed the revolutionary strength of the *"canaille,"* so recently put down in the Commune.[33] Manteuffel pleaded for a conciliatory course vis-à-vis the French—and did so directly to William as well as to Bismarck—and in July 1871, after the first French installments had been paid, he urged the immediate evacuation of three of the occupied *départements.*

While thus meddling in Bismarck's domain, Manteuffel did another risky —and given his prejudices, surprising—thing: he cabled Bleichröder to come and visit him in Compiègne regarding "a most important financial matter." Still ailing in a spa, Bleichröder sent his trusted assistant Lehmann. Bleichröder surmised that Manteuffel wanted expert advice on the modalities of French payment. Instead he asked Bleichröder secretly to invest a fund of 10 million taler which he had saved from French payments for occupation costs. The secrecy was justified: occupation costs were meant to indemnify Germany for actual expenses incurred; they had not been intended as another part of the heavy indemnity. But Bismarck understood the insidious character of an occupation, and as early as December 1870, he had "compared the army of occupation to Caterpillars on a Tree eating their way all over it."[34]

Manteuffel's request surprised Lehmann, Schwabach, and Bleichröder. The tripartite correspondence from those days has survived, much of it in code, so that Bismarck was *Der Reiche* and—in Schwabach's probably improvised code—Manteuffel was *"der goi,"* a term at once contemptuous and unspecific. Bleichröder informed Bismarck of the summons. Too late did he discover that Manteuffel sought to keep Bismarck in the dark about this transaction, which aimed precisely at avoiding the intermediary of "a ministerial account," as General Stosch put it to Bleichröder twenty years later— when he sought to extract a charitable contribution from him.[35] Bleichröder's old friend Keudell, still very closely attached to Bismarck's staff, also claimed credit for having arranged Manteuffel's summons. "I am pleased that this business could be put in your hands, especially on account of the intrigues that took place earlier, because I am certain that the Royal Government cannot expect more valuable and more disinterested services than from your House."[36] Despite Keudell's letter, Bleichröder remained worried lest he had committed a terrible indiscretion by letting Bismarck know of Manteuffel's intention to stash away a tidy military nest egg. He begged Bismarck "not to tell General Manteuffel that I took the liberty of informing you of these developments." Bismarck did not reply, and Bleichröder's anxiety grew. Ten days after his first letter, Bleichröder again wrote Bismarck, "worried about the fate of my humble news," and reporting on a new offer from the Paris Rothschilds concerning France's next payment. After a few days Bleichröder received a laconic reply, acknowledging his letters but giving no assurance of keeping Bleichröder's information confidential; Bismarck also dismissed the Rothschild offer of making payments with French *rente* by noting curtly that similar suggestions had been refused before: "We have no reasons for granting favors [*Zu Gefälligkeiten haben wir keine Ursache*]."[37]

Bleichröder found the whole episode embarrassing, and Schwabach had to reassure him that Bismarck harbored him no ill will and in fact hoped to see him in Varzin as soon as possible. Still, the incident was an early example of the atmosphere of secrecy and uncertainty in which all of Bismarck's subordinates had to operate. In the event, Bleichröder suffered nothing more than some anxious moments, and Manteuffel's savings presumably ended up in some general war chest. The records fail to mention them again.

To return to the indemnity: the French had paid their first installment

on time—and with extraordinary ease: a tribute at once to the perceived solidity of France's credit and to the efficient working of an international banking
consortium. Bismarck had been impressed by this brilliant success—and a
little worried by it. But the indemnity question dragged on—amidst endless
negotiations on official and unofficial levels—for another two years. (The
next great indemnity question, German reparations after World War I, would
have dragged on for sixty years if German default had not put an end to
it after twelve years.) For bankers, millions were at stake, at every stage of
the affair: at the selling of the *rente*, the deposit of monies collected, the transfer of funds, commissions on the way. For the two countries, the normalization
of relations was at stake, and for the French the end of the German Caterpillars.

Right after France's initial payment, in August 1871, the differences be-
tween Manteuffel and Bismarck hardened, as the former negotiated with the
French finance minister and submitted recommendations directly to William.
Bismarck was furious, and Manteuffel unburdened himself to St. Vallier that
Bismarck's anger sprang from his fear that Manteuffel might replace him
and from his reluctance to end the period of tension because of some stock-
exchange maneuvers that he was involved in via his "usual associates, Count
Henckel von Donnersmarck, the Banker Bleichröder etc."[38] Bismarck, of
course, denounced Arnim for similar maneuvers, and it is odd how often rival
German leaders thought that some form of nefarious speculation was at the
bottom of a policy they opposed. If nothing else, these suspicions suggest that
market profiteering was never far from people's minds, but that one was still
ashamed of such preoccupations and most readily projected them onto one's
opponents: Bismarck had no material stake in his French policy.

A day after Manteuffel's confidence to St. Vallier, Bismarck berated the
French chargé in Berlin, M. de Gabriac, at their very first interview. Expressing his anger at French dealings with Manteuffel, Bismarck accused the French
—in August 1871!—of plotting revenge, of being willing to pay 2 billion,
"but when 1874 comes around and the 3 billion fall due, you will make war
on us." Bismarck was his bullying, candid self, and Gabriac noted that it was
Bismarck's style aggressively to put his adversary in the wrong so that he
would be justified in his own hostile designs.[39] It was a time when the French
representatives in Berlin feared that even if France paid 4,999,999,999 francs,
not a single German soldier would leave France until the last franc had been
paid. Did the Germans want their ducats or their pound of flesh—or, as some
French feared, did they want both?[40]

In one of these moments of crisis, in late August 1871, Bismarck used
Bleichröder as his "secret agent" in order to intimidate the French opponents
of Thiers. Keudell, who was with Bismarck and William in Bad Gastein, wrote
Bleichröder about "disquieting" news from France, about revanchist, anti-
Thiers agitation.

> I ask you to leave your friends in Paris in no doubt that we consider the
> situation very serious; that a new government which would inspire less

confidence in us than the present would lead to an immediate increase of the occupation troops, that if it appeared from there as if hostilities were intended we would think it advisable to forestall such a move by an attack from our side, that for us the idea of the resumption of the war—in case the other side does not want to move in peaceful paths—is a common one and that everything is in readiness.

Perhaps through "hints to influential people" in Paris, Bleichröder could prevent unfavorable decisions there: "Perhaps we see things too darkly from here."[41] Keudell made sure that these dark tidings reached Bleichröder and Schwabach so that both men could put pressure on the Paris Rothschilds—who resented it. As always, Bleichröder was the more insistent on carrying out Bismarck's commissions, Schwabach the more reticent, but Bismarck-inspired *démarches* were hardly calculated to heal the rather strained relations between the Paris Rothschilds and Bleichröder. For a while the Rothschilds neither answered nor placed their routine orders with the Berlin House. For once even Schwabach confessed to "fear" that the Rothschilds had taken these letters amiss. It was their business he wanted: "Otherwise, as you know, I have no interest in such matters."[42] Unlike Bleichröder, Schwabach did not covet a political role, which, as this example shows, could hurt business as well as help it.

From 1871 to 1873 Bleichröder played multiple and often conflicting roles. He was Bismarck's adviser on all technical matters pertaining to the indemnity question. At Bismarck's behest, he conducted intermittent, unofficial negotiations with the French. He also sought to keep his special tie with the Rothschilds and to realize his chief goal, to be the German head of any international consortium that would be charged with the final payment of the indemnity. With Bismarck, he often pleaded for a conciliatory course—in the interest of peace, of financial sanity, and in Bleichröder's own interest. To the French in general and the Rothschilds in particular, he often preached the virtues of being more forthcoming because "it cannot be doubted that the flowering of France will begin only when the last German troops have left French soil. . . . The sting of hatred will become tolerable only when the government can cease its payments." Or, as he put it more optimistically: "a major entente of the two nations" could come only after the end of the indemnity question and the withdrawal of German troops.[43] Thiers also thought that "the presence of German troops on our soil has the effect of a foreign substance in a wound."[44]

Bleichröder's role depended on his simultaneous ties to Bismarck and the Rothschilds; still, he paid for this role by experiencing the frustrations of any intermediary. At times, both sides became irritated with him. The Rothschilds accepted Bleichröder's information—while often concealing news from him—shared his anger at the machinations of rivals and interlopers, and pursued their own course. Everybody was out for himself, and the enormity of the stakes and the uncertainty of how the great transaction was to be executed heightened everybody's appetite and suspicion.

In October 1871 the French finance minister, Auguste Pouyer-Quertier, came to Berlin and Bismarck referred him to Bleichröder. The two men discussed the modalities of the next transfer, and the negotiations thus begun were continued in Paris by one of Bleichröder's trusted subordinates, Imelmann. The French were worried over finding acceptable instruments of payment, and Pouyer-Quertier suggested a settlement whereby the House of Bleichröder would receive some 200 million francs in bankers' drafts, provided the German government would accept such drafts as valid payment.[45] Bleichröder sought to interest Bismarck in these plans, but Bismarck tired of his *démarches* and wrote him in January 1872 that his proposals were imprecise and that, moreover, "I can begin to consider the propositions . . . only if the French government takes an official initiative in connection with our negotiations."[46]

This is precisely what Bleichröder urged the Paris Rothschilds to push for and what he hoped the new French ambassador in Berlin would argue for as well. For that post Thiers had selected the Vicomte de Gontaut-Biron— as blue-blooded a conservative nobleman as the new republic could find, if one with little diplomatic experience or sure-footedness in things German. Bismarck complained of his inexperience, but William replied that for him Gontaut-Biron's being "a gentleman of old and noble origin" was far more important. Bleichröder at once asked the Rothschilds to send Gontaut-Biron to him "because I may be of assistance to him as perhaps no one else in Berlin."[47] The two men came to work closely together, and Gontaut-Biron recognized in Bleichröder Bismarck's confidential spokesman; he cultivated the link, the more so as by early 1872 Bismarck saw as few people as possible and, as Gontaut-Biron reported to Thiers, preferred to use intermediaries. It also gradually dawned on the French that Bismarck trusted few of his official subordinates, that he and Arnim had come to hate each other—and that this hatred exaggerated their substantive differences as well. In one of his very first dispatches to Thiers, Gontaut-Biron wrote of "Bleischröder," as he figured throughout their correspondence, as a "very rich banker and very close in his intimacy with Bismarck, whose business he attends to." He also raised the question that was to puzzle foreign representatives for the next two decades: how far to trust Bleichröder. He answered his own question: one's confidence in Bleichröder should be "moderate, but his *démarches* and his communications are certainly known to and authorized by Bismarck and on that account deserve a very special attention." Thiers urged him to listen to Bleichröder, "who is held to have the confidence of Prussia as no one else and from whom one could obtain useful clues that could enlighten us."[48] Repeatedly Thiers went much further and urged Gontaut-Biron to make specific proposals to Bleichröder and to use him in fact as the main interlocutor on all financial matters.

At the end of March 1872, having just seen Bismarck, Bleichröder reiterated his hope for a new French initiative on the method of payment, adding that in return French prisoners in German hands would be quickly released.[49] In April, after the first French initiatives had been taken, Bleichröder, having just seen "my friend," warned Gontaut-Biron and the Rothschilds that Berlin "is not entirely in agreement with Mr. T.'s stance," that is, with his military preparations and his overtures to St. Petersburg. "I think it would be admirable if you . . . would use your well-known influence with T. in order to have him abandon the newly chosen system and in this way to be more accommodating to the ideas of the government here. I ask you . . . to destroy these lines immediately upon perusal"—an injunction the Rothschilds did not heed, even though they scarcely relished any part of the letter.[50]

While Bleichröder was the willing mouthpiece of Bismarck's displeasure, Count Arnim, backed by a German consortium, conducted his own negotiations with the French, and both Bleichröder and the Rothschilds faced the prospect of being left out in the cold. For Bleichröder this was totally unexpected: on May 18 he assured Paris that no decisions would be taken until fall, and on May 19, in obvious desperation, he appealed to Bismarck, who had just begun his rest in Varzin, and informed him that Arnim was negotiating with the French, with Henckel von Donnersmarck at his side and with an anti-Bleichröder clique of bankers in the wings. (Henckel had William's support—a fact calculated to make Bismarck anti-Henckel since at that point king and chancellor were on bad terms.) Henckel, Bleichröder reported, headed a consortium

> to which I do *not* belong! The count now enjoys such powerful support that my position in the great finance operation at whose beginnings Your Highness so graciously called on me is now seriously threatened; I bring this to Your Highness's attention in order to forestall a later justified reproach by Your Highness: "If you had told me this earlier I would have let Count Henckel know that he should work with you in this financial question!"[51]

Bismarck's answer has not been preserved; it was probably inconclusive. Bismarck sought to oblige, when convenient, but these were tangled circumstances where he might have hesitated to push too hard for his private banker. His amanuensis, Lothar Bucher, kept Bleichröder briefed, and when Bleichröder continued to importune Bismarck, Bucher finally rebuked him by saying that none but Bleichröder dared intrude on the chancellor's rest.[52]

At the end of June 1872 France and Germany signed a new convention coordinating French reparation payments and German evacuation plans. In early July Bleichröder complained to Bismarck that Hansemann had been in Paris for ten days and, thanks to Arnim, had been recognized as German agent for the new loan. Consequently, Bleichröder planned to ignore the whole matter but added that "Thiers is troubled because of the last billion and ensuing occupation until 1875 and because of the [occupation] costs. He is afraid of strong opposition in the Chamber—whether true or sham. . . ." Bleichröder added that he had no intention of investing Bismarck's capital in French *rentes*—the very possibility of course suggested that, Bismarck's occasional ranting about the "hereditary enemy" notwithstanding, he still held his earlier view of France's soundness and that he expected to base his investments on nonideological considerations.[53]

Bleichröder's huff did not last long; within a week, with Bismarck's blessings he traveled to Paris, saw Thiers repeatedly, but still complained that the Arnim clique had grabbed everything for itself: "in financial terms, the journey is hardly worthwhile." In his disappointment, Bleichröder could at least strengthen Bismarck's suspicion of Arnim. Bleichröder reported that Thiers feared for his political survival because the French regarded the new convention as even worse than the peace treaty. He warned Bismarck that "after Thiers, painful conditions would prevail . . . it seemed right to sustain the man." This, too, was sound and anti-Arnim advice.* He added that the physiognomy of Versailles was "far more boring" than in 1871; he missed the heady atmosphere of those days.[54]

His visit was far from futile. He seems to have neutralized Arnim's clique and negotiated agreements with the Rothschilds whereby his House would be the leading German representative for a part of the French loan. Relations with the Rothschilds, however, remained strained and costly. In their everyday business, the Rothschilds, for example, demanded the usual interest rate on large short-term deposits—and Bleichröder found it difficult to earn such interest at a time when money was plentiful in Berlin. The Rothschilds apparently threatened to withdraw their business altogether, and Bleichröder responded quickly, deferentially, that he would do whatever he could and would shoulder all sorts of sacrifices in order to keep his tie with his esteemed friends in Paris. The loss of that tie would have discomfited Bleichröder, and the Rothschilds—like Bismarck—liked to remind their clients of their vassalage. In any case, in the final round of the indemnity, Bleichröder played a central and profitable role.

The élan of the French recovery took everyone by surprise, Bleichröder included. After a disastrous defeat and civil war, after a hard peace treaty and despite heavy occupation costs, France rebuilt her army and her economy at an amazing pace. In October 1872 Bleichröder assured Bismarck that France would not be able to pay the total bill by the end of 1873 as Thiers had predicted.[55] In the winter of 1872–1873 Bleichröder was still used to convey Bismarck's occasional bellicosity, and he scared—and then again unscared—Gontaut-Biron by his revelations that Bismarck might yield to military entreaties and not evacuate Belfort on the date originally stipulated.[56] But such was the success of the second French loan and the international consortium to convert French francs into bullion and securities acceptable to Germany that by September 1873 the last sou was paid and the last German

---

* Thiers, in turn, kept urging Gontaut-Biron to stay on close terms with Bleichröder, "who is friendly, who wants to be friendly, and who is the chancellor's man. These last days, it has pleased him to send Mme. Thiers, at whose house he had often dined, some table delicacies that are much esteemed in Germany which have a rather wild taste, a little beyond the capacity of civilized stomachs. Mme. Thiers has thanked him, and I would beg you to handle the enclosed letter, not knowing the exact address of this great financial personage." *Occupation et Libération du Territoire, 1871–1875* (Paris, 1903), II, 179–180. Needless to say, the frequent thank-you notes by Mme. Thiers were couched in different terms. BA.

troops had been withdrawn from French soil—eighteen months ahead of schedule. Thiers had deserved well of the nation. In May 1873, with the successful outcome of his policy assured, the monarchists unseated him. A monarchical restoration, which Bismarck had always opposed, seemed imminent. France remained a great worry.

Bismarck also suspected France's new rulers of conspiring with his Catholic enemies at home. The French, in turn, were never certain that Bismarck might not seek a preventive war, as some of his military leaders desired. In April 1875 a crisis erupted when Bismarck forbade the export of horses to France, German newspapers spoke of "war in sight," and the French appealed to the rest of Europe with expressions of genuine and feigned apprehension; Bismarck backed off, and the threat of war faded away. His motives remained unclear. He may have wanted to clear the air for an entente with France.* In early June, Herbert once again reassured Bleichröder that at present his father saw "no danger whatever to peace."[57] By the end of the year Bleichröder's old friend Goldschmidt from Vienna wrote: "Who would want a world conflagration unless he were out of his mind? . . . [still] there are fools who believe that Bismarck would start a new war with France in order to get French billions."[58] For years the French remained worried about German intentions; Bismarck must have been satisfied when in May 1877 he heard via one of Bleichröder's trusted agents in Paris that despite France's prodigious economic recovery, "the fear of Germany exceeds all imagination! If the German army were to march down the Vosges in the direction of Paris, this would seem the most natural thing in the world."[59]

Bismarck had kept such unfounded fears alive, but with the advent in 1877 of a moderate bourgeois republic in France, his own fears dissipated and in the new European constellation, dominated by the Eastern Question and the quickening pace of imperialism, he sought an entente with France. Bismarck hoped that France could be deflected from her own grievance by "compensations" in the colonial field, by his support of French policy in Rumania and the Near East, by German recognition of her "preeminence" among Latin peoples, based on her superior civilization and her "greater admixture of Germanic blood."[60] It was a time when he went so far as to express his regret to the French ambassador at the annexation of Alsace-Lorraine, which had been forced on him by the military. Bismarck's capacity for blaming others was matched by his flexible, ever self-flattering memory. Bismarck wanted a real understanding with France, for which he was prepared to sacrifice the minor interests of other powers. To the French ambassador he said: "I want you to forgive Sedan as you have forgiven Waterloo."[61] But how could the French forgive what the Germans could not forget?

For this new phase, a change of ambassadors was most desirable, and for Bleichröder a major boon. The republican government recalled Gontaut-

---

* That is the interpretation of A. J. P. Taylor, who added, "like other Germans, Bismarck regarded bullying as the best preliminary to friendship." *The Struggle for Mastery in Europe, 1848–1918* (Oxford, 1954), p. 225.

Biron, whom Bismarck had come to detest because of his alleged responsibility for the war-in-sight crisis and because of his intimacy with Empress Augusta. In his place, the Comte de St. Vallier was sent—a man of equally impeccable blood and conservative views, but far better versed in German affairs. We already noted the success with which he established close connections with Manteuffel, the commander of the German occupation troops. In his mid-forties, a handsome bachelor, fluent in German, a patriot who saw no future in revanche, St. Vallier was an admirable choice. His relations with Bleichröder were probably the closest and the most genuine that Bleichröder had with any diplomat or statesman. The two men saw each other regularly, collaborated continuously, and St. Vallier, being a man of the old school, found it easy to return Bleichröder's solicitude and sentiment. St. Vallier's letters to Bleichröder bespeak a genuine friendship, a genuine care for Bleichröder's health and well-being that few, if any, other men displayed.

A few weeks after St. Vallier's arrival in Berlin, Bleichröder arranged for him to have a long and unusual visit with Bismarck in Friedrichsruh.[62] It was the beginning of a close relationship between Bismarck and St. Vallier. Europe's trouble spot was in the East; after the Congress of Berlin, Bismarck had to keep a wary eye on Russian resentments; in April 1879 St. Vallier saw Bleichröder several times a week in order to find out German policy at a time of rising Austro-Russian tension.[63] After 1880 Bismarck's particular *bête noire,* Gladstone, returned to power. It was a propitious time for improving Franco-German relations, especially if France could be sidetracked into colonial ventures, as in Tunis, or brought into conflict with England over Egypt. St. Vallier understood Bismarck's aims and happened to be in Berlin during the dramatic "second founding" of the Empire. He recognized that the German domestic scene was just as fluid as the international scene—and just as important. He wrote perspicacious reports to the Quai d'Orsay on German domestic politics; only a few of these found their way into the published *Documents diplomatiques français*; they have, however, been used in this account.

Bleichröder figured prominently in these reports. He was cited as Bismarck's authoritative voice, more important even than German officialdom because it was assumed that Bismarck spoke to Bleichröder with particular candor. Bleichröder was also cited time and again as the main expert on Russian finances, on financial details such as the Rothschild loan to Egypt, and as the main mover behind the Rumanian affair.

From the start, St. Vallier found his tenure in Berlin enjoyable and precarious. His connections in Berlin were superb, but his patron in Paris, W. H. Waddington, disappeared, as successive French governments moved to the left. St. Vallier's conservative views became an embarrassing anachronism. As early as June 1879, Bismarck urged St. Vallier to stay at his post, despite the radical tide at home, in order to serve his country; Bismarck assured him that he would never accredit a radical ambassador.[64] Repeatedly St. Vallier turned to Bleichröder for help: if Bismarck would only say the right things to the new government in Paris, St. Vallier would be allowed to stay in Berlin.

Bleichröder mobilized Herbert and Berlin officialdom generally, and Bismarck agreed to use his influence because, as he told Lord Odo Russell, St. Vallier "is the best ambassador that France has ever had in Berlin."[65]

For a time St. Vallier was saved—long enough to reciprocate Bleichröder's favors. In July 1881, in recognition of his help to French prisoners of war, Bleichröder was awarded the cross of commander of the Legion of Honor; it was a signal distinction for the person who ten years earlier had helped to saddle France with a huge indemnity. The scurrilous press in Paris screamed at this honor accorded "to the Germano-Semitic finance vampire, Bleichröder," and sneered that Bismarck's famous watchdog Sultan would be the next recipient. Prince Hohenlohe reported the outcry to Bismarck.[66]

A few months later, Gambetta, once a republican firebrand, now a responsible statesman, came to power and St. Vallier was beyond saving. His post was offered to Baron Courcel, who—after Gambetta's quick fall—thwarted behind-the-scenes maneuvers designed to return St. Vallier to Berlin. French aristocrats considered Berlin a plum, and St. Vallier proved inconsolable as he had to retire to his duties as a mere senator in Paris.[67] He vented his anger in his letters to Bleichröder, whom he repeatedly assured that of all his friends from his Berlin days, only the imperial couple and Bleichröder remained in his affection. St. Vallier's letters are the perfect record of the aristocrat's mounting disgust with plebeian politics, exemplified by the arch-villain, Gambetta, by his "instrument and damned soul," Freycinet, and by the whole crowd of republican leaders who were discrediting France by their pusillanimity in Egypt—while patriots like himself were languishing out of office. His was a shrewd, elegiac conservatism, full of hurt dignity and delicate despair. He regretted Bleichröder's relations with Courcel and with the new politicians in Paris, and a kind of *"et tu"* quality crept into St. Vallier's letters —until in 1886 he died at the age of fifty-two, a broken man, unreconciled to his enforced passivity.

What St. Vallier had sown in the field of Franco-German reconciliation, bourgeois Republicans sought to reap, and Bleichröder quickly adapted to the new men like Jules Ferry and Charles de Freycinet. With Léon Say, a school friend of Alphonse de Rothschild's, he corresponded regularly; as president of the Senate and repeatedly as finance minister, Say was deeply involved in the various monetary conferences of the time, which even then concerned primarily the financial relations between the United States and Europe. From time to time, Bleichröder and Say "conferred" in Marienbad.

Bismarck found French politics confusing, and Bleichröder's commentaries proved useful—the more so as Bismarck's distrust of his ambassadors grew rather than diminished with age. In his hundreds of letters Bleichröder prophesied—often correctly—what would happen or explained the "inside" story of some parliamentary maneuver or market fluctuation. Bismarck read and occasionally annotated these reports. It would be futile to give even a summary of his reports. A few examples must suffice. In early 1882 he correctly foretold the imminent fall of Gambetta and predicted attendant market instability.[68] A few days later he warned Bismarck that the failure of the Union

Générale Bank would involve the imprisonment of some and the impoverishment of other distinguished men of the French right.[69] (It also produced considerable anti-Semitism, as the victims blamed Rothschild machinations for the failure of the bank.) Often he indulged in more general *tours d'horizon*— of which the following from June 1882 was not uncharacteristic.

In Paris, one worries that Freycinet will not be able to stay in power. Even more depressing to the French market than the Egyptian question is the feeling that discord reigns between France and England. The jealousy between the two nations seems close to some climax, and England would like to cut loose from France. To put it mildly, French policy toward the Turks is very infantile.[70]

At issue was the Egyptian question, and Bleichröder's summary of conditions —to modern ears perhaps a little immature itself—approximated Bismarck's own views at the time.

Bleichröder, of course, also briefed French diplomats and statesmen. The international situation was so fluid and Bismarck's conduct often so perplexing that an *explication de texte* or *de geste* proved highly useful. St. Vallier's departure in 1881 coincided with a period when Bismarck intensified his efforts at courting and diverting the French: he found them embroiled with the English in Egypt; he hoped to embroil them with the Italians over Tunis; they involved themselves in Indochina. Bismarck was pleased to see them scatter their energies in new areas while picking up new enemies on the way. Much of the time he was his most benevolent self and genuinely hoped that a Franco-German entente could help to check Gladstone. Briefly, Bismarck toyed with a far-reaching agreement with France that might gradually turn into a new Continental Alliance against England.[71]

Actually Bismarck continually changed keys. As a result, it was extremely difficult for the French to read the many different signals from Berlin. Bleichröder's complicated role makes clear that the French were far more nervous about Bismarck's intentions than Bismarck ever was about the wildest revanchist agitation in France. The French remained scared of German power and puzzled by Bismarck's style, which the French ambassador in 1887 characterized thus: "The alternation of blows and caresses is actually one of the characteristics of the method of dressage applied by Prince Bismarck to the governments that he wants to yoke to his policies."[72] The French knew that Bleichröder often spoke as Bismarck's unofficial voice—but did he always? They had to puzzle out when he was being Bismarck's mouthpiece and when his authentic, private self. Still, they listened and occasionally sneered behind his back.

St. Vallier's successors, Baron de Courcel and Jules Herbette, introduced Bleichröder to successive foreign ministers. In 1883 Baron de Courcel urged the then foreign minister, Challemel-Lacour, to receive Bleichröder, "the banker and confidant of Prince Bismarck whom he uses as an official intermediary with certain ambassadors." The interview took place, and Bleichröder explained Bismarck's "friendly sentiments for France" and his support of French colonial policy. (St. Vallier was chagrined that Bleichröder would see "the enemy" and would say nice things about his successor in Berlin.)[73] On these occasions, Bleichröder played potentate and at times briefed Prince Hohenlohe and the Rothschilds on his mission; at other times, he slipped in and out of Paris, and rumors exaggerated the importance of his mission.[74] A few months later, Bleichröder was again in Paris—this time in connection with his Turkish business—and told the German Embassy that "we must under no circumstances allow Freycinet to come to the fore because he would steer things in a Red direction, which would lead to a social revolution, followed by reaction."[75]

In early 1884 Courcel advised Jules Ferry, the new foreign minister, to receive Bleichröder, with whom he had many "intimate conversations. . . . Although his star has dimmed a little in the recent past, he remains always very well informed, and the nature of his private relations with the Chancellor makes it unlikely that important affairs undertaken by the latter . . . could entirely escape his notice."[76] In the spring of 1884 Bismarck renewed the Three Emperors' Alliance, but sought to reassure France that the sole purpose of that maneuver was to preserve peaceful conditions in the Near East. Accordingly, he dispatched Bleichröder to Paris as his private emissary. We have Ferry's account of Bleichröder's visit: "This crafty old Jew, nearly blind, is the confidant, then, the secret spokesman of the Chancellor. He came to see me 'on a secret, entirely personal mission' . . . [Bleichröder said] the old man wants to say to you that we are friendly, very friendly." Germany, Bleichröder added, wanted still better relations with France but Bismarck was hesitant to say so publicly for fear of weakening Ferry at home. "He sincerely and strongly wants you to stay in power for a long time."* Bleichröder conveyed Bismarck's sense that France should take the lead in Egypt, which, Ferry correctly noted, would embroil France with England, to Bismarck's pleasure. In Turkey, Bismarck offered his discreet help.

"The old crocodile," as Ferry called Bleichröder in his notes on the meeting, then explained—patronizingly—that in his isolated life in Friedrichsruh, Bismarck often exaggerated such things as anti-German articles in obscure French journals, but added: "We push him toward that retreat in order to preserve him for Germany . . . you would not believe how difficult it has become to see him, except for his personal friends like myself. He has not seen . . . the Austrian ambassador for three years." He continued: "The Prince *hates* Gladstone. You cannot imagine to what extent! He does not like his person and he detests his ideas." Bleichröder begged Ferry not to tell anyone of his visit, least of all Hohenlohe. Ferry asked whether Hohenlohe still possessed Bismarck's confidence: "Yes, a certain confidence, not his entire confidence. When you have something private to forward to the Prince

---

* Flattery, too, can often best be conveyed through third parties. An earlier French foreign minister, St. Hilaire, asked Bleichröder to deliver a *"petite démarche"* to Bismarck, adding remarks about Bismarck's "proven genius." St. Hilaire to Bleichröder, 19 Nov. 1881, BA.

Bismarck, I am entirely at your service."[77] Hohenlohe of course found out about Bleichröder's mission, and his distrust of him increased accordingly. He thought Bleichröder was conspiring against him, not realizing that it was probably Bismarck's intention to exploit Bleichröder's weakness for dealing with powerful people. Hohenlohe assumed that Bleichröder was trying to promote the pro-Orleanist sympathies of the Rothschilds.[78] As often in Bleichröder's life—and not without his fault—what struck people as Bleichröder's villainy was really his vanity.

Bleichröder was delighted at the prospect of a "Franco-German entente" and all aglow with his own role in promoting it.[79] In February 1885 Courcel again urged Ferry to receive Bleichröder, whose role, he added, need not be exaggerated, but still "for us he is an intelligent and obliging intermediary. Everything you say to him will be reported very exactly to the German Chancellor." Accordingly, Ferry saw Bleichröder, "the shady confidant [le confident marron]" as he called him, and some years later remembered the conversation as touching on two topics: Bismarck's prospects if and when the crown prince succeeded to the throne and the French involvement in Indochina. On the first, Bleichröder predicted that the crown prince would build Bismarck "golden bridges" to retirement; if these failed, he would force him out some other way. On the second, Bleichröder spoke solicitously about this "unpopular" war in Indochina and France's interest in terminating it quickly. "Would you like Berlin to say a word?" When Ferry bristled, Bleichröder reassured him: "Oh, nothing official. You would not ask anything of the Chancellor; you would simply say what you like in my ear, to me, Bleichröder." Ferry rebuffed him, and saw Bleichröder departing, muttering: " 'I am always there, you know,' he said as he left, groping for his way with his cane, because he is nearly blind, 'you need but say a word to Bleichröder.' "[80] A graphic description of the court Jew shuffling off.

Bleichröder respected Ferry; shortly after this interview, he described Ferry as "the best possible Prime Minister" but thought his fall over Indochina imminent. The war in Indochina did bring about Ferry's downfall, thus removing the best man among the moderate republicans. He lacked "popular appeal," as did the cause of imperialism in far-off places.[81] The hope of a Franco-German entente survived Ferry's fall, but the chances for it grew steadily slimmer. Only strong governments in Paris and Berlin could have sustained such an unpopular course—or, put differently, only strong governments felt sure enough to muffle the jingoist battle drums that supposedly always roused the electorate. In 1886 French nationalist passions centered on a new figure, Boulanger, about whom nothing appeared certain except that he was a general on horseback, with ominous appeal and ambition. He seemed to play on revanchist sentiments and thus added to other strains that doomed the hopes for a Franco-German entente before it ever got properly launched.

Bleichröder favored a pro-French policy long after his master had abandoned all serious hope. In 1885 he acquired an excellent and unsuspected new ally in Paris. Count Münster, one of Bismarck's ablest ambassadors, had been ordered from London, which he loved, to Paris, which he detested—

the fact that the Paris post paid less than London made him angrier still. From Paris, Münster continued to write Bleichröder caustically perspicacious reports, which still today make excellent reading. Even leading French politicians, like Freycinet, appreciated Münster's extraordinary perceptiveness.[82] Likewise, Bleichröder established personal contacts with Ferry's successor, Freycinet, saw him in September 1886, and reported to Bismarck about Freycinet's peaceful intentions and his unhappiness about Boulanger, whom he had made war minister. But Boulanger would have to commit some major blunder before he could be dropped with impunity. Freycinet "would like to be rid of him but does not dare to do anything for fear of falling himself." He was "very excited in regard to Egypt," because Britain was close to declaring a protectorate, which French public opinion would find intolerable—while, Bleichröder added, French holders of Egyptian debt would welcome it. Freycinet raised the specter of other British annexations in the Mediterranean and hoped for Bismarck's support. Finally Bleichröder reported that Freycinet's appointment of his trusted friend and subordinate Jules Herbette as ambassador to Berlin would bring there "a man of extraordinary industry . . . but whether he could fill the post well remains in doubt! Opinions varied." Bleichröder would tell the rest orally.[83] It was Herbette's first assignment outside the Quai d'Orsay; at forty-seven, he was still an unknown. Bleichröder and Freycinet began a correspondence, and Bleichröder sent him "favorable" reports about Herbette.[84]

With Herbette himself, Bleichröder had good relations, though less intimate than with his predecessors. Perhaps Bleichröder was a mite less interested in this "first bourgeois ambassador" from France, as the *National-Zeitung* called Herbette, much to his annoyance.* Bleichröder and Herbette saw each other frequently, and much as they depended on each other, they were a little cautious. Herbette passed on Bleichröder's information to Freycinet, such as Bismarck's continued disinterestedness regarding Egypt, with this aside: "More and more I distrust M. de Bleichröder's sincerity. He plays politics out of an inclination natural to his race and also out of financial interest. Also, he is engaged in business relations with the great bankers of all the countries, whose honest broker he is."[85]

In 1886–1887 the dream of a Franco-German entente that Bleichröder cherished was suddenly replaced by a war scare, the first in a decade. The in-

---

* In fact Herbette complained to Bleichröder about this article in a paper that itself was "an organ of *la haute bourgeoisie*." The French Embassy often asked Bleichröder's intervention in press matters. The most celebrated case of an embassy conflict with the press was the allegation in 1883 that the wife of the French chargé, the Countess d'Aubigny, had been one of the authors of a rather scandalous work, published under the pseudonym Count Vasili, *Berlin Society*. The Comte d'Aubigny wrote a furious letter to Bleichröder—as did St. Vallier, on behalf of the charming countess. Bleichröder had a formal notice inserted in the *National-Zeitung*, and Count d'Aubigny was all gratitude. *Berlin Society*, which contained a distinctly hostile portrait of Bleichröder, caused much tongue-wagging and guessing about possible authors—among them Leonie Schwabach, no less, the wife of Bleichröder's closest associate. The actual author was Princess Catherine Radziwill. Herbette to Bleichröder, 22 Oct. 1886, BA; d'Aubigny to Bleichröder, 28 March and 8 April 1884, BA; Helmuth Rogge, *Holstein und Hohenlohe* (Stuttgart, 1957), pp. 208–210.

ternational scene generally had worsened, with the eruption of the Bulgarian question and the hardening of Britain's position in Egypt, but between France and Germany no new conflict had appeared—except that Boulanger made a great deal of noise, which Bismarck for his own domestic reasons chose to take very seriously. Bismarck had to force an unfriendly Reichstag to accept a new arms bill; a war scare served his purposes.

Count Münster warned Bleichröder in 1886 that Boulanger was the man to watch. At the same time, he never tired of pointing out that while French chauvinism was strong, the desire for peace was stronger still. Republican politics he found disgusting: "*Donnerwetter*, what a country," he once wrote—but still his refrain was peace.[86] Bismarck, however, heard only what he wanted to hear, and when his war minister, Bronsart, reported in December 1886 that a lot of horses were being bought in Schleswig-Holstein, presumably by the French army, Bismarck at once called for an embargo on the export of horses. Such an embargo, he added, "would also have a useful effect in regard to parliament, and aside from its prudential military aspect . . . it would also in case of possible new elections correctly and, for the voters understandably, signify the situation." The cabinet accepted the decree—on such paltry evidence as that in one area some French-speaking agents had ordered horses, allegedly for Belgium! Privately Bismarck also pointed to Russian efforts to get loans in France and repeated his concern that France would wage war as soon as it had won a rapproachement with Russia.[87] Bismarck gradually talked himself into believing in his own specter and took a more bellicose stance. Münster wrote Bleichröder:

> It seems that the belief in war is more popular in Berlin than here, where it becomes clearer all the time that this country does not want war. The Republicans know that the beginning of the war is the beginning of the end of the Republic, and the Monarchists, who otherwise would have wanted war, don't want it because they cannot count on a victory, and they know that defeat would have the most terrifying anarchy as consequence. I am still hoping that once the Reichstag bills are accepted, the saber rattling will stop somewhat.[88]

The real danger, Münster added, came from the east anyway, and Boulanger would be quickly eliminated if German pressure did not keep him in power: no French politican could drop him under German threats.[89]

At the very time when Bismarck plotted the horse edict, on December 23, 1886, Bleichröder hurried to Herbette to assure him that any public agitation in Germany had only the goal of promoting the military bill, "that if this agitation mentioned France, it was only because of the 'impossibility' of mentioning the true cause for all measures, i.e. Russia."[90] (William I would have objected to any public aspersions on Russia.) Perhaps no other single intervention of Bleichröder's was so important or so expeditious as this one, though we do not know whether it was done directly at Bismarck's behest or not. In the ensuing weeks, Bleichröder repeated this message to Herbette. By

January and February 1887 the French had become alarmed at German military preparations; their apprehension mounted when in February 1887 French intelligence seized a dispatch from Bleichröder "that war had been decided upon," and was dependent only on the promise of Russian neutrality.[91] After Bismarck had won the elections, tempers cooled, and he no longer needed Boulanger.

The general, however, followed his own downward course. In February 1889 Bleichröder correctly reported to Bismarck that Boulanger's chances of gaining power were rising again, but added that Boulanger was now taking his indirect advice and cementing relations with the *haute finance*; such a domesticated general would not launch a war against Germany.[92] A few months later, Boulanger fled into exile, having missed his chance at overturning a weak republican government.

In the intricate diplomacy of Bismarck's last three years, France no longer played the central role. What troubled Bismarck was Russian power and the Austro-Russian antagonism; what he feared above all else was a Franco-Russian alliance. The reinsurance treaty with Russia of June 1887 was intended to lessen the danger, as were Bismarck's—and Bleichröder's—repeated assurances to the French that Germany was again entirely pacific. Alternatively, Bismarck threatened both countries, and Bleichröder had every reason to be troubled by German vacillations. His complicated struggles in that period are treated in the context of Bismarck's final desperate years in office.

Bleichröder's special relations with France continued after Bismarck's fall. One of the most irritating of Bismarck's measures against the French had been a passport regulation introduced in 1888 and designed to make French visits to Alsace-Lorraine as difficult as possible. Bleichröder had always opposed it, as had Hohenlohe, the new imperial governor in Alsace-Lorraine, but Bismarck proved obdurate—perhaps to take the edge off military demands for still worse measures. The French were furious, and Count Münster fulminated against the measure: "A mistake from the beginning—one of those mistakes even great men make." Bleichröder urged Bismarck to allow for a temporary suspension of the hardship. In September 1891, with Bleichröder serving as unofficial negotiator between Caprivi and Herbette, the irritant was entirely removed, and men like Herbette and Münster, to whom a Franco-German détente was a political desideratum as well as a source of professional pride, rejoiced and thanked Bleichröder.[93]

In his decades of dealing with France—with ever changing governments and with constantly demanding Rothschilds—Bleichröder reaped profits, honors, and abuse. Often he was an object of suspicion to both Germans and French. He was not a disinterested party and could not be thought such. But it was precisely because he was a banker that he was genuine in his role of mediator or ambassador extraordinary in charge of Franco-German relations: good relations meant good business. Still, people trusted and distrusted him in perhaps equal measure, and in this realm, too, he earned distinction and denigration.

. . .

Bleichröder's connections with France—more varied and more intimate than his connections with any other country—also neatly epitomized his rise. His father had carried out little commissions for the Rothschilds; Gerson became almost their equal. His father, as far as we know, had never been to Paris; Gerson "conferred" at the Quai d'Orsay.

His ties to Britain were less close; he was not fluent in English and never visited the country. His links to the London Rothschilds were not as intimate as with the Paris branch. The British government did not need his financial services, as did the governments of poorer countries. Britain, however, was the only true world power, and her far-flung interests, especially in the Near East and Egypt, were of concern to every international banker. But Britain, beginning in the 1870s, was also a country in serious economic trouble, and her politics, overtly dominated by the rivalry between Disraeli and Gladstone, convulsed by the Irish problem, acquired a new radical potential that alarmed some observers, notably Bismarck. It was a crucial time for Continentals to keep abreast of English affairs.

Britain also had a special aura as a country of unequaled dignity and the repository of honors and distinctions. Many Germans still felt the pangs of an earlier Anglomania. Bleichröder had every reason to cultivate the best possible contacts with England—both public ones that redounded to his standing and private ones that would help him with practical decisions. The reader will remember Bleichröder's appointment as Her Majesty's consul general in Berlin. It was a beginning.

It gave him a formal role to play in the British community in Berlin; it enabled his son to acquire the title of vice-consul at a time when he had disgraced himself in Junker eyes and needed rehabilitation. More important were Bleichröder's exceptionally close ties to Lord Odo Russell, who from 1871 until his death in 1884 was Britain's ambassador in Berlin and by all accounts *primus inter pares* among diplomats there. A favorite of both Bismarck and the crown princess—and the two had few other friends in common—Lord Odo Russell had a wide range of German friends and formed his own shrewd judgment of the German scene. A diplomat of the old school, an aristocrat, a fluent conversationalist in every major European language save Russian, he was as well a man of political sagacity, personal discretion, and "agreeable optimism."[94]

Lord Odo had first met Bismarck in Versailles in 1871; he may have met Bleichröder there too. A year later, he wrote his brother that "Bismarck put his fortune in Bleichröder's hands, who doubled it for him."[95] The Russells also put a part of their fortune in Bleichröder's care, hoping perhaps for a similar windfall. In 1882 Lord Odo wrote him exuberantly: "With unspeakable satisfaction I see from your kind letter that under your loving care and under your skilled experienced direction my private account grows apace and for that I want to express my warmest and most heartfelt thanks. You cannot imagine how pleased I am about it!"[96] A few months after her husband's death, Lady Russell was dissatisfied with the amount left because "I had understood that some of the investments especially latterly had been very advantageous. . . ."[97] Bleichröder also conducted the long negotiations that preceded the purchase of a proper British Embassy in Berlin; when the Russells first arrived the embassy offices were situated in a house, belonging to Count Arnim, that the British shared with the Turkish minister.[98] At Lord Odo's behest, the search had to be conducted incognito—for fear of profiteer prices in Berlin's postwar real estate boom. In the end, Bleichröder arranged for the purchase of the Palais Strousberg, the mansion that the great promoter had built for himself and enjoyed but briefly.

Warm personal relations evolved as well: the Russells were frequent guests at the Bleichröders, and Bleichröder in turn remembered the whole family, including the six children. Lady Russell could count on getting Christmas bouquets of roses and lilacs, and the little Russell children penned their own notes of thanks for their special toys and remembrances.

Most important, of course, the two men constantly exchanged news and views. Bleichröder's name figured frequently in Lord Odo's dispatches home, while for Bleichröder, Lord Odo's candid views on British policy were extraordinarily important.

Bleichröder's other great source on English affairs was Count Münster, German ambassador in London from 1873 on. A Hanoverian nobleman, he "was one among relatively few aristocrats who placed his national ideals above his regional attachments." He worked for Bismarck and had feudal feelings of affection for the Prussian monarch: "I love the dear old man as if he were my father," he wrote Bleichröder after the attempts on William's life.[99] Münster was a conservative *grand seigneur* and a passionate sportsman: he was married to an Englishwoman—with all the doors of English society wide open to him. From 1875 to 1893, first from London and then from Paris, Münster sent Bleichröder a stream of candid letters. The correspondence may have been the more candid because no one suspected this particular connection of Bleichröder's—and even Münster's grandson and recent biographer had no inkling of the close relations, which of course included Bleichröder's banking services.[100]

Münster's letters covered every aspect of European life, *la haute politique* and *la petite histoire*: hints of his secret diplomacy in London during the Russo-Turkish war and a running commentary on the prospects of war and peace. Bismarck was not satisfied with Münster—and not only because Münster had been critical of young Herbert when the latter had been briefly attached to the London Embassy. In fact, Bismarck thought Münster more British than the British, and there were rumors that he sought to replace him, at which point Queen Victoria communicated her concern to William, an intervention hardly calculated to have raised Münster's stock with Bismarck.[101]

Münster was a man of unconcealed biases and attachments; an archconservative, he feared what he thought was the subversive scum of Europe, the socialists in England and Germany, the nihilists and anarchists in Russia. His letters often alluded to this danger and to his private initiatives in combating it:

as when he pushed the British to prosecute German socialist exiles like Joseph Most, assuming correctly that Bleichröder would applaud such initiatives.[102] In all of Münster's letters there was an undertone of pessimism, not unrelated perhaps to his experience of grave illness as a child.[103] In 1877, during the Russo-Turkish war, he predicted an inevitable showdown between Russia and England and wrote Bleichröder of expected British landings at either Constantinople or Gallipoli. In the spring of 1878 he helped to prevent that war and hinted at his laborious efforts at mediating between the British and the Russians. After the Congress of Berlin seemed to have resolved the Eastern Question, his tone briefly changed and he wrote: "I don't see how the peace of Europe can be threatened in the next decade. . . . Politically I am less pessimistic than before." But a few years later, he was back to the old theme, predicting an Anglo-Russian war over Afghanistan and indulging his pessimism over German colonial folly. In 1884 he asked Bleichröder to buy 70,000 marks of a new Russian loan; in April 1885, fearful of war, he wrote Bleichröder, "I would like to use the 70,000 marks invested with you in Russian loan in other ways and would therefore like you to sell that paper immediately, since it can still be done without suffering any loss."[104] This was the most precious kind of intelligence. By being able to see when and why seasoned diplomats moved their funds, Bleichröder had a new gauge of potential trouble.

Bleichröder's connection with Münster was secret and immensely valuable. His most celebrated connection in England was with Disraeli, though perhaps it was more gratifying than immediately useful. The two men met at the time of the Congress of Berlin; Bleichröder had begged Lord Lionel Rothschild for an introduction. Not surprisingly, it is from Disraeli's pen that we have the best description of Bleichröder's feast for the Congress, cited earlier.*

A sparse but important correspondence between the two men ensued. In the Bleichröder Archive, the Disraeli letters have a place of honor: they are not the perfunctory thanks or buy-and-sell orders of a great man, but his authentic and reflective voice.

Bleichröder inaugurated the exchange in October 1878, a few months after he had met Disraeli and a few days after he had conferred with the Russian finance minister: " . . . I shall take the liberty of briefly and critically sketching the financial position of Europe. . . ." Bleichröder concentrated on Russia's finances, which he knew would be of the greatest interest to Disraeli: "Russia requires about 1,400 million rubles to cover the expenses incurred in the East, and must in consequence introduce new taxes which would produce a revenue of 65 to 70 million rubles, so that on these grounds she would be able to make an appeal to European capital." Russia still had 17 million to

---

* From a note of Disraeli's private secretary, Montague Corry, we can infer that Bleichröder lost no time in providing Disraeli with some happy remembrances of that feast: "Twice, since we had the pleasure of enjoying your most agreeable hospitality, Lord Beaconsfield has said to me that your Chateau Lafitte was the finest he ever tasted! So it is no empty phrase to say that your kindness has provided him with a treat which is rare indeed!" Corry to Bleichröder, 6 July 1878, BA.

18 million pounds in foreign balances and hence had no immediate need for a loan. For the time being, she could manage by issuing new notes. "It is of course absolutely certain that in time all values will be depreciated and a certain amount of suspicion awakened; but I must objectively remark that at present Russian finance still enjoys great confidence in Germany and France and in case of another war she could procure 4,000 million to 5,000 million rubles. . . ." Her finances would be shaken, but she could do it.

"In the Austro-Hungarian Empire matters are still worse." The occupation of Bosnia would create new deficits that it would be difficult to cover.

> The crisis in England has hardly yet reached its last stage and the number of its victims and its consequences are not known. . . . I scarcely presume to touch upon foreign politics, as in this field no one can be better informed than Your Lordship; still, a word on the prevailing opinions here may be of some interest. It is supposed that no European war is imminent, at least not in the immediate future: matters in the East are regarded as anything but clear and Russia is disinclined to carry out promptly the decrees of the Berlin Treaty.

Bleichröder concluded with remarks about German domestic politics.

Disraeli's answer in his own hand was prompt and pleasing: "I received with pleasure, and read with much interest your obliging letter, and I hope it will not be the only one, which I shall receive from you." Noting Russia's financial reserves in Europe, he added: "I think the power of Russia to raise a loan will be soon tested if her Government decides on not carrying the Treaty of Berlin into effect." Britain's resolve to have the treaty carried out was a message that Disraeli expected Bleichröder to pass on to Bismarck.[105] At the end of 1878 Bleichröder sent his usual present, which received unusual acknowledgment:

> The caviare, this year, had an additional relish. I think it was the flavor of Peace. —How is our great friend? I hope quite well, and all his amiable family, whom I like very much? I trust he will support me in carrying the Treaty of Berlin into complete effect. His honor, and my own are equally concerned in that. If by the same means, and at the same time, we can preserve our personal honor, and promote the general happiness of mankind, we ought to be satisfied.[106]

The correspondence seems to have lapsed for over a year; in April 1880 Disraeli was turned out of office, and in June he sent his friend and confidant Lord Rowton, the former Montague Corry, to Bleichröder, who replied at once with a long letter about "the unaccountable political change which has taken place in England [and which] has . . . made anything but an agreeable impression here and particularly in the highest quarters." The Whig government, as Bleichröder called Gladstone's cabinet, was thought likely to "involve Europe in unpleasant complications, and the element of uncertainty natural to the party gives rise to a vague feeling of uneasiness abroad." Nor was the prospect of an Anglo-French alliance particularly welcome. But new difficulties might prevent its realization, Bleichröder wrote, alluding no doubt to the problem of Egypt and to Bismarck's determination to exacerbate existing difficulties between England and France. "As regards foreign politics, Mr. Gladstone will be compelled to follow in the path Your Lordship traced out for him, with undesirable vacillations indeed, of which we have had an instance already in the vaunted mission of Mr. Goschen. The Eastern Question would appear destined still to absorb the best attention of the statecraft of the Powers." A breakup of the Turkish Empire would be "a terrible calamity . . . [and] almost sure to lead Europe in a general war." The rest of the letter was again devoted to German domestic affairs and Bismarck's considerable difficulties there. Bleichröder's letters to Disraeli are without the usual note of excessive deference—as if Bleichröder instinctively knew that Disraeli would despise that fawning which Bleichröder's own potentates accepted, indeed expected. A matter of form, perhaps, but indicative of deeper things as well.[107]

Disraeli answered at once—at a time when he was not in the habit of extensive correspondence. Because of the light it sheds on Disraeli and on English politics it deserves to be the only letter cited in its entirety in this book:

Dear Herr von Bleichröder,

Your letter gave me great pleasure and your kind reception of Lord Rowton. I remember your hospitality and your intelligence with unfailing interest. There has been a great change here, but it should not have been so unexpected, as it seems to have been both here and abroad. There never was such a combination of disastrous circumstances as my late government had to encounter: a depressed commerce, a declining revenue, combined with continual seasons of agricultural sterility. How we could carry on affairs as long as we did, seems to me remarkable and we owe that to the devotion and fidelity of the late Parliament.

I do not myself believe, that the English Nation has at all changed its views so far as its external affairs are concerned; only they have suffered so much, and are in so distressed a condition, that they can only think of their hearths and homes. I am not surprised that, with their patience exhausted, they took refuge in change. I should have done so myself.

All my wishes, and all my hopes, now are, that England should maintain peace with honor, and if the new Ministry act in that spirit, I shall support them—But it is difficult to comprehend what they are after, and, perhaps they hardly comprehend themselves. The Cabinet is too large, consists of too many inexperienced men; some of them mere demagogues; their leader, tho' highly gifted, possesses every quality except that of being a leader.

Lord Granville, the Secretary of State, is a gentleman, a statesman, but he has lost the energy of youth, and is, unhappily, visited with some of the infirmities of age; among them extreme deafness. So the management of our external affairs falls much into the hands of the new Under Secretary Sir Charles Dilke, who, until he took office, was an avowed republican, and who is not only the friend, but the pupil, of Gambetta, with whom he is in constant, even daily, correspondence. The new French Ambassador is to work with them.

Here is our danger! Dilke wants to do something *frappant* in foreign affairs, in order to prove, that the Liberals are as patriotic and imperial as the Tories: Gambetta thinks, that if France and England could be seduced into acting together,—about Greece for example—England would get so entangled in feeling with France, that she must become and continue her ally, when the greater question arises and arrives.

This, I take it, is about the real situation of affairs, and I am uneasy, for I feel, that the general peace is endangered.

I am sorry, to hear, that your great friend is so much troubled with his home business, as his commanding intelligence, is, at this moment, required in external matters. I always remember my conversations with him at Berlin with deep interest, and feel for him personally sincere regards. I was glad to hear you were well.[108]

The correspondence continued intermittently until Disraeli's death in April 1881. Not all letters have been preserved. In September 1880 Disraeli sent Bleichröder a short note on the Greek question which began, characteristically, "I am not at all satisfied with the state of affairs." Bleichröder replied by describing Bismarck's Eastern policy and Gladstone's mistakes. In February 1881 Disraeli depicted the predicaments of the Gladstone ministry, and Bleichröder forwarded a copy to Bismarck, who in turn sent it to William, with a covering note that "the former English Prime Minister is in the habit of writing to Herr von Bleichröder rather often." No harm in letting William see an authoritative critique of Gladstone; Bismarck was always afraid of the pro-Gladstone clique at court. Two months later, Disraeli was dead, and Bismarck mourned the one statesman whom he thought his equal.[109]

After Disraeli's death, Bleichröder's relations with Britain became less glamorous again. He advised Lord Goschen on the bimetallist issue, and on the occasion of the German visit of the Prince of Wales, he rendered some discreet services with the German press. He continued to have excellent relations with Lord Odo and his successors; he received gloomy reports from Count Münster and rather breezy accounts from Münster's successor, Count Hatzfeldt. Important news he shared with Bismarck, for, as he once put it: "Given the stormy waves of politics it should be of some interest for Your Highness to get a sense of the dispatches and letters which reached me today from London."[110] Münster hoped for the closest Anglo-German entente, which, he wrote in 1883, Lord Rothschild also sought, as did "most reasonable Englishmen, except for a few ministers." A year later, he wrote that "the overwhelming majority" of Englishmen were pro-German: "I only hope that in our country, too, one will now understand how useful good relations between our two countries are. The Englishman is for us, after all, a lot safer than the Russian or the Frenchman, who, you may say what you wish, is our born enemy." It was a time when Bismarck was wary of the British and once wrote Bleichröder that his ill health kept him away from politics, but added sarcastically, "I am rather curious what will finally develop from the warlike tendency of the colleagues of the peace apostle Bright."[111]

In the last decade of his life, Bleichröder's main concerns about Britain had to do with his own practical interests in the European administration of the Egyptian and Turkish debts. For the rest, he watched with regret the intermittent tension between England and Germany over colonial issues.

Bleichröder's involvement with Russian affairs mirrors the extraordinary growth of his career and influence. In the 1850s and 1860s the interest was primarily economic; beginning with the 1870s, his political connections developed, as successive Russian finance ministers found it useful to consult and negotiate with Bleichröder because of his special place in Berlin. Finally there developed a private correspondence between the czar's ministers and the Jew Bleichröder, a correspondence, unsuspected, that often enough touched on questions of Russian policy and Russian anti-Semitism, which after Alexander II's assassination in 1881 once again became an instrument of official policy. By the end of the 1880s Bleichröder's interests in Russia were so intensive that he risked a protracted disagreement with Bismarck, who wanted, at least temporarily, to obstruct German investment in Russian securities.

German bankers and investors had long regarded the Russian economy as potentially strong but its actual finances as shaky, hence dependent on foreign funds which had to be attracted by the lure of high returns. The House of Mendelssohn had for decades been the leading funnel of German investments to Russia. In the 1850s Bleichröder's partner S. Oppenheim became active in Russian railway construction, and in 1868 Bleichröder joined the Paris-Frankfurt Rothschilds in offering mortgage bonds of the newly founded Russian Bodenkreditverein. Further issues were negotiated, and it has been estimated that in the first ten years these securities alone netted Bleichröder and the Rothschilds a profit of 6,500,000 marks.[112] As we have seen, Bleichröder sold some of these mortgage bonds to his most prominent clientele, Bismarck included, and the operation was but a foretaste of what Russian affairs could net him.

Financial interest implied political concern as well—as did, of course, Bleichröder's role as Bismarck's *homme de confiance*, especially at a time when Russia's war against Turkey threatened the peace of Europe and the fiscal stability of Russia. Once more, Bleichröder built up an extraordinary network of information, which included the British ambassador in St. Petersburg, Lord Loftus, and the German ambassador in London, Count Münster.*

---

* In 1876, at the time of Strousberg's imprisonment and trial in Russia, Lord Loftus "discovered" that he owed Strousberg 15,000 marks, a debt he desperately wanted to keep from the public. Bleichröder obliged at once and helped to hush up the matter—and received useful letters in return which he in turn occasionally forwarded to Bismarck. Lord Loftus-Bleichröder intermittent correspondence, 7 Feb.–21 June 1876, BA; Bleichröder to Herbert von Bismarck, 6 May 1878, FA.

As early as October 1876, Bleichröder informed the Wilhelmstrasse of great Russian armaments; there is some evidence that in 1877 Bismarck promised the Russian government a loan of 100 million to 200 million gold rubles, to be raised by Bleichröder.[113] In the early months of 1878, when the Russian-Turkish war threatened to blow up into an Anglo-Russian war, Bleichröder and the Bismarcks regularly exchanged news on Russian affairs, and Bleichröder repeatedly urged Bismarck to intervene discreetly in St. Petersburg —in order to ensure that the aged Foreign Minister Gorchacov (whom Bismarck detested) be replaced by the sensible "Westerner" Shuvalov and not by a Pan-Slav firebrand like Ignatieff.[114] In the end, Shuvalov's negotiations with the British succeeded in preventing war—a fact that was duly ratified by the Congress of Berlin in the summer of 1878.

Bleichröder's involvement with Russian finances and politics became more intense after the Congress of Berlin. The decisive event for Bleichröder was the one-day stop of the Russian finance minister, General S. A. Greig (a descendant of Scottish emigrants named McGregor), in Berlin in October 1878. Bleichröder sensed the importance of catching Greig before Greig moved to Paris, allegedly for a rest, but in reality, as Bleichröder warned Bismarck privately, "to touch base with the financiers of Europe in order to hear from them in which form or manner European capital would be inclined to participate in the Russian loans that are expected to be raised. I believe it would be of very great interest if I were to succeed in getting together with Greig during his stay here."[115] Bleichröder had been forewarned of Greig's visit by his most important private source in Russia, the Jewish head of the Disconto-Bank in St. Petersburg, A. Sack, who urged him to do all he could to see this not "very intelligent" minister—and to burn the letter after reading it.[116] On October 14 Bleichröder saw Greig; whether with Bismarck's direct help or not is unclear—the indirect help was perhaps sufficient: Greig thought it useful to see Bismarck's financial expert.

The next day Bleichröder told Bismarck about his "long conversation" with Greig, who spoke from "a high pedestal" about Russia's finances, about the credit abroad that sufficed to cover interest payment for at least two years and her solvency at home. Bleichröder questioned Greig's capacity to solve Russia's long-term economic problems.[117] He let others know, too, of his new involvement with Russian affairs. Ten days after the interview, he wrote Disraeli, as we have seen. A short time later, St. Vallier devoted an entire dispatch to the Quai d'Orsay to Bleichröder's conversations with Greig and stressed the political preconditions that Bleichröder had proposed for a loan.[118] All of Europe learned of Bleichröder's talk with Greig.

It was a propitious time to become an expert on Russia, because in the aftermath of the Congress of Berlin Bismarck's mind was filled with apprehension of Russia's likely course. Within Russia, powerful groups seemed to blame Germany for the fact that her military victory had yielded but meager political gains; at the same time Bismarck professed real or feigned concern at Russian armaments. More than that, Germany's projected tariffs threatened Russian grain exports, on which the Russian landed elite depended, and which also supported Russian credit abroad and promoted industrial modernization. German tariffs hurt Russia, even as the influx of German capital helped her. Within limits, Bismarck could use these economic measures as diplomatic weapons as well.[119] In April 1879 he repeatedly discussed Russian affairs with Bleichröder and urged him for the sake of peace to rebuff all Russian entreaties for further loans.[120] Bismarck's hatred for old Gorchacov played a role in his suspicions of Russia, as did his fear that William's pro-Russian leanings could interfere with his own freedom of action. There developed mounting hostility on various fronts. A press campaign exacerbated relations further; the leading Russian papers abruptly ceased their attacks in August 1879 because, as Bleichröder informed the German Foreign Office, the Russian finance minister had warned that a continued campaign would have a "disastrous influence on the price of Russian securities."[121]

Gradually Bismarck determined to press for an Austro-German alliance; he encountered such fierce opposition from William and William's entourage that he was forced once more to resort to his ultimate weapon: the threat of resignation. Why Bismarck should have chosen this course has puzzled historians. The most probable explanation is that he thought an Austro-German alliance would prevent Austria from seeking friends in the West; once Austria was safely hitched to Germany, he could return to a pro-Russian course. The Bleichröder correspondence reflected *contemporary* uncertainty about Bismarck's moves and points to a subsidiary concern: in the summer of 1879 German officials were troubled by the likely resignation of Count Andrássy, the Dual Monarchy's pro-German foreign minister. After Andrássy, Austrian policy might indeed combine a continued anti-Russian policy with a redoubled effort at a Western alliance. In Bismarck's mind, the threats of Russian strength and Austrian desertion reinforced each other—and were further enflamed by his suspicions that a conservative faction at home might hobble his foreign policy. In the event, by October 1879, he overwhelmed William's misgivings and forced a defensive alliance on Austria.[122]

In the ensuing, gradual rapprochement with Russia, Bleichröder played a significant role. His extensive ties with Russian officialdom have not been previously known; they were of symptomatic importance in the history of Russia. Ever since Russia's defeat in the Crimean war, successive rulers had tried to modernize Russia and thus narrow the growing gap between Britain and Germany on the one hand and Russia on the other. Russian manpower was no longer enough; the industrial needs of the army were one reason why in Russia the state played a leading role in promoting economic development. "The central institution of government economic policy was the Ministry of Finance."[123] Russian finance ministers carried a heavy burden: it was their responsibility to provide adequate funds for defense and improvements at a time when, from 1866 to 1885, the army and navy budget amounted to 32 percent of government expenditures and debt servicing to another 28 percent.[124] A succession of able and, on the whole, liberal finance ministers wrestled with these problems, hoping to modernize Russia by introducing Western techniques and attracting Western capital. In their tasks, "the Ministry of Finance preferred to work with Russian Christian capitalists, and as a second best with foreign capitalists, even if some of these were Jews. Russian subjects who were Jews came third in priority. . . ."[125]

Given Bleichröder's double role as banker and agent of Bismarck, it was natural that Russian finance ministers turned to him more and more often. The Jewish question, however, was an ever present shadow. Under Alexander II, Russian Jewry, still restricted to the settlements of the Pale, was able to improve its lot, slowly. The tendency justified a certain amount of optimism, especially if, as in the case of Bleichröder, there was a strong interest in optimism. Bleichröder's own connections with Russia reflected a split within Russian officialdom; those elements who looked upon modernization with fear and horror shunned Jews as well. Those who favored modernization and realized the dependence of Russia on foreign capital both for economic development and for fiscal stability were more favorably disposed toward Jews.

Even before his interview with Greig, Bleichröder had carried on a regular correspondence with one of the leading officials of Alexander's reign, Count P. A. Valuyev. By Russian standards he was a reformist and even something of a liberal; his correspondence with Bleichröder shows him to be a vigorous conservative. In the spring of 1879 he wrote Bleichröder that Russian attacks on Bismarck's diplomacy and on the projected new economic policy of protectionism were unjustified—a veiled criticism of Gorchacov and Russian agrarians, and meant perhaps to placate Bismarck, whose picture he had in his office. Valuyev went on: "With all my heart of course I wish him the best success in Parliament against Lasker & Co. As far as Liebknecht and Bebel are concerned, it is better not to say anything."[126] Both Valuyev and Greig wrote Bleichröder that they placed high hopes in the appointment of Count Saburov as Russian ambassador to Berlin. Valuyev praised Saburov's intelligence and added that the appointment was particularly welcome because Berlin had become the most important post in Europe. Greig spoke of Saburov, a financial expert in his own right, as "intelligent, sympathetic and one of the most fervent admirers of your chancellor and one of the most convinced partisans of the German alliance." Greig added that "our old chancellor [Gorchacov?], whose faults grow with age, has completely disappeared from the scene. He keeps his title, but politically does not exist anymore. . . ."[127] Saburov quickly became an intimate of Bleichröder's and ended up as his client, asking him to invest one deposit, for example, of 250,000 marks "in the surest possible stocks."[128] Holstein thought "the two men were always together" and noted that Bleichröder spread the unlikely story that Saburov's successor in Berlin, Prince Orloff, appointed in 1884, asked Bleichröder for a loan of a million marks almost at once.[129] In any case, Bleichröder and the Russian ambassadors in Berlin were exceptionally close.

No sooner had Bismarck concluded the alliance with Austria than he sought better relations with Russia. Bleichröder was a partner in this endeavor, and his private contacts continued to be supplemented by various financial operations which he concluded with the Russian government to mutual profit. In early 1880 he offered the Russian government an advance of 2 million pounds sterling and became very interested in buying a large block of shares in the Southwestern Railway. After his departure from office, Greig wrote to Bleichröder that "the fact that I inaugurated the official relations of the Imperial Government with your honorable House will remain one of the good memories of my tenure as Minister of Finance."[130] (Bleichröder's son Hans was already counting on his father's receiving a Russian decoration and warned him to hold out for something higher than his rivals had received.)[131] The liberal-minded A. A. Abaza succeeded Greig and continued the private tie to Bleichröder. In turn, Bleichröder sent Bismarck a long memorandum on the dire prospects of Russian finances, on the rumor that Abaza would devalue Russian paper currency by 40 percent, that Alexander II was said to have a fortune of 36 million rubles, all invested in shares payable in gold abroad and not a share payable in Russian rubles. At the very least, Russian difficulties precluded the likelihood of a foreign policy that would cause new "inconveniences and burdens."[132] In June 1881 the Three Emperors' League was reconstituted, and Russo-German relations improved markedly.

In the midst of preparing a new round of reforms, Alexander II was assassinated and succeeded by his more nationalistic, less German-oriented son, Alexander III. Bleichröder at once conveyed his condolences, which, in the name of the czar, Abaza formally acknowledged.[133] The new government adopted a fierce anti-Semitic policy at home, though it continued, now under the able direction of Finance Minister N. K. Bunge, the course of economic modernization. Bleichröder had always been concerned with the lot of his coreligionists and had repeatedly raised the question of their treatment with Russian officials.* Count Valuyev once sought to reassure him on some new legislation but reminded him that the large number of Jews in anarchist circles did indeed create suspicions "of people of Jewish origin."[134] It was one of the ironies of Bleichröder's life that he who detested anarchists and socialists as much as any conservative experienced the added horror of realizing that there were enough Jews among them so that anti-Semites could exploit their presence—even as his own position incited anti-Semitism. The Jew as prominent plutocrat, as middle-class radical à la Lasker, or as desperado anarchist came to be used in the 1880s by different groups as evidence of the mounting Jewish threat.

The new government abandoned Alexander II's policy of gradual relaxation of discrimination and adopted instead a policy of Russification that hit Jews especially hard.[135] Bleichröder made his concern known—a concern that reflected his genuine compassion for his unfortunate brethren and his fear that anti-Semitic measures in Russia could swell the number of so-called Ostjuden in Germany, as indeed the German government also feared. (This was of course a major question—to which we will return later.) In 1881 there were several pogroms, and in March 1882 a new measure barred Jews from

---

* The Paris Rothschilds were also troubled. In May 1880 Baron Alphonse wrote, "I need not tell you how much I am concerned with all that has to do with my coreligionists anywhere in the world." A. de Rothschild to Bleichröder, 3 May 1880, BA.

buying land in the open country. Bleichröder wrote Bismarck, "Jew-baiting, which has begun afresh in Kiev, this time by action of the government, made our stock market, which was in a very favorable mood, close with a setback, especially for Russian securities." On the next day, Bleichröder spoke to Holstein about the renewed anti-Semitism in Russia (did he hope to prod him?), adding that he had just written to Bunge about it, "asking him to bear in mind that in 1868 Rumanian bonds fell by 30 percent because after the first persecution of Rumanian Jewry a committee of Berlin Jews called on their coreligionists throughout the world to discontinue their transactions in these bonds. . . ."[136] Whether he really put it in quite these terms to Bunge we do not know, but Bunge's answer has been preserved and is more elegantly invidious:

> Our legislation in regard to the Jews is defective and the application of the existing laws even more so. If in Germany people belonging to the enlightened class have lacked tolerance, it is natural that this could occur in Russia, where by law the Jews are a nation apart and the collisions have been even stronger . . . but I do not doubt that an equitable solution is possible.[137]

The situation of the Russian Jews deteriorated steadily, both on account of government action and by growing popular anti-Semitism. But far from organizing any boycott, Bleichröder continued to be banker to the czarist government and correspondent of the czar's ministers. He hoped thereby to exert a moderating influence and to strengthen the hands of men like Bunge, who were themselves opposed to the extension of discriminatory—and economically retrograde—legislation.

Throughout the next few years, through various ups and downs in Russo-German relations, Bleichröder retained his link with Russian ministers and informed Bismarck and others of Russian developments. In 1881–1882 he professed to be very bearish on Russian finances. In July 1882, he wrote Bismarck of his "rendez-vous" in Marienbad with Count Shuvalov, who expected the czar to proceed with reforms leading to a constitution and who shared Bunge's favorable assessment of Russian foreign credit. Bleichröder disagreed, because "the European public has become distrustful" and would prefer to sell old rather than buy new Russian securities. As far as Shuvalov himself was concerned, he had no immediate prospect for a ministerial post and above all sought to be ambassador in Berlin.[138]

In 1883 Mendelssohn again placed a Russian loan on the Berlin market; Bleichröder took a dim view of this issue, whether out of disinterested conviction or because he had been left out is unclear. The press denounced the issue, and Bismarck blamed Bleichröder for this hostility. Various papers, including the liberal *Berliner Tageblatt*, pointed out that the very terms of the loan (6 percent payable in gold and 3½ percent discount from purchase price) indicated how shaky Russian finances were—even Rumania could do better. The

Tageblatt, moreover, argued that Germans held enough funds from a government that sought "a war of annihilation [*Vernichtungskrieg*]" against Germany. Bismarck warned the Foreign Office that the official press should not use such language and that Bleichröder, the likely inspirer, ought confidentially to be told that the press articles had neglected to mention "the main reason for the bad financial situation of Russia, i.e., the fact that earlier loans had not been used for productive purposes but exclusively for military needs. . . . Russia was the only power which had to be feared as a possible disturber of the peace, and in case of war nobody could know the result, especially as far as the fate of Poland was concerned." The Polish afterthought may have been an echo of his periodic threats to Russia, involving the restoration of an independent Poland in some form.[139]

From 1883 on, Bleichröder, however, became ever more deeply involved in Russian finances and persuaded himself that his profitable participation in Russian development would also serve to keep German-Russian diplomatic relations on a friendly basis. In 1884, probably at Bismarck's behest, certainly on his assurance "that peace in Europe had been secured, and that Russia would not embark on war," Bleichröder played the leading role in floating a 300 million-mark 5 percent loan for Russia. On Bismarck's order, the Prussian state bank, the Seehandlung, signed for a loan as well—and thus gave it a kind of official imprimatur. Bleichröder reported that the loan was oversubscribed twenty times, an expression "of the complete confidence there is in the pacific assurances of Russia."[140] The operation ended with a row between him and the head of the Seehandlung, creating the suspicion that Bleichröder had earned "a few hundred thousand rubles or so as a special fee."[141] Herbert found it "positively lamentable" to give Russia money "which would only be used for military, naval and propaganda purposes."[142]

Bunge, who had had a distinguished academic career in economics, sent his "homage at the brilliant manner in which you have justified the confidence of the Imperial Government. In attributing to yourself the modest role of godfather to the new loan you are understating the truth. I am happy to recognize that the conception, the initiative, and the conduct of this important affair belong to you almost exclusively."[143] The praise was happily confirmed when the imperial government conferred the Grand Cross of St. Stanislas on Bleichröder—at the very time when he and the prominent Russian banker Horace de Guenzburg were exchanging letters about rising Russian anti-Semitism.[144]

After 1884 Russian affairs became more difficult for Bleichröder. His financial interests continually collided with political realities. In 1885 everybody expected an Anglo-Russian war over Afghanistan ("Count Waldersee looks upon a war between Russia and England in Asia as one of the certainties in store for History"), and in April 1885 Count Münster instructed Bleichröder to sell his 70,000 marks invested in Russian securities. Bleichröder was "very much alarmed and has been sounding his friend the Chancellor as to whether he could not do something to avert the threatened catastrophe." At the same time, he tried to reassure the British that the Russians were not making financial preparations for war, and the British chargé in Berlin commented on Bleichröder's report: "He ought to know the financial situation of Russia well, as he has been so frequently consulted by M. de Giers on the subject and has the best sources of information at his disposal."[145]

On June 3, after a particularly cordial meeting with Bismarck in Varzin, which concluded with Bismarck's embracing Bleichröder, Bleichröder, "according to oral orders," bought 200,000 marks of the latest Anglo-Russian loan; a few days later, Bismarck, still exceptionally cordial, wrote Bleichröder that while he did not believe in some alarming news Bleichröder had telegraphed, he should sell the Russian securities while it could be done without loss. Bleichröder acted accordingly.[146] Later that summer, after Bleichröder had had a conversation with the Russian Foreign Minister Giers, both Bismarck and Bleichröder concurred that an Anglo-Russian war in the fall was inevitable.[147] In the event, this was another war that failed to come off, but the confidential manner in which Bismarck and Bleichröder conferred on these matters infuriated Bismarck's entourage, beginning with his own sons.

From 1886 to 1890 Bismarck's policy toward Russia became more and more problematical, and Bleichröder's simple interests suffered accordingly. Bleichröder's role as banker to Russia at a time of worsening German-Russian relations became a cause célèbre in the final years of Bismarck's rule and in fact deepened the rift between Bismarck and William II. Bleichröder's activities became so intermingled with Bismarck's final crisis that the story must be told in the context of Bismarck's fall. Here it will suffice to say that Bleichröder stuck to his pro-Russian views and in January 1887, in fact, sought to make a personal visit to Russia, as he had in 1883 hoped to send one of his sons there. In the earlier instance, Saburov begged him not to proceed because it would be hard to arrange invitations for private persons, and in the later instance, Sack urged him not to come.[148] It was one thing for Russian ministers of finance to correspond with Bleichröder or to see him in Berlin; it would be quite another for them to see him on their home ground. They could receive his money, not his person. Neither these rebuffs nor Bismarck's hardening attitude made Bleichröder wish to swerve from his course of strengthening his highly profitable Russian connections.

We have followed Bleichröder's role on the international scene, as he played it vis-à-vis the three most important countries of Europe. He had excellent relations elsewhere as well, and he made considerable profits in placing Austro-Hungarian, Serbian, Spanish, Greek, and Italian loans. None of these efforts was without its political significance; for all of them he had to work closely with the German Foreign Office. The interplay among political, military, and economic motives in reaching political decisions was universally assumed but rarely articulated. Bleichröder exemplified it. At times the political pressures and economic temptations coincided, as they did in the case of Austria-Hungary, Serbia, and for a while, Russia; in the 1890s, however,

Bleichröder had to be pushed into bailing out Italian finances in order to keep Italy close to the Triple Alliance—and the reverse of that predicament was of course his rift with Bismarck over his own desire to continue the profitable Russian business. Occasionally, Bleichröder thought the trumps were in his hands—as in his tangled relations with the Rumanians, of whom he thought with the same veiled contempt with which, in turn, so many notables thought of him.

CHAPTER 14

Rumania: The Triumph of Expediency

I care for the Rumanians *as I do for my glass when it is empty*. . . . [Rumanian independence is a matter of indifference, except for the German] Jews, whom I need to coddle, win over and who can be very useful to me in Germany and whom I like to pay in Rumanian money; don't you call that funny money [n'appelez-vous cela de la monnaie de singe]?
—Bismarck to St. Vallier, February 27, 1879

It was one of the most difficult political births, this long-delayed recognition of full Rumanian independence. . . . You can tell yourself that really not a single question went smoothly or simply and that today a whole chaos of terrible complexities lies behind you and that the overcoming and ordering of this chaos and the transition into stable forms was a superhuman test of strength and patience.
—Prince Karl Anton of Hohenzollern-Sigmaringen to his son,
Prince Charles of Rumania, February 27, 1880

According to Bismarck's oft-repeated story, Bleichröder earned his ennoblement in Rumania—a strange place for a German Jew to win Prussian nobility. Out of the Rumanian wilderness, as Bleichröder no doubt thought of it, he drew his greatest honor—and into it, for more than a decade, he poured all his resources. It proved his most complicated venture in foreign affairs.

The Rumanian story illustrates better than any other episode in Bleichröder's life his role as a bridge between worlds that normally remained apart. In miniature, it is also a story that embodies some of the great themes of the nineteenth century: the rise of nationalism, the spread of capitalism, the clash between Western ideals and east European realities. By midcentury Rumania was in the throes of nationalist passion for independence; to gain this independence, Rumanians needed the help and recognition of the Great Powers. For its economic development, most specifically for railroad building, Rumanians lacked native and hence needed foreign capital and expertise. A backward people, the Rumanians needed help—and resented it. At the moment, then, of reaching for independence, Rumanians discovered their dependence on foreign powers, a dependence made more galling when the Great Powers declared that the recognition of Rumanian independence was contingent on her acceptance of Western tenets of equal citizenship for all. This demand, energetically pushed by international Jewry, would have required Rumania to emancipate its exceptionally large Jewish population (a much larger percentage of the total population than anywhere else in central or western Europe), much of which was unassimilated, having recently immigrated to Rumania from Russia, where conditions were still worse. It is also a model in microcosm of what often happens when human (in this case, Jewish) rights and material rights (in this case, the pecuniary advantages of German investors and the political interests of the Great Powers) are pitted against each other. The hope that both were realizable proved illusory; in the end, human rights were bartered away for material gain.

This story—told here for the first time on the basis of new and extensive documentation—coalesced in the person of Bleichröder. In the Rumanian tangle, he was the one man equally committed to the defense of human and material rights. He had to carry out Bismarck's resolve to redeem German investments that seemed lost in an ill-conceived German venture to build Rumanian railroads, and he was a leader in the effort of Western Jewry to protect Rumanian Jews from Rumanian oppression and discrimination. By serving Bismarck in the railroad question, he was for a time in an excellent position to win Bismarck's support for the Jews. All of his connections, loyalties, and dependencies came into play.

For Bismarck, the Rumanian involvement was a never ending annoyance. And yet his policy, so obscure and ultimately so successful, shows him to have been a master of resourceful ruthlessness. It also exemplifies the intertwining of domestic and foreign considerations in the conduct of his diplomacy.

The Rumanian adventure was set in a country that, after a history of unbroken subjugation to the Turks and Russians, sought to establish its independence—which it could do only through the benevolence of the Great Powers. Rumania was one of the pieces coming off the decaying Turkish Empire; its powerful neighbors, Russia and Austria, coveted an independent Rumania as a potential satellite. To exploit the rivalries of the Powers without falling victim to them was no easy task for Rumanians—nor one calculated to call forth the higher virtues of political morality. Expediency was the norm, and all too often deceit the means to success.

Rumania is a nineteenth-century invention. From Roman times on, no such country existed; in the fourteenth century there emerged two principalities, Moldavia and Wallachia, speaking the same language and deriving from the same Latin ancestry, that were subject to the more or less direct rule of the Turks and their Greek subrulers, called Phanariots. From the mid-eighteenth to the mid-nineteenth century, Russia was an intermittent presence in these two principalities, and on the whole its rule was more enlightened than was Turkish suzerainty. After Russia's defeat in the Crimean war, the Concert of Europe decided in the Treaty of Paris of 1856 that the Russian protectorate should end and the two principalities should remain under the suzerainty of Turkey and the protectorate of Europe. The Rumanians clamored for the union of the two principalities and looked to Paris—to their Latin brothers—for help, which was readily granted because Napoleon III saw himself as the protector of nationalities. The protecting Powers, of course, quarreled among themselves and pursued their own purposes. Austria insisted on Rumanian independence from Russia—so that the Austrians could establish a virtual monopoly of influence there. On the other hand, the Austrians were fearful of Rumanian nationalism—which could easily spill over into Hungary, where a large Rumanian population lived. The Rumanians wanted national independence—and attained it step by step, relying on the Great Powers and playing one against the other, as opportunity arose.

This is not the place to present a history of Rumania.[1] For us, it is important to remember that the first ruler over both principalities, Prince Cuza, was deposed in 1866, and that the Rumanian politician Ion Brătianu engineered the selection of Prince Charles of Hohenzollern-Sigmaringen as his successor. Charles belonged to a junior and Catholic branch of the Hohenzollern dynasty; his father had surrendered his sovereignty over the small duchy of Sigmaringen to his royal cousin in Berlin and had in fact entered Prussian service. Charles was a handsome twenty-seven-year-old, ambitious, courageous, and in search of destiny. He wanted to accept the challenge, whatever the risks, and he was encouraged in this by Bismarck. He was more acceptable to all because of his extraordinary pedigree, which linked him not only to the ruling Prussian dynasty but made him a cousin of Napoleon III's as well. Prince Charles knew nothing about his new people, nor his people about him, but his election was ratified in a plebiscite by the impressive and misleading vote of 685,969 for and 224 against him.[2] The Rumanians had long wanted a foreign prince, and obviously his Prussian tie gave Rumania further importance in Bismarck's perspective. Also Charles's dispatch to Rumania set a precedent that in 1870 Bismarck hoped the Spaniards would follow. The exportation of Hohenzollerns would enhance Prussian-German influence.

Prince Charles discovered that the indolent Cuza had left him an unenviable legacy. "Few rulers had had so discouraging a task thrust upon them at the commencement of their occupancy of a throne."[3] Cuza had left empty coffers, a large public debt, officials who had not been paid for six months, and an embryonic civil service that was corrupt and inefficient. Rumanian politicians, anxious to claim for themselves a Western identity and to emphasize their particular kinship with France, drafted a liberal constitution, patterned after the Belgian Charter of 1831. Rumanians wanted to be the model Western offspring, surrounded by infidel Turks and autocratic Russians.

The principles invoked were hard to realize in an economically backward and politically inexperienced country. In the process of constitution-making, the Jewish question erupted. Some Rumanians sought to extend Western principles to Jews, too, and proposed their emancipation. A tremendous outcry ensued, and a new synagogue in Bucharest was burned down. Jews were defined as foreigners, and Article VII of the Constitution stipulated that "only foreigners belonging to a Christian confession can obtain naturalization."[4] In short, Jews were permanently barred from citizenship.

The history of Rumanian Jewry has always been written with more polemics than factuality. Disinterested evidence was hard to come by—beginning with the question of the number and provenance of Rumanian Jews. Estimates for the 1860s varied from 200,000 to 300,000 out of a total population of about 5 million. The Prussian consul in Jassy, the capital of Moldavia, reported to Bismarck in 1869 that a Rumanian government brochure asserting that there were 400,000 Israelites among 5 million Rumanians—or a proportion of 1 to 12½—was wrong; in fact, there were only 230,000 Jews and thus "the proportion of 1 to 19½ is more favorable than in Russia for example."[5] Most of these lived in Moldavia, and most had fled thence from Russia in order to escape the persecutions of Nicholas I. The flood of Jewish immigration came after the Treaty of Adrianople of 1829, which marked the end of the Russo-Turkish war and which offered opportunities of trade and business in lands formerly closed by the Ottomans. Jews were as desperate to leave the miseries of the Russian Pale (which included the ex-Polish lands) as they were attracted to a land of seeming opportunity. Some Jews had moved in from Poland and the Ukraine earlier. Galician Jews they were often called, and the term carried a special, pejorative connotation among all sorts of people, Jews included. In Moldavia the Jews lived apart and according to Rumanian reports did not even speak the language. Indigenous or wealthier Jews, of course, did. Barred from owning land and from most professions, they became artisans and small tradesmen, creditors and innkeepers; Rumanians thought them usurers and promoters of peasant alcoholism. Still more galling for the Rumanians was the fact that by the 1850s in most Moldavian cities, including Jassy, Jews constituted a numerical majority. By 1866 and 1867 Rumanians became more and more restive with even the promise of eventual equality.

After Charles's accession, the Rumanian Chamber began passing new, restrictive legislation concerning Jews. Older prohibitions were revived and new ones added; in 1867 a decree reaffirmed that Jews were barred from holding land, from living in villages, or from owning inns. Local fiat and "spontaneous" outbursts did the rest. In the same year, the Jassy authorities declared the Jewish quarter a health hazard and expelled some Jews, including wealthy ones, as vagabonds. In Galatz, Rumanians sought to expel Jews across the Turkish frontier, but the Turks would not receive them, and some of the victims were left to drown in the Danube.

Rumanian anti-Semitism was different from that of Russia or Hungary. The Rumanian ruling class did not share the common prejudice against business; on the contrary, patterning themselves on the Greeks who had been prominent in the century before independence, the Rumanians became shrewd entrepreneurs, and from the start they saw in the Jews economic rivals—in a way that Hungarian nobles or Russian *dvoryanstvo* did not. In addition, they shared the type of anti-Jewish religious hostility cultivated by the Orthodox Church, which was common to them and the Russians. In short, anti-Semitism in Rumania was constantly nurtured by economic antagonisms—and hence the condition of Jews in Rumania was much worse than it was in Hungary, though significantly less bad than it was in Russia.[6]

The Jews of western Europe made every effort to protect their fellow Jews in the East. In retrospect one can say that the 1860s was a time when the presumption against formal anti-Semitism was strongest in Europe and when the European public would be least indifferent to discriminations and outrages which, it was always said, were worthy of an earlier age of bigotry. The richer and more influential Jews of Europe had established an informal network of cooperation; in an age that was proud of its tolerance and enlightened humanity, they had one great weapon at their disposal: publicity. They used the press to present and indict Rumanian (or, later, Russian) acts of anti-Semitism, and they expected that their liberal readers would have the proper response, that their governments would take formal or informal action, and that the country thus pilloried would feel the pressure of public disapproval. The Jews of western and central Europe were the more determined in their efforts as they realized that Rumania was exceptionally anti-Semitic and uniquely vulnerable to pressure from abroad. Through the press and through private channels, they called attention to Rumanian wrongdoing and appealed to universally accepted principles in order to rouse the European conscience.

From the beginning, Bleichröder was deeply involved in the effort of Jewry to mobilize European opinion against Rumanian anti-Semitism. We have no intimations of his innermost feelings on the subject; even if he had wanted to show reticence and reserve, his powerful friends abroad saw in his connection to Bismarck too important an instrument not to demand his involvement. In May 1867, after the first major outbreak in Jassy, he received a characteristic summons from his friend Moritz von Goldschmidt in Vienna, who no doubt represented the Rothschilds as well: "Because Prussia has primary and greatest influence with the governing Prince in Bucharest, and because Count Bismarck is very tolerant, I am certain that you will attend to this matter. The Vienna Congregation takes a very serious view of this, and for this act of charity, God's reward is certain." A day later, the Prussian ambassador in London, Count Bernstorff, wrote Bismarck: "The Rothschild family is most terribly agitated about the Jewish persecution in Jassy and has urged me to solicit the concern of the Royal Government and to request Your Excellency to take kind steps with the Rumanian Prince on behalf of their coreligionists." Bleichröder also appealed to Bismarck, and thus summoned, the chancellor ordered his consul general in Bucharest to investigate the situation and, "if appropriate, to make forbearing representations to the authorities."[7] The Rumanians, whom Prince Charles thought "the most tolerant of all Christian peoples," were stung by these remonstrances. A few days later, Louis Napoleon wrote Charles: "The affair of the Jews [israélites] has made a strong impression on the public because that persecution, worthy of another age, is viewed as if it were aimed at flattering the low instincts of the masses."[8]* And even Charles's father admonished him to bow to realities: France was Rumania's sole support, Jewish money dominated the French press, and hence the Jewish question would always agitate Paris.[9] All the world was trying to instruct the Rumanians on how to behave to their Jews. The Rumanians, however, proved obdurate pupils and eventually exhausted the passion of their moral tutors.

Bleichröder kept Bismarck informed of further outbreaks. In February 1868 Bismarck assured Adolphe Crémieux, the venerable head of the Alliance Israélite, that he would try to help the Jews in Rumania.[10] The time for aid was at hand. A number of "radical" Rumanian deputies had introduced new legislation that would have deprived the Jews of almost all their civic rights, and the community in Jassy cabled Bleichröder that some local prefects had taken it on themselves to translate parliamentary intent into immediate, terrible reality. The telegram spoke of intended "extermination" and reported that in the district of Bacau "in the space of twenty-four hours 500 Jewish families were expelled from the open countryside and left to wander about aimlessly, wretchedly, without food. The misery is boundless, the misfortune beyond description." In order to dissipate widespread skepticism, Bleichröder asked for and immediately received further details on these incidents. These reports he submitted to Bismarck.[11]

Bismarck's ambassador in London had already telegraphed him "that twelve Rothschilds have requested me urgently to seek the friendly intervention of the Royal Government." Bismarck warned Prince Charles against sanctioning "so annihilating a persecution of this always more useful than dangerous class of the population whose influential coreligionists in all of Europe would turn such a persecution into a dangerous enterprise for the [Rumanian] government." A week later he once more urged the government "to take a strong stand against the Jew-baiting in Moldavia." Bismarck's efforts to have Russia join such informal warnings proved unavailing; in terms that the Rumanians also liked to use, Gorchacov told Prince Reuss, the Prussian ambassador, of his general disinclination "to consider as a crime the measures that the Rumanian Government has taken against the national plague, i.e., the Jews there. . . . If all Jews were Rothschilds and Crémieuxs, then the situation would be different, but under prevailing conditions one could not blame the government if it sought to protect its people against these bloodsuckers."[12] That the Rumanian Jews were no Rothschilds and no saints, that they were not like west European Jews, became a cliché that was invoked time and again for decades; no doubt, the Jews of Jassy were different from the Jews of Paris, but few observers seemed to remember that the people of Bucharest also were different from the people of Paris—and still clamored for their rights.

---

* It was common for enlightened Frenchmen to speak of *israélites* rather than of Jews because the latter term had acquired such a pejorative connotation. Germans spoke of members of the Mosaic Faith or, at times, of *Israeliten*, as did assimilated Jews occasionally. Bismarck rarely bothered with such euphemisms.

It exasperated Charles to have Bismarck, prompted by Bleichröder and the Rothschilds, act the guardian angel of Moldavian Jews, whom Charles viewed as undesirable aliens who by their superior industry and their inferior morals were exploiting his people.[13] The fact that German Jewry, including such prominent men as Bleichröder's friends Freiherr von Oppenheim, Baron Rothschild of Frankfurt, and the writer Berthold Auerbach, bombarded Charles's father, Karl Anton, with pleas on behalf of Rumanian Jews was unlikely to assuage Charles's feelings. Worse, in April 1868, the Jewish leaders made sure that the major papers of Berlin and Vienna carried prominent and scathing attacks on Rumanian Jew-baiting. The campaign proved successful, and Charles informed his father and the world that his government had all along intended to oppose the draft legislation.[14] With the benevolent support of the Great Powers, Jewry succeeded in preventing still harsher laws from being enacted. Some sixty-five years later, the best-known English historian of Rumania gave this rather characteristic summary: "After 1870 the [anti-Semitic] agitation died down, but all through the seventies there were periodical riots and assaults upon the Jews, notably at Vaslui, Ploeşci and Darabani, *which the Alliance Israélite exploited to the full.*"[15]

Bleichröder had done his part, but the Alliance Israélite openly and the Rothschilds covertly probably had a greater impact. The power of French Jewry declined after the defeat of France in 1870, and if Rumanian Jews were to be protected further, a greater effort would have to be made in Berlin. It seemed like a fortunate coincidence for Jewry that precisely at this moment, in 1871, Bismarck begged for Bleichröder's intervention on behalf of German fortunes in Rumania.

Bismarck followed Rumanian affairs from the moment he entered office in 1862. His steady, if contemptuous, attention to Rumania bears out the truth of an earlier observation that Bismarck "was a political chess player who knew how to assess the value of even the small pieces; though he did not primarily play with them, he knew in any case how to keep them in reserve."[16] He followed closely the reports of his consuls in Jassy and Bucharest, and these consular reports, here used for the first time, reflected the position of the European consuls there: they were "the pillars of the European protectorate; and there certainly were no keener observers of this nation in the making."[17]

"These principalities need two things above all else, good elementary schools and passable roads." Or so in 1863 the Prussian consul general defined the problems of Rumania to Bismarck—in terms that are classically applicable to developing countries generally. For reasons of trade and prestige, Rumanian leaders coveted as large a railroad network as possible, and the Prussian consul general supported these plans, which in part, he thought, were directed at breaking the Austro-Hungarian monopoly on Danube shipping.[18] Bismarck, in turn, favored the construction of the projected Rumanian railroad because it would "be in the interest of our commerce."[19]

From the beginning Bismarck's interest in Rumanian railroads was at once commercial and political: no need to allow Austria to extend its influence anywhere, if it could be conveniently avoided. In fact, Prince Charles left for Rumania in the spring of 1866, when Austria and Prussia began mobilizing their troops for the decisive showdown. A Hohenzollern in Austria's rear was an attractive prospect for Bismarck, and he had every reason to support Prince Charles's vigorous concern for the building of railways. The difficulties, however, were great. As in most developing countries, the capital, the machinery, and much of the expertise had to be imported. Various companies from England and Austria evinced an interest; Charles would obviously have a slight preference for a German consortium—such as Bethel Henry Strousberg sought to put together. (Because Rumania had undertaken not to float any further foreign loans, Strousberg proposed that he and his consortium would raise the necessary capital, while the Rumanian government would guarantee the interest.)

Strousberg was the descendant of a Jewish family that had for three or four generations lived in Neidenburg in East Prussia. As a boy, he had converted to Christianity; he spent many years in England, where he made a moderate fortune in journalism, in the insurance business, and even in art exhibitions. He returned to Berlin in 1863 and there began, first for English houses and then on his own, the successful construction of railways in East Prussia. Gradually he extended his empire to mining ventures and the construction of railways abroad.[20]

Strousberg persuaded some well-known Silesian magnates, the dukes of Ratibor and Ujest, as well as Count Lehndorff-Steinort, to join him in forming a consortium. Their names gave the new venture a bright luster. Prince Charles regarded the building of an extensive railroad network "a vital question," and Berlin sent him reassuring reports about Strousberg's reliability. A few weeks later, perhaps as a second thought, Charles sought Bismarck's personal assessment of Strousberg's "seriousness and capacity." Bismarck's reply in his own hand to the Prussian consul general was a classic in evasion:

> You know the situation of Ratibor and Ujest as well as I do. Strousberg has participated repeatedly and skillfully in various railway enterprises and has thereby made some splendid deals; I have of course no opinion about the present condition of his property and can in any case not give an official opinion about the capacities of private individuals because even such an opinion would constitute an indirect guarantee which I cannot undertake for the Royal Government.[21]

Bismarck was so anxious to disclaim all responsibility that he answered at once, without consulting Bleichröder. A year later, on his own initiative, Bleichröder warned Bismarck of Strousberg's likely fate. Referring to Strousberg's efforts to raise funds in Vienna for his Serbian railroads at a time when Austrian finances were in dire straits, Bleichröder added: "The man is very clever, but his manner of undertaking new ventures in order to mend old holes is dangerous, and if he should encounter a [sudden] obstacle, his whole structure may collapse and under its ruins bury millions of gullible shareholders."[22]

The Prussian consuls kept Bismarck posted about the struggle among various foreigners for Rumanian railway concessions. Strousberg's main rival was Count Ofenheim, an Austrian railroad builder who believed that his unprofitable line from Lvov to Cernowitz could be salvaged by extending it through Rumania to the Black Sea. Ofenheim and Strousberg competed for the project—for which the state had no money. A number of prominent Rumanians objected that railways were an expensive investment for the importation of modern evils. More important was the widespread sentiment that foreigners would use railroad concessions to enrich themselves at Rumania's expense and in the process would swamp the country with all manner of undesirable foreigners. Ofenheim would import slovenly Poles, while Strousberg would bring in a Prussian army that would use Rumanian territory to make war on Russia or Turkey. To allay such fears and to promote their own cause, both Ofenheim and Strousberg were busily distributing gold to Rumanian legislators—or so rumor had it. Certainly Prussian consuls believed that the entrepreneurs were distributing and the Rumanian deputies were accepting large favors.[23] Strousberg's consortium entered a cheaper bid than Ofenheim and won Prince Charles's wholehearted support. In the end the government decided on two lines and awarded concessions to both men. By committing his own prestige, Charles finally forced a recalcitrant Chamber in April 1868 to accept the Strousberg concession, and the Senate, having been dissolved on account of its obstruction, did likewise in July 1868.

Strousberg undertook to build several lines (from Roman in the north through Galatz to Bucharest and from there to the Hungarian border), for a total of 942 kilometers. The company was to issue 7½ percent obligations to a maximum of 254,340,000 francs, reckoned at 270,000 francs a kilometer. The issue was to come out in Berlin, under the supervision of an agent of the Rumanian government, who turned out to be a Prussian Oberfinanzrat, Ambronn, an old confidant of Prince Charles's family. The government undertook to guarantee the interest, though there was some ambiguity whether its full responsibility would begin at once or only after the railroad was completed. The agreement stipulated completion by 1872 at the latest.[24]

Strousberg began his new enterprise with great gusto. Like a general exhorting his troops, he addressed his workers in Galatz, admonishing them "not to surrender their Prussian character, not to succumb to German lassitude [Dusel], but to cling to the disciplined, energetic, prudent, and dogged Prussian manner." With such Prussian efficiency, the work would be completed by the end of 1869—or so Strousberg assured the Rumanians.[25] In the meantime, he negotiated for further concessions.

But technical difficulties, Rumanian obstruction, and actual mismanagement gave the lie to Strousberg's effusive optimism. Progress was slower than anticipated, and the rival firm of Ofenheim opened its railway with great fanfare while Strousberg's crew fell ever further behind. By early 1870 J. M. von Radowitz, the new Prussian consul general, arrived in Bucharest. A scion of an old and politically eminent family and a man of superior wit and intelligence, Radowitz was at the beginning of a distinguished diplomatic career. When he left Berlin in January 1870, Bismarck had told him that he was to reckon with Strousberg "as with a power, and in harmony with him to care for the extensive German interests which he represented there." Radowitz met Strousberg before his departure—and disliked him at once. But he realized how all of Berlin had fallen under the spell of this great "operator [*Macher*]": "From the royal princes and the first aristocratic names down to the smallest capitalists, everybody participated in Strousberg's promotions." The great "railway king," as he was also called, lived in flamboyant extravagance; his very ostentation was of course proof of the stability of his ventures. In any case, Radowitz complained at once that Strousberg's affairs cost him more time than anything else in Bucharest, and it was a refrain that Prince Charles, Bleichröder, and others were to echo. Strousberg was to cost many people money, and a few people, by their own estimate, years and years of their lives.[26]

Radowitz reported that a hostile Rumanian press was screaming that foreigners were once again mulcting Rumanians, while hoping all the time that the same foreigners "would buy the press's silence with gold." In Rumania, Prussian emissaries did not succumb to the usual diplomats' temptation of identifying with or defending the host country. They were staggered by what they took to be the venality of Rumanians—and perhaps a greater cultural contrast than between self-conscious Prussian rectitude and Rumanian insouciance in matters of corruption would be difficult to imagine. Radowitz warned that "so excited, so impatient, so highly avaricious a people as the Wallachians" would not wait indefinitely for results from an operation that foreigners were undertaking for their own profit. Radowitz feared that a great wave of anti-German feeling would sweep over Rumania— and cause great embarrassment to Prince Charles and his father because both were thought implicated in the Strousberg affair. Radowitz had already rebuked Strousberg's agent for always pretending that Prince Charles backed every one of Strousberg's moves. He ended his twenty-eight-page report— Bismarck detested long reports—with the hope that at least *some* part of the railroad could be opened soon; then, despite rumors and delays, there would be no real danger to the shareholders. Much would depend on Strousberg's forthcoming visit to Bucharest; if only he would behave circumspectly! Perhaps the Prussian ministry could guide him into more prudent paths.[27]

But the situation went from bad to worse. Strousberg encountered ever new obstacles: every piece of machinery, every track, every skilled laborer had to be imported and brought to the construction site over nonexistent roads. He dismissed his agent and quarreled with his subordinates in Rumania. The "railway king," reported Radowitz, made a practice of treating his men contemptuously but had always been able "to assuage their feelings with cash-jingling satisfaction."[28] There was mismanagement and disaffection in the Strousberg empire.

Radowitz's reports grew more ominous, and Bismarck, though pre-occupied with the Franco-Prussian war, followed the unfolding disaster closely. By the late spring and summer of 1870, Strousberg's shares began to drop, and Radowitz received anxious inquiries from all over Germany about the fate of the venture. He warned Bismarck that a multitude of "small people" stood to lose their savings, though, of course, the "big" people looked no more kindly on a loss of capital. Approximately 50 million taler were at stake, almost all of it in German hands.[29]

By August 1870 the shares had dropped from about 70 to around 43. The market was but a harbinger of further disasters: it was discovered that the Rumanian representative for the railway bond issue, Herr Ambronn, had obliged Strousberg by exchanging gilt-edged securities (a company invest-ment of its assets until it actually needed all the cash for construction ex-penses) for questionable securities issued against Strousberg's other, and increasingly shaky, enterprises. Strousberg was using money earmarked for Rumania to shore up his other ventures in jeopardy.

By September, Ambronn disappeared altogether. His flight confirmed people's worst fears, and Bucharest was outraged. Concurrently, the Moldavian landowners began to charge extravagant prices for their worthless land which Strousberg needed for railway construction. It had been understood that "expropriation committees" would designate the necessary land and decree just compensation for the owners. Instead, prices suddenly shot up, and Rumanian courts upheld the exorbitant demands. Radowitz, more exasperated every day, explained to Bismarck that all foreign representatives in Bucharest agreed that "it was the highest time to think of *serious* measures to save the interests of those under our protection from the steadily worsening corruption of Rumanian justice and officialdom."[30] Bismarck's answer from Versailles was swift and devastating: he ordered Radowitz to adopt the strictest neu-trality and not even to use his personal influence on behalf of German interests. Rebuked and repudiated, Radowitz replied that he would of course heed his new instructions but noted that even Prince Charles had always favored his pressure on the Rumanian ministry.[31]

Bismarck was annoyed by the whole matter, and his restraint bespoke no affection for the Rumanians. Earlier, when Radowitz privately raised the possibility that he needed more than his salary of 8,000 marks to entertain in the way that Prince Charles deemed desirable for the German representa-tive, Bismarck dismissed the plea with the remark that he thought Charles's idea a little infantile: "Such degenerate people cannot be held in check through good dinners but through a few strong battalions."[32] Bismarck's con-tempt for the Rumanians was boundless, and it was no doubt further en-couraged by the wild pro-French sentiment that swept Bucharest at the time of the Franco-Prussian war. To be pro-French was also to be implicity anti-Charles, and the common saying in Bucharest was: "We cannot go to France to fight the Germans, but we shall do it here."[33]

In the fall of 1870 Bismarck was concerned more with Russia's intention to denounce the Black Sea clauses of the Treaty of Paris and the likely repercussions of this on England than with Rumanian affairs. He ordered the

Foreign Office to try to line up Austrian, Russian, and Turkish support for a joint *démarche* in Bucharest and at the same time authorized Radowitz to make informal representations that Prussia could not be indifferent to its interests. Bismarck hoped the other countries would recognize that the collapse of Strousberg would threaten all foreign enterprises in Rumania.[34] His Austrian colleague, Count Beust, adopted a tough line at once, but the czarist government expressed its distrust of Strousberg and refused all cooperation.

The attempted internationalization of Strousberg's troubles came too late. The Franco-Prussian war, meanwhile, depressed the stock market and threatened Strousberg's liquidity—and thus his whole intricate, audaciously built empire of railroads, real estate, and industrial enterprises. In mid-December Strousberg dispatched a desperate plea to Bismarck, who at the time was fighting his own hard battles in Versailles. The great financier was afraid that two weeks hence he would be unable to pay the 2,500,000 taler in semiannual interest on the Rumanian obligations. He claimed that he had already lost 4 million taler by having had to sell securities at low prices in order to maintain his various businesses—some of which were essential for the Prussian war effort. All the Berlin bankers envied and opposed him; hence the state should grant him a loan of 2,500,000 taler against the security of 5 million taler in shares of some of his other enterprises. He thought his request a normal one,

> but it is my misfortune that in the country in which I live and for which I believe I have done a great deal, I have encountered nothing but animosity and odious adversity. . . . Despite the losses incurred during the war, I believe I can designate myself one of the richest men in the land. I attach no weight to this fact, however, because money plays no role with me. . . .[35]

Strousberg also mobilized the duke of Ujest to put pressure on Bismarck—with the surprising result that Bismarck, in a handwritten note, urged the royal government as well as William to help Strousberg. "As far as I know, the livelihood and property condition of many families depend on the several Strousberg enterprises." Strousberg's failure to pay the interest rates would constitute a "calamity."[36]

This willingness of Bismarck's to use state funds to help a private venture—and to do this in the middle of a war—suggests that he was always more accommodating and less doctrinaire in these matters than later historians have believed. It did not take the depression of the 1870s, the formal shift to protectionism in 1879, or the imperialist venture to make Bismarck willing to bail out domestic enterprises in trouble.[37]

Bismarck's colleagues in Berlin demurred. They doubted Strousberg's capacity to repay a loan. Camphausen explained to Bismarck that they agreed that large parts of the Rumanian securities "belonged to little people who were enticed by the lure of relatively high interest and clever publicity to put their savings in this venture. The drop in these papers is very likely to hit some of these people very hard. But I cannot consider such a property loss—which anyone risks who buys speculative issues, and the Rumanian shares must be counted among these—as a calamity which the Royal Government with the help of state credit has an obligation to prevent."[38]

Despite Bismarck's support, Strousberg's last-minute effort to stave off disaster miscarried. The storm that followed was even worse than Bismarck had anticipated. Strousberg announced his inability to pay the semiannual interest on January 1 but promised payment in March. He also alleged that the Rumanian government, having "guaranteed" the interest, was responsible for its payment, while the government insisted that its responsibility was contingent on the completion of the railroads. The shares dropped precipitously, as German investors thought they had been defrauded by the Rumanians, and Rumanians thought that they had once again been defrauded by foreigners, this time abetted by their own dynasty. The situation in Rumania had deteriorated even before this latest blow: the state coffers were still empty; the two parties in parliament were at loggerheads and united only in their hostility to Prince Charles; and the so-called Protecting Powers assured Charles of their benevolent disinterest in Rumanian affairs. Charles was alone—and by late February 1871 his father thought his abdication so likely an event that he already planned alternative domestic arrangements for his son.[39]

The Strousberg affair had all the makings of a grand imbroglio: a huge amount of money was involved (variously estimated at between 150 million and 200 million marks; by comparison, the entire Prussian state debt in 1879 amounted to only 1,300 million marks); the original contract between Strousberg and the Rumanian government had been carelessly drawn up, and thus the issues in dispute proved obscure, leaving infinite room for legal recriminations; mutual distrust was all-pervasive. Germans and Rumanians at least had the solace of their national prejudices: they expected no better from each other. Prince Charles was caught in the middle, without the comfort of easy recriminations. He was blamed by all. No wonder the whole Strousberg affair left him "not an hour's peace."[40] But then it left no peace to anyone who had the misfortune of becoming involved in it. For a while it threatened to blow into a major international crisis.

Bismarck's strategy remained the same as before: he tried to cow the Rumanians by organizing a united front of the major powers in Bucharest. Only the Austrians supported him wholeheartedly. Meanwhile he was put under strong pressure from the German holders of the Rumanian shares; in February they organized themselves and clamored for government help. "The Committee for the protection of the threatened interests of Rumanian railroad obligations" submitted a formal petition to Bismarck duly signed by 580 owners of 2,117,700 taler of such obligations, requesting him to persuade the Rumanian government to pay the guaranteed interest. They explained that "because [Strousberg's] co-concessionaires inspired especially in Silesia such a high degree of certainty and highest trustworthiness," Silesians were most deeply involved. Radowitz estimated that Silesians held nearly half of the 50 million taler invested by Germans.[41] Bismarck realized that not only the pennies of small investors but the large fortunes and credibility of some of the king's most prominent servants were at stake. It would not advance the monarchical cause to have thousands of subjects aggrieved because some of the king's men had lured them into a speculative venture that was tinged with fraudulence.

While the Rumanian parliament was debating the future of the railroad concession, Strousberg served an "ultimatum," as the indignant Radowitz described it. In effect, Strousberg demanded the right to issue new bonds in the name of the Rumanian government in order to pay for his present liabilities, despite the fact that he was supposed still to have a building fund of 9 million taler. He also threatened with vague demands for "indemnities." At the time, Radowitz insisted to Bismarck that Strousberg and not the Rumanian government was responsible for the interest payment; in his memoirs he was to assert the opposite. Radowitz interpreted Strousberg's ultimatum as evidence that he was seeking a way of repudiating his responsibility and blaming the Rumanian government "for an ensuing catastrophe." Worse, Strousberg pretended that the German government would back his demands. Radowitz complained that Strousberg's behavior was "highly incorrect and that the inequities and injuries which he undoubtedly suffered at the hand of the Rumanians could not absolve him from his heavy responsibility for a threatening catastrophe." The only hope was that "in the last minute" Strousberg's co-concessionaires would insist that the interest be paid; after that, a compromise could still be arranged. Without it, the characteristic Rumanian attitude "which thinks it 'patriotic' to harm foreigners as much as possible" would prevail and would lead to complete expropriation. Radowitz had little sympathy for any of the principals in the dispute; he cared for German prestige in Bucharest and for the protection of the small investors.[42]

In the end, the Rumanians unwittingly came to Strousberg's rescue. On March 22 a Rumanian mob broke into the hall where Radowitz and the German colony were celebrating William's birthday. For hours the mob was allowed to run amok. In the ensuing melee several Germans got hurt—while the Rumanian police and army stood idly by. Radowitz was outraged, for in those halcyon days diplomats still regarded civility an enforceable norm. Hours after the event, Radowitz urged Charles to dismiss the entire government—which Charles did. Next, he placed his abdication in the hands of the former regents and asked Radowitz "to implore Bismarck that in the railroad matter the concessionaires should be put under great pressure to pay the January coupons." The prince's honor depended on an acceptable compromise. Even at the moment of abdication, the railroad question was uppermost in Charles's mind.[43]

Eventually, Charles was persuaded to remain on the throne, and a new conservative and, by previous standards, capable government took over. But Bismarck could now be much more brutal than before: the Franco-Prussian war was over, and the Rumanians had supplied sufficient cause for toughness.

He demanded reparations for the outrage committed and threatened the Rumanians with an immediate appeal to their suzerain, Turkey, in case Germany was not given satisfaction. It was a weapon that the Rumanians found most offensive; it reminded them—as it was intended to do—of their legal tutelage vis-à-vis the old Empire. The Rumanians paid, seethingly. Bismarck remembered and used the threat in the next round of trouble.

And still the Strousberg affair dragged on. In the late spring of 1871 the Rumanian government and Strousberg worked out a compromise, but the Rumanian Chamber rejected the plan and promulgated a law that canceled the original concession and decreed the virtual confiscation, with later compensation, of the railways already built. Bismarck was furious and appealed to the sultan for redress; endless complications arose, and Radowitz let off steam by the unusual method of contributing anonymous poems denouncing cheating Rumanians in the pages of the Berlin satirical paper, *Kladderadatsch*.[44] Prince Charles came to believe that Bismarck had launched a "diplomatic campaign [against Rumania]. . . . The question Strousberg is no longer a question *of right* but a question *of force*."[45] But Bismarck had no way of using his superior physical power—a difficulty not unfamiliar to great powers today that have to deal with the outraged and outrageous reactions of a poorer people plotting confiscation.

The immediate issue in this immensely complex question was whether Strousberg or the Rumanians would resume interest payments; if neither, the company would collapse. For Bismarck it was a never ending provocation, made more serious by William's insistence that his aristocratic friends must not be allowed to lose their investments. For the Rumanians it was a question of pride and power; for Prince Charles it became a matter of personal honor—and political survival. If he obliged the Germans, he offended the sensibilities of his own people; if he defended the Rumanians, he would lose German support against Russia and Turkey. No other matter plagued him as much or, as he often said, cost him so many hours of the day or years of his life. It was so tangled a story that later historians dealt with it neither correctly nor objectively.[46]

Bismarck's efforts at hectoring and bullying proved unavailing. He hoped that a concerted international action would force the Rumanians to yield for fear of being cut off from the European capital market. Lord Granville, however, refused all cooperation, because he thought it "a purely commercial issue." Meanwhile, the pressures on Bismarck mounted, as the unfortunate holders of Rumanian bonds organized and appealed to the public via pamphleteering and to the king in quieter and more effective ways.[47] Finally, in the fall of 1871, Bismarck dumped the whole matter on Bleichröder and Adolph Hansemann of the Disconto-Gesellschaft. To the former he explained that the German government was at the end of its tether: "If he [Bleichröder] could succeed in reaching a settlement, 'he would earn God's reward' and he would render his country and the Imperial Government a service that could not be too highly assessed."[48] Bleichröder obliged—and hoped for more mundane rewards.

Bleichröder had followed the Rumanian debacle for some time. In July 1871 Schwabach wrote him about this "mad affair" and reported that one of his clients, Prince Reuss, was worried about his Rumanian investment and annoyed that Bleichröder had urged him not to sell his shares at an earlier time, when the price had not yet fallen as much. Bleichröder also discussed the crisis with William, whose most immediate entourage had a considerable stake in the affair.[49] William's aide-de-camp, Count Heinrich von Lehndorff, was the brother of one of Strousberg's co-promoters. Lehndorff and William were "grateful and reassured" because Bleichröder was taking an interest in the Rumanian affair.[50] Bleichröder hoped to persuade the monarch to translate his benevolent concern for German investors into an active policy. William was bountiful with his thanks and may have given discreet help to some of his paladins.[51]

Bleichröder and Hansemann took charge of the Rumanian horror in October—with what must have been great reluctance. For Bleichröder it proved an eleven-year sentence. For both financiers it required an immense amount of time, patience, and capital. Neither man made a sou, but both received something more precious to Prussian plutocrats than money: ennoblement. In his poetic recital of the Rumanian tangle, cited below, Bismarck asserted that Bleichröder had demanded ennoblement as the price of intervention. He certainly earned it.

Bleichröder and Hansemann had to operate on several fronts simultaneously and agreed to an informal division of labor. Bleichröder served as the chief negotiator with the Rumanians; the German Foreign Office and foreign statesmen regarded him as such. Hansemann looked after the negotiations with Strousberg and, more important, devised the ways and means by which the wretched railroads could actually be built.

It would be wearisome in the extreme to detail the intricacies that followed—*Kladderadatsch* depicted them in an appropriate cartoon. Bleichröder and Hansemann had to found a new joint-stock company to take over the interests of the old Strousberg company; they appealed to the owners of the original bonds to surrender them, and by November 1871 more than 50 million taler's worth of the old obligations had been placed in their hands. The new company had to find an additional 15 million taler with which to complete the railways. It had to reach an agreement with Strousberg (who promised to pay 6 million taler as compensation for the building funds which had been converted into dubious securities and, after a few years, defaulted on his promise),* and had to negotiate a new contract with the Rumanian government, which would in turn have to be ratified by a wildly

---

* Dr. Strousberg himself ended in a Russian jail for bankruptcy in 1875; at the urgings of his old companions, notably Lehndorff-Steinort, the German Foreign Office, under Bismarck's prodding, tried to have Strousberg released, at least long enough to settle his tangled affairs in Germany. William I, who had helped his noble friends, nevertheless disapproved of the company they had kept, and when he heard of Strousberg's conviction greeted the duke of Ujest: "Good day, Dr. Ujest, how is the duke of Strousberg?" Herbert Bismarck to Radowitz, 24 June 1876, GFO: Türkei 104. Marion Gräfin Dönhoff, *Namen die keiner mehr nennt* (Düsseldorf, 1962), p. 186.

suspicious and xenophobic Parliament. To boot, Hansemann, declaring "I cannot build railroads in Rumania," wanted the experienced Royal Austrian Railway Company to take over the actual construction and running of these railways.[52]

Bleichröder had to persuade the Rumanian government to sanction the new plans which he and Hansemann had drawn up. The Rumanian Chamber was particularly incensed at the idea that yet another foreign company would be involved; deputies denounced this new "rape." For Bleichröder it was a struggle between his tenacity and the cunning evasiveness of Rumanian ministers and Parliament.

Bleichröder had several trumps in his hands: he worked hand in glove with Bismarck, whose undiminished anger at the Rumanians occasionally spilled over to Bleichröder as well. The German Foreign Office routinely submitted to Bleichröder its correspondence concerning Rumanian affairs and his efforts there. Bleichröder also managed to orchestrate foreign *démarches* in Bucharest. By conferring with Count Károlyi, the Austrian ambassador in Berlin, he persuaded Vienna to put pressure on the Rumanians. By mobilizing the Paris Rothschilds, he succeeded in having the French government declare in Bucharest that "as one of the Protecting Powers and in order to save the Rumanian government from further complications, it recommends the acceptance of the compromise with Mr. Bleichröder and his companions." Le Sourd, the French consul in Bucharest, who delivered the message, knew that this *démarche* destroyed the Rumanians' last hope for foreign support. A few weeks later, the Rumanian finance minister, Mavrogheni, came to Berlin to establish relations of "mutual trust" with Bleichröder and to discuss the prospects for completing the railways on schedule.[53]

The Rumanians finally capitulated and agreed to let the new German company engage an Austrian company to build the Rumanian railroads that should already have been completed. Even Prince Charles was outraged by German pressure and deeply resentful of Bismarck's high-handedness at mobilizing the power of his state because "some capitalists had thrown their money into an industrial speculation." As far as Charles was concerned, as Lord Granville had said earlier, the matter was a purely commercial one. Charles's father, Prince Karl Anton, though often critical of Bismarck's ruthlessness, rebuked his son: he, too, blamed the Rumanians for defaulting on their guarantee and, more important, admonished him to remember that "at present the Germanic element has the greatest capacity for life and future and that only in a *reasonable* connection [*Anschluss*] with that element can the Rumanians find the basis for remaining masters of their future."[54] Needless to say, this kind of arrogance did not encourage mutual understanding.

The several new conventions were signed in 1872, and the construction of the railways was pushed more efficiently, but there was always a new crisis that required sudden negotiations between Bleichröder and the Rumanians. The main line was completed in May 1873—the very month when the collapse of the Vienna stock market ushered in a new economic crisis for central Europe. The Rumanian railways suffered from the decline in trade, and by 1874, before the last line originally envisioned by Strousberg was put into operation, the Bleichröder-Hansemann Company needed new capital to pay for increased costs.

Bleichröder's attitude on the occasion of this particular crisis can be gleaned from a letter he wrote to Hansemann. It is one of the few letters that has survived; mostly the two friends conversed. Bleichröder reminded Hansemann that his House had already advanced nearly 2 million taler to the new Rumanian Railway Company; according to their original agreement, he assumed that the Disconto-Gesellschaft must have advanced nearly 4 million taler. Bleichröder now categorically refused to advance "even one more taler." It was doubtful, he added, that the money lent to Strousberg would ever be repaid in full. (It was not.) The new needs could be met by the Disconto-Gesellschaft or by the Austrian Railway Company (which Bleichröder thought had always dragged its feet)

or thirdly, and I commend this to your consideration: if neither the Disconto-Gesellschaft nor the Austrian Staatsbahn is ready to make these advances, would this not be the right time to seek new advances from our old associates who ordinarily do not participate in a venture by name only but cannot ever get a high enough percentage share of an enterprise: the Seehandlung, M. A. von Rothschild, Sal. Oppenheim and the Darmstädter Bank. The Seehandlung, which has done so much for Hungary, should be ready with the same amount for Rumania, which is much better off.[55]

Bleichröder's happy thought of enlisting nominal partners seems not to have worked out.

There is every reason to suppose that Bleichröder's potential losses were even greater than the 2 million taler he mentioned to Hansemann. If we can rely on repeated statements that he and Bismarck made to foreign diplomats, it would appear that Bleichröder had lent the great magnates who had fallen in with Strousberg considerable sums of money—against the shaky security of their Rumanian shares. In this way, Bleichröder's own stake in the solution of the Rumanian mess was very considerable indeed.

In the event, Berlin and Bucharest once more fell to wrangling over the terms of the new issue. The same hopeless dance began afresh: Bleichröder pushed Bismarck, who sought to push the other powers to press the Rumanians to oblige, while the Rumanians found the renewed demands insufferable and the pressure humiliating. Prince Charles complained to Bismarck and to his father that the Germans were placing him in an impossible predicament. The Rumanians, he wrote his father in January 1875, were in the midst of negotiating a trade agreement with the Austrians, but "if we do not settle the railway question, then none of the great powers will conclude a treaty with us—Prince Bismarck will see to that."[56] And no sooner was another compromise reached than the Balkan turmoil followed by the

Russo-Turkish war brought on new complications. Bleichröder and Hanse-mann marched from partial success to partial success—and still the fate of German investors remained precarious. By the mid-1870s the income of the existing line dropped sharply, as did the price of the shares. By then, Bleichröder and Hansemann had but one goal: to force the Rumanian government to buy the railways and exchange all outstanding obligations for guaranteed Rumanian state securities. Rumanians balked at this enforced nationalization at a high price, and the affair dragged on for some more years.[57]

While Bleichröder continued his labors on behalf of German Junkers and himself, international Jewry redoubled its efforts to bring help to their op-pressed brethren in the East. The 1870s marked the high point of such efforts. Western Jews, still quite certain of their newly gained and ever stronger position, still untroubled by the first rumblings of a new anti-Semitism in their own countries, resolved to use their power and influence in order to organize collective European pressure on east European governments to improve the lot of the Jewish minorities.

After 1871 the forms of Jewish collaboration changed. The Alliance Israélite was French-dominated, and non-French Jews began to resent the power of Paris in their affairs.[58] By the end of the decade some of Bleich-röder's English correspondents began to make slighting remarks about the Alliance. ("Is not the Alliance Israélite Universelle a gigantic humbug? What influence has it?!")[59] National groups asserted themselves vis-à-vis the Alliance, though it remained an important collective body—important enough even in its declining years to become the symbol of international Jewish power. In fact, the informal cooperation of wealthy Jews corresponding with each other, consulting with their coreligionists in the press and in parliament, and pleading with their respective governments achieved more than did the Alliance. Of all these efforts it has been said, "There was a kind of concert of European Jewry."[60] What appeared to some as a concert struck others as a dissonant conspiracy.

Rumania became a test case for Jewish power. The Rumanians con-tinued to be peculiarly anti-Semitic and peculiarly vulnerable to foreign pressure. In the 1870s Rumania was the prime target; Jewish groups every-where sought to mobilize public opinion so that Rumanian discrimination and anti-Jewish riots would cease. Even American Jewry played a prominent part; through the good offices of the bankers Seligmann, American Jews persuaded President Grant to appoint an American Sephardic Jew, Benjamin Peixotto, as unpaid American consul in Bucharest.

Bleichröder, however, became the main political instrument for Western Jewry. He found himself accountable to Bismarck on the railway tangle and to his fellow Jews on his efforts to win Bismarck's support for Rumanian Jews. It was not an easy role to play, and often all sides were dissatisfied with him. Still, he was in a strategic position—after all, Bismarck continued to need him in Rumania—and for a long time he thought that Bismarck would heed his pleas.

In late March 1872 Bleichröder—freshly ennobled—reminded Bismarck "of the loathsome persecutions which the Jews living in Rumania have repeatedly suffered and now suffer again in Ismail, Kasa, etc. at the hands of the brutal and fanatical masses." He appealed to Bismarck's "well-known humanity" so that Germany would join the protests of the English, French, and Austrian consuls on behalf of these Jews. Bismarck put in the margin of Bleichröder's plea "Fiat," and instructed his consul general to second these *démarches* and to tell Prince Charles

> orally and confidentially what a wretched impression in Germany and in other foreign countries these renewed persecutions of the Jews create . . . the more so as their coreligionists exercise a not inconsiderable influence in the press, in politics, and in far-reaching circles and how therefore any weakness of his government in that regard would weaken Prince Charles personally.

Charles should realize that anti-Semitism was inexpedient—whatever the morality of the matter. Bismarck informed Bleichröder that he had given the appropriate orders in Bucharest.[61]

Bleichröder in turn informed the Alliance Israélite. Paris had congratulated him on his ennoblement, and on the day that he wrote Bismarck he also acknowledged their congratulations: ". . . You may be certain that not the least of my pleasure [about the ennoblement] comes because I see in it a sign that the prejudices against our people are vanishing. I feel myself now all the more obliged to use my insignificant influence on behalf or our oppressed coreligionists in Rumania. . . ." A few days later, he reported that his intervention with Prince Bismarck had "great success" and informed Paris "confidentially" of all that Bismarck had told him.[62]

Bleichröder's private efforts coincided with the founding of a Berlin Committee for Rumanian Jews—its very organization constituted an implicit rebuff to the Alliance. It was a distinguished committee, including the well-known scholar Moritz Lazarus, the popular Jewish writer Berthold Auerbach, and Bleichröder's brother Julius. Bleichröder himself remained aloof, thinking no doubt that he could be most useful in his customary and more congenial behind-the-scene role.[63]

The Berlin Committee boasted to Paris of its successes: a great deal of money had been collected. "Other things will follow. In the next few days, I will send you evidence of our activities in the press. You may already have heard of an anti-Rumanian agitation on the Berlin stock market."[64] The Berlin Committee also urged the organization of an international conference on the subject of Rumanian Jewry; Julius Bleichröder, temporary head of the Berlin Committee, wrote to Paris that such a general conference (which was held in Brussels in the fall of 1872) should deliberate on how "through *united* energies we could strive for a permanent improvement in the material and moral conditions of the Jews in Rumania."[65]

These efforts were widely noticed. The success which Jewry had in arousing gentile opinion can be gauged from a remark made in May 1872 by Lord Odo Russell, Bleichröder's friend, who wrote to the British foreign secretary: "If you can do anything for the protection of the Jews in Rumania you will earn golden Laurels in Germany."[66] Bismarck's Berlin as the champion of Rumanian Jewry—was this the face of a new, liberal Germany, as so many anti-Semites alleged?

It is unnecessary to record all the different efforts of Bleichröder or of Jewry generally. The next great issue came in the mid-1870s, when the Rumanian government wished to conclude trade agreements with the Great Powers—both for commercial reasons and in hopes of gaining a kind of de facto recognition of independence. The key agreement was of course with Germany; the Rumanian Jews appealed to the Berlin Committee to see to it that the treaty stipulated the equality of all religions; otherwise even German Jews engaged in trade in Rumania would be subject to Rumanian restrictions. The Berlin Committee mobilized its parliamentary friends, especially Eduard Lasker, in order to block passage of the treaty unless it stipulated equality. Rumania objected to such a clause, and the German government accepted the liberal position that under the circumstances the treaty should not be signed. The various Jewish groups rejoiced.[67]

Was Jewish pressure the decisive element in shaping Bismarck's policy? In November 1877 Bleichröder wrote a confidential letter to Bismarck in which he expressed "the deepest gratitude of the Rumanian Railway Company for the high protection so benevolently granted; the delay in concluding a commercial treaty enabled us to sign a convention with the Rumanian government" which would hasten a compromise between German creditors and the Rumanian state. Actually, in early 1877 Bismarck used other threats as well in order to make the Rumanians realize that they had no choice but to yield on the railway issue—and had done so at the express request of Bleichröder, who expected the Foreign Office to second his efforts.[68] There is every reason to suppose that in Bleichröder's mind the endless negotiations with the Rumanians over the railways and the pressure over the Jewish question were two separate issues, joined only in his person: by obliging Bismarck in the railroad question he earned a still greater right to claim his protection for the Jews. Did Bismarck see it in the same light? Or when did he perceive the link that was almost implicit in Bleichröder's letter: by being tough on the Jewish question one might force the Rumanians to be compromising on the railroad question? For many years, Bismarck may have seen the two issues as complementary. No doubt he was always more interested in German fortunes and prestige than in Rumanian Jewry, but for a while he was willing to bully the Rumanians on both issues, especially as such bullying coincided with his general political outlook and reflected his contemptuous feeling that the Rumanians and their Jews deserved each other.

In 1876–1878 Bismarck had no particular interest in rebuffing the Jewish community or publicly dissenting from the liberal rhetoric of the West. There were, of course, practical considerations as well. He probably saw in Rumanian Jewry a marginally useful "Germanizing" influence in Rumania.* Most important, of course, was Bismarck's concern for the German investors, and this concern was Bleichröder's "special weapon" in the Jewish question. Sometime in 1878–1879 Bismarck must have come to realize that he could use the international concern over Rumanian Jewry as an instrument by which to coerce the Rumanians on the railroad question. It was a gradual shift in Bismarck's thought, reflecting changed political realities. Bleichröder seems to have been slow in realizing Bismarck's change of priorities that threatened his own hopes.

In the years 1877–1879 Bismarck groped toward a new order in the Reich. The sudden reappearance of the Eastern Question gradually forced Bismarck into fundamental changes in his diplomacy as well. For the Rumanians, the new crisis presented altogether new opportunities and dangers, and hence the tempo of Rumanian developments, including those affecting the fate of Jewry, quickened.

In 1875 the Balkan peoples, except for the Rumanians, revolted against Turkish rule. The Turks suppressed these outbreaks, but the Great Powers hoped to impose on them new reforms that would benefit their Christian subjects. For that purpose an Ambassadors' Conference was summoned to Constantinople in January 1877, and it was a reasonable inference that questions affecting Rumania would be discussed as well. Accordingly the various Jewish bodies concerned with Rumania sought to have the Jewish question placed on the agenda of the Conference.

Bismarck's State Secretary Bülow pledged German support of Jewish claims at the Conference, but the latter came to naught, and by April 1877 Russia declared war on Turkey.[69] The ensuing war dramatized Rumania's plight: she was caught between a decrepit Turkey that still claimed a humiliating suzerainty and an aggressive Russia whose troops had entered Rumanian territory to reach the Turks—and whose minimum war aim was the reconquest of Rumania's northern province of Bessarabia. The Rumanians forced themselves into an uneasy alliance with the potential despoiler, and discovered to their surprise—as did Europe—that the Russians were not so strong nor the Turks so weak as expected. The famous defense of Plevna ("one of the few engagements which changed the course of history") stalled the Russians until December 1877 and brought Rumanian troops into action against the Turks.[70] An armistice was concluded in January, and for the next few months the peace of Europe depended on whether Russia would so moderate her demands on Turkey that Great Britain would desist from de-

---

* In 1888 a new German consul arrived in Jassy and remembered later that "all trade was in the hands of the Jews. By hard work, frugality, economy, and tight cohesion they prevented the rise of the Rumanian traders. . . . I came to know the Jewish trader most thoroughly. Our German export trade found him a valuable instrument and scored brilliant successes thanks to his nimbleness and inventiveness." Wilhelm Ohnesseit, *Unter der Fahne schwarz-weiss-rot: Erinnerungen eines Kaiserlichen Generalkonsuls* (Berlin, 1926), p. 34.

claring war on behalf of Turkey. In the development of this crisis, Bismarck played a major role—as did Bleichröder in the final, concerted effort to force the Great Powers to insist on Jewish equality in the Balkans in any major international settlement of the Eastern Question.

The end of the fighting signaled to international Jewry that the hour for decisive action was at hand. It was generally expected that a peace treaty would recognize Rumanian independence; once Rumania was declared sovereign, the Great Powers would have relinquished their rights to interfere in its internal affairs and, with that, their right to speak up for Rumanian Jewry. Hence the Jews were determined to marshal all their power to have Rumania compelled to grant equality for its Jews as the condition of gaining its independence. What seemed like simple justice to Jews and to liberals— that a new state about to join the ranks of European powers should conform to the principles of toleration and equality before the law as practiced in the West—seemed to Rumanians an outrageous infringement of a nation's right to sovereignty. It was not going to be an easy battle.

Bleichröder was summoned at once. Baron Alphonse de Rothschild put it to Bleichröder with perfect clarity:

> Let me beg you to use all your powerful influence with your government so that the condition of the Jews [in the East] be regulated in a separate article in the peace treaty; otherwise, given the present anti-Jewish sentiment which clearly exists in Rumania, the worst can be expected as regards the fate of the Jews after the war. On the other hand, you can confidently point to the fact that in all those countries which granted Jews equality and a dignified human existence, our coreligionists have been loyal supporters of their government. Considering the tolerant views of Prince Bismarck, it should be easy for you to proceed in the indicated way, and I anticipate with great eagerness the receipt of your reports on a matter which interests me greatly.[71]

It is unlikely that Bleichröder needed such prompting; still, his own initiative began twenty-four hours after he heard from Rothschild. In mid-January Bleichröder proposed that the larger Jewish communities in Germany should petition Bismarck "for intervention by German diplomacy [on behalf] of equal rights for Jews in the proposed new Rumania." He assured the Jewish leaders in Germany that he would be happy "if my humble influence were to succeed in interesting the warm-hearted Prince Bismarck in the cause of our coreligionists in Rumania and, because I know that I stand high in His Excellency's favor, I think we may reckon with a successful outcome."[72] In this way—and much to the surprise of some Jewish leaders—Bleichröder called forth the greatest collective effort that German Jewry had made until that time. Or so the local leader of the Alliance described it, when apologizing to Bleichröder for his earlier skepticism.[73]

The petition was quickly prepared: it asked for Bismarck's continued help so that in the forthcoming negotiations the German government would insist that "Jews in Rumania should receive the same political and civic rights as Christians. As Your Excellency knows from authentic reports, there is hardly a civilized country in Europe in which the Jews are under such pressure and exposed to such ruthless persecution as in Rumania." Bleichröder informed Bismarck of this petition, and within twenty-four hours received assurances from Herbert that his father "would be pleased to receive [the petition] and to accommodate the wishes therein contained."[74] By the end of the month, on Bismarck's behalf, Bülow formally promised the Berlin Jewish community: "The German plenipotentiary will support all efforts which aim at giving all members of every religious group in the countries under consideration the same rights and freedoms which they have constitutionally in Germany."[75] Bismarck's promise of support could not have been more categorical; indeed, it exceeded the petitioner's original demands.

Bleichröder had won the first round. He sent Bülow's answer to the Paris Alliance and added: "You see from the enclosed that I have succeeded in awakening the benevolent interest of our great statesman for our cause. . . ."[76] By this time Bleichröder had clearly moved to the center of the stage, and it was he who orchestrated the entire Jewish effort between mid-January and the actual meeting of the Congress of Berlin in mid-June 1878. He was in constant touch with Jewish groups and with leading statesmen. From Vienna, he heard encouraging reports on Andrássy's response; similar news came from Rome, Amsterdam, and Zürich. St. Vallier assured Bleichröder and Adolphe Crémieux that if there was to be a Congress and if he were at it, he would indeed regard it "as a duty of justice and humanity to seek the means to ameliorate the fate of the Jews [*israélites*] of the Orient, following the old and generous traditions of French policy."[77] The Rothschilds, of course, elicited similar promises in Paris and London. But the initiators of these well-coordinated efforts knew that for once Berlin was the decisive spot, and Berlin was Bleichröder's "turf."

But there was endless wrangling within the Jewish camp as well. Bleichröder received regular reports from various groups in Rumania, where some of the rich Jews of Bucharest were very much opposed to any foreign pressure on "their" government, while the Jews of Jassy, for example, bombarded Bleichröder with their pleas for international action.[78] The Alliance Israélite also thought that before putting further pressure on the Great Powers, the Jews ought to petition the governments of Serbia and Rumania directly. Bleichröder warned against this with unaccustomed vehemence: "I should make clear to you that I do not believe that the fate of our coreligionists in Rumania will ever be improved except by the superior force of the will of Europe. For some weeks now the Rumanian minister of finance has been in Berlin and in many conferences he has always evaded my queries, and I am certain that neither the Rumanian government nor the population has any sympathies for our demands."* To rouse the will of Europe, he continued, it

---

* Bleichröder's friend Moritz von Goldschmidt had put it more dramatically: "In this lovely Rumania, this excrescence rather than protectorate [*Schmutz- nicht Schutzstaat*] of the

would be necessary to demand the equality of all religions, Catholic, Protestant, as well as Jewish.[79] Paris agreed, but even within German Jewry there were powerful voices that warned against the kind of effort that Bleichröder had now embarked upon. In March 1878, for example, the official Jewish publication in Germany warned against pressuring Bismarck, because Rumanians would view such action as "machinations to harm Rumania in the eyes of Europe and to coerce it."[80]

But Bleichröder continued on all fronts. He was still confident of Bismarck's unreserved support—after all, a final settlement of the railroad question had still to be imposed on the Rumanians. In that connection, in April 1878 Bleichröder "received" the Rumanian prime minister, Ion Brătianu, who on the proper occasion made his own demagogic anti-Semitic remarks. Following an understanding with Bismarck, Bleichröder urged Brătianu to "sell" Bessarabia to Russia; presumably, though that remained unstated, such a sale would give Rumania the wherewithal to buy the ill-fated railways. And nothing less than the Rumanian purchase of the railways could ever redeem German investments. Bleichröder urged Bismarck to push in the same direction in Bucharest, though it remains unclear why it was assumed that the Russians would pay for a province they had meant to take in any case. Bleichröder concluded his report to Bismarck: "As far as the Jewish question [Judenfrage] is concerned, Brătianu is quite willing for the Rumanian government to do something; but he seems definitely not to want full emancipation."[81] There is a kind of aseptical distancing implied in Bleichröder's use of the term Judenfrage. Vis-à-vis Bismarck, Bleichröder felt as a fellow diplomat seeking solutions to questions of high policy; vis-à-vis Jews, he felt as a fellow Jew seeking succor for his coreligionists. To Crémieux he gave a much fuller picture of Brătianu's views; Brătianu had implied that he favored the emancipation of native-born Rumanian Jews but "that the immigrant Jews were an immense horde that would become a permanent danger to the Rumanian people, because once in possession of full civic and political rights they would quickly obtain seats in the Chamber in order to control the Rumanian nation."[82] It is odd that Bleichröder understood the paranoid animosities of the Rumanians so well and still assumed that the will of Europe could be imposed upon them.

Whatever his feelings, his efforts were tireless. In May a new German-Rumanian trade agreement, long in preparation, was about to be ratified; at the last moment, the Rumanian government balked at a clause that would have exempted German Jews living in Rumania from the general prohibitions on Jews that prevailed in Rumania, such as restrictions on residence and

---

Great Powers, the poor Jews suffer, nothing is exaggerated, everything is true, and if so far it has not been brought to light, the terrorism of the rulers and the weakness of the consuls are to blame." Goldschmidt hoped that no Jewish business would have any dealings with "these impudent men of power so that they would smother in the filth they call civilization." Actually Goldschmidt had at first been rather skeptical about the claims of Jewish suffering in Rumania but had been convinced by a formal inquiry that the Vienna Alliance had conducted. Goldschmidt to Bleichröder, 30 Jan. 1877, BA.

occupations. The Austrians had signed without insisting on such a clause, and it was Bleichröder's hope—and that of his fellow activists—that the German government would not. Armed with arguments supplied by Bleichröder, Bülow made a strong speech in the Reichstag, arguing that the German government would never tolerate any discrimination against its citizens based on faith; such discrimination ran counter to the German Constitution. The proposed treaty, Bülow contended, would not in fact allow discrimination against the "300 German Israelites" in Rumania. Eduard Lasker and Bleichröder's old companion Wilhelm von Kardorff demurred, fearing that the treaty could sanction such discrimination. There was unanimity in the Reichstag regarding the sanctity of civic equality and sharp denunciation of any thought that Germany would tolerate "second-class citizens." Was there to be such unanimity on this issue ever again in that august body? The Rumanian government refused to budge, and Berlin refused to sign.[83]

It was a great triumph for Jewry. Bleichröder announced to Crémieux: "We are on the eve of emancipation." Crémieux congratulated Bleichröder on "the brilliant success achieved in the Reichstag, thanks to your excellent efforts and those of the Jewish deputies." It was assumed that Germany's action would set a precedent and that all other Great Powers would similarly refuse to sign commercial treaties that sanctioned inequalities.[84]

More and more, Bleichröder emerged as the leader of the Jewish effort; in moments of false modesty, he disclaimed any special eminence and assured Crémieux, for example, that he was but trying "to follow in his footsteps."* No doubt his newly won eminence caused resentment among German Jews, as it did among gentiles. But he began to feel that the mantle of leadership had fallen on him.

On the occasion of Germany's refusal to sign the trade treaty, he wrote the first of his letters to the ninety-four-year-old Patriarch of Jewry, Sir Moses Montefiore, in London. The rejection of the treaty was a "great good fortune." He added that

in my modest way I am following in your footsteps and likewise concern myself with a warm heart for our poor coreligionists on the Danube. I have succeeded in gaining the weighty support of Prince Bismarck for our troubled coreligionists in Rumania, and in accord with his humane outlook he has promised to put his whole weight behind the demand for the equality of all religions at the Congress which we hope will meet soon.

Bleichröder recalled that he had met Sir Moses in his parents' home thirty years earlier.

Sir Moses complimented him on his work and assured him that "Her

---

* As Bleichröder's children followed in the footsteps of Crémieux's children, who converted to Catholicism in the 1840s—a fact that prevented Crémieux from being elected first president of the Alliance Israélite. Bleichröder to Crémieux, 30 June 1878, AI: IDI; see also S. Posener, *Adolphe Crémieux* (Paris, 1934), II, 140–163.

Majesty's Government has expressed its earnest desire to see the principles of justice and religious toleration applied in all their integrity to the Jews of Rumania, and its intention to use its best endeavors to effect this object." The great philanthropist offered to come to Berlin if Bleichröder thought it might be of service to the cause. For the rest, he too remembered his visit to the Bleichröders' on his return from Damascus: "I am delighted to recognize in my friend's son his father's earnest sympathy and active benevolence."[85]

The German refusal to sign the trade agreement served notice on the Rumanians that Berlin would prove obdurate at the all-important Congress. The Congress opened on June 13. It was the greatest gathering of statesmen since Vienna. Bismarck was elected president, and for the first time he found himself in the company of equals: Disraeli and Salisbury, Gorchacov and Shuvalov, and Waddington were there, and so was Andrássy, the handsome, clever Magyar, "who as a person had something extraordinarily winning, a mixture of *grand seigneur* and gypsy."[86] The agenda was long, and the disputes concerning Bulgaria and Bosnia-Herzegovina could still wreck the outcome. The hope, largely achieved, was to find a new alignment of Balkan politics, which would reflect Russia's victory over Turkey and yet not substantially augment Russian power, to which Europe could agree and which would have some chance of enduring. Unlike Vienna, the Berlin Congress was a sober, businesslike affair. The Great Powers wanted to conduct their business swiftly—hence the small powers were heard, if necessary, as special supplicants, but not seen as members. As Disraeli put it, "All questions are publicly introduced and then privately settled."[87]

Bleichröder's office became a kind of headquarters of international Jewry. Everybody met there, and thanks to him, the German press carried long stories about the grievances of Rumanian Jewry and about the petitions served on the Congress. He arranged for the delegates from the Alliance Israélite to see Bülow immediately after the opening of the Congress. He himself conferred with Bismarck about the draft of the main petition, and he saw him again on the day before the opening of the Congress and once more received Bismarck's solemn assurances of support.[88] He saw the other participants, including Disraeli and the charming, cosmopolitan Count Shuvalov, who, unlike his chief Gorchacov, was not unfavorably inclined to the Jewish cause.

For the principals, the Jewish question was obviously marginal, though inescapable. French Foreign Minister Waddington first raised it on June 24 in connection with Bulgaria. That country had fewer than 10,000 Jews, and the Congress ordered that all its citizens, regardless of creed, should enjoy equal rights. The all-important principle had been established where it hurt least; in quick succession, it was extended to eastern Rumelia and Montenegro. When Serbia's turn came, Gorchacov objected. He insisted that there was a distinction between the "cultured Israelites of England and Germany" and the Jews of eastern Europe, who often were "the leeches of their countries." Bismarck rejoined that perhaps Jewish failings were due to the many forms of oppression that Jews had experienced. Waddington and other Western statesmen appealed to the principles of humanity and demanded that new states must recognize the equality of all creeds. The traditional Rumanian rebuttal, that their Jews were foreigners and as such had no rights, was not even considered. On the evening of July 1 the Congress accepted the celebrated Article 44 which in effect demanded that Rumania extend equal political rights, including the right of naturalization, to all its people as a price for the international recognition of its independence.*

Jewry rejoiced. Bleichröder scattered telegrams announcing the great success. In return, he received the most extravagant praise from Western Jewry and from the Jews of Jassy (even a poem likening him to Moses, which he begged them not to publish, as planned). Crémieux cabled "warmest congratulations to an excellent and principal collaborator of so great a work" and Sir Moses Montefiore congratulated him "on the success of your unceasing efforts. . . . I feel sure that with God's blessing all the devoted efforts for the good of our Brethren to which your generous heart has prompted you, and which your great position and influence have enabled you to make in the most influential quarters cannot fail to be attended with the happiest results. . . ."[89] Similar messages poured in from everywhere. At an impromptu meeting of Jewish notables in Bleichröder's home, "those present rose in honor of Bleichröder."[90]

On July 3 Bleichröder entertained the Congress at dinner. Disraeli, Shuvalov, Waddington, Andrássy, Herbert Bismarck—all the great and not so great, except Bismarck, who never attended private functions, were present. An Austrian diplomat wrote home about the "grand dinner at Bleichröder's, the local Rothschild. It was the best dinner I have ever been to."[91] We will note Disraeli's description below (Chap. 17). It was Bleichröder's greatest moment, a fitting climax to what briefly seemed to be the triumphant end of his Rumanian endeavors.

Flushed with victory, Bleichröder sought to press on and wrest from Russia a promise of emancipation as well. To this end, he received Count Shuvalov, the brilliantly successful ambassador to London, and sought to impress on him the need for Russia to adopt the principles of equality that Europe had just decreed for the Balkans. Shuvalov assured him that "he had already repeatedly suggested the emancipation of the Jews in Russia but that until now he had not succeeded; he confidently hoped that after the signing of the peace Russia would give various freedoms to its people, including equality of religion." The two men agreed that Bleichröder should urge Bismarck to put pressure on the Russian ambassador in Berlin to the

---

* The text of the controversial Article 44 read: "In Rumania the distinction of religious creed or confession cannot be brought up against anyone as a motive for exclusion and incapacity, as regards the enjoyment of civil and political rights, admission to public employment and honors, or exercise of different professions or industries. The freedom and open practice of all religions shall be assured to all citizens of the Rumanian state, and also to foreigners, and no obstacle shall be placed in the way of the hierarchic organisation of the various communions, or of their relations with their spiritual chiefs. Citizens of all Powers, merchants or others, shall be treated in Rumania, without distinction of religion, on a footing of perfect equality." R. W. Seton-Watson, *A History of the Roumanians* (Cambridge, 1934), p. 350.

same end. Like Bismarck, Bleichröder was captivated by Shuvalov. He wrote Crémieux and Montefiore "about this noble and high-minded person . . . a man of great intelligence and an equally great heart . . . who would keep his word come what may." Bleichröder anticipated that he would soon become Russian premier.[92]

Montefiore and other Jewish leaders warned Bleichröder against trying to go for broke; Russia was not Rumania, and any effort to coerce Russia would fail. Montefiore imparted his own principles to Bleichröder:

> . . . the best way to obtain the cooperation of the Emperor of Russia and his ministers is to show our confidence in their desire to ameliorate the condition of the Jews. . . . Nor need I impress on your mind the lesson, which history so clearly teaches us, that the social and political condition of a large religious community can only be gradually raised. . . . It also appears to me most important that every effort should be made to induce our wealthier coreligionists in the East to do all that lies in their power to educate and raise their less fortunate Brethren.[93]

It was with a full heart that Jewry thanked the individual statesmen and that Bleichröder organized a particular address of thanks to Bismarck. In the history of Jewry, July 1878 stands out as a moment when because of its own power and influence and by virtue of universally held principles, the fate of Jews in East and West seemed at last safe and propitious. The principle of equality had been formally enshrined; Rumanians had been forced to swallow it, and the presumption of most Western Jews that emancipation would win ever new ground received clear confirmation. No wonder Bleichröder sent the most extravagant of his epistles to Bismarck, a few hours after the Congress had adopted the principle of equality.

> The first sentiment of all those hundreds of thousands who after so many years of oppression and persecution have had their dignity and human rights restored to them is a deep, deep prayer of thanks to the Universal Creator to implore Heaven's Grace for the man who with effective energy and high-mindedness brought the principles of humanity and civilization to their implementation. I can join these prayers today only with a feeble pen. . . . May Your Excellency accept the assurance that no heart has ever beat in deeper devotion or fidelity for Your Excellency than that of . . . Bleichröder.[94]

In more measured tones, the Jewish communities sent their formal thanks as well: "[W]ith joyous pride we view the great deed which took place in Germany's capital city in an Areopagus headed by the Chancellor of the German Reich. . . . Our gratitude is profound, rooted in the confidence that whenever humanity needs a champion, Germany will raise its voice and can never be ignored."[95]

Would Bleichröder have felt quite so content had he known that on his personal letter was written—almost certainly in Bismarck's hand—"*Juden-dank*"? Had he read the story in the *Times* that "Prince Bismarck had consented . . . to lend his powerful aid [to the Jews in Rumania], and the Berlin Israelites promised to fulfill a condition to be placed on his consent—namely, to support the Conservative party on the occasion of the coming elections"?[96] Was anything like this ever spoken of explicitly? Could he have known that a few months later William would remark to a friend: "There were many things decided there [at the Congress] that did not please me; for instance, the emancipation of the Jews in Rumania; but I was sick and was not allowed to do or say anything"?[97] Nor perhaps did Bleichröder and his associates sufficiently heed the warning that the Rumanian foreign minister gave to a Jewish deputation at the time of the Congress: "You are gravely mistaken, however, if you believe that foreign intervention can force us to give you equal rights. We are independent and masters in our own house."[98] On the morrow of the Congress's decisions, a leading Rumanian paper wrote defiantly: "We will not give up Bessarabia; we will not take the Dobrudja, nor shall the Jews have their rights; and we will use force rather than submit to the conditions imposed upon us."[99]

After the first few weeks of exultation, Bleichröder came to realize that his work was far from done, that neither Jews nor Junkers had yet been salvaged. Did he really think that the Rumanians would swallow their anti-Semitic fears and meekly bow to the will of Europe? The answer seems to have been yes—such was his faith in the total efficacy of powerful protection. No one seems to have given much thought to the problem of what to do with a recalcitrant Rumania. Would the Great Powers preserve the solidarity with which they prescribed the principle of equality and collectively withhold recognition from Rumania? Would Bismarck's seeming solicitude for Rumanian Jewry continue at a time when he thought his worst opponents at home were principled liberals, most of whom he dubbed Jews? Would the Great Powers allow the Jewish question to determine their whole policy to Rumania and to the Near East generally? Bleichröder was to discover that the Rumanian affair dragged on and on, and under far less auspicious circumstances than had prevailed before the Congress. Once more, he needed to work simultaneously on several fronts and make sure that his various allies did not desert him. He now became entangled in the most intricate maneuvers and contradictory interests of the Great Powers. As far as Jewry was concerned, he was still the key man, holding in his hands the decisive threads. He felt responsible to them—and gradually saw his leverage declining.

Rumanians of every stripe were at one in their resolution not to give Jews full rights. There was some danger in 1878 that anti-Jewish riots might give vent to these popular feelings.* Prince Charles recognized the near-

* The best-known Rumanian historian, N. Iorga—whose nationalist passion outstripped his historical scrupulosity—put it rather quaintly: "This new humiliation could very easily have

unanimity with which his people opposed the dictate of Europe; his government was willing to make feints in the direction of acceptance, to grant, for example, immediate naturalization to those Jews who had fought in the Rumanian army. The majority in the Chamber opposed all concessions. Nationalist pride and widespread fear of the consequences of Jewish emancipation produced universal obstinacy, disguised by occasional gestures of deferential hypocrisy. The Rumanians simply did not believe that Europe would really insist on these onerous sacrifices. Was it not enough that Rumania surrendered Bessarabia in accordance with the treaty?

At first, Rumanian speculations about Europe's likely indifference seemed justified. Within three weeks of the adjournment of the Congress, Andrássy informed the Rumanian government that realizing the difficulties of implementation, Vienna would soon send a fully accredited minister to Bucharest anyhow.[100] Russia followed suit, and Rumania sent forth the first of a series of emissaries, hoping that Europe would take vague promise for actual performance. Bleichröder and the whole network of Western Jewry now concentrated their efforts on preventing the Great Powers from recognizing Rumania before equal rights had been granted.

In early October 1878 Bleichröder complained to Bülow that the Rumanians had begun to torment the Jews and urged him that recognition of Rumanian independence and of Charles's new title as "Royal Highness" should await the fulfillment of Rumania's treaty obligations. Once again, Bülow made Bleichröder's position his own and instructed German ambassadors accordingly.[101] Bülow was Bismarck's trusted secretary for foreign affairs; he was also a friend of Bleichröder's. His sudden death in October 1879 was to rob Bleichröder of his one ally in Berlin who really believed in the inherent justice of emancipation.

In the fall of 1878 Bleichröder tried to mobilize appropriate pressure in Paris and London. Gradually a common front emerged. Bleichröder urged the eighty-three-year-old Crémieux to intercede with Waddington. The latter gave Crémieux the most categorical assurances that France would not send an envoy to Bucharest until "the Jews had obtained what had been unanimously accorded to them. That is our will and that of Britain, which marches with us in the same path and with the same thought." Disraeli made a similar pledge to Bleichröder in his personal letter: "England is resolved, that the Treaty of Berlin shall be observed, both in spirit and to the letter. I should hardly think that your great friend would be satisfied with any other course." And even before Disraeli's letter, Bismarck had informed the Powers that Germany would withhold recognition until Rumania had fulfilled her obligations. As regards the equality of rights, the Rumanians, embarked on an opposite course, deceived themselves if they thought they would gain recogni-

---

evoked the first anti-Jewish persecutions in Rumania but the ministry was very clever and thus avoided this misfortune." Earlier incidents he tended to blame on the Jews themselves. N. Iorga, *Geschichte des Rumänischen Volkes im Rahmen seiner Staatsbildungen* (Gotha, 1905), II, p. 363.

tion in any case. German public opinion would not accept any other solution. At the end of the month, when Rumania asked the Powers for recognition, Bülow made it clear that the price of recognition was prior emancipation and the establishment of complete religious equality.[102]

But there was hardly a moment of peace for Bleichröder and his associates. Crémieux wrote Bleichröder that he had a "sad presentiment" that the Rumanian machinations would succeed: "*Hélas!* and that will be for you, so devoted to the great cause, a painful sorrow. Your friend M. de Bismarck, on whom we have counted, abandons his position, which should have, and could have, dominated everything and, as he draws closer to the Pope, he backs away from protecting the Jews [*Israélites*]. . . ." Bleichröder, however, could reassure Paris that Bismarck had given him the most clear-cut assurances that Germany would not recognize Rumanian independence until the provisions of the treaty had been fulfilled.[103] From that time forward, with ever greater vehemence, Bismarck appeared as the champion of Rumanian Jews—and only his extravagant anger at the Rumanians could have tipped people off that his true motive was not the disinterested pursuit of principle or even the satisfaction of a domestic pressure group.

In the fall of 1878 Bismarck's firmness blocked all efforts at early recognition. The Italian government, on the other hand, came close to justifying Crémieux's presentiment: it designated a minister for Bucharest, but the pro-Jewish deputies in the Rome parliament thwarted such action—to say nothing of the bristling rebukes that Bismarck administered to the Italians. At a later time, when Italy once again vacillated but returned to the Franco-German fold, Bülow told St. Vallier: "We are charmed to have her rejoin us . . . but experience has taught us not to count on her too much for tomorrow."[104]

Even England weakened—for its own reasons of state. The Rumanians solicitously spread word that Russia had made new demands on them for special military access rights across Rumanian territory; the English, still violently fearful of Russia, sought to bolster Rumanian resistance and hence wanted to proceed with recognition as quickly as possible. Salisbury so informed Waddington and Count Münster. Bismarck reacted with unexpected vigor. Salisbury reported to Russell that "Count Münster has pressed me very earnestly not to recognize Roumania until Jewish disabilities removed. Finding me disinclined to wait, he has pressed French Ambassador to combine with Germany and isolate England on this point."[105] Waddington told the British "that the German government was very stiff in the matter; and that he imagined that Prince Bismarck must have given some pledge respecting it to M. de Bleichröder or some other influential member of the Jewish community at Berlin."[106] Bismarck *was* stiff in this matter and warned would-be deserters from a common front that if they recognized Rumania, Germany would no longer be interested in the execution of the treaty's other provisions.

Actually Bismarck's strategy was far more complicated than that, and its very inscrutability aided its success—a familiar story in Bismarck's statecraft. For almost a year after the Congress of Berlin, he rebuffed all efforts at easing the pressure on Rumania. His policy coincided with his wish to have a close entente with France. But there were other reasons, diplomatic, domestic, and purely personal. The railway question was always in his mind, though he rarely mentioned it in the winter of 1878. At the end of January 1879, for example, Salisbury inquired whether the Powers might not be satisfied with Rumania's granting equal rights to "indigenous non-Christians" —that is, leaving the question of foreign Jews (who usually enjoyed some protection from their country of birth) in abeyance.* The Germans took a high-minded line and lectured the British on the sanctity of treaties and the importance of religious liberty.[107] By the end of February, Bismarck took a more characteristic, bellicose stance. He impressed on Lord Russell "his aversion for the Rumanians in language too violent to be placed on official record. . . . 'He accused them of dishonesty in regard to the stipulations of the Berlin Treaty, of arrogance towards Russia, and of insolence towards Germany, and deplored that they were not within his reach, so as to administer the whipping to them they so richly deserved.' "[108] With dazzling candor, he told St. Vallier that he had said to the Rumanians that "I do not want to hear them mentioned as long as they had not executed the condition fixed by the Treaty of Berlin for their admission to the rank of independent states. . . . I care for the Rumanians *as I do for my glass when it is empty.*" In the Rumanian matter he had a chance to help "the Jews, whom I need to coddle, win over and who can be very useful to me in Germany and whom I like to pay in Rumanian money; don't you call that funny money [n'appelez-vous cela de la monnaie de singe]?"[109] On another occasion, he gave St. Vallier a colorful account of the Rumanian affair and of Bleichröder's role in it.†

Bleichröder also unburdened himself to St. Vallier: "The Rumanians'

---

* A knowledgeable Rumanian Jew wrote Bleichröder that approximately 60 percent of the 250,000 to 300,000 Jews living in Rumania were native-born. He emphasized that exact statistics were impossible to come by. Dr. H. Hirsch to Bleichröder, 10 Feb. 1879, BA.

† St. Vallier reported that Bismarck began by pouring out his anger at the Rumanians, "at the crooks and savages . . . with a liveliness and brutal energy one often encounters in his assessments." The ambassador reported the conversation verbatim: "My other motive [for being anti-Rumanian] has to do with a more private matter which for us, however, has an urgent and distressing character; you are familiar with the Strousberg affair; you know what bloodletting it has inflicted on German capital; close to 200 million francs have been swallowed up in these Rumanian railways which yield nothing and the value of which is hardly one-tenth of the cost; our greatest lords and our bootblacks believed that Strousberg would present them with a gold mine and a great many risked the best part of what they possessed, believing the promises of this adventurer. All that is buried now in the Rumanian mud, and, one fine day, two dukes, one general who is an aide-de-camp, a half-dozen ladies-in-waiting, twice that many chamberlains, a hundred coffeehouse owners and all the cabmen of Berlin found themselves totally ruined. The Emperor took pity on the dukes, the aide-de-camp, the ladies-in-waiting, and the chamberlains, and charged me with pulling them out of the trouble. I appealed to Bleichröder who, on condition of getting a title of nobility which as a Jew he valued, agreed to rescue the Duke of Ratibor, the Duke of Ujest, and General Count Lehndorf [*sic*]; two dukes and an aide-de-camp saved—frankly, that is worth the 'von' bestowed on the good Bleichröder. But the ladies-in-waiting, the cabmen, and the others were left drowning, and even Bleichröder's three Moses [whom he had dredged out of the water] were not so entirely saved but that they have to face each year some nice trial in which they are sued for two or three million marks which they cannot pay since their domains of Ratibor, Ujest, etc. are totally mortgaged in exchange for the

bad faith is such that it has but one objective: to *dupe us* and to *rob us.*"
Prince Charles, though German and a Hohenzollern, "has become worse
than the others, he has made himself a Rumanian in his soul, and in hopes of
gaining popularity, he strives to surpass his subjects in duplicity. I have
furnished Prince Bismarck with certain proof . . . that Charles is at the head
of those who want simultaneously to deceive Europe by sweet words in the
Jewish question and to ruin us in the railway matter." Charles had no intention of accepting the obligations of the treaty; after recognition, the Rumanians
"will continue to persecute the Jews, their slaves and their milk cows, in the
face of a Europe deceived and flouted." As far as the railroads were concerned, Bleichröder explained, the Rumanians were being outrageous. Europe
had invested 400 million francs in that enterprise; 250 million came from
Germany and 150 million from small *rentiers* in France (this rather large
French investment seemed a kind of afterthought or a convenient exaggeration). Most of the German money represented the fortune "of some of our
grands seigneurs and of several personages at the court who, upon the demand
of Prince Bismarck and the wish of the Emperor, I have saved from complete
ruin in lending them large sums against their railroad shares or obligations,
which are now in my hands." The Rumanians had ceased paying interest on
the railroad (in 1877) and were now making efforts to evade the resumption
of payments. The only alternative was the sale of the railroads, but the Rumanians were trying to obstruct the running of the lines and destroy the
matériel in order to buy them for a low price. Like Bismarck, Bleichröder
was ready to sell the railroad to the Russians; but his main concern, he said,
was with the Jewish question. "We have proof that in these two questions
we are confronted by a general conspiracy of all the Rumanians—from the
Prince to the last deputy—against the interests of Europe."[110]

Bismarck's anger mounted as he realized that the whole Rumanian
tangle was getting worse and that his usual weapons seemed ineffective in
this case. It was an open secret in Berlin that the question irritated him more
than any other issue in foreign affairs. In the late spring of 1879 the British
were again pushing for a halfway measure that would clear the way to
recognition while giving only indigenous Jews naturalization. Once again,

---

Bleichröder guarantee. There is but one way for everybody to get out of this trouble and that
it to try to sell the Rumanian railways. . . . [At present] the Rumanian government exploits the
owners' misery with usurious barbarism; by annoyances, injustices, extortions, it wants to force
them to abandon the railways to the government for a crust of bread . . . every day our
German engineers and workers are being beaten, maltreated, imprisoned, cheated, robbed of
everything, and we can do nothing to help them attain justice. That is why I just told you
that I wished I could use naval ships as in Nicaragua to obtain satisfaction; but that is impossible, and neither do I have balloons [*aerostats*] to send in German troops." He urged
the dukes to sell the railways, perhaps to Austria or Russia—for cash because to lend money
to these great defaulters would be a mistake. The dukes thought that Bismarck might object to
the Rumanian railways being sold to Russia, but he had reassured them "that it was a matter
of indifference to me if the Rumanian railways and indeed all of Rumania should fall into
Russian hands." The French ambassador warned the Quai d'Orsay that this was perhaps not
quite so pleasant a prospect for France. 26 Feb. 1879, MAE: CP: Allemagne, Vol. 27.

Bismarck warned that opportunistic deviation in this matter would diminish his interest in the execution of the rest of the treaty. He leaned all the more heavily on the French and told St. Vallier: "The Franco-German entente was the only means . . . to obtain from a small government, made insolent by its weakness, the fulfillment of one of the most important clauses of the Treaty of Berlin."[111] At the end of June Bismarck once again threatened to summon an Ambassadors' Conference in Constantinople, and insisted that if it failed, Turkey should resume its suzerainty over Rumania. Nothing so enraged the Rumanians as this threat.

Bismarck tried every avenue and put some hope in Austrian pressure on Rumania. He spoke to Andrássy of sending German warships through the Dardanelles in order to blockade the Rumanian coast. No wonder Andrássy explained to his consul in Bucharest that the Germans were implacable, though Bismarck's anger was not the result of his "benevolence for the Israelites" (the original phrase was "for the coreligionists of Herr Bleichröder") but of his anger at Rumania's treatment of German material interests. Andrássy's warnings had an effect in Bucharest.[112]

In July 1879 the tempo of negotiations suddenly quickened. On the fifth the special Rumanian Chambers charged with preparing the constitutional changes necessitated by the imposition of Article 44 decided to reaffirm what for long had been the unofficial contention of Rumanians: "that there were not, and that there never had been, any Rumanian Jews; there were merely Jews who had been born in the Principality, but who had never been assimilated either in speech or custom by the Rumanian nation."[113] Hence all Jews were subject to naturalization procedures, and the Chambers insisted that these be done on an individual basis. Prince Charles's government countered this flagrant repudiation of the Treaty of Berlin with a compromise solution of its own, but the Chambers refused to budge, and the government resigned.

Europe was outraged by what a later, pro-Rumanian historian called "proposals which were little short of a challenge to Europe."[114] The Rumanians sought to mollify opinion by painting lurid pictures of what emancipated Jews would do to Rumania. The Austrian consul reported that in the Jewish question the Rumanian government had failed to collect even the most primitive statistical information; everything was arbitrarily presented: "This is surely a main factor in rendering more difficult the solution of the question and to confuse it so that nobody can draw the line between poetry and truth. . . ."[115] The Rumanian Chamber had forced its government to seek an alternative means of appeasing Germany.

The Rumanians sent their finance minister, Dmitri Sturdza, a German-educated statesman with relatively moderate feelings on the Jewish question, to Berlin to negotiate with Bleichröder on the railroad question and with the German government and the French ambassador on the Jewish question. It was known that Bucharest hoped for a compromise: Sturdza's concessions on the railroad question should be balanced by Bismarck's retreat on the Jewish question.[116] He came armed with face-saving concessions from Bucharest: to placate Europe, he proposed that there would be five categories of Jews—essentially embracing those who had been born in Rumania and had in some way, either in education or through military service, distinguished themselves—who would be naturalized at once. On July 8 St. Vallier was told that the German government found these proposals "absolutely inadequate." The French government agreed, and for the rest of the month the two governments consulted on the possibilities of finding a compromise. Sturdza was a resourceful negotiator. He assured Berlin that the Rumanian people would never accept full emancipation, that they considered the Jews "a social scourge," and that if Rumania were forced to accept Article 44, chaos would break out, followed by the resignation of Prince Charles and the immediate reoccupation of Rumania by Russian troops. Indeed, Russian agents were already flooding Moldavia and inciting the population against the pro-Jewish plot of the West; the existence of these Russian agents Bleichröder confirmed independently. It was a clever threat, given England's susceptibilities; it was even more clever than the Rumanians could know, because Bismarck was moving toward an entente with Austria, and Austria would consider a Russian return to Rumania as a grave threat to herself.

Significantly, St. Vallier noted that even Bleichröder agreed that the five proffered categories would cover most of the Jews who really wanted naturalization.* Sturdza also told St. Vallier that the Rumanians were seriously interested in the repurchase of the railways. St. Vallier reminded Waddington how important this was to Bismarck and added that it would be to France, too, because 80 million francs of French capital were involved.[117]

Sturdza and Bleichröder spent all of July haggling over the wretched railroads. Everybody was eager for a solution: Sturdza, because he began to understand that if Rumania settled the railway issue, Bismarck might give up his high-minded stand on the Jews; Bismarck, because he wanted to be rid of the whole Rumanian business; and Bleichröder, because he wanted to cut his losses. Sturdza—whom Bleichröder considered "one of the most decent men in Rumania"—was clever enough to delude Bleichröder into thinking that the Rumanians were more eager to solve the emancipation than the railway business. No doubt, Bleichröder wanted to believe this as well. On July 21 Bleichröder informed Bismarck that negotiations for the purchase of the railways by the Rumanian government had broken down because of Sturdza's insistence that the seat of the new railway company would have to be in Bucharest. "It is impossible for me and my heirs to accept such a responsibility. Financially I have made the greatest possible concessions, but the gentlemen insist on . . . this legal point and over this negotiations have broken

---

* Throughout the fall and winter of 1879–1880, Goldschmidt insisted that the full and immediate emancipation of all Jews in Rumania would be a mistake. He did not think that "*everything* that the Rumanian Jews hoped to achieve could be attained at one time; perhaps it is better that in those countries [*sic*] one does not do violence to the Christian population by full emancipation and thus circumvents excesses, considering that in Austria we have attained the present condition only gradually, and we are, God knows, better people than our Rumanian coreligionists." Goldschmidt to Bleichröder, 5 Feb. 1880 and earlier letters, BA.

off."[118] Dismayed, Bismarck demanded further information on "the nature of the deal that Bleichröder has in mind." If a new company were to have its seat ~till in Berlin, Bismarck feared "that we would have even greater annoyances in the Rumanian railroad affair than before."[119] Radowitz, temporarily at the Foreign Office, sent Bleichröder "very confidential" letters, all breathing Bismarck's sudden impatience—and veiled threats that he would not support the interests of German shareholders indefinitely.[120] Bleichröder hardly needed such admonition. He had his own personal reasons for finding a satisfactory end to the railway tangle and in purely financial matters proved more accommodating than Hansemann. Sturdza was back the next day, and the negotiations resumed. On the Jewish question, Sturdza told Bleichröder that he thought "the principle [of emancipation] had to be recognized, but concerning the modalities further deliberations had to take place." Vague assurances like these and hard bargaining on the railroads kept Bleichröder in Berlin, and he wrote Herbert, who with his father was enjoying the waters of Bad Kissingen: "How intensely important the final settlement of the railway business is for the financial position of my House you can infer from the fact that despite my rather precarious health I prefer to stay here and wait until matters are at a clearer stage before I turn to Homburg for a rest."[121]

After some hard bargaining, Sturdza yielded on the railways, and Bleichröder reported to Bismarck that an agreement was at hand and that Sturdza was off to Bad Kissingen for a rest. Could Bismarck receive him, even for a short audience? Bismarck was most unwilling. Bleichröder had to press the issue, arguing that it would strengthen Sturdza's hand against recalcitrant colleagues in Bucharest; Sturdza himself confided to St. Vallier that he was afraid of Bismarck's hectoring; but finally Bleichröder succeeded in getting a reluctant Bismarck to see an intimidated Sturdza. In a curt telegram, Herbert rebuffed Bleichröder's further request that he should be informed of Bismarck's impressions of the interview; his father, Herbert wrote, had no intention of going into details with Bleichröder at this point.[122]

There was a kind of benevolent deceit in the Bismarcks' discourtesy to Bleichröder. He would have been distressed by what Bismarck told Sturdza— just as Sturdza was heartened. Bismarck spoke of the difficulties which Article 44 posed for Rumania, told how the Article had sprung from French and, of all things, Italian initiative, and how Germany could not oppose it. In such matters, he realized, one had to move in stages, not in a forced march. Still, a small country had to accede to international law, and the Article was part of a treaty and corresponded to general principles that prevailed in all civilized states. He regretted that Rumanians had allowed free Jewish immigration earlier, but now all that they could do was to beat the Jews in economic competition. "To improve German-Rumanian relations it was necessary to get rid of the railroad question." Only then could Rumania receive the full benefit of Germany's friendship, which it needed, wedged as it was between two enemy states.

Bismarck pointed the way to the Rumanians; he did not yet abandon the Jewish question, partly because of his concern for the other Great Powers and, more important, because he meant to have the Jews in reserve in case the Rumanians proved recalcitrant on the railroad question. If the Rumanians were in any doubt about the sentiments in Berlin, a letter of William's to Charles's father should have put them at ease. He had always objected to the emancipation demand but had been out of commission at the time of the Congress: "I know from experience what the Jews in those areas—beginning with Poznania, Poland, Lithuania, and Ukraine—are like—and the Rumanian Jews are said to be even worse! The whole Jewish question was passionately defended by the British. . . . [The English] see in *every* Jew a cultured Rothschild."[123]

The summer of 1879 marked one of those sudden crises in Bismarck's life and career in which his political difficulties took their psychosomatic toll as well. He had at last triumphed in the Reichstag and set a new course at home—only to find that William was adamantly opposed to his vision of a new course abroad. We saw earlier that Bismarck had once again to use his last resource, the threat to resign, in order to make William accept his plan for an Austro-German alliance. In all of this, Rumania always played its irritating role. Bismarck's harassment of Rumania sprang from a combination of personal contempt and *raison d'état*; politically, a closer entente with Austria would require a less bellicose stance vis-à-vis Rumania, which Austria regarded as an outpost, however unreliable, against Russia. Bismarck wanted to be rid of the Rumanian question, and the only thing that still mattered to him was the material interests of German shareholders.

The Rumanians sensed the change of wind; their stalling was beginning to pay off. In August they sent their new foreign minister, B. Boerescu, around Europe, hoping by promise and deception to gain immediate recognition. St. Vallier sent Waddington a report on Boerescu, furnished to him by "an absolutely trustworthy" correspondent of Bleichröder's and picturing the Rumanian as a totally unscrupulous man who had betrayed his political friends and embraced his enemies and whose only consistent view seems to have been that the Jews were Rumania's insufferable plague.[124] On the whole Boerescu's trip was a failure, but it could not have escaped him or his cabinet that at a secret meeting he had had with Bleichröder at Bad Homburg, even Bleichröder had begun to back away from demanding the full implementation of Article 44. Bleichröder asked that the principle of religious liberty should be acknowledged, that Jews born in Rumania and not under foreign protection should obtain citizenship upon reaching majority, and that non-Rumanian Jews should receive citizenship after ten years.[125] Bleichröder wrote Crémieux of his interview with Boerescu and explained that the Great Powers were exceptionally eager to reach a final accord with Rumania. Under these circumstances, he thought, "it is necessary that we should content ourselves at the moment with the implementation at least of a part of our desideratum, hoping that the future would bring the full realization of our program."[126] The Austrian ambassador in Paris thought Boerescu should deal directly with the Alliance Israélite, the true instigator of the campaign behind Article 44.[127]

The two issues now moved to their final resolution. In late September Sturdza returned to Berlin with new and less favorable terms than he had offered Bleichröder and Hansemann earlier, but a satisfactory agreement was initialed on October 3. Bismarck had urged speed; with the Austro-German alliance signed at the end of September, he wanted an end to the Rumanian involvement. The new agreement had yet to be ratified by the Rumanian Parliament; Bismarck made it clear to Bleichröder and Hansemann that he could no longer offer them much protection or diplomatic help. He was trying to disembarrass himself of the entire Rumanian question, which meant saving the railway shareholders—and abandoning the Jews. In any case, on the domestic scene, Jewish liberals had become his special target, and some of his anger may have spilled over.

In October the Rumanian Parliament debated the final wording of a constitutional amendment on the Jewish question. A bill refusing any change in the Constitution was narrowly defeated, and a government bill giving rights of naturalization to indigenous Jews (with a nominal list of one thousand Jews to be naturalized at once, including dead and fictitious persons) was adopted, but fatally weakened by providing for individual naturalization. As the Rumanian Parliament moved to this final travesty of Article 44, Bleichröder wrote the Alliance that he thought Germany wanted Britain and France to take the initiative in opposing recognition; by mid-October he concluded that all had been lost.[128]

The rest is anticlimactic. It would have been hard for Bleichröder to disguise for himself the extent of the defeat. In mid-November he received a confidential report from the German consul in Bucharest, assessing the lot of the Jews under the new arrangements: they were still barred from buying or holding property in the countryside, while practice in the cities varied; they were prohibited from becoming lawyers, pharmacists, or rural innkeepers. They were likely to have the right to settle in town or country "if they possessed wealth."[129] And still Bleichröder wrote the Alliance in Paris—which was beginning to be dissatisfied with him—that he was hoping "to save what could be saved" from earlier hopes, but that in any case, and very surprisingly, the Rumanian Jews seemed satisfied with the new laws of October.[130]

Others were less sanguine. A leader of German Jewry, Ludwig Philippson, the editor of the principal Jewish paper, implored Bleichröder for last-minute efforts to prevent recognition of Rumania "after the dazzling fraud" the Rumanian Parliament had perpetrated. His reasons: "In Germany there are now parties displaying considerable activity with the expressed intention of obtaining retrograde changes in our legislation concerning Jews. . . . If the Signatory Powers recognize this put-up job of the Rumanians as adequate, then these sinister parties in Germany would benefit as well. . . ."[131] Prince Charles's father had similar perceptions, if different emotions:

Every affair has its droll side as well: in Prussia the Protestant *Pastorenpartei* has started with some success an anti-Semitic movement, and the conservative party supports this rather dangerous experiment, whereas at the same time the German government gives or at least has given all aid to the efforts of the Alliance Israélite in Rumania—as if the Oriental Jews were better than the Occidental Jews! . . . If this continues, we may see Jew-baiting here, and then the other Great Powers would have to condemn the German Reich if they want to remain faithful to the demands of the Berlin Treaty![132]

The Rumanians continued to stall on the railroad question. Time and again the Rumanian Parliament sought to revise a convention that Bleich-röder and Sturdza had finally arrived at, and time and again the great stumbling blocks were the guarantees to be offered to the shareholders and the ultimate seat of the new company. Bleichröder had insisted that the shareholders should have a first lien on the Rumanian state tobacco monopoly—which the Rumanians found a humiliating condition. The location of the company's headquarters was also a question of substance and prestige—and proved the most difficult of all.

The Rumanians insisted that the headquarters be in Bucharest; Bleich-röder and Hansemann balked at this, and Bismarck fumed because he wanted the matter settled and would have preferred to have the center of trouble moved to Bucharest. In repeated letters to Bismarck, Bleichröder sought to explain his adamant stance. The question was without clear legal precedent; if the new company were moved to Bucharest at once, German commercial law might no longer be applicable, and Bleichröder (and Hansemann) feared that they could be sued by shareholders for having agreed to a move that might damage the interests of shareholders.[133] On both sides there was immense suspicion. After twelve years of wrangling and deception, it would have been surprising if either side proved particularly forthcoming or benevolent.

To Bismarck's intense annoyance, the railroad question dragged on for another three months. The other powers showed signs of impatience, wishing finally to put the Rumanian quarrel behind them. Bismarck wanted solidarity until the railway issue was settled—and used high-minded arguments about the sanctity of treaties in order to secure his practical ends. Through every possible channel Bismarck sought to put pressure on Bleichröder and Hansemann to conclude the negotiations and to expect no further protection from the government. At the same time, with even-handed anger, he threatened the Rumanians with every weapon left at his disposal. When Bleichröder informed him that Russia and Turkey had served some large and dubious financial demands on Rumania, Bismarck instructed Radowitz to make it clear to the Rumanians that "for the time being we would remain neutral about these financial claims . . . but if they should prove hostile or difficult in the railroad question, we would regard them as political enemies and treat them accordingly and would in particular favor these claims."[134] In the face of such treatment, it is little wonder that Prince Charles complained that "the Berlin gentlemen would like to treat Rumania as if it were Egypt." Of course they did—and did Rumanians cherish foreigners any more than Egyptians did?[135]

At the same time, Bismarck sought to restrain France and England from recognizing Rumania, even though there was general agreement that nothing further could be expected on the Jewish question. He told St. Vallier that a few more weeks of "strangulation would do the Rumanians good, before they were allowed to enjoy an independence which they had done nothing to deserve."[136] At the same time—and with what fine cynicism—the German government told the Rumanian foreign minister that unless they ratified the railway convention at once, the Berlin government would declare "the Jewish question unsolved."[137] Bismarck urged the French and the British to maintain a common front with him on the Jewish question—so that he could pressure the Rumanians on the railway question.[138] He was shamelessly honest at this point: he was unwilling to do anything more for the Jews, but he wanted to keep them in reserve, as a last resort.

But his annoyance mounted, and when, at the end of November, Bleichröder once more and routinely raised the Rumanian issue with Bismarck, Herbert wrote that his father was too ill to be bothered anymore: "In the Rumanian matter he cannot do anything now in any case, and since he always opens and reads all of your letters himself, you would contribute to his recuperation if you did not bring them up for the time being unless they are really important politically."[139] Bleichröder sent him some rare old sherry instead, which he could open with impunity.[140] In truth, it must be said that Bismarck's health was at a precarious low at the time.

But no one shielded Bleichröder from the continued daily press of dealing with the Rumanians. By mid-December the Rumanian Parliament ratified the agreement with certain amendments—that Bleichröder and Hansemann rejected. Another deadlock threatened. Prince Charles thought that "the moment had come when the Emperor should utter the decisive word; especially as regards Bleichröder this would not be without success." Instead, the German government again threatened an end to benevolence, and privately Empress Augusta implored Charles's father to use his influence so that Rumania might at last accept the convention and bury the whole issue. Bleichröder also urged Charles's father to intervene, because the final failure of the proposed settlement would bring about the fall of the Rumanian ministry and "then we find ourselves face to face with chaos."[141]

By February 2, 1880—nearly ten years after Strousberg first defaulted—the Rumanian Parliament voted the original convention with but minor modifications, and Hansemann and Bleichröder formally accepted the new text. There was enormous relief everywhere.

The Rumanians now expected immediate and unconditional recognition; they had been led to believe that this would be Berlin's reward for the price they paid.[142] With Austria's help, which both Germany and Rumania had solicited, the German government prevailed on Waddington to draft an appropriate note by which the Great Powers would communicate their recognition. After some more wrangling about the exact wording, and despite

Rumania's insistence that in return for the railroad settlement the Germans had promised recognition without reservations, a note was prepared that stated that the October legislation (concerning non-Christians) had not "entirely corresponded" to the expectations of the Powers, but "on the other hand, trusting in the will of the Prince's government to come closer and closer in the application of these dispositions to the liberal idea which had inspired the Powers . . . ," these powers now recognized the independence of Rumania.[143] The crisis was over at last, and the statesmen of Europe were relieved. William had long fretted at not being able to send a minister to his princely cousin in Bucharest "because of the affairs of the Jews," and the new French foreign minister, Freycinet, was glad that one of the two major problems he inherited on taking office was settled.[144]

For ten years Bleichröder had labored on the Rumanian question. With what result? He had been ennobled, but his coreligionists in Rumania remained debased. He had celebrated his triumph of 1878, when, with Bismarck's full support, the Powers imposed their liberal principles on Rumania. In the decisive period after the Congress of Berlin, Bismarck gradually understood that the whole Jewish question could be used in order to coerce the Rumanians into a conciliatory course on the railway question. Put more bluntly than he probably ever formulated it for himself, Bismarck welcomed the pro-Jewish efforts as a weapon that he could wield against the Rumanians. By encouraging international support for Jewry, Bismarck fashioned an anti-Rumanian weapon such as he could never have obtained for his Prussian Junkers. Gradually he maneuvered the Rumanians into a situation where they came to understand that if they wanted to continue their oppression of the Jews, they had to pay off German creditors. In short, Bismarck—the "warm-hearted, humane" Bismarck, as Bleichröder had called him—proved cynically adept at using the philo-Semitic and liberal principles of western Europe for his own ends; just as he was about to use the anti-Semitic and illiberal principles of the conservatives at home.* He had used the Jews to bail out the Junkers.

Against the skill and power of this supreme opportunist, the much-vaunted machinations of international Jewry proved entirely unavailing. Indeed, their short-lived triumph in 1878 may have quickened their undoing: they had flaunted their power and hence had become an easier target for the anti-Semitic reaction that set in after the Congress of Berlin—and that exploited both the putative power and the real impotence of international Jewry, as exemplified in the Rumanian story.

By 1913, only 361 Jews had been naturalized in Rumania.[145] Of the others, many emigrated to the United States. They, unlike their richer brethren

---

* In his memoirs, Bismarck's assistant Radowitz put it in a succinct, matter-of-fact way: "In 1879 we had to conclude the wretched railroad business . . . and could do that only in connection with the Jewish and the independence question. We had to put the screws on the Bucharest politicians in that way." Hajo Holborn, ed., *Aufzeichnungen und Erinnerungen aus dem Leben des Botschafters Joseph Maria von Radowitz*, II, *1878–1890* (Berlin and Leipzig, 1925), p. 84.

who stayed behind, saved their descendants from the German scourge that two generations later swept over Europe—and that enshrined anti-Semitism as its principal credo. Bismarck, on the other hand, had thought that one could play with human prejudices as one did with humans themselves: at will and with impunity.

If ever there was an episode in which Bleichröder thought he was moving, while in fact he was being moved, it was the Rumanian tangle. There is no reason to think and almost no evidence to suggest that Bleichröder at any time understood his own role in defeating his own purpose.* Indeed, he was tempted to convert a defeat into a limited victory, as shown by the letter he wrote the Alliance on Crémieux's death, at the moment of the Great Powers' unconditional recognition of Rumania:

> I know, however, that the Great Powers impose on the Rumanian representatives the obligation to pursue emancipation in the sense and spirit of Article 44. The solution of the question thus finds itself in a very favorable phase because those who know the Rumanian situation will recognize as I do that a full and sudden emancipation at a time of agitations that trouble the country and incite the population would have led to the persecution of our coreligionists, whereas in this manner the goal is attained without provoking convulsions in that country which in the first place would have fastened on our friends [*uni en première ligne à nos amis*].[146]

The letter suggests that he tried to minimize the discomfort he must have felt between his expectations in the Rumanian cause and the outcome. There was also a certain blindness that marked Bleichröder's letters. But all blindness contains an element of willing self-deception as well. It was that element of self-deception that so ill-prepared him to live amidst the hidden and not so hidden anti-Semitism of his own country.

---

* The one piece of evidence comes from an avowedly unfriendly and injured source, a Rumanian Jew who belonged to a delegation sent to Berlin in November 1879, at the last minute, to appeal to Bleichröder and to the German government not to abandon the cause of Rumanian Jewry. Bleichröder received them and, according to one member present, told them that until now the German government had demanded the full execution of the Treaty of Berlin: "Still, for every government the immediate interests of one's own country must take precedence over one's concern with the humanitarian ideal. Now the Jewish question gives our Chancellor the opportunity of saving the German treasury several hundred millions which in the hands of your government, regardless of party, are very much endangered. This is a price which does not allow Germany to hesitate to enter into negotiations [over the railway issue]." Bleichröder was also supposed to have told the delegation to negotiate directly with the Rumanian government and to prepare a memorandum for Prince Bismarck. No doubt the Rumanian delegate felt much aggrieved at Bleichröder's sudden "realism" and may have sharpened his words. Quoted in N. M. Gelber's unpublished manuscript on the question of Rumanian Jewry, pp. 228–229, BA.

CHAPTER 15

The Reluctant Colonialist

Believe me, sir, had I such venture forth,
The better part of my affections would
Be with my hopes abroad. I should be still
Plucking the grass to know where sits the wind,
Piring in maps for ports, and piers and roads:
And every object that might make me fear
Misfortune to my ventures, out of doubt
Would make me sad.

—The Merchant of Venice, I, 1

Our colonial efforts suffer from the fact that with us it is rarer for capital and energy to be united in one hand than it is in England. As a rule the German capitalist is unsure of himself, a *homo novus*, who does not yet dare to move toward far-seeing ventures, while energetic entrepreneurial spirit is widely disseminated among our unpropertied. . . . The holders of great German fortunes (unlike their English counterparts) still feel oppressed by the fear that they might lose what they have not yet possessed for a long time. This state of affairs is to a large extent responsible for the fact that we are at a disadvantage vis-à-vis England in the colonial competition. . . . Here is also a reason why in Germany the unpropertied has a far greater grudge against his more propertied fellow citizens than is the case in England, and that the ill will of the majority of the people against the rich minority, especially the bankers, plays a larger role with us than with them. . . . Given that envy is the national evil of the Germans, then one can understand, especially from the human point of view, that for the nonmillionaire the spectacle of a millionaire is indeed not a very pleasant one. . . .

—From a governmental memorandum destined for the press, and corrected in Bismarck's hand, June 1889

Bleichröder reached the height of his power at the very time when Europe entered the last, frenetic phase of its expansion. From the 1870s to the 1890s European powers established or extended their control over large parts of Asia and Africa. By 1900, Europe's rule over the rest of the world had reached its apogee—and began its uncertain retreat.

The causes of this last great wave of imperialism have puzzled and divided historians. Why did the Europeans and the Americans supplement or replace "the imperialism of free trade," an informal rule, with this new and costly system of formal annexation and attempted colonization? The debate over this new imperialism has not been an exercise in disinterested scholarship;

our present political concerns have affected our comprehension of the past. Whereas contemporaries of the imperialist age may have beguiled themselves by thoughts of "civilizing missions," saving souls, or serving their own nation, the apparent consensus of today is that European (and American) imperialism has been the discreditable story of ruthless exploitation, of imposing the false gods of material progress on primitive societies that in retrospect lived happily —or at least contentedly—on the margins of the world, ignorant of the blessings of the machine age and the curse of international rivalries.

Imperialism has acquired a sinister connotation; in the political vocabulary of today it bespeaks iniquity as certainly as does racism—which was associated with it—and as does fascism, which often is seen as a particularly malignant outgrowth of thwarted or threatened imperialism. Among some historians and many ideologists, "the economic taproot of imperialism," as J. A. Hobson called it in his pioneering study of 1902, has become an article of faith. According to this view, the many forms of imperialism (direct rule, indirect rule, economic penetration) have as their prime source the desire for material gain. Hobson even pointed his finger at a special class of people, "the great financial houses," that directed the imperial scramble:

> United by the strongest bonds of organisation, always in closest and quickest touch with one another, situated in the very heart of the business capital of every State, controlled, so far as Europe is concerned, *chiefly by men of a single and peculiar race,* who have behind them many centuries of financial experience, they are in a unique position to manipulate the policy of nations. . . . Finance manipulates the patriotic forces which politicians, soldiers, philanthropists, and traders generate. . . .[1]

A description that seems to fit Bleichröder perfectly—but did he conform to type?

An examination of Bleichröder's response to imperialism should contribute some clarification to the general debate on the mainsprings of imperialism, and, more directly, it should throw some light on Bismarck's short-lived conversion to colonialism, despite his earlier insistence on Germany's nonimperial destiny and despite his later protestations of boredom and indifference. Given Bleichröder's place in Bismarck's world, his views on the imperialist venture are particularly important. How did he respond to the many imperial and colonial temptations that came his way? Did he behave according to schema, did he help push Bismarck into the acquisition of colonies that suddenly gave Germany overseas land five times the size of the Reich itself?

He was certainly aware of the dynamism of expansionism, and he was privy to some of the most crassly material ambitions of imperialists, as we will see in his connection with Leopold II; he was often importuned by merchants and fellow bankers. At the same time, he knew from Count Münster and others that expansionism threatened Germany's good relations in Europe. Bleichröder probably had no theory, no consistent view of imperialism, but in the last fifteen years of his life, he was confronted by a series of decisions, and a scrutiny of these decisions may offer us a clue as to his general attitude toward the profitability and desirability of colonial ventures.

Bleichröder became involved in imperial affairs at an early time. He sensed the significance of Britain's purchase of the Suez Canal shares and of her quickened interest in the Near East and Africa thereafter. More important, he was invited to take a direct interest in one of Germany's first overseas outposts, in Samoa, and King Leopold II of Belgium sought to draw him into his Congo venture from 1878 on.

Germany's stake in the South Pacific had been built up by the venerable Hamburg house of Johann César Godeffroy. "The King of the South Seas" the midcentury head of the firm was called. From the 1830s to the 1870s the Godeffroys had expanded their holdings along the Pacific shores of Central and South America; their own fleet carried on their trade. Their major venture overseas came to be concentrated in the islands of Samoa. There they gradually acquired more than 100,000 acres; their sphere of interest extended over an area of nearly 5,000 miles in length and over 2,000 miles in breadth. The Godeffroys developed plantations, and their agents reported that anything would grow. The main product was copra, the hard kernel of the coconut, which was shipped to Germany, where the oil was extracted, while the rest could be used for animal feed. Some 7,500 to 8,000 tons of copra were exported annually. Mother-of-pearl was collected, sea-island cotton planted, and these and other exotic products gave further substance to the dream of Samoa as a land of boundless bounty.[2]

By the 1860s about 70 percent of the commerce of the South Seas was in German hands. At times, the Godeffroys and the German consuls in Samoa, who were their agents, called on German naval support to cow the divided and despoiled Samoans. Local German interests would have liked to bring Samoa under formal German rule. But other powers had their eyes on Samoa as well, largely for strategic and political reasons. New Zealand and Australia showed a growing concern, which to some extent the British Foreign Office had to make its own. As the United States became a Pacific power, it too had its designs on Samoa, and by the 1870s both Britain and the United States had developed rival positions there. The Godeffroys' private empire was threatened by these formidable intruders and by the continuous turmoil in the native government.[3]

In the late 1870s the Godeffroys had more immediate worries. The profits of Samoa threatened to become their undoing: by investing them in industrial promotions during the *Gründerjahre,* they overextended themselves and by 1873 faced imminent bankruptcy. They were bailed out, partly by the British firm of Henry Schroeder. A few years later, they ran into new trouble, and in order to save at least their Samoan holdings a new company, Deutsche Handels- und Plantagen-Gesellschaft, in which the Godeffroys themselves held only a partial interest, was founded in March 1878. Only some of the shares could be sold; to raise needed capital, the company had to offer the Samoan holdings as collateral for a loan from the English banking house of Baring.[4]

Bleichröder followed all this from a distance; his main contact was with Gustav Godeffroy, who in 1872 left the family firm, though at first he retained some financial interest in it; he became a director of the Norddeutsche Bank in Hamburg—which in turn was a principal shareholder of the semiofficial paper *Norddeutsche Allgemeine Zeitung*—and entered on a patrician political career as well. Among Hamburg merchants and German bankers, Godeffroy was something of a rarity: in the mid-1870s he became a fervent protectionist and a vociferous champion of Bismarck's new economic policy. On the side, he speculated in mining and railway shares, as did the rest of his family— and with the same disastrous results. He complained to Bleichröder, with whom he was on close terms, that he had lost a great deal of money in some iron mines; he hoped to entice Bleichröder to salvage the mines and painted a rosy picture of their future: the United States, he argued, needed vast iron supplies for its railway construction. Bleichröder was lavish with advice, but reticent with his funds.[5]

The new Plantagen-Gesellschaft, however, fared no better than the old Godeffroy firm. By January 1879 the head of Godeffroy appealed to Bülow: the new company needed 2,500,000 marks to survive. Bülow acknowledged the government's longstanding and benevolent interest in the German presence in Samoa, but his response was negative: the same economic conditions that had brought repeated ruin to the Godeffroys made it impossible for any agency of the Reich to raise the sums required. Weeks later, Godeffroy again warned of "the disastrous situation" which the company faced and added, "German ethos and German diligence could in a short time create a veritable Eldorado in the South Seas. . . ."* In July 1879 the Godeffroys asked for a loan of 3 million marks, but it was rejected because the ministry questioned the appropriateness of the state's making such a loan.[6]

On December 1, 1879, the Godeffroys announced their insolvency, and both Bismarck and Bleichröder were at once informed of the event. The Prussian minister in Hamburg wrote Bismarck that the collapse of "the old and reputable House" had caused consternation in the business circles of Hamburg, and on the same day, Gustav Godeffroy informed his associates that the family business, with which he was no longer connected, was unable to meet its obligations. He attached a personal note to Bleichröder, his old "friend and patron," explaining the causes of this "deeply painful family event which kills all my joy in life."[7] The Godeffroys, an old Huguenot family, belonged to the patriciate of Hamburg; they were a kind of Buddenbrooks, and their survival was a matter of concern to the state and the business community. Without having been formally asked for help, Bleichröder wrote to Herbert von Bismarck—who but a week earlier had sharply rebuked him for raising the Rumanian matter at a time when the prince's health was so fragile—about Godeffroy's "very important plantations in the Samoa islands. According to my information, England intends to use the [Godeffroys'] embarrassment

* Of a slightly earlier period, an historian has remarked: "At mid-century the news of a Samoan Eldorado was, at its source, the product of design as well as misjudgment and wishful thinking." R. P. Gilson, *Samoa, 1830–1900: The Politics of a Multi-National Community* (Melbourne, 1970), p. 185.

in order to establish a firm foothold there. If His Highness should have any interest in this matter, I would beg you for a word so that I can have myself thoroughly briefed about the whole matter by the brother, Gustav Godeffroy." Herbert replied at once that while his father's health precluded discussions of the subject, he was interested in Samoa, he would welcome further information from Bleichröder, but that despite his interest he would not on his own initiative make available government funds.[8] The rapidity of Herbert's answer and the totally unsolicited remark about the possibility of government help must have indicated to Bleichröder the chancellor's extraordinary interest in the matter.

Accordingly Bleichröder heeded the insistent pleas of Gustav Godeffroy. To save the South Sea plantations would require little capital and virtually no risk; to allow them to fall to England would weaken or destroy Germany's position in the Pacific. Godeffroy and Bleichröder were in the habit of writing to each other about the proper end of all business: the making of money. But on this occasion, even in his private letter, Godeffroy appealed to Bleichröder in a different vein: "So loyal and influential a man as yourself, one so close to the Chancellor, will see to it that the laurel wreath which our iron Chancellor wound for his brow in the old world will not lose a single, if weighty, leaf in the new world." But Gustav's letter was practical as well as poetic: he urged Bleichröder to get in touch at once with Hansemann and with Hansemann's brother-in-law, Heinrich von Kusserow, the head of the commercial-legal section in the Foreign Office, in order to coordinate efforts for the salvaging of German interests in the South Sea.[9]*

At Gustav's insistence, Bleichröder organized a meeting of the Godeffroys, Hansemann, and himself for Sunday, December 14; by the next day a plan for the founding of a new company was drawn up, in the presence of the head of the Reichsschatzamt, Adolf von Scholz, whom the Foreign Office had ordered to attend the meeting. Stolberg, the interim head of the Foreign Office (Bülow had died suddenly in October 1879), informed Bismarck of the plan: a new company was to be founded, with a capital of 10 million to 12 million marks; but the "prerequisite" was the government's willingness to grant "a subsidiary dividend guarantee, sanctioned by imperial law." Bismarck's laconic marginalia was "How much?" Apparently satisfied by the bankers' formula (the state would guarantee a 4½ percent dividend to the shareholders, with the proviso that the total responsibility of the state would not exceed 300,000 marks annually and that the company would repay all such sums), Bismarck authorized the submission of such a bill to parliament.

By the end of December, William accepted the proposed bill, persuaded

---

* Kusserow has rightly been called a "colonial enthusiast. . . . a disinterested imperialist, one of those men whose imaginations were genuinely fired at the prospect of great overseas dominions under the sway of their country even though they themselves had no economic stake in the colonial world." Henry A. Turner, "Bismarck's Imperialist Venture: Anti-British in Origin?" in *Britain and Germany in Africa*, ed. by Prosser Gifford and Wm. Roger Louis (New Haven, 1967), p. 66. The "disinterested imperialist" played a larger role in empire building than Marxists would allow—the more so as interested imperialists were by no means as plentiful as Marxists later claimed.

that without this initiative, the Samoan holdings would fall to British interests. From start to finish, it had taken Bismarck's government a month to formulate a policy, and the very speed of the decision (at a time when Bismarck's health was at a notoriously low point) and the apparent ease with which it was taken suggests that the government did not think of it as such a radical departure and also seems to bear out in this particular instance the old cliché that empires are acquired in fits of absent-mindedness. Bismarck had taken an important initiative in Samoa; few people at the time could have foreseen that this initiative, whether successful or not, would have a lasting effect on Bismarck's own outlook on imperial ventures.[10]

The government's apparent insouciance did not deter others from taking a very serious view of its plans. The free-trade, mercantile press opposed any possible government intervention, as did Hamburg merchants; one of their newspapers objected that "even if the German government wants to carry on a colonial policy (and all evidence suggests that it is not so inclined) it could not find a more unhappy beginning. Must the nationalization [*Verstaatlichung*] of railroads be followed by the nationalization of overseas speculations?"[11] The free traders saw the projected help to the Godeffroys as an extension of Bismarck's new economic policy of protectionism and heightened state intervention. It is not clear whether Bismarck saw it in this light, because he had always been pragmatic, even cavalier, in making available state help for German firms that had encountered difficulties abroad; no doubt, his protectionist victory of July 1879 made him hesitate even less when the Samoan question arose six months later.

The free traders were not the only ones alarmed. Count Münster, devoted equally to Bismarck and the cause of anticolonialism, bombarded Bleichröder with letters denouncing all governmental efforts in Samoa. In mid-December 1879 he warned against any state guarantee: "The citizens of Hamburg are the worst Germans we have, and they use the imperial government only for their own purpose, if they can." On Christmas Day he wrote, "If one now suddenly begins to carry on colonial policy in the Reichskanzleramt, I would be very sorry indeed. . . ." He hoped that Bismarck would reject his subordinates' ambitions, and Münster gave Bleichröder a list of arguments against German colonialism: the cost was prohibitive, protection of overseas bases would be impossible as long as Heligoland was in British hands, and so on. London banks, such as Barings, moreover, had no interest in acquiring the Godeffroy holdings, and the British government would not lift a finger in order to increase British possessions there: "Hence no colonial nonsense, no Samoa swindle!" In the last two weeks of December Münster wrote Bleichröder five passionate attacks on the proposed Samoan venture, recognizing in it the beginning of a policy he feared. No doubt he hoped Bleichröder would dampen Berlin's ardor and perhaps influence the ailing chancellor as well. Münster's warnings must have carried some weight with Bleichröder.[12]

Bleichröder's friend St. Vallier had long been worried about German interests in Central and South America, in Africa and especially in Morocco, and in the Pacific. He warned Paris of this expansionist tendency and thought that for all its absorption in domestic politics, the German government might annex Samoa as a colony, especially as the crown prince favored this.[13] As soon as St. Vallier heard of Godeffroy's insolvency, he again warned Paris of German intentions in Polynesia that would threaten French interests in Tahiti. France, he thought, should expand its own empire in the South Pacific, and not passively watch German and British expansion. (His appeal to action was a characteristic instance of what might be called preemptive imperialism: expand in order to forestall others. This, too, was an important element in the imperialist dynamic.) To lend weight to his warnings, St. Vallier again emphasized the crown prince's "lively interest" in protecting German possessions in Samoa. The crown prince's apparent involvement in this first colonial question casts some doubt on the often maintained view that Bismarck embarked on colonialism in order to embarrass the pro-British, anticolonial crown prince.

St. Vallier concluded: "Finally I learned yesterday from M. de Bleichröder that he has just formed a great financial company, at the demand of Prince Bismarck . . . and under the patronage and with the support of the government." The new society intended to preserve and expand the threatened Godeffroy holdings.[14]

Bleichröder, Hansemann, and Wallich of the Deutsche Bank did found a new company, the Deutsche Seehandels-Gesellschaft, in February 1880. They took over the Godeffroy interests in Samoa, reached an agreement with the Barings, who were nowhere near as eager to claim their pound of Samoan flesh as the German government pretended, and for the rest waited until the promised state support had been ratified by parliament. The progovernment press intoned patriotism, and St. Vallier thought the whole Samoan affair but a prelude to outright annexation of Samoa and quickened German colonialism everywhere. For him, the mainspring of German expansion was the accelerating emigration from Germany, which kept increasing partly because of "the heavy taxes, the burden of military service, the agricultural and industrial crisis; but, independently of the internal situation and the economic malaise, this disposition [to emigrate] belongs to the adventuresomeness of the German spirit, to the character of the dreamer, to the vagabond imagination of the German, and is destined to continue. . . ."[15] St. Vallier saw Samoa in a much larger perspective, as a test case for Berlin's increasing interest in imperial expansion.

The left-liberal opposition in the Reichstag saw the Samoan bill—so infinitely modest in its financial demands—in a similar light. Bamberger took the lead in attacking this "testing ground" for colonialism, this effort to indulge in imperialism and protectionism while pretending all the while that the national interest demanded such action. By a vote of 128 against, 112 for, and 140 abstaining, the Samoa bill was defeated in April 1880.[16] St. Vallier blamed the defeat on Bismarck's long absence.[17] Actually most of the abstainers had gone to the opening of a new production of *Faust*; they preferred the Faustian spirit on stage rather than in policy.

Bismarck made the most of his defeat. For years he referred contemptuously to "Samoan majorities" in the Reichstag which would sabotage all efforts at expanding governmental aid to German efforts overseas. He had found another "patriotic" stick with which to beat his new worst enemies, the left-liberals. Once more they had proved more loyal to doctrinaire illusions of free trade than to patriotic necessity. Bismarck's continuous effort to help the Godeffroy interests involved him ever more deeply in Samoa until, by 1889, this involvement threatened to bring Germany and the United States to the brink of war.[18]

The defeat of the Samoa bill left Bleichröder and Hansemann free to terminate their salvaging efforts. Instead they devised a different *modus operandi*, encouraged by Bismarck, who in a formal letter to them expressed his pleasure that "in the national interest" the banks would preserve these existing enterprises and thus render a great patriotic service, which would be welcomed by the emperor and all other responsible elements in the Reich.[19] The negotiations about the new company dragged on, made more difficult by the reluctance of the Godeffroys to furnish the necessary data, by the unwillingness of the Seehandlung to continue its cooperation after the defeat of the Samoa bill, and by various and sundry obstacles that brought Bleichröder and Hansemann close to abandoning the whole enterprise. What buoyed them up was Bismarck's continued interest and Hansemann's conviction that "if Samoa falls, then all German interests in the South Sea are lost." After months of trouble, after lawsuits against traducers which they initiated and lost, they finally liquidated in the fall of 1880 the Südsee company they had founded a few months earlier and revived a much-strengthened Deutsche Handels- und Plantagen-Gesellschaft.[20]

Hansemann began to take an ever stronger interest in Germany's position in Samoa and New Guinea.* In some of these efforts he retained Bleichröder's participation; both men headed a New Guinea Consortium in 1884 which a year later received Bismarck's authorization to establish a company protectorate on the (unprofitable) mainland of New Guinea.[21] Bleichröder's name was a guarantee of Bismarck's sanction, but otherwise Bleichröder remained prudently passive. None of the evidence suggests that he took any real interest in this misspeculation. His role in the Samoan enterprise, from start to finish, had been modest and reluctant. According to present-day popular wisdom, he should have been pushing; the evidence suggests that he was being pushed. He was pushed by Gustav Godeffroy—who was a close associate, a director of an important bank, and a man indirectly involved in the negotiations that were then being carried out as to Bleichröder's possible purchase of half the shares in the semiofficial *Norddeutsche Allgemeine Zeitung*.[22] To some

---

* Though there is little, if any, evidence to support the recent contention apropos of Hansemann's activities in New Guinea that he "was captive to . . . [the] belief . . . [that] only colonies . . . could assure German manufacturers of markets for their products, keep emigrating Germans within the German empire, and divert the masses from the appeal of social revolution by providing them with an alternative Utopia." Just as there is no warrant for saying that Hansemann had been the supplicant and Bismarck the wary patron. S. G. Firth, "The New Guinea Company, 1885–1899: A Case of Unprofitable Imperialism," *Historical Studies*, XV (1972), 361.

extent, Bleichröder was a captive of his own power: when "for patriotic reasons" Bismarck became interested in the Samoan holdings of the insolvent Godeffroys, Bleichröder would have compromised his position if he had remained uninvolved. After the defeat of the Samoa bill, General Chauvin wrote him: once it became clear that patriotic men of means would help the chancellor despite this setback, it was no surprise to find Bleichröder's name among them—and in the first place. Chauvin could have added: Bleichröder's absence would have been surprising.[23]

And so Bleichröder participated with a modest sum and negligible enthusiasm; the record shows that he wrote Herbert one letter about Samoa. On issues that mattered to him he was not so reticent. He mobilized none of his friends in parliament or in the press. He was constrained by his business associations and his special relationship with Bismarck to enter the Samoan affair; the initiative was not his, nor did he expand his influence. It is fitting that the great archipelago in the South Sea should have been named after Bismarck. It was Bismarck's interest that maintained and expanded the German presence in the Pacific.

Bleichröder had played a modest role at the first public stirring of German imperialism; he had an important hand in the realization of King Leopold II's gigantic ambition in the Congo. Samoa quickened German imperialism, and King Leopold's gradual acquisition of the Congo was the signal for the partition of sub-Saharan Africa. Bleichröder was a close witness to the rebirth of European imperialism, and he came to know the passion for power, profit, and adventure that propelled imperialism. He saw the scramble, but he was most sparing with his own funds.

In the mid-1870s Bleichröder found a royal friend in Leopold II, king of the Belgians, whom he first met when both were taking the waters at Ostend. Leopold was a repository of all the mixed motives that impelled Europe to launch the last great thrust across the seas: a passionate traveler, an adventurer *manqué*, a man filled with nationalist ambition (in 1861, four years before his accession to the throne, he lamented that Belgium's neutrality limited her European destiny, but added, "the sea washes our coast, the Universe is before us"), in whom the poetry of discovery was supplemented by a growing practicality and rapacity. Free traders at the time might echo Cobden's denunciation of the "bloodstained fetish of Empire," but Leopold contended that colonies were a necessity for Belgian exporters and an imperative of humanitarianism. The slave trade had to be abolished, he claimed—and introduced a new slavery of unimagined cruelty. In a candidly materialistic age, all would-be colonists justified their aspirations in terms of money; Leopold always spoke of the profit that Belgian manufacturers would reap from the acquisition of colonies and new markets. But the merchants remained unconvinced, and more and more Leopold resolved to seek power and profit for himself. In the process of building up what turned out to be the largest private preserve in the history of imperialism, Leopold found Bleichröder a discreet and useful helper. Bleichröder, in turn, was attracted by the royal trappings and impressed by the sovereign voraciousness.[24]

Leopold had traveled far and wide; he had been fascinated by Egypt and the promise of the Suez Canal; he had been to the Far East, and legend has it that he came back from an early trip to the Acropolis with the vow that Belgium must have a colony. He kept the dream after he ascended the throne; tiny, neutral Belgium, with its liberal constitution, offered too little scope for his ambitions—and the fact that his neighbors, like the Dutch, already possessed a huge empire, or like the Prussians had created one in Europe, merely spurred his desire. Leopold scoured the map for a colony; he thought of the South Sea islands and entered into indirect negotiations with the Spanish for the purchase of the Philippines. In 1876 he summoned an international conference on African exploration to Brussels, and the next year he was quick to grasp the significance of Stanley's astounding discovery of the upper Congo River. The center of Africa beckoned. By November 1878 he set up a Studies Committee for the Upper Congo, an innocuously labeled forerunner of the later International Association which came to be the vehicle of his personal rule.[25]* A few days later, in one of his first long letters to Bleichröder, Leopold reverted to a theme they had already discussed at Ostend: "Industry suffers everywhere; it is necessary to create new outlets and to do so in those countries where up until now its products had not penetrated and where public works had not been undertaken. From this double point of view, the African continent deserves our special attention."

Leopold gave a brief exposé of his various projects and for the rest announced the visit of one of his principal aides, Baron Grindl, to give Bleichröder a fuller picture of their plans. "He will tell you how charmed I would be if it proved convenient for you and your friends to take part in our enterprise. . . ." Baron Grindl called on Bleichröder, who declined all enticements to give more than his benevolent interest in the Congolese venture. He and Leopold began a cordial correspondence; Bleichröder reported on the political scene in Germany, on Bismarck's state of mind and health, on the health of the royal family. He added such piquant details as that Pope Leo XIII had commissioned Franz von Lenbach to paint a portrait of Bismarck—a sure sign that a new phase had begun in Vatican-German relations. Bleichröder also invested the funds of Leopold's closest advisers. Leopold wrote less interesting letters in the beginning, but graciously signed them "your friend," or "*votre très affectionné.*"[26]

For some five years Leopold organized his efforts with a certain discretion and dispatch, disguising them all the while by his insistence that the open-

---

* The Brussels Committee was to have national analogues as well, and in November 1878 Gustav Nachtigal, himself a Sahara explorer, established the African Society in Berlin, with the same triple goal as had been formulated in Brussels: the discovery of the still-unknown areas of Africa, their opening to civilization, trade, and commerce, and the peaceful abolition of the slave trade. Nachtigal invited Bleichröder to be a founding member—for the price of 300 marks. But it took a special conversation and several letters to have Bleichröder join— three months later. In 1880 he secretly transferred 40,000 francs from Leopold to the Berlin African Society.

ing of Central Africa was an international task, undertaken for scientific and humanitarian reasons. When Leopold sent Stanley back, the French sent another noted explorer, Savorgnan de Brazza, to explore and claim the northern bank of the Congo. In time, the Portuguese became alarmed as well, and the British, though hopelessly embroiled in Egypt, hoped to block Leopold by siding with Portugal. Once his explorations were completed and the International Association had established itself along the Congo, Leopold needed international recognition of his rule, and in that delicate matter he relied very heavily on Bleichröder. In the Congo, Leopold was operating as a private individual; formally he could not rely on the Belgian diplomats abroad, and Bleichröder became his special envoy in Berlin—the decisive capital for Leopold.

In May 1883 Leopold sent Bleichröder the first of his many requests for help. He began by summarizing the history of the International Association, inspired, he said, by the example of the Red Cross and the ancient knights of Malta and St. John. Over the previous five years, the Association had established a route along the cataracts of the Congo; it had opened up the area to the traders of all nations. "The Association . . . has its own flag and does not pursue a national goal; its agents come from all countries. It has never asked for either protection or financial assistance from any government; it lives off private gifts. . . ." What it now needed was an international act of neutralization which would involve no obligations of any kind from any state:

> The Congo Basin has an immense future; we have opened it. Our work hinders no one and all the world could profit from it. Do you believe, Monsieur le Baron, that the German government, which concerns itself a great deal with industry, with the promotion of its development and with the promotion of general prosperity, would be disposed to recognize the neutrality of our stations? You would oblige me if with your usual skill you could reconnoiter the field and let me have your impressions.[27]

Bleichröder's answer seems not to have survived; Leopold's formula of "neutralization," which later that year was also advanced by a committee of international jurists, was gradually abandoned for something even more commanding: recognition of a new and independent state.

The correspondence seems to have lapsed, but not because the Congo had receded in importance. In fact, Leopold's vast encroachments alarmed all other powers, and the future of Africa suddenly preoccupied the chancelleries of Europe. Leopold's position was most directly challenged by the Anglo-Portuguese Treaty of February 1884, by which the British recognized Portugal's dubious claim to large parts of the Congo. Leopold was troubled and Bismarck furious—in fact, the Anglo-Portuguese Treaty set off a period of unprecedented Anglo-German tension. Bismarck now embarked on his own colonial acquisitions, leaned heavily on the Franco-German entente, and briefly became the arbiter of Africa, as he had intermittently been of Europe.[28]

In the spring of 1884 Leopold secured the United States' recognition of his Association's virtual sovereignty over the Congo; he mollified France by offering her first refusal in case the Association had to liquidate its holdings. His principal goal now was formal recognition, and only Berlin could secure him that. Accordingly, he summoned Bleichröder's help on May 15—in the first of a long series of letters that were destined for Bismarck, via the discreet and unofficial channel of Bleichröder. The next task of the Association, he wrote, was to have the

> Independent State of Central Africa, created under its auspices . . . make its entry into the family of states. We are right now actively engaged in devising a political constitution and in drafting fundamental laws for the new state. We wish that that Constitution should please Germany, whose commercial interests the new state will greatly serve, and every advice, every counsel, that Germany would like to give us, every wish she should communicate to us, will be received by us with the deference it merits.[29]

For the next four months, Leopold bombarded Bleichröder with pleas and suggestions; as the latter wrote Bismarck, "The King of Belgium . . . wishes most fervently for the conclusion of the Congo affair. I replied yesterday that this depended essentially on the Association, which was still hedging on certain binding declarations."[30] For the entire summer, which proved to be the critical phase of the Congo negotiations, Bleichröder was Leopold's principal envoy in Berlin. He briefed both sides and sought to smooth the way for a final settlement. Weekly, sometimes daily, Leopold sent Bleichröder a résumé of his position, and Bleichröder responded with a survey of conditions in Berlin.

In May and early June Bleichröder assured Leopold that the Foreign Office and William had agreed to establish relations with the Association.[31] Leopold in turn promised Bleichröder that "we want the new state not to have any customs barriers at its frontiers," for which purposes, he argued, the Powers ought to agree to a demarcation of the borders.[32] According to Bleichröder, Bismarck insisted on this continued accessibility of the Congo market to German goods. The exports of guns, ammunition, and hard liquor had made extraordinary strides in 1883–1884. The vision of a "German India" in Africa began to gain ground in Germany, and Bismarck thought that a free-trade area in central Africa, ruled by Leopold, would be far more advantageous to German interests than French or Portuguese protectionist rule—to say nothing of possible British inroads. Leopold hoped to use Bismarck's interest to gain French and British recognition as well. After talking with Bismarck, Bleichröder warned Leopold that "as far as England was concerned, no such démarche could be undertaken because the current difficulties between Britain and Germany concern precisely trans-atlantic questions, in a manner that one does not in the least feel like asking even the smallest kindness of England."[33] At the same time, on Leopold's initiative, Bleichröder sought to arrange a meeting between the king and Bismarck, but Bismarck proved evasive. To his Foreign Office,

Bismarck mocked Leopold as "proceeding with such a naïve and demanding egoism as if he were an Italian, who presupposed that everyone would do a great deal *pour ses beaux yeux*, without asking for anything in return."[34]

Leopold was impatient, and Bleichröder had to remind him time and again that Bismarck would settle for nothing less than the most specific guarantees of free trade for Germans for all time to come, that is, even if the rights to the Congo should eventually pass into French hands. In August a special Portuguese envoy appeared in Berlin, and Leopold suspected the worst. Bleichröder was at once mobilized: he was to remind the German government that only Leopold's Association would promise free trade, that the Portuguese would at once raise onerous duties, that only a swift recognition of Leopold's rule could forestall complications. Instructed by Bismarck and the Foreign Office, Bleichröder did not immediately assuage Leopold's fears:

> The propositions made by Portugal are very favorable, I am told, and seek to establish but a few insignificant duties in order to cover the costs of administration. As I have had the honor to explain to Your Majesty, it is necessary for the Association to confirm quickly the guarantee of freedom of trade not only for itself but also for France, its possible successor.

If that were done, "my friends here" would be inclined to propose an international conference to determine the frontiers of the new state.[35] Bleichröder attended to the king's business throughout August. Repeatedly he talked to Hatzfeldt, and on the eleventh he was received by William: "I did not fail to propound the views of Your Majesty," he wrote Leopold.[36] Later that month Bleichröder and his small retinue repaired to the Grand Hotel des Bains in Ostend, one of those palace-hotels where for a heavy price the new plutocracy could approximate the life of the old aristocracy. On the twenty-eighth Bleichröder and his daughter dined with the king at the Royal Pavilion; between courses, they talked of the Congo's destiny.*

In September Leopold sent Bismarck—via Bleichröder—a map of the projected state and pleaded for German recognition which would be copied by the other powers "word for word."[37] At the same time, the Portuguese envoy returned to Berlin, and Leopold anxiously asked for news.[38] Bleichröder was the first to report to Leopold that Bismarck had resolved on the recognition of the new state ("The recognition of the Association is beyond doubt"), though the modalities, particularly as they pertained to the borders, had still to be worked out with France. Finally he wrote on October 6:

---

* A few days later, the *Berliner Börsen-Courier* carried a doggerel about Bleichröder's promenades with the king, which Bleichröder, not displeased, sent Leopold:
> Bei prachtvollem Wetter, zwar stürmisch, doch warm,
> Wird die Nachricht Ihr Blatt int'ressieren:
> Bleichröder geht eben Arm in Arm
> Mit dem König von Belgien spazieren.

At this instant and very confidentially I have received the news that a complete entente has been established between France and Germany in the African question and that in the near future the question of the Congo will be submitted to an international conference. It is nearly certain that this conference will take place in Berlin, probably still in the course of next month.[39]

Bleichröder's news was correct and his work seemed done. A week before the conference opened, Bismarck authorized the formal recognition of the new state. But France remained recalcitrant, and Leopold implored Bleichröder to obtain Bismarck's help: "We want an entente with France, we will make sacrifices to obtain it, but, as you will understand, we cannot go to the point of suicide. France has invented a claim on the left bank of the Stanley Pool . . . ," which would jeopardize the development of the richest province of the new state. Leopold argued that the French threatened the one part of the Congo which might redeem the huge costs of the enterprise. "You know, my dear Baron, that I labor in the general interest, that I am not looking for personal reimbursement for what I have spent, but if, when the Association establishes stations, France comes along and says they are mine, my efforts no longer result in the promotion of the interest of all nations but lead only to satisfy the covetousness of the French."[40]

The conference lasted for three months. Bleichröder played host to it at a grand dinner and offered "magnificent hospitality" to Leopold's representatives.[41] It defined the international principles of free trade and free navigation on which the powers insisted. Both Leopold and Bismarck gained their ends: Leopold had wanted international recognition and Bismarck had wanted a large free-trade area in central Africa—or untrammeled access to this new "German India." Leopold's acquisition, which his own parliament registered with solid indifference, unleashed what a British paper in 1884 already called "The Scramble for Africa." One of the most perceptive of present-day historians of imperialism has written:

> This was the age of European hubris that reached its flamboyant height at the Berlin Congo conference in 1885, when the European powers started the "scramble for Africa" and made it a question of national prestige to plant their colors on every white spot on the map before a rival nation could do the same. . . . In this race in which all rational, economic or humanitarian motives became mere pretexts, every nation carved out for itself immense unknown territories which, as we now know, they were never able really to colonize, organize, or exploit.[42]

Bleichröder had been a midwife to Leopold's ambitions. For months he conducted unofficial negotiations and discreet soundings, necessary supplements to the official exchanges between Brussels and Berlin. Did Bleichröder assess the future of the Congo with the same rosy optimism that Leopold and German publicists affected? The record suggests a far more cautious attitude.

To none of his interlocutors did Bleichröder speak of the Congo in glowing terms. He played a coy or negative role when it came to the financing of the projected Congo railway. (Stanley had pronounced that "without the railroad, the Congo is not worth a penny.") In their conversations in September 1884, Bleichröder had left Leopold under the impression that he would found a company for the opening up of the Congo, including the building of a rail-road.[43] Leopold made occasional allusions to this railroad; Bleichröder made none. Such reticence was not Bleichröder's normal mode of operation. If he had had the slightest financial appetite for building railroads in the Congo, he would have been in an admirable position to press his claims. Instead he waited some five years before he joined—with a minor commitment of his own funds —an international consortium for the construction of a railroad in the Congo.*

After the Berlin Conference and the international recognition of the Congo, Bleichröder and Leopold continued their close relations. In fact, Leopold appealed to Bleichröder's help in yet another matter. In March 1885 Bismarck finally cajoled a recalcitrant Reichstag into granting a large governmental subsidy for the creation of a regular steamship line to the Far East; the Norddeutsche Lloyd was to build the necessary ships and ply the particular route. Repeatedly Leopold appealed to Bleichröder to use his "great influence" to persuade the Lloyd and other lines to select Antwerp as the major continental port. From Ostend Bleichröder wrote Bismarck: "I have repeatedly talked with the King of the Belgians here," who expressed his "most cordial thanks" for Bismarck's help in the Congo and now hoped that German ships would use Antwerp, "the most important harbor for German exports"; otherwise British lines would secure the benefit for themselves. Conveniently, Bleichröder's son Georg was a director of the Lloyd, and in time Bleichröder could report to the king and his equally persistent ministers that the Lloyd ships would call on Antwerp.[44]

Leopold had ample reason to thank Bleichröder "for all the pains that you have had the kindness to take for our affairs. . . . The support which you have given the Association, dear Baron, is very precious, and in expressing my deepest gratitude I would beg you to continue your interest in our work. . . ."[45] The king's gratitude, often and fervently expressed, did not go altogether untapped. The only favor that Bleichröder ever asked of Leopold was readily granted: Bleichröder wanted his pianist-friend, Mme. Grosser, to be invited to give a recital at the royal court. Berlin wags thought that Bleichröder was attracted to Mme. Grosser for more than her musical talents. Such gossip gains

---

* The Bleichröder Archive sheds some light on further connections between Bleichröder and Brussels. In the fall of 1885 Leopold summoned Bleichröder's trusted assistant Gloner to Brussels, but an exchange of telegrams suggests that Bleichröder rejected Leopold's requests; Gloner's coded telegram read: "Just emerged from audience with king, who asked me to send you friendliest regards, all the while regretting your abstention. He is convinced of your good will. . . . I shall be back in the office Sunday morning." Gloner to Bleichröder, 13 Nov. 1885, BA. In 1889 Bleichröder joined the Disconto-Gesellschaft in buying 2 million francs' worth of shares of a projected railroad from Matadi to Stanley Pool; of this sum, Disconto was to take 875,000, and of the remaining sum, which was nominally signed for by Bleichröder, 900,000 would be taken up by other participants. Net result: Bleichröder's maximum financial involvement in the Congo would have amounted to 225,000 francs—a small sum which the archive suggests was further reduced in later negotiations.

a certain credibility when one realizes how much labor went into this special performance.* The king's aide, Count D'Oultremont, took personal charge of Bleichröder's protégée, and the king wrote Bleichröder that "Mme. Grosser is a charming person who plays the piano delightfully. . . . I was happy to confer on Mme. Grosser the title she wanted, and I profit from her willingness to carry these lines to you."[46] It was an amiable reward for Bleichröder's labors, and Mme. Grosser's title, whatever it may have been, must have been one of the more inoffensive by-products of the establishment of Leopold's rule in the Congo.†

While Leopold was consolidating his private hold on the Congo, Bismarck astounded the world by creating a German empire five times the size of the Reich. In 1884–1885, over vast, infertile lands, in areas where few, if any, German interests existed, where few, if any, German citizens had ever trod, the German flag was suddenly planted in order to proclaim German sovereignty. Bismarck's contemporaries were puzzled by the sudden conversion because for so long he had protested his indifference to imperial acquisitions. As early as 1868 he had written Roon that he thought the oft-proclaimed advantages of colonial possessions were an illusion, that private firms would undertake such ventures and that the taxpayer could not be expected to support a policy that would accrue to the benefit of but a few traders. During the Franco-Prussian war some merchants began clamoring for French possessions —Saigon included. Bismarck thought that "for us Germans, colonies would be exactly like the silks and sables of the Polish nobleman who had no shirt to wear under them."[47] Throughout the 1870s he maintained this view—for strategic, political, and economic reasons. The Samoa bill marked the first seeming departure from this policy of restraint, though it still seemed consonant with his view that the German government should merely support, not anticipate, the initiative of German traders. By 1884 he established German colonies in Africa, and in two years acquired far more territory than the boisterous William II with his much-vaunted *Weltpolitik* was to do. By 1886 Bismarck affected boredom and indifference again; his colonial phase was over.

Bismarck's sudden leap across principles and oceans troubled contemporaries and has puzzled historians ever since. In recent years, the debate concerning Bismarck's motives has become livelier and more controversial. It is

* Friedrich von Holstein, that bachelor collector of scandals, wrote Herbert von Bismarck that "your pale [*Bleiche*] friend would like to give [a particular position] to the husband of his beloved, a journalist named Grosser." Holstein to Herbert von Bismarck, 13 Dec. 1883, FA.

† D'Oultremont had no reason to regret his favor to Bleichröder. Years later, he wrote Bleichröder: "At our last interview in Ostend you did me the pleasure of telling me that if a good occasion should present itself for making a small, potentially fruitful, operation, you would gladly offer your good services. As one seems to believe here in a marked and early rise of the ruble, I would be obliged, provided you share this view, if you would try for my account a small operation on this currency." As a prudent man, he specified that he would not want to risk more than a possible loss of 2,000 marks. Three months later, he received 2,000 marks from Bleichröder—the profit from this speculation in rubles which apparently involved no actual outlay of cash on D'Oultremont's part. D'Oultremont to Bleichröder, 7 Dec. 1890 and 31 March 1891, BA.

the context of his decisions that remains at issue: was he primarily thinking of foreign or domestic policy, and if the latter, was he moved primarily by political or economic motives? Was he thinking of colonies as pawns on the European chessboard, were his acquisitions anti-British in intent and also designed to hurt the pro-British (and anti-Bismarck) elements at home, such as the crown prince and the remaining left-liberals? Was he the tool of "monopoly capitalism," as some East German historians have contended, or was he guided by a deeper concern for the economic basis of the regime, threatened as it was by the renewed depression of 1882? Or was it a composite of motives that prompted him to make the break, a commonsensical view propounded by Henry A. Turner, who also points to a general *Torschlusspanik* of the time, "the fear that the gate was rapidly closing and that the last chance was at hand."[48]

It goes beyond the confines of this book to enter this dispute. Obviously Bleichröder's role—our proper concern—is of more than marginal interest. As Bismarck's principal adviser in economic affairs and as his confidant in so many matters, did he fervently support Bismarck's initiatives, did he inspire, indeed did he understand, the putative complexities of Bismarck's economic thought? The manner in which Bleichröder reacted to colonial temptations must shed some light on Bismarck's policies.

Finally the reader must remember the immediate context of Bismarck's move. Bismarck's colonialism reached its apogee in 1884—which was an election year. Successive defeats had embittered him; this time he was determined to crush the left-liberals, who happened to be free-trading anti-colonialists. It was also the year when Leopold sought to realize his claims on the Congo, when the French were embroiled in Indochina, and when the British were still preoccupied in Egypt. The constellation was favorable.

Bismarck's first effort came along the southwest coast of Africa, still independent, where in 1882 a Bremen tobacco merchant, F. A. E. Lüderitz, sought to found a trading establishment and asked for "the protection of the German flag." Lüderitz asked for little, but it was too much for Bismarck. In early 1883 the German government inquired in London whether the British exercised rights of sovereignty in those regions, in which case Germany "would be only too happy to see England extend her efficacious protection to the German settlers in those regions."[49] The British procrastinated for months; in their almost incredible bungling, born of complacency and arrogance, Lord Granville at the Foreign Office and Lord Derby at the Colonial Office must be regarded as the patron saints of Bismarck's empire. Bismarck, always suspicious of Gladstone, came to interpret procrastination as proof of anti-German sentiment, the more so as British inscrutability alternated with pretensions of a British Monroe Doctrine for the whole of South Africa. Between the end of 1883 and April 1884, Bismarck made up his mind to present the British with a *fait accompli*; in April he ordered that Angra Pequeña—Lüderitz's territory—be placed under imperial protection; too late did the British discover that Bismarck no longer held to his earlier and oft-repeated assertions that he was not a colonialist.[50] Too late did they realize that their occupation of Egypt had mortgaged their freedom of action, and that they were caught between the need to buy German support in Egypt and the last-minute demands from South Africa to protect them from German inroads. In a striking phrase, a member of a South African deputation exclaimed to Lord Salisbury: "My Lord, we are told that the Germans are good neighbors, but we prefer to have no neighbors at all."[51] In Polynesia, in Africa, in Central Asia, in the western United States, people and nations suddenly acquired neighbors, and a whole world began to suffer from a premature claustrophobia.

In August 1884 the German flag was hoisted over Angra Pequeña—the first step to imagined greatness, even if knowledgeable men at the time adjudged Southwest Africa unfit even for a penal colony. The British accepted what they could not prevent; in private, Lord Ampthill wrote Bleichröder a few days before the official announcement: "The colonial question has become a triumph for the Chancellor and has put him on a still higher pedestal, if that is possible."[52] Bismarck then redoubled his efforts at a Franco-German entente, with a strong anti-British element as its principal ingredient.[53] In the wake of British distraction in Egypt and Central Asia and with the diplomatic support or indifference of the major continental powers, Bismarck authorized the further acquisitions of large tracts of land (German East Africa, Cameroons, Togoland).

The anti-British element in German colonialism was unmistakable, and Bleichröder heard many echoes of it.* It is well known that Count Münster opposed German expansionism; his letters to Bleichröder were more outspoken than his official communications. In October 1884 he wrote Bleichröder that after seeing Bismarck he thought the chancellor understood "correctly the colonial fanaticism which in Germany dominates those who understand nothing about it." By Christmas Eve 1884 Münster complained of all "the cheap nastiness [*Pöbeleien*]" which Germany was guilty of toward England and which he had to contend with. The nastiness, moreover, was gratuitous: the British, he assured Bleichröder, were not opposed to German colonialism; they even welcomed it as a counterweight to French and American imperialism. "Why our colonial fever has suddenly become mixed with wild chauvinism I would not be able to grasp if I did not know what theory-mongers [*Theoretiker*], what silver-tongued orators, and—in places remote from us—what idealists we Germans are."[54]† What Münster lamented, others welcomed, and

---

* In 1885, a Conservative ministry replaced Gladstone, and its head, Salisbury, took a different view of German imperialism: "I have been using the credit I have got with Bismarck in the Caroline Is. and Zanzibar to get help in Russia and Turkey and Egypt. He is rather a Jew, but on the whole I have as yet got my money's worth." Quoted in Paul M. Kennedy, *The Samoan Tangle: A Study in Anglo-American Relations, 1878–1900* (New York, 1974), p. 48.

† Münster never reconciled himself to German expansionism, and as late as 1890, after Bismarck's fall, he wrote Bleichröder that even "real successes would not convert him" from his opposition to all this "colonial nonsense." Or again: "If Africa, that dark country, did not exist, we diplomats would have little to do. If we had stayed away from there and if the stupid German *Michel* had not stuck his finger in the dark mush [*Brei*], we could now peacefully look on as the English, French, Italians, Portuguese and the Congo-Conference quarrel over it. A role we left to the Russki!!! It was not my fault; you know that." Münster to Bleichröder, 30 June, 26 Dec. 1890, BA.

Peter Saburov, for example, wrote Bleichröder: "We applaud the success of your new colonial policy"—because of its anti-English character.[55]

Bleichröder's varied interests made him see the argument for and against expansionism. Later historians have seen but one side: "Hansemann and Bleichröder . . . played a not unimportant part in winning Bismarck over to a colonial policy." Eugene Staley put it more strongly, asking: "Did the interests and influence of those who wished to place private capital profitably abroad have an important part in [Bismarck's shift to colonialism]? The answer is that they did. The powerful influence of Bismarck's banker friends, von Hansemann and Bleichröder, was exerted in favor of a colonial policy. . . ." Marxist historians see in Bleichröder one of the principal wirepullers of imperialism, and one of them recently labeled Bleichröder as "*kolonialfreudig.*"[56] But was he—or is this one of those assumptions which historians make when fleeting evidence seems to support fixed presumption? Did Bleichröder justify —perhaps partially inspire—Bismarck's oft-expressed exasperation with the timidity of German capital, the unwillingness of Germans to finance overseas risks?*

In any account of German expansionism, Bleichröder's name and capital crop up. Even in the propagandistic preparation for German colonialism Bleichröder's name appeared—indirectly. A German Colonial League was founded in 1882; its argument that colonies would provide vast new markets had a special resonance at a time when another sharp business contraction hit Germany—despite the newly adopted tariffs of 1879.[57] The League's first appeal was signed by some publicists and a few well-known deputies from the National Liberals and the Free Conservatives—Varnbüler and Friedenthal, for example, with whom Bleichröder had close ties. Friedrich Hammacher, a major Rhenish industrialist and National Liberal parliamentarian, was a colonial enthusiast; he was one of the few who articulated the hope that expansion abroad would relieve social tension at home.[58] But Bleichröder did not sign. The bulk of the small membership were relatively unknown *Bürger*; gradually, a few prominent men joined as well, and in 1885 a Berlin chapter was opened. "The few names from the world of industry and banking, politics, and academe represent power elements whose weight had a great impact [*Machtfaktoren deren Gewicht schwer in die Wagschale fiel*]."[59] Among these major figures, the Berlin "*Grossbanken*" were duly represented; Hansemann belonged, as did Schwabach, representing the House of Bleichröder. It is noteworthy, however, that Bleichröder himself did not join—though he was not habitually a nonjoiner or a wallflower who sought to shrink into the background.

---

* German capitalists were not the only ones to exasperate African enthusiasts. Harry Johnston, a protégé of Lord Salisbury's and an explorer himself, wrote to an African hand at the Foreign Office: "British merchants are the most unreasonable of men nowadays—They expect the Government to do everything for them & see no occasion for private enterprise of their own. What they would like is for huge territories like Kilimanjaro to be annexed, opened up, civilised, cleared, swept, & garnished, & then handed over to them to pay a profitable & ready made trade." Wm. Roger Louis, "Great Britain and German Expansion in Africa, 1884–1919," in *Britain and Germany in Africa*, ed. by Gifford and Louis, p. 14.

In the spring of 1884 the German government reverted to earlier plans for the creation of an Overseas German Bank that would facilitate German exports and would break the virtual monopoly which British banks had on regulating this trade. In May 1884 the head of the Reichsbank, Dechend, consulted with the usual intimates: Hansemann, Bleichröder, Siemens, and others. The bankers were interested, but wanted the government to participate as well and expected unprecedented concessions. Bismarck was disappointed, but by the fall contemplated a Government Bank, if private interests continued to demur. Dechend asked Bleichröder for a confidential talk before he would talk to the other bankers. In the end, because of the bankers' caution and Bismarck's other plans, nothing came of the idea.[60]

Bleichröder's name again appeared in connection with Bismarck's first colonial acquisition, Angra Pequeña. As early as June 1884 Bleichröder and Hansemann were rumored to have bought the claims to some putative copper mines in an area close to Lüderitz's possessions. After the establishment of the German protectorate, it turned out that Lüderitz lacked the necessary funds to maintain, let alone develop, his much-coveted possession. In the spring of 1885, to Bismarck's great annoyance, he threatened to sell his interests to a British firm. That would have been a quick, disgraceful end to German colonialism—and would have pricked all those vainglorious promises of new riches. Enter Schwabach, Hammacher, and Hansemann, who more or less coerced an unwilling Lüderitz to sell his possessions to a consortium they would found for the purpose. In April 1885, with Hansemann and Bleichröder again in the lead, a Deutsche Kolonial-Gesellschaft für Südwestafrika was established, with the Bleichröders signing for 200,000 marks out of a total of 800,000 marks. One of the chief propagandists for the new company argued that financial consideration should be set aside in this "patriotic duty." The contributions were, "in a certain sense, a sacrifice."[61] The new company's board of directors included Hammacher, the duke of Ujest—Bleichröder's old associate in losing business—Schwabach, and Georg Bleichröder.[62] Despite certain tax advantages preempted by it, the company faced years of stagnation and unprofitability.[63] A British Embassy official in Berlin remembered Bleichröder's reactions:

> If Angra Pequeña served as a sort of test case for the establishment of a first footing in Africa it was an unprofitable venture. Bleichröder, the banker, afterwards admitted that it had cost him £10,000. Lüderitz had found the place altogether worthless, and did not intend to sink any capital there. The Chancellor had learned that he contemplated offering to sell it to us and, after all the trouble which the settlement had caused him, he was furious. So Bleichröder had to advance the money to keep the little colony going and save Bismarck from a ridiculous position.[64]

Hansemann's biographer, who had married into the family, lamented the fact that Hansemann's patriotic efforts to salvage overseas ventures turned profitable only after his death, in 1903.[65]

Bleichröder learned to dodge the claims of colonialism. Bismarck temporarily supported Carl Peters's scheme for a German empire in East Africa, hoping that it would somehow be governed not by the German state but by a charter company, on the oft-invoked model of the East India or North Borneo Company. For the purpose, a German East Africa Company was founded, but from the beginning Carl Peters's megalomania, workaday incompetence, and steady dearth of funds hobbled it. The government looked for help, but, as one East German historian put it, "the experienced robbers . . . of the finance bourgeoisie" demanded greater security than the state or the company would afford them. The company was finally saved—with the help of William's personal funds as well as those of the Rhineland banker von der Heydt but, contrary to the allegations of later historians, without Bleichröder's assistance.[66] By the summer of 1886 Bismarck himself no longer thought it was necessary to salvage the East African Company: "he could quietly contemplate the collapse of the East African Company without being afraid that our national prestige would suffer from such an event. . . . For our colonial policy he still holds to the guiding principle to follow but not to pave the way for German pioneers." And what could the East African Company do: coffee plantations seemed the only feasible activity that would not compete with domestic German products. "But who should drink all the coffee that can be grown on 30,000 square miles?"[67] The kaiser and Heydt were joined by some prominent Jewish or ex-Jewish Houses: Mendelssohn-Bartholdy, Robert Warschauer and Company, and others—and when the newly constituted company dismissed the cantankerous Peters, his confreres in paranoia complained bitterly against the Jewish conspiracy.[68]

Once Bismarck had given the green light to colonialism, every adventurer and would-be Livingstone sought to stake out a small empire. But costs were prohibitive, and every expedition needed its own special financing. Bleichröder's assistance for such patriotic ventures was often appealed to; he learned to say no.[69] Occasionally he would contribute modest starting sums. In 1884, for example, he gave 1,000 marks to the brothers Denhardt, who for years had explored the land around Witu on the East African coast. In December 1885, Denhardt begged Bleichröder for an interview so that he could report on his progress in opening up for Germany a trading area in what he called "Middle Eastern Africa," encompassing today's Kenya. A few months later he wrote again to Bleichröder and to his assistant Dr. Gloner, pleading for additional help. He had himself collected half of the requisite 500,000 marks to establish a joint-stock corporation for the exploitation of the area; he needed a loan from Bleichröder of at least 50,000 marks and at most 500,000. Without such a loan, he would have to sell out to British interests which were only too eager for the chance, but this of course would prove very disappointing to the German Foreign Office and to colonialism generally. The specter of British rapacity, whether true or not, was the favorite rationalization of the time—much in the manner of appeals to anti-Communism in more recent times. Why, Denhardt asked, did German capital prefer to support non-German ventures abroad and to ignore the claims of German entrepreneurs?[70]

In the end, in December 1887, Prince Hermann zu Hohenlohe-Langenburg, a seasoned "specialist in unsuccessful colonial projects," came to the rescue and organized a Witu Company, to which Bleichröder and a few other dignitaries made a token contribution, and which in the first eighteen months of operations had an income of 4,120 marks.[71]

Even this brief account of Bleichröder's stake in German colonialism makes it clear that from the beginning he was engaged—modestly—in the money-losing business of establishing German colonies overseas. From the first, hesitant move in Samoa to the several colonies in Africa, Bleichröder was always present. More than that, he had helped to establish the greatest empire of the 1880s, Leopold's Congo. He lent his name, his talents, and, with persistent reticence, his money to the cause of colonialism.

Why did he? The simplest answer, implied or assumed in much of Marxist literature, is that he sought to make money. To accept that is to insult Bleichröder's financial intelligence; even his son Hans wrote him in August 1885 that while Bismarck had mishandled his negotiations with the Spaniards regarding the Caroline Islands, which promised to be profitable, to put money into Africa was "nonsense"—the very opposite of the Pacific.[72] Did Bleichröder perhaps believe in the eventual future of the colonies, in their potential to furnish new markets or to produce great mineral wealth? Did he accept any of the standard economic arguments advanced by colonial enthusiasts close to him? The evidence suggests that he did not. Nor did he seem to believe in the recently much-vaunted social-imperialism argument, whereby the activists of the 1880s were supposed to be already aware that somehow German colonialism would "export" and thus perhaps throttle the social question at home. Bleichröder certainly shared an upper-class horror of revolutionaries in general and of Social Democracy in particular. His notion of how to deal with the revolutionaries, however, was a good deal more primitive than the program of the social imperialists: essentially he thought that repression would suffice.* In short, there is no evidence whatever to suggest that Bleichröder at any time accepted any of the arguments, economic or ideological, for German colonialism. His correspondence contains no echo of such sentiments; there is not a single letter from Bleichröder that bespeaks colonial enthusiasm. Münster's jaundiced views were more characteristic of Bleichröder's correspondents than Leopold's self-serving enthusiasm. Bleichröder's actions, on the other hand, while reserved, indicated consistent, modest support of colonialism.

Why did he support German colonialism? First, he probably approximated Bismarck's own pragmatic views on German expansionism. He almost

---

* In April 1883 he wrote King Leopold: "If European politics does not present anything disturbing at the moment, it is because the relations between the powers are excellent, at least judged from externals, still it is necessary to acknowledge that nearly every country is agitated by one or another pressing question, among which the social movement occupies the first rank. The necessity will soon impose itself on all the states to reach a common accord of efficacious measures against these agitators." He discussed the situation, country by country, and expected measures such as the German anti-Socialist law to be an effective remedy. Bleichröder to Leopold II, 23 April 1883, BA.

certainly shared Bismarck's concern that German industry needed free access to overseas markets and that the encroachment of protectionist powers such as France would jeopardize that objective. He may have felt some of the *Torschlusspanik* in regard to colonies which Bismarck and others in the German government felt. If there was to be a race for colonial greatness, the Germans had to be "man enough" to take part and to excel.* Other powers had to be forestalled. Bleichröder certainly believed that German interests abroad deserved protection, as witness his long battle in Rumania. Finally, he was never one to underestimate the arguments of national prestige; perhaps bankers, so keenly aware of their own jockeying for position, understood better than most that prestige reflected and enhanced power. He understood that colonialism might promote Bismarck's violently antiliberal course in an election year, and his own views on the radicals were perhaps more complicated than Bismarck's but no less critical.

A vague consonance of views between Bismarck and Bleichröder probably existed. But most important, Bleichröder supported colonialism because Bismarck and the German government expected him to, because Bismarck was angry enough at the timidity of German merchants in advancing German interests overseas without having to have his private banker disappoint him as well. To ask why Bleichröder supported colonialism, it may be useful to ask what would have happened if he had not: either he or the cause would have been discredited. His presence in a variety of ventures gave respectability and an aura of commercial solidity to them; consistent abstention would have raised doubts about the commercial viability or the political desirability of colonialism. The House of Bleichröder was aware that its acts of omission no less than its acts of commission reflected on Bismarck's intent as well.† Put briefly, Bleichröder was a captive of his prominence; he had to support the government if he wanted to preserve his special position among German bankers.

In this light, Hobson's emphasis on the preeminence of Jewish bankers as supporters of imperialism acquires a different light, at least as applied to German Jews. Their presence, and as I see it, their often reluctant presence, may have been due to their peculiar vulnerability to any kind of national pressure. They were always under a special dispensation to prove their patriotism, and hence least capable of resisting the national argument. This was particularly true of the 1880s, when anti-Semitism reached its height in the Bismarckian era and, ironically enough, in some quarters merged with colonialism itself.

---

* The phrase comes from Joseph Conrad's *Heart of Darkness* and recalls that for explorers, traders, and statesmen the quest for colonies appeared as virile adventure. This, too, was a motive for expansionism that needs to be remembered.

† As an example, consider Schwabach's letter of July 1886 to the German minister in China, explaining why he could not have undertaken any loans to China while she was engaged "in military complications with France." There would have been an "unholy clamor against Germany; because everywhere one is aware—rightly or wrongly, and I even say wrongly—that such a loan would have had the particular *licet* of the Prince." Quoted in Helmuth Stoecker, *Deutschland und China im 19. Jahrhundert* (East Berlin, 1958), p. 279.

The story of Bleichröder, then, bears out Bismarck's oft-forgotten view that German bankers were lamentably reticent in risking their capital in colonial ventures. It bears out as well the contention that Bismarck was not the instrument of rapacious finance-capitalists, but that the bankers were often enough the executors or anticipators of Bismarck's will.* If German colonialism had not sprung up in the 1880s, it is unlikely that Bleichröder or his friends would have invented it.

In part this aloofness must be explained by the eagerness with which they embraced another form of exploitation: the lending of capital under often onerous terms to less developed countries, in the hope of expanding commercial opportunities as well as of reaping profits that were higher than domestic investments afforded. About a month after Bismarck's dismissal, Bleichröder called at the Foreign Office to see Max von Berchem, the driving force of late Bismarckian commercial policy. Berchem summarized their long conversation for the new foreign secretary: Bleichröder had informed him that the German bondholders in Constantinople were satisfied by the new arrangements he had devised and that he hoped that the Imperial Embassy there would continue to support the interests of his House. Berchem remained noncommittal. Next Bleichröder reported that German and Italian financial groups had reached an agreement by which German interests would take over certain Italian operations. "I took the occasion," Berchem reported, "in accordance with the All-Highest instructions to say that His Majesty had been pleased by [Bleichröder's] participation in bringing about this accord." Berchem added that the German government would favor the participation of English *"haute finance"* in this Italian venture, even though Bleichröder thought it unnecessary from the purely financial point of view. Austrian finances came up next, especially as Bleichröder had just returned from Vienna with important information. Next Bleichröder broached the subject of Russian finances; the Russian finance minister, Ivan Alekseyevich Vishnegradski, was thinking of floating a new loan of 300 million marks in order to buy a series of smaller Russian railroads. How would the German government regard such a loan? Berchem thought that Russian holdings in Berlin, having been cut to a third of their former level, should not be increased again. Bleichröder's rejoinder that Vishnegradski's finances were in excellent shape, Berchem countered with the remark: "The shah of Persia also finds himself in splendid condition because he is just as unmindful of the material interests of his country as Mr. Vishnegradski."[73]

A routine conversation about Bleichröder's current interests—which engulfed the world. The *tour d'horizon* touched on the political-commercial relations with Turkey, Austria-Hungary, Italy, Britain, and Russia. At other times, Bleichröder and Berchem or Caprivi discussed the other regions in which

---

* It also recalls Daniel Defoe's assertion in 1711 that it was not the maxim "They that have the Money must have the Management" which was true, but "They that have the Management will have the Money." Quoted in *Essays Presented to Sir Lewis Namier*, ed. by Richard Pares and A. J. P. Taylor (London, 1956), p. 53; I owe this reference to my friend Robert K. Webb.

Bleichröder and the German government had an interest: the countries of eastern Europe, Egypt, Mexico, China, and the United States. Regarding their worldwide interests, Bleichröder and the imperial government kept in closest and mutually advantageous touch, as they had in Bismarck's time.*

It has often been remarked that informal imperialism paid far more handsomely—and ran far fewer risks—than the formal imperialism which consisted of administering and protecting colonies.[74] If the term "imperialism" is extended to mean financial control by one nation or a group of nationals over the fiscal policy of another, then Bleichröder certainly participated in imperial ventures. His wandering interest can also be seen from another perspective: ever since its inception, his House—and that of many other merchant bankers in Europe—had specialized in the handling of government loans. As the century progressed and most advanced nations were able to raise sufficient funds by taxation or by the issuance of loans that required only routine services by bankers, these bankers came to turn to those countries that had not yet sufficiently modernized: old and decrepit empires like the Ottoman Empire or its nominal vassal Egypt, or gradually modernizing but still backward empires like Russia, or new states like Serbia and Bulgaria. Financial independence required a measure of financial know-how, a rational structure of administration and a largely honest bureaucracy, and a modicum of consensus about the rightful needs of the polity. In the absence of these prerequisites, governments were often forced to rely on international bankers for raising the necessary funds to conduct their rudimentary business. The less developed or the more troubled the country, the greater the risk, which had to be offset by higher charges and more onerous conditions; possible profit varied inversely with safety. The greater, too, the need for judgment, for knowing when to pursue a loan and at what price. In this field of dealing with foreign governments—with one's own government always as an interested party—Bleichröder became an internationally recognized authority. A large portion of his fortune derived from this business as well. Bleichröder certainly belonged to that group of "great international bankers—Hobson's vilains—who have always understood that prosperous, independent states make the best clients."[75]

It would be bootless to follow Bleichröder's every foreign venture. Symptomatic examples will suffice. At a remarkably early hour, Bleichröder became involved in the hapless finances of the Ottoman Empire. Between 1854 and 1875 the Ottoman government contracted a foreign debt of 200 million pounds sterling; new loans paid for past loans and present extravagances: it has been estimated that no more than 10 percent "was so used as to increase

---

* The relations between German bankers and the German government were once neatly described by Max Warburg, the great Hamburg financier. His New York partners had sought to interest him in some Japanese loans, and as Warburg noted in his diary, he did "what every good banker does in such cases: I drove to the Foreign Office in Berlin." In short, you consult the Foreign Office before committing your funds abroad. Quoted in Alfred Vagts, "M. M. Warburg & Co. Ein Bankhaus in der deutschen Weltpolitik 1905–1933," *Vierteljahrsschrift für Sozial- und Wirtschaftsgeschichte*, XLV (1958), 302.

the country's economic strength."[76] The sick man of Europe was also the poor man. In 1875 the Ottoman government reduced the interest rate on the outstanding debt by half; a year later it suspended payments altogether. The Balkan rebellions and the Russo-Turkish war finished the job, and even the hardiest of European creditors, whom greed had made gullible, began to despair. Pushed by the Congress of Berlin and the sheerest necessity, the Turkish government, in the famous Decree of Mouharrem of 1881, revamped its entire debt structure and instituted for the first time European control over a part of the imperial revenues. Thus came into existence an international body called the Administration of the Ottoman Public Debt, which was composed of seven delegates, representing the major foreign and domestic debtholders. With the blessings of the German Foreign Office, the House of Bleichröder was selected as having the right to name the German delegate— and thus Bleichröder's word carried some weight on the Bosporus.[77]

After the Congress of Berlin and more especially after Britain's occupation of his province, Egypt, the sultan, Abdul Hamid, became strongly pro-German, and Bismarck, long afraid to commit Germany in the explosive enmities of the Near East, began to relent toward Turkey in the same measure as his concern about Russian hostility mounted. Hence he allowed a few German soldiers to advise the much-battered Turkish army, he favored Germany's growing economic involvement, and he welcomed Bleichröder's watchful eye on Turkish finances.[78] Bleichröder's first representative in Constantinople was Justizrat Primker, who had once been a legal councillor in the German government.

Bleichröder's Turkish appetite grew. Installed in the Public Debt Administration, he sought in 1882 to make common cause with an Austrian consortium, inspired by the ubiquitous Baron Hirsch, to build a railway that would link Turkey and the Austro-Hungarian Empire. Bleichröder apparently hoped for Bismarck's special protection in this venture and asked Hatzfeldt and Radowitz to intervene for him with Bismarck, who refused all protection. Bismarck informed the Austrian government, which was interested in the project, that he must "observe the greatest caution with regard to the negotiations touched on in the Austrian communication, precisely because it contains the name of his own banker, and because [he] unfortunately knows from his own experience how readily the scandalmongers would exploit such a circumstance." In fact, a German paper had already denounced the financial intrigues "of chosen members of the chosen race," who sought to exploit Turkey under the feigned aegis of Germany.[79]

In 1883 the Public Debt farmed out the exploitation of the Turkish Tobacco Revenue to a new company, composed of the House of Bleichröder, the Rothschild-owned Credit-Anstalt in Vienna, and the Imperial Ottoman Bank, and known in brief as the Regie. The Regie had to pay the Debt an annual rental of 750,000 Turkish pounds and had to share profits if and when it recovered more than expenses plus 8 percent.[80] German officialdom congratulated Bleichröder on the success of this operation—and pressed him on whom he should appoint to the Regie. The German ambassador in Constantinople, Radowitz, also a friend and client of Bleichröder's, urged him not to appoint a Mr. Testa, whose close connections with the German Embassy made him unsuitable. "I am certain that you . . . who more than anyone else esteems the work of politics will agree that it is important to keep the necessary instruments pure so that they will lose nothing of their cutting edge." After a far-flung correspondence, Bleichröder accepted Radowitz's candidate, Baltazzi.[81]

But Bleichröder's interests in the Ottoman Empire went even further than playing fiscal viceroy at a distance; he had a modest share of approximately 1,500,000 marks in Baron Hirsch's huge network of Turkish railways. In the winter of 1886 Hirsch decided to sell his vast and strategic holdings. Bleichröder may have been the first to alert Bismarck and the German Foreign Office of this intended and infinitely complicated transaction. In November 1886 Radowitz promised Bleichröder: "If he asks me, I shall always be ready to support your representative here in the defense of the interests of German capital." He added, "Political prospects in general, and in Oriental affairs in particular, you can no doubt understand better in the Behrenstrasse than I can at the Golden Horn."[82]

But even Bleichröder and Bismarck had trouble understanding the Oriental tangle. Before Hirsch could sell the railroads to a consortium he had to reach a financial settlement with the sultan. Bleichröder wrote Bismarck a private note that "for German interests, too, it would be of the most far-reaching importance if a settlement could be reached as soon as possible, preferably through a direct understanding with the Porte because arbitration procedures would necessarily bring about delays."[83]

The governments of Europe were understandably nervous as to the prospective buyer; first rumor had it that the Russians would buy it, and it was Bleichröder's task, via his friend A. I. Sack in St. Petersburg, to ferret out the truth. The Austrian foreign minister, often briefed by Bleichröder, very much wanted Austro-German capital to forestall further French influence at the Porte; the British ambassador in Constantinople also favored a German presence there—as a sure way of fomenting Russo-German antagonism. The fiscal stakes were high: it has been estimated that Hirsch's total profit out of twenty years of building Oriental railways was about 150 million francs—a sizable nest egg, of which a large portion was spent on philanthropic ventures for Oriental Jews. Hirsch acted as a kind of one-man redistributor of Turkish wealth.[84] The political stakes were also high: the Great Powers had a strategic interest in the fortunes of the Porte. If the inflow of new capital were to bring a hitherto uncommitted power, such as Germany, on the scene, the political balance would be affected as well. Bismarck was reluctant to jeopardize his political disinterestedness by the sudden intrusion of massive financial interests, particularly since he thought Turkish finances were a shaky reed to build on.

In February 1888 Schwabach assured the Foreign Office that Hirsch would not find any possible buyers in Berlin; there was little confidence in Turkish solvency, and Bleichröder in fact sought to get rid of the relatively small investment he held.[85] Two months later, Georg von Siemens of the

Deutsche Bank informed the Foreign Office of his interest in the Hirsch shares, since such an arrangement would prevent German capital from flocking to less secure spots (Bismarck appended a question mark at this point) and would forestall greater French interests. But he would want to pursue negotiations with Hirsch "only if the Imperial Government enters no objection from the political point of view." Although Bismarck saw French penetration as a means of promoting Anglo-French rivalry ("England's anti-French interests are useful to us"), he formally approved Siemens's plans, promised diplomatic support, but warned against any assumption that the German government would shield investors from any future complications in the Near East.[86]

It was the opening signal for the decisive German penetration of the Ottoman Empire, carried on under the aegis of Siemens and the Deutsche Bank. Bismarck counseled British or French participation, while the Austrian Foreign Minister Kálnoky bemoaned the "pusillanimity of Austro-German financiers . . . each more wretched than the other."[87] Bleichröder fanned Kálnoky's exasperation with the lack of patriotism on the part of bankers, especially of the Austrian Rothschilds, who showed no great interest in the Turkish business. In the fall of 1888, from Ostend, Bleichröder informed Bismarck that various financiers were there "to confer on the construction of the Asiatic railroads. If Germany should participate, then of course under the condition that German industry should profit through the delivery of railroad material and rails."[88] And if German industry should profit, so would Bleichröder, given his interests in it; banks and industry often had a common stake in foreign ventures, and this linkage is at the heart of what has been called finance capital or finance imperialism.

In 1888–1889, the Deutsche Bank moved in massively: it first arranged a loan for the sultan, which the Anglo-French-dominated Banque Impériale Ottomane had refused to grant. Next it took over and vastly expanded the scope of the Hirsch enterprise; the first, decisive step toward the Berlin-Baghdad Railroad had been taken.

Bleichröder's role had been modest, if pioneering. At a time when hardly any German capital was invested in Turkey, he assumed the leading German role in the international supervision of Turkish finances.[89] He played an equally important and no doubt profitable role in the tobacco Regie—though his involvement in Turkish finances also embroiled him in a wearisome lawsuit, because a German bondholder, the Countess Paumgarten, sued Bleichröder for mismanaging the interests of bondholders. The case went through several instances, and after Bleichröder's death was decided in his favor.[90] The actual building of the new railways in Anatolia was supervised by an engineer, Otto Kapp, who had first concerned himself with Turkish railroads at Bleichröder's behest.[91]

Bleichröder's involvement in Turkish affairs also allowed him to offer patronage to friends, and his last representative in Constantinople was Rudolf Lindau, who after Bismarck's fall found himself unemployed and unappreciated. He assured Bleichröder, "I never forget that it was your friendship that made it possible for me."[92]

While Bleichröder possessed a certain amount of patronage and power on the Bosporus, his more adventurous confreres in western Europe swooped down on Egypt. From the 1850s to the late 1870s, Egypt was like a magnet for adventurers: poor in resources, but rich in dreams, Egypt sought to modernize, as its ruler, Khedive Ismail, tried to enrich his country and himself. Respectable bankers came, as did merchants, and in their wake, speculators and jobbers—and many of them swarmed into a debt-ridden Egypt like so many vultures. Egypt was not only a wonder of financial mismanagement—there was more to it than the khedive's habitual bankruptcy, always exploited by European bankers who sought to squeeze the last drop of possible profit from the Egyptian mess even as the khedive needed to exploit and drive his own starved people. Egypt was also a country of immense strategic importance. Napoleon had dramatized this importance, and in the reign of his nephew, de Lesseps's building of the Suez Canal enhanced and made ineluctable that strategic position.

The leaders of France and Britain saw Egypt as the flawed rock on which rested their empires. Or as Bismarck once put it, in reference to Britain: "Egypt is like the spinal cord of the empire, which connects the backbone with the brain."[93] Beyond the statesmen were bankers and thousands of bondholders, and they too took a passionate interest in the future of the country. From 1875 when Disraeli bought the Suez shares, to the first Rothschild loan in 1878, to the deposition of the khedive in 1880, to the British occupation of 1882—decided on, reluctantly, by Bismarck's enemy Gladstone—and for decades after, the country was trapped in the maelstrom of European politics and finance. In a condition of frustrating dependency, it was a source of fear to itself, a costly temptation to others, a scene where the high-minded learned meanness and the mean turned desperate and cruel.[94]*

Through his correspondence with the Rothschilds and with German officialdom Bleichröder had followed Egyptian affairs—mostly from the perspective of a banker smelling uncertain profit. In June 1882, after the nationalist rebellion had brought chaos to Cairo and with it the likelihood of Anglo-French intervention, Bleichröder reported to Bismarck that "a panic" had hit London and Paris prices, which, since no other political developments had occurred, must be due to the threat to millions of Anglo-French capital in Egypt.[95] German financial interests in Egypt were minimal.† It was, as W. L. Langer put it, "the great Jewish banking-houses of Paris and London—the

---

* Egypt was rich in tales, too; it was current gossip, for example, that the Rothschilds had "made supplication . . . to Bismarck, who ever since his Frankfort days had extended a certain contemptuous protection to the great Hebrew house," in order to have the khedive deposed. Wilfrid Blunt, *Secret History of the English Occupation of Egypt* (London, 1907), pp. 65–66.

† And hard to assess. When the first organ of European control over Egyptian finances, the Caisse de la Dette Publique, was established in 1876, similar to that of Turkey, Germany was not even represented. In April 1884 Lord Granville wrote that "Germany's financial interests in the Caisse did not exceed a miserable million of marks," while in June Bismarck expressed surprise that "one hundred millions of German money was invested in Egyptian securities." Granville was closer to the mark. Edmond George Fitzmaurice, *The Life of Lord Granville* (London, 1905), II, 339; Paul Knaplund, ed., *Letters from the Berlin Embassy, 1871–1874, 1880–1885* (Washington, 1944), pp. 232–233.

Rothschilds, Frühlings, Oppenheims, and Bischoffsheim—[who] floated the loans with heavy discount and took for themselves a fancy commission."[96] In any case, at the time of the British occupation, the public debt had risen to nearly £100 million, the total annual debt charges to £5 million, and the government's total revenue amounted to £10 million.[97] Bleichröder may have had a subsidiary interest, but of minimal significance; it is not clear whether, unlike other German bankers, he would have been eager for a larger share earlier and was rebuffed or whether he shared the general reticence of his fellow bankers.

Matters changed after the British occupation of 1882; Sir Evelyn Baring (later the first Lord Cromer), as British consul general, wielded effective power over Egypt, and in handling the overriding question of how European bondholders could be satisfied without at the same time totally paralyzing the Egyptian economy, he had the assistance of a twenty-six-year-old expert, Edgar Vincent, who in the 1920s, as British ambassador in Berlin, earned the sobriquet "Lord Protector of Germany."[98] The Caisse, under French domination, wanted to collect every sou that some Egyptian official may have contracted, often for money not even received; the British thought the first priority was to create a minimally stable and viable country. Intermittently Bismarck interfered, mostly so as to make the British feel (and resent) their dependence on his good will. After three years of occupation, the British took the first step toward salvaging Egyptian debts by arranging for a new loan of £9,400,000, paying 3 percent (as against the 30 percent that was not unusual a bare ten years earlier), to be guaranteed by the six Powers represented on the Caisse— and for this purpose, the membership of the Caisse was enlarged to include Germany and Russia.

Bleichröder had made his own recommendations to Bismarck on the terms of the loan; he had advocated a 3½ percent rate, which the Foreign Office opposed. Most important, for the new loan of 1885, the first truly respectable loan, the House of Bleichröder was appointed as the sole German disbursement agent (*Couponzahlstelle*).[99] Bleichröder had won for himself a unique place in Germany as far as Egyptian securities went—and no sooner had he done so than he wanted to go further. In the process he overstepped his bounds. In March 1886 he sent a formal petition to Bismarck asking him to instruct the German representative on the Caisse in Cairo that the Bleichröder Bank should be appointed disbursement agent for some of the earlier, the so-called unified and privileged, Egyptian loans as well. Bleichröder argued that the new 3 percent loan had awakened great interest in Egyptian securities among German capitalists, who were inconvenienced by having to present their coupons to the designated Houses in Paris or London. Encouraged by a conversation he had with Bismarck, Bleichröder committed the unusual indiscretion of approaching the German representative, Baron Richthofen, directly; Richthofen replied that he needed Bismarck's formal authorization for such a step, though the Egyptian authorities were well disposed to Bleichröder's plans. In the meantime, Bismarck had consulted Adolf von Scholz, finance minister, who opposed Bleichröder's request: "easy access of Egyptian debentures to the German capital market will bring no benefit to our conditions." Quite aside from increasing the political liability that greater financial involvement in Egyptian values might bring about,

> the government will have to desist from supporting any effort on the part of domestic capital that might seek a higher interest rate abroad, and especially so when the safety of such papers is dubious, as would appear to be the case with the Egyptian papers in question, and the danger of loss of capital or interest seems great. Also it seems necessary to me to reserve domestic capital as much as possible for domestic purposes and enterprises and to keep it serviceable for our own state credit against all eventualities. The pecuniary interests of a few individual bankers could hardly weigh in the balance against these weighty considerations.

Scholz would have opposed the creation of a Berlin agency for the new loan—had he been asked.[100] By his procedure no less than by the substance of his petition, Bleichröder had offended various parts of the German government; on Bismarck's behalf, Geheimrat von Brauer formally rebuked Bleichröder and let it be known in Cairo that Bleichröder had been admonished for "the impropriety of his acts."[101]

Hardly used to such rebukes anymore, Bleichröder was much chagrined—but remarkably tenacious as well. He wrote to Bismarck, in his most grandiloquent manner, concluding: "But I believe I can allow myself the thought that Your Highness would adjudge my conduct more mildly and would spare me the pain that disfavor would cause me," if the circumstances were fully known. He had meant to approach Richthofen indirectly, through a common acquaintance in Cairo, and he had never wanted to interfere with the official conduct of business. The brief explanation, he hoped, would "propitiate" Bismarck.[102] Probably Bismarck's indignation had been exaggerated by his subordinates, ever jealous of Bleichröder. Bismarck himself understood the pull of profit better than most people.

Still, it was an awkward setback for Bleichröder. By chance—more likely by design—his son Hans was in Cairo at the very time of this contretemps; probably more than tourism had brought him there. Other German banks, including Behrens of Hamburg, were pushing similar projects. But Gerson had to bide his time—briefly. In August he appealed directly to the Egyptian government, and in October 1886 he wrote an eight-page letter to Bismarck. He presented a still stronger case: in the interval, even without a German disbursing agent and despite the "painful" necessity of cashing all coupons in Paris or London, Egyptian securities had become immensely popular. The Egyptian government, Bleichröder added, favored the designation of a German agency, and beyond the convenience of investors beckoned the likelihood that such an agency would also end the mediating role of France and England in settling the trade balance between Germany and Egypt. "Not so much because of the advantages that might accrue [to me] and which would have to be reckoned as small, but principally because of the interest of German capital and to secure it the same advantages as are enjoyed by the English and French capitalists I would be pleased and grateful if Your Highness would no longer contest the efforts of the Egyptian government and would empower the German representative on the Caisse de la Dette to support such a motion as soon as it is presented to him."[103] This time the experts of the Foreign Office supported Bleichröder's plea, if for their own reasons. Brauer replied to Bismarck that given the predilection of German capitalists to seek higher interest rates abroad, it would be best to channel such capital into the world market rather than to allow the further accumulation of east European securities. There was already an "appalling" amount invested in Russian securities. Bismarck objected to the Balkan investments as well and instructed the Foreign Office to inform Finance Minister Scholz of the new policy and to authorize Richthofen in Cairo to take the necessary steps.[104]

Scholz was not consulted but merely informed that Bismarck had changed his mind, largely because diversification of German capital abroad would minimize political difficulties: "Apart from the billions of Russian securities in Germany, the German market is inundated to an alarming extent by Austrian, Serbian, Turkish papers."[105] Bismarck had approved Bleichröder's plea *en principe*, but the modalities had to be worked out in Cairo as well as between Cairo and Berlin. Bleichröder had submitted proposals that would entitle him not only to the one-eighth of 1 percent commission, plus expenses, that the Caisse offered the Houses in London and Paris. He hoped as well to make a profit by paying according to the fixed ratio of franc to pound, which would allow him to pocket the proceeds of a more favorable daily exchange rate. After some months of further wrangling and after Berlin had obtained the approval of the British government and the London Rothschilds, Bleichröder was appointed disbursing agent for the earlier loans—though he was obliged to pay German bondholders according to the daily rate. The principal and very substantial profit for the disbursing agent arose from the fact that the funds to be paid to bondholders were deposited with Bleichröder—who could make use of these funds between the date of delivery and disbursement, even if only for a few days; the sums involved were large enough to make this a significant operation. By March 1887 Bleichröder's much enlarged role in Egyptian securities was formally acknowledged.[106]

Bleichröder owed his success not so much to Bismarck's favor as to his gradual reshaping of his foreign policy. By 1886 he intended to be mildly pro-British in Egyptian matters—in part because he was made uneasy by the first stirrings of a Franco-Russian rapprochement. He also sought to deny German capital to Russia. For all these reasons, he favored Bleichröder's augmented role in Egypt—and he favored it so much that by August 1889 he himself invested nearly 150,000 marks in a 4 percent Egyptian loan.[107]

Bleichröder's success was quickly followed by more anguish. In 1888 a new crisis erupted, apparently over the emission of a new loan. Bleichröder's friend and sometime rival in Berlin, Adolph von Hansemann, had intruded, and in unprecedented panic, Bleichröder sent two letters to Hatzfeldt, his client and Germany's ambassador in London, begging him for help in the

Egyptian affair. Hatzfeldt should disabuse the London Rothschilds, who were in collusion with Hansemann, of their high opinion of Hansemann's connections with the German Foreign Office; his own connections with Bismarck were far more important. Bleichröder feared for his preeminence in Egypt, and this was a matter "of the greatest importance to his House"; it prompted his quite unabashed promise to the debt-ridden Hatzfeldt to let him participate fully in the Egyptian loan—and still more fully in the Mexican venture. It was the most anxious SOS of Bleichröder's surviving business correspondence.[108] In the end, his efforts prevailed, and his unique standing remained unbreached.

Bleichröder's extraordinary persistence in Egyptian affairs and his willingness to defend his stand by unusually sharp methods against his closest political and financial allies suggest that he was a formidable antagonist when he thought the stakes justified it. His tenacity in Egypt contrasts forcibly with his modest moves in Germany's own colonies. The Egyptian business fell within his special domain: the servicing of government loans. The profit he made on it—one-eighth of 1 percent commission and the interest on funds deposited—could not have been extravagant, though much of his business was built on such sure income, from hundreds of loans, week by certain week. What really mattered to him, judging from the appeals to Hatzfeldt, was his place in the banking world. In this, banking and politics were similar: prestige and power (or profit) were inseparable, alliances between states as between bankers could all too easily collapse into rivalries, and for both Bismarck and Bleichröder—if on a different scale—constant suspicion was the price of power.*

Bismarck's wish in 1886–1887 to redirect German foreign investment away from its preponderant commitment in eastern Europe reflected short-term political considerations as well as long-term commercial realities. Germany's foreign trade was overwhelmingly located in protectionist markets in Europe; if trade was to develop in new and highly competitive areas, the prior presence of German capital and German banking facilities would help. A British historian has recently argued that in the pre-1914 period "Germany was left with only four geographical areas in which she might win her way in competition—the Near and the Middle East (especially Asia Minor, the Levant, and the Persian Gulf); Equatorial Africa; South and Central America; China and the Far East. In each of these, she was meeting strong competition and making little headway in the decade before 1914."[109]

---

* At roughly the same time, Bleichröder fought just as hard to have the Spanish government appoint him as the sole German agent for the Spanish Debt. He instructed his client, the German minister in Madrid, Count Solms, to secure him that concession from the Spanish government, and Solms reported that the Deutsche Bank and the Mendelssohns were fishing for the same distinction—while he sought to ply the Spanish ministers with expensive entertainment, which was the best way of influencing them, but which he could ill afford. The Spanish finance minister, Solms reported, favored Bleichröder because "you represent the most important House in Berlin." The German government refused to interfere; in the end, Bleichröder received the appointment, and then requested Solms to get him a Spanish decoration as well. In return, Solms continued to get Bleichröder's financial advice, which led Solms to invest in—Egyptian securities. Solms to Bleichröder, 23 Jan. 1885, 24 Jan. 1885, 2 Feb. 1885, 19 March 1885, 10 March 1886, 1 Feb. 1887, BA.

Bleichröder had contributed to the opening of these areas to German influence. His role in the Middle East had been pioneering. In 1888 Bleichröder opened up yet another country to German influence: it was he who organized a major international loan to Mexico at a time when that country's government was desperately looking for European help. Mexico's need was great and European interest minimal; the German minister in Mexico thought that the only guarantee for the healthy development of Mexican politics was the person of President Porfirio Díaz; all other signs were unfavorable. Given everybody's skepticism, Bleichröder could extract singularly advantageous terms for his consortium, which included several British bankers; the banks would provide 10,500,000 pounds sterling to the Mexican government. The guarantee stipulated 23½ percent of the customs revenue; interest was fixed at 6 percent, and the bankers' allowance for expenses was 1¼ percent with an additional ¼ percent commission for the servicing of the loan; the issue price was set at 70 percent of the nominal value. The agreement, moreover, contained a secret clause, granting Bleichröder an option on all future Mexican loans. The bonds were twenty times oversubscribed: "An important factor in their popularity was the high standing of the bankers who participated in the transaction."[110]

Bleichröder had tried to establish for himself a monopoly position in Mexico, as the Rothschilds had done in Brazil—or so the German minister in Mexico reported to Bismarck.[111] A year later, an intense competition for a new Mexican loan ensued, which Bleichröder won—by various means, including, so it was rumored, a secret "commission" to the Mexican finance minister of £300,000.[112] This was a rather common practice then—as it is now. With great effort, Bleichröder maintained his Mexican position, but his heirs gradually forfeited it. His first entry into Mexican affairs coincided with an intensified competition among American, British, and German commercial interests; German trade continued to lag behind the others but would have fared worse without Bleichröder's initiative. In the decade commonly dubbed "the era of Bleichröder," German exports to Mexico increased fourfold. Bleichröder's role, of course, was indirect, neatly symbolized by his gift of two Krupp guns to the Mexican government. It was a way of obliging both the government and the Krupps, whom he had helped to finance and whose search for new markets he supported elsewhere as well.[113]

Bleichröder came to put much stock in the Mexican venture, and he encouraged others to do likewise. It was a hugely profitable business for him. Bismarck followed him into Mexican funds, as he had earlier into Egyptian funds. But Bleichröder also set up his own scheme to persuade the public at large of Mexico's great and rosy future; as we saw, he financed a trip to the United States and Mexico by one of his friends, Paul Lindau, who had offered to write "arresting descriptions" of Mexico. After Bleichröder's death, the Mexican venture became more difficult, and Schwabach quarreled with Sir Ernest Cassel—King Edward VII's banker—over it.[114]

The discrepancy between Bismarck's bold mercantile imagination and the timidity of German capitalists also characterized Germany's relations with China. The first German expedition to China was launched at the very begin-

ning of Bismarck's accession to power in the 1860s and contained a shipful
of young unknowns with distinguished careers ahead of them—men like Radowitz and Max von Brandt, who later became friends of Bleichröder's. Bismarck's interest in China quickened in the 1880s; he too thought that the
Chinese markets beckoned and that German suppliers should meet Chinese
demands for railroads and armaments, whereas there, too, British and American interests were stealing a march on Germany.

In the mid-1880s the usual round of great Berlin bankers formed an
informal "China study group" and dispatched a team of representatives to
China to survey and solicit opportunities. Hansemann also sought to reach an
independent agreement with the London Rothschilds—to whom, from Bleichröder's point of view, he was dangerously close.[115] In 1886 Schwabach wrote
the German minister in Peking, Max von Brandt, an "unofficial" letter, offering the services of the House of Bleichröder for all financial transactions and
for the construction of railways. He reminded Brandt of Bleichröder's connections with the Laurahütte ironworks and the major steamship line, the Nord-
deutscher Lloyd; given these, Bleichröder could meet Chinese needs at least
as well as any German competitor.[116] If Brandt talked to the proper authorities,
he must have met with indifference. In any case, nothing happened.

Bismarck had long hoped that a German overseas bank would be established so that German traders would not always be dependent on settling their
accounts via banks in London and Paris, a procedure that was costly in time
and money. The idea was first broached in 1881, and five years later—when
many German publicists were shouting for a "German Hongkong"—he again
sought to press German bankers to found such an institute.

Bleichröder's characteristic role in this has escaped notice so far. In
September 1887 he reported to Bismarck that the bankers discussing this venture had fallen into hopeless bickering among themselves: "Knowing that
because of the economic interests of Germany the founding of a German-
Chinese Bank is very close to Your Highness's heart, I take the liberty of
suggesting . . . that the promotion of this matter might best be achieved through
a conference, to be called by the director of the Seehandlung, of all those banks
and bankers here who belong to the well-known Seehandlungs-Consortium."
The director of the Seehandlung, Emil von Burchard, was skeptical. Bleichröder's suggestion, he thought, sounded "harmless" but would give the whole
enterprise a governmental character. Burchard sensed the opening wedge for
the usual bankers' demands for state support—and he demurred, pointing out
that in large measure the inability of the bankers to reach an agreement among
themselves had to do with the rivalry of individual bankers. In private conversation, Schwabach confirmed Burchard's suspicion: Bleichröder, the Disconto-Gesellschaft, and the Deutsche Bank had failed to reach an agreement
because of "the sharpened foreign (especially American) competition, because of the lack of safety and solidity of the Chinese business in general,"
and because of differences among themselves concerning the scope of such a
bank. Schwabach then told Burchard that Bleichröder's proposal did aim at
"putting this enterprise, which as a purely *private* promotion does not now
have any chance of realization, on a different basis and to bring it to life

through the participation of *government* funds." Bismarck finally asked a very reluctant finance minister, Adolf von Scholz, to instruct Burchard to call such a meeting.[117]

Within two months and after some opposition among his own ministers, Bismarck accepted Bleichröder's proposal. But the reluctance of the participants—Hansemann, Bleichröder, and Wallich of the Deutsche Bank were the leading members—was so great that the negotiations dragged on for another fifteen months. Hansemann used to explain to the Foreign Office that "we are [too] pedantic" for such enterprises, while Bleichröder insisted that he was already too heavily committed in Europe. Finally, in February 1889, after Bismarck had once again expressed his "warm interest" and his willingness "to make further use of his good offices for the development of the project," the Deutsch-Asiatische Bank was finally founded, with the Disconto-Gesellschaft signing for the largest number of shares, followed by Bleichröder and the Deutsche Bank, by most of the German banks with any foreign interest, and by the Seehandlung, which had been prevailed upon to sign for a token amount.[118]

Once again Bleichröder had assessed correctly—and no doubt contributed to—the extraordinary caution of the German bankers. The first few years of the new bank proved disappointing and seemed to confirm the founders' view that the whole enterprise—in Brandt's disparaging paraphrase of their sentiments—had merely been "a favor to the imperial government." For Bleichröder this particular effort on behalf of German overseas expansion had an unpleasant sequel. A German businessman in China, Carl Paasch, had taken umbrage at his erstwhile friend Brandt, and, after he had returned to Germany, published vicious pamphlets denouncing Brandt's intimate relations with businessmen and vilifying Bleichröder's nefarious influence on the Foreign Office. This particular exercise in paranoid crankiness contributed to Brandt's premature retirement from the Peking ministry (and his subsequent return there as a director of the Deutsch-Asiatische Bank) and further embittered Bleichröder's last years.[119]

Bismarck always took a strong interest in Germany's exports of capital, weighing the political and economic consequences of such exports. At times, the two interests diverged: for economic and commercial reasons, Bismarck hoped to encourage a rechanneling of German investments abroad, so that new markets for German trade would be opened up at the same time. This was especially true of certain overseas investments. But political considerations dictated continued financial support of Germany's allies—and obstruction of her likely enemies, especially Russia. The ever present relations between *haute politique* and *haute finance* became still closer and more complicated after the mid-1880s, as Bismarck's diplomacy ran into ever greater difficulties. More and more, the statesmen of the Great Powers, especially in Germany and France, sought to use their bankers as subsidiary agents of their foreign policy.[120] A few examples from Bleichröder's experience will suffice.

In 1879 Austria-Hungary became Germany's principal ally. Bleichröder had no very sanguine view of the finances of the Dual Monarchy, but took a strong interest in them even before the Alliance.[121] After 1879 he and Hansemann did yeoman service on behalf of the Austrian government. They helped to funnel much German capital into the monarchy, and they capped their efforts in 1881 when the two bankers managed to convert a 400 million Hungarian state loan (*Goldrente*) at 6 percent into a 545 million loan at 4 percent —to the obvious benefit of the Hungarian economy and its prestige. In 1880 Hansemann was rewarded by being made Austrian consul general in Berlin, and both men enhanced their wealth and standing by their services to the Dual Monarchy.[122]

But Bleichröder also knew how to fulfill Bismarck's wishes in a negative (and safe) fashion: he resisted the lure of Balkan profits and left it to rivals to conclude tempting deals that quickly enough turned sour. Serbia was a case in point. From the moment it gained independence in 1878, Serbia was dependent on foreign investments, and almost from the first, the French predominated—largely in the form of Bontoux's famous bank, the Union Générale. A creature of the Vienna Rothschilds, Paul-Eugène Bontoux had turned rival; their unrelenting enmity pursued him to the end, which came in 1882.

Serbia was a political satellite of Austria, and the Austrians would have liked Bleichröder and Hansemann to pick up the Serbian pieces, but the French predominance was quickly reestablished by the appearance of the governmental bank, the Comptoir d'Escompte. In 1884 Bleichröder's former associate Carl Fürstenberg undertook a large Serbian loan and thus brought German investors onto the scene. Bismarck's concern with Serbian finances was further aroused by Serbia's war against Bulgaria in 1885. He demanded details, and Reuss from Vienna and Count Bray from Belgrade gave graphic accounts of French predominance in Serbia: with what infinite charm and worldliness, with what sureness of touch, the French had played on the venality of Serbian officialdom—King Milan included—and how in this fashion they had landed the entire country in a "morass of corruption," with themselves as financial overlords.[123]

In January 1886 Bleichröder had a long interview with the Austrian foreign minister, Count Kálnoky, in which the subject of Serbian finances was discussed at length. Bleichröder's visit (he had seen Bismarck on New Year's Eve, 1885, just before his departure) was part of Bismarck's hitherto overlooked strategy to use the question of Serbian finances in order to test the loyalty of Austria-Hungary. In an extraordinary note to Reuss of December 30, 1885, which has never been published, Bismarck pointed to the intimacy that prevailed between Serbia and France, based on French financial control, supported, however, by the Austrian Länderbank. This intimacy could not be a matter of "indifference" for Germany—given her own likely obligations to Serbia. King Milan's openness to bribes from everywhere, including perhaps the French government, "is not exactly encouraging either." But Reuss's (and presumably Bleichröder's) main task was to sound out Kálnoky on a far more delicate issue:

The question whether Austria judges Serbia's apparent liking for France *with forbearance* or not is not without interest for our relations with Austria. The stronger the chauvinistic element becomes among all parties in France, the more important it is for us to ascertain Austria's position, with which we would have to reckon if against our will we should become involved in a war with the French Republic or with a French monarchy that may have sprung from it.

Bismarck reminded Reuss that Austria had refused to pledge her support in case of such an eventuality—hence it was important to use this case of Serbian involvement with France in order to get a "symptomatic" response which might give Germany some clues as to Austria's likely course.[124] Kálnoky told both Bleichröder and Reuss of his distress at French predominance, which he saw as "systematic despoliation." He was reassuringly contemptuous of Serbian venality, but insisted that the French involvement was solely financial.

The German minister in Belgrade, Count Bray, put the same point succinctly: "In one word: French influence here is extraordinarily powerful and ready to meet any competition, but it is limited exclusively to the financial realm." The French government had not tried to dictate Serbian policies in any way. The French "want to extract from the country whatever life's strength it still possesses. . . . This aim should be reached in the not too distant future." And at that point, the German holders of the Serbian loan would be sorry; when Bismarck read about Carl Fürstenberg and other bankers who had contracted this loan, he scribbled in the margin: "Frivolous people."[125] Bismarck was reassured, and Bray's prediction about the "desolate condition" of Serbian finances proved right. Hopelessly indebted, the Serbian government in the late 1880s tried a new variation on the age-old game of evasion: it delayed interest payment without acknowledging bankruptcy and hoped that bankers, whose securities were accordingly declining, would rush to its rescue. Fürstenberg had a hard time—and Bleichröder could be pleased that he had escaped that particular trap.[126] Like most Balkan capitals, Belgrade liked to call itself the Paris of the East; in matters financial, it could more properly call itself "Little Egypt."

Bleichröder did not escape the Balkan imbroglio altogether. With the Comptoir d'Escompte and the Ottoman Bank, he had helped to finance a branch line in East Rumelia. In July 1888 Bleichröder appealed to Bismarck for immediate help because the Bulgarians had confiscated the railway the instant it had been completed and had arrested most of the personnel. Bismarck replied that he could do nothing in Sofia and that Bleichröder had best mobilize French intervention, since more French than German capital was invested.[127] Undeterred, Bleichröder joined Hansemann later that year to float a large Rumanian loan and thus maintained what to a rival seemed their "strong and almost unassailable position" in Rumania. After Bleichröder's death, the firm collaborated with the Disconto-Gesellschaft in financing the development of the Rumanian oil industry. In 1889 he joined an international consortium for a loan to Greece.[128] These operations were essentially routine for Bleichröder—the bread and butter of his House.

In the last three years of Bismarck's reign, when it became ever more difficult to maintain the fine web of alliances that he had spun, Bleichröder helped him in a case in which the Great Powers used economic weapons for political ends in a particularly flagrant manner. In the 1880s Italy had been drifting ever closer to the Austro-German Alliance, as first signaled by the formation of the Triple Alliance. Various moves, including the visit of Italian officers to Berlin at the end of 1887 to concert plans for an Italian expeditionary force on the Rhine in case of European war, pushed the French into a full-scale attack on Italian finances, which until then they had been most solicitous in shoring up. Encouraged by their government, French banks and investors liquidated their Italian securities, sold their Italian real estate, and by their well-publicized maneuvers helped to precipitate a major crisis in the Italian economy.

On February 15, 1888, the Italian ambassador in Berlin, Count Launay, told Bismarck that Italy's pro-German, anti-French premier, Francesco Crispi, was immensely worried over "a great depression" of Italian funds on the Paris market. Unable to coerce Italy frontally, France had decided on "a silent war" (*une guerre sourde*) in order to punish Italy for her various alliances. Could Bismarck persuade Berlin bankers to help at once? A few days later, "the most famous of all tariff wars" began. It embittered Franco-Italian relations for a decade.[129]

Bismarck summoned Bleichröder, who had long kept a wary eye on Italian finances. Already in 1875 Holstein suggested that Bleichröder should try to replace the Rothschild hold on Italian finances, perhaps together with some British houses. This would free Italy from "dependence on France, whereas . . . a financial obligation to you could perhaps have political benefit for Germany." At that time, Bleichröder turned to Bismarck, and Herbert replied immediately: "That we would like to be accommodating to Italy you know from conversations you have had with my father. Also, at present, as far as he can see, there is no danger whatever to peace."[130] The French hold was preserved; in the fall of 1880 Bleichröder wrote to Bismarck that the Italian government was looking to the Paris Rothschilds for a very large loan to stabilize the lira's international standing. Remembering his earlier conversations with Bismarck, Bleichröder felt safe in urging the Italian ambassador "to remember how important it is that Italy consider her loans in a 'cosmopolitical' fashion and not lay principal emphasis on France alone." Italy should negotiate with England and Germany as well.[131] But the Paris Rothschilds and French banking generally maintained their position in Italy, as Bleichröder could also gather from the fact that from 1880 to 1887 the Paris Rothschilds frequently asked him to transfer millions of francs to the armament firm of F. Krupp on behalf of the Italian government and for the account of the Rothschilds.[132]

But 1888 was different. Bleichröder was no longer soliciting Italian business, but the Italians needed him—and other German houses—for instant support unless their shaky credit structure was to topple altogether, particularly since the French efforts coincided with the onset of an economic depression in Italy.[133] The day after Count Launay's appeal to Bismarck, Schwabach was called to the Foreign Office, Bleichröder having gone from his interview with Kálnoky to a vacation in Nice. Schwabach declared that if the chancellor should deem it desirable, "the House of Bleichröder would be perfectly willing to enter into negotiations with some of its associated firms—in an absolutely secret manner which would not invoke the responsibility of the government at all—in order to counteract the Paris *baisse* through some large purchases of the [Italian] *rente* which it thinks well of." Bismarck's marginalia were curt and to the point: next to Schwabach's offer he wrote "good," and could not "London be taken along?" and next to Schwabach's solicitation of governmental approval, he noted "fiat."[134]

Bleichröder moved in at once: his House bought millions of Italian *rente* within days, and the price was stabilized. But all sorts of complications ensued. Other German bankers—the Darmstädter Bank and the Deutsche Bank—approached the Italian government directly and offered it new loans. Crispi thought that the Paris Rothschilds were using Bleichröder to liquidate their Italian holdings on the Berlin market, and he urged the German government to put pressure on Bleichröder, though it is not clear whether Crispi wanted Bleichröder to stop working for the Rothschilds or merely to buy more for himself. Schwabach's answer was unambiguous: "Whether the Paris Rothschilds were depressing the price of Italian [securities] was a matter of complete indifference to his House. Considering our political interests he was entirely resolved to raise the price of Italian obligations as much as possible." In pursuit of this goal, in the last few days, he had bought 18 million francs of Italian *rente*, 2 million for his private account. Bismarck wanted Launay informed of Schwabach's position, and he assured Crispi that Germany would continue to do all it could to help Italy's finance interests "in its struggle with the Paris Exchange."[135]

In early March 1888 Bleichröder made an offer to the Banca Nationale to form a consortium for the purchase of Italian *rentes*; other German firms used other means and channels to undercut his offer. While Count Berchem rather gloatingly reported to Bismarck on how indebted Crispi and the Italians ought to feel at the help proffered (mostly by Bleichröder), Solms reported from Rome that the leader of a rival German group had declared to him: "Bleichröder is totally excluded. We work together with the Deutsche Bank, the Comptoir d'Escompte in Paris and the Vienna Länderbank. . . ." Bismarck got bored: "I can't bother myself anymore with this money business," he wrote on one of the reports.[136]

But Bismarck could not for long afford boredom with Italian finances. Even after Bleichröder and his associates had stemmed the immediate crisis of 1888, the downturn of the Italian economy continued and led to the failure of successive banks. The state itself was threatened by bankruptcy, and with it, of course, Crispi's government, in whose survival Bismarck had a considerable stake. In 1889 Bleichröder helped to organize another German consortium; in 1890 he led efforts to found "a bank through which special support could be given to public credit—the Instituto di Credito Fondiario."[137] Immediately after Bismarck's fall, Solms wrote Bleichröder that the news had shaken Crispi's position, but that he could be toppled only in the economic realm, where he counted on Bleichröder's support. On the same day, Bleichröder dispatched a telegram to Crispi: "I am happy to be able to announce to Your Excellency that an entente has been concluded between me and a group of banks." Crispi needed Bleichröder's support, and Solms urged Bleichröder to give it.[138] Bleichröder continued his efforts, if reluctantly; he once lectured Ludwig Raschdau, the commercial expert at the Foreign Office (whose father had lost all his money in the Rumanian railways), that Russian loans would be far more advantageous than the Italian business and went so far, according to Raschdau, as to complain of the "unreliability" of the "Italian Jew," presumably Finance Minister Luigi Luzzatti. In the early 1890s, when the private credit structure of Italy was threatened, Bleichröder formed a German consortium, including Hansemann, which, in 1894 with Austrian and Swiss aid, founded the Banca Commerciale Italiano in Milan, with an initial capital of 700 million lira.[139] Its actual founding occurred a year after Bleichröder's death, but it was a fitting climax to his five-year stint on behalf of Italian finances—undertaken, as so much else in Bleichröder's career, both for his own benefit and for that of Bismarck's statecraft. In fact, Bleichröder's Italian venture brought him into close contact with Bismarck's successors—and thus demonstrated the continuity of his ties to the German state, regardless of the ruler at the helm.

As with so many of Bismarck's utterances, his laments about the timidity of German capitalists cannot be taken at face value. Did he believe them himself—or were they intended as so many deflections from the failure of his colonial policy? The older he got and the longer he was in office, the more critical he became of the docile Germans, the more he despised the docility that he himself had taught them. Why not blame German capitalists who had failed to play the role in the colonial field he had envisioned for them? Perhaps they could be held culpable for what Bismarck himself came to regard with ever more jaundiced eyes—the whole colonial episode of the mid-1880s. Or were German capitalists in fact less adventurous than their Western counterparts? Was there some substance to Bismarck's complaint in light of the fact that as late as 1913–1914, 53 percent of German foreign investments were concentrated in European countries—while the comparable figure for Britain was 5 percent?[140]

In the banking world, Bismarck knew Bleichröder best. And did not Bleichröder bear out Bismarck's allegation of a certain timidity? Bankers came to learn that though it may lack glamour, safety is its own reward, whereas the pursuit of great gains usually involves high risks as well. By policy and habit, Bleichröder preferred safety, and safety could be found in dealing with the financial needs of governments—and not with the uncertain future of some African desert. In this, as in so many other ways, Bleichröder was old-fashioned: he distrusted the false lure of colonies, just as he was somewhat reluctant to take full advantage of the immense opportunities that Germany's new industries represented. In the realm of state loans, so attractive to international bankers everywhere and hence so open to the fiercest rivalry, Bleichröder excelled. He battled tenaciously and knew, as did Bismarck in matters of statecraft, that today's archrival could be tomorrow's ally and that, loyalty being a rare virtue in competitive business, an oldtime friend and associate, like Hansemann, could easily join a consortium without or even against Bleichröder. Still, in state loans he could make a sure profit, he could maintain his close tie to his own government, and he could continue to think of himself, as he had in the 1860s, as an auxiliary of *der Chef*. Auxiliary, adviser, supplicant, but never equal, let alone master. In the one instance in which he sought to pit himself against the chancellor's wishes, in the question of enlarging German investments in Russia, Bleichröder was probably right, from both economic and political points of view, but the chancellor, himself embattled, won out. The primacy of the state persisted to Bleichröder's death and beyond.

CHAPTER 16

The Fall of Bismarck

Bismarck's tragedy was that he left a heritage of unassimilated greatness.
—Henry A. Kissinger

Bismarck has had no greater admirer than myself; my wife never read to me a speech or letter or saying of his without my feeling an absolute delight; the world has rarely seen a greater genius, rarely a man of greater courage or character, rarely a greater wit. But one quality he was denied: Magnanimity; the very opposite marks his life and finally took on the repulsive form of most petty malice (without the simultaneously present, infernal humor he would have been unbearable even earlier), and this nonmagnanimity finally ruined him and in this nonmagnanimity is the root of the relative indifference with which even his admirers see him leave.
—Theodor Fontane to Georg Friedlaender, May 1, 1890

Bismarck's system faltered before his demise. In the final years of his reign, all the cracks and weaknesses of his system at home emerged more and more clearly, while his often bullying policy of peace abroad became less and less compatible with the political aspirations of the other Great Powers. The last three years—and especially the last three months—were a period of constant, often desperate improvisations, made more difficult by the gradual weakening of Bismarck's authority at home.

That authority had rested on one unshakeable pillar: the support of William I. Without it, Bismarck's rule would have collapsed long before. It was never an automatic support, and his dependence on it made Bismarck suspicious of all other influences on the king, but for twenty-six years Bismarck won every contest he cared about. Not so with the other segments of German politics; even with his own cabinet in Prussia, he was often embattled (and complained that he had "to ask eight donkeys for permission whenever he wished to eat a spoonful of soup"); he almost never had a secure majority in the Reichstag; he always had to shop for the support of the member governments of the Empire—in short, he thought himself obstructed at every turn, and in his heart of hearts never doubted, as he hinted to the Reichstag in 1882, that absolutism and patriotism were a closer mix than patriotism and the semiconstitutionalism which he himself had introduced.[1]

In 1888 the ninety-year-old William I died, and three months later, his son, Frederick III, followed him into the grave. Frederick, the son-in-law of Queen Victoria and the hope of German liberals, had ascended the throne when already stricken by cancer of the larynx. The putative liberal governed mutely—to be followed by the most verbose of Hohenzollerns. The new monarch, William II, twenty-nine years old, was the antithesis of the old-fashioned Prussian: there was nothing austere or simple about him; he was a complicated man of painful insecurity—his left arm was withered and useless—who sought in pomp and bluster, in vulgar displays of virility, to mask his handicap and to assert what he devoutly believed in: his divine right to rule. But he craved confirmation of that right and yearned to be loved and idolized. Beyond the flawed character was a man of intelligence and vision, determined to set his own stamp on a Germany whose destiny, he thought, was to become a world power, and one universally feared as such. William governed for thirty disastrous years; his power was so great, his influence so pernicious, and his character so decisive that his reign can be read as a reminder that blind forces and structures do not shape everything in the world.

Bismarck and William II were utterly different in thought, experience, and character. Worse, Bismarck had grown accustomed to autocratic power, William was thirsting to be his own master, and sycophants had early on whispered to him that Frederick the Great would not have been great with a Bismarck at his side. To the underlying personal conflict and the growing estrangement between imperious chancellor and imperial upstart, there were substantive conflicts as well, policy choices on which the two men violently disagreed.

With the change of monarchs and the accession of this young and—to many—beguiling monarch, Bismarck's own entourage suddenly found an alternative to rally to, to idolize, to ingratiate themselves with. Bismarck's colleagues, rivals, and subordinates were troubled by his ever more intricate policies, and again substantive disagreement made personal desertion easier. For the last eighteen months of Bismarck's rule, intrigue turned into rank disloyalty, as his own subordinates, especially Holstein, leaked information to his enemies and to foreign powers in order to sabotage his policies. (In private, Holstein lamented the decline of Bismarck's energy and vision, and a corresponding increase in his mendacity, authoritarianism, and unreliability as well as a gradual addiction to morphia—all these symptoms were meant to excuse Holstein's disloyalty.)[2] Years of resentment found their poisonous distillation in those last months.

More important, the final months of Bismarck's rule demonstrated the essential ungovernability of the country he had created. And none saw the terrible implications of this ungovernability more clearly and more fearfully than the chancellor himself. He knew—what so many of William's generation did not—that instability at home and adventurism abroad could doom the German Reich.

For Bleichröder, Bismarck's declining years were excruciatingly hard. In the conservative era of the 1880s, his influence on domestic issues had already begun to decline, even as the resentment of the remaining influence spread. He was still a formidable presence, protected by Bismarck's exceptional trust in him. But as Bismarck's position faded, as the old court gave way to a new court with a new camarilla, Bleichröder's position became shakier. His elaborate system of reciprocal ties and connections weakened and gradually collapsed.

Telegraphing Bleichröder the news of William's death, Count Lehndorff struck the right note: "What should I say. Am undone and destroyed. God help us."[3] Bleichröder had so carefully cultivated the court of William, largely through his relations with Lehndorff; his old client August Count zu Eulenburg had been his link to Frederick's court. All these connections snapped—and what remained was Bleichröder's sense that the new emperor would be different.

Shortly after William's death, Emil Pindter visited Bleichröder and noted maliciously: "In Bleichröder's antechamber always a gay atmosphere: Count Eulenburg is inside, General Count Lehndorff is outside, drinking cognac, and asks, 'Well, August [Eulenburg], can't I get in sometime, too?' These are the pillars of throne and dynasty! ! ! ! Fighting over access to Bleichröder! ! !"[4] As time went on, it became quieter in Bleichröder's antechamber. Lehndorff retired at once, and Eulenburg, though appointed court chamberlain in 1890, never played the same role again; his relations with Bleichröder became less intimate.

At the new court, Bleichröder had no friends. Nor did he think Bismarck had any. (Later, he remembered the time, in spring 1888, when Bismarck, still moved by the occasion, told him that he and the young prince had just exchanged vows of undying loyalty, and Bleichröder supposedly replied: "And you believe in the prince's promise?")[5] Bleichröder had every reason to fear the new monarch. William was an admirer of Bleichröder's old foe Stoecker, and Bismarck had had occasion to rebuke the prince for his public espousal of the anti-Semitic pastor. William was surrounded by fierce anti-Semites—even if in later years, he too had his choice Jews and he too, in turn, became a target of the vicious, cranky type of anti-Semites.

None of this boded well for Bleichröder: he was bound to lose in the realignment of power and careerists. Worse, there were substantive issues dividing new court and old chancellor, issues that became exacerbated by the mounting suspicion on both sides. The kaiser had his own ideas on domestic and foreign policy; he also wished gradually to whittle down Bismarck's power. Bismarck disagreed with all of William's attempted initiatives and mobilized his colleagues against them—and did so the more uncompromisingly as he realized William's wish to strip him of his power.

It was Bleichröder's misfortune to be the central figure in the conflict over foreign policy that divided Bismarck and William. Worse, in defense of his own interests, Bleichröder dissented from the policies of both men. The issue was German-Russian relations, the most complex and most controversial part of Bismarck's foreign policy generally—and the one that in its seeming intractability threatened to undermine Bismarck's entire system.

.   .   .

In the last phase of Bismarck's reign, Russo-German relations dramatized the interconnectedness of politics: in both countries, domestic interests came to put heavy pressure on diplomats and diplomacy; the autonomy of foreign affairs—never a complete reality—was visibly disintegrating. Financial and economic interests came to the fore, as did the strident voices of journalists seeking to influence public opinion. The years 1886–1890 offered a kind of preview of 1911–1914, as nationalist passions rose in Russia and France, and as these passions in turn produced bellicose measures in Germany, the most powerful nation of the continent, made less predictable by its divided authority. The crises of the late 1880s, however, subsided again.

Put most succinctly, Germany was bound to Austria by the alliance of 1879 and by its interest in the survival of the Dual Monarchy; Austria was embattled with Russia in the Balkans, where Bismarck tried to follow an active policy of disinterest, designed to retain the confidence of the two antagonists. After the Congress of Berlin, Russia had growing grievances against Germany—grievances that M. N. Katkov, the clever editor of the *Moscow Gazette*, exploited to the full when he ceaselessly preached that Russia needed not its policy of caution but a "free hand," free, that is, from German constraint. Bismarck feared Katkov, whose political ascendancy coincided with the rise of the revanchist and immensely popular General Boulanger in France.

Bismarck thought that because of the Balkan imbroglio, Germany was like a man between two vicious dogs who would fly at each other as soon as they were unleashed.[6] Bismarck hoped to keep them leashed—and at the same time hoped that Britain and Italy would help Austria contain Russia, leaving him free to conciliate Russia.

Bismarck's Russian policy epitomized his ability to live with ambiguity. He had the strongest reasons for maintaining peaceful relations with Russia; he saw in Russo-German intimacy a bulwark for peace and monarchical solidarity and an obstacle to rebellious Poles and subversive socialists. His worst nightmare was a Russo-French entente—which in the time of Katkov and Boulanger had found its first noisy advocates. Bismarck tried steadily to conciliate and coerce Russia, to woo and bully her into maintaining close relations. He had few illusions about the possibility of permanently restraining the two dogs in the Balkans or of preventing the Russian dog from pairing off with its French counterpart. He had no illusion at all about the frivolous stupidity of some of Germany's military chieftains who saw salvation in a preemptive strike against Russia. As he put it to his ambassador in Vienna in 1888: "The most brilliant victories would not avail: the indestructible empire of the Russian nation, strong because of its climate, its desert, its frugality, strong also because of the advantage of having but *one* frontier to defend, would *after* its defeat remain our sworn enemy, desirous of revenge, just as today's France is in the West."[7] From the mid-1880s on, Bismarck's worries about relations with Russia deepened. More frequently than before, he chose a tough stance, hoping to intimidate the expansionist party there. Unlike the military in Berlin, he rejected the notion of a permanent hostility between the two countries and hence rejected the lure of a quick solution.

Bismarck's Russian policy was understood by few of his underlings and supported probably by none. The most celebrated saboteur was Holstein, who covertly collaborated with the anti-Russian party in Berlin and Vienna. William eventually sided with Bismarck's critics, and here emerged the central, divisive issue between emperor and chancellor—a conflict with the security of the Reich at stake and combining substantive disagreement with personal suspicion and enmity.

Bleichröder was in the middle of that conflict. His interests were simple: with his role in the great loans of the 1880s, Bleichröder had joined Mendelssohn and Hansemann as one of the chief bankers to Russia. The profits of loans and conversions were exceptionally large, and the outlook was for an ever expanding business because Russia's needs were great and her economic potential immense. Bleichröder, moreover, assumed an identity of interests between himself and the Reich. In 1884 Bismarck had urged him to promote the Russian loan, and Bleichröder thought that Germany's continued leading role in Russian finances enhanced its influence. But by 1886 the wind changed; other economic interests were clamoring for a hard line against Russia, and political-military considerations militated against facilitating credit to Russia.

The issue proved one of world-historical significance and hence justifies a short digression. In the 1880s Russia was embarked on the costly course of industrialization and of building a railroad network that would connect its vast expanse. Russia had insufficient domestic capital and hence was dependent on foreign investments—which could be attracted by a high rate of interest plus the prospect of Russian economic growth. Russian methods of borrowing abroad were costly and cumbersome, and successive finance ministers under Alexander III sought to rationalize the process by consolidating the myriad of small debts that had been issued on a short-term, high-interest basis. By such rationalization, the Russian treasury stood to cut down on its huge debt payments.

Germany had become Russia's chief supplier of capital. Approximately 20 to 25 percent of German export capital had gone to Russia; by January 1887 it was estimated that more than 2 billion marks' worth of Russian securities were in German hands.[8] This huge amount constituted well over half of Russia's total indebtedness abroad. Trade between the countries had been on an equally intense basis until the 1880s, when for nationalist and commercial reasons Russia raised her tariffs (even as Germany had done in 1879), to the great disadvantage of German industrial exports. In short, fiscal and commercial interests diverged.

For Bleichröder, the Russian connection was a source of vast profit and great political prestige. He had not been the first to enter the Russian field (the Mendelssohns had done that), and the competition for it was intense. But Bleichröder had a special advantage and knew how to play it. The

Russians appreciated his tie to Bismarck and came to refer to the "Bismarck-Bleichröder consortium."[9] Bleichröder's name obviously added kudos to Russian securities in Germany, and he had persuaded some of his best-known clients, Bismarck included, to invest their money in Russian funds.[10] His fame spread, and the United States minister to Russia attributed to Bleichröder the great success of the 1884 loan, which had attested "the recovery of Russian credit."[11] The Russians were pleased, and in 1885 the czar bestowed the Order of St. Stanislav on Bleichröder. The precondition of Bleichröder's further success was Bismarck's benevolent support; without it, German bankers would be in trouble, and Bleichröder doubly so.

Russo-German relations, however, deteriorated, and by the fall of 1886, as we saw in Chapter 13, Bismarck warned Bleichröder that he had lost faith in the permanence of good relations with Russia.* Bleichröder quickly saw that deteriorating political relations had their financial consequences as well. For years he had warned Bismarck that Russia could turn to France for its capital needs; in December 1886 he discovered that the Russians sought to raise a 500 million-franc loan in Paris, and he expected that the Paris banks would ask for his participation. He rushed to Bismarck's assistant in the Imperial Chancellery, Franz von Rottenburg, with the news, seeking Bismarck's approval and support for his participation: "What should I do? It cannot please the Prince if Russia gets money from Paris; he has told me repeatedly that financial relations between two countries are the surest basis for political contacts. If I refuse, moreover, Russia will be annoyed and the Chancellor wants to avoid that. . . ."

Rottenburg thought that Bleichröder, afraid of losing "the millions which this affair would yield him," sought some gesture of support from Bismarck which would demonstrate to German investors that Bismarck backed Bleichröder's renewed venture in Russian securities. Rottenburg stalled, wishing to shield Bismarck, who was resting in Friedrichsruh. On his own initiative, he told Bleichröder: "That financial relations do not necessarily lead to political intimacies, we have learned the hard way, through our own experience. If it were true, then we would virtually be welded to Russia."[12] Bismarck did indeed prefer noninvolvement, and Bleichröder's insistent calls on Rottenburg—late at night and on Christmas Day—proved frustrating. Worse, Herbert wanted him taunted as well and ordered Rottenburg to tell Bleichröder of the czar's recent remarks about the "damned Jews"; Rottenburg reported that Bleichröder "was not angry about the czar's remark; he smiled and whispered, 'frivolous man.' With a loan in sight, he will swallow even worse things."[13] Rottenburg's reports about Bleichröder were always harsh; a year before, he had invented some wild story in order to excuse himself to Herbert for receiving Bleichröder. And still, he was friendly with Bleichröder and found his Christmas Day interview rewarding: "*Der Bleiche*

---

* Nervous vigilance was part of statecraft. In August 1886 Bismarck heard it rumored that the Russian government had ordered 4,000 kilos of tincture of iodine from Schering. Iodine was commonly used to keep wounds sterile; "disquieted" by such warlike purchases, Bismarck ordered an immediate, discreet investigation. Rottenburg to Foreign Office, 18 Aug. 1886, GFO: I.A.A.a. 50, adh, secreta, vol. 3a.

gave me a lecture about all of European politics; perhaps some of it is of interest to Bismarck."[14] A week after telling Bleichröder not to participate, Bismarck ordered him to do so—or else the Russians would blame his aloofness on the chancellor's opposition.[15] In the end nothing came of that particular loan.

Bismarck's vacillation and sudden reversal should have prepared Bleichröder for worse to follow. As part of his intricate foreign policy (in early 1887, Bismarck tried to create an Anglo-Austrian combination to contain Russia that would leave him free to adopt a friendly stance toward Russia, as manifested in the secret Reinsurance Treaty between the two powers signed in June), Bismarck began a systematic campaign against Russian finances. His motives were many: he sought to intimidate Russia and deny her credit, but he also sought to punish her for a whole series of economic measures that had hurt German interests. Because of new tariffs, German industrialists suffered a major slump in their exports to Russia; other legislation restricted their right to conduct business there. German agrarians feared that a further expansion of the Russian rail network would augment grain exports to Germany. Bismarck may also have wanted to warn Russia's new finance minister, Ivan Alekseyevich Vishnegradski, who was known as a nationalist and protectionist. (Bleichröder had been reassured by his Russian friend A. Sack that Vishnegradski, though known as a protégé of Katkov's, was also a heavy investor in Sack's bank, a practical person unlikely to follow Katkov's absurd schemes.)[16] Moreover, Bismarck was genuinely concerned that there was too much Russian money in German hands, and in the summer of 1887 he authorized a press campaign against Russian securities. Russian values dropped by 5 percent, and in October the London *Economist* commented: "The Russian financiers must be well aware that the German market is as good as closed to them for a long period to come."[17]

In October 1887 Bleichröder himself was charged with warning Shuvalov against taking German peacefulness for granted. By November, egged on by Herbert and despite pleas from Bleichröder, Bismarck went even further. On November 10 he issued the famous *Lombardverbot* which ordered the Reichsbank to cease accepting Russian securities as collateral for loans.[18] The move was symbolic and dramatic rather than immediately effective; people assumed it would be a temporary measure; if maintained, it would obviously diminish investors' confidence in all Russian securities. But it was an offensive move, the more so as it was promulgated a week before Alexander III's visit to Berlin. In some ways, it was a variation on an old tactic of Bismarck's: to bully an opponent into friendship. In this instance, the tactic boomeranged, because France was eager to supplant Germany's fiscal presence in Russia—in fact, as we have seen, the first steps in that direction had already been taken.*

Bleichröder was distressed by Bismarck's "*Finanzkrieg*" against Russia. It depressed the value of all existing Russian securities and made it virtually

---

* The *Economist* commented on the conjunction of *Lombardverbot* and imperial visit— in a manner poignant to present-day readers: "It is not pleasant when the Russian Treasury wants money so pressingly, to find its loans formally banned on the most accessible Bourse

impossible for German bankers to undertake new operations. The exodus of Russian securities from Germany to France began almost at once, and Bismarck's goal of having less German money in Russian securities was quickly reached. Bleichröder thought it all a great mistake, and behind the scenes worked for a change of policy. Obviously Russian officialdom held him peculiarly responsible for Bismarck's actions. Bismarck explained to him that he had been "very dissatisfied" with his interview with Alexander III. In December Bleichröder wrote Bismarck that news from St. Petersburg made it clear "that the czar does not want war. . . . Russia's hostile attitude toward Austria is unmistakable, and the troop concentrations along the Austrian border are unquestionably intended to incite Austria."[19] The *Lombardverbot* transcended Bleichröder's personal interest: Paris now competed for the lucrative Russian business, just as Bleichröder had always warned, and in the process of this historic shift from Berlin to Paris the most intense rivalries among banking houses took place as well.

In the ensuing struggles, Bleichröder had his own secret tie to the Russian finance minister, a tie that linked him to one of the fascinating minor characters of the underworld of European politics. Bleichröder had overt as well as secret links to Elie de Cyon, alias Ilya Fadeyevich Tsion. Cyon was a Russian Jew, born in 1843, a distinguished professor at the St. Petersburg Academy of Medicine, a student of Virchow and Claude Bernard, driven out by angered radical students. In 1876 Cyon emigrated to France, changed his name and appropriated the aristocratic "de," began a journalistic career there as editor of *Le Gaulois*, and succeeded his patron, Mme. Adam, as director of *Nouvelle Revue*; in 1880 he was made a chevalier of the Legion of Honor. By the late 1880s he was widely known as a friend and an agent of Katkov's, presumed therefore to be anti-German; in February 1887 the new Russian finance minister, Vishnegradski, called Cyon to St. Petersburg to help him develop new ties with the Paris market. In the late 1880s and early 1890s Cyon was taken for what he himself said he was: a promoter of the Franco-Russian alliance, of which he also became the first historian.

From 1887 on, Cyon also had the closest ties to Bleichröder. (As early as 1884 he approached Bleichröder with the extraordinary suggestion that the latter help finance a newspaper that Cyon and Katkov would edit jointly; if Bleichröder would finance it, it would support close Russo-German relations. Bleichröder rejected the invitation, and in 1893 Bülow lamented the fact that the French had been "less prudish. It is better to sacrifice a few millions than to make real concessions.")[20] On his way back from Russia, Cyon stopped off in Berlin to brief Bleichröder on his misson, which included the establishment of the first direct tie between the Paris Rothschilds and the Russian finance minister. Bleichröder in turn assured Cyon of Bismarck's peaceful intentions.[21]

Cyon found his relations with Bleichröder profitable—in the literal

---

by order of the German Chancellor. These courts, living as they do from hand to mouth, and in constant pecuniary difficulties, are compelled to think of finance in a way which seems to Englishmen, whose Government is never in difficulties, rather degrading." 26 Nov. 1887, p. 1490.

sense of the word—and hence continued them for the next three years. At the end of May 1887 Cyon wrote Bleichröder that "since the 20th of May I am in the service of the [Russian] Finance Ministry as official for extraordinary missions. All major affairs will thus go through my hands." He also assured him of his continuing gratitude for Bleichröder's former—and unexplained—services and promised to remember these in the future. Bleichröder wanted to make sure of Cyon's services and by return mail offered him a commission in advance of a particular transaction which Cyon was to negotiate; Cyon accepted the advance of 1,200,000 francs, provided he would be allowed to pay interest on the advance until the commission had been actually earned. Such delicacy![22] There followed a steady stream of letters and coded telegrams from Cyon to Bleichröder, first from Paris and then, in the summer of 1887, from St. Petersburg, whence he had again been summoned by Vishnegradski in order to help him break the Berlin monopoly on Russian loans—or so the French perceived his mission, which was also the occasion of his renouncing his French and reassuming his Russian citizenship. From there, he warned Bleichröder that the German press campaign against Russian securities was jeopardizing Bleichröder's interests at a time when the outlook for Russo-German deals was again propitious; at the same time, Cyon publicly attacked Bismarck as the instigator of this press campaign, and Bleichröder transmitted to Cyon Bismarck's denials of these charges.[23] To Bleichröder, Cyon always appeared as the friend of Russo-German relations. In Russia Cyon was always the proponent of a Franco-Russian entente and the champion of Katkov—who died that summer, hoping that Cyon would become his successor as editor and defender of Russian nationalism.

Cyon preferred to work for Russia and himself in Paris. For the next two years, he supplied Bleichröder with inside information about the negotiations between Vishnegradski and competing French and German bankers. At times, Cyon had to be "laconic" because "my entire correspondence is opened at the demand of G. [presumably Giers, foreign minister and special target of Katkov]." He warned Bleichröder that in Russia he was considered an accomplice of Bismarck's hostile policy, carried on despite Russia's peaceful disposition.[24]

Cyon served many masters in order to serve himself. Everybody knew him; everybody suspected him. In April 1887—at the very time when Bleichröder was paying Cyon for services yet to be performed—Bismarck asked Bernhard von Bülow, the German chargé d'affaires in St. Petersburg (and later German chancellor), about Cyon and received this classic answer: "Decent and patriotic Russians consider the journalist Cyon as a mendacious and venal Jew with revolutionary tendencies. Still, Cyon is an intimate friend of Katkov. This merely proves that Katkov is either crazy or himself a cryptorevolutionary."[25] Giers told the story that Alexander III once referred to Cyon as "a canaille . . . a bad man."[26] The French police meanwhile suspected Cyon of pro-German leanings, emphasized his frequent attacks on the venality of the French press and parliament, and thought him capable of serving all manner of "discreet and shady needs" at the Russian Embassy in Paris. In 1889 he was implicated in charges that Bismarck had tried to establish direct links with Boulanger via Bleichröder and Cyon. He acknowledged his relations with Bleichröder, but denied the charge. Some doubts remain.[27] At the end of the 1890s he wrote a polemical attack on Vishnegradski's successor, Count Witte, and lost his Russian citizenship because of it. The Germans expelled him for anti-Bismarck pamphlets, the French refused his plea for renaturalization (they were afraid of offending their Russian friends: Cyon became a victim of the very entente he helped to promote), and he finally settled down in Switzerland, with occasional, furtive visits to Paris to see his mistress. He died in 1912, helped by the sacraments of the Church, received a Church funeral, and carried with him to his grave the secret of why so promising a scientist should have so squandered his gifts and talents.[28]*

From 1888 to 1890 Bleichröder was caught up in Russian affairs, which became more and more complex and demonstrated in microcosm the hazards that Bleichröder faced in a world so intricately interconnected. As a banker, he wished to maintain his tie to Russia; as Bismarck's confidant, he could ill afford to ignore, let alone defy, the chancellor's wishes—which themselves proved vacillating, motivated as they were by shifting considerations. Meanwhile, the price of Russian securities declined in Berlin and, at lower prices, they gradually found their way into French hands. In May 1888 Bleichröder was credited with stopping the slow erosion of the ruble in Berlin and thus served his own interests and those of Russia.[29]

All through the spring of 1888 he sought to persuade Bismarck to change his anti-Russian policy, but to no avail. Bleichröder was chafing at the bit, angry and puzzled at Bismarck's tight rein. At times, he thought that the anti-Russian course was due to the pressure of Prussian agrarians; at other times he thought Bismarck wanted to inhibit Russian armaments. Bleichröder was impressed by neither argument and told the French ambassador in May: "I understand absolutely nothing of Prince Bismarck's present policy, and I am wondering where we are headed."[30]

For about seven months Bismarck proved unbudgeable. In July 1888—at the very time of William's accession to the throne and the first serious negotiations between Vishnegradski and French banks—he began to relent. By the fall of 1888 French and German bankers flocked to St. Petersburg and vied with one another to obtain a loan. Bleichröder dispatched Schwabach,

---

* The final police report on the subject of his possible renaturalization, submitted to the 2d Bureau of the Cabinet, offers some clues—and an extraordinary insight into the police view of conventional morality: "It is probable that he stood to realize large benefits from these diverse operations [including the Panama scandal], but we have learned nothing unfavorable that would cast doubt on his probity. M. de Cyon has always lived extremely well. . . . As to his conduct, it is not irreproachable, but it corresponds—or almost corresponds—to that of the majority of rakes of our time. Although married and father of a family, he has had mistresses and particularly has maintained relations with an actress, Marie Legoult, from whom he has a child which he receives at his home." Préfecture de Police, Archives de la Seine, Paris, 28 May 1895.

but apparently with a variety of projects instead of precise propositions; Cyon explained Schwabach's failure: "Vishnegradski is a mathematician, and he has a certain instinctual disinclination against anything that is not submitted to him clearly and in definite figures."[31] As rival negotiations were proceeding in St. Petersburg, Bleichröder sought to win Bismarck's formal sanction for his participation in a Russian loan.

In October Rottenburg informed Bleichröder twice that Bismarck wanted "to accommodate" Russia, and did not object to the proposed arrangement, provided that the total value of Russian securities in German hands would remain unchanged and that the public would in no way be encouraged to invest in funds that Bismarck did not deem "safe."[32] Was it the securities that he thought unsafe or the pro-Russian publicity? In the same month, Bleichröder discussed his Russian schemes with Bismarck in Friedrichsruh, but a few days later wanted still further reassurance. Finally, Rottenburg wrote him a "very confidential" and very stern letter, reminding him that he had just conversed with Bismarck in Friedrichsruh about this matter and that it was time to leave Bismarck in peace:

> Moreover, His Highness would hardly find it compatible with his official position to express his views about this matter in writing. In accordance with my personal view I should point out to you that [to conclude] a Russian loan at the moment when at least two Russian army corps are moving close to the Austrian frontier and when the front lines are receiving strong material reinforcements would generally create the impression of a war loan.

This would be particularly alarming to Rome and Vienna. "You are yourself . . . so perspicacious in political matters that it is not necessary for me to direct your attention to this aspect of the matter."[33]

In the event, Bleichröder did not benefit from Bismarck's reluctant change of heart. By late 1888 a French consortium, headed by the Banque Paris et Pays Bas and excluding the Rothschilds, beat out their long-established German counterparts, and Vishnegradski signed with them. They offered a 500 million-franc loan on the Paris market, and while Mendelssohn and Fürstenberg's Berliner Handelsgesellschaft participated in this offering, Bleichröder was shut out. The loan was a political sensation and a financial triumph: for the first time French *rentiers* discovered the attractiveness of solid Russian bonds with their high yield compared to the seemingly uncertain securities of their own country, buffeted as it was by political storms and financial scandals. The immediate profits for the participating banks had been nearly 11 million francs. Bleichröder had every reason to mind his exclusion and to mend his fences.[34]

Bismarck now veered back to a more pro-Russian policy, and in March 1889 Bleichröder took part in a Russian loan. In April he and Hansemann— on behalf of what used to be called the Rothschild consortium—negotiated for a major conversion operation in Berlin. The Paris Rothschilds took the occasion to hector Bleichröder, instructing him to await their initiative, to be patient because even if later the Russians demanded a higher price of emission "our profit consists of the margin, and we do not care what the base of that margin is, as long as the base is safe and certain." Moreover, Baron Alphonse complained, German haste appeared unseemly, since most of the new securities would have to be sold in the Paris market; the Germans had been unloading their Russian holdings continually. Hansemann and Bleichröder pushed negotiations anyhow and by the end of May, on behalf of the Rothschild consortium—though with themselves taking 26 percent each and the Rothschilds apparently having to be satisfied with much less than the 33 percent they had stipulated—signed an agreement with Vishnegradski. It called for a huge conversion of 250 million marks of old 5 percent Russian railroad shares for new shares at 4 percent; the Russian state had become a virtual guarantor of these shares, which at once made them appear more attractive and allowed the Russian state to effect savings because of the lower interest rate. The German press welcomed these operations, which it was assumed Bismarck had approved. In fiscal terms, the conversion was a success, and Bleichröder and Hansemann pocketed the lion's share of profits. Bleichröder, however, became the sole target of unprecedented abuse. His last great Russian enterprise also proved to be his greatest political liability at home.[35] For him, they were Pyrrhic profits.

Almost at once, the Bleichröder conversion, as it was always referred to, became the focus of the first great battle between Bismarck and William, egged on by his ambitious, anti-Semitic advisers. Waldersee, Holstein, and company were furious at this service to Russia at a time when they thought war was inevitable and desirable. They wanted to make war with, not money from, Russia, and at the very least, they wanted Bismarck's *Finanzkrieg* continued with new severity. They had no difficulty in feeding William's anger; he had turned from being Russophile to being Russophobe and was determined to teach Bismarck a lesson in statecraft that he would not forget. To William's party, the issue seemed starkly drawn: they were defending Germany's national interests, which Bismarck had allowed his Jew to injure for the sake of his profit.

William was certain that the operation would save the Russians 20 million marks annually in interest, that this would strengthen their credit, augment their war chest, and tempt them to hurl themselves against Germany. He demanded that Bismarck stop the conversion, either by direct pressure on Bleichröder or by indirect pressure on the Berlin stock market so that it would not list the new Russian securities. It was widely rumored that in a letter to Bismarck he accused Bleichröder of being "a *Canaille* without a fatherland who thinks only of his business deal."[36] Bismarck would not budge and replied: "I cannot . . . influence his [Bleichröder's] affairs, because for services which cost him money he always expects counterservices which I am unable to perform. The press is more easily in a position to scare off

Berlin bankers and foreign entrepreneurs, and it is already active in this direction." The conversion, moreover, would not enhance Russia's military potential, while the official interdiction of it would jeopardize Russo-German relations and the peace of Europe.[37] But Bismarck had another reason for not affronting Russia at that moment. He was at the height of a conflict with Switzerland over its toleration of subversives and had just put together a concerted effort by Germany, Austria, and Russia to put pressure on Switzerland. Bismarck advised the kaiser that "he considered Social Democracy more dangerous than strengthening Russia for war through loans"—a striking phrase.[38] In the end, the Berlin market did authorize the listing of the new issues and the immediate threat of William's dismissing Bismarck because of Bleichröder, a spectacle Holstein solicitously conjured up for Herbert, faded.[39]

But the conflict remained: it was too good an issue for the emperor's party to let go of it. It appealed to all those noble souls who thought bankers corrupt and Jews "without a fatherland"; it appealed to the many officials who resented Bleichröder's influence and who thought that at a minimum the affair could force a break between Bleichröder and Bismarck, humiliating to both men. Herbert played an ambiguous role. To the kaiser's most intimate friend, Philipp Eulenburg, he wrote: "I, too, would like to wreck the handi-work of those gangsters of bankers who are helping to give lower interest to the Russians, but I am unfortunately rather powerless in this matter."[40] Having thus identified himself with the emperor's cause, he carefully explained to Rantzau the origin of William's fury; Bismarck's enemies

> have told His Majesty, what unfortunately is true—that Bleichröder is everywhere spreading the lie that the Chancellor was not opposed to the conversion and that through years of inconsiderate mendacity on Papa's account, Bleichröder had established such a position at the Berlin Bourse that all the other marketeers [*Börsianer*] believed him that his transactions had been approved by the government, *otherwise he would not engage in them.* For years, I would have liked Papa to have dismissed this dangerous Jew as his banker, he is too inconsiderate a liar, and Papa has had more trouble and annoyance through him than he himself knows; when this money-grubbing Semite can earn a few millions, then he could not care less what happens to Papa or the Fatherland.

Bismarck saw this letter and noted in the margin apropos of Bleichröder's not caring: "Who would?"[41] But Bismarck's even-handed contempt of humankind could not avail against his foes: they hammered away at the near-treason of Bismarck's Jew Bleichröder.

Bismarck's most implacable foe was Count Waldersee, who in 1888 had been appointed by his friend William II to succeed Moltke as chief of the general staff. Just before, Bismarck had confided to Bleichröder that he thought Waldersee would have to be removed from Berlin.[42] Waldersee was a political general *par excellence*, determined to dictate policy, preferably by becoming Bismarck's successor. He was certain that Germany was headed for a "world war" and should strike first, preferably against Russia.[43] Waldersee and Bismarck had quarreled in the past, and Waldersee now used Bleichröder as a wedge to divide chancellor and emperor.

When William wanted Bleichröder attacked in the press, Waldersee insisted that "this would no longer be enough; the Chancellor himself must intervene. If the Jews know that he is definitely against [the Russian loan], then they will keep their hands off; if not, not." William next berated Herbert for Bleichröder's sins, and Herbert, with understandable irritation, replied, "But Your Majesty knows that I have no relations with him at all." William rejoined, "I know that, but I do not care about it, because he goes in and out of your father's house."[44] William also ordered Rudolf Lindau, a subordinate of Herbert's and a close acquaintance of Bleichröder's, to denounce Bleichröder's Russian schemes. Lindau now served William's wishes quite often and hence had no compunction about attacking Bismarck's banker and his own brother's benefactor. Lindau used some articles written by Carl Fürstenberg, Bleichröder's former protégé and now head of the Berliner Handelsgesellschaft, which had been left out of the Russian operation.[45] It was hard times for everyone.

Bismarck encouraged the government press to attack Bleichröder's schemes, while Bleichröder's journals (the *National-Zeitung* and *Berliner Börsen-Courier*) supported the Russian operation. William was satisfied with the press agitation, and the rift between him and Bismarck was formally closed.[46] Still, Bismarck was furious at Waldersee, and in the summer of 1889, the *Norddeutsche Allgemeine Zeitung* attacked Waldersee as a warmonger meddling in foreign policy. Indignant, Waldersee wrote the war minister, Verdy du Vernois, a scathing indictment of the man behind this campaign: "The whole press scandal was started because the attempt was made by the Very Highest Office to prevent the conversion loan; it originated therefore with people whose financial interests were threatened, with the 'Group Bleichröder,' i.e., with Jews and Jew-companions, and with those who find it troublesome that His Majesty should express or realize his own views."[47] For the next few months, Waldersee scattered his venom freely, attacking the Bismarck-Bleichröder axis as viciously as he could. Years later, when writing his memoirs, he admitted that his attacks on "Bismarck's relations with Bleichröder may have been greatly exaggerated" and decided for that reason—and perhaps out of fear of a libel suit—to delete the most offensive passages from publication.[48] Judging from what *was* published, we may assume that Waldersee was indeed stoking his anti-Bismarck campaign with ferocious anti-Semitism. Waldersee claimed success: Bleichröder's conversion loan of 1889, he wrote, marked the point at which the emperor "in his heart broke with Bismarck, father and son. . . . From then on, the emperor was only play-acting with the Chancellor."[49]

Bleichröder, then, was deeply involved in the struggles preceding Bismarck's fall. He had always been the favorite target of anti-Bismarck

450 GOLD AND IRON

scribblers;* the kaiser's party now used him for the same purpose. His power was attacked at the moment of its decline: clearly Bismarck brushed aside Bleichröder's objections to his Russian policy. In matters of such importance, Bleichröder's influence was limited. It is ironic to think that he was most vilified when he had passed his zenith—and when he was pursuing a policy that, serving his private interests, also would have benefited his country. Bismarck's anti-Russian course precipitated the financial prelude to the Franco-Russian Alliance, which Bismarck rightly had always feared as the gravest threat to Germany. It is probable, however, that in time Russia would have struck up a new economic and political relationship with France in any case.†

Bleichröder knew that he had acquired some very powerful enemies, and he may even have sensed that his very existence widened the gulf between emperor and chancellor. His "friends"—Holstein, Pindter, Rudolf Lindau, et al.—readily briefed him on the latest maneuvers against him. He saw the division of authority, and at the height of the controversy between William and Bismarck over his Russian projects Bleichröder uttered the lament which in different form was to be the standard lament of William's reign: "But I have to know whether Bismarck governs or *who governs!*"[50]

Bleichröder's choice was obvious. He wanted Bismarck to govern.** Sentiment and self-interest dictated the same policy: to do everything to preserve Bismarck's rule. Loyalty aside, Bleichröder knew William to be a friend of fierce anti-Semites. Bismarck's enemies were his enemies, only more so. Ironically, the greatest contribution Bleichröder could have made to Bismarck's cause was his own political extinction. That price Bleichröder neither could nor would pay.

The Russian loan controversy was but a prelude to Bismarck's final crisis—at which Bleichröder was again present, as he had been in Versailles

* And of course remained so: in the fall of 1889, Bleichröder received the Order of St. Anne from the czar, and several papers "seized the opportunity to criticize the lack of patriotism of Israelites who are not abashed to offer their credit to the aggrandizement of Germany's enemies." Hansemann was also decorated—but not abused. Ministerium für Handel und Gewerbe to von Richthofen, 9 Oct. 1889, DZA: Potsdam: Königl. Polizei Präsidium, Acta betreffend Gerson Bleichröder, Rep. 30; *Le Moniteur de Rome*, 13 Oct. 1889, newspaper clipping in GFO: Russland 71, Nr. 1, Bd. 5.

† Hans-Ulrich Wehler, usually so insistent on the importance of long-term trends, takes the older view that the Bismarckian system was to blame for the Alliance and cites as evidence the famous remark by Russia's conservative foreign minister, Giers, that "Bismarck drove us into the hands of France, especially by his financial measures." But what else would Giers have said in 1893 to the German ambassador? See H.-U. Wehler, *Krisenherde des Kaiserreichs 1871–1918* (Göttingen, 1970), pp. 178–180.

** He had been worried about Bismarck's departure for some time. In May 1888, during Frederick III's short reign, he pleaded with Bismarck not to resign because he disagreed with Crown Prince William's views. Following well-rehearsed lines from Holstein, Bleichröder told Bismarck, "Your Highness, when a pair of horses stampede, is it better for the coachman to be hurled from his box or to remain in his seat where he can still control them a little?" Norman Rich and M. H. Fisher, eds., *The Holstein Papers*, (Cambridge, 1957), II, 374–375.

at the beginning of Bismarck's rule in Germany. In the fall and winter of 1889, while Bismarck was ruminating in Friedrichsruh and the kaiser was on an imperial tour of the Near East, from which he flashed Bismarck fatuous messages about his triumphs, the political situation steadily deteriorated.

In 1887, by exploiting the specter of Boulangist *revanchisme* and Katkov's anti-German campaign, Bismarck invoked a terrible war scare and produced "patriotic" elections. The parties of the right, Conservatives, Free Conservatives, and National Liberals, formed the governing *Kartell*, and for the only time in the 1880s Bismarck had something like a parliamentary majority behind him. It would have been hard to preserve that uneasy alliance; it seems likely that Bismarck deliberately hastened its demise. By his maneuvers, the *Kartell* went into the elections of February 1890 in total disarray—and emerged beaten. The National Liberals and Free Conservatives lost half their seats; the Radicals doubled and the Socialists trebled theirs. It was a rout, and Bismarck's earlier plan for a Conservative-Center coalition now appeared to be the only possible solution. It was not one that appealed to William or his advisers.

After the elections of February 20, Bismarck pursued his *politique du pire*, exacerbating all existing conflicts in order to appear again, as he had in the beginning, as the indispensable leader. Within days of the election, he charted a collision course with the new parliament; he hinted that the princes had made the Reich and that they could unmake it, too; he toyed with scrapping the Constitution that he himself had designed. Others in Berlin preferred to scrap the architect of that Constitution.

By early March, Bleichröder was deeply worried. On a trip to Vienna, he told his friend and client the German ambassador, Prince Henry VII of Reuss, that Bismarck's fall was a distinct possibility. To Bleichröder it appeared as "the end of the world." He also identified Waldersee as Bismarck's chief enemy.[51]

Bleichröder rushed back to Berlin. Between March 6 and 13, Bismarck sent for him on three separate occasions.[52] Bleichröder may have seen Bismarck at other times as well; he certainly saw his entourage. On March 7 he stayed for an hour and a half; it was then that they decided to embark on the largest financial transaction of Bismarck's life, and Bleichröder commenced to sell his state securities. Bleichröder pleaded with Bismarck not to resign, and the two men discussed a strategy for survival. Bismarck hoped to force the kaiser to accept a coup d'état or a Center-Conservative coalition—either would have robbed him of his independence. Bleichröder now offered—or Bismarck asked him—to produce Windthorst, the leader of the Center, as he had produced him the last time Bismarck had seen him, in 1879.[53]

Bleichröder had long cultivated close relations with some of the leading Catholics. He was particularly close to Windthorst, as we know, and to Prince-Bishop Kopp. Both Windthorst and Kopp were among the critics of Catholic anti-Semitism—otherwise they described opposite ends of the Catholic spectrum. Kopp was an ecclesiastical diplomat, who mediated between Leo XIII and Bismarck, and who was skeptical about the "democratic" tendencies in the Center party. Bismarck rewarded this conservative bishop with an appointment to the Prussian upper house, where Kopp continued his policy of accommodation and conciliation with the state. Bleichröder knew both men, and now hoped to use them for Bismarck's defense. Kopp "seems to have played a vital role throughout the [chancellor] crisis as a link between the government and the Center Party." Kopp also tried to persuade William of the Center's reliability.[54]

Kopp was an accomplished diplomat, a true prince of the Church assigned to a delicate diocese—that of Breslau, which contained not only Catholic Silesians, with their fervent German patriotism, but millions of Poles, devout believers in God and Poland. His correspondence with Bleichröder, extant for the period after 1887, although clearly begun earlier, reveals him as a man of charm and friendliness. His letters invariably express his "yearning" to see Bleichröder, his "deepest, greatest admiration." In the first three months of 1890, when Bismarck's fate was being decided, Kopp called on Bleichröder often because he had "many important things" to tell him.[55] In March 1890 he wrote five times asking to be received, and he sometimes called without writing first. Kopp's repeated praise of Bleichröder's benevolence may well have also referred to material things, perhaps in the form of substantial help to diocesan charity.

On March 9 Bleichröder talked to Windthorst, and the next day he saw Bismarck. Despite Holstein's warning that such a conference would be dangerous, Bleichröder arranged for the two leaders to meet on March 12.[56] Bismarck was his candid self: he began the interview by announcing that the kaiser was about to dismiss him. Windthorst wanted him to stay, and Bismarck said he could do so only with Center support. They discussed the price of such support; had a compromise been reached, it would have marked a major upheaval in German politics. Windthorst asked for the repeal of all remaining Kulturkampf legislation and for independent control of education. Bismarck sounded conciliatory, but Windthorst wondered whether he still had the power to force through such concessions. On the other hand, Windthorst suspected that Bismarck's successor would have still less power, and after Bismarck's fall, he remarked, "for our purposes, at least, he left too early." Windthorst emerged from the meeting, warning Rottenburg that it must be kept entirely confidential, for publicity would hurt Bismarck; he told someone else, "I have come from the deathbed of a great man."[57]

The famous interview hastened the end. Bismarck's enemies, including probably the state secretary of the interior, Boetticher, quickly alerted William that the meeting had taken place. The newspapers were full of stories about Windthorst's "Bleichröder visit" with Bismarck, as the meeting came to be called.[58] Three days after the interview William dragged Bismarck out of bed and scathingly rebuked him for having received Windthorst. Bismarck bristled, and matters ended, as they often did in imperial Germany, with a veiled reference to putative enemies of the Reich. This time William blamed Bismarck for dealing with "Jews and Jesuits who are always under one cover." William, incensed at Bismarck's independent political maneuvering, felt further outraged that Bismarck's Jew should have been centrally involved. As the kaiser's chief confidant put it, Bismarck acknowledged Bleichröder's role, explaining that Bleichröder was his banker and that "Jews generally were a useful part of human society through whom he had successfully conducted other and even more important affairs, even with foreign cabinets." "Bleichröder . . . had always been a thorn in the Kaiser's side."[59] At the end of their violent quarrel, William asked for Bismarck's resignation.

The crisis dragged on for a few more days. To the end, Bleichröder kept hoping that the worst could be averted and so informed the Paris Rothschilds.[60] On the seventeenth Bleichröder saw Bismarck again; he now realized that Bismarck's dismissal was but a matter of hours or days, and on his return, Pindter found him "very excited, sobbing, with anginal pain."[61] Bleichröder tried to persuade William's entourage that Bismarck should at least remain as foreign minister, to no avail. At Holstein's behest, he apparently tried to persuade Bismarck to have Herbert stay in the Foreign Office—also to no avail.[62]

On the seventeenth, the emperor twice asked for the chancellor's resignation. The die was cast; the Bismarckian era was over. To the end, Bleichröder had played a leading role. In the uncertainty of the final weeks, he was a center of activity and intrigue. Various men and factions sought to use his easy access to Bismarck, but his efforts on Bismarck's behalf proved abortive. If anything, he had become a marginal liability. For at the end of Bismarck's reign—as at the birth of the Empire in Versailles—the very figure of Bleichröder had produced the open manifestation of the latent anti-Semitism of the German elite. In 1889–1890 it appeared at the pinnacle of political society, at the court itself, and it was used as a weapon against Bismarck, who until then had thought that he could use Jews and anti-Semites, as he used most other mortals: to his own advantage and with impunity.

Bleichröder's tears were genuine. For twenty-eight years he had been close to Bismarck, and however difficult proximity to that titanic figure might have been at times, it gave Bleichröder the sense and substance of his own importance; it was part of his identity. The slights and sufferings were forgotten; forgotten, too, that like so many subordinates, he had complained that Bismarck was "inconsiderate and squeezed people like lemons."[63] What remained was sorrow that his tie to power had snapped, that his habit of serving greatness had been broken. Bismarck's fall was Bleichröder's fall, too; his special sun had set. The tears were for himself.

Bleichröder's friends certainly assumed that condolences were in order. On hearing the news, Baron Rothschild wrote from Paris that Bleichröder could hardly lament Bismarck's resignation more than the Paris family did:

> It is inappropriate for us to speak out in favor of the German Chancellor. Still, if you have an opportunity to see him we beg you to tell him that in the interest of world peace we deeply regret his departure, because we are convinced that to a large extent its maintenance in the

last years was his doing. If we nevertheless do not think that peace is threatened, then this chiefly reflects our confidence that it will be possible for the Prince, given his great influence, to work behind the scenes on behalf of peace, as he has done before.[64]

The ubiquitous Cyon wrote: "The great events of the last few days have . . . undoubtedly caused you great pain. Your friend of thirty years' standing departs from political life at the very moment when his remaining at the top in Germany was considered a guarantee of peace even among his most embittered enemies abroad."[65] The German ambassador in Rome wrote Bleichröder that Prime Minister Crispi felt Bismarck's departure as a great personal and political blow.[66] Letters from elsewhere in Europe brought the same message. Europe grieved far more than Germany did.

In Berlin there was relief and exhilaration that the autocrat had finally gone; there was pleasure at seeing the discomfiture of Bismarck and Bleichröder. An old friend of the Bismarcks', Baroness Spitzemberg, wrote on the day of the dismissal: "As far as the [Bismarck] family is concerned, now it will suffer—not without justice—the nemesis for the brutality and cruelty with which it ground so many people, great and small, into the dust: but the spectacle will not be pleasant. My God, what meanness will now appear after all the Byzantine servility of former days."[67]

Obviously Bleichröder's standing was impaired, and in April 1890 Pindter noted: "Bleichröder is almost entirely uninformed now. His sole confidant is Count Eulenburg; the ambassadors seem to be withdrawing, too; of course, Bleichröder is no longer Bismarck."[68] The anti-Bismarck scramble, the precipitous shift of loyalties to the new rulers, left Bleichröder stranded.

But not for long. Bleichröder was not without political resiliency himself, and his personal loyalty to Bismarck did not inhibit his efforts to form close relations with the new rulers. Some men, like Holstein, drew much closer again to Bleichröder after Bismarck's fall; he had become less of a threat to Holstein, and hence they could resume, indeed go beyond, former intimacy. Holstein now addressed Bleichröder as "esteemed friend," and the two men continually exchanged news. He remained on good relations with State Secretary Boetticher, whom Bismarck had come to despise as a traitor;* he developed new ties to rising stars like Alfred von Kiderlen-Wächter and Ludwig Raschdau as well as to the new foreign secretary, Baron Marschall von Bieberstein, and he was in steady contact with their assistants.[69] He con-

---

* In 1891 the following story appeared in the press, probably leaked by Bismarck himself: some years earlier, Boetticher's father-in-law, an official of the Reichsbank, had mismanaged, perhaps misappropriated, official funds, and at Bismarck's request, Bleichröder and other bankers helped Boetticher with sums reported at either 350,000 or a million marks. Later, Bismarck gave Boetticher the same amount, probably out of the Welfenfond, so that the bankers could be paid off. It was a murky story, and Bleichröder was appalled that Bismarck would leak it so as to blacken Boetticher's name. Bismarck repeated the story in his memoirs, without mentioning Bleichröder's role. *Bismarcks Grosses Spiel. Die geheimen Tagebücher Ludwig Bambergers*, ed. by Ernst Feder (Frankfurt, 1932), p. 462; Helmuth Rogge, *Holstein und Hohenlohe* (Stuttgart, 1957), p. 357; *GW*, XV, 481; Robert Nöll von der Nahmer, *Bismarcks Reptilienfonds* (Mainz, 1968), pp. 190–201.

tinued to consult with the government, assuming that no government would want to dispense with his news or opinions. A large part of his relationship with Bismarck had been functional, and the banker took it as a matter of course that he would have some entrée to any government. In December 1891 Kardorff, at the height of his career, noted that he had visited Bleichröder, "who is always well informed. He assured me that Caprivi enjoyed the Kaiser's esteem because he did everything the latter wanted. . . ."[70]

Bleichröder was something of a bridge between the new, collective government and the deposed autocrat. There was nothing but suspicion between Berlin and Friedrichsruh. Bismarck did everything he could to embarrass the new rulers, convinced that they were undoing his work. The latter, unreasonably afraid of his return to power, did everything to obstruct him. Bleichröder proved an intermittent, useful intermediary, who also scotched all rumors of a possible reconciliation between Bismarck and the emperor. According to Bleichröder, Bismarck had said that if he ever sought such a reconciliation, his wife would divorce him. Earlier, Bleichröder had remarked that Bismarck hated his enemies unto the fourth generation, but Johanna hated them unto the thousandth.[71]

In exile, Bismarck appreciated Bleichröder even more—and more openly. Bleichröder's loyalty and solicitude never wavered. He maintained the closest links with the fallen chancellor. On the morning after the Bismarcks' arrival in Friedrichsruh, their trusted doctor, Schweninger, telegraphed Bleichröder: "Prince and Princess slept well, feel fresh and well."[72] Most people in Berlin were glad not to have to worry anymore about Bismarck's peevish health. On the second day of his exile, Bismarck celebrated his seventy-fifth birthday—and Bleichröder was of course among the few well-wishers. The two men had a long talk, and Bismarck explained that what had wounded him most deeply was the kaiser's duplicity in pretending to the world that his parting from Bismarck had been amicable.[73]*

Bleichröder continued to be privy to Bismarck's thoughts. They continued to correspond with each other, to see each other, to exchange news—and to trust each other. Bismarck was afraid that their very intimacy invited surveillance; in June 1890 a letter from Bleichröder was lost, and Bismarck demanded a careful investigation at the Berlin and Friedrichsruh post offices. "There is the suspicion," wrote Bismarck's secretary, at his master's behest, "that in this matter there was design at some office, be it here or, more probably, in Berlin, and that such a thing could recur. One does not think here that all Berlin offices would necessarily be free of inquisitiveness concerning the correspondence between His Highness and yourself."[74] Bismarck's fear showed what importance he attached to his correspondence with Bleich-

---

* At the moment of Bismarck's dismissal, William published a letter to him, creating him duke of Lauenburg and promising him a life-size picture of his sovereign. Of the new title, Bismarck said he would use it when he wanted to travel incognito; of the life-size picture, we have no comment but can guess. A month later, William sent Schweninger an extravagant message, ordering him to continue to look after Bismarck's health and from time to time send the kaiser reports about it. Horst Kohl, ed., *Bismarck-Regesten* (Leipzig, 1892) II, 499; William to Schweninger, 24 April 1890, DZA: Merseburg: Rep. 89 H, Zivilkabinett XXIII, 12ff.

röder. He knew from his own experience that it was easy to order the surveillance of someone's correspondence, and he always thought his enemies were as ruthlessly resourceful as he was. Then again, it flatters the vanity of deposed rulers to think that they are the bugbears of their successors.

Bleichröder visited Bismarck regularly and always received a cordial welcome. Bismarck was eager for news and often asked for Bleichröder's "expert opinion" on such controversial matters as Caprivi's new trade agreements.[75] When they met, the two men talked of the present and reminisced about the past. They also discussed Bismarck's investments. At times, Bleichröder offered his advice, as in June 1890, when he urged Bismarck to moderate his press polemics. Bismarck replied, "When I am attacked, I hit back; otherwise I cannot sleep."[76] A few days later, Bismarck gave a five-hour interview to *Le Petit Journal* and asked Bleichröder to send him a copy of the published version. Bleichröder told Pindter that he would have wished for "a little more reticence on the Prince's part."[77]*

Because of Bleichröder's close ties with Bismarck, Berlin dignitaries still sought him out; Bleichröder's reports about Bismarck's views and plans made the rounds, often enough reaching William's ears.[78] Occasionally he mediated between Bismarck and his former associates or acquaintances who feared that Bismarck had broken with them. Perhaps the most poignant example was Kopp, who complained to Bleichröder that the Bismarck press was attacking him for no just cause. "Although the conduct of the press is a matter of indifference to me, I am not insensitive to the judgment of the Prince." The charge that he had favored Polish agitation was untrue:

> It is, unfortunately, part of the difficulty of my position that I am simultaneously cast in the role of benefactor and enemy of Polish aspirations. . . . It is untrue that I concern myself with elections or with influencing the Center party. . . . To compromise through political undertakings the clerical responsibilities which have been entrusted to me contradicts my conception of my position and my duty.

Given Bleichröder's benevolence, Kopp assumed he would know how to use this "candid exposition. . . . I do not want the Prince to get the idea that I forget the past—loyal to that memory, I remain always in grateful admiration."[79] A few weeks later, upon Kopp's receipt of the red hat, Bismarck wrote him a warm note of congratulations, assuring him of his unchanged sentiments.[80]

Bismarck was grateful that Bleichröder remained one of the faithful

---

* In the interview, Bismarck was his new irenic self: Germany was totally satiated: "we want to run no risks." Toward France he was especially solicitous—so much so that the editor concluded: "More than at any other time in his life, M. de Bismarck is today the necessary guardian of the peace." Bismarck lamented his personal predicament: "I spent forty-three years ridding myself of my habits as a rustic *gentilhomme*; it is very hard for me to become a farmer again; politics took hold of me and will not let go . . . [but] I am forgetting that I have nothing more to do." *Le Petit Journal*, 29 May 1890.

few during his exile. There was little that he could offer him now; he knew that Bleichröder's loyalty bespoke a genuine regard which Bismarck returned with warmth. In 1893, Bismarck recalled that Bleichröder, whatever his personal life might have been like, "toward me, he had always proven himself as a selfless, extremely intelligent, circumspect and efficient businessman, with great refinement of thought." Bismarck then mentioned all of Bleichröder's services and concluded: "In short, I am personally obliged and grateful to him." To a journalist Bismarck was to have remarked that Bleichröder showed him, even in retirement, "a devotion and a gratifying loyalty that could serve as a model for our patriotic Christian countrymen."[81]*

The finely calibrated forms of address in Bismarck's letters reflected this greater intimacy. In the two years before Bleichröder's death, Bismarck's letters began with "Esteemed friend" and ended, almost always, with "*Der Ihrige*," a formula reserved for colleagues and old friends, like Lucius von Ballhausen and Maybach. He wrote, "Esteemed friend, your warm congratulations and your charming [birthday] present attest anew your feelings of friendship for me and as such are of the highest value to me."[82] Bismarck reciprocated by sending Bleichröder a signed picture of himself for Christmas and by extending his solicitude to Bleichröder's children. They, too, were now invited to Friedrichsruh and given a warm, if not uncritical, welcome.

Bismarck often voiced concern about Bleichröder's health. A few weeks before Bleichröder's death, he wrote: "I was happy to see from your letter that your health is satisfactory or, as you say, bearable, and hence I hope that with the coming of milder weather you will give my wife and me the pleasure of visiting us here again."[83] It was Bismarck's last letter to Bleichröder. After Bleichröder's death, Bismarck wrote Schwabach: "In Mr. von Bleichröder I did indeed lose someone who was my true friend under all changing circumstances. I am glad that the conditions of the Banking House will remain the same, and I am counting on continuing in the future the relations which for so many years I have had with the firm."[84] At Bleichröder's funeral Bismarck was represented by his daughter and by a very large wreath. It was his last, public token of respect and friendship for Bleichröder.

For Bismarck, life became ever lonelier as he lived first in Varzin and after 1894 in Friedrichsruh. He had himself said of his departure from Berlin: "A state funeral with full honors."[85] There were real deaths to follow: his

---

* Not that gratitude could not be alternated with malice, especially when such malice was opportune. In talking to an anti-Semitic editor in August 1890, Bismarck made his most contemptuous remarks about Bleichröder: "I know exactly what kind of man Bleichröder was and what he did, all sorts of things and passions which such people with little cultivation, without a strong moral fundament, and in opulent enjoyment of their immeasurable wealth are wont to do. But I could not and should not have treated him ill because that would have violated my inherited views of obligatory *noblesse*." He praised Bleichröder's financial services, which he had rendered without receiving anything in return, without getting any state secrets: "That Bleichröder would have liked [such secrets] and perhaps gave himself airs to third parties about being the Bismarck-banker I know, but that is part of the race and of business. I could not have altered that even if I had changed my banker." *GW*, IX, 86–87.

amanuensis Lothar Bucher, his banker, and Johanna in 1894; the world grew still around him. His infirmities increased. Death came in 1898, years after he had ceased to live.

In his memoirs Bismarck neglected to mention Bleichröder, and Bismarck's editors and biographers followed suit by pretending that Bleichröder was a person of minimal, marginal importance. In his lifetime, his allegedly evil influence was often exaggerated; posthumously, he was condemned to undeserved obscurity. But Bleichröder had probably sensed what we now know: that for a third of a century he had played a major role in Bismarck's Germany, that he helped to shape that Germany, and that its chancellor had grown dependent on him. What he probably did not understand was that the peculiar combination of his successes and his humiliations was symptomatic of the deeply flawed relations of Germans and Jews.

PART THREE

THE ANGUISH OF ASSIMILATION

CHAPTER 17

The Jew as Patriotic Parvenu

But one of the most senseless things in this wide world is the serious treatment of the problem of guilt, at least so it seems to me. It's not the uttering
of reproaches that seems to me senseless; certainly when one is in distress
one utters reproaches in all directions (although of course not in direst
distress, for then one utters no reproaches); it's also comprehensible that one
takes such reproaches to heart at the time of agitation and turmoil; but that
one should consider it possible to argue about it as about any ordinary
arithmetical problem which is so clear that it produces results for daily
conduct, this I don't understand at all. Of course you are to blame, but then
your husband is also to blame and then you again and then he again, since it
cannot be otherwise in the living together of human beings, and the blame
piles up in endless succession until it reaches the grey Original Sin, but what
use can it be for my present day or for the visit to the doctor in Ischl to
rummage about in eternal sin?

—Franz Kafka, *Letters to Milena*

Bleichröder's success was swift and extraordinary, as was Germany's.
It was brittle, as was Germany's. The career of Gerson Bleichröder mirrored some of the fundamental processes of the two worlds he
belonged to, one by birth, the other by desperate desire. He was a Jew by
birth, a German by choice. For years he thought that he could combine both
worlds, that a private and loosening association with the Jewish world would
not be incompatible with a public and ever greater role in the German world.
In fact his middle years described the moment of the least troubled amalgamation of German and Jewish society; his declining years marked the first
organized repudiation of that amalgamation, and his very success was taken
as a warrant for repudiation.

The story of Germany's rise in the nineteenth century is familiar. After
centuries of disunity, the nation was united—from above, its birth inextricably
intertwined with the will of its leaders to maintain the essence of authoritarian
government. The nation, barely unified, was divided by the forces of
modernization, by the full onslaught of industrial capitalism, which placed
the traditional ruling classes in economic jeopardy and the *Bürgertum* in fear
of rising socialism. Bismarck and Bleichröder were both a symbolic and a
functional team that sought to buttress the old classes—by protecting them
economically and by reaffirming the supremacy of their values and code of
life—and to deprive an already intimidated middle class of its political will.

Bleichröder, ennobled, did not strive after some independent patrician style of life, but became a plutocratic copy of an earlier feudal caste. And the caste, which owed so much to him, resented him for being plutocratic and inauthentic.

The German-Jewish amalgamation reflected the particular path that German society took in the nineteenth century, a path significantly different from that of France, Britain, and Holland. Emancipation was granted grudgingly, and the emancipators assumed that Jews, inferior to Christians, would improve themselves morally—by conversion preferably. The emancipators could not know that the lifting of barriers would be followed by the rapid conversion of a relatively closed community to a dynamic society in which opportunities would abound and new fortunes would challenge ancient privilege. Emancipation lifted barriers, but it was the modernization of society, the sudden possibilities of attaining eminence through education and wealth (*Bildung und Besitz*), that gave the Jews the unanticipated chance of leaping ahead. The Jews in Germany profited from the possibilities of social mobility; so did other Germans. But mobility meant freedom for some, and terrible dislocation, psychic and social, for others. As Jews excelled in the economic realm, the uprooted, disadvantaged groups, often in direct experience of and competition with Jewish traders and creditors, harked back to the old emancipators' wish that Jews would improve themselves—by which the emancipators meant a moral improvement. By the 1870s the detractors claimed that the Jews, far from becoming "improved," that is, German, had reduced Germans to their base level, had infected them with their materialistic mode. From the mid-1870s on, a new group of anti-Semites took the Jew as symbol and profiteer of modernity, of liberalism and capitalism. The fact that German liberalism was weaker than and ideologically different from its Western counterpart and that the German *Bürgertum* never acquired the self-confidence and historic importance of the French or British bourgeoisie meant that the Jewish community did not have a liberal shield that would defend their rights as part of a code of universally recognized human rights. The continued moral sway of an impoverished and greedy warrior-agrarian class meant that the subject of money was overladen by hypocrisy and taboos—more so than in other countries where similar sentiments existed in somewhat muted form. Preoccupation with money is not edifying; the denial of its importance or the yearning for some idyllic past where honor or virtue, not money, determined rank is a congenial but, as the German case showed, dangerous delusion. From the 1880s on, German nationalism acquired an aggressive, xenophobic character; it was even more intolerant of pluralism or of minorities that were at once cohesive at home and had special ties abroad than was illiberal nationalism elsewhere. Other countries had similar prophets of illiberal nationalism, but their resonance among the leading classes of society was greater in Germany than elsewhere.[1]*

This is a sketch of some of the historic forces that shaped Bleichröder's

---

* I have further developed some of these thoughts in an essay, "The Burden of Success," in a volume in honor of Lionel Trilling, to be published in 1977 by Basic Books.

life and times. He was but dimly aware of these larger ramifications of his career; few men understand the currents that dominate their time. Bleichröder's vision—except in matters financial—was no sharper than that of most of his contemporaries. It ill-equipped him to understand the particular circumstances and forces that shaped the German-Jewish life in common. He could not understand why the Germans treated their Jews with such seeming changeability; perhaps no other people mixed hospitality with hostility in quite the same, confounding manner.* Bleichröder was the merchant-prince of Berlin; he rose to heights that no Jew and few commoners before him attained; amidst respect, obsequiousness, and whispered abuse, he was received everywhere in German society—usually at the back door. Not grasping the past or the ambiguous present, he could not possibly foresee the future. He did what most men do: extrapolate from the present; he saw a world of ever easier amalgamation, of Jews accepted in society, and, if need be, protected by the state. There was cause for optimism in the 1860s and 1870s: surely the future belonged to integration and assimilation, to his kind of Jew whom the state rewarded with ennoblement. Jew-baiting was a relic of the past, an unfortunate anachronism.[2] The historic conditions of his life were impossible for him to comprehend; he had a partial perception of his own subjective experience.

You are equal, said the law. You are more than equal, said Bleichröder's patent of nobility, bestowed by Bismarck and the king. You are less than equal, said the gentile world, and behind his back whispered: "filthy Jew . . . with his Jewish money . . . and Talmudic wisdom . . . Jew pig."[3] You are not one of them, said the inner voice; you and your tribe *are* inferior to the people among whom you live—and yet superior in matters of intelligence, acumen, shrewdness, hard work. The world remembered deicide and evil; the self, aspiring to acceptance, still had shreds of faith that Jews, after all, were God's chosen people. On one thing Jews and Germans in the modern era agreed: there was a world of difference between them, and the legal assertion of equality merely compounded the unease of intercourse.

To be sure, some Jews felt this unease more strongly than others. At midcentury most of Germany's half-million Jews still lived in an invisible ghetto by preference, they lived near each other, they worked with one another, they married each other. In the era of legal emancipation—the last

---

* In a much-noted book of the 1880s, published under a pseudonym but generally attributed to Princess Catherine Radziwill, a chapter was devoted to "Mr. von Bleichröder and the Princes of Finance." It begins: "Berlin is not Paris. In the capital of the new German Empire, as in Russia, prejudices still exist that have long since disappeared in France. Among these prejudices, one must include a certain repugnance to shake the hand of a Jew in front of a witness or to go to his house or to receive him at one's own. It is deliberate that I say before a witness, because in the intimacy of a tête-à-tête all these little scruples evaporate. There is no city in the entire world where the children of Israel are more repulsed by society or where that society makes greater use of them." Comte Paul Vasili, *La Société de Berlin* (Paris, 1884), pp. 152–153.

disabilities were removed in 1869—and growing assimilation, they gradually ventured across these invisible lines and entered the gentile world in schools and universities, as traders and draftees, as doctors and scientists, as bankers, journalists, and lawyers.

Bleichröder epitomized an important moment in the tangled, tragic history of Germans and Jews. The foremost mercantile Jew of his era, his life demonstrated the heights to which Jews could aspire—as well as the pain and the precariousness of the ascent. Bleichröder—the friend of Bismarck and the correspondent of kings, the financier of great enterprises and the material savior of impoverished aristocrats—proved how profitable German-Jewish coexistence could be for both parties. His achievements were prodigious, as was his social success. He won a degree of recognition and importance unprecedented in the history of German Jewry. He clearly embodied the possibilities of success and integration. But the history of a community cannot be written in terms of outward behavior or success—least of all the history of German Jewry. The core of conduct and behavior lay in the attitudes of people, unconscious as well as conscious, tacit as well as overt. As Bleichröder rose from his near-ghetto origin to being ennobled, his attitudes changed as well: like so many of his fellow Jews, he developed the most intense loyalty to the state, which dispensed and extracted favors. To the state, he proved that Jews were exceptionally useful, almost a kind of surrogate bourgeoisie. He also saw the state as a protector from anti-Semitic predators.*

In Bleichröder's life the German Jews found a super-size portrait of themselves; many of the ways and values of Jewry, especially of prosperous Jewry, were mirrored in this man.† Where almost all Jews profited from the establishment of the new Reich, Bleichröder's gains were unique; where almost all Jews became eager patriots, indeed superpatriots, in the new Reich, Bleichröder's attachment to Bismarck personified this loyalty. Where most Jews continued to regard the state as a potential benefactor, Bleichröder demonstrated that it could grant important favors and could at times even be mobilized on behalf of threatened or maltreated Jews at home and abroad.

But Bleichröder's life exemplified the other side of this profitable coexistence as well. At times his relationship to authority embodied subservience

---

* As Ludwig Börne put it much earlier: "Because I was born without a fatherland, my desire for a fatherland is more passionate than yours, and because my birthplace was not bigger than the *Judengasse* and everything behind the locked gates was a foreign country to me, therefore for me now the fatherland is more than the city, more than a territory, more than a province. For me only the very great fatherland, as far as its language extends, is enough." Quoted in Robert M. Berdahl, "New Thoughts on German Nationalism," *AHR*, LXXVII (1972), 78–79.

† Throughout this part I occasionally speak of "German" Jewry, despite the fact that there were significant differences in the conditions of Jewish life in the different states of the new Reich. I am also aware that within the Jewish community there were great differences as to wealth, status, outlook. Roughly two-thirds of German Jewry lived in Prussia, and most of my remarks will approximate their experience.

and obsequiousness. He begged when he could have petitioned; he petitioned when he could have demanded; he proved yielding when he should have been obdurate. He was vain when he should have been proud. He was munificent in offering gifts to benefactors and friends and lavish in contributions to public charities. The giver is twice blessed, it says; but in Bleichröder's case, the giving was complicated not only by the usual expectation of reward but by a sense that charity was a vocational necessity, a tacit tribute.[4]

More than any other German Jew of his time, Bleichröder lived on the fringes of the gentile world. By his usefulness and ennoblement, he had unique entrée to the highest strata of German society. He was the only Jew who was *hoffähig*, presentable at court. Some honors bring humiliations in their train. He desperately sought to be accepted by that society; the greater the resistance he incurred, the stronger his desire to succeed. And success had to be visible—hence the hunt after decorations, the ostentation of his feasts, the solicitude with which he sought to make his entertainment the finest in Berlin. Bleichröder was a parvenu in a double sense: both his money and his gentility were of recent origin. The life of a parvenu is never pleasant or edifying; to be a Jewish parvenu—or pariah merchant-prince—in German society was peculiarly difficult.

Bleichröder encountered various types of hostility. There was the "gentle," behind-the-back anti-Semitism of many of his friends, the inevitable sneer about some "Jewish" solecism. There was the social disdain of some aristocrats, the repeated rebuffs, say, of Bleichröder's eagerly tendered invitations. There were the break with Herbert von Bismarck and the anti-Semitic pranks of Herbert's entourage. Perhaps Bleichröder overlooked their slights; perhaps he was impervious to them. His children, as we will see, achieved nothing and wanted everything; to their failures he could not be impervious. They embraced Protestantism—even as they abjured the Protestant ethic, that unquestioned acceptance of the gospel of work that was the lodestar of their father's life.

Nor could he overlook the rising storm of anti-Semitism in Germany, which took him as its prime target. Anti-Semitic scribblers and carefully organized movements fastened on him as the archetypical profiteer of emancipation and *Gründertum*. During the last twenty years of his life he received honors and abuse in equal measure, and what in retrospect is most extraordinary is that the men who honored him and profited from him did nothing to protect him. He was left to cope alone with his enemies; occasionally he petitioned king and chancellor for protection of all of Jewry. When Bismarck moved, he did so not for Bleichröder or Jews or justice, but because he saw that some of the attacks were directed against his own person and against property. He considered both sacrosanct.

Bleichröder's dominant feelings as German Jew were undoubtedly satisfaction and security. He had come far and he was safe. But his rise and that of his coreligionists did not go unchallenged; the backlash, as we would call it today, became stronger and stronger in the last years of his life. For a long time, his faith in the state, in the "warm-hearted" Bismarck, quieted his fears and left him hoping that anti-Semitism would vanish again.*

The attacks on him and his kind strengthened that curious sense of inferiority which he felt qua Jew. By fervently embracing the values of an elite that defined his kind as an outsider, by seeking to mold his life in accordance with these dominant values and customs, he condemned himself and his children to perpetual vulnerability. Genuine acceptance by the highest levels of German society was a mirage that lured Gerson and his children ever deeper into a wilderness of unrealizable ambitions from which there was no return.

Could Gerson have chosen differently? His brother Julius did choose a different path, as we will see. In judging Gerson† one must remember the character of German society to which he was trying to assimilate; in a sense, ennoblement was a command performance. A new role was thrust upon him —even if he had thirsted after it. He thought of himself as a trailblazer. Other Jews, equally favored, would follow him, but for the time being he had to be his own model. Nor were his expectations altogether unrealistic. The rise of German Jewry had been so spectacular that the hope of ever greater integration seemed reasonable. Lines between Germans and Jews were crossed: in friendship and in marriage. For the successful, acceptance seemed possible; lingering prejudices could be ignored (and reciprocated); was there not also deeply entrenched antagonisms between Protestants and Catholics, between Prussians and Bavarians?

It is not the hope of integration and acceptance that surprises in Gerson: it is the manner in which the goal was pursued. But men much younger than himself, born when anti-Semitism was on the rise again, "yearned to be not merely a guest, to be regarded not as a stranger. Not as an invited guest, nor as one tolerated out of pity and kindliness, nor, worst of all, as one admitted because his hosts have consented to ignore his race and descent."[5] And there was reason for the hope: an English observer in Berlin in the early 1870s was much impressed by the eminence of the Jews and by their standing among gentiles: "In reality, the Berlin Christian is a far more tolerant being than his English coreligionist."** Bleichröder was not alone in his illusions and ambitions.

* It is ironic that in the year of Bleichröder's death, the nineteen-year-old Chaim Weizmann uttered one of the most scathing indictments of Jewish blindness concerning German anti-Semitism. Addressing the director of the Jewish seminary at which he was teaching and outraged by that director's confidence that Germans would cease being anti-Semitic once they had "their eyes opened to the excellent qualities of the Jews," Weizmann cried out: "Herr Doktor, if a man has a piece of something in his eye, he does not want to know whether it is a piece of mud or a piece of gold. He just wants to get it out." Weizmann, *Trial and Error* (New York, 1949), p. 32.

† In this part, I speak of Gerson, partly to distinguish him from his brother Julius. The contrast between the brothers is an essential part of Gerson's story, as the conflict between Christian and Thomas Buddenbrook was a central theme in *Buddenbrooks*. Gerson is to suggest the private person, not the public figure playing roles.

** Shephard Thomas Taylor, *Reminiscences of Berlin during the Franco-German War of 1870–71* (London, 1885), p. 238. Taylor spoke thus of Jewish wealth: ". . . whilst the Christians of Berlin have, as a rule, to bear the burden and heat of the day, a disproportionate share of the material loaves and fishes falls to the lot of the more fortunate Jew. . . . [The Jews]

One must beware, however, of ascribing to Bleichröder feelings and sensitivities that may have been alien to him. His innermost feelings are nowhere recorded: he left no diary, and only a few of his letters have an intimate or candid content. He apparently was obtuse, insensitive to many slights, filled with the feeling that his wealth, position, and intelligence were shields enough against attacks from below. Obtuseness was probably the key to social success—just as intelligence was the condition of his material success. He had none of the sensibility of a Heine; he was not even as psychologically aware as a Carl Fürstenberg or a Walther Rathenau.* Whatever misgivings or fears he had could be assuaged with the common hope that emancipation had just begun and that anti-Jewish prejudice would wither away as Germans came to realize the great usefulness of Jews. In his simple assumption of continued progress, he mirrored the attitude of many of his rich coreligionists. Reality, however, was much harder. There was something cruelly symbolic even in Gerson's blindness: he could not see the dangers as he staggered into a world full of hidden and not so hidden hatreds.

Bleichröder's faith in the future was shared by his fellow Jews. However divided on other issues, most Jews were as one in thinking that the new Reich, coming on the heels of full emancipation, heralded a new era for them. They exuded pride about things German, to the discomfort of their coreligionists elsewhere; Bleichröder's Prussian patriotism irritated the Paris Rothschilds as early as 1866. (This loyalty and pride persisted, and as late as 1916 a French observer noted: "Still today, Prussians, Saxons, Badensians,

---

inhabit the best houses in the best quarters of the town, drive about the parks in the most elegant equipages, figure constantly in the dress circle at the opera and theatres, and in this and other ways excite a good deal of envy in the minds of their less fortunate Christian fellow-citizens." Taylor continued that in England there would be far greater animus against Jews if they held a similiar position; the whole problem, he thought, would disappear because "it would almost seem as if the end of Judaism were near at hand in Berlin." By this he meant that the traits of Jewishness were on the decline. Pp. 236, 237, 241.

* Given the paucity of information, then, it may be useful to record how others felt in situations that Bleichröder could not have escaped. In 1898, in pursuit of his Zionist goals, Theodor Herzl visited an old friend of Bleichröder's, Count August Eulenburg, on the latter's estate at Liebenberg. He described his complicated feelings, beginning with his reception at the railway station by the count's coachman: "I am probably the first Jew he has ever driven. . . . Here I was in the midst of Spielhagen's world, the landed gentry, who had been spoken of in the circle in which I used to live, among scoffing Jewish liberals, with nothing but hatred, fear, and derision. The noteworthy thing about the episode is that I am by no means coming to them as a submissively fawning assimilationist, but as an upstanding Jew. . . . The Count came out at once. He was in hunting costume, and it seemed to me the first thing he did was to take stock of my clothes. . . . Naturally, as a member of a race which he considers a higher one, he feels superior to me. But how can I resent it when I consider the wretched way in which precisely the 'higher' Jews—that is, the kind he has contact with, if any—behave toward our idealistic cause? Incidentally, he does seem to acknowledge the fact that one can associate with the Jew Herzl." It was a time when Herzl was hoping for German support of a Zionist settlement in Palestine, and Eulenburg had indicated William's interest in establishing a German protectorate. Herzl noted in his diary: "The protectorate! Many will shake their heads over it. But I believe the only right course is to accept it gratefully. . . . To live under the protection of this strong, great, moral, splendidly governed, tightly organized Germany can only have the most salutary effect on the Jewish national character." *The Complete Diaries of Theodor Herzl,* ed. by Raphael Patai (New York and London, 1960), II, 687, 688, 693.

Württembergers, and Bavarians exist in Germany. Only the Jews are exclusively German. From north to south, from east to west, they constitute the armature of the empire.")[6] But their loyalty, their love, and their superpatriotism were not requited.* For that the prejudices remained too strong, and the resentments grew rather than diminished.

This is not the place to give even the briefest history of anti-Semitic feelings.[7] Anti-Semitism was an old prejudice sanctioned by religion (the Jews seen as having Jesus's blood on their hands), confirmed by the enforced physical apartness of the Jews, as they pursued their own religious life in the ghettos to which they were banished. Law and custom excluded them from most crafts; by gentile intent and acquired skill, Jews became the "pariah-capitalists" of earlier generations.[8] The Jew as Shylock is a familiar story—and a complicated one, as Shakespeare's Shylock should remind us.

Emancipation removed most legal disabilities, but informal disabilities remained, as did prejudices. There had always been an anti-Mammon component to anti-Semitism, and, as we noted, in the new Germany, as capitalism spread, so did the revulsion against it. Aristocrats continued to have "house Jews" to conduct their business for them, and thus expressed at once disdain for the pursuit and the pursuer—and a feeling that Jews excelled in this field.

As we will see, the liberal interlude of relative tolerance proved brief. The nation-state had given Jews rights that the older *Ständestaat* had withheld. But Jews, emancipated from disabilities and competing in German life, aroused a fierce reaction, and the nation-state, especially in Germany, acquired a new, violent intolerance for any form of deviance or pluralism. From the 1870s on, nationalism became antiliberal, and the Jew—once the sinner against the faith—became the insidious plotter against the nation.[9] In the politics of cultural despair, a compound of nationalism, antimodernity, and anticapitalism, the Jew was the symbol of evil. After 1870 there gradually spread the notion that this alien force was part of a vast international conspiracy "set on ruining and then dominating the rest of mankind."[10]

Jews had their own set of prejudices and feelings, and these too showed remarkable persistence amidst outward change. First, even the most assimilated Jews believed that Jews were a distinct group, originally held together by a common faith, common rites, common suffering; as these shared experiences waned, certain characteristics, formed in an earlier era, remained. One looked, thought, felt Jewish—whether one wanted to or not. But what was this quality of being Jewish? Among Jews, as among Protestants, religion gradually withered, as the belief in science undermined faith in the supernatural. In an age of enlightenment, what survived of the Jewish religion? And were these remnants worth the constant reminders of apartness, of latent hostility?

Liberal Protestants thought not; they believed that Jews should sacrifice

---

* The rich patriotic Jews were often called *Kaiser-Juden,* and Chaim Weizmann depicted them harshly as being "more German than the Germans, obsequious, superpatriotic, eagerly anticipating the wishes and plans of the masters of Germany." *Trial and Error,* p. 143.

their now tenuous faith on the altar of a common German humanity. They expected that Jews would gladly pay for the privilege of emancipation by giving up their religion. Enlightenment views of Judaism as especially obscurantist—and these views certainly informed Marx's violent anti-Semitism—came to be fused with a rising nationalism so that even the most tolerant, liberal Protestants could not accept the Jews' religious apartness.* Many Germans hoped for this surrender of Judaism not because they disliked Jews but because they disliked pluralism and were made uneasy by a group that still had a great deal of internal cohesion.

The lot of the Jews was not easy for them to understand. As Bleichröder's life demonstrates, their condition changed at various times, often in subtle and uncertain ways. Gentile expectations that Jews would redeem the gift of emancipation by conversion were rarely articulated between 1830 and 1880. Jews assumed that they could have the rights of emancipation *and* their Germanized version of apartness. Was it not enough that they now conducted their services in German? Was it not enough that they felt German? Could they not be integrated fully as German citizens of Jewish—or as the common euphemism of the time had it, Mosaic—faith? Still, as Walther Rathenau remarked as late as 1911: "In the adolescent years of every German Jew occurs that painful moment which he remembers all his life: the first time when he becomes fully conscious that he has entered the world as a second-class citizen and that no achievement and no service can liberate him from this condition."[11] Perhaps the way out was baptism; anti-Semitic pressure pushed some in this direction and restrained others. To cite Rathenau once more: would a Jew not hesitate to surrender the spiritual legacy of his ancestors in order to acquire material benefits—even if he had long since accepted the Christian ethics? Would conversion not be tantamount to accepting a "Prussian *Judenpolitik*, the premises of which are retrograde, false, inappropriate, and immoral"?[12] Remaining Jewish was often a matter of honor, not a religious conviction; a change of faith smacked of opportunism, though genuine religious sentiments inspired some conversions. Among religiously indifferent Jews the choice to convert to an equally indifferent or "liberal" Protestantism involved a difficult choice among conflicting impulses. Some Jews, perhaps, may have felt as the old French lady who, when asked why she did not convert, answered: "J'ai trop peu de religion pour en changer."[13]

Hostility from the outside world, then, confirmed some Jews in their

* See Karl Marx, "On the Jewish Question," *Early Texts*, ed. by David McLellan (Oxford, 1971), esp. pp. 108–114; at a time when the early Marx is so often celebrated, his remarks on the Jewish question from that same period need to be considered. A popular prejudice was put in a philosophical context when Marx exclaimed: "What is the secular cult of the Jew? Haggling. What is his secular god? Money. Well, then, an emancipation from haggling and money, from practical, real Judaism would be the self-emancipation of our age" (p. 110). It is sometimes forgotten—or considered irrelevant—that Marx was the son of a converted Jew, a descendant of a distinguished rabbinical family; he married into an aristocratic family. Do none of these facts have a bearing on his rather aristocratic loathing of Jews as capitalists—or of capitalists as Jews? And is it altogether a negligible accident that his polemics were often peppered with crude racial epithets, such as calling Lassalle "a Jewish nigger"?

apartness and led others to redouble their protestations of Germanness, and for many it did both. Especially for those who felt German and shared their compatriots' reverence for the fatherland, and who felt a genuine identification with German culture coupled with an almost complete estrangement from Jewish customs, it was a part of their predicament that they could not speak freely or collectively about their condition: to do so would be to underscore their separate identity. This hobbled all collective and individual efforts at defense against the rising tide of anti-Semitism. It is an ironic coincidence that in the year of Bleichröder's death, in 1893, the Jews did found their first defense organization, thus abandoning their earlier reliance on state benevolence.[14]

Bleichröder's own life and family mirrored some of the conflicting possibilities that a German Jew faced. The temptations of assimilation, of course, were greater for the rich and successful Jews than for their less prosperous brethren. Gerson himself always believed that he could be both a German and a Jew, and he hoped that his personal eminence and conservative commitment would serve his own and his group's interests. At an earlier time, he would have been called a *Hofjude*; at a later time, and among a different people, he might have been called an Uncle Tom. His brother, Julius, took a different tack: he championed liberal causes and led Jewish defense efforts. Gerson's children converted. Julius's did not. Many Jews undoubtedly wished that they could shed their Jewishness—but how? A few thought that baptism was the answer; others hoped for a kind of silent acclamation of acceptance. Where so many sought such divergent goals, it is hardly surprising that the German-Jewish community was torn by inner conflicts and tensions.

As a group, German Jews were highly self-conscious—and stingingly self-critical. Jewish *Selbsthass* was a common characteristic and Jewish anti-Semitism more than a mordant oxymoron. They lived in a society that held them inferior, even contemptible. They did not escape the degradation of the downtrodden, the self-inflicted wound of assimilating the dominant group's judgment of onself and one's kind. Their self-disdain reflected and reinforced their own sense of inferiority vis-à-vis the Germans. Ludwig Bamberger, next to Lasker Germany's chief Jewish parliamentarian, thought that "Jewish" characteristics comprised: "pushiness and tactlessness, greed, insolence, vanity and title-chasing, 'intellectual parvenuism' and servility."[15] The Jews were boastful even in their self-criticism.

Yet centuries of suffering and surviving persecution burned something like pride into their collective self-consciousness—and contempt for their persecutors. They thought ill of themselves—yet were proud that they belonged to a tough, intelligent people that could include self-criticism among its virtues. Even the most assimilated Jew, though wishing for nothing more than gentile acceptance, would upon occasion or provocation—even if only to himself—mutter "goy," that clannish word of contempt for the outsider, the insensitive soul. If one word can hope to capture the spiritual travail of German Jewry, it would be ambivalence. They were ambivalent about themselves, ambivalent about their fellow Germans; perhaps ambivalence was a form of realism, but German Jews were not particularly realistic. Ambivalence was a large component of the psychic cost which German Jews had to pay for their extraordinary successes.

From full legal emancipation in 1869 to its revocation in 1933 was but a lifetime: what an astounding transformation took place in that period! It has become a sentimental commonplace to dwell on Jewish contributions to German life. There probably was no other European country where Jews played so diverse and prominent a role as in Germany. How can one account for this moment of success—and in some fields, of uniquely fruitful collaboration—amidst such hostility and ambivalence?

Heine once said that Jews are like the people among whom they live, only more so. The story of German-Jewish coexistence confirms this; Germans and Jews were not opposites alternately attracting or repelling each other. To understand Bleichröder it is necessary to recall a few of these common characteristics, including those that were generally esteemed and those that would have been regretted if they had been noticed. Necessity had taught Jews the virtue of *Tüchtigkeit*—efficiency with a special aura—and certainly Germans had long cultivated it. Germans and Jews were a serious, sober, thorough people; they formed close family ties and infused their lives with a certain ritualized warmth and sentimentality. Educated Germans and Jews shared an extraordinary appreciation for learning: they respected the living scholar and they revered the cultural heritage of the past. There were many more shared values, but to list them is perhaps less instructive than to mention those shared attitudes about which both groups were far less aware.

Because both Germans and Jews had a long history of disunity, of uncertain nationhood, their sense of identity was precarious. What other people asked themselves as often as did the Germans: What is German? To which the emancipated Jews added: What is Jewish? The *Reichsdeutsche* answered by developing a harsh, strident supernationalism, and German Jews often chimed in. The precarious sense of identity was related to another characteristic which had many deeper causes: the lack of civic responsibility, the underdeveloped sense of citizenship, the prevalence of political servility. Kant had thought that the Enlightenment would lead Germans out of their *Unmündigkeit*, their nonage. But politically Germans were kept in an often disguised servitude; they did not even know that Bismarck's authoritarianism or the kaiser's intermittent Caesarism limited their freedom. Psychological predispositions coincided with harsh political reality to deprive Germans of the experience of freedom. Bamberger once exclaimed: "This people is not born to be free," but he did not realize that this applied *a fortiori* to many of his German coreligionists.[16] (In the 1860s, when asked what vice he hated most, Karl Marx replied "servility"—and continued to denounce followers who disagreed in the most vulgar and authoritarian terms.)[17] Both Germans and Jews were given to a kind of pompous subservience, which could lead to servility as well as to sudden leaps of utopian dreams about imperial destiny or social regeneration. Germans and Jews had a peculiar talent for quick alternation of mood; during the Second World War, Churchill put it in pithy extravagance: "The Hun is either at your throat or your knees"—a behavior that German anti-Semites often attributed to Jews. It is a common characteristic of what we have come to call the authoritarian personality.

Bleichröder exemplified many of these shared traits. Like many of his rich coreligionists, he was intensely patriotic and conservative. Still, the richest man in Germany was déclassé, at the margins of several worlds. For all his wealth and power, his mentality reflected the civic uncertainties of Germans and Jews. He also demonstrated that subservience paid and, in his case, paid handsomely. But his life showed the darkest side of the German-Jewish amalgam as well: abuse, attack, uncertainty, cowardice, and corruption.

Bleichröder's life shows the respectable world of German society; it also illuminates the subterranean world of nastiness, intrigue, and incessant suspicion. The rich no less than the poor experience human meanness. In imperial Germany a powerful Jew was a magnet for all the latent malice of that society.

Bleichröder's beginnings were relatively uncomplicated. He was born and raised a Jew—and that fact alone imposed some certainties on his life. To be a Jew in Prussia in the 1820s and 1830s was still a fairly simple matter; Jewishness implied a faith and a moral code, the observance of certain rites and prohibitions, and above all it offered a fairly tight fellowship. The outside world was still sufficiently alien and hostile to enjoin fidelity to one's own kind. As a boy of ten, in 1832, Bleichröder could not have imagined his ascent to the ranks of the Prussian nobility. For Gerson that was as remote as the moon.

It would have been unthinkable for Bleichröder not to marry a Jew. Marriage in any case was a simpler business in his day than in ours, or in the days of his children. A choice for life, it was often made by parental fiat and in accordance with financial considerations, terminable only in rare and suspect cases. That Gerson, aged twenty-seven, had the proper regard for the seriousness of the step can be inferred from a report he sent to his father from an inspection trip of eligibles, a *Brautschau*, in Vienna. Old Samuel had recommended a look at the Lippmann daughters, and Gerson, at first uncertain which was the oldest, discovered she was ugly and repulsive. The family was "*gemütlich*," and he could have felt at home: "Still the girl could have been swimming in millions—I would not want to ask for her hand. Self-respect is my motto, and I would have to be ashamed in my innermost soul to bring you such a daughter." He promised next to inspect the Mark girl in Breslau, "because I am used happily to accommodate myself to your wishes." But he was skeptical about that prospect, too, and added "you must persuade yourself that pecuniary conditions alone cannot lead me to make a decision which would make me and with me another being unhappy for *ever*." The father put an "agreed" next to that.[18]

In the end, as we saw, he married Emma Guttentag, whose father was a banker in Breslau. We know little about her. Gerson's social ascent was harder on her than on him. There was always some gossip about this plain woman, at once vain, demanding, and gauche. Disraeli left a devastating picture, cited below; others remembered her more kindly.

Bleichröder led his life as a good Jew. By 1864 he had become a member of the directory (*Vorstand*) of the Jewish community in Berlin—a clear sign that he was a respected figure in Berlin Jewry.[19] He observed some of the customs and all the holidays, and he was generous in his contributions to Jewish causes. To his friends, like Oppenheim, he sent old prayer books as presents.[20] There is no reason to suppose that in the first forty or so years of his life the thought of altering his religious ways ever occurred to him. He was too deeply rooted in these ways, and his intimate relations with the loyally Jewish Rothschilds confirmed his own commitment. Indifference, let alone apostasy, was unthinkable.

Jewishness, of course, had long since ceased to be an exclusive loyalty. Among German Jews, loyalty to their faith and to their monarch had long coexisted, as it did in most European countries.* Before the Revolution of 1848, German Jewry was politically quiescent, as were most Germans. Heine's radicalism found few followers. Rich Jews of course tended to be even more conservative than their brethren, and it was symptomatic of this tradition that in 1846 Gerson's older friend Abraham Oppenheim was a conservative candidate for election to the Cologne city council.[21] The Revolution of 1848 brought a large number of Jews on the political scene, overwhelmingly of course on the liberal side. The failure of that revolution led to a renewed secession of Jews from politics that ended with the advent of the so-called New Era in 1858; Jews now tended to make common cause with the liberal-bourgeois parties.[22]

Bleichröder followed a different path. He retained his conservative leanings, as did some other rich Jews. He was loyal to the dynasty that had already protected and honored his ancestors and himself; after his tie with Bismarck, he had but one loyalty, and that was to the chancellor. Undoubtedly he hoped for further favors; so did men even better placed than himself. We noted earlier Carl Meyer von Rothschild's fawning request to Bismarck for yet another decoration. If a mighty Rothschild could thus stoop to be raised, how much more natural for a Bleichröder to prostrate himself before Prussian power. The Rothschilds, after all, were a world

---

* Even if few Jews could rival Ludwig Philippson's fervent homage to Frederick William III on the occasion of his birthday in 1837: "I am a Prussian. Therefore the third of August is a holy, blessed day for me. My King was born on that day. One God and one King. . . . He is King of all that is Prussian. And Prussian I am, even if also Jewish." Philippson was editor of the main Jewish newspaper, *Allgemeine Zeitung des Judentums*. Quoted in Jacob Toury, *Die politischen Orientierungen der Juden in Deutschland. Von Jena bis Weimar* (Tübingen, 1966), p. 21.

power, a universally recognized dynasty upon whom many monarchs had bestowed favors. Bleichröder was a mere beginner.

By the 1860s, Bleichröder's success depended on his relations to the Rothschilds and to Bismarck. To the traditional political piety or *Staatsfröm-migkeit* of prosperous Jewry came Bleichröder's personal ties to the most extraordinary German statesman of all times. Tradition and special opportunity, then, pointed to ever greater attachment to the state; with time, a form of Prussian chauvinism and German nationalism took hold of Bleichröder as well. The new sentiment was everywhere in the ascendancy, and Bleichröder absorbed it as he felt himself more and more a part of the Bismarck establishment. By the time he was hobnobbing with the victors in Versailles, his conversion to German nationalism was complete, whether he realized the stages of conversion or not.

Bleichröder's new Germanism obviously quickened his desire to have his status as a German unambiguously recognized. Most Germans had what has sometimes been called "buttonhole panic"; they were afraid of buttonholes and chests that were bare of decorations. Shame at nudity takes many forms, and what is a fig leaf for some is a big, bejeweled medal for another. We have already followed Bleichröder's successful hunt after titles: the first order came in 1858, Geheimer Kommerzienrat eight years later, the Iron Cross in 1871, and finally the unique ennoblement in 1872. "Soon your chest will not be big enough to hold all these high orders from various potentates," wrote friend Oppenheim—himself not uncovetous of these honors.* And indeed he accumulated orders from Bavaria, Austria, Russia, France, Brazil, and other countries. They bespoke appreciation for services rendered; later ages found more vulgar ways to achieve the same end.

The trouble with these outward honors was that they never satisfied for long: there were always others to be coveted. That was hard on both psyche and pocketbook. Honors implied greater visibility, and greater visibility meant not only greater expense but greater vulnerability to the malice of the envious. As Oppenheim wrote Bleichröder when the latter received the Iron Cross: "Recently, you have been showered with distinctions and you are greatly envied."[23] His brother Julius, by way of contrast, seemed relatively indifferent to the trappings of title; his descendants tell us he was proud of leading a much simpler life than Gerson, and in 1898, when he was offered the title of Kommerzienrat, he refused with a certain hurt dignity because the honor had come too late.

Gerson was different. He hungered after every honor in sight—and perhaps rationalized his appetite by thinking that these distinctions redounded to Jewry's benefit as a whole. He was paving the way for others; he was securing positions of influence that would help his brethren. Certainly this

---

* In fact, in 1871, Oppenheim's wife begged Bleichröder to try to secure an Iron Cross for her son, who had been promised one for his services in France but apparently had been frozen out. Henriette Oppenheim to Bleichröder, 28 Feb. 1871. Also Oppenheim to Bleichröder, 12 March 1871 and 19 Jan. 1875, BA.

is what Oppenheim felt at his ennoblement: "This is a triumph for all our coreligionists."[24] In 1885, when Queen Victoria reluctantly, at last, gave Nathaniel Rothschild a hereditary peerage, "English Jews greeted [the news] with almost delirious joy . . . the emancipation of the Jews in England was at last really complete."[25] Gerson probably felt with something of the same pride that he was garnering honors for his people.

But his situation was more complicated than Nathaniel's. Bleichröder won honors in a country where, beginning in the mid-1870s, anti-Semitic sentiments were on the rise again, where the pressure for social conformity was great, and where eccentricity was far less prized than in England. The expectation was that Bleichröder would conform—and there was nothing he desired more. But attempted conformity prompted resentment and mockery, and as he and his family sought to approximate German customs and values, he became slightly estranged from his own people without being accepted by those he sought to join. He met success and frustration in equal measure. Worst of all, he was a butt of ridicule. Malicious people liked to tell of the great feast that Bleichröder ordered to celebrate his ennoblement; he had asked a high official in the court for a list of eligible officers, but added: "Leave out the nonnoble [bürgerliche] gentlemen; we want to be entirely among ourselves."[26] Apocryphal perhaps, but not unsymptomatic. A variant of this story was published in provincial newspapers; Bleichröder reprimanded a captain who had brought a bourgeois officer to one of his feasts: "My friend, we cannot sink that low." At the captain's signal, the officers rose and left—not to return until Bleichröder's formal apology, which was duly tendered. An informal ban was retained, and officers no longer attended the house of this "arrogant Jewish Geldprotzen."[27]

Some such incident must have occurred, even before his ennoblement. Baroness Spitzemberg confirmed that some alleged "silliness" of Bleichröder's led the finest regiments in town to boycott the house; in February 1872, because of their absence, no "formal ball" could be held. But such was the occasion and the guests (including Princess Bismarck) that the dance was a great success even if "tails [rather than uniforms] predominated rather more than usual in Berlin." Spitzemberg was a keen observer of the Berlin scene and indignant at some of the restrictions still visited on cultured Jews, such as Moritz Lazarus. On the other hand, she shared with most people a distaste for a certain kind of moneyed Jew. Recording a pleasant evening at the home of Bleichröder's friend and rival, Hansemann, she noted that the company was "gut bürgerlich, no stock-market Jews and plutocratic snobs."[28] Even before his ennoblement, indeed before his stay in Versailles, Bleichröder entertained the titled (and often dull) society—and excluded his own relatives and most Jews.[29] It was not something that a Spitzemberg would overlook: it was ugly, and it confirmed every prejudice against the parvenu. The aristocrat is proud of his ancestors and family; the parvenu is ashamed of them. Of course, inviting one's Jewish relatives would not have pleased the German aristocracy either. But Bleichröder's phony "exclusiveness" grated on gentiles and Jews alike, and obviously became much worse after his rebirth as *von* Bleichröder.

The police files of 1874 contain this report:

> Mr. von Bleichröder, who since his elevation to nobility almost bursts with pride and who publicly no longer entertains his former friends and associates, keeps himself apart from them even in his walks: on his promenades in the Sieges-Allee [Berlin's fashionable avenue along the Tiergarten] he walks on the western side instead of on the eastern with the great majority of promenaders, who are almost all Jews. Asked why he walked on the other side, he is supposed to have answered that the eastern side smelled too much of garlic. Several of Bleichröder's former acquaintances heard of this remark and a few days ago took him to task for it on the promenade, and things did not go too smoothly then.[30]

Whether literally true or not, the police report suggests a classic case of the arriviste—who never arrives. Bleichröder implicitly repudiated his past, distanced himself from his former friends and from his own kind, and used the culinary-olfactory discriminant—garlic was *the* common characteristic which German anti-Semites always ascribed to Jews—in order to emphasize his own higher, sweetly scented status.

A psychologist may offer another—and illuminating—explanation. Bleichröder was gradually groping for new roles and a new identity. There was the public scramble for acceptance, but there may also have been the less conscious striving for a new identity to replace the old identity as Jew. He wanted to be a major figure in Bismarck's Christian world, and his ostentatious role as repository of secrets was one way of asserting his new identity. By the same token, Bleichröder's insistence on a new identity might have enraged those of his Christian enemies who had projected onto him "entities from [their] psychic world," and by projecting them to the outside could better protect themselves from these inner threats. In that way, the Christian had a stake in Bleichröder's Jewish identity and suffered a psychic threat as Bleichröder sought to minimize the difference between himself and his Christian milieu.[31]

Berlin was full of gossip that rang the changes on this theme. Bleichröder was acquiring a reputation for vanity and falseness among Jews and anti-Semites alike. In 1876 Schwabach reported to Gerson that a journalist had asked him whether it was true that Gerson was about to assume the name of Baron Gütergotz (his estate); Schwabach had replied that he thought it highly improbable, "because one does not give up the name of Bleichröder if one is called that."[32] The very existence of such a rumor is suggestive. Most people would have agreed with Felix Bamberg, a friend of Bleichröder's, who wrote to Prince Karl Anton of Hohenzollern-Sigmaringen: "Bleichröder does not belong to the more modest people."[33]

But Bleichröder was as much lured into the gentile world as he was pushing. He sought a style of life appropriate to his new station. Wealth and nobility enjoined a show of eminence. Gerson sought to excel, as the Rothschilds had always done, as all princes of wealth did. In the process he did things that were risible and craven. Again, his was only an exaggerated version of what most rich Germans did at the time: the plutocrats aped the impoverished aristocracy, and their willing subservience facilitated the aristocrats' continued social hegemony. In France, by contrast, the bourgeoisie evolved its own style, not free of aristocratic desires and, according to novelists and observers, not particularly edifying, but bourgeois values, not aristocratic values, permeated the nation.[34]

Bleichröder's fortune demanded conspicuous consumption. Toward the end of his life, his annual income was officially estimated at 2,000,000 to 2,200,000 marks—the equivalent of twice that many dollars today. According to unofficial estimates, his income in 1892 amounted to 3,340,000 marks and his total fortune to between 36 million and 40 million marks.[35] In Berlin he was the richest man by far; in the Reich, only Alfred Krupp was thought his equal. He had to live up to his own wealth. Or as a contemporary wrote in a much-noted work on Berlin society: "[He] is one of the most intelligent men of our time; his vision in questions of politics and finance is superb. He foresees events even before the circumstances which must give rise to them have appeared. . . . And still, he does not have the necessary moral strength to dominate one weakness: his wish at any price to play another role in high society than that of a moneybag [*sac à millions*]."[36]

Other Jews and other plutocrats had a similar desire—all over the capitalistic world. It was especially hard in Berlin where a British observer noted that "commerce, industry and finance [had not] yet found a way into the reception rooms of privilege. A certain number of excellencies would indeed attend the gargantuan banquets offered by the great banker Bleichröder . . ." In Berlin there was little that could be called "Society," and hence such Jewish salons as Leonie Schwabach's were much esteemed.[37] Bleichröder thought that his sumptuous feasts would attract the great. As Maxe von Arnim, countess of Oriola, herself a *grande dame* with a salon that included artists and writers, noted in the early 1870s: Bleichröder "liked to give sumptuous dinners to which he invited the highest dignitaries, in whose midst he was then the only non-German [*Nicht-Germane*]." (It is ironic to note that the anti-Semitic scribblers insisted that the countess herself had married into a Portuguese family of Jewish descent.) As an example, she cited the time when the old Moltke invited himself to her house with the explanation: "I must. Because I have just declined an invitation from Bleichröder with the explanation that I had already accepted yours."[38] Or as the mythical Count Vasili wrote in 1884: "Berlin society is divided into two camps—those who go to Bleichröder while mocking him, and those who mock him but do not go."[39]

Those who came had to be rewarded. The diplomatic corps was always well represented, as was German officialdom. These notables were always "on call," and they knew that *chez* Bleichröder "matters of state and stomach were admirably mixed."[40] Bleichröder's feasts were renowned, as he wished them to be. The well-known writer Ludwig Pietsch, whom Bleichröder had repeatedly helped, once explained to Emma that the *Vossische Zeitung* had turned down his account of a recent feast of hers. But he wanted her to know that he was "not blind or deaf to the magic of the feast in your hospitable house. In taste, greatness, and glamour it surpassed anything that I have ever seen in a private house."[41] More important is the testimony of Disraeli, himself no stranger to the trials of assimilation. From the Congress of Berlin he reported to Queen Victoria:

> July 3, 1878—The great banker of Berlin is Mr. Bleichröder. He was originally Rothschild's agent, but the Prussian Wars offered him so great opportunities, that he now almost seems to rival his former master. He has built himself a real palace, and his magnificent banqueting hall permitted him to invite the whole of the Plenipotentiaries and the Secretaries of Embassy and the chief Ministers of the Empire. All these last were present, except Prince Bismarck, who never appears, except occasionally at a Royal Table. Mr. Bleichröder, however, is Prince Bismarck's intimate, attends him every morning, and according to his own account, is the only individual who dares to speak the truth to His Highness. The banqueting hall, very vast and very lofty, and indeed the whole of the mansion, is built of every species of rare marble, and, where it is not marble, it is gold. There was a gallery for the musicians, who played Wagner, and Wagner only, which I was very glad of, as I have rarely had an opportunity of hearing that master. After dinner we were promenaded through the splendid saloons—and picture galleries, and a ballroom fit for a fairy tale, and sitting alone on a sofa was a very mean-looking little woman, covered with pearls and diamonds, who was Madame Bleichröder and whom he had married very early in life, when he was penniless. She was unlike her husband, and by no means equal to her wondrous fortune.[42]

Facts and fantasy are beautifully mixed, as befits a novelist and creator of the mysterious banker-figure Sidonia.

The feasts were meticulously planned operations. What anguish, what cost must have gone into these productions—at which host and guests played games of social deception.[43] Everything had to be of unsurpassed quality: guests, victuals, entertainment. Exotic food was imported from the far corners of Europe, and the police department had to assign two officers to regulate traffic. Competitive ostentation produced extravagance and monuments of garishness. The Bleichröder Archive contains a letter from the conductor of the royal orchestra, Benjamin Bilse, in which he declined to perform at one of these fetes because he and his orchestra liked neither the place assigned to them nor the fact that their playing was to take place simultaneously with a croquet game. In the end, he did play.[44] Taste, sureness of touch, and the creation of the right ambiance are qualities that no amount of money could provide.

Bleichröder's feasts were amply talked about and attended. The court Chaplain, Adolf Stoecker, angered by them and by their occurrence during Lent, cited them specifically in his remonstrance to the king. Theodor Fontane, incomparable chronicler of Prussian society, knew of the Bleichröders; his wife and Gerson had been playmates as children, and at the end of their lives the two men exchanged greetings and gifts. Fontane once wrote that real wealth had always impressed him and that the power of the great captains of industry had always awed him:

> Since youth, everything great has had magic for me; I succumb to it without envy. But the "bourgeois" is only a caricature of it; he makes me angry in his pettiness [*Kleinstietzigkeit*] and his constant desire to be admired for nothing. Father Bourgeois let himself be painted for a thousand taler and expects that I take the mess [*Geschmiere*] as a Velásquez. Mother Bourgeois has bought herself a lace mantilla and treats the purchase as an event. Everything that is procured or "presented" is offered up with a glance that says "How fortunate for you to be able to eat of *this* cake, to drink of *this* wine." Everything is childish overestimation of a way of life and of an economy that is just as much a two-bit existence [*Sechserwirtschaft*] as my own. . . . A piece of bread is never two bits, a piece of bread is something sublime, is life and poetry. But a roast goose with special wine and eclairs, if the hostess beams and deludes herself into thinking that for two hours she has torn me away from my everyday existence, that is two bits in itself and doubly so because of the sentiments that come with it. The bourgeois does not know how to give because he has no idea of the nought of his gift.[45]*

Bleichröder's sublime feasts, costing thousands and thousands of marks, never quite lost some of this two-bit quality.

But wealth had to be displayed in more enduring forms as well. Philanthropy ranked high among Bleichröder's obligations, as it did with the Rothschilds, as it did with the rich everywhere. Exceptions proved the rule. Gerson's son Hans happened to be in London when Lionel Rothschild died; Hans wrote back that "few people genuinely mourned because Lionel did not know how to make himself liked and did next to nothing for the poor."[46] Charity was a kind of conscience money or a form of self-glorification, but the fact remains that the bounty of the rich—for whatever mixture of motives—provided (inadequate) medical and social services for the sick or orphaned and enhanced the cultural well-being of the prosperous. Bleichröder was no exception: he gave publicly and privately; he gave to Germans,

---

* By contrast, among austere Prussian aristocrats, children were forbidden to praise (let alone criticize) food; it was not talked about, and trespasses were punished by a humiliating slap in the face. Or so a fine historian remembered an experience from childhood. Joachim von Dissow, *Adel im Übergang* (Stuttgart, 1962), p. 27. Dissow's work is one of the few memoirs we have of the life of old Prussian families.

Jews, and foreigners; he was forever being solicited. The list of his donations was prodigious. He must have been gratified but hardly surprised by Ludwig Pietsch's remark that "thanks to your magnanimity, your achievements benefit all of humanity."[47]

His philanthropy was indeed ecumenical. He contributed to the poor and the sick of all denominations: from Catholic hospitals in Berlin to the Hebrew Orphan Asylum in New York. He helped to build an Anglican church in Berlin, a synagogue in Ostend, a Protestant church in a Rhenish village because Admiral Stosch begged him to contribute to it, and a Catholic church in the Mark Brandenburg. The *Katholische Volkszeitung* publicized Bleichröder's largesse: "To Geheimrat von Bleichröder I go when all else fails," a Catholic priest was quoted as saying. And he went away with 9,000 marks for the completion of his church.[48]

Royalty could be especially demanding. The crown princess was anxious to have a richly appointed English church in Berlin and, as the true daughter of Queen Victoria, had her chamberlain write Bleichröder that she had heard that he might make yet another contribution to the church, which was to be opened, amidst great fanfare, on her birthday. He had already made "a magnificent donation" before the cornerstone was laid; did he have any further, specific amount in mind? Would he like to give the organ—"one could affix a dedicatory plaque to it."[49] Bleichröder obliged, and the world took note.* Nobility extracted—as well as obliged.

In fact, the pleas of the great often extracted largesse, as the former minister Friedenthal, who had done Bleichröder various favors, wrote in 1889: "After not troubling you as a beggar in the many years of our friendship, I must now become unfaithful to that habit." A German rest home in Nice, much favored by the empress, needed "*large* gifts."[50] And so it went, year in, year out: petitions from the powerful to the wealthy. It was, in truth, a form of taxation. Bleichröder spent millions on charity, and Princess Marie Radziwill spoke for many when she lamented his death: "Bleichröder died; he is generally mourned and his disappearance pains me; he was very beneficent, helped me greatly in the work of our Catholic hospital, and I owe him much. The whole financial world is very much agitated in Berlin. Bleichröder was the Rothschild of our capital."[51]

Even in death Bleichröder could not escape the shadow of the Rothschilds. If he gave much, they gave more; if he was famous, they were legendary. In some ways, they had made him—and his feelings toward them were correspondingly ambivalent. But he followed them—and in some cases, joined them—in steady philanthropic support to fellow Jews.

Just as Bleichröder had to compete with the Hansemanns and the

---

* The *Jewish Chronicle* of London commented: ". . . the first, as also the principal, gift in aid of this object was a donation of £1,500 from Baron von Bleichroeder, the British Consul-General in Germany. Although this handsome contribution is doubtless given by the Baron in his official capacity, at the same time the fact will not be lost sight of that he is a Jew, a circumstance which will enhance the value of the gift in the eyes of those who gladly hail such occurrences as tending to cement the bonds of good feeling between men of all creeds. Such acts of mutual sympathy are not unknown in this country . . ." 2 Feb. 1883.

Siemenses in German philanthropy, so he had to keep up with the other leading patrons of Jewish causes. It was a bond that tied him, for example, to the patriarch of Jewish philanthropists, Sir Moses Montefiore, with whom Bleichröder exchanged news on Jewish affairs until Montefiore's death in his 101st year. Montefiore had made a fortune as a young man, retired from business in his forties, and spent some sixty years in the cause of his coreligionists in Europe, Russia, and the Near East. Bleichröder was not about to emulate such singlemindedness, but he cared about Montefiore's approval and was solicitous to gain it. He had a host of exacting models.

A great deal of money went to east European Jewry. Bleichröder supported the far-flung activities of the Alliance Israélite, including a school in Jerusalem; when sending a thousand francs to it, Bleichröder added in a letter to the Alliance that he would like to know whether "the emigration of Israelites from Russia is still continuing. . . ."[52] He sent the Alliance money for destitute Jews in Baghdad and Morocco, quite aside from helping those closer to home. We have already seen his massive and ultimately unsuccessful efforts on behalf of Rumanian Jewry. Of the first Lord Rothschild it was said that "in return [for his munificence], he received not so much devotion (for that is a quality impossible in argumentative Jews) as apotheosis: and in the East End of London and the teeming ghettos of Eastern Europe, he became a legend in his lifetime."[53] Nobody could compete with the Rothschilds, but Bleichröder also was a name to be reckoned with wherever Jewry was in distress.

Charity and politics were often intertwined. Like others, Bleichröder was concerned about the steadily worsening lot of Russian Jewry; in 1891, for example, the Rothschilds everywhere thought that renewed pogroms constituted a breach of promise on the part of Russia. Large numbers of Jews were fortunate enough to escape; at the height of this kind of mass exodus, Bleichröder estimated that seven hundred refugees a day were arriving in Berlin, a totally implausible figure. He assured the British ambassador that "for a considerable time already he had done everything he could to prevent the emigration of these destitute Jews to England." He had ordered the Central Committee in charge of Jewish refugees to warn against emigration to Britain, where "the labor market was already saturated." He had suggested that these refugees be sent to Palestine or America— because obviously these *Ostjuden* were no more welcome in Germany than in Britain. The exchange between Bleichröder and Sir Edward Malet was duly published in the *Times* in June 1891.[54]

Help to the ghettos was a natural for Bleichröder; but he also wanted to play the Maecenas of German culture. It was a favorite role for German Jews to play: it was their tribute—in every sense of the word—to the greatness of the German spirit. He befriended a host of struggling writers and artists. He helped to endow museums like the Germanisches Museum in Nürnberg, supported exhibitions, paid for the collection of patriotic memorabilia. His greatest single contribution was to medicine: in 1890, anonymously but in memory of his parents, he gave Robert Koch, the discoverer of the tuberculosis bacillus, a choice plot of sixteen acres in Berlin and a million marks for the construction of a new hospital and for the treatment of destitute patients with Koch's new therapy.[55]

It was a huge amount for that time, and about 3 percent of his capital; it was also a token of the growing support that science derived from the business world. Such was Bleichröder's reputation that his friend Paul Lindau wrote him that as soon as he had heard of the anonymous gift to Koch he knew that Bleichröder must have been the donor.*

But Medici-like, the rich also seek to leave proper mementos of their own persons. Bleichröder commissioned Germany's foremost portrait painter, Franz von Lenbach, to paint a picture of Bismarck—and some years later, he asked Lenbach to paint his own portrait. Bismarck liked to tell the story that Lenbach charged twice as much for Bleichröder's portrait as for Bismarck's, and when asked why, Lenbach replied that he *enjoyed* painting the chancellor. Bleichröder paid him 30,000 marks for a portrait that took Lenbach three years to complete.[56] Bleichröder had another picture painted by Emile Wanters for 17,000 francs. With the renowned official sculptor of Berlin, Reinhold Begas, and especially with Mrs. Begas, Bleichröder maintained amicable relations—or so her letters would suggest. The rich have ever sought to decorate themselves with the friendship of artists; Bleichröder's name was also linked romantically with a pianist, "sweet Mrs. Grosser," as Grete Begas called her, though, we know nothing about the nature of their relationship. Bleichröder commissioned Begas to design a family mausoleum; Begas obliged and proposed something of Carrara marble. He estimated the cost at 75,000 marks—at a time when the annual income of well over 70 percent of the population was under 900 marks.[57] A Bleichröder had to plan for a dignified and memorable exit.

To say nothing of devising a dignified and comfortable presence: as in Dickens's great caricature of Podsnappery, Bleichröder's life was carefully planned and regulated. One senses little of the improvised or the impetuous in his life with its steady rhythm of work, travel, and restorative *Kur*. He worked long, long hours, and even on Saturdays and Sundays he received his important clients or confidants, called on Bismarck or entertained, and always attended to his correspondence. Pleasure, sports, any kind of escape from business, was alien to Bleichröder's style. He helped artists and engaged them, he went to concerts, but he seems to have been aesthetically illiterate.

The one common weakness among the rich of that day was food— the one sense that this repressive, work-oriented society would allow itself to indulge. Bleichröder had long known that delicacies also made excellent gifts; in the early 1850s Abraham Oppenheim had him scurry around at Christmas time to find fresh asparagus. Other orders followed—from

---

* In the same year as Bleichröder's gift, Fontane wrote: "*At least here in Berlin*, all freedom and higher culture has been mediated for us primarily by rich Jewry. It is a fact one has to accept finally, and as an artist or a literary person, one has to accept it with pleasure (because without it, we could not exist at all)." *Briefe Theodor Fontanes*, 2nd series, (Berlin 1909), II, p. 245.

Oppenheim, from the Rothschilds, sometimes from the court. The ordinary out of season, the exotic in all seasons, and everything of the highest quality —that was the aim. The ultimate treat was caviar, that great delicacy from the far-off Caspian Sea, so exquisite to the taste, so easy to digest, and so difficult to get fresh. Bleichröder had his own couriers bring it to Berlin. In the course of his life, Bleichröder must have bought several tons of it, mostly as presents for others, some destined for his own table as well. Gerson also had a special fondness for fruit and ordered it from all over Europe. In those days, the procuring of delicacies was still an exercise in individual ingenuity: there was no refrigeration, and in Berlin, unlike Paris, the luxury shop was hardly known yet. Food, then, was a universal pastime, and one that Jews may have been especially keen on.

The concern with food was not unconnected with the tremendous concern for health. Quite aside from particular illnesses—and Bleichröder suffered from a cruel illness that finally left him blind—one worried about one's health, one's digestion, one's nerves, one's doctors. People at the time had an intuitive sense of how psyche and body suffered reciprocally, and their letters usually sounded melancholy about their health. Bismarck's complaints, as we know, were legion. Some twenty years before his death, Schwabach wrote Gerson that he was a dying man.[58] The great antidote to these maladies, real and hypochondriacal, was the *Kur*, the annual overhauling of the machinery, the great cleansing of the body, which had become a ritual for rich Europeans. The *Kur* was a serious business, though carried on in some spa of great beauty. One drank the waters, one dieted, one suffered deliciously—and often recuperated in a *Nachkur*.

As in everything else, there was a hierarchy of spas. As a young man, Bleichröder went to the less fashionable places like Franzenbrünn. In time, he went to the great ones, like Gastein or Ostend and again and again to Marienbad.* Even during the *Kur*, Bleichröder continued his business; the spa was to some extent a functional cross between the golf course and the club. A casino was usually provided as well, to satisfy the gambling instincts of the rich. Important people from all over Europe assembled and exchanged news. Bleichröder was especially diligent: every morning, the department heads of his House dispatched reports to him, and his son Hans or his partner Schwabach would send private and supplementary news. Even without the telephone, he was never far away from his business.

The *Kur*, part ritual, part status symbol, was essentially a means for healthy people to survive their unhealthy ways. Real sickness was something

---

* Sir Isaiah Berlin told me that in the early 1920s in Marienbad people were still singing a popular song about Bleichröder. According to another oral report, Russian soldiers in the First World War had a battle song about marching against Bleichröder. One of the leading resident doctors of Marienbad remembered Gerson at the end of his many years at Marienbad "slowly moving along the promenade, completely blind, eyes protected by dark glasses, cumbersome gait, dragging feet, supported on the arm of his secretary, or more often, on the arm of a beautiful woman, a typical example of the old dictum that money alone does not buy happiness." Dr. E. Heinrich Kisch, *Erlebtes und Erstrebtes* (Stuttgart and Berlin, 1914), pp. 268–269.

else again, and only good doctors could help. Drugs were still in their early, presynthetic stage, and the skill of doctors played a decisive role. Bleichröder had a host of famous doctors, some successively, others concurrently. In the spring and summer of 1871 he suffered a collapse, affecting his general condition and his digestion, but most especially his right eye. For years he had suffered from glaucoma, and this condition suddenly worsened with an ulcerated infection of the vitreous body—perhaps as a consequence of all his exertions. In 1870 he consulted the well-known Professor Graefe, who in turn recommended his best assistant, Dr. Evers. Evers assured Bleichröder that absolute rest in healthy surroundings "would have a beneficial effect on your nervous system, somewhat disturbed by illness and overwork."[59] By the fall of 1871 he had improved, but his eyes grew progressively worse. In later years, he also suffered from insomnia and a mild case of diabetes.[60]

He had ample reason, then, to consult the best doctors, and he sought out the most famous as well. On occasion, he consulted Billroth, the world-famous surgeon in Vienna, or Bergmann, a great internist in Berlin. He went to every eye specialist he could find. After the two assassination attempts on William I, he cultivated close relations with William's private physician, Dr. von Lauer. Through Lauer, Bleichröder could supply the monarch with all the special delicacies he might want, and it was from Lauer that Bleichröder received direct news of the king's condition. Lauer was one of Bleichröder's physicians until in his eighties he retired from active practice. At the same time, Bleichröder consulted Dr. Frerichs, at whose disposal he once put his estate in Gütergotz, and in return he received the most solicitous medical attention and the promise of the only thing even a Bleichröder needed: "a friendship of depth, loyalty, and feelings, always ready for sacrifices, in good and bad days . . . something that in our days becomes rarer and rarer and which can be appreciated only by someone who, like you, dear friend, has a deeply sensitive heart."[61] For years, Bleichröder offered Frerichs's advice and services to Bismarck, convinced—correctly—that for a long time Bismarck was not getting the proper medical care.*

To have the best of everything was always Bleichröder's aim. As models, he had the Rothschilds and the indigenous nobility; he sought to adopt a style of life consonant with their expectations. His Ferrières was Gütergotz; he liked it there, far from the bustle of Berlin. For the rest, despite his unlimited resources, he cultivated no great eccentricity; he left no monument of individuality or great taste—he had a passion for business and politics. Beyond that he was a limited, perhaps even a timid man, afraid to assert his inclinations or his taste.

---

* In 1883, a young doctor, Ernst Schweninger, took over and gained an immediate hold on Bismarck who would finally heed the demands of medical prudence and dietary moderation. "At their first meeting, Bismarck said roughly: 'I don't like being asked questions.' Schweninger replied: 'Then get a vet. He doesn't question his patients.'" A. J. P. Taylor, *Bismarck* (New York, 1955), p. 196.

To raise children is rarely easy, and to raise children amidst luxury is doubly hard. For the young, the lure of pleasure supplants the sting of necessity: why work, save, deny oneself something, when the coffers are full and one's parents live in ostentatious splendor? A strong paternal model, backed by a strict ethos and some version of the Protestant ethic, may overcome the temptations that afflict the affluent young. But Shaw's solution—that a big business like the Undershaft armament works should in each generation be inherited by a foundling—is an ingenious commentary on the difficulty of bequeathing talent as well as money to one's natural heirs. Parental timidity and social uncertainty are likely to compound the difficulties. The Rothschilds and the Rockefellers were exceptions, able to impose their ethic on the young; Bleichröder was not.

The troubles began early, and rather innocently. Hans, the eldest, was not a likable boy; in 1865, when he was twelve, his tutor complained to the father that Hans lacked "the simple, natural honesty and kindness" of his younger brother, Georg, "and other children sense this lack at once. It is much to be regretted that between the two boys there is so little mutual love."[62] Such accounts are rare in an incomplete business archive, and the Bleichröder Archive is especially meager in this respect. We have a few letters from Hans to his father and fewer still from the third son, James, named after the great Paris Rothschild.

Hans's letters suggest a disagreeable disposition: as a teenager he asked his vacationing parents to buy him a special cane—in Berlin none was good enough. He was querulous and heartless—as an occasional reference to a superannuated servant or other aides would suggest. By the time he was in his late twenties, despite his formal association with his father's bank and his wide travels in Europe and America, he was filled with lassitude and ennui, concerned with his health and *Kur*—in short, the spoiled scion of Mammon, with no passion beyond indulgence. The wish to be someone other than he was injured his identity and self-respect still further; but parental money and parental model had done their corrupting work even earlier.*

What would Gerson have expected of his sons? To some extent, what most fathers of the time expected: a replica of himself: hard work, success, prominence, the reputation of moral probity and religious commitment. He was disappointed time and again.

None of the sons learned to work. Hans entered his father's business as a very young man, resented continued paternal supervision, and repeatedly apologized for having aroused his father's displeasure by his indifferent

---

* The terrible portrait of debauched wealth and falseness that Thomas Mann depicted in "The Blood of the Walsungs" suggests something of the atmosphere in which Hans luxuriated and suffered. It is a story of the degeneracy of the son and daughter of a banker-father whose Jewishness was not explicitly acknowledged but is patent nevertheless. At the behest of his wife's Jewish father, Thomas Mann withdrew the story after its first appearance. In *Buddenbrooks* and elsewhere as well, Mann suggested the unpleasantness of Jewish *nouveaux riches* without labeling them as such.

work habits. As a twenty-six-year-old, he promised his father that he would mend his ways and give no further ground for dissatisfaction. At another time, he reported that he was working from eight-thirty to six-thirty with but half an hour for lunch. All he wanted, Hans insisted, was to be his own master; in 1881 he became a partner in the firm.[63] Difficulties remained; inevitably Hans was overshadowed by his father. In his simultaneous, pathetic desire for independence and his excessive protestations of filial love ("In childish love, your loyally devoted son," he wrote as a twenty-four-year-old) we hear echoes of Herbert Bismarck's difficulties with his father. It is not easy to be a famous father's favorite, destined to feel smothered by the father's authority *and* dependence.

And yet how much easier for Herbert than for Hans! Herbert at least knew what was expected of him and had no doubts about conduct, bearing, and career. Gerson's children, on the other hand, reflected their father's complicated ambitions and loyalties. They received conflicting signals from him: on the one hand, Bleichröder was a dedicated worker; on the other, he put a great premium on externals, on keeping up with society. In Bleichröder's life there was always a functional relation between social role and work. His children pursued acceptance as an end in itself.

It was natural that Bleichröder should want his children to have advantages that had been denied him. But beyond that lay the world of special distinctions and values, of honors and titles, which in German society was still so intricate and so important. What Bleichröder wanted for his children was that they should enjoy *standesgemässe* acceptance in the gentile world while retaining some loyalty to Jewry. Under the best of circumstances, it would have been a little like squaring the circle.

We know that he brought up the children to observe the Jewish holidays: whether belonging meant more than that or for how long they observed the high holidays, we do not know. Bleichröder had put a distance between himself and the Jewish community. He never denied his origins, and to the last he retained his status as intercessor, but he rarely identified himself openly with the Jewish community. Letters would suggest that he mostly worshiped at home, a princely custom which for him seemed the more convenient because of his blindness.*

We have seen Bleichröder's own struggle for acceptance, and it was natural for him to offer his children what he could: wealth and connections. The boys went to Gymnasium and university—without distinguishing themselves. (Hans apparently made himself so obnoxious that he had to be moved from one Gymnasium to another.) What mattered to the children socially was acceptance in the exclusive fraternities: Bleichröder tried hard to place Hans with the distinguished Saxo-Borussian fraternity, in vain, at least in the beginning. Anti-Semites alleged that repeatedly he shirked the

---

* The loveliest room in Ferrières had been a private synagogue (old families in their ancestral homes usually had a private chapel), until in the 1950s after the present owner's marriage to a Christian, the château was renovated, and the synagogue turned into a family library, called the hunting room.

obligatory duel, in short, that he was a coward.[64] The younger sons may have been more fortunate.

But the highest prestige in imperial Germany came from military distinction: which regiment one served in, with what rank, and above all whether one had become a reserve officer or not. Hans did well in the beginning; he served with the Royal Hussars of Bonn and even received the coveted commission of reserve officer. It was the kind of thing that German youth had printed on their visiting cards, for it was their most important credential. It bespoke manly prowess, *Schneidigkeit*, and above all it attested a man's acceptance of patriotic, feudal values.[65] Even in the 1870s it was a rarity for a Jew to become a reserve officer; Hans made it, thanks to his father's ennoblement and influence.

In the first public scandal to hit the Bleichröder family, Hans lost his rank of lieutenant of the Guards. Details are blurred, but it seems that on the day of the second assassination attempt on William I, on June 2, 1878, Hans appeared in uniform before the royal castle, amidst the milling, sorrowful crowd, in the company of one or several women of ill repute—variously described as hussies or whores. He was charged with conduct unbecoming to an officer, placed before a court of honor, and dismissed from the regiment. The sentence of a court of honor was traditionally kept secret, and hence considerable mystery shrouded the charge and the sentence.[66]

Bleichröder was mortified: it would have been hard to think of a worse lapse or a worse moment for it in his own career. The anti-Semitic agitation, with himself as one of its prime targets, was steadily rising; the Congress of Berlin was about to open, and Bleichröder was in the midst of his efforts on behalf of Rumanian Jewry. It was also the time when, for a brief moment, Bleichröder flirted with the idea of running for parliament. Hans was cashiered in August; it was a terrible disgrace—and one difficult to hush up.[67]

Bleichröder hoped for royal clemency. In February 1879, after William had recovered, Bleichröder sent Bismarck a draft of his petition to William, begging the king to appoint Hans to the Landwehr or militia so that despite the sentence of the court of honor he could wear the king's coat again. If this could not be granted, Bleichröder added, he himself might have to leave Germany. The humiliation would be too great for him to bear.

We do not know whether the final version carried this drastic ultimatum, but at least it served notice on Bismarck how desperate his banker was. Years later, Bismarck remembered only that Bleichröder had appealed to him in vain: "He would have given his dearest possession—his first ten million—for a silver *portépée*."[68] Bleichröder, who had endured all manner of abuse and denigration, could not envision life in Germany with his son dishonored, deprived of the right to wear a uniform.*

Gerson mobilized all his friends and connections. On May 26, 1879,

---

* In the first part of *The Sleepwalkers*, Hermann Broch drew a satirical picture of the symbolic importance of the uniform in the life of a Prussian officer. Bleichröder's plea reminds us that the uniform was the ultimate protection against the social inadequacy which Germans and Jews seem to have felt.

he wrote Bismarck that the clemency petition would be presented to His Majesty the next day by Lehndorff,

> and if Your Highness should have the graciousness to drop a few words in favor of this petition, Your Highness could be certain of my deepest gratitude. I surrender myself to the consoling hope that if my son should have been remiss in particular against the person of the All-benevolent Master then His Majesty will be all the more ready to decide on an act of personal charity.[69]

There is no record of an answer.

Counts Eulenburg and Lehndorff delivered the petition into the hands of the monarch and gave it their "urgent support."[70] Perhaps Bismarck did bestir himself on behalf of Bleichröder, and an old client, General E. L. von Albedyll, chief of the military cabinet and since 1871 "at the elbow of the king-emperor," promised his support. For years, Albedyll had troubled Bleichröder about his wife's investments, and here was his chance to reciprocate.[71] But the king was in no hurry. Even if he had been inclined to forgive such indelicacy, he had to contend with men who had been waiting for a proper pretext to get rid of Hans. Not long after the episode, Herbert von Bismarck in fact boasted to some English friends, Charles Dilke included, of how Hans was eliminated.

> To the whole table he [Herbert] stoutly maintained that it was right that no Jew should be admitted into the Prussian Guards or into clubs. One man at the table said: "But you had a Jew in the Guards"; to which Bismarck replied: "We precious soon hunted him out." The man hunted out [Dilke continued] was the son of Prince Bismarck's banker, the Rothschilds' agent, British Consul at Berlin, and Bismarck's confidential adviser at the time of the treaty of Versailles.[72]

Herbert—with his particular hatred of Bleichröder—was here giving vent to the new, tougher attitudes that were coming in vogue in the early 1880s. Hans had been one of the last Jews to become a reserve officer in the Prussian army; between 1885 and 1914 no Jews were so promoted. The Prussian officer corps and government did not deem Jews worthy of this honor, and their de facto exclusion at the top encouraged the new anti-Semitism at the bottom. Equality before the law did not mean equality in the army—if only because the army thought itself above the law.[73]

Bleichröder kept working on his son's rehabilitation. In July 1879, with considerable difficulty, he persuaded the British Foreign Office to appoint Hans as Her Majesty's vice-consul at Berlin.[74] By the end of the year, Bleichröder complained to Bismarck that he still had received no reply from the king.[75] In the end, the king seems to have taken the unusual step of setting aside the sentence of the court of honor, but Hans could never rejoin his old regiment.[76] Nor did he receive any other commission.

The incident confirmed Hans's disdain for exertion. In apologizing for his bad mood, which he knew annoyed his father, he wrote:

> I regret that I lack the strength of character to become master of this nervous dejectedness, but the misfortune which hit me [in 1878] has affected my spirits very deeply and hence I have repeatedly wanted to ask you to send me far away into the world and to leave me to my own fate. Now that I am alone [in Berlin] I am slowly recovering my self-confidence and hope honestly still to achieve something in the way of business because I am not more stupid than the average, and geniuses rarely fall from heaven, but I must be allowed to be my own master. . . .[77]

With Hans so humiliated, Gerson was busy making sure that the second offspring would get into the right regiment. The usual triumvirate of Eulenburg, Lehndorff, and Albedyll was mobilized—successfully.[78] In 1882 the youngest son, James, had to be taken care of. This time a Colonel Rosenberg plotted the strategy, assuring Bleichröder that he saw no reason why "a man who is capable and comes from a family so devoted to the crown should not be made an officer." Others, Rosenberg warned, felt differently, and considerable finesse would be required. He would do his best, and Bleichröder should appeal to the crown prince: Albedyll, he assumed, would be benevolently neutral. After ten months of maneuvering and the departure of some unnamed enemy, a new reserve officer was born.[79]

Military rank was the surest entrée to imperial society; marrying into a good Christian family was another, and conversion was the third and most radical way. The Bleichröder children, as we will see, tried all avenues. They were at once tempted by the gentile world and tempting to it. Their wealth made them desirable, and their sensuality made them easy prey of their own appetites and other people's greed. Rumors and scandals abounded.

How far people thought that Bleichröder might go in the way of assimilation became evident in 1881, when the prominent *Pester Lloyd* of Budapest carried a big story under the headline "Conversion to Catholicism":

> For some time now a rumor has been making the rounds in Berlin that the family Bleichröder is about to convert to Catholicism. The *Deutsche Landes-Zeitung* informs us that its recent story [concerning the conversion] . . . has now been confirmed in Rome. We could disclose even more, but we refrain because the matter touches such intimate family concerns.

The *Reichsbote* added that one of the Bleichröder sons was about to marry a Catholic, the daughter of Count Paul Hatzfeldt.[80] Bleichröder's friends thought the rumor credible. Consul Felix Bamberg wrote to Prince Karl Anton of Hohenzollern-Sigmaringen that according to German and

Italian papers "Herr von Bleichröder together with his entire family are expected in Rome in order to enter the Catholic Church."[81]

No clue to the origin of this widely circulated rumor has been uncovered. For anyone who knew Bleichröder and knew of his connections with the Rothschilds the story must have seemed highly improbable. But it was implausible for another reason. The normal pattern for Prussian Jews was to convert to Protestantism, and it is hard to imagine why people would have thought that Bleichröder would commit apostasy in order to become a member of yet another suspect minority; certainly his friend Bismarck viewed Catholics with reserve. Bleichröder's conversion to either Protestantism or Catholicism would have created a sensation in Europe; in the event, nothing happened, and his descendants took the easier, more conventional step to Protestantism.

At the end of that same year, 1881, Emma Bleichröder died suddenly. Whatever their innermost relations may have been, they had come to complement each other harmoniously, and Gerson felt bereft. Condolences poured in and were preserved in his archive. Edmond de Rothschild, for example, wrote that he knew of the "tenderness" that filled Gerson's heart "for this sweet companion of your life who extended to you all the love which you deserved." Edmond intended no ambiguity and continued that in such moments of anguish "only religious feeling can offer some help; I know how serious yours is, and I have confidence that your piety will support you in this terrible trial."[82]

The funeral was a gala affair—or so it was reported in a provincial paper.

> Frau von Bleichröder died totally unexpectedly. . . . To the end she had been extraordinarily robust and healthy; her small and graceful figure made her seem very youthful, even though she was in her early fifties. She was a charming, benevolent, and modest woman, not dazzled by the glitter of her fortune. . . . The large congregation . . . [at the Bleichröder home] was visibly moved . . . by the speech of the Jewish minister, supported by the magnificent choir from the Synagogue. The high aristocracy and the diplomatic corps were present, including Princess Bismarck and Lady Ampthill.

The court was formally represented as well.[83]

Bleichröder made a special donation in her name to a Catholic hospital which enjoyed the empress's patronage; in return he received Augusta's gracious commendation:

> I cannot delay expressing my sincere thanks for your benevolence, which, by being so closely linked to the memory of your wife, is doubly valuable. Through your kind mediation, her loving nature, which so many poor people came to appreciate, proves efficacious even after her passing away, and I can understand still better now that this

loss leaves the most painful gap in your life and the lives of your children—a gap that can never be filled.[84]

As we will see, Emma's death coincided with another crisis that Bleichröder faced at this time. The threat that an earlier indiscretion might be divulged had Bleichröder teetering at the edge of public scandal. The contradictions of his life sharpened: eminence and respectability on the outside, fear and threatened sordidness in private, public acclaim and whispered abuse, the desire for a happy patriarchal family life and the reality of ever growing loneliness and filial indifference.

Bleichröder's children did not do him proud. Absorbed in their own affairs, content to spend his money, they neglected him in his last years of lonely infirmity. He minded—the more, perhaps, as he recalled his own conduct toward his parents. Shortly after Emma's death, he indulged in reminiscences which his secretary transcribed. He painted scenes of a happy childhood: hard work, close companionship, his mother occasionally reading aloud from the novels of Cooper or Bulwer; in the summer, the family rented a house in Pankow until Gerson could buy his father an estate in the village of Bukow. With "touching piety" Gerson talked of his mother, whom he remembered as the embodiment of the ideal woman and who had died when he was still quite young. He recalled his devotion to his father, who was so modest that he would rent but never buy the carriage that was needed to bring him from his summer home to the office in Berlin. On one of his father's last birthdays, Gerson gave him a proper carriage. He remembered his father's tears of gratitude. These memories, revived perhaps by Emma's death, are the most personal testimony we have. Gerson clearly had a sentimental side, and to his son Hans he wrote a little later that he had paid "dear visits" to his parents' graves and that during the high holidays "I will attend to my prayers in the usual manner and will not forget you."[85] For all his millions and his prominence, he may at times have envied Julius, whose life was more harmonious, closer to the old roots.

Recollections of his own past prompted a rare complaint about his own children. "The boss noted," his secretary continued,

that in the education of his own children he had come to recognize, with the best intention and reflection, that a different method would be more appropriate for the present age, and hence he did not tie them to the house, gave them even in their younger years greater freedom, and did not so anxiously shield them from all contact with the modern world. I meant well, but now I have to recognize that I was wrong.

And the secretary added: "Must he not from time to time have a feeling of loneliness? Are there not days when he barely sees or talks to one of his four children, when none takes the time to keep him company?"[86]

But Bleichröder was a forgiving father; he was also a man who believed that "if you have to play the fool, play the kind fool, not the angry fool."[87]

His children neglected him, and at times they disgraced him; he apparently showed no anger. What probably aggrieved him most was that his children embraced Protestantism and abandoned his own values; they repudiated him, and he continued to cherish them.

His two surviving letters to Hans from the mid-1880s bespeak exceptional warmth, and he signed them "your always loving, faithful father."[88] His special love was attached to his youngest child and only daughter, Else, called Elschen or *Töchterchen*. She, too, experienced celebrated slights; according to an oft-repeated, oft-distorted story, at her first court ball the officer corps cut her, and she "was therefore in grave peril of being a wall-flower. . . . However, the crown prince told [Count Bernstorff, officer of the guard and later ambassador to Washington] to dance with the lady. . . . The crown prince was well aware that I, like him, regarded anti-Semitism as a stain on the escutcheon of German culture."[89] In frequent anti-Semitic retelling, the story focused not on the crown prince's gesture but on the officers who so gallantly humiliated a young girl, thus protecting their Prussian honor.[90]

This was the milieu in which the younger Bleichröders grew up—and which they sought to escape. In 1887 Else married a Baron Bernhard von Uechtritz; the marriage was terminated almost at once, amidst the inevitable gossip about the baron, who had acquired a dowry of 2,500,000 marks, and about Else, who had acquired an aristocratic name. In 1889 she married Rudolf von Biedermann-Tourony, a converted Jew from Vienna. The marriage took place in the Dreifaltigkeitskirche in Berlin—for the net sum of 45 marks. (The bill has been preserved in the Bleichröder Archive.)[91] What strange, ambivalent feelings old Gerson must have had during this Christian ceremony. Bleichröder bought the young couple a large estate near Breslau; he was pleased by his new son-in-law and to his friend Rudolf Lindau he punned: "In truth, the groom is a thoroughly sober [*biederer*] man. I have no doubt that the union of the two will lead to a true happiness." He was pleased, too, that they had been formally invited to the Bismarcks'. Shortly before his death, he wrote to Lindau: "I have my daughter, son-in-law, and enchanting grandchild with me, and I am content in the very depth of my heart."[92] He yearned to be a Jewish patriarch, surrounded by a loyal, loving, and obedient family. Fate placed him closer to Lear.

His first grandchild, Hans, Jr., was born in 1888—out of wedlock. Hans—not long after his misadventures with the army—struck up a close but not exclusive liaison with Marie Brebeck, the daughter of a gentile launderer. In 1892 another grandson, Werner, was born, also out of wedlock. In 1904 Hans, now a partner in the House of Bleichröder, married Marie, and Hans, Jr., now sixteen—in a characteristic Bleichröder gesture—threw a champagne party for his classmates to celebrate his newly won legitimacy.[93]

In 1888 Bleichröder's youngest son, James, married the nineteen-year-old Harriet Alexander, daughter of a prosperous Hamburg Kommerzienrat. The ceremony took place in the St.-Petri Church in Hamburg. Bleichröder lived to see two grandchildren from that marriage, too; he assumed that James was happy in a large and elegant country estate in Klein-Drehsa in Saxony. James's marriage, richly spiced with affairs and scandals, also ended in divorce.

To the outside world, Bleichröder appeared to be a man blessed by success and good fortune. General Chauvin congratulated him in 1879 on a celebration in his house: "There may be other banking firms in Germany that have enjoyed as long an existence, but few could claim such a magnificent success, and that is your special merit." Bismarck's aide Christoph Tiedemann, in his New Year's greeting for 1885, wrote that for someone so fortunate as Bleichröder, one could only send one's best wishes for his good health.[94] The truth was more complicated. He was a lonely and maligned man. His children did little to overcome his loneliness. His enemies did much to augment it.

CHAPTER 18

The Hostage of the New Anti-Semitism

You and I belong to a race which can do everything but fail.
—Disraeli to Leonard Montefiore, ca. 1870

B leichröder's Jewishness dominated his life. In his last twenty years, there could have been but few days when he was not reminded in some way or other that he belonged to a minority, detested when it was wretched and detested anew when it was prospering. In the first four decades of his life, his Jewishness and his Germanness rarely collided, but he could live in and mediate between both worlds. In the 1870s, after his ennoblement, he sought to translate his new honor into social reality. He suffered snubs, rebuffs, indignities, both private and public. In the 1880s the anti-Semitic whisperings in Bismarck's entourage became even more common, and after his wife's death, Bleichröder—for a variety of reasons—moderated his social ambitions. It was enough to have influence, some form of power, without flaunting social prominence as well. In many ways, his life mirrored the cycle of German-Jewish relations: he rose to eminence in the halcyon days of the 1850s and 1860s, and he came to greatness and grief in the subsequent decades.

As we have seen, Bleichröder was always exposed to what might be called fashionable or acceptable anti-Semitism, a residue of snobbery and suspicion toward a people adjudged to be different, mercenary, and intrinsically inferior. So pervasive was this sentiment and seemingly so natural and unmalevolent that few Germans would have scrupled to acknowledge it. In truth, most of Bleichröder's best friends were anti-Semites. That same type of anti-Jewishness existed in France, Britain, the United States, indeed the whole civilized world. "Nice" people thought Jews, with but a few exceptions, not "our kind." Jews were not admitted as social equals in clubs or in other places of institutionalized camaraderie; one might have them in one's family, provided they were especially endowed—with talent or money. It was a residual prejudice, entrenched most firmly in the socially prominent, whether liberals or conservatives, republicans or monarchists.

In Germany in the 1870s, however, the picture changed: radically and, in a sense, lastingly. Anti-Jewish sentiments and feelings persisted, but they were supplemented by and partly transformed into a new anti-Semitic dogma and agitation. The very term "anti-Semitism" was first invented in Germany in the 1870s and came to connote a principled unshakeable hostility to Jews and the intent to translate that hostility into political action which would curb their power or remove their presence.[1] After two decades of relative public silence, the "Jewish question" was raised loudly and insistently—and in many quarters. There were many variations on anti-Semitism, but at the core of all was the belief that the pariahs had become the true power in the new Germany, that Jews were not only despicable but mortally dangerous—because Germans were peculiarly vulnerable to Jewish subversion. From the beginning to the end of German anti-Semitism was this paranoid fear of the power of the Jews: at first, they were depicted as the economic masters of the Germans, but gradually, and long before Hitler, there developed the myth that Jews had the power to destroy the German character, to corrupt Germans, economically, morally, eugenically, sexually.

For this new anti-Semitism, Bleichröder was the principal witness. By virtue of his visibility and power, he offered an extraordinary target, the more so as his way of life provided easy ammunition to detractors. His was a name to reckon with, a name that conjured up envy and suspicion. He embodied all that the socially aggrieved came to detest: he was a Jew with legendary wealth and power, a parvenu and plutocrat unsettling the traditional order of rank. He seemed to fit all the stereotypes of the anti-Semites: the Jew as promoter and plotter, as corrupter and perpetual wirepuller, the Jew, in short, as a man of devious power—and it was Jewish power that made gentiles uneasy and anti-Semites frantic. He had amassed his fortune by stockjobbing, in defiance of that sacred principle that a man should earn his daily bread. There was a violent anticapitalistic element in the new anti-Semitism; Bleichröder, the international banker, the respectable usurer, was proof of all the iniquities of Jews and capitalists.*

Bleichröder, as we will see, found it difficult to cope with these attacks. When Bleichröder, the friend and pseudoequal of the great, became the target of the gutter, the elite maintained an embarrassed silence. Worse, its own "polite" anti-Semitism acquired a more vicious tone, as Bismarck's entourage demonstrated. The unwillingness of the elite to condemn Bleichröder's traducers or anti-Semitism in general was a premonition of things to come, as was Bleichröder's own uneasy defense. Worst of all, the very government that used Bleichröder in myriad ways and on whose benevolent pro-

---

* In his study of "The Paranoid Style in American Politics," Richard Hofstadter emphasizes "the quality of pedantry": "One of the impressive things about paranoid literature is precisely the elaborate concern with demonstration it almost invariably shows. One should not be misled by the fantastic conclusions that are so characteristic of this political style into imagining that it is not, so to speak, argued out along factual lines. The very fantastic character of its conclusions leads to heroic strivings for 'evidence' to prove that the unbelievable is the only thing that can be believed. . . . But respectable paranoid literature not only starts from certain moral commitments that can be justified to many non-paranoids but also carefully and all but obsessively accumulates 'evidence.' " *The Paranoid Style in American Politics and Other Essays* (New York, 1965), pp. 35–36.

tection he counted seemed to abandon its neutrality toward Jews and came to adopt, at least temporarily, anti-Semitic attitudes and actions. At best the state maintained a malign neglect of Jews; at worst, it condoned or initiated actions (on the recruitment of the officer corps, for example) that confirmed the status of Jews as second-class citizens.

Through it all, Bleichröder remained a Jew. He continued to intercede for his coreligionists at home and abroad. For all his entrée to Christian society, for all his yearning for acceptance, he did not follow his children to Protestantism. He had many reasons for not abjuring a faith that had formed him in a way that it did not form his children. He was also a shrewd man, who weighed his moves carefully, and in pondering conversion he intuitively might have felt that the rewards were not commensurate with the price. As Ludwig Börne, who had converted in 1818, exclaimed: "It is like a miracle! I have experienced it a thousand times and still it remains ever new. Some accuse me of being a Jew, others forgive me for being a Jew, still others praise me for it, but all of them reflect upon it."[2] Bleichröder reflected on his Jewishness and knew that the world around him would always reflect on it, regardless of what he might do.

Bleichröder's experience also reminds us of the ambiguity of the term "anti-Semitism." After the holocaust, how could it be otherwise? For some thirty years after Auschwitz, the term "anti-Semitism" was used at once more loosely and more ominously than ever before. It came to be thought that any criticism of Jews, past or present, was anti-Semitic and that all past anti-Semitism, especially all German anti-Semitism, had prepared the way for the final tragedy. Thus—and for entirely understandable and perhaps largely unconscious reasons—the collectivity of pre-1933 Jewry received a kind of implicit, retroactive immunity. Clearly, whatever lapses or collective faults European Jewry may have been guilty of, these were incommensurable with the final horror the Nazis visited upon their victims. The dead shielded their ancestors. But the very incommensurability of Jewish conduct and Nazi response could also serve as a spur for a frank and fearless study of the earlier period.

Perhaps the term itself is inadequate. Does it make sense to lump together the apostles of hate like Paul de Lagarde, who already in the 1870s called for the extermination of Jews, and such men as Theodor Fontane or Jacob Burckhardt, who warned that unless Jews became less visible and demanding they might be overwhelmed by disaster? Should the same term be used for a fanatic who lives in a world of calculating fantasy—like Ahlwardt or Drumont—and the businessman or politician who has Jewish friends but harbors as well a latent suspicion of Jews which from time to time erupts in some anti-Semitic remark?* In Europe and America the anti-Jewish impulse,

---

* The dictionary definition of the term suggests its umbrella quality: "opposition to, prejudice or discrimination against, or intolerance of Jews, Jewish culture, etc." Funk and Wagnalls, *Standard College Dictionary*, New York, 1963, p. 65.

the sense of Jews as a separate and suspect people, with some virtues and many vices, was endemic.* In most countries, however, mass movements designed to combat Jews or Jewish influence did not flourish, except fleetingly, until the 1930s. In short, anti-Jewish sentiment was common even among people who later became defenders of Jewish rights, but anti-Semitism as a concerted effort to translate anti-Jewish sentiment into political action achieved importance principally in Germany and Austria.†

The history of Bleichröder also suggests the inadequacy of certain theories about the causes of anti-Semitism. To take but one celebrated example: Jean-Paul Sartre's contention that "if the Jew did not exist, the anti-Semite would invent him. . . . [T]he anti-Semite . . . creates the Jew" echoed much enlightened opinion—even if his conclusion that only in socialist countries will anti-Semitism cease makes for grim reading today.[3] Bleichröder was a hostage of the anti-Semites. They could not have created him; his power, his connections, and his lapses were not inventions of the anti-Semites. What the anti-Semites did—as we will see—was to convert the particular into the general, the accidental into the innate, and to leap from fact to fantasy; they insisted that individual acts proved the existence of a preconceived pattern of conspiracy. Defense against such attacks is almost impossible.

Lastly, one obvious point must be recalled. Bleichröder and most of his fellow Jews did not believe that the sudden upsurge of anti-Semitism could really threaten their newly won constitutional rights of legal equality. Troubled and bewildered though they were by anti-Semitism, they assumed it would decline. They certainly did not think that it would grow into an ever more potent political instrument. No one in 1880 could have imagined a Hitler, any more than in 1933 people could have imagined an Auschwitz. There

---

* Historians have always fastened on organized anti-Semitism; a comparative study of latent, informal anti-Semitism in different European countries would be a difficult but immensely rewarding venture. As a mere instance of this latent anti-Semitism, consider the description of John Maynard Keynes when, at the Peace Conference in Paris, Lloyd George suddenly berated the French finance minister, Klotz, who refused to allow the Germans to pay for food imports with gold; Klotz wanted the gold saved for reparations. "Do you know Klotz by sight?—a short, plump, heavy-moustached Jew, well groomed, well kept, but with an unsteady, roving eye. . . . Lloyd George had always hated him and despised him; and now saw in a twinkling that he could kill him. Women & children were starving, he cried, and here was M. Klotz prating and prating of his 'goold.' He leant forward and with a gesture of his hands indicated to everyone the image of a hideous Jew clutching a money bag. His eyes flashed and the words came out with a contempt so violent that he seemed almost to be spitting at him. The anti-Semitism, not far below the surface in such an assemblage as that one, was up in the heart of everyone. Everyone looked to Klotz with a momentary contempt and hatred. . . ." J. M. Keynes, *Essays and Sketches in Biography* (New York, 1956), p. 229.

† The world around 1890 or 1900 was full of the kind of prejudice that surfaced in Eleanor Roosevelt and that surprises us in her—because she became such a resolute fighter against every racial or religious prejudice; in 1904, however, she inquired of Franklin whether on his first day at Columbia Law School "you found any old acquaintances or had only Jew Gentlemen to work with!" And of Felix Frankfurter she wrote: "an interesting little man but very Jew." Or again: "The Jew party [was] appalling. I never wish to hear money, jewels and . . . sables mentioned again." Joseph P. Lash, *Eleanor and Franklin* (New York, 1971), pp. 135, 214.

were many reasons in the 1870s and 1880s to think that Jews would continue to make steady progress—quite aside from the perfectly human desire to indulge in optimism.

In the early 1870s a new type of anti-Semitism was emerging, different from the traditional, ritualistic, largely religious anti-Semitism of earlier times.* Old-fashioned anti-Semites disliked and despised Jews; the new anti-Semites despised *and* feared Jews—or at least preached fear of them. The new dogma insisted that Jews had combined in a conspiracy to achieve domination over Germans, that Jewry as such—and no longer individuals—constituted a mortal threat to the German people. In the decade of the 1870s this view of the world became a powerful force in Germany. We are here concerned with Bleichröder's place in this new ideology, but we must ask as well how this ideology came to gain credence and respectability in so short a time.

It has often been said that the great depression, which began in 1873 and was perceived as a consequence of fraudulent speculation, spawned the new ideology—as it did in other countries, including the United States.[4] A later, still worse depression has been similarly blamed for the rise of National Socialism, but in both cases the historian's fallacy of misplaced concreteness may be at work. In the 1870s other factors played a major role as well, and it was precisely this confluence of events and sentiments that favored the rise of this new dogma. In the 1870s German society was in the grip of change and people suddenly began to perceive the baneful consequences of modernization. The glorification of the unified nation continued the exaltation of 1871, but it was also the secular faith appropriate to a modernizing society.[5] Moreover, the battle between the Christian state and the Christian churches, the Kulturkampf, injured specific interests and unsettled many minds. The 1870s, then, was a period of turmoil in the economic, spiritual, and ideological realm. Whence was the new state bound, what was the character of the new society, and who would determine the new direction and the new character?

Amidst all this change and travail, it was incontrovertible that the place of Jews in Germany *had* changed and changed dramatically. Perhaps never before in Europe had a minority risen as fast or gone as far as did German Jews in the nineteenth century. Their success was made possible by emancipation and facilitated by the great economic transformation; it was a rise that corresponded to Jewish customs and ambitions and was distorted by re-

* Obviously there were some voices that never stopped lamenting the presence and influence of Jews. Bismarck's friend Hermann Wagener was one of these, and in 1862 he wrote: "The Jewish tribe has indeed a different blood from the Christian peoples of Europe, a different body, a different constitution, other affects and passions, and with his physical constitution is connected his alienness [*Fremdschaft*]." Unable to create his own home, the Jew "yearns for the domination of others, for their suppression and exploitation. . . . If we add to these peculiarities the thick, fat skin and the volatile, mostly disease-inclined blood, we see before us the Jew as white Negro, but the robust nature and the capacity for physical work of the Negro are missing and are replaced by a brain which by size and activity bring the Jew close to the Caucasian peoples." Quoted in Dr. Wilhelm Bauer, *Deutsche Kultur von 1830 bis 1870*, in *Handbuch der Kulturgeschichte*, ed. by Dr. Heinz Kindermann (Potsdam, 1937), pp. 216–217.

maining, tacit disabilities. Jews, previously excluded from the mainstream of German life, pounced on the new opportunities and proved perhaps more strikingly than any other group the dynamic possibilities of having "careers open to talent." In 1871 Jews constituted only 1.25 percent of the German population, but their place in German society could hardly be gauged by that figure. Excluded from some fields, they flocked to and prospered in others. In midcentury the Jews of Berlin constituted 2 to 3 percent of the total population; about half the early entrepreneurs of that city were Jewish. In 1881 Berlin Jews made up 4.8 percent of the population, .4 percent of the civil servants, 8.6 percent of its writers and journalists, 25.8 percent of those engaged in the money market, and 46 percent of its wholesalers, retailers, and shippers. In many cities in Silesia, Jews constituted about 4 percent of the population and paid more than 20 percent of the taxes—an index of their disproportionate income. In 1871, 43 percent of the inhabitants of Hamburg earned less than 840 marks a year, but only 3.4 percent of the Jews belonged to this group. And by the 1880s, a member of the British embassy in Berlin had the impression that "the capital of the country was rapidly passing into the hands of a limited number of Jews of enormous wealth, as industry encroached upon the old agricultural interest."[6]

Traditional Jewish veneration for learning plus the new promise of social reward gave Jews a particular incentive to excel in German education. As a consequence, they were disproportionately represented in Gymnasiums and universities; by the mid-1880s, nearly 10 percent of all students enrolled at Prussian universities were Jewish—or seven times their proportionate number in the population. The disproportion was even higher in large-city Gymnasiums, and the anti-Semitism of secondary school teachers, made more virulent by their occupational resentment at being so close to and yet so inferior to university teachers, may also have been related to the palpable presence of so many Jewish children in their classes.

In short, the Jews were disproportionately active in large cities, in commerce, and in professions that generally assured them an income and an influence far greater than those of the German population at large. Bleichröder was merely the visible exemplar of this new role, and after his sojourn in Versailles and his ennoblement in 1872, he symbolized as well the link between new plutocracy and power. Given the antecedent sentiments in Germany about Jews, about business, and about social values generally, it would have been astonishing if the sudden rise of Jewry had not evoked resentment.

The rise of Jewry coincided with a general change in the life and ethos of the new Germany—a change which many people lamented. One did not have to be an anti-Semite to find bourgeois standards or capitalistic values objectionable. The novels and diaries of this time testify to this revulsion. The novelist Friedrich Spielhagen, for example, tried to expose the meanness, corruption, and ugliness of a newly moneyed society. The greatest trick of the anti-Semites was to fasten this antibourgeois sentiment, endemic in Europe, onto the Jews, and by insisting that Jews were responsible for the new values and new ways, they gave some specious logic to their charge that Germany had been *verjudet*.

Aside from capitalism, some men despaired of the tone and spirit of the new Empire. In 1872, in his great polemic against David Friedrich Strauss, Friedrich Nietzsche warned that German hubris after the victory over France could lead "to the extirpation of the German spirit." In a similar vein, if more narrowly political and vitriolic, Constantin Frantz, son of a Lutheran pastor and an admirer of Bismarck's turned critic, inveighed against the moral decay of the new Reich, which in 1872 he attributed to the all-pervasive spirit of the triumphant National Liberals. On them he blamed "the turning away from Christianity and the turning to a new paganism," the rule of mendacity and Mammon: "Truly the whole world is full of deceit." Berlin, full of the vices of modernity, had lost its claim "to be the metropolis of the German spirit." After 1866, he said, a new arrogance had taken hold of the Germans, but they surpassed the French only in "stock-market swindling and speculation horrors." The exaltation of Mammon and Realpolitik heightened the conflict between the rich and the poor and would increase the power of socialism. "We have won external peace, but not internal contentment."[7] For Frantz in 1872, the enemy was the National Liberal spirit embodied in the excrescences of unbridled capitalism and in the amoral politics of Bismarck. The Jews did not figure in this indictment, but four years later—and the shortness of the interval suggests the rapidity with which anti-Semitic thought became current coinage—he wrote: "Who actually governs in the new Reich? and what have the victories of Sadowa and Sedan achieved, for what purpose the booty of billions, why the battle for culture [*wozu wird Kultur gekämpft*], if not above all for the promotion of Jewish domination?"[8] In 1878 he argued that the state had become a vehicle of Jewish domination and soon "will not even be able to mint coins, but will have to leave this, too, to the bankers and in future Bleichröder or Rothschild will appear on our currency. . . . Indeed it might be best if this were already so, for then everyone would know who governs in present-day society."[9]

The growing consciousness of corruption facilitated the acceptance of the new anti-Semitism. Frantz had not invented the charge. In February 1873 Eduard Lasker had pointed to the collusion between government and promoters. The crash of 1873 gave dramatic proof of all the charges of corruption and provided an ideal atmosphere in which conspiratorial theories could flourish. Given the presumption of corruption, it was easy to suppose and insinuate that the Bleichröder-Bismarck link attested corruption as well, that Bismarck would never have worked with and rewarded a Jew if he had not drawn illicit benefit from the association.

The charges of corruption appealed to a multitude of aggrieved groups and classes that suffered from the consequences of change without understanding its causes. At the time of the Kulturkampf, orthodox Protestants and Catholics feared for their spiritual hegemony and their material power; they began to feel displaced, homeless. The Junkers, increasingly impoverished, feared the rise of the new plutocracy and objected to Bismarck's dalliance with the new business class. Artisans were threatened by factories and displaced by new businessmen, and the working class, suffering already from all manner of exploitation, including terrible housing conditions, was threatened by unemployment—which in turn raised the specter of another Commune, this time in Berlin.

In the 1870s, as we have seen, conservative suspicion of Bismarck was at its height, but a frontal attack on the head of state and the idol of the people would have been difficult. How better to blacken Bismarck's name than by suggesting that he was the victim of an unscrupulous conspiracy—and by pointing at Bleichröder, suggesting that Bismarck was not an innocent victim? Bismarck's own cherished principle of *do ut des* made this seem plausible; and against this background of plausibility, clever scribblers could insinuate that the Bismarck-Bleichröder tie, reeking of illicit profit, somehow stood for all of Bismarck's curious dealings with Jewry. Nothing is more unsettling to people than the oft-repeated charge that their miseries are due to corrupt officials in the pay and under the spell of concealed conspirators wielding the real power. What Bismarck's enemies were suggesting was that the chancellor was under the influence of a Jewish conspiracy, which was masterminded by Bleichröder. "Enmity toward Bismarck and struggle against the Jews were one and the same issue in these circles."[10] All that was needed was some substantiation, because great conspiratorial theories—and history is full of them—need some anchorage in recognizable reality. To provide the necessary evidence—and the standards of truth were modest— was the work of three men, Otto Glagau, Otto von Diest-Daber, and Rudolph Meyer.

Otto Glagau was a professional journalist who, in December 1874, started a series of articles on corruption and capitalist promotion in the *Gartenlaube*, a family journal of low-brow taste and vast circulation. At the time, the magazine sold 460,000 copies, and its readership was close to 2 million.[11] Glagau concocted a clever polemic, disguised as instant history and discreetly spiced with anti-Semitism. The bulk of the series, later published as two volumes in several editions, was an exposé of the system of company promotion, of who spawned what corporations with what fraudulent claims and under what cover of aristocratic respectability. Glagau pointed to the interlocking directorates who controlled these new creations, to the prominent names that gave dignity to them; he placed S. Bleichröder and the Disconto-Gesellschaft at the head of the list as "chief promoters." He described Bleichröder's various creations and creatures, especially his close association with Kardorff and Hatzfeldt.[12] By ironic asides and occasional innuendos, Glagau stressed the role of Jews, but his fiercest invectives came only after his first articles had been privately and publicly attacked for reviving medieval prejudices and for spreading intolerance. The editor of the *Gartenlaube* was also put under all sorts of pressure. Then Glagau lashed back and in a few deft strokes of alarmist exaggeration sought to give a terrifying picture of Jewish domination.

No longer should false tolerance and sentimentality, cursed weakness and fear, prevent us Christians from moving against the excesses, excrescences, and presumption of Jewry. No longer can we suffer to see the Jews push themselves everywhere to the front and to the top, to see them everywhere seize leadership and dominate public opinion. They are always pushing us Christians aside, they put us up against the wall, they take our air and our breath away. . . . The richest people in Berlin are Jews, and Jews cultivate the greatest pretense and the greatest luxury, far greater than the aristocracy or the court. It is Jews who in the main fill our theaters, concerts, opera halls, lectures, etc. . . . It is Jews who primarily engineer the elections to the Diet and the Reichstag. . . . God be merciful to us poor Christians.

In these angry rebuttals, he claimed for the first time that 90 percent of the promoters and marketeers (*Börsianer*) were Jews.[13]

Bleichröder had reason to be distressed; Glagau had mixed all sorts of truths and falsehoods; Bleichröder had not been one of the greatest promoters, but he did have his confreres in press and parliament. Glagau had tarred Bleichröder with the brush of corruption, had somehow linked his name with some of the worst excesses of the period—with Strousberg, for example, whom Bleichröder himself had warned against. And he had done all this in a journal of mass circulation. The rest Glagau left to his fellow sniffers of corruption.

Glagau was followed by a conservative politician, Franz Perrot, who in the summer of 1875 wrote several sensational articles in the *Kreuzzeitung*. (We have already discussed these "New Era" articles in a different context; Perrot labeled the economic policy of Bismarck and Delbrück as "*Judenpolitik*"—and identified "the dominant banker" Bleichröder as the chief instigator of policies designed to profit Bleichröder and his fellow Jews.)[14] The *Kreuzzeitung*, distinguished less for its intellectual tone than for its clientele, was the voice of Protestant orthodoxy, and many of Bleichröder's clients read it. Bismarck's advice that he should disclaim *all* influence on government policy offered neither solace nor an acceptable solution.[15] In the end, Bleichröder suffered in silence, while Bismarck's later attack on the *Kreuzzeitung* proved futile. His erstwhile colleagues in conservatism did not repudiate their paper—instead they continued to oppose Bismarck's policies. The charges in fact spread, and Bismarck was certain that assiduous gossips spread slander to the innermost circles of the court and had reached the ears of his chief enemy, Queen Augusta.

In the meantime, leading Catholic papers echoed these attacks. One of them wrote: "Whosoever makes laws in our country and has the decisive voice in finance, science, art, and the press has Semitic blood in his veins."[16] After the "New Era" articles in the Protestant paper, the major Catholic daily, *Germania*, launched its series denouncing the prevailing "*Judenwirtschaft*" and demanding a boycott of Jewish firms. Jewish financiers were condemned for subscribing to the French war loan in 1870 while having been reluctant to take up the loan of the North German Confederation. The Jews, in short, were unpatriotic, something the Catholics were often accused of. The temptation to pay back the liberals—and for liberals, always read Jews—was too great for *Germania*: "The Kulturkampf, too, is in fact and in many of its manifestations exclusively a consequence of the Jew-business. On account of the Kulturkampf, too, we are pleased that the Jewish problem has for some time now been posed clearly and decisively."[17] Or again: "the true 'Kulturkampf,' directed not against the religion of the Jews, not against Jewry as such, but against the Jewish spirit which threatens Christianity and the German character and against the Jewish money domination which is the death of our national prosperity, has become an urgent necessity and fortunately has already become widely popular."[18] *Germania* hinted at what another anti-Bismarck writer put quite blatantly: "It has oftentimes been assumed by conservatives and by eminent Centrists that Prince Bismarck undertook the Kulturkampf, which is equally harmful to the Catholic and the Protestant church, in order to deflect public attention from his connection with Bleichröder and its consequences."[19] The provincial Catholic press spread the same message.

Catholic anti-Semitism had deep roots, going back many centuries; it would have taken remarkable self-restraint for Catholics not to voice their anti-Semitism at the very moment when Jews for the first time in history really did present a force against them. No wonder Bleichröder sought the friendship of Windthorst and Prince-Bishop Kopp, both of whom tried to moderate Catholic anti-Semitism.

Orthodox Protestants and angry Catholics echoed the theme of Jewish domination which Wilhelm Marr, one of the first racial, avowedly nonreligious anti-Semites, was elaborating at the time. In his oft-reprinted pamphlet entitled "The Victory of Jewry over Germanism," written in 1873, Marr proclaimed: "The historic fact that Israel has become the *leading social-political power* of the nineteenth century is plainly visible. *To dejudaize [entjuden] ourselves* is already beyond *our physical and intellectual strength*." German weakness had allowed Jews to gain this power, to become "the dictators of the state financial system." Marr reveled in despair: "The *Jewish Caesarism* is but a question of time. . . . World domination belongs to Semitism."[20] The fear that demonstrable Jewish preeminence proved hidden Jewish *domination* was the mainspring of the new anti-Semitism.

Most publicists, however, were less fatalistic; they sought individual culprits and corrupters. Among these publicists, Otto von Diest-Daber came to play a prominent role. The son of a Prussian general decorated with the Pour le Mérite, Diest-Daber had been a Landrat in the Rhineland and a conservative deputy in the Prussian Diet; from the mid-1860s on, he became increasingly disaffected. As a Landrat he had discovered that the rich were buying their sons' way out of the army, and he was quick to press charges of corruption. Soon he hit guilty and innocent alike and was launched on a career of calumny. In the war of 1870 he volunteered as a fifty-year-old and served as captain; he was promised but never received the Iron Cross, first class—he was forever a disappointed man, convinced that the world was rotten. He smelled sin and corruption everywhere—and occasionally uncovered traces others failed to see.[21]

He had tangled with Bismarck in 1868, alongside other disgruntled conservatives. In the early 1870s he bombarded Bismarck with missives imploring him to sever his ties to Jews and financiers. For Diest-Daber, Bismarck's complicity with Mammon was personified by his link to Bleichröder—which Bismarck's disgruntled assistant Thile had first revealed to him in 1870. Bismarck came to know of this leak and called Thile "a dangerous man . . . quite incapable."[22] Diest and others were outraged that Bismarck in his moment of triumph had forsaken his old friends, betrayed his old creed, and surrounded himself with Jews and liberals. Bismarck in turn thought Diest-Daber and his ilk "envious and disgruntled *Standesgenossen*"—an uncharitable half-truth. His critics were cranky, envious, and sometimes mad, but they gave voice to a far greater resentment than Bismarck understood at the time. He was closer to the mark when in the same context he observed that "it is a peculiarity, if not of all people then certainly of the Germans, that the discontented person is more diligent and busier than the contented, the covetous more ambitious than the satisfied." His enemies, he thought, were more active than his supporters, and the former were motivated not by principle but "by ambition . . . or by resentment over political and confessional adversities."[23]

Diest-Daber was certainly busy. Years later, he claimed that in 1874 he talked with Field Marshal Moltke and discovered that Germany's foremost military hero also believed that "Mammonism" and the world of promoters were endangering the new Reich. Moltke agreed with Diest that the "money power must be combated because it plays into the hands of socialism. He regretted Prince Bismarck's intimate relations with Bleichröder and the fact that he gives this Jew power of attorney to administer his property. One must try to break this influence and to separate Bismarck from Bleichröder." At the same time, Diest saw Field Marshal Manteuffel, who, not surprisingly, was also indignant at the Bismarck-Bleichröder tie.[24] Backed by such eminence, Diest opened his campaign against Bleichröder.

The names Moltke and Manteuffel have hitherto not been mentioned in connection with the anti-Semitic campaign against Bismarck; to be sure, Diest was rather free with the truth, and perhaps these conversations were figments of his imagination. But there is good reason to suppose they actually occurred as described. We have seen the anti-Semitic undercurrent at the headquarters in Versailles. Austere military men like Moltke had little use for the pomposity of new wealth; they clung to the old pieties and foresaw ruin in Mammonism and in the secularism implicit in the Kulturkampf. Moltke had still other credentials for his antimaterialist attitude; a translator of Shakespeare, he had aesthetic objections to the new plutocracy as well. Certainly, the military contempt for much that we call modern is an important theme of the last hundred years. What Moltke in his hauteur felt, scribblers propagated, often to their own advantage.

As we will see, the nature of the attacks varied, but they were all focused on Bleichröder and they all operated with innuendos, insinuations, and lies. The technique was to dip known facts into common prejudice and marvel at the monster that emerged. Bleichröder *was* Bismarck's Jewish banker and confidant, and there was a common presumption that Jews were generically unscrupulous and avaricious. It seemed plausible that Bismarck would have burdened himself with this Jew only for extravagant profit. On the other hand, Bleichröder's many connections made it easy to depict him as a terrible spider. What is clear is that the paranoid flair of these writers led them to intuit something of Bleichröder's importance.

As early as 1874, Diest wrote a polemic against the new materialism as having bred socialism; the "golden hydra" had to be destroyed. He sent a copy of this pamphlet, "*Geldmacht und Sozialismus,*" to Bismarck, avowing that he was still his supporter.[25] For a time, he hoped to free Bismarck from this hydra, but failing that, he set out to prove that Bismarck had drawn vast profit from his connection with the head of the hydra, Bleichröder. In 1876 he published a pamphlet on the moral basis of the state which contained the central charge of that first campaign, thereafter often repeated, that the chancellor had granted certain privileges to a Bleichröder-led consortium which in 1870 had founded the Preussische Central-Bodenkredit-Aktiengesellschaft, that Bleichröder had made a huge profit on this, and that Bismarck in his private capacity had been amply rewarded as well. Diest alleged that Bleichröder had assigned Bismarck shares in the company at an issue price of 108, which were then sold at the stock market for 128, for a profit to Bismarck of 83,000 taler. A further charge was that Bleichröder managed to give Bismarck an annual return of 18 percent on his capital. No doubt Bismarck would have liked such windfalls, if they had been legitimately won, but Bleichröder performed no such miracles. One can imagine Bismarck's wrath at being vilified for a gain he never made. Diest implicated other notables as well, especially Kardorff.[26]

A whole series of suits and countersuits developed. Endless complications arose, and a macabre note was added by the suicide of a Geheimrat von Wedemeyer, Diest's chief purveyor of news and, like Diest, a paranoid failure from the aristocratic underworld. Diest's charges were repeated in an embittered anti-Bismarck paper, *Reichsglocke,* edited by Rudolph Meyer. In February 1877 Meyer was sued for libel, and Bleichröder was the chief witness at the celebrated trial. In order to authenticate his evidence, Bleichröder had to divulge his role as Bismarck's banker and adviser. To the testimony already cited in Chapter 12, he added: "How little Prince Bismarck had time to care for his private concerns can perhaps be gleaned from the fact that he asked me some time ago whether he owned or had ever owned shares of the Preussische Central-Bodenkredit-Aktiengesellschaft." Bleichröder carefully checked the matter and established that Bismarck had never owned such stock, had never made any profits whatsoever from this enterprise, and that "all contrary allegations I declare to be malicious slander." He had owned mortgage bonds, not shares, of the company, but these were a nonspeculative investment.[27] Bleichröder's refutation, repeated under oath, is fully borne out by the regular statements that have been preserved in the Bismarck Archive. The trial ended with Meyer's conviction, but Bismarck's close tie to Bleichröder had been publicly acknowledged.

Diest-Daber's turn in court came in May 1877; again Bleichröder testified and "rather sharply disposed of Diest's cross-examination," as he wrote Herbert Bismarck. He had threatened Diest with a slander suit if he were to repeat the allegation that one of Bleichröder's employees had given secret information in exchange for a 10,000-taler bribe. Diest prevaricated, while Bleichröder's stance evoked his friends' "admiration."[28] Several days later, Bleichröder wrote Herbert Bismarck that Diest had received a prison sentence of a mere three months, and attributed this lamentably "mild sentence" to the timidity of his co-witnesses, among them Bismarck's former secretary Thile and Carl Meyer Rothschild. Hansemann, another witness, also regretted this leniency, and Herbert agreed that the penalty given Diest was indeed rather mild: "I do not know what motivated the judges in their sentence!"[29]

Not surprisingly, Diest found a three-month sentence anything but mild. In 1878 he sued Bismarck, who insisted that as a general of the cavalry he had the right to have the case tried in military court. At yet another trial, Schwabach testified—the House of Bleichröder was always involved.[30] Earlier a military court of honor had ordered that Diest must resign his cavalry captaincy and surrender his uniform.* The two punishments together confirmed Diest in his sense that he was a victim of persecution, a martyr for truth. For years he hounded courts and high personages, protesting his innocence, accusing others of plotting against him, while launching his own outrageous accusations against all and sundry—and always against Bismarck and Bleichröder. Bismarck's banker had become his private phobia, and he echoed some and invented other charges of perjury against Bleichröder. After Bleichröder's death, Diest published a summary of his long-drawn-out war against Bismarck and Bleichröder, a summary full of facts and fantasy, liberally spiced with endless laments about his own suffering. There was something pathetic in his paranoia, and one could muster some sympathy for the man if he had been less bellicose. But no sooner had he won his much-coveted pardon from William II, which allowed him to wear his uniform again, than he became embroiled with Georg von Bleichröder, after Gerson's death, about his father's alleged wrongdoing.[31] Diest was one of those persons from the underworld of politics who were destined to suffer and make suffer.

In the camp of antiliberal muckrakers, Rudolph Meyer was perhaps the most fascinating and versatile. Earlier a university student of the natural sciences and of political economy, a friend of Karl Rodbertus and Hermann Wagener, a close acquaintance of Karl Marx and August Bebel, Meyer was convinced that the rise of the proletariat was the greatest social phenomenon of the time. His ideal was a social monarchy, dedicated to the material in-

---

* In the Diest papers there is a petition by Diest's wife to the king, begging him to restore her husband's rank. To support her case, she cited an episode from Diest's life which in a sentence evokes the moral world of her time—so different from ours: "When his father lay on his deathbed in terrible agony and the loyal son stood by him day and night and cried out in deepest devotion: 'If only I could suffer for you, die for you,' the father replied, 'Not that, my child, you must still serve and benefit your fatherland.'" Meta von Diest to William I, 12 June 1877, DZA Potsdam Reichskanzlei, Angriffe des Diest-Daber auf den Fürsten Bismarck und Rahabilitierungsgesuche, No. 401, Band 1.

terests of the lower classes and shielded by a common religious faith.* An admirer of Bismarck's foreign policy, he detested what he thought was Bismarck's support of self-serving, corrupt Manchesterism. For years he hoped to wean Bismarck from his liberal associates. But Bismarck would not listen—and in 1877 Meyer published a massive exposé of the links between corrupt businessmen and corrupt politicians. It was a serious, powerful work, rich in detail, clear and bitter in tone—and with venom against Bismarck, who had spurned his pleas. The chief culprits were unbridled capitalism and Jewry, and the identity of the two was conveniently located in the figure of Bleichröder. Having contended that the influence of the stock market extended to William, Meyer added: "Through the most influential of Berlin's distinguished businessmen, Herr G. Bleichröder, the stock exchange . . . always has access to Bismarck, something that not even foreign ambassadors could claim, and all that remained to be done was to corrupt parliament as well."[32] Bleichröder's link with Bismarck epitomized Meyer's thesis that "a company of political businessmen and 'industrious' politicians had constituted itself in Germany which penetrated parliaments, which by all sorts of devices won the upper echelon of the civil service for its own purposes, which attained influence everywhere, and thus promoted an economic policy which served only its own interests and even these in a shortsighted manner."[33]

In the midst of an unprecedented depression, this charge of collusion, corruption, and stupidity proved popular. Meyer turned Bismarck's favorite weapon against him: he accused Bismarck of condoning such

> corruption of the upper classes of society . . . that that society has become easy prey for social democracy. . . . Blame rests with the man who never once used his immense power to check this decay. Anyone who like Prince Bismarck puts the stamp of his character on his age and who claims the right to do so is responsible for the kind of stigma which our society carries on its forehead.[34]

Meyer's chief witness against Bismarck was again Bleichröder. As Bismarck's "*Hausfreund*," guilty of "scandalous greed and dirty business practices," Bleichröder was depicted as the evil genius of Bismarck's policies. "It is well known that Prince Bismarck understands nothing of economic matters." Hence he allowed Bleichröder to administer the Welfenfond investment, to manipulate the Reichsbank, to promote countless semifraudulent enterprises. Bleichröder's name appeared on almost every page, and yet he was charged with few specific wrongdoings; it was all done by insinuation, by the appearance of exactitude. But why had Bismarck allowed Bleichröder this extraordinary influence, why had he thus abetted the rise of socialism? At the very

---

* Meyer once put his views rather crisply: "Whoever takes religion from the people is a criminal, but if that person belongs to the propertied classes he is a fool as well—because whoever takes heaven away from the people will have to give them the earth." *Deutsche Landeszeitung*, 25 July 1871, quoted in Kurt Feibelmann, *Rudolf Hermann Meyer* (Würzburg, 1933), p. 38.

beginning of his book, Meyer referred to Diest-Daber's charge that Bismarck had benefited from Bleichröder's promotions; Meyer cautiously added that these charges had not yet been authenticated: "Should they be proven, then the Jew-domination under which Germany has in fact smarted for years would be explained in the most painful but sufficient manner."[35] This was a typical sleight of hand: if a particular allegation should be proven correct, then a fantasy—Jewish domination—which by its sweeping character was past proof would be "explained." In the event, the charge against Bismarck was proven false, but the fantasy lived on, its creators no doubt waiting for some other validation.

Meyer had an uncanny sense of Bleichröder's power: if Bismarck

> grasps the hand of Europe's most avaricious and most notorious promoter, receives him as a daily guest, then it is natural that the idolaters of all classes who anxiously study how Bismarck clears his throat and how he spits should think it an honor to have the most intimate relations with the head of this ring [of corruption]. No wonder that court nobles and court marshals, chiefs of protocol and court ladies, should confide their savings to him and should sit at his table. . . . There is no statesman in all of Europe who maintains such friendly relations with a rising representative of Mammonist presumption as does Prince Bismarck with his house-Jew Bleichröder.[36]

Some two hundred pages of this kind of slander cum revelation proved highly effective; it also sufficed to bring Meyer to court. He was sentenced to eighteen months in prison for insulting Bismarck and other ministers; his book was suppressed. Meyer chose exile instead, and filled with still greater rage, he continued his attacks against *"Das System Bismarck* which had condemned the German people to a condition of servility without analogy in the civilized world. . . ."[37] Meyer's jumble of facts and fiction, charged with fear and venom, prefigured some of the later radical attacks from the right; in his own way, he also prefigured the closeness between the radical right and the radical left. Not for nothing was Meyer acquainted with Marx, and in the 1890s he wrote various articles for the Marxist journal *Neue Zeit.* Anti-Semitism at the time was indeed the immoral equivalent of socialism— just as socialism perhaps was the surrogate for anti-Semitism among the working class. No wonder anti-Semites thought Karl Marx a major figure in the Jewish conspiracy: he had devised a doctrine that deflected proletarian anger from his own people.

We have now seen the chief ingredients of this new poisonous brew: anticapitalism disguised as anti-Semitism, with a dash of Germanic socialism added. August Bebel often quoted the saying that "anti-Semitism is the socialism of imbeciles."[38] A telling phrase—and characteristically optimistic. To say that anti-Semitism was the faith of fools is to see but a partial truth. Anti-Semitism was also the protest of aggrieved and violent men who felt uprooted, homeless, dispossessed. Only by remembering the deficiencies of liberal, capitalistic, essentially secular culture and the grievances that it engendered can one understand why anti-Semitism and later fascism proved so enormously enticing. To say it was the faith of fools obscured the fact that people wanted a faith and thought official culture barren cant. In the 1870s a strong movement against liberalism in politics, capitalism in economics, and Judaism in society sprang up, and at the end of the decade in Germany it was given added strength because the government itself embraced an antiliberal course. From then on, the gutter and the government had common foes.

The new anti-Semitism has to be seen in yet another context; beginning with the 1870s, racism came to be a popular and xenophobic myth, made respectable by the trappings of scientism. The Jew (or the nonwhite) came to be seen as biologically, hence irredeemably, inferior; not all anti-Semites were racists nor all racists anti-Semites. Racism gave a kind of scientific credibility to the long-cherished popular view that Jews could be recognized by specific physical characteristics: dark, greasy hair; hooked nose; thick, sensuous lips; short, obese body. (Bleichröder fitted none of these, and yet people often referred to his Jewish physiognomy.) It was a fashionable current of thought which affected even those who did not embrace it. Bismarck, for example, was full of racist twaddle at times, and yet it would be wrong to think that he subscribed to racism. It was part of his vocabulary, not to be ignored, as it has been, nor to be pounced upon as a new key. Racism was simply one more respectable reason for suspecting Jews.

Bleichröder had become a favorite target of the underworld. He was probably puzzled and worried by these incessant attacks; nor did the lawsuits allow him to ignore them.* Still, he may have regarded this sniping from below as a nuisance inherent in his high position—the great carry their own cross. He could take comfort from the fact that his friend Bismarck was his fellow sufferer. There was something bittersweet for him about all this talk linking Bleichröder and Bismarck—and Bleichröder perhaps pushed aside the other, even more frequent linkage of himself and Jewry. In any case, until the end of the 1870s, anti-Semites were even less socially acceptable than their victims, the Jews. The anti-Semites were outsiders, troublemakers, anti-Bismarck cranks; they lacked dignity and decorum. In an amazingly short time, they were to gain both.

---

* On the other hand, even a rabbi, writing to him on behalf of two Jews who had lost their money in one of Bleichröder's promotions, warned him of the dangers he was running for himself and others if his mercantile honor were to be sullied: "When the time comes, you will not be able to appear before the sight of our Lord with your millions, which you will leave behind as earthly possession, but what matters before the highest seat of judgment is whether we have preserved our *honor unbesmirched*, we will be assayed only in that regard, and if we are found wanting, then we will be *mercilessly banished*." But even on earth there are risks, as Bleichröder must know how "often and heartlessly men of other faiths . . . speak of israelite bloodsuckers and usurers." It is for Bleichröder to insure that he give no substance to such charges. Dr. Landsberger (Landesrabbiner) to Bleichröder, 24 Apr. 1877, BA.

The decisive change came in 1878–1880, the years when Bleichröder was hoping that Rumania would accept the principle of civic equality, the necessary condition for Jewish survival and success. It was precisely during the denouement of the Rumanian situation that Bismarck's own politics changed. In 1878–1879 he abandoned his alliance with the National Liberals and embraced a new conservative course. In matters concerning Rumanian Jews, Bleichröder had thought Bismarck "warm-hearted and tolerant." But by 1879 Bismarck's chief enemies at home were the Progressives, whose leaders were largely Jewish. He was "warm-hearted" no more; in fact, he became more and more tolerant of the anti-Semites and realized their usefulness in his embittered struggle with the Progressives. He was always swayed more by his enemies than by his friends; Jewish prominence among his enemies put a great strain on his gradually acquired neutrality toward Jews. Would Bleichröder's pleas on behalf of German Jews find as sympathetic a hearing with Bismarck as his earlier pleas on behalf of Rumanian Jews? It is always easier to be high-minded at the expense of others.

By 1879 it became clear that the atmosphere in the Reich had changed. In that year two dignitaries with impeccable credentials warned in decorous tones against the Jewish danger and thus legitimized the existence of "a Jewish question." One was Adolf Stoecker, court chaplain and hence regarded as representative of crown and church, and the other was Heinrich von Treitschke, widely hailed as Prussia's greatest historian and as an ornament of the University of Berlin. The unmatched prestige of pastor and professor—the guardians of national morality—brought respectability to the campaign against Jews and Liberals. Stoecker and Treitschke had probably been emboldened by the government's switch, and their agitation in turn emboldened others. There had been a kind of primitive idealism in the cries from below; the new message transposed the essence of the earlier campaign into the "higher" reaches of Germanic-Christian thought.

Stoecker's path to anti-Semitism was in itself symptomatic. Born poor, he was able to enter the Protestant ministry only because of great parental sacrifices. He was an army chaplain in the Franco-Prussian war, and his patriotic fervor earned him an appointment as court chaplain in Berlin. The office had a prestigious aura; in fact, other chaplains were much closer to the court. His post gave him ample time to study life in Berlin: he was appalled by the secularism of the rich and the socialism of the poor—both manifesting a terrible decline of the church. Reared in poverty, he saw no reason why the poor should not retain their faith in church and country; in 1878 he founded the Christian-Social Workers' party, in order to woo the workers with a new social gospel that would replace Marxism. His party was to be an adjunct of the Conservative party, and his reforms harked back to the old patriarchal tradition. He was the first cleric to go into Berlin's working-class districts in search of souls and votes; his colleagues preferred safer districts. But even his "powerful personality and captivating eloquence" could not prevail against socialist dogma.[39] Berlin workers were not to be won by sweet words or promises; they remembered that the church had been monolithic in its support of the established order. In the elections of 1878, Stoecker's party fared disastrously. It received less than 1 percent of the Berlin votes.[40]

Stoecker drew the obvious lessons from his defeat. He began preaching his anticapitalist gospel cum nationalism to a different clientele, to the unorganized shopkeepers and artisans, to men who felt themselves victimized by the new plutocracy. A new audience dictated new tactics. For a while Stoecker hesitated to join the anti-Semitic chorus; finally, in September 1879, he addressed a mass meeting on "Our Demands on Modern Judaism" and found himself launched on a profitable course at last.*

Stoecker sounded all the traditional warnings about the sway of Jewry— and did so in a restrained, seemly fashion, more in sorrow than in anger. It was the only possible stance for a good Christian. In that first speech, he expressed regret that the liberal press talked about everything—except the Jewish Problem. His demands on Jewry struck an ironically reasonable note, and many conservative Jews voiced similar views.[41] He asked of Jews a little more modesty, a little more tolerance, a little more equality—in other words, demands that paraphrased and mocked the traditional demands the Jews had served on gentiles. He added ominously: "Israel must renounce its aim of becoming the master of Germany," it must cease being "an irreligious power" that, having lost its own faith, now seeks to subvert Christianity. Hence the demand for more tolerance. Jews should cease living off Christian labor— hence the demand for more equality. Stoecker also wished for fewer Jews. Berlin had 45,000 Jews, as many, he claimed wrongly, as lived in France and England altogether. The old refrain was still there: too many Jews, too powerful, too foreign. That was why he regarded "modern Jewry as a great danger for the life of the German people." That was why he demanded various restrictions on Jews; otherwise "the cancer from which we suffer will grow." For all the apparent restraint, here was the archetypical formulation: the Jew as the mortal threat. If his modest demands were not met, he warned, the more radical enemies of the Jews would triumph and resort to far tougher means—a self-fulfilling prophecy.[42]

Stoecker's anticapitalist line had already alarmed some of Berlin's affluent people; his attack on the Jews seemed but an intensification of a dangerous theme. A few days after his first foray against Jews, Bleichröder was urged by his friend Kardorff to warn Bismarck to dissociate himself publicly from Stoecker, for otherwise people would think him a protector of Stoecker's.[43] There was good reason for Kardorff to fear that the public

---

* As Stoecker's Nazi biographer, Walter Frank, described the new audience: "The small tradespeople and the small proprietors were joined by the educated middle class, by the officer corps, civil service, and academic youth. To the extent that they were not also enchained by financial indebtedness, they felt themselves threatened in their social status by the rise of the economically more powerful Jewry, which knew superbly how to turn its financial power into *Bildung* and its *Bildung* into power; their views on vocation and social class, which had grown up in close connection with the Prussian military state, also brought them into opposition to mercenary Judaism which rejected these views." Walter Frank, *Hofprediger Adolf Stoecker und die christlichsoziale Bewegung*, 2nd. ed. (Hamburg, 1935), pp. 76–77.

might regard Bismarck as Stoecker's patron: was he not campaigning violently against such men as Lasker and Bamberger, whom in private he identified as "the Semites"?[44] Kardorff was sensitive to the dangers of silence, but he made no public statement himself—ever—and he almost certainly did not write Bismarck directly. Surely this would have been one time when Bleichröder would have welcomed gentile initiative.

Bleichröder waited. He still had enough to do on behalf of Rumanian Jewry. But a few weeks later, the second blow fell, in the form of Treitschke's attack in the influential *Preussische Jahrbücher*. He too inveighed against the predominance of Jews and their subversion of German ideals. Both men professed as much worry about German weakness as about Jewish strength; for Treitschke, an attack on the Jews was but a reassertion of his devotion to the German state, to the pure nationalism which should sustain that state. Jews were outsiders; if they wanted to enjoy the full privileges of German citizenhood, they should abjure their separateness and embrace Christianity— though there were plenty of anti-Semites who warned against encouraging racially degenerate people to obtain privileges by feigning apostasy.[45] But neither Treitschke nor Stoecker was a racist; all that Treitschke asked for was a Christian German nation. Outsiders were enemies, clever and unscrupulous outsiders were worse enemies—hence, in Treitschke's famous peroration: "The Jews are our misfortune."[46]

With one blow, Treitschke had given respectability to anti-Semitism. He had made it a part of German patriotism; he had wrapped an old prejudice in a new cloak of idealism. In his celebrated annual lectures on politics he repeated his deprecations—and from that time on, anti-Semitic rabble-rousers could count on either a sympathetic echo from above or at least a divided, equivocal response from the established classes. In Treitschke's wake could sail all sorts of other groups—among them German students who excluded Jews from their fraternities and adopted anti-Semitic principles in their national organization. German students have a long history of championing illiberal causes. Treitschke raised anti-Semitism from the gutter; he gave public dignity to old sentiments and new phobias. In impeccable patriotism, he drowned liberal beliefs in tolerance. After Treitschke, there was something virtuous about being anti-Semitic.

Treitschke's article aroused a major controversy—but mostly among Jewish scholars. They answered in a variety of ways, defensively and aggressively; one such rebuttal, by an historian, seems to allude to Bleichröder: "Christian circles are insufficiently acquainted with the great mass of average Jewish city dwellers who live in peaceful, middle-class diligence without the pretentious luxury of the moneyed aristocracy and without the filthy degeneracy of usury and peddling." (One of Treitschke's protagonists at once pounced on this reminder of the "good Jew" or the "quiet Jew," by insisting that "the title of banker hides the cheat, that of businessman the jobber—and everywhere, as far as it is possible, the usurer. The title is Sunday finery.")[47] Treitschke inspired much Jewish soul-searching, and one mighty rejoinder from his great liberal colleague, Theodor Mommsen, who foresaw the evil that Treitschke had let loose. Mommsen's defense was eloquent, his warning against a "civil war" of Christians against Jews prophetic; his peroration was a plea to those Jews who had lost their strong religious beliefs to embrace Christianity—and thus to join fully the German nation and prevailing international civilization. The nation-state, he explained, hates all vestiges of particularism. In short, even he saw conversion as the belated price of emancipation.[48]

Like many rich Jews, Bleichröder probably hoped that the new anti-Semitism (still with its anticapitalistic edge) would vanish again.* But Bleichröder was not allowed to play the ostrich for very long. For that he was too prominent; sooner or later he would always be singled out. In June 1880, at one of Stoecker's mass rallies, heckled by socialists who claimed that for two thousand years the Church had done nothing to help the lot of the lower classes, Stoecker shot back in a characteristic effort at deflection: "Why do you demand social assistance from the clergy alone? Why never from the Jews? Herr von Bleichröder has more money than the entire Protestant clergy put together."[49]

It was too much for Bleichröder. He had endured all sorts of lies and vilifications passively, but he was stirred to immediate action by this public incitement—by a court chaplain—against his fortune, which probably did exceed that of all Protestant pastors put together. Within the week he dispatched a petition to William I: "I dare call for Your . . . Majesty's high patriarchal protection for myself, but not only for myself, rather for a whole class of loyal subjects of Your Majesty, who surely are not useless citizens of the state." Nor were the Jews the only target. Stoecker was turning "the bitter struggle against the Jews, [into] a social struggle against property as such." He had already publicly accused Bleichröder of having amassed 7 million taler from usury, "by cheating Christians. . . . My name is now on the tip of every Christian-social agitator's tongue; it is invoked not only as a target for persecution but is branded as the prototype of all capital, of the stock market, of all prosperity, and of all evil." Bleichröder understood his predicament and his defenselessness. Were he to sue Stoecker, it would only fan the scandal. The public authorities, on the other hand, had offered him no protection. On the contrary, the public assumed that "influential men in higher circles" protected the agitators. But the Christian-social agitation differed from Social Democracy only "by being more dangerous because more practical. . . . The mass of the people is being stirred to its very depth." If this goes on, he warned, any accident would suffice to unleash a movement that then no man could control. In clumsy, elliptical language, Bleichröder hinted that at that point and with deepest anguish he might have to leave the fatherland.

---

* He must have sent reassuring missives to his friends abroad; Moritz von Goldschmidt wrote that he wished he could agree with Bleichröder's sense that Stoecker was "not dangerous, as you put it, but [his agitation] coincides in a peculiar way with the poison-tree speech of your minister Maybach." Goldschmidt to Bleichröder, 3 Dec. 1879, BA.

He warned that the agitation against him was but "the beginning of the misfortune of a terrible social revolution" that would threaten all society. Bleichröder's petition ended with an appeal to the monarch's "patriarchal heart and high wisdom to find ways to preserve His subjects and His state from ruin."[50] The petition was involuted and awkward; the style betrayed both the haste of the drafting and the embarrassment of the author.*

Bleichröder's petition marked the second time that he made this threat of self-exile, and it deserves some reflection. Bleichröder must have seen the threat as a weapon, perhaps in tacit imitation of Bismarck's functional threats of resignation. Would the king want to lose so useful a servant as Bleichröder? Would he want the world to know that Germany's most prominent Jew had chosen exile? But there is more than a threat here: must we not read it as an acknowledgment, perhaps but partially conscious, of Bleichröder's concern lest he become homeless? He had come to be more German than Jew; his adult life had been a wager based on the simple reciprocity: I serve the state and the state protects me. If that *do ut des* collapsed, Bleichröder's role would be annihilated and his business would suffer. Would the state really leave him the special target of mass agitators? His whole role, his identity, depended on being the protected Jew who could use his special status, on occasion and in his own way, in order to intercede on behalf of his less fortunate coreligionists. Threat aside, there is a poignant, probably but half-perceived truth to Bleichröder's lament that without protection he might have to leave the country he loved and served and prospered in.†

Bleichröder's petition became the focus of a prolonged controversy within the government. How would the Prussian government adjudicate between its leading Jew and the court chaplain, whose faith and fidelity to the crown seemed exemplary? What was said and done—and more important, what was not said and done—offer an extraordinary insight into the thoughts and presuppositions of officialdom when confronted by the anti-Jewish agitation of the day.

Bleichröder sent a copy of his petition to Bismarck: "I would rejoice if you were to agree with its contents."[51] There is no trace of a written acknowledgment. Was he afraid to indulge Bleichröder's nervousness or was it inconvenient to write a letter that would perforce have to touch on the sub-

---

* Walter Frank comments that Bleichröder's "complaint in its mixture of Oriental Byzantinism, timidity and hidden threat as well as in its inadequate German was not without appeal for the cultural historian and the psychologist." No doubt it is a revealing document, but the mixture Frank ridicules characterized more than Bleichröder's style; except for the somewhat idiosyncratic German, it was the style of the German *Bürgertum* generally. Frank, *Stoecker*, pp. 85–86.

† Bleichröder was probably right in thinking that his threat of emigration was his last resort. In 1908 a high court dignitary at William II's court reminisced: "My father is certainly a strong Conservative, but in the Jewish question he cannot close his eyes to the fact that our policy with regard to it is not only narrow-minded and unjust, but demoralizing. We are injuring ourselves by gradually forcing some of the best, most enterprising, and wealthiest families out of the country, and are courting danger by driving the Jews into opposition." Count Robert Zedlitz-Trutzschler, *Twelve Years at the Imperial German Court* (London, n.d. [1924?]), pp. 217–218.

stance of the delicate matter? It is in fact an extraordinary comment on the Bismarck-Bleichröder tie that there is not a single Bismarck letter that has survived or a recorded conversation between the two men that touched on the subject of German anti-Semitism. There is no known letter of Bleich-röder's to foreign friends—to the Rothschilds or Disraeli, for example—in which he said: "My warm-hearted friend is appalled by the new anti-Semitic agitation." At the moment it was fortunate for Bleichröder that Bismarck had little use for Stoecker, who was attacking the government as well. Political anti-Semitism, moreover, had been used against Bismarck for nearly a decade; he had reason to be wary of it.

Nor was William likely to be pro-Stoecker. Among other reasons, he, too, had his favorite Jewish banker—though he probably disliked having to choose between Jew and pastor. In September the *Berliner Börsen-Courier*, a paper notoriously close to Bleichröder, reported correctly that William had received Bleichröder in Ems and had intimated to him his disapproval of Stoecker. Other papers copied the story. At that point, Stoecker fired off a petition to William, referring to the notice in the *Börsen-Courier*: "that purely Jewish sheet . . . the vilest of Berlin, perhaps of all of Europe," which sought to depict William as "an enemy of the German movement." Stoecker begged William not to repudiate his fight against Jewry, especially since it was not directed against all Jews but "only against frivolous, usurious, cheating Jewry, which indeed is the misfortune of our people." He acknowledged that he had once mentioned Bleichröder by name "in the most harmless way. . . . *And Herr von Bleichröder is indeed a pillar of Jewish predominance.* Every year during Lent he takes the liberty of giving a ball just before Holy Week; and unfortunately almost all court and state officers go to that feast. But such happenings create the most painful impression among our people."[52] After this letter it became all the harder for William to remain neutral. He asked Bismarck and Robert von Puttkamer, the new and archconservative Prussian minister of public worship and instruction, for advice. The two men differed; Puttkamer was sympathetic to Stoecker, if a little uneasy about his mixing of priesthood and politics. Bismarck wanted him prosecuted under the anti-Socialist laws. In the summer of 1880 Bleichröder's cause seemed likely to prevail.

Bismarck always abhorred the priesthood in politics; he was specifically annoyed at Stoecker's criticism of the government's social policy and at his "socialist" pleas for higher taxes for the rich. (Here Stoecker was touching a raw nerve of Bismarck's.) Moreover, he thought Stoecker was attacking the wrong Jews. Sounding a major new theme, Bismarck complained to Puttkamer that in regard to the Jewish question it was wrong to assume that

> with us it is the *rich* Jews who exert a great influence on the press. It may be different in Paris. Not moneyed Jewry [*Geldjudentum*] but the political-reformist Jewry [*Reformjudentum*] makes itself important in our press and our parliamentary bodies. The interests of moneyed Jewry are more readily tied to the preservation of our state institutions and

cannot do without them. It is propertyless Jews who have little to lose and much to gain

that are dangerous and capable of allying themselves with all manner of subversive opposition, socialism and Stoecker included.[53]

It was another way of saying that rich Jews were useful and conservative; ordinary Jews were liable to be radical or subversive. It was a crude class analysis: Jewry, Bismarck seems to suggest, was not so much united by religion as divided by class. The anti-Semites might drive rich Jews into the radical camp—hence Stoecker's socialist anti-Semitism deserved a rebuff. There was a payoff in protecting Jews against a demagogue like Stoecker; it would keep rich Jews on his side and perhaps diminish the attractiveness of liberalism for other Jews.* On the other hand, he probably thought that "a little anti-Semitism" might make the rich Jews still more pliable; in any case, a strong denunciation of anti-Semitism as such would affront his new supporters, the conservatives. Given all these pressures and being totally immune to any principled argument, he leaned toward an ad hoc solution: administer a sharp rebuke to Stoecker for his incitement to class discord.

In mid-November Bismarck still inveighed against the "Jewish proletariat" in press and parliament and thought that Stoecker's agitation was driving right-thinking, rich Jews into the arms of the Progressives.[54] This became a major and persistent theme for Bismarck—and one that Bleichröder came to echo.

Bismarck assured Puttkamer that it was not Stoecker's anti-Jewish attacks which had prompted his intervention: "For me, in his speeches and agitation, *the Socialist element* is far more decisive *than the anti-Semitic.*"[55] No doubt, this is how Bismarck felt—but it was also an excellent argument to appease Puttkamer, who was most reluctant to take any legal action against Stoecker. To prosecute Stoecker under the anti-Socialist laws would please Bismarck's Jewish constituency without offending the anti-Semites. It was a Bismarckian solution.

Puttkamer was less fastidious in discriminating among Jews; he liked no variety of them and found license for his prejudice in Treitschke's judg-

---

* Bismarck was not the only one to recognize the conservative character of nineteenth-century Jewry. Disraeli lets his Jewish banker Sidonia remark: ". . . If you permit men to accumulate property, and they use that permission to a great extent, power is inseparable from that property, and it is in the last degree impolitic to make the interest of any powerful class to oppose the institutions under which they live. The Jews, for example, independent of the capital qualities for citizenship which they possess in their industry, temperance, and energy and vivacity of mind, are a race essentially monarchical, deeply religious, and shrinking themselves from converts as from a calamity, are ever anxious to see the religious systems of the countries in which they live, flourish. . . ." Despite their radical stance at times, ". . . the Jews are essentially Tories." A reassuring fact, given that Disraeli also contends they hold vast, secret power. *Coningsby or, The New Generation* (New York, 1961), pp. 302–303. Nietzsche put it thus: "The power of the middle classes is then upheld by means of commerce, but above all, by means of money-dealing: the instinct of great financiers is opposed to everything extreme—on this account the Jews are, for the present, the most *conservative* power in the threatening and insecure conditions of modern Europe." *The Will to Power*, (Edinburgh, 1910), vol. II, aphorism 864, p. 303.

ment. Before Puttkamer and Bismarck could agree on a joint opinion to William, the Stoecker affairs became enmeshed with the more general outburst of anti-Semitism in the fall of 1880. Anti-Semitism suddenly emerged as a major political issue, and as a consequence Bismarck's views toward Stoecker changed abruptly.

As happens so often to would-be reformers, Stoecker was quickly outflanked by more radical agitators. In the fall of 1880 various anti-Semitic groups began a huge and unprecedented campaign to collect signatures for a petition to the government, demanding that the legal equality of Jews be abridged, that Jews be barred from positions of public authority, and that Jewish immigration be curtailed. The controversy over the Jewish question suddenly reached a new intensity, and some people, Bleichröder's friend St. Vallier among them, thought the Jews themselves were responsible for the ever louder agitation.*

In November 1880 the right-wing Progressive deputy, Dr. Hänel, supported by prominent colleagues like Virchow, Rickert, and Richter, put the anti-Semitic petition on the Prussian Diet's agenda and solicited the government's views regarding its demands "that aim at the elimination of the complete constitutional equality of Jews."[56] The Progressives hoped that the government would repudiate anti-Semitism even before the petition was submitted—or, failing that, that the government's tacit support of anti-Semitism could be exposed.

Instantly Bismarck's mood became transformed. The fury and decisiveness of his response have hitherto not been noticed. From Friedrichsruh, he thundered against this "unjustified Progressive presumption . . . frivolous . . . impertinent." He urged his colleagues to ignore the interpellation; when he discovered that it could not be ignored, he warned that in public "even the least" support for Stoecker from the side of the government would have to be avoided. The ministry accepted this, and Puttkamer merely made the in-

---

* In November 1880 the Comte de St. Vallier devoted a special report to the anti-Semitic campaign in Germany: "The German press and, following its example, the foreign press, has for some time been much concerned with a campaign against Jews undertaken by a section of public opinion, a bizarre campaign more in keeping with the ideas of the Middle Ages than of our own era." The attack started a year earlier, launched by Stoecker and directed against "the rapid and successive usurpations of the Jewish race." In dramatic detail, St. Vallier recapitulated Stoecker's charges of Jewish monopoly and pointed to the newly organized Anti-Semitic League as lending further support to Stoecker's cause. The League, composed of churchmen, professors, other prominent members of society, and even some liberals, was preparing a petition to submit to the government, demanding restrictive laws against Jews "recalling the persecutions of the 14th and 15th centuries." The government remained unimpressed, but among parliamentarians, professors, and writers "a considerable reaction" had set in that was defaming the new League. A press polemic had begun, with all the important papers defending the Jews, only five or six papers attacking them. Without this hubbub, St. Vallier wrote, the anti-Semitic agitation would disappear completely and the persistence of the press can only be explained by the fact that "the publishers and editors of the principal papers are nearly all Jewish. They are pleading *pro domo,*" hoping to arouse opposition to anti-Semites everywhere. St. Vallier concluded by explaining that his very mention of so "local and ephemeral" a subject came only from his realization that the Paris press, served by its Berlin correspondents, who were also mostly Jewish, had exaggerated this affair. St. Vallier to St. Hilaire, 16 Nov. 1880, MAE: Allemagne, Vol. 38.

teresting reservation that he would have to speak "if it should be said that the Stoecker affair were a consequence of the Puttkamer system." Against such an allegation he would have to defend himself—and his very anticipation of such a charge is significant, as is his use of the term "system" for his administration.[57]

The two-day debate suddenly demonstrated the dominance and self-confidence of the anti-Semites—and the isolation of the Progressives and the defensiveness of their arguments. Hänel explained the reasons for his interpellation, pointing to the anti-Semitic agitation designed to curb Jewish rights and reminding the Diet of the principles so recently enacted by the Congress of Berlin and championed by Bismarck. Were these principles to be violated in Germany? Admitting the many unpleasant characteristics of the Jews, Hänel called for the affirmation of their legal rights, nevertheless, and warned that anti-Semitism had already taken a most perfidious turn by embracing racism, by this irredeemable condemnation of individuals by the accident of their descent. Racism, he argued, was anti-Christian. The Prussian vice-chancellor spoke a few aseptic sentences, culminating with the statement that "the state government does not intend to have the constitutional arrangements changed." He said nothing about the agitation; no wonder that Virchow called the answer "correct, but frigid to the very core." The Conservative and most of the Center spokesmen heaped abuse and admonitions on the Jews: endless variations on the charges that by usury and cheating, Jews had attained a predominant position in the German economy to the detriment of all other sectors, that in other realms of public life Jews had also reached an equally pernicious power. Hänel's reference to the Congress of Berlin was rebuffed as demonstrating "the immeasurable *international* power which this tiniest minority in all countries has already won." The odious role of Jews no longer needed to be argued; it had become axiomatic. A Conservative spokesman called for "the emancipation of the Christians."* A Center deputy aired deep animosity when he said that Catholics had originally supported Jewish emancipation, despite the many offensive traits of Jews, and in the last ten years had "earned the most extreme and most violent enmity and persecution precisely from these quarters." Windthorst took a more moderate line, calling for an end to all anti-Jewish and anti-Catholic agitation.

The record of the two debates gives a grisly picture of the atmosphere of the occasion: the anti-Semitic catcalls, the vicious sarcasm, the pent-up hatred. The tone of the debate was more ominous than the words themselves.[58]†

---

* The imagery of Stoecker's peroration told all: "Gentlemen, recently a corpse was found in a district not far from here. The corpse was examined—and at hand were a Jewish district physician, a Jewish surgeon, a Jewish judge, a Jewish barrister—only the corpse was German. [Much laughter.] Gentlemen, we do not want this fate for Berlin or for the other great cities; we want to keep our people alive through its own vital strength, and be assured that in this effort the people stands behind us." *Die Judenfrage: Verhandlungen des preussischen Abgeordnetenhauses über die Interpellation des Abgeordneten, Dr. Hänel* (Berlin, 1880), p. 138.

† The London *Times* carried this report: "What degree of interest was manifested in the debate may be judged from the fact that . . . before its commencement all the galleries were

It was not a glorious moment for the Prussian parliament or a reassuring moment for German Jewry. A sense of futility overcame Bleichröder's friend Berthold Auerbach.* Ludwig Bamberger thought of emigrating.[59] Eça de Queiroz, a foremost Portuguese novelist, by no means blind to Jewish vice and power, was appalled by the government's response:

> It leaves the Jewish colony unprotected to face the anger of the large German population—and washes its ministerial hands, as Pontius Pilate did. It does not even state that it will see that the laws protecting the Jews, citizens of the Empire, are enforced; it merely has the vague intention, as vague as a morning cloud, of not altering them *for the moment*.[60]†

Bleichröder had expected a very different outcome: on the day of the debate, he wrote Bismarck: "The agitation concerning the Jewish question is very intense here, but with today's session of the Diet it will come to an end."[61] Just before the debate, he had been given assurances—or thought he had—that the government would take a strong stand against the anti-Semitic agitation. He communicated his optimism to the London Rothschilds in two letters, which they forwarded to Disraeli:

---

filled to overflowing. The present controversy is one in which all are deeply interested and in which all are partisans, though comparatively few have the courage to proclaim their attitude towards it by word or deed. . . . The Court box and the diplomatic gallery became crowded betimes. Among the general public . . . there was noticeable a strikingly preponderating number of men and women with a distinctively Hebrew cast of features. Even the outer pavement was thronged with persons, disappointed in their endeavor to get inside . . . while some of the evils against which the very debate was directed were curiously manifested upon a smaller scale in the street without. Several of those rather idle but ingenious gentlemen, of undeniable Eastern extraction, who drive a roaring trade with Opera tickets Unter den Linden had managed . . . to possess themselves of several entry cards granted the general public, which they now successfully sought to dispose of at fabulous rates . . . all of which reminds one of Prince Bismarck's simile of the hunter who winged his arrow against an eagle with a feather torn from its own breast." *Times*, 22 Nov. 1880.

* The aged Jewish writer Auerbach, who had spent his whole literary life among Germans and cherished his Germanness, sat through the parliamentary debate, embittered and enraged. "Have I lived in vain?" he exclaimed. When he wanted to answer Stoecker a few months later, Lasker persuaded him to desist. Anton Bettelheim, *Berthold Auerbach* (Stuttgart, 1907), p. 376.

† Eça de Queiroz went on to explain: "the motive of this anti-Semitic fury is simply the growing prosperity of the Jewish colony. . . . High finance and small business are both in [Jewish] hands. . . . In the liberal professions he absorbs everything: he is the lawyer with more briefs and the doctor with more patients. . . . But if the Jew's wealth irritates him [the German], the show the Jew makes of his riches absolutely maddens him. . . . [The Jews] always talk loud as if treading a conquered land. . . . They cover themselves with jewels, all the trappings of their carriages are of gold, and they love vulgar and showy luxury. . . . In Germany, the Jew has slowly and stealthily gained possession of two great social forces—the Exchange and the Press. . . ." Eça de Queiroz then lists all the social and economic grievances of Germans which in the old days Bismarck would have dispelled by a war. War was no longer feasible, and "therefore, with little chance of a war, Prince Bismarck distracts the starving Germans' attention—by pointing to the prosperous Jew. Naturally he does not allude to the death of Our Lord Jesus Christ. But he speaks of the millions of Jews and the power of the Synagogue. And this explains the government's strange and disastrous declaration." *Letters from England* (Athens, Ohio, 1970), pp. 51–55.

With regard to the interpellation about the Jewish question, the Government will state in reply that the petition has not yet come into their hands, but they will declare even now that they would never violate the Constitution which grants equal rights to all citizens, no matter what religious creed they belong to.

On discussing the interpellation, Government will also declare that they regret to the utmost the excesses that have been committed. What is, however, still more important is that the Emperor will declare himself within a few days that He is entirely opposed to all such objectionable agitation.

This declaration is all the more important as the belief has spread among the Public that this persecution of Jews has been favorably looked upon in the highest circles. The Emperor would most likely make this declaration in the form of an answer to my humble petition of June last, authorizing me to publish his reply. I much regret that it has been found impossible to bring Court Chaplain Stoecker under the operation of the Socialist Law, this law referring solely to the Socialist Democrats and not to agitations of another nature. I hope that this very much to be lamented matter will come to an end with the Parliamentary discussion.

The next day he wrote:

Today's sitting of Parliament is not yet over. I have only to confirm the information I sent you yesterday, viz.: that the government have in short but precise terms pointed out the Constitutional position which they have taken up with regard to this matter. No doubt they will further declare that they regret exceedingly the excesses which have been committed. . . .

I believe that the result will be favorable to the Jews and that the agitation will cease.

None of Bleichröder's expectations came true; his dismay would have been infinitely greater if he had known that Rothschild added these devastating comments to Disraeli:

There is no doubt that Bleichröder himself is one of the causes of the Jewish persecution. He has been employed so often by the German Government that he has become arrogant and forgets that he is very often merely "a trial balloon."

There are also a great many other reasons which we can discuss at full length when we meet again; among them the constant influx of Polish, Russian, and Rumanian Jews who arrive in a state of starvation and are socialists until they become rich.

The Jews also are proprietors of half the newspapers particularly of those papers which are anti-Russian. A good deal of money has no doubt been sent from St. Petersburgh to stimulate this persecution.

I hear also that Madame von Bleichröder is most disagreeable and haughty.[62]

A wretched picture of Bleichröder—and of the Rothschilds.*

The government did not condemn the excesses—not with one syllable. Had Bleichröder been misled by the government so as to prevent him from marshaling his forces? It would have been easy to do, because he would have heard what he wanted to hear, and it would have been consonant with what he knew about Bismarck's intended response to Stoecker. Or perhaps Bismarck and his colleagues decided to harden their stand at the last moment. In 1880 Bismarck was neither anti-Semitic nor clearly philo-Semitic: he had a wide spectrum of views about Jews, some favorable because of their proven usefulness and power, many unfavorable, both from residual animosity and because of their oppositional stance. The Progressive interpellation suddenly forced a decision from him; he acted under pressure, which always incited his anger. The needle—to cite his earlier metaphor—had to stop swinging somewhere. In that week in November 1880 it stopped at a decidedly anti-Semitic point. It had been an improvised decision; it was also a decision of some magnitude. It set a precedent. More: after such an improvised decision, the mind comes to rearrange its own preceding thoughts—in accordance with the action taken. This is what happened to Bismarck and to German officialdom. The spectrum of views on Jews narrowed. The Progressives had accomplished the very opposite of what they intended: the government line had become more illiberal, and in a semiofficial release to the press, the government boasted of the new line:

> . . . the object unreflectingly aimed at by the Progressives through the interpellation—namely, a condemnation of the so-called anti-Semitic movement by the House of Deputies—has not in the least degree been reached. . . . The strength of the movement has been revealed by the debate, . . . and from the consciousness of strength gained . . . it will be more likely to derive fresh courage than to feel in any way disheartened.[63]†

The London *Times* reported a general agreement in Berlin "that the ruling Powers are inclined to wink at, if they do not openly encourage, a movement

---

* The Rothschilds seem to have a certain penchant for blaming Jews for anti-Semitism. In 1875 Carl Meyer Rothschild wrote Bleichröder: "As for the anti-Semitic feelings, the Jews themselves are to blame, and the present agitation must be ascribed to their arrogance, vanity, and unspeakable insolence." Precisely a hundred years later, Baron Guy de Rothschild said publicly: "The largest single dangers to the Jewish community are often the Jews." Did the Rothschilds—with their unmatched wealth and power—contribute nothing to anti-Semitism? Rothschild to Bleichröder, 16 Sept. 1875, B.A.; *New York Times*, 30 March 1975.

† A sober book anonymously published in Vienna under the title *Fürst Bismarck und der Antisemitismus* (2d printing; Vienna [Hugo Engel], 1886), p. 143, contended that the worst anti-Semites regarded Bismarck "as their silent but most helpful chief [*Oberhaupt*]," and despite all their violent deeds and words *"until now to the best of our knowledge no single authentic utterance of the German Chancellor has appeared that he disapproves of all this, certainly not a public statement"* (italics in original).

aiming at stemming the rising tide of Semitic power and influence in the Empire."[64] And still, the government had acted correctly enough so that the Progressives could not exploit its tacit support of anti-Semitism. In fact, anti-Semitism belonged to the enemies of the Progressives—and the politics of Germany was dominated by their enemies.

Bleichröder must have been disappointed, however much he may have tried to disguise the defeat. He may have found minor solace in the fact that at the time of the parliamentary debate, seventy-five Berlin notables issued a declaration denouncing the anti-Semitic agitation as injurious to national unity. Jews had "brought honor and profit to the fatherland." Germans should rid themselves of medieval fanaticism and cherish "the legacy of Lessing. Already we can hear the cry for discriminatory legislation and for the exclusion of Jews from this or that trade or profession, honor, or position of confidence. How long will it be until the herd clamors for this too?" The signatories included leading members of the university and the city administration, a few businessmen, and one pastor with a previous record of rebelliousness; many of the signers were well-known Progressives.[65] Not one of Bleichröder's friends and clients signed it—not one of those upright nobles like Lehndorff, Hatzfeldt, Kardorff, who had so often protested their gratitude and friendship. Nor did they launch their own public appeal—so as not to be tainted by collaborating with the left. Privately, orally, the one or the other may have assured Bleichröder of his concern, though we have no record of it. Publicly the debate was between anti-Semites and Progressives, with the broad middle doing what it usually does—nothing. Many people may have shared William's sentiments when he remarked at the end of November that he did "not approve the activities of Court Chaplain Stoecker . . . but that the whole matter would disappear . . . and the hubbub is useful to make the Jews a little more modest."[66]

If there was one refrain around 1880 among Christians and Jews alike, it was this yearning for "the modest Jew." It sprang from different motives and it meant different things, but it always implied the vague hope for less visibility, less gaudiness, less audibility. The cultivated Jewish doctor—with his harmonious relations to Christian patients—the quiet Jewish scholar or writer, wished for the modest Jew on aesthetic and prudential grounds. Berthold Auerbach wrote in 1877: "Of course, there is much that Jews can be blamed for, on both sides of the Atlantic.* Above all, they lack quiet cultivation, that self-contentment through self-improvement and internal ennoblement. There is an addiction to ostentation and pompous showing off, especially among Jewish women." Were there not corresponding traits among newly rich Christians? he asked.[67] In early 1880, also in a letter, Jacob Burckhardt warned:

---

* He wrote this letter to Friedrich Kapp, German democrat and exile in America, apropos of the "monstrous incident," when Hilton, a hotel owner in Saratoga Springs, barred the New York banker Seligmann because he was a Jew. It was an incident that caused an enormous stir among American and European Jewry.

To the Semites I recommend a great deal of sagacity and moderation, and even then I do not believe that the present agitation will die down again. . . . . The Semites will particularly have to atone for their totally unjustifiable interference in all sorts of affairs, and newspapers will have to rid themselves of their Semitic editors and journalists if they want to survive. Such a thing [anti-Semitism] can break loose suddenly and contagiously from one day to the next.[68]

Burckhardt's call for "modesty" expressed the Conservatives' wish that liberal Jews become less powerful, but it also expressed the fear that a social animus might engulf and destroy Jews far beyond anything that a "gentle" anti-Semite would want.

We must reckon with the thought, so common among observers of the 1880s, that at the beginning of the new anti-Semitism there was certainly some relation between the conduct and prominence of the Jews and the gathering backlash. In the long run, probably, fantasy, racism, or paranoia would have triumphed over fact in any case, but most people do not think of "the long run," wishing rather to prosper and survive in the short run, guided by selective memories from the past. Hence many Jews took it as axiomatic that their efforts at self-defense also demanded efforts at self-improvement— and the consciousness of that need did not ease the uncertainties surrounding self-defense.[69]

"The modest Jew" also reminds us again that anti-Semitism and anti-capitalism were inextricably intertwined in the beginning. The immodest Jew was usually the wealthy Jew, and the wealthy Jew was the product of capitalism—in German *Vulgäridealismus* usually called materialism in order to suggest a deformation of the spirit rather than the workings of an economic order.[70]

And finally "the modest Jew" recalls the countless descriptions of Germans and foreigners alike on how immodest, how loud and arrogant, the Germans of the new Reich were, especially when on foreign soil. (And many German Jews, perhaps subconsciously, still felt that they were perpetually on foreign soil.)* The Germans detested what unconsciously appeared to them as Jewish caricatures of their own gracelessness, of their own social unease. And finally and most importantly, Bleichröder's life exemplified the power of anti-Semitism in another way: his faults or lapses were always labeled *Jewish* faults; the association of Jewishness and nega-

---

* In this connection, consider the single instance of John Maynard Keynes's description of his German counterparts in the negotiations over the feeding of German civilians in early 1919; at the time Keynes did everything he could to help the Germans and mitigate the hatred of the Allies: "Meanwhile the Germans met us. . . . Erzberger, fat and disgusting in a fur coat, walked down the platform to the Marshal's saloon. With him were a General and a Sea-Captain with an iron cross around his neck and an extraordinary resemblance of face and figure to the pig in *Alice in Wonderland*. They satisfied wonderfully, as a group, the popular conception of Huns. The personal appearance of that race is really extraordinarily against them. Who knows but that it was the real cause of the war!" Keynes, *Essays and Sketches in Biography*, p. 202.

tive characteristics was endemic. Christians committed individual trespasses; Jews committed trespasses typical of their people.

The government had still to answer Bleichröder's petition; the parliamentary debate had harmed him and favored Stoecker's cause. Before it, Bismarck had wanted to throw the anti-Socialist law at Stoecker, and even William had spoken about him to Puttkamer "in an embittered fashion." Stoecker's clerical superior thought that he was not long for the court chaplaincy.[71] The debate changed everything, especially for Bismarck. He no longer thought that Puttkamer and he should submit separate opinions to William. After several more blasts about Stoecker's unforgivable pleas for progressive taxation, Bismarck suddenly pulled back and in light of the parliamentary debate renounced his earlier "sharper demands. . . . The attacks which Richter, Rickert, and associates were not ashamed to launch decided my father," wrote Herbert Bismarck, "to express himself less severely regarding Stoecker. . . . To do nothing that could be construed as agreeing with the worst enemies of the government" was Bismarck's motive for treating Stoecker with sudden leniency.[72] As against his passionate hatred of the Progressives, Bismarck's ambiguous and aseptic views about Jews carried little weight. If his detested enemies spoke on behalf of Jewry, then Bismarck could not do likewise—not even in the faintest, most indirect fashion. With friends like the Progressives, known later as the *Judenschutztruppe*, the Jews could count on having powerful enemies.

In early December Bismarck and Puttkamer finally submitted their joint report to William. They objected to Stoecker's meetings that "incited to class hatred and made unfulfillable promises," and they urged the monarch to issue "a serious warning against stirring up ill will and divisiveness." William's final draft was gentler still; he merely expressed his "disapproval" that Stoecker should have specified certain large fortunes and should have criticized the government's social policy. He admonished him "to preserve the peace among all classes of my subjects, as befits a good pastor."[73] It was a rebuke, but one that even a less bellicose person than Stoecker could live with, and it avoided the Jewish question altogether.

William took even longer to answer Bleichröder's petition. In late December Bleichröder complained to Bismarck that the monarch still had not answered him; once more Bismarck had to prod Puttkamer, who thought that a curt acknowledgment would suffice for Bleichröder. Seven months after his original petition and at Bismarck's insistence, Bleichröder finally received a six-line reply from the court, with the information that the monarch had made "appropriate" remarks to Stoecker.[74] With that laconic circumlocution, the case was closed. Did Bleichröder ever think that if this was the treatment vouchsafed the leading Jew, his less distinguished coreligionists would fare still worse?

We know that Bleichröder was troubled by the sudden eruption of popular anti-Semitism, as was the whole Jewish community in Germany and outside. His own standing with international Jewry would suffer if German anti-Semitism became a lasting force. At the time of his petition to William, in June 1880, he reported to Moses Montefiore about the new anti-Semitic movements. Bleichröder probably agreed with the patriarch's confident reply that, despite the seriousness of the situation, "I cherish the hope that through prudence and discretion on our part and through enhanced enlightenment, based on the principles of humanity, on the part of the non-Jews, an influence on the existence of our brethren can still be achieved."[75] Bleichröder certainly believed in prudence and discretion. Montefiore was not the only one to write him about German anti-Semitism, and he may have been reassured by foreign solicitude, even as his patriotism was probably outraged by the aspersions that foreigners felt free to cast on Germans. As early as 1875, his old friend Moritz von Goldschmidt had written to him, with some concern: "Tell me sometime why the *risches* [anti-Semitism] with you blows up again so much. A sad phenomenon in a state that concerning clerical matters is as enlightened as Prussia." For years Goldschmidt badgered Bleichröder for news about the new German anti-Semitism; in November 1880 he wrote of his "unease" about the anti-Semitic League: "Is there no will in the *highest reaches* to deal with Stoecker and consorts?"[76] Alphonse de Rothschild from Paris—with whom Bleichröder often discussed the sufferings of coreligionists in such semibarbarous countries as Russia or Morocco—also commiserated with him right after the parliamentary debate: "In regard to the Jews it is really most regrettable that your government takes such an ambiguous stand and that it wants to make political capital out of a question that is really not suited for that. We regret this stance—inconsonant with the spirit of our age—all the more as we are quite unable to have any influence on decisions there."[77] A dig at Bleichröder's own impotence—or, more likely, an acknowledgment that Rothschild power, so effective in countries that needed their money, had met its match in imperial Germany? The Jews of Europe were concerned because they sensed that German anti-Semitism could have immediate repercussions in their own countries.

It is hard to reconstruct Bleichröder's innermost reaction to the sudden resurgence of anti-Semitism. If he had not been singled out as a chief target, he too might have been tempted to blame the agitation on the misconduct of other Jews—on "pushy Jews" from below, or on the rising number of *Ostjuden*, with their un-Germanic speech and customs, or on the liberal Jews who attacked Bismarck. At the time, Bleichröder's one-time friend Ludwig Bamberger warned that well-situated Jews did not understand the seriousness of the attacks on Jewry; he may have had Bleichröder in mind.[78]

Bleichröder continued the path of prudence and petition; not Gerson, but his brother Julius played an active role in a committee of notables, established by a distinguished Jewish gathering on December 1, 1880, to plan a defense against the anti-Semitic movement and to promote "Jewish self-improvement."[79] Gerson kept aloof from such public ventures.

Bleichröder's own response to the events of 1880 was to reaffirm his governmental loyalty; he took pains to emphasize that he did not belong to oppositional Jewry, that his ties to the liberal press were much exaggerated. He was particularly anxious to disavow any connection with the *Berliner*

Börsen-Courier and planted a story to that effect in the authoritative *Norddeutsche Allgemeine Zeitung*. He explained this move to Tiedemann, saying that it "would promote the separation of the *conservative* Jewish elements from those of the Progressive party." Tiedemann in turn informed the Bismarcks of this maneuver, adding that he thought Bleichröder should be encouraged in this, despite some inaccuracies in the presentation of the particular case. Herbert agreed.[80]

Bleichröder had two goals: he wanted Bismarck and German officialdom to know that he remained a staunch conservative but that the rising anti-Semitism, generally thought to be sanctioned by the government, would lead "all Jews save him" to vote for the Progressives. He assured people that he had no connection with the liberal press; when Holstein expressed surprise, because everybody thought he "dominated" the *Börsen-Courier*, Bleichröder asked who thought this, and Holstein replied: "You might as well ask where a leper has a spot." Time and again, Bleichröder expressed his dismay "at the progress of the anti-Semitic movement," which would end up driving all his coreligionists into the Progressive camp.[81] He was trying to appear as the good Jew—and at the same time, to warn the government that its apparent support of anti-Semitism would defeat its political purposes.

Bleichröder had a good sense of timing. William's gentle reproof to Stoecker had not calmed the anti-Semitic agitation; on the contrary, it was on the increase in Germany and in eastern Europe. Bismarck was confronted by an upswing in anti-Semitism and an increasing number of Jews who, convinced of his own complicity in anti-Semitism, were leading an anti-Bismarck faction within the German *Bürgertum*.[82] It was a good time to remind Bismarck that some Jews were still in the conservative fold.

In 1881 popular outbursts against Jews erupted, the most notable being in Neustettin, near Bismarck's home in Varzin, where, after an anti-Semitic rabble-rouser had delivered a particularly bitter diatribe against Jews, the local synagogue was burned down, and the town's leading Jews were accused of committing arson so that they could collect the insurance to pay for a new one.[83] This time the government did forbid anti-Semitic speeches in Pomerania and West Prussia.[84] In April 1881 a petition, carrying 250,000 signatures and demanding legal restrictions on Jewish immigration and public employment, was delivered to Bismarck. A year later, a wave of pogroms inaugurated the reign of Alexander III in Russia; at a cabinet meeting in May, Bismarck discussed the ensuing threat of Jewish immigration from the East and urged measures that would keep "undesirable elements" out of Germany. At the suggestion of Interior Minister Eulenburg, the cabinet ordered special patrolling of the borders with Russia so that "persons who looked undesirable" should be kept out. Bismarck added that in the Upper Silesian district of Oppeln, where many Jews had fled, anyone who clearly lived off usury should be expelled.[85] For the Berlin Jews, too, this threatened immigration had long been a delicate issue, and at one point Berlin spokesmen warned the Alliance Israélite in Paris that they would suspend all collaboration with the Alliance if it continued to encourage Russian Jews to pass through the German capital.[86]

The most important issue for the Jews, however, was the emergence in 1881 of anti-Semitism as a major weapon in national politics. In the general regrouping that had taken place in the decisive years 1878–1880, the National Liberals finally split, and the left wing, led by Ludwig Bamberger and Eduard Lasker—two Jews whom Bismarck came to loathe—formed a new party. It made no difference that gentiles were among the so-called Secessionists, and that indeed a mainstay of the Deutsche Bank, Georg Siemens, belonged to it as well. Bismarck dubbed his enemies "Ministry Gladstone" and thought it Semitic. The chancellor precipitated the first test in 1881, when he called for new elections at which he hoped to crush the Bamberger-Lasker faction. Stoecker and his associates bent every effort to wrest Berlin from the hands of Progressives and Jews; Stoecker himself was the Conservative candidate against Virchow. Bill Bismarck threw himself into the campaign, exuding his father's hatred for the Secessionists and Progressives. Bismarck, however, saw the complexity of the issue and wrote his son: "Stoecker's election is highly desirable: first, as the nonelection of his opponent [Virchow] and, second, because he is an extraordinary, pugnacious, useful comrade-in-arms"; but then warned him against *openly* supporting Stoecker because that would suggest endorsement of previous anti-Semitic activities which Bismarck could not countenance.[87] Months earlier, Eugen Richter, the leader of the Progressives, had pointed to the new tacit alliance: "the [anti-Semitic] movement is beginning to attach itself to Prince Bismarck's coattails, and although he does not want it and occasionally lets his press blame it for excesses, its leaders continue to snuggle up to him and to refer to him, just like noisy children eagerly surrounding their father."[88]

The Conservatives and the anti-Semites made common cause: their avowedly anti-Semitic campaign netted them some additional votes, but the anti-Bismarck forces scored an unprecedented victory. Progressives and Secessionists did extremely well; the Progressives retained their seats in Berlin, gained thirty-three new seats in the country, and won nearly a 70 percent increase in popular votes.[89]

Anti-Semitism had not paid off—and Bismarck distanced himself from it, discreetly. Hardly was the election over when he authorized Behrend, his business associate in Varzin, to publish the gist of a conversation they had had, in which Bismarck had said: "I most decidedly disapprove of this fight against Jews." In the rest of the conversation, published only in 1895, he denounced with particular vigor any discrimination based on descent: "Someday one could attack Germans of Polish or French descent with the same right and claim that they were not Germans." He also assured Behrend that he would never agree to any limitation of the constitutional rights of Jews.[90] A year earlier and during the parliamentary debate such a statement would have had an extraordinary impact; in 1881 in some obscure provincial paper it meant relatively little. But the consequences of this impassioned campaign were important: in political crises, respectable conservatives had no compunction about using anti-Semitic demagoguery. Second, Jews now found that they had but one ally, the Progressives and the Secessionists, the true liberals of Germany, who happened to be the chief target of Bismarck's hatred. As a consequence, Bismarck and Bleichröder, who had hoped to keep Jews in the conservative camp, now found them gravitating to the left, less by choice than by necessity. In subsequent elections, even the National Liberals occasionally supported anti-Semitic candidates in order to oppose Progressives; after 1881 the majority of German Jews voted for the left-liberal parties. Gerson's brother Julius openly belonged to that majority.[91] Once again, two hostile groups pushed each other into positions that confirmed their fears and prejudices. The dynamics of repulsion led Jews to vote for the left, which in turn gave fresh impetus to the anti-Semites.

These events afford an extraordinary perspective on how the German government, Bismarck, and Bleichröder reacted to the first outburst of political anti-Semitism. In those months, responses were set that lasted for a very long time. The government's refusal to take an unequivocal stand against anti-Semitic agitators lent further respectability to the agitation and foreshadowed later prevarication and concealed discrimination on the part of the government. In the 1880s the Bismarck regime began a policy of covert discrimination against Jews; it was a policy that the civil service continued under William II.[92] And Bismarck's own role in setting this new policy was far more decisive than has previously been noted.

Bismarck's moral insouciance hid a more complicated opportunism. Anti-Semitism was no part of his creed; he had come to discover the usefulness of Jews to the state and to himself. There was, moreover, a presumption against extreme demagoguery, partly because of concern over foreign reaction.[93] On the other hand, Bismarck lacked the principles that would automatically shield him from the temptation of political anti-Semitism. He had no basic commitment to what we call civil rights; he had no attachment to any kind of equality; the very idea affronted him. At best he had come to accept the civic equality of Jews, but if his enemies were to make an issue of the imperfectness of this equality in practice, he would rather discredit his enemies than in any way admit that they might be calling attention to a justified grievance.

The French have a saying, *"Les amis de nos amis sont nos amis."* Bismarck lived by the view that the enemies of his enemies must be his friends— especially if they were effective. Put differently, for Bismarck all people and all things were pawns.

The early phase of political anti-Semitism suggests as well that it was not simply a device of the ruling classes to fend off the lower classes. Anti-Semitism had failed as an issue that would entice proletarian socialists, but it proved useful in a fight against a segment of the propertied elite, that is, the liberals; it was an issue that conservatives hoped would attract some elements of the lower middle class to patriotic, right-wing parties.

In March 1884, a few months before the next Reichstag election, the Secessionists and the Progressive party fused to form the Freisinnige Partei, often translated as Radical party. The new organization stood for old-fashioned liberalism that opposed Bismarck's state socialism and for constitutional reform that opposed his dictatorial ways—and thus stood for all the things he most detested. "Like a rabid bull, Bismarck pounced on this new enemy, made dangerous by its strength and its relations to the Crown Prince."[94]

The stage was set for another electoral flirtation with anti-Semitism. Bleichröder apparently sensed this and once more turned to William with a petition, less personal in character, more revealing in substance, than his previous effort. On May 21, 1884, he wrote the monarch about "the political situation . . . into which Jews are being forced by the anti-Semitic agitation. I am no politician and do not presume to have a judgment about political matters." But the anti-Semitic agitation had been gaining strength; it had tried to win favor with the government and the Conservative party, and some of the Conservative leaders "already call the worst anti-Semitic agitators 'their dear and esteemed friends.' " The anti-Semites believed that government leaders favored them; they noticed that the government seemed to accept anti-Semitic support in parliament. Conservatives had gradually come to echo anti-Semitic sentiments. "This development . . . must drive the Jews out of the Conservative party. The more they are rebuffed by the Conservative party, the more strongly they are driven toward the liberal parties, including their extreme manifestations, Progressives and Radicals." In short, the Jews were being driven into opposition "because they find only among Liberals un-ambiguous recognition of and respect for their rights and defense against malicious attacks. I know from a most reliable source that considerable energies and funds which were originally earmarked for the conservative cause have been offered by Jews to Liberals only out of anxiety about the anti-Semitic movement." Bismarck placed a question mark next to the phrase about funds originally set aside for Conservatives.

Bleichröder assured the monarch that among his Jewish subjects there were at least as many with a conservative outlook as among gentiles, but they faced a terrible dilemma. In the 1881 election in Berlin, for example, the Conservatives ran anti-Semitic candidates: "I faced the choice between the anti-Semite who reviles me, my birth, and my family in the most shameless fashion and the Progressive. I concluded that I had to abstain from the election." Others had similar experiences, even outside Berlin: "Thus because of anti-Semitism we Jews have to a considerable extent been morally excluded from exercising our electoral rights." Even some gentiles, Bleichröder added, found it repugnant to vote for Conservatives who were also anti-Semitic. The next elections offered no better prospect, and Bleichröder ended with a plea and a promise:

If the anti-Semitic movement, however, could be banished, then I am certain that the Jews in deepest gratitude for deliverance from great pain and liberated from this unnatural pressure would use all their energies and means in order to express in the elections their truly patriotic be-liefs for Emperor and Reich and Government. We trust Your Majesty's high wisdom and love for all German subjects to find those paths that would lead to the welfare of the fatherland and its citizens.[95]

There was much truth to Bleichröder's petition; the anti-Semites did think the government silently favored them. The bulk of German Jewry was being rebuffed, and a man like Bleichröder was becoming politically homeless. As far as we know, Bleichröder never wavered in his refusal to support anti-Semitic Conservatives. Not all rich Jews, not even Bleichröder's intimates, maintained a similar course. A year after Bleichröder's petition, the Alliance Israélite in Paris received the following report from Berlin: "At a recent primary election in Berlin, Bleichröder's associate, Schwabach, gave his vote for the *anti-Semitic* elector, even though Julius Bleichröder, brother of Baron Bleichröder, was the designated liberal elector." The German correspondent added that Schwabach had recently been suggested as the head of a German branch of the Alliance Israélite: "Nice setup [*Netter Zustand*]."[96]

The upsurge of anti-Semitism troubled and divided Jewry. In the past, the state had protected them. And now—after years of emancipation and after so many Jews had become Germanized internally—the state would sanction, indeed covertly exploit, anti-Semitic agitation. For Bleichröder, whose whole life had been predicated on his close relationship to the government and its great leader, the events of the early 1880s must have been painful. He recognized the danger and resorted to the traditional strategy of defense, to humble, private petition to the monarch.

If any Jew in Germany could plead the case of Jewish usefulness to the state, it was Bleichröder. And still, there was something pathetically inadequate in his supplication: first, he overestimated the power of the king to banish the new uproar. There was no magic wand by which the king could scatter all anti-Semitic thoughts and sects, though government repudiation would of course have robbed anti-Semitism of its respectability, and many Germans would have hesitated to surrender to the new phobia if the government had not tacitly licensed it. But, worse, if Bleichröder had to base his appeal to the government on the grounds of German self-interest alone, then others—frightened conservatives, for example—could argue that anti-Semitism did pay, that the events of the late seventies and early eighties had shown it to be a popular diversion. The only transcendental principle the Jews could appeal to was the liberal belief in equal rights and toleration; but Bleichröder did not think in such terms, and German officialdom regarded such principles as un-Germanic twaddle. There was no generally accepted principle of the polity that would at least theoretically condemn anti-Semitic agitation. Liberal Jews could appeal to liberal tenets—even if German liberals were retreating from the notion that Jews would have both equality as citizens and separate identity as a religious community.[97] Public denunciation of the government or open opposition to it could not have occurred to Bleichröder; it would not have been consonant with his character or perceived interest. Bleichröder's one remaining argument was the inexpediency of anti-Semitism; unedifying, uncertain, but perhaps not altogether unrealistic; perhaps it was the only argument that counted for anything in Bismarck's Germany. And if that failed, then, as Bleichröder repeatedly intimated, there was only homelessness, "at home" or abroad.

There is no record of William's answer or of any intergovernmental discussion of Bleichröder's new petition. But in the mid-1880s anti-Semitism did abate. Bismarck needed new political alignments and found Stoecker an embarrassment. After successive electoral defeats, Bismarck in 1887 put together the *Kartell*, a combination of the Conservatives and the National Liberals. For the latter, Stoecker's role as a leading Conservative was an affront, and Bleichröder allegedly bought off an anti-Semitic candidate so that Jews and liberals could vote for the *Kartell.** The charge that Bleichröder had used his wealth to corrupt the electoral process was frequently repeated and embellished.[98]

Bismarck, on the other hand, was more troubled by Stoecker's friends than by his liberal enemies. In the winter of 1887 Stoecker drew ever closer to yet another anti-Bismarck cabal, that headed by Alfred von Waldersee. Waldersee, in turn, persuaded the emperor's grandson, Prince William, to take a friendly interest in Stoecker. Bismarck's attacks on "protestant Windthorsts" made young William pull back, leaving him with the first stirrings of anti-Bismarck resentment. Stoecker's stock fell continuously: during the brief reign of the liberal Frederick III, anti-Semitism was regarded as a real danger to the land, and at that point, and for his own reasons, it was Bismarck who saved him from dismissal. In the end, even William, once he had ascended the throne, did not wish to identify himself with the divisive Stoecker. In March 1890 William dismissed Bismarck, in April, Stoecker. But Stoecker had played his role in dignifying anti-Semitism. Others continued it in still more radical fashion, with Bleichröder still as the priceless target. In the beginning of the anti-Semitic agitation, Bleichröder was its star witness. If he had not existed, the anti-Semites could not have invented him. He was a hostage until anti-Semitism was so prevalent a phobia that it no longer needed him as evidence.

---

* In the new controversy between Bismarck and Stoecker, Bleichröder's name cropped up at once. For the critical election of 1887 the *Kartell* nominated a Catholic, Christoph Joseph Cremer, to run against Eugen Richter, the leader of the Progressives, in the latter's Berlin constituency. Cremer, a friend and associate of Stoecker's and allegedly the author of *Germania*'s anti-Semitic article in the mid-seventies, might well have embarrassed Liberal or Jewish sensibilities. He withdrew just before the election, amidst rumors that Bleichröder had paid 10,000 marks to eliminate Cremer. Richter and Stoecker alluded to these rumors, and Cremer finally published a pamphlet, "The Alleged 10,000 Marks of Herr von Bleichröder," in which he argued that he had not personally received any money from Bleichröder, but that there was nothing immoral about Bleichröder's supporting causes he favored: "One should start with the thought that Herr von Bleichröder might be at least a National Liberal or a Free Conservative. Or should he in the end be still more 'conservative' now that he has incorporated his daughter into the Silesian nobility through marriage and repeatedly suffered the news to go about that he himself had become Christian." What is surprising, Cremer claimed, was not that Bleichröder might have given 10,000 marks to a *Kartell* committee, but that he did not give 100,000 or 200,000 marks. By this time, however, Cremer's real enemy was Stoecker—and that too was symptomatic, because German anti-Semites were forever quarreling among themselves, as were, at times, their victims. Christoph Joseph Cremer, "Die angeblichen 10,000 Mark des Herrn von Bleichröder" (Berlin, 1889), *passim*.

CHAPTER 19

The Embittered End

... and yet for aught I see,
they are as sick that surfeit with too much
as they that starve with nothing.

—*The Merchant of Venice*, I, ii

A nti-Semitism was not the only cross Bleichröder had to bear. But it was mean and omnipresent, and it made all other unpleasantness still harder to cope with. Bleichröder suffered the afflictions of the rich; not a day without some request for help, whether from a prestigious charity or an impecunious stranger who had heard of Bleichröder's legendary benevolence. Sometimes other methods were applied. At the time of the anti-Semitic agitations, Bleichröder became the repeated victim of blackmail attempts. At the end of November 1880 Bleichröder received three anonymous letters demanding various, rather modest, sums, ranging from 1,500 to 3,000 marks to be deposited at prearranged places; in case of refusal, a member of his family would be killed. At about the same time, a former journalist asked for 500 marks or he would reveal some terrible scandal. In April 1881 the liberal *Berliner Tageblatt* published a compressed version of some of these threats, under the headline "A Nihilistically Tainted Blackmail Attempt." Bleichröder was furious at the publicity and at once complained to his friend Guido von Madai, the police chief of Berlin.[1] Madai had tried earlier to keep blackmail attempts from reaching the press. In the same winter of 1880, Bleichröder's daughter, Else, was subjected to threats or impertinences, and Madai promised to provide an unobtrusive police escort for her.[2]

At the end of the eighties, some woman sought to blackmail Bleichröder by threatening to divulge that her husband had had an adulterous affair with Else. Bleichröder turned the matter over to the public prosecutor, and a court sentenced the woman to three months' imprisonment; the anti-Semitic press carried the news.[3] Bleichröder's wealth and prominence brought him both protection and danger.

Bleichröder's relations to Madai are of more than symptomatic significance. Madai himself was something of a shadowy figure, as befits the head of the police, whom the socialists, in particular, loathed and thought of as "in reality, the *Reichspolizeiminister*," in charge, among other things, of censorship.[4] One writer has called him "a reactionary in the worst sense of the word" and a patron of Stoecker's, whereas some of the anti-Semitic scribblers of the time accused him of being a Jew and of having close relations with Jews, especially with Bleichröder.[5] Madai's letters to Bleichröder are remarkably intimate; they often begin with "Dear friend and benefactor [*Gönner*]." As always, the relation was based on reciprocal favors. Bleichröder sent gifts to Madai's wife and contributions to her charities; more important, he saved Madai's son, Conrad, from the consequences of his own shiftlessness. Penniless, jobless, in utter desperation, Conrad wrote to Bleichröder that he had left the position his father had got for him—because the employer was a "democrat incarnate." But Conrad could not admit this to his father; Bleichröder obliged and thus protected the boy "from the most terrible misfortune. . . . I would work day and night if only to win the love of my parents"—but there were no jobs in the depression and Bleichröder's help was crucial.[6] Father Madai, in turn, gave Bleichröder occasional information and tried—unsuccessfully—to "extract" the Crown Order, third class, for Bleichröder's father-in-law on the occasion of the latter's golden wedding, but Interior Minister Eulenburg refused because golden weddings were deemed insufficient reasons for decorations.[7] Madai also provided special police guards for Bleichröder's various feasts. Bleichröder was importuned by some of Madai's lieutenants; the record suggests that Bleichröder, along with other bankers such as Mendelssohn and Warschauer, "supported" several police lieutenants with small sums of 300 marks for unspecified returns.[8]

But Madai's principal role consisted of help in the greatest of Bleichröder's private troubles. For the last twenty-five years of his life Bleichröder was involved in a terrible scandal that combined—as happened so often in that century—charges of adultery with efforts at blackmail. Bleichröder, the pillar of respectability, came close to being indicted for perjury. His police file carries some notations about it, and a thick dossier of the Justice Ministry contains most of the formal material. A host of scurrilous pamphlets provided the public with lurid details and with grave charges of perjury and corruption. The only thing that eluded the courts then and the historians now is the complete truth of the case; we know enough, however.

The incontrovertible facts are few, simple, and sordid. Beginning in 1868, a Berlin divorcee named Dorothee Croner made financial demands on Bleichröder on the grounds that her marriage had broken up after her husband had discovered Bleichröder in her house. Much later it became clear that the court had granted Mrs. Croner a divorce because of her husband's adultery and designated him as the sole guilty party. Once the woman's demands began, Bleichröder turned to Polizeidirektor von Drygalski and police lieutenant Hoppe in order to arrange for some kind of accommodation. It was convenient for Bleichröder to be represented by police officials, and Hoppe continued in his service for many years—a fact known to Hoppe's chief and Bleichröder's friend Madai. In return for money received and further funds promised—the exact amounts remained in dispute—Croner consented to go off to Copenhagen, whence she was formally escorted by one of Drygalski's subordinates, a member of the criminal police, Hugo von

Schwerin. In the early 1870s she was back in Berlin and, according to Hoppe's official account, tried constantly to have her regular payments raised: "She used every opportunity she could find in order to sustain and increase the nervous excitement of Herr von Bleichröder . . . and did this by writing him long letters once or even twice a day or by suddenly appearing at his side during his walks."[9] Her game of alternately threatening and begging led to equally alternating responses—intermittent largesse interspersed with occasional efforts at starving her out by cutting off funds altogether. In January 1875 Bleichröder's legal intermediary, Dr. Kalisch, died, and from June of that year we have the first extant letter of Madai to Bleichröder about this affair.[10] At a later time, Madai acknowledged that "Bleichröder had called on my personal intervention in regard to the constant, unbearable annoyances and begging requests of Mrs. Croner: I did no more, however, than to have her call on me and to give her a serious warning."[11] No doubt, the personal intervention of the Berlin police chief must have had some inhibiting effect on her.

But not for long and not enough. In April 1880 she brought a civil suit for 18,000 marks against Bleichröder, alleging that they had had intimate relations in 1865–1866, that these had led to her divorce, that through Dr. Kalisch, Bleichröder had agreed in a written contract to pay her thirty taler a month and twenty-five taler on the four high Jewish holidays each year until her death—as well as provide certain benefits to her children.* The sums were trivial—as much as Madai was paying his least expensive informant.[12] As a part of this settlement, Croner had promised not to reveal the affair to Bleichröder's wife. The weakness of her case lay in the fact that her copy of the alleged agreement had mysteriously disappeared. In the ensuing investigation—apparently in the absence of all publicity—Bleichröder took two oaths; the first oath (*Editionseid*) avowed that he did not have a copy of said agreement and the second (*Erfüllungseid*) had this awkward text: "I swear that it is not true that I signed a document which said that in exchange for the claimant's not revealing her alleged affair with me to my wife I would promise to pay her for the rest of her life thirty taler monthly, etc." On the basis of these oaths and the court's view that a "leading businessman . . . with such business acumen" would not sign his name to a document that was meant to guarantee secrecy, Croner's case was dismissed. The public prosecutor sent her a detailed review of the case, emphasizing that it would be unlikely that "the accused, one of the foremost businessmen of our time," would have been so "foolish" as to give her written evidence of something he wanted her to keep quiet.[13]

The public prosecutor drew the only possible inference from these proceedings: that Bleichröder did in fact have illicit relations with Croner,

---

* The second provision suggests strongly that she was Jewish. Did the stipulated payments on the high holidays hark back to the traditional ritual of the Day of Atonement that provides that if a transgressor repents and offers his apologies to the transgressed and if, nevertheless, the offended party still bears a grudge, the sinner is no longer to blame? This interpretation was suggested to me by my friend Jay Winter.

that he had in fact made substantial payments to her, and that he had received help from the highest quarters in the Prussian police.[14] There is no way in which the historian can arrive at different conclusions. It is extraordinary that Bleichröder—so infinitely solicitous about social standing—would have an affair with a woman who, according to everyone's account, lacked all beauty, charm, and standing; when he first met her, he probably was unaware of the fact that in the late 1850s she had been already sentenced to three months' imprisonment for blackmail. Court documents described her as an illiterate. The man who could afford the choicest luxuries apparently indulged in a brief affair with a woman who was plain, stupid, and mean—attributes that unkind gossips occasionally fastened on his wife as well. There is no accounting for taste in adultery; we may surmise that Bleichröder had hoped for a discreet *Seitensprung*, as the Germans call it. Discreet, Dorothee Croner was not—and for a few moments of illicit indulgence Gerson suffered years of blackmail, gossip, and finally scurrilous publicity. A less rich man, a less prominent citizen, could have escaped with less pain.

The two oaths he swore settled the first phase of legal proceedings and opened the way to endless, ever worsening complications. Croner felt aggrieved and at that very moment was joined by one of those perfect cranks from the underworld who combine paranoia, self-righteousness, and infinite resentment with a cunning sense of personal profit. In 1880 Hugo von Schwerin was dismissed from the criminal police because of alleged complicity with gamblers; his own version of course was different and attested his total innocence.[15] He thought himself a victim of a frameup. Dismissal from the police—without pension—did not open doors to other employment, and in his anger and despair Schwerin apparently remembered his brief assignment on behalf of Bleichröder's protectors to transport Croner to Copenhagen. He now rallied to her cause—for likely profit, because he was to receive 10 percent of all that she extracted from Bleichröder, and for certain revenge, because Schwerin thought he could make miserable the lives of his former bosses and of Bleichröder. An additional psychic reward would be to pose as the defender not so much of Croner, with whom allegedly he was living at the time, but as the defender of unsullied Prussian justice—so clearly violated in this case.

Joined by Schwerin, Croner in 1883 demanded that the public prosecutor open perjury proceedings against Bleichröder on the ground that his second oath in 1881 had been untruthful. Obviously perjury was a grave charge—and a conviction would have brought imprisonment and would have ruined Bleichröder's life and career. The public prosecutor opened renewed investigations, summoned witnesses to testify under oath, and in November 1883 ruled that there was insufficient evidence for prosecution. Schwerin and Croner sought to win a reversal of this decision by appealing directly to the highest court of appeal (Kammergericht), but in the midst of these preliminaries, Croner formally withdrew her petition (*Antrag*) because she was now convinced of "the accused's innocence." After full deliberation, the court decided that there was insufficient evidence to press charges and dropped the case.[16]

It would be hard to account for Croner's sudden conversion without assuming that Bleichröder managed to persuade her that to assert his innocence would be profitable to her, too. According to never denied rumors, Bleichröder's intermediary was a former employee of his and ex-Lord Mayor of Berlin, Weber, who gave Croner 75,000 marks.* The only trouble was that she refused to give Schwerin his 10 percent, thus leaving him more aggrieved than ever. Bleichröder's intermediaries finally persuaded a reluctant Schwerin to accept 6,000 marks from Bleichröder directly—a deal that Schwerin himself acknowledged.[17] But the 6,000 marks further incited Schwerin's outraged conscience. Single-handedly he now took over the defense of Croner and the prosecution of Bleichröder. He was certain that corruption in high places had protected Bleichröder, that justice had been aborted. From 1884 on, the Bleichröder file in the Prussian Ministry of Justice was swelled with petitions from Schwerin; he fired off angry pleas to public prosecutors and judges, to Puttkamer and Friedberg, to William I and to the crown prince— all of them, in his insolently obsequious tone, suggesting that he, Schwerin, unjustly dismissed from his post, was the sole guardian of the sanctity of law. Gradually he escalated his charges, alleging that Bleichröder had profited from the highest judicial protection. The documents reveal, though Schwerin could not have known it at the time, that the minister of justice, Heinrich von Friedberg, did take a personal interest in the matter and demanded direct reports with special dispatch. Obviously Friedberg's subordinates knew that Bleichröder also enjoyed the special confidence of Bismarck. Prosecutors and judges believed that Bleichröder had made misleading statements in 1881, that some sort of agreement had been drawn up by Kalisch to settle Croner's demands, but none thought that there was sufficient evidence to convict Bleichröder of perjury. (Bleichröder, after all, had sworn that *he* had not signed any agreement; he had said nothing about his agent, Kalisch.) There was no malfeasance of justice—only a large whiff of favoritism solicitously kept alive for years by Schwerin and others.

The highest reaches of the government had to contend with Schwerin's allegations. William had to be briefed, Friedberg and Puttkamer carried on an official correspondence, and the crown prince asked whether Schwerin's allegations were not slanderous, hence liable to prosecution. But this, too, was denied because private petitions were traditionally exempt from prosecution.[18] The subterranean agitation continued for some time.

In early 1884 even the Council of Ministers discussed the affair. Bleichröder had invited the whole cabinet to dinner, but Friedberg felt "obliged to warn people off Bleichröder for the moment, because a discreditable case

---

* According to a letter of Croner's to the justice minister in 1896, she received 6,000 marks annually from 1884 to 1893 via former Lord Mayor Weber and was left destitute when Weber reduced and finally stopped payments after Bleichröder's death. Croner to Schonstedt, 30 April 1896, DZA: Merseburg: Justiz-Ministerium, Untersuchung wider den Geh. Kommerzienrath v. Bleichröder. Littr. 8, No. 764.

against him was pending." Friedberg—whom Holstein alleged to have been a distant relative of Bleichröder's—gave the cabinet a full briefing on the case, with particular mention of the fact that Croner had moved the perjury charge from an unwilling Department of Public Prosecutions to the courts themselves—a fact which to Holstein suggested collusion between the public prosecutors under Friedberg's supervision and Bleichröder, but which could also be read as an indication that Croner had been enabled to exhaust all legal means. A week later, Bleichröder repeated his invitation, and Friedberg now accepted because "the woman had withdrawn her accusation." Holstein's own commentary is instructive and perhaps symptomatic. He notes "Friedberg's anxiety. . . . First of all, for fear that Bleichröder, a Jew, might cause a scandal in this age of anti-Semitism, the public prosecutor's office is prevented from functioning." (Friedberg was a converted Jew.) In short, Holstein also believed that justice had been tampered with; he, too, thought Bleichröder guilty, because an innocent man would have insisted on a full airing of the accusations instead of bribing Croner to withdraw the case. But Bleichröder might have been legally innocent and still shunned the scandal of a public trial.

Holstein also noted, with great anger, that Bismarck's son-in-law, Rantzau, "for fear of annoying His Highness," refused to tell Bismarck about the Bleichröder case and the cabinet's discussion of it. Instead, at the height of the trouble, Bleichröder was invited to Friedrichsruh and could thus "bolster his prestige. . . . [He came] back radiant."[19] Since Holstein knew the story, we can trust him to have spread it. If Holstein suspected Bleichröder's guilt and official collusion, others probably harbored similar suspicions. It was too good a case for anti-Semites to keep quiet.

From 1884 to 1886 Schwerin contented himself with petitions about Bleichröder's alleged perjury, interspersed with petitions for his own reinstatement. He received no satisfaction, and by the end of the decade, and especially after Bismarck's dismissal, he made common cause with the leader of the anti-Semites, Hermann Ahlwardt, who, like Schwerin, was a moralist from the underworld. Before discovering the sacred cause of anti-Semitism, Ahlwardt—for embezzling funds—had been dismissed from his post as principal of a school.[20] Embroiled in many fights and adept at smear tactics, Ahlwardt made the anti-Bleichröder campaign his own. Part two of his opus, "The Desperate Struggle Between the Aryan Peoples and Judaism," published in 1891, was entitled "The Oath of a Jew" and consisted of sixty-four pages of documents and commentary that could have been supplied only by Schwerin. In Ahlwardt's hands, surmise and hearsay hardened into fact, and the result was a seemingly authentic story of lechery, perjury, and corruption that added up to a perfect formula for an anti-Semitic best seller. After presenting "facts" (including the story that in 1866, during the Austro-Prussian war, Bleichröder made Croner carry secret messages hidden between her breasts to the Frankfurt Rothschilds), he ended with the necessary anti-Semitic message: "Purge Jews from our judicial system [*Hinaus mit den Juden aus unserer Justiz*]: Otherwise, *Finis Germaniae*." Once more, the

Bleichröder story demonstrated the evil power of Jewry, but the villain was the dismissed chancellor: in 1871 "Bismarck gave Germany over to the *Grossjuden*, who sucked it dry."[21] Ahlwardt, a Reichstag deputy, had accused Bleichröder of perjury and the judicial authorities, and especially "the Jew" Friedberg, of collusion. His pamphlet sold thousands of copies and "created an enormous sensation."* It constituted an unmistakable challenge to Bleichröder and to the authorities.

Ahlwardt's charges had immediate echoes. The leading Socialist paper, *Vorwärts*, reported the Bleichröder story as evidence of the corruption of a capitalist society:

> We are not interested in the private love affairs of the Baron von Bleichröder, of this petty chieftain of the stock market, this leader of the dance around the golden calf. But in his little work, Ahlwardt accused the Berlin police of having helped Bleichröder to disguise and suppress this scandal. . . . This touches the public interest. It is a question whether the security authorities did in fact assist a wealthy man—we do not care whether he is a representative of circumcised or uncircumcised capital.

Were Ahlwardt's charges of police collusion, backed by putative documentary evidence, true or not? If the police did what Ahlwardt had alleged, "this would be an obvious violation of the law, a gross endangering of public safety, a flagrant misuse of official power, and the most forthright intervention of the courts should be a self-evident consequence."[22] Earlier, Franz Mehring had taken note of Ahlwardt's charges in the Socialist *Neue Zeit*:

> Especially the fact that a Jewish big capitalist committed perjury in order to avoid paying alimony to a dismissed *maîtresse* and that some police officers assisted him in his dirty private affairs of getting rid of the inconvenient witness has been verified to such a high degree of probability that it is not quite comprehensible why there is no official investigation of the evidence which, after all, is a little disparaging for the "God-fearing Empire of piety."[23]

What the socialists viewed from the perspective of class justice, the anti-Semites saw from the perspective of racial justice. In the 1890s Ahlwardt was leading a resurgent anti-Semitic movement, and his charges of perjury and collusion proved irresistibly appealing to his following. At times, the charges became even more fanciful; a police agent reported that at an anti-Semitic rally in Berlin, with 1,800 people in the audience, a Dr. Ax charged that a Jewish doctor had tried to poison Croner—with all necessary ghoulish details supplied. Another speaker brought the house down when

---

* Ahlwardt knew that he often was rather light-hearted with the truth and once replied, when asked for proof of some allegation: "If I cannot prove something, then I just assert it." Hellmut von Gerlach, *Von Rechts nach Links* (Zürich, 1937), p. 114.

he shouted: "Lock up the Jews in their old alleys before they lock you up in a Christian quarter."[24] Hundreds of meetings echoed these charges, scores of newspapers and broadsheets scattered them about, and the government received regular petitions that the case against Bleichröder should be reopened at once—because the statute of limitations would render him immune after 1891. The fact that at one point the police confiscated Ahlwardt's brochure and prosecuted him added a whiff of martyrdom to the case.[25]

In the fall of 1891, amidst all this hubbub, several members of the cabinet investigated the case, and the justice minister formally requested opinions from the public prosecutor and the attorney general (Oberstaatsanwalt) whether Ahlwardt's new evidence warranted a reopening of the case. The press, both the scurrilous and the respectable papers, got wind of this request and spread reports that a new prosecution was likely to take place.

In the event, the chief public prosecutor, having once more scrutinized all the evidence, subpoenaed some witnesses and, noting the disappearance of certain documents from the early 1880s which Ahlwardt reproduced in his pamphlet, concluded that nothing had been adduced which would justify reopening the case. He remembered that Bleichröder's failure to meet Ahlwardt's explicit provocation with a suit was "striking," but could probably be attributed to his fear of enlarging the scandal. He saw no way of acquiring sufficient evidence which would convince a court that Bleichröder had sworn a false oath. Given the "peculiarity" of the case and the failure of all previous efforts to present incontrovertible evidence, he counseled against reopening it now.[26] The prosecutor and finally the minister of justice concurred, and at the end of October 1891 it was formally decided not to reopen the case.[27]

For Bleichröder, this must have been small comfort. He had lived under the cloud, sometimes more ominous, sometimes less, for too many years. A few friends commiserated with him. In December 1890 Paul Lindau wrote Bleichröder of the horrible indignities both men were being subjected to. "You too have had the misfortune to collide with the worst rabble of the world."[28] But most associates kept an embarrassed silence, as did Bleichröder himself.

The storm did not abate, even after the cut-off date for prosecution, and despite all efforts of the justice minister to maintain "the most extreme secrecy."* The *Norddeutsche Allgemeine Zeitung* carried an official denial that new investigations had led to a reopening of the case; the opposite had been decided.[29] An anonymously published pamphlet—almost certainly written by Schwerin himself—appeared in January 1893 under the title "Schwerin und Bleichröder." Its message was simple:

---

* In 1892 in Leipzig appeared yet another anonymous, anti-Semitic pamphlet, actually by Balder, "Die Wahrheit über Bismarck: Ein offenes Wort an die deutsche Nation," which repeated all the old canards about Bleichröder's fraudulent dealings on Bismarck's behalf: "Via Bismarck, Bleichröder reached power and prestige, via Bleichröder, Bismarck reached the same—a couple of worthy contemporaries" (p. 117). The pamphlet also charged that Bleichröder controlled fifty newspapers and had amassed a fortune of 700 million marks.

Barons, counts, princes and many a highest state dignitary curry favor with him [Bleichröder]—*so far* has the German people come through the acceptance of a foreign race, corrupted for millennia, which cherishes the money bag as god and fraud as religion. Pull yourself together, German people, and fight for a Germanic administration of law— otherwise you are lost for all time.[30]

The rest of the pamphlet was in a similar vein, bolstered by countless documents from earlier proceedings. It is likely that Bleichröder still saw this— as did of course the police and the various ministries.

Neither public agitation nor private blackmail efforts ceased. Countless articles and innuendos kept the case alive. Dorothee Croner returned to Berlin in the winter of 1892–1893 and found yet another "protector" who was willing to become a prosecutor of Bleichröder. Even her daughter entered the fray and petitioned for a perjury trial against Bleichröder. It too was formally rejected.[31] The *Volks-Zeitung* brought the news that the recently returned Croner had once again turned to the public prosecutor—after her demands for several hundred thousand marks from Bleichröder had remained unanswered. She alleged that Bleichröder had given her 40,000 marks in 1891 to silence her, but that her current husband had stolen a fourth of that amount. The paper ran the story on February 18, 1893, under the appropriate headline: "An Old Story in a New Edition."[32]

The public innuendos embittered Bleichröder's life to the very end. At the same time, until a few days before his death, he maintained his public role, conferred with ministers, and entertained notables.[33] He was active to the last, despite increasing infirmities. The final public attack on him occurred on February 18, 1893. On the next day, after a short illness, Bleichröder died, of a pulmonary edema, at the age of seventy-one.

All the ambiguities of his life marked his end as well. He was given a lavish funeral. The Prussian *Heroldsamt* received a full report about the final honors rendered the deceased nobleman. Bleichröder's mansion had been transfigured into a dignified house of mourning. "A black flag at half-mast on top of his *Palais*," exquisite palms and flowers everywhere, busts of Bleichröder, Bismarck, and William, at the foot of the coffin four cushions with his orders and medals—and on top of the coffin, the wreaths from the family, a palm branch set in flowers from Bismarck, and two wreaths from the British Embassy. "Baron Alphonse de Rothschild had dispatched a special courier from Paris with a gigantic wreath, made up half of violets and half of Marshal Niel roses." Minister Boetticher and Count Lehndorff contributed magnificent palms; business firms vied with one another to have the best floral arrangement. The knights of the Iron Cross placed a wreath near the coffin as well. Attending the ceremony were the diplomatic corps and members of the government, the high bureaucracy, and the international business community; Rabbi Maybaum gave a long eulogy in which he listed Bleichröder's great achievements but primarily praised those traits and deeds that made clear that "according to his strength he overcame the great dangers of wealth. We emphasize here in the first place his piety for his parents. He missed but few services in the synagogue when the deceased were remembered, and when he established a foundation, he dedicated it to the memory of his parents—may they rest in God."[34] "An imposing funeral procession" finally made its way past Bleichröder's place of birth to the Jewish cemetery in the Schönhauser Allee, and there he was laid to rest according to Jewish rites. Thus ended the last and greatest ceremony— almost a state occasion, as recorded in the official report.[35]

The newspapers carried long eulogies: "One of Germany's most magnanimous men, a philanthropist in the most sublime sense of the word. . . . [The German financial world] has lost its foremost representative." The principal Jewish paper sounded a cautious note:

> With Gerson von Bleichröder's death ends a full and successful life but also a life that was not shielded from the sorrow and troubles of human existence. . . . Such great material successes are not attained without hard struggle, without envy and other animosities pursuing and devastating one's life. Gerson von Bleichröder experienced this to the utmost, and in other ways, too, fate hit him hard and repeatedly.[36]

What was not recorded in the *Heroldsamt* or in the papers was an official note in the police files, sent in by Count Eulenburg: "Bleichröder's heirs are very much worried that anti-Semitic demonstrations" might disrupt the funeral procession; they were also afraid that a vicious pamphlet on the death of the "most wretched Jew" would be distributed along the route to the cemetery.* The Police chief, Richthofen, made the necessary arrangements; special protection was discreetly mobilized, and the ceremony passed without incident. On the next day, Bleichröder's heirs sent 100,000 marks to Berlin's mayor, for public purposes and in honor of the deceased.[37]

Bleichröder was laid to rest with full honors, but still needful of the state's protection. For services rendered, the Prussian Crown and German Reich had amply rewarded him. Only the sense of belonging and security, only the sense of safe acceptance, had been withheld. And that perhaps is the essence of the anguish of assimilation.

---

* Nor was the family's concern entirely unjustified. A Protestant church paper was out-raged at how on the occasion of his death "the entire Jewish press celebrated Gerson von Bleichröder as a *Saint*," forgetting all the grave charges pending against him. The paper sought to expose "the mendacious obeisances of a mendacious age." *Allgemeine evangelische-lutherische Kirchen-Zeitung*, 21 March 1893, quoted in *Sigilla Veri, Lexikon der Juden* (Erfurt, 1929), "Bleichröder," p. 646.

Epilogue: The Fall of a Family

The thought precedes the deed as the lightning the thunder. German thunder is of true German character: it is not very nimble, but rumbles along somewhat slowly. But come it will, and when ye hear a crashing such as never before has been heard in the world's history, then know that at last the German thunderbolt has fallen. At this commotion the eagles will drop dead from the skies and the lions in the farthest wastes of Africa will bite their tails and creep into their royal lairs. There will be played in Germany a drama compared to which the French Revolution will seem but an innocent idyll.

—Heinrich Heine, *Religion and Philosophy in Germany*

Working out whether to get out today or whether you have still got till tomorrow requires the sort of intelligence with which you could have created an immortal masterpiece a few decades ago.

—Bertolt Brecht, *Flüchtlingsgespräche*

Bleichröder's public legacy, the House bearing his name, continued to play a preeminent role in Berlin—but a decline, at first barely noticeable, set in soon after his death. Other private banks suffered a similar fate; the *Grossbanken* pushed them aside or swallowed them up.[1] The intimate connections between the House of Bleichröder and the German government weakened after Gerson's death. The business was carried on by Julius Schwabach as senior director (*Seniorchef*); Hans von Bleichröder, Gerson's eldest son, who had worked in his father's House since 1881, was an active partner, though his inclination to work grew neither with age nor with responsibility.

Still, S. Bleichröder remained a firm of worldwide repute. It was one of the elite private banks in Europe, active on an ever wider front in line with Germany's new *Weltpolitik*. Together with old associates, such as the Disconto-Gesellschaft, the Rothschilds, Mendelssohns, and others, Bleichröder participated in loans to governments in financing a host of ventures in Europe, Asia, Africa, and America. It continued to have a dominant position in Rumanian finances as well as in Italy and Mexico; in New York, still in Gerson's lifetime, the firm of Ladenburg, Thalmann and Company came to be a de facto Bleichröder property.[2] Schwabach belonged "to those eminent representatives of this international *haute finance* who ignored frontiers." In the many joint ventures of French and German banks between 1898 and 1914, the Bleichröder House occupied a leading place. Bankers on both sides of the Rhine preferred to pursue their quiet, profitable forms of peaceful cooperation even at a time when their respective governments drifted ever further apart.[3]

We know less about the bank after Gerson's death; there are no private papers that survived from the Schwabach era, and the bank itself lost much of its independent prominence. It retained its distinguished clients in Germany and its preeminence abroad. In 1897 Julius Schwabach celebrated the fiftieth anniversary of his entry into the House of Bleichröder. He marked the occasion, so the police reported, by making charitable gifts of 100,000 marks, though the only known recipient was the Jewish Reform-gemeinde in Berlin, which received 20,000 marks. He was generous to the Jewish community, but his children all left the faith and converted to Protestantism. Schwabach's annual income was estimated at 2,500,000 marks, his total wealth at 27 million. On this anniversary the government declined to grant him a further decoration. He died a year later.[4]

Even in Schwabach's lifetime, Gerson's children played a marginal role in the House. Hans was a member, James was a silent partner—with a participation of 14 million marks, according to the police file. Between 1896 and 1903 the police estimated James's wealth to have increased from 16 million to 22 million (an indication, presumably, of the prosperity of the bank), and his annual income in 1903 was estimated at 800,000 marks.* For a time Georg was a sleeping partner as well.

To some extent the House lived on its past glory, even while Julius Schwabach was alive. Its international reputation declined, as can be inferred from a letter that Max Warburg wrote to his brother Paul in New York, to the effect that Schwabach had bitterly complained about having been "entirely passed over" in connection with an issue of Illinois Central bonds. Max urged his brother to discuss the matter of Bleich-röder's future participation in American affairs with Kuhn, Loeb and Company even while lamenting the marked decline in the quality of the bank's managers after Gerson's death: "it is still our first Jewish banking House; moreover the matter acquires great interest for us, because I am told that

---

* Of James it was reported that he belonged to the conservative Bund der Landwirthe which, unlike its competing, more populistic organization, the Bauernbund, accepted Jews—reluctantly. It certainly was also very active in anti-Semitic agitation. "Über die Reichstags-wahlen," *Historisch-politische Blätter* (1893), II, 60. In the same year, another Bleichröder descendant acquired political notoriety at the other end of the spectrum. The liberal Julius Bleichröder had a son-in-law, Leo Arons, who was a socialist, the major financial supporter of the revisionist *Sozialistische Monatshefte*, and a Privatdozent in physics at the University of Berlin. A fierce controversy developed over whether so "subversive" a man should have the right to teach, and the issue finally resulted in a special law called *lex* Arons. For an East German account of the affair, see Dieter Fricke, "Zur Militarisierung des deutschen Geisteslebens im wilhelminischen Kaiserreich: Der Fall Leo Arons," *Zeitschrift für Geschichtswissenschaft*, VIII (1960), 1069–1107.

Bleichröder has for some time been on bad terms with Behrens"—as were the Warburgs.[5]

For the next three decades, the bank continued under the direction of Schwabach's son, Paul, who had originally planned a different career. He had studied history and written a creditable thesis on seventeenth-century French tax administration. In 1896, at the age of twenty-nine, he entered the Bleichröder bank and, two years later, after his father's death, assumed its direction. Almost immediately, the aged Bismarck summoned him to Friedrichsruh—and reminisced about the better life of the past, spoke harshly of William II and the Conservatives who in 1890 had deserted him, touched briefly on the continuing financial ties between the Bleichröder bank and himself, and then ended his interview—one of his last—by saying: "I still have two wishes: I would like to see Varzin again and I would like one more time to lose myself in cold champagne."[6] Four months later, Bismarck died.* The link between the Bismarck family and the Bleichröder bank survived intact until the 1930s.[7]

Paul Schwabach soon came to play a major role in Berlin society; he had an easier entrée to it than Gerson had had. In 1893, when he applied for a reserve officer's commission, his regiment plied the Berlin police with various questions, of which the first—and presumably most important—was: "Is the family of Julius Leopold Schwabach still of the Mosaic faith?" The answer came forthwith that while the parents were of the Mosaic faith "the three sons have all converted to the evangelical church"—the word "faith" having been crossed out in the original and "church" substituted.[8] With that hurdle overcome and after his marriage in 1896 to Ellinor Schröder, daughter of a prominent Hamburg banker, Paul could begin his social career.

The Schwabachs maintained a glittering salon in Berlin, where diplomats and officialdom congregated, and an exclusive country estate in Kerzendorf, where special friends, like Carl Fürstenberg, were frequent visitors.[9] Paul rose to great social eminence. In 1907 he was ennobled; just before, he had helped William II to purchase an estate on Corfu. Now both men had their place in the sun, and Paul's social presence became greater still, a fact that the shipbuilder Albert Ballin "detested . . . [because] the social ambitions of wealthy Jews only increased anti-Semitism."[10] But Schwabach, close friend of Holstein, occasional guest at William's table and hunting parties, no longer felt his Jewishness—even if others remembered it. Still, the problem of reconciling Jewish ancestry with a passion for assimilation proved inescapable for Schwabach and his heirs, as it did for the Bleichröder clan; it dominated and ruined their lives.

Like Gerson, Paul found diplomacy irresistible. Unlike Gerson, Paul was most discreet in executing his various missions to foreign statesmen and bankers, including of course the Rothschilds. At various times, particularly

---

* Of his grave, the *New York Times* reported: "The wreaths are extremely beautiful. That from Count and Countess von Bismarck is inscribed 'Bill and Sibylle.' That from the Bleichröder Bank was so large that it needed a whole carriage in itself." 3 Aug. 1898.

during the several Moroccan crises, Schwabach counseled moderation and was used by Berlin officials to transmit private messages of peaceful intent to French and British statesmen. He was closest to the British Rothschilds and to his boyhood friend Sir Eyre Crowe, whose anti-German sentiments Schwabach had no inkling of. He was an ardent patriot, but not an uncritical chauvinist or expansionist. At the beginning of the war he rejoined his regiment; later he was attached to the German occupation authorities in Belgium and tried to save the life of Edith Cavell.[11] International bankers, with their wish for peace, played a secondary role in wartime Berlin. Paul dissented from the expansionist programs of many industrialists; he was an opponent of unlimited submarine warfare ("I do not know for certain," he wrote in May 1917, "whether it was really Herr von Bethmann Hollweg who was responsible for the delay in the U-boat war. If so, he would have deserved well of the fatherland, and it would be hard to overestimate his service").[12]

Paul was not an uncritical admirer of the kaiser's regime; he complained of its Byzantinism and was alarmed by the power-drunk Pan-Germans. But the collapse of imperial Germany came as a terrible blow to him, as it did to most Germans. In 1918 he joined the Democratic party, though he probably drifted to the right again thereafter. In 1921 he celebrated his twenty-fifth year at S. Bleichröder and remembered Gerson as the first German to recognize and embody the close ties between politics and finance: "Herr von Bleichröder knew that the activities of the individual businessman, if they were to be fruitful, could never be separated from the common ground of the fatherland."[13] It was his own conception as well, and, throughout Weimar, he retained his close ties with men of power and importance. Through his close friendship with Frau von Lebbin, he fell heir to the papers of one of Gerson's most malicious friend-foes, Fritz von Holstein. After the war he resumed his international correspondence, tried to persuade British statesmen and bankers that beggaring Germany would wreck Europe, and in May 1925 wrote to an English associate that Bolshevism was the greatest danger:

> It follows, from what I have said, that nothing can help except a change of the political and economical [sic] system in Russia, and I should think that, if all the European cabinets followed an energetic policy, forming so to say a single front, they ought to find a method by which a change would be brought about in Russia. In speaking of a change I do not suppose that the Czar should be called back to the throne; the form of government is of little avail, rather a detail; what concerns us, is the economical system.[14]

Anti-Bolshevism ill-prepared him for the mortal danger at home.

At the time of his twenty-fifth anniversary in the firm, Paul made some condescending remarks about Hans and Georg Bleichröder, who had been his original partners "but who were mostly otherwise engaged."[15]

(In 1902 Georg, a great sports enthusiast, was killed in an automobile accident. Hans died in 1917.) Indeed, his own role was the more important as Bleichröder's own progeny continued its rapid decline into decadence, debauchery, and sloth. Gerson's sons made a mockery of his traditions.* Of all the wretched affairs that his sons indulged in, perhaps James's relations with a woman named Flora de Saint Riquier may be taken as symptomatic. For a long time he lived with this woman almost twenty years younger than himself, who had a considerable, if unsavory, reputation in Berlin. Her mellifluous name was fraudulent; she was born the daughter of a Jewish horsedealer in Berlin, named Heymann, was adopted in 1889 by a convicted embezzler named von Hochberg, and was fleetingly and uncertainly married to a Frenchman in England by the fine name of Saint Riquier. The police surmised that "the adoption through von Hochberg to attain noble status as well as the marriage to Saint Riquier took place on Bleichröder's prompting."[16] In the end, James married Flora and sought to have Berlin society accept her; after a few years she walked out on him, taking her extravagant jewelry with her to her next escapade with a South American diplomat. The press dutifully reported these doings.[17] James's sons sought to become reserve officers, and during the Great War, James himself became a cavalry captain of the home reserves, and one of his sons was killed in battle, "at the head of his company." Just before the war his daughter had married Jordan von Campe, scion of an old Prussian family.[18]

The next generation was no more distinguished. Anti-Semites called Hans, Jr., "the type of *jeunesse isidorée*." He, too, was a full-time ladies' man, and his most celebrated love was for Princess Sophia of SachsenWeimar, who in 1913 shot herself because her parents opposed her marriage to Hans. They also barred Hans from attending the funeral.[19]

The decline of the Bleichröder family was even more rapid than its rise. It is a familiar story: families have often been corrupted and destroyed by wealth. Perhaps the temptations in German society were greater than elsewhere. To fight these temptations a sense of family and above all a sense of self are necessary. But the young Bleichröders yearned to be what they were not and could never be, and thus had wealth but little self-esteem. As it was, sensuality dissipated ambition, and the father's labors paid for the children's license. All this has a familiar ring among plutocrats—but the setting and ultimate denouement were unique.

It had been hard for the bank to survive the economic storms of the postwar years. The public prestige remained high, and in 1923, the hardest of postwar years for the German economy, the firm celebrated its one hundred and twentieth anniversary. After that, a rapid decline set in. In the mid-1920s, after a rather sordid lawsuit, the Bleichröder heirs—principally

---

* With one important exception: They continued his munificence in promoting medical research. In May 1914, the family Bleichröder, as it was identified in the announcement, gave a million marks to the Berlin internist Friedrich Kraus and to the Berlin Charité hospital for the "treatment of needy patients, including especially those from the middle classes," in new methods of physical therapy. F. Kraus, "Bleichröderstiftung," *Deutsche Medizinische Wochenschrift*, 14 May 1914, p. 1023.

Curt von Bleichröder, son of James—were eliminated from the family business, and for a while Paul hoped to run it alone. But the firm was in desperate need of new capital and new talent. An early association with the Munich bank of H. Aufhäuser proved unsatisfactory; in 1931, amidst the great economic crisis, a close identity of interests was established with Gebrüder Arnhold, a flourishing, well-administered Dresden bank, founded in 1864, and from 1875 to 1926 under the commanding leadership of Georg Arnhold. By comparison, S. Bleichröder had become a shadow of itself. In the same year, Paul sold his shares of the Wolff Telegraph Bureau to the Reich government, thus ending a tie that had existed for over sixty years.[20]

Hitler's accession to power finally led to the extinction of the bank through the process of Aryanization. In 1938 the bank ceased to exist in Germany—and a new firm bearing the name Arnhold and S. Bleichroeder came to be established first in London and then in New York, where an ancient name has won new eminence. The prospering of the new firm was in no small measure due to the distinguished contribution of F. H. Brunner, once a leading member of the Berlin bank and the salvager of the Bleichröder Archive.

The firm's decline and disappearance was the tangible consequence of Hitler's rise to power. The utter incomprehension and moral confusion of so many of the Bleichröder-Schwabach heirs was the intangible side. Having cut themselves off from Judaism and having so unreservedly embraced German values, how were they to respond to the new regime which decreed that in the eyes of the Nazi law converts to Christianity were still Jews? The harshest blow fell on Paul von Schwabach's son, Paul, Jr., a serious, capable person very much in love with the charming descendant of an old Prussian family, Carmen von Wedel. The Nürnberg Laws forbade marriage, and Paul, driven desperate, filed a special petition in February 1936 as *Halbarier* to the minister of the interior, asking for permission to marry the girl he loved. He even sought to mobilize men of influence to put pressure on Rudolf Hess. Schwabach tried to get David Lloyd George to intervene directly with Hitler, but he declined, as did several other Englishmen. In June 1937 his petition was refused. Reluctantly he tried—with the help of Alfred Duff Cooper and Duncan Sandys—to obtain permanent residence in Britain. In the midst of these plans, the thirty-five-year-old Paul died suddenly after a very short illness—so that prominent Swiss newspapers spoke of suicide out of a broken heart. This was probably untrue, but his will to live and his ability to comprehend the world had been fatally diminished.[21]

The elder Schwabach never recovered from the death of his friend, partner, and son. His life—in the private as in the public realm—was shattered; nor could he comprehend the horrors around him. In one of his last letters, written a few weeks before his death and just after the Munich Agreement, he complained bitterly—about the Versailles Treaty, drawn up by a constant alternation of "dumbheads and wretched knaves [*Lumpen*]. Among the latter, I give Clemenceau and Wilson pride of place."[22] He died a few days after the Nazi pogroms of November 1938.

Some of Gerson's grandchildren escaped abroad; others sought to escape by a different route, through petition and submission. The files of the German Ministry of the Interior contain a letter of January 7, 1942, from Curt von Bleichröder, a son of James's first marriage. In it he appeals to Minister of the Interior Frick for exemption from the new law enjoining Jews to wear the yellow star and from deportation and "beyond that to give me a chance through *Arisierung* to find a useful place again as officer." As justification, he cites his service as reserve officer in the front lines during the Great War and the fact that he was thrice wounded. "At the first national uprising after the war, 'the Kapp-*Putsch*,' I was at my post [*zur Stelle*]." As a member of the *Stahlhelm*, he took part in the "storming of the *Vulkan-Werft* in Stettin." One of his brothers was killed at the front and another, Edgar, was shot down in action. His father, James, though fifty-five at the time, did military service as cavalry captain. Curt's letter was signed: "Heil Hitler!" Edgar, in turn, made a separate plea, largely based on the testimony of two "Pg's" (party members), as the Nazi lingo, used by Edgar, had it. Their testimony was to prove Edgar's support of the Nazi movement. One of these party members, Edgar wrote, "insists that he entered the party in 1930, moved by my propaganda." The same party member offered to testify that Edgar had been aware of his racial past and had always meant to effect his "*Arisierung*." A Frau Bechstein—presumably of the Bechstein piano manufacturers—formally pleaded with Frick on behalf of Curt, but the final decision was made by SS Obersturmbannführer Adolf Eichmann. On May 7, 1942, Eichmann's office turned down the requests; the Bleichröders were Jews, especially "in light of the repeated declarations [*Willensäusserung*] of the Führer regarding the treatment of such petitions." Because they had been injured in the First War, they would be exempt from deportation to the East; "but it is intended that in the process of a final settlement [*Bereinigung*] of the Jewish question in the Reich territory they would be placed in a ghetto for old people [*Altersghetto*] within the Reich territory."[23]

The degradation that these supplications bespeak needs no commentary. They are almost too neatly symbolic. In the nakedness of their desperate deference, they seem so utterly unambiguous—and yet, however much Gerson's own deference is mirrored in this final act of self-abasement, one must remember as well that these brothers sought to save their lives amidst a chaos that was approaching an unbelievable catastrophe.

In the event, they saved themselves by fleeing to Switzerland, where the Red Cross gave Curt a coat, for he was penniless. Their sister, Baroness von Campe, was deported to a camp in Riga in August 1942, as a "Jewess."[24] After the end of the war various members of the then-scattered family fell into a bitter dispute over the disposition of the Bleichröder heritage.[25] The final item in the bizarre story of the Bleichröder Bank in the maelstrom of German history was the announcement carried in the *New York Times* that the granddaughter of the chief partner of Arnhold and S. Bleichroeder in New York was to marry a great-grandson of Otto von Bismarck. It would finally have signaled the union in equality between S. Bleichröder and the

Bismarcks—to be achieved only after two wars and two revolutions. In due course, the engagement was annulled. Cupid spoiled what Clio wanted. The story of Bleichröder has no happy ending.

There is no epitaph for Bleichröder. His was a story of achievement, triumph, ruin, of vain hopes torn apart by the tides of history. He was a part of the great transformation of German society; his life—his successes and his sufferings—mirrors the dynamism and the faulted character of that society.[26] The multiplicity of his public roles made him a leading figure of his time, and yet even his private life was dominated by his confused struggle with a society that was at once hostile and enticing. He was both master and slave of his society. The richest man in Germany was not the freest— far from it. His story is the story of hubris, in him and against him, of golden chains that blinded men to iron servitude. There are lessons in his life far greater than his influence or fortune ever were: they are his lasting monument.

NOTES

Introduction

1. *Troilus and Cressida*, V, 10.
2. Max Weber, *Wirtschaft und Gesellschaft. Grundriss der verstehenden Soziologie*, 5th ed. (Tübingen, 1972), p. 531.
3. *The Portable Veblen*, ed. by Max Lerner (New York, 1950), p. 475.
4. Memorandum of Dr. Rittscher, quoted in Kalman Stein, "The Labor Movement in Lübeck 1866–1914. An Alternative Model for the Development of Social Democracy," a Columbia University doctoral dissertation in history, 1976.
5. Werner Jochmann, a German historian, recently observed: "It was impulses emanating from German historiography that gave rise in the nineteenth century to the inception and subsequent flowering of the discipline of Jewish studies. Yet German historiography itself never saw fit to devote even the slightest attention to the history of an active minority living predominantly in Europe at the time" ("The Jews and German Society in the Imperial Era," *LBY*, 20 [1975], p. 5). In 1911 Werner Sombart wrote his controversial *Die Juden und das Wirtschaftsleben*, while Max Weber made scattered and significant remarks about the role of Jews in capitalism and in German society, but unfortunately never treated the subject systematically in all its complexity, as he could have done so masterfully.
6. Lionel Trilling, *The Liberal Imagination. Essays on Literature and Society* (New York, 1950), p. 212.
7. Friedrich Nietzsche, *Beyond Good and Evil. Prelude to a Philosophy of the Future*, trans. by Walter Kaufmann (New York, 1966), p. 80.
8. Richard Hofstadter, *The American Political Tradition and the Men Who Made It* (New York, 1948), p. viii.
9. Lionel Trilling, *Sincerity and Authenticity* (Cambridge, Mass., 1972), p. 15.

1 / First Encounter: Junker and Jew

1. Lysbeth W. Muncy, *The Junker in the Prussian Administration under William II, 1888–1914* (Providence, 1944), p. 15.

2. Jacob Jacobson, ed., *Die Judenbürgerbücher der Stadt Berlin, 1809–1851* (Berlin, 1962), pp. 108, 494.
3. Jacob Katz, *Out of the Ghetto: The Social Background of Jewish Emancipation, 1770–1870* (Cambridge, Mass., 1973), pp. 26, 61, 80–81.
4. On the court Jew, see Heinrich Schnee, *Die Hoffinanz und der moderne Staat: Geschichte und System der Hoffaktoren in deutschen Fürstenhöfen im Zeitalter des Absolutismus*, 3 vols. (Berlin, 1953–1955); and Selma Stern, *The Court Jew* (Philadelphia, 1950).
5. Hermann Samter, "Fünf Generationen. Die Geschichte der Familie Bleichröder," *Gemeindeblatt der jüdischen Gemeinde zu Berlin*, June 16, 1935.
6. On this, see Dietrich Eichholtz, *Junker und Bourgeoisie vor 1848 in der preussischen Eisenbahngeschichte* (East Berlin, 1962).
7. S. Bleichröder to Paris Rothschilds, 18 April, 5 May, 5 and 6 Nov. 1838, 9 Jan. 1839, RA.
8. S. Bleichröder to Baron James, 16 Sept. 1840, 9 Jan. 1843, RA.
9. S. Bleichröder to London Rothschilds, 14 Sept., 11 Nov., 15 Dec. 1831, RA, London; Samuel Bleichröder to Frankfurt Rothschilds, 8 May 1848, BA.
10. I owe this information to David S. Landes, who obtained the material from the London Rothschilds. S. Bleichröder to London Rothschilds, 8 Oct. 1831, RA, London.
11. S. Bleichröder to Paris Rothschilds, 17 July 1840, RA.
12. S. Bleichröder to Baron James, 28 Feb. 1843, RA.
13. See Hugo Rachel, Johannes Papritz, and Paul Wallich, *Berliner Grosskaufleute und Kapitalisten*, Vol. III: *Übergangszeit zum Hochkapitalismus, 1806–1856* (Berlin, 1967), pp. 126–27.
14. S. Bleichröder to Baron Anselm Solomon, 17 Nov. 1839, RA.
15. S. Bleichröder to Baron James, 14 June 1843, RA.
16. Hajo Holborn, *A History of Modern Germany, 1840–1945* (New York, 1969), p. 122.

17. Theodore S. Hamerow, *The Social Foundations of German Unification, 1858–1871: Ideas and Institutions* (Princeton, 1969), ch. 1 *passim*, and p. 31; David S. Landes, *The Unbound Prometheus: Technological Change and Industrial Development in Western Europe from 1750 to the Present* (London, 1969), ch. 4; Hermann Münch, *Adolph von Hansemann* (Munich, 1932).

18. Abraham Oppenheim to Bleichröder, 12 July 1855, 5 June 1859, BA.

19. See Münch, *Hansemann*, pp. 77–78; Helmut Böhme, *Deutschlands Weg zur Grossmacht: Studien zum Verhältnis von Wirtschaft und Staat während der Reichsgründungszeit, 1848–1881* (Cologne and Berlin, 1966), pp. 57–82.

20. Leo Tolstoi, *Anna Karenina* (New York, 1939), I, 309.

21. *GW*, XIV¹, 14.

22. *Ibid.*, p. 58.

23. *Ibid.*, p. 16.

24. *Ibid.*, p. 179.

25. Even the most sensitive portrayals of Bismarck such as Otto Pflanze's essay, "Toward a Psychoanalytical Interpretation of Bismarck," *AHR*, 77 (1972), 419–44, and Henry A. Kissinger's "The White Revolutionary: Reflections on Bismarck," *Daedalus*, 97 (1968), 888–924, pay a great deal of attention to Bismarck's extraordinary religious conversion and almost no attention to the impact of 1848.

26. *Gedanken und Erinnerungen von Otto Fürst von Bismarck* (Stuttgart, 1898), I, 31–32. Hereafter cited as *Gedanken*.

27. *GW*, XIV¹, 150.

28. *Gedanken*, I, 72.

29. *GW*, XIV¹, 187; and quotation in Pflanze, "Psychoanalytical Interpretation," p. 424.

30. *GW*, XIV¹, 228.

31. *Ibid.*, p. 214.

32. *Ibid.*, p. 213.

33. *Ibid.*, p. 222.

34. Egon Caesar Conte Corti, *Das Haus Rothschild in der Zeit seiner Blüte, 1830–1871* (Leipzig, 1928), pp. 334–50.

35. *Ibid.*, pp. 290–319; Erich Eyck, *Bismarck: Leben und Werk*, 3 vols. (Erlenbach-Zürich, 1941–1944), I, 197–200; Karl Demeter, "Aus dem Kreis um Bismarck in Frankfurt am Main," *FBPG*, 48 (1936), 294–326; quoted in Böhme, *Deutschlands Weg*, p. 56.

36. Corti, *Haus Rothschild*, pp. 353–55, and *GW*, I, 278.

37. *Gedanken*, I, 200–206.

38. *GW*, III, 343.

39. *GW*, XIV¹, letters of January 1851, esp. 25 Jan. 1851, p. 191.

40. *Gedanken*, I, 191.

41. Professor Wolfram Fischer was kind enough to supply me with the date of Bleichröder's move; his source was *Allgemeiner Wohnungs-Anzeiger* . . . for 1860, 1861, and 1863.

42. The drafts of Wagner and Cosima Bülow can be found in RA.

43. Delbrück to the Police Chief, 22 Sept. 1861, and Police report on Bleichröder, 4 Oct. 1861, BLHA: Königl. Polizei-Präsidium, Acta betreffend Gerson Bleichröder, Rep. 30. On the title of Kommerzienrat, see Hartmut Kaelble, *Berliner Unternehmer während der frühen Industrialisierung. Herkunft, sozialer Status und politischer Einfluss* (Berlin, 1972), 273–75.

2 / Bismarck's Struggle for Survival

1. Quoted in Wilhelm Bothe, *Bismarcks Kampf mit dem preussischen Parlament 1862 bis 1866* (Breslau, 1932), p. 14. The best recent work on the constitutional conflict in Prussia is Heinrich August Winkler, *Preussischer Liberalismus und Deutscher Nationalstaat: Studien zur Geschichte der deutschen Fortschrittspartei, 1861–1866* (Tübingen, 1964); see also Eugene N. Anderson, *The Social and Political Conflict in Prussia, 1858–1864* (Lincoln, Nebr., 1954).

2. Holborn, *Modern Germany*, p. 141.

3. Bleichröder to Baron James, 11 March 1862, BA.

4. Böhme, *Deutschlands Weg*, pp. 116–120.

5. Recent historians, notably Böhme, have emphasized the coincidence of material interests between government and opposition—a fact that earlier historians tended to neglect. But the present exaggerated emphasis tends to underestimate the feeling of hopelessness generated by the 1862 situation: the deadlock could not have been overcome unless the terms of the conflict were redefined, something which none of the participants before Bismarck was able to do.

6. *GW*, XIV¹, 228.

7. The Bismarck literature is of course boundless. More than 7,000 works are listed in *Bismarck-Bibliographie. Quellen und Literatur zur Geschichte Bismarcks und seiner Zeit*, ed. by Karl Erich Born (Cologne, 1966). A good recent bibliography may be found in Walter Bussmann, *Das Zeitalter Bismarcks, 1852–1890* (Frankfurt am Main, 1968); and still one of the best analyses of Bismarck's views in 1862 is in chapters 2 and 3 of Egmont Zechlin, *Bismarck und die Grundlegung der deutschen Grossmacht* (2d ed.; Stuttgart, 1960), though he too slights Bismarck's necessary concern with material interests in politics.

8. The Bismarck literature, as mentioned before, is overwhelming. Aside from other works already mentioned, I found Gustav Schmoller's "Vier Briefe über Bismarcks sozial-politische und volkswirtschaftliche Stellung und Bedeutung," in *Zu Bismarcks Gedächtnis*, ed. by Gustav Schmoller, Max Lenz, and Erich Marcks (Leipzig, 1899), remarkably perceptive.

9. *GW*, II, 142.

10. Quoted in Zechlin, *Bismarck*, p. 369.

11. Kissinger makes a similar argument in his "The White Revolutionary," *Daedalus*, 97 (1968), 888–924.

12. Quoted in Robert Blake, *Disraeli* (London, 1966), p. 430.

13. Zechlin, *Bismarck*, pp. 369–75.

14. *APP*, III, 131–32.

15. *GW*, XIV¹, 223.

16. Leopold von Ranke, *Tagebücher*, ed. by Walther Peter Fuchs (Munich-Vienna, 1964), pp. 139–40.

17. *GW*, XIV¹, 223.

18. *GW*, IV, 28–33.

19. On this episode, see the spirited essay by Ludwig Dehio, "Bismarck und die Heeresvorlagen der Konfliktszeit," *HZ*, 144 (1931), 31–47.

20. Theodore S. Hamerow, *The Social Foundations of German Unification, 1858–1871: Struggles and Accomplishments* (Princeton, 1972), pp. 158–59.

21. Schmoller, "Vier Briefe," p. 17.

22. Jacob Toury, *Die politischen Orientierungen der Juden in Deutschland: von Jena bis Weimar* (Tübingen, 1966), p. 115.

23. A recent sociological study of the parliament of 1862 estimated that more than 80 percent of the Diet's members were wealthy, either by income or by capital. Adalbert Hess, *Das Parlament das Bismarck widerstrebte: zur Politik und sozialen Zusammensetzung des preussischen Abgeordnetenhauses der Konfliktszeit, 1862–1866* (Cologne and Opladen, 1964), p. 56.

24. Bleichröder to Baron James, 24 Sept. 1862, RA.

25. Quoted in Otto Pflanze, *Bismarck and the Development of Germany: The Period of Unification, 1815–1871* (Princeton, 1963), p. 177.

26. Bleichröder to Baron James, 30 Dec. 1862; 18, 24 Jan. 1863, RA.

27. *Ibid.*, 25 Jan., 9 Feb. 1863, RA.

28. Zechlin, *Bismarck*, p. 436; Bleichröder to Baron James, 21 Feb. 1863, RA.

29. Heinrich von Sybel, who in 1863 attacked Bismarck for his Polish policy, later wrote this representative *laudatio*: "by interfering against the Polish insurrection she [Prussia] secured the true friendship of Russia." Sybel, *The Founding of the German Empire by William I* (New York, 1890–1898), III, 431. A notable exception is of course A. J. P. Taylor, *Bismarck: The Man and the Statesman* (New York, 1955), pp. 65–66, who in this instance, as in so many others, overturned conventional views. See also Pflanze's judicious summary, *Bismarck*, pp. 185–89.

30. Bleichröder to Baron James, 21 Feb. 1863, RA.

31. H. Schulthess, ed., *Europäischer Geschichtskalender, 1860–1940* (81 vols.: Nördlingen, 1861–1941), *1863*, pp. 123–24; and Irmgard Goldschmidt, *Der polnische Aufstand von 1863 in den Verhandlungen des Preussischen Abgeordnetenhauses* (Cologne, 1937).

32. Roon to Bismarck, 1 March 1863, DZA: Merseburg: Zitelmann Nachlass.

33. Bleichröder to Baron James, 28 Feb. 1863, RA.

34. I. Goldschmidt, *Der polnische Aufstand*, p. 29; *APP*, III, 239–335 *passim*.

35. Bleichröder to Paris Rothschilds, 22 Feb., 9 and 10 March, 9 April 1863, RA.

36. Cf. Herbert Rothfritz's important study, *Die Politik des Preussischen Botschafters Grafen Robert von der Goltz in Paris, 1863–1869* (Berlin-Grünewald, 1934); and Otto Graf zu Stolberg-Wernigerode, *Robert Heinrich Graf von der Goltz. Botschafter in Paris 1863–1869* (Berlin, 1941).

37. Bleichröder to Paris Rothschilds, 15 May 1863, RA.

38. *GW*, XIV², 639.

39. Cf. Pflanze, *Bismarck*, pp. 192–212.

40. *Gedanken*, I, 287.

41. Bleichröder to Baron James, 17 May 1863, RA.

42. Schulthess, *Geschichtskalender, 1863*, pp. 130–31.

43. Quoted in Bothe, *Bismarcks Kampf*, p. 49.

44. See Pflanze, *Bismarck*, pp. 207–12.

45. Bleichröder to Paris Rothschilds, 24 May 1863, RA.

46. Quoted in Hamerow, *German Unification . . . Struggles*, p. 164.

47. Bleichröder to Paris Rothschilds, 24 May 1863, RA.

48. *Ibid.*, 9 and 3 June 1863, RA.

49. Quoted in Bothe, *Bismarcks Kampf*, p. 52.

50. On the "crisscrossing of doctrines and practices during the era of national unification" as exemplifying "the new statecraft of opportunism," see Hamerow, *German Unification . . . Struggles*, p. 192 and ch. 5 *passim*, as well as Böhme, *Deutschlands Weg*, pp. 120–38.

51. Bleichröder to Paris Rothschilds, 9 June 1863, RA.

52. *Ibid.*, 28 Sept. 1863, RA.

53. Hans-Joachim Schoeps extols Bismarck's achievement, which he thought no other Prussian statesman could have duplicated. "Der Frankfurter Fürstentag und die öffentliche Meinung in Preussen," *GWU*, 19 (1968), 73–90.

54. Bleichröder to Baron James, 1 May 1863, RA.

55. Bleichröder to Paris Rothschilds, 29 Sept. 1863, RA.

56. *Ibid.*, 19 Nov. 1863, RA.

57. *Gedanken*, I, 297–98.

58. Robert von Keudell, *Fürst und Fürstin Bismarck: Erinnerungen aus den Jahren 1846–1872* (Berlin and Stuttgart, 1901), pp. 194–95.

59. The Bleichröder and Bismarck archives contain many requests from either side for an interview. As one example, we may take Bleichröder's letter to Bismarck, 24 Feb. 1864 (FA), in which he asked for an appointment because he had received a new letter. From a letter to Baron James, we know that he did see Bismarck the next day, and we may safely assume that Bleichröder saw Bismarck even more often that he reported to Baron James.

60. *GW*, V, 474.

61. *GW*, VII, 66.

62. Fritz Hellwig, *Der Kampf um die Saar, 1860–1870: Beiträge zur Rheinpolitik Napoleons III* (Leipzig, 1934), pp. 152–56. According to Hellwig, Bleichröder's proposal was discussed by the cabinet.

63. Hans-Joachim von Collani, *Die Finanzgebarung des preussischen Staates zur Zeit des Verfassungskonfliktes, 1862–1866* (Düsseldorf, 1939), p. 26. Cf. also Pflanze's unsatisfactory account, *Bismarck*, p. 263.

64. Schulthess, *Geschichtskalender, 1863*, pp. 146–47.

65. Bleichröder to Baron James, 21 Dec. 1863, RA.

66. *SBHA*, 15 Jan. 1864, IX, pp. 525–38.

67. Lothar Wickert, ed., *Theodor Mommsen-Otto Jahn: Briefwechsel, 1842–1868* (Frankfurt, 1962), p. 302. Mommsen applied the *Faust* quotation to Bismarck even after the latter's dismissal in 1890.

68. Károlyi to Rechberg, 22 Jan. 1864, HHSA: PA III: Preussen.

69. Bleichröder to Baron James, 21 Dec. 1863, RA.

70. Bleichröder to Paris Rothschilds, 29 Jan. 1864, RA.

71. Kenneth Bourne, *The Foreign Policy of Victorian England, 1830–1902* (Oxford, 1970), pp. 107–10. See also Keith A. P. Sandiford, "The British Cabinet and the

Schleswig-Holstein Crisis, 1863–1864," *History*, 58 (1973), 360–83.

72. Collani, *Die Finanzgebarung*, pp. 26–27.

73. Paul H. Emden, *Money Powers of Europe in the Nineteenth and Twentieth Centuries* (London, 1937), p. 397.

74. Bleichröder to Baron James, 4 Feb. 1864, RA.

75. Bleichröder to Paris Rothschilds, 17 and 19 Feb. 1864, RA.

76. For Bismarck's meeting with Bodelschwingh, see Horst Kohl, ed., *Fürst Bismarck: Regesten zu einer wissenschaftlichen Biographie des ersten deutschen Reichskanzlers*, 2 vols. (Leipzig, 1891–1892), I, 222–24.

77. Oswald Schneider, *Bismarcks Finanz- und Wirtschaftspolitik* (Munich, 1912), pp. 1–3.

78. *Denkwürdigkeiten aus dem Leben des General-Feldmarschalls Kriegsministers Grafen von Roon*, 4th ed., 3 vols. (Breslau, 1897), II, 210, 214–15.

79. Bleichröder to Paris Rothschilds, 25 Feb. 1864, RA.

80. Bleichröder to Bismarck, 14 March 1864, SA.

81. Christopher Hibbert, *Garibaldi and His Enemies: The Clash of Arms and Personalities in the Making of Italy* (Boston, 1966), pp. 338–44.

82. Bleichröder to Baron James, 14 March 1864, RA.

83. Collani, *Die Finanzgebarung*, p. 27.

84. *Ibid.*

85. Bleichröder to Paris Rothschilds, 5 May 1864, RA.

86. Bleichröder to Bismarck, 6 May 1864, FA.

87. Original-Protokolle über die Sitzungen des Preussischen Staats-Ministeriums, 12 June 1864, DZA: Merseburg: Rep. 90a.

88. Collani, *Die Finanzgebarung*, p. 29.

89. *Ibid.*, pp. 29–30.

90. *Ibid.*, p. 31.

91. Chotek to Rechberg, 14 June 1864, HHSA: PA III: Preussen.

92. Wolfgang Zorn, "Wirtschafts- und sozialgeschichtliche Zusammenhänge der deutschen Reichsgründungszeit (1850–1879)," in H.-U. Wehler, ed., *Moderne deutsche Sozialgeschichte* (Cologne and Berlin, 1966), pp. 254–70.

93. Original-Protokolle über die Sitzungen des Preussischen Staats-Ministeriums, 6 July 1864, DZA: Merseburg: Rep. 90a.

94. *Ibid.*, 12 July 1864.

3 / Between the Throne and the Gallows

1. Pflanze, *Bismarck*, p. 237.

2. Lionel Trilling, ed., *The Selected Letters of John Keats* (New York, 1951), p. 92.

3. The phrase comes from Rudolf Stadelmann, *Das Jahr 1865 und das Problem von Bismarcks Deutscher Politik* (Munich, 1933), p. 41.

4. He was presumably referring to the petition of Arnim-Boitzenburg, which demanded either annexation or the establishment of a Prussian Protectorate. It received "20,000 signatures, chiefly from conservatives and right-wing liberals." Pflanze, *Bismarck*, p. 266.

5. Bleichröder to Baron James, 13 May 1864, RA.

6. *Ibid.*, 7 Sept. 1864, RA.

7. *GW*, IV, 545.

8. *Ibid.*, p. 484.

9. *Ibid.*, p. 554.

10. Bleichröder to Bismarck, 3 Aug. 1864, DZA: Merseburg: Keudell Nachlass.

11. Roon, *Denkwürdigkeiten*, II, 258.

12. Bleichröder to Baron James, 9 Dec. 1864, RA.

13. Roon, *Denkwürdigkeiten*, II, 268.

14. Bleichröder to Baron James, 26 Oct. 1864, RA.

15. Pflanze, *Bismarck*, p. 271.

16. Roon, *Denkwürdigkeiten*, II, 326–27, 387–88.

17. *GW*, X, 235–41.

18. Schulthess, *Geschichtskalender, 1865*, pp. 156–66; and Collani, *Die Finanzgebarung*, p. 31.

19. *GW*, X, 252.

20. Bleichröder to Keudell, undated June 1865; Keudell to Bleichröder, undated June 1865, BA. Bleichröder to Baron James, 5 and 9 June 1865, RA.

21. *DPO*, IV, 371–82.

22. *Ibid.*, p. 387.

23. *GW*, V, 95.

24. *APP*, V, 700.

25. *Ibid.*, p. 701.

26. Hermann von Goldschmidt, *Einige Erinnerungen aus längst vergangenen Tagen* (Vienna, 1917), pp. 7–13.

27. Chester W. Clark, *Franz Joseph and Bismarck: The Diplomacy of Austria before the War of 1866* (Cambridge, Mass., 1934), p. 212.

28. Goldschmidt to Bleichröder, 1 March 1865, BA.

29. *Ibid.*, 7 March 1865, BA. A copy of this letter, without the name of sender or recipient, was found in the files of the Prussian Foreign Office and was reprinted in *APP*, V, 753–54, where it was misdated 14 March 1865. Apparently Bleichröder had sent a copy of Goldschmidt's letter to Bismarck, who in turn had passed it on to Thile with the comment "for the files."

30. Goldschmidt to Bleichröder, 9 March 1865, BA.

31. *Ibid.*, 11 March 1865, BA.

32. Keudell to Bleichröder, 14 and 16 March 1865, BA.

33. *APP*, V, 752–54.

34. Goldschmidt to Bleichröder, 11 March 1865, BA.

35. *DPO*, IV, 606.

36. Bleichröder to Baron James, 19 March 1865, RA.

37. *DPO*, IV, 638.

38. *Ibid.*, p. 733.

39. Protocol der Conseils-Sitzungen, Kronrat, 19 June 1865, DZA: Merseburg: Rep. 90a.

40. Münch, *Hansemann*, pp. 81–82.

41. Bleichröder to Baron James, 5 June 1865, BA.

42. Keudell, *Fürst und Fürstin Bismarck*, p. 211.

43. *GW*, XIV², 697.

44. Adolf Beer, *Die österreichische Handelspolitik im 19. Jahrhundert* (Vienna, 1891), pp. 332–33; and Clark, *Franz Joseph and Bismarck*, p. 278.

45. John C. G. Röhl, "Kriegsgefahr und Gasteiner Konvention. Bismarck, Eulenburg und die Vertagung des preussisch-österreichischen Krieges im Sommer 1865," in *Deutschland in der Weltpolitik des 19. und 20. Jahrhunderts*, ed, by Imanuel Geiss and Bernd Jürgen Wendt (Düsseldorff, 1973), pp. 89–103, bases his argument on unpublished Bismarck letters to Fritz Eulenburg.

46. *GW*, XIV², 699.

47. Röhl, "Kriegsgefahr," p. 97.

48. *Ibid.*, p. 98.

49. Alexander Bergengruen, *Staatsminister August Freiherr von der Heydt* (Leipzig, 1908), pp. 40–53, and police report of 18 Dec. 1865, on Bleichröder's activity on behalf of the Cologne-Minden Railroad: BLHA: Königl. Polizei-Präsidium, Acta betreffend Gerson Bleichröder, Rep. 30. Hamerow, *German Unification . . . Struggles*, pp. 24–27.

50. Bleichröder's original memorandum of 20 Dec. 1862, which has never before been noted, together with other documents relating to the Cologne-Minden Railroad, is contained in the files of the Ministerium der öffentlichen Arbeiten, DZA: Merseburg: Rep. 93C.

51. Schulthess, *Geschichtskalender, 1865*, p. 174; others claim August 10 as the date the contract was signed and therefore fail to see its full implications for Bismarck's policy.

52. Collani, *Die Finanzgebarung*, pp. 40–41.

53. *GW*, V, 240.

54. Roon, *Denkwürdigkeiten*, II, 354–55.

55. Chotek to Mensdorff, 12 Aug. 1865, HHSA: PA III: Preussen.

56. Bleichröder to Bismarck, 19 July 1865, DZA: Merseburg: Zitelmann Nachlass.

57. *APP*, VI, 318.

58. Röhl, "Kriegsgefahr," p. 102.

59. Friedrich Ferdinand Graf von Beust, *Aus drei Viertel-Jahrhunderten: Erinnerungen und Aufzeichnungen, 1809–1885* (Stuttgart, 1887), I, 279.

60. *GW*, V, 271.

61. Chotek to Mensdorff, 15 Sept. 1865, HHSA: PA III: Preussen.

62. Goldschmidt to Bleichröder, 25 Sept. 1865, BA.

63. Böhme emphasizes this point, but adduces insufficient evidence. *Deutschlands Weg*, chapters 2 and 3, *passim*.

64. *DPO*, V¹, 4.

65. Stadelmann, *Das Jahr 1865*, p. 54.

66. Schwabach to Paris Rothschilds, 11 Sept. 1865, BA.

67. *GW*, V, 299.

68. *Ibid.*, pp. 309, 316.

69. Bertrand Gille, *Histoire de la Maison Rothschild*, 2 vols. (Paris, 1965–1967), II, *1848–1870*, p. 449, and Kohl, *Bismarck-Regesten*, I, 265.

70. *APP*, VI, 420.

71. Stadelmann, *Das Jahr 1865*, pp. 16–17.

72. On the Austrian loan, see Lawrence D. Steefel, "The Rothschilds and the Austrian Loan of 1865," *JMH*, 8 (1936), 27–39; for the loan in the context of French policy, see the fine study by E. Ann Pottinger, *Napoleon III and the German Crisis, 1865–1866* (Cambridge, Mass., 1966), pp. 42–47.

73. Goldschmidt's letter is not included in the BA, but see Clark, *Franz Joseph and Bismarck*, p. 312.

74. *DPO*, V¹, 52.

75. Eyck, *Bismarck*, II, 105.

76. Roon, *Denkwürdigkeiten*, II, 380, 319.

77. Chotek to Mensdorff, 7 Oct. and 20 Nov. 1865, HHSA: PA III: Preussen.

78. *GW*, X, 256.

79. *SBHA*, 19 Jan. 1866, I, pp. 15–31.

80. Eyck, *Bismarck*, II, 118.

81. Roon, *Denkwürdigkeiten*, II, 420.

82. Julius Heyderhoff, ed., *Deutscher Liberalismus im Zeitalter Bismarcks. Eine politische Briefsammlung* (2nd ed., Osnabrück, 1967), I, 273.

83. Bleichröder to Paris Rothschilds, 3 Feb. 1866, RA.

84. *GW*, X, 209.

85. *Ibid.*, p. 264.

86. *APP*, VI, 615, 617.

87. Heyderhoff, *Deutscher Liberalismus*, I, 286.

88. Roon, *Denkwürdigkeiten*, II, 400–401.

89. Collani, *Die Finanzgebarung*, p. 45.

90. Goldschmidt to Bleichröder, 11 and 18 Feb. 1866, BA.

91. Heinrich Friedjung, *Der Kampf um die Vorherrschaft in Deutschland, 1859–1866* (Stuttgart, 1897–1898), I, 165. It is clear that Hohenthal was warned of a Prussian invasion in case of war. His source may have been a high Prussian officer rather than Bleichröder— or perhaps both. *DPO*, V¹, 267, 273–74.

92. *DPO*, V¹, 253, 400–401.

93. Goldschmidt to Bleichröder, 17 March 1866, BA.

94. *Ibid.*, 20, 26, 31 March, and 1 May 1866, BA.

95. Clark, *Franz Joseph and Bismarck*, pp. 375–79.

96. Quoted in Richard Millman, *British Foreign Policy and the Coming of the Franco-Prussian War* (Oxford, 1965), p. 13.

97. Fritz Löwenthal, *Der preussische Verfassungsstreit, 1862–1866* (Munich, 1914), p. 276.

98. Quoted in Walter Reichle, *Zwischen Staat und Kirche: Das Leben und Wirken des preussischen Kultusministers Heinrich v. Mühler* (Berlin, 1938), p. 174.

99. Baron James to Bleichröder, 25 May 1862, RA.

100. Corti, *Haus Rothschild*, pp. 422–28; Pottinger, *Napoleon III*, p. 123, on Rothschild's lament, and pp. 82–105, on French expectations of Austrian victory; for similar German sentiments, see Böhme, *Deutschlands Weg*, pp. 197–207.

101. Bleichröder to Baron James, 16 Feb. 1866, RA.

102. Cf. Hellwig, *Der Kampf*, pp. 161–62.

103. *DPO*, V¹, 215–16.

104. Bleichröder to Bismarck, 9 March 1866, FA.

105. Bodelschwingh to Bleichröder, 12 March 1866, BA.

106. Bleichröder to Paris Rothschilds, 17 March 1866, BA.

107. Schulthess, *Geschichtskalender, 1866*, p. 167; and Hellwig, *Der Kampf*, p. 170.

108. Reichle, *Mühler*, p. 172.

109. *APP*, VI, 728.

110. *GW*, V, 415.

111. *APP*, VI, 731–32.

112. *GW*, V, 451.

113. *APP*, VI, 645.

114. Reichle, *Mühler*, p. 173.

115. Béhaine to Bleichröder, 7 April 1866, BA.

116. Bleichröder to Baron Lionel Rothschild, 11 and 13 April 1866, RA, New Court Archive. These letters were shown to Professor Landes, who prepared summaries of them, which he kindly gave me. The London Rothschilds declined to make more than a few letters and a few additional transcriptions available.

117. Jürgen Schuchardt, "Die Wirtschaftskrise vom Jahre 1866 in Deutschland," *Jahrbuch für Wirtschaftsgeschichte*, II (East Berlin, 1962), 91–141.

118. Reichle, *Mühler*, p. 173.

119. *OD*, VIII, 78.

120. Baron James to Bleichröder, 3 and 15 April 1866, BA; Bleichröder to Baron James, 18 April 1866, RA.

121. Hellwig, *Der Kampf*, pp. 225, 169.

122. *GW*, V, 474–75.

123. Few historians have noted this cabinet session. Preussisches Staats-Ministerium, Staats-Ministerial Sitzungs-Protokolle, 2 May 1866, DZA: Merseburg: Rep. 90a.

124. It is interesting to note that on 28 Aug. 1866 the state ministry urged that the question be reopened, and that on 16 Jan. 1867 the cabinet recommended to the king that because of changed conditions the project of selling the mines should be dropped. Staats-Ministerial Sitzungs-Protokolle, 28 Aug. 1866, and 16 Jan. 1867, DZA: Merseburg: Rep. 90a. Most of the archival material pertaining to the Saar mines in those years, filed under mining (Rep. 89 and 90), has been lost during or after World War II.

125. Hellwig, *Der Kampf*, pp. 174–75.

126. Goldschmidt to Bleichröder, 18 May 1866, BA.

127. Auszüge aus den Protokollen der Conseil- und Staats-Ministerial Berathungen, 3 May 1866, GFO: I.A.A.a 27, Vol. 1.

128. Rudolf von Delbrück, *Lebenserinnerungen 1817–1867*, 2 vols. (Leipzig, 1905), II, 370.

129. Schulthess, *Geschichtskalender, 1866*, p. 169. Alfred Stern, *Geschichte Europas von 1848 bis 1871* (Stuttgart and Berlin, 1923), III, 468.

130. Bleichröder to Paris Rothschilds, 2 May 1866, RA.

131. Georg Buss, *Die Berliner Börse von 1865–1913* (Berlin, 1913), p. 116.

132. Delbrück, *Lebenserinnerungen*, II, 371–72.

133. Löwenthal, *Preussischer Verfassungsstreit*, p. 275; cf. also Heinrich von Poschinger, ed., *Aktenstücke zur Wirthschaftspolitik des Fürsten Bismarck*, 2 vols. (Berlin, 1890–1891), II, 84–85.

134. Bleichröder to Baron Lionel Rothschild, 4 and 7 May, RA, New Court Archive.

135. Goldschmidt to Bleichröder, 5 and 11 May 1866, BA.

136. Benary to Bleichröder, 11 and 22 May 1866, BA.

137. The archives of the Prussian Foreign Office contain a note from Bleichröder to Bismarck, dated 9 May 1866, transmitting an important letter from Vienna. The letter has been lost or perhaps filed elsewhere, but may well have been from Benary or Goldschmidt. DZA: Merseburg: I.A.A.l. 41. sec.

138. Gordon A. Craig, *The Battle of Königgrätz: Prussia's Victory over Austria, 1866* (Philadelphia and New York, 1964), p. 6. This is a superb study of the battle and its significance.

139. Collani, *Die Finanzgebarung*, p. 45.

140. Münch, *Hansemann*, p. 116.

141. Bergengruen, *Heydt*, p. 327; Schulthess, *Geschichtskalender, 1866*, p. 169.

142. Collani, *Die Finanzgebarung*, p. 49.

143. *Ibid.*, p. 53.

144. Goltz to Bismarck, 21 May 1866, DZA: Merseburg: I.A.A.l. 41. sec.

145. Bleichröder to Rothschild, 26 May 1866, RA.

4 / A Banker's Share in Bismarck's Triumph

1. Zechlin, *Bismarck*, p. 341.

2. Keudell, *Fürst und Fürstin Bismarck*, pp. 263–64.

3. Heyderhoff, *Deutscher Liberalismus*, p. 312; Eyck, *Bismarck*, II, 203–4; Karl Twesten, *Was uns noch retten kann. Ein Wort ohne Umschweife* (Berlin, 1861), pp. 24, 52.

4. *GW*, VII, 131.

5. *GW*, XIV², 623.

6. *GW*, VII, 132.

7. Bergengruen, *Heydt*, pp. 322–24.

8. Cf. Heydt's memoranda, 1 Jan. 1865, 15 Feb. 1866, BA.

9. *GW*, IV, 373; V, 349–50; Otto Becker, *Bismarcks Ringen um Deutschlands Gestaltung*, ed. by Alexander Scharff (Heidelberg, 1958), 114–17.

10. Schuchardt, "Die Wirtschaftskrise," *Jahrbuch für Wirtschaftsgeschichte*, 2 (1962) 113.

11. Heydt to Bleichröder, 16 and 18 May, 1866, BA.

12. Auszüge aus den Protocollen der Conseil- und Staats-Ministerial Berathungen, 4 June 1866, GFO: I.A.A.a 27, Vol. 1.

13. Münch, *Hansemann*, p. 27.

14. *Ibid.*, p. 117.

15. Memorandum corrected in Bismarck's hand, June 1889, DZA: Potsdam: Reichskanzlei, Handel und Gewerbe, No. 18, Vol. 6.

16. Pflanze, *Bismarck*, p. 321.

17. Golo Mann, "The Second German Empire: The Reich That Never Was," in E. J. Feuchtwanger, ed., *Upheaval and Continuity: A Century of German History* (Pittsburgh, 1974), p. 31.

18. Quoted in Gustav Adolf Rein, *Die Revolution in der Politik Bismarcks* (Göttingen, 1957), p. 144.

19. Baudissin to Bleichröder, 22 May 1866, BA.

20. Oppenheim to Bleichröder, 14 and 21 June 1866, BA.

21. Bleichröder to Bismarck, 19 and 20 June 1866, FA; Heinrich von Poschinger, ed., *Erinnerungen aus dem Leben von Hans Viktor von Unruh* (Stuttgart, 1895), pp. 241-43.

22. For Bismarck's conversation with Unruh in 1866, see Poschinger, *Unruh*, pp. 243-50; for his conversation of 1859, *GW*, VII, 37-40; for his talk with the crown prince, *GW*, VII, 137.

23. Bleichröder to Paris Rothschilds, 21 June 1866, BA.

24. Bleichröder to Paris Rothschilds, 19 June 1866, RA.

25. Heyderhoff, *Deutscher Liberalismus*, p. 307.

26. Bleichröder to Paris Rothschilds, 25 June 1866, RA.

27. Bleichröder, Note, 29 June 1866, SA. On the Schönhausen Archive (SA), see ch. 12, note 14.

28. Craig, *Battle of Königgrätz*, p. 26.

29. *Ibid.*, pp. 163-64.

30. A familiar exclamation, quoted in Adam Wandruszka's excellent *Schicksalsjahr 1866* (Graz, 1966), p. 13.

31. See Karl Heinrich Höfele, "Königgrätz und die Deutschen von 1866," *GWU*, 17 (1966), 393-416.

32. Bleichröder to Bismarck, 4 July 1866, DZA: Merseburg: Keudell Nachlass.

33. *GW*, VI, 120.

34. Rein, *Die Revolution*, p. 148; Eduard von Wertheimer, *Bismarck im politischen Kampf* (Berlin, 1930), pp. 236-37.

35. *GW*, V, 537-38.

36. Bleichröder to Paris Rothschilds, 3 July 1866, RA.

37. Holborn, *Modern Germany*, p. 135; draft of a letter by Nicolas Kiss to Bismarck, 21 May 1866, Kossuth Nachlass, Budapest, National Archives I, 4405.

38. Bismarck's draft, 5 July 1866, DZA: Merseburg: I.A.A.l. 41. sec., and *GW*, VI, 37.

39. Wandruszka, *Schicksalsjahr*, p. 177.

40. Bleichröder to Bismarck, 8 July 1866, DZA: Merseburg: Keudell Nachlass.

41. *GW*, VI, 20.

42. Horst Kohl, ed., *Bismarck-Jahrbuch 1894-1899*, 6 vols. (Leipzig, 1894-1899), IV, 186.

43. Bleichröder to Bismarck, 18 July 1866, DZA: Merseburg: Keudell Nachlass.

44. Richard Schwemer, *Geschichte der freien Stadt Frankfurt a.M.*, Vol. III²: *1814-1866* (Frankfurt a.M., 1918), p. 349 and chs. 8, 9, *passim*.

45. Quoted in *ibid.*, p. 344.

46. Bleichröder to Keudell, 23 July 1866, DZA: Merseburg: Keudell Nachlass.

47. *GW*, VI, 63, 90; Eyck, *Bismarck*, II, 268-72.

48. Bismarck to Bleichröder, 25 July 1866, BA.

49. Schwemer, *Frankfurt*, p. 383.

50. Bleichröder to Paris Rothschilds, 8 July 1866, RA.

51. For the further course of the negotiations, see Schwemer, *Frankfurt*, ch. 9.

52. Bismarck to Bleichröder, 18 July 1866, BA.

53. Keudell to Bleichröder, 19 July 1866, BA.

54. Bleichröder to Keudell, 23 July 1866, DZA: Merseburg: Keudell Nachlass.

55. *Ibid.*

56. Cf. Bleichröder to Keudell, 29 June 1866, *ibid.*; Kohl, *Bismarck-Regesten*, I, 291.

57. Keudell, *Fürst und Fürstin Bismarck*, p. 367.

58. Bleichröder to Bismarck, 8 July 1866, DZA: Merseburg: Keudell Nachlass.

59. Schulthess, *Geschichtskalender, 1866*, p. 175; and Gerhard Ritter, "Die Entstehung der Indemnitätsvorlage von 1866," *HZ*, 114 (1915), 18-64.

60. Bleichröder to Paris Rothschilds, 8 Aug. 1866, RA.

61. Kissinger, "The White Revolutionary," *Daedalus*, 97 (1968), 888-924.

62. See "The Political Consequences of the Unpolitical German," in my *The Failure of Illiberalism: Essays on the Political Culture of Modern Germany* (New York, 1972), esp. pp. 11-15.

63. Quoted in Becker, *Bismarcks Ringen*, p. 258.

64. *GW*, VII, 140.

65. Goldschmidt to Bleichröder, 1 Aug. 1866, BA.

5 / Bismarck's Purse and Bleichröder's Place

1. Moritz Busch, *Tagebuchblätter* (3 vols., Leipzig, 1899), II, 65.

2. See Charlotte Sempell, "Unbekannte Briefstellen Bismarcks," *HZ*, 207 (1968), 609-16.

3. Michael Werner, ed., *Begegnungen mit Heine: Berichte der Zeitgenossen* (Hamburg, 1973), II, 241.

4. Quoted in Alfred Vagts, "Bismarck's Fortune," *CEH*, 1 (1968), 203-33. Vagts' article is one of the first serious summaries of Bismarck's financial dealings. It is necessarily incomplete and leans heavily on Ulrich Küntzel's rather inaccurate *Die Finanzen grosser Männer* (Vienna and Düsseldorf, 1964), pp. 447-511.

5. Sempell, "Briefstellen Bismarcks," pp. 609-13.

6. Bleichröder to Bismarck, 3 May 1859, SA and subsequent statements of account.

7. Küntzel, *Die Finanzen*, p. 477.
8. Bleichröder to Bismarck, 4 April 1859, 11 Jan. 1861, SA.
9. *Ibid.*, 11 April 1861.
10. Oppenheim to Bleichröder, 8 and 12 Nov. 1861, BA.
11. Bleichröder to Bismarck, 22 Jan. 1862, SA.
12. Küntzel, *Die Finanzen*, p. 478.
13. Bleichröder statement, 31 Dec. 1863, SA.
14. SA: Bleichröder file.
15. Bleichröder to Bismarck, 6 May 1863, SA.
16. *Ibid.*, 5 April 1864; statement of account, April-Sept. 1864.
17. Bleichröder to Bismarck, 12 Sept. 1864; statement, 31 May 1865, BA.
18. Bleichröder to Bismarck, 23 Nov. 1863, FA; Bleichröder to Zitelmann, 4, 5, 8 Dec. 1863, DZA: Merseburg: Zitelmann Nachlass. Bleichröder's other letters to Zitelmann were apparently lost; the Nachlass is lamentably thin.
19. Annual Statement, 31 Dec. 1866, SA.
20. Bleichröder to Bismarck, 4 July 1867, SA.
21. *Ibid.*, 12 July 1867.
22. Kohl, *Bismarck-Regesten*, I, 311–12.
23. *GW*, XIV², 725.
24. *Ibid.*, p. 729.
25. Ernst Westphal, *Bismarck als Gutsherr: Erinnerungen seines Varziner Oberförsters* (Leipzig, 1922), p. 12; Arnold Oskar Meyer, *Bismarck. Der Mensch und der Staatsmann* (Stuttgart, 1949), pp. 382–89.
26. A. O. Meyer, *Bismarck*, p. 382.
27. The words in quotation marks were in English in the original, *GW*, XIV², 761, 753.
28. *Ibid.*, pp. 727, 739.
29. Bernhard von Puttkamer to Bismarck, 28 Sept. 1867, BA.
30. *GW*, XIV², 725.
31. Westphal, *Bismarck*, p. 20.
32. *Ibid.*, pp. 48–49.
33. Busch, *Tagebuchblätter*, I, 468.
34. *Johanna von Bismarck. Ein Lebensbild in Briefen (1844–1894)* (Stuttgart, 1915), p. 215.
35. Bleichröder to Bismarck, 6 Sept. 1868, SA.
36. *Ibid.*, 6 Nov. 1867.
37. *Ibid.*, 6 Sept. 1868.
38. *Ibid.*, 15 Sept. 1868; also *GW*, XIV², 762.
39. See Münch, *Hansemann*, pp. 298–333; Siegfried von Kardorff, *Wilhelm von Kardorff: Ein Nationaler Parlamentarier im Zeitalter Bismarcks und Wilhelms II, 1828–1907* (Berlin, 1936), pp. 89–95.

40. Statement, July-December 1868, SA.
41. Bleichröder to Bismarck, 1 July, 31 Dec. 1869, SA.
42. Bleichröder to Paris Rothschilds, 25 Jan. 1868, RA.
43. Münch to Beust, 25 Sep. 1869, HHSA: PA III: Preussen.
44. Busch, *Tagebuchblätter*, I, 467.
45. Bleichröder to Bismarck, 25 Nov. 1869, SA.
46. Graf Hugo Lerchenfeld-Koefering, *Erinnerungen und Denkwürdigkeiten* (Berlin, 1935), p. 254.
47. Puttkamer to Bismarck, 28 Nov. 1867, 15 Jan. 1868, BA.
48. Puttkamer to Bismarck, 25 Nov. 1868, BA.
49. Bleichröder to Bismarck, 12 July 1867, 6 Sept. 1868, SA.
50. Struck to Bleichröder, 29 April 1870, BA.
51. Becker, *Bismarcks Ringen*, p. 185.
52. On the later phases of this, see Münch, *Hansemann*, pp. 138–48.
53. Julius to Gerson Bleichröder, 29 March 1864, April 1868, 1 June 1869, 2 July 1870, BA.
54. Police Report, 4 Oct. 1861, BLHA: Königl. Polizei-Präsidium, Acta betreffend Gerson Bleichröder, Rep. 30.
55. Baron James to Bleichröder, 8 May 1864, BA.
56. Bleichröder to Paris Rothschilds, 14 Oct. 1867, RA.
57. Goldschmidt to Bleichröder, 27 Aug. 1866, BA.
58. Bleichröder to Paris Rothschilds, 10 Nov. and 18 Dec. 1866, RA.
59. Bleichröder to Paris Rothschilds, 6 June 1868, RA.
60. Richard Freiherr von Friesen, *Erinnerungen aus meinem Leben* (Dresden, 1880), II, 305–6.
61. Bleichröder to Rothschild, 10 Nov. 1866, RA.
62. Kaskel to Bleichröder, 18 July 1866, BA.
63. Friesen, *Erinnerungen*, p. 340.
64. Bleichröder to Rothschilds, 18 and 22 Oct., 8 and 16 Nov., 1 and 17 Dec. 1866, RA.
65. Bleichröder to Rothschilds, 8 Nov. 1866, RA.
66. Saxon Minister in Berlin to Bleichröder, 15 Feb. 1870, BA.
67. Friesen, *Erinnerungen*. pp. 351–52.
68. Hans Philippi, "Zur Geschichte des Welfenfonds," *Niedersächsisches Jahrbuch für Landesgeschichte*, n.s., 31 (1959), 190–99; Eberhard Naujoks, "Bismarck und die Organisation der Regierungspresse," *HZ*, 205 (1967), 69.

69. Bleichröder to Bismarck, 1 Oct. 1869, SA.

70. *GW*, XIV², 762.

71. Bergengruen, *Heydt*, pp. 367–69; Bleichröder to Bismarck, 15 Oct. 1869, SA.

72. Bleichröder to Bismarck, 6 and 21 Nov. 1869, SA.

73. Friedrich Zunkel, *Der Rheinisch-Westfälische Unternehmer 1834–1879: Ein Beitrag zur Geschichte des deutschen Bürgertums im 19. Jahrhundert* (Cologne and Opladen, 1962), pp. 118–22.

74. Report to Bismarck, 18 Dec. 1865, BLHA: Königl. Polizei-Präsidium, Acta betreffend Gerson Bleichröder, Rep. 30. Also Bismarck to Itzenplitz, 26 Dec. 1865, Justizministerium, Bundesarchiv Koblenz. I owe this reference to Dr. Fred Grubel of the Leo Baeck Institute in New York.

75. Letter to Police Chief, 1 and 7 March, 20 May 1867, BLHA: Königl. Polizei-Präsidium, Acta betreffend Gerson Bleichröder, Rep. 30.

76. F. Eulenburg to Bleichröder, 7 May 1867, BA.

77. Zunkel, *Rheinisch-Westfälische Unternehmer*, p. 314.

78. Letters, 27 Aug., 15 and 16 Oct., 10 Nov. 1868, BLHA: Königl. Polizei-Präsidium, Acta betreffend Gerson Bleichröder, Rep. 30.

79. Memorandum to Bleichröder, 10 Oct. 1870, 31 March 1871, BA.

80. Rothschild to Bismarck, 12 Nov. 1863 (italics in original), SA; Rothschild to Bismarck, 30 Dec. 1863, SA.

81. August Eulenburg to Philipp Eulenburg, 31 May 1890, Bundesarchiv, Koblenz: Eulenburg Papers. I owe this reference to John Röhl.

82. Unfortunately, only a few letters have survived, though these are unusually suggestive. On Bismarck and Nesselrode, cf. Julius Heyderhoff, ed., *Im Ring der Gegner Bismarcks* (Leipzig, 1943), pp. 134, 191.

83. Nesselrode to Bleichröder, 17 July 1866; 21 May, 3 and 6 July 1867, BA.

84. Heinrich Otto Meisner, ed., *Denkwürdigkeiten des General-Feldmarschalls Alfred Grafen von Waldersee* (3 vols.; Stuttgart and Berlin, 1922–1923), I, 10.

85. Brandt to Bleichröder, 28 March 1870, BA.

86. Lasker to Bleichröder, 19 Dec. 1869, and 11 March 1870, BA.

87. Röder to Bleichröder, 4 May 1867, 28 March 1869, 26 Jan. 1870, BA.

88. *Ibid.*, 2 April 1870.

89. Rudolf Vierhaus, ed., *Das Tagebuch der Baronin Spitzemberg. Aufzeichnungen aus der Hofgesellschaft des Hohenzollernreiches* (Göttingen, 1960), p. 15.

90. *APP*, X, 223–24.

91. *Papiers et correspondance de la famille impériale* (Paris, 1870), I, 230–34. On Stoffel, see Vierhaus, *Spitzemberg*, p. 122.

92. Cf. Gille, *Maison Rothschild*, I: *Des Origines à 1848*, pp. 467–88, for a brief account of the Rothschilds' phenomenal social success.

93. Keudell to Bleichröder, 3 Jan., two letters, 11 Jan. 1868, BA.

94. F. Eulenburg to Bleichröder, 25 April 1869, BA.

95. Keudell to Bleichröder, 28 Dec. 1866, BA.

96. Receipt, 4 Oct. 1868, BA.

97. Vierhaus, *Spitzemberg*, p. 88.

6 / The Third War

1. Bleichröder to Rothschild, 22 March 1867, RA.

2. Benary to Bleichröder, 11 April 1867, BA.

3. Goldschmidt to Bleichröder, 26 April 1867, BA.

4. Brandeis to Bleichröder, 1 May 1867, BA.

5. Keudell to Bleichröder, 7 May 1867, BA.

6. Brandeis to Bleichröder, 16 May 1867, BA.

7. Bleichröder et Bismarck, 25 July 1867, FA. My italics.

8. Lehmann to Bleichröder, 14 Aug. 1867, BA.

9. Bleichröder to Bismarck, 2 Oct. 1868, SA.

10. *APP*, X, 223–24.

11. *Papiers de la famille impériale*, I, 230–34.

12. Busch, *Tagebuchblätter*, I, 303.

13. Münch to Beust, 13 March 1869, HHSA: PA III: Preussen.

14. Pflanze, *Bismarck*, ch. 17, "The Failure of the National Movement."

15. Münch to Beust, 9 Oct. 1869, HHSA: PA III: Preussen.

16. Lothar Gall, *Der Liberalismus als regierende Partei. Das Grossherzogtum Baden zwischen Restauration und Reichsgründung* (Wiesbaden, 1968), pp. 467–71.

17. *GW*, VI, 166–68; on this question, see Josef Becker, "Bismarck und die Frage der Aufnahme Badens in den Norddeutschen Bund im Frühjahr 1870. Dokumente zur Interpellation Laskers vom 24. Februar 1870," *Zeitschrift für die Geschichte des Oberrheins*, 119 (1971), 427–70.

18. Wimpffen to Beust, 21 May 1870, HHSA: PA III: Preussen.

19. Keudell, *Fürst und Fürstin Bismarck*, p. 419.

20. *GW*, VI², 202–3.

21. For a recent summary of the international repercussions of the Spanish turmoil, see Richard Konetzke, "Spanien, Die Vorgeschichte des Krieges von 1870 und die Deutsche Reichsgründung," *HZ*, 214 (1972), 580–613.

22. The Hohenzollern candidacy and the origins of the Franco-Prussian war have been the subject of great and still continuing controversy. The best recent summaries are Josef Becker, "Zum Problem der Bismarckschen Politik in der Spanischen Thronfrage 1870," *HZ*, 212 (1971), 529–607; and S. William Halperin, "The Origins of the Franco-Prussian War Revisited: Bismarck and the Hohenzollern Candidature for the Spanish Throne," *JMH*, 45 (1973), 83–91. The best work on all aspects of the war is Michael Howard's superb *The Franco-Prussian War: The German Invasion of France, 1870–1871* (New York, 1961).

23. Wimpffen to Beust, 19 March 1870, HHSA: PA III: Preussen.

24. Lawrence D. Steefel, *Bismarck, the Hohenzollern Candidacy, and the Origins of the Franco-German War of 1870* (Cambridge, Mass., 1962), p. 39.

25. Pflanze, *Bismarck*, p. 449.

26. J. Becker to author, 17 Oct. 1969. Bleichröder's involvement has been repeatedly alleged without evidence; see, for example, Bastian Schot, "Die Entstehung des Deutsch-Französischen Krieges und die Gründung des deutschen Reiches," in Helmut Böhme, ed., *Probleme der Reichsgründungszeit 1848–1879* (Cologne and Berlin, 1968), p. 276.

27. Brandt to Bleichröder, 9 July and 22 May 1870, BA.

28. Bleichröder to Rothschild, 25 and 29 June 1870, RA.

29. Bleichröder to Bismarck, 26 June 1870, SA.

30. Bismarck to Bleichröder, 1 July 1870, BA.

31. Bismarck to Bleichröder, 1 Oct. 1874, BA.

32. Bleichröder to Rothschild, 5 July 1870, RA.

33. John Morley, *The Life of William Ewart Gladstone* (Revised edition in 1 volume; New York, 1921), II, p. 325.

34. Hermann Oncken, *Die Rheinpolitik Kaiser Napoleons III von 1863 bis 1870 und der Ursprung des Krieges von 1870/71* (Stuttgart, 1926), III, 416. Georges Bonnin, ed., *Bismarck and the Hohenzollern Candidature for the Spanish Throne. The Documents in the German Diplomatic Archives* (London, 1957), p. 228, reprints a Bleichröder telegram that preceded this letter by a few hours; the word

Abberufung is mistranslated as "resignation" instead of "recall."

35. Bleichröder to Bismarck, 8 July 1870, FA.

36. Bleichröder to Rothschild, 6 July 1870, RA.

37. Bleichröder to Bismarck, 9 July 1870, GFO: Spanien 32. Also Bonnin, *Bismarck*, pp. 237–38.

38. Johanna von Bismarck to Bleichröder, BA.

39. *GW*, VI², 349.

40. Bleichröder to Rothschild, 11 July 1870, RA.

41. Corti, *Haus Rothschild*, p. 441.

42. Robert Howard Lord, *The Origins of the War of 1870: New Documents from the German Archives* (Cambridge, Mass., 1924), pp. 163, 178–80.

43. Waldersee to Brandt, 8 July 1870; Brandt to Bleichröder, 9 July 1870, BA. Cf. also Meisner, *Denkwürdigkeiten . . . Waldersee*, I, 75.

44. Perponcher to Bleichröder, 12 July 1870, BA.

45. *GW*, VI², 353.

46. On Bismarck's diplomatic counteroffensive on July 12 and 13, cf. William L. Langer's brilliantly probing essay, "Bismarck as Dramatist," in *Studies in Diplomatic History and Historiography in Honour of G. P. Gooch*, ed. by A. O. Sarkissian (London, 1961), pp. 199–216.

47. Lord, *Origins of the War*, pp. 60–61, 196.

48. Kriegstagebuch Herbert Bismarck, FA, Kapsel 28, 12 July 1870; I am grateful to Dr. Klaus-Peter Hoepke, who helped edit Herbert Bismarck's correspondence and who made this excerpt available to me.

49. See Langer, "Bismarck," and the recent brief summary in Jochen Dittrich, "Ursachen und Ausbruch des deutsch-französischen Krieges 1870–71," in *Reichsgründung 1870–71*, ed. by Theodor Schieder and Ernst Deuerlein (Stuttgart, 1970), pp. 88–91.

50. Howard, *Franco-Prussian War*, p. 57.

51. Münch, *Hansemann*, pp. 89–96; Hamerow, *German Unification . . . Struggles*, pp. 400–403.

52. Wimpffen to Beust, 13 Aug. 1870, HHSA: PA III: Preussen.

53. Goldschmidt to Bleichröder, 13, 19 July and 20 Aug. 1870, BA.

54. On this transformation of national sentiment, see Karl Heinrich Höfele, "Sendungsglaube und Epochenbewusstsein in Deutschland 1870–71," *Zeitschrift für Religions- und Geistesgeschichte*, 15 (1963), 265–76.

55. *Bismarck's Pen: The Life of Heinrich Abeken*, edited from his letters and journals by his wife, trans. by Mrs. Charles Edward Barrett-Lennard and M. W. Hoper (London, 1911), p. 292.

56. Otto Becker, *Bismarcks Ringen*, p. 797.

57. Wacker to Foreign Office, 5 Aug. 1870, GFO: Frankreich 70. Cf. also Walter Lipgens, "Bismarck, die öffentliche Meinung und die Annexion von Elsass und Lothringen 1870," *HZ*, 199 (1964), 64.

58. Thile to Keudell, 4 Aug. 1870; Keudell to Thile, 16 Aug. 1870, GFO: Frankreich 70; Günter Richter, *Friedrich von Holstein: Ein Mitarbeiter Bismarcks* (Lübeck and Hamburg, 1966), pp. 33–34.

59. Bernstorff to Foreign Office, 4 Aug. 1870, GFO: Frankreich 70: Geheim.

60. *Letters from Paris, 1870–1875*, written by C. de B., a political informant to the head of the London House of Rothschild, trans. and ed. by Robert Henrey (London, 1942), p. 72.

61. Perglas to Bleichröder, 29 July 1870, BA; Rudolf Lenz, *Kosten und Finanzierung des Deutsch-Französischen Krieges 1870–1871. Dargestellt am Beispiel Württembergs, Badens and Bayerns* (Boppard am Rhein, 1970), pp. 82–84.

62. Eberhard Weis, "Vom Kriegsausbruch zur Reichsgründung," *Zeitschrift für bayerische Landesgeschichte*, 33 (1970), 806–8.

63. Cf. Keudell to Bleichröder, 27 March 1872, quoted in Wilhelm Schüssler, "Das Geheimnis des Kaiserbriefes Ludwig II," *Geschichtliche Kräfte und Entscheidungen, Festschrift für Otto Becker* (Wiesbaden, 1954), p. 209. For a more cautious view of the connection between Prussian subsidies and the *Kaiserbrief*, see Hans Rall, "Bismarcks Reichsgründung und die Geldwünsche aus Bayern," *Zeitschrift für bayerische Landesgeschichte*, 22 (1959), 408–9.

64. Hans Philippi, review, *Niedersächsisches Jahrbuch für Landesgeschichte* n.s. 40 (1968), 194–97.

65. Otto Becker, *Bismarcks Ringen*, p. 798.

66. Augustus Loftus, *The Diplomatic Reminiscences of Lord Augustus Loftus, 1862–1879*, 2 vols. (London, Paris, and Melbourne, 1894–1895), I, 317–18.

67. Bleichröder to Keudell, 13 Aug. 1870, DZA: Merseburg: Keudell Nachlass.

68. Bleichröder to Baron Alphonse, 9 Sept. 1870, RA.

69. Bleichröder to London Rothschilds, 6 May 1871, RA, London.

70. Bleichröder to Mendel, 3 Dec. 1870, BA.

71. Bleichröder to Keudell, 13 Aug. 1870, DZA: Merseburg: Keudell Nachlass; Kurt

Rheindorf, *England und der deutsch-französische Krieg 1870–1871* (Bonn and Leipzig, 1923), pp. 44–45; Loftus, *Reminiscences*, I, 318; Bleichröder to Rothschild, 5 Sept. 1870, RA.

72. Bleichröder to Rothschild, 2 and 3 Sept. 1870, RA; Bleichröder to London Rothschilds, 2 Sept. 1870, RA, London; Münch, *Hansemann*, p. 90.

73. Bleichröder to Baron Alphonse, 19 Aug. 1870, RA; Brandeis to Bleichröder, 26 Aug. 1870, BA.

74. *Ibid.*, 7 Sept. 1870, BA.

75. All of Bleichröder's letters dated after September 15 bore a Rothschild stamp: "reçu à Paris, 18 février 1871"; RA.

76. Queen Elizabeth to Bleichröder, 3 Oct. 1870, BA.

77. Cf. the letters of 28 Dec. 1870 of the Central Committee of the German League for Relief to wounded or sick soldiers, BA.

78. L. Schneider, *Aus dem Leben Kaiser Wilhelms, 1849–1873*, 2 vols. in 1 (Berlin, 1888), II, 132–34.

79. William to Bleichröder, 28 Nov. 1870, BA.

80. Schneider to Bleichröder, 13 Jan. 1871, BA.

81. Johanna von Bismarck to Bleichröder, 30 Sept. 1870, BA.

82. Johanna von Bismarck to Bleichröder, 22 Nov. 1870, BA.

83. Schneider to Bleichröder, 19 Aug. 1870, BA.

84. Howard, *Franco-Prussian War*, pp. 227–28.

85. Schneider to Bleichröder, 22 Sept. 1870, BA.

86. Schneider, *Leben Kaiser Wilhelms*, II, 257.

87. Quoted in Busch, *Tagebuchblätter*, I, 217.

88. Howard, *Franco-Prussian War*, pp. 347–48.

89. *GW*, XIV², 793

90. Paul Hatzfeldt, *Hatzfeldts Briefe. Briefe des Grafen Paul Hatzfeldt an seine Frau, 1870–71* (Leipzig, 1907), p. 72. Busch, *Tagebuchblätter*, I, 214–15.

91. Cf. letters from Schneider to Bleichröder, BA.

92. Keudell to Bleichröder, 5 Sept. 1870, BA.

93. Cf. letters by Perponcher, Radziwill, Winterfelt; Bleichröder list of presents; Eulenburg to Bleichröder, BA.

94. Paul Bronsart von Schellendorff, *Geheimes Kriegstagebuch 1870–1871*, ed. by Peter Rassow (Bonn, 1954), p. 349.

95. Bleichröder to Keudell, 5 and 13 Aug. 1870, DZA: Merseburg: Keudell Nachlass.

96. Keudell to Bleichröder, 16 Aug. 1870, BA.

97. *GW*, VI², 442 ff.

98. Keudell, *Fürst und Fürstin Bismarck*, pp. 448–50.

99. *Der Briefwechsel zwischen Friedrich Engels und Karl Marx*, ed. by A. Bebel and Ed. Bernstein (Stuttgart, 1913), IV, 316.

100. The literature on the annexation question is immense; the recent controversy was sparked by Lipgens, "Bismarck," pp. 31–112. See also Lothar Gall, "Das Problem Elsass-Lothringen," in *Reichsgründung 1870–71*, ed. by Schieder and Deuerlein, pp. 366–85; for a review of the post-Lipgens literature, see p. 367.

101. Howard, *Franco-Prussian War*, pp. 181–82.

102. *GW*, VI², 454–55.

103. Howard, *Franco-Prussian War*, pp. 220–22.

104. On Bismarck's earlier press campaign, see Lipgens, "Bismarck," pp. 31–112.

105. Bleichröder to Keudell, 14 Aug. 1870, DZA: Merseburg: Keudell Nachlass.

106. Bleichröder to Keudell, 10 Sep. 1870; Keudell to Bleichröder, 11 Sept. 1870, GFO: Frankreich 70.

107. Bernstorff to Bismarck, 12 Sept. 1870, *ibid*. Bismarck may have been struck by the analogy because he spoke often and well of America in those days.

108. Mendel to Bleichröder, 13 Sept. 1870, BA. Unfortunately, Mendel's subsequent letters—till the end of December 1870—are not in the Bleichröder Archive, presumably because Bleichröder passed them on to the Foreign Ministry.

109. Keudell to Bleichröder, 29 Sept. 1870, BA.

110. Bronsart von Schellendorff, *Kriegstagebuch*, pp. 93–94.

111. Keudell to Bleichröder, 29 Sept. 1870, BA.

112. Thile to Bismarck, 14 Oct. 1870, GFO: Frankreich 70.

113. *Ibid.*, 26 Oct., 8 and 21 Nov. 1870.

114. Keudell to Bleichröder, 20 Oct. 1870, BA.

115. Bleichröder to Keudell, 28 Oct. 1870, DZA: Merseburg: Keudell Nachlass.

116. Goldschmidt to Bleichröder, 20 Aug. and 21 Oct. 1870, BA.

117. Schweinitz to Bismarck, 25 Oct. 1870, GFO: Frankreich 70. Keudell to Bleichröder, 3 Nov. 1870, BA.

118. *Ibid.*, 3 Nov. 1870, and 12 Dec. 1870, BA.

119. *Ibid.*, 13 Dec. 1870, BA. Cf. *Heinrich Abeken*, p. 297.

120. *GW*, VI², 625–28.

121. Keudell to Bleichröder, 18 Dec. 1870, BA.

122. Bleichröder to Bismarck, 13 Dec. 1870, FA.

123. On the anti-Bismarck and anti-German mood of the time, cf. Lipgens, "Bismarck," pp. 84–88; and W. E. Mosse, *The European Powers and the German Question 1848–1871. With Special Reference to England and Russia* (Cambridge, 1958), ch. 11, *passim*; Lord Odo Russell reported at this time to Granville, the Foreign Secretary, that he would no longer be surprised to see Bismarck "change the map of Europe far more than the Emperor Napoleon was expected to do," and he added "we must be prepared for many disagreeable surprises." *Ibid.*, p. 354.

124. Keudell to Bleichröder, 5 Sept. and 26 Nov. 1870, BA.

125. *Ibid.*, 12 Dec. 1870.

126. Bleichröder to Bismarck, 13 Dec. 1870, FA.

127. Albrecht von Stosch, *Denkwürdigkeiten. Briefe und Tagebuchblätter*, ed. by Ulrich von Stosch (Stuttgart, 1904), p. 227.

128. Cf. Mendel to Bleichröder, 29 Dec. 1870 and 1, 2, 8, 9, 14, 20, 21, 25 Jan. 1871, BA. Mendel also regularly briefed the Prussian Ambassador, Bernstorff, at this time.

129. Keudell to Bleichröder, 23 Jan. 1871, BA.

7 / Hubris in Versailles

1. For a recent summary of the conflict, see Eberhard Kolb, "Kriegführung und Politik, 1870–71," *Reichsgründung, 1870–71*, ed. by Schieder and Deuerlein, pp. 95–118, esp. pp. 95, 99, and 113.

2. Quoted in Hamerow, *German Unification . . . Struggles*, p. 419.

3. Richard Millman, *British Policy and the Coming of the Franco-Prussian War* (Oxford, 1965), p. 217.

4. Busch, *Tagebuchblätter*, I, 77.

5. *Ibid.*, I, 236; II, 161.

6. Lipman to Philippson, 21 Dec. 1870; Philippson to Bleichröder, 23 Dec. 1870, BA.

7. *GW*, VII, 479.

8. Stosch, *Denkwürdigkeiten*, p. 230.

9. Busch, *Tagebuchblätter*, II, 110.

10. *Ibid.*, p. 125.

11. Brandt to Bleichröder, 1 Feb. 1871; Richard Wentzel to Bleichröder, 31 Jan. 1871; Bülow to Bleichröder, 30 Jan. 1871, BA.

12. Busch, *Tagebuchblätter*, II, 155; Abeken to Bleichröder, 6 Feb. 1871, BA.

13. *GW*, VI², 691.

14. Stosch, *Denkwürdigkeiten*, p. 232.

15. Bleichröder to Paris Rothschilds, 12 Feb. 1871, RA.

16. Wimpffen to Beust, 13 Aug. 1870, HHSA: PA III: Preussen.

17. The reference to the precedent of 1815 is taken from the unpublished essay by David S. Landes, "The Great Indemnity."

18. *GW*, XIV², 793.

19. Auszüge aus den Protokollen der Conseil- und Staats-Ministerial Berathungen, 26 Sept. 1870, GFO: I.A.A.a. 27, Vol. I.

20. Oppenheim to Bleichröder, 20 Oct. 1870, BA.

21. Oppenheim to Bleichröder, 23 and 31 Jan. 1871, BA.

22. Auszüge aus den Protokollen der Conseil- und Staats-Ministerial Berathungen, 8 Feb. 1871, GFO: I.A.A.a. 27, Vol. I.

23. In this connection, it must regrettably be noted that Hans Herzfeld's *Deutschland und das geschlagene Frankreich, 1871: Friedensschluss, Kriegsentschädigung, Besatzungszeit* (Berlin, 1924), presents a tendentious account of peacemaking in 1871 in order to contrast German magnanimity with French meanness.

24. Hermann Oncken, ed., *Grossherzog Friedrich I von Baden und die deutsche Politik von 1854–1871: Briefwechsel, Denkschriften, Tagebücher* (2 vols.; Stuttgart, 1927), II, 365.

25. Meisner, *Denkwürdigkeiten . . . Waldersee*, I, 162.

26. Bronsart von Schellendorff, *Kriegstagebuch*, p. 348.

27. Oppenheim to Bleichröder, 14 Feb. 1871, BA.

28. Schwabach to Paris Rothschilds, 11 Feb. 1871, RA.

29. Brandeis to Bleichröder, 17 Feb. 1871, BA.

30. Bleichröder to Brandeis, 20 Feb. 1871, RA.

31. Lehmann to Bleichröder, 20 Feb. 1871, BA.

32. On Thiers, see Theodore Zeldin, *France, 1848–1945*, Vol. I: *Ambition, Love, and Politics* (Oxford, 1973), pp. 606, 610.

33. *GW*, VI², 705–6.

34. A. R. Allinson, ed., *The War Diary of the Emperor Frederick III, 1870–1871* (London, 1927), p. 312.

35. Meisner, *Denkwürdigkeiten . . . Waldersee*, I, 162; Busch, *Tagebuchblätter*, II, 169.

36. Loftus, *Reminiscences*, I, 328.

37. Jules Favre, *Gouvernement de la défense nationale du 29 janvier au 22 juillet 1871*, (Paris, 1875), III, 96.

38. *Ibid.*, pp. 96–97.

39. Allinson, *War Diary of the Emperor*, p. 313.

40. Rheindorf, *England und der Krieg*, pp. 156–57.

41. Allinson, *War Diary of the Emperor*, p. 325; and Corti, *Haus Rothschild*, pp. 446–53.

42. *GW*, VI², 708; Veit Valentin, *Bismarcks Reichsgründung im Urteil englischer Diplomaten* (Amsterdam, 1937), 452–55.

43. *GW*, XIII, 218.

44. See unidentified newspaper clipping in BA, and *Kölner Zeitung*, 23 Feb. 1871.

45. Keudell to Bleichröder, 20 Feb. 1871, BA.

46. Cf. Bleichröder to Paris Rothschilds, 17 Feb. 1871, asking that 1,800 francs be paid to Mr. Moulton, Hatzfeldt's father-in-law, RA. See also Hatzfeldt, *Briefe*, p. 73 and *passim*.

47. Bronsart von Schellendorff, *Kriegstagebuch*, pp. 348–49, 360–63.

48. Hermann Baumgarten and Ludwig Jolly, *Staatsminister Jolly* (Tübingen, 1897), p. 212.

49. Hatzfeldt, *Briefe*, p. 314; Keudell, *Fürst und Fürstin Bismarck*, p. 475; Kolb, "Kriegführung," p. 117.

50. Lehmann to Bleichröder, 20 Feb. 1871, BA.

51. Mendel to Bleichröder, 12 March 1871, BA.

52. Goldschmidt to Bleichröder, 9 and 18 March 1871, BA.

8 / A New Baron in a New Berlin

1. Quoted in Höfele, "Sendungsglaube und Epochenbewusstsein," *Zeitschrift für Religions- und Geistesgeschichte*, 15 (1963), 267.

2. Vierhaus, *Spitzemberg*, p. 121.

3. *From Max Weber: Essays in Sociology*, ed. by H. H. Gerth and C. Wright Mills (New York, 1946), p. 391.

4. Vierhaus, *Spitzemberg*, p. 127.

5. Akademie der Künste (Berlin), *Aspekte der Gründerzeit, 1870–1890* (Catalogue of Exhibit, 1974), pp. 45–46.

6. See my "Money, Morals, and the Pillars of Society," in *The Failure of Illiberalism*, esp. pp. 27–30.

7. *Berliner Städtisches Jahrbuch für Volkswirtschaft und Statistik*, Vol. 32 (Berlin, 1913), section B, p. 3; Vol. 4 (Berlin, 1878), p. 15; Vol. 15 (Berlin, 1890), p. 8.

8. *Carl Fürstenberg. Die Lebensgeschichte eines deutschen Bankiers, 1870–1914*, ed. by Hans Fürstenberg (Berlin, 1931), pp. 64–65.

9. Quoted in Gerhard Masur, *Imperial Berlin* (New York, 1970), p. 74.

10. *Ibid.*

11. Robert Michels, *Probleme der Sozialphilosophie* (Leipzig, 1914), p. 150; see also

Robert M. Berdahl's "New Thoughts on German Nationalism," *AHR*, 77 (1972), 65–70.

12. Michels, *Probleme*, p. 151.

13. Schwabach to Bleichröder, 14 Sept. 1871, BA.

14. Walter Bagehot, *Lombard Street: A Description of the Money Market* (New York, 1897), p. 267.

15. Hans-Ulrich Wehler, *Bismarck und der Imperialismus* (Cologne and Berlin, 1969), p. 97.

16. See Alfred Rubens, "The Rothschilds in Caricature," The Jewish Historical Society of England, *Transactions, 1968–1969*, 22 (1970), 76–87.

17. Fürstenberg, *Lebensgeschichte*, p. 56.

18. Ottmar von Mohl, *Fünfzig Jahre Reichsdienst. Lebenserinnerungen* (Leipzig, 1921), p. 46. Bismarck's father had spent many winters in Berlin at 53 Behrenstrasse, and Bismarck himself lived at various times of his life at 20 and 60 Behrenstrasse. See Dr. Georg Schmidt, *Schönhausen und die Familie von Bismarck* (Berlin, 1897), pp. 156, 167, 172.

19. Mohl, *Fünfzig Jahre*, p. 72.

20. See Georg Schweitzer's "Berliner Börse," in *Berliner Pflaster. Illustrierte Schilderungen aus dem Berliner Leben*, ed. by M. Reymond and L. Manzel (Berlin, 1891), p. 325.

21. Even Nietzsche, at the end of a clear philo-Semitic passage, wrote: "And perhaps the young stock-exchange Jew is altogether the most disgusting invention of mankind." Friedrich Nietzsche, *Werke*, ed. by Karl Schlechta (Munich, n.d.), I, 686.

22. Schwabach to Bleichröder, 11 Sept. 1871, BA.

23. Guttentag to Bleichröder, 13 Aug. 1871, BA.

24. Bismarck to Eulenburg, 8 March 1872, DZA: Merseburg: Königl. Herolds-Amt, Acta betreffend von Bleichröder: VI. B. 154.

25. Adels-Brief, 8 March 1872, *ibid*.

26. Lamar Cecil, "The Creation of Nobles in Prussia, 1871–1918," *AHR*, 75 (1970), 757–95.

27. *Allgemeine Zeitung des Judentums*, April 16, 1872.

28. Cf. *GW*, VIII, 462; Fürstenberg, *Lebensgeschichte*, p. 58.

29. Winifred Taffs, *Ambassador to Bismarck. Lord Odo Russell* (London, 1938), p. 302.

30. Fürstenberg, *Lebensgeschichte*, p. 57. Also Bleichröder to Bismarck, 22 Jan. 1871, SA.

31. Bleichröder to Bismarck, 13 March 1872, FA.

32. *GW*, XIV², 818–19.

33. Hillfried to Bleichröder, 13 Jan. 1873, BA.

34. Vierhaus, *Spitzemberg*, p. 16.

35. Quoted in Heinz Gollwitzer, *Die Standesherren. Ein Beitrag zur deutschen Sozialgeschichte* (Göttingen, 1964), p. 325.

36. Draft for a heraldic emblem, 21 March 1872, and undated description of it, DZA: Merseburg: Königl. Herolds-Amt, Acta betreffend von Bleichröder: VI. B. 154.

37. Georgiana Blakiston, *Lord William Russell and His Wife, 1815–1846* (London, 1972), pp. 337–38.

38. Lord Odo Russell to Viscount Enfield, 28 Sept. 1872, PRO: FO, 64/749.

39. Note by Granville, *ibid.*, 8 Oct. 1872.

40. Russell to Bleichröder, 12 Oct. 1872, BA.

41. Bleichröder to Bismarck, 21 Oct. 1872, FA. Also Bismarck's formal notification to Oberpräsident of Province of Brandenburg, 26 Nov. 1872, BLHA: Königl. Polizei-Präsidium, Acta betreffend Gerson Bleichröder, Rep. 30.

42. *Ibid.*, 17 Dec. 1870, 4 Oct. 1873, and 5 Nov. 1873: Bleichröder's applications re: Bavarian, Italian, and Brazilian decorations; 13 Dec. 1872: notification that Bleichröder's application to wear Saxon and Austrian decorations has been granted.

43. Schwabach letters of 8 Sept. 1871, 1 Oct. 1877, 6 Feb. 1878, *ibid.*, Acta betreffend Julius Leopold Schwabach, Rep. 30.

44. Kühlow notes, BA.

45. Roon, *Denkwürdigkeiten*, III, 358. It is not out of character that Roon's descendants recorded the fact of his having sold Gütergotz, but not the name of the buyer.

46. Information on sale prices from letter of Gerhard Küchler, Chairman, Landesgeschichtliche Vereinigung für die Mark Brandenburg, e. V., to author, 24 Feb. 1973.

47. On Gilly's remodeling of Gütergotz, see Hans Herzfeld, ed., *Berlin und die Provinz Brandenburg* (Berlin, 1968), p. 564.

48. Cf. Hans Rosenberg, "Die Pseudo-demokratisierung der Rittergutsbesitzerklasse," in *Moderne deutsche Sozialgeschichte*, ed. by Hans-Ulrich Wehler (Cologne and Berlin, 1966), pp. 287–308.

49. Roon to Bleichröder, 9 June 1875, BA.

50. Siebert to Bleichröder, 12 and 23 July 1883, BA.

51. Bleichröder to Bismarck, 13 Aug. 1877, SA.

52. Schneider to Bleichröder, 22 Aug. 1877, and several preceding letters, BA. M. Goldschmidt to Bleichröder, 15 Aug. 1877; he enclosed a clipping from *Neue Freie Presse*, 13 Aug. 1877, BA.

53. Fürstenberg, *Lebensgeschichte*, p. 91.

54. Marie von Bunsen, *Die Welt in der ich lebte. Erinnerungen aus glücklichen Jahren 1860–1912* (Leipzig, 1929), p. 49.

55. Mohl, *Fünfzig Jahre*, p. 87.

56. Alois Braudl, quoted in Karl Heinrich Höfele, ed., *Geist und Gesellschaft der Bismarckzeit (1870–1890)* (Göttingen, 1967), p. 221.

57. Theodor Fontane, *L'Adultera* (Berlin, 1891), p. 1.

58. Ernst Ludwig von Gerlach, *Aufzeichnungen aus seinem Leben und Wirken 1795–1877*, ed. by Jakob von Gerlach, Vol. II: *1848–1877* (Schwerin, 1903), p. 361.

9 / Imperial Style in Politics and Economics

1. On the functional use of his threat of resignation, see Michael Stürmer, "Staatsstreichgedanken im Bismarckreich," *HZ*, 209 (1969), 566–615.

2. *GW*, XIV^2, 921.

3. Russell to Salisbury, 15 April 1878, PRO: FO, 64/904, no. 269 secret.

4. K. Th. Zingeler, *Karl Anton Fürst von Hohenzollern* (Stuttgart and Leipzig, 1911), pp. 224, 226.

5. Lucius von Ballhausen, *Bismarck-Erinnerungen* (Stuttgart and Berlin, 1921), p. 236.

6. Friedrich Curtius, ed., *Denkwürdigkeiten des Fürsten Chlodwig zu Hohenlohe-Schillingsfürst*, (Stuttgart and Leipzig, 1907), II, 367.

7. Bleichröder to Bismarck, 20 Dec. 1872, FA.

8. *Ibid.*, 11 Dec. 1874, FA.

9. *Ibid.*, 11 and 19 Dec. 1874; cf. also Ernst Rudolf Huber, *Deutsche Verfassungsgeschichte seit 1789* (Stuttgart, 1969), IV, 1053–57, on the founding of the Reichsbank.

10. Bleichröder to Bismarck, 25 Oct. 1876, SA.

11. *Ibid.*, 3 Oct. 1877.

12. Wehler, *Bismarck*, p. 57. Helmut Böhme, "Big Business, Pressure Groups and Bismarck's Turn to Protectionism, 1873–1879," *Historical Journal*, 10 (1967), 221.

13. Imelmann to Bleichröder, 5 Sept. 1871, BA.

14. See the famous exposure of fraudulence, Otto Glagau, *Der Börsen- und Gründungs-Schwindel in Berlin*, 4th ed. (Leipzig, 1876), *passim*, which lists no other Bleichröder promotion.

15. 1 Oct. 1877, BLHA: Königl. Polizei-Präsidium, Acta betreffend Julius Leopold Schwabach, Rep. 30.

16. Dr. Manfred Pohl, "Die Deutsche Bank in der Gründerkrise (1873–1876)," *Deutsche Bank, Beiträge zu Wirtschafts- und Währungsfragen und zur Bankgeschichte*, no. 11, 1973.

17. The best rapid survey of the boom and the subsequent depression can be found in Wehler, *Bismarck*, esp. pp. 53–84.

18. I have discussed the cultural impact of the depression in my *Failure of Illiberalism*, pp. 26–57, and in "Capitalism and the Cultural Historian," in . . . *From Parnassus: A Volume of Essays for Jacques Barzun*, ed. by Dora B. Weiner and William R. Keylor, to be published by Harper & Row in the winter of 1976.

19. Thomas Mann, *Buddenbrooks. Verfall einer Familie* (Berlin, 1928), p. 209.

20. I owe this point to Otto Pflanze. *GW*, VI^3, 58–60.

21. See Helmut Böhme, "Big Business," pp. 224–25.

22. Bleichröder to Bismarck, 25 July 1873, 27 July 1874, SA.

23. Kardorff, *Kardorff*, pp. 22–25.

24. *Ibid.*, pp. 87, 86–115, and *passim*.

25. Kardorff to Bleichröder, 6 July 1871, BA.

26. Kardorff to Bleichröder, 18 Jan. 1876, BA.

27. Friedenthal to Bleichröder, 29 Oct. 1877, BA.

28. Kardorff to Bleichröder, 1 April 1887, BA; see also Kardorff, *Kardorff*, pp. 192–93, for a different account of his financial straits, ignoring Bleichröder's role altogether and making no mention of the connection between Kardorff's personal fortune and his support of a particular legislation.

29. From April through July 1887, there were ten letters to Bleichröder dealing with Kardorff's tangled affairs, BA.

30. Kardorff to Bleichröder, 18 Aug. 1875, BA.

31. Oppenheim to Bleichröder, 24 June 1875, BA.

32. *Kreuzzeitung*, 29 June 1875, returned by H. von Bismarck to Bleichröder, BA.

33. Kardorff to Bleichröder, 3 July 1875, BA.

34. Bleichröder to H. von Bismarck, 29 June 1875, FA.

35. H. von Bismarck to Bleichröder, 1 July 1875, BA. An earlier draft, corrected by the chancellor himself, is to be found in the Bismarck Archive. At the time, Otto von Bismarck was also contemplating a suit against the *Kreuzzeitung* but hesitated because the paper might benefit from a "sensational trial." *GW*, VI^3, 61–62.

36. Bleichröder to H. von Bismarck, 5 July 1875, FA.

37. Lucius, *Bismarck*, p. 78.

38. Bismarck to Delbrück, 23 Oct. 1875, GFO: I.A.A.a. 50, Vol. I.

39. Kardorff to Bleichröder, 29 Aug. 1875, BA.

40. Oppenheim to Bleichröder, 31 Oct. 1875, BA.

41. Bleichröder to Bismarck, 7 Nov. 1875, SA.

42. Rothschild to Bleichröder, 13 Feb. 1876, BA.

43. Delbrück to William, 31 Aug. 1875, DZA: Merseburg: Zivilkabinett, Rep. 89H III, Vol. 6; see also for extensive intragovernment correspondence concerning Oppenheim's petition of 30 June 1875.

44. Ivo Nikolai Lambi, *Free Trade and Protection in Germany, 1868–1879* (Wiesbaden, 1963), pp. 115–16.

45. Kardorff to Bleichröder, 6 Feb. 1876, 15 Sept. 1877, BA.

46. Rothschild to Bleichröder, 16 April 1876, BA.

47. *Ibid.*, 9 Oct. 1876.

48. *Ibid.*, 17 April 1876.

49. Lucius, *Bismarck*, pp. 76–78, 87.

50. Lucius to Bismarck, 2 July 1876, GFO: I.A.A.a. 50, Vol. II.

51. Kardorff, *Kardorff*, pp. 100–101.

52. A. Oppenheim to Bleichröder, 4 Sept. 1876, BA.

53. Rothschild to Bleichröder, 27 Oct. 1876, BA.

54. Eulenburg to Bismarck, 25 Oct. 1876, GFO: I.A.A.a. 50, Vol. I.

55. Bismarck to Bleichröder, 31 Jan. 1877, BA; Bleichröder to Bismarck, 31 Jan. 1877, FA.

56. Bleichröder to Bismarck, 30 April 1877, FA.

57. Fürst Nikolai Orloff, *Bismarck und Katharina Orloff. Ein Idyll in der hohen Politik* (Munich, 1936), p. 164.

58. A. J. P. Taylor, *Bismarck*, p. 137.

59. Lucius, *Bismarck*, p. 110.

60. Kohl, *Bismarck-Regesten*, II, 140.

61. Lucius, *Bismarck*, p. 137.

62. Bismarck to William, 7 Oct. 1876, DZA: Merseburg: Zivilkabinett, Rep. 89H III, Vol. 6.

63. Karl W. Hardach, *Die Bedeutung wirtschaftlicher Faktoren bei der Wiedereinführung der Eisen- und Getreidezölle in Deutschland 1879* (Berlin, 1967), who stresses this point.

64. Christoph von Tiedemann, *Sechs Jahre Chef der Reichskanzlei unter dem Fürsten Bismarck*, 2nd ed. (Leipzig, 1910), p. 355.

65. Varnbüler to Bismarck, 29 June 1877, GFO: I.A.A.a. 50, Vol. II.

66. Varnbüler to Bleichröder, 20 June 1875, 29 Oct. 1879, 19 Nov. 1879, BA.

67. Bülow to Bismarck, 25 Dec. 1877, DZA: Potsdam: Reichskanzlei, Akten betreffend die deutsche Handels- und Wirtschafts-Reform 1877–1888, No. 408 Vol. 1.

68. Schwartzkopf to Bleichröder, 4 June 1877, BA.

69. Bleichröder to H. von Bismarck, 4 June 1877, FA.

70. H. von Bismarck to Bleichröder, 6 June 1877, BA.

71. *GW*, VI³, 85; H. A. Bueck, *Der Centralverband deutscher Industrieller* (Berlin, 1902), I, 177–79.

72. Varnbüler to Bismarck, 29 June 1877, GFO: I.A.A.a. 50, Vol. II.

73. Bleichröder to Bismarck, 2 Feb. 1878, SA.

74. Louis Meyer to Bleichröder, 1 and 15 March 1878, BA.

75. Bleichröder to Bismarck, 4 March 1878, SA.

76. Bleichröder to Bismarck, 4 March 1878, SA; Huber, *Deutsche Verfassungsgeschichte*, IV, 145; *Gedanken*, II, 179, 188–98.

77. Lucius, *Bismarck*, p. 134.

78. Tiedemann, *Sechs Jahre*, pp. 235–44.

79. *GW*, VI³, 156.

80. Tiedemann, *Sechs Jahre*, pp. 249, 252.

81. Bismarck to Bleichröder, 25 Jan. 1878, BA; Bleichröder to Bismarck, 1 Feb. 1878, FA.

82. H. von Bismarck to Bleichröder, 20 May 1878, BA; Bueck, *Centralverband*, I, 364–65; *GW*, VI³, 111–12.

83. Bleichröder to H. von Bismarck, 21 May 1878, 18 May 1878, FA; Kardorff, *Kardorff*, pp. 139–41.

84. *Gedanken*, II, 188–97.

85. Bleichröder to Bismarck, 11 May 1878, SA.

86. A letter of Bleichröder, 23 May 1878, addressed to a "Geheimrat" and preserved in the SA; probably the letter was addressed to Bleichröder's friend Christoph von Tiedemann, who was chief of the imperial chancellery.

87. Eduard Lasker, *Fünfzehn Jahre parlamentarischer Geschichte, 1866–1880* (Berlin, n.d.), p. 141.

88. Eyck, *Bismarck*, III, 227.

89. August Bebel, *Aus meinem Leben*, II (Stuttgart, 1911), 418; Paul Wentzcke, ed., *Im Neuen Reich, 1871–1890. Politische Briefe aus dem Nachlass liberaler Parteiführer* (Bonn and Leipzig, 1926), p. 215.

90. Bueck, *Centralverband*, I, 373.

91. Beutner to Bleichröder, 20 May and 1 June 1878, BA.

92. *Ibid.*, 12 and 13 June 1878.

93. *Denkwürdigkeiten . . . Hohenlohe*, II, 234–35.

94. Tiedemann, *Sechs Jahre*, p. 252.

95. Bleichröder to Beutner, 6 July 1878, BA; Bleichröder's letter was returned to the files with a notation that Beutner had already left Berlin.

96. Beutner to Bleichröder, 28 June 1878, 4 July 1878; Freiherr von Swaine to Beutner, 29 June 1878, BA; Bleichröder to H. von Bismarck, 2 July 1878, FA.

97. H. von Bismarck to Rantzau, 28 July 1878, SA.

98. See Ernest Hamburger, *Die Juden im öffentlichen Leben Deutschlands. Regierungsmitglieder, Beamte und Parlamentarier in der monarchischen Zeit, 1848–1918* (Tübingen, 1968), pp. 269–84, for an excellent sketch of Lasker's career.

99. H. von Bismarck to Bleichröder, 8 July 1878, BA.

100. Rantzau to Bleichröder, 28 July and 4 Aug. 1878, BA.

101. H. von Bismarck to Rantzau, Aug. 1878, SA, courtesy of Dr. Hoepke.

102. Bismarck to Regierungspräsident Bötticher in Flensburg, 11 Aug. 1878, and Bismarck to Count Stolberg, 1 Sept. 1878, DZA: Potsdam: Reichskanzlei, Reichstagswahlen, Candidatur der Grafen Herbert and Wilhelm von Bismarck, No. 3, Vol. 1.

103. Blank to Bleichröder, 30 June 1878, BA.

104. Copy of Bleichröder to Blank, 3 July 1878, BA.

105. Draft, 8 July 1878, on Centralverband stationery, and copy of Bleichröder to Blank letter, 3 July 1878, BA. It is perhaps worth noting that Bleichröder must have asked Beutner to return to him documents relating to his candidacy; otherwise they would not be in the Bleichröder Archive today. Perhaps he wanted to remove all evidence of this abortive effort.

106. Blank to Bleichröder, 13 July 1878, BA.

107. Rudolph Meyer, *Politische Gründer und die Corruption in Deutschland* (Leipzig, 1877), pp. 34–35.

108. Richard Wentzel to Bleichröder, 6 Aug. 1878, BA.

109. Bleichröder to Bismarck, 19 July 1878, GFO: I.A.A.a. 50, Vol. 3.

110. Wehler, *Bismarck*, pp. 92–93, argues the opposite.

111. Hardach, *Bedeutung*, p. 193.

112. Kohl, *Bismarck-Regesten*, II, 171–72.

113. St. Vallier to Waddington, 8 Jan. 1879; for an elaboration of Bismarck's views on the railroad question, cf. *ibid.*, 8 April 1879, MAE: Allemagne, Vol. 27, 28.

114. Meyer to Bleichröder, 26 March 1878, BA.

115. E. Hüsgen, *Ludwig Windthorst*, 3rd ed. (Cologne, 1911), p. 272.

116. Meyer to Bleichröder, 13 Dec. 1878, BA.

117. Erich Eyck, *Bismarck and the German Empire* (London, 1950), p. 205.

118. Windthorst to Bleichröder, 28 March 1879, BA.

119. Meyer to Bleichröder, 6 April 1879, BA.

120. St. Vallier to Waddington, 8 and 22 April 1879, MAE: Allemagne, Vol. 28; Windthorst to Bleichröder, 13 April 1879, BA.

121. A. von Eulenburg to Bleichröder, 3 April 1879, BA.

122. Meyer to Bleichröder, 16 May 1879, BA.

123. E. Nolte to Windthorst, 2 July 1879, BA.

124. Vierhaus, *Spitzemberg*, p. 178.

125. Meyer to Bleichröder, 4 May 1879, BA.

126. St. Vallier to Wadington, 8 April 1879, MAE: Allemagne, Vol. 28.

127. Kohl, *Bismarck-Regesten*, II, 188.

128. Lucius, *Bismarck*, pp. 158-59.

129. St. Vallier to Waddington, 2 July 1879, MAE: Allemagne, Vol. 29.

130. St. Vallier to Waddington, 5 July 1879, *ibid.*

131. *GW*, XII, 117–28.

132. Orloff, *Bismarck*, p. 168.

133. St. Vallier to Waddington, 15 July 1879, MAE: Allemagne, Vol. 29.

134. Bleichröder to Bismarck, 3 Dec. 1879, SA.

135. Bleichröder to H. von Bismarck, 12 Dec. 1879, FA.

136. Memorandum, H. von Bismarck, 14 Dec. 1880, GFO: I.A.A.a. adh. secr.; and Bismarck to William, 12 July 1879, DZA: Merseburg: Zivilkabinett, Rep. 89H III, Vol. 7.

137. On this, see James J. Sheehan, *The Career of Lujo Brentano* (Chicago, 1966), chs. 3-4.

138. Ralf Dahrendorf, *Society and Democracy in Germany* (New York, 1967), p. 39; Alfred von der Leyen, *Die Eisenbahnpolitik des Fürsten Bismarck* (Berlin, 1914), is still indispensable; see also Rudolph Morsey, *Die Oberste Reichsverwaltung unter Bismarck, 1867–1890* (Münster, 1957), pp. 139–60, and Karl Marx-Friedrich Engels, *Werke* (East Berlin, 1962), XIX, 172–75.

139. Franz Perrot, *Bismarck und die Juden*, ed. by L. Feldmüller-Perrot (Berlin, 1931), p. 63.

140. Bleichröder to Bismarck, 25 July 1873, SA.

141. Bismarck to Bleichröder, 13 Aug. 1873, BA.

142. Morsey, *Reichsverwaltung*, p. 143.

143. *Ibid.*, pp. 143–46.

144. Kurt Grunwald, "Europe's Railways and Jewish Enterprise," *LBY*, 12 (1967), 201.

145. D. Oppenheim to Bleichröder, 2 Feb. and 9 May 1875, BA.

146. *Ibid.*, 5 June 1876.

147. Bleichröder to Bismarck, 11 Dec. 1877, SA.

148. Morsey, *Reichsverwaltung*, p. 153; *GW*, VI³, 96.

149. Fürstenberg, *Lebensgeschichte*, p. 72.

150. Rothschild to Bleichröder, 22 June 1876, BA.

151. Hans Bleichröder to Gerson von Bleichröder, 26 July 1877, BA.

152. Goldschmidt to Bleichröder, 14 Nov. 1877, BA.

153. Bleichröder to Bismarck, 8 June 1876, SA.

154. Bleichröder to Bismarck, 16 Dec. 1878, SA; on the rates of interest, see A. Sartorius von Waltershausen, *Deutsche Wirtschaftsgeschichte, 1815–1914*, 2nd ed. (Jena, 1923), p. 298.

155. H. von Bismarck to Wilhelm von Bismarck, 11 Jan. 1879, SA, courtesy of Dr. Hoepke.

156. Cohn to Bleichröder, 25 Jan. 1879, BA.

157. Prince Henry XII of Reuss to Bleichröder, 1 Dec. 1878 and 2 May 1879; Lehndorff to Bleichröder, 15 July 1879; A. Eulenburg to Bleichröder, 29 Aug. and 20 Nov. 1879, BA. Bleichröder to Bismarck, 1 and 12 June 1879, SA.

158. Bleichröder to Bismarck, 3 June 1879, SA.

159. Friedrich Jungnickel, *Staatsminister Albert von Maybach* (Stuttgart, 1910), pp. 73–81.

160. Killisch to Bleichröder, 6 Dec. 1877, BA.

161. Undated Pro Memoria in Angelegenheit der Verstaatlichung der Rhein-Nahe-Eisenbahn, BA.

162. Bleichröder to Bitter, 14 June 1880; Bitter to Bleichröder, 28 June 1880; Bleichröder to Bitter, 29 June 1880, BA.

163. Bleichröder to Bitter, 29 June 1880; 5 July and 5 Sept. 1880, BA.

164. SBHA, 11 Jan. 1881, I, pp. 896–904.

165. Undated memorandum, BA.

166. See entries 16 Nov. 1880, 4 May 1881, 30 June 1881, 8 Aug. 1881, account 24 Jan. 1884, SA; cf. also Jungnickel, *Maybach*, pp. 90–91.

167. Leyen, *Eisenbahnpolitik*, p. 129; Jungnickel, *Maybach*, p. 92.

168. Johannes Ziekursch, *Politische Geschichte des neuen deutschen Kaiserreiches*, (3 Vols.; Frankfurt, 1925–1930), II, 374; in pp. 357–75, Ziekursch calls attention to these remarks in the 1880s; Stürmer, "Staatsstreichgedanken," analyzes them as a necessary part of the Bismarckian system.

169. Boetticher to Bleichröder, 10 Sept. 1887 and 11 Jan. 1888, BA; Bleichröder to H. von Bismarck, 7 Dec. 1879, FA.

170. Wentzcke, *Im Neuen Reich*, p. 383.

171. Lucius, *Bismarck*, pp. 306–7; Bleichröder to Bismarck, 17 Dec. 1884, FA. Morsey, *Reichsverwaltung*, pp. 115–6.

172. *GW*, XII, 146–48.

173. Cf. the excellent summary of Bismarck's corporate ideas in Ralph H. Bowen, *German Theories of the Corporative State* (New York, 1947), pp. 148–56.

174. Quoted in Hans Rothfels, ed., *Otto von Bismarck. Deutscher Staat* (Munich, 1925), p. 387.

175. St. Vallier to Barthelemy Saint Hilaire, 1 Nov. 1880, MAE: Allemagne, Vol. 38.

176. Rothfels, *Bismarck*, p. 414.

177. Bleichröder to Bismarck, 29 Sept. 1880, FA.

178. Cf. Walter Vogel, *Bismarcks Arbeiterversicherung* (Braunschweig, 1951), pp. 34–50, 138.

179. Lange to Bismarck, 3 Nov. and 4 Dec. 1885, SA.

180. Wilhelm von Scholz, ed., *Staatsminister Adolf von Scholz, Erlebnisse und Gespräche mit Bismarck* (Stuttgart and Berlin, 1922), pp. 36, 60, 70–71.

181. Norman Rich and M. H. Fischer, eds., *The Holstein Papers*, Vols. I–III (Cambridge, 1955–1961), II, 56–57.

182. Schulthess, *Geschichtskalender, 1884*, p. 60.

183. Bleichröder to Bismarck, 24 May 1884, SA.

184. *Holstein Papers*, II, 227–28. Schulthess, *Geschichtskalender, 1884*, p. 63; *GW*, VIII, 511.

185. Quoted in Hans Goldschmidt, *Das Reich und Preussen im Kampf um die Führung* (Berlin, 1931), p. 69.

186. St. Vallier to Freycinet, 7, 8, 13 April 1880, MAE: Allemagne, Vol. 34.

187. *GW*, XIV², 917–18.

188. Hans Philippi, *Preussen und die braunschweigische Thronfolgefrage, 1866–1913* (Hildesheim, 1966); Stewart A. Stehlin, *Bismarck and the Guelph Problem, 1866–1890: A Study in Particularist Opposition to National Unity* (The Hague, 1973), ch. 6.

189. Lerchenfeld-Koefering, *Erinnerungen*, p. 165; Hans Philippi, "König Ludwig II. von Bayern und der Welfenfond," *Zeitschrift für bayerische Landesgeschichte*, 23 (1960), 90.

190. *Holstein Papers*, III, 104.

191. *Holstein Papers*, II, 75–80.

192. *Ibid.*

193. On the million marks, cf. Philippi, "König Ludwig," p. 94; Philippi's article accepts uncritically the Holstein testimony and occasionally cites evidence inadequately.

194. Pfister to Bleichröder, 14 and 23 Feb. 1884, BA.

195. *GW*, XIV², 949–50.

196. Draft letter, Bleichröder to Pfister, 26 April 1884, BA.

197. Pfister to Bleichröder, 19 June 1884, BA; also Philippi, "König Ludwig," pp. 95–96.

10 / Greed and Intrigue

1. On frugality, as well as the aristocratic life in general, see one of the few good accounts we have: Joachim von Dissow, *Adel im Übergang. Ein kritischer Standesgenosse berichtet aus Residenzen und Gutshäusern* (Stuttgart, 1961), p. 24.

2. Lionel Trilling, *Sincerity and Authenticity* (Cambridge, Mass., 1972), p. 37.

3. Max Weber, *Gesammelte Politische Schriften* (Munich, 1921), p. 14.

4. I have developed this theme further in an essay on "German Landed Elites," to be published in *European Landed Elites,* ed. by David Spring (Baltimore: Johns Hopkins University Press, in press). See also the important essay by Hans Rosenberg, "Die Pseudo-demokratisierung," in H.-U. Wehler, ed., *Sozialgeschichte,* pp. 287–308.

5. Dissow, *Adel,* p. 25.

6. Charles Dickens, *Our Mutual Friend* (New York, 1960), p. 134.

7. Thomas Mann, *Buddenbrooks,* p. 49.

8. Theodor Fontane, *Briefe an Georg Friedlaender,* ed. by Kurt Schreinert (Heidelberg, 1954), p. 2.

9. As the merest example, see *ibid.,* p. 305; and Lord Howarth of Penrith, *Theatre of Life, 1863–1905,* Vol. I (London, 1935), p. 84.

10. Lucius, *Bismarck,* pp. 21, 56; see also A. O. Meyer, *Bismarck,* pp. 485–505 *passim.*

11. *GW,* XIV², 85.

12. Kardorff, *Kardorff,* p. 114.

13. Lucius, *Bismarck,* p. 78; *GW,* XV, 343–355; and Gerhard Ritter, *Die preussischen Konservativen und Bismarcks deutsche Politik 1858–1871* (Heidelberg, 1913), esp. pp. 361–78.

14. Lucius, *Bismarck,* p. 111; see also Heyderhoff, *Im Ring, passim.*

15. Kardorff, *Kardorff,* p. 112.

16. Heyderhoff, *Im Ring,* p. 22.

17. Lucius, *Bismarck,* p. 28.

18. *Holstein Papers,* II, 64–65, 228.

19. *Denkwürdigkeiten . . . Hohenlohe,* II, 120.

20. Hatzfeldt to Bleichröder, 15 April 1878, BA; see also the perceptive comments

in Lerchenfeld-Koefering, *Erinnerungen,* pp. 229–33.

21. For an informative article on the entourage which, however, ignores the unpleasant atmosphere, see Hans Goldschmidt, "Mitarbeiter Bismarcks im aussenpolitischen Kampf," *Preussische Jahrbücher,* 235 (1934), 29–48 and 125–56.

22. Walter Bussmann, ed., *Staatssekretär Graf Herbert von Bismarck. Aus seiner politischen Privatkorrespondenz* (Göttingen, 1964), p. 15.

23. Hans Goldschmidt, "Mitarbeiter Bismarcks," p. 30.

24. Bussmann, *Herbert von Bismarck,* p. 71.

25. *Holstein Papers,* II, 103.

26. *Ibid.,* p. 131.

27. Graf Anton Monts, *Erinnerungen und Gedanken des Botschafters,* ed. by Karl Friedrich Nowak and Friedrich Thimme (Berlin, 1932), p. 50.

28. Vierhaus, *Spitzemberg,* p. 17.

29. Bussmann, *Herbert von Bismarck,* p. 71.

30. *Ibid.,* pp. 71–73.

31. The best treatment of it can be found in George O. Kent, *Arnim and Bismarck* (Oxford, 1968); see also Norman Rich, "Holstein and the Arnim Affair," *JMH,* 28 (1956), 35–54; and Bussmann, *Herbert von Bismarck,* pp. 15–17. By using the Bleichröder and Bismarck Archives, I have been able to go beyond Kent's account.

32. *GW,* XIV², 844.

33. Kent, *Arnim,* p. 83; Rich, "Holstein," p. 42.

34. Landsberg to Bleichröder, 5 and 11 March 1874, BA.

35. Kent, *Arnim,* p. 97.

36. Bleichröder to Bismarck, 10 July 1872, BA.

37. Kent, *Arnim,* p. 98; Norman Rich, *Friedrich von Holstein: Politics and Diplomacy in the Era of Bismarck and Wilhelm II* (2 vols., Cambridge, 1965), I, 77–78; Bussmann, *Herbert von Bismarck,* pp. 73–75; Morsey, *Reichsverwaltung,* p. 122; Heinrich Spiero, *Rudolf Lindau* (Berlin, 1909), p. 7. See also the excellent essay by Eberhard Naujoks, "Rudolf Lindau und die Neuorientierung der Auswärtigen Pressepolitik Bismarcks (1871–1878)," *HZ,* 215 (1972), esp. pp. 299–318.

38. Bleichröder to Bismarck, 13 Oct. 1873, GFO: II B.10, Vol. V. Werner Pöls, "Bleichröder und die Arnim-Affäre," *HZ,* 211 (1968), 65–76, missed this letter and did not see the full range of Landsberg-Bleichröder correspondence. Bleichröder's involvement was even greater than Pöls assumed.

39. Landsberg to Bleichröder, 12 April

1875; undated, probably 20 Nov. 1875; and 19 Nov. 1880, BA.

40. *Ibid.*, 3 Feb. 1873.

41. Jean Bouvier, *Les Rothschilds* (Paris, 1960), pp. 184–86.

42. *Holstein Papers*, III, 33.

43. Landsberg to Bleichröder, 10 Oct. 1873, BA; also, Bleichröder to Bismarck, 13 Oct. 1873, GFO:II B.10, Vol. V.

44. *GW*, XV, 346.

45. Paul Knaplund, ed., *Letters from the Berlin Embassy: Selections from the Private Correspondence of British Representatives at Berlin and Foreign Secretary Lord Granville, 1871–1874, 1880–1885* (Washington, 1944), p. 91.

46. Landsberg to Bleichröder, 14 Jan. 1874, BA.

47. Kent, *Arnim*, p. vi.

48. Landsberg to Bleichröder, 4 March 1874, BA.

49. *Ibid.*, 5 and 11 March 1874.

50. Bleichröder to Bismarck, 6 March 1874, SA.

51. Undated letter, Landsberg to Bleichröder, probably from early March 1874, BA.

52. Landsberg to Bleichröder, 29 April 1874, BA.

53. *Ibid.*, 14 April 1874.

54. The original Landsberg-Bleichröder letter, 12 May 1874, is in BA; a copy is in the Bleichröder file in the Bismarck Archive, under letters addressed to Herbert, FA.

55. Landsberg to Bleichröder, 20 May 1874, BA.

56. Lucius, *Bismarck*, pp. 65–66.

57. Landsberg to Bleichröder, 20 May 1874, BA.

58. *Ibid.*, 27 May 1874.

59. Bleichröder to Bismarck, 2 and 27 July 1874, SA.

60. Kent, *Arnim*, pp. 144–53.

61. *Ibid.*

62. Bleichröder to Bismarck, 4 Oct. 1874, SA.

63. Landsberg to Bleichröder, 6 Oct. 1874, BA. *Der Arnim'sche Prozess* (Berlin, 1874), pp. 25–26.

64. Kent, *Arnim*, pp. 160–61; Pauly to Bismarck, 8 Dec. 1874, BA; *Der Arnim'sche Prozess*, p. 217.

65. Bülow to William I, 26 Dec. 1874, DZA: Merseburg: Zivilkabinett, Rep. 89H VI, Vol. 3b, v. Arnim.

66. Bleichröder to Bismarck, 15 Dec. 1874, FA; on Bleichröder's letter informing Bismarck that Landsberg would return to Paris, unless the Chancellor wanted to see him, Bismarck scribbled: "Dr. L. tonight 9 p.m."

67. *Denkwürdigkeiten . . . Hohenlohe,*

II, 141; the English translation of this work is lamentable.

68. Lerchenfeld-Koefering, *Erinnerungen,* p. 82.

69. Kent, *Arnim*, p. 172.

70. Landsberg to Bleichröder, 12 March and 18 June 1875, BA.

71. *Ibid.*, 24 Oct. 1875.

72. Schwabach to Bleichröder, 6 June 1876, BA.

73. Landsberg to Bleichröder, undated letter, probably March 1874, BA; *Denkwürdigkeiten . . . Hohenlohe*, II, 120.

74. Landsberg to Bleichröder, 27 May 1874; *Denkwürdigkeiten . . . Hohenlohe*, II, 123.

75. Landsberg to Bleichröder, 20 Nov. 1875, BA.

76. For the best assessment of Holstein's role, see Rich "Holstein."

77. Landsberg to Bleichröder, 21 April 1876, BA; also Rich, *Holstein*, I, 162–73.

78. Undated letter, after 1890, BA.

79. *SBHA*, 7 Feb. 1873, II, p. 940. See also Lasker's earlier speech, *ibid.*, 14 Jan. 1873, I, pp. 521–47.

80. Bleichröder to Bismarck, 7 Feb. 1873, FA.

81. Wolfgang Saile, *Hermann Wagener und sein Verhältnis zu Bismarck* (Tübingen, 1958), pp. 114–22; Ritter, *Preussischen Konservativen*, p. 370.

82. Kardorff, *Kardorff*, p. 96.

83. *GW*, XIV², 828.

84. Hermann Wagener, *Erlebtes: Meine Memoiren aus der Zeit von 1848 bis 1866 und von 1873 bis jetzt* (2 vols. in one; Berlin, 1884), II, 58; Saile, *Wagener*, pp. 122–24.

85. Lucius, *Bismarck*, p. 116.

86. Johanna von Bismarck to Bleichröder, 23 Nov. 1876, BA.

87. Wagener to Bleichröder, 6 Dec. 1876, BA.

88. *Ibid.*, 4 Dec. 1876, 13 and 28 Feb. 1877.

89. *Ibid.*, 24 June 1880; Saile, *Wagener*, p. 129.

90. Morsey, *Reichsverwaltung*, p. 248.

91. Lerchenfeld-Koefering, *Erinnerungen*, p. 120.

92. *Hatzfeldt Briefe*, p. 256.

93. Rich, *Holstein*, I, 9–10.

94. *Hatzfeldt Briefe*, p. 275 .

95. *Ibid.*, p. 310. Hatzfeldt ended his letter with these four dots.

96. Bleichröder to Hatzfeldt, 23 Nov. 1871, HN. Dr. Gerhard Ebel, Bad Nenndorf, has been editing the political correspondence of Hatzfeldt, and we exchanged Hatzfeldt and Bleichröder letters. On the founding of the Laurahütte, see also the scurrilous but

informative Glagau, *Börsenund Gründungs-Schwindel*, pp. 85–86.

97. Hatzfeldt to Bleichröder, 13 Nov. 1871, BA.

98. Bleichröder to Hatzfeldt, 29 Jan. 1872, HN; and Glagau, *Börsen- und Gründungs-Schwindel*, pp. 200–201.

99. Hatzfeldt to Bleichröder, 9 Feb. 1872, BA.

100. Kardorff, *Kardorff*, p. 96.

101. Bleichröder to Hatzfeldt, 18 Jan. 1872, HN; Hatzfeldt to Bleichröder, 5, 10 Jan. and 13 July 1872, 1 Jan. 1873, BA.

102. Bleichröder to Hatzfeldt, 9 Aug. 1873, HN.

103. *Ibid.*, 22, 24 March and 5 April 1873.

104. *Ibid.*, 28 Feb. 1874 and 6 March 1875.

105. *Ibid.*, 6 March 1875.

106. Hatzfeldt to Bleichröder, 13 March 1875, BA.

107. Bleichröder to Hatzfeldt, 31 March 1876, HN.

108. Hatzfeldt to Bleichröder, 13 Sept. 1876, 24 Sept. 1877, HN.

109. Hatzfeldt to Bleichröder, 4 March 1878, BA.

110. *Ibid.*, 15 April 1878.

111. See also Holstein's laudatory comments about Hatzfeldt's mission in Madrid, *Holstein Papers*, I, 193; Bleichröder to H. von Bismarck, 28 April 1878, FA.

112. H. von Bismarck to Bleichröder, 29 April 1878, BA.

113. *Holstein Papers*, III, 44.

114. Bleichröder to Bismarck, 30 Jan. 1879, SA.

115. *Denkwürdigkeiten* . . . *Hohenlohe*, II, 278–79.

116. Bleichröder to H. von Bismarck, 31 Oct. 1879, FA.

117. H. von Bismarck to Bleichröder, 2 Nov. 1879, BA.

118. Bussmann, *Herbert von Bismarck*, pp. 96–97; Helmuth Rogge, *Holstein und Hohenlohe* (Stuttgart, 1957), pp. 149–50.

119. Holstein to Bleichröder, 1 Jan. 1880 (?), BA.

120. Bleichröder to Bismarck, 1 Aug. 1880, FA; H. von Bismarck to Bleichröder, 2 Aug. 1880, BA; Bleichröder to H. von Bismarck, 19 Aug. 1880, FA.

121. H. von Bismarck to Rantzau, 31 Aug. 1880, SA; Rogge, *Holstein*, pp. 89, 149–50; Bussmann, *Herbert von Bismarck*, pp. 95–96; Rantzau to Foreign Office, 10 and 11 Nov. 1880, GFO: I.A.A.a. 50 adh. secr., Vol. III.

122. Rogge, *Holstein*, pp. 104–5; Deutsches Montagsblatt, 2 Feb. 1880, in FA; *Holstein Papers*, II, 31.

123. *The Times*, 15 Oct. 1885.

124. Morsey, *Reichsverwaltung*, pp. 119–120.

125. Moritz Busch, *Bismarck: Some Secret Pages of His History* (3 vols.; London, 1898), III, 67, 73–4. Cf. also Hajo Holborn, ed., *Aufzeichnungen und Erinnerungen aus dem Leben des Botschafters Joseph Maria von Radowitz*, 2 vols. (Leipzig, 1925), II, *1878–1890*, p. 204.

126. Bussmann, *Herbert von Bismarck*, pp. 139–41.

127. *The Times*, 16 Oct. 1885.

128. Bleichröder to Hatzfeldt, 21 Nov. 1885, HN; Hatzfeldt to Bleichröder, 7 Oct. 1885, BA.

129. Bleichröder to Hatzfeldt, 5 Aug. 1882, HN.

130. Bussmann, *Herbert von Bismarck*, p. 142.

131. Hatzfeldt to Bleichröder, 5 Nov. 1885, BA.

132. *Ibid.*, 17 and 27 Sept., 11 Oct. 1889; Bussmann, *Herbert von Bismarck*, p. 546.

133. Bleichröder to Hatzfeldt, 2 March, 7 and 9 April 1888, HN; Hatzfeldt to Bleichröder, 30 Jan. 1889, BA.

134. Hofrath Bork to Bleichröder, 26 July 1878, BA.

135. Count Perponcher to Bleichröder, 6 and 13 Dec. 1878, BA.

136. Freiherr Hermann von Eckardstein, *Lebenserinnerungen und Politische Denkwürdigkeiten* (Leipzig, 1919), I, 35–40.

137. William II, *My Early Life* (London, 1926), p. 89.

138. Graf Harry Kessler, *Gesichter und Zeiten. Erinnerungen* (Berlin, 1962), pp. 79–80.

139. Lehndorff to Bleichröder, 23 Nov. 1875; 8 and 19 Nov. 1878; 15 July 1879; 10 Oct. 1880; 31 March 1885, BA.

140. *Ibid.*, 21 July 1877, 5 May 1880, 29 Nov. 1881.

141. William I to Bleichröder, 6 July 1884, BA. I have not been able to track down the shadowy Gabrielle de Karsky—or de Karski, as she signed her letters. She had a home in Warsaw and presumably was Polish.

142. On the Radziwill attachment, see Erich Marcks, *Kaiser Wilhelm I* (8th printing, Munich and Leipzig, 1918), pp. 29–34; and Kessler, *Gesichter*, pp. 45–46.

143. *Holstein Papers*, III, 128.

144. Bleichröder to William I, 18 Aug. 1884, with notation from William I to Bleichröder, 19 Aug. 1884, BA; William I to Bleichröder, 20 Aug. 1884, BA; Coumont to Bleichröder, 4 Oct. 1884, BA.

145. Gabrielle de Karski to Bleichröder, 11 Feb. (no year—probably 1885), BA.

146. *Ibid.*, 5 Sept. (no year—probably 1885).

147. *Ibid.*, 28 Dec. (no year—probably 1885).
148. William I to Bleichröder, 27 Aug. 1886, BA.
149. H. von Bismarck to Bleichröder, 19 Sept. 1876, BA.
150. *Aus 50 Jahren. Erinnerungen des Fürsten Philipp zu Eulenburg-Hertefeld* (Berlin, 1923), p. 95. Eulenburg was Herbert's closest confidant at that time, and his account is the most authentic we have. See also Louis Snyder, "Political Implications of Herbert von Bismarck's Marital Affairs, 1881, 1892," *JMH*, 36 (1964), 155–69.
151. *Aus 50 Jahren*, p. 93.
152. *Ibid.*, pp. 102, 105.
153. Bleichröder to Bismarck, 13 April 1881, FA.
154. BA.
155. Bleichröder to H. von Bismarck, 5 July 1881; H. von Bismarck to Bleichröder, 6 July 1881; Bleichröder to H. von Bismarck, 8 July 1881, BA.
156. Nachlass Boetticher, Bundesarchiv, Koblenz. Dr. John Röhl was kind enough to send me this.
157. Kardorff to Bleichröder, 20 June 1881, BA.
158. H. von Bismarck to Wilhelm von Bismarck, 9 Aug. 1882, FA, courtesy of Dr. Klaus-Peter Hoepke, the assistant editor of Bussmann, ed., *Herbert von Bismarck*.
159. *Holstein Papers*, III, 104–5.
160. Rantzau to H. von Bismarck, 11 Aug. 1882, FA, courtesy of Dr. Hoepke.
161. See, for example, Rantzau to H. von Bismarck, 21 Oct. 1886, FA, courtesy of Dr. Hoepke.
162. *Holstein Papers*, II, 57.
163. *Ibid.*, p. 277.
164. Bleichröder to Bismarck, 24 May, 3 and 9 Aug. 1882, SA; Wilhelm von Bismarck to Bleichröder, 7 and 8 June 1882, BA.
165. Bucher to Bleichröder, 16 Nov. 1872, BA.
166. Bismarck to Bleichröder, 17 July 1882, BA.
167. Bleichröder to Bismarck, 3, 7, 9 Aug. 1882, SA; also *GW*, XIV², 950.
168. H. von Bismarck to Wilhelm von Bismarck, 9 Aug. 1882; Rantzau to H. von Bismarck, 7 Oct. 1882, FA, courtesy of Dr. Hoepke; Bussmann, *Herbert von Bismarck*, p. 210.
169. *GP*, VI, 355.

11 / The Fourth Estate

1. Rudolf Morsey, "Zur Pressepolitik Bismarcks. Die Vorgeschichte des Pressedezernats im Auswärtigen Amt (1870)," *Publizistik*, I (1956), 180.

2. *GW*, XII, 349.
3. See Lenore O'Boyle's excellent "The Image of the Journalist in France, Germany, and England, 1815–1848," *Comparative Studies in Society and History*, 10 (1968), 302–12.
4. It has only been in recent years that Bismarck's relations with the press have been scrutinized. The outstanding work for the early years is Eberhard Naujoks, *Bismarcks Auswärtige Pressepolitik und die Reichsgründung, 1865–1871* (Wiesbaden, 1968); see also Naujoks, "Bismarck und die Organisation der Regierungspresse," *HZ*, 205 (1967), 46–81. Other studies by Irene Fischer-Frauendienst and Rudolf Morsey are listed below. R. Nöll von der Nahmer, *Bismarcks Reptilienfonds* (Mainz, 1968), is an unreliable and unscholarly work.
5. Otto Groth, *Die Zeitung. Ein System der Zeitungskunde*, Vol. II (Mannheim, 1929), p. 199.
6. Graham Storey, *Reuters: The Story of a Century of News-Gathering* (New York, 1951), pp. 3–31.
7. Cf. Naujoks, "Regierungspresse," pp. 46–81.
8. Paul Lindau, *Nur Erinnerungen* (2 vols.; Berlin, 1916–1917), I, 234–41.
9. Cf. an undated memo almost certainly by Richard Wentzel from 1869, BA. Cf. also Eberhard Naujoks for a slightly different but unpersuasive version: "Bismarck und das Wolffsche Telegraphenbüro," *GWU*, 14 (1963), 19–20.
10. Wentzel memo, BA. Cf. also Dr. Stieber, *Denkwürdigkeiten: Aus seinen hinterlassenen Papieren*, ed. by Leopold Auerbach (Berlin, 1884), pp. 246–47, who described the 1865 agreement, but concealed the 1869 agreement.
11. See the original agreement to form Continental Telegraph Company, 22 May 1865, BA.
12. Naujoks, "Wolffsche Telegraphenbüro," pp. 19–20.
13. Julius Fröbel to Bismarck, 6 Feb. 1869, DZA: Merseburg: A.A.I. Rep. 4. No. 721, Geheimes Staatsarchiv, Generalia. See also Julius Fröbel, *Ein Lebenslauf: Aufzeichnungen, Erinnerungen, und Bekenntnisse* (2 vols.; Stuttgart, 1890–1891), I, 521–22, for mention of Reuter's efforts, but not of his private letter to Bismarck.
14. Keudell to Bleichröder, 20 Feb. 1869, BA.
15. *Ibid.*, 23 April 1869.
16. Wentzel to Bleichröder, 24 April 1869, BA.
17. Cf. contract of 10 June 1869, approved by Bismarck on 11 June, DZA: Merseburg: A.A.I. Rep. 4. No. 721, Geheimes Staatsarchiv, Generalia.

18. Rosenberg to Bismarck, 10 March 1870, ibid.

19. Irene Fischer-Frauendienst, Bismarcks Pressepolitik (Münster, 1963), p. 29.

20. Quoted in O'Boyle, "Journalist," p. 305.

21. Storey, Reuters, p. 53.

22. Knaplund, Letters from the Berlin Embassy, p. 101.

23. Hans Philippi to author, 20 April 1970.

24. Philippi, "Zur Geschichte des Welfenfonds," Niedersächsisches Jahrbuch, n.s., 31 (1959), 190–99.

25. Eberhard Naujoks, "Eine Abrechnung über den Welfendonds (1. April–31. Dezember 1869)," Publizistik (1969), I, 16–29.

26. Keudell to Bleichröder, 29 Jan. 1868, BA.

27. Wentzel to Bleichröder, 2 Aug. 1871, BA.

28. Reuter to Bleichröder, 29 Dec. 1874, copy of Wentzel to Reuter, 1 Jan. 1875, BA.

29. Bleichröder to Bismarck, 20 Feb. 1875, DZA: Merseburg: A.A.I. Rep. 4. No. 721, Geheimes Staatsarchiv, Generalia.

30. Bülow to Bleichröder, 23 Feb. 1875, BA.

31. Bülow memorandum, 10 March 1875, DZA: Merseburg: A.A.I. Rep. 4. No. 721, Geheimes Staatsarchiv, Generalia.

32. Continental Telegraph Company to Bleichröder, 30 Dec. 1875, BA.

33. Bosse memorandum, 4 March 1879, DZA: Merseburg: A.A.I. Rep. 4. No. 721, Geheimes Staatsarchiv, Generalia.

34. Wentzel to Bleichröder, 4 June and 24 Nov. 1879; and draft treaty marked 5 Feb. 1880, BA.

35. Holstein to Bleichröder, 28 Aug. 1880, BA.

36. Cf. Naujoks, "Wolffsche Telegraphenbüro," pp. 26–28.

37. Havas and Reuter made further attempts to buy out Wolff; the last such effort occurred in 1889 and again ended in failure. Eduard Lebey to Bleichröder, 28 March 1889, BA.

38. Busch, Tagebuchblätter, I, 304; Naujoks, Bismarcks Auswärtige Pressepolitik, p. 333.

39. Bismarck to Camphausen, 14 Jan. 1872, DZA: Merseburg: A.A.I. Rep. 4. No. 721, Geheimes Staatsarchiv, Generalia.

40. See Naujoks, "Lindau," HZ, 215: 299–344, passim.

41. Copy, Agreement between Prussian State Ministry and Continental Telegraph, 4 March 1872, DZA: Merseburg: A.A.I. Rep. 4. No. 721, Geheimes Staatsarchiv, Generalia.

42. Schlesinger to Bleichröder, 11 June 1877, BA.

43. Schlesinger to Bleichröder, 9 May 1878, BA.

44. Holstein Papers, II, 140–41.

45. Government memorandum, 2 Feb. 1876, GFO: I.A.A.a. 33.

46. Undated and unsigned Pro Memoria, giving the history of the negotiations in 1872 and subsequently. DZA: Merseburg: A.A.I. Rep. 4. No. 721, Geheimes Staatsarchiv, Generalia.

47. Bleichröder to Bucher, 21 Feb. 1876, including Schlesinger to Bleichröder, 19 Feb. 1876, GFO: I.A.A.a. 33.

48. Unsigned Pro Memoria, 1 March 1876, ibid.

49. Bleichröder to Bismarck, 15 March 1876, SA.

50. Bucher to Bleichröder, 12 April 1876, BA.

51. Hans von Bleichröder to Bleichröder, 20 April 1876, BA.

52. Protocol signed by Bleichröder, Schlesinger, and Wentzel, 14 April 1876, DZA: Merseburg: A.A.I. Rep. 4. No. 721, Geheimes Staatsarchiv, Generalia.

53. Bleichröder to Bucher, 21 April; Bucher to Bleichröder, 27 April 1876, ibid.; Naujoks, "Lindau," 308–9.

54. Schlesinger to Bleichröder, 19 April 1876; and Englische Correspondenz, 29 April 1876, BA.

55. Camphausen to Bismarck, 26 Feb. 1878, also 28 Feb. 1878, marked secret, DZA: Merseburg: A.A.I. Rep. 4. No. 721, Geheimes Staatsarchiv, Generalia.

56. Schlesinger to Bleichröder, 9 May 1878, BA.

57. Tiedemann, Sechs Jahre, pp. 298–99.

58. St. Vallier to Waddington, 26 Feb. 1879, MAE: Allemagne, Vol. 27.

59. German thoroughness and Nazi polemics are combined in the survey of the press and Jewry in Walter Heide, ed., Handbuch der Zeitungswissenschaft (Leipzig, 1940–1943).

60. GW, VII, 66.

61. See the detailed account in Naujoks, Bismarcks Auswärtige Pressepolitik, pp. 68–78.

62. Bamberg to Bleichröder, 24 Sept. 1879, BA.

63. Ibid., 13 Sept. 1880.

64. Etienne to Bleichröder, 3 May 1876, BA.

65. Hertzka to Bleichröder, 20 Feb. 1880, BA; Goldschmidt to Bleichröder, 3 March 1880, BA.

66. G. von Bunsen and Rudolf von Gneist to Bleichröder, 3 April 1877, BA.

67. Schwabach to Bleichröder, 4 July 1876, BA.

68. Paul Lindau to Bleichröder, 16 Dec. 1890, 16 March and 15 May 1891, BA.

69. On Sonnemann, see Hamburger, Juden

im öffentlichen Leben, pp. 311–21. Also St. Vallier to Waddington, 9 Oct. 1878, MAE: Allemagne, Vol. 25.

70. Sonnemann to Bleichröder, 11 June 1875, 10 Feb. 1877, BA.

71. Bleichröder to Bismarck, 11 and 21 Dec. 1880, FA.

72. Bussmann, *Herbert von Bismarck,* p. 196; Busch, *Tagebuchblätter,* III, 40.

73. See the very active correspondence between Hersdörfer and Bleichröder, covering the years from 1875 to 1880, in BA; Bussmann, *Herbert von Bismarck,* p. 177; and Kurt Koszyk, *Deutsche Presse im 19. Jahrhundert. Geschichte der deutschen Presse* (Berlin, 1966), II, 151–52.

74. Glagau, *Börsen- und Gründungs-Schwindel,* pp. 316–17.

75. Killisch von Horn to Bleichröder, 5 Dec. 1877, BA.

76. *Ibid.,* 20 and 24 Oct. 1879.

77. Groth, *Die Zeitung,* II, 193, 574–77; Münch, *Hansemann;* Koszyk, *Deutsche Presse,* II, 291; see also Franz Mehring, *Gesammelte Schriften* (Berlin, 1960), II, 396–97.

78. Betzold to Bleichröder, 9 April 1870, BA; on the fascinating Betzold, see Eckardstein, *Lebenserinnerungen,* I, 240–46.

79. Franz-Xaver Kraus, *Tagebücher* (Cologne, 1957), p. 618; and Koszyk, *Deutsche Presse,* II, 182.

80. Joachim Boehmer, "Die Norddeutsche Allgemeine Zeitung," *Zeitungswissenschaft,* I (1926), 56, 73, 92, 103.

81. Bussmann, *Herbert von Bismarck,* p. 387; and Busch, *Tagebuchblätter,* II, 570.

82. H. von Bismarck to Rantzau, 9 Aug. 1878, FA, courtesy of Dr. Werner Pöls. See also Bussmann, *Herbert von Bismarck,* pp. 99–101.

83. See Hermann Hofmann, *Fürst Bismarck, 1890–1898* (Stuttgart, 1914), I, 76–90.

84. Pindter to Bleichröder, 8 Aug. 1880, BA; Goldschmidt to Bleichröder, 20 May 1882, BA.

85. *GW,* VI³, 198–99.

86. Ohlendorff to Bleichröder, 8, 9, 16, 18 Dec. 1880, BA; Tiedemann to Bleichröder, 27 Dec. 1880, BA; Fischer-Frauendienst, *Pressepolitik,* p. 170.

12 / The Prince Enriched

1. *GW,* XV, 346–47.

2. *GW,* XIV², 821. Bismarck mentioned 85,000 taler, but the actual amount proved to be 87,500 taler. On the present size of Friedrichsruh, see *Hamburger Abendblatt,* 31 January 1976.

3. Bleichröder to Bismarck, 1 May 1884, SA.

4. *GW,* XIV², 820–21.

5. According to the report of Bleichröder's assistant; Siebert to Bleichröder, 15 July 1871, BA.

6. Bismarck to Keudell, 15 July 1871, Dr. C. Dietrici to Keudell, 3 Aug. 1871, SA. On per capita income, see Walther G. Hoffmann, *et al., Das deutsche Volkseinkommen, 1851–1957* (Tübingen, 1959), p. 39.

7. Bezirks-Commission für Berlin, 20 Oct. 1871, SA.

8. 15 March 1877, SA.

9. Kardorff, *Kardorff,* p. 107.

10. *GW,* XII, 103.

11. Taylor, *Bismarck,* p. 112.

12. The various accusations and the subsequent trial will be discussed below in chapter 18; for an uncritical repetition of the charge, see *Der Spiegel,* 31 March 1965, p. 67.

13. 1 Jan. 1881, 31 Oct. 1890, SA.

14. These and subsequent figures are taken from Bleichröder's financial statements to Bismarck which I found in three packets, labeled Schönhausen Archiv, stored in the attic over the present Prince Bismarck's riding stables. Bleichröder sent monthly, quarterly, semiannual, and annual statements to Bismarck, not all of which have survived. He occasionally sent lists of his portfolio, and some of these have survived. A few of Bleichröder's statements are to be found in the Bleichröder Archive at Harvard University.

15. Cf. Böhme, *Deutschlands Weg,* pp. 320–44; on the general conditions of the early 1870s.

16. Bleichröder to Bismarck, 4 Aug. 1872, SA.

17. Böhme, *Deutschlands Weg,* pp. 341–45.

18. Bleichröder to Bismarck, 25 July 1873, SA.

19. Bismarck to Bleichröder, 22 Aug. 1874, BA.

20. Bleichröder to Bismarck, 25 Aug. and 2 Sept. 1874, SA.

21. Bismarck to Bleichröder, 1 Oct. 1874, SA.

22. *GW,* VIII, 212, 383.

23. On Peter Shuvalov, cf. Hugh Seton-Watson, *The Russian Empire* (Oxford, 1967), p. 378; also R. W. Seton-Watson, *Disraeli, Gladstone and the Eastern Question,* new ed. (Edinburgh, 1962), p. 40.

24. Johanna von Bismarck to Bleichröder, 29 Sept. 1875; Jenny Fatio to Bleichröder, 31 Oct. 1875, BA.

25. Bleichröder to H. von Bismarck, 2 Oct. 1875, FA.

26. *GW,* VIII, 383.

27. Cf. handwritten note on Bleichröder letter.

28. Bleichröder to Bismarck, 11 June 1885, SA.

29. *Ibid.,* 8 and 14 March 1890, SA.

30. J. C. G. Röhl, *Germany Without Bismarck: The Crisis of Government in the Second Reich* (Berkeley, 1967), pp. 52–55.

31. So Herbert reported to Lord Rosebery, in English, on 30 March 1890; Bussman, *Herbert von Bismarck*, p. 567.

32. Bleichröder to Bismarck, 4 and 7 June 1890, SA.

33. Bismarck to Bleichröder, 23 July 1891, BA.

34. *GW*, XII, 365.

35. *GW*, XIV², 909.

36. *GW*, XIV², 834.

37. A. O. Meyer, *Bismarck*, p. 446; Westphal, *Bismarck*, p. 12.

38. See A. O. Meyer, *Bismarck*, p. 382, on land hunger.

39. Westphal, *Bismarck*, p. 56.

40. *GW*, XII, 374.

41. Siebert to Bleichröder, 15 July 1871, BA.

42. Bleichröder to Bismarck, 12 Nov. 1873, SA; Bismarck to Bleichröder, 16 Nov. 1873, BA.

43. Bleichröder to Bismarck, 20 Oct. 1879, plus draft in Bismarck's hand concerning purchase, SA.

44. *Ibid.*, 1, 2, 6, 20 Dec. 1882, SA.

45. Bleichröder's statement, 31 Dec. 1883, SA.

46. Bismarck to Bleichröder, 25 Aug. 1872, BA.

47. Quoted in Vagts, "Bismarck's Fortune," *CEH*, I, 213.

48. Bussmann, *Herbert von Bismarck*, p. 459; H. von Bismarck to Rantzau, 2 July 1887, FA, courtesy of Dr. Hoepke.

49. Bismarck to Bleichröder, 29 Oct. 1880, BA. He sought to save Ritsch's face. Four years later, Bleichröder twice reported on this man, who by then had become a regular grain speculator in the commodity market and was reported to have lost a million marks. Bleichröder to Bismarck, 30 June and 11 Aug. 1884, SA. See also Westphal, *Bismarck*, p. 112.

50. Bleichröder to Bismarck, 24 Jan. 1881, SA.

51. A. O. Meyer, *Bismarck*, pp. 448–49.

52. Old insurance claim, Vaterländische Feuer-Gesellschaft to Lange, 24 Nov. 1882, BA; Bleichröder to Bismarck, 27 Feb. 1883, SA; Wilhelm von Bismarck to Bleichröder, 21 Dec. 1882, BA.

53. Westphal, *Bismarck*, pp. 49, 54.

54. Bleichröder to H. von Bismarck, 8 July 1876, FA.

55. H. von Bismarck to Bleichröder, 9 July 1876; Drews to Bleichröder, 9 July 1876, BA.

56. Bleichröder to H. von Bismarck, 11 and 13 July 1876, FA; Bismarck to Bleich-

röder, 6 Aug. 1876; H. von Bismarck to Bleichröder, 12 Oct. 1876, BA.

57. Bleichröder to Bismarck, 2 Aug. 1876, SA.

58. Bismarck to Bleichröder, 6 Aug. 1876, BA.

59. *Ibid.*, 3 Oct. 1876.

60. Bleichröder to Bismarck, 9 and 10 Oct. 1877, SA.

61. Bismarck to Bleichröder, 3 Dec. 1877, BA; Bleichröder to Bismarck, 8 Dec. 1877, SA.

62. Bleichröder to H. von Bismarck, 10 Jan. 1878; Bleichröder to Bismarck, 5 Feb., 2 Oct., and 4 Nov. 1878, all in SA.

63. Wilhelm von Bismarck to Bleichröder, 13 Jan. 1879, BA.

64. Bleichröder to H. von Bismarck, 16 Jan. 1879; Bleichröder to Bismarck, 15 Jan. 1879, SA.

65. Bleichröder to H. von Bismarck, 11 Nov. 1879, SA.

66. H. von Bismarck to Bleichröder, 25 Dec. 1879, BA.

67. *Ibid.*, 31 Dec. 1879.

68. Bleichröder statement, no date [1883]; Wilhelm von Bismarck to Bleichröder, 30 Jan. 1885, BA; Rantzau to Bleichröder, 26 Sept. 1888; Bernhard Behrend to Bleichröder, 1 Oct. 1888; Rottenburg to Bleichröder, 7, 22, 25, 27 Oct., 5 Nov. 1888, BA; Kohl, *Bismarck-Regesten*, II, 492.

69. Westphal, *Bismarck*, p. 55; and *GW*, VIII, 489.

70. *GW*, VIII, 423–24. See Otto Jöhlinger, *Bismarck und die Juden* (Berlin, 1921), pp. 105, 129.

71. *GW*, XII, 106.

72. Copy of memo in Wilhelm von Bismarck's hand, 6 Feb. 1882, BA.

73. Lange to Bleichröder, 20 July 1882, BA.

74. *Ibid.*, 21 Aug. 1886, 6 Nov. 1887.

75. Hibernia to Bleichröder, 29 March 1890, BA.

76. Böhme, *Deutschlands Weg*, pp. 318–19, 508.

77. Bleichröder to Bismarck, 1 Jan. 1879, 6 Jan. 1880, Jan. 1884, SA.

78. Bleichröder memorandum, addressed to Dr. Gloner, 1 Feb. 1891, BA.

79. Taylor, *Bismarck*, p. 251.

80. Rottenburg to Bleichröder, 21 May 1890, BA.

81. Vagts, "Bismarck's Fortune," p. 230.

82. Quoted in Kohl, *Bismarck-Jahrbuch*, VI, 399.

83. Various account statements, Bleichröder to Bismarck, 1885–1890, SA; see also *Holstein Papers*, II, 204–5.

84. *Holstein Papers*, II, 178, 181, 277;

Küntzel, *Die Finanzen*, pp. 483–84; *Vossische Zeitung*, 23, 24, 25 March 1885, DZA: Merseburg: Zivilkabinett, Standeserhöhungen des Fürsten von Bismarck, Rep. 89H XXIII, No. 12f.

85. Various account statements, Bleichröder to Bismarck, 1885–1890, SA; see also *Holstein Papers*, II, 204–5; Bismarck to William I, 13 June 1885, DZA: Merseburg: Zivilkabinett, Standeserhöhungen des Fürsten von Bismarck, Rep. 89H XXIII, No. 12f.

86. Vierhaus, *Spitzemberg*, pp. 218–19; *Holstein Papers*, II, 178–79, also n. 87. Lerchenfeld-Koefering, *Erinnerungen*, p. 255.

87. *Holstein Papers*, II, 82.

88. *GW*, XIV², 900–1.

89. Lucius, *Bismarck*, p. 382.

90. Ernst Feder, ed., *Bismarcks Grosses Spiel. Die Geheimen Tagebücher Ludwig Bambergers* (Frankfurt a.M., 1932), p. 333.

91. Vagts, "Bismarck's Fortune," p. 216.

92. *GW*, XII, 348, 371.

93. Wilmowski to Bleichröder, 17 May 1890, and Bismarck to Bleichröder, 22 May 1890, BA; Bleichröder's accounts, 31 Dec. 1890 and official tax assessment notice, 8 March 1890, SA; Hellmut von Gerlach, *Von Rechts nach Links* (Zurich, 1937), pp. 96–101. On income-tax estimates in Prussia, see Gerd Hohorst, Jürgen Kocka, and Gerhard A. Ritter, *Sozialgeschichtliches Arbeitsbuch. Materialien zur Statistik des Kaiserreichs, 1870–1914* (Munich, 1975), p. 106.

13 / The World of Banking and Diplomacy

1. The phrase was Lord Ampthill's, 20 Nov. 1881, Knaplund, *Letters from the Berlin Embassy*, p. 235.

2. Kardorff, *Kardorff*, p. 108.

3. There is of course a vast literature on the dimensions of foreign policy and on the inadequacy of the older type of diplomatic history. In 1954, one of the masters of diplomatic history, Pierre Renouvin, called both for greater attention to economic and financial factors in the study of diplomatic history and for "prudence" in assessing causal relations; "L'histoire contemporaine des relations internationales; orientation de récherches," *Revue Historique*, 211 (1954), esp. 234–42. Eckart Kehr pioneered studies in the domestic origins of German foreign policy—a subject laden with taboos at the time—and Hans-Ulrich Wehler has given much currency to the notion of the "primacy of internal policy." See, for example, Kehr, *Der Primat der Innenpolitik. Gesammelte Aufsätze zur preussisch-deutschen Sozialgeschichte im 19. Jahrhundert*, ed. by Hans-Ulrich Wehler (Berlin, 1965). See also the sane and succinct statements by Lionel Robbins, *The Economic Causes of War* (London, 1939), and by James Joll, *1914. The Unspoken Assumptions*, an inaugural lecture (London, 1968).

4. Knaplund, *Letters from the Berlin Embassy*, p. 193. Goldschmidt to Bleichröder, 27 Nov. 1879, BA.

5. *GP*, VI, 165.

6. Knaplund, *Letters from the Berlin Embassy*, p. 256.

7. See Herbert Feis, *Europe: The World's Banker, 1870–1914* (New Haven, 1930), p. 160.

8. Bleichröder to Bismarck, 3 Feb. 1880, SA.

9. *GP*, V, 320.

10. *DDF*, II, 482; Rottenburg to Bleichröder, 28 Nov. 1882, BA.

11. *GP*, VI, 165, 169.

12. Bleichröder to Bismarck, 8 Aug. 1877, SA.

13. See Morsey, *Reichsverwaltung*, pp. 104–122; and Monts, *Erinnerungen*, pp. 39–53.

14. Knaplund, *Letters from the Berlin Embassy*, p. 208.

15. Bussmann, *Herbert von Bismarck*, p. 477.

16. *Ibid.*, p. 268.

17. *GP*, VI, 343.

18. Martin Winckler, *Bismarcks Bündnispolitik und das europäische Gleichgewicht* (Stuttgart, 1964), p. 31.

19. William Flavelle Monypenny and George Earle Buckle, *The Life of Benjamin Disraeli, Earl of Beaconsfield*, new and rev. ed. (2 vols.; New York, 1929), II, 1202.

20. Arthur von Brauer, *Im Dienste Bismarcks* (Berlin, 1936), pp. 206–77, Münster to Bleichröder, 8 June 1878, BA.

21. H. von Bismarck to Rantzau, 17 Oct. 1887, FA, courtesy of Dr. Hoepke.

22. *Holstein Papers*, II, 131; Bussmann, *Herbert von Bismarck*, p. 476.

23. Winfred Sühlo, *Georg Herbert Graf zu Münster* (Hildesheim, 1968), p 140; Zara S. Steiner, *The Foreign Office and Foreign Policy, 1898–1914* (Cambridge, 1969), p. 174.

24. The literature on European diplomacy in Bismarck's time is vast and ever-increasing. Monographs abound, great synthetic reconstructions are few and mostly inadequate. The best studies are William L. Langer, *European Alliances and Alignments, 1871–1890*, 2nd ed. (New York, 1956); A. J. P. Taylor, *The Struggle for Mastery in Europe, 1848–1918* (Oxford, 1954); and Pierre Renouvin, *Histoire des relations internationales*, Vol. VI: *Le XIXᵉ siècle*, Part 2, *De 1871 à 1914* (Paris, 1955). A useful survey of the general literature is in Allan Mitchell, *Bismarck and the French Nation, 1848–1890* (New York, 1971), and in Andreas Hillgruber, *Bismarcks Aussenpolitik* (Freiburg,

1972), while Hans-Ulrich Wehler's *Bismarck und der Imperialismus* bolsters a particular thesis with a masterly command of the sources and of secondary accounts.

25. *DDF*, VII, 4.

26. Taffs, *Ambassador to Bismarck*, p. 66.

27. Taylor, *Mastery in Europe*, p. 255.

28. St. Hilaire to Bleichröder, 3 Jan. 1883; Münster to Bleichröder, 1 Jan. 1884, BA.

29. Taffs, *Ambassador to Bismarck*, p. 70; Blake, *Disraeli*, p. 613; and St. Vallier to Waddington, 24 and 25 April 1878, MAE: Allemagne, Vol. 22.

30. Münster to Bleichröder, 21 Jan. 1890, BA.

31. David S. Landes, "The Great Indemnity," unpublished mss., covering the period through the first loan in June 1871.

32. Waldersee to Bismarck, 1 July 1871, GFO: Frankreich 70.

33. On this see Henri Doniol, *M. Thiers Le Comte de Saint Vallier Le Général de Manteuffel* (Paris, 1897). I have also used the Manteuffel Nachlass in Merseburg, which contains a full record of St. Vallier's fascinating letters to Manteuffel—a source hitherto not used, I believe.

34. Knaplund, *Letters from the Berlin Embassy*, p. 34.

35. Stosch to Bleichröder, 16 April 1892, BA.

36. Keudell to Bleichröder, 25 July 1871, BA.

37. Bleichröder to Bismarck, 22, 24, 25, 28, 31 July 1871; Bismarck to Bleichröder, 10 Aug. 1871, GFO: Frankreich 70.

38. *DDF*, I, 60.

39. *DDF*, I, 61–65.

40. Le Duc de Broglie, *La Mission de M. de Gontaut-Biron à Berlin*, 2nd ed. (Paris 1896), p. 22.

41. Keudell to Bleichröder, 28 Aug. 1871, BA.

42. Schwabach to Bleichröder, 30 Aug., 5 and 9 Sept. 1871, BA.

43. Bleichröder to Rothschild, 29 Sept., 29 Dec. 1871, RA.

44. Hans Herzfeld, *Deutschland und das geschlagene Frankreich*, p. 127.

45. Imelmann to Bleichröder, 7 Dec. 1871, BA, for an almost verbatim record of these negotiations.

46. Bismarck to Bleichröder, 6 Jan. 1872, BA.

47. *Occupation et Libération du Territoire, 1871–1875, Correspondances* (2 vols.; Paris, 1903), I, 131; Bleichröder to Rothschild, 29 Dec. 1871, RA.

48. *Occupation et Libération*, I, 157, 170. It is characteristic of the historical treatment of Bleichröder that in this invaluable collection

of documents pertaining to Franco-German relations, his name is mentioned constantly and the close relation between Gontaut-Biron and Bleichröder is amply evidenced, while in the more or less hagiographic account of Gontaut-Biron's tenure in Berlin, Broglie, *La Mission*, Bleichröder is mentioned only in passing, pp. 26, 27. But then, does it enhance a man's reputation to have worked with the Court Jew? See also *DDF*, I, 132–33.

49. Bleichröder to Rothschild, 24 March 1872, RA.

50. *Ibid.*, 20 April 1872; Broglie, *La Mission*, pp. 26–27.

51. Bleichröder to Bismarck, 19 May 1872, GFO: Frankreich 72.

52. Bucher to Bleichröder, 16 and 17 June 1872, BA.

53. Bleichröder to Bismarck, 4 July 1872, FA.

54. Bucher to Keudell, 12 June 1872, BA; Bleichröder to Bismarck, 10 July 1872, FA.

55. Bleichröder to Bismarck, 21 Oct. 1872, FA.

56. *Occupation et Libération*, II, 162 ff, 266 ff.

57. H. von Bismarck to Bleichröder, 10 June 1875, BA.

58. Goldschmidt to Bleichröder, 27 Dec. 1875, BA.

59. Landsberg to Bleichröder, 6 May 1877, BA.

60. GP, III, 395–96; also see the entirely inadequate "Beginnings of a German-French Understanding, 1878–1885," in *GP*, III, 379–454.

61. Taylor, *Bismarck*, p. 214.

62. H. von Bismarck to Bleichröder, 7 Feb. 1878, BA.

63. *DDF*, II, 469–73, 477–78, 481–82.

64. *Ibid.*, p. 526.

65. *Ibid.*, III, 243.

66. Hohenlohe to Bismarck, 25 July 1881, and enclosure of *L'Unité Nationale*, 26 July 1881, GFO: Frankreich 87.

67. Hohenlohe to Bismarck, 13 Feb. 1882, *ibid.*

68. Bleichröder to Bismarck, 2 Feb. 1882, *ibid.*

69. *Ibid.*, 6 Feb. 1882.

70. Bleichröder to Bismarck, 17 June 1882, SA.

71. See Taylor, *Mastery in Europe*, pp. 281–303.

72. *DDF*, VI, 440.

73. *DDF*, V, 49; St. Vallier to Bleichröder, 12 Oct. 1883, BA.

74. Rogge, *Holstein*, p. 132.

75. Bussmann, *Herbert von Bismarck*, p. 175.

76. *DDF*, V, 212.

77. *Ibid.*, pp. 242–44.
78. Rogge, *Holstein*, pp. 205–6, 210; St. Vallier to Bleichröder, 22 March 1884, BA.
79. Bleichröder to Hatzfeldt, 10 Jan. 1885, BA.
80. *DDF*, V, 566–67.
81. Bleichröder to Karl Anton von Hohenzollern-Sigmaringen, 30 March 1885, HS; Gordon Wright, *France in Modern Times* (Chicago, 1960), p. 310.
82. C. de Freycinet, *Souvenirs, 1878–1893*, 7th ed. (Paris, 1913), pp. 438–39.
83. Bleichröder to Bismarck, 26 and 29 Sept. 1886, GFO: Frankreich 87.
84. Freycinet to Bleichröder, 8 Oct. and 29 Nov. 1886, BA.
85. *DDF*, V, 342–43.
86. Münster to Bleichröder, 9 Feb. 1886, 31 Dec. 1885, BA.
87. Bismarck to Bronsart, 22 Dec. 1886; cabinet meeting, 23 Dec. 1886, DZA: Potsdam: Reichskanzlei, Akten betreffend Angelegenheiten der auswärtigen Politik im Allgemeinen, No. 1, Vol. 2.
88. Münster to Bleichröder, 1 Jan. 1887, BA.
89. *Ibid.*, 10 Feb. 1887.
90. *DDF*, VI, 397.
91. *Ibid.*, p. 453.
92. Bleichröder to Bismarck, 22 Feb. 1889, GFO: Frankreich 105, Nr. 3a.
93. *DDF*, VII, 660–63, 683. Herbette to Bleichröder, 13, 15, 19 Aug., 24 Sept. 1891; Münster to Bleichröder.
94. Comte Charles de Moüy, *Souvenirs et Causeries d'un Diplomate* (Paris, 1909), p. 114. In 1881, Lord Russell was created Lord Ampthill.
95. Odo Russell to Arthur Russell, 3 April 1872, Russell Papers, PRO, courtesy of Sir Alec Randall.
96. Ampthill to Bleichröder, 5 Jan. 1882, BA.
97. Emily Ampthill to Bleichröder, 21 Sept. 1884, BA.
98. Taffs, *Ambassador to Bismarck*, p. 4.
99. Holborn, *Modern Germany*, pp. 193–94; Münster to Bleichröder, 11 May 1878, BA.
100. Herbert von Nostitz, *Bismarcks unbotmässiger Botschafter. Fürst Münster von Derneburg (1820–1902)* (Göttingen, 1968), does not mention Bleichröder, nor do several recent monographs.
101. St. Vallier to Waddington, 25 April 1879, and St. Vallier to Freycinet, 30 May 1880, MAE: Allemagne, Vol. 28, 35.
102. Münster to Bleichröder, 31 March 1881, BA.
103. His grandson and unsatisfactory biographer, Nostitz, stresses his illnesses; *Bismarck unbotmässiger Botschafter*, pp. 19–25.
104. Münster to Bleichröder, 17 July

1878, 7 March 1879, 12 May 1884, and 4 April 1885, BA.
105. Bleichröder to Beaconsfield, 24 Oct. 1878, Disraeli Papers, Hughenden Manor (Buckinghamshire); Beaconsfield to Bleichröder, 2 Nov. 1878, BA. In this and subsequent Disraeli letters, I have left the original punctuation.
106. Beaconsfield to Bleichröder, 5 Jan. 1879, BA.
107. Bleichröder to Beaconsfield, 10 June 1880, Hughenden Manor.
108. Beaconsfield to Bleichröder, 16 June 1880, BA.
109. *Ibid.*, 24 Sept. 1880; Bleichröder to Beaconsfield, 6 Oct. 1880, and 1 March 1881, Disraeli Papers, Hughenden Manor. Bleichröder to Bismarck, 19 Feb. 1881, GFO: England 69; Bismarck to William, 19 Feb. 1881, *ibid.*
110. Bleichröder to Bismarck, 10 Oct. 1880, BA.
111. Münster to Bleichröder, 23 Oct. 1883, 1 July 1884, BA; Bismarck to Bleichröder, 6 Aug. 1882, BA.
112. On this and other details, see Joachim Mai, *Das deutsche Kapital in Russland, 1850–1894* (East Berlin, 1970), esp. pp. 74–77; in his thoroughly researched study, Mai used some of the Bleichröder material which Prof. Landes and I gave to the DZA in return for permission to use their archives and to have some files microfilmed. His crude Sovietphilia, however, is almost a caricature of what can happen to a German scholar entrapped by an ideological system backed by political power.
113. *Ibid.*, p. 115.
114. Bleichröder to H. von Bismarck, 28 April 1878, Bleichröder to Bismarck, 16 May 1878, FA.
115. Bleichröder to Bismarck, 5 Oct. 1878, SA.
116. Sack to Bleichröder, 21 Oct. 1878, BA. On Sack see Fürstenberg, *Lebensgeschichte*, pp. 109–10, who deals extensively with the life of prewar Russian bankers.
117. Bleichröder to Bismarck, 15 Oct. 1878, FA.
118. St. Vallier to Waddington, 8 Nov. 1878, MAE: Allemagne, Vol. 24.
119. On this, see also Hans-Ulrich Wehler, *Krisenherde des Kaiserreichs, 1871–1918* (Göttingen, 1970), pp. 163–80.
120. *DDF*, II, 469–73, 477–78.
121. Memorandum naming Bleichröder as source of information, 31 Aug. 1879, GFO: Russland 65, adh. 1, Vol. 1.
122. A. Eulenburg to Bleichröder, 21, 24, 29, 31 Aug. 1879; Lehndorff to Bleichröder, 24 Sept. 1879, BA.
123. Hugh Seton-Watson, *Russian Empire*, p. 517.

124. See the general survey in Theodore H. von Laue, *Sergei Witte and the Industrialization of Russia* (New York, 1963), p. 22 and ch. 1, *passim*.

125. Hugh Seton-Watson, unpublished lecture, "Nationalism, Supra-Nationalism and Repression in Central Europe."

126. Valuyev to Bleichröder, 7 March 1879, BA; Bruce Waller, *Bismarck at the Crossroads: The Reorientation of German Foreign Policy after the Congress of Berlin, 1878–1880* (London, 1974), p. 125.

127. Valuyev to Bleichröder, 23 Jan. 1880; Greig to Bleichröder, 9 May 1880, BA.

128. Saburov to Bleichröder, Feb. 1882, BA.

129. *Holstein Papers*, II, 83.

130. Greig to Bleichröder, 12 Nov. 1880, BA.

131. Hans von Bleichröder to Bleichröder, 6 and 8 Aug. 1879, BA.

132. Bleichröder to Bismarck, 25 Nov. 1880, FA.

133. Abaza to Bleichröder, 15 March 1881, BA.

134. Valuyev to Bleichröder, 23 April 1880, BA.

135. Hugh Seton-Watson, *Russian Empire*, pp. 493–96.

136. *Holstein Papers*, II, 16–17.

137. Bunge to Bleichröder, 30 March 1882, BA.

138. Bleichröder to Bismarck, 20 July 1882, SA. Also 16 Aug. 1881 and 21 March 1882, GFO: Russland 71.

139. Rantzau to Foreign Office, 5 Dec. 1883, *ibid.*; Dieter Friede, *Der Verheimlichte Bismarck* (Würzburg, 1960), pp. 167–68.

140. Knaplund, *Letters from the Berlin Embassy*, p. 392; Bleichröder to Prince Karl Anton of Hohenzollern-Sigmaringen, 9 May 1884, HS.

141. *Holstein Papers*, II, 131.

142. *Holstein Papers*, III, 107.

143. Bunge to Bleichröder, 1 May 1884, BA.

144. Horace de Guenzburg to Bleichröder, 10 Aug. 1883, BA.

145. Münster to Bleichröder, 4 April 1885, BA; Knaplund, *Letters from the Berlin Embassy*, pp. 396, 395.

146. Bleichröder to Bismarck, 5 and 11 June 1885, SA; Bismarck to Bleichröder, 9 June 1885, BA; *Holstein Papers*, II, 202–3.

147. *Ibid.*, p. 230.

148. Saburov to Bleichröder, May 1883, BA; Sack to Bleichröder, 24 Jan. 1887, BA.

14 / Rumania: The Triumph of Expediency

1. The standard work in English is R. W. Seton-Watson, *A History of the Rou-manians: From Roman Times to the Completion of Unity* (Cambridge, 1934), which deals with our part of the story in a summary and rather pro-Rumanian manner; for the founding of Rumania, see also the spirited work by T. W. Riker, *The Making of Roumania: A Study of an International Problem, 1856–1866* (London, 1931).

2. R. W. Seton-Watson, *Roumanians*, p. 315.

3. Riker, *Roumania*, p. 554.

4. R. W. Seton-Watson, *Roumanians*, p. 347.

5. Consul in Jassy to Bismarck, 24 Dec. 1869, GFO: Türkei 24. Simon Dubnow, *Die neueste Geschichte des jüdischen Volkes. Das Zeitalter der ersten Reaktion und der zweiten Emanzipation (1815–1881)*, Vol. IX of *Weltgeschichte des jüdischen Volkes von seinen Uranfängen bis zu seiner Gegenwart*, trans. from Russian by Dr. A. Steinberg (Berlin, 1929), p. 483, spoke of 200,000, while others, including Bleichröder's informants, mentioned 300,000.

6. I am grateful to Hugh Seton-Watson for reading an earlier version of this chapter and for comments on Rumanian anti-Semitism on which I based some of my own remarks.

7. Goldschmidt to Bleichröder, 26 May and 1 June 1867, BA. Bernstorff to Bismarck, 27 May 1867; Bismarck to St. Pierre, 28 May 1867, GFO: Türkei 24.

8. *Aus dem Leben König Karls von Rumänien. Aufzeichnungen eines Augenzeugen* (4 vols.; Stuttgart, 1894–1900), I, 210.

9. *Ibid.*, p. 213.

10. Bismarck to Crémieux, 22 Feb. 1868, Rumanian Jews, AI:ID2.

11. Israelitische Gemeinde Jassy to Bleichröder, 6 and 10 April 1868, BA.

12. *APP*, IX, 821, 835; Bernstorff to Bismarck, 27 March 1868; Reuss to Bismarck, 28 May 1868, GFO: Türkei 24.

13. *Aus dem Leben König Karls*, I, 257.

14. A. von Oppenheim to Karl Anton, 28 March 1868; Carl Freiherr von Rothschild, 8 April 1868; B. Auerbach to Karl Anton, 7, 24, and 26 April 1868; *Börsenzeitung*, 20 April 1868; *Neue Freie Presse*, 4 April 1868, HS.

15. R. W. Seton-Watson, *Roumanians*, p. 350 (my italics).

16. Hajo Holborn, *Deutschland und die Türkei, 1878–1890* (Berlin, 1926), p. 1.

17. Riker, *Roumania*, p. vii.

18. St. Pierre to Bismarck, 15 Aug. 1863, DZA: Merseburg: A.A.II. Rep. 6. No. 4205, Geheimes Staatsarchiv, Rumänische Eisenbahnen.

19. Bismarck to St. Pierre, 29 Sept. 1863, *ibid.*

20. After his downfall in Russia in 1876, Strousberg wrote an interesting apologia called

Dr. Strousberg und sein Wirken (Berlin, 1876).

21. *Aus dem Leben König Karls* I, 243; Keyserling to Bismarck, 13 March 1868; Bismarck to Keyserling, 15 March 1868, DZA: Merseburg: A.A.II. Rep. 6. A4205, Geheimes Staatsarchiv, Rum. Eisenbahnen.

22. Bleichröder to Bismarck, 6 Nov. 1869, SA.

23. Jorring? (from Jassy) to Bismarck, 22 March 1868; Keyserling to Bismarck, 5 June 1868, DZA: Merseburg: A.A.II. Rep. 6. A4205, Geheimes Staatsarchiv, Rum. Eisenbahnen.

24. Radowitz to Bismarck, 8 April 1870, *ibid.*; Münch, *Hansemann*, pp. 149–50.

25. Blücher to Foreign Office, 21 Sept. 1868, DZA: Merseburg: A.A.II. Rep. 6. No. 4205, Geheimes Staatsarchiv, Rum. Eisenbahnen.

26. Holborn, *Radowitz*, I, 189 ff.

27. Radowitz to Bismarck, 8 April 1870, DZA: Merseburg: A.A.II, Rep. 6. A4205, Geheimes Staatsarchiv, Rum. Eisenbahnen.

28. Münch, *Hansemann*, pp. 157–58; Radowitz to Bismarck, 22 April 1870, DZA: Merseburg: A.A.II., Rep. 6. No. 4205, Geheimes Staatsarchiv, Rum. Eisenbahnen.

29. Radowitz to Bismarck, 6 May 1870, *ibid.*

30. *Ibid.*, 2 Oct. 1870.

31. *Ibid.*, 21 Oct. 1870.

32. Holborn, *Radowitz*, I, 196.

33. *Aus dem Leben König Karls*, II, 159.

34. Bismarck to Foreign Office, 9, 11 Nov. 1870, DZA: Merseburg: A.A.II. Rep. 6. No. 4205, Geheimes Staatsarchiv, Rum. Eisenbahnen.

35. Strousberg to Bismarck, 13 Dec. 1870, *ibid.*

36. Bismarck to Camphausen, 23 Dec. 1870, *ibid.*

37. For a different view, see Wehler, *Bismarck*, pp. 215–23.

38. Camphausen to Bismarck, 31 Dec. 1870, DZA: Merseburg: A.A.II. Rep. 6. No. 4205, Geheimes Staatsarchiv, Rum. Eisenbahnen.

39. *Aus dem Leben König Karls*, II, 144–170.

40. Heinrich Steubel, *Das Verhältnis zwischen Staat und Banken auf dem Gebiete des Preussischen Anleihewesens von 1871–1913* (Berlin, 1935), p. 34; *Aus dem Leben König Karls*, II, 203.

41. Radowitz to Bismarck, 10 March 1871, DZA: Merseburg: A.A.II. Rep. 6. No. 4205, Geheimes Staatsarchiv, Rum. Eisenbahnen.

42. *Ibid.*; Holborn, *Radowitz*, I, 215.

43. Radowitz to Bismarck, 24 March 1871, DZA: Merseburg: A.A.II. Rep. 6. No. 4205; Geheimes Staatsarchiv, Rum. Eisen-

bahnen. Holborn, *Radowitz*, I, 217–22; and *Aus dem Leben König Karls*, II, 174–78.

44. Holborn, *Radowitz*, I, 231, and *Kladderadatsch*, 30 July and 13 Aug. 1871.

45. *Aus dem Leben König Karls*, II, 213.

46. In part, this may arise from the fact that no previous historian has looked at the archival record. As an example of misinformation, consider the opinion of the best English historian of Rumania: "Bismarck's uncompromising support of the *louche* Strousberg has always remained somewhat of a mystery, and attempts have been made to explain it by the fact that the latter was a dependent of the great Berlin banking house of Bleichröder, upon whom Bismarck relied almost unreservedly in all financial questions." R. W. Seton-Watson, *Roumanians*, pp. 330–31. The account in Münch's *Hansemann*, pp. 148–67, is also misleading.

47. Gabriac to Rémusat, 12 Aug. 1871, MAE: Allemagne Vol. 1.

48. Münch to Beust, 9 Oct. 1871, HHSA: PA III: Preussen.

49. Schwabach to Bleichröder, 31 July and 15 Aug. 1871, BA.

50. Lehndorff to Bleichröder, 24 and 25 Dec. 1871, BA.

51. Bleichröder to Bismarck, 26 Aug. 1872, FA.

52. Münch, *Hansemann*, pp. 154 ff.

53. Bismarck note, 24 Jan. 1872; Bucher to Bleichröder, 16 June 1872, BA; Thielau to Bismarck, 28 Dec. 1871, 7 Jan. 1882; Abeken to William I, 25 April 1872, GFO: Türkei 104.

54. *Aus dem Leben König Karls*, II, 246.

55. Bleichröder to Hansemann, 1 April 1872, BA, Bleichröder Privatbüro.

56. *Aus dem Leben König Karls*, II, 414.

57. Münch, *Hansemann*, pp. 158–60.

58. On this, see Zosa Szajkowski, "Conflicts in the Alliance Israélite Universelle and the Founding of the Anglo-Jewish Association, the Vienna Allianz and the Hilfsverein," *Jewish Social Studies*, 19 (1957), 29–50.

59. H. Guedalla to Bleichröder, 23 Feb. 1880, BA; Guedalla was Sir Moses Montefiore's companion and was married to his niece.

60. Dr. Lloyd P. Gartner's excellent study, "Romania, America, and World Jewry: Consul Peixotto in Bucharest, 1870–1876, *American Jewish Historical Quarterly*, 58 (1968), 54.

61. Bleichröder to Bismarck, 30 March 1872; Bismarck to Thielau, 2 April 1872; Bismarck to Bleichröder, 2 April 1872, GFO: Türkei 24.

62. Bleichröder to Alliance Israélite, 30 March and 6 April 1872, AI:ID 1.

63. On the Berlin Committee, see N. M. Gelber, "The Intervention of German Jews at the Berlin Congress, 1878," *LBY*, 5 (1960),

223, and his unpublished manuscript on the same subject, which he was kind enough to lend to Prof. Landes.

64. Dr. S. Neumann to N. Leven, 10 May 1872, AI:IA1.

65. Julius Bleichröder to Alliance Israélite, 16 Aug. 1872, *ibid.*

66. Knaplund, *Letters from the Berlin Embassy*, p. 63.

67. Gelber, "Intervention," pp. 225–27; Berlin Committee to Alliance Israélite, 24 April, 20 July, 22 Aug. 1876, AI:IA1.

68. Bleichröder to Bismarck, 13 Nov. 1877, FA.

69. Gelber, "Intervention," p. 227.

70. Taylor, *Mastery in Europe*, p. 245.

71. Rothschild to Bleichröder, 12 Jan. 1878, Lettres Partic. Allemagne, RA.

72. Quoted in Gelber, "Intervention," p. 229.

73. Dr. S. Neumann to Bleichröder, 4 June 1878, BA.

74. H. von Bismarck to Bleichröder, 7 Feb. 1878, BA.

75. Copy of Bülow's letter, 28 Feb. 1878, BA.

76. Bleichröder to Alliance Israélite, 4 March 1878, AI:ID1.

77. Alliance Israélite, Vienna, to Bleichröder, 1 Feb., 6 and 26 March 1878, BA. St. Vallier to Waddington, 27 March 1878, MAE: Allemagne, Vol. 22.

78. Daniel to Bleichröder, 13 March 1878, BA.

79. Bleichröder to Alliance Israélite, 21 Feb. 1878, AI:ID1.

80. *Allgemeine Zeitung des Judentums*, 5 March 1878.

81. Bleichröder to Bismarck, 10 April 1878, FA.

82. Bleichröder to Crémieux, 12 Feb. 1878, AI: ID1.

83. *SBHA*, 14 May 1878, III, pp. 1314–25; Lasker to Bleichröder, 18 May 1878; Bülow to Bleichröder, 22 May 1878, BA.

84. Bleichröder to Crémieux, 19 May 1878, AI:ID1. Isidore Loeb to Bleichröder, 20 and 29 May 1878, BA.

85. Bleichröder to Sir Moses Montefiore, 23 May 1878; Sir Moses to Bleichröder, 5 June 1878, BA.

86. Holborn, *Radowitz*, II, 28.

87. Quoted in R. W. Seton-Watson, *Disraeli, Gladstone*, p. 434.

88. Bülow to Bleichröder, 15 June 1878, BA; Gelber, "Intervention," pp. 236–38.

89. Crémieux to Bleichröder, 2 July 1878; Sir Moses Montefiore to Bleichröder, 2 and 11 July 1878, BA.

90. Gelber, unpublished mss., p. 87.

91. *Ibid.*, p. 87c. Alexander Novotny,

Quellen und Studien zur Geschichte des Berliner Kongresses, Vol. 1 (Graz and Cologne, 1957), 115.

92. Bleichröder to Montefiore, 9 July 1878, BA; Bleichröder to Crémieux, 9 July 1878, AI:ID1.

93. Montefiore to Bleichröder, 28 July 1878, BA.

94. Bleichröder to Bismarck, 2 July 1878, FA.

95. Leaders of Berlin Community to Bismarck, 11 July 1878, DZA: Potsdam: Reichskanzlei: Akten betreffend Angelegenheiten der auswärtigen Politik im Allgemeinen, No. 1, Vol. 1.

96. *The Times*, 4 July 1878.

97. Catherine Radziwill, *The Empress Frederick* (New York, n.d.), p. 150.

98. Quoted in Gartner, "Romania," p. 111.

99. *The Times*, 5 July 1878.

100. Andrássy to Consul Stadler, 8 Aug. 1878, HHSA: PA XVIII: Rumänien.

101. Waller, *Bismarck at the Crossroads*, pp. 58–59. Waller sets the final phase of the Rumanian story in the context of Bismarck's diplomacy; his account of the railway entanglement and the Jewish question is very compressed and repeats the common error that Adolph Hansemann was Jewish.

102. Bleichröder to Alliance Israélite, 31 Aug., 16 and 18 Sept. 1878, AI:ID1; Alliance Israélite to Bleichröder, 4 Sept. 1878, BA; Beaconsfield to Bleichröder, 2 Nov. 1878, BA; Bülow to German ambassadors, 6 Oct. 1878, GFO: Türkei 24.

103. Crémieux to Bleichröder, 12 Oct. 1878, BA; Bleichröder to Alliance Israélite, 14 Oct. 1878, AI:ID1.

104. St. Vallier to Waddington, 12 April 1879, MAE: Allemagne, Vol. 28.

105. Salisbury to Russell, 22 Nov. 1878, PRO: FO, 64/900, no. 499.

106. Quoted in W. N. Medlicott, "The Recognition of Roumanian Independence, 1878–1880," *Slavonic Review*, 11 (1933), 369. Medlicott's is the best study of the question, but "viewed from the angle of British foreign policy" (p. 355). Even he made serious mistakes about Bismarck's motives and Bleichröder's role in the Rumanian affair: "The question of the treatment of the Jews became dangerously entangled with the question of the railways, partly because many of the subordinate officials of the railway in Roumania were German Jews, partly because a controlling interest in the railways had been taken by the great Jewish bankers, Hansemann [*sic*] and Bleichröder, with whom Bismarck's personal and political ties were becoming increasingly intimate" (p. 356).

107. Medlicott, "Roumanian Independence," pp. 573–75.

108. *Ibid.*, p. 574.

109. St. Vallier to Waddington, 27 Feb. 1879, MAE: Allemagne, Vol. 27.

110. *Ibid.*, 24 and 12 April 1879, Vol. 28.

111. *Ibid.*, 28 June 1879, Vol. 29.

112. Waller, *Bismarck*, p. 169; Andrássy to Hoyos, 6 July 1879, HHSA: PA XVIII: Rumänien.

113. Medlicott, "Roumanian Independence," p. 577.

114. R.W. Seton-Watson, *Roumanians*, p. 351.

115. Hoyos to Andrássy, 9 July 1879, HHSA: PA XVIII: Rumänien.

116. Hoyos to Andrássy, 16 July 1879; also Bosizio to Andrássy, 15 Aug. 1879, *ibid.*

117. St. Vallier to Waddington, 19 July 1879, MAE: Allemagne, Vol. 29.

118. Bleichröder to Bismarck, 21 July 1879, FA.

119. H. von Bismarck to Radowitz, 23 July 1879, GFO: Türkei 104.

120. Radowitz to Bleichröder, 11, 25 July 1879, BA.

121. Bleichröder to Bismarck, 22 July 1879; Bleichröder to H. von Bismarck, 28 July 1879, FA. This letter negates Waller's assertion that by July Bleichröder "had . . . recovered the money personally advanced to the railway company" (*Bismarck*, p. 171).

122. Bleichröder to H. von Bismarck, 25, 28 July 1879; H. von Bismarck to Bleichröder, 26, 29 July 1879, BA; St. Vallier to Waddington, 28 July 1879, MAE: Allemagne, Vol. 29.

123. *Aus dem Leben König Karls*, IV, 233–37.

124. St. Vallier to Waddington, 28 July 1879, MAE: Allemagne, Vol. 29.

125. Medlicott, "Roumanian Independence," p. 584.

126. Bleichröder to Crémieux, 11 Aug. 1879, AI:IDi.

127. Beust to Foreign Office, Vienna, 26 Aug. 1879, HHSA: PA XVIII: Rumänien.

128. Bleichröder to Alliance Israélite, 1, 3, 18 Oct. 1879, AI:IDi.

129. Rotenhein to Bleichröder, 25 Nov. 1879, BA.

130. Bleichröder to Alliance Israélite, 16 Nov. 1879, AI:IDi.

131. Phillipson to Bleichröder, 25 Nov. 1879, BA.

132. *Aus dem Leben König Karls*, IV, 288–89.

133. Bleichröder to Bismarck, 12, 13 Dec. 1879, GFO: Türkei, 104.

134. H. von Bismarck to Radowitz, 18 Nov. 1879, *ibid.*

135. *Aus dem Leben König Karls*, IV, 251.

136. Quoted in Medlicott, "Roumanian Independence," p. 587.

137. *Aus dem Leben König Karls*, IV, 272.

138. St. Vallier to Waddington, *DDF*, II, 597–98.

139. H. von Bismarck to Bleichröder, 28 Nov. 1879, BA.

140. *Ibid.*, 21 Dec. 1879.

141. *Aus dem Leben König Karls*, IV, 276–80.

142. Szecheny to Haymerle, 31 Jan. 1880, HHSA: PA XVIII: Rumänien.

143. *Aus dem Leben König Karls*, IV, 294; Haymerle to Austrian embassies, 5, 7, 11 Feb. 1880; Beust to Vienna, 12 Feb. 1880, HHSA: PA XVIII: Rumänien.

144. St. Vallier to Freycinet, 14 March 1880, Freycinet to St. Vallier, 16 June 1880, MAE: Allemagne, Vol. 33, 34.

145. Gartner, "Romania," p. 112.

146. Bleichröder to Alliance Israélite, 14 Feb. 1880, AI:IDi.

15 / The Reluctant Colonialist

1. J. A. Hobson, *Imperialism: A Study* (Ann Arbor, Mich., 1965), pp. 56–59, my italics.

2. R. P. Gilson, *Samoa, 1830–1900: The Politics of a Multi-National Community* (Melbourne, 1970), p. 259.

3. Paul M. Kennedy, *The Samoan Tangle: A Study in Anglo-American Relations, 1878–1900* (New York, 1974), p. 28 and ch. 1, *passim*.

4. Helmut Washausen, *Hamburg und die Kolonialpolitik des deutschen Reiches, 1880 bis 1890* (Hamburg, 1968), pp. 55–57; and Kurt Schmack, ed., *J. C. Godeffroy & Sohn, Kaufleute zu Hamburg. Leistung und Schicksal eines Welthandelshauses* (Hamburg, 1938), *passim*.

5. Gustav Godeffroy to Bleichröder, 24 March, 15 June 1879, BA.

6. Godeffroy to Bülow, 25 Jan., 1 Feb. 1879; Bülow to Godeffroy, 6 Feb. 1879; Godeffroy to Bülow, 9 March 1879, DZA: Potsdam: Ausw. A. Rep. VI, Handels- und Schiffs-Sachen: Australien.

7. Wentzel to Bismarck, 1 Dec. 1879, *ibid.*; Godeffroy to Bleichröder, 2 Dec. 1879, BA.

8. Bleichröder to H. von Bismarck, 5 Dec. 1879, FA; H. von Bismarck to Bleichröder, 7 Dec. 1879, BA.

9. Gustav Godeffroy to Bleichröder, 10 Dec. 1879, BA.

10. Stolberg to Bismarck, 17 Dec. 1879; Bismarck to Stolberg, 21 Dec. 1879; Philipsborn to Bismarck, 25 Dec. 1879, Philipsborn to William, 31 Dec. 1879, DZA: Potsdam: Ausw.

A., Rep. VI, Handels- und Schiffs-Sachen: Australian; Münch, *Hansemann*, p. 224. See also Eugene Staley, *War and the Private Investor. A Study in the Relations of International Politics and International Private Investment* (Chicago, 1935), pp. 109–27. On Samoa, see also Mack Walker, *Germany and the Emigration, 1816–1885* (Cambridge, Mass., 1964), pp. 206–13. Also on Samoa, Robert Louis Stevenson, *A Footnote to History: Eight Years of Trouble in Samoa* (New York, 1901), passim.

11. *Reform*, 13 Dec. 1879, Nr. 296, newspaper clipping in DZA: Potsdam: Ausw. A., Rep. VI, Handels- und Schiffs-Sachen: Australien; Washausen, *Hamburg*, p. 58.

12. Münster to Bleichröder, 16, 20, 25, 31 Dec. 1879, BA.

13. St. Vallier to Waddington, 14 July, 21 Nov. 1878, MAE: Allemagne, Vol. 24, 25.

14. *Ibid.*, 8 and 27 Dec. 1879, Vol. 31.

15. St. Vallier to Freycinet, 27 March 1880, *ibid.*, Vol. 33.

16. See Wehler, *Bismarck*, p. 219, also pp. 215–25; Rudolf Ibbeken, *Das aussenpolitische Problem, Staat und Wirtschaft in der deutschen Reichspolitik, 1880–1914* (Schleswig, 1928), p. 44.

17. St. Vallier to Freycinet, 28 April 1880, MAE: Allemagne, Vol. 34.

18. Kennedy, *Samoan Tangle*, ch. 2.

19. Bismarck to Bleichröder and Hansemann, 7 May 1880, DZA: Potsdam: Ausw. A. Rep. VI, Handels- und Schiffs-Sachen: Australien; a part of this letter is reproduced in facsimile in Münch's *Hansemann*.

20. Hansemann to Hohenlohe, 29 July 1880, DZA: Potsdam: Ausw. A. Rep. VI, Handels- und Schiffs-Sachen: Australien; Hansemann to Bleichröder, 14 Aug. 1880, BA.

21. On this, see S. G. Firth, "The New Guinea Company, 1885–1899: A Case of Unprofitable Imperialism," *Historical Studies*, 15 (1972), 361–77; Wehler, *Bismarck*, pp. 391–400; and Münch, *Hansemann*, pp. 226–46.

22. See chapter 11.

23. Chauvin to Bleichröder, 9 April 1880, BA.

24. É. Banning, *Mémoires Politiques et Diplomatiques: Comment fut fondé le Congo* (Paris and Brussels, 1927), p. xiv; W. L. Langer, *European Alliances*, p. 284.

25. Ruth Slade, *King Leopold's Congo: Aspects of Race Relations in the Congo Independent State* (London and New York, 1962), pp. 35–39; and Neal Ascherson, *The King Incorporated: Leopold II in the Age of Trusts* (London, 1963), pp. 39–58.

26. Leopold II to Bleichröder, 5 Dec.

1878, BA; Marcel Luwel, "Gerson von Bleichröder, l'ami commun de Leopold II et de Bismarck," *Afrika-Tervuren*, 8 (1963), 93–110, based in part on the Bleichröder Archive, presents a summary of their relationship.

27. Leopold II to Bleichröder, 4 May 1884, BA.

28. On the diplomacy of this period, see Langer, *European Alliances*, pp. 299–307.

29. Leopold II to Bleichröder, 15 May 1884, BA.

30. Bleichröder to Bismarck, 6 Aug. 1884, SA.

31. Luwel, "Bleichröder," p. 98.

32. Leopold II to Bleichröder, 1 June 1884, BA.

33. Luwel, "Bleichröder," pp. 99–100.

34. Quoted in Robert S. Thomson, *Fondation de l'état indépendant du Congo. Un chapitre de l'histoire du partage de l'Afrique* (Brussels, 1933), p. 182.

35. Luwel, "Bleichröder," p. 103.

36. *Ibid.*, p. 104.

37. Leopold II to Bleichröder, 8 Sept. 1884, BA.

38. *Ibid.*, 16 Sept. 1884.

39. Luwel, "Bleichröder," p. 106.

40. Leopold II to Bleichröder, 29 Nov., 12 Dec. 1884, BA.

41. *Ibid.*, 29 Oct. 1884.

42. Herbert Lüthy, "Colonization and the Making of Mankind," *JEH*, 21 (1961), 487.

43. See Banning, *Mémoires*, pp. 24–25.

44. Schulthess, *Geschichtskalender, 1885*, pp. 55–62; Wehler, *Bismarck*, pp. 239–57; Leopold II to Bleichröder, 20 Aug., 31 Oct., 24 Dec. 1885, BA; Bleichröder to Bismarck, 8 Sept. 1885, SA.

45. Leopold II to Bleichröder, 12 Nov., 12 Dec. 1884, BA.

46. D'Oultremont to Bleichröder, 28 Nov. 1884; Leopold II to Bleichröder, 29 Nov., 12 Dec. 1884, BA; Coumont to Bleichröder, 3 Oct. 1884, BA.

47. Busch, *Bismarck*, I, 552.

48. By now the literature of the subject is immense. Aside from the older works, such as Mary E. Townsend, *The Rise and Fall of Germany's Colonial Empire, 1884–1918* (New York, 1930), the basic and magisterial work is that of Hans-Ulrich Wehler, *Bismarck und der Imperialismus*, a mine of material, marshaled to show that Bismarck's policy sprang principally from domestic considerations, reflecting the underlying economic realities. Wehler's book has itself evoked a sub-literature of criticism; his strong emphasis on the "social-imperialist" basis of Bismarck's policies has attracted particular criticism. On this, see Paul M. Kennedy, "German Colonial Expansion: Has the 'Manipulated Social Imperi-

alism' been Ante-dated?," *Past and Present*, 54 (1972), 134–41. See also the more flexible interpretations by Henry A. Turner, "Bismarck's Imperialist Venture: Anti-British in Origin?" in *Britain and Germany in Africa: Imperial Rivalry and Colonial Rule*, ed. by Prosser Gifford and Wm. Roger Louis (New Haven, 1967), pp. 47–82, esp. p. 51; Walker, *Germany*, pp. 203–4; also A. J. P. Taylor's provocative but now much criticized study, *Germany's First Bid for Colonies, 1884–1885: A Move in Bismarck's European Policy* (London, 1938); and Fritz Ferdinand Müller, *Deutschland—Zanzibar—Ostafrika 1884–1890* (East Berlin, 1959).

49. Turner, "Bismarck's Imperialist Venture," p. 57.

50. Knapland, *Letters from the Berlin Embassy*, pp. 87–89, 119.

51. Langer, *European Alliances*, p. 296.

52. Lord Ampthill to Bleichröder, 3 July 1884, BA.

53. A. J. P. Taylor claimed that Bismarck's "first bid for colonies" was essentially a diplomatic maneuver to find a viable ground for a Franco-German entente; Turner has painstakingly refuted this thesis: "Actually, just the opposite was the case: Bismarck's advances to France were the result of his colonial policy, not its cause." Turner, "Bismarck's Imperialist Venture," p. 77. If anything, the study of Bleichröder would suggest that a rapprochement between France and Germany had been actively envisioned on both sides of the Rhine from 1878 on.

54. Münster to Bleichröder, 17 Oct., 24 Dec. 1884, BA.

55. Saburov to Bleichröder, 9 Dec. 1884, BA.

56. W. O. Henderson, *Studies in German Colonial History* (London, 1962), p. 46; Staley, *War and the Private Investor*, pp. 431–32; Müller, *Deutschland*, p. 425; D. K. Fieldhouse, *Economics and Empire, 1830–1914* (Ithaca, 1973), p. 331 and part I, *passim*. See also Benjamin J. Cohen, *The Question of Imperialism: The Political Economy of Dominance and Dependence* (New York, 1973), for a general discussion.

57. Wehler, *Bismarck*, pp. 163–68.

58. Alex Bein, *Friedrich Hammacher, 1824–1904* (Berlin, 1932), pp. 88–90.

59. Wehler, *Bismarck*, p. 165.

60. *Ibid.*, pp. 236–38; Dechend to Bleichröder, 23 Aug. 1884, BA.

61. Wehler, *Bismarck*, pp. 282–85; Bein, *Hammacher*, pp. 92–93.

62. Schwabach, 18 June 1885, BA.

63. Münch, *Hansemann*, pp. 246–48.

64. Sir James Rennell Rodd, *Social and*

Diplomatic Memories, 1884–1893 (London, 1922), I, 65.

65. Münch, *Hansemann*, pp. 246–48.

66. On this, see Kurt Büttner, *Die Anfänge der deutschen Kolonialpolitik in Ostafrika* (East Berlin, 1959), pp. 104–5; Müller, *Deutschland, passim*; and Wehler, *Bismarck*, pp. 343–67.

67. Rottenburg to Berchem, 17 July 1886, GFO: I.A.A.a. 50, adh. secr., Vol. III.

68. Müller, *Deutschland*, pp. 174–76. On Peters' twisted person and the appropriateness of this nationalist psychopath as exemplar of German colonialism, see the caustic and perceptive comments by Wehler, *Bismarck*, pp. 337–39.

69. As an example, see the plea by a German explorer of the Gold Coast who likened his discoveries to those of Stanley, and who wrote from Accra, sick and penniless, begging for a loan of 2,000 marks. Krause to Bleichröder, 2 Nov. 1887, BA.

70. Müller, *Deutschland*, p. 297; Denhardt to Bleichröder, 14 Dec. 1885, 13 May 1886; also Denhardt to Gloner, 13 May 1886, BA.

71. Wehler, *Bismarck*, pp. 369–70.

72. Hans von Bleichröder to Bleichröder, 31 Aug. 1885, BA.

73. Berchem memo, 29 April 1890, GFO: Russland 71. On Berchem, see Wehler, *Bismarck*, p. 237.

74. See John Gallagher and Ronald Robinson, "The Imperialism of Free Trade," *The Economic History Review*, 6 (1953), 1–15, which deals with the English case, but has a bearing on Germany as well.

75. David S. Landes, "Some Thoughts on the Nature of Economic Imperialism," *JEH*, 21 (1961), 505.

76. Feis, *Europe*, p. 313.

77. Donald C. Blaisdell, *European Financial Control in the Ottoman Empire* (New York, 1929), pp. 1–107, *passim*. Albert Wuarin, *Essai sur les Emprunts d'états et la protection des droits des porteurs de fonds d'états étrangers* (Geneva, 1907), p. 225.

78. Holborn, *Deutschland*, p. 46; Knaplund, *Letters from the Berlin Embassy*, p. 230; for a popular account of the Sultan and the growth of German influence in his Empire, see Joan Haslip, *The Sultan: The Life of Abdul Hamid* (London, 1958), pp. 189–205.

79. *Holstein Papers*, II, 18, 23; Kurt Grunwald, *Türkenhirsch: A Study of Baron Maurice de Hirsch, Entrepreneur and Philanthropist* (Jerusalem, 1966), pp. 46–47.

80. Blaisdell, *European Financial Control*, pp. 113–14.

81. Radowitz to Bleichröder, 6 Oct. 1883,

undated letter, 1883; Hohenlohe to Bleichröder, 1 Nov. 1883, 20 April 1884; Prince Henry VII of Reuss to Bleichröder, 10 Nov. 1883, BA; Testa to Bleichröder, 6 Oct. 1883; Rantzau to Bleichröder, 27 Oct. 1883, BA.

82. Bauer, Memo, 26 Jan. 1887; Bleichröder to Bismarck, 30, 31 Jan. 1887, GFO: Türkei 144; Radowitz to Bleichröder, 20 Nov. 1886, BA.

83. Bleichröder to Bismarck, 14 Jan. 1888, BA.

84. See Grunwald, *Türkenhirsch*, pp. 58–62, and *passim*.

85. Schwabach to Foreign Office, 15 Feb. 1888, GFO: Türkei 144.

86. Karl Helfferich, *Georg von Siemens. Ein Lebensbild aus Deutschlands grosser Zeit*, Vol. III (Berlin, 1923), pp. 28–29.

87. Reuss to Bismarck, 20 Dec. 1888, GFO: Türkei 144; Bleichröder to Hatzfeldt, 15 Aug. 1888, BA.

88. Bleichröder to Bismarck, 8 Sept. 1888, SA.

89. Feis, *Europe*, p. 318.

90. For details, based on material originally supplied by the House of Bleichröder, see Wuarin, *Les Emprunts d'états*, pp. 223–35.

91. Helfferich, *Siemens*, III, 46; see pp. 15–132 for Siemens' part in the railroad construction.

92. Rudolf Lindau to Bleichröder, 22 Jan. 1893, BA; Fürstenberg, *Lebensgeschichte*, p. 236.

93. Busch, *Bismarck*, III, 52.

94. No one has caught the complexities, at once financial, political, and human, of the entire story of Egyptian dependence better than David S. Landes in his justly renowned *Bankers and Pashas: International Finance and Economic Imperialism in Egypt* (London, 1958). Unfortunately, there is no comparable study of Egypt after the British occupation. But see Mathilde Kleine, *Deutschland und die ägyptische Frage, 1875–1890* (Greifswald, 1927); Charles Issawi, "Egypt since 1800: A Study in Lop-sided Development," *JEH*, 21 (1961), 1–25; Wolfgang J. Mommsen, *Imperialismus in Ägypten* (Munich, 1961); and William L. Langer, *European Alliances*, ch. 8. See Ronald Robinson and John Gallagher, *Africa and the Victorians: The Official Mind of Imperialism* (London, 1961), for the central role of Egypt in British thought and strategic planning.

95. Bleichröder to Bismarck, 19 June 1882, SA.

96. Langer, *European Alliances*, p. 254.

97. Arthur E. Crouchley, *The Economic Development of Modern Egypt* (London, 1938), p. 145.

98. Emden, *Money Powers*, p. 399.

99. Memorandum of Arthur von Brauer, 19 April 1885; Bleichröder to Bismarck, 20 April 1885, GFO: Aegypten 5.

100. Bleichröder to Bismarck, 24 March 1886; Derenthall to Bismarck, 6 April 1886; Scholz to Bismarck, 10 April 1886, GFO: Aegypten 5, adh. 1.

101. Brauer to Derenthall, 14 April 1886, *ibid.*

102. Bleichröder to Bismarck, 13 April 1886, *ibid.*

103. *Ibid.*, 1 Oct. 1886.

104. Brauer memorandum, 6 Oct. 1886, *ibid.*

105. Brauer to Scholz, 12 Oct. 1886, *ibid.*

106. Schmidt to Bismarck, 22 and 29 Nov. 1886; Hatzfeldt to Bismarck, 28 Jan. 1887; German Correspondent in Cairo to Foreign Office, 20 Feb. 1887, *ibid.*

107. Bleichröder to Bismarck, account statement, 31 Dec. 1889, SA.

108. Bleichröder to Hatzfeldt, 7, 9 April 1888, BA.

109. D. C. M. Platt, *Latin America and British Trade, 1806–1914* (London, 1972), p. 101.

110. Edgar Turlington, *Mexico and Her Foreign Creditors* (New York, 1930), p. 213. Also Friedrich Katz, *Deutschland, Diaz, und die Mexikanische Revolution* (East Berlin, 1964), p. 100. Also Freiherr von Zedtwitz, German minister to Mexico, to Raschdau, 26 Dec. 1888; and the memorandum, Mühlenberg, 5 Feb. 1898, GFO: Mexico 1, courtesy of Alfred Vagts.

111. Quoted in F. Katz, *Deutschland*, p. 100.

112. *Ibid.*, p. 103.

113. *Ibid.*, pp. 107, 131; Wehler, *Bismarck*, p. 226; see also Platt, *Latin America*, pp. 298–302.

114. Sir Ernest Cassel to Bleichröder, 1 Dec. 1893, BA.

115. The major work on German penetration of China is Helmuth Stoecker, *Deutschland und China im 19. Jahrhundert. Das Eindringen des deutschen Kapitalismus* (East Berlin, 1958), which was able to draw on the remnants of the German ministers' archives in Peking. See also Wehler, *Bismarck*, p. 409; and Münch, *Hansemann*, p. 218.

116. H. Stoecker, *Deutschland und China*, pp. 193–94, 279–80; the Bleichröder Archive, unfortunately, contains no letters from Brandt for the later period, and Stoecker cites but this one letter; given his desire to trace the role of German "exploiters" in China, it is a likely inference that no other letter survived in the Peking archive.

117. Bleichröder to Bismarck, 9 Sept.

1887; Schwartzkoppen memo, 17 Sept. 1887; *Reichskanzlei*, memo, on meeting with Schwabach, n. d.; Bismarck to Scholz, instructions, 5 Oct. 1887, DZA: Potsdam: Reichskanzlei, Akten betreffend überseeische Dampferlinien, Handelsverbindungen und Kolonien, No. 18, Vol. 4. The *Reichskanzlei* material seems not to have been used by Stoecker.

118. H. Stoecker, *Deutschland und China*, pp. 207–8; Münch, *Hansemann*, pp. 215–20; Ludwig Raschdau, *Unter Bismarck und Caprivi. Erinnerungen eines deutschen Diplomaten aus den Jahren 1885–1894* (Berlin, 1939), p. 18.

119. H. Stoecker, *Deutschland und China*, pp. 261–62; Carl Paasch, *Ein deutscher Pentateuch: Rüstzeug zum Kampfe gegen das Judenthum. Für Politiker und Abgeordnete aller Parteien* (Leipzig, 1892).

120. The first effort to deal with this question was Jacob Viner's "International Finance and Balance of Power Diplomacy, 1880–1914," reprinted in his *International Economics* (Glencoe, 1951), pp. 49–85. See also Ibbeken, *Staat und Wirtschaft*. Neither study uses archival material.

121. Vienna Rothschilds to Bleichröder, *passim*, BA.

122. See Münch, *Hansemann*, pp. 111–113, 196–98. Münch was married to Hansemann's granddaughter, and his biography, however scrupulous, is colored by his own relation to the man he depicts as "Germany's first banker," p. 88.

123. Bleichröder to Bismarck, 14 Oct. 1884; Reuss to Bismarck, 28 March 1882 and 5 Jan. 1886; GFO: Serbien 7.

124. Bismarck to Reuss, 30 Dec. 1885, *ibid.*; largely in Bismarck's own hand; italics in original.

125. Bray to Bismarck, 21 Jan. 1886; Foreign Office, memo, 15 Jan. 1886, *ibid.*

126. *Ibid.*, 7 Dec. 1888; Fürstenberg, *Lebensgeschichte*, pp. 278–98; Feis, *Europe*, pp. 258–68.

127. Bleichröder to Bismarck, 17 July 1888; memoranda 19 and 22 July 1888; telegram 21 July 1888; Rantzau to Brauer, 28 July 1888, GFO: Türkei 133 adh. 22.

128. Bülow to Bismarck, 5, 18 June 1888, GFO: Rumänien 4; also Helfferich, *Siemens*, III, 4; Le Maistre to Bismarck, 18 May 1889, GFO: Griechenland 44. *Die Entwickelung der rumänischen Petroleum-Industrie und die Beteiligung der Disconto-Gesellschaft und des Bankhauses S. Bleichröder daran*. This article, not otherwise identified, published apparently around 1907, is part of BA.

129. Langer, *European Alliances*, pp. 447–448; Staley, *Private Investor*, pp. 92–93; Viner, "International Finance," pp. 59–63; Launay to

Bismarck, 15 Feb. 1888, GFO: Italien 73 secr. Shepard B. Clough, *The Economic History of Modern Italy* (New York, 1964), p. 117.

130. Holstein to Bleichröder, 5 June 1875; H. von Bismarck to Bleichröder, 10 June 1875, BA.

131. Bleichröder to Bismarck, 1 Sept., 1, 4 Oct. 1880, FA.

132. Copies, Rothschild to Bleichröder, 1880–1887, RA.

133. Clough, *Modern Italy*, p. 126.

134. Launay to Bismarck, 15 Feb. 1888; memo, 16 Feb. 1888, GFO: Italien 73 secr.

135. Berchem to Bismarck, 29 Feb. 1888; Rottenburg to Bismarck, 1 March 1888; Bismarck to Solms, 3 March 1888, *ibid.*

136. Berchem to Bismarck, 21 March 1888; Solms to Bismarck, 30 March 1888; Launay to Bismarck, 7 March 1888, *ibid.*

137. Feis, *Europe*, p. 238; Clough, *Modern Italy*, pp. 124–32; Münch, *Hansemann*, pp. 204–6.

138. Solms to Bleichröder, 3 April 1890, BA; Gina Luzzato, *L'economia italiana del 1861 al 1914*, Vol. 1: *1861–1894* (Milan, 1963), p. 244.

139. Münch, *Hansemann*, p. 206; Feis, *Europe*, p. 239; Ludwig Raschdau, *Unter Bismarck*, pp. 188–89, and his *Wie ich Diplomat wurde: Aus dem Leben erzählt* (Berlin, 1938), p. 9.

140. Staley, *War and the Private Investor*, p. 11.

16 / The Fall of Bismarck

1. *GW*, XII, 390.

2. *Holstein Papers*, II, *passim*, esp. 362, 369.

3. Lehndorff to Bleichröder, 10 March 1888, BA.

4. 29 March 1888, p. 7 of "Gespräche mit und über Gerson von Bleichröder in den Jahren 1888–1890. Aus den Tagebüchern von Emil Friedrich Pindter," prepared by his grandson, Joachim Pindter (of Freiburg), and given to me by him.

5. Elie de Cyon, *Histoire de l'entente Franco-Russe, 1886–1894* (Paris, 1895), p. 379.

6. Langer, *European Alliances*, p. 370.

7. Quoted in Peter Rassow, *Die Stellung Deutschlands im Kreise der Grossen Mächte, 1887–1890* (Mainz, 1959), p. 211.

8. Mai, *Das deutsche Kapital*, pp. 131, vi, 195.

9. Bussmann, *Herbert von Bismarck*, p. 196.

10. In view of the popularity of Russian securities among Bleichröder's clients, the recent summary assertion by an East German historian that Prussian Junkers had always

"looked with disfavor" on capital exports to agrarian countries that competed with Germany needs careful reexamination. The contention that because of his industrial interests Bleichröder turned against Russian investments is also contradicted by the evidence. Sigrid Kumpf-Korfes, *Bismarcks "Draht nach Russland"* (East Berlin, 1968), pp. 125, 154.

11. U.S., Department of State, *Diplomatic Papers, 1884*, pp. 449–50.

12. Rottenburg to Rantzau, 16 Dec. 1886, FA, courtesy of Dr. Pöls.

13. Rottenburg to Rantzau, 24 and 25 Dec. 1886, FA.

14. *Holstein Papers*, II, 253; Rottenburg to Rantzau, 26 Dec. 1886, FA.

15. *Holstein Papers*, II, 327.

16. Sack to Bleichröder, 24 Jan. 1887, BA.

17. *Economist*, 45 (15 Oct. 1887), 1306; René Girault, *Emprunts russes et investissements français en Russie, 1887–1914. Récherches sur l'investissement international* (Paris, 1973), p. 141.

18. Kumpf-Korfes, *"Draht nach Russland,"* p. 157.

19. *Deutsches Montagsblatt*, 28 Nov. 1887, newspaper clipping in GFO: Deutschland 122, No. 1a 4. Bleichröder to Bismarck, 1 Dec. 1887, FA, courtesy of Dr. Pöls.

20. Redern (Paris Embassy) to Bismarck, 10 Sept. 1886, GFO: Frankreich 105, No. 2; Bülow to Eulenburg, 13 March 1893, Eulenburg Nachlass, courtesy of Dr. John Röhl.

21. Cyon *L'entente Franco-Russe*, pp. 302–7.

22. Cyon to Bleichröder, 29 May and 4 June 1887, BA.

23. *Ibid.*, 24 July 1887. Cyon, *L'entente Franco-Russe*, pp. 349–50.

24. Cyon to Bleichröder, 24 Feb. 1888, BA.

25. Bülow to Bismarck, 13 April 1887, GFO: Frankreich 105, No. 2.

26. Schweinitz to Foreign Office, 19 March 1887, GFO: Russland 91, No. 1.

27. Préfecture de Police, Archives de la Seine, Paris, BA 1023; also Cyon, *L'entente Franco-Russe*, pp. 395–405.

28. Until now, Cyon has been remembered as a scientist or an historian-journalist; the *Encyclopedia Judaica* (1971), for example, records only his distinguished scientific career, while his name has cropped up among historians as an agent of Katkov. I became interested in Cyon because of his relations with Bleichröder and tracked down additional information in the German Foreign Office and the French police files. I am grateful to Professor George F. Kennan of the Institute for Advanced Study in Princeton for several conversations we have had on Cyon and on Franco-Russian relations generally. I am also very much indebted to him for letting me read several chapters in manuscript of his forthcoming work on the Franco-Russian Alliance of 1894.

29. Girault, *Emprunts russes*, pp. 156–58.

30. Pindter, "Gespräche," 1 Jan., 7 April, 12 and 17 May 1888; *DDF*, VII, 131.

31. Cyon to Bleichröder, 6 Nov. 1888, BA.

32. Rottenburg to Bleichröder, 3 and 6 Oct. 1888, BA.

33. *Ibid.*, 9 Nov. 1888.

34. Girault, *Emprunts russes*, pp. 159–70.

35. *DDF*, VII, 431. Kumpf-Korfes, *"Draht nach Russland,"* pp. 165–71; Mai, *Das deutsche Kapital*, pp. 151–53; Alphonse de Rothschild to Bleichröder, 8, 10, 23 April 1889, BA.

36. Pindter, "Gespräche," 26 June 1889, p. 21.

37. Kumpf-Korfes, *"Draht nach Russland,"* pp. 166–67.

38. Richard Hertz, "Der Fall Wohlgemuth," *Historische Vierteljahrschrift*, 31 (1939), 760.

39. Bussmann, *Herbert von Bismarck*, p. 537.

40. H. von Bismarck to Eulenburg, 24 June 1889, Eulenburg Nachlass, courtesy of Dr. John Röhl.

41. Bussmann, *Herbert von Bismarck*, pp. 540–41.

42. Rogge, *Holstein*, p. 330.

43. Martin Kitchen, *The German Officer Corps, 1890–1914* (Oxford, 1968), ch. IV and p. 68.

44. Meisner, *Denkwürdigkeiten . . . Waldersee*, II, 55.

45. See J. C. G. Röhl, "The Disintegration of the *Kartell* and the Politics of Bismarck's Fall from Power, 1887–1890," *Historical Journal*, 9 (1966), 79; Fürstenberg, *Lebensgeschichte*, pp. 244–46.

46. Rich, *Holstein*, I, 253; Raschdau, *Unter Bismarck*, p. 18.

47. Meisner, *Denkwürdigkeiten . . . Waldersee*, II, 66–67.

48. *Ibid.*, p. 112.

49. *Ibid.*, pp. 54–55. See also Langer, *European Alliances*, p. 496.

50. Pindter, "Gespräche," 18 June 1889, p. 20, italics mine.

51. H. O. Meisner, ed., *Aus dem Briefwechsel des Generalfeldmarschalls Alfred Grafen von Waldersee*, Vol. I, (Stuttgart, 1928), p. 351.

52. Bismarck to Bleichröder, 6, 10, and 13 March 1890, BA.

53. Pindter, "Gespräche," 8 March 1890, p. 28. I have based my summary of Bismarck's last maneuvers on Röhl's *Germany without Bismarck*, ch. 1.

54. On Kopp, see Franz Schnabel's sensi-

tive study, "Kardinal Kopps Bedeutung für den politischen Katholizismus in Deutschland," *Abhandlungen und Vorträge, 1914–1965,* ed. by Heinrich Lutz (Freiburg, 1970), pp. 1–13; Rudolf Morsey, "Die deutschen Katholiken und der Nationalstaat zwischen Kulturkampf und Ersten Weltkrieg," *Historisches Jahrbuch,* 90 (1970), 31–64; Röhl, "Disintegration of the *Kartell,*" p. 86; Wilhelm Schüssler, *Bismarcks Sturz* (Leipzig, 1922), pp. 159–60.

55. Kopp to Bleichröder, 23 March 1890, BA.

56. Röhl, "Disintegration of the *Kartell,*" p. 87; Pindter, "Gespräche," 8 March 1890, p. 28.

57. Bachem Nachlass, folio, 63, Stadtarchiv Cologne. I owe these references to Dr. John Röhl; cf. also Eyck, *Bismarck,* III, 588.

58. Kardorff, *Kardorff,* p. 223. Bleichröder's mediation was widely known but there was much speculation about who had instigated it. The question was again discussed in the *Vossische Zeitung* of 28 Nov. 1891; Bismarck sent Bleichröder a copy of the paper and it was preserved in the BA. See also *GW,* IX, 336–37.

59. Eulenburg, *Aus 50 Jahren,* p. 234; *GW,* VIII, 696.

60. Rothschild to Bleichröder, 19 March 1890, BA.

61. Pindter, "Gespräche," 17 March 1890, p. 30.

62. *Holstein Papers,* III, 332.

63. Hohenlohe, *Denkwürdigkeiten,* II, 120.

64. Rothschild to Bleichröder, 19 March 1890, BA.

65. Cyon to Bleichröder, no date, BA.

66. Solms to Bleichröder, 3 April 1890, BA.

67. Vierhaus, *Spitzemberg,* p. 272.

68. Pindter, "Gespräche," 12 April 1890, pp. 32–33.

69. Kiderlen to Bleichröder, 1891–1892, BA; Raschdau to Bleichröder, 1891, BA; Caprivi to Bleichröder, 1 Feb. 1892, BA; 9 Dec. 1890, Memo, GFO: Deutschland 131.

70. Kardorff, *Kardorff,* p. 247.

71. Raschdau, *Unter Bismarck,* p. 155; Ludwig Reiners, *Bismarck gründet das Reich, 1864–1871* (Munich, 1957), II, 263.

72. Dr. Schweninger to Bleichröder, 30 March 1890, BA.

73. Pindter, "Gespräche," 7 April 1890, pp. 31–32.

74. Chrysander to Bleichröder, 17 June 1890, BA.

75. Bismarck to Bleichröder, 9 Dec. 1891, BA.

76. Pindter, "Gespräche," 15 May 1890, p. 33.

77. Chrysander to Bleichröder, 30 June 1890, BA; Pindter, "Gespräche," 2 June 1890, p. 34.

78. Rogge, *Holstein,* p. 364.

79. Kopp to Bleichröder, 11 Sept. 1892, BA.

80. *GW,* XIV², 1008.

81. *GW,* IX, 336; Samter, "Fünf Generationen," *Gemeindeblatt der jüdischen Gemeinde zu Berlin,* June 16, 1935.

82. Bismarck to Bleichröder, 7 April 1891, BA.

83. Bismarck to Bleichröder, 3 Feb. 1893, BA.

84. Bismarck to Schwabach, 23 Feb. 1893, BA.

85. Taylor, *Bismarck,* p. 253.

17 / The Jew as Patriotic Parvenu

1. This is a highly compressed version of a vast subject. I have dealt with the central theme in earlier studies, especially *The Politics of Cultural Despair: A Study in the Rise of the Germanic Ideology* (Berkeley, 1961); *The Failure of Illiberalism*; and most recently in my "Comments," *LBY,* 20 (1975), 79–83. Indispensable in any effort to locate the Jewish story in its proper German context are Leonard Krieger, *The German Idea of Freedom: History of a Political Tradition* (Boston, 1957); and Ralf Dahrendorf, *Society and Democracy in Germany* (New York, 1967).

2. See Felix Gilbert, ed., *Bankiers, Künstler und Gelehrte. Unveröffentlichte Briefe der Familie Mendelssohn aus dem 19. Jahrhundert* (New York, 1975), p. xxxvii, for a similar observation about the Mendelssohn family.

3. *Holstein Papers,* III, 104; Bussmann, *Herbert von Bismarck,* pp. 71, 73; Curtius, *Denkwürdigkeiten . . . Hohenlohe,* II, 234.

4. German Jews generally stressed their special vocation for charity. Toury, *Die politischen Orientierungen der Juden in Deutschland,* pp. 147–48.

5. Jacob Wassermann, *My Life as German and Jew* (New York, 1933), p. 24.

6. Quoted in Hamburger, *Juden im öffentlichen Leben,* pp. 551–52.

7. The literature on this subject is abundant. We now have studies on anti-Semitic thought such as George Mosse, *The Crisis of German Ideology* (New York, 1964), and Norman Cohn, *Warrant for Genocide* (London, 1967); on anti-Semitic organizations and politics, such as Peter Pulzer, *The Rise of Political Anti-Semitism in Germany and Austria* (New York, 1964), Paul Massing, *Rehearsal for Destruction: A Study of Political Anti-Semitism in Imperial Germany* (New York, 1949), and Richard S. Levy, *The Downfall of the Anti-Semitic Political Parties in Imperial Germany* (New Haven, 1975); on the setting of anti-Semitism, see Hannah Arendt, *The Ori-*

gins of Totalitarianism (New York, 1951); on liberal Protestantism and Jewry, see Uriel Tal, *Christians and Jews in Germany: Religions, Politics, and Ideology in the Second Reich, 1870–1914* (Ithaca, 1975); and on organized Jewish self-defense, see Ismar Schorsch's *Jewish Reactions to German Anti-Semitism, 1870–1914* (New York, 1972). We still need a comprehensive study of the German Jewish community from emancipation in 1869 to extinction in 1944; there is little even to compare to Michael R. Marrus's stimulating work, *The Politics of Assimilation: A Study of the French Jewish Community at the Time of the Dreyfus Affair* (Oxford, 1971).

8. The phrase is Max Weber's in *The Protestant Ethic and the Spirit of Capitalism* (New York, 1958), p. 271.

9. On the transformation of nineteenth-century anti-Semitism, see especially Eleonore Sterling, *Er ist wie Du. Aus der Frühgeschichte des Antisemitismus in Deutschland (1815–1850)* (Munich, 1956).

10. Cohn, *Warrant for Genocide*, p. 16.

11. Walther Rathenau, *Gesammelte Schriften*, Vol. I (Berlin, 1918), pp. 188–89.

12. *Ibid.*, p. 190.

13. Quoted in Marrus, *Politics of Assimilation*, p. 61.

14. On the foregoing, see especially Schorsch, *Jewish Reactions*.

15. Compiled by Toury, *Politischen Orientierungen*, p. 151.

16. Bamberger, p. 286.

17. W. Blumenberg, "Ein Unbekanntes Kapitel aus Marx' Leben. Briefe an die holländischen Verwandten," *International Review of Social History*, 1 (1956), 107–8.

18. Gerson Bleichröder to S. Bleichröder, 8 June 1850, BA.

19. A. Oppenheim to Bleichröder, 19 March 1864, BA.

20. *Ibid.*, 19 Sept. 1858.

21. Toury, *Politischen Orientierungen*, p. 16.

22. *Ibid.*, p. 111.

23. Oppenheim to Bleichröder, 12 March 1871, BA.

24. *Ibid.*, 24 March 1871.

25. Cecil Roth, *The Magnificent Rothschilds* (London, 1939), p. 125.

26. *Sigilla Veri. Lexikon der Juden* (Erfurt, 1929), s.v. "Bleichröder," p. 638.

27. *Neue Allgemeine Zeitung für Franken und Thüringen*, 25 April 1879, BA.

28. Vierhaus, *Spitzemberg*, pp. 132, 136, 138.

29. *Ibid.*, p. 88.

30. Police report, 16 Jan. 1874, FA, courtesy of Allan Mitchell.

31. I owe this paragraph to the striking observations made by David J. De Levita, *The Concept of Identity* (Paris and The Hague, 1965), pp. 86–95, 187–89, where he discusses the role of "secrets" and the projective character of anti-Semitism.

32. Schwabach to Bleichröder, 20 April 1876, BA.

33. Bamberg to Carl Anton, 5 Oct. 1883, HS.

34. See the richly suggestive work by Theodore Zeldin, *France, 1848–1945*, Vol. I; see also Ernest K. Bramstedt, *Aristocracy and the Middle-Classes in Germany: Social Types in German Literature, 1830–1900*, rev. ed. (Chicago, 1964), *passim*.

35. Memorandum, 9 Oct. 1888, BLHA: Königl. Polizei-Präsidium, Acta betreffend Gerson Bleichröder, Rep. 30; Rudolf Martin, ed., *Jahrbuch des Vermögens und Einkommens der Millionäre in Preussen* (Berlin, 1912), pp. 138 ff.

36. Comte Paul Vasili, *La Société de Berlin* (Paris, 1884), pp. 156–57.

37. Sir James Rennell Rodd, *Social and Diplomatic Memories*, p. 60. On this whole question, see Lamar Cecil, "Jews and Junkers in Imperial Berlin," *LBY*, 20 (1975), 47–58; he somewhat underrates the self-sufficiency of gentile society.

38. *Maxe von Arnim, Tochter Bettinas/ Gräfin von Oriola*, ed. by Johannes Werner (Leipzig, 1937), pp. 269–79, 205; on Countess Oriola, see Vierhaus, *Spitzemberg*, pp. 137–38.

39. Vasili, *La Société de Berlin*, p. 158.

40. On the serious side of entertainment, see the testimony of a retired Baden diplomat, Eugen von Jagemann, *Fünfundsiebzig Jahre des Erlebens und Erfahrens, 1849–1924* (Heidelberg, 1925), p. 209.

41. Ludwig Pietsch to Emma von Bleichröder, 7 March 1879, BA.

42. Monypenny and Buckle, *Disraeli*, II, 1202.

43. The great novelists of the last century have depicted these feasts and the deceptions they occasioned. For our purposes, consider—as mere examples—Charles Dickens, *Our Mutual Friend*, esp. Book 1, ch. 2, and Anthony Trollope, *The Way We Live Now*, ch. 59.

44. Bilse to Bleichröder, BA.

45. Quoted in Herbert Roch, *Fontane* (Berlin, 1962), pp. 107–8.

46. Hans von Bleichröder to Bleichröder, 3 June 1879, BA.

47. Pietsch to Bleichröder, 26 Dec. 1879, BA.

48. *Katholische Volkszeitung*, No. 53, 5 March (no year), BA.

49. Seckendorff to Bleichröder, 30 Oct. 1885, BA; Taffs, *Ambassador to Bismarck*, p. 374.
50. Friedenthal to Bleichröder, 26 April 1889, BA.
51. Princesse Marie Radziwill, *Lettres de la Princesse Radziwill au Général de Robilant, 1889–1914*, Vol. I: *1889–1895* (Bologna, 1933), p. 152.
52. Bleichröder to Alliance Israélite, 11 Jan. 1882, AI:IIB13.
53. Roth, *Magnificent Rothschilds*, pp. 126–27.
54. Münster to Caprivi, 3 June 1891, and Metternich to Caprivi, 20 June 1891, GFO: Russland 73.
55. Gossler to Bleichröder, Robert Koch to Bleichröder, and *Norddeutsche Allgemeine Zeitung*, 2 Dec. 1890, BA.
56. *GW*, IX, 476; and Lenbach receipt, 10 Aug. 1882, BA.
57. Werner Sombart, *Die Deutsche Volkswirtschaft im neunzehnten Jahrhundert* (Berlin, 1927), p. 648; Begas to Bleichröder, 23 June 1882, BA.
58. Schwabach to Bleichröder, 15 May 1876, BA.
59. Professor Graefe to Bleichröder, 20 May 1870; Dr. Evers to Bleichröder, 9 July 1871; also Evers's medical report, 29 Aug. 1871; Dr. Herzberg to Bleichröder, 19 Aug., 2 Sept. 1871, BA.
60. Dr. Frerichs to Bleichröder, 31 July 1881, BA.
61. Lauer to Bleichröder, 1 Jan. 1889; Dr. Frerichs to Bleichröder, 8 Sept. 1883, BA.
62. Dr. A. Eberhard to Bleichröder, 6 Aug. 1865, BA.
63. Hans von Bleichröder to Bleichröder, 14 Aug. 1878, BA.
64. Dr. Eberhard to Bleichröder, 6 Aug. 1865; Laur to Bleichröder, 20 Oct. 1875, BA.
65. On the reserve officer, see the classic essay by Eckart Kehr, "Zur Genesis des Königlich Preussischen Reserveoffiziers," in *Der Primat der Innenpolitik*, ed. by H.-U. Wehler, pp. 53–63; and Gordon Craig, *The Politics of the Prussian Army, 1640–1945* (Oxford, 1955), pp. 237–38.
66. *GW*, IX, 86.
67. Hans von Bleichröder to Bleichröder, 14 Aug. 1879, BA.
68. See copy of the draft in the FA; the original of the draft seems to have been lost; *GW*, IX, 86.
69. Bleichröder to Bismarck, 26 May 1879, SA.
70. Eulenburg to Bleichröder, 27 June 1879, BA; Lehndorff to Bleichröder, 27 May 1879, BA.
71. Albedyll to Bleichröder, 8 and 16 Oct.

1875 and others, BA; and Craig, *Prussian Army*, p. 225.
72. Stephen Gwynn and Gertrude M. Tuckwell, *The Life of the Rt. Hon. Sir Charles W. Dilke, Bart., M.P.*, Vol. I (New York, 1917), p. 432.
73. See Werner T. Angress's excellent "Prussia's Army and the Jewish Reserve Officer Controversy Before World War I," *LBY*, 17 (1972), 19–42.
74. Foreign Office to Bleichröder, 28 July 1879, PRO: FO, 62/944.
75. Bleichröder to Bismarck, 29 Dec. 1879, FA.
76. *Sigilla Veri*, "Bleichröder," p. 653.
77. Hans von Bleichröder to Bleichröder, 14 Aug. 1879, BA.
78. Lehndorff to Bleichröder, 19 Jan. 1889, BA.
79. Rosenberg to Bleichröder, 27 Jan., 13 June, 19 Oct. 1882, BA.
80. *Pester Lloyd*, 19 Feb. 1881.
81. Bamberg to Carl Anton, 20 Feb. 1881, HS.
82. Philipsborn to Bleichröder, 3 Dec. 1881; Edmond de Rothschild to Bleichröder, 1 Dec. 1881, BA.
83. *Hannoverscher Courier*, 12 Dec. 1881, BA.
84. Empress Augusta to Bleichröder, 4 Jan. 1882, BA.
85. Kühlow notes, 17 and 22 May 1882; Bleichröder to Hans von Bleichröder, 28 Sept. 1884, BA.
86. Kühlow, 17 May 1882, BA.
87. Fürstenberg, *Lebensgeschichte*, p. 57.
88. Bleichröder to Hans von Bleichröder, 28 Sept., 19 Oct. 1884, BA.
89. *The Memoirs of Count Bernstorff* (London, 1936), p. 12.
90. *Sigilla Veri*, "Bleichröder," p. 656.
91. 8 June 1889, BA.
92. Bleichröder to Rudolf Lindau, 3 Dec. 1890, 30 Nov. 1892, Bundesarchiv: Koblenz, Kl. Erw., 310.
93. This and subsequent tidbits I owe to Dr. Joachim Sprinz, longtime German consul in Nice, who had been a close companion of Hans and Werner. He was called a Bleichröder companion or *Begleiterscheinung*. I saw him in June 1967, and am grateful for his help.
94. Chauvin to Bleichröder, 25 Aug. 1879; and Tiedemann to Bleichröder, 31 Dec. 1884, BA.

18 / The Hostage of the New Anti-Semitism

1. For a brief history of the term and its substance, see Thomas Nipperdey and Reinhard Rürup, "Antisemitismus," in *Geschichtliche Grundbegriffe. Historisches Lexikon zur*

politisch-sozialen Sprache in Deutschland, ed. by O. Brunner *et al.*, I (1972) pp. 129–53, now reprinted in Rürup, *Emanzipation und Antisemitismus. Studien zur "Judenfrage" der bürgerlichen Gesellschaft* (Göttingen, 1975).

2. Quoted in Schorsch's *Jewish Reactions*, p. 5.

3. Jean-Paul Sartre, *Portrait of the Anti-Semite* (London, 1948), pp. 10, 120.

4. The link between depression and the new anti-Semitism, long assumed, has been most emphatically asserted in Hans Rosenberg, *Grosse Depression und Bismarckzeit* (Berlin, 1967), pp. 88–117. For a brief critique of Rosenberg, in light especially of Uriel Tal's analysis of the intellectual origins of the new anti-Semitism, see Hermann Greive, "Zu den Ursachen des Antisemitismus im Deutschen Kaiserreich von 1870–71," *Judaica*, 27 (1971), 184–92. For the link between depression and anti-Semitism in America, see John Higham, "Antisemitism in the Gilded Age," *Mississippi Valley Historical Review*, 43 (1957), 559–78; and Richard Hofstadter, *The Age of Reform* (New York, 1955), pp. 77–81. See also my "Money, Morals, and the Pillars of Society," in *Failure of Illiberalism*.

5. See the perceptive comments of R. M. Berdahl on German nationalism, *AHR*, 77: 65–80.

6. Kaelble, *Berliner Unternehmer*, pp. 79–80. Also Schorsch, *Jewish Reactions*, esp. pp. 14–15; Monika Richarz, "Jewish Social Mobility in Germany during the Time of Emancipation (1790–1871)," *LBY*, 20 (1975), 69–77. Sir James Rennell Rodd, *Social and Diplomatic Memories*, p. 56.

7. Constantin Frantz, *Die Religion des Nationalliberalismus* (Leipzig, 1872), pp. v, 59, 213, 217, 221, 235–37.

8. Quoted in Nipperdey and Rürup, "Antisemitismus," p. 137.

9. Quoted in Pulzer, *Political Anti-Semitism*, p. 78.

10. Kurt Wawrzinek, "Die Entstehung der deutschen Antisemitenparteien (1873–1890)," *Historische Studien*, 168 (1927), 11.

11. Hermann Zang, *"Die Gartenlaube" als politisches Organ* (Würzburg, 1935), p. 14.

12. Glagau, *Börsen- und Gründungs-Schwindel*, p. 24.

13. *Ibid.*, pp. xxx, 150; xxv, 30.

14. Wawrzinek, "Entstehung," p. 9.

15. *Ibid.*, pp. 9–11.

16. Quoted *ibid.*, p. 12.

17. Quoted in Walter Boehlich, ed., *Der Berliner Antisemitismusstreit* (Frankfurt, 1965), p. 56; Massing, *Rehearsal for Destruction*, pp. 14–15.

18. *Germania*, 10 Sept. 1875, quoted in Nipperdey and Rürup, "Antisemitismus," p. 142.

19. Otto von Diest-Daber, *Bismarck und Bleichröder. Deutsches Rechtsbewusstsein und die Gleichheit vor dem Gesetze* (Munich, 1897), pp. 40–41.

20. W. Marr, *Der Sieg des Judenthums über das Germanenthum, Vom nicht confessionellen Standpunkt aus betrachtet* (Bern, 1879), pp. 33, 46, 48. Italics in original.

21. Richard Lewinsohn, *Das Geld in der Politik* (Berlin, 1931), pp. 43–45.

22. Busch, *Bismarck*, II, 312.

23. *Gedanken*, II, 160.

24. Diest-Daber, *Bismarck und Bleichröder*, pp. 4–6.

25. Otto von Diest-Daber, *Berichtigung von Unwahrheiten in den Erinnerungen des Fürsten Bismarck und Deutsches Rechtsbewusstsein* (Zurich, 1899), p. 8, and Diest-Daber to Bismarck, 11 Oct. 1874, DZA: Potsdam: Reichskanzlei, Angriffe des Diest-Daber auf den Fürsten Bismarck und Rehabilitierungsgesuche, No. 4.1, Vol. 1.

26. Kardorff, *Kardorff*, pp. 101–5; Diest-Daber, *Bismarck und Bleichröder*, p. 10 and *passim*.

27. Kardorff, *Kardorff*, p. 107.

28. Landsberg to Bleichröder, 1 June 1877, BA.

29. Bleichröder to H. von Bismarck, 25 and 28 May 1877, FA; H. von Bismarck to Bleichröder, 27 May 1877, BA.

30. Court's decision, 28 March 1878, DZA: Potsdam: Reichskanzlei, Angriffe des Diest-Daber auf den Fürsten Bismarck und Rehabilitierungsgesuche, No. 4.1, Vol. 1; and Kardorff to Bleichröder, 27 Oct. 1877, BA.

31. Kardorff, *Kardorff*, p. 110; Diest-Daber, *Bismarck und Bleichröder*, pp. 106–201. See also Diest-Daber, *Berichtigung*, *passim*.

32. Rudolph Meyer, *Politische Gründer*, p. 27.

33. *Ibid.*, p. 2.

34. *Ibid.*, p. 200.

35. *Ibid.*, p. 4.

36. *Ibid.*, pp. 77, 104, 185, 200–201.

37. Rudolph Meyer, *Briefe und sozialpolitische Aufsätze . . .*, I, pp. 709, 740; also *Politische Gründer*, p. 202; Kardorff, *Kardorff*, pp. 106–7.

38. Hermann Bahr, *Der Antisemitismus. Ein internationales Interview* (Berlin, 1894), p. 12.

39. So Baroness Spitzemberg described him at a later date; Vierhaus, *Spitzemberg*, p. 386.

40. Pulzer, *Political Anti-Semitism*, p. 92.

41. On Jewish self-criticism at the time, see Schorsch, *Jewish Reactions*, pp. 47–48, and Michael A. Meyer, "Great Debate on Antisemitism: Jewish Reaction to New Hostility in Germany, 1879–1881," *LBY*, 11 (1966), 164.

42. See Adolf Stoecker, *Christlich-Sozial. Reden und Aufsätze* (Bielefeld and Leipzig, 1885), pp. 143–54.

43. Kardorff to Bleichröder, 30 Sept. 1879, BA.

44. Lucius, *Bismarck*, pp. 163–64.

45. Cf. my *Politics of Cultural Despair*, p. 140.

46. See Boehlich, *Antisemitismusstreit*, p. 11; also Andreas Dorpalen, *Heinrich von Treitschke* (New Haven, 1957), and the excellent summary of the significance of Treitschke's attack in Hamburger, *Juden im öffentlichen Leben*, pp. 99–100.

47. Boehlich, *Antisemitismusstreit*, pp. 76, 190.

48. Theodor Mommsen, *Reden und Aufsätze* (Berlin, 1905), pp. 410–26.

49. Walter Frank, *Hofprediger Adolf Stoecker und die christlichsoziale Bewegung* (Hamburg, 1935), p. 85.

50. Bleichröder to William I, 18 June 1880, DZA: Potsdam: Reichskanzlei, Angelegenheiten der Juden, No. 16, Vol. 1.

51. Bleichröder to Bismarck, 18 June 1880, *ibid.*

52. Goldschmidt to Bleichröder, 23 Sept. 1880, BA. Frank, *Stoecker*, pp. 89–90; see also draft of letter in DZA: Merseburg: Stoecker Nachlass.

53. *GW*, VI³, 199; also draft of this letter in DZA: Potsdam: Reichskanzlei, Angelegenheiten der Juden, No. 16, Vol. 1.

54. Bismarck to Tiedemann, 15 Nov. 1880, *ibid.* See also Lucius, *Bismarck*, p. 216.

55. Bismarck to Tiedemann, 21 Nov. 1880, DZA: Potsdam: Reichskanzlei, Angelegenheiten der Juden, No. 16, Vol. 1; Frank, *Stoecker*, p. 96.

56. 13 Nov. 1880, Hänel Interpellation, DZA: Potsdam: Angelegenheiten der Juden, No. 16, Vol. 1.

57. H. von Bismarck to Tiedemann, 17 and 18 Nov. 1880; Tiedemann to H. von Bismarck, 19 Nov. 1880, *ibid.*

58. *Die Judenfrage. Verhandlungen des preussischen Abgeordnetenhauses über die Interpellation des Abgeordneten, Dr. Hänel* (Berlin, 1880), p. 211 and *passim.*

59. On Bamberger, see Stanley Zucker, "Ludwig Bamberger and the Rise of Anti-Semitism in Germany, 1848–1893," *CEH*, 3 (1970), 332–52.

60. Eça de Queiroz, *Letters from England* (Athens, Ohio, 1970), p. 47.

61. Bleichröder to Bismarck, 20 Nov. 1880, GFO: I.A.A.a. 50, Vol. III.

62. Guy de Rothschild to Disraeli, 22 Nov. 1880, Hughenden Manor, B/XXI, R/263, plus enclosures. I owe this reference to my colleague Marvin Swartz.

63. Quoted in *The Times*, 25 Nov. 1885.

64. *Ibid.*, 23 Nov. 1880.

65. Pulzer, *Political Anti-Semitism*, pp. 337–38; Hans Liebeschütz, *Das Judentum im deutschen Geschichtsbild von Hegel bis Max Weber* (Tübingen, 1967), pp. 341–42; Boehlich, *Antisemitismusstreit*, pp. 202–4.

66. *Denkwürdigkeiten . . . Hohenlohe*, II, 307.

67. Anton Bettelheim, *Berthold Auerbach* (Stuttgart, 1907), p. 375.

68. *Jakob Burckhardts Briefe an seinen Freund Friedrich von Preen, 1864–1893* (Stuttgart and Berlin, 1922), p. 137.

69. On this, see Schorsch, *Jewish Reactions*, pp. 47–48 and *passim.*

70. On *Vulgäridealismus*, see my *Failure of Illiberalism*, pp. 17–19.

71. Tiedemann to H. von Bismarck, 19 Nov. 1880, DZA: Potsdam: Reichskanzlei, Angelegenheiten der Juden, No. 16, Vol. 1.

72. H. von Bismarck to Tiedemann, 29 Nov. 1880, *ibid.*

73. Bismarck and Puttkamer to William 4 Dec. 1880, William's draft, 27 Dec. 1880, *ibid.*; and Frank, *Stoecker*, p. 100.

74. Bleichröder to Bismarck, 29 Dec. 1880, FA; Wilmowsky to Bleichröder, 26 Jan. 1881, DZA: Potsdam: Reichskanzlei, Angelegenheiten der Juden, No. 16; Vol. 1.

75. Montefiore to Bleichröder, 13 June 1880, BA. Franz Kobler, ed., *Jüdische Geschichte in Briefen aus Ost und West* (Vienna, 1938), p. 352.

76. Goldschmidt to Bleichröder, 29 Sept. 1875, 5 Nov. 1880, BA.

77. Alphonse de Rothschild to Bleichröder, 4 Dec. 1880, BA.

78. Boehlich, *Antisemitismusstreit*, p. 176.

79. M. A. Meyer, "Great Debate on Antisemitism," p. 169. Ingrid Belke, ed., *Moritz Lazarus und Hermann Steinthal. Die Begründer der Völkerpsychologie in ihren Briefen* (Tübingen, 1971), p. 154.

80. Tiedemann to H. von Bismarck, 31 Dec. 1880, DZA: Potsdam: Reichskanzlei, Angelegenheiten der Juden, No. 16, Vol. 1.

81. Holstein to H. von Bismarck, 22 Dec. 1880, FA, courtesy of Dr. Hoepke.

82. Zucker, "Ludwig Bamberger," pp. 338–350.

83. Schulthess, *Geschichtskalender, 1881*, p. 31; Puttkamer report, 22 May 1881, also 21 Aug. 1881, DZA: Potsdam: Reichskanzlei, Angelegenheiten der Juden, No. 16, Vol. 1.

84. Schorsch, *Jewish Reactions*, p. 39.

85. Königl. Staatsministerium, 22 May 1882, DZA: Potsdam: Reichskanzlei Angelegenheiten der Juden, No. 16, Vol. 1.

86. Berlin Committee to Alliance Israélite, 29 Dec. 1881, AI:IA1.

87. Frank, *Stoecker*, pp. 109–10.
88. Quoted in Massing, *Rehearsal for Destruction*, p. 37.
89. Gustav Seeber, *Zwischen Bebel und Bismarck* (East Berlin, 1965), p. 77.
90. *Die Post*, 6 Nov. 1881, newspaper clipping in DZA: Potsdam, Reichskanzlei, Angelegenheiten der Juden, No. 16, Vol. 1; *GW*, VIII, 423–24.
91. Police reports 8 May 1894 and 31 Dec. 1897, BLHA: Königl. Polizei-Präsidium, Acta betreffend Julius Bleichröder, Rep. 30; also Hamburger, *Juden im öffentlichen Leben*, pp. 136–38; Toury, *Politischen Orientierungen*, pp. 182–85.
92. Marjorie Lamberti, "The Prussian Government and the Jews: Official Behavior and Policy-Making in the Wilhelminian Era," *LBY*, 17 (1972), 17.
93. Jöhlinger, *Bismarck und die Juden*, pp. 43–45, argues this point.
94. Johannes Ziekursch, *Politische Geschichte des Neuen Deutschen Kaiserreiches*, Vol. II: *Das Zeitalter Bismarcks* (Frankfurt, 1927), p. 366.
95. Bleichröder to William, 12 May 1884, DZA: Potsdam, Reichskanzlei, Angelegenheiten der Juden, No. 16, Vol. 1.
96. Sigismund Simmel to Isidore Loeb, 6 Nov. 1885, AI:IAI.
97. See Tal, *Christians and Jews, passim*.
98. Christoph Joseph Cremer, *Die angeblichen 10,000 Mark des Herrn von Bleichröder* (Berlin, 1889), pp. 3, 7, 17, 21.

19 / The Embittered End

1. Bleichröder to Madai, 10 April 1881, and subsequent report, BLHA: Königl. Polizei-Präsidium, Acta betreffend Gerson Bleichröder, Rep. 30.
2. Madai to Bleichröder, 26 Sept. 1879; Dec. 1880, BA.
3. *Staatsbürger-Zeitung*, 5 Sept. 1889, newspaper clipping in BLHA: Königl. Polizei-Präsidium, Acta betreffend Gerson Bleichröder, Rep. 30.
4. Dieter Fricke, *Bismarcks Prätorianer. Die Berliner politische Polizei im Kampf gegen die deutsche Arbeiterbewegung (1871–1898)* (East Berlin, 1962), p. 62.
5. Jöhlinger, *Bismarck und die Juden*, pp. 46–47; Carl Paasch, *Der Jüdische Dämon* (2 vols. in 1; Leipzig, n.d. [1891?]), p. 145. Also Hermann Ahlwardt, *Die Prozesse Manché und Bleichröder* (Leipzig, 1891), I, 4.
6. Conrad Madai to Bleichröder, 18, 24 March 1877, BA.
7. Madai to Bleichröder, 18, 22 June 1879, BA.
8. Hans von Bleichröder to Bleichröder, 3, 24 July 1880, BA.

9. Hoppe, 22 Nov. 1884; also Madai to Puttkamer, 4 Dec. 1883, DZA: Merseburg: Justiz-Ministerium, Untersuchung wider d. geh. Kommerzienrath v. Bleichröder, Littr. B, No. 764.
10. Madai to Bleichröder, 11 June 1875, BA.
11. Madai to Puttkamer, 4 Dec. 1883, DZA: Merseburg: Justiz-Ministerium, Untersuchung wider d. geh. Kommerzienrath v. Bleichröder, Littr. B, No. 764.
12. Fricke, *Bismarcks Prätorianer*, p. 53.
13. Copy, Staatsanwalt to Croner, 13 Nov. 1883, DZA: Merseburg: Justiz-Ministerium, Untersuchung wider d. geh. Kommerzienrath v. Bleichröder, Littr. B, No. 764.
14. Report, Erster Staatsanwalt des Königl. Landgerichts to Oberstaatsanwalt des Königl. Kammergerichts, 15 Oct. 1891, *ibid*.
15. *Schwerin und Bleichröder: Edelmann und Jude* (Dresden, 1893), *passim*. This pamphlet was written either by or for Schwerin.
16. Oberstaatsanwalt to Justice Minister Friedberg, 12 Feb. 1884, DZA: Merseburg: Justiz-Ministerium, Untersuchung wider d. geh. Kommerzienrath v. Bleichröder, Littr. 8, No. 764.
17. *Schwerin und Bleichröder*, p. 82.
18. Personal Adjutant Oberstleutnant Sommerfeld to Friedberg, 30 Dec. 1884, DZA: Merseburg: Justiz-Ministerium, Untersuchung wider d. geh. Kommerzienrath v. Bleichröder, Littr. B, No. 764.
19. *Holstein Papers*, II, 84–85, 93–94; Bussmann, *Herbert von Bismarck*, pp. 210–13.
20. Pulzer, *Political Anti-Semitism*, pp. 112–13.
21. Hermann Ahlwardt, *Der Eid eines Juden* (Berlin, 1891), pp. 45, 61.
22. *Vorwärts*, 10 July 1891, newspaper clipping in BLHA: Königl. Polizei-Präsidium, Acta betreffend Gerson Bleichröder, Rep. 30.
23. *Neue Zeit*, 27 July 1890; quoted in Massing, *Rehearsal for Destruction*, p. 266.
24. Politische Polizei, 28 Oct. 1891, BLHA: Königl. Polizei-Präsidium, Acta betreffend Gerson Bleichröder, Rep. 30.
25. Ahlwardt, *Prozesse Manché*, p. 8. As yet another example of these broadsheets, see Dr. Erwin Bauer, *Der Fall Bleichröder* (Leipzig, 1891).
26. Der Erster Staatsanwalt to Oberstaatsanwalt, 15 Oct. 1891, DZA: Merseburg: Justiz-Ministerium, Untersuchung wider d. geh. Kommerzienrath v. Bleichröder, Littr. B, No. 764.
27. Justizminister, draft of memorandum, 29 Oct. 1891, *ibid*.
28. Paul Lindau to Bleichröder, 3 Dec. 1890, BA. Lindau was being publicly vilified

for all sorts of lapses of good taste and for exercising a kind of dictatorship over the Berlin stage. Paasch, *Jüdische Dämon*, II, 125 ff.

29. 51st Polizei-Revier, 13 Oct. 1891; *Norddeutsche Allgemeine Zeitung*, 23 Oct. 1891; DZA: Merseburg: Justiz-Ministerium, Untersuchung wider d. geh. Kommerzienrath v. Bleichröder, Littr. B, No. 764.

30. *Schwerin und Bleichröder*, p. vii.

31. Königl. Kammergericht, 1 Feb. 1892, DZA: Merseburg: Justiz-Ministerium, Untersuchung wider d. geh. Kommerzienrath v. Bleichröder, Littr. B, No. 764.

32. *Volks-Zeitung*, 18 Feb. 1893, newspaper clipping, *ibid.*

33. Kardorff, *Kardorff*, p. 278.

34. *Berliner Börsen-Zeitung*, 22 Feb. 1893, *Berliner Tageblatt*, 22 Feb. 1893, newspaper clippings in DZA: Merseburg, Königl. Herolds-Amt., Acta betreffend von Bleichröder, VI. B. 154.

35. Quoted in Peter Deeg, *Hofjuden* (Nuremberg, 1939), pp. 454–57.

36. *Internationales Bank- und Handels-Journal* (Vienna), 20 Feb. 1893, BA. *Allgemeine Zeitung des Judentums*, 24 Feb. 1893.

37. Police report, 21 Feb. 1893, BLHA: Königl. Polizei-Präsidium, Acta betreffend Gerson Bleichröder, Rep. 30; also BA.

Epilogue: The Fall of a Family

1. David S. Landes, "The Bleichröder Bank: An Interim Report," *LBY*, 5 (1960), 211.

2. Fürstenberg, *Lebensgeschichte*, p. 117.

3. On Bleichröder's role in Franco-German cooperation, see the important work by Raymond Poidevin, *Les relations économiques et financières entre la France et l'Allemagne de 1898 à 1914* (Paris, 1969), p. 83 and *passim*.

4. Memoranda, 12, 15 May 1897, BLHA: Königl. Polizei-Präsidium, Acta betreffend Julius Leopold Schwabach, Rep. 30.

5. Max M. Warburg to Paul Warburg, 22 Oct. 1898, Warburg Archive, courtesy of J. A. Sherman. Permission to quote *this* excerpt of the letter was granted by Eric M. Warburg, letter to author, June 9, 1976.

6. Paul H. von Schwabach, *Aus meinen Akten* (Berlin, 1927), p. 334.

7. *Ibid.*, p. 330; and personal information from F. H. Brunner.

8. Regiment's inquiry, 4 Jan. 1893; Polizei-Präsidium's answer, 11 Feb. 1893, BLHA:

Königl. Polizei-Präsidium, Acta betreffend Schwabach, Rep. 30.

9. Fürstenberg, *Lebensgeschichte*, p. 399.

10. Lamar Cecil, *Albert Ballin: Business and Politics in Imperial Germany, 1888–1918* (Princeton, 1967), p. 109, and his "Jews and Junkers," *LBY*, 20: 47–58.

11. *The Times*, 19 Nov. 1938.

12. Schwabach, *Aus meinen Akten*, p. 313; also Friedrich Thimme, "Auswärtige Politik und Hochfinanz. Aus den Papieren Paul H. von Schwabachs," *Europäische Gespräche*, 7 (1929), 317–18.

13. Schwabach, *Aus meinen Akten*, p. 386.

14. *Ibid.*, p. 440.

15. *Ibid.*, p. 387.

16. Police memorandum, 1 April 1903, BLHA: Königl. Polizei-Präsidium, Acta betreffend James von Bleichröder, Rep. 30.

17. Police memorandum, 24 April 1909; *Die Wahrheit*, 24 April 1909, newspaper clipping, *ibid.*

18. Regiments' inquiries, 5 Dec. 1913, 12 Jan. 1917; *Berliner Zeitung am Mittag*, 13 June 1913, newspaper clipping, *ibid.*

19. Jagemann, *Fünfundsiebzig Jahre*, p. 271.

20. Emden, *Money Powers*, p. 254; Siegmund Kaznelson, ed., *Juden im deutschen Kulturbereich*, 3rd ed. (Berlin, 1962), pp. 725–26; Modris Eksteins, *The Limits of Reason* (Oxford, 1975), p. 76.

21. Fully documented in BA. Dr. Sprinz also spoke of suicide to me.

22. Paul von Schwabach to F. H. Brunner, 18 Oct. 1938, BA. The entire Schwabach-Brunner correspondence is a poignant reminder of how varied was the response to Nazism and how uniform the suffering.

23. Curt von Bleichröder to Reichsminister des Innern, Frick, 7 Jan. 1942; Edgar von Bleichröder to Adjutant des Reichsministers des Innern, 23 Jan. 1942; Adjutant des Reichsministers des Innern to Reichssicherheitshauptamt, attention of SS-Obersturmbannführer Eichmann, 29 Jan. 1942; Reichsführer SS und Chef der deutschen Polizei, 7 May 1942, Reichsministerium des Innern, Bundesarchiv, Koblenz: R 18/5246.

24. Information from Dr. Sprinz. Letter from International Tracing Service to author, 28 June 1976.

25. Copy of U. S. Court of Restitution Appeals of the Allied High Commission for Germany, 23 Nov. 1953, case no. 611, BA.

26. Dahrendorf, *Society and Democracy in Germany*, ch. 4.

ACKNOWLEDGMENTS

This book has had a long history and accordingly has put me under many great obligations. Without the help of individuals and institutions, both here and in Europe, this book could not have been written.

In the first instance I would have liked to express my gratitude to F. H. Brunner, of Arnhold and S. Bleichroeder, New York, who brought the Bleichröder Archive to New York and put it at the disposal of David S. Landes. In time, Mr. Brunner and I became well acquainted and I learned a great deal from his practical wisdom and wide experience. He died before the book he had so hoped to see was completed, but I was able to show him almost every chapter in draft form, and I benefited from his criticism.

It was my friend David Landes who first invited me to join him in this enterprise. After a rapid look at the Bleichröder Archive, I was persuaded of its importance, and accepted his suggestion of collaboration. That was two decades ago, and at the time we both envisioned a short book, quickly executed.

We started work in 1960 at the Banque Rothschild in Paris. In 1961 and 1962 we traveled to the archives of the German Democratic Republic and we worked together in Vienna and Budapest. It had been our intention to divide the work so that the economic aspects would be Landes' domain and the social and political fields would be mine. Gradually our schedules diverged, and in 1970 he decided to suspend his work on Bleichröder in order to pursue other urgent tasks. Before and after that date, I profited from his superb knowledge of nineteenth-century history, his sure judgment of things historical and human, and his familiarity with business archives. We shared each other's research and read each other's chapters; he has always been generous with his counsel and help. In 1973 he read an early draft of this book and in 1974 a few chapters of a much altered version.

From the beginning, I received indispensable help from institutions which made the far-flung research for this book possible. In 1960–61 I went on a sabbatical to Paris, thanks to a fellowship from the Social Science Research Council. The Council for Research in the Social Sciences of Columbia University provided further assistance in the form of several summer grants and of funds that helped me to defray microfilm expenses. The Dunning Fund of Columbia's Department of History made it possible for me to turn some of the most important microfilms into xerox reproductions.

I would also like to acknowledge the generosity of the custodians of various archives. First and foremost I wish to thank the Banque Rothschild in Paris for giving us access to its incomparable holdings; my thanks go to Bertrand Gille, Pierre Dupont-Ferrier, and to Baron Guy de Rothschild, who at a much later date also gave me permission to visit the Château de Ferrières. I am grateful to the recently deceased Prince Otto von Bismarck of Friedrichsruh, who in 1961 and 1967 allowed me to consult invaluable Bleichröder material. Finally I wish to thank the officials of the Political Archive of the Foreign Office of the Federal Republic of Germany, especially its late head, Dr. Ullrich, and throughout the years of research, Dr. Sasse and Dr. Weinandy. My particular gratitude goes to the directors of the Deutsches Zentralarchiv in Potsdam and Merseburg, Dr. Lötzke and Dr. Weltsch, who went out of their way to make our stay in the archives pleasant and productive. I wish to thank the custodians of all the other archives listed above as well. I owe a special debt to Kenneth E. Carpenter, the curator of the Kress Library at Harvard University. The Columbia University libraries have been exemplary in their help to an insistent supplicant. The Royal Library of the Hague was particularly helpful as well.

Access to these and other archives was made possible by further grants: in 1966 I received a fellowship from the American Council of Learned Societies that allowed me to spend a sabbatical at Oxford, where I enjoyed the hospitality and stimulation of Nuffield College and St. Antony's College. The European Institute of Columbia University gave me repeated grants for travel and clerical assistance; I remain grateful to the encouragement of its first director, Philip E. Mosely.

In the long process of research I received aid from several friends and colleagues. At a critical juncture and in pursuit of essential material, I obtained decisive help from Hans-Ulrich Wehler and Bernhard Vogel, currently minister of education in the Rhineland-Palatinate. Without the assistance of Georges Castellan in Paris I doubt that we would have been able to work in the archives of the German Democratic Republic. I also received help from Peter Rassow, Walter Bussman, and Victor Brombert. I am especially indebted to Wolfram Fischer, who responded to my queries with expert and expeditious answers. I suffered what all American scholars of European history must suffer at one time or another: the distance from archives or libraries that one unexpectedly needs. I received much help in the form of additional material on Bleichröder that colleagues happened to come upon in their own research and generously offered to share with me. I think especially of John Röhl, Klaus-Peter Hoepke, Alfred Vagts, and additionally of Marvin Swartz, J. A. Sherman, Allan Mitchell, Werner Pöls, Otto Pflanze, and Eberhard Naujoks. I am also grateful to Rudolf Bleichröder, of Samuel Montagu & Co. Limited, London, who was kind enough to share with me his recollections of the families of Gerson and Julius Bleichröder.

For much of the writing of the book I was able to take refuge in several scholarly havens. In 1969–70, with the help of a fellowship from the John Simon Guggenheim Memorial Foundation, I spent a year at the Institute for Advanced Study in Princeton. In 1972–73 I was at the Netherlands Institute for Advanced Study, where, under the watchful eye of Dr. Misset and the solicitude of Els Glastra van Loon-Boon, the first European institute of interdisciplinary work has been established. During the same year the Rockefeller Foundation invited David Landes and me to spend a short but profitable time at the Villa Serbelloni.

Many friends and colleagues discussed my work with me, and I would like to thank in particular: Jacques Barzun, Sir Isaiah Berlin, William Diebold, Jr., Albert O. Hirschman, George F. Kennan, David De Levita, and Walter Sokel. Some of my friends criticized individual chapters at an early stage: Peter Kenen, Arthur Mitzman, Hugh Seton-Watson, and Rudolf Vierhaus. Leonard Krieger read the revised first part of the book, and his comments sharpened my own thoughts while encouraging me as well. I gave the completed manuscript to Felix Gilbert, Christoph M. Kimmich, Robert K. Webb, and Jay Winter, and I am deeply grateful for their willingness to take on such a formidable assignment in the midst of their own work. Their criticisms improved the manuscript in many important ways. Felix Gilbert, with his fine sense for the European past and his grasp of the historian's responsibility, read the Introduction as well; even earlier, we had countless conversations from which I benefited immeasurably. The Introduction was also read by David Rothman and Ismar Schorsch, and finally by Ralf Dahrendorf. It is now nearly twenty years since we were both fellows at the Center for Advanced Study in the Behavioral Sciences, and everything that I have written and done in the intervening years has borne the mark of his thought and of our friendship.

Over the years I have had help from a succession of research assistants, among them Vojta Mastny, Martin Landy, Hans Torke, Larry Abrams, Arthur Doppelt, and Martin Newhouse; in the summer of 1974 I had the good fortune of enlisting Deborah Roberts, a classicist at Yale, as library sleuth, typist, and whimsical commentator on the foibles of this book. The bulk of the manuscript was typed, with admirable skill and patience, by Ene Sirvet; earlier Ineke Veilbrief-van Egmond and Ruth Earman helped in the transcriptions of notes. At the end of the work Michelle Kehmi proved a great help with the mechanics of preparing the notes. For the last ten months I could count on the patient and resourceful help of Katharina J. Zimmer; in the final stages of getting the manuscript ready for publication her help was gallant and indispensable.

I am deeply grateful to my friend and editor, Ashbel Green, without whom the book would have been longer still, marred by more lapses of various kinds. His inspiring mixture of sound advice and forbearance has been an extraordinary boon.

The book was written and revised over a long and difficult period. The important years for its composition coincided with an upheaval that shook Columbia University, which had been my intellectual home for the preceding twenty-five years; it demanded and deserved my fullest commitment. It was also a period of great personal losses. Hajo Holborn, who had always been a friend and mentor, died in 1969. My two oldest friends and colleagues,

Richard Hofstadter and Henry L. Roberts, died shortly thereafter. In the last five years Lionel Trilling, long a teacher and friend, took a vital interest in my book. Beyond all else, he had a glowing commitment to work which continually reinforced me. He died a few months ago. I would like to think that the traces of their thought and inspiration can be found in this book.

During these last years, the support of my family has sustained me. The dedication records my greatest and least tangible debt; for years my wife understood and accommodated the book, and in ways too subtle for me to describe she willed its end. My children also aided me in many and complementary ways. My son, Fred, from a literary vantage point, helped me to see events and sentiments in a new perspective; at the very end he made me grapple with some obstinacies of the Introduction. My daughter, Katherine, herself an historian, read galley proofs with me, and in the process her groans of exasperation were as splendidly helpful as her many superb suggestions for improvements.

I have received abundant help. It has been a daunting experience and any errors of judgment or of fact are mine.

FRITZ STERN

Rochester, Vermont
July 28, 1976

BIBLIOGRAPHY

In the interests of economy I have decided against listing every file in every archive that I have consulted. The list would be long; the files I quoted are of course identified in the preceding notes. I also thought it tedious to list all the books that I have read. The books and articles I quoted are listed in the preceding notes. The list offered here is intended as an acknowledgment of some of the books that were of particular value to me either in deepening my understanding of the central themes of this book or in broadening my outlook in regard to its historic setting. It is an incomplete list, but I hope it may be helpful to some readers. It is an invidious task to prepare such a selection, and I am afraid that unwittingly I may have omitted some works that in fact should have been included.

As I mentioned in the introduction and as must have been evident in the text and notes, I found the great novels of the last century and the plays of Ibsen and Shaw of immense value. I believe it was more than pleasure that has led me to read and think about the novels of Stendhal, Balzac, Flaubert, Dickens, Trollope, Thomas Mann, and Theodor Fontane.

For an understanding of society in the 1870s, I found the pages of *Kladderadatsch* particularly illuminating.

Arendt, Hannah, *The Origins of Totalitarianism*. New York, 1951.

Berdahl, Robert M., "New Thoughts on German Nationalism," *AHR*, 77 (1972), 65–70.

Blake, Robert, *Disraeli*. London, 1966.

Böhme, Helmut, *Deutschlands Weg zur Grossmacht: Studien zum Verhältnis von Wirtschaft und Staat während der Reichsgründungszeit, 1848–1881*. Cologne and Berlin, 1966.

Born, Karl Erich, ed., *Bismarck-Bibliographie. Quellen und Literatur zur Geschichte Bismarcks und seiner Zeit*. Cologne, 1966.

Bussmann, Walter, ed., *Staatssekretär Graf Herbert von Bismarck. Aus seiner politischen Privatkorrespondenz*. Göttingen, 1964.

Craig, Gordon A., *The Politics of the Prussian Army, 1640–1945*. Oxford, 1955.

De Levita, David J., *The Concept of Identity*. Paris and The Hague, 1965.

Dissow, Joachim von, *Adel im Übergang. Ein kritischer Standesgenosse berichtet aus Residenzen und Gutshäusern*. Stuttgart, 1961.

Eyck, Erich, *Bismarck: Leben und Werk*, 3 vols. Erlenbach-Zürich, 1941–1944.

Fischer, Wolfram, *Wirtschaft und Gesellschaft im Zeitalter der Industrialisierung. Aufsätze, Studien, Vorträge*. Göttingen, 1972.

Freud, Sigmund, *Civilization and its Discontents*, 4th ed. London, 1949.

Fürstenberg, Hans, ed., *Carl Fürstenberg. Die Lebensgeschichte eines deutschen Bankiers, 1870–1914*. Berlin, 1931.

Gilbert, Felix, ed., *Bankiers, Künstler und Gelehrte. Unveröffentlichte Briefe der Familie Mendelssohn aus dem 19. Jahrhundert*. New York, 1975.

Hofstadter, Richard, *The Age of Reform*. New York, 1955.

———, *The Paranoid Style in American Politics and Other Essays*. New York, 1965.

Holborn, Hajo, *Germany and Europe: Historical Essays.* New York, 1970.
——, *A History of Modern Germany, 1840–1945.* New York, 1969.
Howard, Michael, *The Franco-Prussian War: The German Invasion of France, 1870–1871.* New York, 1961.
Joll, James, *1914. The Unspoken Assumptions,* an inaugural lecture. London, 1968.
Kaelble, Helmut, *Berliner Unternehmer während der frühen Industrialisierung. Herkunft, sozialer Status und politischer Einfluss.* Berlin, 1972.
Katz, Jacob, *Out of the Ghetto: The Social Background of Jewish Emancipation, 1770–1870.* Cambridge, Mass., 1973.
Kehr, Eckart, *Der Primat der Innenpolitik. Gesammelte Aufsätze zur preussisch-deutschen Sozialgeschichte im 19. Jahrhundert,* ed. by Hans-Ulrich Wehler. Berlin, 1965.
Kissinger, Henry A., "The White Revolutionary: Reflections on Bismarck," *Daedalus,* 97 (1968), 888–924.
Landes, David S., *Bankers and Pashas: International Finance and Economic Imperialism in Egypt.* London, 1958.
——, "Some Thoughts on the Nature of Economic Imperialism," *JEH,* 21 (1961), 496–512.
——, *The Unbound Prometheus: Technological Change and Industrial Development in Western Europe from 1750 to the Present.* London, 1969.
Langer, William L., *European Alliances and Alignments, 1871–1890,* 2nd ed. New York, 1956.
Lüthy, Herbert, "Colonization and the Making of Mankind," *JEH,* 21 (1961), 483–95.
Marx, Karl, *Manifesto of the Communist Party; The Eighteenth Brumaire of Louis Bonaparte; The Civil War in France; The Class Struggles in France, 1848 to 1850.*
Münch, Hermann, *Adolph von Hansemann.* Munich, 1932.
Petersdorff, Hermann von, and others, eds., *Bismarck: Die Gesammelten Werke,* 15 vols. in 19, Berlin, 1923–1933.
Pflanze, Otto, *Bismarck and the Development of Germany: The Period of Unification, 1815–1871.* Princeton, 1963.
——, "Toward a Psychoanalytical Interpretation of Bismarck," *AHR,* 77 (1972), 419–44.

Rich, Norman, and Fischer, M. H., eds., *The Holstein Papers,* vols. I–III. Cambridge, 1955–1961.
Rürup, Reinhardt, *Emanzipation und Antisemitismus. Studien zur "Judenfrage" der bürgerlichen Gesellschaft.* Göttingen, 1975.
Rosenberg, Hans, *Grosse Depression und Bismarckzeit.* Berlin, 1967.
Sartre, Jean-Paul. *Portrait of the Anti-Semite.* London, 1948.
Schorsch, Ismar, *Jewish Reactions to German Anti-Semitism, 1870–1914.* New York, 1972.
Taylor, A. J. P., *Bismarck: The Man and the Statesman.* New York, 1955.
——, *The Struggle for Mastery in Europe, 1848–1918.* Oxford, 1954.
Trilling, Lionel, *The Liberal Imagination: Essays on Literature and Society.* New York, 1950.
——, *Sincerity and Authenticity.* Cambridge, Mass., 1972.
Toury, Jacob, *Die politischen Orientierungen der Juden in Deutschland: Von Jena bis Weimar.* Tübingen, 1966.
Vierhaus, Rudolf, ed., *Das Tagebuch der Baronin Spitzemberg. Aufzeichnungen aus der Hofgesellschaft des Hohenzollernreiches.* Göttingen, 1960.
Walker, Mack, *Germany and the Emigration, 1816–1885.* Cambridge, Mass., 1964.
Weber, Max, *Gesammelte Politische Schriften.* Munich, 1921.
——, *Wirtschaft und Gesellschaft. Grundriss der verstehenden Soziologie,* 5th ed. Tübingen, 1972.
Wehler, Hans-Ulrich, *Bismarck und der Imperialismus.* Cologne and Berlin, 1969.
——, *Krisenherde des Kaiserreichs, 1871–1918.* Göttingen, 1970.
——, ed., *Moderne deutsche Sozialgeschichte.* Cologne and Berlin, 1966.
Zeldin, Theodore, *France, 1848–1945,* Vol. I: *Ambition, Love, and Politics.* Oxford, 1973.
Ziekursch, Johannes, *Politische Geschichte des Neuen Deutschen Kaiserreiches,* 3 vols. Frankfurt, 1925–1930.
Zunkel, Friedrich, *Der Rheinisch-Westfälische Unternehmer 1834–1879: Ein Beitrag zur Geschichte des deutschen Bürgertums im 19. Jahrhundert.* Cologne and Opladen, 1962.

Index

ABOUT THE AUTHOR

A recognized authority on modern Europe, Fritz Stern is Seth Low Professor of History at Columbia University. Born in Germany in 1926, he came to the United States in 1938. He holds three degrees from Columbia, where he has taught for three decades. He has also taught at Cornell, Yale, Free University of Berlin, and the University of Konstanz in West Germany. He is the author of *The Politics of Cultural Despair* and *The Failure of Illiberalism*, the editor of *The Varieties of History*, and co-editor, with Leonard Krieger, of *The Responsibility of Power*. He was a member of the Institute for Advanced Study at Princeton, 1969/70, and of the Netherlands Institute for Advanced Study, 1972/73; he has been awarded fellowships by the Guggenheim Foundation, the American Council on Learned Societies, and the Center for Advanced Study in the Behavioral Sciences at Stanford. He is now working on a book on contemporary Europe, supported by a Ford Foundation grant. A member of Phi Beta Kappa, he is on the Editorial Advisory Board of *Foreign Affairs*. He lives in New York with his wife, Margaret, and is the father of two children.

VINTAGE POLITICAL SCIENCE AND SOCIAL CRITICISM

V-568   **ALINSKY, SAUL D.** / Reveille for Radicals
V-736   **ALINSKY, SAUL D.** / Rules for Radicals
V-726   **ALLENDE, PRESIDENT SALVADOR AND REGIS DEBRAY** / The Chilean Revolution
V-286   **ARIES, PHILIPPE** / Centuries of Childhood
V-604   **BAILYN, BERNARD** / Origins of American Politics
V-334   **BALTZELL, E. DIGBY** / The Protestant Establishment
V-571   **BARTH, ALAN** / Prophets With Honor: Great Dissents & Great Dissenters in the Supreme Court
V-791   **BAXANDALL, LEE (ed.) AND WILHELM REICH** / Sex-Pol.: Essays 1929-1934
V-60   **BECKER, CARL L.** / The Declaration of Independence
V-563   **BEER, SAMUEL H.** / British Politics in the Collectivist Age
V-994   **BERGER, PETER & BRIGITTE AND HANSFRIED KELLNER** / The Homeless Mind: Modernization and Consciousness
V-77   **BINZEN, PETER** / Whitetown, USA
V-513   **BOORSTIN, DANIEL J.** / The Americans: The Colonial Experience
V-11   **BOORSTIN, DANIEL J.** / The Americans: The Democratic Experience
V-358   **BOORSTIN, DANIEL J.** / The Americans: The National Experience
V-501   **BOORSTIN, DANIEL J.** / Democracy and Its Discontents: Reflections on Everyday America
V-414   **BOTTOMORE, T. B.** / Classes in Modern Society
V-742   **BOTTOMORE, T. B.** / Sociology: A Guide to Problems & Literature
V-305   **BREINES, SIMON AND WILLIAM J. DEAN** / The Pedestrian Revolution: Streets Without Cars
V-44   **BRINTON, CRANE** / The Anatomy of Revolution
V-30   **CAMUS, ALBERT** / The Rebel
V-966   **CAMUS, ALBERT** / Resistance, Rebellion & Death
V-33   **CARMICHAEL, STOKELY AND CHARLES HAMILTON** / Black Power
V-2024   **CARO, ROBERT A.** / The Power Broker: Robert Moses and The Fall of New York
V-862   **CASE, JOHN AND GERRY HUNNIUS AND DAVID G. CARSON** / Workers Control: A Reader on Labor and Social Change
V-98   **CASH, W. J.** / The Mind of the South
V-555   **CHOMSKY, NOAM** / American Power and the New Mandarins
V-248   **CHOMSKY, NOAM** / Peace in the Middle East? Reflections on Justice and Nationhood
V-815   **CHOMSKY, NOAM** / Problems of Knowledge and Freedom
V-788   **CIRINO, ROBERT** / Don't Blame the People
V-17   **CLARKE, TED AND DENNIS JAFFE (eds.)** / Worlds Apart: Young People and The Drug Problems
V-383   **CLOWARD, RICHARD AND FRANCES FOX PIVEN** / The Politics of Turmoil: Essays on Poverty, Race and The Urban Crisis
V-743   **CLOWARD, RICHARD AND FRANCES FOX PIVEN** / Regulating the Poor: The Functions of Public Welfare
V-940   **COBB, JONATHAN AND RICHARD SENNETT** / Hidden Injuries of Class
V-311   **CREMIN, LAWRENCE A.** / The Genius of American Education
V-519   **CREMIN, LAWRENCE A.** / The Transformation of the School
V-808   **CUMMING, ROBERT D. (ed.)** / The Philosophy of Jean-Paul Sartre
V-2019   **CUOMO, MARIO** / Forest Hills Diary: The Crisis of Low-Income Housing
V-305   **DEAN, WILLIAM J. AND SIMON BREINES** / The Pedestrian Revolution: Streets Without Cars
V-726   **DEBRAY, REGIS AND PRESIDENT SALVADOR ALLENDE** / The Chilean Revolution
V-638   **DENNISON, GEORGE** / The Lives of Children
V-746   **DEUTSCHER, ISAAC** / The Prophet Armed
V-748   **DEUTSCHER, ISAAC** / The Prophet Outcast
V-617   **DEVLIN, BERNADETTE** / The Price of My Soul